Second Canadian Edition

BUSINESS

Ricky W. Griffin
Texas A&M University

Ronald J. Ebert
University of Missouri

Frederick A. Starke
University of Manitoba

Prentice Hall Canada Inc., Scarborough, Ontario

Canadian Cataloguing in Publication Data

Griffin, Ricky W.
        Business

2nd Canadian ed.
Includes index.
ISBN 0-13-378845-8

1. Industrial management. 2. Business enterprises.
3. Industrial management – Canada. 4. Business
enterprises – Canada. I. Ebert, Ronald J.
II. Starke, Frederick A., 1942–   . III. Title.

HD31.G75 1996   658   C95-931562-4

© 1996 Prentice-Hall Canada Inc., Scarborough, Ontario
A Viacom Company

Prentice-Hall, Inc., Englewood Cliffs, New Jersey
Prentice-Hall International (UK) Limited, London
Prentice-Hall of Australia, Pty. Limited, Sydney
Prentice-Hall Hispanoamericana, S.A., Mexico City
Prentice-Hall of India Private Limited, New Delhi
Prentice-Hall of Japan, Inc., Tokyo
Simon & Schuster Asia Private Limited, Singapore
Editora Prentice-Hall do Brasil, Ltda., Rio de Janeiro

ISBN 0-13-378845-8

Acquisitions Editor: Patrick Ferrier
Developmental Editor: Dawn du Quesnay
Copy Editor: Deborah Burrett
Production Editor: Mary Ann Field
Production Coordinator: Deborah Starks
Permissions/Photo Research: Karen Taylor/Alene McNeill
Cover Design: Monica Kompter
Cover Image: The Image Bank/Roy Wiemann
Page Layout: Steve Lewis

Original edition published by Prentice-Hall, Inc.
A Division of Simon & Schuster
Englewood Cliffs, New Jersey
Copyright © 1996, 1993, 1991

1 2 3 4 5 VH 00 99 98 97 96

Printed and bound in USA

Send comments by e-mail to
collegeinfo_pubcanada@prenhall.com

OVERVIEW

CONTENTS

4 Business Ethics, Social Responsibility, and Business Law   81

5 Managing the Business Enterprise   117

Part Three
Managing Human Resources 205

8 Planning for and Developing Human Resources 207

9 Motivating, Satisfying, and Leading Employees 235

Part Four
Managing Production   295

Part Five
Managing Marketing   381

16 Pricing and Distributing Goods and Services   455

Part Six
Managing Financial Issues 495

17 Understanding Accounting Issues   497

18 Understanding Money and Banking ... 527

19 Financial Decisions and Risk Management ... 555

20 Understanding Securities and Investments   591

Part Seven
Meeting Business Challenges   623

21 Business-Government Relations   625

22 Understanding International Business   647

23 Managing Computers in Business   679

PREFACE

This is the second Canadian edition of *Business*. Our goals in this edition are the same as those in the first edition: to excite and inform students about today's business world, and to support instructors with an interesting and attractive book that explains the basic ideas that beginning business students must learn.

Naturally, the Second Canadian Edition maintains the strengths that made the first edition so successful. First of all, it is a well organized text, flowing logically from one concept to another. This of course is critical if students are to understand the complexities and dynamics of Canadian business, though unfortunately it is not always the case in the texts available in the market today. Second, the text maintains its strong global focus. International Report boxes and end-of-part international case studies inform and provoke thought about business practices in Western and Eastern Europe, Asia, and the United States, giving students an international perspective in which to place their new knowledge of Canadian business. Third, boxed features throughout the text present the practical side of Canadian business. The above-mentioned International Report and Canadian Business Scene boxes provide practical examples that bridge the gap between theory and practice. Last but definitely not least, the book retains its inviting, full-colour design, replete with interesting photographs depicting life in all aspects of the business world. The attractive layout, photos, and meaningful use of colour help get and hold students' attention, and make the experience of learning about business more enjoyable.

Changes to the Second Edition

This edition incorporates changes that were suggested by professors and students who used the first edition. It also includes changes that were suggested by reviewers. Most chapters contain a new opening case describing a real Canadian company and the challenges and opportunities it faces. Many new boxed inserts, end-of-chapter cases, and end-of-part cases are also included in this edition. These boxed inserts and cases, which describe real Canadian business firms in action, are arranged in two themes: "The Canadian Business Scene" and "International Report."

New Features

There are three new features at the end of each major section of the text: two video cases based on the CBC series *Venture*, a "Building Your Business Skills" exercise, and a "Careers in Business" discussion. Each of these are described in more detail later in this Preface.

Chapters Containing Significant Revisions

Several chapters have been significantly revised to take into account new developments in the modern business world. These include

Chapter 1:   Several new boxed inserts have been added dealing with international business. The increased emphasis on international business in this and other chapters is a continuing theme in this revised edition.

Chapter 2:   The recent changes in the cooperative movement and the implications of those changes for the cooperative as a form of business ownership are included in this chapter.

Chapter 7: This chapter presents new information on entrepreneurship in Canada and a profile of a famous Canadian entrepreneur. It also contains information on entrepreneurship in the former communist countries, and explains the difficulties these entrepreneurs have.

Chapter 8: Several new trends in human resource management are discussed in this chapter, including the trend toward freelancing, the use of video technology to screen job applicants, and the dramatic changes that are taking place in the management of Japanese companies (additional changes in the Japanese management system are discussed in Chapter 9).

Chapter 11: The material in this chapter has been reorganized and updated. New information is presented on the latest developments in operations management, including cellular layouts, flexible manufacturing, and soft manufacturing.

Chapter 13: New material has been included on several popular strategies for improving productivity. These include value-added analysis, benchmarking, cause-and-effect diagrams, ISO 9000, and re-engineering.

Chapter 14: A new section focusing on organizational buying describes industrial, institutional, government, and reseller markets and how they differ from consumer markets. A new section dealing with international marketing examines each of the elements of the marketing mix—product, place, promotion, and price.

Chapter 15: The section on developing new products has been extensively revised and new information is presented. A new section has also been added dealing with promotional practices in small businesses.

Chapter 16: New material on the Canadian retailing and distribution sectors includes a discussion of the "wheel of retailing" concept, the dramatic changes in retailing caused by firms like Wal-Mart entering Canada, and new technology which allows better tracking of items in the distribution system.

Chapter 17: Because more and more Canadian companies are involved in exporting and importing goods and services, there is an increased need to focus on international accounting. New material on this important subject is presented in this chapter.

Chapter 18: An interesting new section on international currency evaluation is presented in this chapter. A new boxed insert in Chapter 22 on the rapidly declining value of the Russian ruble complements this discussion.

Chapter 19: The discussion of the role and functions of the financial manager has been extensively revised and updated.

Chapter 22: This chapter has been extensively reorganized and updated. New material on free trade agreements in North and South America is included, as well as information on the rise of international business, the new global economy, and major world marketplaces.

Chapter 23: Rapid developments in computer technology continue unabated. This chapter presents new information on object-oriented technology, groupware, new developments in office automation, executive information systems, the Internet, and the virtual office.

Organization of the Text

The text is organized into seven sections as follows:

Part I: Introducing the Contemporary Business World

This section introduces students to the basic ideas underlying business activity. Chapter 1 describes how business activity is oriented toward making a profit by satisfying consumer needs. Several types of economic systems are also described. Chapter 2 focuses on the different forms of business ownership—sole proprietorships, partnerships, corporations, and cooperatives—that can be used to run a business. Chapter 3 describes how the interrelationship of business firms with consumers, the work force, and government presents both challenges and opportunities for businesses. In Chapter 4, the impact of ethics, social responsibility, and business law are discussed.

Part II: Managing the Business Firm

The chapters in this section focus on the general management activities that are necessary in business firms. Chapter 5 introduces the functions of management—planning, organizing, leading, and controlling—and the three basic types of management skills—technical, human relations, and conceptual. Chapter 6 focuses in detail on the planning and organizing functions. In Chapter 7, general management principles are applied to small business.

Part III: Managing Human Resources

The chapters in this section focus on the most important resource in business firms: people. Chapter 8 describes the activities that are necessary in order to recruit, hire, train, and compensate the company's human resources. Chapter 9 deals with managerial activities that are necessary to motivate and lead employees so that they are both satisfied and productive. Chapter 10 presents information on Canadian labor unions, and the way that unions affect management activity.

Part IV: Managing Production

This section describes those managerial activities which are necessary to convert raw materials into finished products and services that are needed by consumers. Chapter 11 focuses on the production of goods, while Chapter 12 deals with the "production" of services. In Chapter 13, the crucial issue of productivity and quality is examined.

Part V: Managing Marketing

The chapters in this section explain the key activities that are carried out by marketing managers. Chapter 14 introduces the "4 Ps of marketing"—product, place, promotion, and price. Other activities—such as marketing research and the study of consumer behavior—help marketing managers carry out the marketing function effectively. Chapter 15 looks in detail at the development and promotion of products, while Chapter 16 focuses on pricing and distributing goods and services.

Part VI: Managing Financial Issues

This section introduces students to the key financial aspects of business firms. Chapter 17 describes the accounting function and the financial statements that accountants generate for managers and investors. In Chapter 18, the role of money and the various financial intermediaries in Canada are examined. Chapter 19 focuses on the role of the financial manager, as well as the various sources of funds available to business firms. Chapter 20 looks at securities markets and the buying and selling of stocks, bonds, and other investments.

Part VII: Meeting Business Challenges

The final section of the text addresses three major issues that business firms must deal with. Chapter 21 explains how government decisions can affect business firms, and how these two major forces in the Canadian economy must adapt to each other. Chapter 22 describes the critical area of international business and free trade, and the various levels of involvement in international business that are possible. The text concludes with Chapter 23, an assessment of how computers are affecting business firms.

Major Features of the Text

Each chapter in this text contains the following features to stimulate student interest in, and understanding of, the material which is being presented about business:

Part Opener

At the beginning of each of the seven parts of the book is a brief outline introducing the material that will be discussed in that part. By revealing the rationale for the structure of the part, it gives students a glimpse of the "big picture" as they head into a new area of the business world.

Chapter Materials

Each *chapter* contains several features that are designed to increase student interest and understanding of the material being presented. These features are as follows:

Learning objectives.   A list of learning objectives is found at the beginning of each chapter. These guide students in determining what is important in each chapter.

Chapter outline.   An outline of the topics to be discussed is presented on the first page of the chapter. This will help students see the logical flow of ideas in the chapter.

Opening case.   Chapters 2 through 23 begin with a one-page description of an incident that happened in a real Canadian company. The subject matter of this opening case is relevant to the material being presented in that chapter. This helps the student bridge the gap from theory to practice.

Boxed inserts.   Each chapter contains 3–6 boxed inserts describing activities in Canadian or international companies. These inserts are designed to clearly show students how theoretical concepts are put into actual practice by business firms. There are two types of boxes: "The Canadian Business Scene" (which focuses on Canadian businesses) and "International Report" (which focuses on examples of business activity from around the world).

Examples.   In addition to the boxed inserts, each chapter contains numerous examples of how businesses operate. These examples will further help students understand actual business practice in Canada and elsewhere.

End-Of-Chapter Material
Several important pedagogical features are found at the end of each chapter. These are designed to help students better understand the material that was presented in the chapter. The features are as follows:

Summary of key points.   The material in each chapter is concisely summarized to help students understand the main points that were presented in the chapter.

Case studies.   Each chapter concludes with two case studies which focus on real Canadian or international companies. These cases are designed to help students see how the chapter material can be applied to a real company that is currently in the news. At the end of each case, there are several questions which guide students in their analysis.

Key terms.   In each chapter, the key terms that students should know are highlighted and defined in the text, repeated in the margin, listed at the end of the chapter (with page references), and collected in the glossary at the end of the book.

Study questions and exercises.   There are three general types of questions here: questions for review (straightforward questions of factual recall), questions for analysis (requiring students to think beyond simple factual recall and apply the concepts), and application exercises (requiring students to visit local businesses or managers and gather additional information that will help them understand how business firms operate).

Building your business skills.   This new feature is an in-depth exercise that allows students to examine some specific aspect of business in detail. The exercise may ask the student to work individually or in a group to gather data about some interesting business issue and then develop a written report or a class presentation based on the information that was gathered.

End-Of-Part Material
Each part concludes with several additional pedagogical features. These are designed to help the student master the material and think analytically about it.

Video cases.   These are an exciting feature new to this edition. There are two video cases at the end of each part; each case is based on a recent CBC *Venture* episode. (A videotape containing the 14 episodes that are summarized in the text is available for textbook adopters.) The instructor can show the episode in class and then either have a class discussion using the questions at the end of the written case as a guideline, or ask students to turn in a written assignment which contains answers to the questions at the end of the case. This approach to teaching will add a major new dynamic to classes.

International case study.   These international cases are designed to help students think about business in international terms. Specific questions are included at the end of the case to guide class discussion or serve as material for written student assignments. All international cases from the first edition have been replaced and updated.

Experiential exercise.   These exercises, which typically require one or two hours to complete, are set up so that students can "experience" a realistic business situation and thereby gain increased understanding of business.

Careers in business.   Students have a keen interest in the kinds of jobs they might take when they leave college or university. This new feature provides information about careers that are available, occupations which are in high demand, pointers on interviewing for jobs and preparing a résumé, and other related career information. This should be of great practical use to students.

Supplementary Material

For the Instructor

CBC Videos.   This collection of hand-picked CBC video clips is perhaps the most dynamic of all the supplements you can use to enhance your classes. Prentice Hall Canada and CBC have worked together to bring you the best and most comprehensive Canadian video package available in the college market. Containing clips from the CBC series *Venture*, these tapes have extremely high production quality, present substantial content, and are hosted by well-versed, well-known anchors.

Test Item File.   Contains nearly 2000 questions. For each chapter there are approximately 50 multiple choice questions, 25 true-false questions, and 10 essay questions. Also available in computerized format on 3.5" disks.

Instructor's Manual and Video Guide.   Contains suggestions on how to use the text effectively. It also includes transparency masters, suggested lecture outlines, answers to end-of-chapter questions and end-of-part case studies, as well as answers to video case study questions.

Electronic Transparencies.   Overhead masters of selected graphic illustrations from the text. Also available in full-colour Powerpoint electronic format. Colour acetates available in limited quantities—to qualified adopters only.

For the Student

Study Guide.   This guide will enable students to review the introductory business concepts presented in the text. It will also help them gain insight into the application of these concepts.

E–Z Write Business Plan Writer Software.   This exceptionally easy-to-use software, available on a 3.5" disk for IBM and compatibles, provides a template for a complete business plan, and includes examples of financial documents on Lotus templates. This invaluable supplement will be packaged with the Study Guide.

Contemporary Views.   *The Financial Post* and Prentice Hall Canada have joined together in an exclusive arrangement to produce a student edition of *The Financial Post*, tailored to business students. Through this program, the core subject matter provided in the text is supplemented by a collection of specially chosen, time-sensitive articles from one of Canada's most distinguished business newspapers. These articles demonstrate the vital, ongoing connection between what is learned in the classroom and what is happening in Canada and the world around us, and are updated annually. This free supplement comes shrinkwrapped to the text.

Acknowledgements

We owe special thanks to the acquisitions editor, Patrick Ferrier, to the development editor, Dawn du Quesnay, and to the production editor, Mary Ann Field.

The following individuals helped by reviewing the manuscript:

David Hunter of Humber College and William Martello of the University of Calgary.

Their comments were carefully considered and implemented wherever possible.

Frederick A. Starke
1996

TO STUDENTS

We started to call this section "How to Make an A." However, in this age of litigation, we decided to take a more conservative approach and instead explain how we think you can get the greatest value from this text.

First, it is important to recognize that business is a complex and dynamic field in which you are likely to encounter many new concepts and terms. You may find yourself disagreeing with some things. On the other hand, avoid the pitfall of believing that everything you find in this book—and in the study of business—is simply common sense. If this were the case, the statistics on business failure discussed in Chapter 7 would be quite different.

The starting point in any class is your instructor's course outline. Read it thoroughly and make sure you understand all the objectives and course requirements.

You should always read assigned chapters before coming to class. First read carefully through the chapter objectives and reflect on what the chapter will be about. Then, as you read the text, keep the objectives in mind (perhaps looking back at them occasionally) to see how they are being developed. Make notes about important points and anything you do not understand. Use the figures, tables, and photos to amplify the text material. Use the marginal notes to acquaint yourself with vocabulary.

When you reach the end of the chapter, read the summary carefully and make sure you understand all the things it lists. Use the review questions to test your recall of important points. And make sure you know the meanings of all the key terms. Use the cases as your instructor assigns.

When you go to class, listen carefully to what your instructor says about the assigned material. You might highlight ideas from the text as your instructor discusses them. Be sure to take notes on points covered in class that are not in the book.

As well, be sure to ask questions about any point you do not understand. All too often, students don't ask questions for fear of looking silly. In our opinion, there is no such thing as a silly question from someone who wants to learn.

After class, spend more time with the chapter. Read through it again, noting other things you are learning. And if there are still points you do not understand, see your instructor during her or his office hours.

Be aware, too, that you have access to the same kinds of information that most business people use to manage their business lives. Publications such as *Canadian Business, The Globe and Mail, The Financial Post,* and *The Report on Business Magazine* contain valuable information about the nature of business in Canada. The CBC television series *Venture* also presents useful information about the dynamics of Canadian business activity. As you use this text and gain a sense of the workings of the business world, try to think about what you read and see and hear from the full range of information sources available to you.

Will all this work get you an A? Maybe, but regardless of the effect it has on your grade in the course, this process will greatly enhance your learning and get you off to a good start on your future career in business.

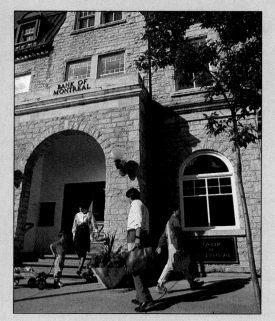

Part One

*I*NTRODUCING THE CONTEMPORARY BUSINESS WORLD

In Chapters 1–4, you will read about four situations that may seem at first glance to have little in common: the reunion rock concert called Woodstock II, an employee buyout at Great Western Brewery, a major change at Fishery Products International, and the waste management activities of Philip Environmental Inc.

Woodstock II and Philip Environmental provide a service, while Great Western Brewery and Fishery Products International provide a physical product. Great Western Brewery is a small firm, but Philip Environmental is very large. In spite of these and other differences, these situations have a common thread: they are all business situations where people are trying to make a profit by providing a product or a service to customers. Each case tells a part of the story of our contemporary business world.

Part One, Introducing the Contemporary Business World, provides a general overview of business today, including its economic roots, its legal structure, its current challenges, and its ethical problems and opportunities.

■ We begin in **Chapter 1, Understanding the Canadian Business System,** by examining the role of business in the economy of Canada and other market economies.

■ Then, in **Chapter 2, Setting Up Business in Canada,** we explore the various forms of business ownership in Canada and look briefly at the history of Canadian business.

■ In **Chapter 3, Recognizing Business Trends and Challenges,** we consider the wide range of issues confronting businesses in Canada and throughout the world.

■ Finally, in **Chapter 4, Business Ethics, Social Responsibility, and Business Law,** we look at how individual ethics and corporate social responsibility develop and affect the firm's environment and its customers, employees, and investors.

1

Understanding the Canadian Business System

LEARNING OBJECTIVES

After studying this chapter, you will be able to

■ Define the nature of Canadian business and its goals.

■ Differentiate between types of economic systems based on the way each one controls and uses the factors of production.

■ Describe how demand and supply in markets affect resource distribution in Canada.

■ Identify the elements of private enterprise and various degrees of competition in the Canadian economic system.

■ Explain the criteria used to assess how well the Canadian economy meets its goals.

CHAPTER OUTLINE

OPENING CASE

"This Is Not 1969"—Doing Business at Woodstock II

"If you build it, they will come." These words, paraphrased from the popular movie *Field of Dreams*, apply equally well to the Woodstock concerts of 1969 and 1994. Both events featured three days of rock music, partying, and mud in upstate New York. When entrepreneurs Michael Lang, Joel Rosenman, and John Roberts were all in their mid-20s, they formed a partnership called Woodstock Ventures and produced the original 1969 Woodstock festival in the town of Bethel, New York. They managed to launch their enterprise for about $3 million. However, although a three-day ticket cost just $18, gate crashers outnumbered paying customers, and despite a legendary crowd of "half a million strong," the promoters lost money on the concert investment itself. Ultimately—years later—they broke even thanks to royalty payments generated by the trademarked Woodstock logo.

In 1994, the original partners joined forces with promoter John Scher, head of Polygram Diversified Ventures, to stage a 25th-anniversary concert on a farm near Saugerties, New York. The cost this time topped $30 million. Then again, this time the promoters planned to sell 250 000 tickets priced at $135 each. Millions more in underwriting dollars came from corporate sponsorships. Lead sponsor Pepsi-Cola, for example, spent about $5 million on Woodstock '94, and more than 1 million bottles of Pepsi were sold or given away during the three days of the festival. Häagen-Dazs spent about $1 million and used the concert to introduce a new flavor. Apple Computer, Continental Airlines, and Vermont Pure Water were also million-dollar sponsors. MTV established a special home-shopping program to sell $1 million in concert memorabilia. Other sources of income included royalties from movies, videos, and audio recordings of the concert. Finally, fees from pay-per-view TV broadcasts in 27 countries were expected to bring in an estimated $5 million to $8 million.

The approach to "Woodstock II," then, was a big-business approach. Not surprisingly, it soon became the source of criticism from various quarters. Critics charged, for example, that the overt commercialization of the event—for instance, an "official t-shirt" was available for sale—violated the communal spirit of '69. In response, promoter Scher noted that Marlboro, Coors, and Budweiser were turned down as sponsors. "This is 1994," he declared. "This is not 1969. What everything costs is hundreds of times what it cost in 1969. Had we taken the beer sponsorships and liquor and tobacco ads that were offered us, we probably could have lowered the ticket price to $25."

Defenders of the organizers also pointed out that, in the 25 years between Woodstock I and II, rock music itself has become very big business. Among the 50 groups scheduled to appear were such trend-setting newcomers as Nine Inch Nails. Others—including Santana, Joe Cocker, and Crosby, Stills and Nash—had also appeared

at the original Woodstock. In any case, veteran performers and newcomers alike were lured to Woodstock II by the promise of performance fees of $250 000 or more. (By comparison, The Who, now one of the legends of rock 'n' roll, had received $11 200 for their 1969 festival appearance.) Admittedly, some newer "alternative" musicians worried that fans would regard an appearance at Woodstock to as evidence of "selling out" to the mainstream industry. In the end, however, enlightened economic self-interest seemed to emerge as a common theme among musicians of every different inclination. "To be quite frank," admitted Trent Reznor of Nine Inch Nails, "we were offered a lot of money. We don't have sponsorships; this way we can fund the rest of our tour." Reznor's view was echoed by Mike Cirnt, bassist for Green Day. Woodstock, he admitted, was "really corporate," but that's one of the reasons we're playing. It's helping us make up a lot of the money we've lost touring, being out there keeping our ticket prices low."

However, despite the appeal of both new music and old, tens of thousands of tickets remained unsold just prior to the concert date. Demand was dampened somewhat by the requirement (to encourage car pooling) that tickets be sold in blocks of four. In addition, some ticket buyers were confused because a rival concert—billed as "Bethel '94—The Reunion at Yasgur's Farm"—was set for the same weekend at the actual site of the 1969 Woodstock festival. The promoters of the Saugerties concert slapped rival organizers with an $80 million lawsuit. Even more lackluster demand for tickets—priced at $94.69—eventually forced cancelation of Bethel '94. Finally, when the Saugerties organizers repackaged tickets to sell in pairs, sales picked up, ultimately approaching the 200 000 mark.

When the weekend of Woodstock '94 finally arrived, a crowd estimated at 350 000 witnessed an event that, according to most, lived up to the Woodstock legend. Even after the mud has dried, however, the "idealism vs. capitalism" debate continues. One 40-something baby boomer registered his Woodstock complaint on the Internet: "I refuse to participate in something I believe is nothing more than making money off people's lust for the past." Not surprisingly, promoter Michael Lang has a different view of Woodstock '94. "In a lot of ways, it turned out to be very much like '69. The audience wanted a Woodstock, and it made one," he said. ◆

Supply and demand, competition and profitability, even social responsibility and threats in the legal environment—as in the tale of Woodstock II, these and a host of other forces are the main themes in stories of success and failure that are told over and over again in the annals of business enterprise throughout the world. As you will see in this chapter, those forces are also the key factors in the Canadian economy. You will also see that although the world's economic systems differ markedly, the standards for evaluating success or failure are linked to a system's capacity to achieve certain basic goals.

What do you think of when you hear the word *business*? Does it conjure up images of huge corporations like Canadian Pacific and Alcan Aluminum? Smaller companies like your local supermarket? One-person operations like the barbershop around the corner? Indeed, each of these firms is a **business**— an organization that produces or sells goods or services in an effort to make a profit. **Profit** is what remains after a business's expenses have been subtracted from its revenues. Profits reward the owners of businesses for taking the risks involved in investing their money and time.

The prospect of earning profits is what encourages people to open and expand businesses. Today businesses produce most of the goods and services that we consume, and they employ many of the working people in Canada. Profits from these businesses are paid to thousands upon thousands of owners and shareholders. And business taxes help support governments at all levels. In addition, businesses help support charitable causes and provide community leadership.

In this chapter, we begin your introduction to Canadian business by looking at its role in our economy and society. Because there are a variety of economic systems found around the world, we will first consider how the dominant ones operate. Once you have some understanding of different systems, you can better appreciate the workings of our own system. As you will see, the effect of economic forces on Canadian businesses and the effect of Canadian businesses on our economy produce dynamic and sometimes volatile results.

business
An organization that seeks to earn profits by providing goods and services.

profit
What remains (if anything) after a business's expenses are subtracted from its sales revenues.

Global Economic Systems

A Canadian business is different in many ways from one in China. And both are different from businesses in Japan, France, or Peru. A major determinant of how organizations operate is the kind of economic system that characterizes the country in which they do business. An **economic system** allocates a nation's resources among its citizens. Economic systems differ in who owns and controls these resources, known as the "factors of production."

economic system
The way in which a nation allocates its resources among its citizens.

Factors of Production

factors of production

The resources used to produce goods and services: natural resources, labor, capital, and entrepreneurs.

natural resources

Items used in the production of goods and services in their natural state, including land, water, minerals, and trees.

labor

The mental and physical training and talents of people; sometimes called human resources.

capital

The funds needed to operate an enterprise.

The basic resources a business uses to produce goods and services are called **factors of production**. They include natural resources, labor, capital, and entrepreneurs.[1] Figure 1.1 illustrates the factors of production.

Land, water, mineral deposits, and trees are good examples of **natural resources.** For example, Imperial Oil makes use of a wide variety of natural resources. It obviously has vast quantities of crude oil to process each year. But Imperial also needs the land where the oil is located, as well as land for its refineries and pipelines.

The people who work for a company represent the second factor of production, **labor**. Sometimes called *human resources,* labor is the mental and physical capabilities of people. Carrying out the business of such a huge company as Imperial requires a labor force with a wide variety of skills ranging from managers to geologists to truck drivers.

Obtaining and using material resources and labor requires **capital**, the funds needed to operate an enterprise. Capital is needed to start a business and to keep the business operating and growing. Imperial's annual drilling costs alone run into the millions of dollars. A major source of capital for

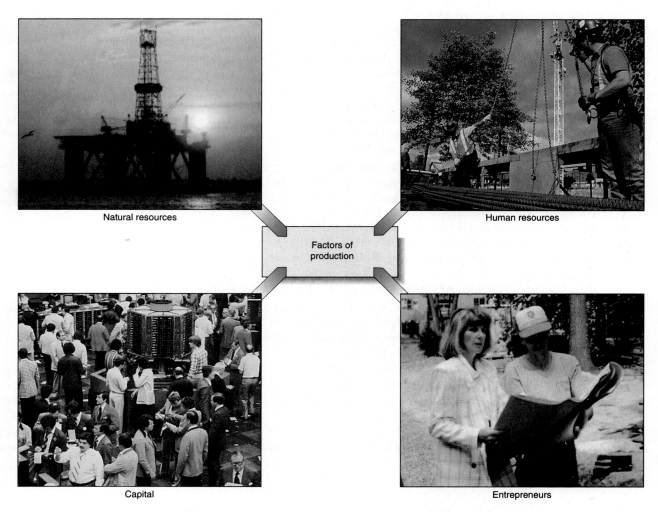

Natural resources

Human resources

Factors of production

Capital

Entrepreneurs

Figure 1.1

Factors of production are the basic resources a business uses to create goods and services. The four basic factors used are natural resources, labor, capital, and entrepreneurs.

most businesses is personal investment by owners. Personal investment can be made either by the individual entrepreneurs or partners who start businesses or by investors who buy stock in them. Revenues from the sale of products, of course, is another and important on-going source of capital. Finally, many firms borrow funds from banks and other lending institutions.

Entrepreneurs are those people who accept the opportunities and risks involved in creating and operating businesses. They are the people who start new businesses and who make the decisions that allow small businesses to grow into larger ones. Murray Pezim, Conrad Black, and the Griffiths family are well-known Canadian entrepreneurs. The Sky Freight Express video case on page 114 describes how the factors of production were used by entrepreneur Michael Talker when he started a courier service.

entrepreneur
An individual who organizes and manages natural resources, labor, and capital to produce goods and services to earn a profit, but who also runs the risks of failure.

Types of Economic Systems

Different types of economic systems manage the factors of production in different ways. In some systems, ownership is private; in others, the factors of production are owned by the government. Economic systems also differ in the ways decisions are made about production and allocation. A **planned economy**, for example, relies on a centralized government to control all or most factors of production and to make all or most production and allocation decisions. In **market economies**, individuals—producers and consumers—control production and allocation decisions through supply and demand. We will describe each of these economic types and then discuss the reality of the *mixed market economy*.

Planned Economies.   The two most basic forms of planned economies are communism and socialism. As originally proposed by the 19th-century German economist Karl Marx, **communism** is a system in which the government owns and operates all sources of production. Marx envisioned a society in which individuals would ultimately contribute according to their abilities and receive economic benefits according to their needs. He also expected government ownership of production factors to be only temporary: Once society had matured, government would "wither away" and the workers would gain direct ownership.

Most Eastern European countries and the former Soviet Union embraced communist systems until very recently. During the early 1990s, however, one country after another renounced communism as both an economic and a political system. Today, Cuba, North Korea, Vietnam, and the People's Republic of China are among the few nations with avowedly communist systems. Even in these countries, however, planned economic systems are making room for features of the free-enterprise system from the lowest to the highest levels. In Cuba, for example, special shops once reserved for diplomats are now patronized by Cubans from all walks of life. Here, they can buy goods that the severely troubled government systems cannot supply. Moreover, they use money earned from a variety of free-market activities (which are, technically, illegal). For example, the stores themselves are surrounded by paid bicycle parking lots, carwashes, and stalls selling home-grown produce and homemade handicrafts. All of this street-corner commerce reflects a rapid growth in private enterprise as a solution to problems that a centralized economy has long been unable to solve.[2]

As the box "China Moves Warily Toward Capitalism" shows, the People's Republic of China has begun to permit private ownership, promote competition, and encourage innovation. Unlike the now-defunct Soviet Union (which loosened political bonds first and economic ones later), the leaders of China have kept a tight rein on political freedom, but have loosened the economic bonds.

planned economy
An economic system in which government controls all or most factors of production and makes all or most production decisions.

market economy
An economic system in which individuals control all or most factors of production and make all or most production decisions.

communism
A kind of planned economy in which the government owns and operates all industries.

While we can identify different types of economies, the distinctions between them are becoming increasingly blurred. Previously planned economies in Eastern Europe, for example, are moving toward a market system. The woman shown here is selling decorated eggs on the street. China still uses a planned economy, but more and more elements of capitalism are becoming evident. In Canada, capitalism has always allowed farmers to decide what they would grow and how much to sell it for. Of course, capitalists aren't protected from failure, a concern that people in planned economies seldom have to confront.

Their private enterprise is humming, stock exchanges have opened, new forms of private property have been created, and the country is experimenting with its first bankruptcy law. But the balance between central planning and the market economy is not yet clear. China is in effect abandoning its communist ideology in favor of a more capitalistic one, but it is doing so very quietly.[3]

socialism

A kind of planned economy in which the government owns and operates the main industries, while individuals own and operate less crucial industries.

In a less extensively planned economic system called **socialism**, the government owns and operates only selected major industries. Smaller businesses such as clothing stores and restaurants may be privately owned. Although workers in socialist countries are usually allowed to choose their occupations or professions, a large proportion generally work for the government. Many

International Report

CHINA MOVES WARILY TOWARD CAPITALISM

China's province of Guangdong (formerly known as Canton) ranks fifth among China's 30 provinces in terms of population, but it ranks first in exports, industrial production, and foreign investment. Billboards tout Coke, Pepsi, and Head & Shoulders Shampoo. In the early 1980s, Guangdong became a laboratory for experiments with capitalism. Since then, hundreds of manufacturing firms in nearby Hong Kong have shifted some or all of their production to the province. The economic alliance of Chinese neighbors links the sophistication, management skills, and marketing know-how of Hong Kong's population with the low-cost production base of Guangdong's citizens. Labor costs are 80 percent lower in Guangdong than in Hong Kong.

China's experiments with capitalism came after years of disastrous attempts to put all production under government control. Communally run farms were the first organizations to be modified to provide incentives for individual farmers, and these formed the nucleus of China's return to small-scale private enterprise. In 1987, the country's southern coastal district was designated as a "scout" to explore new roads to an open, market-oriented economy.

Joint ventures with western firms are very popular in Guangdong, with over 10 000 undertaken so far. Avon Products Inc. began selling cosmetics in China in 1990; its initial sales were four to six times its estimates.

But China's movement toward capitalism is not without problems. While free-enterprise experiments have been going on for about 15 years, state-owned enterprises still dominate, employing over 100 million workers and supporting pensions paid to another 20 million. The effort to integrate free enterprise into a planned economy is plagued with problems. Consider conditions in Wuhan, a city of 7 million people.

While China has mostly deregulated cotton prices, it still maintains a quota system to support its huge textile industry. Under the quota system, Communist party managers can buy cotton for their textile mills at about $920 per metric ton. Critics charge, however, that buyers then underreport their purchases and sell the surplus on open world markets at about twice the price—$1800. Supplies are also diverted to small local cotton mills, where labor is cheaper and taxes go uncollected. Naturally, at the mills for which the cotton was originally intended, shortages become critical. The No. 1 Cotton Mill in Wuhan has been completely shut down for weeks at a time, and 9000 workers are often in danger of being unemployed for longer stretches. The director of the factory acknowledges that, ironically, the culprits are inspired by the profit motive: "This is the problem," he explains, "that you have in the transition from a planned to a market economy."

Meanwhile, 70 000 out of 90 000 workers at Wuhan Iron and Steel Co. have been shifted to jobs at smaller subsidiary firms. Once guaranteed salaries and pensions by the state, they have been informed that their futures now depend on the profitability of their new employers. "We are helping the workers mount a horse and leading it a short distance and hoping it will gallop," explains the president of Wuhan Steel.

In 1997, China will become the new owner of the former British Crown Colony of Hong Kong. The success of the Hong Kong-Guangdong expermiment, as well as other capitalist initiatives in China, will play a large part in determining how far China will go in its experiment with capitalism.

---

government-operated enterprises are inefficient, since management positions are frequently filled based on political considerations rather than ability. Extensive public welfare systems have also resulted in very high taxes. Because of these factors, socialism is generally declining in popularity.[4]

In Israel, even the kibbutz concept is being questioned. In a kibbutz, members contribute their services in producing goods and then share equally in the resources that are generated. The emphasis is on teamwork and absolute equality. But at Kibbutz Ein Ziwan, a monument to socialist values, several historic practices (communal cars, central dining facilities) have been abandoned because they are no longer affordable. In addition, the kibbutz will soon take a dramatic step: paying people based on how productive they are, rather than on the equal-sharing basis of the past. Other kibbutzim are also considering taking this step.[5]

Market Economies.   A *market* is a mechanism for exchange between the buyers and sellers of a particular good or service. To understand how a *market* *economy* works, consider what happens when a customer goes to a fruit stand to buy apples. Let's say that while one vendor is selling apples for $1 per pound, another is charging $1.50. Both vendors are free to charge what they want, and customers are free to buy what they choose. If both vendors' apples are of the same quality, the customer will buy the cheaper ones. But if the $1.50 apples are fresher, the customer may buy them instead. In short, both buyers and sellers enjoy freedom of choice.

Market economies rely on markets, not governments, to decide what, when, and for whom to produce. **Capitalism** provides for the private ownership of the factors of production. It also encourages entrepreneurship by offering profits as an incentive. Businesses can provide whatever goods and services and charge whatever prices they choose. Similarly, customers can choose how and where they spend their money.[6] Businesses that produce inefficiently or fail to provide needed or desired products will not survive. At least that is the theory in "pure" market economies.

capitalism

A market economy; an economic system in which markets decide what, when, and for whom to produce.

Mixed Economies.   The economic systems we have described differ greatly from each other, but the fact is that no country in the world today has a purely communistic, socialistic, or capitalistic economy. As already noted, for example, the People's Republic of China has begun encouraging some entrepreneurial activity. Both England and France maintain government control of some industries but allow free market operations in others. Government planners in Japan give special assistance to "sunrise industries"—those expected to grow. In Canada, the federal government regulates many aspects of business. And many utilities are owned by provincial governments. Thus, most of the world's countries have a **mixed economy** in which one of the basic economic systems dominates but elements of the other systems are present as well.

mixed economy

An economic system with elements of both a planned economy and a market economy; in practice, typical of most nations' economies.

Basis of the Canadian Economic System

Understanding the complex nature of the Canadian economic system is essential to understanding Canadian businesses. In the next few pages, we will examine the workings of our market economy in more detail. Specifically, we look at markets, demand, supply, the business cycle, private enterprise, and degrees of competition.

market

An exchange process between buyers and sellers of a particular good or service.

demand

The willingness and ability of buyers to purchase a product or service.

Markets, Demand, and Supply

In economic terms, a **market** is not a specific place, like a supermarket, but an exchange process between buyers and sellers. Decisions about production in a market economy are the result of millions of exchanges. How much of what product a company offers for sale and who buys it depends on the laws of demand and supply.

Basically, **demand** is the willingness and ability of buyers to purchase a product or service. **Supply** is the willingness and ability of producers to offer a good or service for sale. The **law of demand** states that buyers will purchase (demand) more of a product as its price drops. For example, assuming you like corn chips, you are likely to buy more and more of them as the price drops. At a price of 50 cents for the "large, economy-size" bag, you and other chip lovers would buy them in large quantities. This is the kind of thinking that motivated Michael Talker to start Sky Freight Express. Conversely, the **law of supply** states that producers will offer more for sale as the price rises. Corn chip makers, for example, would make more chips if you and other buyers would pay $5.00 for each large bag.

supply

The willingness and ability of producers to offer a good or service for sale.

law of demand

The principle that buyers will purchase (demand) more of a product as price drops.

law of supply

The principle that producers will offer (supply) more of a product as price rises.

A market is an exchange process between buyers and sellers of a particular good or service. For example, a customer exchanges money with a retail grocer for products such as breakfast cereal or toothpaste.

In the market for any product, the laws of demand and supply interact to set a market, or **equilibrium,** price and quantity on which buyers and sellers agree. Figure 1.2 shows this result as the intersection of the demand and supply curves (which are straight lines in this case). Notice that at a price of $1.50, buyers will purchase and Amaizing Chips will supply 300 bags of chips per week.

If Amaizing chose to make any other number of bags of chips, the result would be an inefficient use of resources and lower profits. For example, if Amaizing supplies 400 bags and tries to sell them for $1.50 each, consumers will leave a **surplus** of 100 bags on the shelf. Amaizing will lose the money it spent making those chips. If Amaizing supplies only 200 bags, it will "lose" the extra money it could have made by making 100 more. Even though consumers will pay $2.00 per bag for 200 bags because of the **shortage,** Amaizing earns only $4000 ($2.00 × 200 bags) instead of $4500 ($1.50 × 300 bags). Thus Amaizing, like all businesses, must constantly try to find the right combination of price and quantity supplied to maximize its profits.

This simple example involves only one company, one product, and a handful of buyers. Obviously, the Canadian economy is far more complex. Thousands of companies sell hundreds of thousands of products to millions of buyers every day. But in the end, the result is much the same—companies try to supply the quantity and selection of goods that will earn them the largest profits.

equilibrium
The price and quantity of a product at which the quantities demanded and supplied are equal.

surplus
A situation in which supply exceeds demand at a given price.

shortage
A situation in which demand exceeds supply at a given price.

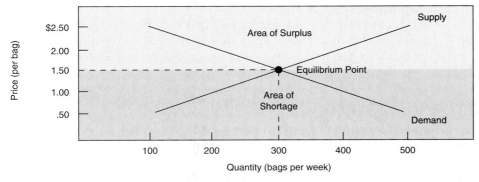

Figure 1.2
A market is governed by the laws of demand and supply. Buyers will purchase more corn chips as the price drops. In contrast, suppliers will produce more corn chips as the price increases. The laws of demand and supply interact to create an equilibrium price and quantity.

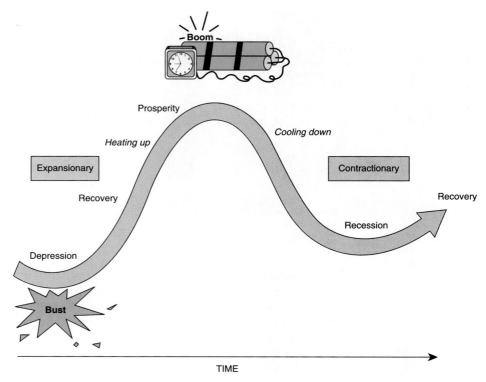

Figure 1.3
The business cycle.

The Business Cycle

business cycle

The fluctuation in the level of economic activity that an economy goes through over time.

The **business cycle** is the fluctuation in the level of economic activity that an economy goes through over time.

The business cycle can be divided into four stages: prosperity, recession, depression, and recovery. The *expansionary* phases are recovery and prosperity. A new business like Sky Freight Express is more likely to be successful if it starts up during the expansionary phases of the business cycle. The *contractionary* stages are recession and depression. During recessions, companies cut back on items like executive travel. At GM Canada, for example, employees have been told to travel less and use the phone more. At McDonald's Restaurants, 300 managers travelled to a convention in Montreal in car pools rather than by air.[7]

Periods of expansion and contraction can vary from several months to several years. As shown in Figure 1.3, a slowdown need not result in a depression if the recovery gets underway before the economy tumbles too far down.

Private Enterprise

private enterprise

An economic system characterized by private property rights, freedom of choice, profits, and competition.

In his book *The Wealth of Nations,* first published in 1776, economist Adam Smith argued that a society's interests are best served by **private enterprise** —allowing individuals within that society to pursue their own interests without governmental regulation or restriction. He believed that because of self-interests, the "invisible hand of competition" would lead businesses to produce the best products they could as efficiently as possible and to sell them at the lowest possible price. Each business would unintentionally be working for the good of society as a whole.

Market economies have prospered in large part due to private enterprise. As Adam Smith first noted, private enterprise requires the presence of four elements: (1) private property rights, (2) freedom of choice, (3) profits, and (4) competition.[8] These elements are shown in Figure 1.4.

Private Property.   Smith maintained that the creation of wealth should be the concern of individuals, not the government. Thus, he argued that the ownership of the resources used to create wealth must be in the hands of individ-

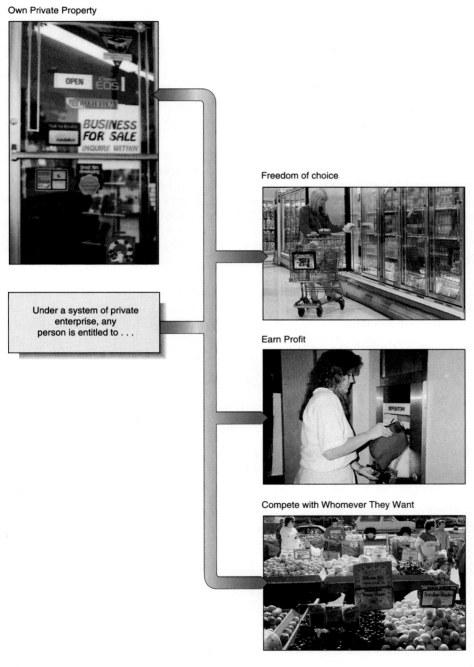

Figure 1.4
A free enterprise system is based on four basic elements. In such a system, all people are entitled to own private property, to choose what to buy and sell, to earn profit, and to compete with whomever they want.

private property

The right to buy, own, use, and sell an item.

uals, not the government. Individual ownership of property is part of everyday life in Canada. You or someone you know has bought and owned automobiles, homes, land, or stock. The right to **private property**—to buy, own, use, and sell almost any form of property—is one of the most fundamental aspects of capitalism. Most of us take private property for granted. Yet, in some countries you could not own a business even if you had the money to pay cash.

freedom of choice

The right to choose what to buy or sell, including one's labor.

Freedom of Choice. **Freedom of choice** means that you can try to sell your labor to whomever you choose. You can also choose which products to buy. Freedom of choice further means that producers of goods and services can usually choose whom to hire and what to make. Under normal circumstances, the government does not go to a manufacturing firm for example, and tell it what kinds of products to make.

Profits. What a company chooses to produce will, by definition, be affected by the *profits* it hopes to make. A business that fails to make a profit must eventually close its doors. The majority of small businesses fail within the first five years of their existence.[9] But the lure of profits leads some people to give up the security of working for someone else and assume the risks of entrepreneurship.

Canadian corporate profits as a percentage of Gross Domestic Product (GDP) have been declining. In 1940, for example, average pretax profits were over 12 percent of GDP, but by 1990 they had dropped to just over 7 percent. Wages, on the other hand, have steadily risen, from 48 percent of GDP in 1940 to over 56 percent in 1990. Corporate income taxes have declined to 12 percent of federal tax revenues in 1988 from 22 percent in 1964.[10]

competition

The vying among businesses in a particular market or industry to best satisfy consumer demands and earn profits.

Competition. If profits motivate individuals to start businesses, **competition** for resources and customers motivates individuals to operate their businesses efficiently. In order to gain an advantage over their competitors in the marketplace, businesses must produce their goods and services for as little as possible and sell them for as much as possible. However, if they are quite successful and their profits are unusually high, other firms will sense an opportunity and also enter the market. The ensuing competition between these firms will drive the prices down. To continue to make a profit, each business must constantly look for more efficient ways to make its products, as well as for new and/or improved products.

Degrees of Competition

Not all industries are equally competitive. Economists have identified four basic degrees of competition within a private enterprise system—pure competition, monopolistic competition, oligopoly, and monopoly. Figure 1.5 illustrates these four degrees of competition.

pure competition

A market or industry characterized by a very large number of small firms producing an identical product so that none of the firms has any ability to influence price.

Pure Competition. In order for **pure competition** to exist, firms must be small in size, but large in number. In such conditions, no firm is powerful enough individually to influence the price of its product in the marketplace.

First, in pure competition the products offered by each firm are so similar that buyers view them as identical to those offered by other firms. Second, both the buyers and sellers know the price that others are paying and receiving in the marketplace. Third, the firms involved in a purely competitive situation are small, which makes it relatively easy for a firm to go into or out of business.

Under pure competition, price is set exclusively by supply and demand in the marketplace. Sellers and buyers must accept the going price. Despite

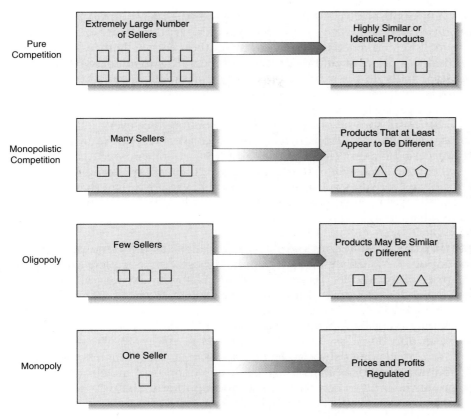

Figure 1.5
There are four basic degrees of competition in a private enterprise system.

some government price-support programs, agriculture is usually considered to be a good example of pure competition in the Canadian economy. The wheat produced on one farm is essentially the same as wheat produced on another farm. Both producers and buyers are well aware of prevailing market prices. Moreover, it is relatively easy to get started or to quit producing wheat.

Monopolistic Competition.   In **monopolistic competition**, there are fewer sellers than in pure competition, but there are still many buyers. Sellers try to make their products at least appear to be slightly different from those of their competitors by tactics such as brand names (Tide and Cheer), design or styling (Ralph Lauren and Izod clothes), and advertising (as done by Coke and Pepsi).

   Monopolistically competitive businesses may be large or small, because it is relatively easy for a firm to enter or leave the market. For example, many small clothing manufacturers compete successfully with large apparel makers. Product differentiation also gives sellers some control over the price they charge. Thus Ralph Lauren Polo shirts can be priced with little regard for the price of Eaton's shirts, even though the Eaton's shirts may have very similar styling.

Oligopoly.   When an industry has only a handful of sellers, an **oligopoly** exists. As a general rule, these sellers are almost always very large. The entry of new competitors is restricted because a large capital investment is usually necessary to enter the industry. Consequently, oligopolistic industries (such as the automobile, rubber, and steel industries) tend to stay oligopolistic.

monopolistic competition
A market or industry characterized by a large number of firms supplying products that are similar but distinctive enough from one another to give firms some ability to influence price.

oligopoly
A market or industry characterized by a small number of very large firms that have the power to influence the price of their product and/or resources.

Oligopolists have even more control over their alternatives than do monopolistically competitive firms. However, the actions of any one firm in an oligopolistic market can significantly affect the sales of all other firms. When one reduces prices or offers some type of incentives to increase its sales, the others usually do the same in order to protect their sales. Likewise, when one raises its prices, the others generally follow suit. As a result, the prices of comparable products are usually quite similar.

Since substantial price competition would reduce every seller's profits, firms use product differentiation to attract customers. For example, the four major cereal makers (Kellogg, General Mills, General Foods, and Quaker Oats) control almost all of the cereal market. Each charges roughly the same price for its cereal as do the others. But each also advertises that its cereals are better tasting or more nutritious than the others.[11] Competition within an oligopolistic market can be fierce.

monopoly
A market or industry with only one producer, who can set the price of its product and/or resources.

natural monopoly
A market or industry in which having only one producer is most efficient because it can meet all of consumers' demand for the product.

Monopoly.   When an industry or market has only one producer, a **monopoly** exists. Being the only supplier gives a firm complete control over the price of its product. Its only constraint is how much consumer demand will fall as its price rises. Until 1992, the long-distance telephone business was a monopoly in Canada, and cable TV, which has had a local monopoly for years, may lose it if telephone companies and satellite broadcasters are allowed into the cable business.[12]

In Canada, laws such as the *Competition Act* forbid many monopolies. In addition, the prices charged by "natural monopolies" are closely watched by provincial utilities boards. **Natural monopolies** are industries where one company can most efficiently supply all the product or service that is needed. For example, like most utilities, your provincial electric company is a natural monopoly because it can supply all the power (product) needed in an area. Duplicate facilities—such as two nuclear power plants, two sets of power lines, and so forth—would be wasteful.

Consumers often buy products under conditions of monopolistic competition. For example, there are few differences between different brands of toothpaste, cold tablets, detergents, canned goods, and soft drinks.

Assessing the Canadian Economic System

Thus far we have noted that nations employ a variety of economic systems. We naturally think our economic system works better than those used in other countries. We point with pride to our high standard of living and to our general prosperity. Yet, leaders in other countries believe just as strongly that their systems are best. So how do we really know that our system works as well as we think? To assess the effectiveness of an economic system objectively, we must consider the society's goals, its record in meeting those goals, and the interaction of governmental and non-governmental forces within the economy.

Economic Goals

Nearly every economic system has as its broad goals stability, full employment, and growth. Economies differ in the emphasis they place on each and their approach to achieving them.

Stability.   In economic terms, **stability** is a condition in which the balance between money available and goods produced remains about the same. As a consequence, prices for consumer goods, interest rates, and wages paid to workers change very little. Stability helps maintain equilibrium and predictability for business people, consumers, and workers.

The biggest threat to stability is **inflation**. Inflation is a period of widespread price increases throughout the economic system. Annual inflation in Canada was around 10 percent in the late 1970s and early 1980s but slowed significantly in the early 1990s. The box "Coping with Inflation" describes some of the difficulties that several countries have recently faced because of high inflation. Figure 1.6 shows how inflation has varied over the years in Canada.

stability

A situation in which the relationship between the supply of money and goods, services, and labor remains constant.

inflation

A period of widespread price increases throughout an economic system.

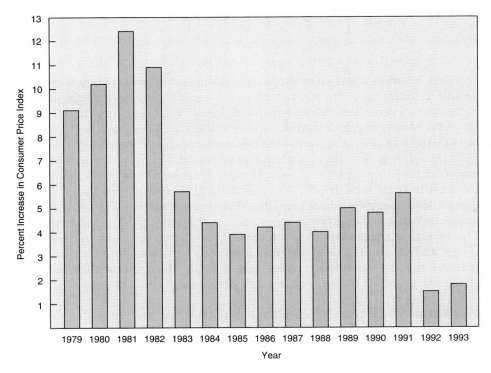

Figure 1.6
In the last few years the rate of price increases in Canada has levelled off.

International Report

COPING WITH INFLATION

For most of the twentieth century, Canadians have taken for granted that inflation will not be a serious problem. While the annual inflation rate in Canada occasionally creeps up to 10 or 12 percent, this is nothing compared to the 500 percent experienced in Brazil in 1994, and the 4200 percent experienced in Argentina in 1989.

Argentina attempted to fight inflation by swapping its nearly worthless austral for a new peso valued at one to one with the U.S. dollar. By doing this, they hoped to develop a currency that Argentines could believe in. But conditioned as they were to high inflation, businesses initially continued to raise prices even after the new currency had been introduced. Over time, however, the inflation rate has gradually come down, and by 1994 was in the neighborhood of 120 percent per year. Unfortunately, the new peso is overvalued by as much as 40 percent, and purchasing power is lower than it was before the plan was introduced. Many people who were formerly part of the middle class have been pushed into the lower class.

Brazil's annual inflation has exceeded 100 percent each year for the last decade. Recently, the rate has climbed even higher, exceeding 500 percent according to some indexes. These high rates have been caused primarily by chronic government deficits and excessive government spending. Individuals cope with these high rates using various strategies. One popular method is to pay by cheque and date the cheque as much as 10 days later. On the tenth day, the person takes the money from an interest-bearing account and puts it in an empty chequing account. But even these strategies may not help. Doctors note that the number of heart and stroke victims was up 20 percent in 1993, and they think that high inflation is the culprit because it increases the stress that people feel.

Like Argentina, Brazil is making a concerted effort to get inflation under control by introducing a new currency (the *real*, pronounced ray-AL) and tying it to the U.S. dollar. Unlike Argentina, there is no law guaranteeing convertibility of one real for one dollar, nor is there any law that forbids the central bank from printing money not backed by reserves. The expectations of Brazilians are crucial to the success of the plan. If they think the government will not back up the plan if the going gets tough, then the country is likely to experience a new round of inflation soon.

These stories of high inflation in other countries may come as a surprise to Canadians. Inflation in Canada dropped to very low levels in the early 1990s, and by the middle of 1994 *deflation*—a decline in price levels—was experienced for the first time since 1955, as consumer prices fell by 0.2 percent. Lowered prices were caused in part by reductions in government tobacco taxes, and by the invasion of retail discounters like Wal-Mart into Canada.

Yet inflation is not necessarily bad. Stability can cause stagnation and a decline in innovation. The onset of inflation is usually a sign of growth. Initially, higher prices cause businesses to expand, hire new workers, pump more dollars into advertising, and introduce new and exciting products and services. New businesses also start up to take advantage of the prosperity.

Inflation is not the only threat to economic stability. Suppose that a major factory in your town closes. Hundreds or even thousands of workers would lose their jobs. If other companies in the area do not have jobs for them, these unemployed people will reduce their spending. Other local businesses will thus suffer drops in sales—and perhaps cut their own workforces. The resulting **recession**, characterized by a decrease in employment, income, and production, may spread across the province and the nation. A particularly severe and long-lasting recession, like the one that affected much of the world in the 1930s, is called a **depression**.

recession

The part of the business cycle characterized by a decrease in employment, income, and production.

depression

A particularly severe and long-lasting recession like the one that affected the world in the 1930s.

Full Employment.   Full employment means that everyone who wants to work has an opportunity to do so. In reality, full employment is impossible. There will always be people looking for work. These people generally fall into one of four categories.

Some people are out of work temporarily while looking for a new job, a situation known as *frictional unemployment*. A skilled engineer who has just quit her job but who will find a new job soon is in this category. Other people are out of work because of the seasonal nature of their jobs, a situation known as *seasonal unemployment.* Farm workers and construction workers, for example, may not work much in the winter. Sometimes people are out of work because of reduced economic activity, a situation known as *cyclical unemployment.* For example, many oil field workers in Alberta lost their jobs during the petroleum glut of the late 1980s. Some regained their jobs when stability returned, while many others moved to jobs in other industries. Finally, some people are unemployed because they lack the skills needed to perform available jobs, a situation known as *structural unemployment.* A steel worker laid off in a town looking for computer programmers falls into this category.

Because of the many reasons for unemployment, the rate of unemployment has varied greatly over the years, as Figure 1.7 shows. And because full employment is essentially impossible, our real goal is to minimize unemployment. High unemployment wastes talent and is a drain on resources that must be allocated to unemployment-associated welfare programs. Higher welfare costs, in turn, result in higher taxes for everyone.

Growth.   A final goal of our economic system is **growth**, an increase in the amount of goods and services produced by our own resources. In theory, we all want our system to expand—more businesses, more jobs, more wealth for everyone. In practice, growth is difficult without triggering inflation and other elements of instability. However, an extended period of no growth may eventually result in an economic decline—business shutdowns, a loss of jobs, a general decrease in overall wealth, and a poorer standard of living for everyone.

growth
An increase in the amount of goods and services produced using the same resources.

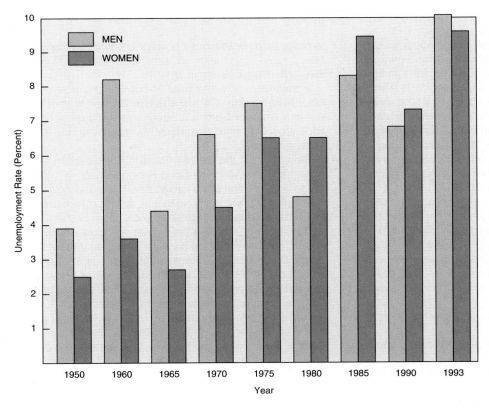

Figure 1.7
There has been a gradual upward trend in unemployment rates, with women having higher rates than men in several recent years.

For many decades, Canada experienced growth rates in excess of most nations. More recently, however, countries such as South Korea, Taiwan, Japan, and Germany all had higher growth rates than Canada, in part because they became increasingly more efficient at producing goods and services.[13]

This should not lead us to be depressed about Canada's economic prospects. Canada has a strong economy in the minds of others (see the box "The Outlook for Canada").

Measuring Economic Performance

In order to judge how well an economic system is achieving its goals, economists use one or more of the following measures: standard of living, gross national product, productivity, the balance of trade, and national debt.

standard of living
A measure of a society's economic well-being.

Standard of Living.   The **standard of living** is a measure of a society's economic well-being. It helps us to observe the change in a society's well-being over time and to compare one society's well-being with that of another. Canadians have become used to expecting their living standards to increase as time goes on. But we may be entering a period when living standards will

The Canadian Business Scene

THE OUTLOOK FOR CANADA

Outsiders often see more positive things about Canada than Canadians do. The Organization for Economic Cooperation and Development (OECD), for example, views Canada as a high-performing economy in need of some fine tuning. This contrasts sharply with the view of many Canadians that our international competitiveness is woefully inadequate. The International Monetary Fund (IMF) is also an admirer. It says that Canada will be the fastest growing economy among the "Group of Seven" (G-7) industrial countries, and we will have lower inflation rates than everyone except Japan.

While there are areas of concern in Canada's economy (high national debt, large annual budget deficits, a fluctuating dollar, and high taxes), the many positive aspects should not be overlooked. Most fundamentally, Canada is positioning itself in areas that are going to be the wave of the future, including electronics, telecommunications, health care, and financial services. Consider these facts:

- Canada's electronics industry is larger than its pulp-and-paper industry.
- More Albertans work in financial services than in the oil and gas industry.
- More workers in British Columbia are involved in telecommunications than in the entire forest industry.

Even Michael Porter, the Harvard University professor who wrote a report that was critical of Canada's international competitiveness, is quick to admit that Canada has already made major adjustments on the way to getting its economic house in order.

Foreign investors also seem to see Canada more positively than many Canadians do. Robert Hormats, vice-chairman of Goldman Sachs International of New York, says that, relative to other countries, Canada is in pretty good shape.

One cloud on the horizon: Canada's credit rating was downgraded by Moody's Bond Rating Service in 1995; that may discourage some foreign investment and increase the interest rate we will have to offer to attract investors.

Perhaps Canadians are self-critical because they live next to the U.S., which is the richest economy on earth. What Canadians may not consider is that our productivity and Gross Domestic Product (GDP) per capita are 94 percent of that in the U.S. In addition, Canadians enjoy advantages in other important areas. Medical coverage in Canada is widely available at a cost of 9 percent of GDP; in the U.S., millions of people are excluded and yet the cost is still 12 percent of GDP. In Canada, 8.6 percent of children live in poverty; in the U.S., the figure is 19.8 percent. The murder rate in Canada is 2.2 per 100 000 people; in the U.S., the rate is 8.3 per 100 000 people. A recent United Nations quality-of-life study rated Canada as the second-best place in the world to live.

not increase at all. Infometrica, an Ottawa-based economic consulting firm, predicts that in real terms, consumer disposable income will show no increase at all for the 1990s.[14]

Gross National Product.   If you add up the total value of all the goods and services produced by an economic system during a one-year period, the sum is the system's **gross national product**, or **GNP**. GNP is a useful indicator of economic growth because it allows us to track an economy's performance over time. Canada's GNP was over $687 billion in 1993.

Because inflation and other factors can change the value of the dollar, however, we compare economies based on an adjusted figure called **real gross national product**. Real GNP is GNP that is adjusted for inflation and changes in the value of a country's currency. The United States has the highest real GNP per capita of any industrial nation in the world (almost $21 000 U.S.). Meanwhile, real GNP per capita in Japan is only slightly over $14 000. Other countries with relatively high real GNP per capita include Canada (almost $19 000), Norway (almost $17 000), and Germany (almost $15 000).

Productivity.   As a measure of economic growth, **productivity** describes how much is produced relative to the resources used to produce it. That is, if Mind Computers can produce a personal computer for $1000 but Canon needs $1200 to produce a comparable computer, Mind is more productive. The box "Productivity Problems at Canadian National Railways" describes how productivity ideas are used to compare business firms. Chapter 13 provides a detailed look at productivity.

Balance of Trade.   Another commonly used measure of economic performance is the **balance of trade**, the total of a country's exports to other countries minus its imports from other countries. A positive balance of trade is generally considered to be favorable because new money flows into the country from the sales of exports. A negative balance is less favorable because money is flowing out of the country from the purchase of imports. Canada has enjoyed a favorable balance of trade since the mid-1970s, but the balance is favorable only because Canada exports so much to the United States. Our balance of trade with most other countries is unfavorable.

National Debt.   Like a business, the government takes in revenues (primarily in the form of taxes) and has expenses (military spending, social programs, and so forth). For the last several years, Canada has been running a **budget deficit**: It has been spending more money than it has been taking in. This deficit has created a huge **national debt**—the amount of money that Canada owes its creditors. We discuss this in more detail in Chapter 3.

Managing the Canadian Economy

The government manages the economic system through two sets of policies. **Fiscal policies** refer to the collection and spending of government revenues. Tax policies, for example, can function as fiscal policy to increase revenues. Similarly, budget cuts (for example, closing military bases) function as fiscal policy when spending is decreased.

Monetary policies focus on controlling the size of the nation's money supply. Working primarily through the Bank of Canada (the nation's central bank), the government can influence the ability and willingness of banks throughout the country to lend money. It can also influence the supply of money by prompting interest rates to go up or down. A primary goal in recent years has been to adjust interest rates so that inflation is kept in check.

gross national product (GNP)
The total of all goods and services produced by an economic system during a one-year period.

real gross national product
Gross national product adjusted for inflation and changes in the value of a country's currency.

productivity
A measure of efficiency that compares how much is produced with the resources used to produce it.

balance of trade
The total of a country's exports (sales to other countries) minus its imports (purchases from other countries).

budget deficit
The result of the government spending more in one year than it takes in during that year.

national debt
The total amount of money that Canada owes its creditors (presently over $550 billion).

fiscal policies
Policies by means of which governments collect and spend revenues.

monetary policies
Policies by means of which the government controls the size of the nation's money supply.

The Canadian Business Scene

PRODUCTIVITY PROBLEMS AT CANADIAN NATIONAL RAILWAYS

According to a special report by its own accounting department, Canadian National Railways runs one of the least competitive railways in North America. The major findings of the study are as follows:

1. CN has substantially more employees and twice as many administrators as the typical major railway in the U.S.
2. Expenses are increasing at CN, but decreasing at U.S. railroads.
3. Since 1988, revenues have steadily fallen at CN, but have steadily risen in the U.S.
4. Labor costs were the largest component of CN's expenses, with over 45 percent of each revenue dollar going to meet payroll obligations (U.S. railroads averaged only 28 percent).

There are some differences between Canadian and U.S. railroads that might explain these numbers. For example, CN operates under difficult winter conditions that most U.S. railroads don't have to cope with. As well, CN operates more miles of track than most U.S. railroads, and much of this track does not get a lot of use. However, the Burlington Northern Railroad operates 6400 more kilometres of track than CN, yet has only 4500 administrators (CN employs over 11 000 administrators).

In one of the most important indicators of labor productivity—revenue ton miles (RTM) per employee—CN finished in last place. This measure is computed by taking the tons of freight carried, multiplying that figure by the number of miles it was carried, and then dividing by the number of employees. CN's RTM was 2.54, which is less than half of what U.S. railroads averaged. The statistics for administrative employees are even more distressing. For every administrative employee, CN generated less than one-third of the U.S. average of RTM's.

One interesting finding emerged from this study: CN has far fewer train engineers than the typical U.S. railroad—6561 compared with the average of 9379 for U.S. railroads. It also has the smallest number of locomotives per train (2.56 versus 3.38 for U.S. railroads), and they pull the largest number of cars per locomotive.

Summary of Key Points

Organizations that produce or sell goods or services to make a profit are called businesses. Profit is the difference between a business's expenses and its sales revenues.

An economic system is the way a nation distributes its resources to its citizens. Economic systems differ in terms of who owns and/or controls the four basic factors of production: material resources, labor, capital, and entrepreneurs. In planned economies, government controls all or most factors. In market economies, individuals control the factors. Generally speaking, communist and socialist countries have planned economies. Capitalism is based on a market economy. Most countries today have mixed economies dominated by one of these systems but including elements of the others.

The Canadian economy is strongly influenced by markets, demand, and supply. Demand and supply work together to set a market, or equilibrium, price and quantity.

The Canadian economy is founded on the principles of private enterprise: private property rights, freedom of choice, profits, and competition. Degrees of competition include pure competition, monopolistic competition, oligopoly, and monopoly.

The basic goals of the Canadian economic system include stability, full employment, and growth. The standard of living, gross national product, productivity, the balance of trade, and the national debt are measures of how well an economy has met these goals.

Filofax—Back from the Brink

The six-ring Filofax binder is one of the legendary products that have come out of Britain. It was a "must-have" for British vicars and army officers during the 1920s and then a status symbol for yuppies in the 1980s. In the 1990s, the users are typically women who are trying to cope with a busy schedule of children and work.

Filofax grew slowly over many years under the direction of Grace Scurr, who started at the firm as a temporary worker and rose to the position of chairwoman. She left the company in the 1960s. Sales were less than $200 000 per year in the early 1980s, when the company was bought by David Collischon. Soon a bewildering array of new binders were being offered by the company. When Filofax binders became a Yuppie in-product, Collischon found that he could raise prices and still increase sales. At one point, Filofax binders were selling for twice as much as other functionally equal binders.

By the mid-1980s, annual sales had increased to nearly $30 million, and the company had expanded from a hus-band-and-wife operation to one with 250 employees. The company went public in 1987, but problems began in 1988 when sales began to decline. A management consultant was brought in to help solve the problem. He discovered that the company had lost sight of its customers needs and had to return the basics that had made it successful for so many years. The company abandoned many of its product lines and in the 1990s has refocused on price-conscious consumers. Much of the manufacturing work is now contracted out, and the work force has been cut from 250 to 75. The consultant is continually looking for ways to cut costs further.

These and other actions have restored the company to profitability. Sales in 1993 exceeded $40 million and profits topped $6 million.

CASE QUESTIONS
1. How are the factors of production used at Filofax?
2. How does Filofax illustrate the strengths of the private enterprise system? The weaknesses? ◆

University Pizza

You have just arrived home from a hard day of classes and you settle down to read the evening newspaper. You note with interest an article about a provincially supported university that is selling pizza and is making a lot of money doing so. The vice-president of the university is quoted: "We got involved in this business because the provincial legislature has sharply reduced our funding, so, we are exploring creative ways to make up for the lack of public funds." The vice-president goes on to say that the more money the university makes from its business activities, the less money students will have to pay for tuition. According to the article, students are generally supportive of the idea.

The article also notes that several retail merchants are not happy that the university is running a business. They argue that the university is being supported by public money and that it should stick to educating students and not compete with private sector firms. The provincial legislature is also interested; a private member's bill, rumored to be ready for introduction, would prohibit any university from getting involved in retail sales that "can reasonably be expected to create a significant level of general competition with private stores."

CASE QUESTIONS
1. Explain how the concept of business opportunity applies in this case.
2. How would you respond to the argument by retailers that the university should not be in the business of selling products?
3. If you were a member of the provincial legislature, would you support the proposed legislation banning university involvement in retail sales? Why or why not? ◆

Key Terms

business	capitalism	private property	growth
profit	mixed economy	freedom of choice	standard of living
economic system	market	competition	gross national product
factors of production	demand	pure competition	(GNP)
natural resources	supply	monopolistic competition	real gross national
labor	law of demand	oligopoly	product
capital	law of supply	monopoly	productivity
entrepreneur	equilibrium	natural monopoly	balance of trade
planned economy	surplus	stability	budget deficit
market economy	shortage	inflation	national debt
communism	business cycle	recession	fiscal policies
socialism	private enterprise	depression	monetary policies

Study Questions and Exercises

Review Questions

1. What are the factors of production? Is one more important than the others? If so, which one? Why?
2. What are the major characteristics of a market economy? How does a market economy differ from a planned economy?
3. Explain the differences in the four degrees of competition and give an example of each. (Do not use the examples given in the text).
4. Why is productivity important? Why is inflation both good and bad?

Analysis Questions

5. Select a local business and identify the basic factors of production that it uses. Now identify the factors used by your college or university. What are the similarities and differences?
6. In recent years, many countries have moved from planned economies to market economies. Why do you think this has occurred? Can you envision a situation that would cause a resurgence of planned economies?
7. Identify a situation in which excess supply of a product led to decreased prices. Identify a situation in which a shortage led to increased prices. What eventually happened in each case? Why?

Application Exercises

8. Choose a locally owned and operated business. Interview the owner to find out what factors of production the business uses and its sources for acquiring them.
9. Visit a local shopping mall or shopping area. List each store you see and determine what degree of competition it faces in that environment. How do other businesses compete to market goods or services?
10. Go to the library and read about ten different industries. Classify each according to degree of competition.

Building Your Business Skills

Goal

To encourage students to understand how the competitive environment affects a product's price.

Situation

Suppose that you open an ice-cream parlor in a community that has three other ice-cream shops within an area of four city blocks. During the first six months, you charge $1.50 for each ice-cream cone—the same price as your competitors. Just as summer begins, however, one competitor drops the price to $1.25. Within a week, the others follow suit. Your break-even price per cone is $1. You are thus concerned about getting into a price war that may destroy your business.

Method

Divide into groups of four or five people. The mission of each group is to develop a general strategy for handling the competitors' price changes. In your discussion, take the following factors into account:

- how the demand for your product is affected by price changes

- the number of competitors selling the same or a similar product
- the methods you can use—other than price—to attract new customers.

Analysis

Develop specific pricing strategies based on the following situations:

- Within a week after dropping the price to $1.25, one of your competitors raises the price back to $1.50.
- Two of your competitors drop their prices further—to $1 a cone. As a result, your business drops by 30 percent.
- On August 1, at the height of the summer season, one of the stores that dropped its price to $1 goes out of business. Of the remaining stores, one holds the price at $1 while the other sells cones for $1.25.

Follow-up Questions

1. How is it possible to create a demand for your product through inducements that are not price-related, including customer service, store environment, and location?
2. Is it always in a company's best interest to feature the lowest prices?

2

Setting Up Business in Canada

LEARNING OBJECTIVES

After studying this chapter, you will be able to

- Identify the major forms of business ownership.
- Discuss sole proprietorships and partnerships and identify their advantages and disadvantages.
- Describe the structure and operation of corporations.
- Identify several special forms of business ownership.
- Describe three recent innovations in business ownership form.
- Trace the history of business in Canada.

CHAPTER OUTLINE

OPENING CASE

Employee Buyouts—Good News and Bad News

During the past few years, the idea of employee buyouts has become increasingly popular in both Canada and the U.S. In the U.S., for example, several of the largest firms in the commercial airline industry—United, TWA, and Northwest—recently became employee-owned. At United, the pilots and machinists unions now own 53 percent of the company. In exchange, they made concessions like agreeing to a no-strike clause.

In Canada, there are several prominent examples of employee buyouts. The most famous is probably the buyout of the Temiscaming, Quebec, forest products plant in 1972. International Paper sold the mill to the Quebec government, which kept a 40 percent stake and sold the rest to managers and an investment company. The mill has been profitable ever since. In 1991, the Ontario government helped finance a deal that allowed workers to save the Kimberly-Clark mill at Kapuskasing, Ontario. The workers paid $12.5 million for 52 percent ownership. Skeptics doubted whether the deal would be as successful as Temiscaming, but they were proved wrong. In its first quarter of operations, the mill made a profit of nearly $500 000. At Algoma Steel, employees bought a 60 percent ownership in the company as part of a bailout deal by the Ontario government.

An interesting, but less well-known case, is that of Great Western Brewery. In 1990, Molson Cos. Ltd. decided to close the Carling O'Keefe brewery in Saskatoon. The company offered to transfer workers to other plants, but Don Ebelher, the maintenance chief at the brewery, and 14 other workers bought the plant because they felt they would have more job security working for themselves. Each person put up between $50 000 and $100 000 for the 25 percent equity required. The rest of the money came from a loan through Saskatchewan's Economic Development Corp. Ebelher is now Great Western's CEO.

In this employee-owned company, employee initiative is high, consultation and teamwork are facts of life, the management structure is very flat, and everyone takes pride in their work because they own the company. The firm still needs managers, but they behave quite differently than their predecessors. They work much more closely with production workers and often discuss ways to improve the way that work is done. In a traditional organization, this typically wouldn't happen. The marketing manager at Great Western, Jack White, says that consultation with employees has made him a better manager. The company has four managers instead of the 12 it had when it was owned by Molson. The total number of employees has dropped from 65 to 55.

Interestingly, the workers are represented by a union. Why have a union in an employee-owned company? The local union president says that because Canadian brewing has traditionally been dominated by unions, there is still a competitive advantage to be gained by shipping products with a union label. But employees in this company have not demanded big wage increases because, as owners, they are keeping the financial health of the company in mind.

Problems exist in employee-owned firms, just as they do in traditionally-owned businesses. At Great Western, for example, demand for the new company's product exceeded expectations, so workers felt they had to work long hours and scrape together left-over assembly line parts in order to increase production. Some employees routinely work 60- or 70-hour weeks. But after these problems had been solved, the company's beer lost its novelty status in the marketplace, and its market share declined from its original 20 percent down to 8 percent. At present, the plant is operating at less than 50 percent capacity.

Difficulties are also evident in other employee-owned firms. In the U.S. airline industry, employee buyouts have occurred typically in financially troubled companies. But with the intense competition in that industry and the large losses currently being experienced by the airlines, it is not clear whether employee ownership can lead to improved financial performance.

At Algoma Steel, bonuses for top executives were cancelled in 1994 even though the company made a $16 million profit for the first quarter. Workers had given up $3 an hour as part of the original employee buyout plan, and the president felt that it would be inappropriate for him to take a large bonus after the workers had made big sacrifices. So he gave up his $400 000 bonus. A recent employee survey strongly favored limiting the compensation of top executives. If lowered compensation makes it harder for the firm to attract top quality executives, company performance may decline.

Some employee-owned firms have found that they do not have the financial resources to achieve desired goals. Relcon Ltd., which makes electronic drives that regulate the speed of electric motors, became an employee-owned firm way back in 1960 when the founder of the firm died and the employees bought out his interest. Although the firm was profitable, it was never able to crack export markets because it didn't have the money to do so. But when it was taken over by Siemens AG, the German electronics giant, it suddenly had the necessary resources to become a player on the international scene. ◆

In this chapter we will consider the dynamics of business ownership in Canada. After you understand the major types of business structures—and some special forms—you can appreciate how business organizations have evolved throughout the history of Canada.

Types of Business Organizations

All business owners must decide which form of legal organization—a sole proprietorship, a partnership, a corporation or a cooperative—best suits them and their business. Few decisions are more critical, since the choice affects a host of managerial and financial issues, including income taxes and the owners' liability. In choosing a legal form of organization, the parties concerned must consider their likes, dislikes, and dispositions, their immediate and long-range needs, and the advantages and disadvantages of each form. Seldom, if ever, does any one factor completely determine which form is best.[1]

Sole Proprietorships

As the very first legal form of business organization, **sole proprietorships** date back to ancient times. They are still the most numerous form of business in Canada. Despite their numbers, however, they account for only a small proportion of total business revenues in this country.

sole proprietorship
A business owned (and usually operated) by one person who is personally responsible for the firm's debts.

Because most sole proprietorships are small, often employing only one person, you might assume that all are small businesses. However, sole proprietorships may be as large as a steel mill or as small as a lemonade stand. Some of Canada's largest companies started out as sole proprietorships. Eaton's, for example, was originally a one-man operation founded by Timothy Eaton. One of Canada's biggest sole proprietorships is the Jim Pattison Group, with sales of $3 billion and 15 000 employees (see the boxed insert on page 179). Figure 2.1 summarizes the basic advantages and disadvantages of the sole proprietorship form of ownership.

Advantages.   Freedom is the most striking feature of sole proprietorships. Because they alone own their businesses, sole proprietors need answer to no one but themselves. They can also maintain a high level of privacy, since they are not required to report information about their operations to anyone.

Sole proprietorships are simple to form. Sole proprietors often need only put a sign on their door in order to go into business for themselves. They are also easy to dissolve. Rock concerts or athletic events may be organized as sole proprietorships by individuals who then dissolve the business entity when the event is over.

Low start-up costs are yet another attractive feature of sole proprietorships. Legal fees are likely to be low, since some sole proprietorships need only register the business with the provincial government in order to make sure that no other business bears the same name. Some proprietorships do need to take out licences, however. For example, restaurants and pet shops need special licences.

Sole proprietorships also offer tax benefits for new businesses likely to suffer losses before profits begin to flow. Tax laws permit sole proprietors to treat the sales revenues and operating expenses of the business as part of their personal finances. Thus, a proprietor can cut taxes by deducting any operating losses from income earned from sources other than the business.

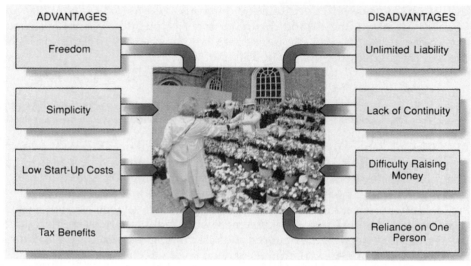

Figure 2.1
The most popular form of business ownership in Canada is the sole proprietorship. There are both advantages and disadvantages to this form of ownership.

Since most businesses lose money at the beginning, this tax situation is very helpful to entrepreneurs starting up.

unlimited liability
A person who invests in a business is liable for all debts incurred by the business; personal possessions can be taken to pay debts.

liquidate
Sell the assets of a business.

Disadvantages.   One major drawback of sole proprietorships is their **unlimited liability**. A sole proprietor is personally liable for all debts incurred by the business. Bills must be paid out of the sole proprietor's own pocket if the business fails to generate enough cash. Otherwise, creditors can step in and claim the proprietor's personal possessions, including a home, furniture, and automobile. (Actually, the law does protect some of the proprietor's assets, but many can be claimed). The impact of unlimited liability is described in the box "Unlimited Liability at Lloyd's of London."

Another disadvantage is lack of continuity. A sole proprietorship legally dissolves when the owner dies. The business can, of course, be reorganized soon after the owner's death if a successor has been trained to take over the business. Otherwise, executors or heirs must **liquidate** (sell the assets of) the business.

Finally, a sole proprietorship is dependent upon the resources of a single individual. If the proprietor has unlimited resources and is a successful manager, this characteristic is not really a problem. In most cases, however, the proprietor's financial and managerial limits constrain what the organization can do. Sole proprietors often find it hard to borrow money not only to start up, but also to expand. Banks often reject such applications, fearing that they will not be able to recover the loan if the sole proprietor becomes disabled. Often, would-be proprietors must rely on personal savings and loans from family for start-up funds.

Partnerships

A partnership is established when two or more individuals agree to combine their financial, managerial, and technical abilities for the purpose of operating a company for profit. The partnership form of ownership was developed to overcome some of the more serious disadvantages of the sole proprietorship.

International Report

UNLIMITED LIABILITY AT LLOYD'S OF LONDON

Lloyd's of London is one of the most famous insurance companies in the world. It began operations several centuries ago by insuring British merchant ships. The individuals who invest in Lloyd's are called "names." These names have unlimited liability, i.e., they are liable for any losses incurred by the company. Their liability for losses is not limited to their original investment, but rather to the amount of money they have. Thus, their personal property can be seized to pay off their liabilities.

Why would a person invest in a company like Lloyd's when they know they will have unlimited liability? Because historically such investments have yielded good returns. Traditionally, names have been wealthy people who could afford to take the occasional loss. But during the go-go 1980s, many new names were recruited who were not wealthy (but had dreams of wealth). When their involvement brought losses instead of profits, they lost everything they owned. The British press played up cases of names being forced to move out of expensive homes that had been in the family for generations, but many poorer people have also lost their homes.

Why has Lloyd's suddenly run into financial difficulty?

The answer is that changing times are threatening the company. It is becoming clear that an insurance system designed in 1600 cannot cope with certain 20th-century realities—natural disasters, terrorism, pollution, industrial accidents, and a trend toward increasing litigation.

All of these factors have sent insurance claims sky-high. During the last three years, for example, Lloyd's lost a total of $12 billion. In that same period, the number of names has fallen from 27 000 to 19 000. Several members who were part of a group of names that lost $800 million committed suicide. Another group of names from Canada have sued the company, alleging fraud, to prevent Lloyd's from seizing their assets to make good on claims.

In April 1993, Lloyd's CEO David Rowland introduced a plan that would end the company's tradition of unlimited liability and allow corporations to become new members with limited liability. But existing names will continue to have unlimited liability. Late in 1994, the group suing Lloyd's won a lawsuit which said they had been the victims of negligence by professionals in the insurance market. The judgment against Lloyd's could total as much as $1 billion.

There are several different types of partnerships. (See Table 2.1.) Our discussion, however, focuses on the most common type—the **general partnership**.

Partnerships are often an extension of a business that began as a sole proprietorship. The original owner may want to expand, or the business may have grown too big for a single person to handle. Many professional organizations, such as legal, architecture, and accounting firms, are also organized as partnerships. Figure 2.2 summarizes the advantages and disadvantages of the partnership form of organization.

general partnership
A business with two or more owners who share in the operation of the firm and in financial responsibility for the firm's debts.

Advantages.   The most striking feature of general partnerships is their ability to grow by adding talent and money. Partnerships also have a somewhat easier time borrowing funds than do sole proprietorships. Banks and other lending institutions prefer to make loans to enterprises that are not dependent on a single individual.

Like a sole proprietorship, a partnership is simple to organize, with few legal requirements. Even so, all partnerships must begin with an agreement of some kind. It may be written, oral, or even unspoken. Wise partners, however, insist on a written agreement to avoid trouble later. This agreement should answer such questions as

- Who invested what sums of money in the partnership?
- Who will receive what share of the partnership's profits?
- Who does what and who reports to whom?
- How may the partnership be dissolved? In that event, how would leftover assets be distributed among the partners?

TABLE 2.1   Types of Partnerships and Partners

Types of Partnerships

General partnership	All partners have unlimited liability for the firm's debts.
Limited partnership	This partnership has at least one general partner and one or more limited partners. The latter's liability is limited to their financial investment in the firm.

Types of Partners

General partner	Actively involved in managing the firm and has unlimited liability.
Secret partner	Actively participates in managing the firm and has unlimited liability. A secret partner's identity is not disclosed to the public.
Dormant partner	Does not actively participate in managing the firm. A dormant partner's identity is not disclosed to the public. Has unlimited liability.
Ostensible partner	Not an actual partner but his or her name is identified with the firm. Usually an ostensible partner is a well-known personality. Promotional benefits accrue from using his or her name for which the person is usually paid a fee. Has unlimited liability.
Limited partner	Liability is limited to the amount invested in the partnership.

■ How would surviving partners be protected from claims by surviving heirs if a partner dies?

Although it helps to clarify how partners relate to each other, the partnership agreement is strictly a private document. No laws require partners to file an agreement with some government agency. Nor are partnerships regarded as legal entities. In the eyes of the law, a partnership is nothing more than two or more persons working together. The partnership's lack of legal standing means that Revenue Canada taxes partners as individuals.

Disadvantages.   As with sole proprietorships, unlimited liability is the greatest drawback of general partnerships. By law, each partner may be held personally liable for all debts incurred in the name of the partnership. And if any partner incurs a debt, even if the other partners know nothing about it, they are all liable if the offending partner cannot pay up. For example, right after two men formed a partnership to operate a car wash, their equipment severely damaged a customized van. The owner sued for damages. One partner lacked the funds to cover the loss, even though the partnership agreement specified that he was responsible for equipment liability claims. Fortunately, the other partner agreed to pay half the damages and to loan the money to his partner for the other half.

Another drawback is often lack of continuity. When one partner dies or pulls out, a partnership may dissolve legally, even if the other partners agree to stay. The dissolving of a partnership, however, need not cause a loss of sales revenues. If they wish, the surviving partners can quickly form a new partnership to retain the business of the old firm.

ADVANTAGES   DISADVANTAGES

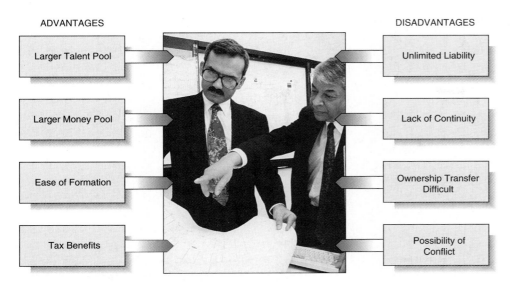

Larger Talent Pool		Unlimited Liability
Larger Money Pool		Lack of Continuity
Ease of Formation		Ownership Transfer Difficult
Tax Benefits		Possibility of Conflict

Figure 2.2
Partnerships are fairly common in professional organizations.

A related drawback is the difficulty of transferring ownership. No partner may sell out without the other partners' consent. Also, a partner who wants to retire or to transfer his or her interest to a son or daughter must receive the other partners' consent. Thus, the life of a partnership may depend on the ability of retiring partners to find someone compatible with the other partners to buy them out. Failure to do so may lead to forced liquidation of the partnership.

Finally, a partnership provides little or no guidance in resolving conflict between the partners. For example, suppose one partner wants to expand the business rapidly and the other wants it to grow slowly. If under the partnership agreement the two are equal, it may be difficult for them to decide what to do. Conflicts can involve anything from personal habits like smoking to hours of operation to managerial practices.

Corporations

Another very common form of business ownership is the **corporation**. Almost all larger businesses in Canada use this form. As Figure 2.3 shows, corporations dominate the manufacturing sector. (See also Table 2.2.)

When you think of corporations you probably think of giant businesses like General Motors of Canada or BCE. The very word *corporation* suggests bigness and power. Yet, the tiny corner newsstand has as much right to incorporate as does a giant oil refiner. And the newsstand and oil refiner have the same basic characteristics that all corporations share: legal status as a separate entity, property rights and obligations, and an indefinite lifespan.

A corporation has been defined as "an artificial being, invisible, intangible, and existing only in contemplation of the law."[2] As such, corporations may

- Sue and be sued.
- Buy, hold, and sell property.
- Make and sell products to consumers.
- Commit crimes and be tried and punished for them.

corporation
A business considered by law to be a legal entity separate from its owners with many of the legal rights and privileges of a person; a form of business organization in which the liability of the owners is limited to their investment in the firm.

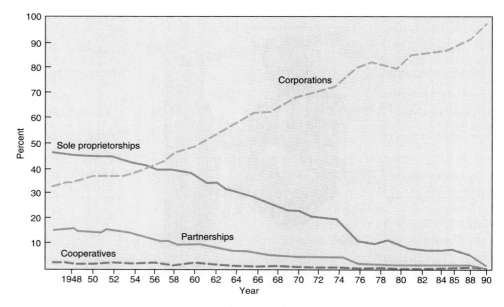

Figure 2.3
Percentage distribution of manufacturing establishments by form of ownership.

Corporations can be found in both the private and the public sector in Canada, although our emphasis is on the private sector. We discuss Crown (government) corporations in Chapter 21.

Formation of the Corporation.   The two most widely used methods to form a corporation are federal incorporation under the *Canada Business Corporations Act* and provincial incorporation under any of the provincial incorporations acts. The former is used if the company is going to operate in more than one province; the latter is used if the founders intend to carry on business in only one province.

Except for banks and certain insurance and loan companies, any company can be federally incorporated under the *Canada Business Corporations Act*. To do so, Articles of Incorporation must be drawn up. These articles include such information as the name of the corporation, the type and number of shares to be issued, the number of directors the corporation will have, and the location of the company's operations. All companies must attach the word "Limited" (Ltd./Ltée) or "Incorporated" (Inc.) to the company name to indicate clearly to customers and suppliers that the owners have limited liability for corporate debts. The same sort of rules apply in other countries. British firms, for example, use PLC for "public limited company" and German companies use AG for "Aktiengesellschaft" (corporation).

Provincial incorporation takes one of two forms. In certain provinces (British Columbia, Alberta, Saskatchewan, Manitoba, Ontario, Newfoundland, Nova Scotia, and the two territories), the registration system or its equivalent is used. Under this system, individuals wishing to form a corporation are required to file a memorandum of association. This document contains the same type of information as required under the *Canada Business Corporations Act*. In the remaining provinces, the equivalent incorporation document is called the letters patent. In Quebec, a corporation may be formed either by issuing a letters patent or by drawing up articles of incorporation. The specific procedures and information required vary from province to province. The basic differences between these incorporation systems is that the registration system forms corporations by authority of parliament, while the letters patent system forms corporations by royal prerogative.

Shares of Stock and Shareholders' Rights.   Corporations can raise money by selling shares in the business—**stock**—to investors, who then are known as **shareholders.** Shareholders are the owners of a business. Business profits are distributed among shareholders in the form of **dividends.** Managers who run a corporation also serve at the discretion of the shareholders. The nature of the relationship between the shareholders, the board of directors, and management has been the focus of much recent discussion.[3]

Why do corporations sell stock? Besides the obvious reason already noted—to raise money—stock makes for an easy transfer of ownership in a corporation. Shareholders can sell their shares to anyone who is willing to buy them (unless the stock certificates say that shareholders must offer to sell them to the corporation first).

Corporate stock may be either preferred or common. **Preferred stock** guarantees those who own it a fixed dividend, much like the interest payment earned in a savings account. Preferred shareholders have priority, or preference, over common shareholders as to dividends and also to assets if a business liquidates. Many major corporations issue preferred stock; few small corporations do.

In contrast, **common stock** usually pays dividends only if the corporation makes a profit. Holders of common stock have the last claim to any assets if the company folds. Dividends on common stock, like those on preferred stock, are paid per share. Thus, a shareholder with ten shares receives ten times the dividend paid a shareholder with one share. Unlike preferred stock, however, common stock *must* be issued by every corporation, big or small.

Preferred shareholders generally do not have voting rights. Common shareholders *always* have voting rights, with each share of common stock carrying one vote. When investors cannot attend a shareholders' meeting, they can grant to someone who will attend authority to vote the shares. This procedure, called voting by **proxy**, is the way almost all individual investors vote.

stock
A share of ownership in a corporation.

shareholders
Those who own shares of stock in a company.

dividend
A part of a corporation's profits paid out per share to those who hold its stock.

preferred stock
Shares whose owners have first claim on the corporation's assets and profits but who usually have no voting rights in the firm.

common stock
Shares whose owners usually have last claim on the corporation's assets (after creditors and owners of preferred stock) but who have voting rights in the firm.

proxy
A legal document temporarily transferring the voting rights of a shareholder to another person.

TABLE 2.2   The Top Ten Corporations in Canada, 1994
(ranked by sales)

Company	Sales (in billions)
1. General Motors of Canada Ltd.	$24.9
2. BCE Inc.	21.6
3. Ford Motor Co. of Canada Ltd.	20.1
4. Chrysler Canada Ltd.	15.7
5. George Weston Ltd.	13.0
6. Alcan Aluminum Ltd.	11.2
7. Ontario Hydro	8.7
8. The Thomson Corp.	8.6
9. IBM Canada Ltd.	8.4
10. Imasco Ltd.	8.1

Ownership of common stock does not automatically give an individual the right to act for the corporation or to share in its management. (Many management personnel do own stock, however.) The only way that most shareholders can influence the running of a corporation is to cast their votes for the board of directors of the corporation once a year. In most cases, however, shareholders' votes are meaningless, since corporations offer only one slate of directors for election.

Even when shareholders have choices, the number of shareholders may mean little real power for individual owners. For example, Noranda has thousands of shareholders, but only a handful of them have enough votes to have any effect on the way the company is run.

board of directors

A group of individuals elected by a firm's shareholders and charged with overseeing, and taking legal responsibility for, the firm's actions.

Board of Directors.   By law, the governing body of a corporation is its **board of directors**. The directors choose the president and other officers of the business and delegate the power to run the day-to-day activities of the business to those officers. The directors set policy on paying dividends, on financing major spending, and on executive salaries and benefits. For example, the board of directors can fire the CEO if the board does not agree with the CEO's business decisions. However, in most cases a board of directors will support the CEO.

Large corporations tend to have large boards with as many as 20 or 30 directors. Smaller corporations, on the other hand, tend to have no more than five directors. Usually, these are people with personal or professional ties to the corporation, such as family members, lawyers, and accountants.

inside directors

Members of a corporation's board of directors who are also full-time employees of the corporation.

Many boards have outside as well as inside directors. **Inside directors** are employees of the company and have primary responsibility for the corporation. That is, they are also top managers, such as the president and

Corporations hold annual meetings with their shareholders. At such meetings, managers summarize what the corporation accomplished during the last year, announce plans for the coming year, and answer questions from individual shareholders. Shareholders also elect new members to the board of directors.

executive vice president. **Outside directors** are not employees of the corporation in the normal course of its business. Attorneys, accountants, university officials, and executives from other firms are commonly used as outside directors. The basic responsibility of both inside and outside directors is the same, however—to insure that the corporation is run in a way that is in the best interests of the shareholders.

Directors also are legally responsible for corporate actions, and they are increasingly being held responsible for their actions (see the box "Hot Seats on the Board of Directors"). For example, a group of shareholders sued the entire board of Microsoft Corporation because the company's failure to meet its profits projections caused the price of its stock to plummet.[4] Boards communicate with shareholders and other potential investors through the corporation's annual report, a summary of the company's financial health.

Officers.   Although board members oversee the corporation's operation, most of them do not participate in day-to-day management. Rather, they hire a team of top managers to run the firm. As we have already seen, this team, called *officers*, is usually headed by the firm's **chief executive officer**, or **CEO**, who is responsible for the firm's overall performance. Other officers typically include a *president*, who is responsible for internal management, and *vice presidents*, who oversee various functional areas like marketing or operations. Some officers may also be elected to serve on the board, and in some cases, a single individual plays multiple roles. For example, one person might serve as board chairperson, CEO, and president. In other cases, a different person fills each slot.

Public Versus Private Corporations.   Some corporations are public, others private. A **public corporation** is one whose stock is widely held and available for sale to the general public. Anyone who has the funds to pay for them can go to a stockbroker and buy shares of Brascan, George Weston, or Canadian Pacific. The stock of a **private corporation,** on the other hand, is held by only a few people and is not generally available for sale. The controlling group may be a family, employees, or the management group. Eaton's and Bata Shoes are private corporations.

Most new corporations start out as private corporations, because few investors will buy an unknown stock. As the corporation grows and develops a record of success, it may decide to issue shares to the public as a way to raise additional money. Apple Computer is just one example of a corporation that "went public." McCain Foods is a large private corporation that has been experiencing problems because of a feud between two of the McCain brothers, Wallace and Harrison. In 1994, they began serious discussions about how to take their company public.[5] Figure 2.4 summarizes the advantages and disadvantages of corporations, both public and private.

Advantages of the Corporation.   Limited liability is the most striking feature of corporations. That is, the liability of investors is limited to their personal investments in the corporation. In the event of failure, the bankruptcy courts may seize a corporation's assets and sell them to pay debts, but the courts cannot touch the personal possessions of investors. Limited liability may be the main reason that many businesses incorporate, but limited liability is meaningless in some cases. For example, if all your personal assets are tied up in a business, then limited liability offers you little protection.

Another advantage of a corporation is continuity. Because it has a legal life independent of its founders, a corporation can continue to exist and

outside directors
Members of a corporation's board of directors who are not also employees of the corporation on a day-to-day basis.

chief executive officer (CEO)
The person responsible for the firm's overall performance.

public corporation
A business whose stock is widely held and available for sale to the general public.

private corporation
A business whose stock is held by a small group of individuals and is not usually available for sale to the general public.

The Canadian Business Scene

HOT SEATS ON THE BOARD OF DIRECTORS

In former years, it was not uncommon for individuals to be appointed to the board of directors by the "old-boy network" to rubber-stamp decisions made by company executives. But those days are fast disappearing. Directors are increasingly chosen based on their background and for the ways they can contribute to the success of the firm. Board members are also involved in the decision-making process.

Korn/Ferry International, an executive search firm, conducted a survey of Canadian CEOs and found that 95 percent of them felt that if a board member is not doing an adequate job, the CEO should be able to ask for the board member's resignation. Causes listed included insufficient interest in the job, poor attendance at board meetings, inadequate contribution at board meetings, and a change in the person's business position during their term on the board.

Accepting a director's post in the 1990s means more hard work than in the past. There are typically four to six board meetings per year, and preparation for each one can take up to 24 hours of work. Because of this, directors are getting larger fees than they used to. Average annual compensation for many directors now exceeds $15 000.

Changes in board composition are also evident. A survey by the Conference Board of Canada shows that the percentage of women sitting on boards has more than doubled since 1984. However, it still stands at only 5.8 percent. Most women who are board members are "outside" directors, not employees of the company. This is consistent with the general trend away from appointing top-level executives to the board.

Many investors feel that board members are not independent enough to make objective decisions. Directors usually see themselves as being chosen by management (usually the CEO), so they feel a responsibility to management but not to the shareholders. If problems arise, board members often give managers only a slap on the wrist. They also seem reluctant to reduce management salaries when the firm is doing poorly. And when takeover bids come along, board members often reject them, even if the takeover would benefit the shareholders. Board members reject these bids so they can maintain their power and position.

The threat of liability suits from unhappy shareholders has forced board members to take their responsibilities more seriously. The collapse of the Canadian Commercial and Northlands banks in Alberta in the 1980s led to lawsuits totalling $1.5 billion against directors of those banks. Ontario's new hazardous waste legislation puts the responsibility on directors to make sure that their corporation does not damage the environment. To counter this pressure, board members are asking corporations to provide liability insurance. A survey by the Conference Board of Canada revealed that 16 percent of the companies surveyed had experienced at least one legal action against their directors, and some had had as many as 15 legal actions. More than 70 percent of Canadian companies pay for liability insurance for their directors.

Shareholders have shown increased willingness to vote out board members if they feel a poor job is being done. At Sherritt Gordon Ltd., one shareholder group accumulated more than 5 percent of the company's stock and then made a bid to elect a new slate of directors. The group claimed that the board of directors had failed to take proper steps to deal with potential problems regarding oversupply in the Canadian fertilizer industry. At the special meeting, the dissident shareholders were successful in voting out the existing board members and installing their own people.

In other firms, board members have been sued, with shareholders claiming that the board members failed to fulfill their duties. For example, ten ex-directors of Peoples Jewellers Ltd. are involved in a $35 million lawsuit that alleges that the directors failed to disclose risks associated with a bond issue which was sold to the public in 1990. The directors could be forced to pay out of their own pocket if the judgment exceeds the $10 million in liability insurance that covers them. Liability fears such as this have caused directors to leave financially troubled companies like PWA and Westar Mining Ltd.

All of these challenges come at a time when the role of the board of directors is more important than ever. In an era of intense global competition, strategic leadership is absolutely essential. This will mean that big changes will have to occur in the way that boards operate. The "old code" of keeping the board in the background and letting management set strategy and operate the company will have to be replaced with a "new code" which requires board members to be actively involved in confronting problems the firm is facing.

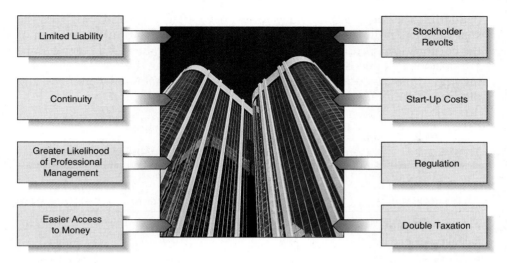

Limited Liability	Stockholder Revolts
Continuity	Start-Up Costs
Greater Likelihood of Professional Management	Regulation
Easier Access to Money	Double Taxation

Figure 2.4

Corporations dominate the Canadian business system. Like sole proprietorships and partnerships, the corporate form of ownership has several advantages and disadvantages.

grow long after the founders have retired or died. In theory, a corporation can go on forever.

Most corporations also benefit from professional management. In a sole proprietorship, a single person typically owns and manages the business. In most corporations, on the other hand, professional managers run the company but do not necessarily own any part of it.

Finally, corporations have a relatively easy time raising money. By selling more stock, they can expand the number of investors. In addition, the legal protections afforded corporations and the continuity of such organizations tend to make bankers more willing to grant loans.

Disadvantages of the Corporation.   Ease of transferring ownership, one of the corporation's chief attractions, can also complicate the life of its managers. For example, one or more disgruntled shareholders in a small corporation can sell their stock to someone who wants to control the corporation and overthrow its top managers. Gaining control of a large corporation by this method is a complicated and expensive process, partially because of the large number of shareholders and partially because of the large sums of money involved. Amid the takeover environment of the 1980s, some shareholders of large firms succeeded. Philip Morris took over both General Foods and Kraft against their wishes and then combined them to form Kraft General Foods.[6] We discuss this interesting topic in more detail in Chapter 3.

Forming a corporation also costs more than forming either a sole proprietorship or a partnership. The main reason is that someone who wants to incorporate must meet all the legal requirements of the province in which it incorporates. Corporations also need legal help in meeting government regulations. Corporations are far more heavily regulated than are proprietorships and general partnerships.

The greatest potential drawback of the corporate form of organization, however, is **double taxation**. A corporation must pay income taxes on its profits, and then shareholders must pay income taxes on the dividends they receive from the corporation. Unlike interest expenses, dividends are not tax

double taxation

A corporation must pay taxes on its profits, and the shareholders must pay personal income taxes on the dividends they receive.

deductible for corporations. They come out of after-tax profits. So, from the shareholder's point of view, this procedure amounts to double taxation of the corporation's profits. By contrast, sole proprietorships and partnerships are taxed only once, since their profits are treated as the owner's personal income. Table 2.3 compares the various forms of business ownership, using different characteristics.

TABLE 2.3   A Comparison of Three Forms of Business Ownership

Characteristic	Sole Proprietorship	Partnership	Corporation
Protection against liability for bad debts	low	low	high
Ease of formation	high	high	medium
Permanence	low	low	high
Ease of ownership transfer	low	low	high
Ease of raising money	low	medium	high
Freedom from regulation	high	high	low
Tax advantages	high	high	low

Cooperatives

cooperative

An organization that is formed to benefit its owners in the form of reduced prices and/or the distribution of surpluses at year-end.

A **cooperative** is an organization that is formed to benefit its owners in the form of reduced prices and/or the distribution of surpluses at year-end. The process works like this: suppose some farmers believe they can get cheaper fertilizer prices if they form their own company and purchase in large volume. They might then form a cooperative, which can be either federally or provincially chartered. Prices are generally lower to buyers and, at the end of the fiscal year, any surpluses are distributed to members on the basis of how much they purchased. If Farmer Jones bought 5 percent of all co-op sales, he would receive 5 percent of the surplus.

Voting rights are different from those in a corporation. In the cooperative, each member is entitled to one vote, irrespective of how many shares he or she holds. This system prevents voting and financial control of the business by a few wealthy individuals. Table 2.4 shows the top ten Canadian cooperatives.

Some large cooperatives have recently decided to become publicly traded companies. In 1994, SaskPool delegates voted 80 percent in favor of trading their shares on the Toronto Stock Exchange, thus giving up their status as a cooperative. United Grain Growers had made the same move a year earlier, and it was able to raise $34 million in its first year as a corporation. Other grain cooperatives like Manitoba Pool Elevators may follow suit. The ability to sell shares of stock will give the grain companies extra capital to invest in food processing, but farmers say they will lose control of the grain companies, and that more and more power will fall into the hands of managers.[7]

**TABLE 2.4   The Top Ten Cooperatives in Canada, 1994
(ranked by revenues)**

Cooperative	Revenues (in millions)
1. Saskatchewan Wheat Pool	$2088
2. Federated Co-operatives Ltd.	1984
3. Coopérative fédérée du Québec	1489
4. XCAN Grain Pool	1395
5. Alberta Wheat Pool	1174
6. Agropur, coopérative agro-alimentaire	1015
7. Agrifoods International Cooperative Ltd.	883
8. Calgary Co-operative Association Ltd.	500
9. Manitoba Pool Elevators	495
10. Co-op Atlantic	470

Types of Cooperatives.   There are hundreds of different cooperatives, but they generally function in one of six main areas of business:

- Consumer cooperatives—These organizations sell goods to both members and the general public (e.g., co-op gasoline stations, agricultural implement dealers).
- Financial cooperatives—These organizations operate much like banks, accepting deposits from members, giving loans, and providing chequing services (e.g., credit unions).
- Insurance cooperatives—These organizations provide many types of insurance coverage, such as life, fire, liability (e.g., the Cooperative Hail Insurance Company of Manitoba).
- Marketing cooperatives—These organizations sell the produce of their farm members and purchase inputs for the production process (e.g., seed and fertilizer). Some, like Federated Co-operatives, also purchase and market finished products.
- Service cooperatives—These organizations provide members with services, such as recreation.
- Housing cooperatives—These organizations provide housing for members, who purchase a share in the cooperative, which holds the title to the housing complex.

In numbers of establishments in Canada, cooperatives are the least important form of ownership. However, they are of significance to society and to their members; they may provide services that are not readily available or that cost more than the members would otherwise be willing to pay. The box, "An Uncooperative Cooperative," describes how important some cooperatives are.

International Report

AN UNCOOPERATIVE COOPERATIVE

It is ironic that Japan, often praised for its efficiency in business, has one of the most inefficient agricultural industries in the world. The average Japanese pays far more for wheat, beef, and rice than the average Canadian does. Strong protectionist laws that have restricted imports of rice and beef cost Japanese buyers over $61 billion—about 4 percent of personal consumption—in 1986.

Who has reaped the profits from this gouging of the Japanese consumer? Not Japanese farmers. The typical farming family earns only about $24 000 per year from agriculture—less in real terms than 10 years ago. Little wonder, then, that the number of Japanese who are full-time farmers has fallen 40 percent in the past 15 years.

If the farmers are not profiting from Japanese protectionism, then who is? The answer is the national farmers' cooperative, Nokyo. Over the past decade, Nokyo has increased its assets to $447 billion and its staff to 380 000, making it the nation's largest employer except for the Japanese government. To understand Nokyo's power, you need to understand its pervasive influence on Japanese farm life. Nokyo is the primary maker of farm loans in Japan and a major insurer of farmers and their property. Many Japanese farmers wind up buying their trucks and tractors from Nokyo outlets and filling them at Nokyo gas stations. So complete is Nokyo's control of farming community life that few farmers will take the risk of buying fertilizer and farm equipment from other sources—despite Nokyo's much higher prices. As one rice farmer notes, "When you live in a small town, you figure you will lose more socially bucking the system than you will gain in financial terms."

Nokyo has entrenched itself in Japanese culture primarily because of the votes it controls. Because seats in the Japanese Diet (parliament) have not been redistributed to correspond to the population shift to the cities in recent decades, Nokyo still fills a substantial percentage of the seats belonging to the ruling Liberal Democratic Party. In return for voting for Nokyo-backed candidates, farmers have received ever-increasing subsidies.

Nevertheless, there are indications that Nokyo's days of power may be drawing to a close. Pressured by the international economic community, Japan's government has agreed to lift many restrictions on agricultural products, including beef and citrus. Japanese ministers have even begun to hint that imported rice—that much-venerated staple of Japanese life—may not be too far off (perhaps in another ten years). A government-sponsored commission recently issued a report condemning Nokyo for overcharging Japanese farmers and for concentrating too much on its financial operations and too little on its obligation to provide technical assistance to farmers.

Change seems likely at a higher level as well. Redistricting is likely to reduce the parliamentary seats controlled by Nokyo supporters. At the same time, more political power will pass into the hands of city dwellers, who are apt to favor policies reducing the prices they pay for consumer goods.

Other Forms of Business Ownership

In recent years, several other forms of business ownership have become popular. Significant among these are employee-owned corporations, strategic alliances, subsidiary and parent corporations, and institutional ownership.

employee stock ownership plan (ESOP)
An arrangement whereby a corporation buys its own stock with loaned funds and holds it in trust for its employees. Employees "earn" the stock based on some condition such as seniority. Employees control the stock's voting rights immediately, even though they may not take physical possession of the stock until specified conditions are met.

Employee-Owned Corporations

As we saw in the opening case, corporations are sometimes owned by the employees who work for them. While many smaller corporations are owned by the individuals who founded them, there is a growing trend today for employees to buy significant stakes of larger corporations. The current pattern is for this ownership to take the form of **employee stock ownership plans** or **ESOP**.

An ESOP is essentially a trust established on behalf of the employees. A corporation might decide, for example, to set up an ESOP to stimulate employee motivation or to fight a hostile takeover attempt. The company first secures a loan, which it then uses to buy shares of its stock on the open market. A portion of the future profits made by the corporation is used to pay off the loan. The stock, meanwhile, is controlled by a bank or other trustee. Employees gradually get ownership of the stock, usually on the basis of seniority. But even though they might not have physical possession of the stock for awhile, they control its voting rights immediately.

Workers at Algoma Steel Corp., for example, will have a 60 percent ownership in the company. The shift to employee ownership in this instance is part of a bailout deal by the Ontario government. In the U.S., there is a noticeable trend toward employee ownership in the commercial airline industry. Northwest, TWA, United, and Southwest all recently turned to employee ownership as they restructured.[8]

Strategic Alliances

A **strategic alliance**, or joint venture, involves two or more enterprises cooperating in the research, development, manufacture, or marketing of a product. Companies might choose to engage in, say, a joint venture for several reasons. One major reason is that it helps spread the risk. For example, the national oil company of Nigeria and Chevron Oil were both interested in building a new type of drilling platform to search for oil in swampy areas. The platform was so expensive, however, that the companies were afraid to build it on their own. They decided to each contribute half the costs and share in its use. Thus, each firm decreased its own risks.

Another reason for joint ventures is that each firm thinks it can get something from the other. For example, Toyota and General Motors recently agreed to jointly own and manage an automobile assembly plant in California. General Motors had not been able to operate the plant profitably alone, and had actually shut it down. But they eventually realized that they could learn more about the Japanese approach to management by working with Toyota. And the Japanese, in turn, got access to an assembly plant in the U.S. without having to invest millions of dollars in a new one. Examples of other joint ventures are described in the box "Strategic Alliances."

strategic alliance
An enterprise in which two or more persons or companies temporarily join forces to undertake a particular project.

Subsidiary and Parent Corporations

Still another important trend in business ownership is the growing number of subsidiary and parent corporations, some of which are listed in Table 2.5. A **subsidiary corporation** is one that is owned by another corporation. The corporation that owns the subsidiary, in turn, is called a **parent corporation**. The establishment of parent and subsidiary relationships can offer a number of benefits.

subsidiary corporation
One that is owned by another corporation.

parent corporation
A corporation that owns a subsidiary.

TABLE 2.5   Parent/Subsidiary Relations

p = parent, s = subsidiary

p PepsiCo	**p Grand Met**
s Pepsi-Cola	s Pillsbury
s Frito-Lay	s Alpo
s Kentucky Fried Chicken	s Heublein
s Pizza Hut	
s Taco Bell	**p Dylex**
	s Tip Top Tailors
p Unilever	s Harry Rosen
s Lever Brothers	s Big Steel Man
s Lipton	s Fairweather
s Minnetonka	s Bi-Way
s Chesebrough-Pond's	s Thrifty's

One benefit is that the assets and other resources of one corporation can be protected from claims against the other. It also allows unrelated businesses to have their own images, their own strategies, and so forth. For example, most people do not realize that Kentucky Fried Chicken and Pizza Hut are owned by the same company—PepsiCo. This arrangement allows Pepsi-Cola to battle Coca-Cola, and Pizza Hut to battle Pizza Inn. And if one business falters, PepsiCo can sell it without great damage to the image or reputation of its other businesses.

Institutional Ownership

institutional investors

Organizations like mutual and pension funds which purchase large blocks of company stock.

Most individual investors do not own enough stock to exert any influence on the management of big corporations. In recent years, however, more and more stock has been purchased by **institutional investors** such as mutual funds and pension funds. Because they control enormous resources, these investors can buy huge blocks of stock. Occasionally, institutional investors may expect to be consulted on major management decisions. Mutual funds are discussed in Chapter 20.

International Report

STRATEGIC ALLIANCES

Strategic alliances are becoming very common in international business. The motivation behind strategic alliances is often global position. That is, how can your firm best sell its products or services in distant markets without spending excessive amounts of money doing it?

A recent Ernst & Young survey of 822 Canadian high-tech companies found that 41 percent were involved in some form of strategic alliance, more than half with foreign firms. Most of the firms had more than one strategic alliance, suggesting that their first experience had been positive.

Allelix Biopharmaceuticals Inc. and Glaxo Canada Inc. are working together to develop pharmaceuticals to combat osteoporosis. Graham Strachan, CEO of Allelix, says that strategic alliances are particularly necessary in the pharmaceutical field because of the high expense and long lead times encountered in developing new products. Although the connection is with Glaxo Canada, its parent is Glaxo Holdings PLC of the U.K. (sales over $6 billion). If Allelix develops a worthwhile product, it will have a lot of market clout through Glaxo Holdings PLC.

Molson Co. Ltd. and Elders IXL Ltd. of Australia formed a strategic alliance called Molson Breweries. The stated goal is to increase sales in the U.S., but the arrangement will also increase Molson's chance to crack the U.K. market. Elders owns Courage Ltd., one of the top U.K. brewers. Since all the big British brewers own pub chains, the only way to gain entry into the market is to set up distribution deals with companies that already have a foothold.

However, not all joint ventures are successful. Cascades Inc., the Quebec paper company, disassociated itself from a partnership with Groupe Pinault SA of France to operate a French newsprint company. The reason given for the breakup was "conflicting philosophies."

Noranda Forest Inc. planned to build a $1 billion pulp mill in Tasmania in partnership with the Australian company North Broken-Hill. The project was shelved when the Australian government imposed tougher pollution regulations. Noranda Forest Inc. management felt that North Broken-Hill had handled the environmental issue poorly because of its inexperience in the area.

Another strategic alliance was developed between Canadian yacht maker C & C Industries and the Dutch powerboat builder Neptunus Shipyard BV. The Dutch firm was running its plant at capacity and decided it wanted to build boats in North America so it wouldn't have to ship them across the Atlantic. The Canadian firm was looking for some way to sell its products in Europe. A customer of the Dutch firm who lived in Toronto played the role of matchmaker. After negotiations, the two companies signed a contract in 1989 which had C & C building $6 million worth of powerboats for Neptunus. Unfortunately, C & C went into receivership a few months later.

A Brief History of Business in Canada

Canadian business has not always had the variety of complex structures we have just discussed. Indeed, a look at the history of business in Canada shows a steady development from sole proprietorships to the complex corporate structures of today. In this section, we will trace the broad outlines of the development of business in Canada. Table 2.6 highlights some of the specific events in Canadian business history.[9]

TABLE 2.6   Some Important Dates in Canadian Business History

1490	English fishermen active off the coast of Newfoundland	1896	First large pulp and paper mill in Canada opened at Sault Ste. Marie
1534	Account of first trading with Native peoples written by Jacques Cartier	1907	First issue of *The Financial Post*
1669	*Nonsuch* returns to London with a cargo of furs from Hudson Bay area	1920	First ship-plate steel mill in Canada opens in Sydney, Nova Scotia
1670	Hudson's Bay Company founded	1917–1922	Creation of Canadian National Railways
1730–1740	Hat-making industry arises in Quebec and is stifled by French home officials	1926	U.S. replaces Great Britain as Canada's largest trading partner
1737	Compagnie des forges du St. Maurice formed to produce iron	1927	Armand Bombardier sells first "auto-neige" (forerunner of the snowmobile)
1779	North West Company forms	1927	Canadian Tire begins operations in Toronto
1785	Molson brewery opens		
1805	First Canadian paper mill built at St. Andrew's, Quebec	1929	Great stock market crash
		1929–1933	Great Depression
1809	First steamboat (the *Accommodation*) put into service on the St. Lawrence River by John Molson	1930	Canadian Airways Limited formed
		1932	Canadian Radio Broadcasting Corporation formed. (It became the CBC in 1936.)
1817	Bank of Montreal chartered		
1821	Hudson's Bay Company and North West Company merge	1935	Bank of Canada begins operations
		1937	Canadian Breweries Limited is formed
1830–1850	Era of canal building	1940	C.D. Howe appointed as Minister of Munitions and Supply
1836	First railroad train pulled by a steam engine		
		1945	Argus Corporation Limited formed
1855	John Redpath opens first Canadian sugar refinery in Montreal	1947–1951	Early computer built at the University of Toronto
1856	Railroad trains begin running between Toronto and Montreal	1947	Leduc Number 1 oil well drilled in Alberta
1857–1858	First oil well in Canada drilled near Sarnia, Ontario	1949	A.V. Roe (Avro) makes Canada's first commercial jetliner
1850–1860	First era of railroad building	1964	Volvo of Sweden begins assembling cars in Nova Scotia
1861	Toronto Stock Exchange opens		
1869	Eaton's opens for business in Toronto	1965	Auto Pact signed with the U.S.
1879	National Policy implemented; raised tariffs on foreign goods to protect and encourage Canadian manufacturers	1969	Canada becomes world's largest potash producer
		1980–1986	Dome, Canadair, and Massey-Ferguson receive financial assistance from the federal government
1885	Last spike driven to complete the Canadian Pacific Railroad		
1897–1899	Klondike gold rush	1989	Free trade agreement with U.S. comes into effect
1880–1890	First western land boom	1993	North American Free Trade Agreement comes into effect

The Early Years

Business activity and profit from commercial fishing were the motivation for the first European involvement in Canada. In the late 1400s, ships financed by English entrepreneurs came to the coast of Newfoundland to fish for profit. By the late 1500s, the Newfoundland coast was being visited by hundreds of fishing vessels each year.

Beginning in the 1500s, French and British adventurers began trading with the Indians. Items such as cooking utensils and knives were exchanged for beaver and other furs. One trading syndicate made over 1000 percent profit on beaver skins sold to a Paris furrier. Trading was aggressive and, over time, the price of furs rose as more and more Europeans bid for them. Originally the fur trade was restricted to eastern Canada, but by the late 1600s, *coureurs de bois* were travelling far to the west in search of new sources of furs.

European settlers who arrived in Canada in the sixteenth and seventeenth centuries initially had to farm or starve. Gradually, however, they began to produce more than they needed for their own survival. The governments of the countries from which the settlers came (notably England and France) were strong supporters of the mercantilist philosophy. Under *mercantilism*, colonists were expected to export raw materials like beaver pelts and lumber at low prices to the mother country. These raw materials were then used to produce finished goods like fur coats which were sold at high prices to settlers in Canada. Attempts to develop industry in Canada were thwarted by England and France who enjoyed large profits from mercantilism. As a result, Canadian manufacturing was slow to develop.

The Factory System and the Industrial Revolution

Industrial Revolution

A major change in goods production that began in England in the mid-eighteenth century and was characterized by a shift to the factory system, mass production, and specialization of labor.

factory system

A process in which all the machinery, materials, and workers required to produce a good in large quantities are brought together in one place.

mass production

The manufacture of products of uniform quality in large quantities.

specialization

The breaking down of complex operations into simple tasks that are easily learned and performed.

British manufacturing took a great leap forward around 1750 with the coming of the **Industrial Revolution**. This revolution was made possible by advances in technology and by the development of the **factory system**. Instead of hundreds of workers turning out items one at a time in their cottages, the factory system brought together in one place all of the materials and workers required to produce items in large quantities, along with newly created machines capable of **mass production**.

Mass production offered savings in several areas. It avoided unnecessary duplication of equipment. It allowed firms to purchase raw materials at better prices by buying large lots. And most important, it encouraged **specialization** of labor. No longer did production require highly skilled craftspeople who could do all the different tasks required to make an item. A series of semiskilled workers, each trained to perform only one task and supported by specialized machines and tools, greatly increased output.

In spite of British laws against the export of technology and manufacturing in North America, Canadian manufacturing existed almost from the beginning of European settlement. Modest manufacturing operations were evident in sawmills, breweries, grist mills for grinding grain, tanneries, woollen mills, shoemaker's shops, and tailor's shops. These operations were so successful that by 1800, exports of manufactured goods were more important than exports of fur.

With the advent of steam power in the early 1800s, manufacturing activity began to increase rapidly. By 1850, more than 30 factories—employing more than 2000 people—lined the Lachine Canal alone. Exports of timber to England in 1850 were 70 times greater than what they were in 1800. The demand for reliable transportation was the impetus for canal building in the mid-1800s and then the railroad-building boom in the mid- and late-1800s.

The Entrepreneurial Era

One of the most significant features of the last half of the nineteenth century was the emergence of entrepreneurs willing to take risks in the hope of earning huge profits. Adam Smith in his book *The Wealth of Nations* argued that the government should not interfere in the economy, but should let businesses function without regulation or restriction. This laissez-faire attitude was often adopted by the Canadian government. As a result, some individuals became immensely wealthy through their aggressive business dealings. Some railway, bank, and insurance executives made over $25 000 per year in the late 1800s, and their purchasing power was immense. Entrepreneurs such as Joseph Flavelle, Henry Pellatt, and John MacDonald lived in ostentatious mansions or castles.

The size and economic power of some firms meant that other businesses had difficulty competing against them. At the same time, some business executives decided that it was more profitable to collude than to compete. They decided among themselves to fix prices and divide up markets. Hurt by

In the eighteenth century, the home crafts industry provided our young nation with clothing and foodstuffs. During the nineteenth century, machinery such as the cotton gin changed the way the world worked. Today, automation continues to alter our work lives and the types of products that are available to us.

these actions, Canadian consumers called for more regulation of business. In 1889, the first anti-combines legislation was passed in Canada, and legislation regulating business has increased ever since.

The Production Era

The concepts of specialization and mass production that originated in the Industrial Revolution were more fully refined as Canada entered the twentieth century. The Scientific Management Movement focused management's attention on production. Increased efficiency via the "one best way" to accomplish tasks became the major management goal.

production era
The period during the early twentieth century when businesses focused almost exclusively on improving productivity and manufacturing methods.

Henry Ford's introduction of the moving assembly line in the U.S. in 1913 ushered in the **production era.** During the production era, less attention was paid to selling and marketing than to technical efficiency when producing goods. By using fixed work stations, increasing task specialization, and moving the work to the worker, the assembly line increased productivity and lowered prices, making all kinds of products affordable for the average person.

During the production era, large businesses began selling stock—making shareholders the owners—and relying on professional managers. The growth of corporations and improved production output resulting from assembly lines came at the expense of worker freedom. The dominance of big firms made it harder for individuals to go into business for themselves. Company towns run by the railroads, mining corporations, and forest products firms gave individuals little freedom of choice over whom to work for and what to buy. To restore some balance within the overall system, both government and labor had to develop and grow. Thus, this period saw the rise of labor unions and collective bargaining. We will look at this development in more detail in Chapter 10. The Great Depression of the 1930s and World War II caused the federal government to intervene in the economic system on a previously unimaginable scale.

Today, business, government, and labor are frequently referred to by economists and politicians as the three *countervailing powers* in our society. All are big. All are strong. Yet, none totally dominates the others.

The Sales and Marketing Eras

By the 1930s, business's focus on production had resulted in spectacular increases in the amount of goods and services for sale. As a result, buyers had more choices and producers faced greater competition in selling their wares. Thus began the so-called **sales era**. According to the ideas of this time, a business's profits and success depended on hiring the right salespeople, advertising heavily, and making sure products were readily available. Business firms were essentially production- and sales-oriented, and they produced what they thought customers wanted, or simply what the company was good at producing. This approach is still used by firms that find themselves with surplus goods that they want to sell (e.g., used-car dealerships).

sales era
The period during the 1930s and 1940s when businesses focused on sales forces, advertising, and keeping products readily available.

Following World War II, pent-up demand for consumer goods kept the economy rolling. While brief recessions did occur periodically, the 1950s and 1960s were prosperous times. Production increased, technology advanced, and the standard of living rose. During the **marketing era**, business adopted a new philosophy on how to do business—use market research to determine what customers want, and then make it for them. Firms like Procter & Gamble and Molson were very effective during the marketing era, and continue to be profitable today. Each offers an array of products within a particular field (toothpaste or beer, for example), and gives customers a chance to pick what best suits their needs.

marketing era
The period during the 1950s and 1960s when businesses began to identify and meet consumer wants in order to make a profit.

The Finance Era

In the 1980s, emphasis shifted to finance. In the **finance era** there was a sharp increase in mergers and in the buying and selling of business enterprises. Some people now call it the "decade of greed." As we will see in the next chapter, during the finance era there were many hostile takeovers and a great deal of financial manipulation of corporate assets by so-called corporate raiders. Critics charged that these raiders were simply enriching themselves and weren't creating anything of tangible value by their activity. They also charged that raiders were distracting business managers from their main goals of running the business. The raiders responded that they were making organizations more efficient by streamlining, merging, and reorganizing them.

finance era
The period during the 1980s when there were many mergers and much buying and selling of business enterprises.

The Global Era

The last few years have seen the continuation of technological advances in production, computer technology, information systems, and communication capabilities. They have also seen the emergence of a truly global economy. Canadians drive cars made in Japan, wear sweaters made in Italy, drink beer brewed in Mexico, and listen to stereos made in Taiwan. But we're not alone in this. People around the world buy products and services from foreign companies.

While it is true that many Canadian businesses have been hurt by foreign imports, numerous others have profited by exploring new foreign markets themselves. And domestic competition has forced many businesses to work harder than ever to cut costs, increase efficiency, and improve product and service quality. We will explore a variety of important trends, opportunities, and challenges of the global era throughout this book.

Summary of Key Points

All businesses must decide on a form of legal organization. The most common forms are the sole proprietorship, the general partnership, the corporation, and the cooperative. Each has several advantages and disadvantages.

Sole proprietorships, the most common business form, consist of one person doing business with no legal charter. While they offer the owner great freedom and are easy to form, they also present high financial risks. Partnerships are merely proprietorships with multiple owners.

Corporations are owned by those who hold stock in the company. These shareholders share in the company's profits and elect a board of directors to oversee the professional managers who run the company. Stock in some corporations is widely held by the public; stock in other firms is limited to a small, private group. The corporate form is used by most large businesses because it offers financial protection to investors, but it is a complex legal entity.

Cooperatives are formed to benefit their owners in the form of reduced prices or the distribution of surpluses from operations. Each shareholder has only one vote regardless of the number of shares he or she owns.

New forms of business ownership are also becoming more important. Examples are employee stock ownership plans (ESOPs), strategic alliances, and subsidiary and parent corporation relationships.

Modern Canadian business structures reflect a pattern of development over centuries. Throughout much of the colonial period, sole proprietors supplied raw materials to English and French manufacturers. The rise of the factory system during the Industrial Revolution brought with it mass production and specialization of labor, but companies continued to be owned as sole proprietorships or partnerships. This pattern continued during the entrepreneurial era, in which some key businessmen built giant business firms. As companies grew during the production era, successfully emphasizing increased output, the corporate form of business organization became popular. During the sales and marketing eras, businesses, focusing on sales staff, advertising and the need to produce what consumers most want, continued to prefer the corporate form. In the 1980s the focus shifted to finance, and there was an increase in corporate mergers as well as the buying and selling of business enterprises.

The most recent shift has been toward a global economic outlook where businesses produce and market products and services around the world with little regard for national boundaries. The global era promises to be a major challenge for managers throughout the 1990s.

CONCLUDING CASE 2-1

A Piece of the Rock

Rock'n' roll may be here to stay, but ownership of the Hard Rock Cafes has proven a bit more transitory. It started innocently enough. In 1970, Isaac Tigrett was convinced that London was ready—even eager—for hamburgers, chicken, and ribs. Never having run a restaurant, Tigrett took as a partner Peter Morton, who was then operating a London restaurant called the Great American Disaster. Each of them put up $5000. They borrowed another $35 000 from a European bank, and, in June 1971, the first Hard Rock Cafe was ready to roll.

The restaurant was a success virtually from the day it opened its doors. Would-be customers lined up inside and outside the Cafe, waiting to get in. Celebrities such as Jack Nicholson and Dustin Hoffman could often be found playing the pinball machines there. T-shirts and sweatshirts bearing the Hard Rock Cafe emblem became the "in" souvenir for tourists and locals alike.

By 1982, however, Tigrett and Morton had agreed to disagree and to dissolve the partnership. Morton accepted $800 000 for his share in the London restaurant. He also retained the rights to operate Hard Rock Cafes in the Western U.S., Australia, Brazil, Israel, Venezuela, and parts of Canada. Tigrett got the London operation and rights everywhere else in the world.

Morton promptly opened successful branches of the Hard Rock Cafe in Los Angeles, San Francisco, and Chicago. Meanwhile, Tigrett opened cafes in Stockholm, Reykjavik, and New York City.

The New York City Cafe, in particular, showed Tigrett's marketing genius. To attract crowds (and help defray expenses), Tigrett took two partners—Yul Brynner and Dan Aykroyd. Much of the $3.6 million it cost to open in

New York went into decor. The bar, 12 metres long, is shaped like a Fender Stratocaster guitar. Mementos of rock stars past and present cover the walls: one of Jimi Hendrix's hats, a drum played by Ringo Starr, a guitar from Eric Clapton, a costume from Bette Midler. Despite the high start-up cost, the New York operation also proved immensely profitable. In 1984, that restaurant took in $7 million, of which $1.2 million was profit. That made for a healthy 17 percent profit margin in an industry that averaged only 4.2 percent.

To finance continued expansion, though, Tigrett needed more capital. Thus in 1987, Tigrett's portion of the Hard Rock Cafes "went public," offering shares in the company for sale to the public. Despite some gloomy predictions by stock analysts, the public gobbled up Hard Rock's offering.

The success of Tigrett's 1987 stock offering also attracted the attention of Pleasurama, the British leisure group. In 1988, Pleasurama purchased Tigrett's operations for $100 million. A year later, Pleasurama fell victim to a hostile takover by Mecca Leisure. Mecca, in turn, was swallowed up in 1990 by an even larger firm, Rank Organization.

What lies ahead for the Hard Rock? Peter Morton hopes to strike it lucky in Las Vegas, where Hard Rock is opening a 326-room hotel and casino—with an 82-foot-high electric guitar on its roof. Meanwhile, Robert Earl, who took over the British end of Hard Rock's operations for Rank, has recently opened a new restaurant in New York City called Planet Hollywood. As its name suggests, Planet Hollywood (designed by the set designer for the movie *Batman*) features mementos of film stars past and present—including the motorcycle ridden by Arnold Schwarzenegger in *Terminator 2*.

CASE QUESTIONS
1. What were the benefits of the Tigrett-Morton partnership? What were the disadvantages?
2. Who do you think benefited most from the breakup of the Tigrett-Morton partnership?
3. If you had had sufficient capital, would you have gone into partnership with Tigrett to open a New York operation? Why or why not?
4. Do you think Isaac Tigrett made the right decision in selling his operation to Pleasurama? Why or why not?
5. In which of the two halves of the Hard Rock Cafes would you rather be a shareholder? Why?   ◆

CONCLUDING CASE 2-2

A Tough Annual Meeting at Petro-Canada

The mood of Petro-Canada shareholders at the 1992 annual meeting was grim. Of the 1500 shareholders present, 80 percent were also Petro-Canada employees. They had watched the price of Petro-Canada shares drop dramatically during the last few months, and they were not happy. Many had taken out loans from the company to buy their shares; these loans had to be repaid in one year. One employee had bought 5000 shares and was sitting on a loss of more than $20 000. These employees knew that company executives (who had also taken out loans to buy stock), had been given a much better loan deal than employees—top executives were given 10 years to repay their loans.

There was other bad news. The Friday before the annual meeting, the company had announced that 660 jobs would be cut and 1000 retail gas stations closed. As well, an anonymous letter had been circulating around the company the week before the meeting. Essentially, it said that Bill Hopper would have to "face the music" at the annual meeting for all the misery that was evident at Petro-Canada. The letter made allegations about Hopper's extravagent lifestyle and his use of corporate jets, limousines, and a personal chef. The letter concluded with an exhortation to boo Hopper off the stage at the annual meeting.

As Hopper walked onto the stage at the annual meeting, the atmosphere was hostile. He introduced himself and the other executives in a repentant, low-key, serious tone. He noted the difficulties the company had been having and said the results were the worst in his 37 years in the business. He acknowledged that the firm lost $598 million in the last fiscal year.

Then, to the surprise of many, he announced that salaried employees in the resource division would be cut by 40 percent and that corporate staff would also be cut. These actions would reduce Petro-Canada's payroll to less than 5000 (it had been 10 000).

During the question period, the first person drew applause by suggesting that management take a 10–15 percent wage cut. The next questioner represented the United Church of Canada; he wanted to know about Petro-Canada's activities in Myanmar. Another shareholder (who was also applauded) said if Hopper presented the same kind of results next year, he should look to his "golden parachute."

After the meeting, shareholders aggressively questioned members of the board of directors one-on-one, indicating that Hopper was the real problem at Petro-Canada. The directors defended him, noting that the oil industry was in bad shape. After the meeting had broken up, the directors went to the Petro-Canada Tower for lunch. In previous years, the lunch was a lavish spread, but this time they ate sandwiches.

Bill Hopper had apparently survived the meeting unscathed. But a few months later, he was fired as the CEO of Petro-Canada.

CASE QUESTIONS
1. What kind of liability do shareholders in Petro-Canada have, given the poor performance of the company?
2. What responsibility does the Board of Directors have for the problems at Petro-Canada?
3. Obtain a copy of the latest Petro-Canada annual report. What has happened to the company since the president was fired?   ◆

Key Terms

sole proprietorship	common stock	double taxation	factory system
unlimited liability	proxy	cooperative	mass production
liquidate	board of directors	employee stock ownership	specialization
general partnership	inside directors	plan (ESOP)	production era
corporation	outside directors	strategic alliance	sales era
stock	chief executive officer	subsidiary corporation	marketing era
shareholders	(CEO)	parent corporation	finance era
dividend	public corporation	institutional investors	
preferred stock	private corporation	Industrial Revolution	

Study Questions and Exercises

Review Questions

1. What are the comparative advantages and disadvantages of the three basic forms of business ownership?
2. Why might a corporation choose to remain private? Why might a private corporation choose to go public?
3. What are the primary benefits and drawbacks to serving as a limited partner in a partnership?
4. Are joint ventures limited to corporations, or can individuals also enter into joint ventures?
5. Why is it important to understand the history of Canadian business?

Analysis Questions

6. Locate two annual reports and review them. Identify the specific points in the reports that the board of directors are communicating to the shareholders.

7. Go to the library and identify four major joint ventures beyond those discussed in the text. Is one of the parties likely to benefit more than the other?
8. How can you, a prospective manager during the global era, better prepare yourself now for the challenges you will face later in this decade?

Application Exercises

9. Interview a manager in a sole proprietorship or general partnership. Based on your talks, what characteristics of that business form led to the owner choosing it?
10. Interview the owner of a corporation. Based on your talks, what characteristics of that business form led to the owner choosing it?

Building Your Business Skills

Goal

To encourage students to evaluate the form of business ownership that is best for a specific small business.

Situation

Suppose that you want to open a business in a suburban community. You will provide music lessons to children and musical entertainment at parties and community events. You will also sell musical instruments and sheet music. Although you will run the business yourself, you need four additional employees to service customers and to maintain inventory and facilities. Although you naturally expect to succeed, you also expect to lose money during the first two years of operation.

Method

Working in groups of four or five, consider how the following factors would influence your decision to operate your business as either a sole proprietorship or a private corporation:

■ treatment of taxable income
■ liability for unpaid business debts
■ liability for injury to customers (remember, most of your customers are children)
■ legal steps required to set up the business.

Follow-up Questions

1. Suppose that the music store is very successful and that within five years you own a chain of ten stores. How would your analysis of the preceding factors change as your business expands?
2. Were liability concerns or tax concerns more important in your choice of business structure?
3. If as a sole proprietor you decide to take in a partner, would you be more likely to form a partnership or a private corporation? What type of partnership would you choose?

3

Recognizing Business Trends and Challenges

LEARNING OBJECTIVES

After studying this chapter, you will be able to

- Describe three major trends that affect the nature of business today.
- Explain how and why government has regulated businesses in the past and why it has elected to deregulate some industries.
- Discuss changes in the labor pool and their effect on business.
- Describe changes in consumer rights and demographics and their impact on Canadian business.
- Identify and discuss five major business challenges of the 1990s.

CHAPTER OUTLINE

OPENING CASE

Coping with a Sea Change

Fishery Products International Ltd. was created in 1983 by the federal and provincial governments out of seven bankrupt fishing companies. It became Canada's largest fishing company. In 1988, it recorded revenues of $366 million, employed 8000 Newfoundlanders, owned 15 processing plants and 70 trawlers, and processed 140 000 tonnes of cod, flounder, and groundfish annually. It was a vertically integrated company, involved in both fish harvesting and fish processing.

In 1992, all of this activity was threatened when the federal government imposed a moratorium on cod fishing because stocks were so depleted. By 1994, only two of the 15 processing plants were operating, the company had sold 25 of its trawlers, and 6000 employees had been laid off. But in spite of predictions that the company would go under, it has survived by making the painful decision to shift its focus away from fish harvesting and toward fish trading and processing. It now processes fish that have been caught in other parts of the world.

During the downsizing, vice-president Ernest Bishop was called into the president's office and told that he would be heading up the department that would be responsible for finding fish worldwide. Since then, he has discovered that there are lots of fish in foreign seas, particularly off the east coast of Russia. He has arranged deals to process pollock from Alaska, flatfish from Iceland, and cod from Norway into fish sticks and fish dinners. He now juggles time zones and fights jet lag; he spends nearly half his time outside Newfoundland in his quest for fish to process. In a great irony, he has discovered that there is a worldwide glut of groundfish, causing their price to drop by 15 per cent. The company will dramatically increase the tonnage of groundfish that are processed.

As part of its overall plan to cope with the collapse of the local fishery, the company has also acquired Clouston Foods, a seafood trading company which buys shrimp, salmon, scallops, and lobster in Ecuador, Brazil, New Zealand, and Indonesia. It has also purchased the U.S. food service business of its rival National Sea Products Ltd. of Halifax.

Chairman Vic Young says that if the company had not made these changes, its revenues would have fallen to only $100 million a year. Instead, sales soared to over $600 million in 1993. But there are still problems. The company lost $15 million in 1993 because of trawler write-offs of $20 million. The 6000 workers who were laid off have little hope of working in the fishing industry for the remainder of this decade, and Young has been forced into the public spotlight when announcing plant closings. Worker frustration runs high, particularly when they see Russian trawlers unloading foreign fish at the Fortune, Newfoundland docks. They worry that even if the cod fishery recovers, Fishery Products might continue to rely on cheap foreign fish.

◆

Fishery Products International Ltd. was presented with a major challenge when the moratorium on cod fishing was imposed. The firm's struggle to adapt is not unique. Today, nearly every company must contend with shifts in its relationships with its competitors, the government, its workforce, and its customers as the result of a change in its external environment.

In this chapter, we explore the trends and challenges facing business firms. We first examine how the rapid pace of change affects business activity. We then examine how businesses interact with various segments of the economy—government, the work force, and consumers. The chapter concludes by discussing five major challenges that business firms are trying to deal with in the 1990s.

Business and Change

Some of the trends and challenges confronting Canadian businesses are internal to the organizations themselves. Among the most pressing of these shifts are the growth of high technology, a move from manufacturing to information services, and an increase in mergers and acquisitions.

The Impact of High Technology

One major trend that has affected virtually every aspect of business is the development and spread of high technology. A **high-technology (high-tech)** firm spends more on research and development and employs more technical employees than the typical manufacturing firm. The term "high-tech" may conjure up images of computers and robots. For example, high-tech robots produced by Fanuc Corporation, a Japanese firm, are used in virtually all automobile plants today. Firms that make these products are definitely high-tech. But so are firms in the aircraft, pharmaceuticals, biotechnology, and communications industries.

High-tech has not, however, been the utopia originally envisioned. It has not created the number of new jobs that many economists originally predicted. Some of the production jobs it has created have been in foreign factories. Many workers trained for industrial jobs have also been unable or unwilling to make the transition to high-tech jobs. Finally, many entrepreneurs who rushed into the high-tech area did so with poorly conceived plans and were unsuccessful. Even firms like IBM, Digital Equipment Corp., and Wang have had to cut staff and reorganize in the face of declining profits. Still, high-tech is clearly with us to stay and will have an increasingly important role in our economy.[1]

high technology
As applied to businesses, a firm that spends more on research and development and employs more technical personnel than the average manufacturing firm.

From Manufacturing to Information Services

Developments in high technology have also contributed to another change in the business world. In recent years, the manufacturing sector—long the backbone of Canada's economy—has decreased as an employer of workers, while the service sector has grown. This growth is clearly illustrated in Figure 3.1. In 1950, only 42 percent of Canadians were employed in services-producing industries; by 1993, the figure was over 72 percent. No wonder, then, many have begun to say that Canada has a **service economy**.

Not all service industries have grown as much as others, though. While employment in traditional service industries such as construction, restaurants, hotels, and repair services has grown as a percentage of total employment, **information services** is the area of greatest growth of late. Information services personnel include lawyers, accountants, data processors, computer

service economy
A reference to the growing importance of services, rather than products, as the major contributor to the Canadian economy.

information services
Service industries that provide information in return for a fee. Examples include law, accounting, and computer processing.

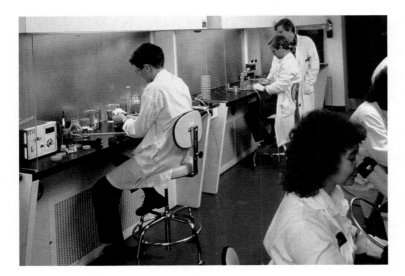

Whether they are producing a product or a service, high technology is increasingly affecting all business firms.

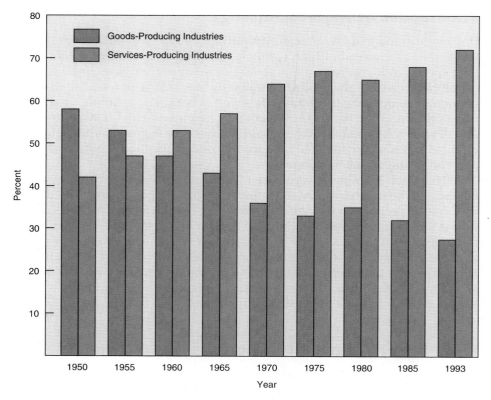

Figure 3.1
Proportion of employment in goods- and services-producing industries.

operators, financial analysts, office personnel, and insurance agents—all those who spend their day working on or with information.

This sector has grown for many reasons. An increasing need to acquire and manage information in a highly competitive marketplace is a prime factor. Another reason is the increasing government regulation of business. With more government regulations, companies have had to hire more people to read the regulations and to construct and implement policies that comply with the regulations. Filling out government forms is another major task.

The Rise of Mergers and Acquisitions

acquisition

The purchase of a company by another, larger firm, which absorbs the smaller company into its operations.

merger

The union of two companies to form a single new business.

In Chapter 2, we saw that businesses today buy and sell other companies like farmers used to buy and sell produce. An **acquisition** is simply the case of one firm buying another. In contrast, a **merger** is a consolidation of two firms. In the case of an acquisition, one firm (usually the larger) buys the other (the smaller). The transaction is similar to buying a car that then becomes your property. In a merger, on the other hand, the firms are usually more similar in size and the arrangement is more collaborative. CN and CP, for example, developed a proposal to merge their Eastern Canadian freight networks because there wasn't enough business to support both railroads in eastern Canada. Price Co. and Costco Wholesale Corp. merged their operations. And in the U.S., Martin Marietta and Lockheed merged to form the world's largest defence company.[2]

After a merger or acquisition, three things can happen. One possibility is that the acquired company will continue to operate as a separate entity.

Even though Trilon Financial Corporation bought London Life Insurance several years ago, the insurance company has continued to operate autonomously. Another possibility is that the acquired business will be absorbed by the other and simply disappear. Finally, the two companies may form a new company. For example, when Warner and Time merged in 1989, they formed a new company called Time-Warner.

As shown in Figure 3.2, mergers can take many forms. When the companies are in the same industry, as when Ford purchased Jaguar or Price and Costco merged, it is called a **horizontal merger**. When one of the companies is a supplier or customer to the other, it is called a **vertical merger**. Finally, when the companies are unrelated, it is called a **conglomerate merger**.

A merger or acquisition can take place in one of several different ways. In a **friendly takeover**, the acquired company welcomes the acquisition, perhaps

horizontal merger
A merger of two firms that have previously been direct competitors in the same industry.

vertical merger
A merger of two firms that have previously had a buyer-seller relationship.

conglomerate merger
A merger of two firms in completely unrelated businesses.

friendly takeover
An acquisition in which the management of the acquired company welcomes the firm's buyout by another company.

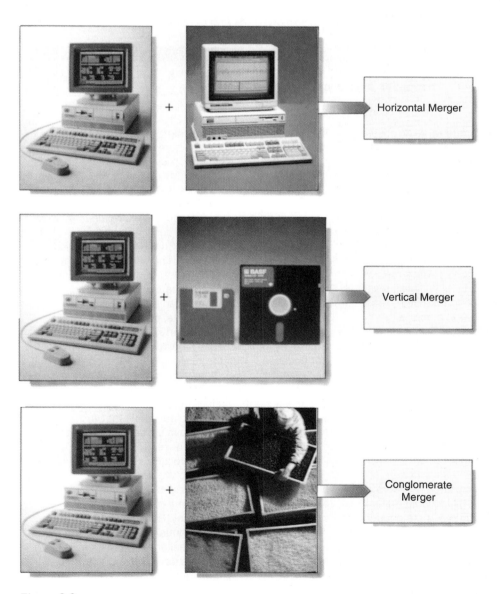

Figure 3.2
There are several different types of mergers. The three most common types are horizontal, vertical, and conglomerate mergers.

hostile takeover

An acquisition in which the management of the acquired company fights the firm's buyout by another company.

poison pill

A defence management adopts to make a firm less attractive to a hostile suitor in a takeover bid.

because it needs cash or sees other benefits in joining the acquiring firm. But in a **hostile takeover**, the acquiring company buys enough of the other company's stock to take control, even though the other company opposes the takeover. Philip Morris's takeovers of General Foods and Kraft were both hostile.[3]

A **poison pill** is a defence management adopts to make a firm less attractive to a current or potential hostile suitor in a takeover attempt. The objective is to make the "pill" so distasteful that a potential acquirer will not want to swallow it. For example, a pill adopted by Inco gave shareholders the right to buy Inco stock or the acquirer's stock at a 50 percent discount if more than 20 percent of Inco stock were acquired by a group without approval of Inco's board of directors. The box "Poison Pills Are Back" describes this idea in more detail.

The Canadian Business Scene

POISON PILLS ARE BACK

During the 1980s, terms like "corporate raider," "hostile takeover," and "poison pill" came into wide usage. In the late 1980s, for example, Garfield Emerson, a Canadian pioneer in poison pills, developed a takeover defence for Maclean-Hunter Ltd. that allowed its shareholders to buy more Maclean-Hunter stock at half price if another firm acquired more than 10 percent of Maclean-Hunter's stock. In the recession of the early 1990s, it seemed that these ideas were falling out of favor and that a more conservative business environment was returning. But there has been a resurgence of some 1980s-style activities like poison pills. Consider the following cases.

When MDC Corp. of Toronto tried to take over Regal Greetings and Gifts Inc., Regal adopted a poison pill, or shareholder rights plan, that would allow Regal to flood the market with cheap shares of its stock. This would make it much more expensive for another company to take over Regal. When MDC heard of this ploy, it requested the Ontario Securities Commission to stop Regal from using its poison pill.

In a similar case, Pharma Patch PLC of Ireland tried to take over Cangene Corp. of Toronto. Cangene produces two biological products that are designed to detect and fight infections. Cangene introduced a poison pill which allowed its existing shareholders who were not sympathetic to the takeover bid to buy large numbers of cut-rate shares of Cangene's stock. This would make it much more difficult for Pharma Patch to acquire enough shares to gain control of Cangene.

Time-Warner Inc. adopted a poison pill defence to keep its largest shareholder, Seagram Co. Ltd., from acquiring more than 15 percent of Time-Warner's stock. The pill allowed Time-Warner shareholders to exercise lucrative stock rights if the 15 percent threshhold was exceeded by Seagram. Seagram later decided to sell its shares and invest elsewhere.

The most recent highly publicized poison pill case was the one in which Royal Oak Mines Inc. tried to take over Lac Minerals Ltd. When faced with this threat, Lac adopted a poison pill which allowed the directors of Lac to sell new shares at a 50 percent discount. This made it very expensive for Royal Oak to gain controlling interest, so they asked the Ontario Securities Commission to squelch the poison pill and threatened to withdraw their takeover offer if their request was not granted. In the end, all the maneuvering was irrelevant, because Lac finally agreed to a friendly takeover by American Barrick Resources.

As these cases demonstrate, poison pills are generally developed as a reaction to an outside takeover threat. But Nova Corp. proposed a poison pill to its shareholders, not because it was the target of a hostile takeover, but because it might be sometime in the future. Nova said the poison pill would protect shareholders, but Fairvest Securities Corp., a shareholder rights advocate organization, sent out a "shareholder alert" that argued that Nova's poison pill gave Nova's board of directors too much latitude in accepting or rejecting takeover offers. Nova put on a major public relations blitz and eventually got shareholders to agree to the poison pill.

At John Labatt Ltd., management proposed a poison pill which would have made it more difficult for an outsider to take over the company. But shareholders rejected the proposal at the 1994 annual meeting after an institutional money manager questioned the wisdom of management's expansion plans. Of the 57 poison pill proposals made by managers in Canadian companies, this is the first one to be rejected.

A hostile takeover often involves the practice of paying **greenmail**. In this situation, investors (called *raiders*) acquire large blocks of stock, threaten a hostile takeover, then let the target company buy back their stock at a price that gives the raiders a substantial profit.

The Economic Council of Canada published a study showing that the profits of companies that have been targets of takeovers are as likely to rise as they are to fall. About 40 percent became more profitable after being taken over, while another 40 percent became less profitable.[4]

Because of the potential for monopolies to arise, the government has become increasingly vigilant regarding mergers and acquisitions. As you will see in the next section, this is but one of the areas where business is affected by the government.

greenmail
A buyback of stock at a large profit to one or more investors who are threatening a hostile takeover of a firm.

Business and Government

In just one week in January 1989, three super-mergers were announced (Imperial Oil-Texaco Canada, Molson's-Carling O'Keefe, and Canadian Airlines International-Wardair). In 1992, Air Canada and Canadian Airlines International also announced their intention to merge. The government of Canada intervened in the Air Canada-Canadian Airlines case, and required evidence that Air Canada was the only firm that was available to merge with Canadian Airlines (the proposed merger eventually fell through). Ottawa also blocked the proposed merger of Maple Leaf Mills and Ogilvie Mills on the grounds that it would have given the combined companies too much control of the Canadian milling market.[5] It also rejected the proposal by Canadian Pacific to buy Canadian National's operations east of Winnipeg because that would have left much of the country with only a single rail operator. In the U.S., when PepsiCo announced plans to acquire Seven-Up and Coca-Cola Co. said it would buy Dr. Pepper, the government intervened and blocked both mergers. If those mergers had been approved, 81 percent of the soft-drink market would have been in the hands of two companies.

Government Regulation of Business

Government regulates business for a variety of reasons, chiefly to protect competition and to meet the nation's social goals.

Protecting Competition.   One key reason for government to regulate business is to ensure competition. Government regulation in this area protects both consumers and other businesses. As we saw in Chapter 1, competition is crucial to a market economy. Laws against monopolies preserve competition and mean companies will strive to offer goods that meet consumers' expectations at a reasonable price. Similarly, without government restrictions, a large business with vast resources could cut its prices so low and advertise so much that smaller firms lacking equal resources would be forced to close.

In cases when for some reason a monopoly is desirable, government regulation seeks to prevent companies from price gouging. For example, telephone, utility, and cable television rates are controlled by federal and provincial agencies. Government regulation is also common in industries where only limited competition exists. Fears that oligopolies such as the trucking, airline, and railroad industries will collude on prices have led the federal government at various times to set rates in these industries. Fears of the power of television and radio stations have been used to justify government rules and pressure on these organizations to run public service ads and to give equal time to opposing views. We will discuss the area of government control of business in more detail in Chapter 21.

Meeting Social Goals.   Another reason for the regulation of business is to help meet social goals. Social goals promote the general well-being of our society. In several areas, business activities and social goals overlap.

In Canada, as in any market economy, consumers must have money to purchase goods and services. But our sense of fairness dictates that the ill should be treated, regardless of their ability to pay. Toward this end, Canada has maintained a public health-care system with wide access. Public immunization programs have inoculated millions of Canadians against TB, polio, and even the flu.

Another social goal—a safe workplace—has also generated extensive government regulation of businesses. Each province has workplace health and safety legislation to assure worker safety. In addition, worker compensation programs require businesses to contribute to a fund that pays workers who have been injured on the job.

Federal and provincial governments also regulate industrial pollution and countless other aspects of business in order to "protect" the public. Federal laws regulate banks, stock sales, and automotive emissions. Provinces license physicians, insurance salespeople, and barbers. And local ordinances establish where garbage can be dumped and who can serve liquor. Indeed, thousands of laws regulate every aspect of business in Canada today. When Michael Talker, the founder of Sky Freight Express, started an air courier service, he discovered that the company and its pilots had to be certified by Transport Canada before they were allowed to start operations.

The Move Toward Deregulation and Privatization

deregulation
A reduction in the number of laws affecting business activity.

In recent years government involvement in business has decreased through deregulation and privatization. **Deregulation** means a reduction in the number of laws affecting business activity and in the powers of government enforcement agencies. In most cases, deregulation frees the corporation to do what it wants without government intervention, thereby simplifying the task of management.

Meeting social goals is a continuing challenge to business. Immunization programs such as the one shown here are set up to help prevent the spread of diseases. Business often contributes to such programs and/or helps manage them.

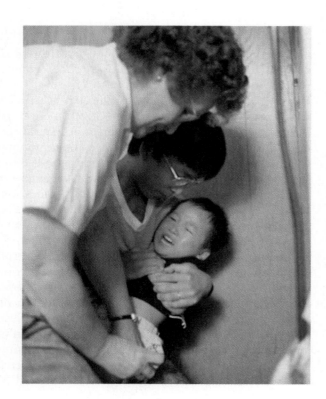

Deregulation is evident in many industries, including airlines, pipelines, banking, trucking, and communications.

Deregulation of the Canadian airline industry has meant that the government no longer dictates how many airlines there will be and where and when they will be allowed to fly. When the government decided to deregulate, it was predicted that there would be a 2 to 3 percent increase per year in demand for air travel spaces. Instead, demand increased 13-18 percent in most places and up to 50 percent in some. Since much of this demand is squeezed into the morning and evening rush hours, airports are having difficulty handling it. There are too few runways and air traffic controllers. This has led to suggestions that the government should get back into regulating the airline industry. The government does not want to do this.[6]

Before deregulation in 1985-86, regulated pipelines bought and sold gas at prices fixed by government. Exports were tightly controlled. Deregulation freed prices and exports and encouraged direct contracts between producers and consumers. Because prices were freed in a period of oversupply, they fell. Before 1986, natural gas cost more than $2.50 per thousand cubic feet; by 1991, it had fallen to less than $1.25. Producers are producing and exporting more gas than formerly but revenues are stagnant. The transition to a free market has been painful.[7]

Banks have also been deregulated and are now selling government securities in their branches and offering a much wider array of financial services than previously. This same trend is evident in other countries as well. Banks are not the only financial organizations on the move because of deregulation. Merrill Lynch Canada, a securities firm, has applied for a licence to operate a bank subsidiary. This is the first time a brokerage firm has applied for a Canadian bank licence. The company feels that if banks are allowed to expand into securities, securities firms should be allowed to expand into banking.

Deregulation in the trucking industry has forced many poorly-run firms out of business. Those that remain must be very competitive if they are to survive. In the communications business, the historic decision by the CRTC to allow competition among long-distance telephone companies has made long-distance calls cheaper, but it has also created some confusion for both business and residential customers.

Privatization refers to the transfer of activities from the government to the private sector. The Federal government has sold several corporations, including Air Canada, Teleglobe Canada, and Canadair Ltd. Provincial governments are also selling off businesses, for example, the Ontario Transportation Development Corp., Manitoba Oil and Gas Corp., Pacific Western Airlines (sold by the Alberta government), and Nova Scotia Power Inc. There is increasing talk about privatizing provincial hydroelectric utilities, particularly in Quebec and Newfoundland.[8]

Privatization does not only involve the selling of businesses. In some provinces, private business firms contract to manage hospitals and other health care institutions previously operated by government employees. Terminal Number 3 at Lester B. Pearson International Airport in Toronto, which opened in February 1991, was built and is operated by a private firm.

Privatization has had some unexpected outcomes. For example, executives at former Crown corporations have gotten some large wage increases because the government had put a ceiling on wages for various management positions. When the organization is privatized, salaries go up to reflect the average pay scale in the private sector. Another example of unexpected outcomes is contained in the box "It's A New World."

Canada is not the only country where privatization is taking place. In Mexico, for example, 900 of the 1200 state corporations have been privatized.[9] Telephone companies in Mexico, New Zealand, and Argentina have also been privatized. In France, the government is privatizing 21 key state-controlled

privatization
The transfer of activities from the government to the public sector.

The Canadian Business Scene

IT'S A NEW WORLD

For 70 years, the province of Alberta held a monopoly on the sale of liquor. The 202 stores in the province were neat, orderly, and boring. Alberta Liquor Control Board (ALCB) employees all wore tan shirts and brown pants. In 1993, the government suddenly announced that it was getting out of the retail liquor business. By doing so, it would save $65 million each year in salaries and operating costs; it would also get another $58 million from the sale or lease of the old government stores.

Within a year, 500 private stores had opened up, some leasing old ALCB sites. People from all walks of life have tried their hand at selling liquor, and almost 4000 private sector jobs have been created. But the Alberta Liquor Store Retailers Association (ALSRA) thinks a shakeout is coming. Competition is heating up, and price wars have pushed some owners to bankruptcy.

Consider the experience of Skip Bromley who opened Calmar, Alberta's first retail liquor store. The old government store in the town averaged more than $900 000 in revenue annually, and Bromley figured he would do very well. Indeed, business was brisk for the first few weeks, but then a competitor popped up next door, then another one across the street. Bromley found himself working long hours to keep his business going; his profit margin also dropped as he was forced to reduce prices to cope with the competition. He closed up shop a few months later.

His story is not unusual. David Paulgaard also had big plans when he opened his store in Calgary. But within a short time, six competitors opened up shop within a five-kilometre radius. He says his markups are very low and profits are minimal.

The privatization of liquor sales was made without any public consultation. The day before privatization was announced, only a handful of people in the province knew it

was coming. Within a few months, almost all of the former employees lost their jobs. The ALCB now restricts itself to the role of wholesaler, importer, and tax collector.

Considerable confusion accompanied privatization. A law was hastily passed that kept large grocery chains like Safeway from selling liquor in their stores. Instead, they were required to build stand-alone sites. This was the result of a fierce lobbying effort by ALSRA, which argued that privatization was supposed to benefit small business, not big business.

The new owners in the retail trade have a lot of complaints. Some say that they can't make a decent profit, even on sales of $7-8 million. They also say that customers notice that prices are higher than when the government ran the stores.

The retailers are not the only ones complaining. Local distillers and brewers say a new tax introduced by the province has cut into their profits, too. Drummond Brewing Co. managed to get a 9 percent share of the Alberta market by selling inexpensive beer. But the new tax has added 21 cents per litre to its price, and sales of the beer have dropped. The president of the firm says that privatization completely negated the firm's corporate strategy. Privatization also created a "one-way trade lane" into Alberta because producers in other provinces can ship their liquor to Alberta, but other provinces have maintained existing trade barriers keeping Alberta beer out.

Privatization forced Highwood Distillers Ltd. to expand its international focus, and its efforts are paying off. Prior to privatization, it exported about 1000 cases to foreign markets. After privatization, it shipped over 13 000 cases. Unfortunately, it also incurred the biggest loss in its history because of the one-way trade lane and the new government tax.

companies in an attempt to reduce the deficit and energize the economy. Firms to be sold include the nation's third largest bank, a large chemical company, and a large oil company. Privatization is a world-wide phenomenon, and it will lead to the dismantling of much of the government involvement in business that has developed during the 20th century. It is estimated that between 1993 and 1995 well over $100 billion dollars will be raised in equity markets by governments as they privatize some of their organizations.[10]

lobbyist

A person hired by a company or an industry to represent its interests with government officials.

How Business Influences Government

As shown in Figure 3.3, businesses attempt to influence the government through lobbyists, trade associations, and advertising. A **lobbyist** is a person hired by a company or industry to represent its interests with government

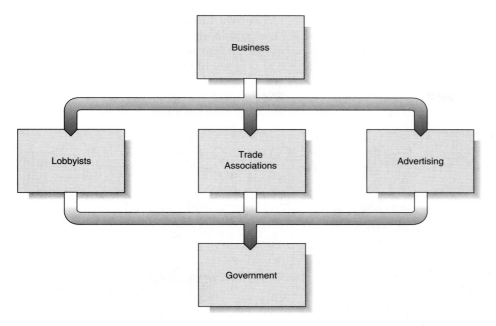

Figure 3.3
Business influences the government in a variety of different ways.

officials. The Canadian Association of Consulting Engineers, for example, regularly lobbies the federal and provincial governments to make use of the skills possessed by private sector consulting engineers on projects like city water systems. Some business lobbyists have training in the particular industry, public relations experience, or a legal background. A few have served as legislators or government regulators.

The Lobbyists Registration Act came into effect in 1989. Lobbyists must register with the Registrar of Lobbyists so that it is clear which individuals are being paid for their lobbying activity. For many lobbying efforts, there are opposing points of view. The Canadian Cancer Society and the Tobacco Institute present very different points of view on cigarette smoking and cigarette advertising.

Employees and owners of small businesses that cannot afford lobbyists often join **trade associations**. Trade associations may act as an industry lobby to influence legislation. They also conduct training programs relevant to the particular industry, and they arrange trade shows at which members display their products or services to potential customers. Most publish newsletters featuring articles on new products, new companies, changes in ownership, and changes in laws affecting the industry.

trade association
An organization dedicated to promoting the interests and assisting the members of a particular industry.

Business and the Work Force

Because workers are an important resource to every company, relations with the work force are an important dimension of the contemporary business world.

Changing Demographics of the Work Force

The statistical makeup—the demographics—of the Canadian labor force has changed gradually over the years. As Figure 3.4(a) illustrates, the work force has grown steadily throughout the twentieth century.

The Graying Work Force.   As shown in Figure 3.4(b), the work force has been getting older. In 1921, for example, the median age of the Canadian population was under 24 years; by 1993, it had risen to over 33 years. The median age continues to rise and could be as high as 50 by the year 2036. In

(a) Canadian work force, 1911-1993, selected years.

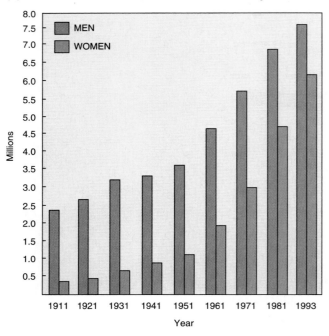

(b) Median age of the Canadian population.

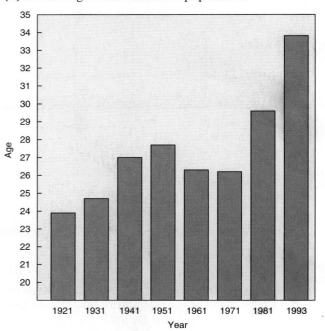

(c) Employment participation for men and women, 1921–1993, selected years.

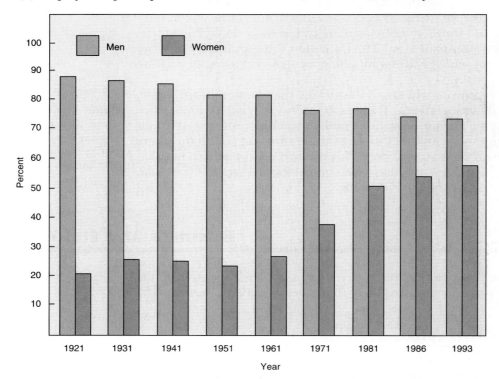

Figure 3.4

1981, the largest age bracket was the group between 15 and 24. Population projections show that by 2006 the largest group will be the 40-49 age bracket and by 2031 it will be the 70-74 age bracket. These are dramatic changes. Business firms will have to cope not only with slower population growth but also with people's changing needs as they age.

Companies that produce baby food have already experienced problems because of the declining number of babies. In the future, companies that sell products to people in their twenties will find that market declining significantly. On the other hand, increased opportunities will be available to firms selling goods and services to older people.

Women in the Work Force.   The growing number of women in the work force is another trend that has had a significant impact on business. As Figure 3.4(c) shows, in 1921 only 20 percent of the female population worked outside the home. By 1993, the figure had risen to almost 60 percent.

There are many reasons for the increased number of women working outside the home. Faced with rapid increases in the prices of goods and services during the 1970s, many couples found that they needed two incomes to maintain their standard of living. In addition, the women's movement and the greater number of women attending and graduating from colleges and universities have provided more career options for women.

The large percentage of women in all types of careers has had and will continue to have a major impact on business. For example, many companies are having to address the problem of child care in order to retain valuable trained personnel. Women working outside the home are also providing more marketing opportunities for business. For example, in recent years there has been increased demand for convenience foods that require little preparation, such as microwavable dinners and frozen pizzas. Products like telephone

The increased number of women working outside the home has resulted in more demand for the services provided by day-care centers.

The Canadian Business Scene

WHATEVER HAPPENED TO LEISURE?

It seems preposterous to suggest that late twentieth-century Canadians have less leisure time than our predecessors did 80 years ago. The official work week today is 38 hours; in 1910, it was 50 hours. Most households now have washing machines, TVs, VCRs, microwave ovens, and other "labor saving" devices. And we read about the "leisure industry" that has grown up in the last 20 years. At the same time, more and more people are reporting that they are spending more time working than ever before.

In one study, 90 percent of the respondents said they did not take part in leisure activities because they did not have enough time or energy. Many people seem to feel vaguely uneasy about participating in leisure activities. Decima president Allan Gregg says that the "Protestant work ethic" is in turmoil. People say they want more leisure, but they cannot stop working long enough to enjoy it. Individuals choose work over leisure,

even though doing so prevents them from enjoying the fruits of their labor.

A typical executive, for example, is "plugged in" to new technology the moment he or she wakes up. Meetings are arranged on the cellular car phone on the way to work, and faxes are received in the car, at home, and at the office. A computer at both the home and the office allows the executive to work constantly. On vacation, the executive takes along a laptop computer and receives daily faxes from the office. The amount of work has expanded to fill the technology available.

The overwhelming majority of Canadians spend their free time watching television. Others spend time doing activities as varied as bird watching and bungee jumping. But virtually no one simply stops working to think, to read, or to savor silence. The introspection that occurs during real leisure may be either frightening or boring, and neither of these is an attractive prospect.

---

answering machines and home computers have increased in popularity, partially because of two-career families. Restaurants and home-cleaning services have benefited too. There has also been increased demand for professional "gear" for working women: business attire, briefcases, and the like. The fact that women are no longer caring for children full-time has even created a new industry—the day-care industry. The box "Whatever Happened to Leisure?" describes other changes that are affecting business.

Business and Consumers

consumer movement

Activism on the part of consumers seeking better value from businesses.

consumer rights

The legally protected rights of consumers to choose products, to safety when using products, to be informed about any potential risk from a product, and to be heard in the event of problems with a product.

Businesses have had to adjust to an increase in the power of the consumer. Gone are the days of *caveat emptor,* "let the buyer beware." A business following that dictum today is apt to face boycotts, lawsuits, and government intervention. Consumer tastes and preferences are also more complex than in the past.

Activism on the part of consumers seeking better value from businesses—the **consumer movement**—has altered the way many businesses conduct themselves. While the consumer movement traces its roots back to the turn of the century, Ralph Nader's much publicized attack on unsafe cars being produced by General Motors (*Unsafe at Any Speed,* 1965) really gave consumerism its momentum.

Over the last decade, legislation has broadened **consumer rights** considerably. In particular, legislation now essentially guarantees consumers the right to choose the products they desire, the right to safety in the products they purchase, the right to be informed about what they are buying, the right to choose, and the right to be heard in the event of problems. As a result, most products today come with extensive instructions as to their use and, in the case of food products, a detailed list of their ingredients. Most products also have a guarantee or warranty, and many list telephone numbers or addresses to contact in the event of problems. We will consider these and related issues more fully in Chapter 14.

Challenges of the 1990s

Given the nature and complexities of today's business environment, it is not surprising that Canadian business faces a number of critical challenges. As Figure 3.5 shows, five of the most important challenges are productivity, federal budget deficits, free trade, pollution, and technology.

In Search of Higher Productivity

As we saw in Chapter 1, productivity is a measure of our economy's success. It is also the measure of a business's success, since it reflects the efficiency with which a company uses resources. A company that uses fewer resources (whether of materials, management, or labor) to make the same number of products as another firm is more efficient. While Canadian workers are very productive, intense domestic and foreign competition has caused managers to look closely at ways to improve productivity even further. The complex nature of the productivity problem and attempted solutions are discussed in Chapter 13.

Federal Budget Deficits

A **federal deficit** occurs when federal government expenditures are greater than federal revenues in a given year. Defence, social welfare, and interest on government debt are kinds of federal expenditures. Federal revenues come mostly from personal and corporate income tax. Figure 3.6 shows Canada's federal surpluses and deficits for recent years.

 The series of annual deficits in the last 10 to 15 years has added up to a staggering total *federal debt*. The Canadian government owes its creditors over $550 billion. These creditors include Canadian and foreign citizens, as well as business firms. The cost of servicing the debt (interest payments) is the government's largest single expenditure and accounts for about one-quarter of all federal government spending.

 The deficit has been increasing at an alarming rate in recent years. From Confederation (1867) to 1981, the total accumulated debt was only

federal deficit
The situation that occurs when federal expenditures are greater than federal revenues in a given year.

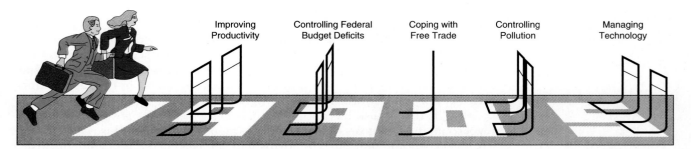

Figure 3.5
Five basic challenges of the 1990s.

Improving Productivity   Controlling Federal Budget Deficits   Coping with Free Trade   Controlling Pollution   Managing Technology

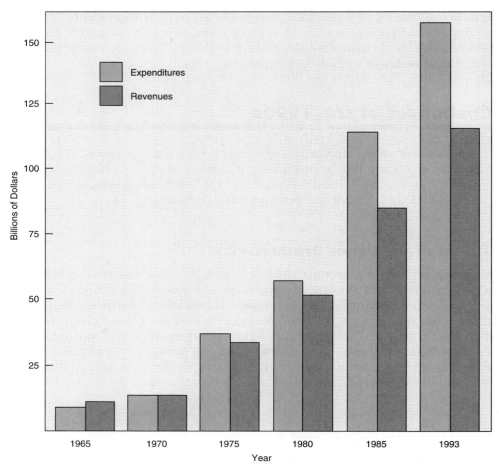

Figure 3.6
Federal government expenditures and revenues, 1965-1993.

$85.7 billion. But since 1981, *annual* deficits have been in the $20-$40 billion dollar range. In 1994, a Dominion Bond Rating Service Ltd. report said that the federal and provincial governments of Canada will face further downgrading of their credit ratings if they do not reduce their deficits. The report said the governments are on a debt treadmill, with interest payments from past borrowings making it difficult to lower deficits.[11]

The deficit affects both Canadian consumers and Canadian business firms. The government must borrow more and more money each year to finance the debt along with the current year's deficit. Canada borrowed money more often in international markets than any other nation in the period 1989–94. Of all bonds issued in international markets during that period, Canada ccounted for 31 percent of the total. The U.S. accounted for only 19 percent.[12] Because the supply of money available for lending at any given time is limited, the government finds itself competing with consumers, businesses, non-profit organizations, and local and provincial governments for borrowed money. This huge demand in the face of limited supply puts upward pressure on interest rates.

The deficit also has an impact in other ways. If the government raises personal income taxes in an attempt to reduce the deficit, this reduces consumer spending and business firms will sell less. If the government raises corporate taxes, business firms will have less profit to distribute to shareholders or to reinvest in the firm for future growth.

Coping with Free Trade

In recent years there has been a rapid globalization of competition. In addition to the mature industrial economies of North America, Western Europe, and Japan, newly industrialized countries like South Korea, Singapore, Hong Kong, and Taiwan have become serious rivals for export sales. Canadian firms no longer can take domestic markets for granted because of this competition.

Why have so many foreign companies been more successful of late than their Canadian competitors? Some pay their employees lower wages. Some have employees who accomplish more in an equal amount of time. Lower safety standards and pollution controls in many foreign countries mean lower costs of producing goods. Fewer "paperwork" requirements means that foreign companies do not have to employ as many accountants and lawyers—a substantial savings.

Some countries fail to honor patents. Brazilian companies, for example, have copied computer designs and now sell these "clones" throughout Latin America. Even Japanese companies have copied computer circuits, although in the late 1980s they agreed to stop this practice. Like the former Soviet Union, Eastern European bloc nations actually employed spies to steal technology. In all these cases, the foreign companies did not have to spend money on research and development of the product, so they did not have to include that cost in the price of their product.

Many countries have complex rules that restrict the import of goods. Some impose tariffs (taxes) on our products. Others have complex "inspection" procedures that cost Canadian companies time and money.

The free trade agreement with the U.S., as well as NAFTA, have resulted in much new domestic competition for Canadian firms. They have also, however, resulted in competitive opportunities in the U.S. and Mexico that did not exist before.

As you can see, the international trade problem is a complex one. These and related issues of international business are explored more fully in Chapter 22.

The Continuing Challenge of Pollution

Ecology is the relationship between living things and their environment. It includes conservation of resources, recycling of used resources, and pollution control. Pesticides, oil spills, smog, chemical dumping, solid wastes, noxious fumes, and radioactive waste all pollute our air, water, and land. **Pollution** is the contamination of the natural environment by the introduction of harmful substances that endanger our health and quality of life.

ecology
The relationship between living things and their environment.

pollution
The contamination of the natural environment by the introduction of harmful substances.

The activities of some business firms do pollute the environment. Water, air, and land pollution are all evident in Canada. Mercury emission in the English-Wabigoon and Spanish river systems in northern Ontario, acid rain, air pollution in the area surrounding Sudbury, and unsightly landfill sites around major cities are all examples of pollution.

In some cases we blame business for pollution that is caused by consumers. Because consumers demand convenient packaging of beverages, we have aluminum pop-top cans. But it is consumers, not businesses, who create litter through improper disposal of the used cans.

In other cases the problem lies with the way the good or service is made. For example, chlorofluorocarbons are used as coolants in refrigerators and air conditioners and for making plastic foams. When they rise from the earth, they set off chemical reactions in the stratosphere that rapidly destroy ozone. It is the ozone layer that protects us from the sun's ultraviolet radiation.

The dilemma for business and government is that emphasizing pollution control in a single industry may result in that industry's output being non-competitive internationally. If other countries do not have the same pollution standards Canada has, their firms will have a lower cost structure; therefore they will be able to undercut the prices of Canadian firms. A similar situation exists for individual companies in an industry. If one company buys pollution control equipment and other companies do not, then the innovating company will have costs that are uncompetitively high.

Today we have laws covering air, solid waste, and water pollution. We also have laws against pollution by pesticides, noise, toxic substances, and hazardous wastes. It is becoming more and more obvious that pollution is a global problem that must be dealt with globally. The World Bank, which makes loans to countries for economic development, has established firm guidelines on how bank projects should avoid or minimize damage to tropical forests, watersheds, and wildlands.[13]

Increased concern about the ecology has also created numerous opportunities for new products. An entire industry has grown up to sell products that reduce air and water pollution. Devices to process smokestack emissions and waste before it is released into water sources are products for which markets have developed. We will explore the issue of pollution in more detail in Chapter 4.

Technology: Friend or Foe?

technology

The application of science that enables people to do entirely new things or perform established tasks in new and better ways.

Technology is the application of science that enables people to do entirely new things or perform established tasks in new and better ways. Consider the following examples:

- After studying the movement of the human foot in minute detail, Canstar Sports Inc. developed the Micron Mega skate, which is now worn by 70 percent of NHL players.[14]
- Improved technology in automobile engines by Honda and Mitsubishi has resulted in 20 percent increases in gas mileage with no loss of power. The engines also emit 20 to 30 percent less carbon dioxide. A Honda Civic, for example, will get 100 kilometres per 5.8 litres of gas in city driving.[15]
- Alcan has developed a ceramic and aluminum composite called Duralcan, which the company is confident will be widely used in automobile manufacturing by the year 2000. The material is already being used in mountain bikes with rave reviews; a bike built with Duralcan weighs less than half as much as a bike built with the standard steel frame.[16]
- Inco Ltd. and Ainsworth Electric Co. are cooperatively developing a new communications technology that may revolutionize mining. It will allow miners to operate heavy machinery to drill, load, and transport ore deep beneath the earth by punching keyboards on the surface. The first test of the system was at Inco's Copper Cliff North nickel mine in Sudbury; it increased productivity by 20 percent.[17]

research and development (R&D)

Activities that are intended to provide new products, services, and processes.

Business firms must embrace technological change so that their processes, products, and product features will not become obsolete. They must also be ready to respond to the competitive effect of such technology. If a firm is aggressive, it will be the first to introduce a new, cheaper way to make its "Product X." It might also introduce "Product X-Mark II" with features that make a competitor's Product Y obsolete. Any of these objectives requires substantial investment in research and development (R&D). **R&D** refers to those activities that are necessary to provide new products, services, and processes. It usually requires a large investment in laboratories, equipment, and scientific talent.

Canada's R&D efforts have lagged behind those of other industrialized economies (see Figure 3.7). When we take into account the fact that the GNP of countries like Japan, the U.S., and Germany is much higher than the GNP of Canada, it means that R&D spending (and employment) in Canada is only a fraction of what it is in other industrialized countries. Only a small number of firms do R&D in Canada, and the top 25 firms account for over half of all R&D.

Technology and Social Problems.   Dealing with technology and its role in modern society will continue to be a major business challenge of the 1990s. Is high technology friend or foe to Canadians and Canadian businesses? Critics fear that automated machinery will replace traditional jobs. They predict a depersonalized society in which people become numbers to a computer that receives telephone calls, handles banking transactions, maintains the temperatures in our homes, and even answers the doorbell.

Defenders of technology point to its promised benefits. New genetically engineered seeds that will increase agricultural production for a hungry world are now entering the market. New vaccines that may help win the battle against cancer and certain viruses are in development. And new employment opportunities in safer environments than the hot and dangerous steel mills of the past are a reality for many today.

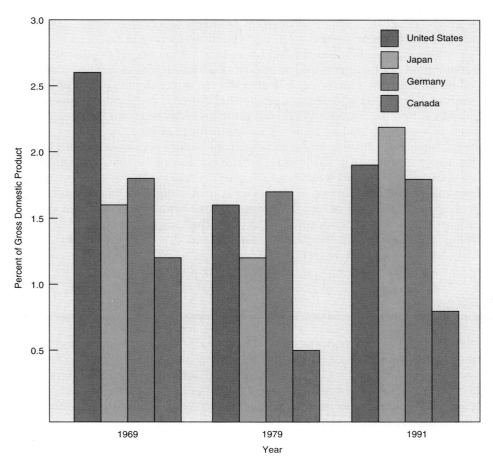

Figure 3.7
Gross expenditure for industrial R&D as a percentage of gross domestic product.

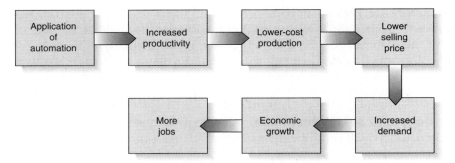

Figure 3.8
Automation and unemployment.

Technology and Unemployment.   Ever since machines became important in the production process, there has been concern that they would take over the work done by humans and that massive unemployment would result. Does automation cause unemployment? The best answer to this question is that automation does cause unemployment in the immediate area where it is applied but, overall, automation creates far more jobs than it takes away. The reasoning behind this conclusion is shown in Figure 3.8.

Competition motivates business firms to find better or cheaper ways to produce products. A company may introduce a new production technology to get the benefits of greater efficiency. This new technology will reduce production costs. Some workers will be needed to operate the new technology, but others will not be needed at all because of the increased productivity the new technology brings. With lower-cost production, the company is able to sell its products at a lower price. Generally speaking, the lower the price of a product, the greater the demand; increased demand for goods in general results in economic growth. With economic growth comes an increase in demand for workers and an increase in the number of jobs.

This is how automation affects unemployment society-wide, but it may not apply in a specific situation. Consider a company that is planning to open a highly automated factory with only 25 supervisory and maintenance personnel. The new factory will replace a nearly obsolete factory, which at present employs 300 workers. The company must face the problem of the unemployed workers. Economic theory says that improved technology will, in the long run, benefit the whole economy. But this theory gives little comfort to those who will be out of jobs.

Summary of Key Points

Business, the government, labor, and consumers represent four countervailing powers that influence and are influenced by one another. Over the last two decades, the influence of labor has stabilized, while consumer influence has been on the rise. The business world has also had to contend with a shift from manufacturing to information services, the advent of high technology, and increased merger activity.

Government regulates business in order to promote competition and to help achieve social goals. Recent years have seen a trend toward deregulation and privatization, but businesses continue to use lobbying and trade associations to influence government.

Changing demographics in the labor force have influenced how business managers deal with the work force and with consumers. The most notable of these changes are an aging population and more working women. Consumer-rights activism has forced businesses to be sensitive to consumer complaints.

Businesses face a variety of challenges in the 1990s. Foremost among these are the need to increase productivity, to reduce the federal budget deficit, to regain a competitive edge in international trade, to behave responsibly with respect to industrial pollution, and to harness technology.

CONCLUDING CASE 3-1

Challenges for Canada's Airlines

Air Canada and Canadian Airlines International (CAI) have been locked in an intense competitive struggle for the past few years. And things are not going to get any easier. The two face a host of challenges in the era that lies ahead. Both airlines simply must become more efficient if they are to survive.

Both companies have become involved with large U.S. airlines in an attempt to ensure their futures. While this will improve their chances for survival, it will likely mean many lost jobs. Both Air Canada and CAI have already cut 25 percent of their employees since 1990, and the remaining employees have taken wage cuts ranging from 5-15 percent.

Increasing the efficiency of operations is an important item for the airlines. Consider these examples:

- Air Canada discovered that by cutting the amount of time its aircraft sit on the ground between flights, it can get 40 more minutes of flying time each day for each plane. This creates the equivalent of seven additional 137-seat planes.
- Baggage handling is another area where improvements can be made. Reducing baggage handling mistakes cuts the cost of shipping late bags to angry travellers and also reduces the turnaround time between stops.
- At CAI, flight attendants collect menus from passengers. If they don't, the cleanup crews will throw them out. Since each menu costs 30 cents, the savings add up.

- Air Canada is transferring most of its information systems department to a new company; the move will save the firm between $10 and $20 million annually.

Once all the efficiency-enhancing moves have been made, Canadian air carriers will be among the most efficient in the world. But they still face the problem of how to increase revenues. Fare wars have been very common in the 1990s, and the industry has had excess capacity. With the tightening up of operations, fewer seats will be available, and the airlines may be able to raise fares somewhat.

Another trend that will have to be dealt with is the decline in business travellers. All companies have been on a cost-cutting binge over the last few years, and business executives are simply not flying as much as they used to. So, the airlines will be focusing more on leisure travellers in their bid to increase revenues. Unfortunately, leisure travellers are turning more and more to charter services to meet their needs. Over the past three years, charter carriers have increased their share of the intercontinental market from 2 percent to 20 percent.

CASE QUESTIONS
1. Are there other steps that Air Canada and Canadian Airlines International can take to meet the challenges facing them? Explain.
2. What role has the government played in the challenges facing the two companies? (Read the opening case in Chapter 6 before answering this question.) ◆

Is Free Trade Good or Bad for Canada?

Wayne McLeod is president of CCL Industries Inc., a company that makes aluminum cans and other packaging for consumer products. Like many of his fellow executives, in the late 1980s, McLeod was a strong supporter of the free trade agreement. But since the agreement has taken effect, CCL's market share has dropped from 50 percent to 3 percent, and 70 percent of the company's assets are now located outside Canada. (This situation is the reverse of what it was before free trade.) The company has created no new jobs in Canada because of free trade.

While most firms have not been so dramatically affected, there is growing concern that the free trade agreement may not be such a good deal for Canada after all. The problem is that disentangling the impact of free trade from other negative factors is difficult. Factors such as high interest rates, adversarial labor relations, high taxes, and a fluctuating Canadian dollar interact and make it difficult to tell just what the impact of the free trade agreement really is. The unexpected severity of the 1991–93 recession is another big factor affecting Canada's economy.

Supporters of free trade argue that Canada's economy would be in even worse shape without free trade. Other countries would have stopped investing in Canada if they hadn't seen evidence that we were moving along with the international tide of freer trade. Thomas d'Aquino, president of the Business Council on National Issues, argues that Canada did the right thing by signing the free trade agreement. The agreement has revitalized Canadian CEOs and caused them to embrace the idea of international competition. It has also enhanced the perception in other countries that Canadian business "has what it takes."

Some unexpected changes have taken place that could not have been predicted before free trade but which have negatively affected Canada's ability to compete. For example, the dramatic increase in the Canadian dollar (from $0.77 U.S. in October, 1987, to $0.89 in November, 1991) reduced Canada's ability to sell in the U.S. But then the dollar fell to $0.72 U.S. by 1995. If the Canadian dollar eventually rises to parity with the U.S. dollar (and there is a persistent rumour circulating that an unwritten rule in the Canada-U.S. free trade agreement says that it should), the situation will become even more difficult for Canada. On the other hand, the more recent decline of the Canadian dollar to about $0.75 U.S. should reduce the negative impact somewhat.

Because the Canadian business establishment was such a strong supporter of free trade, little significant criticism of the agreement is being heard from that quarter. The business community expected some positives and some negatives from free trade, but so far the negatives are coming faster than expected. Some of these negatives, however, are surely caused by the recession and not by free trade.

CASE QUESTIONS
1. Explain how the rise in the value of the Canadian dollar reduced the ability of firms in Canada to sell their products in foreign countries.
2. What would happen if the Canadian dollar was equal in value to the U.S. dollar?
3. Explain why is it so difficult to determine the impact of free trade on Canada. Give a specific example.
4. All things considered, has free trade been beneficial or harmful to Canada?

◆

Key Terms

high technology
  (high-tech)
service economy
information services
acquisition
merger
horizontal merger

vertical merger
conglomerate merger
friendly takeover
hostile takeover
poison pill
greenmail
deregulation

privatization
lobbyist
trade association
consumer movement
consumer rights
federal deficit
ecology

pollution
technology
research and
  development (R&D)

Study Questions and Exercises

Review Questions

1. Identify three significant internal forces that businesses must now contend with.
2. Why does the government feel the need to regulate business?
3. In what ways do businesses attempt to influence government? What ethical implications can be drawn regarding these actions?
4. Why is productivity such an important issue today?
5. What are five major hurdles facing business in the 1990s?

Analysis Questions

6. Using periodicals such as the Globe and Mail and Canadian Business, identify six recent mergers.

Determine whether each was hostile or friendly. Also classify each as horizontal, vertical, or conglomerate.

7. Locate three examples of instances in which you believe business has been more responsive to consumer expectations recently than it was in the past.
8. What do you see as the appropriate role of technology in the future? In general, will it improve or harm our society? Should it be regulated? If so, how?

Application Exercises

9. Interview a local bank manager. Identify ways in which deregulation of the banking industry has made banking more risky and more profitable.
10. Visit a local manufacturing company. Identify ways in which it has been affected by high technology.

Building Your Business Skills

Goal

To help students see how the five general challenges of the 1990s that are mentioned in the chapter have impacted Canadian business firms.

Situation

Assume that you are a management consultant. The vice-president of planning for a large manufacturing firm has approached you about doing a consulting project which would identify some of the major strategic issues that are facing manufacturing firms in Canada. The vice-president wants to know how managers in a variety of manufacturing firms have been affected by challenges such as increasing productivity, reducing federal budget deficits, increasing exports, reducing pollution, and coping with rapid changes in technology. The vice-president also wants to know what managers in other firms are doing to meet these challenges.

Method

Divide the class into groups of three. Have each group interview a manager in a manufacturing firm. Your goal is to determine how the issues of productivity, budget

deficits, international trade, pollution, and technology have impacted the firms of the managers you are interviewing, and what these managers think can be done to meet the challenges. In your interviews, ask the managers to rank these five challenges in order of importance. Also, ask the managers for specific examples of how these challenges have impacted their firm and any specific plans they may have for meeting the challenges.

Have all groups present a summary of their data, and then have a class discussion about the overall findings.

Follow-up Questions

1. What challenges did managers identify as particularly important?
2. Are some challenges important for all firms, while others are important only to some? Why might this be?
3. Have some challenges become more significant in recent years? Have some challenges become less significant?
4. What are the most common ways that companies try to meet these five challenges?

Business Ethics, Social Responsibility, and Business Law

LEARNING OBJECTIVES

After studying this chapter, you will be able to

- Explain how individuals develop their personal codes of ethics and why ethics are important in the work place.
- Distinguish social responsibility from ethics and trace the evolution of social responsibility in modern Canadian business.
- Describe how the concept of social responsibility applies to environmental issues and to businesses' relationship with customers, employees, and investors.
- Identify four general approaches to social responsibility and the steps needed for a firm to take on the maximum responsibility.
- Explain how issues of social responsibility and ethics relate to small businesses.
- Identify the sources of law.
- Explain the requirements for a valid contract and the remedies for breach of contract.
- Compare the agency-principal and bailor-bailee relationships.
- Outline the main points of the law of property, including the role of warranty.

CHAPTER OUTLINE

Waste Not, Want Not

Enzo Fracassi came to Canada from Italy in 1965. He earned a living hauling sand and scrap steel out of Hamilton steel mills and foundries, and trucking sand and gravel for the construction industry. His sons Allen and Philip worked evenings and weekends. When the business failed in the late 1970s, the two sons borrowed money, bought some dump trucks from the receiver, and started in again hauling sand from a foundry. On the last run of each day, they dumped the sand in their own yard and hand-picked the scrap steel out of it to resell it. Since they had to pay a dumping fee for the sand at a landfill, the more steel they picked out, the lower the fee would be.

From this simple beginning a large firm has grown. From his office on Brant Street, Philip looks out at a waste transfer station that now stands on the site where his house used to be. The waste transfer station is an important part of the brothers' plan to change the view of waste management from a "haul-and-dump" mentality to a new focus on recycling and service. Their goal: to turn industrial waste into industrial fuel and raw materials.

Philip Environmental (PE) is now an integrated waste management conglomerate that has four divisions: (1) solid waste management (hauling and dumping industrial waste), (2) resource recovery (scrap metal recycling), (3) hazardous waste (oil and solvent recycling), and (4) environmental services (consulting services). With annual revenues of $400 million, the company is 20 times larger than it was just four years ago.

Consider a typical example of PE activity: Furnace dust is a reddish metallic powder that is a by-product of steel mills. PE collects it and hauls the dust to a transfer station. It then shakes the dust through screens to remove any impurities like scrap iron, wood, or trash. The scrap iron is sent to PEs resource recovery division, while trash goes to the solid waste division. Then the dust is mixed with other additives to make it suitable for use in cement kilns.

PE has a lot of waste to work with. Each year, Canada and the U.S. together generate over 400 million tonnes of garbage and nearly 200 million tonnes of hazardous waste. The result is a $145 billion industry that deals with waste management. But it's a risky business, what with environmental demands rising, more restrictive laws being passed, the threat of liabilities, and increased difficulty in operating landfill sites.

These problems have not slowed down the Fracassi brothers. They have created a company that offers everything from consulting services and recycling to landfilling and emergency cleanup of toxic wastes. The Fracassi's see their business as more like manufacturing and processing than simple waste hauling. They manufacture products from raw materials provided in the waste they collect. Their goal is to offer companies one-stop-shopping for waste management, with an emphasis on recycling. PE's contract with St. Lawrence Cement is illustrative of its approach. PE sells the cement company waste oil and solvent which St. Lawrence burns in its kilns. PE also sends St. Lawrence sludge collected from, say, Redpath Sugars, as well as foundry sands and steel-mill furnace dust which St. Lawrence uses in the production of cement.

The key to success is cross-selling the services of each PE company to the clients of all the rest. For example, Waxman Resources (a PE subsidiary) might send tin-plated copper scrap it picks up to Metal Recovery Industries (another PE subsidiary) for de-tinning. Cross-selling allows PE subsidiaries to sell clients on a wider range of services and keep the competitors away by stressing the one-stop-shopping approach.

But PE must cope with three problems. First, the amount of waste that is produced in North America is declining. This means fewer raw materials are available for companies like PE. Second, competition is increasing. Not only are there several large U.S. firms that dwarf PE, but PE's customers may become its competitors as they move toward recycling their own waste and keeping the savings for themselves. Third, environmental pressure is building to limit the amount of waste PE can take to its landfill sites. Because PE is trying to acquire additional landfill sites, environmentalists are not convinced the company has a real commitment to recycling. But industry experts say that it is more profitable to haul and dump (if you own the landfill) than it is to recycle, so PE has an incentive to do more landfill work. ◆

In the last chapter, several trends and challenges facing business were described. Philip Environmental is an example of a firm that has been able to
benefit from the challenge of coping with pollution. In this chapter—the
last of four that introduce you to the contemporary business world—we
look closely at business ethics and social responsibility. At one time, these issues were not considered very important. But times have changed, and the
practices of today's business firms are in the spotlight. As you will see, managers are faced with a variety of ethical dilemmas, and business firms must
address many issues of social responsibility.

The Nature of Ethics in the Workplace

Just what is ethical behavior in business? You will find as many answers as
people you ask, because **ethics**—standards or morals regarding what is right
and wrong or good and bad—are highly personal.

    Ethics vary greatly from person to person and from situation to situa-
tion. They are based on our society's ideas of right and wrong. Ethics vary from
culture to culture. And within our cultural standards, we all develop our own
personal "code of ethics" that accommodates differences within societal standards. For example, Western society generally considers stealing or bribery
as "wrong" and patriotism and giving as "right." In other cultures, however,
different ethical standards exist. It is important to realize, then, that what
constitutes ethical and unethical behavior is determined partially by the individual and partially by the cultural context in which it occurs.

    Because ethics are both personally and culturally defined, differences
of opinion can genuinely arise as to what is ethical or unethical. For example,
many people who would be appalled at the thought of shoplifting a candy bar
from a grocery store routinely take home pens and pads of paper from their
offices, seeing these items almost as a part of their pay. Other people believe
that if they find money on the sidewalk it is okay to keep it. Still other people
view themselves as law-abiding citizens but have no qualms about using radar
detectors to avoid speeding tickets. In each of these situations, people will
choose different sides of the issue and argue that their views are ethical.

ethics

*Individual standards or moral
values regarding what is right
and wrong or good and bad.*

Influences on Ethics

Aside from situational factors, what makes different people's codes of ethics
vary so much? Figure 4.1 shows the most common influences on an individual's ethics and behavior: family and peers (and the values they convey)
and experiences.

    Families—especially parents—have the first chance to influence a
child's ethics. Parents usually put a high priority on teaching their children
certain values. In many families, these values include religious principles.
Most parents also try to teach their children to obey society's rules and to
behave well toward other people. The so-called *work ethic*—the belief and
practice that hard work brings rewards—is learned in the home. Children
who see their parents behaving ethically are more likely to adopt high ethical standards for themselves than are the children of parents who behave
unethically. Teenagers are particularly likely to reject the verbal messages
of parents who do not practise what they preach.

Figure 4.1
An individual's ethics are determined by a number of different factors. Three of the most basic determinants are family, peers, and experiences.

As children grow and are exposed more to other children, peers begin to have more influence on ethical behavior. Indeed, the values of the group may become far more important than those of the larger society. Although such beliefs and behavior are most talked about in the case of juvenile delinquent gangs, they also apply to the business world. Many unethical (and even criminal) business behaviors are fostered by a company environment in which such practices are acceptable (at least until the company gets caught).

Finally, experiences can increase or decrease certain types of ethical behavior and beliefs about what is right and wrong. A child punished for telling lies learns that telling lies is wrong. Likewise, a company president who goes to jail for misrepresenting the company's financial position will probably have a new understanding of business ethics. But the manager who gets away with sexually harassing an employee will be more likely to see nothing wrong with it and do it again.

The Canadian Business Scene

SUCCEEDING WITH ETHICAL BUSINESS BEHAVIOR

Today, as never before, Canadians are demanding ethical behavior from business managers. Defenders of business behavior may be somewhat justified in charging that business people today are under fire for behavior that for decades was "not only accepted, but ... actually encouraged." Nevertheless, to survive and prosper in the long run, business people today *must* pay attention to ethical issues.

Experts in the area of business ethics have a number of recommendations for executives and entrepreneurs seeking to develop truly ethical behavior in their firms:

■ *Ethics are transmitted from the top down.* Unless top management is committed to ethical behavior—and *acts* in an ethical manner—those below will not follow suit. It is critical that companies consider the ethical views of applicants applying for management positions.

■ *Just as companies create written goals for their profit expectations, so must firms create written goals and codes for ethical behavior.* Written codes are especially important in large firms and firms that have had ethical difficulties in the past.

■ *Vague statements of ethical behavior are useless.* Ethical codes must be as specific as possible, outlining probable ethical situations for employees of the company and appropriate responses.

■ *Companies need to monitor conformance with the ethical code with the same frequency and vigor as they do conformance with financial goals.* Ethical "auditors" must understand a manager's responsibility for economically satisfactory outcomes, but should not tolerate severe deviations from the firm's ethical code.

■ *Employees must be accountable for their actions.* Make compliance with the most crucial aspects of the code a condition of employment. Warn, demote, or fire employees who violate these restrictions.

■ *When managers are rewarded only for profitability, they tend to ignore ethicality.* Reward managers for conforming to ethical standards.

■ *Managers may be uncertain as to which behavior(s) is/are ethical in many situations, especially those that arise suddenly.* Managers should be encouraged to discuss such situations with colleagues and employees, since consensus opinion in a firm of ethically committed individuals has a high chance of being ethically correct.

Turning around the ethical behavior of a firm is not easy, but it can be done. Indeed, given the current business climate, it *must* be done.

Company Policies and Business Ethics

In recent years, the general public has become increasingly concerned about the behavior of Canadian business leaders. A 1990 survey by Decima Research showed that 45 percent of Canadians consider business leaders unprincipled. The comparable figure ten years earlier was 20 percent.[1] As illegal and/or unethical activities by managers have caused more problems for companies, many firms are taking steps to encourage their employees to practise more acceptable behavior.[2] The box "Succeeding With Ethical Business Behavior" offers further guidelines.

Perhaps the single most significant thing a company can do is to demonstrate top management's support for ethical behavior. The importance of top management support is demonstrated in the box "To Bribe or not to Bribe." Many companies have adopted written codes of ethics that clearly state the firm's intent to conduct business ethically. Figure 4.2 (on p. 87) shows the code of ethics adopted by Great-West Life Assurance.

A lively current debate concerns the degree to which business ethics can be "taught" in schools. Not surprisingly, business schools have been important participants in such debates. But companies also need to educate employees. More and more firms are taking this route, offering ethics training to their managers. Imperial Oil, for example, conducts workshops for employees that emphasize ethical concerns. Their purpose is to help employees put Imperial's ethics statement into practice.

International Report

TO BRIBE OR NOT TO BRIBE

Business executives occasionally must make difficult decisions that have important ethical implications. Consider the following situations:

■ David Brink is the chairman of Murray & Roberts Holdings of South Africa. On one of its housing construction projects in the Sudan, the company experienced a problem when payments for work done didn't come through as expected. A government official indicated that he could start the money flowing again if the company would pay him a "commission." The company refused and took the matter to the World Court. Although it took 12 years to get a decision, the case was settled in the company's favor.

■ Jean-Pierre van Rooy is president of Otis Elevator Co. of Farmington, Connecticut. When mobsters in St. Petersburg, Russia approached the Otis operation and asked for "protection" money, the company refused, even though they knew that several other companies— including Coca Cola and Pepsi—had had their operations firebombed after refusing to pay. Otis has a strict company policy of not paying bribes, so it has simply tightened security around its St. Petersburg plant and is hoping for the best.

The experiences of Brink and van Rooy are not unusual in the world of international business. While speaking at a conference on business ethics, the secretary general of Interpol, the world police intelligence network, noted that the tolerance for dishonesty is increasing in both the advanced and developing countries of the world. Managers are therefore likely to be faced at some point in their career with demands that they pay bribes to someone in order to facilitate work. Since corruption is common in international business, the main fear among managers is that they will lose important business contracts if they take a tough stand against paying bribes or commissions. But both Brink and van Rooy don't accept that argument. Brink says that while his company has lost some contracts because they wouldn't pay bribes, they are better off without that business; van Rooy also feels that his company has not suffered because of its strict anti-corruption policy.

Some observers estimate that U.S. business firms lost more than $400 billion worth of business because of strict anti-corruption laws there. The U.S. Foreign Corrupt Practices Act bans all commissions and bribes, but it applies only to U.S.-based companies. Attempts are currently underway to get the 24-member Organization for Economic Cooperation and Development to support a stronger anti-corruption agreement, but there is considerable resistance in other countries to imposing rules like those by which U.S. corporations have to abide. Other critics say such a measure will not work because corruption is so common in much of the world.

One international banker advises his clients that bribes are a way of life in Russia, and if they want to do business there they will have to go along with paying bribes. Corruption was common under the old communist regime in Russia. For example, people paid bribes to get their children into good schools or to jump the line to buy a refrigerator. Surprisingly, things have gotten worse since the collapse of communism. In the first 9 months of 1994, more than 70 000 bribery and extortion cases were opened. A presidential report said that one-third of all retail trade earnings goes for corrupt purposes. Russian consumers therefore pay a 33 percent "tax" for bribery. Nearly half the respondents in a recent poll said they had been forced to pay a bribe to a government official. Bribery has become so common that the newspaper *Komsomolskaya Pravda* compiled a price list of Moscow bribes (e.g., the bribe needed to obtain a Moscow residency permit and the right to purchase an apartment is around $35 000).

The greatest hope in raising the level of ethical behavior lies with individual managers, particularly those at the top management level. If the chief executive sanctions anything illegal, this will send the wrong message to the firm's employees. Conversely, if the chief executive is high-profile about being very ethical, this not only models correct behavior to employees, it may actually discourage bribe requests from outsiders because they know where the company stands.

The Nature of Social Responsibility

social responsibility
A business's collective code of ethical behavior toward the environment, its customers, its employees, and its investors.

Ethics affect how an individual behaves within a business. But **social responsibility** affects how a business behaves as an entity on its own toward other businesses, customers, investors, and society at large. Like ethics, social responsibility is individualistic (for the firm, not a person), since it must attempt to balance different commitments. For example, in order to

---

Guiding Principles — The Great-West Life Assurance Company

1. Great-West Life's management recognizes that, to prosper, the company must serve its clients, staff members and sales representatives, shareholders, and the community at large, with integrity and according to the highest standards of conduct.

2. We will maintain an environment of trust in, and respect for, the dignity of the individual. We will strive to select superior people. We will build and maintain a dynamic organization through an open and participative style of management. We will give staff members and sales personnel every opportunity to make the most of their abilities and reward them according to their contribution to meeting our objectives.

3. We will distribute our products and services in the best interests of our clients through distribution systems that are contemporary, innovative, and socially responsible.

4. Our investment program will carefully balance the quality, terms, and rate of return on our investments. We will strive to achieve a consistently superior rate of return to meet our overall financial objectives and obligations to our clients.

5. We will find new and better ways to serve our clients by offering products and services that are both contemporary and innovative to satisfy their changing needs and desires. We will maintain their goodwill by meeting our commitments to them both in spirit and letter with particular emphasis upon the financial management and security of their funds.

6. We will work to increase the long-term value of shareholders' investment to maintain our reputation as a sound and growing financial institution.

Figure 4.2
Ethical principles at Great-West Life Assurance Co.

behave responsibly toward its investors, a company must try to maximize its profits. But a responsibility toward its customers means that it must produce safe goods or services. In their zeal to respond to investors, companies sometimes step over the line and act irresponsibly toward their customers. Hertz Rent-A-Car was recently charged with overcharging its corporate customers and filing bogus insurance claims for damages. The video case on p. 115 describes the activities of Ethicscan, an organization that monitors the social responsibility of business firms.

Just as an individual's personal code of ethics is influenced by many factors, so is a firm's sense of social responsibility. To a large extent social responsibility depends on the ethics of the individuals employed by a firm—especially its top management. But social responsibility can also be forced from outside by government and consumers. How a firm behaves is also shaped by how other firms in the same country and industry behave and by the demands of investors.

The Evolution of Social Responsibility

The concept of social responsibility has evolved in three identifiable phases.[3] The first was the entrepreneurial era of the late nineteenth century (see Chapter 2). The businesses run by these entrepreneurs had tremendous economic power. But abuses of that power brought public outcries. It was during this era that ordinary citizens and government first became concerned about business methods. This concern manifested itself in the nation's first laws forbidding certain ways of doing business.

The second phase in the evolution of social responsibility occurred during the Great Depression. Many people in the 1930s blamed business greed and lack of restraint for the loss of their jobs as businesses closed. Out of the economic turmoil emerged new laws that attempted to define an expanded role for business in protecting and enhancing the general welfare of society.

Finally, the social unrest of the 1960s and 1970s brought new charges that business is a negative force in our society. Government regulation again increased, forcing health warnings on cigarettes, stricter environmental protection standards, and a host of other restrictions. Many businesses, too, responded by demonstrating a stronger social conscience.

Some observers today suggest that we are entering a fourth era of social responsibility. In this era, an increased awareness of the global economy and heightened campaigning on the part of environmentalists and other activists have combined to make many businesses more sensitive to their social responsibilities.

Areas of Social Responsibility

In defining its sense of social responsibility—or having it defined—most firms must confront four issues. As Figure 4.3 shows, these issues concern an organization's responsibility toward its environment, its customers, its employees, and its investors.

Responsibility Toward the Environment

pollution

The injection of harmful substances into the environment.

One critical area of social responsibility involves how the business relates to its physical environment. As noted earlier in Chapter 3, **pollution** has been and continues to be a significant managerial challenge. Although noise pollution is attracting increased concern, air pollution, water pollution, and land pollution are the subjects of most anti-pollution efforts by business and governments.[4]

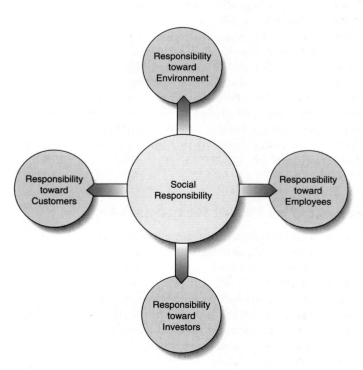

Figure 4.3
There are four basic areas of social responsibility.

Air Pollution.　　Air pollution results when a combination of factors converge to lower air quality. Large amounts of chemicals such as the carbon monoxide emitted by automobiles contribute to air pollution. Smoke and other chemicals emitted by manufacturing plants also help to create air pollution.

Legislation has gone a long way toward controlling air pollution. Under new laws, many companies have had to install special devices to limit the pollutants they expel into the atmosphere. Such clean-up efforts are not without costs, however. The bill to private companies for air pollution control devices runs into billions of dollars.

Even with these devices, however, acid rain remains a problem. **Acid rain** occurs when sulphur pumped into the atmosphere mixes with natural moisture and falls as rain. Much of the acid rain damage to forests and streams in the eastern United States and Canada has been attributed to heavy manufacturing and power plants in the midwestern United States.

Acid rain poses a dilemma in social responsibility for businesses. Current technologies to greatly reduce sulphur pollution are so costly that they would force many businesses to close. Such a move would cause major financial losses for investors and for laid-off employees, not to mention the loss of crucial services. The business challenge is to find ways to significantly reduce the sulphur—and thus the acid rain—without incurring costs that are too high to bear.

Water Pollution.　　For years, businesses and municipalities dumped their waste into rivers, streams, and lakes with little regard for the effects. Thanks to new legislation and increased awareness on the part of businesses, water quality is improving in many areas. Millar Western Pulp Ltd. built Canada's first zero-discharge pulp mill at Meadow Lake, Saskatchewan. There is no discharge pipe to the river, no dioxin-forming chlorine, and next to no residue. Dow Chemical built a plant at Fort Saskatchewan that will not dump any pollutants into the nearby river.[5]

Land Pollution.　　Two key issues are associated with land pollution. The first issue is how to restore the quality of land damaged and abused in the past. This issue is particularly important in areas where strip mining has jeopardized the safety of nearby residents.

A second, but no less important, issue is how to prevent such problems in the future. Changes in foresting practices, limits on types of mining, and new forms of solid waste disposal are all attempts to address this issue, although such changes are often opposed. As we saw in the opening case, a whole new industry—**recycling**—has developed as part of increased consciousness about land pollution. RBW Graphics, for example, uses a process that cleanses paper fibers and other impurities from ink recovered from printing presses. The system saves the company 35 000 kilograms of ink annually. This ink used to be transported to a dump. Instead, recycling saves the company $175 000 each year.[6]

Other business firms are also reducing what they send to city dumps. The Royal York Hotel in Toronto, for example, has installed machinery that extracts 70 percent of the moisture from organic waste. The hotel has reduced the amount it sends to the dump by 50 percent. Ramada Renaissance in Toronto has bought a refrigerator that stores waste which will ultimately become animal food. The hotel anticipates it will reduce its waste sent to the dump by 75 percent.[7] Bell Canada has reduced the amount of garbage it generates each day from 800 kilograms to 22 kilograms at its Etobicoke, Ontario, location.[8]

An especially controversial problem centers on toxic waste disposal. **Toxic wastes** are dangerous chemical and/or radioactive byproducts of various manufacturing processes. Because toxic waste cannot usually be processed into harmless material or destroyed, it must be stored somewhere. The problem is—where? Few people want a toxic waste storage facility in their town.

acid rain
A form of pollution affecting the eastern United States and Canada as a result of sulphur expelled into the air by midwestern power and manufacturing plants.

recycling
The reconversion of waste materials into useful products.

toxic waste
Pollution resulting from the emission of chemical and/or radioactive byproducts of various manufacturing processes into the air, water, or land.

Various organizations aggressively monitor business activity that might lead to pollution. For example,

■ Greenpeace sent a letter to 60 Canadian and foreign investment dealers making the case that the dealers should advise their clients not to invest in Canadian Mining and Energy Corp. because of environmental concerns.[9]

■ A group of Canadian shareholders has criticized Placer Dome Inc. for its open pit copper mine on Marinduque Island in the Philippines.[10]

■ The Task Force on the Churches and Corporate Responsibility (TFCCR) and Probe International have publicly criticized Canadian firms like Atomic Energy of Canada Ltd. (selling a food irradiator to Thailand), Petro-Canada (road building in the Ecuadorian rain forest), and Brascan Ltd. (exploration rights for tin in areas of Ecuador conflicting with Native land claims).[11]

■ Because those who own the land can be forced to pay to clean it up, the Royal Bank refuses to lend money to some types of companies (e.g., waste oil firms) until an environmental audit has been carried out. When Dominion Barrel and Drum went bankrupt, for example, it left behind thousands of contaminated barrels on 21 hectares of land. The firm's creditor, the Federal Business Development Bank, decided not to foreclose on the land when it found that it would cost over $1 million—more than what the land was worth—to clean it up.[12]

Many business firms are now acting to reduce various forms of pollution. However, as the box "Living Up To Environmental Expectations" shows, the

Toxic waste disposal and clean-up have become increasingly important areas of debate and concern in recent years.

The Canadian Business Scene

LIVING UP TO ENVIRONMENTAL EXPECTATIONS

Over the last few years, business firms have learned some hard lessons about the environmental movement in Canada. In spite of increased spending on pollution control equipment and greater sensitivity to environmental concerns, companies are finding that consumers and environmental groups can be difficult to satisfy. Chemical giant Dow Chemical and the fast-food wonder McDonald's are two firms that have experienced such frustrations.

Dow Chemical

Dow has long been a target of environmentalists, both because of the kinds of products it produces and because of some well-publicized chemical spills. One of the most famous occurred in 1985 when the company was responsible for a massive spill of perchloroethylene into the St. Clair River. That incident galvanized the company into aggressively confronting its pollution problem and, in the last few years, it has spent millions of dollars as part of its plan to drastically reduce pollution. At its Sarnia plant, for example, Dow has embarked on a ten-year, $100 million project to keep waste waters inside the plant. The company has also steadily increased environmental spending in general. It has pledged $20-$25 million to cut its air emissions in half by 1995. Teams of workers at its various plants systematically check equipment to assess the potential for leaks and spills before they happen.

But all this activity is not enough for environmental groups such as Pollution Probe, Greenpeace, and the Walpole Island First Nation Council. They want Dow to stop making certain chemicals altogether because ending their production will automatically solve the pollution problem. But "sunsetting" (stopping production of certain chemicals) is highly controversial. Dow makes considerable profits from manufacturing chemicals such as chlorine and is reluctant to stop producing it. Environmentalists, on the other hand, would like to see production of a whole range of chemicals ended almost immediately.

McDonald's

McDonald's has also had its share of environmental frustrations. Ironically, McDonald's is a company that has long been environmentally conscious. When McDonald's started operations in 1955, public health was a major concern and many fast-food restaurants were sanitary danger zones. McDonald's made a commitment to freshly prepared food of uniform quality wrapped in disposable paper. In the 1960s, environmentalists began to focus on litter. McDonald's pressured its franchisees to clean up all the garbage within a square block of each restaurant.

By the 1970s, legislation prompted McDonald's to address what type of disposable packaging it should use. Because environmentalists were concerned about the number of trees being cut down to fulfill its packaging

needs, the firm adopted the plastic polystyrene foam container (the "clamshell"). But by the mid-1980s, environmentalists were denouncing polystyrene on three grounds: the manufacture of polystyrene creates harmful toxic emissions; the use of chlorofluorocarbons in the manufacturing process damages the ozone layer of the earth; plastic polystyrene is not biodegradable.

McDonald's responded to these concerns by changing the manufacturing process to eliminate the need for chlorofluorocarbons and to reduce the toxic emissions produced. In answer to the issue of biodegradability, McDonald's noted that polystyrene makes up only three-tenths of 1 percent of landfill by weight whereas paper and cardboard make up 35 percent of the total weight. Nonetheless, in spite of polystyrene's low impact on landfill sites, McDonald's stated that it wanted to be environmentally sound and so would recycle polystyrene.

The company committed over $5 million dollars to recycling, including building a recycling plant. Hoping to get a "green housekeeping" seal of approval, McDonald's signed a cooperation agreement with the Environmental Defense Fund (EDF) that gave the EDF complete access to McDonald's records. But, as McDonald's learned, the EDF was totally opposed to polystyrene in any form, recycled or not.

At about the same time, McDonald's began receiving large numbers of letters from consumers who didn't like the polystyrene clamshells. When the head of the EDF refused to join McDonald's senior environmental officer at a press conference, the company decided that its recycling plan just wasn't going to work. It replaced the clamshell with thin paper wrappers.

McDonald's seems to be in a no-win situation. Now the company is under fire from environmentalists who claim that paper waste is even worse than polystyrene. They accuse McDonald's of reneging on its commitment to recycling for public relations reasons rather than for environmental reasons. They also quote from a study McDonald's had used originally to defend polystyrene, a study which showed that greasy paper is almost impossible to recycle.

McDonald's decisions affect other businesses as well. When Lily Cups, the supplier of polystyrene, lost the clamshell business, it had to lay off 46 workers. It also had to scramble to buy paper-product machinery to fulfill its contract with McDonald's for coffee cups. McDonald's vice-president of environmental affairs says that the company is fed up with taking all the heat alone. He notes that other companies do less than McDonald's for the environment, yet they never get bad press.

The basic lesson that can be learned from McDonald's experience is that all the parties involved—government, business, environmentalists, suppliers—have to collaborate on environmental issues if the outcome is to be positive.

road to environmental purity is not easy. Under the Canadian and Ontario Environmental Protection Acts, liability for a business firm can run as high as $2 million per day. To protect themselves, companies must prove that they showed diligence in avoiding an environmental disaster such as an oil or gasoline spill.[13] The Environmental Choice program, sponsored by the federal government, licenses products that meet environmental standards set by the Canadian Standards Association. Firms whose products meet these standards can put the logo—three doves intertwined to form a maple leaf—on their products.[14]

Responsibility Toward Customers

Social responsibility toward customers generally falls into one of two categories: providing quality products and pricing those products fairly. As with the environment, firms differ in their level of concern about responsibility to customers. Yet unlike environmental problems, customer problems do not require expensive technological solutions. Most such problems can be avoided if companies obey the laws regarding consumer rights and illegal pricing practices.

consumerism

A social movement that seeks to protect and expand the rights of consumers in their dealings with businesses.

Rights of Consumers.   Much of the current interest in business responsibility toward customers can be traced to the rise of consumerism. **Consumerism** is a form of social activism dedicated to protecting the rights of consumers in their dealings with businesses.

Consumers have several rights. First, they have the right to safe products. For example, when you buy a new paint sprayer, it must be safe to use for spraying paint. It must come with instructions on how to use it, and it must have been properly tested by its manufacturer. Dow Corning Corp. halted production of silicone breast implants after questions were raised about the product's safety. Critics claimed the company continued to market the product even though evidence existed that there were problems with silicone. The price of Dow's stock dropped over ten dollars when the market heard the news.[15]

Second, consumers have the right to be informed about all relevant aspects of a product. Food products must list their ingredients. Clothing must be labeled with information about its proper care. And banks must tell you exactly how much interest you are paying on a loan. Cereal companies have come under fire recently for some of the claims they have made about the oat bran content of their cereals, as well as its likely effects.

Third, consumers have a right to be heard. Many companies today have complaints offices. Retailers like Kmart offer a money-back guarantee if consumers aren't satisfied. On many of its products Proctor & Gamble puts a toll-free number that consumers can call if they have questions or complaints. When companies refuse to respond to consumer complaints, consumer protection agencies such as the Better Business Bureau and consumer interest groups such as the Airline Passengers Association may intervene.

Finally, consumers have a right to choose what they buy. Central to this right is free and open competition among companies. In times past, "gentlemen's agreements" were often used to avoid competition or to divide up a market so that firms did not have to truly compete against each other. Such practices are illegal today and any attempts by business to block competition can result in fines or other penalties.

Interfering with competition can also mean illegal pricing practices. **Collusion** among companies—getting together to "fix" prices—is against the law. Polar Plastic Ltd. of Montreal pled guilty to conspiring to fix prices of disposable cups, glasses, and cutlery in the U.S. market. Although secret meetings and phone conversations took place between executives of competing companies as they tried to fix prices, the conspiracy was not successful.[16]

collusion

An illegal agreement among companies in an industry to "fix" prices for their products.

Responsibility Toward Employees

Organizations also need to employ fair and equitable practices with their employees. Later, in Chapter 8, we describe the human-resource management activities essential to a smoothly functioning business. These same activities—recruiting, hiring, training, promoting, and compensating—are also the basis for social responsibility toward employees. A company that provides its employees with equal opportunities for rewards and advancement without regard to race, sex, or other irrelevant factors is meeting its social responsibilities. Firms that ignore their responsibility to employees leave themselves open for lawsuits. They also miss the chance to hire better and more highly motivated employees.

Some progressive companies go well beyond these legal requirements, hiring and training the so-called hard-core unemployed (people with little education and training and a history of unemployment) and those who have disabilities. The Bank of Montreal, for example, sponsors a community college skills upgrading course for individuals with hearing impairments. The Royal Bank provides managers with discrimination awareness training. Rogers Cablesystems Ltd. has begun to provide individuals with mobility restrictions with telephone and customer-service job opportunities.[17] Bell Canada employs more than 1000 people with disabilities (2 percent of its permanent work force). But, in Canada, over 50 percent of those with physical disabilities are still unemployed.[18]

In addition to their responsibility to employees as resources of the company, firms have a social responsibility to their employees as people. Firms that accept this responsibility make sure that the workplace is safe, both physically and emotionally. They would no more tolerate an abusive manager or one who sexually harasses employees than they would a gas leak.

Business firms also have a responsibility to respect the privacy of their employees. While nearly everyone agrees that companies have the right to exercise some level of control over their employees, there is great controversy about exactly how much is acceptable in areas like drug testing and computer monitoring. When Canadian National Railways instituted drug testing for train, brake, and yard employees, 12 percent failed. Trucking companies have found that nearly one-third of truckers who have been involved in an accident are on drugs.[19]

Employees are often unaware that they are being monitored by managers who are using new computer technology. Computer software firms even sell programs called "Spy" and "Peek" to facilitate monitoring. This type of monitoring increases employee stress levels because they don't know exactly when the boss is watching them. A lawsuit was brought against Northern Telecom by employees who charged that the firm installed telephone bugs and hidden microphones in one of its plants.[20]

Respecting employees as people also means encouraging ethical behavior. Too often, individuals who try to act ethically find themselves in trouble on the job. This problem is especially true for **whistle-blowers**, employees who detect an unethical, illegal, and/or socially irresponsible action within the company and try to end it.

For example, Ross Gray, formerly a vice-president at Standard Trustco Ltd., was dismissed from his position after he "blew the whistle" on illegal activities at the company. The company claimed that Gray had participated in the illegal activities. He filed a wrongful dismissal suit against the firm.[21]

In a socially responsible company, whistle-blowers can confidently report their findings to higher-level managers, who will act or forward the report to someone who can. However, in many firms, whistle-blowers are penalized for their efforts and find themselves demoted or even fired. A few of these individuals persist, taking their cases to the media or to government agencies. But employees in companies that discourage whistle-blowing more often choose to keep silent, to the loss of both business and society.

whistle-blower
An individual who calls attention to an unethical, illegal, and/or socially irresponsible practice on the part of a business or other organization.

Responsibility Toward Investors

It may sound odd to say that a firm can be irresponsible toward investors, since they are the owners of the company. But if the managers of a firm abuse its financial resources, the ultimate losers are the owners, since they do not receive the earnings, dividends, or capital appreciation due them. Managers can act irresponsibly in several ways.

Improper Financial Management.   Occasionally, organizations are guilty of financial mismanagement. In other cases, executives have been "guilty" of paying themselves outlandish salaries, spending huge amounts of company money for their own personal comfort, and similar practices. Creditors can do nothing. Even shareholders have few viable options. Trying to force a management changeover is not only difficult, it can drive down the price of the stock, a penalty shareholders are usually unwilling to assign themselves.

cheque kiting
The illegal practice of writing cheques against money that has not yet arrived at the bank on which the cheque has been written, relying on that money arriving before the cheque clears.

Cheque Kiting.   Other practices are specifically illegal. **Cheque kiting**, for instance, involves writing a cheque against money that has not yet arrived at the bank on which it is drawn. In 1993, E. F. Hutton and Co. was convicted of violating kiting laws on a massive scale: In a carefully planned scheme, company managers were able to use as much as $250 million every day that did not belong to the firm. Managers would deposit customer cheques for, say, $1 million into the company account. Knowing that the bank would collect only a percentage of the total deposit over the course of several days, they proceeded to write cheques against the total $1 million.

insider trading
The use of confidential information to gain from the purchase or sale of stock.

Insider Trading.   Another area of illegal and socially irresponsible behavior by firms toward investors is the practice of **insider trading**. Insider trading occurs when someone uses confidential information to gain from the purchase or sale of stocks. Most of these cases have occurred in the United States. In one highly publicized case, Ivan Boesky, a professional Wall Street trader, was convicted of insider trading. An acquaintance of Boesky's, Dennis Levine, worked for Drexel Burnham Lambert, an investment banking firm. When Levine heard of an upcoming merger or acquisition, he passed the information along to Boesky. Boesky, in turn, bought and sold the appropriate stocks to make huge profits, which he then split with Levine. In one especially profitable instance, Boesky used Levine's information about Nestlé's plans to buy Carnation stock to earn over $28 million in profits.[22]

Misrepresentation of Finances.   Irresponsible and unethical behavior regarding financial representation is also illegal. All corporations are required to conform to generally accepted accounting practices in maintaining and reporting their financial status. Sometimes, though, managers project profits far in excess of what they truly expect to earn. When the truth comes out, investors are almost always bitter. Occasionally, companies are found guilty of misrepresenting their finances to outsiders.

parking
The illegal and complex practice of shifting funds between countries to avoid taxes

Parking.   Yet another illegal practice, **parking** involves complex shifts of funds between countries to avoid taxes. Companies that do this may keep two sets of financial records to facilitate a parking scheme. One is the "public" set, the other a "private" set for the eyes of certain managers only. The private records help managers keep tabs on the funds.

The safety of workers is an important consideration for all organizations. The required use of hardhats, for example, is designed to protect workers from head injuries.

Implementing Social Responsibility Programs

Thus far, we have discussed social responsibility as if consensus exists on how firms should behave in most situations. In fact, dramatic differences of opinion exist as to the appropriateness of social responsibility as a business goal. As you might expect, some people oppose any business activity that cuts into profits to investors. Others argue that responsibility must take precedence over profits.

Even people who share a common attitude toward social responsibility by businesses may have different reasons for their beliefs. Some opponents of such activity fear that if businesses become too active in social concerns, they will gain too much control over how those concerns are addressed. They point to the influence many businesses have been able to exert on the government agencies that are supposed to regulate their industries. Other critics of business-sponsored social programs argue that companies lack the expertise needed. They believe that technical experts, not businesses, should decide how best to clean up a polluted river for example.

Supporters of social responsibility believe that corporations are citizens just like individuals and therefore need to help improve our lives. Others point to the vast resources controlled by businesses and note that since businesses often create many of the problems social programs are designed to alleviate, that they should use their resources to help. Still others argue that social responsibility is wise because it pays off for the firm.

Max Clarkson, formerly a top-level business executive, is now the director of the Centre for Corporate Social Performance and Ethics at the University of Toronto. He says that business firms that have a strong consciousness about ethics and social responsibility outperform firms that don't. After designing and applying a social responsibility rating system for companies, he found that companies that had the highest marks on questions of ethics and social responsibility also had the highest financial performance.[23]

Approaches to Social Responsibility

Given these differences of opinion, it is little wonder that corporations adopt a variety of postures when making decisions about social responsibility. Four common approaches are discussed below.

social-opposition approach
The stance of a firm that makes a conscious decision not to observe regulatory and standard business practice guidelines to social responsibility.

Social-Opposition Approach.   A firm that takes a **social-opposition approach** is one that does as little as possible in the area of social responsibility. While few in number, these organizations attract banner headlines when caught and make all businesses look bad. When they cross the line and behave irresponsibly, or even illegally, they try to cover it up and deny any wrongdoing. These organizations usually know what they are doing and make conscious decisions that most people would recognize as not being in the best interest of society.

social-obligation approach
A conservative approach to social responsibility in which a company does only the minimum required by law.

Social-Obligation Approach.   The **social-obligation approach** is consistent with the argument that profits should not be spent on social programs. The company that uses this approach does the minimum required by government regulation and standard business practices, but nothing else.

Tobacco companies exemplify this approach. They did not put health warnings on their packages and did not drop television advertising until forced to do so by the government. In other countries that lack such bans, Canadian and American tobacco companies still advertise heavily and make no mention of the negative effects of smoking.

social-reaction approach
A moderate approach to social responsibility in which a company sometimes goes beyond the minimum required by law on request.

Social-Reaction Approach.   Firms using the **social-reaction approach** go beyond the bare minimums if specifically asked. For example, many companies will match employee contributions to approved causes. Others sponsor local hockey teams. But someone has to knock on the door and ask.

social-response approach
A liberal approach to social responsibility in which a company actively seeks opportunities to contribute to the well-being of society.

Social-Response Approach.   Firms that adopt the social response approach actively seek opportunities to contribute to the well-being of society. McDonald's, for example, has worked with children's hospitals and local communities to establish Ronald McDonald Houses to provide lodging for families of seriously ill children hospitalized away from home

Ronald McDonald House helps the families of children who are in hospital care. It is supported by McDonald's and is an excellent example of socially responsible behavior by a business corporation.

The Body Shop, a franchise chain that sells soaps, salves, balms, foot massagers, and other beauty products, tries to be socially responsible in everything it does. Its cosmetics are all natural and are not tested on animals. The containers are recyclable and refundable. The Body Shop features window displays that are given to "causes," for example, to Friends of the Earth or the World Wildlife Fund. Each store is involved in a community project to which staff must devote an aggregate of four paid hours a week. The Body Shop recently raised $45 000 for the World Wildlife Fund of Canada.[24]

Corporations in Canada give about 10 percent of all money given to charity. But they give less than one-half of 1 percent of pretax profits to charity. The most generous industries are metal mining, clothing, and machinery; the least generous are oil, transportation equipment, and wood. Eighty percent of Canadians feel that business should give to charity.[25]

Managing Social Responsibility Programs

Making a company truly socially responsible in the full sense of the social-response approach takes an organized and managed program. In particular, managers must take four steps to foster social responsibility, as shown in Figure 4.4.

First, social responsibility must start at the top. Without this support, no program can succeed. Top managers must make the decision that they want to take a stronger stand on social responsibility and develop a policy statement outlining their commitment.

Second, a committee of top managers needs to develop a plan detailing the level of support to be directed toward social responsibility. Some companies set aside a percentage of profits for social programs. Levi Strauss, for example, has a policy of giving 2.4 percent of its pretax earnings to worthy

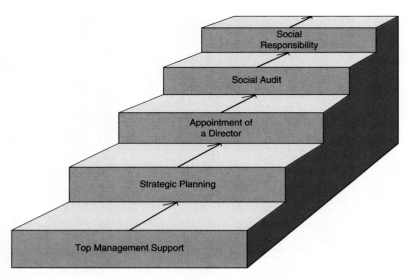

Figure 4.4
Establishing a social responsibility program involves four basic steps.

causes. Managers also need to set specific priorities. Should the firm train the hard-core unemployed or support the arts, for example?

Third, one specific executive needs to be given the authority to act as director of the firm's social agenda. Whether this is a separate job or an additional responsibility, this individual must monitor the program and ensure that its implementation is consistent with the policy statement and the strategic plan.

Finally, the organization needs to conduct occasional social audits. A **social audit** is a systematic analysis of how a firm is using funds earmarked for its social-responsibility goals. Consider the case of a company whose strategic plan calls for spending $100 000 to train 200 hard-core unemployed people and subsequently to place 180 of them in jobs. If at the end of one year the firm has spent $98 000, trained 210 people, and placed 175 into jobs, an audit will confirm the program as a success. But if the program cost $150 000, trained only 90 people, and placed only ten of them in jobs, the audit will reveal the program's failure. A failure should signal the director and the committee to rethink the program's implementation and/or their choice of priorities.

social audit

A systematic analysis of how a firm is using funds earmarked for social-responsibility goals and how effective these expenditures have been.

Social Responsibility and the Small Business

Although many of the examples in this chapter illustrate responses to social responsibility and ethical issues by big business, small businesses face many of the same questions.

As the owner of a garden supply store, how would you respond to a building inspector's suggestion that a cash payment would expedite your application for a building permit? As the manager of a nightclub, would you call the police, refuse service or sell liquor to a customer whose ID card looks forged? Or as the owner of a small laboratory, would you actually call the board of health to make sure that it has licensed the company you want to contract with to dispose of the lab's medical waste? Is the small manufacturing firm justified in overcharging a customer by 5 percent whose purchasing agent is lax? Who will really be harmed if a small firm pads its income statement to help get a much-needed bank loan?

Can a small business afford a social agenda? Should it sponsor hockey teams, make donations to the United Way, and buy light bulbs from the Lion's

Club? Is joining the Chamber of Commerce and supporting the Better Business Bureau too much or just good business? Clearly, ethics and social responsibility are decisions faced by all managers in all organizations, regardless of rank or size. One key to business success is to decide in advance how to respond to these issues.

The Role of Law in Canadian Society

Law is the set of rules and standards that a society agrees upon to govern the behavior of its citizens. Both the British and the French influenced the development of law in Canada. In 1867, the British North America (BNA) Act created the nation of Canada. The BNA Act was "patriated" to Canada in 1982 and is known as the Constitution Act. As we will see in Chapter 21, this act divides legislative powers in Canada between the federal and provincial governments.

law
The set of rules and standards that a society agrees upon to govern the behavior of its citizens.

Sources of Law

The law in Canada has evolved and changed in response to our norms and values. Our laws have arisen from three sources: 1) customs and judicial precedents (the source of common law), 2) the actions of provincial and federal legislatures (the source of statutory law), and 3) rulings by administrative bodies (the source of administrative law).

Common law is the unwritten law of England, derived from ancient precedents and judges' previous legal opinions. Common law is based on the principle of equity, the provision to every person of a just and fair remedy. Canadian legal customs and traditions derive from British common law. All provinces except Quebec, which uses the French Civil Code, have laws based on British common law, and court decisions are often based on precedents from common law. That is, decisions made in earlier cases that involved the same legal point will guide the court.

common law
The unwritten law of England, derived from precedent and legal judgments.

Statutory law is written law developed by city councils, provincial legislatures, and parliament. Most law in Canada today is statutory law.

statutory law
Written law developed by city councils, provincial legislatures and parliament.

Administrative law is the rules and regulations that government agencies and commissions develop based on their interpretations of statutory laws. For example, Consumer and Corporate Affairs Canada develops regulations on false advertising using federal legislation.

administrative law
Rules and regulations that government agencies develop based on their interpretations of statutory law.

The Court System

In Canada, the judiciary branch of government has the responsibility of settling disputes among organizations or individuals by applying existing laws. Both provincial and federal courts exist to hear both criminal and civil cases. The Supreme Court of Canada is the highest court in Canada. It decides whether or not to hear appeals from lower courts.

Business Law

Business firms, like all other organizations, are affected by the laws of the country. **Business law** refers to laws that specifically affect how business firms are managed. Some laws affect all businesses, regardless of size, industry, or location. For example, the Income Tax Act requires businesses to

business law
Laws that specifically affect how businesses are managed.

The Supreme Court decides whether or not to hear appeals of lower court rulings. Its decision is final.

pay income tax. Other laws may have a greater impact on one industry than on others. For example, pollution regulations are of much greater concern to Inco than they are to Lawson Travel.

Business managers must have at least a basic understanding of seven important concepts in business law:

- contracts
- agency
- bailment
- property
- warranty
- torts
- negotiable instruments.

Contracts

contract

An agreement between two parties to act in a specified way or to perform certain acts.

Agreements about transactions are common in a business's day-to-day activity. A **contract** is an agreement between two parties to act in a specified way or to perform certain acts. A contract might, for example, apply to a customer buying a product from a retail establishment or to two manufacturers agreeing to buy products or services from each other. A valid contract includes several elements:

- *an agreement*—All parties must consciously agree about the contract.
- *consideration*—The parties must exchange something of value (e.g., time, products, services, money, etc.).
- *competence*—All parties to the contract must be legally able to enter into an agreement. Individuals who are below a certain age or who are legally insane, for example, cannot enter into legal agreements.
- *legal purpose*—What the parties agree to do for or with each other must be legal. An agreement between two manufacturers to fix prices is not legal.

The courts will enforce a contract if it meets the criteria described above. Most parties honor their contracts but, occasionally, one party does not do what it was supposed to do. **Breach of contract** occurs when one party to an agreement fails, without legal reason, to live up to the agreement's provisions. The party who has not breached the contract has three alternatives under the law in Canada: 1) discharge, 2) sue for damages, or 3) require specific performance.

An example will demonstrate these three alternatives. Suppose Barrington Farms Inc. agrees to deliver 100 dozen long-stemmed roses to the Blue Violet Flower Shop the week before Mother's Day. One week before the agreed-upon date, Barrington's informs Blue Violet that it cannot make the delivery until after Mother's Day. Under the law, the owner of the Blue Violet can choose among any of the following:

Discharge.   Blue Violet can also ignore its obligations in the contract. That is, it can contract with another supplier.

Sue for Damages.   Blue Violet can legally demand payment for losses caused by Barrington's failure to deliver the promised goods. Losses might include any increased price Blue Violet would have to pay for the roses or court costs incurred in the damage suit.

Require Specific Performance.   If monetary damages are not sufficient to reimburse Blue Violet, the court can force Barrington's to live up to its original contract.

Agency

In many business situations, one person acts as an agent for another person. Well-known examples include actors and athletes represented by agents who negotiate contracts for them. An **agency-principal relationship** is established when one party (the agent) is authorized to act on behalf of another party (the principal).

The agent is under the control of the principal and must act on behalf of the principal and in the principal's best interests. The principal remains liable for the acts of the agent as long as the agent is acting within the scope of authority granted by the principal. A salesperson for IBM, for example, is an agent for IBM, the principal.

Bailment

Many business transactions are not covered by the agency-principal relationship. For example, suppose you take your car to a mechanic to have it repaired. Because the repair shop has temporary possession of something you own, it is responsible for your car. This is a **bailor-bailee relationship**. In a bailor-bailee relationship, the bailor (the car owner) gives possession of his or her property to the bailee (the repair shop) but retains ownership of the item. A business firm that stores inventory in a public warehouse is in a bailor-bailee relationship. The business firm is the bailor and the warehouse is the bailee. The warehouse is responsible for storing the goods safely and making them available to the manufacturer upon request.

The Law of Property

Property includes anything of tangible or intangible value that the owner has the right to possess and use. **Real property** is land and any permanent buildings attached to that land. **Personal property** is tangible or intangible

breach of contract
When one party to an agreement fails, without legal reason, to live up to the agreement's provisions.

agency-principal relationship
When one party (the agent) is authorized to act on behalf of another party (the principal).

bailor-bailee relationship
When a bailor, a property owner, gives possession of the property to a bailee, a custodian, but retains ownership of the property.

property
Anything of tangible or intangible value that the owner has the right to possess and own.

real property
Land and any permanent buildings attached to that land.

personal property
Tangible or intangible assets other than real property.

assets other than real property. Personal property includes cars, clothing, furniture, money in bank accounts, stock certificates, and copyrights.

Transferring Property.   From time to time, businesses and individuals need to transfer property to another person or business. A **deed** is a document that shows ownership of real property. It allows the transfer of title of real property.

A **lease** grants the use of an asset for a specified period of time in return for payment. The business or individual granting the lease is the lessor and the tenant is the lessee. For example, a business (the lessee) may rent space in a mall for one year from a real estate development firm (the lessor).

A **title** shows legal possession of personal property. It allows the transfer of title of personal property. When you buy a snowmobile, for example, the former owner signs the title over to you.

Warranty

When you buy a product or service, you want some assurance that it will perform satisfactorily and meet your needs. A **warranty** is a promise that the product or service will perform as the seller has promised it will.

There are two kinds of warranties—express and implied. An **express warranty** is a specific claim that the manufacturer makes about a product. For example, a warranty that a screwdriver blade is made of case-hardened steel is an express warranty. An **implied warranty** suggests that a product will perform as the manufacturer claims it will. Suppose you buy an outboard motor for your boat and the engine burns out in one week. Because the manufacturer implies by selling the motor that it will work for a reasonable period of time, you can return it and get your money back.

Because opinions vary on what is a "reasonable" time, most manufacturers now give limited time warranties on their products. For example, they will guarantee their products against defects in materials or manufacture for six months or one year.

Torts

A **tort** is a wrongful civil act that one party inflicts on another and that results in injury to the person, to the person's property, or to the person's good name. An **intentional tort** is a wrongful act intentionally committed. If a security guard in a department store suspects someone of shoplifting and uses excessive force to prevent him or her from leaving the store, the guard might be guilty of an intentional tort. Other examples are libel, embezzlement, and patent infringement.

Negligence is a wrongful act that inadvertently causes injury to another person. For example, if a maintenance crew in a store mops the floors without placing warning signs in the area, a customer who slips and falls might bring a negligence suit against the store.

In recent years, the most publicized area of negligence has been product liability. **Product liability** means that businesses are liable for injuries caused to product users because of negligence in design or manufacturing. **Strict product liability** means that a business is liable for injuries caused by their products even if there is no evidence of negligence in the design or manufacture of the product.

Negotiable Instruments

Negotiable instruments are types of commercial paper that can be transferred among individuals and business firms. Cheques, bank drafts, and certificates of deposit are examples of negotiable instruments.

---

deed

A document that shows ownership of real property.

lease

A document that grants the use of an asset for a specified period of time in return for payment.

title

A document that shows legal possession of personal property.

warranty

A promise that the product or service will perform as the seller has promised it will.

express warranty

A specific claim that a manufacturer makes about a product.

implied warranty

An assumption that a product will perform as the manufacturer claims it will.

tort

A wrongful civil act that one party inflicts on another.

intentional tort

A wrongful act intentionally committed.

negligence

A wrongful act that inadvertently causes injury to another person.

product liability

The liability of businesses for injuries caused to product users because of negligence in design or manufacture.

strict product liability

The liability of businesses for injuries caused by their products even if no evidence of negligence in the product's design or manufacture exists.

negotiable instrument

Types of commercial paper that can be transferred among individuals and business firms.

The Bills of Exchange Act specifies that a negotiable instrument must

- be written
- be signed by the person who puts it into circulation (the maker or drawer)
- contain an unconditional promise to pay a certain amount of money
- be payable on demand
- be payable to a specific person (or to the bearer of the instrument).

Negotiable instruments are transferred from one party to another through an endorsement. An **endorsement** means signing your name to a negotiable instrument; this makes it transferable to another person or organization. If you sign only your name on the back of a cheque, you are making a *blank* endorsement. If you state that the instrument is being transferred to a specific person, you are making a *special* endorsement. A *qualified* endorsement limits your liability if the instrument is not backed up by sufficient funds. For example, if you get a cheque from a friend and want to use it to buy a new stereo, you can write "without recourse" above your name. If your friend's cheque bounces, you have no liability. A *restrictive* endorsement limits the negotiability of the instrument. For example, if you write "for deposit only" on the back of a cheque and it is later stolen, no one else can cash it.

endorsement

Signing your name to a negotiable instrument making it transferable to another person or organization.

Summary of Key Points

Individual codes of ethics are derived from societal standards of right and wrong, and from peer values and experiences. Because ethics affect the behavior of individuals on behalf of the companies that employ them, many firms are adopting formal statements of ethics. Company-sponsored training is aimed at giving employees practice in making decisions in keeping with these policies.

Social responsibility is the firm's—not the individual's—response to the larger society's needs. Until the second half of the nineteenth century, businesses often paid little attention to these needs. Since that time, public pressure and government regulations have forced businesses to consider the public welfare, at least to some degree.

Social responsibility requires firms to minimize their pollution of the air, water, and land. Social responsibility toward customers requires firms to price products fairly and to respect customers' rights to make informed choices about safe products and to have their complaints rectified. Social responsibility toward employees requires firms to respect workers as resources and as people. Social responsibility toward investors requires firms to manage their resources and to honestly represent their financial status. All socially responsible behavior involves some costs to the firm. But it can also benefit the firm in terms of better community relations, more repeat-customer business, more qualified and motivated employees, and greater investor interest.

Companies approach social responsibility in many ways; these include an obstructive social-opposition stance, the legal minimum requirement of the social-obligation approach, a more moderate social-reaction approach on request, and an open-handed social-response approach. The last approach requires careful management. Drafting a policy statement, developing a detailed plan, appointing a director to implement the plan, and conducting social audits to check the plan's success are all necessary.

Employees of small businesses face many of the same ethical questions as do employees of larger firms. Small businesses must confront the same areas of social responsibility and the same need to decide on an approach to social responsibility as do larger firms. The differences are primarily in scale.

Law comprises the standards, principles, and rules a society establishes to govern the actions of its members. Common law grows out of previous judicial decisions and is based on precedent. Statutory law is codified, or written, law. It is enacted by city councils, provincial legislatures, and parliament. Administrative law is developed by government agencies and commissions. Business law is that body of law that pertains particularly to business activities.

A contract is a mutual agreement between two or more people to perform or not perform certain acts. To be valid, a contract must include an agreement, consideration, competence of the parties to the contract, and a legal purpose. If there is a breach of contract, the remedies are discharge, suing for damages, and specific performance.

The law of agency focuses on the legal duties of two parties who engage in an agency-principal relationship. The law of bailment is concerned with the surrender of personal property by one party to another with the expectation that the property will be returned in the future.

The law of property distinguishes between real property and personal property. In the sale of property the question of warranty often becomes important. The two kinds of warranty are express warranty and implied warranty.

A tort is a wrongful act that injures a person's body, property, or good name. The most common type of tort in business is negligence. The concept of product liability is considerably broadened by the concept of strict product liability.

A negotiable instrument is a piece of paper that is evidence of a contractual relationship and can be transferred from one person or business to another. Cheques and certificates of deposit are examples of negotiable instruments.

CONCLUDING CASE 4-1

The Industrial Spies Who Came in from the Cold

José Ignacio López de Arriortua did what millions of workers do each year—he changed jobs. But there was nothing ordinary about José López's job switch: Shortly after he left General Motors for Volkswagen, GM charged him with industrial espionage.

For nine months, López had headed GM's huge purchasing operation. Originally hired to slash $4 billion from GM's bill for automotive parts, he held a job that put him in the center of key strategy decisions and financial forecasts. For one thing, José López handled on a daily basis the kind of top secrets that would in large part determine GM's success throughout the 1990s. Indeed, two days before announcing his resignation, López had attended an international strategy meeting at GM's Opel subsidiary in Germany. During the meeting, he was introduced to GM Europe's model plans, sales projections, and financial forecasts up to the year 2000. He also watched Opel prototypes being put through their paces on Opel's Dudenhofen track.

Fearing that López had taken confidential information away from the European strategy meeting, GM demanded written confirmation that López "had not taken any documents" with him "pertaining to [GM's] present and future corporate plans." Fueling GM's deepest fears were

Volkswagen's subsequent efforts to lure away other GM employees. With López's help, Volkswagen had indeed tried to recruit more than 40 managers at Opel and GM, often enticing them with offers of doubled salaries. Before an injunction put a stop to its recruiting forays, VW had succeeded in hiring away seven key GM executives.

Although VW has denied allegations of industrial espionage and corporate raiding, the charges have left both López and the German carmaker under a legal and ethical cloud. That cloud became heavier when the district attorney of Darmstadt, Germany, discovered confidential GM documents at the home of a former GM executive who had, like López, defected to VW. At stake for Volkswagen is the public's perception of company ethics—an intangible factor that could affect the firm's sales. When a German polling organization asked 1000 Germans what they thought of the López affair, 65 percent believed that there was "something to" the allegations, while only 7 percent deemed them unfounded. Although Volkswagen hired López to cut costs and help return the company to profitability, it may have set itself up for failure if consumers react negatively to perceived unethical conduct. It may be a classic case, says Ian I. Mitroff, head of the crisis-management unit at the University of Southern California, where "the solution to one difficulty puts you into even worse problems." The potential problem for Volkswagen is fairly clear—the loss of public trust.

Finally, there is at least one more irony in the López affair. During his nine-month tenure at General Motors, López is charged with having leaked proprietary information from one supplier to another—actions that were in fact tolerated by GM. Suppliers who had been given blueprints of top-secret technology were able to underbid companies that had spent millions on research and development. As a result of these actions, 110 key automotive suppliers have ranked GM last among its industry peers in professionalism, cooperation, and communication. That vote constitutes an astounding fall for a purchasing department once considered the most professional and ethical in the auto industry.

CASE QUESTIONS
1. As a result of López's resignation, GM CEO John F. Smith Jr. decided to require all top officers to sign formal contracts restricting their ability to work for a com-

peting company for three years after leaving GM. How do you feel about this contract provision?
2. In your opinion, does an employee have an ethical responsibility to maintain the confidentiality of information gained on the job with one company when taking a job with a competing firm?
3. Should Volkswagen be concerned with the public's reaction to the López affair?
4. GM allowed López to reveal suppliers' proprietary information in order to elicit lower bids. In effect, says Carnegie Mellon management professor Gerald C. Meyers, "when it's used for GM, it's a boon. When it's used against them, it's a terrible thing." Considering its behavior, did GM demonstrate a double standard in its reaction to the López affair?
5. The ethics of both VW and GM were called into question by the López affair. How will the ethical misjudgments of both companies affect their relationship with customers, suppliers, and employees? ◆

CONCLUDING CASE 4-2

MacMillan-Bloedel vs. Greenpeace

Greenpeace, an environmental activist organization, and MacMillan-Bloedel (MB), the forest products giant, are not getting along these days. Recently, Greenpeace pressured two of MBs European customers to cancel contracts for $8 million worth of pulp. Greenpeace targeted MB after a prolonged confrontation in 1993 between MB loggers and environmentalists at Clayoquot Sound, an old-growth rain forest on the west side of Vancouver Island.

When Clayoquot Sound first became an issue, the province formed a committee to get all the interested parties together. The idea was to reach a consensus on logging. The environmentalists walked out early in the process, but the rest of the committee continued on for over a year until they too reached a deadlock. The provincial government then decided to designate nearly half of the land as wilderness, which means it is unlikely ever to be logged.

Environmentalits were unhappy even with this concession. A demonstration in Victoria in 1993 turned into a riot, and set the stage for the summer-long attempts to block logging crews from going to work.

MB has used court injunctions to keep demonstrators from blocking roads into the timber. More than 700 people were arrested and charged, including four European leaders of Greenpeace. But MB apparently won the public relations battle. A poll showed that 60 percent of the people in B.C. supported logging on Clayoquot Sound.

Bob Findlay, the CEO of MB, anticipates that Green-

peace will continue to pursue its goal of blocking MB from clear-cutting and harvesting old-growth forests, in spite of an independent report that the practice does not have significant effects on the ecology. Another pulp industry executive says that Greenpeace's goal is to end industrial forestry world-wide.

Executives at MacMillan say that they will not back down. In fact, they are becoming more aggressive in defending their position. A consultant to the paper industry recommends that the entire industry go on the offensive. He recommends that pulp industry representatives show up whenever Greenpeace does, so that Greenpeace's claims can be effectively countered.

MB has tried to counter negative publicity about Clayoquot by publishing an environmental report along with its annual report. It portrays the company as serious about meeting its environmental obligations. It has trained loggers to identify fish spawning streams and it has reduced the effluent at all its pulp and paper mills below mandated levels. It is also replanting practically everything it cuts.

CASE QUESTIONS
1. What difficulties will MacMillan encounter as it tries to balance its responsibilities towards its customers, employees, investors, and the environment?
2. Can these disagreements be resolved? Explain.
3. What does MacMillan-Bloedel need to do to be considered an environmentally responsible company? ◆

Key Terms

ethics	parking	contract	warranty
social responsibility	social-opposition approach	breach of contract	express warranty
pollution	social-obligation approach	agency-principal	implied warranty
acid rain	social-reaction approach	relationship	tort
recycling	social-response approach	bailor-bailee relationship	intentional tort
toxic waste	social audit	property	negligence
consumerism	law	real property	product liability
collusion	common law	personal property	strict product liability
whistle-blower	statutory law	deed	negotiable instrument
cheque kiting	administrative law	lease	endorsement
insider trading	business law	title	

Study Questions and Exercises

Review Questions

1. What factors influence the development of an individual's personal code of ethics?
2. What are the major areas of social responsibility that organizations need to be concerned about?
3. List the four rights of consumers.
4. What are the four basic approaches to social responsibility that an organization might choose to adopt?
5. Compare and contrast common, statutory, and administrative law.

Analysis Questions

6. What kind of wrongdoing would most likely prompt you to become a whistle-blower? What kind of wrongdoing would be least likely to prompt you? Why?

7. In what ways do you think your personal code of ethics might clash with the operations of some companies?
8. If you were a shareholder in a corporation, which of the four approaches to social responsibility would you like to see applied by company management? Why?

Application Exercises

9. Identify a local business and observe its operations. Identify the ways in which the firm is a potential or actual polluter and how the company addresses its pollution problems.
10. Find a newspaper or magazine account of a contract dispute between two parties. Identify the major issues in the dispute. How does the information in this chapter on contract law apply to the case?

Building Your Business Skills

Goal

To encourage students, as future employees, to apply the concept of corporate social responsibility to their rights to privacy.

Situation

As an employee of the Widget Manufacturing Co., you are concerned that your employer is undertaking activities that infringe on your right to privacy. Specifically, you suspect that your employer is invading your privacy in the following ways:
- by requiring drug testing
- by reading your medical records
- by listening to your office phone conversations
- by reading your electronic mail
- by asking questions about your personal habits
- by listening to your voice-mail messages.

Method

Step 1: Working with four other students, research your privacy rights in each of the areas listed above. In your analysis, be certain to separate ethical and legal issues. For example, although it may be unethical for your employer to read your electronic mail, your research may tell you that he or she has the legal right to do so.

Step 2: Using the information gathered in your research, write a short employee-rights handbook that explains the privacy rights of Widget Manufacturing Co. employees and the employer's responsibilities with regard to these rights.

Follow-up Questions

1. Do you think that employee surveillance will become an increasingly important ethical concern in the future? Why or why not?
2. Although the law may not always protect an employee's privacy, in your opinion do companies have the ethical responsibility to respect certain privacy rights?

PALLISER FURNITURE CORPORATION

Palliser Furniture Corporation began operations in 1933 in the Winnipeg suburb of North Kildonan when Albert A. DeFehr started a woodworking company in the basement of his home. Building step-stools, planters, ironing boards, and clothes racks, Mr. DeFehr's new company began with a very modest output of three pieces per day. Now, over 60 years later, the company has become the largest furniture manufacturer in Canada, and is managed by Albert's three sons—Frank, Art, and Dave.

Having been significantly influenced by his Christian home and church upbringing, Palliser President Art DeFehr had deliberately made it a priority to integrate volunteer service involvements into his business career. Art had worked under the auspices of the Mennonite Central Committee on two separate assignments in Bangladesh in 1975, and later in Thailand, in 1980. These two involvements had introduced him to Asia, not only as a place of need, but also as a place of opportunity. A Harvard M.B.A., Art sensed the strategic opportunity emerging from the countries of the Pacific Rim. One such country was Taiwan.

Taiwan is situated in the far western Pacific at the crossroads of Northeast and Southeast Asia. The island has an area of 22 240 square kilometres inhabited by almost 20 million people. The national language is Mandarin, but English is one of the more commonly spoken foreign languages. The climate is described as subtropical with an average annual temperature of between 21.7 and 24.1 degrees Celsius for the northern and southern parts of the island, respectively.

There were over 200 furniture manufacturers in Taiwan. These were concentrated along the country's southwest coast. Some of these companies manufactured unfinished component parts, while others manufactured completely finished "showroom-ready" furniture.

During a visit to Taiwan on one of his Asian services tours, Art had recognized the emergence of the Taiwanese furniture manufacturing industry. Eager to learn, the Taiwanese manufacturers were developing quickly to a position of parity with their North American counterparts.

However, what he had also observed was that the mindset of most of the North American buyers was not evolving proportionately to the growth of the Taiwanese manufacturers' expertise.

The DeFehr brothers visited Taiwan to explore the country's potential as a supplier of complementary furniture products and accessories. Visits to about 20 Taiwanese furniture manufacturing plants during a whirlwind tour of the country had quickly convinced the brothers of Taiwan's potential as a supplier of complementary products. The country's exchange rate of $0.25 (U.S.) only served to sweeten the opportunity even more.

It was decided after their initial visit that Palliser would start cautiously, beginning with only about six dealers. Gradually, it hoped, the suppliers would grow to about a dozen. Likely inclusions in the initial supplier pool were Yeh Brothers of Kaohsiung, Sanyu Manufacturers of Pingtung (east of Kaohsiung), and Hwaung Manufacturers of Hsinchu. Products initially targeted for export to Canada included unpainted wood designs for assembly in dining room china cabinet fronts, and fully finished black lacquer end tables. Operations were targeted to begin in late 1986.

McGill professor Henry Mintzberg, in his popular article, "The Manager's Job: Folklore and Fact," had observed that one of the key roles senior management played was that of liaison. Explained most simply, this meant that the executive was responsible for building and maintaining a network of relationships with the external environment that were necessary to ensure the effective functioning of the organization. One such contact was Yan Kee Suppliers of Taiwan Inc. On one of his last evenings in the country, Art had set aside time for dinner and socializing with the company president. The evening had been intended to be an evening of network development and thus far had gone very smoothly.

But suddenly Art DeFehr felt uneasy. Two attractive Taiwanese women had just sat down at their table and now looked expectantly toward Art and his host. His host's subtle smile to the two women as they sat down seemed to indicate that their visit was not unexpected.

Art DeFehr had often heard the old adage "When in Rome, do as the Romans," but he now wondered if Palliser's dealings in Taiwan meant accepting what one company salesman had called "booze, broads, and bribes." Was accepting these offers a necessary part of doing business in Taiwan? He also wondered whether he should challenge a national custom. He wondered further whether this *was* the custom. He contemplated further what effect his response would have on future business dealings. A precedent was about to be set.

The DeFehr's had always tried to integrate their religious convictions into the daily business dealings of Palliser Furniture. But now, Art wondered whether growth into Taiwan would force the company to compromise its ethical principles. He had often heard of "palms being greased" in one way or another. If most of Palliser's competitors were involved in such dealings (as his host implied), maybe this was just a part of doing business in Taiwan. He also wondered if he could be offending his host by turning down his offer.

His mind jumped ahead to a possible future situation where one of his employees would be confronted with the same situation. Should he leave employees to decide what their response would be, or was it Art's responsibility to provide direction on what was acceptable in business dealings?

He thought further. Were the traditional conservative Christian convictions that Palliser held becoming outdated in the global marketplace? A scene from "Fiddler on the Roof" came to mind. The scene involved the story's central character Tevye, who discovers that some of his age-old Jewish traditions are no longer sustainable in an ever-changing world. Were Palliser's ethics no longer sustainable?

As these thoughts raced through Art DeFehr's mind, he was jolted back to reality by his Taiwanese host, who said "I thought you might enjoy some 'companionship' for the evening." His host waited for Art DeFehr's reply.

CASE QUESTIONS
1. What is Art DeFehr's motivation in trying to arrange a business deal with furniture companies in Taiwan?
2. What new challenges will Palliser Furniture face if it becomes involved with Taiwanese furniture companies?
3. What are the sources of ethics for Art DeFehr?
4. As president of Palliser, what responsibility does Art DeFehr have in modelling ethical behavior for his employees? What impact will his decision in this situation have on employees?
5. What should Art DeFehr do?

Experiential Exercise:
Meeting the Challenge of Modern Business

OBJECTIVE

To help students understand the complexities facing businesses as they seek to act responsibly toward their shareholders, their employees, and their communities.

TIME REQUIRED

45 minutes
    Step 1: Individual activity (to be completed before class)
    Step 2: Small-group activity (25 minutes)
    Step 3: Class discussion (20 minutes)

PROCEDURE

Step 1: Read the following case regarding the Wright Pen Company.

For over seven generations, the Wright Pen Company has been the proud maker of writing implements, beginning with quill pens. Today the firm makes fountain pens, ballpoint pens, rolling ball and felt-tipped pens, and refills for most of its pens. Since its founding by Jess Wright, the company has also prided itself on never having laid off its workers and on always being a good "corporate citizen." Funds from the Wright Pen Company have provided scholarships for local students, built the Wrightville Center for the Arts, and supported a wide variety of local charities.

Now, however, the management at Wright Pen Company finds itself with a dilemma. For years, the firm has dumped the waste products from its ink-making operation into the Effluvia River, which runs alongside its plant. Unfortunately, recent studies show liver cancer rates five times higher among Wrightville residents than in the general population. Federal tests indicate that the water in the Effluvia River may be a contributing factor.

The options open to the Wright Pen Company are as follows:

Option 1: Make no changes in operations at this time. The evidence that has been presented is preliminary, and Wright Pen is not the only source of waste dumped into the river.

Option 2: Install a new waste-disposal system that would eliminate questionable substances from the waste being dumped by Wright Pen. As the chart indicates, however, this system would add to Wright's costs, forcing it to either reduce dividends to shareholders or to raise prices, which would lower sales and could force staff cutbacks.

Option 3: Close the ink-making plant and arrange to have these products made overseas where pollution controls are not so stringent and where labor costs are lower.

What Do You Think Wright Pen Company Should Do?

Step 2: The instructor will divide the class into small groups. Each group is to complete the grid on the next page and decide on the best overall course of action for Wright Pen Company.

COSTS/PROFITS CHART

DECISION-MAKING GRID

	Under Current System	Under New Waste System
Cost of 1 ballpoint pen refill	.13	.23

Profit on one ballpoint
   pen refill
      at current $.29 ea.
      at $.39 ea.
	.16
	.26
		.06
		.16

Number of refills
   sold annually
      at current $.29 ea.
      at $.39 ea.
	2 500 000
	1 170 000	

Annual profits
      at current $.29 ea.
      at $.39 ea.
	$400 000
	$304 000
		$150 000
		$187 200

	Option 1	Option 2	Option 3
Probable effect on shareholders			
Probable effect on employees			
Probable effect on community			

Step 3: One member of each small group will present the group's conclusions to the class.

QUESTIONS FOR DISCUSSION

1. Why did different groups arrive at different answers? At the same answers?
2. How did your small group discussions reveal some of the problems partners face in making decisions for a partnership?

CAREERS IN BUSINESS
It's Not Just a Job...

"What do you want to be?"

Throughout your life, you've probably heard this question over and over. Perhaps you already know the answer. But if you don't, you're not alone. Many people spend years searching for an answer, moving from job to job and working for company after company. Indeed, most people today wind up working for more than one firm and holding more than one position over the course of their career.

Most experts agree that the people with the most successful careers are those who make an effort to plan them. And just as a career is a lifelong progression, so career planning should not be limited to the search for your first job. Rather, it is a process that should occur throughout your working life. If you have not already begun to plan your career, now is the time to start.

One of the purposes of this book is to help you plan and manage your career. To that end, you will find a special two-page discussion at the end of each part of this text that addresses one or more aspects of careers and career planning. Since the first step in any sound planning process is the gathering of information, we begin by looking at the job market you will probably face when you graduate—which fields are expanding, which are shrinking.

OVERALL JOB OUTLOOK

During the 1960s and 1970s, many businesses grew rapidly. They built new facilities, hired new employees, and expanded their operations in many directions. In the 1980s, however, increased global competition forced many firms to cut back, a trend that continued with the recession of the early 1990s. Virtually every industry was affected to some extent—airlines and retailers, computer manufacturers and car makers all felt the pinch. Many shut down plants and laid off thousands of workers. Even firms such as IBM, which long had "no-layoff" policies, found themselves with no alternative. As a result, university and college graduates in the late 1980s and early 1990s faced an especially tight job market. As the economy has begun to bounce back, however, many companies are cautiously beginning to hire again.

JOB PROSPECTS BY FIELD AND OCCUPATION

Despite the general upturn, there remain important differences in job prospects. Table 1 categorizes job prospects by field as either good, fair, or poor for the next decade. Employment prospects are considered *good* when projections are for more job openings than candidates for those jobs. Jobs in business health care are included in this

Table 1 Job Prospects by Field

Fields with Good Employment Prospects
Business—management, accounting, marketing, finance, operations
Computer and information sciences—systems analysis, programming
Engineering—chemical, mechanical, and civil engineering and drafting
Health care—medicine, nursing-home and hospital administration
Physical sciences—biology, chemistry

Fields with Fair Employment Prospects
Architecture and landscape design
Communication technologies—writing, broadcasting
Education—teaching and administration
Protective services—fire fighting, law enforcement

Fields with Poor Employment Prospects
Foreign languages
Parks and recreation
Public affairs
Social sciences—psychology, sociology, social work
Visual and performing arts

category. Employment prospects are considered *fair* when the number of job openings is projected to be roughly the same as the number of candidates interested in those job openings. Careers in communications and architecture fall into this category. And employment prospects are considered *poor* when the number of job openings is expected to be smaller than the number of candidates for those jobs. Psychology and sociology are two fields with poor employment prospects.

Even within specific fields, prospects for some positions are brighter than they are for others. Table 2 illustrates projected growth in key managerial and professional jobs. Of the jobs listed, positions for mathematical and computer scientists are increasing the most rapidly, while employment for college and university teachers is increasing least rapidly. You may also be interested to know that one recent survey identified the 20 "hot track" careers for the 1990s and beyond as: international accountant, software developer, management consultant, environmental engineer, financial planner, health services administrator, human-resources director, corporate-bankruptcy lawyer, quality manager, international marketer, internist, fund-raising director, geriatric nurse, paralegal, chef, specialty store buyer, pharmaceutical representative, biomedical researcher, special education teacher, and recycling coordinator.

Table 2   Job Prospects by Occupation

Occupation	Rate of Increase, 1990–2005
Mathematical and computer scientists	73%
Registered nurses and other health therapists	43%
Lawyers and judges	34%
Primary, secondary, and special education teachers	30%
Health diagnosticians	29%
Executives, administrators, and managers	27%
Engineers	26%
Natural scientists	26%
Technical specialists	23%
College and university teachers	19%

JOB OUTLOOK FOR BUSINESS-RELATED FIELDS

In this text, we are naturally most concerned with the prospects for employment in the business sector. While business is included in the overall "good prospects" category, it is important to note that within the general field of business there are considerable variations in employment prospects. Table 3 lists specific employment prospects within business. While manufacturing jobs often pay better than service jobs, most growth in the business community of late has been—and is expected to continue to be—in the service sector, especially in business-to-business services and in the health-care industry.

INTERNATIONAL JOB PROSPECTS

Students today are increasingly interested in international job opportunities. Part of the allure of an international job is the prospect of traveling to exotic countries, living in interesting places, and dealing with different kinds of people. However, an "international" job sometimes means

Table 3   Job Prospects in the Business World

Jobs with Good Prospects
 Manufacturing or production management
 Information systems
 Quality management
 Computer information technology
 Tax accounting

Jobs with Fair Prospects
 Public accounting
 Auditing
 General management
 Marketing and sales
 Human-resources management
 Hotel and restaurant management
 Retailing
 Insurance
 International management

Jobs with Poor Prospects
 Banking
 Advertising
 Securities sales
 Consulting
 Retail buying
 Financial administration
 Administration of not-for-profit organizations

nothing more than working—in Canada—for a foreign-owned firm such as General Electric or IBM. Most entry-level international jobs fall into this category.

If you are committed to an international career, however, openings are available, and the number of truly international jobs—those involving extensive travel or even relocation to other nations—is expected to rise in the decades to come. In general, entry-level jobs in the arena include sales positions and export brokers and import merchants. Senior managers in many areas are also candidates for international reassignment—usually after they've mastered another tongue in which to talk business.

Video Case I-I

SKYFREIGHT EXPRESS*

Michael Talker hung up the phone and heaved a heavy sigh. He was attempting to get his new company, Sky Freight Express, up and running but was encountering one problem after another. Talker, president of the start-up air carrier had moved to Canada from Israel 14 years ago. He had worked as a professional engineer for several years until recently, when he had been laid off.

Michael's strategy was to service a small, but potentially very lucrative, market niche. This niche involved same-day delivery of packages between Toronto and the two more easterly cities of Ottawa and Montreal. Until recently this service had been provided by industry giants Air Canada and Canadian Airlines. These two airlines charged premium fees: for delivering a small package door-to-door Air Canada was reported to be charging $72.00. Given these comparatively high prices, Talker perceived the possibility of a low-price niche opportunity in this market. Spurred on by his vision he proceeded to take out a commercial loan that allowed him to acquire a $70 000 aircraft that the courier service could use in flying between the three cities.

In the months leading up to the start-up of operations Talker operated on a shoestring budget. Nonetheless, things had been moving along quite well; he had launched an advertising campaign for the company and its cut-rate pricing strategy throughout much of the Toronto courier community. He had also signed up a handful of pilots who would operate the aircraft through its courier runs.

Recently though, he had encountered several problems. First, he discovered that the company and its pilots required certification by Transport Canada. Added to this was the discovery that the process could take up to 90 days to complete. To make matters even worse, two of his pilots had bailed out on him just before Transport Canada was to carry out official certification test flights with the company. As a result, Talker was forced to delay the test rides until he was able to secure replacement pilots.

A second problem then surfaced as a result of this regulatory delay. Michael had banked his operation on local courier services in each of the three cities supplying him with a steady flow of parcels. Now, one of these courier services announced to Michael that they would not advertise SkyFreight's services until the airline was actually up and flying.

A third major complication arose when Talker discovered tensions flaring between these local couriers. Some couriers were pushing for higher prices than the rock bottom $29.95 that Michael had built his business plan around. One courier was even reported to have marked its rate up to $65.00 per parcel. This created a real problem for SkyFreight Express. If the prices the SkyFreight-allied air couriers were charging the public were too high. the company's perceived price advantage would evaporate. However if SkyFreight's prices were perceived by the couriers as being too low, they would not bother to use the company's services.

Michael felt overwhelmed by these recent developments. He had never expected that the decision to start up a business would be so complex. Given this recent spate of setbacks and his commitment to commence operations on March 7, he wondered what actions he could take to keep his dream alive.

Study questions:

1. What is a factor of production? What are the factors that Michael needs to get SkyFreight Express up and flying?
2. What are the laws of supply and demand? Explain SkyFreight Express's strategy in terms of these laws.
3. What is the difference between a sole proprietorship, a partnership, and a limited corporation? If Michael Talker wanted to take on a partner, what characteristics would you advise him to look for in a partner?
4. What is meant by the business cycle? How would you expect the business cycle to impact on the operations of a company like SkyFreight Express? What, if anything, could Michael Talker do to minimize the impact of the business cycle on his company?

---

* This case is based on the *Venture* episode broadcast on May 1, 1994.

Video Case I-II

ETHICSCAN*

Just over five years ago David Nitkin began operating a business venture known as Ethicscan. The company operates in a very unusual and specialized market niche: reporting on the corporate responsibility of Canada's business community. The very existence of companies like Nitkin's indicate a fundamental shift in societal expectations. Not only are corporations expected to

make a profit—they are also expected to obey the law and act in an ethical way in all their dealings.

Ethicscan's initiatives have not met with unanimous approval, with one observer accusing the company of "dishing out...dirt" on Canada's companies. One business journalist, Terry Corcoran of *The Globe & Mail,* has even gone so far as to describe David's company as "a confused soup of goody goodiness." Commenting further, Corcoran states that neither Nitkin nor anyone else should attempt to steer a corporation's ethical values since "a corporation and a corporate executive [are] not in the business of making society a better place. [Rather] corporations are in the business of making money, and they have to make money and operate within a legal framework, and it is the legal framework that gives them, to a major degree, their ethical guidelines."

Nitkin's company publishes its newsletter, *The Corporate Ethics Monitor,* six times per year. The 16-page publication has about 300 subscribers, each of whom pays $300 per year. According to David, the vast majority of subscribers are corporations who want to be kept abreast of what is on the leading edge of responsible corporate behavior and social reporting. Each issue of the *Monitor* focuses on a particular industry; recent issues have zeroed in on the airline, oil, and department store industries respectively. In one recent issue on Canada's banks, Nitkin gave low marks to the Canadian Imperial Bank of Commerce for its inadequate maternity leave. The bank

eventually changed its policies, with Nitkin assuming some of the credit for having put the bank under pressure. More recently, David has been keeping an eye on the bank's policies on making loans to environmentally-risky companies.

As a result of Ethicscan's success, Nitkin has been able to launch a very successful consulting service. Through the service he is often hired by corporations to perform an "ethics check," which is like a credit check, on any potential companies a firm is considering dealing with. Quig Tingley of the British corporation, *The Body Shop,* sees Nitkin's help as invaluable. According to Tingley, protecting the company's sterling public image is a key company objective. Therefore it is essential that "[the *Body Shop* not] end up buying baskets from someone who's manufacturing them in a slave labor camp."

Study questions:

1. What is meant by the phrase *corporate social responsibility*? How far does corporate social responsibility extend? In what ways might a publication like *Corporate Ethics Monitor* influence the way in which a corporation defines its responsibilities?
2. What basic trends are reshaping the way business is done? Of all of these trends, which would explain the existence of a company like Ethicscan?
3. What are the different approaches a company can take toward its social responsibilities? How do you think managers representing each approach would be likely to view Ethicscan?
4. What are some practical strategies that a company can undertake in order to "manage for social responsibility"? In what ways can the work of Ethicscan aid in managing for social responsibility?

* This case is based on the *Venture* episode broadcast on January 16, 1994.

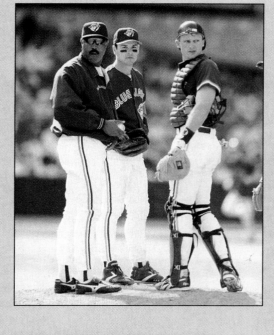

Part Two

*M*ANAGING THE BUSINESS FIRM

Sam Bronfman, Rhys Eaton, and Robyn and Rhona MacKay are four of the people you will read about in the cases that open Chapters 5–7. These people all manage business organizations. Seagrams and Canadian Airlines are very large, while MacKay's Ice Cream is small. But the common thread among these managers is their ability to carry out the basic functions of management in a skillful and inventive way.

Part Two, Managing the Business Firm, provides an overview of business management today. It includes a look at the various types of managers, the special concerns of managing small businesses, the ways in which managers set goals for their companies, and how a business's structure affects its management and goals.

■ We begin in **Chapter 5, Managing the Business Enterprise,** by examining what managers do, how they do it, and the different levels of management in the modern corporation.

■ In **Chapter 6, Planning and Organizing,** we explore the planning function of management and look closely at various levels of strategic planning in business. We also examine the different ways that a company can structure itself and the effects of these structures on management styles and decision-making within the firm.

■ Finally, in **Chapter 7, Running the Small Business,** we explore the role of small businesses and franchises in the Canadian economy—what they do, why they succeed or fail, and how they are owned and managed.

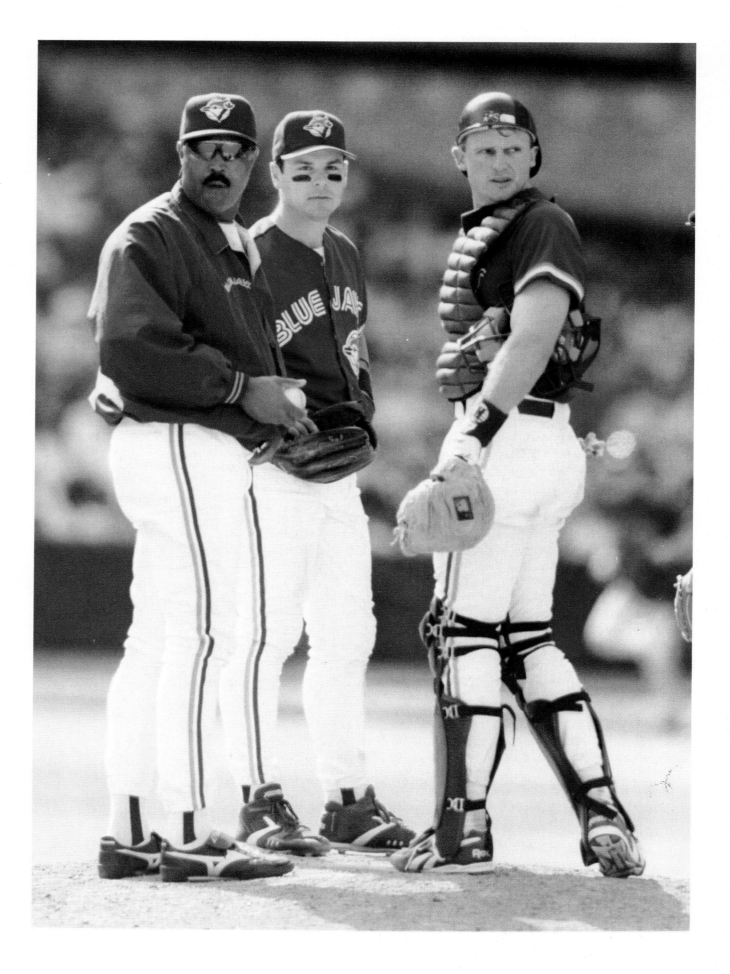

5

Managing the Business Enterprise

LEARNING OBJECTIVES

After studying this chapter, you will be able to

- Describe the four activities that comprise the management process.
- Identify and discuss kinds of managers by level and area.
- Discuss the three basic managerial skills.
- Identify ways in which managerial skills may be acquired and three ways in which companies recruit managers.
- Distinguish between managerial styles and explain how styles are influenced by the situation and the corporation's culture.

CHAPTER OUTLINE

Opening Case: Managing Growth in a Big Way

The Management Process
    Planning
    Organizing
    Leading
    Controlling

Kinds of Managers
    Levels of Management
    Areas of Management

Basic Management Skills
    Technical Skills
    Human Relations Skills
    Conceptual Skills

Becoming a Manager
    Preparing for Management
    Where Organizations Find Managers

Corporate Cultures and Management Styles
    Corporate Culture
    Management Styles

Concluding Case 5-1: Leading the League

Concluding Case 5-2: Can-Mark
    Manufacturing

Managing Growth in a Big Way

Sam Bronfman got his start in business by running liquor over the back roads of Saskatchewan and loading it into the stripped-down cars of U.S. bootleggers in the 1920s and 30s. He did nothing criminal because selling liquor was legal in Canada, but it was a risky business (his brother-in-law was shot and killed by a rumrunner). After Prohibition ended in the U.S. in 1933, Sam expanded the company on both sides of the border, diversifying into the oil business along the way.

By the 1950s, some of the Bronfman clan lived in Montreal and some in New York. One of Sam's sons, Charles, is best known to Canadians as the original owner of the Montreal Expos. The other son, Edgar Sr., took over from Sam in 1971. His son, Edgar Jr., has become the key figure in the company in the 1990s. The $6 billion empire he runs is a far cry from his grandfather's first efforts in rural Saskatchewan.

Edgar Jr. started with the company in 1982. He was an assistant in the office of the president for three months, then went on his first operational assignment in Europe. He came back in 1984, and improved his corporate credentials by restructuring the company and cutting U.S. staffing levels. He became president and CEO in 1989. He gets credit for most of the major decisions that have recently made the company successful. These include the purchase of Martell SA (a maker of fine French cognac, which gave Seagram's its entree into the Chinese market); the acquisition of Tropicana Products Inc. (which diversified the company into the growing market for health beverages); and the sale of seven mediocre brands (which focused the company on more profitable brands).

Edgar has both an artistic and business temperament. He is friends with some well-known show business types, including actor Michael Douglas. At work, he believes in setting goals, motivating his people, and then delegating authority to them. He describes his management style as a "light grip on the throat." Other describe him as very disciplined and creative. Still others say he is distant, aloof, and even condescending.

One of Edgar's high profile actions was to pay more than $2 billion for 15 percent of Time Warner Inc. The executives at Time Warner were not sure what Edgar was up to. Seagram had been buying shares secretly on the open market for some months before it informed Time Warner of what it was doing. Usually this suggests that an unfriendly takeover attempt is in the works. Time Warner responded with a poison pill which prevented anyone who acquired more than 15 percent of the stock to do so without making an all-cash offer. But then Edgar took an even more startling action—he sold Seagram's stake in Time-Warner *and* DuPont and invested several billion dollars in MCA, the entertainment giant.

For his part, Edgar says he is simply trying to build up shareholder value by getting involved in a good strategic investment. This is precisely what his father did some years ago when he converted the family's $2.3 billion worth of oil holdings into a 24 percent stake in DuPont (which is now worth $10 billion). Edgar Jr., in fact, regularly mentions the DuPont investment as proof that Seagram's is willing to make large investments without trying to take over the company.

Edgar also says that, although he is proud of what his father and grandfather have done, his work must stand on its own merits. He could, like his father, make an essentially passive investment that doesn't dramatically change the nature of Seagram, or he can, like his grandfather, seize a great opportunity and lay the fonundation for a vast new empire. (The video case "Edgar Bronfman Jr." on p. 202 gives additional information about this top manager.) ◆

Edgar Bronfman is one of millions of managers worldwide who work in business firms. In this chapter, we explain how these managers differ from industrial engineers, accountants, market researchers, production workers, secretaries, and other people who work in business firms. Although we will focus on managers in business firms, managers are necessary in many other kinds of organizations—colleges and univiersities, charities, social clubs, churches, labor unions, and governments. The president of the University of Toronto, the prime minister of Canada, and the executive director of the United Way are just as much managers as the president of MacMillan Bloedel.

We begin by describing the basic functions that all managers must perform, as well as the different levels where managers are found in business firms. We then describe the various skills that managers must possess and how individuals get to be managers. We conclude by describing what corporate culture is, and how it affects the style of leadership that managers use.

The Management Process

Management is the process of planning, organizing, leading, and controlling an enterprise's financial, physical, human, and information resources in order to achieve the organization's goals of supplying various products and services. Thus, the CEO of Walt Disney Productions, Michael Eisner, is a manager because he regularly carries out these four functions as films are being made. Actors like Bette Midler or Tom Selleck, while they may be the stars of the movies, are not managers because they don't carry out the four functions of management.

The planning, organizing, leading, and controlling aspects of a manager's job are interrelated, as shown in Figure 5.1. But note that while these activities generally follow one another in a logical sequence, sometimes they are performed simultaneously or in a different sequence altogether. In fact, any given manager is likely to be engaged in all these activities during the course of any given business day. To understand why, you need to know more about each activity. The box "What Do Managers Actually Do?" gives some explanation of the dynamic nature of managerial jobs.

management
The process of planning, organizing, leading, and controlling a business's financial, physical, human, and information resources in order to achieve its goals.

Planning

Determining what the organization needs to do and how to best do it or get it done means **planning**. Planning itself involves a series of activities by managers. First, managers need to determine the firm's goals. Next, they need to develop a comprehensive strategy for achieving those goals. Goal setting and strategic planning are the subject of Chapter 6.

planning
That portion of a manager's job concerned with determining what the business needs to do and the best way to achieve it.

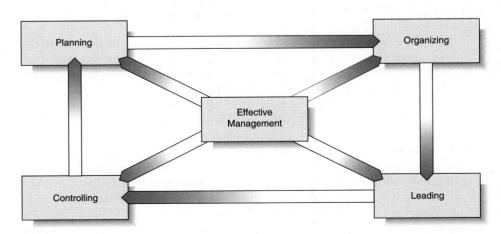

Figure 5.1
The management process.

The Canadian Business Scene

WHAT DO MANAGERS ACTUALLY DO?

Most business textbooks state that managers plan, organize, direct, and control. These terms are very general and do not describe specific activities in a manager's day. Henry Mintzberg of McGill University conducted a detailed study of the work of five chief executive officers and found the following.

1. *Managers work at an unrelenting pace.* Attending formal and informal meetings, making telephone calls, responding to incoming mail, and dealing with subordinates who need attention uses up all the time available during the typical workday. Executives frequently take work home in the evenings.

2. *Managerial activities are characterized by brevity, variety, and fragmentation.* Half of all managerial activities in Mintzberg's study were completed in less than nine minutes, and only 10 percent took more than one hour. Telephone calls averaged only six minutes. Desk work and unscheduled meetings lasted on average 15 and 12 minutes, respectively.

3. *Managers have a preference for "live" action.* Managers emphasize work activities that are current, specific, and well defined. Processing mail was seen as a burden because it generally didn't help the manager get current information. Of the 40 routine operating reports that the managers received during the study, only two elicited a written reaction.

4. *Managers are attracted to the verbal media.* Verbal interaction accounted for 78 percent of the five managers' time (scheduled meetings—59 percent; un-

scheduled meetings—10 percent; tours—3 percent; and telephone calls—6 percent). The written media accounted for only 22 percent of the managers' time. Managers are attracted to "soft" information, such as gossip, hearsay, and speculation, because today's rumor may be tomorrow's fact.

Mintzberg believes that a manager's job can be described as ten roles that must be performed. The manager's formal authority and status give rise to three **interpersonal roles:** 1) *figurehead* (duties of a ceremonial nature, such as attending a subordinate's wedding); 2) *leader* (being responsible for the work of the unit); and 3) *liaison* (making contact outside the vertical chain of command). These interpersonal roles give rise to three **informational roles:** 1) *monitor* (scanning the environment for relevant information); 2) *disseminator* (passing information to subordinates); and 3) *spokesperson* (sending information to people outside the unit).

The interpersonal and informational roles allow the manager to carry out four **decision-making roles:** 1) *entrepreneur* (improving the performance of the unit); 2) *disturbance handler* (responding to high-pressure disturbances, such as a strike at a supplier); 3) *resource allocator* (deciding who will get what in the unit); and 4) *negotiator* (working out agreements on a wide variety of issues like the amount of authority an individual will be given).

The video case "Earth Buddy" on p. 203 gives some idea of the excitement and frustration that are present in managers' jobs.

---

decision making

That portion of a manager's job concerned with choosing among alternative courses of action to reach a desired goal.

Part of all management processes, but an especially crucial part of the planning step, is **decision making**. Decision making involves choosing the best course of action for a particular situation. Figure 5.2 illustrates the basic steps in decision making.

First, the manager must recognize the need for a decision, define the problem, gather facts, and identify some alternative solutions. For example, when Michael Eisner was appointed CEO of Walt Disney Productions, he realized that the company had grown stagnant after Walt Disney died. He defined the problem as a need for redirection, used subordinate-gathered data to support his contentions, and developed several possible paths that could be taken.

Next, the manager must evaluate each alternative and select the best one. Eisner chose to develop Disney as a complete entertainment provider, including TV, movies, and theme parks, and associated businesses (such as hotels and products with pictures of Disney characters). He then used the Imagineers (a combination think-tank and carpentry shop) as well as a strategic planning group to determine the costs and benefits of his plans. Finally, the manager must implement the chosen alternative and periodically follow up and evaluate the effectiveness of that choice. Eisner carefully assesses how his changes are affecting the company's performance.

Figure 5.2
Steps in managerial decision making.

Organizing

The second basic managerial activity, **organizing**, means determining how to best arrange resources and jobs to be done into an overall structure. Disney keeps each of its businesses somewhat independent and somewhat interdependent. Each business has its own management team, and the president of each business has considerable autonomy in running it. But many major decisions and those affecting several businesses (such as licensing Mickey Mouse T-shirts for sale at Disney World) are made at the corporate level. Groups such as the Imagineers also work for all Disney businesses. We will explore organizing in Chapter 6.

organizing
That portion of a manager's job concerned with structuring the necessary resources to complete a particular task.

Leading

The activities involving interactions between managers and their subordinates to meet the firm's objectives are known as **leading** (or directing). By definition, managers have the power to give orders and demand results. Leading, however, goes beyond merely giving orders. Leaders attempt to guide and motivate employees to work in the best interests of the organization. For example, Michael Eisner's plans for Disney require tens of thousands of people to execute them. We discuss leadership more fully in Chapter 9.

leading
That portion of a manager's job concerned with guiding and motivating employees to meet the firm's objectives.

Controlling

The fourth basic managerial activity, **controlling**, means monitoring the firm's performance to make sure that it stays on track toward its goals. At Disney, Eisner's use of the Imagineers and the strategic management group and his decision to keep movie budgets low have kept the firm's profits growing.

controlling
That portion of a manager's job concerned with monitoring the firm's performance and, if necessary, acting to bring it in line with the firm's goals.

Figure 5.3 shows the basic control process. The process begins with standards, or goals, the company wants to meet. For example, if the company wants to increase sales by 20 percent over the next ten years, an appropriate standard might be an increase of around 2 percent each year. Managers must then measure actual performance regularly and compare this performance to the standard. If the two figures agree, the organization will continue its present activities. If they vary significantly, though, either the performance or the standard needs adjusting. For example, if sales have increased 2.1 percent at the end of the first year, things are probably fine. On the other hand, if sales have dropped by 1 percent, something needs to be done. The original goal may need to be lowered, more may need to be spent on advertising, and so forth.

The video case "Earth Buddy" on p. 203 clearly shows what happens when the controlling function is not properly carried out.

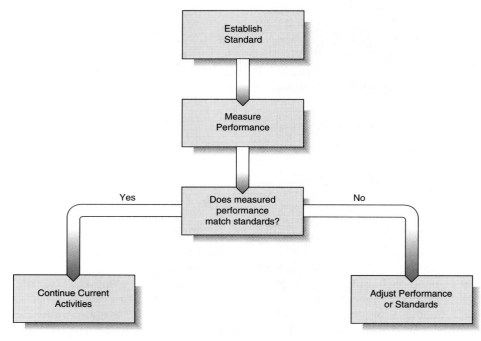

Figure 5.3
Steps in the control process.

Kinds of Managers

Although all managers plan, organize, lead, and control, not all managers have the same degree of responsibility for each activity. Moreover, managers differ in the specific application of these activities. Thus we can divide managers by their *level* of responsibility or by their *area* of responsibility.

Levels of Management

The three basic levels of management are top, middle, and first-line management. As Figure 5.4 shows, in most firms there are more middle managers than top managers and more first-line managers than middle managers. Moreover, as the categories imply, the power of managers and the complexity of their duties increase as we move up the pyramid.

top managers

Those managers responsible for a firm's overall performance and effectiveness and for developing long-range plans for the company.

Top Managers.   The fairly small number of executives who guide the fortunes of most companies are **top managers**. Common titles for top managers include President, Vice President, Treasurer, Chief Executive Officer (CEO), and Chief Financial Officer (CFO). Michael Eisner is a top manager for Disney, and Edgar Bronfman is a top executive for Seagram. Top managers are responsible to the board of directors and shareholders of the firm for its overall performance and effectiveness. They set general policies, formulate strategies, oversee all significant decisions, and represent the company in its dealings with other businesses and government.[1]

middle managers

Those managers responsible for implementing the decisions made by top managers

Middle Managers.   Although below the ranks of the top executives, **middle managers** occupy positions of considerable autonomy and importance. Titles such as Plant Manager, Operations Manager, and Division Manager are typical of middle-management slots. The producer of a Disney film is a middle

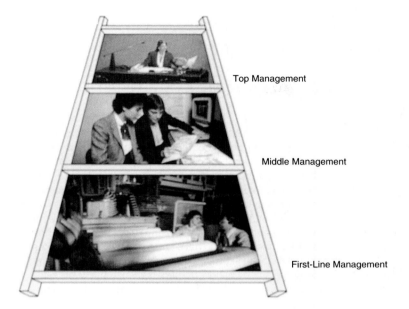

Figure 5.4
Most organizations have three basic levels of management.

Top Management

Middle Management

First-Line Management

manager. In general, middle managers are responsible for implementing the strategies, policies, and decisions of the top managers. For example, if top management decides to bring out a new product in 12 months or to cut costs by 5 percent, middle management will have to decide to increase the pace of new product development or to reduce the plant's work force. With companies increasingly seeking ways to cut costs, however, the job of middle manager has lately become precarious in many large companies. Labatt's laid off 120 middle managers when it developed a new corporate strategy. Air Canada also recently dropped 400 managers.[2] See the box "Pyramids, Downsizing, and Pancakes" for more information on this trend.

First-Line Managers.   At the bottom of the management hierarchy are **first-line managers** who supervise the work of employees. First-line managers hold titles such as Supervisor, Office Manager, and Foreman. The supervisor of Disney's animation department is a first-line manager. First-line managers tend to spend most of their time working with and supervising the employees who report to them. Some have entered the firm without a college or university degree or have been promoted from within the company.

first-line managers

Those managers responsible for supervising the work of employees.

Areas of Management

Within any large company, the top, middle, and first-line managers work in a variety of areas including marketing, finance, operations, human resources, and information. Figure 5.5, shown on p. 127, illustrates this relationship.

Marketing Managers.   Marketing includes the development, pricing, promotion, and distribution of a product or service. **Marketing managers** are responsible for getting products and services to buyers. Marketing is especially important for firms dealing in consumer products, such as Procter & Gamble, Coca-Cola, and Sun Ice. These firms often have large numbers of marketing managers at various levels. For example, a large firm will probably have a vice-president for marketing (top manager), regional marketing managers

marketing managers

Those managers responsible for developing, pricing, promoting, and distributing goods and services to buyers.

The Canadian Business Scene

PYRAMIDS, DOWNSIZING, AND PANCAKES

Most businesses have traditionally been organized in the shape of a pyramid. The largest number of workers formed the base, and fewer and fewer people occupied positions as one neared the apex of the pyramid.

But intense competition, both domestically and internationally, has forced businesses to find new ways to structure themselves. The two most publicized strategies that have been used are downsizing (cutting the scope of an organization's operations) and flattening the organizational pyramid so that it has fewer levels of management.

While many companies have decided that downsizing is the way to increase efficiency, it can cause serious problems. For example:

- When headquarters staff are let go during downsizing, line managers find that they have an increased workload.
- Anticipated cost savings often do not materialize.
- Employee productivity often stays the same or declines after downsizing.
- Employee morale usually drops after downsizing.

In previous recessions in Canada, employment levels in white collar jobs did not decline nearly as much as blue-collar jobs. But in the latest recession, downsizing led to the elimination of entire levels of management in some firms. In the 1990s, many firms are looking more like pancakes than pyramids.

What is the pancake company like? First, there are far fewer middle managers. Second, and perhaps more important, the role played by middle managers has been fundamentally redefined. No longer charged with the responsibility of controlling and making decisions, middle managers are now expected to delegate down and encourage their staff to make decisions.

For some, this change has meant new-found freedom

and increased autonomy. Working in a "participatory" structure, these managers now have easy access to top executives, can get decisions made more quickly, and can focus on more aspects of the business. Those who thrive on change seem particularly well suited to the flattened organizational structure.

On the negative side, however, these changes have required tremendous sacrifices. Many people have lost their jobs. And managers who have survived the cuts experience the stress of working with a new set of rules. The most common complaint by middle managers is extreme overwork.

Stresses and pressures increase when the streamlining processes are not well planned. Eliminating layers of management does not by itself ensure increased profits. Careful study of which jobs can be eliminated and a clear definition of a company's goals are critical ingredients to successful reorganization.

In spite of the difficulties involved, many companies that have flattened their management structure say the rewards have been worth the effort. Management teams, in which managers work with colleagues from other sections of the company, have proven very effective. The team approach gives managers first hand knowledge of how and where the company is most efficient and profitable.

Moving managers around an organization to broaden their understanding of the company's business has also proven successful. Their value to the company increases and managers benefit personally by finding new opportunities to use their talents. The continued challenge of doing something new builds enthusiasm and creativity.

Is the thinning of middle management only a trend? Probably not. Most experts agree that the pressures of global competition and improved bottom lines will only intensify in the coming years. This means that streamlined organizations are here to stay.

(middle managers), and several district sales managers (first-line managers). A marketing person often rises to the top of this type of corporation.

In contrast, firms that produce industrial products such as machinery and janitorial supplies tend to put less emphasis on marketing and to have fewer marketing managers. However, these firms do not ignore marketing altogether. In recent years, law firms and universities have also come to recognize the value and importance of marketing. For a detailed look at marketing, see Chapters 14-16.

financial managers

Those managers responsible for planning and overseeing the financial resources of a firm.

Financial Managers.   Management of a firm's finances, including its investments and accounting functions, is extremely important to its survival. Nearly every company has **financial managers** to plan and oversee its financial

Figure 5.5
Organizations require managers from a wide variety of areas to be effective. The most common areas are marketing, finance, operations, human resources, and information.

resources. Levels of financial management may include a vice-president for finance (top), division controller (middle), and accounting supervisor (first-line). For large financial institutions like the Bank of Montreal, First City Trust, and Burns Fry, effective financial management is the company's reason for being. No organization, however, can afford to ignore the need for management in this area. Chapters 17-20 treat financial management in detail.

Operations Managers.   A firm's operations are the systems by which it creates goods and services. **Operations managers** are responsible for production control, inventory control, and quality control, among other duties. Manufacturing companies like Steelcase, Bristol Aerospace, and Sony need operations managers at many levels. Such firms typically have a vice-president for operations (top), plant managers (middle), and foremen or supervisors (first-line). In recent years, sound operations management practices have also become increasingly important to service organizations, hospitals, universities, and the government. Operations management is the subject of Chapters 11-13.

operations managers
Those managers responsible for controlling production, inventory, and quality of a firm's products.

Human Resource Managers.   Every enterprise uses human resources. Most companies have **human resource managers** to hire employees, train them, evaluate their performances, decide how they should be compensated, and, in some cases, deal with labor unions. Large firms may have several human resource departments, each dealing with specialized activities. Imperial Oil, for example, has separate departments to deal with recruiting and hiring, wage and salary levels, and labor relations. Smaller firms may have a single department, while very small organizations may have a single person responsible for all human resource activities. Chapters 8-10 address issues involved in human resource management.

human resource managers
Those managers responsible for hiring, training, evaluating, and compensating employees.

information managers

Those managers responsible for the design and implementation of systems to gather, process, and disseminate information.

Information Managers.   A new type of managerial position appearing in many organizations is **information manager**. These managers are responsible for designing and implementing various systems to gather, process, and disseminate information. Dramatic increases in both the amount of information available to managers and in the ability to manage it have led to the emergence of this important function. While relatively few in number now, the ranks of information managers are increasing at all levels. Federal Express, for example, has a Chief Information Officer. Middle managers engaged in information management help design information systems for divisions or plants. Computer systems managers within smaller businesses or operations are first-line managers. Information management is discussed in Chapter 23.

Other Managers.   Some firms have more specialized managers. Chemical companies like CIL have research and development managers, for example, whereas companies like Petro Canada and Apple have public relations managers. The range of possibilities is endless; the areas of management are limited only by the needs and imagination of the firm.

Basic Management Skills

The success people enjoy in managerial positions is limited by their skills and abilities. As we noted in the section on planning, decision making is an important skill in all areas of management. Three other types of skills—technical, human relations, and conceptual—are also basic to good managers.

Technical Skills

technical skills

Skills associated with performing specialized tasks within a firm.

Skills associated with performing specialized tasks within a company are called **technical skills**. A secretary's ability to type, an animator's ability to draw a cartoon, and an accountant's ability to audit a company's records are all technical skills. People develop their technical skills through education and experience. The secretary, for example, probably took a keyboarding course and has had many hours of practice both on and off the job. The animator may have had training in an art school and probably learned a great deal from experienced animators on the job. The accountant earned a university degree and, possibly, professional certification.

As Figure 5.6 shows, technical skills are especially important for first-line managers. Most first-line managers spend considerable time helping employees solve work-related problems, monitoring their performance and training them in more efficient work procedures. Such managers need a basic understanding of the jobs they supervise.

As a manager moves up the corporate ladder, however, technical skills become less and less important. Top managers, for example, often need only a cursory familiarity with the mechanics of basic tasks performed within the company. Michael Eisner, for example, freely admits that he can't draw Mickey Mouse or build a ride for Disney World.

Human Relations Skills

human relations skills

Skills associated with understanding and working well with other employees.

Skills associated with understanding and getting along with other people are called **human relations skills**. Such skills are a necessary ingredient for managerial success in most settings. For example, a manager with poor human re-

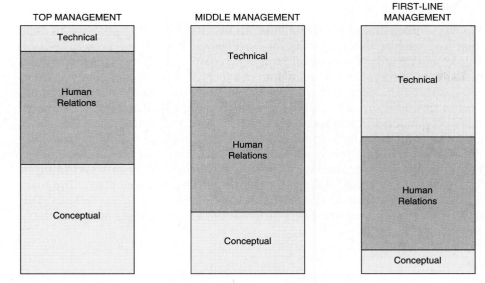

Figure 5.6
Different levels in an organization require different combinations of managerial skills.

lations skills may face conflict with subordinates, find that valuable employees quit or transfer, or have poor morale among those employees who stay. In contrast, a manager with good human relations skills is more likely to manage conflict properly, keep valuable employees, and maintain good morale.

As shown in Figure 5.6, human relations skills are important at all levels, although slightly more important for middle managers. Middle managers must often act as a bridge between top managers and first-line managers as well as with managers from other areas of the organization.[3]

First-line managers spend a considerable portion of their time supervising the work of operating employees. And a significant portion of this time may be devoted to training. For example, this supervisor is teaching an employee how to operate a new piece of equipment.

Conceptual Skills

conceptual skills
Skills associated with abstract thinking, problem diagnosis and analysis, and future planning.

Finally, **conceptual skills** include the ability to think in the abstract, to diagnose and analyze different situations, and to see beyond the present. For example, when Steve Wozniak and Steve Jobs created the first personal computer in a garage, it required that they both use technical skills. Wozniak was interested only in the technical side of the problem and saw no commercial opportunities. Jobs, however, recognized the bigger picture and pushed hard for mass production and marketing of their new "toy." The result? Apple Computer.

Conceptual skills help managers see new market opportunities. They help managers understand when to push ahead and when to retreat. They help managers better deal with the causes of their successes and failures. The need for conceptual skills differs at various management levels. Top managers depend the most on conceptual skills, first-line managers the least. This difference results from the basic differences in the purposes of these jobs.

Becoming a Manager

The skills of management are not easily acquired by would-be managers. Nor can organizations easily identify people who possess these skills. As you will see in this section, both the training and the recruiting of managers are complex operations.

Preparing for Management

At one time, managers simply started at the "bottom" (in many cases, a plant or warehouse) and worked their way to the "top." While such a career path is still possible, the increasing complexity of management makes people who follow it a rare breed. Today more than ever before, managers are acquiring their skills and abilities through a cyclical process of education, experience, and then more education.

Most managers start learning their basic skills in university or college classrooms.

Education.   The most common starting point for contemporary Canadian managers is a B. Comm. degree from a university or a college degree in business administration. Many people leave school with this degree and start their careers. Their learning, however, is not complete. More and more people eventually return to school to get a masters of business administration (MBA) degree.[4] Even managers who do not earn an MBA usually go through corporate training programs. Many attend management development programs and seminars sponsored by universities or private training companies. Learning is a lifelong process for most managers.

Experience.   Education is not the only route into management. In some companies, managers—especially first-line managers—may have little or no advanced education. They have earned their positions strictly on the basis of experience. This pattern is common in heavy manufacturing industries such as steel and automobile production.

Experience is also necessary for those with degrees who want to get ahead. After completing their degree(s), most people today accept an entry-level position in a large company, go to work in a family-owned business, or start their own business. As their careers progress, they gain much valuable experience. In larger companies, for example, most management trainees go through formal training programs and work in a variety of areas to gain a broader perspective. As the box "Home Sweet Home" notes, however, experience is no guarantee of success.

Where Organizations Find Managers

Just as there are different paths to management, companies acquire new managers in different ways. Firms have three basic sources of new managers: the academic world, the company itself, and other companies.

Recruiting from Colleges and Universities.   Colleges and universities are a major source of new managers. Large firms like Sears, the Bank of Montreal, Canadian Pacific, and Noranda hire hundreds of new graduates as managers every year. Often they start graduates from community colleges and universities as first-line managers. MBAs may be able to start at the lower levels of middle management.

The primary advantages of this source are that the managers are young and have been exposed to the latest ideas. On the other hand, they frequently lack experience and a proven track record. Businesses that adopt this strategy must invest in effective campus recruiting strategies and be prepared to develop future managers over a longer period of time.

Promoting from Within.   Another common source of managers is the firm itself, especially one or two layers below where the new managers are needed. Promotion from within offers many advantages. Recognizing that they have a chance to advance within the company motivates lower-level employees to do their best. Employees who are promoted from within also come with a track record. The firm has its own data on the individual's performance and accomplishments.

International Report

HOME SWEET HOME

In this global age, an international business needs its top managers to have practical experience in foreign operations, so managers with such experience will advance further and faster, right? Not necessarily.

After years of sending managers to facilities around the world, companies are rethinking their policies. At the heart of this shift is the very high cost of sending residents abroad. A manager who costs the company $100 000 per year in Canada can cost three times that if shipped to England for a year.

Even with the "extras" that managers often receive when they go overseas, today, more than ever before, middle- and upper-level managers are reluctant to take posts abroad.

For many managers, foreign branches are still just branches of the company. Many branches at home and abroad are understaffed and/or underequipped. Managers also lose the chance to interact formally and informally with top management at the corporation's headquarters. As a result, they may have little influence on staffing and pay decisions that affect their operations.

Another factor in accepting a position abroad is its effect on the manager's family. A manager's spouse is often unable to get a work permit and/or a job in a foreign land. Children must adapt to schooling in a different culture.

(Actually, this problem is an even greater hurdle for Japanese managers posted abroad, since their children may miss the all-important Japanese cramming sessions in preparation for brutal university-entrance exams.) Every member of the family will have to adjust to cultural differences, in some cases including a different language.

An even greater hurdle to getting Canadian managers overseas is that it often does not pay off for the manager in the long run. Those who accept a foreign post may find themselves all but forgotten by their superiors when they return home expecting promotions and new challenges. Many find themselves relegated to unexciting areas of the company and, ironically, often to areas that have no need of the international expertise these managers now have.

In light of their own costs and employees' reluctance, many firms have sharply curtailed the number of managers they send to foreign posts. Instead, they are filling more and more management positions abroad with local employees. Managers who do go abroad often insist on knowing to what position they will return—and making sure it will be meaningful. No matter how far they roam, it seems that managers want to be sure that they can go home again.

Of course, if someone from middle management is promoted to an executive position, someone else must be found to fill the middle-management position. Promotion from within tends to perpetuate current practices and ideas, giving less opportunity for innovation. In addition, these promotion decisions are sometimes seen as being too political, making other employees resentful or damaging their morale.

Hiring Away from Other Organizations.   Finally, some managers are hired away from other businesses. Contacts with talented managers willing to consider alternative opportunities can come from a manager's own network or through professional recruiting firms, commonly referred to as "headhunters."

As with the other options, hiring away from other firms has both advantages and disadvantages. The company may be able to get more talented people than are available internally. Already-trained managers mean a savings to the organization. Hiring from outside may inject fresh ideas and creativity. On the other hand, insiders passed over in favor of an outsider may feel resentful and leave. The newcomer may not fit into the company. Thus, the managers in charge of attracting human resources need to consider carefully the pros and cons of each source as they develop their human resource strategy.

Corporate Cultures and Management Styles

Recruiting new managers is a tricky business. Companies cannot rely solely on an individual's academic degrees and work experience in making a hiring or promotion decision. They must also consider the prospective manager's style and how it will fit into the company's style.

Corporate Culture

Consider the following story, which details an interesting development in the relationship between employee behavior and corporate values:

■ In 1989, Microsoft programmer Wes Cherry wrote a software program duplicating the game solitaire. Originally designed to amuse people as they learned Microsoft's new Windows software, Solitaire became such a hit that since 1990 the company has packaged it with nearly 50 million copies of Windows. To the consternation of many companies, however, Solitaire has become a nuisance and even a threat to productivity. According to one survey, about 42 percent of office computer users admit to playing games at their desks. Some organizations have banned game playing, and some have even removed programs from company-owned computers. Meanwhile, other companies actually endorse computer games. Managers in these offices see them as contributing to productivity because they help to reduce stress.[5]

corporate culture

The shared experiences, stories, beliefs, and norms that characterize a firm.

This story shows that just as every individual has a unique personality, so every company has a unique identity—its corporate culture. **Corporate culture** is the shared experiences, stories, beliefs, and norms that characterize an organization. Various corporate cultures can be effective. What is important to managers is establishing and maintaining a strong, clear culture.[6]

At Toyota's Cambridge, Ontario, plant, for example, the corporate culture stresses values, principles, and trust. It also emphasizes customer satisfaction. For each employee, the next person down the production line is the customer. The culture is one of continuous improvement *(kaizen)*.[7]

A company may consciously change its culture to improve its performance. Bata Shoes, long a traditional marketer, now stresses that it will not be satisfied with Canada's high prices to consumers. It advertises that its prices are as low as or lower than those in the U.S. The new corporate culture is also oriented to providing shoes to customers very quickly.

When two firms with different cultures merge, both have to adjust. For example, Baker-Lovick and McKim Advertising Ltd. were both purchased by BBDO Worldwide, a U.S. agency. But Baker-Lovick and McKim have completely different cultures. McKim is conservative and does not seek publicity, while Baker-Lovick loves the limelight. The new merged firm is likely to become more like Baker-Lovick in the future.[8] The box "Melding Two Cultures" describes the adjustments in culture that were necessary in two other Canadian firms.

The Canadian Business Scene

MELDING TWO CULTURES

The merger of two firms with different corporate cultures presents both problems and opportunities. Consider the experiences of two Canadian firms.

Relcon Ltd.
In the 1940s, George Rumble founded a firm called Rumble Equipment. When he died in 1960, his employees bought out the firm and renamed it Relcon. The company's main product—electronic drives that precisely control the speed of electric motors—was successful in the Canadian market, but the firm did not have the resources necessary to become an international success. The culture at the firm was very relaxed and informal; the employees thrived on a loose structure and collaborative management, symbolized by the round table in the boardroom. Decision making was often "by the seat of the pants."

That easygoing culture changed when Relcon was acquired by Siemens AG, the German electronics giant. One employee says "there was profound culture shock." Under Siemens' control, rigid structures and job descriptions now exist for all employees. Employees who formerly shifted back and forth between several different jobs now find themselves doing much more highly focused work. Relcon used to make a relatively small number of electronic drives and inspect every one of them before shipping. But now the factory has become a high-volume manufacturing facility. Much more emphasis is therefore being placed on statistical analysis of operations, and every aspect of the work is being measured much more carefully than formerly.

As a result of the acquisition, the culture of Relcon has become much more methodical and bureaucratic. The new president has taken a cautious approach when introducing these changes. He says that when you merge two cultures, you must do it slowly because you want to get the best out of both companies, not the worst. Most employees seem to agree that things are going well, and they are happy that their international visibility has increased since they were acquired by Siemens.

Triathlon Vehicle Leasing.
Triathlon was one of the biggest Canadian firms in the car and truck leasing business. In 1994, it was acquired by GE Capital Fleet Services, part of the giant General Electric empire. Rolf Ruegg from Brussels, Belgium was appointed as the new unit's leader. To smooth the transition, an "integration" team was set up with representatives from all affected departments. The team met every week so that department representatives could air their concerns and keep their people up to date on changes that were taking place. The team identified various challenges and opportunities that were facing the new unit.

A major issue was differences in the cultures of the two organizations. Triathlon, which was proud of its people and its closeness to its customers, had a traditional hierarchical structure. It felt that it was being swallowed up by a multinational giant. GE employees, by contrast, were used to a flat organization structure (only four levels of management), lots of empowerment, an informal management style, and casually dressed staff. The integration team grappled with these and other issues and also made the decision to let about 100 people go. "Assimilation exercises" were run for the employees that remained.

All the people in the new company are striving to meld two different cultures. That may be tougher than some of the technological changes that are also being introduced as part of the merger.

Corporate culture is an important ingredient in organizational success. Japanese companies have been quite successful in building strong cultures by creating shared experiences and values among their employees. The executives in the upper right photo are participating in a traditional purification ceremony at 4:30 in the morning. Later in the day they will remember this common experience as they work together.

Forces Shaping Corporate Culture. A number of forces shape corporate cultures. First, the values held by top management help set the tone of the organization and influence its business goals and strategies. For example, after Wozniak and Jobs founded Apple Computer, their laid-back approach and disdain for formality permeated the entire company. Even an older firm like Ford still bears traces of its founder. Most of Ford's top executives remain "car people," often engineers by training and background, rather than financial experts.

The firm's history also helps shape its culture. Championship banners line the Montreal Forum, reinforcing the message that the Canadiens are winners. Maintaining a corporate culture draws on many dimensions of business life. Shared experiences resulting from norms sustain culture. Thus, working long hours on a special project becomes a shared experience for many employees. They remember it, talk about it among themselves, and wear it as a badge of their contribution to the company.

Stories and legends are also important. Walt Disney has been dead many years now, but his spirit lives on in the businesses he left behind. Quotations from Disney are affixed to portraits of him throughout the company's studios. And Disney's emphasis on family is still visible in corporate benefits such as paying for spouses to accompany employees on extended business trips. In fact, employees are often called "the Disney family."

Finally, strong behavioral norms help define and sustain corporate cultures. For example, a strong part of the culture at Hewlett-Packard Canada is that everyone wears a name tag and that everyone is called by his or her first name.

Communicating the Culture. To use the corporate culture for the betterment of the organization, managers must accomplish several tasks that all depend on effective communication:

- Managers themselves must have a clear understanding of the culture.
- Managers must transmit the culture to others in the organization. Communication is thus one of the aims in training and orientation for newcomers. Another way of communicating the culture is to develop a clear and meaningful statement of the organization's mission.
- Managers can maintain the culture by rewarding and promoting those who understand it and who work toward maintaining it.

Management Styles

As you might expect, corporate cultures affect not only which people a company hires but also the styles of individual managers. Many styles are possible, depending on the manager and the circumstances.

The Continuum of Management Styles.   As Figure 5.7 shows, management styles run the gamut from autocratic to democratic to free-rein. Most managers do not fall clearly into any one neat box. But these three major types of management styles point to very different types of responses to problems. Studying them should help you to identify tendencies in the managers you will interact with in business and may help you identify the style that best suits you as a manager.

Managers who adopt an **autocratic style** simply issue orders and expect those beneath them to obey unquestioningly. Two well-known Canadian executives—Robert Campeau (Campeau Corp.) and Laurent Beaudoin (Bombardier Inc.)—are cited in the business press as being autocratic leaders.[9]

Probably the best example of an autocratic style is a military commander on the battlefield. The autocratic style allows for rapid decision making, since no one else is consulted. However, subordinates of autocratic managers often feel frustrated and angry at their lack of input.

autocratic style
A management style characterized by the manager making all decisions and issuing orders without the input of subordinates.

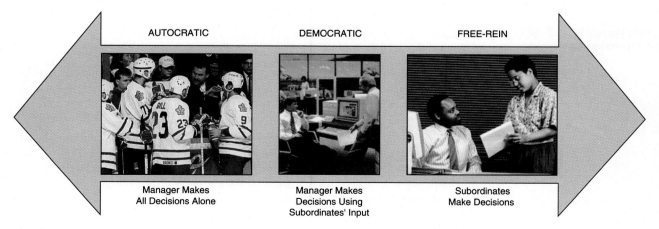

AUTOCRATIC   DEMOCRATIC   FREE-REIN

Manager Makes   Manager Makes   Subordinates
All Decisions Alone   Decisions Using   Make Decisions
                        Subordinates' Input

Figure 5.7
A wide variety of management styles can be used.

democratic style
A management style characterized by the manager making decisions that take into account the input of subordinates.

In contrast, managers who adopt a **democratic style** ask their subordinates for suggestions before making decisions. Charles Hantho (Dominion Textiles) and Robert Hamaberg (Standard Aero) are both democratic managers. Jean Chretien, the prime minister of Canada, is also a person who delegates a lot of authority to subordinates to make decisions. Robert Findlay, CEO of MacMillan-Bloedel Ltd., came up through the ranks in a very hard-nosed company, but his style is very consultative. He works in a glassed-in fishbowl of an office where the staff feels comfortable enough to drift in and out without knocking.[10]

There is a trend to delegate more authority to subordinates. At the Canadian Passport Service, passport examiners until recently have been limited to checking only routine matters in passport applications. Under a new employee empowerment program, examiners have been given increased discretion to decide on more complex matters regarding passport applications.[11]

free-rein style
A management style characterized by the manager allowing subordinates to make most decisions.

Finally, managers who adopt a **free-rein style** serve as advisors but allow subordinates to make most decisions. A person chairing a local committee of volunteers to raise funds for a new library may find a free-rein style most effective. The free-rein style can increase creativity, helping a firm or other organization find new solutions. However, not all subordinates have the necessary background to make all decisions.

The Contingency Approach.   Because each management style has its strengths and weaknesses, most managers use a variety of styles depending on the situation. Even the most democratic of managers will adopt an autocratic style if it becomes necessary. Flexibility has not always been a part of management styles or management actions, however. For most of this century, managers tended to believe that problems had only one best solution. Thus, if raising pay reduced turnover in one plant, experts assumed that the same technique would work equally well in another plant.

contingency approach
The philosophy that the appropriate managerial behavior in any situation is dependent (contingent) on the unique characteristics of the situation.

More recently, however, managers have begun to adopt a **contingency approach** to problem-solving. That is, they have started to see appropriate managerial behavior in any situation as dependent, or contingent, on elements of that situation. This change in outlook has resulted from the increasing recognition of the complexity of managerial problems—and solutions. In our example above, the contingency approach recognizes that pay raises may reduce turnover when workers in a plant have been badly underpaid but may have little effect when workers feel they are well paid but ill-treated by their managers. In the latter case, training managers in human relations skills may be the solution. The point of the contingency approach is that there are multiple paths to solving a problem.

Summary of Key Points

Management is the process of planning, organizing, leading, and controlling a variety of resources in order to achieve the firm's goals. Planning is determining what the company needs to do and how best to do it or get it done. Decision making is an integral part of planning. Organizing is developing a structure of tasks and patterns of authority so as to accomplish the firm's goals. Leading activities involve the interactions between managers and their subordinates. Controlling is the process of monitoring the firm's performance to make sure it stays on track toward its goals.

Managers can be differentiated in two ways. By level, there are top, middle, and first-line managers. By area, there are marketing, financial, operations, human resource, information, and other kinds of managers. Top managers set policies, formulate strategies, and oversee all of a firm's major decisions. Middle managers implement these strategies, policies, and decisions. First-line managers carry out these strategies, policies, and decisions as they work with and supervise employees. Managers at all levels may be found in all areas of a company.

Three basic management skills are necessary for success. Technical skills are needed to perform specialized tasks within the organization. Human relations skills include understanding and getting along with other people. Conceptual skills help a manager to think in the abstract, to diagnose and analyze different situations, and to see beyond the present. Individuals may acquire managerial skills in many ways. However, most go through a cyclical process of education, experience, more education, and then more experience.

When businesses need to hire new managers, they find them at colleges and universities, in the lower ranks of the firm, and/or in other companies. Recent graduates offer a fresh perspective but need experience to become good managers. In-house personnel may be highly motivated and fit in well but may tend to reprise old ideas. Managers hired away from other firms often bring new ideas but may alienate existing employees.

Corporate culture is the shared experiences, stories, beliefs, and norms that characterize a company. A strong, well-defined culture can help a business reach its goals and influence management styles. Management styles range from autocratic to democratic to free-rein. But, in keeping with the contingency approach, most managers adapt their style to fit the specific situation.

CONCLUDING CASE 5-1

Leading the League

Paul Beeston is the CEO of the Toronto Blue Jays. His associates think that, like Tom Hanks in the Movie *Big*, he walks a fine line between crazy kid and top-notch executive. Beeston, who is legendary for his commitment to the organization, started as the team's first full-time accountant and rose through the ranks to become president in 1989. He arrives at work between 7 and 7:30 a.m. each day, and hasn't taken a vacation in four years. With the team's 1992 and 1993 World Series victories and its profitable condition, Beeston has much of which to be proud.

Beeston works closely with exectuvie vice-president Pat Gillick. Beeston handles the administration and balances the books, while Gillick monitors the team's on-the-field performance. Beeston is very much into signing players like Dave Winfield, Roberto Alomar, and George Bell to big-time deals. He has a reputation as a tough but fair negotiator. He responds to fan outrage at high player salaries by saying that baseball players need a good environment to work in. The Blue Jays' salary budget for 1992 was over $40 million.

Beeston is continually under pressure to perform, i.e., to win. This is not a simple matter, since the club has 25 often temperamental ballplayers. It is necessary continually to find new players through the scouting system and to keep those players coming through the system.

CASE QUESTIONS
1. What skills of management does Paul Beeston need to be effective? How have these changed over the years as he moved from accountant to CEO?
2. Briefly describe how each of the functions of management are carried out by Paul Beeston.
3. Is being CEO of a baseball team much different than being CEO of a manufacturing firm? Explain.
4. How is Beeston's job similar to the job of CEO at CN Railways? How is it different?

◆

CONCLUDING CASE 5-2

Can-Mark Manufacturing

Henry Friesen was a supervisor at Can-Mark Manufacturing, a company which produced a variety of consumer goods. Recently, Friesen had been put in charge of a group of nine people who were to produce the company's latest addition to its product line. The production process for the new product required state-of-the-art equipment, and the company's industrial engineers had just completed a lengthy series of tests to determine reasonable production standards for the new machines.

The production line experienced trouble right from the start. The workers had difficulty getting the machines to work and rejects were running substantially above the level that was considered acceptable. One afternoon, as Friesen was sitting in his office wondering how to resolve this problem, the plant superintendent, Peter Jansen, appeared at his door. Friesen invited him in and the following conversation took place:

Jansen: Henry, what's the problem with our new line? You know this product is high profile, and I'm already getting pressure from the vice-president. He says the new product is crucial to our company, and he wants these production flaws corrected immediately. There's a lot of demand out there for this product, and we've got to get production volume up.

Friesen: After talking to the workers, I'm convinced the production standards are out of line. My people are very motivated and experienced, but they can't meet the standards the engineering people have set.

Jansen: But our engineers have a very good reputation for setting realistic job standards.

Friesen: I know that, but this time they've made a mistake. This state-of-the-art equipment we're using is more difficult to work with than they could have imagined.

Jansen: We've got to get output on this line up to standard or we'll both be in trouble with top management.

At this point, one of Friesen's workers entered his office and told him of yet another problem with the new equipment, so Friesen had to cut the meeting short. For the rest of the day his discussion with Jansen weighed heavily on his mind.

CASE QUESTIONS
1. Explain how the decision making process in Figure 5.2 applies in this situation. What should Henry Friesen do?
2. What level of management does Henry Friesen occupy? What does this imply about the relative emphasis he should place on technical, human relations, and conceptual skills?
3. Explain the practical impact of the leading and controlling functions in this situation.
4. How does the culture of this organization impact on Henry's job as a manager?

◆

Key Terms

management	top managers	human resource	corporate culture
planning	middle managers	managers	autocratic style
decision making	first-line managers	information managers	democratic style
organizing	marketing managers	technical skills	free-rein style
leading	financial managers	human relations skills	contingency approach
controlling	operations managers	conceptual skills	

Study Questions and Exercises

Review Questions

1. Relate the basic managerial skills to the four activities in the management process. For example, which skill(s) is (are) most important in leading?
2. What are the major areas of management found in most organizations?
3. What are the three sources of new managers?
4. Why has the contingency approach become so important?

Analysis Questions

5. Select any group of which you are a member (company, family, club, etc.). Explain how planning, organizing, leading, and controlling are practised.
6. Identify managers by level and area at your college or university.
7. In what kind of company are technical skills for top managers more important than human relations or conceptual skills? Are there organizations in which conceptual skills are not important?
8. Using the management style continuum explained in this chapter, which style do you think you would most likely adopt if you became a manager?

Application Exercises

9. Interview a manager of a local company. Identify that manager's job according to the level and area of management. Show how planning, organizing, leading, and controlling are part of his or her job. Inquire about the manager's education and work experience. Which management skills are most important for this job?
10. Compare and contrast the corporate cultures of two businesses in your community in the same industry (for example, a Sears department store and a Costco warehouse.)

Building Your Business Skills

Goal

To encourage students to understand the link between achieving organizational goals and managing the corporate culture.

Situation

Suppose that you are part of Taligent, an IBM/Apple Computer joint venture whose mission is to develop a new operating system to compete with Microsoft and Nexis. Besides formidable technical challenges, you must also find a way for the diametrically opposed corporate cultures from IBM and Apple to coesixt. IBM, for example, is a hierarchical organization that moves ideas systematically up the corporate ladder, where they are approved and refocused before coming back down again in the form of strategic plans. Apple, on the other hand, has a collegial culture the empowers employees to make important decisions at all levels.

Method

Step 1: Place yourself in the position of an IBM executive assigned to Taligent. What are the advantages and disadvantages that the IBM culture brings to the group in the following areas:

■ *Decision making:* At IBM, the decision-making process is both crucial and deliberate, as is the collection and reporting of hard data.
■ *Administrative support:* IBM executives are used to working with groups of dedicated support personnel who help them complete assignments but who also insulate them from the distractions of various events in the company.
■ *Dress code:* Blue business suits are an IBM tradition.

Step 2: Place yourself in the position of an executive from Apple Computer working on Taligent and perform the same analysis. What advantages and disadvantages does Apple's corporate culture bring to the project in the same areas:

■ *Decision making:* While the pace of work is faster because decisions are made at all levels at Apple, the emphasis on empowerment over hierarchy can lead to anarchy—or at least to confusing communications. Moreover, decisions at Apple are often guided more by company folklore than by hard data.
■ *Administrative support:* With fewer support personnel, Apple is a "leaner" organization than IBM.
■ *Dress code:* The dress code at Apple is less formal and more relaxed than at IBM.

Step 3: As a class, divide into groups of four or five. Discuss your analysis of the effects of the IBM and Apple corporate cultures on the success of Taligent.

Follow-up Questions

1. What cultural factors are likely to create the most serious problems for the joint venture?
2. How should team managers handle the cultural differences that will inevitably emerge among IBM and Apple employees?

6

Planning and Organizing

LEARNING OBJECTIVES

After studying this chapter, you will be able to

- Identify the purposes of goal-setting by businesses and the three levels of goals.
- Describe the planning process.
- Discuss three levels of strategic plans.
- Distinguish between tactical and operational plans and show how each helps to implement strategic plans.
- Discuss the elements that influence a firm's organizational structure.
- Identify and describe the building blocks of organizational structure.
- Describe how authority is delegated in centralized and decentralized organizations and between line and staff departments.
- Explain the operation and importance of the informal organization.

CHAPTER OUTLINE

OPENING CASE

Dogfight over Canadian Skies

As the blue jet slowly taxied out to the runway, a red jet passed it, going in the opposite direction. The pilot of the blue jet received a salute from the pilot of the red plane—a middle finger salute. This incident typifies the intense competition and strong feelings that exist between Canada's two premier air carriers—Air Canada and Canadian Airlines International (CAI). It also illustrates the difficulty of planning in an industry characterized by intense competition and government regulation.

That CAI is flying at all is a source of amazement to many industry observers. Its problems have been extensively reported during the last four years. In a video made for employees, the company president explained how external factors had caused CAI to incur significant losses in the early 1990s. The Gulf War in 1991, for example, caused a dramatic increase in fuel prices, and this increased operating expenses. The recession of 1991-1992 was longer and more severe than expected, and this reduced demand for air travel. This, in turn, generated less cash from operations than planned, so the company had to borrow money. But this increased interest costs.

To make matters worse, CAI was dealt another setback when Japan Airlines decided to bow out of an agreement to share the costs of Toronto-to-Tokyo flights. JAL did this because it was losing money on joint service operations.

There were several possible solutions to CAI's troubles. One was to get involved in some sort of joint venture with another airline. In 1992, American Airlines offered to invest $246 million in CAI, with the understanding that CAI would join American's Sabre reservation system. But CAI was already involved in Gemini, a reservation system that it jointly ran with Air Canada. When Gemini heard about CAI's plan, it sued for $1 billion, claiming that if CAI withdrew from the Gemini system, it would no longer be viable.

Another possibility was merging with arch-rival Air Canada. But as merger talks began, the federal Bureau of Competition expressed serious concerns that a merger would create a monopoly in air travel for Air Canada. The Competition Tribunal required CAI to demonstrate that Air Canada was the only serious buyer.

As another possibility, CAI asked the four western provinces and the federal government for a $190 million bailout. The request came at about the same time a federal report concluded that there should be no airline bailouts. Nevertheless, the government finally agreed to give $50 million if CAI would reduce its scope of operations and lay off some people.

In April 1993, the federal tribunal ruled that CAI could not leave the Gemini system, but that decision was reversed in November 1993. The National Transportation Board (NTB) also approved CAI's proposed partnership with American Airlines, and concluded that it would not result in undue control of CAI by American Airlines. American Airlines has now invested the $246 million that it originally proposed, and CAI is on a stronger financial footing.

Air Canada is very unhappy because the NTB's decision increases the threat of job losses. The ill will generated by the dispute was apparent during hearings before the Competition Tribunal. At those hearings, an internal Air Canada plan to frustrate CAI's withdrawal from Gemini came to light. The document suggested that Air Canada work with Gemini to prevent CAI from leaving the system. To add insult to injury, Air Canada was required to pay about $18 million to American Airlines for breach of contract in an unrelated case.

What does the future hold? If the events of the past few years are any indication, the turmoil in the airline industry will continue. In the last decade the two airlines have lost a total of $2 billion. CAI now employs 25 percent fewer employees than it did in 1990. Both airlines will have to cut costs, increase revenues, improve service, and somehow differentiate themselves from each other. They can do this by cutting the amount of time an aircraft spends on the ground between flights. This increases the time a plane can be in the air; every 40 minutes of additional flying creates the equivalent of seven 137-seat planes. Reducing baggage handling mistakes also cuts costs. Achieving these efficiencies will challenge the planners at both organizations.

The most recent financial information on Air Canada and CAI is promising. Air Canada made a profit in 1994, and CAI has sharply reduced its losses.   ◆

Commercial airline companies, like other businesses, occasionally have difficulty planning. Planning is a crucial activity for both profit-oriented businesses and for non-profit organizations such as schools, government agencies, religious and charitable organizations, the military, and unions. Planning is a basic function of management.

This chapter is divided into two major parts. In the first part, we look at the steps in the planning process and at strategic planning. In the second part, we focus on organizational structure. The structure of an organization helps it organize work in order to achieve goals set during the planning process.

The Planning Process

Managers at all levels in a business carry out the planning process. The process includes the following steps (see Figure 6.1):

- set organizational goals
- identify the gap between actual and desired positions
- develop plans to achieve objectives
- implement the plans
- evaluate planning effectiveness

Set Organizational Goals

Goals are the results that an organization wants to achieve. (We use the terms "objectives" and "goals" synonymously.) Goals should have a time frame and be specific, measurable, challenging, and accepted by the person who must achieve them.

goals
Results the organization wants to achieve.

Goals focus employee attention on tasks that are consistent with the organization's mission, assist in allocating resources, and help managers assess performance. Unitel Communications Inc. set a goal to capture 5 percent of the residential and business long-distance phone market within three years of its startup and 16 percent by its tenth year of operation.[1] Xerox Corp. set a goal to begin competing in the rapidly expanding field of document processing because it promises higher profit margins than traditional photocopying.[2] Shell Canada Ltd. has adopted the goal of changing its fossil fuel companies to energy companies that will put as much effort into solar and wind power as they do into oil and gas exploration.[3]

The goals of each company differ, depending on the company's purpose and mission. Every enterprise has a **purpose**—a reason for being. Businesses seek profits for their owners, universities seek to discover and transmit new

purpose
The company's reason for being in business.

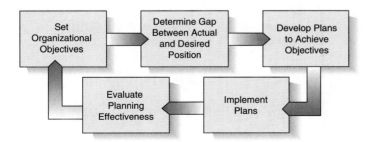

Figure 6.1
The planning process.

mission

How the company will achieve its purpose.

long-term goals

Goals over extended periods of time, usually five or more years into the future.

intermediate goals

Goals over a period one to five years in the future.

knowledge, and government agencies seek to help the public. As well, every enterprise has a **mission**—a view of how it will achieve its purpose.

To illustrate the difference between purpose and mission, consider the similarities and differences between Timex and Rolex. Both companies have the same purpose—to make money by selling watches—but they have very different missions. Timex emphasizes low-cost, reliable watches that can be purchased anywhere from Kmart to Shopper's Drug Mart. Rolex, on the other hand, sells high-priced, high-quality fashion watches only through selected jewelry stores.

No matter what a company's purpose and mission, it must set long-term, intermediate, and short-term goals. Figure 6.2 shows the hierarchy of these goals and how they are established.

Long-term goals are goals expected to be achieved over extended periods of time, typically five years or more. Great-West Life might set a long-term goal of increasing its number of life insurance customers by 3 percent over the next five years. Master Card might set a long-term goal of doubling the number of merchants who accept its cards during the next ten years.

Goals that involve the period from one to five years ahead are called **intermediate goals**. Companies usually have several intermediate goals related to different areas. For example, marketing's intermediate goal might be to increase sales 3 percent in two years. Production's intermediate goal might be to decrease overhead expenses by 6 percent in four years. Human resources might seek to cut turnover by 10 percent in two years. Finance might aim for a 3 percent increase in return on investment in three years.

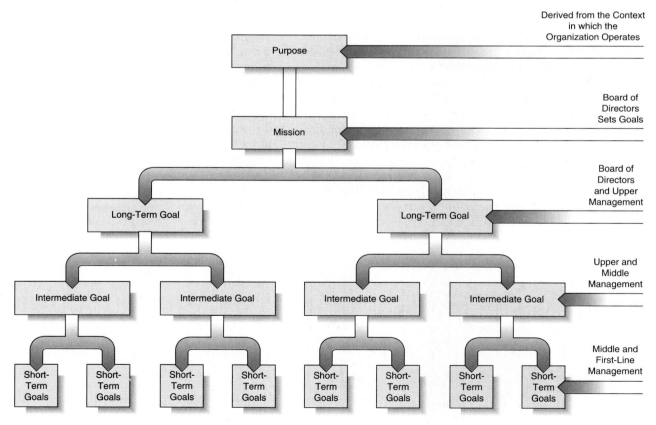

Figure 6.2
Businesses pursue a hierarchy of goals.

Finally, companies need goals for the near future, less than one year hence. Like intermediate goals, these **short-term goals** are developed for different areas. Increasing sales 2 percent this year, cutting costs by 1 percent next quarter, and reducing turnover by 4 percent over the next six months are all short-term goals.

short-term goals
Goals in the near future, usually less than one year.

Within any company, managers at different levels are responsible for setting different kinds of goals. The firm's purpose is largely determined by the context in which it operates—that is, the environment in which it markets its products. The board of directors generally defines the firm's mission. Working in conjunction with the board, top managers then usually set long-term goals. These same managers typically work closely with middle managers to set intermediate goals. Finally, middle managers work with first-line managers to set and achieve short-term goals. All of these different goals must be integrated so that everyone in the organization is pulling in the same direction.

To manage the planning process, many firms have adopted a **management by objectives (MBO)** approach.[4] MBO is a system of collaborative goal setting that extends from the top of the organization to the bottom. Managers meet with each of their subordinates individually to discuss goals. This meeting usually occurs annually and focuses on the coming year. The box "MBO at Investors" describes how this process works at a large Canadian company.

management by objectives (MBO)
An approach to management control and employee motivation in which a manager and an employee cooperatively establish goals against which the employee is later evaluated.

Identify the Gap Between Actual and Desired Positions

In the second step of the planning process, managers must determine how well organizational objectives are being achieved. The focus may be on the entire company, a department within the company, or an individual within a department. Consider the following examples:

1. A year-end financial analysis of the company will determine whether the company reached its profitability objectives.
2. At the end of a recruiting period, a department can assess whether it reached its hiring objective of four new people.
3. An annual performance appraisal of an individual will tell the boss and subordinate whether the subordinate reached his or her goals for the year.

These examples assume that both managers and subordinates will behave rationally when they measure progress toward objectives. This step will be difficult to carry out if measuring performance creates fear and resentment in subordinates, or if objectives have not been stated clearly. Once these problems are overcome, managers can decide what plans are needed to close the gap between the desired and actual objective.

Develop Plans to Achieve Objectives

As we have seen, objectives focus on the results the organization wants to achieve. **Plans**, by contrast, focus on the activities that must be performed to achieve the objectives, on the person or group who will carry these activities out, and on the deadline for their completion. There are many types of plans, including strategic plans, operational plans, single-use plans, and standing plans, as we shall see later in this chapter.

plans
Activities that must be performed if goals are to be achieved.

Implement Plans

The steps that we have discussed so far—setting objectives, determining the gap between the desired and the actual, and developing plans to achieve objectives—all require managers to think about what is to be accomplished.

The Canadian Business Scene

MBO AT INVESTORS GROUP FINANCIAL SERVICES INC.

Sales representatives at Investors Group Financial Services sell a wide range of financial services including mutual funds, investment certificates, insurance programs, pension plans, annuities, and tax-sheltered plans. The company has financial planning centres in every major metropolitan area of Canada, and employs over 3000 salespeople. It has the largest direct salesforce of any company in the financial services sector.

Investors has used MBO since 1974 to motivate its sales force in selling financial services. The MBO process begins when the vice-president of sales develops general goals for the entire sales force. These goals may be based on last year's performance, or on a desired growth over last year's performance. This sets the stage for Planning Week, which is held annually in 73 regional centres across Canada during the first week of December. The purpose of Planning Week is to give salespeople a chance to (1) review their personal, career, and financial accomplishments, (2) relate their individual results to the goals of the whole company, and (3) think through personal, career, and financial goals for the coming year.

During Planning Week, sales reps meet with their division managers and set specific sales objectives for the next year. This process involves 5 steps:

1. *Determine franchise operating costs.* Since each sales rep in essence owns a franchise, the first step is to calculate what it will cost to operate the franchise during the upcoming year.

2. *Determine personal requirements.* Each salesperson decides how much money he or she needs to meet living expenses in the upcoming year.

3. *Determine total financial requirements.* The costs from steps 1 and 2, plus a profit requirement, determine the sales rep's total financial requirements for the year.

4. *Develop an activity plan.* The sales rep prepares a plan of action to reach the goals set in steps 1–3. This involves setting goals for the number of contacts and presentations the sales rep will have to make in order to reach the dollar sales goal.

5. *Measure productivity.* This involves completion of a detailed MBO summary sheet showing the sales rep's monthly production in the year just ended, as well as goals for each month's production in the upcoming year.

Once these 5 steps are completed, division managers meet with salespeople and come to a consensus about what the sales rep's goals will be. Each division manager then forwards the proposed objectives for his or her division to the appropriate regional manager. This process continues all the way up to the vice-president of sales, who gives final approval to the overall sales objectives of the company for the upcoming year.

On occasion, a salesperson will set a goal that a manager considers either too low or too high. When this happens, negotiation between the salesperson and the manager takes place to find a goal that is satisfactory to both. The company has found that resolving problems through negotiation early in the process helps to prevent serious disagreements later on.

Recognition and rewards are an important part of the MBO process. For example, sales production of $2 million per year qualifies the salesperson for the Millionaire plaque; sales of $8 million qualifies the person for a diamond ring. Most salespeople earn an award of some type, and they are publicly recognized for their achievement. Each salesperson feels that he or she is making a positive contribution to the company.

About 75 percent of Investors' salespeople conscientiously fill out the MBO forms, and it has made a noticeable difference in their sales performance. A few salespeople, however, view MBO as a game of paper shuffling, and for them, it is probably not very helpful. In such cases, managers try to "sell" MBO to their staff, rather than trying to force it on them.

Investors has found that MBO is well suited to its sales function. The goals of salespeople can be stated in quantitative terms, and the sales reps can easily tell whether they have reached their goals. The company has also found that salespeople often set much more challenging goals for themselves than they would have in the absence of MBO. All of this impacts favorably on the bottom line—Investors profitability continued uninterrupted right through the recession of 1991–1993.

At some point, however, this thinking must be converted into action. It is here that many managers encounter problems because implementing plans involves introducing change. And introducing any change, including new plans, is likely to meet with resistance from employees. Managers must address this opposition before the plans begin taking effect if they are to be successful in carrying out the planning function.

Managers usually work together to set goals and determine corporate strategy. These activities take a great deal of time but are critical to the success of any organization.

Evaluate Planning Effectiveness

A plan is effective if it helps an organization reach its objectives. Consider the issue of corporate policies. Suppose a firm has a policy that purchasing agents may not accept gifts from suppliers if those gifts unduly influence their purchasing behavior. Such a policy is effective if it motivates purchasing agents to buy supplies that are best for the company. The plan is ineffective if it causes purchasing agents to spend time trying to figure out how to get around the policy. Gauging the effectiveness of plans can be frustrating, especially if plans deal with the entire firm or have a long-term impact. It is easy to judge a plan intended to make the company the industry leader in sales, but it is much harder to measure the effectiveness of a plan to develop the most creative work force in the industry.

Managers need to recognize that plans may not be achieved as expected and that they may need to be altered. **Contingency planning** attempts to identify in advance important aspects of the business or its market that might change. It also defines how the company will respond to those changes.

Suppose, for example, that a company develops a plan to create a new business. It expects sales to increase at an annual rate of 10 percent for the next five years and develops a marketing strategy for achieving that level. But suppose that sales have increased by only 5 percent by the end of the first year. Does the company abandon the business, invest more in advertising, or wait to see what happens in the second year? Any of these alternatives is possible, however, things will go more smoothly if managers have decided in advance what to do in the event of lower-than-expected sales. Contingency planning helps managers do exactly that.

contingency planning
A plan that attempts to identify in advance important aspects of a business or its market that might change and to define how the firm will respond in the event of those changes.

crisis management

Managing an unexpected emergency by making an immediate response to it.

Managing an unexpected emergency requiring an *immediate* organizational response is also part of planning. A highly publicized case of effective **crisis management** involved the pain reliever Tylenol. The makers of Tylenol, Johnson & Johnson, have been praised for their response to two incidents where Tylenol was found to contain cyanide. As soon as J&J learned of this, it removed all Tylenol from retail stores. Managers made themselves available to the media and embarked on an education program to inform the public of the steps the company was taking to ensure consumer safety.

Formulating Strategic Plans

corporate strategy

A plan stating what businesses a corporation does and does not wish to enter.

A **corporate strategy** is a plan decided by a firm's top management that outlines which businesses a firm will become involved with and which ones it will avoid. While planning is more concerned with the "nuts and bolts" of setting goals, choosing tactics, and establishing schedules, strategy is much broader in scope. It describes what the organization as a whole intends to do, and how it intends to respond to new challenges and opportunities.

MacMillan-Bloedel, for example, has made the strategic decision to get out of making and selling pulp, and will focus only on those businesses where it is already a major player. The backbone of the company in the future will be building materials.[5]

strategy formulation

The developing of a long-range plan for meeting goals.

Managers devote a great deal of hard work, attention, and creativity to formulating different strategies—ways to meet their companies' goals at all levels. **Strategy formulation** is a special kind of planning which focuses on the overall organization. It involves three basic steps: (1) setting strategic goals, (2) analyzing the company and its environment, and (3) matching the two.[6] As the box "Planning for Success" notes, this kind of assessment is central to any sound business plan.

Setting Strategic Goals

strategic goals

Long-term goals derived directly from the firm's mission.

Strategic goals are long-term goals derived directly from the firm's mission statement. For example, one of the first things new CEO George Fisher did at Kodak was to set several strategic goals. One strategic goal called for renewed emphasis on film marketing and processing, one called for eliminating several peripheral businesses, and still another stressed the need to speed up the introduction of new technology. Kodak also plans to sell more film overseas: After all, Fisher reasons, about half the people in the world have yet to experience the pleasure of taking their own pictures.[7]

Analyzing the Organization and Its Environment

environmental analysis

Scanning the environment for threats and opportunities.

Environmental analysis involves scanning the environment for threats and opportunities. New products and new competitors, for example, are both *threats*. So are new government regulations, imports, changing consumer tastes, and hostile takeovers. In formulating its new strategy, for instance, Kodak saw opportunities for growth in the film market and recognized that technology was changing so fast that it had to get that technology to market much faster than planned. It also saw increased competition from its biggest rival, the Japanese firm Fuji.

organizational analysis

Analyzing the firm's strengths and weaknesses.

Meanwhile, managers also must undertake an **organizational analysis** to understand a company's strengths and weaknesses better. *Strengths* might include surplus cash, a dedicated workforce, an ample supply of managerial talent, technical expertise, or little competition. The absence of any of these strengths could represent an important *weakness*. Kodak, for example, saw that although it was doing fine in research and development, translating breakthroughs into new products was taking a long time.

Matching the Organization and Its Environment

The final step in strategy formulation is matching environmental threats and opportunities against corporate strengths and weaknesses. The matching process is the heart of strategy formulation: More than any other facet of strategy, matching companies with their environments lays the foundation for successfully planning and conducting business.[8] Kodak managers, for example, decided that the firm needed to concentrate on its core business, photographic equipment and supplies. Thus it began selling its other businesses, such as a software manufacturer and a consumer-credit division.

The Canadian Business Scene

PLANNING FOR SUCCESS

Have you ever thought of starting your own small business? Many Canadians have taken the plunge successfully. But many more have failed. What separates the winners from the losers? Often it's a matter of planning. And sound small business planning begins with a formal plan that answers key questions.

What kind of business will this be and where will it be located? Be specific. Don't just say you're going to go into the clothing business. If you plan to open a shop selling designer bridal gowns in the newly chic downtown area, say so.

What is the market like and how will you fit in? Research into the industry, local conditions, and competitors for your proposed business is a must.

What special skills or experience do you and your partners bring to the business? Most small business people choose something they have long been interested in. Note your business degree, your partner's apprenticeship with a clothing designer, and your work as buyer for a local department store.

How do you plan to market your company? Too often, small business people fail to develop detailed, concrete marketing plans. This is the place to describe your store layout and explain why it will help your business succeed. You also need to plot your advertising and promotion, including costs.

What special problems will you face? Assessing potential difficulties now lets you work out solutions in advance. For example, knowing that June, August, and December are the big months for weddings will enable you to plan for extra sales help in busy months and for special sales promotions in slow months.

How do you plan to finance the business? To start a new business, you need—at a minimum—enough to cover all your costs (including your living expenses) for six months. Since it can take two to three years to break even, aim for three times that amount.

What do you expect your revenues and costs to be? Again, be specific. Estimate as accurately as possible total sales and costs for the first year and the first five years of the business. In addition, calculate what you will have to pay out each month and what receipts you can expect in that same month. Finally, note exactly when you expect to break even.

What are your long-term plans? Do you plan to open branches? Move to a larger store? Expand your operation to include other products? How will you achieve these goals?

Answering questions such as these and drawing up a formal business plan offer many benefits. First, doing so forces you to really think through your proposed business. Second, it provides objectives against which to check your progress. Third, it gives prospective investors (such as banks) concrete information on which to base decisions and thus affects your potential financing. And finally, it can serve as a sales tool in some industries. For example, if you are opening your own advertising agency, your plan can tell potential clients about your background and philosophy.

If all this sounds like a lot of work, you're right. But remember, it's only the start!

Levels of Strategic Plans

As Figure 6.3 illustrates, firms typically have three strategy levels: corporate, business, and functional.

Corporate Level Strategy

The strategic management process at the corporate level establishes the strategy for the whole organization. In a small organization, the corporate strategy may be the only one, but in larger organizations it serves as the umbrella or comprehensive strategy for the whole organization. The board of directors and top managers usually establish the corporate strategy, and set objectives for and approve strategic decisions made at lower levels. Strategic decisions at this level are usually long-term, affect the overall direction of the organization, and involve large commitments of resources, especially financial resources.

Business Unit Level Strategy

strategic business unit (SBU)

The smallest operating division with authority to make its own strategic decisions.

A **strategic business unit (SBU)** is the smallest operating division of an enterprise that is given authority to make its own strategic decisions within corporate guidelines. An example of an SBU at C-I-L Inc. is the operation for lawn fertilizer bagged for the home market. Large chemical companies such as C-I-L Inc. produce several chemical products. One division produces fertilizer and within this division the producers of bagged lawn fertilizer would be an SBU.

Functional Level Strategy

A functional level strategy refers to the strategic management process within departments such as marketing, production, finance, research and development, and human resources. This level focuses on the efficiency and effectiveness of operational areas such as purchasing, maintenance, and cost accounting; the

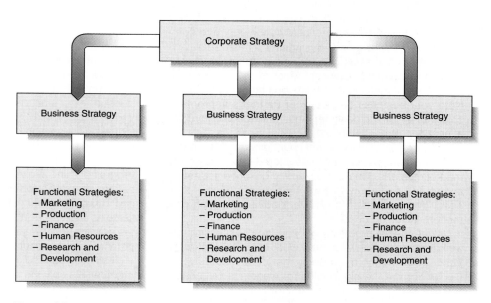

Figure 6.3
Three levels of strategy.

results are usually quantifiable. Objectives and strategies are established for each function; the time allowed for implementing the strategies and fulfilling the objectives is the shortest of any level.

Strategic Options

There are many strategic options a firm might choose. Several of the most well-known are described briefly below.

Generic Options

Generic strategies fall into one of three broad categories: cost leadership, differentiation, and focus.[9] **Cost leadership** occurs when an enterprise strives to have the lowest costs in the industry. Most enterprises in the resource industries base their strategies on cost leadership since the prices of the products are often established in markets over which they have no control. Canadian newsprint producers, for example, must control costs and find supplies of raw materials that will enable them to be cost leaders.

When pursuing a strategy of **differentiation**, an organization tries to provide goods or services that are distinctive from those of its competitors. Many consumer products firms try to differentiate, or distinguish, their products from others through distinctive advertising or packaging. Calvin Klein clothing is an example of a differentiated product.

When a **focus**, or niche, strategy is used, the business concentrates on serving a particular market segment, or niche. An enterprise choosing the focus strategy might be able to establish its niche on the basis of either cost leadership or differentiation.

cost leadership
Striving to have the lowest costs in the industry.

differentiation
Striving to provide products that are distinctive from those of competitors.

focus
Concentrating on serving a particular market segment.

Internal Growth Options

Market penetration occurs when an enterprise tries to increase the market share of its existing products or services in their present markets, usually through greater marketing efforts. By contrast, **market development** means introducing existing products into new geographic areas. Kodak has increased sales in foreign markets, including Japan, in an effort to develop new markets. **Product development** takes place when enterprises attempt to increase sales by improving or modifying their existing products or services for either existing or new customers.

market penetration
Seeking to increase market share in the firm's present market.

market development
Introducing existing products into new geographic areas.

product development
Improving existing products for current or new customers.

Integration Options

There are two basic integration options: vertical or horizontal. With **vertical integration** the corporation can seek ownership or control of a supplier, or it can seek ownership or control over a firm's distribution or retailers. **Horizontal integration** occurs when a company purchases or increases control over another enterprise in the same business (i.e., a competitor).

vertical integration
When a firm seeks ownership or control of its supplier or retailers.

horizontal integration
When a company buys or increases control of a competitor.

Diversification Options

Concentric diversification involves adding new but related products or services to an existing business. Both CP Rail and Canadian National diversified into trucking, an activity clearly related to railway operations.

concentric diversification
Adding new but related products or services to an existing business.

conglomerate diversification
Adding unrelated products or services.

Adding unrelated products or services is called **conglomerate diversification**, or conglomerate merger. Bell Canada decided to diversify by forming BCE Inc., which acquired interests in such unrelated businesses as trust companies, pipelines, and real estate.

cooperative strategies
Joint ventures, alliances, networks, strategic partnering, and strategic networks.

Cooperative Options

Cooperative strategies, which may take the form of joint ventures, alliances, networks, strategic partnering, and strategic networks, have become more popular in the past decade. In each case, enterprises establish a collaborative arrangement for sharing or splitting managerial control in a particular undertaking.

stabilization
Maintaining revenues and profits.

retrenchment
Increasing efficiency through asset reduction or cost cutting.

liquidation
Selling the enterprise's assets and ceasing to exist.

Stabilization and Retrenchment Options

Strategic options do not always entail growth. The **stabilization** option is designed to maintain revenues and profits. Growth may occur but strategic decisions are only made gradually. In **retrenchment**, efforts are made to increase efficiency through asset reduction or cost cutting. **Liquidation** involves selling the enterprise's assets and ceasing to do business.

Implementing Strategic Plans

Once a firm has formulated its strategic plans, it must implement them. Implementation usually requires a series of tactical and operational plans.

Tactical Plans

tactical plans
Specific short-run action plans to intermediate action plans for achieving strategic goals.

Short-run to intermediate plans that parallel strategic goals, but on a narrower scale, are called **tactical plans**. Figure 6.4 depicts the general relationship between strategy and tactics. Note that strategic goals relate to higher levels of management and have long time frames. Tactical plans are more narrowly focused at the middle levels of management and have shorter time frames.

For example, McDonald's is currently undergoing a dramatic expansion in Europe. The decision and general planning that set this course was a strategic goal. However, because each foreign market is different, McDonald's developed a tactical plan for each one. The tactical plans address local market conditions, government regulations, local competition, and so forth. As a result, McDonald's restaurants in Switzerland sell beer. In France, they also sell wine. In West Germany, pork sandwiches are very popular.

Operational Plans

operational plans
Highly detailed short-run plans for performing specific tasks necessary to the achievement of strategic goals.

Even more specific and focused than tactical plans are a company's **operational plans**. Operational plans relate to specific activities that need to be performed in a fashion consistent with other plans. Single-use plans and standing plans are the two main types of operational plans.

single-use plans
Operational plans for carrying out activities not likely to be repeated in the future, such as a program or a project.

Single-Use Plans. Activities not likely to be repeated in the future need **single-use plans**. When Black & Decker bought General Electric's small-appliance business for $300 million, it acquired 150 products. Black & Decker had only three years to convert all the products to its own name and design—the biggest brand-name switch in history. To carry out the changeover Black & Decker developed a comprehensive single-use plan.

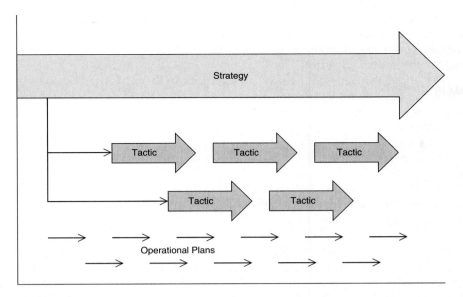

Figure 6.4
Operational plans are derived from tactical plans, which follow from strategies.

Standing Plans. In contrast to single-use plans, **standing plans** relate to activities that are carried out regularly. Policies, standard operating procedures, and rules and regulations are all standing plans.

General guides for action are called *policies*. For example, a department store might issue credit cards only to people with stable employment, a local address, a good credit rating, and a set minimum income. This profile represents the store's policy. People who fail to meet one or more of the criteria will routinely be denied credit, while those who meet all the minimums will be approved.

Slightly more narrow in scope, *standard operating procedures (SOPs)* outline general steps to be followed in carrying out a policy. In the example of the credit card, an SOP might dictate that when a credit application is received at the department store, a credit analyst must check to see that it meets each of the criteria. If it does, the SOP might require credit personnel to create a file for the applicant, place the application and credit history inside it, and then mail a credit card to the individual.

Finally, the narrowest of all plans, *rules* and *regulations*, govern specific questions, issues, and circumstances. The department store might have a rule that the maximum credit limit for a new cardholder is $750 and that this limit cannot be raised for at least six months.

standing plans
Operational plans for carrying out activities that are a regular part of a business's operations.

The Structure of Business Organizations

Exactly what do we mean by the term organizational structure? In many ways, a business is like an automobile. All automobiles have an engine, four wheels, fenders and other structural components, an interior compartment for passengers, and various operating systems including those for fuel, braking, and climate control. Each component has a distinct purpose but must also work in harmony with the others. Automobiles made by competing firms all have the same basic components, although the way they look and fit together may vary.

Similarly, all businesses have common structural and operating components, each of which has a specific purpose. Each component must fulfill its own purpose while simultaneously fitting in with the others. And, just

organizational structure

The specification of the jobs to be done within a business and how those jobs relate to one another.

organization chart

A physical depiction of the company's structure showing employee titles and their relationship to one another.

chain of command

Reporting relationships within a business; the flow of decision-making power in a firm.

like automobiles made by different companies, how these components look and fit together varies from company to company. Thus, **organizational structure** is the specification of the jobs to be done within a business and how those jobs relate to one another.

Every institution—be it a for-profit company, a not-for-profit organization, or a government agency—must develop the most appropriate structure for its own unique situation. What works for Air Canada will not work for Revenue Canada. Likewise, the structure of the Red Cross will not work for the University of Toronto.

What accounts for the differences? An institution's purpose, mission, and strategy affect its structure. So do size, technology, and changes in environmental circumstances. A large manufacturing organization operating in a dynamic environment requires a different structure than a small service firm, such as a video rental store or barber shop.

Most businesses prepare **organization charts** that illustrate the company's structure and show employees where they fit into the firm's operations. Figure 6.5 shows the organization chart for a hypothetical company. Each box represents a job within the company. The solid lines that connect the boxes define the **chain of command**, or the reporting relationships within the company. Thus, each plant manager reports directly to the vice president for production who, in turn, reports to the president. When the chain of command is not clear, many different kinds of problems can result.

An actual organization chart would, of course, be far more complex and include individuals at many more levels. Indeed, because of their size, larger firms cannot easily draw a diagram with everyone on it.

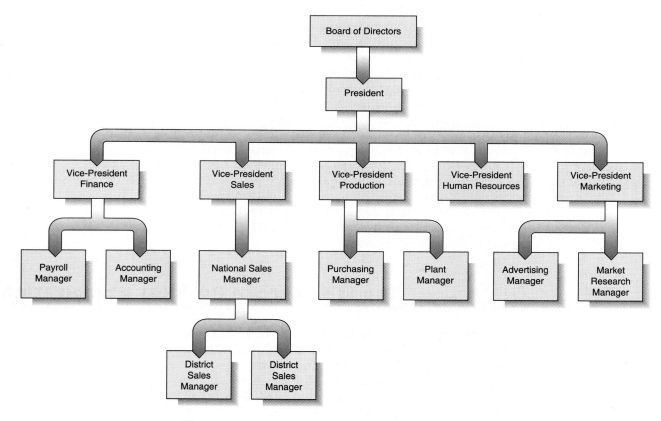

Figure 6.5
An organization chart shows key positions in the organization and interrelationships among them.

Basic Organizational Structures

A glance at the organization charts of many organizations reveals what appears to be an infinite variety of structures. However, closer examination shows that most of them fit into one of two basic categories: functional or divisional. As business has become more globalized, more and more firms are adopting an international organizational structure. These three structures are described below.

The Functional Structure

The functional structure is the oldest and most commonly used. In the **functional structure**, the various units in the organization are formed based on the functions that must be carried out to reach organizational goals. The functional structure makes use of departmentation by function. An example of a functional structure is shown in Figure 6.5. The advantages and disadvantages of the functional structure are summarized in Table 6.1.

functional structure

Various units are included in a group based on functions that need to be performed for the organization to reach its goals.

TABLE 6.1   Advantages and Disadvantages of a Functional Structure

Advantages	Disadvantages
1. Focuses attention on the key activities that must be performed.	1. Conflicts may arise among the functional areas.
2. Expertise develops within each function.	2. No single function is responsible for overall organizational performance.
3. Employees have clearly defined career paths.	3. Employees in each functional area have a narrow view of the organization.
4. The structure is simple and easy to understand.	4. Decision making is slowed because functional areas must get approval from top management for a variety of decisions.
5. Eliminates duplication of activities.	5. Coordinating highly specialized functions may be difficult.

The Divisional Structure

The functional structure's disadvantages can make it inappropriate for some companies. Many companies have found that the divisional structure is more suited to their needs. The **divisional structure** divides the organization into several divisions, each of which operates as a semi-autonomous unit and profit center. In 1990, Alberta's Conservative government unveiled a new divisional structure and a new name for Alberta Government Telephones (AGT). The new organization is called Telus Corporation and is patterned after Montreal-based BCE. It oversees the telecommunications activity of seven operating companies, including AGT.

divisional structure

Divides the organization into divisions, each of which operates as a semi-autonomous unit.

As we shall see later in this chapter, divisions in organizations can be based on products, customers, or geography. Whatever basis is used, divisional performance can be easily assessed each year because the division operates as a separate company. Firms with this structure are often called *conglomerates*.

The advantages and disadvantages of the divisional structure are summarized in Table 6.2.

TABLE 6.2   Advantages and Disadvantages of a Divisional Structure

Advantages	Disadvantages
1. Accommodates change and expansion.	1. Activities may be duplicated across divisions.
2. Increases accountability.	2. A lack of communication among divisions may occur.
3. Develops expertise in the various divisions.	3. Adding diverse divisions may blur the focus of the organization.
4. Encourages training for top management.	4. Company politics may affect the allocation of resources.

International Organization

Many businesses today manufacture, purchase, and sell in the world market. Thus a number of variations on basic organizational structure have emerged. Moreover, as competition on a global scale becomes more complex, companies often find that they must experiment with the ways in which they respond.

For example, at Club Méditerranée, an international French-based firm that provides vacation sites (called "villages") around the world, each village manager used to report both to a country manager and to a number of different directors. Directors worked out of company headquarters, and each director had primary responsibility for some facet of Club Med operations and marketing. This structure, however, proved less than satisfactory. Club Med prides itself on providing village arrangements that reflect various *local* atmospheres—a difficult feat for directors to achieve from remote locations. To solve this problem, the company adopted a different form of organization. A major component of the new structure involved sending operations and marketing staff to specific geographic regions.

For similar reasons, other firms have developed a wide range of approaches to international organizational structure. Whirlpool, for example, purchased the appliance division of the Dutch electronics giant N.V. Philips and as part of its international organization structure now makes the cooling coils for its refrigerators at its new plant in Trento, Italy.[10] Other companies, such as Levi Strauss, handle all international operations through separate international divisions. Still others concentrate production in low-cost areas and then distribute and market globally. Some firms, such as Britain's Pearson PLC (which runs such diverse businesses as publishing, investment banking, and Madame Tussaud's Wax Museum), allow each of their businesses to function autonomously within local markets. Finally, some companies adopt a truly global structure in which they acquire resources (including capital), produce goods and services, engage in research and development, and sell products in whatever local market is appropriate, without any consideration of national boundaries.

The Building Blocks of Organizational Structure

Whether a business is large or small, the starting point in developing its organizational structure is determining who will do what and how people performing certain tasks can most appropriately be grouped together. Job specialization and departmentalization represent the basic building blocks of all businesses.

Specialization

The process of identifying the specific jobs that need to be done and designating the people who will perform them leads to **job specialization**. In a sense, all organizations have only one major "job"—say, making a profit by manufacturing and selling men's and boys' shirts. But this job, of course, is broken into smaller components. In turn, each component is assigned to an individual. Consider the manufacture of men's shirts. Because several steps are required to produce a shirt, each job is broken down into its component parts—that is, into a set of tasks to be completed by a series of individuals or machines. One person, for example, cuts material for the shirt body, another cuts material for the sleeves, and a third cuts material for the collar. Components are then shipped to a sewing room, where a fourth person assembles the shirt. In the final stage, a fifth person sews on the buttons.[11]

job specialization
The use of individuals with specialized skills to perform specialized tasks within a business.

Specialization and Growth. In a very small organization, the owner may perform every job. As the firm grows, however, so does the need to specialize jobs so that others can perform them. To see how specialization can evolve in an organization, consider the case of Mrs. Fields Cookies. When Debbi Fields opened her first store, she did everything herself: bought the equipment, negotiated the lease, baked the cookies, operated the store, and kept the records. As the business grew, however, Fields found that her job was becoming too much for one person. She first hired a bookkeeper to handle her financial records. She then hired an in-store manager and a cookie baker. She herself concentrated on advertising and promotions. Her second store required another set of employees—another manager, another baker, and some salespeople. While Fields focused her attention on other expansion opportunities, she turned promotions over to a professional advertising director. Thus the job that she once did all by herself was increasingly broken down into components and assigned to different individuals.

Job specialization is a natural part of organizational growth. As the box "Di-Vine Madness" points out, it is neither a new idea nor limited to factory work. It carries with it certain advantages—individual jobs can be performed more efficiently, the jobs are easier to learn, and it is easier to replace people who leave the organization. On the other hand, if job specialization is carried too far and jobs become too narrowly defined, people get bored, derive less satisfaction from their jobs, and often lose sight of how their contributions fit into the overall organization.

Departmentalization

Jobs must first be appropriately specialized. Then they must be grouped into logical units, a process called **departmentalization**. Departmentalization may occur along customer, product, process, geographic, or functional lines, or a combination of these.

departmentalization
The grouping of jobs into logical units.

Customer Departmentalization. Most general department stores such as Eaton's and the Bay are divided into a men's department, a women's department, a hardware department, and a number of other departments, each targeted to a specific category of customer. **Customer departmentalization** makes shopping easier by providing identifiable store segments. A customer shopping for a baby's playpen can head straight for the Children's Furniture Department. Customer departmentalization also allows the store to group products when arranging for purchases, deliveries, and sales. The business benefits from the efficiencies this kind of organization offers, while customers get better service.

customer departmentalization
Departmentalization according to the type of customer likely to buy a given product.

International Report

DI-VINE MADNESS

Once a year, for three days in November, the Burgundy region of France goes a little mad. These days, known as *Les Trois Glorieuses* (The Three Glorious Ones), are part of a traditional celebration marking the final harvesting of grapes. Over the course of the three days, pickers and chateau owners alike will make merry, eating wonderful food and, of course, drinking glass after glass of Burgundy wine.

Les Trois Glorieuses are just a taste of the full-bodied traditions surrounding French winemaking. Laws dating to the Napoleonic Era and a built-in aversion to change have left many aspects of the French wine industry virtually unaltered since Roman Catholic monks brewed the first modern wines centuries ago.

At the bottom of the social barrel are the *vendangeurs*—the pickers. In some areas of France, machines now pick the grapes. But in areas like Burgundy and Champagne, where plots are small and vines grow in close-set rows, handpicking is still necessary. Supervising the vendangeurs is the *vignon*. Typically a man with years of experience, the vignon also oversees all planting, weeding, and pruning of the vines throughout the year.

Unlike in Spain and Portugal, where workers still crush the grapes by stomping on them, French vineyards use machines to crush the grapes. Then, under the watchful eye of the *cellarer,* the juice (and skins in the case of red wines) is transferred into fermenting vats.

Left to its own devices, grape juice begins to ferment almost at once. Winemakers keep fermentation from changing the juice to vinegar by adjusting the oxygen supply and the temperature of the juice. At this point the *chef de cave* enters the picture in person. Traditionally, a chef de cave is a combination technical expert and chief operating officer. In addition to overall responsibility for the winery's operation, this is the person whose highly skilled palate dictates the ultimate taste of the wine.

Over the course of months, the chef de cave will taste the fermenting juice and test it for remaining sugar. At last the moment comes—it is time to end the fermentation.

The juice is drawn off, leaving behind a fair amount of residue. But the wine is still clouded with sediment. To remove these "lees," vintners draw the wine through pipes to other casks in a process called "racking" that may be repeated several times. Gelatin, egg white, or a similar substance may be used to settle out remaining sediment, a process called "fining." Only then is the wine bottled.

Sparkling wines like champagne require a few extra steps—and specialists. After an initial fermentation, the unracked, unfined wine is placed in specially reinforced bottles with a small amount of sugar and yeast. The champagne will then lie on its side for months or even years. When the winery is ready to release the champagne for sale, it must clear out any residue. But because it is carbonated and already in bottles, ridding champagne of sediment is more complex than filtering still wines.

The process begins by placing the bottles in special racks. Each day a *remueur* turns each bottle a quarter of the way around and ever so slightly closer to upside down, until the neck is pointing almost straight down and the sediment has collected there. The neck of the bottle is then frozen. An expert *disgorgeur* quickly pops out the cork and removes the sediment. The disgorgeur's assistant tops off the bottle with some of the same champagne (and sometimes some sugar) and inserts a fresh cork, all in a matter of seconds.

At last the wine, be it still or sparkling, is ready to go to market. But no self-respecting chateau sells direct to any individual short of the Queen of England. Instead, France's wine houses go through intermediaries known as *courtiers* (wine brokers) and *negotiants* (wine wholesalers). Courtiers travel across the country, tasting and evaluating wines and establishing prices for them. Local negotiants, who ship French wines to the four corners of the globe, can place orders only through the courtiers, who get a 2 percent commission. Critics charge that the system is cumbersome and out-of-date. But one negotiant counters, "For years I've heard that we have an obsolete, dying system. The only problem is, no one has come up with anything better."

---

product departmentalization

Departmentalization according to the specific good produced.

process departmentalization

Departmentalization according to the production process used to make a good.

Product Departmentalization.   Unlike retailers, manufacturers do not usually find customer departmentalization a useful organizational structure. Some opt for **product departmentalization**, dividing the company according to the specific good produced.

Process Departmentalization.   Other manufacturers favor **process departmentalization**, dividing the company according to the production process used. Vlasic, a pickle maker, has separate departments that transform cucumbers into fresh-packed pickles, pickles cured in brine, or relishes.

Geographic Departmentalization.   Some firms may be divided according to the area of the country—or even the world—they serve. This is known as **geographic departmentalization**. Concluding Case 6-2 at the end of the chapter describes a company that is structured along geographic lines.

Functional Departmentalization.   Finally, many service and manufacturing companies develop departments based on a group's functions or activities—**functional departmentalization**. Such firms typically have a production department, a marketing and sales department, a personnel department, and an accounting and finance department. These departments may be further subdivided, as a university's business school may be subdivided into departments of accounting, finance, marketing, and management.

Advantages of Departmentalization.   Assuming that a company is departmentalized logically, the firm benefits from such divisions of its activities. Departmentalization facilitates both control and coordination, and top managers can more easily see how the various parts of the organization are performing.

For example, departmentalization allows the firm to treat each department as a **profit center**, a separate unit responsible for its own costs. By assessing the profits from the sales in a particular area—perhaps men's clothing—Sears can decide whether to expand or curtail its promotion in that area. Similarly, the profitability of Old Dutch potato chips will affect decisions about whether to increase or decrease expenditures on that product. Vlasic may consider automated equipment if the productivity of the relish production line is much lower than that of the fresh-packed line.

geographic departmentalization
Departmentalization according to the area of the country or world supplied.

functional departmentalization
Departmentalization according to a group's functions or activities.

profit center
Treatment of a division of a corporation as if it were a separate company with regard to its individual profitability.

Many department stores are departmentalized by product. Concentrating different products in different areas of the store makes shopping easier for customers.

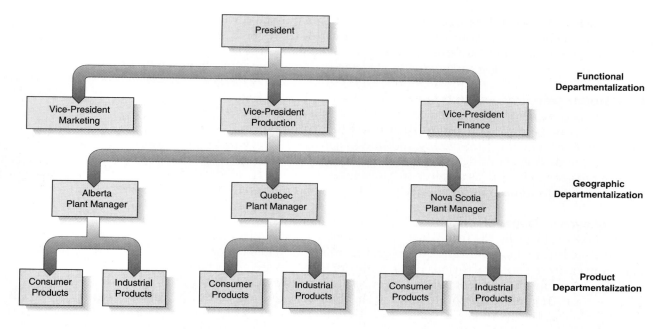

Figure 6.6
Most organizations use multiple bases of departmentalization. This organization, for example, is using functional, geographic, and product departmentalization.

Because different forms of departmentalization offer different advantages, larger companies tend to adopt different types of departmentalization at various levels of the corporation. For example, the company illustrated in Figure 6.6 uses functional departmentalization at the top level. Its production department is divided along geographic lines, while its marketing unit is departmentalized by product group.

Responsibility and Authority

responsibility
A duty to accomplish assigned tasks.

authority
The right to make decisions necessary to accomplish certain tasks.

delegation
The assignment of a task, responsibility, and/or authority by a manager to a subordinate.

accountability
The liability of a subordinate in the event of non-performance of a task.

As you might expect, arguments may develop over who is supposed to do what and who is entitled to do what within a company. In any company with more than one person, the individuals involved must work out an agreement about responsibilities and authority. **Responsibility** is a duty to perform an assigned task. **Authority** is the right to make decisions necessary to complete the task. The buyer for men's clothing is responsible for purchasing the men's wardrobe that will be sold in the upcoming season and has the authority to make those purchases.

Delegation and Accountability

Unless all those involved in a company are equal partners, issues regarding delegation and accountability must also be addressed. **Delegation** begins when a manager assigns a task to a subordinate. The subordinate then has the responsibility to accomplish that task and is **accountable** for its completion. If the subordinate does not perform the assigned task properly and promptly, the manager may demand a good reason why or may penalize the subordinate.

Subordinates sometimes cannot complete a task because their managers have not also delegated the necessary authority. Such employees face a dilemma: they cannot do what the boss demands, but that boss will probably still hold them accountable. Successful managers surround themselves with a team of strong subordinates and then delegate sufficient authority to those subordinates to get the job done. There are four things to keep in mind when delegating:

- decide on the nature of the work to be done
- match the job with the skills of subordinates
- make sure the person chosen understands the objectives he or she is supposed to achieve
- make sure subordinates have the time and training necessary to do the task.

Centralization and Decentralization.   In every organization, management must decide how to distribute authority throughout the hierarchy. **Centralization** occurs when top management retains the right to make most decisions that need to be made. In a highly centralized organization, the CEO makes most of the decisions, and subordinates simply carry them out. For example, Cedric Ritchie, the CEO of the Bank of Nova Scotia, knew all the details of the bank's operations and made many decisions that CEOs of other banks delegated to subordinates.[12]

centralization
Occurs when top managers retain most decision making rights for themselves.

Decentralization occurs when top managers delegate the right to make decisions to the middle and lower levels of the management hierarchy. At General Electric's Bromont, Quebec, plant, for example, every effort has been made to get employees involved in a wide range of decision making.[13] Traditional jobs like supervisor and foreman do not exist at the plant, and all hiring is done by committees made up of workers. Some workers spend only 65 percent of their time on production work; the other 35 percent is spent on training, planning, and in meetings. At Hymac Ltée., a Laval, Quebec, producer of pulp processing machinery, managers encourage employees to meet with customers to determine how Hymac can serve them more effectively.[14]

decentralization
Occurs when lower-and middle-level managers are allowed to make significant decisions.

Span of Control.   The distribution of authority in an organization also affects how many people work for any individual manager. The number of people managed by one supervisor is called the **span of control**. Employees' abilities and the supervisor's managerial skills help determine whether the span of control is wide or narrow. So do the similarity and simplicity of tasks performed under the manager's supervision and the extent to which they are interrelated. For example, by eliminating two layers of management, the president of the Franklin Mint recently increased his own span of control from 6 to 12.

span of control
The number of people managed by one manager.

When several employees perform either the same simple task or a group of interrelated tasks, a wide span of control is possible and often desirable. For instance, because all the jobs are routine, one supervisor may well control a whole assembly line. Moreover, each task depends on another: If one station stops, everyone stops. Having one supervisor ensures that all stations receive equal attention and function equally well. In contrast, when jobs are not routine, or when they are prone to change, a narrow span of control is preferable.

Not surprisingly, decentralized companies use wide spans of control and require few layers of management. The result is often called a *flat organizational structure*. On the other hand, centralized authority means that a firm relies on narrow spans of control, multiple layers of management, and a *tall organizational structure*.

Line and Staff Authority

staff experts
Employees with technical training in areas like accounting or law.

line managers
Managers in the regular chain of command.

line organization
All positions are line positions.

Staff experts are people who have specialized training in technical areas like law, market research, industrial safety, and accounting. Staff experts are not in the chain of command and generally have no authority. Instead, they give advice to line managers based on their technical knowledge. **Line managers** are in the regular chain of command of the organization. They receive advice from staff experts and have the authority to decide whether they will implement the advice.

In a **line organization**, all the positions are line positions. There is a direct line of authority from the top of the firm to the bottom. Each level in the organization is subordinate to the one above it, and there are no advisory specialists. Each department is involved in activities geared toward the primary goal of the firm. In a manufacturing firm, for example, production, marketing, and finance are the primary functions (look back to Figure 6.6).

In the line organization, authority and responsibility are clear, and each subordinate has only one boss. The line structure works well as long as an organization is small. But as a firm grows, functional managers acquire more subordinates. These subordinates may be doing diverse tasks, and managers may find it difficult both to keep up with the latest technical developments in all these areas and to perform their day-to-day administrative duties. When the firm reaches this point, it may have no alternative but to move to a line-staff structure.

line-staff organization
One which has both line managers and staff experts.

A **line-staff organization** has both line managers and staff experts. The line-staff structure recognizes that certain functions in an organization (the line functions) are directly related to the organization's reason for existence, while other functions (staff functions) support the line functions. In the Canadian Forces, for example, the line officers are those who actually engage in battle. Staff officers perform functions such as military intelligence that support the activities of the line officers. At Iron Ore of Canada, the line managers oversee the extraction and marketing of iron ore. Staff managers like safety officers support the line managers by making sure that the mines are safe so that production operations can be carried out.

Staff members, therefore, aid line departments in making decisions but do not have the authority to make final decisions. Suppose, for example, that the Fabrication Department at Clark Equipment has an employee with a drinking problem. The manager of the department could consult a human-resources staff expert for advice on handling the situation. The staff expert might suggest that the worker stay on the job but enter a counseling program. But if the line manager decides that the job is too dangerous to be handled by a person whose judgment is often impaired by alcohol, that decision will prevail.

The distinction between line and staff is clear if we keep in mind the goals of the particular organization. At Aluminum Company of Canada, personnel is a staff function because it supports the primary functions of producing and marketing aluminum. However, at an employment agency like Office Overload, personnel is a line function because the primary goals of the firm are hiring and providing personnel. The legal staff at Canadian National Railways is a staff function, but at a law firm like Shewchuk & Associates, the legal staff is a line function.

committee and team authority
Authority granted to committees or work teams that play central roles in the firm's operations.

Committee and Team Authority

Recently, more and more organizations have started to use **committee and team authority**—authority granted to committees or work teams that play central roles in the daily conduct of the firm's operations. A committee, for example, may consist of top managers from several major areas. If the work of the committee is especially important, and if the committee will be working for an extended time, the organization may even grant it special authority as a decision-making body that goes beyond the individual authority possessed by each of its members.

At the operating level, many firms today are also using *work teams*—groups of operating employees empowered to plan and organize their own work and to perform that work with a minimum of supervision. As with permanent committees, the organization will usually find it beneficial to grant special authority to work teams so that they may function more effectively.

Project Organization: Another Variation on Authority.   A typical line or line-staff organization is characterized by unchanging vertical authority relationships. It has such a setup because the organization produces a product or service in a repetitive and predictable way. Procter & Gamble, for example, produces millions of tubes of Crest Toothpaste each year using standardized production methods. The company has done this for years and intends to do so indefinitely.

But some organizations find themselves faced with new product opportunities or with projects that have a definite starting and end point. These organizations often use a project structure to deal with the uncertainty encountered in new situations. **Project organization** involves forming a team of specialists from different functional areas of the organization to work on a specific project.[15] A project structure may be temporary or permanent; if it is temporary, the project team disbands once the project is completed and team members return to their regular functional area or are assigned to a new project.

Project organization is used extensively by Canadian firms, for example, in the construction of hydroelectric generating stations like those developed by Hydro-Québec on La Grande River, and by Manitoba Hydro on the Nelson River. Once the generating station is complete, it becomes part of the traditional structure of the utility. Project organization has also proven useful for coordinating the many elements needed to extract oil from the tar sands. Project management is also used in other kinds of tasks, including shipbuilding, construction, military weapons, aerospace, and health care delivery.[16] The box "Project Management at Genstar" describes how this form of organization works, and how authority issues are decided.

Some companies use a **matrix organization**, which is a variation of project structure in which the project manager and the regular line managers share authority. When a project is concluded, the matrix is disbanded. IBM, for example, has a line-staff structure overall, but it used a matrix organization to develop the original PC. The matrix was disbanded when the PC succeeded.

A problem with the matrix structure is that employees have two bosses—their regular line boss *and* the project manager. Employees may therefore receive conflicting orders. These and other problems have caused some firms that used to like the matrix structure to move away from it. For example, Digital Equipment Company's president, Robert Palmer, announced in 1994 that "matrix management at our company is dead."[17]

project organization
An organization that uses teams of specialists to complete specific projects.

matrix organization
A project structure in which the project manager and the regular line managers share authority until the project is concluded.

The Canadian Business Scene

PROJECT MANAGEMENT AT GENSTAR SHIPYARDS LTD.

Genstar Shipyards Ltd. is a Vancouver firm that specializes in the custom building and repair of icebreakers, research vessels, ferries, tugs, and barges. In peak periods, it delivers a new ship every two months. The value of the ships varies from a low of about $2 million for a small tugboat to a high of nearly $60 million for a state-of-the-art icebreaker. Construction periods for ships range from four months to two years.

Project management is really the only structure that makes sense for shipbuilding. Since time is of the essence in every construction contract, and since costs must be closely monitored, a project structure is necessary.

The shipyard has an operations manager who is responsible for the overall shipbuilding activity. Two project managers (PMs) report to the operations manager. Each ship the company builds is treated as a project, and the two PMs are responsible for seeing that projects are finished on schedule, to specification, and within budget. Some projects employ up to 400 people, so the PM's job may have a major administrative component.

The PM is responsible for the development of a master schedule for each vessel's design and construction. He or she identifies personnel and equipment that are necessary to complete the job, and interacts with all departments involved in the project. Once the master schedule has been set, the PM is responsible for seeing that the schedule and the budget are met. After the ship is built and launched, the PM oversees its trial run and delivery to the owner.

The PM has the authority to decide the construction sequence on the project as well as the number of workers that will be assigned to each phase of the project. These decisions are made after consulting the project plans. Workers on the project report to a supervisor. If the PM and the supervisor disagree about who should be assigned to a project, the PM can appeal to the superintendent (the supervisor's boss). The PM usually prevails on staffing issues.

Other areas of potential disagreement also exist. For example, a supervisor might think work on some part of a ship's construction ought to be done in one way, while the PM thinks it should be done in some other way. If the disagreement is a question of sequencing of the work, the PM will usually prevail; if the disagreement is about specific trade practices, the supervisor will generally win out. As another example, a supervisor may try to assign more tradespeople to a project than the PM thinks are necessary. The supervisor may be trying to create a cushion in meeting the construction schedule. In these cases, the PM usually wins out because the total project schedule and budget must be kept in mind, whereas the supervisor may be thinking only of the work that a particular crew is doing.

The PM does not have the authority to hire, lay off, or fire workers; this is the responsibility of the supervisor. The PM works with the supervisor to determine when the work force should be increased or decreased. The PM also has the authority to approve payment to outside sources from which the company has purchased materials.

To be effective, the PM requires interpersonal skills (the ability to instill enthusiasm in workers), administrative skills (the ability to keep the project on schedule and within budget), and technical skills (the ability to communicate with the technically skilled people who are working on the project).

The Informal Organization

formal organization

The specified relationships between individuals, their jobs, and their authority, as shown in the company's organizational chart.

informal organization

A network of personal interactions and relationships among employees unrelated to the firm's formal authority structure.

grapevine

An informal communications network that carries gossip and other information throughout an organization.

So far we have focused on the **formal organization** of businesses—the part that can be seen and drawn in chart form. But organization within any company is not limited to the organization chart and the formal assignment of authority. Frequently, the **informal organization**—the everyday social interactions among employees—alters a company's formal structure.

One of the most powerful informal forces in any firm is the grapevine. The **grapevine** is an informal communications network that carries gossip and other information throughout the organization. As the box "Heard It Through the Grapevine" notes, the grapevine can be a useful source of information—if you take it with a grain of salt.

When its reports are accurate, the grapevine can serve a company by supplying information more rapidly than formal channels can. For example, if employees see an ambulance pull up to the plant, they will use the grapevine to find out if someone has had an accident. Long before the personnel

The grapevine is a powerful informal communication network in most organizations. These workers may be talking about any number of things—an upcoming deadline on an important project, tonight's football game, the stockmarket, rumors about an impending takeover, gossip about forthcoming promotions, or the weather.

The Canadian Business Scene

HEARD IT THROUGH THE GRAPEVINE

Faster than a speeding bullet—that's the office grapevine. But how accurate it is? Should you listen to it, or is it just so much gossip?

Today many experts advise tuning to the grapevine's message. They note that the grapevine is often a corporate early warning system. Ignoring this valuable source of information can leave you the last to know that you're about to get a new boss, or that you have a potentially fatal image problem. Even personal information about co-workers and superiors can be useful in helping you interact positively with these individuals.

Do consider both the source and the message carefully, though. Most office gossip has at least some kernel of truth to it. But as "facts" get passed down from person to person, they can get twisted out of shape. In other cases, those passing on news will deliberately alter it, either to advance their own goals or to submarine someone else's chances. Experts also warn that listening to and passing on information damaging to someone's reputation can backfire, harming your credibility and making you a target for similar gossip.

In general, the more detailed the information, the less likely it is to be true. Likewise, beware the hush-hush "don't quote me on this" rumor. (Cynics claim that the better the news, the less likely it is to be true, too.) But the higher the source, the greater the likelihood that the grapevine has the real story. Don't reject information from "lower" sources, however. Many an executive secretary can provide valuable insights into a corporation's plans.

An interesting phenomenon of office communication occurs when individuals responsible for formal information systems, such as newsletters, press briefings, and memoranda, spread a somewhat different story on the grapevine. Which should you believe? Today it is so common for a corporate executive to publicly deny rumors of layoffs one day and hand out pink slips the next that no one even raises an eyebrow. The grapevine, unconcerned with public image and long-range schemes, cuts to the heart of the matter.

The grapevine is not infallible, however. In addition to miscommunication and attempts by some people to manipulate it for their own ends, it may carry rumors with absolutely no basis in fact. Such rumors are most common when there is a complete lack of information. Apparently, human nature abhors such a vacuum and fills it. Baseless rumors can be very hard to kill, however.

department can issue an announcement, the grapevine can supply the news that a pregnant worker had her baby early. Similarly, advance word of impending changes in the company's operations can help employees adjust mentally—and even physically (by getting a new job elsewhere, for example)—before the actual shift. The informal organization also facilitates networking and **mentoring**, which can enhance the career development of individuals and promote organizational effectiveness.

mentor

A manager who guides the careers of subordinates by offering them advice, providing them with training and expanded responsibility, and otherwise assisting them in gaining promotions.

Some companies encourage the informal exchange of information.[18] For example, 3M sponsors clubs for 12 or more employees to try to enhance communication across departments. Other companies have physically arranged offices and other facilities to be more conducive to informal communications. One bank moved two departments to the same floor in an attempt to encourage intermingling of the employees. These companies believe informal communications can stimulate discussions that solve organizational problems.

On the down side, informal communications can also cause problems. They can play an instrumental role in office politics that put the interests of individuals ahead of those of the firm. Likewise, a great deal of harm can be caused if distorted or inaccurate information flows through the grapevine. For example, if the grapevine is carrying false information about impending layoffs, valuable employees may act quickly (and unnecessarily) to look for employment elsewhere.

Summary of Key Points

The planning process involves setting organizational goals, identifying the gap between actual and desired positions, developing plans to achieve the objectives, implementing the plans, and evaluating planning effectiveness.

Goals provide businesses with direction and guidance, assist in the allocation of resources, help define the corporate culture, and enable managers to assess performance. Long-term, intermediate, and short-term goals refer to plans for various periods of time, from five years or more in the future to less than a year hence. The board of directors sets long-term goals in conjunction with top management. Middle managers work with top managers to set intermediate goals and with first-line managers to set short-term goals.

Management by objectives helps in the planning process by getting subordinates and their supervisors to set clearly defined, agreed-upon goals for the short run that are consistent with the company's broader, long-term goals.

Formulating strategy is a multistep process. First, strategic goals are set. Next, environmental threats and opportunities are assessed along with corporate strengths and weaknesses. Finally, the environment and the company are matched.

Strategic planning is needed on the corporate, business, and functional levels. The corporate level is concerned with the industries in which a firm decides to compete. Overall business-level strategies include strong growth, slow growth, and retrenchment. Functional strategies address the business's marketing, finance, production, human resource, and research and development activities.

Tactical plans specify short- and intermediate-term actions designed to address narrow portions of a strategic plan. Operational plans address specific programs and projects that must be completed to further the firm's tactical and strategic plans.

Every business requires structure to operate. Organizational structure varies according to the mission, strategy, environment, technology, and size of a firm. It can be drawn as an organization chart showing the chain of command and relationships among various positions.

The basic organizational structures are functional and divisional structures and international organizations. In the functional structure, the various departments in the firm are formed based on the key tasks the firm must perform (e.g., in a manufacturing firm, these are marketing, finance, and production). In a divisional structure, the various units are divided into divisions, each of which is a semi-autonomous unit and profit center. International organizational structures have emerged because businesses today manufacture, purchase, and sell in the world market. These structures take many different forms in response to the complexities of global competition.

The building blocks of organizational structures are job specialization and departmentalization. As a firm grows, it usually has a greater need for people to perform specialized tasks. It also has a greater need to group types of work. Common forms of departmentalization include customer, product, process, geographic, and functional. Large businesses usually use more than one form of departmentalization.

Responsibility is a duty to perform a task; authority is the power to make decisions. In a centralized organization, only a few individuals in top management have real decision-making authority. In a decentralized organization, much authority is delegated to lower-level management. In areas in which both line and staff departments are involved, line departments generally have authority to make decisions, while staff departments have a responsibility to serve as advisors.

The informal organization is a system of personal relationships and interactions among employees unrelated to the formal organization shown in a firm's organization chart. The informal organization can have a major effect on a company's operations and must be taken into account by managers. In particular, the grapevine can help a business get information to its employees more quickly, and/or it can be a source of disruption.

Johnson & Johnson—The Decentralized Empire

As CEO of Johnson & Johnson, Ralph Larsen likens his job to that of an orchestra conductor: He supplies inspiration and direction to the individuals whom he leads while allowing them the creative freedom to make beautiful music. At J&J, beautiful music—or, in any case, profit—is now flowing from the offices of the presidents of the 166 separately chartered companies that make up the decentralized corporate empire. These companies include Advanced Care Products, Janssen Pharmaceutical, Johnson & Johnson Consumer Products, McNeil Consumer Products, and Ortho Pharmaceutical. They manufacture such all-time sales superstars as Tylenol, Band-Aid, and Johnson's Baby Powder.

The top managers of all J&J companies are encouraged to act independently—to make financial, marketing, research, and development decisions as if they were accountable to no one but the corporate board of directors. Ultimately, of course, J&J presidents are accountable to Larsen and his team. For all practical purposes, however, they rarely run into their corporate bosses—a situation that suits Larsen fine. He believes that the J&J approach "provides a sense of ownership and responsibility for a business that you simply cannot get any other way."

Decentralization is a longstanding tradition at J&J. It issues from the conviction of Robert Wood Johnson, the son of the company founder, that small, decentralized units were more manageable and could react more quickly to market changes. The experiment began in the 1930s, when the younger Johnson encouraged Ethicon Inc., a sutures maker, and Personal Products Co., a feminine-hygiene products manufacturer, to operate as independent units.

That tradition continues today throughout Johnson & Johnson: Strategy flows upward to corporate headquarters rather than the other way around. Operating under a relatively flat organizational structure, the 166 operating company presidents report directly to 19 company group chairmen. In turn, chairmen report to three sector chairmen representing J&J's pharmaceutical, professional, and consumer divisions. Finally, the three sector chairmen report directly to Larsen.

Although decentralization has long been quite profitable for J&J, the practice has not been without its share of problems. There have, for example, been occasional mistakes—sometimes costly, sometimes embarrassing—that might have been avoided with guidance from corporate headquarters. Decentralization has also created certain overhead problems. For instance, some back-office functions, including computer services, purchasing, accounts payable, and payroll processing, tend to be duplicated across 166 different operations. Not surprisingly, this latter problem has

shown up in J&J's bottom-line costs. For example, at Merck & Co., a drugmaker with a more centralized organizational structure, overhead amounts to 30 percent of sales. Overhead at J&J equals 41 percent of sales.

Seeing the need to trim expenses, Larsen has begun pooling back-office functions. He has also launched other projects to consolidate operations at J&J divisions. In this respect, says Larsen, centralization makes sense: "If customers have questions about a delivery, they don't have to call the baby company, then our consumer-products organization, and so on. They make one phone call to one person who specializes in delivery, and no matter where the problem is, that person takes care of it."

While some observers believe that Larsen's consolidation plans may undermine the very fabric of J&J's decentralized culture, Larsen is convinced that he is merely correcting an imbalance in a decentralized system that has gotten (temporarily) out of hand. For example, he has trimmed the number of companies in J&J's European professional-products division from 28 to 18—a more manageable and ultimately more profitable number.

Despite such moves, however, Larsen is committed to the values that have defined J&J for nearly 60 years, including independence and the freedom to be innovative in research, marketing, and staffing. "We will never give up the principle of decentralization, which is to give our operating executives ownership of a business," said Larsen. "They are ultimately responsible."

CASE QUESTIONS

1. How is decision making at Johnson & Johnson affected by the company's decentralized organization?
2. There is another decentralization problem at J&J: Presidents who make mistakes are quickly swept out of the organization. In your opinion, should these upper-level managers receive more support from corporate headquarters when mistakes are made? Why or why not?
3. The following statement was made by Marvin L. Woodall, president of J&J Interventional Systems Co.: "I'm almost never distracted by Johnson & Johnson management." How do you suppose the CEO of a highly centralized organization would react to such a comment?
4. Why are Larsen's attempts to reduce overhead costs so important to J&J? In your opinion, do his actions undermine the company's tradition of decentralization?
5. Describe the characteristics of a person who would enjoy working for a decentralized company like J&J. What kind of person would prefer working for a company with a more centralized system?

◆

Corporate Structure at Bata Ltd.

Bata Ltd. has its headquarters in Toronto. It has 66 000 employees, 6300 shoe stores, and operates in 68 countries. Bata sells more than 1 million pairs of shoes each day. In an industry that must quickly sense and act upon footwear trends, Bata's enormous size means that it must work hard to be responsive to changes demanded by the market.

The company is departmentalized by territory, with divisions operating in Europe, Africa, the Far East, and South America. Each region is headed by a regional executive. In spite of its international operations, Bata has not been considered a global corporation in the usual sense of the term. It is not a vertically integrated production and marketing company. In fact, the company's products vary from region to region in accordance with the local population's wants and needs. The result is that the company is a "multidomestic" operation, with each subsidiary operating more or less autonomously.

The economics of the footwear industry have changed in recent years, and Bata has been running to keep up with companies such as Reebok International Ltd. and Nike. Reebok and Nike manufacture shoes in low cost areas like Korea, Taiwan, and China and then use a central office to market and distribute them. Bata, by contrast, operates factories around the world, gearing its production to the local population. This arrangement has led to poor integration of its operations.

Recognizing the need to change, the company has embarked on a major streamlining. Even though Bata has been highly decentralized, it still had excess layers of management at head office. The first step in revamping the operation was to flatten the organizational pyramid so that changes in the market could be responded to more quickly. The restructuring has meant great improvements, according to Tom Bata, Jr. He noted that having a series of executives in Toronto resulted in duplication and power struggles. The restructuring means that there is now just one layer of managers between top management and the managers in the various countries where Bata operates.

The shift has meant an increase in power and responsibility for the managers remaining in the hierarchy, and a decrease in the amount of time key figures spend politicking and selling their ideas to the entrenched hierarchy. Now, the four managers who make up the international head office are out of the country 60-70 percent of the time.

The company has evolved into a "horizontal corporation," a term used by Harvard Business School professor Michael Porter to describe corporations that must resolve both global and local interests. The horizontal corporation is based on the premise that the old-style multinational company is too rigid, too hierarchical, and too attuned to the interests of the "home country." Horizontal corporations stress lateral decision making and a common set of shared ideas, not the vertical chain of command.

CASE QUESTIONS
1. On what basis is Bata departmentalized? What are the advantages and disadvantages of this type of departmentalization?
2. Contrast Bata's structure with its competitors' (Nike and Reebok). Why was Bata's structure disadvantageous for it?
3. Speculate on how the "horizontal corporation" idea might work in practice at Bata.

Key Terms

goals	differentiation	organizational structure	authority
purpose	focus	organization chart	delegation
mission	market penetration	chain of command	accountability
long-term goal	market development	functional structure	centralization
intermediate goal	product development	divisional structure	decentralization
short-term goal	vertical integration	job specialization	span of control
goal optimization	horizontal integration	departmentalization	staff experts
management by	concentric	customer	line managers
objectives (MBO)	diversification	departmentalization	line organization
plans	conglomerate	product	line-staff organization
contingency planning	diversification	departmentalization	committee and team
crisis management	cooperative strategies	process	authority
corporate strategy	stabilization	departmentalization	project organization
strategy formulation	retrenchment	geographic	matrix organization
strategic goal	liquidation	departmentalization	formal organization
environmental analysis	tactical plan	functional	informal organization
organizational analysis	operational plan	departmentalization	grapevine
strategic business unit	single-use plans	profit center	mentor
cost leadership	standing plans	responsibility	

Study Questions and Exercises

Review Questions

1. Why is goal setting an important part of business planning? Can organizations function without goals?
2. What are the steps in the basic planning process?
3. What are the three general levels of strategy?
4. What is an organization chart? What purpose does it serve?
5. Why is a company's informal organization important to its operations?

Analysis Questions

6. How can organizations integrate long-term, intermediate and short-term goals?

7. Identify five operational plans at your college or university.
8. Compare and contrast the functional and the divisional approaches to organizational structure.

Application Exercises

9. Interview a manager of a local service business such as a fast-food restaurant. Identify what types of tasks are delegated. Is the appropriate authority also delegated in each case?
10. Select a local organization with which you have some familiarity. Go through the four steps of strategy formulation for that organization.

Building Your Business Skills

Goal
To encourage students to understand the role of the grapevine in business firms, and to learn how to deal with rumors that spread through the grapevine.

Situation
Suppose that as a department manager, you learn that a rumor is spreading through the grapevine that the company is planning to close your facility at the end of the month, thereby laying off dozens of employees. The rumor is not true. You want to stop it but are not sure what to do.

Method
Evaluate the pros and cons of the following strategies for stopping the rumor.

Strategy 1: When you first hear the rumor, issue a formal memo denying everything but giving no additional information.

Strategy 2: As you happen to see them in the office, talk with employees and reassure them that the rumor is false.

Rather than dealing with the rumor in detail, talk about it in general terms.

Strategy 3:
- When you first realize that a rumor is starting, try to track down its sources.
- Evaluate the damage being caused by the rumor.
- Plan a counterattack by gathering all the facts about the rumor and where it has spread.
- Confront the rumor by using concrete evidence to refute it; if necessary, bring in experts to support the refutation; directly state that the rumor is false and that spreading lies is damaging and unfair.

Follow-Up Questions
1. Which type of rumor is more difficult to contain—a rumor contained within an organization or one that has spread to competitors, customers, and other external groups?
2. Why do you think that the informal communication network holds such power in business organizations?

Running the Small Business

LEARNING OBJECTIVES

After studying this chapter, you will be able to

■ Identify the role of small business in the Canadian economy.

■ Define a small business.

■ Describe an entrepreneur and explain why some people start their own businesses.

■ Describe the ways in which someone can become a small business person.

■ List some of the challenges of starting a small business.

■ Relate the functions of management to the operation of a small business.

■ Describe the assistance provided to small business, in particular, the help from government.

CHAPTER OUTLINE

Major sections of this chapter were written by Robert W. Sexty.

OPENING CASE

Passing the Torch

In 1949, Jimmy MacKay started a small dry goods store and butcher shop in Cochrane, Alberta. When the new highway bypassed the main street in the 1950s, he started selling ice cream cones to keep drawing customers to the store. Eventually demand for ice cream became so great that he focused completely on it. As the years passed, his young children began working in the store. The business was run informally, and deals were made on the basis of a handshake.

When Jimmy died in 1983, two of his daughters—Robyn and Rhona—wanted to carry on with the business. They knew how to serve ice cream and balance the cash register, but they knew very little about other important aspects of managing a small business, including managing employees. But they felt passionately about the business, and thought they should try to continue in it. Few people thought they could make a go of it.

Initially, they had serious troubles, particularly in establishing their credibility in the business and in maintaining the high quality of the ice cream. After their ice cream supplier began to cut corners on quality, they replaced their father's verbal agreements with written ones that explicitly stated the level of product quality that suppliers had to provide. The sisters also studied ice cream technology, and travelled as far away as Pennsylvania to talk to other people who were knowledgeable about ice cream.

Over time, Robyn and Rhona developed a good understanding of the ice cream business. They no longer simply sell ice cream cones. They bought the building their father rented, and they renovated it. They expanded into higher-margin products like chocolate and cappuccino. They have also expanded their manufacturing operations by selling to premium ice cream retailers in both Alberta and B.C. Today the business employs three times the number of people it used to, and very few of them

are family members. Employees are now trained in how to stack a cone as well as the intricacies of making ice cream. The employees are able to answer customer inquiries about what makes the ice cream so good.

Over a quarter of a million tourists visit the town of Cochrane every year, and many of these visit MacKay's Cochrane Ice Cream Ltd. The store has become an important part of the local economy because its presence has encouraged others to establish businesses such as restaurants and arts and crafts shops.

The sisters have given serious thought to the future of the business. Since they are financially conservative, do not like debt, and take on only what they can manage themselves, they decided not to open an ice cream store in Calgary. They have decide to pursue controlled growth, rather than risk losing control of their business. So they opened another retail store near their ice cream shop; that store sells chocolates manufactured by a Calgary firm. ◆

Every year, thousands of people like Robyn and Rhona MacKay launch new business ventures. These individuals, called entrepreneurs, are essential to the growth and vitality of the Canadian economic system. Entrepreneurs develop or recognize new products or business opportunities, secure the necessary capital, and organize and operate businesses.

In this chapter we first define the term "small business," describe the role of the entrepreneur, and note the advantages and disadvantages of owning a small business. Alternative approaches to becoming a small business owner (including franchising) are noted, as are the challenges facing entrepreneurs. The chapter concludes with a description of the various sources of assistance that are available to small business owners.

If you are aware of the challenges you will encounter as an entrepreneur, you are more likely to avoid the classic problems small business owners face. It is easy to start a business, but to operate one at a profit over a period of years requires the knowledge and application of the fundamentals of management. This chapter is designed to give you realistic expectations about small business management.

Small Business in Canada

The Canadian media pay considerable attention to the activities of large business enterprises but often neglect the fact that small businesses are thriving and are making a significant contribution to the economic well-being of Canadians. A small business may be a corporation, sole proprietorship, or a partnership. Small businesses include those operated by professionals, such as doctors, lawyers, and accountants, and self-employed owners, such as mechanics, television technicians, and restauranteurs. They are found in virtually every industry and are particularly prominent in the retail trade. In numbers, small business is the dominant type of business in Canada. According to Statistics Canada, small business enterprises account for about 98 percent of the 900 000 enterprises in Canada and for about 19 percent of total business revenue.

History has shown that major innovations are as likely to come from small businesses or individuals as from big businesses. Small firms and individuals invented the personal computer, the stainless-steel razor blade, the transistor radio, the photocopying machine, the jet engine, and the self-developing photograph. They also gave us the helicopter, power steering, automatic transmissions, air conditioning, cellophane, and the 19-cent ballpoint pen.

The degree of small business varies across different industries. As shown in Figure 7.1, small business firms are dominant in the construction and retailing industries, but not so dominant in manufacturing. About 6 out of every 10 Canadians employed in the private sector work in a firm with less than 500 employees.

During the past few years, small businesses have been net creators of jobs, while large firms have been net job destroyers. Companies with fewer than 20 employees added jobs at a 26 percent rate and cut them at an 18 percent rate, for an 8 percent net gain. Companies with more than 500 employees added jobs at a 6 percent rate and cut them at a 7 percent rate, for a one percent loss.[1]

The value of small business to Canada's economy has been recognized by the federal and provincial governments with the establishment of small business departments and lending institutions catering to these enterprises. Government agencies sponsor awards to recognize entrepreneurs or enterprises that have performed in an outstanding manner. An example of one such award is the Canada Awards for Business Excellence. Begun in 1984 by the federal government, these awards were created to acknowledge exceptional business achievements, ones that contribute to Canada's competitiveness in national and international business. The awards are given each year to honor extraordinary performance in various categories of business activity including entrepreneurship and small business.

The Increase in Small Business Activity

The reasons for the increase in small business activity are as follows:
1) Big businesses offer less job security since layoffs are more likely. Growing numbers of employees are also dissatisfied with working for large organizations that are impersonal and where efforts of employees often go unrecognized.

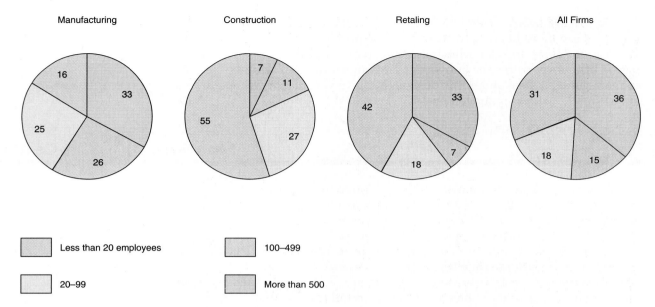

Manufacturing   Construction   Retaling   All Firms

Less than 20 employees   100–499

20–99   More than 500

Figure 7.1
Employment distribution by enterprise size.

2) Many large companies and government departments are being reduced in size, creating opportunities for subcontracting work and consulting services. Former employees often leave their employment and start businesses to provide these services.

3) For most of the past 15 years, it has been easier to start a small business than previously. The economy has grown, especially the service industries that require less investment to enter.

4) Persons who are self-employed earn almost 50 percent more on average than persons who are employees. Small business is financially attractive.[2]

Small Business Defined

small business

An independently owned and operated business not dominant in its field of operations.

There are almost as many definitions of small business as there are books on the topic. Two approaches will be used here to define a small business: one based on characteristics and the other based on size. A **small business** is one that is independently owned and operated and is not dominant in its field of operations. It possesses most of the following characteristics:

- Management of the firm is independent. Usually the managers are also the owners.
- An individual or a small group supplies the capital and holds the ownership.
- The area of operations is usually local, and the workers and owners live in the same community. However, the markets are not always local.
- The enterprise is smaller than others in the industry. This measure can be in terms of sales volume, number of employees, or other criteria. It is free of legal or financial ties to large business enterprises.
- The enterprise qualifies for the small business income tax rate under the Canada Income Tax Act.

A common type of small business in Canada is the convenience store. It attracts customers from its immediate area with its long hours of operation and the product lines it carries.

The size of a small business and how the size should be measured are matters of debate. Two common measures are sales revenues and the number of employees. The Canadian government's Small Business Office in conjunction with Statistics Canada defines a small business as having less than $2 million in annual sales. Various government agencies also use numbers of employees to define small business. However, this number differs widely among government agencies: the federal Ministry of State for Small Business stipulates 50 or fewer, the Federal Business Development Bank says 75 or fewer, and Statistics Canada uses numbers ranging from 100 to 1500 for manufacturing industries, and 50 for service industries.

For our purposes, a small business is one that is independent and smaller than the main enterprises in an industry, generally employing one to 1500 people. The video case "Earth Buddy" on page 203 describes a typical small business in Canada.

Describing the Entrepreneur

Persons who start and operate business firms are called **entrepreneurs.** **Entrepreneurship** refers to an individual's willingness to take advantage of business opportunities and to assume the risk of establishing and operating a business.

The typical entrepreneur is about 42 years old, as compared with the typical employee, who is about 34 years old. An increasing number of women are becoming entrepreneurs, and they now account for half the increase in new business owners each year. Women typically are more conservative than men in running a small business, and their failure rate is lower than for men.[3]

entrepreneur
One who starts and operates a small business.

entrepreneurship
An individual's willingness to assume the risks of establishing and operating a business.

Dozens of studies have identified common traits among entrepreneurs. A researcher at the University of Western Ontario compiled a list of many of the characteristics identified by these studies, including assertiveness, challenge seeking, charismatic, coping, creative, improvising, opportunistic, preserving, risk taking, self-confident, tenacious, venturesome, and oriented toward achievement and action.[4] An Ontario government report, *The State of Small Business*, found that the main reasons for starting a business were:

- The need to achieve or the sense of accomplishment. Entrepreneurs believe that they can make a direct contribution to the success of the enterprise.
- The need to be their own boss and to control their time.
- The perceived opportunity in the marketplace to provide a product or service.
- The wish to act in their own way or have the freedom to adapt their own approach to work.
- The desire to experience the adventure of independence and a variety of challenges.
- The desire to make money.
- The need to make a living.[5]

The motivations of successful entrepreneurs include having fun, building an organization, making money, winning in business, earning recognition, and realizing a sense of accomplishment.[6] The box "Jimmy Pattison— Canadian Entrepreneur Extraordinaire" describes the career of one of Canada's best-known entrepreneurs.

Entrepreneurship has both benefits and costs. On the positive side, entrepreneurs get a tremendous sense of satisfaction from being their own boss. They also enjoy successfully bringing together the factors of production (land, labor, and capital) to make a profit. Perhaps the greatest benefit, however, is that entrepreneurs can make a fortune if they have carefully planned what the business will do and how it will operate.

On the negative side, entrepreneurs can go bankrupt if their business fails. Customers can demand all sorts of services or inventory that small businesses cannot profitably supply. Entrepreneurs must work long hours and often get little in return in the first few years of operation. An entrepreneur may find that he or she is very good at one particular aspect of the business—for example, marketing—but knows little about managing the overall business. This imbalance can cause serious problems. In fact, poor management is the main reason businesses fail.

Finding Information on Small Business

Many sources of information on small business are available. The following represent the main resources.

Small Business Textbooks.   There are several Canadian textbooks on small business and entrepreneurship.[7] And of course, many others are written in other countries, especially the United States.

Books Profiling Canadian Entrepreneurs.   Many books have been published on successful (and some unsuccessful) Canadian entrepreneurs. Examples include Gould's *The New Entrepreneurs: 80 Canadian Success Stories*, Barnes and Banning's *Money Makers: The Secrets of Canada's Most Successful Entrepreneurs*, and Fraser's *Quebec Inc.: French Canadian Entrepreneurs and the New Business Elite*.[8]

Magazines.   Two Canadian publications are devoted to small business and entrepreneurship. *Profit: The Magazine for Canadian Entrepreneurs*, published

The Canadian Business Scene

JIMMY PATTISON—CANADIAN ENTREPRENEUR EXTRAORDINAIRE

Most 65-year old Vancouverites like to have a relaxed breakfast and read the newspaper. Not Jimmy Pattison, one of Canada's most famous entrepreneurs. It's 9 a.m., and he has been in his office since 6 a.m. He has already gone through his mail and phone messages, solved a potential crisis, and talked to a businessman from Thailand who wants to do a deal. In spite of his great wealth, Pattison has no intention of slowing down.

The Jim Pattison Group, one of Canada's largest sole proprietorships, had sales last year of $3 billion and employed 15 000 people. Jimmy Pattison started out in the 1950s selling pots and pans door to door. He knew he could make enough money to live on if he sold just one set of pots and pans each day. He also learned that he could sell one set if he could just get three evening appointments to make his sales pitch. To get those three evening appointments, he had to knock on about 30 doors. Then he discovered that if he whistled while going door to door, he only had to make 22 house calls to get three appointments. So that's what he did.

In 1961, he began selling cars. Over the years he became involved in numerous other ventures. Now his one-man conglomerate owns 12 car franchises, a Caribbean bank, Ripley's Believe-It-Or-Not, Overwaitea food stores, outdoor signs, Gold Seal fishery products, and Westar Group Ltd., to name just a few. The company's biggest investments in the next few years will be in B.C. and Alberta. Expansion into the U.S. is also planned. In the 1980s, the company did no business in the U.S., but now the U.S. accounts for 20 percent of company sales. He is also thinking of expanding into Mexico.

Pattison is obviously in charge of the company. His inner circle includes six executives specializing in law, tax, accounting, insurance/administration, cash management, and deal-making. He says being a private company allows him to take a long-run perspective. He says that as long as he keeps his banker happy, things run smoothly. One of Pattison's biggest recent challenges has been to "renew" the company by recruiting a younger generation to replace his colleagues. Most of the new top executives come from the operating divisions. One is only 29 years old.

Pattison says he has only sales skills, but those have served him well throughout his career. He notes that sales requires hard work, and it forces you to relate to people. Those two elements are crucial for success. He also learned in selling that having the door slammed in your face teaches you to handle setbacks and disappointments. He learned not to take no for an answer.

nine times a year by CB Media Ltd., is a practical magazine oriented toward business people. A more academic publication is the *Journal of Small Business and Entrepreneurship,* published quarterly by the Centre for Entrepreneurship, Faculty of Management, University of Toronto, for the International Council for Small Business Canada. In addition, there are many magazines and journals published in the United States.

Small Business Centers or Institutes.   Dozens of centers and institutes, usually located at colleges or universities, provide assistance to small businesses. Examples are the P.J. Gardiner Small Business Institute at Memorial University of Newfoundland, the Centre for Entrepreneurship at the University of Toronto, and Business Consulting Services at the University of Saskatchewan.

Small Business Organizations.   Several organizations have been formed to represent the interests of small business. The largest is the **Canadian Federation of Independent Business (CFIB)**, a nonprofit, nonpartisan political action group, or lobby, representing the interests of small and medium-sized business to governments. The CFIB has about 75 000 members. Its stated objectives are to promote and protect a system of free competitive enterprise in Canada and to give the independent entrepreneur a voice in laws governing business and the nation. A similar organization is the Canadian Organization for Small Business, operating in western Canada. Numerous provincial groups also exist.

Canadian Federation of Independent Business (CFIB)
A nonprofit, nonpartisan lobby group representing small and medium-sized businesses.

Government and Private Agencies.   Information is also available from government and private bodies including small business departments in provincial governments, the "Small Business Network" in Willowdale, Ontario, and the Business Information Centre of the Federal Business Development Bank. Many chartered banks have booklets and brochures on various topics related to small business.

Becoming a Small Business Owner

Most people become involved in a small business in one of four ways: they take over a family business, they buy out an existing firm, they start their own firm, or they buy a franchise. There are pros and cons to each approach.

Taking over a Family Business

Taking over and operating one's own family business poses many challenges. There may be disagreement over which family member assumes control. If the parent sells his or her interest in the business, the price paid may be an issue. The expectations of other family members is typical of how managing such an organization can be difficult. Some may consider a job, promotion, and impressive title their birthright, regardless of their talent or training. Choosing an appropriate successor and ensuring that he or she receives adequate training, and disagreements among family members about the future of the business are two problem areas. Sometimes the interests of the family and those of the enterprise conflict. As a result, family enterprises often fail to respond to changing market conditions. The challenges faced in running such an organization are summarized in Figure 7.2.

A family business also has some strengths. It can provide otherwise unobtainable financial and management resources because of the personal sacrifices of family members; family businesses often have a valuable reputation or goodwill that can result in important community and business relationships; employee loyalty is often high; and an interested, unified family management and shareholders group may emerge.

Buying an Existing Enterprise

Because a family-run business and other established firms are already operating, they have certain advantages for the purchaser: the clientele is established, financing might be easier because past performance and existing assets can be evaluated, experienced employees may already be in place, and lines of credit and supply have been established. An entrepreneur who buys someone else's business, however, faces more uncertainty about the exact conditions of the organization than a person who takes over his or her family's operation.

The acquisition of an existing enterprise may have other drawbacks: the business may have a poor reputation, the location may be poor, and an appropriate price may be difficult to ascertain.

Starting a Business

This approach is likely the most challenging to becoming a small business owner, for there is no existing operation, no established customers, and no history in the form of financial or marketing records upon which to base decisions. Consequently, acquiring financing can be difficult; investors, either lenders

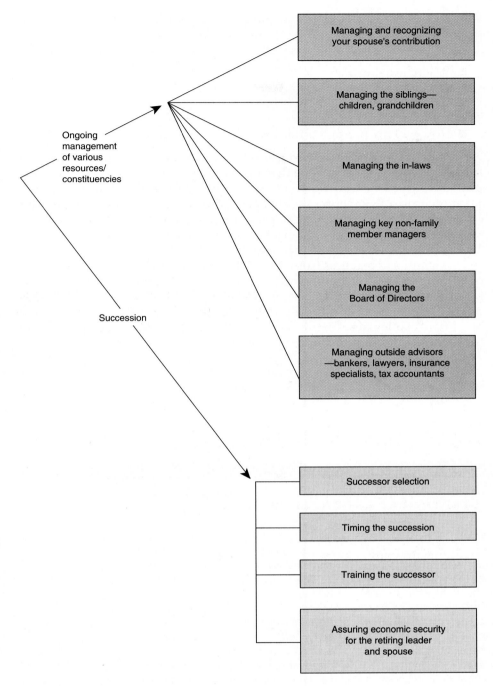

Figure 7.2
Family-owned business leader's key challenges.

or shareholders, have to be convinced of the enterprise's viability. Beginning a new enterprise usually means spending large amounts of money before sales or revenues materialize. Overall, new businesses pose a higher risk and greater uncertainty than established organizations since the business venture is unproven and the competence of the entrepreneur is most likely unknown.

The risks of starting a business from scratch are, not surprisingly, greater than those of buying an existing firm. Success or failure depends on identifying a genuine business opportunity—a product for which many customers will pay well but which is currently unavailable to them. To find openings, entrepreneurs must answer the following questions:

- Who are my customers?
- Where are they?
- At which price will they buy my product?
- In what quantities will they buy?
- Who are my competitors?
- How will my product differ from that of my competitors?

microenterprise

An enterprise that the owner operates part-time from the home while continuing regular employment elsewhere.

Many new businesses start as **microenterprises**—enterprises operated from the home part-time while the entrepreneur continues to work as a regular employee of another organization (see the box "Starting as a Microenterprise). Sometimes such a business is operated in partnership with others. The obvious advantage of beginning as a microenterprise is that the entrepreneur can test his or her idea before quitting regular employment. This approach is being used increasingly by Canadians.

Beginning a business from scratch has its benefits. An entrepreneur can create the image for the business he or she wants and is unrestricted by past reputation or policies. The owner has the flexibility to decide how big or small the operation is to be and has the chance to start small and grow at a manageable pace. Finally, an entrepreneur has the freedom to choose the location and building decor.

The Canadian Business Scene

STARTING AS A MICROENTERPRISE

Studies of entrepreneurship estimate that up to 50 percent of small businesses begin as "microenterprises." Two types of people start businesses with this approach: those with full-time employment outside the home who operate the business in off-hours and homemakers starting on a small scale to supplement a spouse's or partner's income. By the year 2000, it is estimated that 40 percent of the work force will operate full-time from their homes, either by operating microenterprises or by telecommuting.

An example of a micro or home office business is Lori M Consulting in Toronto. It was formed by Lori Molmar, an executive with the Federation of Women Teachers' Association of Ontario. She left that job to set up a business in her home as an interior designer and environmental gerontologist. The cost of operating from her home was lower and she even built an addition to accommodate the business.

A key source of microbusiness opportunities is the increased use of outside services by business and government. Even small and medium-sized businesses are hiring consultants to provide some services, thus avoiding the obligations of hiring full-time employees. Microenterprises have also grown because of the overall growth in the service industry and the computerization and increased affordability of office equipment.

The principal benefits of microenterprises are the following: their start-up and operating costs are low; little financial risk is encountered if the business fails; the work environment is casual; family responsibilities can be accommodated; and the hours of operation can be tailored to an individual's schedule. But such businesses also have disadvantages: the owners may feel isolated, having little, if any, social interaction with others; family and friends may cause distractions and disruptions; a productive working environment may not be available; and self-discipline is required to keep working and not be distracted.

Home Inc.: The Canadian Home-Based Business Guide is a guide to microenterprises; the Canadian Federation of Independent Business has also studied the trend because it encourages entrepreneurship. The National Home Business Association has a data base of over 10 000 home-based entrepreneurs from all over Canada. This association provides a package of services to members that includes group rates on health insurance, educational seminars, a referral service to promote members' services, and discounts from stationery and equip-

Buying a Franchise

Contrary to popular belief, franchising did not begin with the 1950s boom in fast-food franchises like McDonald's. Rather, its beginnings date back to the early 1800s. Not until 1898, however, when General Motors began franchising retail dealerships, did modern franchising begin in earnest. Similar systems were created by Rexall (pharmacies) in 1902, Howard Johnson (restaurants and, later, motels) in 1926, and many oil, grocery, motel, and fast-food franchisers in the early twentieth century.

One of the fastest ways to establish a business is to buy a franchise. Franchising has continued to increase in economic importance (see the box "Just Like Home"). **Franchising** involves drafting a contract between a manufacturer and a dealer that stipulates how the manufacturer's or supplier's product or service will be sold. The dealer, called a **franchisee**, agrees to sell the product or service of the manufacturer, called the **franchisor**, in return for royalties. Franchising organizations well-known in Canada include Holiday Inn, McDonald's, College Pro Painters, Weight Watchers, Kentucky Fried Chicken, Midas Muffler, and Canadian Tire.

The franchising arrangement can be beneficial to both the franchisee and the franchisor. The franchisee enjoys the following benefits:

- *Recognition.* The franchise name gives the franchisee instant recognition with the public.
- *Standardized appearance of the franchise.* Customers know that consistency exists from one outlet to another.
- *Management assistance.* The franchisee can obtain advice on how to run the franchise effectively.
- *Economies of scale in buying.* The head office of the franchise buys in large volume and resells to the franchisee at lower prices than he or she could get buying alone.
- *Promotional assistance.* The head office of the franchise provides the franchisee with advertising and other promotional material.

The franchisee is not the only party who gains in franchising. The franchisor enjoys the following benefits:

- *Recognition.* The franchisor is able to expand its area of operation by signing agreements with dealers in widely dispersed places.

franchising

A contract between a manufacturer and a dealer that stipulates how a product or service will be sold.

franchisee

The dealer who agrees to sell the product or service.

franchisor

The manufacturer of the product or service.

Franchising is very popular in Canada. It offers individuals who want to run their own business an opportunity to establish themselves quickly in a local market.

International Report

JUST LIKE HOME

It could be any Canadian city. On one corner sits a McDonald's restaurant. On another is a Kentucky Fried Chicken shop. Down the street is a 7-Eleven convenience store. A Budget Rent-A-Car outlet sits next to a Holiday Inn. Yes, it could be anywhere in Canada. But it's not. It's Tokyo, Japan.

Despite its reputation as an insular culture, Japan has embraced a number of franchising overtures. Probably the most successful chain to franchise in Japan is 7-Eleven stores, thanks largely to its major Japanese franchisee, Ito Masatoshi. He now operates 3800 7-Eleven stores. A savvy marketer, Masatoshi appealed to single urban residents stranded by the early closing hours of traditional Japanese grocery stores.

Japan is just one of many nations providing new markets for the franchise concept. Today, more and more franchisors are selling or opening operations from Fiji to France, from Moscow to Malaysia. Canada has more franchises than any nation outside the United States and most of these franchises are with U.S. firms.

U.S. franchisors like Kentucky Fried Chicken and McDonald's have dominated international markets for years. But NAFTA has created opportunities for Canadian franchisors to move into Latin America. Yogenfruz (frozen yogurt), Ceiling Doctor (home repairs), Pizza Pizza Ltd., and Cara Operations Ltd. have already gained some success in Mexico.

A common language is not enough to ensure success for franchises. Cultural differences have kept sales in the United Kingdom low. For example, ComputerLand stores has sold only 20 of 60 planned franchises in the U.K. British residents simply do not impulsively buy computers they see in store windows as their North American cousins do. Fast-food franchises have fared especially badly because most Britons prefer not to spend their spare cash eating out in such places.

Undeterred, many firms are looking closely at continental Europe for franchising opportunities. The new European Community's rules will make it much easier for foreign firms to franchise their operations while still maintaining reasonable control over product offerings. The demise of communism in eastern Europe and the dissolution of the Soviet Union also provide new areas for franchising. Formerly only joint ventures with the national governments were possible. Certainly franchising provides an excellent opportunity for citizens in these nations to gain expertise in marketing and other capitalist necessities. However, as some observers have noted, only the largest franchisors—those who can afford to accept a small initial fee and wait for the profits to come in—will be able to take advantage of this new franchising potential. Smaller franchisors will have to wait until the Eastern European countries develop stable economies, currencies, and individual entrepreneurs who have substantial cash to invest.

Those who have succeeded in international franchising offer a few basic rules. First, do your market research and make sure your product or service will fit into the culture. Gymboree, which franchises developmental play programs for preschoolers and their parents, has turned down Japanese investors because its centers require a great deal of space—something in short supply in Japan. Second, be patient. It may take ten years for foreign stores to start showing a profit. Third, find a reliable partner. Toys 'R' Us entered into a joint venture with McDonald's to use the latter's expertise to open new toy stores in Japan. Finally, be prepared to be flexible. One frozen yogurt maker found interest—and sales—picking up when it offered a green-tea flavor in Japan.

- ■ *Promotion savings.* The various franchisees can decide on local advertising efforts; this arrangement saves the franchisor money on wasted coverage in areas where it does not have a franchise.
- ■ *Franchisee payments.* The franchisees pay the franchisor for the right to operate their franchises.
- ■ *Attention to detail.* Since franchisees own their franchises, they are motivated to do a good job and to sell the franchisor's product or service aggressively.

Franchising has facilitated the growth of small business in Canada. The financial and management assistance franchisees can receive from the franchisor removes many of the risks that typically face small business owners. In fact, whereas about 80 percent of all small businesses fail within five years, less than 20 percent of franchises fail in the same period.

Franchising, however, does have its shortcomings. Not all the franchises on the market are as successful as McDonald's. Many entrepreneurs are uninterested in becoming franchisees because the franchisor is able to regulate their behavior too closely. They would rather start their own business and take whatever risks are necessary in return for the freedom to do what they want.

Challenges for the Entrepreneur

Starting and operating a business enterprise is challenging: financing must be obtained, the enterprise must be carefully managed, and assistance must often be found. The box "Entrepreneurship in the Former Soviet Union" describes some of the problems faced by entrepreneurs in formerly communist countries.

Financing the Small Enterprise

The amount of capital needed to start a small business prevents some people from becoming entrepreneurs. However, sources of funding are available, and a list is given in Table 7.1. It should be noted that some sources are more likely than others to provide money. Lenders may or may not lend money to entrepreneurs, depending upon whether the enterprise is just beginning or is ongoing.

TABLE 7.1   Principal Sources of Funds for Small Business Enterprises

Debt Sources
These are funds borrowed by the enterprise. They may come from:
   The entrepreneur who may loan money to the enterprise
   Private lenders, that is, individuals or corporations
   Financial institutions such as banks, credit unions, trust companies, and
      finance companies. Such borrowing may be by the enterprise but
      guaranteed by the entrepreneur or secured against other nonbusi-
      ness assets of the entrepreneur
   Trade credit, that is, the delayed payment terms offered by suppliers
   Government agencies, for example, the Federal Business Development
      Bank
   The selling of bonds or debentures (usually only done when the enterprise
      is larger)

Equity Sources
This money is invested in the enterprise and represents an ownership in-
terest. It comes from:
   The entrepreneur's personal funds
   Partners, either individuals or corporations
   Family and friends
   Venture capitalists
   Governments
   The selling of shares to the public (usually only done when the enterprise
      is larger)
   Employees who may participate in a stock purchase plan or simply invest
      in the enterprise.

Retained Earnings
Profits, that is, funds generated from the operation of the business, can be
either paid to the owners in dividends or reinvested in the enterprise. If retained or reinvested, profits are a source of funds.

International Report

ENTREPRENEURSHIP IN THE FORMER SOVIET UNION

Malgorzata Daniszewska was an insider in communist Poland. Her husband was a government minister—the chief spokesman for the government of General Wojciech Jaruzelski. Although everyone expected her to espouse the party line, she never fully embraced the economic principles of communism. Therefore, it was not surprising that when the old regime crumbled, Daniszewska was ready to take on the risks and seek the rewards of capitalism. She was also in a position to spread the word to other would-be entrepreneurs in Poland. After buying *Firma*, a government-owned monthly business magazine, Daniszewska decided to deliver a strong pro-business message to the Polish populace. She choose to deliver her message symbolically: She set up a shoeshine stand—a symbol disdained by the communists as one of the worst forms of capitalist exploitation—on a Warsaw street. The public relations ploy—which made Daniszewska the first person to shine shoes in Warsaw since World War II—called attention to her serious capitalist theme: Private business is the future for Poland, and if it is good enough for an ex-bureaucrat's wife, it is good enough for other Poles who want to better their lives.

Daniszewska is one of the thousands of Polish entrepreneurs who are helping to transform their country's economy. Their efforts to establish a new private-enterprise system are moving in the right direction and, in the process, encouraging economic growth. While some other East European economies are actually shrinking in the post-communist era, Poland's gross domestic product grew by a modest but promising 1 percent in 1992. It is expected to grow another 3 percent annually through the mid-1990s. Although this growth has been aided somewhat by Western investment, its backbone consists of small and medium-sized Polish businesses.

Poland's new generation of entrepreneurs has had to struggle to learn the basics of capitalism. Many who took off in the pursuit of profits before they understood the responsibilities of running businesses are already bankrupt. Admittedly, many failures were due not simply to lack of knowledge, but to a shortage of capital that has sent interest rates sky high.

Entrepreneurs are also active in other countries that used to be run by communists:

- In newly unified Germany, while a million East Germans have flooded into the wealthier, happier

West, some 250 000 West Germans have headed to the "Wild East" for business opportunity. With backing from an investor-partner, for example, Albrecht Wendt leased 2000 acres of prime farmland from an elderly farmer who did not want to sign yet one more extension of a cooperative agreement left over from the communist era. Wendt has the land for 18 years, and his interest payments are subsidized by the government.

- In the city of Skoda in the Czech Republic, the most admired entrepreneur in town is Multi Dekor, who does a handsome business providing furnishings for the new shops of fellow entrepreneurs.

- In Saratov, Russia, where he has built a successful trucking business, rampant crime and police corruption require Vladimir Tyrin to employ 70 armed security guards among his 183 employees. In fact, Tyrin has now diversified: He hires out his private security force to other fledgling firms that cannot otherwise protect themselves. "You need connections, money, intellect, energy, and hard work," explains Tyrin. "We got the armored personnel carrier just to be on the safe side."

- Arpad Kovacs runs a dress making shop in Budapest. He lives in relative luxury, but he has to cheat on his taxes in order to do so. He is supposed to pay 70 percent of his profits in taxes, but he understates his sales volume so that he ends up paying about 45 percent. Many entrepreneurs claim losses for their businesses even when the business makes a profit.

Funds for Starting a Business.   The most likely sources of financing are the personal funds of individuals, in particular, the entrepreneurs themselves. Some government agencies may provide assistance funds for startup and so might chartered banks if they think that the proposed business has promise.

Funds for an Ongoing Business. After the enterprise has operated for some time, other services are more likely to be used, if a good financial reputation has been established. Sources include trade credit (that is, the delayed payment terms offered by suppliers), chartered banks, trust companies, and venture capitalists. Another source of funds is profits from the business. Entrepreneurs seldom pay themselves all the profits generated by the enterprise. Some profits are reinvested in the enterprise and are called **retained earnings.**

Managing Funds. In Table 7.1, each source is identified as debt or equity. **Debt** refers to borrowed funds that require interest payments and must be repaid. **Equity** refers to the money, or capital, invested in the enterprise by individuals or companies who become owners, and to profits reinvested. In the case of small enterprises, the entrepreneur is often the sole owner. The challenge for entrepreneurs is to keep the amount of funds borrowed and funds invested in ownership in balance. If an enterprise relies upon debt too heavily, interest payments might become burdensome and could lead to the failure of the enterprise.

Investors who invest equity obtain ownership and have some influence on the firm's operations. If investors own 51 percent or more of the firm's equity, they could control the enterprise. As enterprises require funds to grow, this diminishing of control frequently cannot be avoided.

retained earnings
Profits reinvested in an enterprise.

debt
Borrowed funds that require interest payments and must be repaid.

equity
Money invested in the enterprise by individuals or companies who become owners.

Managing the Small Enterprise

Small business owners must be familiar with many of the concepts, theories, and practices associated with the four management functions: planning and decision making, organizing, influencing, and controlling.

Planning in Small Enterprises. Although the planning process in a small business may not be formalized, it is necessary for its successful startup and operation. When a business begins, the suppliers of any funds will require a business plan as outlined in Table 7.2. The components of the business plan are also appropriate for ongoing enterprises. Aspects of the planning process outlined in Chapter 6 would be utilized by entrepreneurs as would the components of strategic management. Entrepreneurs still have to make managerial decisions about all aspects of the business's operations although the process will not be as formalized as in a larger enterprise.

Organizing in Small Enterprises. Some degree of organizing is necessary even in the smallest enterprise, and the significance of this management function increases as the enterprise grows. When the enterprise grows, departments will have to be established, managers and other employees hired, authority delegated, and an organizational structure arranged.

Influencing in Small Enterprises. This management function may be irrelevant when the enterprise is a one-person operation. But as the enterprise grows, motivation, leadership, communication, managing conflict and change, and creating a suitable corporate culture take on increasing importance. Entrepreneurs often have trouble in the influencing role. The dominant characteristics of these people—independence and ambition—do not always lend themselves to performing well as an influencer over others. The traits that enable an entrepreneur to get started and to become successful are not necessarily those needed to manage the efforts of employees. Many entrepreneurs are weak in human resource management and have problems with recruiting and retaining good employees.

TABLE 7.2   A Business Plan

The contents of a business plan vary depending upon the information required by the financial institutions or government agencies. Some entrepreneurs develop plans as a personal guide to check on where they are or want to be. The following are the components that might be included in such a plan:

Cover Page
Contains the enterprise's name, address, telephone numbers, and key contacts.

Table of Contents

Executive Summary
A brief statement, usually about one page long, summarizing the plan's contents.

Background/History of the Enterprise
A concise outline of when and how the enterprise got started, the goods or services it sells, and its major suppliers and customers.

Management
Background information on the entrepreneur and other employees, especially other managers (if there are any).

Marketing Assessment
Descriptions of the products or a service profile, the results of any market research, a market description and analysis, an identification of competition, and an account of the marketing strategy.

Production Assessment
A brief description of the production process, the technological process employed, quality requirements, location and physical plant, and details of machinery and equipment.

Financial Assessment
A review of the capital structure and the money needed to finance the business. Usually includes a projected balance sheet, profit and loss statement, and a cash flow forecast. Lenders might also require details of loan collateral and a repayment proposal.

Research and Development (R&D)
For many enterprises, R&D is important and a statement of what is planned would be included. There might also be an assessment of the risks anticipated with any new products or ventures.

Basic Data
Data on the enterprise's bankers, accountants, lawyers, shareholders (if any), and details of incorporation (if applicable).

Appendices
The following might be attached to a plan: detailed management biographies, product literature, evaluation of assets, detailed financial statements and cash flow forecast, and a list of major contracts.

Controlling in Small Enterprises.   Entrepreneurs must somehow monitor what is happening to their business. Relying on intuition or hunch is unsatisfactory. In fact, most investors in an enterprise insist that control mechanisms be in place. Financial control techniques are by far the most common, but ways to secure feedback on marketing, production, and human resources are also employed. The video case "Earth Buddy" on p. 203 describes a controlling problem that emerged when raw materials were not available for production when they were needed.

Transitions in Management

As the discussion of management functions shows, changes in how a business is managed occur as the enterprise grows. Models of small business growth have been developed that help explain these changes in management.[9] Table 7.3, gives examples of the shift in management approaches necessary as a small enterprise develops.

The launch stage covers the preparatory activities as well as the actual startup, while the survival stage is the initial period of operation (up to five years) in which many enterprises fail. During expansion, the organization passes the break-even point, and success appears to be more likely. Finally, the maturity stage involves slowed or slight growth and might be referred to as a "comfort" stage where success is assured. Maturity is not necessarily the end of growth for a business. Expansion opportunities are still sought and diversification is considered, sometimes through taking over or merging with other enterprises.

During these stages, the firm changes from being entrepreneurial to being professionally managed. This change usually happens once the business employs between 50 and 100 people. That is, the entrepreneurial approach to management where one individual dominates shifts to a professional management style with several top, middle, and supervisory managers necessary to operate the enterprise.

TABLE 7.3   Growth Model for Small Enterprises

Characteristics	Launch	Survival	Expansion	Maturity
Key Issues	Development of business "idea" Raising funds Obtaining customers	Generating revenues Breaking even	Managing and funding growth Obtaining resources Maintaining control	Expense control Productivity Consideration of diversification and other expansion
Management Style	Entrepreneurial, individualistic, direct supervision	Entrepreneurial, allows others to administer but supervises closely	Delegation, coordinative, but still entrepreneurial Monitoring	Decentralization, reliance on others
Organizational Structure	Unstructured	Simple	Functional, centralized	Decentralized functional/product
Product/Market	Single line and single market	Single line and market but increasing diversity	Wider product range and multiple markets	Several product lines, multimarket and channels
Main Sources of Funds	Owners, friends, and relatives	Owners, suppliers (trade credit), banks	Banks, new partners, retained earnings, secured long-term debt	Retained earnings, long-term debt, shareholders

The Survival of Small Business

Numerous statistics on the survival rate of small businesses have been compiled. The following data are representative:

- About 13-15 percent of all business enterprises disappear each year.
- One half of new businesses fail in the first three years. After that the failure rate levels off.
- After ten years, only 25 percent of businesses are still in existence.
- The average life span of small enterprises is 7.25 years.
- Female entrepreneurs have a survival rate about twice as high as that of males.[10]

The low survival rate need not be viewed as a serious problem, since failures are natural in a competitive economic system. In some cases, enterprises are poorly managed and are replaced by more efficient and innovative ones. In recent years, more enterprises have started than have failed, indicating the resiliency of small business and entrepreneurs.

Reasons for Success

Four factors are typically cited to explain the success of small business owners:

1. *Hard work, drive, and dedication.* Small business owners must be committed to succeeding and be willing to put in the time and effort to make it happen. Long hours and few vacations generally characterize the first few years of new business ownership.
2. *Market demand for the product or service.* If the area around a college has only one pizza parlor, a new pizzeria is more likely to succeed than if there are already 10 in operation. Careful analysis of market conditions can help small businesspeople assess the reception of their products in the marketplace.
3. *Managerial competence.* Successful small businesspeople have a solid understanding of how to manage a business firm. They may acquire competence through training (by taking courses in small business management at a local college), experience (by learning the ropes in another business), or by using the expertise of others.
4. *Luck.* Luck also plays a role in the success of some firms. For example, after one entrepreneur started an environmental clean-up firm, he struggled to keep his business afloat. Then the government committed a large sum of money for toxic waste clean-up. He was able to get several large contracts, and his business is now thriving.

Reasons for Failure

Small businesses collapse for a number of reasons (see Table 7.4). The entrepreneur may have no control over some of these reasons (for example, weather, fraud, accidents), but he or she can influence most items on the list. This is the main reason an entrepreneur should learn as much as possible about management.

TABLE 7.4   Causes of Small Business Failure

Poor management skills
poor delegation and organizational ability
lack of depth in management team
entrepreneurial incompetence, such as a poor
    understanding of finances and business markets
lack of experience

Inadequate marketing capabilities
difficulty in marketing product
market too small, nonexistent, or declines
too much competition
problems with distribution systems

Inadequate financial capabilities
weak skills in accounting and finance
lack of budgetary control
inadequate cash flow forecasts
inadequate costing systems
incorrect valuation of assets
unable to obtain financial backing

Inadequate production capabilities
poorly designed production systems

old and inefficient production facilities and
    equipment
inadequate control over quality
problems with inventory control

Personal reasons
lost interest in business
accident, illness
death
family problems

Disasters
fire
weather
strikes
fraud by entrepreneur or others

Other
mishandling of large project
excessive standard of living
lack of time to devote to business
difficulties with associates or partners
government policies change

Assistance for Entrepreneurs and Small Business Enterprises

In the Canadian economic system, the existence of small enterprises is considered desirable for a number of reasons, including the employment it provides, the innovations it introduces, and the competition it ensures. To help entrepreneurs through the hazards of starting up and operating a new business, substantial assistance is available. Government is the main source of assistance, but other sources are also available. Various sources of assistance are summarized in Table 7.5.

In spite of the numerous government assistance programs, small business owners are not happy with government involvement in small business. A 1993 *Financial Post* survey revealed that just 5 percent of small business owners felt that a government program had helped them start their business. By contrast, 46 percent felt that government policies and regulations (e.g., excessive paper work requirements and red tape) have caused them to cut back their business operations. Small business owners also said that government assistance programs are not as effective as they used to be. Small business owners rank managerial competence as most important in promoting growth. Government assistance is ranked last.[11]

TABLE 7.5   Summary of Assistance for Small Business

Government Assistance

Industry Canada is the department in the federal government responsible for small business and has many programs to promote entrepreneurship. Provincial governments also have numerous programs.

The National Entrepreneurship Development Institute was established as a non-profit organization to serve as a clearing house for information about entrepreneurship.

Taxation policy allows small business to pay lower levels of taxes than other enterprises.

The Federal Business Development Bank (FBDB) administers the Counselling Assistance for Small Enterprises (CASE) program which offers one-on-one counselling by experienced people to thousands of entrepreneurs each year.

The Small Business Loans Act (SBLA) encourages the provision of term loan financing to small enterprises by private sector institutions by guaranteeing the loans.

The Program for Export Market Development shares the cost of efforts by business to develop export markets.

Incubators and technology centers operate across Canada. Incubators are centers where entrepreneurs can start their business with the assistance of counselling services. Federal government funds support technology centers that evaluate innovations under research and development.

Schools for Entrepreneurs funded by government but operated by the private sector prepare prospective entrepreneurs by training them in all aspects of small business. An example is the Regina Business and Technology Centre.

Private Sector

The Canada Opportunities Investment Network (COIN) is a computerized national investment match making service operated through Chambers of Commerce. This service brings potential entrepreneurs together with people who might be willing to supply them with capital.

Banks and other financial institutions not only lend money but also provide advice to entrepreneurs.

Venture capitalists finance high risk enterprises to which others are unwilling to lend money. Business angels are a special category of private venture capitalists who invest in new, high-risk enterprises that they feel should be supported even though no one else will.

Consultants and numerous publications exist to answer questions.

The Canadian Federation of Independent Business (CFIB) is the largest of the organizations formed to protect the interests of small business. It is a non-profit, nonpartisan group, or lobby, which represents the interests of about 75 000 small and medium size enterprises.

Summary of Key Points

The Canadian economy relies upon a business enterprise system to provide the goods and services needed by consumers. In turn, the business enterprise system relies upon entrepreneurs, persons who start and operate small businesses. New business startups provide new products for consumers, competition for established enterprises, and increased employment opportunities for Canadians. The business system is continuously evolving, and small businesses are the source, or beginning, of that system.

Throughout the 1980s, the small business sector grew substantially and received recognition for its role in the business system. Governments increased their efforts in assisting small businesses as did banking and educational institutions. As a result, we know much more about the challenges facing entrepreneurs who want to start a business, and the difficulties of operating a business. We have also learned about the traits or characteristics of persons who are entrepreneurs. There are now many sources of information available on small business.

A person can become involved in a small business by taking over a family business, buying an existing enterprise, starting a business from scratch, or purchasing a franchise. Each has advantages and disadvantages. The business person faces several challenges regardless of the way he or she becomes an entrepreneur. It can be difficult to identify the appropriate sources of funds and then to acquire the financing necessary to start and continue a business.

Another challenge relates to the management capabilities and knowledge necessary to succeed in business. There are many aspects of managing the business that relate to the concepts, theories, and practices associated with the four management functions of planning, organizing, influencing, and controlling. These functions apply to small business as they do to any organization. A particular challenge to small business is the transition necessary from an entrepreneurial style suitable when the business begins to a more professional approach when the business's size increases.

Not all small businesses survive. The failure rate is high for numerous reasons. Governments and other institutions are making efforts to improve the chances of success by supplying funds, lowering taxation rates, and providing advice on all aspects of operation including the management of people and technology. However, small business should not be coddled so much that it cannot fail. Failure is a characteristic of the business system and will occur when businesses do not supply the goods and services wanted by consumers.

CONCLUDING CASE 7-1

Business Is Blooming

Grower Direct Inc. is Canada's largest importer of roses, with sales of $25 million. It sells long-stemmed roses for $9.99 a dozen at 126 franchised stores across Canada (in Quebec it is called Jardins Direct). It is able to sell roses at a low price because it is vertically integrated all the way back to the farm. Owner Skip Kerr is part of a joint venture on a farm near Quito, Ecuador that produces 4 million roses each year. Flowers are shipped to a company-owned facility in Miami, Florida where they are quality tested. They are then delivered by truck to franchisees' retail stores.

Grower Direct has grown rapidly because it has sold franchises. Franchisees pay $20 000 for an exclusive territory, plus $30 000–50 000 to outfit a store equipped with walk-in coolers. Once the outlet is up and running, the franchisee pays head office $40 for each box of 300-500 flowers shipped to their store.

While the franchising concept has allowed Grower Direct to rapidly increase its total sales, there are potential problems with the franchising concept. In Toronto and Vancouver, for example, several franchisees broke away from the company, claiming that they had to pay too much for their flowers from the franchisor and could buy them more cheaply in Toronto. But, as long as they were part of the franchise, they were forced to buy their flowers from Grower Direct. A court case dealing with some of the terms of the franchise agreement is pending.

Kerr agrees that franchisees can get flowers cheaper elsewhere than they can from Grower Direct, but he says these flowers are of much lower quality. He says he never has bought low quality flowers, and he never will. One Toronto franchisee, who took over a Grower Direct franchise, discovered that she could buy flowers on the local market for about half the price that Grower Direct was charging her as a franchisee. She now owns a non-franchised store.

One franchisee who owns 11 Grower Direct franchise outlets says being a franchisee is very restricting. Franchisees often have ideas about how to improve the business, but they must operate the way the franchisor dictates. Other franchisees accept the restrictions because they want to run a business outlet where they can be their own boss.

CASE QUESTIONS
1. Do franchisees really own their own business?
2. Do the benefits of being a franchisee outweigh the costs (e.g., restrictions put on franchisees by the franchisor)? Explain.
3. How might a franchisor address complaints from franchisees that they are being overly restricted in how they are allowed to operate? ◆

CONCLUDING CASE 7-2

GeoVision Systems Inc.

GeoVision Systems Inc. of Ottawa was a pioneer in computer software called geographical information systems (GIS), automated map making that turns maps into "spatial data bases." The company was formed by Douglas Seaborn in 1984 when it was spun off from SHL Systemshouse Inc., of which he was one of the founders. Systemshouse experienced financial problems in 1984, and GeoVision was formed with about 20 employees.

Competition from large American companies was very intense. An R & D program assisted by federal tax credits was undertaken to explore new applications, allowing GeoVision to be competitive. The company was successful in developing new products, many of which were sold to municipal governments and utility companies. Sales grew from $2 million in 1984 to more than $20 million in 1991. The GIS appeared to be a growing market.

The company decided to increase its presence in the U.S. through a major sales and marketing effort. Problems arose when managers and salespeople were hired who were not familiar with GIS and GeoVision's technology,

which was among the most complicated in the industry. The U.S. business grew but some customers were dissatisfied with the service they were receiving. Other problems arose, including the departure of the U.S. manager and the termination of a partnership with IBM because that company was in financial difficulty. GeoVision expanded by purchasing a company in Wisconsin for the primary purpose of forging the links with IBM.

Customers began to worry about GeoVision's financial viability and whether it would survive. In mid-1993, GeoVision went into receivership in both the U.S. and Canada. The technology and assets of GeoVision were taken over by Systemshouse in October 1993.

CASE QUESTIONS
1. GeoVision provides an example of which approach to starting a business?
2. In your view, what went wrong with GeoVision?
3. Could the problems have been anticipated? Explain. ◆

Key Terms

small business
entrepreneurs
entrepreneurship

Canadian Federation of
Independent Business
(CFIB)

microenterprise
franchising
franchisee

franchisor
retained earnings
debt
equity

Study Questions and Exercises

Review Questions

1. Why has the number of small businesses in Canada increased?
2. What are the characteristics of a small business?
3. What are the characteristics of an entrepreneur?
4. What are the advantages and disadvantages of the following ways of becoming involved in a small business: taking over a family business, buying out an existing business, starting a business from scratch, and buying a franchise?
5. What are the causes of small business failure?

Analysis Questions

6. Why are small businesses important to the Canadian economy?
7. Why would a person want to become involved in a microenterprise instead of going into business full-time?

8. Why do small businesses fail despite all the assistance available? Should we be concerned about these failures?

Application Exercises

9. Interview a person who is involved in a family business to identify the management challenges he or she faces. Check your findings against the key challenges identified in Figure 7.1. Write the Canadian Association of Family Enterprises for more information at 10 Prince Street, 3rd Floor, Toronto, ON, M4W 1Z4.
10. Research a business that you are interested in and prepare a plan for starting it. Use the contents of a business plan listed in Table 7.2. Develop a complete, professional business plan using the EZ-Write Plan Writer disk that accompanies the *Study Guide* for this text or may be purchased separately.

Building Your Business Skills

Goal

To encourage students to explore the opportunities for small business in exporting products overseas.

Situation

Suppose that you are the owner of a small manufacturing firm and that you have been frustrated in your attempts to increase sales. Your company, which makes roll-up doors for beverage trucks, enjoys a 50-percent market share, but a slowdown in the beverage market has left you with little room for expansion in Canada. You decide to explore the possibility of exporting your product to foreign markets.

Method

Working in groups of four or five, research sources of assistance for small businesses involved in export trade.

Follow-Up Questions

1. Judging from your research, what is the most difficult hurdle usually faced by small business exporters?
2. What position should a small firm be in before it considers exporting its products overseas? Consider such factors as years in business, depth of management, Canadian sales, and financial assets.

EASTERN EUROPE: THE LONG AND WINDING ROAD

With millions of residents who have never seen a VCR or a microwave oven, who have never viewed a TV commercial or a billboard, the formerly communist nations of Eastern Europe are either the greatest opportunity ever for the modern capitalist or a disaster waiting to happen.

Virtually everyone acknowledges that establishing capitalism in Eastern Europe will not be easy. Indeed, the list of potential problems is staggering. Most of the nations in that region lack all or most of the following:

- Laws that protect private property and guide the establishment of contracts.
- Standardized accounting procedures—or, for that matter, *any* accounting procedures to speak of.
- Banks.
- Stock and bond markets.
- Convertible currency (currency that can be exchanged for the currencies of other countries).

These gaps cannot be filled overnight; Western cultures have spent centuries developing these systems. Moreover, continued political and economic turmoil in Eastern Europe has led to a pattern in which many internal laws, tax regulations, and restrictions on foreign trade are here today and gone tomorrow.

People, the lifeblood of any business, are also a problem for Eastern Europe. In very short supply are three groups most Westerners take for granted:

- Entrepreneurs.
- Experienced business managers.
- Highly productive and skilled workers.

Even more daunting is the fact that there is absolutely no precedent for the privatization of an entire nation's worth of companies. The largest privatization effort to date, in Chile, involved fewer than 500 companies, most of which were simply restored to the same private owners from whom they had been seized by an earlier government a decade before.

In contrast, Poland alone has several hundred thousand enterprises to convert to private ownership. And virtually none of the millions of factories and shops in the nations of the former Soviet Union even existed before the Bolshevik revolution of 1918 and the advent of communism.

Having promised to privatize their nations rapidly, leaders of many Eastern European countries now find themselves caught in a bind—whom can they get to buy these companies? Foreign firms are wary, both because of the political and economic turmoil in the region and because of the difficulties of assessing the worth of Eastern European businesses.

Nor can these nations rely on sales at home. Private citizens have already bought many of the small shops in Poland, Hungary, and the Czech Republic, and will probably run all the nation's shops and service industries before too long. But selling large manufacturing facilities to the citizens of the country for cash isn't possible, simply because the total assets of all the people of each nation are not great enough to buy all the firms of that nation.

Attempts to turn over businesses to the existing managers and workers have created other problems. Where managers have been given control, some have "sold" their firms to outside buyers—"dummy companies" they themselves own—at very low prices. When managers are elected and controlled by workers and worker councils, they tend to keep payrolls full and workers content at the expense of improving operations and making profits.

The experiences of Polamp, the Polish national light bulb maker, illustrate some of these problems. With the collapse of the Soviet Union, its primary customer, Polamp fell on hard times. Its general manager, Jerzy Kedzierski, tried to put together a consortium of investors, including himself, to buy the company, only to be shot down by the Ministry of Industry. After a five-week management course at the University of Pennsylvania's Warton School of Business and Economics, he returned with a radical plan to slash costs, unload such frills as holiday homes owned by the company, and convert the plant's 2.75 hectares into a technological park. The workers' council, irate that the plan would cost 700 jobs, vetoed it and fired Kedzierski.

Poland continues to forge ahead. Both Poland and the Czech Republic are developing plans to give all or most of their population the equivalent of shares in the nation's industries. While this scheme may settle ownership questions, it leaves unaddressed the more crucial issue of who has the ability to *run* these businesses.

Part of the solution to this problem lies in the efforts under way to train Eastern Europeans in the basics of capitalism and business management. This is being done in two ways. One approach has been for business schools in Canada and the U.S. to develop cooperative arrangements with educational institutions in Eastern Europe. Canadian and American professors go to various Eastern European sites for four to six weeks and conduct classes in marketing, management, finance, information systems and so on for managers and professors at Eastern European universities.

A second approach is for newly graduated MBA's from Canada and the U.S. to work for a year or so in an Eastern European country. They live on local wages and in local housing while helping advance the practice of management in the area where they are living. They also get valuable international experience which should benefit their own careers.

Attracted by the prospect of new markets, sparse competition, and low wages, a number of large Western and Japanese businesses have shown a willingness to invest in Eastern European firms that make such basics as cars, glass, processed food, and soap—industries in which turning a profit will largely be a matter of upgrading facilities. Both Procter & Gamble and Unilever have acquired detergent companies in Eastern Europe. General Electric has a controlling interest in Tungsram (the Hungarian light bulb maker), and Volkswagen has a major holding in Skoda automotive plants in the Czech Republic.

In addition, many companies have announced plans to produce their products in Eastern European plants, where labor is relatively cheap. GM, Ford, Suzuki, and Mazda already have plants operating there, as do Coca-Cola and ABB (the Swedish-Swiss maker of heavy industrial equipment and locomotives). McDonald's much-publicized restaurant in Moscow is expected to be just the tip of the iceburger.

Making and introducing new products to these new markets is also on the agenda for a number of Western firms. Making their presence known may be a problem, though. Western businesses have a wealth of knowledge about marketing to share with the partners in joint ventures, but one of the primary marketing tools—advertising—poses problems. Dozens of advertising agencies have set up offices in the old Eastern Bloc, but most are simply gathering information for their clients and preparing simple, straightforward print ads. Apparently, communist governments' use of television and radio to blast propaganda has led many Eastern Europeans to associate these media with lies—naturally, an association most businesses wish to avoid.

Digital Equipment Corporation (DEC) was pleasantly surprised to find that it's already well known in Eastern Europe, albeit for the wrong reasons. Over the years, the governments of the Soviet Republics came to know and prize DEC's VAX minicomputers. (In fact, the theft problem was so widespread that an unidentified DEC engineer arranged for the silicon chip at the heart of these computers to include a microscopic message in the Cyrillic alphabet: "VAX. For Those Who Care Enough To Steal the Very Best.") Thus, DEC has a built-in customer base of people who not only know and like VAX computers, but who are also trained in the software that runs these machines. As a result, since the end of communist rule in Eastern Europe, DEC has entered into a number of joint ventures there—including some with former DEC-clone makers.

What lies ahead in Eastern Europe? It's too soon to tell. But given the prospect of profits to be made, both history and capitalist theory agree that someone, somehow, will get businesses running there.

CASE QUESTIONS
1. Which of the four activities of the managerial process do you think will be hardest for Eastern Europeans to implement? Why?
2. If you were the general manager of a Hungarian shoe manufacturer, what goals would you set for the firm in the short run? In the long run?
3. Pick a large Canadian firm and explain how and why it might choose to operate in the former Soviet Union.
4. Given the problems facing Eastern Europe—inflation, unemployment; political, religious, and ethnic strife; and lack of management, to name a few—would you expect to characterize these nations as communist, socialist, or capitalist five years from now? Why?

Experiential Exercise:
Reorganizing for More Efficient Growth

OBJECTIVE

To help students see how changes in a company's business operations may require changes in its organizational structure.

TIME REQUIRED

45 minutes
  Step 1: Individual activity (to be completed before class)
  Step 2: Small-group activity (25 minutes)
  Step 3: Class discussion (20 minutes)

PROCEDURE

Step 1: Read the following case regarding the firm of T. Wilder Industries.

T. Wilder Industries was started twenty years ago with a mission of producing and selling moderately priced clothing for large and tall women. Initially, such clothing was the only product T. Wilder made. Also, like most clothing companies at the time, it sold its products through department and specialty stores. Then, 15 years ago, T. Wilder branched out and began making clothing for big and tall men. Ten years ago, the firm decided to offer a full range of sizes, from the smallest women's petites to the largest men's portly longs. Five years ago, the firm added a line of children's clothing. This year, the company opened a series of company-owned stores to sell its goods directly to the public.

   As the organization grew, Thea Wilder, founder and chief executive officer of T. Wilder Industries, simply added new vice-presidents to the organizational structure she started with. Because all vice-presidents (see list on facing page) report directly to her, however, Wilder now finds this structure unwieldy. Not only must she directly manage too many people, but she is also forced to make far too many decisions. This problem will escalate if, as management plans, the company begins to manufacture and sell accessories for men and women five years from now.

How Should T. Wilder Industries Be Organized?

Step 2: The instructor will divide the class into small groups. Each group is to
  a. Decide on a new organizational structure for T. Wilder Industries.
  b. Develop a new organization chart for the firm.
  c. Identify each position as line or staff.
  d. Write a new mission statement for T. Wilder Industries.

Step 3: One member of each small group will present the group's proposal for reorganization to the class.

QUESTIONS FOR DISCUSSION

1. Which individuals would you expect to oppose your proposed reorganization most strongly and why?
2. How would your proposed reorganization work if T. Wilder Industries were to enter the home draperies market ten years hence? What if it entered the consumer electronics market (televisions, VCRs, etc.) instead?

VICE-PRESIDENTS AND THEIR PERSONNEL

Vice-Presidents (Senior Mgmt.)	Middle Management	First-Line Mgmt./ Technicians	Others
Big & Tall Women's Design		2 designers	1 clerical
Big & Tall Women's Sales and Marketing	1 sales manager 1 marketing mgr.	30 sales reps 3 marketers	8 clerical
Big & Tall Women's Manufacturing		3 supervisors 2 schedulers	300 line 3 clerical
Big & Tall Men's Design		1 designer	1 clerical
Big & Tall Men's Sales and Marketing	1 sales manager 1 marketing mgr.	25 sales reps 3 marketers	6 clerical
Big & Tall Men's Manufacturing		2 supervisors 1 scheduler	200 line 2 clerical
Petite Women's Design		1 designer	1 clerical
Petite Women's Sales and Marketing	1 sales manager 1 marketing mgr.	15 sales reps 2 marketers	4 clerical
Petite Women's Manufacturing		2 supervisors 1 scheduler	150 line 2 clerical
Regular Women's Design		3 designers	2 clerical
Regular Women's Sales and Marketing	1 sales manager 1 marketing mgr.	40 sales reps 5 marketers	9 clerical
Regular Women's Manufacturing		5 supervisors 3 schedulers	450 line 4 clerical
Regular Men's Design		2 designers	2 clerical
Regular Men's Sales and Marketing	1 sales manager 1 marketing mgr.	30 sales reps 3 marketers	6 clerical
Regular Men's Manufacturing		3 supervisors 2 schedulers	300 line 3 clerical
Children's Design		1 designer	1 clerical
Children's Sales and Marketing	1 sales manager 1 marketing mgr.	25 sales reps 2 marketers	5 clerical
Children's Manufacturing		2 supervisors 1 scheduler	200 line workers
Retail Stores	4 district mgrs.	38 store mgrs.	175 clerks 5 clerical
Finance	2 supervisors	4 accountants	7 clerks
Computer Services		2 programmers/ analysts	20 order entry
Personnel		4 recruiters	5 clerical
Warehousing		5 supervisors	50 workers

CAREERS IN BUSINESS
Reality Check

Combined with your studies in the classroom, real-world experience can both provide you with an excellent grounding for your working years and guide you in selecting the path that's right for you. Indeed, some professions—including medicine and public accounting—require "hands-on" training before an individual can be licensed.

But even if your chosen (or contemplated) occupation doesn't require practical experience, you are well advised to get some before seeking your first job. There are many ways in which you can gain experience. Some of your options include part-time work, volunteer work, internships, cooperative education, and getting to know people in your field (networking).

PART-TIME AND VOLUNTEER WORK

Many students have to work during the school year to make ends meet. Many others have the financial resources that allow them not to work. But the fact that you don't have to work doesn't mean that you *can't* work. Getting a part-time job during the school year and/or working summers is a great way to gain insights into different occupations.

The key is to find work now that is related to the work you think you'd like to do in the future. For example, if you think you might want to work in retailing, consider getting a part-time job in a local clothing, music, or sporting goods store. If you think you might want to be a lawyer, apply for a clerical job in a law office. If you think banking might be your forte, apply for a part-time job in a local bank. Even if you are doing only a routine clerical job, you will still gain some appreciation for what the people in that line of work do. If you are interested in a career in international business, take advantage of the summers to broaden your international horizons.

Volunteer work is another useful avenue for learning about different career paths. If you think the medical profession is your calling, volunteer at a local hospital. Serving as a teacher's aide in a local high school can help you gain insights into the teaching profession. Churches, charities, and museums also depend on volunteer assistance and can provide valuable career insights now and prepare you for a full-time, paid career in the future. For example, one woman who joined a neighborhood association to help "sell" her partly restored neighborhood to potential buyers found herself with multiple job offers to sell real estate—and the skills to earn a good living.

During the summer, if you need a paying job and can't find one in your chosen field, you might want to consider taking two jobs instead of one. That is, accept a part-time paying job outside your area of interest, but then put in unpaid time at a nonprofit or for-profit organization in your chosen field.

Besides helping you learn more about potential careers, part-time and volunteer work while you are in school will send a message to prospective employers later that you are industrious, inquisitive, and highly motivated. All of these traits are considered assets in potential employees. Moreover, learning to balance work and school will help you focus your energies, plan your time, and prioritize different tasks.

INTERNSHIPS

One special form of work/study deserves special mention: the internship. An internship is essentially a temporary full-time position in an organization. Most internships are set up for the summer months. The intern spends the summer working on special project, as a member of a team, or as an assistant to a manager in the organization. For example, an accountant might work as an intern in an accounting firm, a finance student might work as an intern in a bank, and a restaurant management intern might work as an intern in a food services firm. Although some small firms offer internships, most internships are set up at large firms.

Internships come in a variety of forms. Some are set up by schools, while others are lined up by students, either on their own or with the help of the campus placement office. Some firms pay interns for their services. Others offer only the chance to learn.

If your school offers an internship program, visit the appropriate office and find out what's involved. If your school does not offer an internship program, contact firms in the appropriate industry and offer your services. Be sure to spell out what you are interested in learning and stress that the organization will receive something for its efforts (your work), all while contributing to your education.

Most organizations want to interview internship candidates before making their decision. During the interview, don't forget to find out as much about the organization and what you will be doing as an intern as you possibly can. Among the most important things to learn are:

■ *Whom* will you work with? Will you spend much time working and interacting with other interns? Will you have any interactions with managers other than those to whom you will be assigned?

■ *What* will your duties be? Will you be working on an ongoing project or a special project? What skills will you develop during the internship? What will be the outcome of your work? Will it be a report? A presentation to the managers?

■ *Where* (in what city) will you be working? Will you be working in an office, a factory, a sales office? Will you be working in a single department or in several departments?

■ *How* will you be compensated? Will you receive a formal evaluation at the end of the internship? Will you be paid? If so, how much? Will any of your expenses be paid? (This is an especially important consideration if you will incur significant commuting expenses.) Will you receive any university or college credits for your internship? Will the organization consider hiring you later if you do a good job during your internship?

COOPERATIVE EDUCATION

Some colleges—and businesses—are so committed to the importance of internship that they have formalized it as an ongoing cooperative education program. In such programs, students complete some core courses, then alternate between semesters of full-time study and semesters of full-time work.

NETWORKING

Finally, you can get another perspective on—and possibly even a boost up into—a career path by networking, or making contacts with people who might be influential in helping you get a position later. You can establish such contacts in a variety of ways. Start by joining clubs or associations on campus like the Marketing Club or the Management Society. Also consider joining professional associations. Attend all local meetings of whatever associations you join.

Career fairs, which are usually sponsored by student organizations, also present excellent opportunities. At these fairs, companies send recruiters to campus to meet students and explain what their organizations do. Meeting such people can be of considerable help later. Attending campus speeches and talks by visitors from the business community is also a good way to meet people.

If you work part-time, volunteer, and/or land an internship, everyone you meet in that organization should become a part of your network. Even if your bosses during your internship cannot offer you a job later, they will pass your name on to their contacts if you have done a good job for them. As you seek contacts for your network, don't overlook your own classmates, who may be able to introduce you to others in your field. You may end up working with them later on down the line!

Video Case II-I

EDGAR BRONFMAN JR.*

When Edgar Bronfman Jr. took over the reins as the new chief executive officer of Seagram's, he faced a major executive challenge. The company had been started by Edgar's grandfather, Sam Bronfman, in the 1920s in Montreal. It was taken over by Edgar's father, Edgar Sr., and his Uncle Charles, who together had run the company until Edgar Jr.'s June 1, 1994 appointment as the company's chief executive officer.

Seagram's is a large Montreal-based multinational corporation. The company is best known for its production and marketing of such premium liquor brands as Chivas Regal and Martell Cognac, which it markets in over 150 countries worldwide. In addition to its distilling operations Seagrams is also involved in the manufacturing of such well known consumer products as Tropicana orange juice.

Seagram's has grown to its current size of $11 billion in assets by utilizing both internal development and external acquisition strategies. Two recent acquisitions included the company's decision to commit to a 24.3 percent share of the Canadian operations of the U.S. chemical giant du Pont, as well as a 15 percent share of the New York-based communications conglomerate Time-Warner. Even more recently, the company has sold its interest in both these companies and has invested in MCA, the entertainment company.

The company's operations are also effectively diversified across a range of different national markets with approximately 80 percent of annual revenues coming from activities outside the North American marketplace. One example of the firm's aggressive international orientation is its recent initiative in the Peoples' Republic of China. Only three years ago the company had no sales in China; as of June 1994 approximately 15 percent of the firm's cognac sales came from mainland China alone.

Edgar Bronfman Jr.'s early career history was atypical of the traditional corporate executive. He had opted to leave the family fold at age 15 to seek opportunities in the entertainment industry, where he eventually worked with such performers as Jack Nicholson and Dionne Warwick. In his late 20s he returned to the family business, where he has since been involved in a variety of managerial assignments. There are a number of similarities and differences between Edgar Jr. and the man he succeeded, his father Edgar Sr. Both men are characterized by a reliance on gut instinct and a willingness to take risks. However, compared to his father, the younger Bronfman is more oriented to the people issues of the operation.

Study questions

1. What skills must every manager possess? How does the need for these skills vary according to the manager's level in the company? What does this suggest concerning the skills that Edgar Bronfman will need to possess as Seagram's CEO?
2. Chapter 5 describes several different management styles. Describe each of these styles in your own words. Which of these best describes Edgar Bronfman's management style?
3. What are the differences between corporate-, business-, and functional-level strategy? Which of these three types of strategy should Edgar Bronfman be most concerned with? Which should he be least concerned with? Why?
4. What are the basic strategic options that a business can consider pursuing? Which of these options has Seagram's attempted?

---

* This case is based on the *Venture* episode first broadcast on June 19, 1994.

houghts of bankruptcy, scandal and personal disaster raced through Anton Rabie's mind as he faced the prospect that loomed before him. The buying office of the U.S. retail giant, K mart, appeared to be having second thoughts about placing an order with Anton's fledging manufacturing company. The product Anton's company hoped to sell K mart was a novelty product called Earth Buddy that Anton, together with four of his closest friends, had developed for the retail fad market.

The Earth Buddy was manufactured by stuffing sawdust and grass seed inside a nylon stocking. The stocking was then decorated with two eyes, glasses, a nose and mouth and placed in a colorful cardboard box. After purchasing an Earth Buddy the customer watered it and then watched as it sprouted its grassy toupee in the ensuing weeks.

To date Anton and his four business cohorts had sold thousands of Earth Buddies to several of the largest retail operations in Canada, including Zellers. Tremendous demand for the product had netted the company nearly $400 000 profit in only four short months of operation.

With this healthy momentum behind them, Anton and company had set their collective sights on even bigger targets south of border in the huge U.S. market. Combining persistence with panache, he had recently enticed K mart U.S. to consider placing an order for 500 000 units. This order was several times larger than anything the company had handled to date.

The K mart order was not without its problems, however. Foremost was K mart's insistence on the order's timely delivery. This was a problem because of the comparatively small-scale runs the company was used to. Producing half a million buddies was almost inconceivable. Further complicating the demand for timely delivery was K mart's unwillingness to make a firm written commitment to the order. This resulted in Anton's company having to begin the manufacture of the order on speculation that the written purchase order would be forthcoming.

Faced with these two uncertainties Anton and his friends decided to risk all and began manufacturing hundreds of thousands of Earth Buddies in the hope that the K mart order would actually materialize. In order to realize their objective of 500 000 units, the company needed to produce about 16 000 units each day. This production objective required Michelle and Ben, the two manufacturing managers, to hire and train an additional 140 employees.

In the early weeks of manufacturing the order another problem had surfaced: raw material stockouts. Secure, sufficient, and balanced supplies of each of the key raw inputs were not always on hand. At one point, a shortage of sawdust had resulted in most of the company's production employees having to be sent home early and in a shortfall of several thousand finished buddies.

However, the worst problem associated with the K mart order was its perpetual uncertainty. While Anton had been assured of a purchase order from the U.S. giant, he still had not received written confirmation of K mart's commitment to the sawdust-based pals. With the majority of the order now complete, Anton felt both relieved and worried. What if the K mart order fell through? Fresh out of business school, he had only limited experience in dealing with giant corporations and the giant orders they placed. What, if anything, could he do to secure the K mart order?

Study questions

1. What are the four functions of management? How are these functions carried out differently in a small business?
2. Why, according to Table 7.4 do small businesses fail? Which of these appears to be most relevant to the manufacturers of Earth Buddy?
3. How are strategic plans formulated? How effectively have Anton and his friends formulated their company's strategy?
4. What are the different growth stages a small business goes through? What stage would you place Anton's company in? In terms of this model, what do you think are the major growth challenges that Anton and his friends will encounter within the next five years?

* This case is based on the *Venture* episode first broadcast on December 11, 1994.

WHAT Is
SELF-ESTEEM

BELIEF IN SELF
PRIDE IN SELF
SELF IMAGE

Part Three

Part Three

Managing Human Resources

You will read about several timely and complex human resource management issues in the opening cases of the chapters in this section—restructuring and relocating Crown Life Insurance Company, attempts to achieve labor peace at MacMillan Bloedel, and working toward labor-management cooperation at various companies in Canada. In the difficult circumstances in which Canadian business firms have found themselves in the 1990s, it is even more important that the firm's human resources be managed effectively.

Part Three, Managing Human Resources, provides an overview of the relationship between managers and their employees, including managers' attitudes, the activities of managers responsible for human resource management, the special relationship between management and labor unions, and the role of the government in labor-management issues.

■ We begin in **Chapter 8, Planning for and Developing Human Resources,** by exploring the activities of assessing employee needs and training, promoting, and compensating employees.

■ Then, in **Chapter 9, Motivating, Satisfying and Leading Employees,** we examine the reasons why firms should establish good relations with their employees and how managers' attempts to maintain productivity can affect their relations with employees.

■ Finally, in **Chapter 10, Dealing With Organized Labor,** we look at the development of the union movement in Canada, why and how workers organize, and how government legislation has affected workers' rights and abilities to organize.

8

Planning for and Developing Human Resources

LEARNING OBJECTIVES

After studying this chapter, you will be able to

■ Define human resource management and explain why businesses must consider job-relatedness criteria when managing human resources.

■ Discuss how managers plan for human resources.

■ Identify the steps involved in staffing a company.

■ Describe ways in which managers can develop workers' skills and deal with workers who do not perform well.

■ Explain the importance of wages and salaries, incentives, and benefits programs in attracting and keeping skilled workers.

■ Describe how laws regarding employment equity, pay equity, and worker safety affect human resource management.

OPENING CASE

Restructuring in a Big Way

In 1989, senior managers at Crown Life Insurance Co. began considering moving to a smaller center as part of a drive to cut operating costs. A southern Ontario site had been considered most likely, but when two Regina businessmen offered to inject $250 million into the company if it would move to Saskatchewan, their offer was accepted.

The company's first priority was to maintain "business as normal" while it transferred staff, hired new people, and put up a building in Regina. The move took two years in total, and there were dramatic changes in the work force. Of the 1300 people who worked in Toronto, only 300 took up the offer to go west. The company hired an additional 700 people locally in Regina or from other centers in Canada, the U.S. and Europe.

Most of the new people hired in Regina were well-educated, but many had little or no experience in the insurance industry. The average age of the company's workforce dropped, from the mid-30s in Toronto to the mid-20s in Regina. One underwriter who moved from the Toronto office says the new workers are more enthusiastic about their work.

Major changes also occurred in internal company operations. During the move, top management discovered that many work processes had never been properly documented, so employees had to prepare detailed descriptions of what was involved in their jobs. While documenting work processes, it was determined that there could be greater incentive for workers to be customer oriented, so ways of dealing with customers were totally reviewed. Statements of customer accounts are now issued by a production department, and customer service representatives work exclusively with clients. Travel claims and accounts payable activity has also been streamlined to cut costs and increase service levels.

What has been the result of the move? The company is handling the same amount of business as before, but with 20 percent fewer employees. And top management believes that even more work can be handled without adding additional people as technology and systems are enhanced. Annual operating costs are $25 million lower than they were before the company moved, and the company is now much

more flexible. Workers do not have a preconceived notion of how much work they should do in a day, nor do they resist new ideas because of the old "we've always done it that way" excuse. Human resources vice-president Pamela McIntyre observes that she doesn't hear people in the company say things like "we've always done it that way." That's because they've only been doing it that way for a short time.

The challenge facing the company now is to build on the low-cost structure it has created. President Brian Johnson wants the company to be among Canada's top five insurance companies in terms of new business that is generated. Part of the plan to achieve the goal is to focus even more closely on the customer, providing products that can be tailored to fit exactly the requirements of the individual. While the primary sales distribution network remains the agent/broker network, the company also uses other methods of distribution. These include strategic alliances with other organizations, such as banks and property and casualty insurers, financial centres, worksite marketing and direct marketing. ◆

When Crown Life Insurance moved its operations halfway across Canada, it had to spend considerable time recruiting, hiring, and training new employees. In this chapter, we consider the formal systems that companies use to develop and maintain an effective work force. These systems focus on defining the jobs that need to be done; ensuring that appropriate workers are hired and oriented to their new jobs; training, appraising, and compensating employees; and providing appropriate human resource services to employees.

Foundations of Human Resource Management

Human resource management involves developing, administering, and evaluating programs to acquire and enhance the quality and performance of people in a business. Human resource specialists—sometimes called personnel managers—are employed by all but the smallest firms. They help plan for future personnel needs. They recruit, train, and develop employees. And they set up employee evaluation, compensation, and benefits programs.

But in fact all managers are personnel managers. Managers of production, accounting, finance, and marketing departments choose prospective employees, train new workers, and evaluate employee performance. As you will see in this section, all managers must be aware of the basis of good human resource management—job-relatedness and employee-job matching.

Job-Relatedness and Employee-Job Matching

According to the principle of **job-relatedness**, all personnel decisions, policies, and programs should be based on the requirements of a position. That is, all criteria used to hire, evaluate, promote, and reward people must be tied directly to the job they perform. For example, a policy that all secretaries be young women would not be job-related since neither youth nor femaleness is essential in performing secretarial work. Such a policy represents poor human resource management because the company loses the chance to hire more experienced help and to consider skilled men for the position. On the other hand, a policy of hiring only young women to model teenage girls' clothing would be job-related and would thus reflect sound human resource management.

Fundamental to the concept of job-relatedness—and to human resource management in general—is the idea of matching the right person to the right job. The direct result of good human resource management is the close match of people, skills, interests, and temperaments with the requirements of their jobs. When people are well matched to their jobs, the company benefits from high rates of employee performance and satisfaction, high retention of effective people, and low absenteeism. All personnel activities relate in some fashion to the employee-job match. Job matching may not be easy, as shown in the box "Mismatch in Jobs and Skills."

Planning for Human Resources

Just as planning for financial, plant, and equipment needs is important, so too is planning for personnel needs. As Figure 8.1 shows, such planning involves two types of activities by managers—job analysis and forecasting.

Job Analysis

Job analysis is the detailed study of the specific duties required for a particular job and the human qualities required to perform that job. For simple, repetitive jobs, managers might ask workers to create a checklist of all the duties they perform and the importance of each of those duties for the job. In analyzing more complex jobs, managers might combine checklists with interviews of job holders to determine their exact duties. Managers might also observe workers to record the duties they perform.

Using the job analysis, human resource managers can develop **job descriptions**. A job description outlines the objectives, responsibilities, and

human resource management
The development, administration, and evaluation of programs to acquire and enhance the quality and performance of people in a business.

job-relatedness
The principle that all personnel decisions, policies, and programs should be based on the requirements of a position.

job analysis
A detailed study of the specific duties in a particular job and the human qualities required for that job.

job description
The objectives, responsibilities, and key tasks of a job; the conditions under which it will be done; its relationship to other positions; and the skills needed to perform it.

The Canadian Business Scene

MISMATCH IN JOBS AND SKILLS

There is a "mismatch" problem in Canada—people have skills the market no longer wants, and companies have needs that unemployed people cannot satisfy. The Canadian Labour Market and Productivity Centre estimates that 22 percent of the unemployed have skills that didn't match their former employers' needs. Interestingly, this figure is down from the 64 percent estimate in 1989. However, during the 1990s, the matching problem is likely to worsen again as companies become ever more demanding in what they want in employees.

The mismatch problem is obvious in a field like information technology. In an industry that relies almost solely on human brainpower and creativity, companies are in desperate need of computer programmers, software developers, and computer scientists. Canadian universities graduated one-third *fewer* computer scientists in 1990 than they did in 1986. Yet some graduates had difficulty finding employment because they were not trained to deal with computer networks, servers, workstations, and other new developments. During this same period, university enrollment increased 12 percent, with the number of students studying history increasing 59 percent, and sociology 31 percent. Neither of these areas are promising in terms of available jobs.

Why have students not become interested in information technology? Attitudes and perceptions probably play a negative role. Computer experts are often portrayed as socially inept individuals who are "nerds" or "geeks." There is still something in Canadians that allows people to dismiss careers in technology as uninteresting.

But this is only part of the reason that a mismatch problem exists. There is also a growing recognition that we must change the way people are trained. Education should be a lifetime experience, not merely something that ends when a person graduates from some school. Pressure to change and adapt comes from the workplace as companies adopt new technologies to deliver new services. Employees who were hired in the 1960s or 1970s may not want to adapt to the new realities.

Honeywell Ltd. is just one firm that has had to come to grips with some unpleasant new realities. Its Toronto plant, which makes instrumentation for heating and cooling equipment, found that customers were demanding that the firm be certified under the ISO 9000 international quality program. This meant that Honeywell would have to introduce just-in-time inventory, total quality management, and self-directed work teams. But when the company looked at its work force, it found that only half had English as their first language, and that many had not finished high school.

Before the workers could cope with the new demands being imposed on the company, they needed to be trained. This gradually evolved into a "learning for life" program, which involved English, math, and computer courses. Employees were also trained in production and inventory management, total quality, and communication skills. Part of the training was provided at Humber College in Toronto. Each year, Humber sells about $30 million worth of education to private sector firms like Kodak Canada and John Labatt Ltd.

The mismatch problem will be solved when people on the job market have a total mix of characteristics—analytic abilities, practical skills, and flexibility—to encompass the full range of what companies are looking for. A recent Conference Board of Canada study asked employers what they were looking for in employees. Some of the things—teamwork, ability to think, ability to communicate—can be taught in school. But others—positive attitudes, responsibility, and adaptability—are more difficult to develop in educational programs.

One firm has taken advantage of this mismatch. Atlantic Computer Institute was founded on the idea that students often come out of universities over-educated and under-trained. The Institute trains them in computer technology in an intensive 11-month program. Graduates of the Institute find jobs in software writing, local-area network support, and writing technical manuals.

Another way to cope with potential mismatches is a co-op program. Under this system, university students alternate between taking classes and working for a business firm. The University of Victoria, for example, operates a year-round schedule, alternating "job semesters" with traditional classes. When students graduate, they are often hired by the firm they worked for during the co-op program.

job specification

The specific skills, education, and experience needed to perform a job.

key tasks in a job. It also describes the conditions under which the job will be done, the relationship of the job to other positions, and the skills needed to do the job. The skills, education, and experience necessary to fill a position make up the **job specification**.

Job analysis and the resulting job descriptions and specifications are the foundations of effective human resource management. They serve as tools

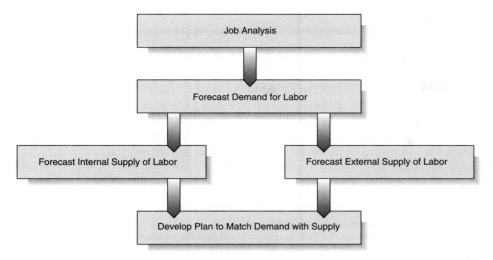

Figure 8.1
Planning for human resources.

in hiring personnel for specific positions, as guides in establishing training programs, and as sources of comparison in setting wages. But most important, by defining job requirements objectively, they allow managers to make personnel decisions in keeping with the principles of job-relatedness.

Forecasting

Once they have analyzed the nature of their needs, managers must forecast their needs. Managers need to forecast both their demand for employees of different types and the likely supply of such employees in the short term (less than one year), intermediate term (one to five years), and long term (over five years). Only then can they formulate specific strategies for responding to any potential employee surplus or shortage. As in any forecast, however, the manager's true purpose is to minimize major surprises, not to predict future needs exactly.

In forecasting *demand*, managers must take into account their businesses' plans for growth (if any). They must also figure in the normal rate of turnover and the number of older employees nearing retirement, among other factors. In forecasting *supply*, managers must consider the complexity of the job and which current employees could be promoted to fill higher positions. But they must also predict whether the labor market for a particular job will be in a state of surplus or shortage.

Managing a forecasted need for fewer employees also requires careful consideration. Although some firms simply lay off employees during slow periods, the corporate culture of other companies prohibits or limits such behavior. For example, when IBM needed to reduce its work force in the late 1980s, the firm used early retirement incentives and retraining programs instead of layoffs. Some of its cutbacks in the 1990s, however, have involved layoffs and outright terminations.

In an attempt to avoid layoffs, business firms are increasingly hiring contract workers to complete specific projects rather than hiring traditional full-time workers. When the project is over, the contract worker moves on to complete another contract at a different firm.

Staffing the Organization

Once managers have decided what positions they need to fill, they must find and hire individuals who meet the job requirements. Staffing of the corporation is one of the most complex and important aspects of good human resource management. In this section, we will consider how businesses fill positions from both outside and inside the organization. Sometimes personnel must be recruited and chosen from the outside. As well, decisions must be made about employee promotions to fill vacancies within the organization.

TABLE 8.1 The Top Ten Employers in Canada, 1994 (ranked by number of employees)	
Company	**Number of Employees**
1. BCE Inc.	116 000
2. George Weston Ltd.	77 100
3. Imasco Ltd.	65 800
4. Canada Post Corp.	62 878
5. McDonald's Restaurants of Canada	60 000
6. Hudson's Bay Co.	56 500
7. Semi-Tech Corp.	50 000
8. The Thomson Corp.	48 600
9. Laidlaw Inc.	40 000
10. Sears Canada Inc.	39 310

External Staffing

A new firm has little choice but to acquire staff from outside itself. Established firms may also turn to the outside to fill positions for which there are no good internal candidates, to accommodate growth, or as a way to bring in fresh ideas. Such external staffing can be divided into two stages: recruitment and selection.

recruitment

The phase in the staffing of a company in which the firm seeks to develop a pool of interested, qualified applicants for a position.

Recruitment.   In the first step, the company needs to develop a pool of applicants who are both interested in and qualified for the open positions. The purpose of **recruitment** is to generate a large number of potential employees. Thus, successful recruitment focuses only on the most basic qualifications of a job.

For example, recruitment ads for a financial analyst might require applicants to hold an MBA degree with an emphasis on finance. But requiring a degree from a particular school will unnecessarily restrict the number of applicants. Recruitment specifications should always be clearly job-related.

Companies have many options in recruiting employees, depending in part on the nature of the job. As we will discuss in more detail later in this chapter, current employees may be recruited to fill openings within the firm. In seeking outside applicants, businesses may visit high schools, vocational schools, colleges, and universities. In some cases, labor agreements may specify that new employees be found using the labor union's membership rolls. Of course, many companies advertise in newspapers or trade publications or seek the help of public and private employment agencies. Word of mouth and personal recommendations are often factors in the hiring of top

An in-depth interview with a prospective employee is often part of the recruiting process, particularly for managerial jobs.

management personnel. Even unsolicited letters and resumes from job seekers can produce the right person for a job.

When recruiting, firms must be careful not to violate anti-discrimination laws. The key federal anti-discrimination legislation is the ***Canadian Human Rights Act*** of 1977. The goal of this act is to ensure that any individual who wishes to obtain a job has an equal opportunity to compete for it. The act applies to all federal agencies, federal Crown corporations, any employee of the federal government, and business firms that do business interprovincially. Thus, it applies to such firms as the Bank of Montreal, Air Canada, Telecom Canada, Canadian National Railways, and many other public and private sector organizations that operate across Canada. Even with such wide application, the act affects only about 10 percent of Canadian workers; the rest are covered under provincial human rights acts.

The *Canadian Human Rights Act* prohibits a wide variety of practices in recruiting, selecting, promoting, and dismissing personnel. The *Act* specifically prohibits discrimination on the basis of age, race and color, national and ethnic origin, physical handicap, religion, gender, marital status, or prison record (if pardoned). Some exceptions to these blanket prohibitions are permitted. Discrimination cannot be charged if a blind person is refused a position as a train engineer, bus driver, or crane operator. Likewise, a firm cannot be charged with discrimination if it does not hire a deaf person as a telephone operator or as an audio engineer.

These situations are clear-cut, but many others are not. For example, is it discriminatory to refuse women employment in a job that routinely requires carrying objects with a mass of more than 50 kilograms? Ambiguities in determining whether discrimination has occurred are sometimes circumvented by using the concept of "**bona fide occupational requirement**."

Canadian Human Rights Act
Ensures that any individual who wishes to obtain a job has an equal opportunity to apply for it.

bona fide occupational requirement
When an employer may choose one applicant over another based on overriding characteristics of the job.

An employer may choose one person over another based on overriding characteristics of the job in question. If a fitness center wants to hire only women to supervise its women's locker room and sauna, it can do so without being discriminatory because it established a bona fide occupational requirement.

Even after referring to bona fide occupational requirements, other uncertainties remain. Consider three cases: Would an advertising agency be discriminating if it advertised for a male model about 60 years old for an advertisement that is to appeal to older men? Would a business firm be discriminating if it refused to hire someone as a receptionist because the applicant was overweight? Would a bank be discriminating because it refused to hire an applicant whom the human resources manager considered would not fit in because of the person's appearance?

We might speculate that the advertising agency is not discriminating, the business firm might or might not be discriminating, and the bank could probably be accused of discrimination, but we can't be sure. The human rights legislation cannot specify all possible situations; many uncertainties remain over what the law considers discriminatory and what it considers acceptable. Nevertheless, the spirit of the legislation is clear, and managers must try to abide by it.

Enforcement of the federal act is carried out by the Canadian Human Rights Commission. The commission can either respond to complaints from individuals who believe they have been discriminated against, or launch an investigation on its own if it has reason to believe that discrimination has occurred. During an investigation, data are gathered about the alleged discriminatory behavior and, if the claim of discrimination is substantiated, the offending organization or individual may be ordered to compensate the victim.

Each province has also enacted human rights legislation to regulate organizations and businesses operating in that province. These provincial regulations are similar in spirit to the federal legislation, with many minor variations from province to province. All provinces prohibit discrimination on the basis of race, national or ethnic origin, color, religion, sex, and marital status, but some do not address such issues as physical handicaps, criminal record, or age. Provincial human rights commissions enforce provincial legislation.

Employment Equity Act of 1986

Federal legislation that designates four groups as employment disadvantaged—women, visible minorities, aboriginal people, and people with disabilities.

The ***Employment Equity Act of 1986*** addresses the issue of discrimination in employment by designating four groups as employment disadvantaged—women, visible minorities, aboriginal people, and people with disabilities. Companies covered by the *Act* are required to publish statistics on their employment of people in these four groups.

The Bank of Montreal recently became the first company outside the U.S. to win a prestigious award for promoting women's careers. Women represented over half of executive level promotions at the bank in 1993. The Bank of Montreal has introduced initiatives such as flexible working hours, a mentoring program, a national career information network, and a gender awareness workshop series.[1]

Companies are increasingly making provisions for disabled employees. At Rogers Cablevision, a division of Rogers Communications Inc., a large workplace area was completely redesigned to accommodate workers who were either visually disabled or in wheelchairs. Special equipment was also installed—a large print computer for workers with partial sight, and a device which allows blind workers to read printed materials.[2]

selection

The process of sorting through a pool of candidates to choose the best one for a job.

Selection.   Once a pool of applicants has been identified, managers must sort through those individuals and select the best candidate for the job. **Selection** is by no means an exact science, since it is difficult to predict any given individual's behaviors and attitudes. Nevertheless, it is an important process. Hiring the wrong employee is costly to the firm and is unfair to that individual.

To reduce the element of uncertainty, personnel experts and other managers use a variety of selection techniques. The most common of these methods, as shown in Figure 8.2, are applications and resumes, screening interviews, ability and aptitude tests, reference checks, on-site interviews, and medical, drug, and polygraph tests. Each organization develops its own mix of selection techniques and may use them in any order.

The application form, used for almost all lower-level jobs, asks for information about the applicant such as background, experience, and education. A resume is a prepared statement of the applicant's qualifications and career goals, and is commonly used by people seeking managerial or professional positions.

In many cases, companies receive several applications or resumes for a job opening. Human resource personnel must narrow the field, first on the basis of the applications and then by holding screening interviews. In these ways, clearly unqualified individuals are weeded out, especially walk-in applicants for low-level jobs who simply do not have the required job skills. Line managers (those with hiring authority) then interview qualified applicants at greater depth. Other people in the hiring manager's department may also interview job candidates. In some companies, potential subordinates of the prospective employee are included in the interview process.

During both types of interviews, the interviewer asks questions about the applicant's background and qualifications. The interviewer must be careful to address only job-related issues. For example, a female applicant cannot be asked whether she plans to marry or have a family. Such questions can further sex discrimination. In addition to asking questions, interviewers also provide information about the company and answer any questions applicants may have.

For some positions, ability or aptitude tests may be part of the initial screening process.[3] When Toyota hired workers for its Cambridge, Ontario,

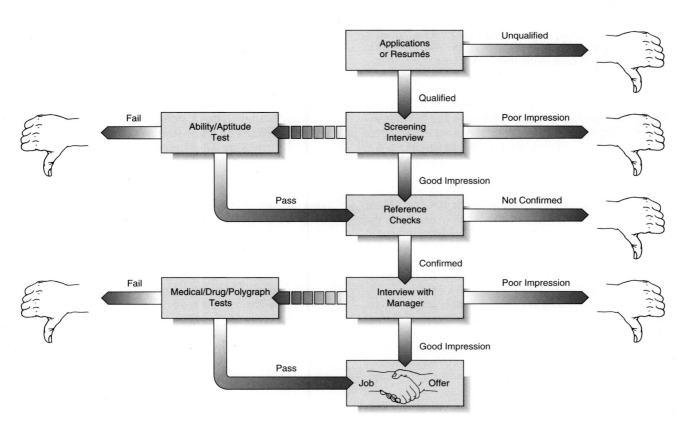

Figure 8.2
General steps in the selection process.

plant applicants were put through a series of tests to determine their math, verbal, and communication skills and their ability to work on a team. Even though most of the workers hired had never worked for an automobile firm before, they are now producing the highest-rated car in North America.[4] A new way to screen job applicants is described in the box "Screen Test."

Regardless of the type of test used, it must meet two conditions. First, the test must be job-related. A company cannot, for example, ask an applicant for a secretarial job to take a test on operating a forklift. It is clearly appropriate, however, to ask the person to take a typing test. The second requirement of an employment test is that it must be a valid predictor of performance. That is, there must be evidence that people who score well on the test are more likely to perform well in the job than are people who score poorly on the test. A test used for selection must not serve as a basis for discrimination against anyone for reasons unrelated to the job.

Another step used in employee selection is to check references. Reference checks often provide little useful information about an applicant's personality

The Canadian Business Scene

SCREEN TEST

Finding, screening, and hiring new employees can be a big expense for companies. It can cost $5000–$10 000 to hire a clerical person, and much more to hire a top manager. In this cost-conscious era, companies are always ready to consider alternatives to the traditional hiring techniques.

One such promising new technique is video assessment. Potential new hires view videos that show a series of realistic work situations (portrayed by actors). For example, one scenario shows an assistant to a department manager who is trying to convince the supervisor of the word-processing pool to give his job top priority because the boss wants some last-minute changes made in a report. The supervisor refuses and the assistant goes back to the boss asking him to intercede. At the end of each situation the viewers choose one of four courses of action to resolve the problem shown in the video. The test administrator then uses the computer to score candidate choices (much like a university or college instructor would grade student exams).

Video assessment is fast, reliable, cheap, and versatile. It also lets managers screen more extensively for jobs at the lower levels in the organization. Improving selection at entry level jobs should mean better customer service and greater chances for promotion from within. Video assessment can also give management greater insight into employee strengths and weaknesses before they are hired, and this can help the company solve long-standing problems like high turnover.

Video assessment evolved from assessment centers, which have been in use for more than 30 years (see the description later in this chapter). While assessment centers do get results, they are high-cost operations (up to $5000 for each person who is assessed). Videos are cheap by comparison. They take about an hour to complete and cost between $25 and $100. Canadian firms using video assessment include Weyerhaeuser, Reebok, Northern Telecom, Eaton's, and BC Hydro.

But care must be taken when using video assessment. If a company simply buys a ready-made video from a consulting firm it may get lax about doing its homework—stating the specific knowledge, skills, and motivation needed to do various jobs. Mindlessly using video assessment could, for example, cause a company to hire a salesperson who is good at "cold calls" when what they really needs is a salesperson who is good at maintaining existing accounts.

Another potential problem is that managers don't have a stake in selection criteria the way they do when they interview people. Some companies overcome these limitations by using multiple methods. Weyerhaeuser used both video assessment and an assessment center to hire a supervisor for a sawmill. Some companies also use video assessment for ongoing training purposes. At Reebok, employees view the videos on a regular basis in training and development sessions.

because applicants usually list as references only people likely to say good things about them. Even former employers may be reluctant to say negative things, fearing a lawsuit. But crosschecks can confirm information about an applicant's experience or education. For example, if you tell an interviewer that you graduated with a B. Comm. (Honors), a quick call to the student records office of your university can verify the truth of your statement.

Once a number of applicants have been interviewed and checked out, the manager will make a hiring decision. Before a job offer is actually made, however, some companies require an extra step—a physical exam, a polygraph test, and/or, increasingly, a drug test.[5] These tests are designed to protect the employer. For example, a manufacturer afraid of injuries from workers hurt on the job might require new employees to have a physical examination. The company gains some information about whether the employees are physically fit to do the work and what (if any) preexisting injuries they have. Polygraph (lie detector) tests are largely illegal now, and drug tests are also coming under fire. However, some companies still use one or both as insurance against theft or drug abuse by employees.

Internal Staffing: Promotions

No matter how careful it is, the selection process of new applicants cannot compare with a company's knowledge of its current employees. It is not surprising that many firms prefer to "hire from within"—to promote or transfer existing staff members—whenever possible.

Some firms that historically have practiced promotion from within are rethinking that strategy. IBM, for example, has had only 6 CEOs in its history, all of whom were appointed after they had spent many years working their way up the hierarchy at IBM. But with the replacement of John Akers with outsider Louis Gerstner, the company will have an easier time breaking with tradition as it works to solve its massive problems.[6] Futhermore, promotion from within can cause disputes, especially in family-owned businesses. The video case "Family Business" on p. 292 indicates how this can be a problem.

Handling of promotions and job changes varies from company to company. Some firms use **closed promotion systems** in which managers decide which workers will even be considered for a promotion. In such companies, promotion decisions tend to be made informally and subjectively and to rely heavily on the recommendations of an employee's supervisor. Closed systems remain popular, especially in small firms, because they minimize the time, energy, and cost of making promotion decisions.

Other firms maintain **open promotion systems** in which available jobs and their requirements are posted. Employees who feel they possess the qualifications fill out applications, take tests, and interview with managers, much as if they were outside applicants. Open systems allow individual employees to have more say in their career paths. The democratic nature of such systems may also contribute to higher employee morale. But an open system can be time-consuming and expensive. Resources must be spent processing, interviewing, and screening internal applicants.

In addition to open and closed systems, some promotions are determined in part by seniority. Employees with more years of service in the company receive the promotions. This pattern—a standard feature of many union contracts—assures that those promoted have experience. It does not guarantee promotion of the most competent candidate, however. Changes in the Japanese system—where seniority has been very important—are described in the box "Changing the Rules of Employment in Japan."

closed promotion system
An internal promotion system in which managers choose the workers who will be considered for a promotion.

open promotion system
An internal promotion system in which all employees are advised of open positions and may apply for those positions if they want.

International Report

CHANGING THE RULES OF EMPLOYMENT IN JAPAN

Until recently, if you were a Japanese male working full time for a large Japanese corporation, you had a job for life, no matter how well or how poorly you performed. You also received a guaranteed income tied solely to seniority. In many ways, you were the envy of unionized workers all over the world.

These halcyon days, however, are coming to an end for many Japanese workers. Faced with the worst economic slump since World War II, Japanese companies are rethinking lifetime-employment and seniority-based wage policies. They are now examining policies that would enable them to become more responsive to economic conditions. According to Peter Morgan, an economist at Merrill Lynch Japan, Japanese companies are currently carrying two million more workers than they need, and their competitive positions in the world market are suffering as a result.

Mazda Motor Corp. is one Japanese firm which recognizes lifetime employment as an unaffordable luxury but which remains unwilling to release white-collar workers. The financially strapped company recently transferred several hundred managers from offices to assembly lines for three-month periods to perform jobs normally handled by contract workers. Hiroshi Matsuo, a personnel department manager who now unloads auto parts, reacted typically to the change: "Why should I protest?" he asks. "When we consider Mazda's current situation, with an excess of office workers, perhaps this situation is necessary."

Japanese companies are also moving away from seniority-based pay in favor of merit pay. For example, about 4500 managers at Honda are now on a performance-based merit-pay system. For the first time, highly rated employees can earn as much as $10 000 more than poor performers. Under the traditional seniority system, achievers and laggards alike were paid strictly according to seniority—on length of service to the company rather than on the quality of their work. Indeed, the link between seniority and income is still so strong at Fujitsu Ltd., Japan's largest computer company, that older subordinates often receive more money than talented younger bosses.

The economic downturn may make lifetime employment and seniority-based compensation luxuries that Japanese companies are no longer willing to support. Ironically, Canadian and American companies—once viewed as fat and unresponsive by the Japanese—now command leaner and more flexible organizations and, in many industries, are leading the way back to profitability.

Developing the Work Force

One of the first things that newcomers participate in is their orientation to the organization. It then falls to personnel experts and other managers to maintain and enhance the employee-job match and employees' performance on the job. Toward this end, some companies have instituted training and development programs on many levels. In addition, every firm has some system for performance appraisal and feedback that helps managers and employees assess the need for more training.

Orientation

orientation
The initial acquainting of new employees with the company's policies and programs, personnel with whom they will interact, and the nature of the job.

The purpose of the **orientation** is to help employees learn about and fit into the company. At one level, the orientation can focus on work hours, parking priorities, and/or pay schedules. People may simply watch films, read manuals, and be introduced to new co-workers. At another level, orientation can indoctrinate the worker into the corporate culture and provide valuable insights into how to succeed.

Employee Training and Development

After orientation, the new employee starts to work. However, both old and new employees may receive training or be enrolled in a development program.

Such training generally occurs for one of two reasons: to make up for some deficiency or to give the employee a chance to acquire skills needed for promotion. GM Canada, for example, recently spent $24 million on employee training as part of a program to increase quality levels at its Canadian plants.

Statistics Canada reports that 16 percent of Canadian adults cannot read the majority of written material they encounter in everyday life, and that 22 percent do not have the reading skills to deal with complex instructions. Companies like Northern Telecom and CCL Custom Manufacturing are finding that they have to train workers because the equipment they must use is increasingly complex.[7] A study by the Conference Board of Canada found that large companies spend an average of $475 per year on training employees. This amount is only half as much as American firms spend, and American companies, in turn, spend only a fraction of the amounts that Japanese firms spend.[8]

Many companies are reluctant to retrain older workers, fearing that they are uninterested in training or that the company will not recoup its training investment because the workers have only a few years left in their careers. But Kenworth, the heavy truck manufacturer, found that after it trained a group of older workers, productivity rose nearly 20 percent, and the time spent correcting manufacturing defects dropped from about 40 hours per truck to less than 10.[9]

The reasons for training and development differ, as do the methods used. The most common methods are on-the-job training, off-the-job training, management development programs, networking/mentoring, and assessment centers.[10]

On-the-Job Training.   As the term suggests, **on-the-job training** is training that occurs while the employee is actually at work. Ford Motor trained 140 workers for a year to work in a new aluminum casting plant in Windsor, Ontario. Because workers need to know many jobs (e.g., melting aluminum and molding and cleaning engines), they needed a lot of training.[11] Much on-the-job training is unplanned and informal, as when one employee shows another how to use the new photocopier. Someone needs some help, so it is provided.

In other cases, on-the-job training is quite formal. For example, secretaries may learn to operate a new word-processing system at their desks. The advantages of on-the-job training are that it occurs in the real job setting and can be done over an extended period of time. The biggest disadvantage is that distractions on the job site may make training difficult.

Off-the-Job Training.   In contrast, **off-the-job training** is performed at a location away from the work site. It may be at a classroom within the same facility or at a different location altogether. For example, refresher courses are offered for managers of McDonald's 600 Canadian restaurants at the Canadian Institute of Hamburgerology; training videotapes are also shown to restaurant workers.[12] Coffee College is a two-week cram course run by Second Cup Ltd., Canada's largest retailer of specialty coffee. During their stay at Coffee College, franchisees and managers learn a lot of details about coffee. They also learn how to hire workers, keep the books, detect employee theft, and boost Christmas sales.[13]

The advantage of off-the-job training is that the instructor can focus intensively on the subject without interruption and in a controlled environment. On the other hand, many off-the-job locations are artificial and lack the realism necessary to really learn more about the job. Many companies therefore do both. The workers at Circo Craft Co. Inc., a maker of printed circuit boards, spent an average of 71 hours in training in 1993. Some of the training was on-the-job and some was off-the-job.[14]

on-the-job training
Those development programs in which employees gain new skills while performing them at work.

off-the-job training
Those development programs in which employees learn new skills at a location away from the normal work site.

management development programs

Those development programs in which current and prospective managers learn new conceptual, analytical, and problem-solving skills.

Management Development Programs.   These programs are targeted specifically at current or future managers. In contrast to regular training, which focuses on technical skills, **management development programs** try to enhance conceptual, analytical, and problem-solving skills. Most large organizations have management development programs. Some programs are run in-house by managers or training specialists. Others take place at management development centers on university campuses. Still others require managers to get completely away from the work place and study certain subjects intensively. For example, Decision Dynamics is a two-week management development program conducted at a resort hotel on Lake Winnipeg. A well-conceived strategy for developing managerial talent is almost mandatory if an organization is to prosper.

Management development programs are built around a variety of techniques. The *lecture method* is useful for presenting facts. It is therefore a good way to inform managers about things like the meaning of new laws that regulate business activity. In the *case method*, participants are given a problem situation to analyze and solve. *Simulation techniques* require trainees to act out realistic business situations to give them practice in decision making. In *role playing*, each trainee is given a specific role to read and act out. The aim here is to create a realistic situation and then have the trainees assume the roles of a specific person in that situation.

networking

Informal interactions among managers for the purpose of discussing mutual problems, solutions, and opportunities.

Networking and Mentoring.   In addition, some management development also takes place informally, often through processes known as networking and mentoring. **Networking** refers to informal interactions among managers for the purpose of discussing mutual problems, solutions, and opportunities. Networking takes place in a variety of settings, both inside and outside the office—for example, at conventions and conferences, meetings, business lunches, social gatherings, and so forth.

A mentor is an older, more experienced manager who sponsors and teaches younger, less experienced managers. The mentoring process helps younger managers learn the ropes and benefit from the experiences, insights, and successes (and failures) of senior executives. Networking and mentoring may be especially useful for female and/or minority managers: These individuals may have fewer role models and may be more likely to benefit from greater interaction with experienced managers.

assessment center

A series of exercises in which management candidates perform realistic management tasks while being observed by appraisers.

Assessment Centers.   An **assessment center** is a series of exercises in which management candidates perform realistic management tasks under the watchful eyes of expert appraisers. Each candidate's potential for management is assessed or appraised.

A typical assessment center might be set up in a large conference room and go on for two or three days. During this time, managers and potential managers might take selection tests, engage in management simulations, make individual presentations, and conduct group discussions. In a program like this the assessors look to see how each participant reacts to stress or to criticism by colleagues. They also watch to see which candidates emerge as leaders of the group discussions.

performance appraisal

A formal program for comparing employees' actual performance with expected performance; used in making decisions about training, promoting, compensating, and firing.

Performance Appraisal

Performance appraisals are formal evaluations of how well workers are doing their jobs. Every company assesses the performance of its employees in some way, even if it is only the owner telling the only employee, a receptionist, "Good job. You're getting a raise." In larger firms, the process is more extensive. A formal performance evaluation system generally involves a regularly scheduled written assessment. The written evaluation, however, is only one part of a multistep process.

The appraisal process begins when a manager makes job performance expectations clear to an employee. The manager must then observe the employee's performance. If the standards are clearly defined, a manager should have little difficulty with the next step—comparing expectations with actual performance. For some jobs, a rating scale like that illustrated in Figure 8.3 is useful. This comparison forms the basis for a written appraisal and for decisions about any raise, promotion, demotion, or firing of the employee. The final step in the appraisal process is for the manager to meet with the employee to discuss the appraisal.

When job performance expectations are based on the actual requirements of the job, formal appraisals benefit both the company and workers. The company is protected from lawsuits charging unfair treatment. It also has a reasonably objective basis on which to compare individuals for promotions.

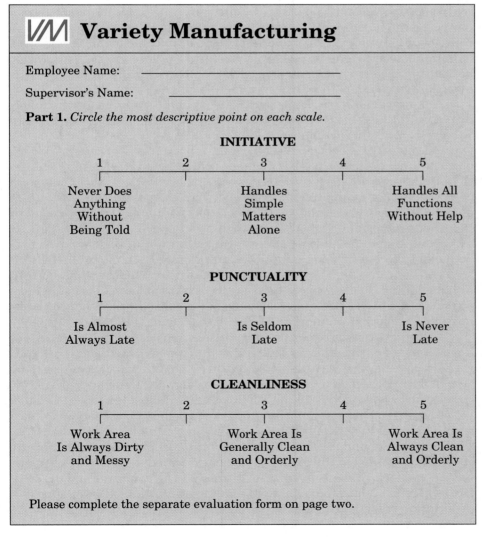

Figure 8.3
Graphic rating scales such as this one are common methods of performance appraisal.

Workers benefit from clear goals to work toward and knowledge of how well they are doing. They often feel that such systems are fairer than subjective evaluations. Objective performance appraisal may be difficult in family-owned businesses, as the "Family Business" video case shows.

Terminating and Demoting Workers.   Written appraisals are especially important when a business must fire or demote employees either because of poor worker performance or because the firm is reorganizing or is in economic trouble. Whether the worker or the company is the problem, demoting or firing employees is one of the duties a manager least wants to perform. For example, managers who dismiss subordinates as part of a downsizing may become very depressed themselves as they think about all the people whose jobs they terminated. The task may be made easier by writing a glowing recommendation or securing a good severance arrangement for an employee let go because of company changes. And when the employee is causing a problem, a systematic process can help the manager—and the employee.

Most companies with formal systems have a step-by-step process of warnings and punishments leading up to dismissal. For the first warning, the manager might talk informally to the employee, expressing disappointment over the problem—poor job performance or attendance, for example. To protect itself from lawsuits, many companies require managers to give the offending employee a written warning. An employee causing a problem can also expect to hear about it during a formal appraisal. At that time, the manager will specify certain changes that the employee must make or lose the job. This system not only protects the company, it also lets employees know that their jobs are in jeopardy and offers them a chance to do better.

If a problem persists, a manager may have little choice but to discipline, demote, or dismiss the employee. Disciplinary actions—such as suspending a worker from the job without pay for several days—are usually taken only when the employee's behavior is dangerous or disruptive. For example, someone who strikes a fellow worker might be sent home to "cool off."

demotion

Reducing the rank of a person who is not performing up to standard.

Demotions are most often used when managerial personnel fail to meet expectations. For example, a sales manager who is performing poorly may be demoted to sales representative. Demoted managers are often humiliated by this downgrading and seek jobs elsewhere.

termination

Firing an employee who is not performing up to standard.

Finally, in extreme cases, outright **termination** of the employee may be the only recourse. For example, a salesperson who continually falls far short of the established quota may be a drag on corporate profitability. Although firing is never pleasant, managers of companies with sound human resource policies can take some solace in knowing that, by the time such a dismissal takes place, the employee should be expecting it.

Companies must now be extremely careful when dismissing employees. For example, a general manager at Jumbo Video Inc., who was fired when he refused to take a large pay cut, was awarded more than $226 000 in damages. The manager had earlier signed a contract containing certain stipulations which the company later tried to void because of financial problems. The judge ruled that the company had reneged on the contract.[15] The box "The World of Unjust Dismissal" gives further information on the issue of employee dismissal.

alternate dispute resolution

The employee and the company agree to submit their dispute to binding arbitration.

Employees and employers are beginning to use **alternate dispute resolution** (ADR) with increasing frequency. Suppose an employee is dismissed and feels that it is a wrongful dismissal. The employee and the company agree to submit the dispute to binding arbitration with no appeal of the decision possible. This saves both parties considerable time and money.[16]

The Canadian Business Scene

THE WORLD OF "UNJUST DISMISSAL"

Legislation on unjust dismissal was added to the Canada Labour Code in 1978. It covers nonunionized, nonmanagement employees in federally regulated industries such as banking, transportation, and telecommunications and is designed to provide a cheap, fast, and effective route for employees to appeal an unfair firing without having to go to court.

An employee who thinks he or she has been unjustly fired files a complaint with Labour Canada. If the complaint is judged worthwhile, the employer is contacted and asked to give the reason why the employee was fired. A Labour Canada inspector then reviews the case and tries to persuade the two parties to agree. If the parties cannot agree, the case is sent to an adjudicator who either upholds the dismissal or orders the employee reinstated. If either side disputes the judgment, it can request a judicial review.

The legislation requires that the employee be given the benefit of the doubt whenever possible. The company must prove it had "just cause" in firing the person. Since adjudicators do not have to base their decisions on precedent, it is difficult for a company to predict the outcome of a complaint.

Critics of the legislation point to cases in which they feel poor decisions were made. Consider the case of a Canadian Imperial Bank of Commerce employee who was fired because of her off-hours associations. Police burst into her apartment at precisely the time five men were dividing the loot from a robbery at a nearby CIBC branch. The Labour Canada adjudicator who reviewed the case ruled that the bank did not have "just cause" for firing her because she had not done anything wrong herself. CIBC was ordered to give her back pay. A bank supervisor at another bank got her job back even after she admitted that she had planned to steal customers' money. A consumer credit officer in another firm was reinstated despite his conviction on weapons charges.

Because of the time and risk involved, many employers settle before the adjudication stage. Nearly 75 percent of the 600 complaints that are brought annually are resolved before they get to adjudication and another 10 percent are resolved before the adjudicator's report. Critics of the legislation argue that the cost of the procedure and the potential for reinstatement give "daring" employees an incentive to complain. They would like to see more training of adjudicators, transcriptions of proceedings, and adjudicators given the right to award costs against a frivolous complaint.

Even prominent managers may go to court over wrongful dismissal. Robert Campeau, who took Campeau Corp. to the edge of bankruptcy, is asking for damages of $10 million from the company. He claims his employment was improperly terminated when he was fired as CEO of Campeau. When Joel Bell was fired as head of Canada Development Investment Corp., he received $3.3 million in a wrongful dismissal suit.

Compensation and Benefits

A major factor in retaining skilled workers is a company's **compensation system**—what it offers employees in return for their labor. Wages and salaries are a key part of any compensation system, but most systems also include features such as incentives and employee benefits programs. We will explore each of these elements in this section. Bear in mind, however, that finding the right combination of elements is complicated by the need to make employees feel valued while simultaneously keeping company costs to a minimum. Thus, compensation systems are highly individualized, depending on the nature of the industry, the company, and the types of workers involved.

compensation system
What a firm offers its employees in return for their labor.

Wages and Salaries

Wages and salaries are the dollar amounts paid to employees for their work. **Wages** are dollars paid for time worked. Workers who are paid by the hour receive wages. Canadian manufacturing workers are among the highest paid workers in the world. Only German workers receive higher wages.[17]

wages
Dollars paid based on the number of hours worked or the number of units produced.

salary

Dollars paid at regular intervals in return for doing a job, regardless of the amount of time or output involved.

Salary is the money an employee receives for getting a job done. An executive earning $100 000 per year may work five hours one day and fifteen the next. Such an individual is paid to get a job done rather than for the specific number of hours or days spent working. Salaries are usually expressed as an amount to be paid per year but are often paid each month or every two weeks.

In setting wage and salary levels, a company must consider several factors. First, it must take into account how its competitors compensate their employees. A firm that pays less than its rivals may soon find itself losing valuable personnel.

Within the company, the firm must also decide how wage and salary levels for different jobs will compare. And within wage and salary levels, managers must decide how much to pay individual workers. Two employees may do exactly the same job, but the employee with more experience may earn more, in part to keep that person in the company and in part because the experienced person performs better. Some union contracts specify differential wages based on experience. Note that the basis for differential pay must be job-related, however, not favoritism or discrimination.

Incentive Programs

incentive program

Any program in which a company offers its workers additional pay over and above the normal wage or salary level in order to motivate them to perform at a higher-than-normal level.

The term **incentive programs** refers to special pay programs designed to motivate high performance. The use of incentive programs increased in the 1980s, largely because of concern for productivity.

Sales bonuses are a typical incentive. Under such a program, employees who sell a certain number or dollar amount of goods for the year receive a special payment. Employees who do not reach this goal earn no bonus. Similarly, *merit salary systems* link raises to performance levels in non-sales jobs. For example, many baseball players have clauses in their contracts that pay them bonuses for hitting over .300, making the All-Star game, or being named Most Valuable Player. Executives commonly receive stock options and bonuses as an incentive. The box "Compensation at the Top" deals with the sometimes controversial issue of compensation levels of top executives.

gain-sharing plan

An incentive program in which employees receive a bonus if the firm's costs are reduced because of greater worker efficiency and/or productivity.

Some incentive programs apply to all employees in a firm. **Gain-sharing plans** distribute bonuses to all employees in a company based on reduced costs from working more efficiently. Palliser Furniture Ltd. introduced a gain-sharing plan that rewards employees for increasing production. Any profit resulting from production above a certain level is split 50-50 between the company and the employees.[18]

profit-sharing plan

An incentive program in which employees receive a bonus depending on the firm's profits.

Profit-sharing plans are based on profit levels in the firm. Profits earned above a certain level are distributed to employees. Stock ownership by employees serves as an incentive to lower costs, increase productivity and profits, and thus increase the value of the employees' stock.[19]

Comparable Worth

In spite of recent advances, women still earn less than men. A 1994 Statistics Canada report shows that women who work full-time earn about 72 percent of what men do ($28 350 vs. $39 468). Single women earn 99 percent of what single men earn. Back in 1969, women earned 59 percent of what men did. The most recent gains by women occurred because men lost four of every five jobs that disappeared during the recession of the early 1990s. Most top jobs in both the public and private sector continue to be held by men, and women continue to be concentrated in the lower paying clerical and secretarial positions.[20]

comparable worth

A legal idea that aims to pay equal wages for work of equal value.

Comparable worth is a legal concept that aims at paying equal wages for jobs that are of comparable value to the employer. This might mean

The Canadian Business Scene

COMPENSATION AT THE TOP

Top executives in Canada can earn well over $500 000 per year. Some earn over $1 million, and a few earn even more. Some illustrative salaries for top Canadian managers in 1992 are as follows:

- Robert Smith (American Barrick) $4.5 million
- Edgar Bronfman (Seagram) 3.7 million
- Anthony Petrina (Placer Dome) 2.6 million
- Desmond Hudson (Northern Telecom) 2.3 million
- William Holland (United Dominion) 1.0 million

In addition to high compensation when they are working for a company, executives may also receive large compensation when they leave. When Paul Stern resigned as president and CEO of Northern Telecom, for example, the company came up with a severance package that totalled approximately $3 million. This included two years' salary and benefits, 10 years of credited service to his pension plan, and the purchase of his home.

Some business firms will end up paying large sums of money to executives after they retire. An executive who earned a large salary during his or her time with the company may represent a liability to the company of more than $5 million dollars (assuming that the executive lives for 15 years after he or she retires).

In spite of these large numbers, the compensation of top Canadian managers does not appear to be out of line in comparison to what executives in other countries are paid. A 1991 compensation study by Towers Perrin showed that the average compensation for CEOs heading up companies with sales of about $250 million was as follows:

Country	CEO Compensation
U.S.	$747 500
France	448 500
Italy	421 300
Canada	407 600
UK	399 600
Japan	371 800
Germany	364 500

While Canadian salaries are higher than those of top executives in Japan and Germany, they are much lower than those in the U.S.

Besides the question of absolute salaries paid to top executives, there is the issue of whether their salaries should move up and down in relation to their company's performance. Does this happen? Sometimes, but it is not hard to find cases where executive salaries go up while company profit goes down. For example, in a year when Imperial Oil's profit fell 37 percent, the chairman's total compensation package went up 12 percent. Similar situations were evident in other companies, including Bell Canada Enterprises, Canadian Occidental Petroleum, Canadian Pacific, and Westcoast Transmission Co. Ltd.

Recent Statistics Canada data show that the average hourly paid worker in Canada earns slightly more than $20 000 per year. Are the large differences in compensation between hourly workers and CEOs warranted? How do we determine what a top executive is worth? Those who defend large executive salaries suggest an instructive comparison with professional sports, where one superstar can make a team. A similar argument might be made that a particular CEO could make a company. As in professional sports, a business firm may have little alternative but to pay a seemingly large salary to a top manager.

A key issue in this debate is the determination of executive performance. Unlike a professional superstar—whose performance stats are objective and easily measured—a top executive operates in an environment of considerable uncertainty. How should executive performance be measured? Ideally, the board of directors should clearly indicate the goals they want the company to achieve (for example, a certain level of competitiveness or quality), and then reward the CEO for achieving those goals. Unfortunately, many boards do not have the confidence or insight to set such goals. They may also be reluctant to deal firmly with CEOs on the issue of salary. But shareholders have no such reluctance, and they increasingly are demanding a say in executive compensation decisions.

Ontario's new pay disclosure rules require that the compensation of top executives be disclosed. This will allow pension fund managers to gauge how well executive pay matches company performance. In recent years, these pension funds have shown a willingness to put pressure on companies to change their management practices and improve their performance. And pension funds themselves are subject to scrutiny. The Ontario Teachers Pension Plan Board disclosed the salaries of its top five executives, but only after a teacher in the district had fought for two years to get the board to disclose salaries.

The recession of the early 1990s put the brakes on executive compensation to some extent. A survey conducted by Hay Group management consultants showed that 40 percent of CEOs received no increase at all in 1993. Still, to many critics, it is simply not "right" that top executives receive 20, 50, or even 100 times more than their workers receive. They argue that it is unethical to pay top executives $1 million or $5 million a year for what they do.

comparing dissimilar jobs, such as those of nurses and mechanics or secretaries and electricians. Proponents of comparable worth say that all the jobs in a company must be evaluated and then rated in terms of basic dimensions such as the level of skill they require. All jobs could then be compared based on a common index. People in different jobs that rate the same on this index would be paid the same. Experts hope that this will help to reduce the gap between men's and women's pay.

Critics of comparable worth object on the grounds that it ignores the supply and demand aspects of labor. They say, for example, that legislation forcing a company to pay people more than the open market price for their labor (which may happen in jobs where there is a surplus of workers) is another example of unreasonable government interference in business activities. They also say that implementing comparable worth will cost business firms too much money. A study prepared for the Ontario Ministry of Labour estimated that it would cost approximately $10 billion for the public and private sectors in Ontario to establish equitable payment for jobs of equal value. Yet the cost defence cannot be easily used. In one case, the Quebec Human Rights Commission ruled that 24 female office employees of the Quebec North Shore Paper Company were performing work of equal value to that done by male production workers. The company was required to increase the secretaries' salaries by $701 annually and give them over $1000 in back pay.[21]

Benefits Programs

benefits

What a firm offers its workers other than wages and salaries in return for their labor.

A growing part of nearly every firm's compensation system is **benefits** programs—compensation other than wages and salaries. Benefits now often comprise over half a firm's total compensation budget. Most companies are

Benefits are an important part of most compensation programs. Some are provided by the employer while others are mandated by the government. A new parental leave provision allows either parent to take up to ten weeks of paid leave after the birth or adoption of a child.

required by law to provide workers' compensation, holiday pay, and Canada Pension Plan and unemployment insurance contributions. Most businesses also voluntarily provide extended health, life, and disability insurance. Many also allow employees to buy stock through payroll deductions at a slightly discounted price. In the 1980s, many firms began to provide vision care and dental benefits to employees. Some even provide free legal services to employees.

As the range of benefits has grown, so has concern about containing their cost. Businesses are experimenting with a variety of procedures to cut benefits costs, while maintaining the ability to attract, retain, and maintain the morale of employees.[22] One new approach is the use of **cafeteria benefits**. These plans provide a set dollar amount in benefits and allow employees to pick among alternatives. Employees at Toyota's Cambridge, Ontario, plant are given the opportunity once each year to structure their benefits packages. For example, they can give more weight to dental coverage if they have young children, or to life insurance or disability coverage, depending on their circumstances.[23] More and more firms are using "temporary" workers on a long-term basis. Since they are not covered by most companies' benefits plans, temporary workers allow businesses to keep staff levels high and benefits costs low.

Rising benefits costs have also made managers more aware of the need for businesses to communicate with their employees about benefits. Often, employees do not fully understand—and thus appreciate—their benefits. Personnel specialists can increase employees' awareness about their benefits by providing clearly written handbooks and by holding meetings in which workers can get answers to their questions about benefits.

cafeteria benefits
A flexible approach to providing benefits in which employees are allocated a certain sum to cover benefits and can "spend" this allocation on the specific benefits they prefer.

Employee Safety and Health.   Employee safety and health programs help to reduce absenteeism and labor turnover, raise productivity, and boost morale by making jobs safer and more healthful.

Government regulations about employee safety are getting stricter. Ontario, which loses more than 7 million working days yearly because of on-the-job injuries, has passed amendments to the Ontario *Occupational Health and Safety Act*. Officers and directors of companies will be held personally responsible for workplace health and safety and will be punishable by jail terms and fines for permitting unsafe working conditions.[24]

Some industrial work—logging, construction, fishing, and mining—can put workers at risk of injury in obvious ways. But other types of work—such as typing or lifting—can also cause painful injuries. **Repetitive strain injuries** (RSIs) occur when workers perform the same functions over and over again. These injuries disable more than 200 000 Canadians each year and account for nearly half of all work-related time loss claims. The box "Repetitive Strain Injuries" describes successful efforts by some firms to cope with this problem.[25]

repetitive strain injuries
Injuries that occur when workers perform the same functions over and over again.

In Canada, each province has developed its own workplace health and safety regulations. The purpose of these laws is to ensure that employees do not have to work in dangerous conditions. These laws are the direct result of undesirable conditions that existed in many Canadian businesses at the close of the nineteenth century. While much improvement is evident, Canada still has some problems with workplace health and safety. In one study of six western industrialized nations, Canada had the worst safety record in mining and construction and the second worst record in manufacturing and railways.

The Ontario Occupational Health and Safety Act illustrates current legislation in Canada. It requires that all employers ensure that equipment and safety devices are used properly. Employers must also show workers the proper way to operate machinery. At the job site, supervisors are charged with the responsibility of seeing that workers use equipment properly. The act also requires workers to behave appropriately on the job. Employees have the right to refuse to work on a job if they believe it is unsafe; a legal procedure exists for resolving any disputes in this area.

The Canadian Business Scene

REPETITIVE STRAIN INJURIES

In recent years, there has been considerable publicity about repetitive strain injury (RSI). One reason RSI is increasing is that the average age of the workforce is increasing, and older people are more prone to RSI. The recession of the early 1990s was also a culprit; workers with the least seniority were laid off first, and those that remain are much older. In some manufacturing plants, the *average* worker is over 50 years of age.

When Snap-On Tools of Canada opened a new factory, worker complaints about shoulder and arm injuries increased to the point where the company's workers' compensation premiums were threatening to double. The injuries were occurring because workers had to lift heavy objects, work at a high rate of speed, and use tools that were positioned awkwardly above or below shoulder level.

At the peak of its problems, a safety engineer from the Industrial Accident Prevention Association contacted the company and offered to help solve the problem. After a thorough investigation, several major changes were introduced. Supervisors and workers were trained in occupational health and safety matters, daily work routines were changed (workers now switch jobs every two and one-half hours), and work stations were improved so that workers could raise or lower items to be worked on at a

comfortable level. After the program had been instituted, only seven worker compensation claims were filed over the course of a year (just 0.3 per cent of total hours worked at the plant). Product quality also increased because workers did not have to struggle to do their jobs.

Other companies have instituted similar changes to reduce RSI. At Chrysler Corporation's Jefferson North plant, for example, air guns that drive screws are specially designed to reduce carpal tunnel syndrome, a particularly bad type of RSI. A machine also raises heavy aluminum sheets so that workers are spared lifting which could lead to injury.

At Cuddy Food Products, the sole supplier of poultry products to McDonald's, as many as 44 workers per month became disabled from repetitive strain injury. The company instituted a plan to redesign how workers performed their jobs and trained people to avoid injuries. During one nine-month period after the training, not a single repetitive strain injury was reported. At CP Rail, injuries were reduced 50 percent when employees did ten minutes of warm-up exercises before beginning work.

RSI is not limited to manufacturing plants. Many workers who type all day or who do repetitive filing work in office settings also suffer from RSI.

In most provinces, the Ministry of Labour appoints inspectors to enforce health and safety regulations. If the inspector finds a sufficient hazard, he or she has the authority to clear the work place. Inspectors can usually come to a firm unannounced to conduct an inspection.

Retirement.   Some employees are ready for retirement much earlier than others. But because most retirement plans are based on an employee's age, some workers who should retire earlier stay on the job while others, who are still useful workers, leave before they would like to. This policy is short-sighted. A compromise is to grant year-to-year extensions to productive employees who want to continue working but who have reached retirement age. Recently several workers in different locations across Canada have successfully challenged mandatory retirement rules. Their employers must allow them to work even though they are past the traditional retirement age. More and more executives will be staying on past the age of 65, partly because the company needs their expertise and partly because the idea of mandatory retirement at age 65 has become outdated.

Many personnel departments provide pre-retirement counselling. Special educational programs inform people who are about to retire about important retirement-related matters like Social Insurance benefits, Canada Pension Plan provisions, investments, and second careers inside or outside the firm. In a sense, such pre-retirement counselling is the final step in the human resource department's overall employee career management program.

Miscellaneous Services.   Human resource departments also provide many other services, which vary widely among firms. These range from setting policies to deal with allegations of sexual harassment on the job to helping employees arrange car pools.

At Levac Supply Ltd. of Kingston, Ontario, one employee harassed another with derogatory remarks over a 14-year period. In spite of the fact that the Ontario Human Rights Code excludes companies from liability in the case of sexual harassment (as long as they make a reasonable effort to stop the harassment), a board of inquiry ruled that the company was jointly responsible with the employee who had actually done the harassing. The woman who was harassed was awarded $48 273 in a settlement.[26]

Time and circumstances greatly affect the nature of human resource work. For example, a firm may experience a big decrease in one department's workload and a big increase in another department's workload. The human resource department might help the two department managers to shift workers between departments, help arrange retraining if that is needed, or help to develop a plan for sharing the available work among employees—shorter work weeks for all workers or layoffs in order of seniority.

Human resource departments in many firms help to develop flexible work schedules. Flextime, as opposed to fixed working hours, makes it easier for many workers, especially working mothers, to enter the labor force. The concept of flextime is discussed in more detail in Chapter 9. Although it may present some scheduling problems, flextime also makes it possible for some employees to work full-time instead of having to settle for part-time work.

Increasing numbers of companies are providing pre-retirement counselling services to employees. This counselling provides both financial and lifestyle information to those employees who are nearing retirement.

Summary of Key Points

Human resource management involves developing, administering, and evaluating programs to acquire and enhance the quality and performance of people in a business. Good managers always bear in mind the principle of job-relatedness—that human resource decisions and policies should be based on the requirements of a job. Managers who apply this principle and match the right employee to the right job produce satisfied, effective workers.

Planning for future human resource needs entails several steps. Conducting a job analysis enables managers to create detailed, job-related job descriptions and specifications. Managers must then forecast supply and demand for the types of workers they will need. Only then can managers devise strategies to match supply with demand.

Staffing a business may involve hiring from outside the company. Such external staffing requires the company first to recruit applicants and then to select from among the applicants. Companies must ensure that they do not discriminate against candidates during this phase of the process. The selection phase typically includes interviewing, testing, and checking the references of applicants. Whenever possible, however, many companies prefer to fill positions internally, by promoting existing personnel.

If a company is to get the most out of its workers, it must develop those workers. Nearly all employees undergo some initial orientation process. Many also acquire new skills through on-the-job training, off-the-job training, and/or management development programs. Performance appraisals help managers decide who needs training and who should be promoted. Appraisals also tell employees how well they are doing at meeting expectations. Employees who continually fail to meet performance or behavior expectations may be disciplined, demoted, or terminated.

Compensation programs include wages and salaries, incentives, and benefits for workers. By paying its workers as well as or better than competitors do, a business can attract and keep qualified personnel. Incentive programs such as sales bonuses, gain-sharing, and profit-sharing can also motivate existing personnel to work more effectively. Benefits programs may increase employee satisfaction but are a major expense to businesses today.

In hiring, training, compensating and/or firing workers, managers must obey many laws. Equal employment opportunity and equal pay laws forbid discrimination other than that based on legitimate job requirements. Controversy over what constitutes discrimination in paying men and women who hold different jobs is a current issue. Managers are also required to provide employees with a safe working environment.

Up and Out

Donovan Retzlaffe, chairman and chief executive officer (CEO) of Lanark Products Ltd., announced on July 1, 1994 that he had reluctantly accepted the resignation of the firm's vice-chairman, Lorenzo Valli. In his announcement, Retzlaffe indicated that Valli had served the firm well and had been a "rock of Gibraltar" during the 49 years he had worked there.

The rise of Valli from mailroom clerk to vice-chairman is the stuff that legends are made of. Valli constantly said that there was nothing more important than loyalty to the firm. He joined Lanark in 1945 at the age of 19. He began working in the mailroom, and over the next 43 years gradually worked his way up the corporate ladder until he became vice-chairman in 1988. Valli fondly remembers the time that the company loaned him $4500 in 1963 to pay some legal bills that he had incurred. Valli was a no-nonsense, simple man. When he stepped down, he still lived in the same modest home that he had purchased in 1965.

Although the public announcement indicated that Valli had resigned, insiders at Lanark knew that he had actually been asked to leave because his management style was just too "abrasive" for the new image Lanark Products Ltd. was cultivating. It was also widely believed that there was a basic personality conflict between the CEO and Valli, even though the two had been working closely together for about 10 years. Some senior managers expressed the view that the company should never have given Valli the position of vice-chairman if they thought his style was too abrasive.

The "resignation" of Valli had some industry observers worried because of other events at Lanark. Employment statistics in early 1994 showed that nearly half of Lanark's upper management personnel had been with the firm for less than two years. This was partially the result of rapid expansion of the firm's activities. There had also been a rather large number of middle level managers leaving the firm. Although the reasons weren't completely clear, there were indications that they were not happy with the new direction of the firm.

CASE QUESTIONS
1. Do you think that Lanark Ltd. treated Valli fairly in asking him to resign after 49 years of service?
2. Was his dismissal handled properly? How would you have handled the situation?
3. If you were the CEO of Lanark Ltd., would you be concerned that nearly half the top managers had been with the firm for less than two years? If you were concerned, what would you do about it? How would you go about determining if there is a problem with the middle level of managers? ◆

Freelancing

When people think about careers, they usually think of going to work full-time for a company and, if they like it, staying at that company for many years. In fact, until recently the notion of "lifetime employment" was touted as the wave of the future. Even if a person didn't stay at one firm, the idea still was that the person would work full-time for a company for at least a few years.

But times are changing. A growing number of workers are becoming freelancers—individuals who contract with a company for a set period of time, usually until a specific project is completed. After the project is completed, the freelancer moves on to another project in the firm, or to another firm. Statistics Canada estimates that 30 percent of working adults are doing non-standard work like freelancing.

Why is this happening? The main reason is that competitive pressures are forcing firms to reduce their costs and increase their productivity. The current buzzword is "flexibility" and this can often be achieved by hiring freelancers to solve specific company problems. This allows a firm to maintain a minimum number of full-time workers and then supplement them with freelancers.

Some people freelance because they can't get full-time work with one company, but others freelance by choice. Accomplished freelancers can control their own destiny, make above-average incomes, and have a strong sense of flexibility and freedom. Typically, freelancers don't get paid company benefits like full-time workers do, but pressures are building to change this. In 1994, the province of Saskatchewan became the first in Canada to require companies to pay contract and part-time workers at least some benefits.

Many banks and insurance companies have trouble seeing the needs of contract workers. To them, it may appear that the contract worker is not really employed on a steady basis because they work for so many different companies. Creative Arts Management Service is a firm that fills this void. It offers business advice, financial planning, budgeting, and legal services for contract workers. The firm takes the view that freelancing, if properly planned and executed, is the best security in the new economy of the 1990s.

While the work of technical or professional employees is often contracted out to freelancers, the *management* of various functions may also be contracted out. The Halifax District School Board contracted out the management of custodial services for the district's 42 schools to ServiceMaster Canada Ltd. The school district expects to save more than half a million dollars each year. And Manpower Temporary Services manages a packaging department for a pharmaceutical firm that sometimes numbers up to 130 people, and sometimes as few as 70, depending on demand. A Manpower manager is on site at the pharmaceutical firm; she recruits the temporary workers, does some of the necessary training, conducts performance appraisals of temporary workers, and handles the payroll.

Management experts predict that freelancing will increase in importance. With the massive layoffs that have been evident in recent years, workers are beginning to realize that job security is not provided by large firms. Rather, security comes from having confidence in your own knowledge and skills, and marketing yourself in innovative ways. Freelancing has been facilitated by the recent advances in information technology, since workers do not necessarily have to be at the workplace in order to do their work.

There are both positive and negative aspects to the idea of non-standard work. From the worker's perspective, those with marketable skills will find that non-standard work will result in high pay and satisfying work. For those without marketable skills, non-standard work will likely mean part-time work in low-paying service jobs. Those individuals who lack either the ability or interest to capitalize on non-standard work will find that there is much uncertainty in their careers.

From the organization's perspective, a conclusion about the value of non-standard work means weighing the value of long-term employee loyalty and commitment against the benefits of the increased flexibility that is possible with part-time freelancers.

CASE QUESTIONS

1. What kind of people are most likely to want freelance work?
2. What are the pros and cons of freelance work from the individual's perspective? From the organization's perspective?
3. Is it unethical to hire freelancers in order to avoid paying company benefits to them?   ◆

Key Terms

human resource management	bona fide occupational requirement	management development programs	wages
job-relatedness	*Employment Equity Act*	networking	salary
job analysis	selection	assessment center	incentive program
job description	closed promotion system	performance appraisal	gain-sharing plan
job specification	open promotion system	demotion	profit-sharing plan
recruitment	orientation	termination	comparable worth
Canadian Human Rights Act	on-the-job training	alternate dispute resolution	benefits
	off-the-job training	compensation system	cafeteria benefits
			repetitive strain injury

Study Questions and Exercises

Review Questions

1. Why is a good employee-job match important? Who benefits more, the organization or the employee? Why?
2. Identify as many advantages and disadvantages as you can for internal and external staffing. Under what circumstances is each more appropriate?
3. Why is formal training so important? Why not just let people learn about their jobs as they do them?

Analysis Questions

4. How are overtime wages different from and similar to incentive program payments?
5. Select a job currently held by you or a close friend or relative. Draw up a job description and job specification for this position.
6. Did you have to take a test to be admitted to school? How valid do you think your score was as a predictor of academic success? Why?

7. What benefits do you consider most and least important in attracting workers? In keeping workers? In motivating workers?
8. Have you or anyone you know been discriminated against in a hiring decision? Was anything done about it?

Application Exercises

9. Interview a human resource manager at a local company. Select a position for which the firm is currently recruiting applicants and identify the steps in the selection process.
10. Obtain a copy of an employment application. Examine it carefully and determine how useful it might be in making a hiring decision.

Building Your Business Skills

Goal
To aid students in understanding the importance, cost, and complexity of benefits packages in contemporary organizations.

Situation
Suppose you are a human resources director and the president of your organization has asked you to look at ways to cut costs in the area of benefits. You are, however, to avoid sacrificing the quality of benefits that your organization currently offers. You know that cutting costs will require some compromises, but you are determined that you will not subtract anything from the present benefits package without also adding something. You are determined that employees will not feel cheated.

Method
Divide the class into teams, each of which is responsible for researching employee benefits at a nearby organization. One team should be assigned to research the college or university where you are studying.

Step 1
Arrange an interview with the human resources director at the organization that you have chosen to study. Ask for a summary of benefits available, the cost to the organization for each benefit offered, and some of the supporting documentation that is distributed to employees.

Step 2
Arrange a separate interview with an employee at the same organization—one who does not work in human resources. Ask the interviewee what he or she does and does not like about the firm's benefits package.

Step 3
Compare your findings with those of other teams.

Follow-Up Questions

1. Were you surprised at the range and cost of benefits typically available to employees?
2. Given what you now know about benefits packages, how would you approach the task that your superior assigned to you? Where would you make cuts? What compromises might you strike?
3. Do you think that organizations do enough to communicate with their employees about the financial implications of their benefits?

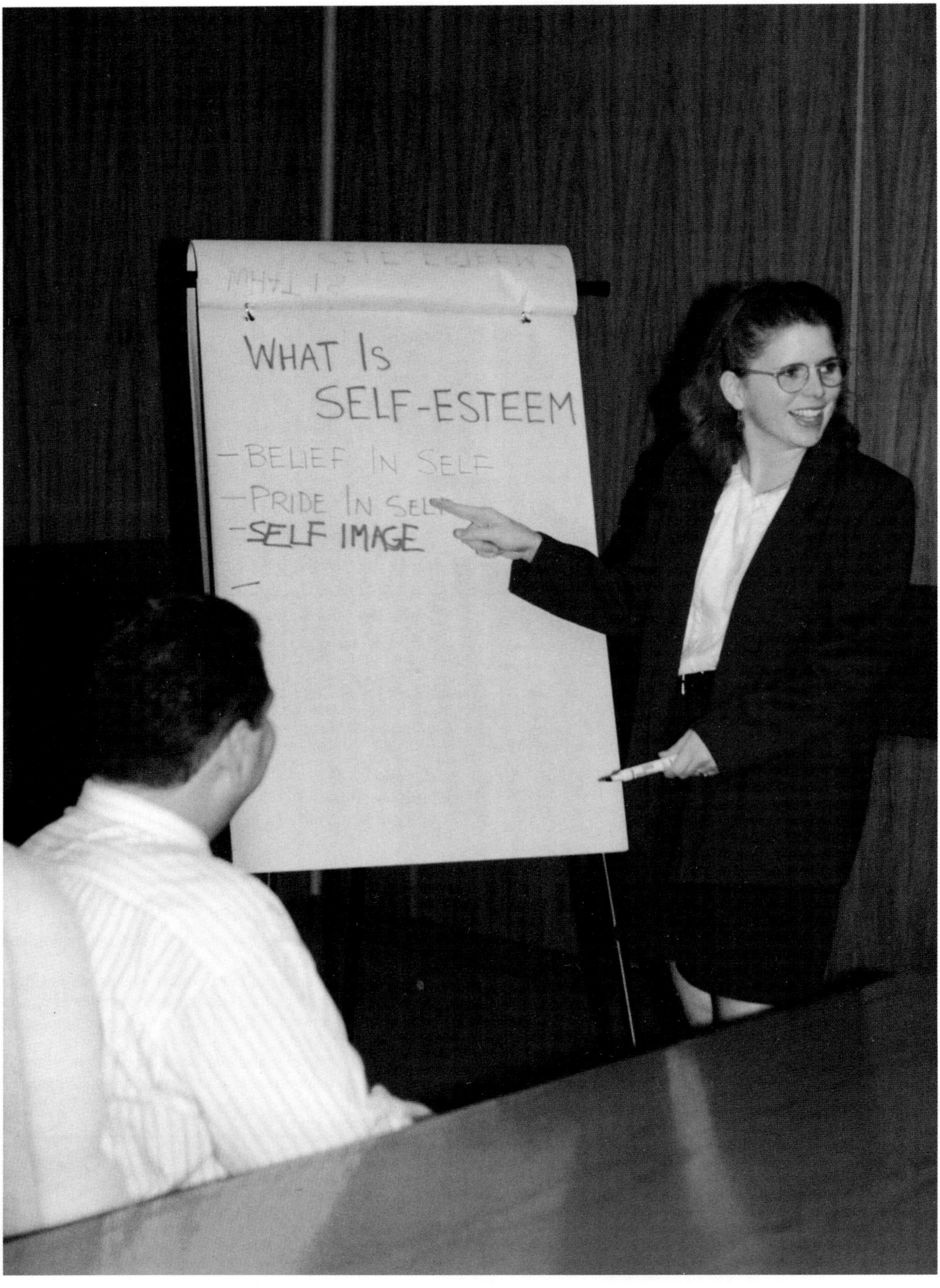
WHAT IS
SELF-ESTEEM
—BELIEF IN SELF
—SELF IMAGE

9

Motivating, Satisfying, and Leading Employees

LEARNING OBJECTIVES

After studying this chapter, you will be able to
- Discuss the importance of good human relations.
- Identify and summarize various theories of employee motivation.
- Describe strategies for improving employee satisfaction.
- Explain the role of leadership in human relations.

CHAPTER OUTLINE

Opening Case: Making Peace with the Work Force

The Importance of Good Human Relations in Business
Job Satisfaction and Employee Morale
Why Businesses Need Satisfied Employees
Job Satisfaction and Dissatisfaction Trends

Motivation in the Workplace
Classical Theory and Scientific Management
The Hawthorne Studies
Contemporary Motivation Theories

Strategies for Enhancing Job Satisfaction
Reinforcement and Punishment
Management by Objectives
Participative Management
Job Enrichment and Redesign
Modified Work Schedules

Motivation and Leadership in the 1990s

Concluding Case 9-1: Motivating the Sales Force

Concluding Case 9-2: Teamwork or Dirty Work?

Making Peace with the Work Force

In the 1980s, forestry giant MacMillan Bloedel went through a traumatic time of downsizing, closing mills, shutting down machines, and reducing its work force by 25 000 people. Today it is a very 90s company—trim size, a big presence in the Japanese market, and many innovative products coming from its mills and laboratories. Despite all of its restructuring, however, the company still lost money in 1991 and 1992, and still suffers from competitive disadvantages. A Price-Waterhouse survey showed that the labor cost component of a tonne of pulp from the BC coast was $129, compared to $94 for eastern Canada and $84 for the southern U.S. And the company still suffers from outdated human resource practices, which hamper its drive to become more competitive.

Labor relations have never been particularly good at the company. On three different occasions in the 1980s the company experienced wildcat (unauthorized) strikes. Each time, the company sued the union for lost revenue, and each time they won cash awards and workplace concessions. The regional vice-president of the union says that there is not a lot of trust in the relationship between workers and the company. Further compounding the problem was a remark by the company's president in 1990 that the problems with the Canadian work force meant that the company would be expanding operations only in the U.S.

To resolve its many problems, the company is embarking on a strategy to get its workers more involved in decision making. Several new ideas have been introduced by management, including the following:

- Production plans and financial data are now shared with workers at regular intervals.
- Division managers take union reps on trips to competing mills to show them just how competitive the market has become.
- Joint union/management committees encourage suggestions from workers on how productivity can be improved.

But much distrust remains. At the Port Alberni mill, management and workers struck a deal where the company would spend $5 million to extend early-retirement benefits, and the union would institute much more flexible working arrangements. For example, in the past, if a millwright wanted to work on a pump and needed pipes disconnected, the millwright had to wait for a pipefitter to disconnect the pipes. Now, a worker can do as much of a job as he or she is able to do. Unfortunately, the Port Alberni agreement is falling apart because of poor communication and misunderstood goals. The workers were supposed to "pay back" the $5 million in increased productivity, but the goals that were set have not been reached. As a result, the company has announced that it will shut down part of the mill and another 200 jobs will be lost.

The agreement ran into difficulty because the workers thought they were going to get new investment in the plant and more jobs. The company thought the workers were agreeing to be more cooperative. Workers are now being warned that workplace reforms contain no guarantees. The union has responded by promising to be much less cooperative in the future.

There are still difficulties at Port Alberni. During a strike in 1994, the provincial labor board ruled that workers from TNL Construction should be allowed to cross the picket line. When they tried, a riot ensued. Union officials said the company "set up" the union and caused the trouble by contracting for TNL to do work for the company.

The company has been more successful at the Chemainus mill on Vancouver Island. There, employees are organized into work teams and meet with management each week to make sggestions for improving operations. A gain-sharing program was instituted and started paying out bonuses for productivity. In 1992, for example, each worker received an $11 500 bonus. Company management, concerned because the payout to workers reflected the falling Canadian dollar and skyrocketing lumber prices far more than it did increases in worker productivity, demanded that the plan be redesigned. If properly handled, a gain-sharing program can benefit both the company and workers. The company says that 30 percent of the division's sales increase in 1992 was caused by increased productivity.

Attitude adjustments are still necessary. While the company talks of teamwork and flexibility, it still threatened to sue the union for a one-day wildcat strike over company plans to discontinue bus service for workers. For its part, the union says it is willing to talk aobut increasing the company's competitiveness, but it interprets every initiative as a threat to the status quo. Perhaps the company has discovered the key to better employee relations—money. For people to produce more, they must see some personal benefit in doing so.   ◆

MacMillan-Bloedel is not the only company that is having difficulties with its workers. As competitive pressures have increased during the 1990s, many companies have tried to increase worker productivity. But many workers simply feel that they are being asked to work harder for the same money.

Because the firm's human resources are its most important asset, managers must effectively motivate, lead, and satisfy employees. In this chapter, we will explore the reasons why satisfied employees are an asset to any company. We will also consider some of the approaches managers have taken to satisfy employees over the years. Increasingly, companies are looking for ways to enhance workers' job satisfaction and to develop managers with the leadership skills to meet both employee and corporate goals.

The Importance of Good Human Relations in Business

Human relations refers to the interactions between employers and employees and their attitudes toward one another. In this section, we will explore ways to define good human relations and some of the reasons they benefit businesses.

human relations
Interactions between employers and employees and their attitudes toward one another.

Job Satisfaction and Employee Morale

One way to assess human relations in a firm is by workers' job satisfaction. **Job satisfaction** is the pleasurable feeling experienced from doing your job well, whether you are a mail carrier, retail clerk, bus driver, or business executive. Employees with high job satisfaction are also likely to have high employee morale. **Morale** is the mental attitude that employees have about their workplace. It reflects the degree to which employees perceive that their needs are being met by the job.

job satisfaction
The pleasure and feeling of accomplishment employees derive from performing their jobs well.

morale
The generally positive or negative mental attitude of employees toward their work and work place.

Why Businesses Need Satisfied Employees

When workers are enthusiastic and happy with their jobs the organization benefits in many ways. Because they are committed to their work and the organization, satisfied workers are more likely to work hard and try to make useful contributions to the organization. They will also have fewer grievances and are less likely to engage in negative behaviors (e.g., complaining, deliberately slowing their work pace, etc.). Satisfied workers are also more likely to come to work every day and are more likely to remain with the organization. So, by ensuring that employees are satisfied, management gains a more efficient and smooth-running company.

Empowerment of employees is the buzzword of the 1990s. It means motivating and energizing employees to create high-quality products and to provide bend-over-backwards service to customers so that the firm is more competitive. It means eliminating whole layers of traditional management that exist simply to control people. Properly used, it can reduce absenteeism and turnover and increase quality and productivity.[1]

empowerment
Motivating employees to produce high quality products.

Just as the rewards of high worker satisfaction and morale are great, so are the costs of job dissatisfaction and poor morale. Dissatisfied workers, for example, are far more likely to be absent due to minor illnesses, personal reasons, or a general disinclination to go to work. Low morale may also result in high turnover. Some turnover is a natural and healthy way to weed out low-performing workers in any organization. But high levels of turnover have many negative consequences, including numerous vacancies, disruption in production, decreased productivity, and high retraining costs.

Job Satisfaction and Dissatisfaction Trends

The picture of Canadian industry shows mixed results when companies try to give employees what they want and to keep them on the job. Consider the following:

■ A survey of 2300 workers by the Wyatt Co. of Vancouver found that three-quarters of Canadian workers are satisfied with the content of their job, but fewer than half are happy with the way they are managed. Workers felt that management did not show genuine interest in them and did not treat them with dignity. Managers, on the other hand, felt that they *did* treat workers with dignity. Perhaps most disconcerting of all, fewer than one-third of those surveyed felt that promotions were based on merit. The longer they had been with a company, the more cynical they were about this issue.[2]

■ Another survey of 1631 employees from 94 companies across Canada and the U.S. found that, while employees are optimistic and committed to their work, they also feel frustrated because they have no control over what happens in their job. Most employees feel that their abilities are not used to the fullest extent. They want direction and measurable goals.[3]

■ Based on responses from 7000 private- and public-sector workers, a Conference Board of Canada survey found the following:

> One-third of employees felt that caring for children or elderly parents limited their career advancement.
> One-eighth had left an employer because of family responsibilities.
> Seventeen percent had turned down promotions.
> Twenty-five percent had turned down transfers.
> Women were four times as likely as men to report conflicts in home and work responsibilities.[4]

All categories of employees—professional, clerical, management, and hourly—feel less secure in their jobs than just a few years ago. This pattern stems in part from cutbacks and layoffs experienced throughout industry in recent years. Many large corporations have announced plant closings, putting thousands of employees out of work. Not surprisingly, workers are likely to feel decreased commitment and job satisfaction. Employees at small firms are generally more content with their lot, a situation explained in the box "When Good Things Come in Small Places." But it may be difficult to motivate some employees in family-owned firms—they know they will never control the firm because they are not part of the family. The video case "Family Business" on p. 292 addresses this question of succession in family-owned businesses.

Many workers are also dissatisfied with their salaries. Some, for example, do not think that pay is fairly distributed within their company. A large majority of nonmanagement employees do not believe that pay increases are linked directly to performance. Many workers think they are underpaid compared to people in other companies. The box "Workplace Blues" on p. 240 describes how many workers feel about their job and the company they work for.

Motivation in the Workplace

motivation

The set of forces that causes people to behave in certain ways.

Although job satisfaction and morale are important, employee motivation is even more critical to a firm's success. As we saw in Chapter 5, motivation is one part of the managerial function of directing. Broadly defined, **motivation** is the set of forces that cause people to behave in certain ways. For example, while one worker may be motivated to work hard to produce as much as possible, another may be motivated to do just enough to get by. Managers must understand these differences in behavior and the reasons for them.

The Canadian Business Scene

WHEN GOOD THINGS COME IN SMALL PLACES

Most small companies do not pay as well as larger firms. They often cannot offer the benefits—especially pension plans—that are standard features at giant corporations. In many cases, they do not offer the chance for advancement to be found in a bigger company.

Why, then, do surveys consistently find that employees of small businesses are happier about their lot than corporate workers? The answer appears to lie in the old adage that "money isn't everything."

Chief among the reasons people give for enjoying their positions in small companies is the opportunity to make a difference. Especially in very small firms, virtually every employee has access to the top managers. With access comes the ability to take ideas for change and improvements to the people who can make them happen.

Many managers and employees of small businesses also enjoy the challenge of making a new business succeed. In place of the square-peg/square-hole jobs in larger companies, small firms welcome people with the ability and willingness to take on all sorts of projects.

The diversity of work attracts some managers away from large corporations, despite the lower pay at small firms. Increasingly, such managers are taking lateral (same job level) moves to smaller companies for the opportunity to gain broader experience. Then, with new skills, they return to the corporate world at higher levels and higher salaries.

People do differ in their satisfaction with small companies, however. Not surprisingly, satisfaction with a small company is often directly linked to an individual's position within that company. In general, the higher the level, the higher the satisfaction. Line workers, who tend to suffer the downside of low pay without getting the benefit of challenging work, are most apt to work for a small firm only because it is conveniently located.

At the other end of the scale, professional staff such as lawyers, accountants, and scientists enjoy the greatest challenges and feel the greatest satisfaction with their jobs. Salespeople, a positive breed by nature, fairly gush with enthusiasm for the flexibility of small companies. "If you have to change a policy to make a customer happy, it's easier," notes one sales representative for a small firm.

What about the managers? For many, small companies are a mixed blessing. Company owners who won't share decision-making power can be a source of frustration. Lack of opportunity for advancement—where do you go in a family-run firm with nine family members heading the departments?—drives many out. Managers at small companies are no less likely than their corporate counterparts to change jobs.

Over the years, many theories have been proposed to address the issues of motivation. In this section, we will focus on three major approaches to motivation in the workplace that reflect a chronology of thinking in the area: *classical theory* and *scientific management, behavior theory,* and *contemporary motivational theories*.

Classical Theory and Scientific Management

According to the so-called **classical theory of motivation**, workers are motivated solely by money. In his book *The Principles of Scientific Management* (1911), industrial engineer Frederick Taylor proposed a way for both companies and workers to benefit from this widely accepted view of life in the workplace.[5] If workers are motivated by money, Taylor reasoned, then paying them more would prompt them to produce more. Meanwhile, the firm that analyzed jobs and found better ways to perform them would be able to produce goods more cheaply, make higher profits, and thus pay—and motivate—workers better than its competitors.

Taylor's approach is known as **scientific management**. His ideas captured the imagination of many managers in the early twentieth century. Soon, plants across Canada and the U.S. were hiring experts to perform **time-and-motion studies**. Industrial-engineering techniques were applied to each facet of a job

classical theory of motivation
A theory of motivation that presumes that workers are motivated almost solely by money.

scientific management
Analyzing jobs and finding better, more efficient ways to perform them.

time-and-motion studies
The use of industrial-engineering techniques to study every aspect of a specific job to determine how to perform it most efficiently.

The Canadian Business Scene

WORKPLACE BLUES

Lately, many business journals have reported on the demoralization of business managers. The low morale reported by so many middle managers in the 1990s is the result of job losses, a vastly increased workload for those who remain on the job, and a feeling that their work world is completely beyond their control.

Middle managers increasingly perceive that top management has no "game plan" other than to draw enormous salaries for themselves (see the box on Executive Compensation in Chapter 8). The logical consequence is that many white-collar workers now have attitudes toward "the brass" that are more cynical than they were in the past.

"Loyalty between the corporation and its managers extends only as far as the next paycheque now," mourns one formerly committed manager. "In my career, I gave up a lot of personal plans—anniversary parties, vacations, and so on—for the sake of the company. I wouldn't do that today because I've realized all the loyalty and sacrifice was going one way only." Instead, more and more middle managers are turning to smaller companies, hoping not only to gain a real voice in operations, but also to escape the frenetic world of the large corporation.

Corporations benefit when demoralized managers move on. Low morale in the workplace has been linked to low productivity for reasons ranging from work avoidance (such as hanging out at the water cooler) to job avoidance (such as calling in sick) to sabotage (both physical sabotage of company property and "emotional" sabotage of other workers).

What can a company with low morale do? The buzzword in business today is "empowerment"—giving workers at all levels a feeling that they *can* control things, that they *do* make a difference. One of the quickest ways to empower employees is to make them part owners of the business, a route many companies (including such industry giants as Avis) have taken successfully. Giving teams of employees full authority over meaningful projects from start to finish can also build commitment to the firm. Conducting frequent surveys of employee attitudes, soliciting employee input, and—most importantly—*acting on that input* have given companies such as Hyatt an edge in attracting and keeping valued staff.

In the long run, though, rebuilding morale will require rebuilding both trust and communication between upper management and those below. Those searching for the source of the current morale problem need look no further than the one place where few seem to realize there *is* a morale problem: the executive suite. Despite widespread press reports of low morale, 91 percent of CEOs at major companies said morale among middle managers in their companies was "excellent" or "very good." Is anybody up there listening?

---

piecework system

Paying workers a set rate for each piece of work produced.

in order to determine how to perform it most efficiently. These studies were the first "scientific" attempts to break down jobs into easily repeated components and to devise more efficient tools and machines for performing them.

As for compensation, Taylor's *differential percent system* was a new twist on the standard **piecework system** by which a worker was paid a set rate per piece completed. For example, a worker in a garment shop might receive 25 cents for each sleeve stitched. Under Taylor's system, however, workers who fell below a specified quota were paid at a certain level—a different percent—per piece. Those who exceeded the quota got higher pay, not just for the extra pieces but for all the pieces they completed.

Taylor's approach enjoyed much initial success among manual laborers. In many heavy industries, management was willing to pay greater wages for significant increases in productivity. Henry Ford, for example, was eventually able to build cars more rapidly and cheaply than any other automaker, in large part by paying his workers *more than double* the usual wage. Ultimately, however, the scientific management system began to show flaws resulting from its failure to see that factors other than money often contribute to job satisfaction.

The Hawthorne Studies

One of the first challenges to the classical theory of human relations management came about by accident. In 1925, a group of Harvard researchers began a study at the Hawthorne Works of Western Electric. Their intent was to examine the relationship between changes in the physical environment and worker output, with an eye to increasing productivity.

The results of the experiment at first confused, then amazed, the scientists. Increasing lighting levels improved productivity but so did lowering lighting levels. And against all expectations, raising the pay of workers failed to increase their productivity. Gradually they pieced together the puzzle. The explanation for the lighting phenomenon lay in workers' response to attention. In essence, they determined that almost any action on the part of management that made workers believe they were receiving special attention caused worker productivity to rise. This result, known as the **Hawthorne effect**, had a major influence on human relations management, convincing many businesses that paying attention to employees is indeed good for business.

But, as the scientists also found, the Hawthorne effect has limits. Even a pay raise is not enough to get people to work harder if they have an informal consensus that such behavior is inappropriate. For example, they found that workers in a wiring room received constant criticism from their peers when they exceeded the group norm for output. Eventually, most got the message and decreased their production to the established level. This result has led businesses to pay greater attention to the informal organization within their companies (see Chapter 6) and to recognize that human relations management is not a perfect solution.[6]

Hawthorne effect

The tendency for workers' productivity to increase when they feel they are receiving special attention from management.

The Hawthorne studies were an important step in developing an appreciation for the human factor at work. These women worked under different lighting conditions as researchers monitored their productivity. To the researchers' amazement, productivity increased regardless of whether the light was increased or decreased.

Contemporary Motivation Theories

Following the Hawthorne studies, managers and researchers alike focused more attention on the importance of good human relations in motivating employee performance. Stressing the factors that cause, focus, and sustain workers' behavior, most motivation theorists are concerned with the ways in which management thinks about and treats employees. The major motivation theories include the *human-resources model*, the *hierarchy of needs model*, *two-factory theory*, *expectancy theory*, *equity theory*, and *good-setting theory*.

The Human-Resources Model: Theories X and Y.   In an important study, behavioral scientist Douglas McGregor concluded that managers had radically different beliefs about how best to use the human resources at a firm's disposal. He classified these beliefs into sets of assumptions that he labeled "Theory X" and "Theory Y."[7] The basic differences between these two theories are highlighted in Table 9.1.

TABLE 9.1   Beliefs about People at Work

Theory X and theory Y convey very different assumptions about people at work.

Theory X	Theory Y
1. People are lazy.	1. People are energetic.
2. People lack ambition and dislike responsibility.	2. People are ambitious and seek responsibility.
3. People are self-centered.	3. People can be selfless.
4. People resist change.	4. People want to contribute to business growth and change.
5. People are gullible and not very bright.	5. People are intelligent.

Theory X

A management approach based on the belief that people must be forced to be productive because they are naturally lazy, irresponsible, and uncooperative.

Theory Y

A management approach based on the belief that people want to be productive because they are naturally energetic, responsible, and cooperative.

Managers who subscribe to **Theory X** tend to believe that people are naturally lazy and uncooperative and must therefore be either punished or rewarded to be made productive. Managers who incline to **Theory Y** tend to believe that people are naturally energetic, growth-oriented, self-motivated, and interested in being productive.

McGregor generally favored Theory Y beliefs. Thus he argued that Theory Y managers are more likely to have satisfied, motivated employees. Of course, Theory X and Y distinctions are somewhat simplistic and offer little concrete basis for action. Their value lies primarily in their ability to highlight and analyze the behavior of managers in light of their attitudes toward employees.

Maslow's Hierarchy of Needs Model.   Psychologist Abraham Maslow proposed that people have a number of different needs that they attempt to satisfy in their work. He classified these needs into five basic types and suggested that they are arranged in the hierarchy of importance shown in Figure 9.1. According to Maslow, needs are hierarchical because lower-level needs must be met before a person will try to satisfy those on a higher level.[8]

- *Physiological needs* are necessary for survival; they include food, water, shelter, and sleep. Businesses address these needs by providing both comfortable working environments and salaries sufficient to buy food and shelter.
- *Security needs* include the needs for stability and protection from the unknown. Many employers thus offer pension plans and job security.

GENERAL EXAMPLES   ORGANIZATIONAL EXAMPLES

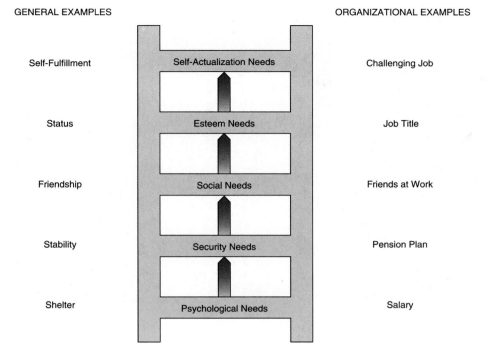

Self-Fulfillment   Self-Actualization Needs   Challenging Job

Status   Esteem Needs   Job Title

Friendship   Social Needs   Friends at Work

Stability   Security Needs   Pension Plan

Shelter   Psychological Needs   Salary

Figure 9.1
Maslow's hierarchy of human needs provides a useful categorization of the different needs people have.

- *Social needs* include the needs for friendship and companionship. Making friends at work can help to satisfy social needs, as can the feeling that you "belong" in a company.
- *Esteem needs* include the need for status and recognition as well as the need for self-respect. Respected job titles and large offices are among the things that businesses can provide to address these needs.
- Finally, *self-actualization needs* are needs for self-fulfillment. They include the needs to grow and develop one's capabilities and to achieve new and meaningful goals. Challenging job assignments can help satisfy these needs.

According to Maslow, once one set of needs has been satisfied, it ceases to motivate behavior. This is the sense in which the hierarchical nature of lower- and higher-level needs affects employee motivation and satisfaction. For example, if you feel secure in your job, a new pension plan will probably be less important to you than the chance to make new friends and join an informal network among your co-workers. If, however, a lower-level need suddenly becomes unfulfilled, most people immediately refocus on that lower level. Suppose, for example, that you are seeking to meet your esteem needs by working as a divisional manager at a major company. If you learn that your division—and consequently your job—may be eliminated, you might very well find the promise of job security at a new firm as motivating as a promotion once would have been in your old company.

Maslow's theory recognizes that because different people have different needs, they are motivated by different things. Unfortunately, research has found that the hierarchy varies widely, not only for different people but across different cultures.

Rewards are an important determinant of employee motivation. Because this woman's outstanding performance was recognized and rewarded, she is likely to continue to work hard. Good working conditions may also motivate employees. This clean, organized office helps workers do their jobs.

two-factor theory

A theory of human relations developed by Frederick Herzberg that identifies factors that must be present for employees to be satisfied with their jobs and factors that, if increased, lead employees to work harder.

Two-Factor Theory.   After studying a group of accountants and engineers, psychologist Frederick Herzberg concluded that job satisfaction and dissatisfaction depend on two factors: *hygiene factors*, such as working conditions, and *motivating factors*, such as recognition for a job well done.[9]

According to **two-factor theory**, hygiene factors affect motivation and satisfaction only if they are *absent* or *fail* to meet expectations. For example, workers will be dissatisfied if they believe that they have poor working conditions. If working conditions are improved, however, they will not necessarily become *satisfied*; they will simply be *not dissatisfied*. On the other hand, if workers receive no recognition for successful work, they may be neither dissatisfied nor satisfied. If recognition is provided, they will likely become more satisfied.

Figure 9.2 illustrates two-factor theory. Note that motivation factors lie along a continuum from *satisfaction* to no satisfaction. Hygiene factors, on the other hand, are likely to produce feelings that lie on a continuum from *dissatisfaction* to *no dissatisfaction*. While motivation factors are directly related to the work that employees actually perform, hygiene factors refer to the environment in which they perform it.

This theory thus suggests that managers should follow a two-step approach to enhancing motivation. First, they must ensure that hygiene factors—working conditions, clearly stated policies—are acceptable. This practice will result in an absence of dissatisfaction. Then they must offer motivating factors—recognition, added responsibility—as means of improving satisfaction and motivation.

Research suggests that two-factor theory works in some professional settings, but it is not as effective in clerical and manufacturing settings. (Herzberg's research was limited to professionals—accountants and engineers only.) In addition, one person's hygiene factor may be another person's motivating factor. For example, if money represents nothing more than pay for time worked, it may be a hygiene factor for one person. For another person, however, money may be a motivating factor because it represents recognition and achievement.

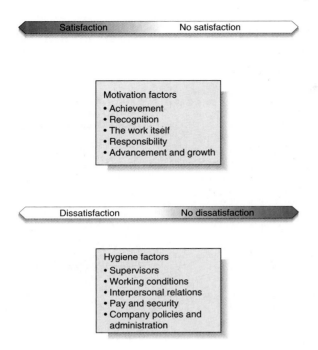

Figure 9.2
According to two-factor theory, job satisfaction
depends on two factors.

Expectancy Theory.   **Expectancy theory** suggests that people are
motivated to work toward rewards which they want *and* which they believe
they have a reasonable chance—or expectancy—of obtaining.[10] A reward
that seems out of reach, for example, is not likely to be motivating even if it
is intrinsically positive. Consider the case of an assistant department manager
who learns that a division manager has retired and that the firm is looking for
a replacement. Even though she wants the job, she does not apply for it
because she doubts that she would be selected. She also learns that the firm
is looking for a production manager on a later shift. She thinks that she
could get this job but does not apply because she does not want to change
shifts. Finally, she learns of an opening one level higher—full department
manager—in her own division. She may well apply for this job because she
both wants it and thinks that she has a good chance of getting it.

Figure 9.3 shows a simplified expectancy model. As you can see, this
theory holds that motivation leads to effort, whose success depends on both
an employee's ability and the environment in which he or she is working.
Effort also leads to various outcomes. The employee ultimately places a value
on each of these outcomes—say, relatively desirable or undesirable. That
value will determine the employee's level of motivation and the quality of
the effort that he or she will put forth.

Expectancy theory also helps to explain why some people do not work as
hard as they can when their salaries are based purely on seniority: Because they
are paid the same whether they work very hard or hard enough to get by,
there is no financial incentive for them to work harder. In other words, they
ask themselves, "If I work harder, will I get a pay raise?" and conclude that the
answer is no—that they expect not. Similarly, if hard work will result in one or
more *undesirable* outcomes—say, a transfer to another location or a promotion
to a job that requires travel—employees will not be motivated to work hard.

expectancy theory
The theory that people are motivated to work toward rewards which they want and *which they believe they have a reasonable chance of obtaining.*

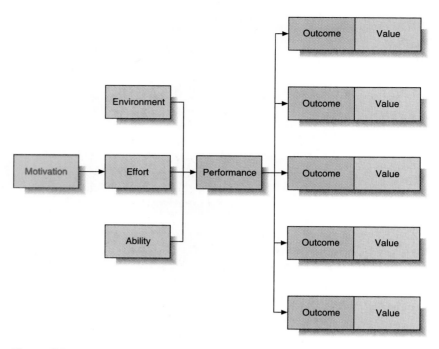

Figure 9.3
Expectancy theory suggests that obtainable rewards motivate people more than rewards that appear to be out of reach.

equity theory

The theory that people compare (1) what they contribute to their job with what they get in return, and (2) their input/output ratio with that of other employees.

Equity Theory.   **Equity theory** focuses on social comparisons—people evaluating their treatment by the organization relative to the treatment of others. This approach says that people begin by analyzing what they contribute to their jobs (time, effort, education, experience, and so forth) relative to what they get in return (salary, benefits, recognition, security). The result is a ratio of contribution to return. Then they compare their own ratios to those of other employees. Depending on their assessments, they experience feelings of equity or inequity.[11]

For example, suppose a new college graduate gets a starting job at a large manufacturing firm. His starting salary is $25 000 per year, he gets a compact company car, and he shares an office with another new employee. If he later learns that another new employee has received the same salary, car, and office arrangement, he will feel equitably treated. If the other newcomer, however, has received $30 000, a full-size company car, and a private office, he may feel inequity.

Note, however, that the two ratios do not have to be the *same*—they need be only *fair*. Let's assume, for instance, that our new employee has a bachelor's degree and two years' work experience. Perhaps he learns subsequently that the other new employee has an advanced degree and ten years' experience. After first feeling inequity, our new employee may now conclude that his comparison person is actually contributing more to the organization. The other employee is equitably entitled, therefore, to receive more in return.

When people feel that they are being inequitably treated, they may do various things to restore fairness. For example, they may ask for raises, reduce their effort, work shorter hours, or just complain to their bosses. They may also rationalize their situation ("management succumbed to pressure to promote a woman"), find different people with whom to compare themselves, or leave their jobs altogether.

Good examples of equity theory at work can be found in professional sports. Each year, for example, rookies are signed to lucrative contracts. No sooner is the ink is dry than veteran players start grumbling about raises or revised contracts.

Goal-Setting Theory.   **Goal-setting theory** describes the kinds of goals that better motivate employees. In general, effective goals tend to have two basic characteristics. First, they are moderately difficult: While a goal that is too easy does little to enhance effort and motivation, a goal that is too difficult also fails to motivate people. Second, they are specific. A goal of "do your best," for instance, does not motivate people nearly as much as a goal like "increase profits by 10 percent." The specificity and clarity of this goal serves to focus attention and energy on exactly what needs to be done.[12]

An important aspect of goal setting in the employee's participation in the goal-setting process. When people help to select the goals that they are to work toward, they tend to accept them more readily and are more committed to achieving them. On the other hand, when goals are merely assigned to people with little or no any input on their part, they are less likely to adopt them.

goal-setting theory
The theory that people perform better when they set specific, quantified, time-framed goals.

Strategies for Enhancing Job Satisfaction

Deciding what motivates workers and provides job satisfaction is only part of the manager's battle. The other part is to apply that knowledge. Experts have suggested—and many companies have instituted—a wide range of programs designed to make jobs more interesting and rewarding and the work environment more pleasant. In this section, we will consider five of the most common types of programs: reinforcement and punishment, management by objectives, participative management, job enrichment and re-design, and modified work schedules.

These employees are part of a quality circle that is discussing ways to improve work methods and thereby increase productivity.

Reinforcement and Punishment

Many companies try to alter workers' behavior through systematic rewards and punishment for specific behaviors. Rewards, or positive reinforcement, can be used to increase the frequency of desired behaviors. For example, paying large cash bonuses to salespeople who exceed their quotas will cause them to work even harder in the future to exceed their quotas again. New incentive reward systems at B.C. Tel, Drexis Inc., and the Toronto SkyDome all rely on positive reinforcement (see the box "Incentives and Motivation").

Punishment, on the other hand, is used to get people to change their behavior by giving them unpleasant consequences. Employees who come to work late repeatedly may need to be suspended or have their pay docked to change their behavior in the future. When the National Hockey League fines or suspends players found guilty of drug abuse, it is seeking to change their behavior in the future.

Sometimes punishments may be necessary. Most managers dislike punishing unacceptable behavior, in part because workers may respond with anger, resentment, hostility, or retaliation.

Extensive reinforcement works best when people are learning new behavior, new skills, and new jobs. As they become more adept, rewards can become more infrequent. Managers generally like giving rewards and placing a positive value on a person's good behavior, since these actions make for positive employer-employee relationships. Moreover, rewards are more likely to motivate workers and increase their job satisfaction than are punishments.

There are some limitations on using rewards to shape workers' behavior. Rewards will only work if people:

- believe they can perform better by making an effort.
- believe that they will receive rewards for performing better.
- want the rewards the company offers for performing better.

Management by Objectives

In Chapter 6, we described a technique for managing the planning process called *management by objectives*, or *MBO*. While MBO is mainly concerned with helping managers implement and carry out their plans, it can serve other purposes as well.

One very important benefit of using MBO is improved human relations. For example, when employees sit down with their managers to set goals for the coming year, they learn more about the organization's goals, come to feel that they are an important part of the team, and see how they can improve the company's performance by working toward their own goals.

The year-end assessment of goal attainment and rewards can also improve human relations. Assuming managers are using the MBO system properly, employees should come away from these meetings understanding the value of their contributions and with a fair and equitable reward. Thus, MBO can help employees satisfy a variety of needs and can also facilitate their perceptions of fairness. Investors Syndicate has enjoyed considerable success with its MBO program (refer to the box on p. 146).

Participative Management

participative management
A method of increasing employees' job satisfaction by giving them a voice in how they do their jobs and how the company is managed.

Another popular technique for promoting human relations is **participative management.** Simply stated, participative management involves giving employees a voice in how they do their jobs and how the company is managed. Such participation should make employees feel more committed to the goals of the organization because they help shape them.

The Canadian Business Scene

INCENTIVES AND MOTIVATION

Canadian companies have begun to realize that offering incentives beyond the normal benefits can result in creative ideas as well as large increases in employee productivity. These incentives may be monetary or nonmonetary. Consider the following:

- At B.C. Tel, a suggestion system was implemented that gives cash rewards to employees for ideas that generate revenue or save the company money. The employee receives 10 percent of the money saved or the revenue generated. Employees have received up to $20 000 for ideas.
- Drexis Inc. recently flew 12 employees and their families to Disney World as a reward for increasing sales by over 100 percent in one year.
- Proctor & Redfern Ltd., a consulting engineering firm, lets high achievers serve on committees with senior executives, represent the firm at outside functions, or enroll in development courses for which the company pays the bill.
- Avatar Communications Inc. sent employees on a weeklong Outward Bound expedition into the wilderness. The trip had both reward and motivational components.
- Pitney Bowes Canada Ltd. sent 60 of its top salespeople and their spouses to Hong Kong after they achieved 135 percent of their sales quota; salespeople who achieved 112 percent received a trip to San Diego.
- At Cloverdale Paint, employees who come up with innovative ideas to improve customer service receive a personal letter from the president and a coffee mug or T-shirt bearing the company logo. The best idea submitted each quarter earns the originator a restaurant gift certificate worth $50. The employee who makes the best suggestion of the year receives $200 and an engraved plaque presented at a workplace ceremony.
- Manitoba Telephone System instituted a suggestion system called IDEA$PLUS, which gives employees cash awards of up to $10 000 for good ideas.
- Employees at the Toronto SkyDome are given coupons for exceptional service, such as finding a lost child or repairing a broken seat. The coupons can be used to accumulate points which can be redeemed for prizes.
- Emery Apparel Canada Inc. conducts an annual "Oscar" awards ceremony. With great hoopla, the CEO asks for the envelope with the name of the winner of the top award. Last year, a 12-year employee won the award for figuring out (on her own time) how to satisfy a customer's difficult request.
- At Ford Motor Company, workers are rewarded for suggestions that save the company money. For example, when a metal press operator found a way to save on the amount of sheet metal used in floor panels, the company gave back to the worker $14 000 of the $70 000 saved. A recent study shows that activity like this has an effect—it takes workers at Ford one-third less time to build a car than workers at GM.

Incentives are important for top managers as well. The higher a manager is placed in a firm, the more likely it is that a good chunk of the manager's pay will be performance-based. A Conference Board of Canada study of executive compensation in Canada showed that up to 40 percent of top executives' total compensation comes in the form of incentives. For lower-level managers, the figure was 20 percent, and for other employees it was 10 percent. Top managers in the U.S. often receive up to 60 percent of their total compensation in the form of incentives. Most Canadian companies have set up some type of incentive plan for their senior executives.

Incentive systems must be carefully developed or they will not motivate employee behavior in the desired direction. In addition to the usual sales and profit goals, firms are beginning to look at incentive systems that reward managers for achieving goals like effective downsizing, increasing environmental consciousness, and improving the corporate culture. A decision must also be made about whether the incentive system will be directed at individual employees or groups. Historically, incentives have been directed at individuals, but with the new emphasis on teamwork in organizations, this is changing. Now, a group may get an incentive if it gets a new product launched on time.

Incentive systems must be used with care because they may unintentionally motivate employees to engage in undesirable behavior. For example, stockbrokers are often given bonuses for making sales of mutual funds. Super salespeople may be given trips to exotic locations in return for making their sales goals. This may motivate the salesperson to push a product or service that really doesn't meet the customers' needs.

Some employees prefer a democratic, or supportive, leader. A survey at B.C. Telecom, for example, showed that people with a supportive boss missed less work, were less tense, felt more secure, and were more confident about their ability to get ahead in the company. Supervisors who got negative ratings usually were inflexible, supervised their workers too closely, and didn't communicate useful information to them.[13]

Japanese companies like Honda have been especially effective at practising participative management. And participative management has become more popular in recent years in Canada, partly from imitating the Japanese and partly as businesses and labor unions have become increasingly cooperative. At CP Express and Transport, for example, truck drivers were allowed to decide how to spend $8 million on new equipment.[14] The box "The Japanese Management System" describes some of the strong and weak points of that system.

International Report

THE JAPANESE MANAGEMENT SYSTEM

In the 1980s, the Japanese management system was all the rage. At its most basic, the system contained the following elements:

1. *Lifetime employment.* Employees stay at one firm for their entire career instead of changing jobs as is common in Canada. Seniority is the basis for promotion.

2. *Temporary employees.* Large Japanese firms have many temporary employees, most of them female. If a downturn occurs, these employees are the first to be laid off. Women act as a buffer to protect men's jobs.

3. *Participative decision making.* When an important decision is to be made, everyone who will feel its impact is involved in the decision-making process. A decision is made only after a consensus is reached.

4. *Management training.* An emphasis on company loyalty underlies much management training in Japan. Training is oriented toward groups instead of individuals, and is designed to encourage team spirit.

5. *Other characteristics.* The Japanese management system also emphasizes daily exercise for employees at the work site, pep talks by supervisors, identical uniforms for workers and managers, no unions, nonspecific job classifications, and company outings for employees and their families.

This system has served Japan well over the years. In fact, until recently it was thought that this system made Japan a formidable competitor in world markets. But things have changed dramatically in just a few short years. The 1990s have not been a happy time for Japanese managers and workers. During 1992-94, Japan found itself in a major recession, and industrial output declined for 23 consecutive months, the longest decline on record.

Consumer confidence is weak, unemployment is rising, GNP is declining, and the lifetime employment and seniority ideas are coming under fire.

And now, another problem has appeared. In the past, most of the emphasis in Japanese companies was on training factory workers to carry out their tasks in an efficient manner. But in the process, not enough attention was paid to the productivity of *office workers*. Only a few office workers have personal computers, and it is not unusual for four or five workers to share a phone. The sense of order that pervades the factory is absent in the office.

When times were good in the 1980s, the excess office staff was not noticeable. But the deep recession of the 1990s has made the problem very clear. Japanese managers are now realizing that no amount of economizing in the factory can make up for overstaffed offices. One management consultant estimates that Japan's big public companies have between 12 and 20 percent too many middle managers.

Japanese companies are beginning to address the problem of overstaffing. Many companies have reduced the hiring of college graduates, and are hoping that attrition will eventually solve the problem of overstaffing. Others are using the carrot-and-stick approach. At Honda Motors, for example, the seniority system is being replaced with a merit system. Employees will now be judged on the basis of how well they meet six-month goals set by their managers. Those who do not perform well will end up in lower paying jobs.

Toyota Motor is trying to shock its white-collar workers into being more productive. Each department has been asked to give up 20 percent of its employees to task forces that will identify new business opportunities and explore ways to improve white collar productivity.

At one level, employees may be given decision-making responsibility for certain narrow activities, such as when to take their lunch breaks, how to do their jobs, and so forth. At a broader level, employees are also being given a say in more significant issues and decisions. One popular technique to encourage participative management is the **quality circle,** a group of employees who meet regularly to consider solutions for problems in their work area. Great West Life, for example, has reported success with its quality circle program. Quality circles are explored in detail in Chapters 11 and 13.

While some employees thrive in participative management programs, they are not for everyone. The key is for managers to provide employees with opportunities to participate in decision making only to the extent that they want to participate. If employees really would prefer not to be involved, they should not be forced.

quality circle
A technique for maximizing quality of production. Employees are grouped into small teams that define, analyze, and solve quality and other process-related problems within their area.

Job Enrichment and Redesign

While MBO programs and participative management can work in a variety of settings, job enrichment and job redesign programs can increase satisfaction only if a job lacks motivating factors to begin with.

Job Enrichment Programs.   Based on the two-factor theory discussed earlier, **job enrichment** attempts to add one or more motivating factors to a situation. For example, job rotation programs add to growth opportunities by rotating an employee through various positions in the firm. Workers gain new skills and a broader overview of their work that allows them to contribute to the firm in more ways.

Other job enrichment programs focus on increasing responsibility or recognition. At one company, a group of eight typists worked in isolated cubicles. Their job involved taking calls from any of dozens of field sales representatives and typing up service orders. They had no client contact; if they had a question about the order, for example, they had to call the sales representative. They also received little performance feedback. Interviews with these workers suggested that they were bored with their jobs and did not feel valued. As part of a job enrichment program, each typist was paired with a small group of designated sales representatives and became a part of their team. Typists were also given permission to call clients directly if they had questions about the order. Finally, a new feedback system was installed to give the typists more information about their performance. As a result, their performance improved and absenteeism decreased markedly.[15]

job enrichment
A method of increasing employees' job satisfaction by extending or adding motivating factors such as responsibility or growth.

Job Redesign Programs.   In some ways an extension of job enrichment, **job redesign** is even more application-oriented and recognizes that different people want different things from their jobs. By restructuring work to achieve a more satisfactory person-job fit, job redesign can motivate individuals who have a high need for growth or achievement.[16] Three typical ways of implementing job redesign are to combine tasks, to form natural work groups, and to establish client relationships.

Combining tasks enlarges a job and increases its variety, making workers feel that their work is more meaningful. In turn, workers are more motivated. For example, the job done by a computer programmer who maintains computer systems might be redesigned to include some system design and development work. The programmer is then able to use additional skills and is involved in the overall system package.

People who do different jobs on the same project are good candidates for *natural work groups.* On the one hand, these groups help employees get an overview of their jobs and see their importance in the total structure. On the

job redesign
A method of increasing employees' job satisfaction by improving the worker-job fit through combining tasks, creating natural work groups, and/or establishing client relationships.

One part of job redesign programs is to establish client relationships. This mechanic is explaining to a customer why she needs to have her air filter changed. Such personal contact often motivates employees to work harder because they can see how their work benefits customers.

other hand, these groups help management, and the firm in general, because the people working on a project are usually the most knowledgeable about it and are thus able to solve problems related to it. Quality circles are natural work groups.

To see how natural work groups affect motivation, consider a group where each employee does a small part of the job of assembling radios. One person sees his job as attaching red wires while another sees hers as attaching control knobs. The jobs could be redesigned to allow the group to decide who does what and in what order. The workers can exchange jobs and plan their work schedules. Now they all see themselves as part of a team that assembles radios.

A third way of redesigning a job is to *establish client relationships*—to let employees interact with customers. This approach increases the variety of a job. It also gives workers greater feelings of control over their jobs and more feedback about their performance. Lotus Development Corp. uses this approach as a means of granting necessary independence to creative employees: Instead of responding to instructions from marketing managers on how to develop new products, software writers are encouraged to work directly with customers. Similarly, software writers at Microsoft watch test users work with programs and discuss problems with them directly rather than receive feedback from third-party researchers.

Modified Work Schedules

As another way of increasing job satisfaction, many companies are trying out different approaches to working hours and the work week. Several types of modified work schedules have been tried, including flextime, the compressed workweek, telecommuting, and workshare programs.

Flextime.   Some modifications involve adjusting a standard daily work schedule. **Flextime** allows people to pick their working hours. Figure 9.4

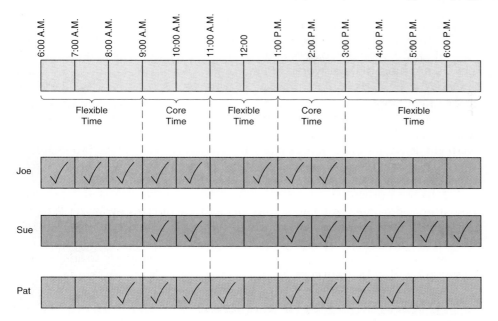

Figure 9.4
Flextime schedules include core time, when everyone must be at work, and flexible time, during which employees can set their own working hours.

illustrates how a flextime system might be arranged and how different people might use it. The office is open from 6 a.m. until 7 p.m. Core time is 9 a.m. until 11 a.m. and 1 p.m. until 3 p.m. Joe, being an early riser, comes in at 6 a.m., takes an hour lunch between 11 and 12, and finishes his day by 3 p.m. Sue, on the other hand, prefers a later day. She comes in at 9 a.m., takes a long lunch from 11 a.m. to 1 p.m., and then works until 7 p.m. Pat works a more traditional day from 8 a.m. until 5 p.m.

Flextime programs give employees more flexibility in their professional and personal lives. Such programs allow workers to plan around the work schedules of spouses and the school schedules of young children, for example. The increased feeling of freedom and control over their work life also reduces individuals' levels of stress.

Companies can also benefit from flextime programs. In large urban areas, flextime programs reduce traffic congestion that contributes to lost work time. Companies benefit from the higher levels of commitment and job satisfaction among workers in such programs. 3M Canada and National Cash Register are among the companies that have adopted some form of flextime. A survey of 1600 Canadian companies showed that nearly half of them had some type of flextime program.

The Compressed Workweek.   In the **compressed workweek**, employees work fewer days per week, but more hours on the days they do work. The most popular compressed workweek is 4 days, 10 hours per day, but some companies have also experimented with 3 days, 12 hours per day. The "weekend worker" program at 3M Canada in London, Ontario offers workers 12 hour shifts on Saturdays and Sundays only, and pays them the same wage as if they had worked normal hours Monday through Friday. There is a long waiting list to transfer to weekend work.[17]

Tellers at the Bank of Montreal in Oakville Place work long days (up to 14 hours), but enjoy a short work week. Some tellers work 7 a.m. to 9 p.m.

flextime
A method of increasing employees' job satisfaction by allowing them some choice in the hours they work.

compressed workweek
Employees work fewer days per week, but more hours on the days they do work.

Thursday and Friday, and 7:30 a.m. to 5:30 p.m. Saturdays. Others work Monday to Wednesday for 14 hours each day. Employees like the system because it allows them to do personal errands during the day on the weekdays they do not have to be at work.[18]

telecommuting

Allowing employees to do all or some of their work away from the office.

Telecommuting.   A third variation in work design is **telecommuting**, which allows people to do some or all of their work away from their office. The availability of networked computers, fax machines, cellular telephones, and overnight delivery services makes it possible for many independent professionals to work at home or while travelling. More and more Canadian workers do a significant portion of their work outside their conventional offices.[19]

Telecommuting helps employees avoid driving a long way to work, but they often report feeling isolated and lonely. To avoid this problem, B.C. Tel and Bentall Development Inc. jointly developed a satellite telecommuting office in Langley, B.C. It allows workers who used to have to commute to Burnaby or Vancouver to reduce their travel time considerably and still be able to interact with other workers.[20]

But telecommuting may not be for everyone. Would-be telecommuters must ask themselves several important questions: "Can I meet deadlines even when I'm not being closely supervised? What will it be like to be away from the social context of the office five days a week? Can I renegotiate family rules, so my spouse doesn't come home expecting to see dinner on the table just because I've been home all day?"

Another obstacle to establishing a telecommuting program is convincing management that it will be beneficial for everyone involved. Telecommuters may have to fight the perception—from both bosses and co-workers—that if they are not being supervised, they are not working. Managers are often very suspicious about telecommuting, asking "How can I tell if someone is working when I can't see them?"

worksharing (job sharing)

A method of increasing employee job satisfaction by allowing two people to share one job.

Workshare Programs.   A fourth type of modified work schedule, **worksharing** (also called **job sharing**), also benefits both employee and employer. This approach essentially allows two people to share one full-time job. For example, at Steelcase, two talented women in the marketing division both wanted to work part-time. By each working two and a half days a week, they get their wish and the job gets done. In other cases, one person might work mornings and the other afternoons.

Short-run worksharing programs can help ease experienced workers into retirement while training their replacements. Worksharing can also allow students in university co-op programs to combine academic learning with practical experience.

Long-run worksharing programs have proven a good solution for people who want only part-time work. For example, five people might decide to share one reservationist's job at Air Canada with each working one day a week. Each person earns some money, remains in the job market, and enjoys limited travel benefits.

Motivation and Leadership in the 1990s

Motivation and leadership remain critically important areas, but as times change, so do the ways that managers motivate and lead their employees.

On the motivation side, today's employees want rewards that are often very much different from those that earlier generations desired. Money, for example, may not be the prime motivator for most people. In addition, because businesses today cannot offer the degree of job security that many workers want, motivating employees to strive toward higher levels of performance requires skillful attention from managers.

The diversity inherent in today's workforce also makes motivating worker behavior more complex for managers. The reasons for which people work encompass more goals than ever before, and the varying lifestyles of diverse workers means that managers must first pay closer attention to what their employees expect to get for their efforts and then try to link rewards with job performance.

Today's leaders are also finding it necessary to change their own behavior. As organizations become flatter and workers more empowered, managers find it less acceptable to use the autocratic approach to leadership. Instead, many are becoming more democratic, functioning more as "coaches" than "bosses"; in other words, just as an athletic coach teaches athletes how to play and then steps back to let them take the field of competition, many leaders now try to provide workers with the skills and resources to perform at their best before backing off to let them do their work with less oversight and supervision. The box "Leading for Success" outlines some rules followed by successful managers.

The Canadian Business Scene

LEADING FOR SUCCESS

Today, every business is looking for leaders. Individuals who can manage demand for and supply of a company's products are no longer enough. Companies need and want people who can lead them into new areas and into a newly competitive world. But where will these leaders come from? Experts are sharply divided over whether leadership can be taught, at least in the classroom. They do agree on some of the basic qualities of a leader, however.

- *A leader has vision and sets goals.* Vision is the ability to see into the future, as it were, to see where the company can go and how it can get there. Leaders clearly state not only the firm's mission but also the goals and objectives that will enable subordinates to realize this mission.
- *A leader takes risks.* Change and failure are threatening to most people, especially the traditional manager. Leaders see changes as opportunities and failures as lessons learned.
- *A leader hires leaders.* Self-confident leaders are not afraid of hiring other leaders or of grooming subordinates to become leaders. Leaders *are* afraid of hiring mediocre managers.
- *A leader delegates.* In today's competitive world, no one can do it alone. By definition, a leader is a person who has followers.
- *A leader trusts and is loyal to subordinates.* Trust begets trust and loyalty begets loyalty. A manager

who takes a raise while cutting staff is no leader. Leaders are willing to work shoulder to shoulder with subordinates. They view their subordinates not as "resources" to be manipulated but as people to be inspired. Leaders also have a degree of expert knowledge that inspires confidence and trust in their decisions.

- *A leader shares the glory.* Wise leaders recognize that praise is the most effective motivator ever devised. It takes minimal time and effort—only a bit of consideration—to reap huge long-term benefits.
- *A leader takes responsibility.* Managers may get away with blaming subordinates for failures. Leaders know "the buck stops here."
- *A leader is congruent.* "Do as I say, not as I do," is as poor an approach to motivating employees as it is to teaching children.
- *A leader has standards.* Ethical behavior starts at the top. To be looked up to, a leader must set—and follow—high ethical standards. In setting standards for subordinates, leaders know that people generally live up (or down) to the expectations of them.
- *A leader is consistent.* Leaders do not believe they are infallible. They are flexible enough to adapt to new information and circumstances. But they do not bend with every breeze. They stay on course and in focus.

Summary of Key Points

Good *human relations*—the interactions between employers and employees and their attitudes toward one another—are important to business because they lead to high levels of *job satisfaction* (the degree of enjoyment that workers derive from their jobs) and *morale* (workers' overall attitude toward their workplace). Satisfied employees generally exhibit lower levels of absenteeism and turnover; they also have fewer grievances and engage in fewer negative behaviors.

Views of employee motivation have changed dramatically over the years. The *classical theory* holds that people are motivated solely by money. *Scientific management* tried to analyze jobs and increase production by finding better ways to perform tasks. The *Hawthorne studies* were the first to demonstrate the importance of making workers feel that attention is being paid to their needs.

The *human-resources model* identifies two kinds of managers: *Theory X managers*, who believe that people are inherently uncooperative and must be constantly reinforced, and *Theory Y managers*, who believe that people are naturally responsible and self-motivated to be productive.

Maslow's *hierarchy of needs model* proposes that people have a number of different needs (ranging from physiological to self-actualization) that they attempt to satisfy in their work. People must fulfill lower-level needs before seeking to fulfill higher-level needs. *Two-factor theory* suggests that if basic hygiene factors are not met, workers will be dissatisfied; only by increasing motivating factors can companies increase employees' performance.

Expectancy theory holds that people will work hard if they believe that their efforts will lead to desired rewards. *Equity theory* says that motivation depends on the way employees evaluate their treatment by an organization relative to its treatment of other workers. *Goal-setting theory* focuses on the motivational impact of individual goals that are established by both supervisors and workers.

Managers can use several strategies to increase employee motivation and satisfaction. The principle of *reinforcement*, or *behavior modification theory*, holds that reward and punishment can control behavior. *Rewards*, for example, constitute positive reinforcement when they are tied directly to desired or improved performance. *Punishment* (using unpleasant consequences to change undesirable behavior) is generally less effective.

Management by objectives (a system of collaborative goal setting) and *participative management and empowerment* (techniques for giving employees a voice in management decisions) can improve human relations by making employees feel like part of a team. *Job enrichment, job redesign*, and *modified work schedules* (including *flextime*, the *compressed workweek, telecommuting*, and *work-share programs*) can enhance job satisfaction by adding motivating factors to jobs in which they are normally lacking.

Effective *leadership*—the process of motivating others to meet specific objectives—is an important determinant of employee satisfaction and motivation. To effectively motivate employees, managers need to assess situations carefully, especially to determine the desire of subordinates to share input or exercise creativity.

Motivating the Sales Force

Mary Kay Cosmetics was begun by Mary Kay Ash. Sales have increased from $198 000 in 1963 to $613 million in 1993. The company employs 300 000 salespeople, all but 2000 of whom are women.

The typical Mary Kay saleswoman starts at the bottom by buying a makeup kit for about $100. She then phones friends, organizes parties in her home, and sells them makeup for about twice what she paid for it. She also recruits new saleswomen and receives a percentage of what they sell. Each saleswoman buys direct from head office at the same price. There is no cap on how much a woman can make. The most successful make over $200 000 per year.

How does the company motivate these salespeople? By giving them recognition, not just cash. Each year thousands of Mary Kay Cosmetics saleswomen attend a three-day rally called Seminar. At this rally, saleswomen are recognized for their achievements in selling. They receive compliments and gifts ranging from small tokens to the legendary pink Cadillac. At this annual rally, the emphasis is on recognizing accomplishments. Emotional compensation is just as important as financial compensation. Company-paid trips are seen as particularly desirable. One group of winners won a trip to London. The high point of the trip came when Harrods was closed for an hour so the group could shop in private.

Recognition from Mary Kay Ash seems to be what many saleswomen crave the most. She personally crowns four Queens of Seminar—women who have excelled at sales or recruiting. She kisses the winners, pats their hands, and presents them with roses. She also tells her own life story of how she started out poor in 1937 and, after seeing how women were treated by business firms (a man received a promotion she should have received), she decided, at age 45, to start her own company that would treat women right.

Husbands are very much in evidence at the annual Seminar, and recently one salesman even received a pink Cadillac for his selling achievements. But it is clear that the event is for the saleswomen. The company stresses that the wife's business is a proprietorship, not a partnership. It belongs to her, not to the couple. At the Seminar, the general view is conveyed that the husband's responsibility is to support his wife's career. In a videotape directed to husbands, Mary Kay Ash stresses that woman was created to stand alongside man as his equal.

CASE QUESTIONS
1. What is the relative emphasis on money vs. recognition as a motivational tool at Mary Kay Cosmetics?
2. Would the kind of recognition given at this company motivate workers in other kinds of business firms?
3. Are there any shortcomings in the way Mary Kay Cosmetics motivates salespeople?   ◆

Teamwork or Dirty Work?

To proponents, it's a chance for Canadian firms to increase productivity and become competitive in global markets once more, and for workers to use their brains as well as their backs. But to opponents, it's just another management attempt to speed up production at the expense of workers' jobs, earnings, and health. It's the latest in Japanese imports: the team concept.

Actually, the idea of using teams of workers trained in all phases of constructing a product is not original to the Japanese. British, Swedish, and American firms have experimented with the team concept for over 40 years.

In a traditional assembly line, an individual worker performs only one specified task. Over the years, the worker builds up seniority and is then allowed to apply for better paying or easier jobs in the company. Assembly line workers are, in turn, supervised very closely by first-line managers.

In contrast, the team concept breaks down job distinctions. All members of a team are "cross-trained" to perform every necessary function to produce a good or service. Teams also solve minor problems as they arise. Individuals who show the most leadership within the team—not necessarily those with the most seniority—are promoted.

These radical departures disturb both managers and workers in many companies. First and foremost on the minds of both groups is the issue of power. Managers in industries such as automobiles and steel—which are trying hardest to institute teamwork—are accustomed to giving orders and having them carried out. The need to share power and to ask for suggestions instead of issuing commands is difficult for many managers. First-line managers are particularly likely to resist such changes since, under the team concept, far fewer of such managers are needed.

On the other side of the fence, some workers see the team concept as transferring responsibility but not authority. In many places, managers of the team still dictate the problem to be solved and the parameters for solving it. Teams may be put in a position of choosing to increase production either by using less safe methods or by rejecting fewer flawed pieces.

Part of this problem no doubt stems from differences between Japanese and Canadian workers. Japanese workers do not expect a voice in management and the teamwork system devised in Japan makes no provision for it. To get Canadian workers to "buy into" working harder for their employers, companies have had to face worker demands for greater input into management. Any shift will take years to effect.

Even the job rotation aspect of the team concept has been called into question. Some workers like the chance to change assignments: "I used to switch jobs for half a day with one of my buddies just because we were bored. [Job rotation] makes the day go by faster." But others disagree sharply: "Being able to do six monotonous jobs is no more fulfilling than being able to do one," says one worker.

Although some labor unions support the team concept when management is willing to link it to guarantees of job security, a very vocal minority see it as another in a long series of union-busting attempts by industry. The Canadian Auto Workers, for example, opposes teamwork partnerships between labor and management. In particular, they dislike the fact that unions are being forced to bid against each other for jobs. They point to GM's decision to close a more productive non-team plant and keep open a less productive pro-team plant.

CASE QUESTIONS
1. What are the differences between the new team concept and the old assembly-line concept?
2. What problems might a company encounter when it tries to implement the team concept?
3. Can labor and management ever really be a team, or is there a fundamental difference in goals between workers and managers?
4. Is the team concept just a gimmick to allow management to get more work out of workers or to "bust" unions? Even if it is a gimmick, might there be advantages for workers?

♦

Key Terms

human relations
job satisfaction
morale
empowerment
classical theory of
  motivation

scientific management
time-and-motion studies
piecework system
Hawthorne effect
Theory X
Theory Y

two-factor theory
expectancy theory
equity theory
participative management
quality circle
job enrichment

job redesign
flextime
compressed workweek
telecommuting
worksharing (job sharing)

Study Questions and Exercises

Review Questions
1. Do you think most people are satisfied or dissatisfied with their work? Why?
2. Compare and contrast the hierarchy of human needs and the two-factor theory.
3. How can participative management programs enhance employee satisfaction?
4. In what type of situations might a manager be primarily autocratic (boss-centered)? In what type of situations might a manager be primarily democratic (subordinate-centered)?

Analysis Questions
5. Some evidence suggests that people fresh out of college or university initially show high levels of job satisfaction. Their job satisfaction drops dramatically in their late twenties, but gradually increases again as they get older. What might account for this pattern?
6. As a manager, how could you apply each of the theories of employee motivation discussed in this chapter? Which would be easiest to use? Which would be hardest? Why?

7. Suppose you were an employee and realized one day that you were essentially dissatisfied with your job. Short of quitting, what might you do to improve things for yourself?
8. List five important Canadian managers of today who are also great leaders. Give reasons why you chose the five.

Application Exercises

9. Go to the library and research a manager and/or owner of a company in the early twentieth century and a manager or owner of a company in the last decade. Compare and contrast the two in terms of their leadership style and their view of employee motivation.
10. Interview the manager of a local manufacturing company. Identify as many different strategies for enhancing job satisfaction at that company as you can.

Building Your Business Skills

Goal

To encourage students to analyze the profile of Linda J. Wachner, CEO of Warnaco, in terms of the methods she uses to motivate, satisfy, and lead employees.

Situation

Linda J. Wachner took control of Warnaco, a maker of intimate apparel and menswear, after a hostile takeover in 1986. In 1991, she took the company public. The following first-person profile appeared in *Fortune* magazine in December 1992:

> When we took over, I had worked in the company 22 years earlier in a much lower position, and a lot of the same people were still there. So I had to get the people comfortable with me in the first 90 seconds. At the same time I had to change things radically. The company very badly needed new direction, and it needed new thinking and enthusiasm.
>
> What we did was impose a philosophy we call "Do it now." If we didn't make our people understand that the consumers are our bosses and make them look where the consumers are going and what they will want to buy in five years and ten years, we would not have been able to set the new direction.
>
> So we changed. And that started at the top. The corporate office used to be 200 people—now it's seven. We invited 100 people of the existing management group to buy equity in the new Warnaco. We gave them the chance to buy stock and helped them finance their investment....
>
> Then we got them to focus on four key things. In a public company, everybody's looking at earnings per share. But in a private company, in a leveraged buyout like ours, you're driven by cash. You've got to get your people to think about cash. Our focus was on cash flow EBIT [earnings before interest and taxes], innovative ideas, and distribution. Each level of management had to make objectives geared to those four goals. I didn't try to reach consensus, because that's not really my way. I gave people the direction....
>
> The biggest obstacle to change we encounter is keeping people's energy up. I have enormous energy. I'm a morning person and an afternoon person and an evening person. And I will stay up for two or three days in a row to get it done.
>
> I don't ask others to keep my work schedule but I want to keep them focused on the same goal. When they are falling down saying, "Gee, I can't do it anymore," you've got to pick them up and say, "Yes you can, and here's why." It's getting them to dream the dream.
>
> Once they're dreaming the dream and they see it in return on their own equity, how do you continue keeping the energy up? Success is a positive reinforcement. Every time we have a little success, we bring people together and we say, "Look, this is what we've done." So we've been able to build energy and momentum in people.... Don't get me wrong, getting these successes hasn't been easy. And some people felt that the pressure to succeed was too great. Some people left. So we said, "Okay, if you can't meet the goal or if you can't get under the limbo rack, goodbye, and we don't hold it against you." But of the 100 people we put in equity almost seven years ago, 86 are still here and have a major financial stake in the company.
>
> One other interesting observation came out of this experience: A lot of people want to be led.
>
> When people have a good leader who instills team spirit, and they live in an environment that demands excellence, energy, and keeping up of momentum in order to achieve a goal, then they want to stay, or, if they leave, they want to come back. While I'm pleased to say that we are building a first-rate company, it's even more exciting that we've built a world-class team.

Method

Working together with four or five other students, analyze the elements of Wachner's leadership style. In your analysis, consider the following factors:

- Wachner's focus—or lack of it—on job satisfaction and morale
- her views on employee motivation
- her conviction that financial rewards are the ultimate motivator
- her management style
- her views on leadership.

Follow-Up Questions

1. How would you assess Wachner's ability to motivate, satisfy, and lead employees?
2. In your opinion, what are her leadership strengths? Her weaknesses?

10

Dealing with Organized Labor

LEARNING OBJECTIVES

After studying this chapter, you will be able to
- Explain why workers unionize.
- Trace the evolution of unionism in Canada.
- Describe the major laws governing labor/management relations.
- Identify the steps in the collective bargaining process.
- Discuss the future of unionism in Canada.

CHAPTER OUTLINE

Labor-Management Cooperation

Organized labor in Canada has the same problem that management has: cheap offshore competition. Like business firms, the Canadian labor movement has been trying to deal with the harsh realities of the new global economy. One response is to merge several unions. For example, three unions merged to form the Communications, Energy and Paperworkers Union of Canada. Mergers allow unions to cut internal costs, improve service, and gain clout at contract renewal time.

Other unions have tried raiding. The Canadian Autoworkers and the United Steel Workers, for example, are maneuvering to absorb smaller unions in areas like fishing and health care. Some unions have put more money into organizing drives in an effort to increase membership. Still others have joined with government and business firms to create councils that retrain laid-off workers or upgrade worker skills.

But the strategy gaining the most attention at the moment is cooperation with management. While unions still see themselves as adversaries of management, they don't see warfare as productive. The Communication and Electrical Workers of Canada (CWC), for example, has adopted a policy of cooperating with restructuring and training efforts introduced by management, as long as management includes the union in the change process. So, when Inglis Ltd. decided that the assembly lines in its plant would be replaced with small teams of workers, union reps opened up the bargaining process to more of the union membership, and didn't raise objections to the company's plan to make the work cells more flexible. Management responded by promising not to close the factory as long as its productivity stayed at the desired level. Workers on the teams were given additional responsibility and received information about the company's financial position. The result was more efficient and happier employees. Unfortunately, workers were not able to achieve the productivity levels that management wanted, and the plant was closed in 1994.

The response of Inglis workers is not the usual one to changes introduced by management. And it does raise this important question: how should the labor movement respond to the massive changes that are taking place as a result of globalization, increased competition, and computer technology? Some industry observers argue that unions and companies simply must create a new partnership if they are to survive. Strategic alliances between labor and management may be the way to go.

But this will require very large changes in attitudes. Whether unions should cooperate with management and play a role in "wealth creation" is a very controversial subject. In 1989, delegates at the Canadian Auto Workers convention passed an anti-partnership resolution condemning the new order of labor relations. While some prominent unionists reject any notions of cooperation, others are more pragmatic and see it as the wave of the future.

The new approach is typified by events at Ford Motor Co. After a contentious strike back in 1982, both the union and management agreed to a truce. As part of an effort to improve union-management relations, several union members visited a Japanese car plant to see how labor relations worked there. Then Ford set up a tent in the plant parking lot in Oakville and filled it with company financial data that the workers could look over. Later, plant managers and union reps started meeting once a week to work out problems. While tensions have not completely disappeared, there is a much more cooperative attitude on both sides. Management shares information with the union, and the union responds by solving minor problems before they result in grievances.

Perhaps the most promising development on the labor-management cooperation front is a new emphasis on jointly-supported training. The Canadian Steel Trade Employment Congress (CSTEC) is jointly funded by labor, management, and the federal government; it lobbies on behalf of industry as well as pushing retraining of unemployed steelworkers. More than 8 000 displaced steelworkers have taken training in literacy, computer programming, and environmental technology. The CSTEC has had a job replacement rate of 63 percent.

The Sectoral Skills Council is an industry-labor group designed to establish a training "culture." So far, over 50 plants and 22 000 workers from six different unions belong. Recently, technicians who had to assemble equipment for installation in an Ontario nuclear plant took two weeks of paid classroom training to learn how to do it properly.

Zehrs Markets, a grocery chain, and the United Food and Commercial Workers, the union its workers belong to, jointly manage a training center to upgrade and broaden employee skills. The training center mixes classroom and on-the-job training for meat cutters, bakers, clerks, and produce managers. Because of the training, workers' promotability is increased. ◆

In this chapter we will examine various aspects of labor-management relations in Canada. We will begin by considering how and why workers have chosen to band together in the past as well as what laws regulate these organizations and labor-management relations. We will then explore the interaction of worker organizations and management in areas such as compensation, employee performance, and workers' grievances. Finally, we will take a look at the future of labor organizations in Canada.

Why Workers Unionize

Over two thousand years ago, the Greek poet Homer wrote, "There is a strength in the union even of very sorry men."[1] Although there were no labor unions in Homer's time, his comment is an apt expression of the rationale for unions. **Labor unions** are groups of individuals working together to achieve job-related goals, such as higher pay, shorter working hours, and better working conditions.

Labor unions arose in this country as a way to force management to deal collectively with employees in a more humane and fair manner. In the nineteenth and early twentieth centuries, working hours were long, pay was minimal, and working conditions were often unsafe. Workers had no job security and minimal benefits. Many companies employed large numbers of children and paid them poverty wages (see the box "Child Labor"). If people complained, they were fired.

Unions forced management to listen to the complaints of all workers rather than to just those few brave enough to speak out.[2] The power of unions comes from collective (group) action. **Collective bargaining** is a process through which union leaders and management personnel negotiate common terms and conditions of employment for those workers represented by the unions.

labor unions
Groups of individuals who work together to achieve shared job-related goals.

collective bargaining
The process through which union leaders and management personnel negotiate common terms and conditions of employment for those workers represented by the union.

The Canadian Business Scene

CHILD LABOR

During the nineteenth century young children were hired to work in factories at very low wages and under extremely poor working conditions. Because most of them were denied the chance to attend school, they remained unskilled. Improvements in these conditions came slowly.

The founding conference of the Canadian Labour Union in 1873 supported a resolution to prohibit the employment of children under ten in manufacturing establishments where machinery was used. In 1886, the *Ontario Factory Act* was passed. It prohibited the employment of boys under 12 years and girls under 14, and set a limit of 60 hours of work per week for women and children.

During the twentieth century, major advances have been made. At present, the federal government and all provinces have passed child labor laws. The *Canada Labour Code* allows the employment of individuals under the age of 17 years only if they are not required to attend school under the laws of their province of residence and if the work is unlikely to endanger their health or safety. In addition, no one under 17 is permitted to work during the hours from 11:00 P.M. to 6:00 A.M.

The Development of Canadian Labor Unions

The earliest evidence of labor unions in Canada comes from the maritime provinces early in the nineteenth century. Generally, these unions were composed of individuals with a specific craft (e.g., printers, shoemakers, barrel-makers). Most of these unions were small and had only limited success. However, they laid the foundation for the rapid increase in union activity that occurred during the late nineteenth and early twentieth centuries.

A succession of labor organizations sprang up and just as quickly faded away during the years 1840-1870. In 1873, the first national labor organization was formed—the Canadian Labour Union. By 1886, the Knights of Labor (a United States-based union) had over 10 000 members in Canada. The Canadian labor movement began to mature with the formation of the Trades and Labour Congress in 1886. The TLC's purpose was to unite all labor organizations and to work for the passage of laws that would ensure the well-being of the working class.

The growth of labor unions began in earnest early in the twentieth century as the concept of organized labor gradually came to be accepted. Within the ranks of labor, various disputes arose that resulted in numerous splits in labor's ranks. For example, there was concern that United States-based unions would have a detrimental effect on Canadian unions. The Canadian Federation of Labour was formed in 1908 to promote national (Canadian) unions over U.S. unions. These and other disputes (such as how communists in the movement should be handled) often led to the creation of rival union organizations that competed for membership. By 1956, these disputes had been largely resolved, and the two largest congresses of affiliated unions—the Trades and Labour Congress and the Canadian Congress of Labour—merged to form the Canadian Labour Congress. This amalgamation brought approximately 80 percent of all unionized workers into one organization. Table 10.1 highlights some of the important events in Canadian labor history.

The Canadian Labour Congress (CLC), formed in 1956, brought the majority of unionized workers in Canada into one organization.

TABLE 10.1   Some Important Dates in Canadian Labor History

1827	First union formed: boot and shoemakers in Quebec City
1840-1870	Many new unions formed; influenced by U.S. and British unions
1871	Formation of Toronto Trades Assembly; composed of five craft unions; went out of existence a few years later
1873	Canadian Labour Union formed; objective was to unite unions across Canada
1879	First coal miners union in North America formed in Nova Scotia
1881	The U.S.-based Knights of Labor enter Canada
1883	Canadian Labour Congress formed; lasted until 1886
1886	Canadian Trades and Labour Congress formed; later became known as the Trades and Labour Congress of Canada (TLC)
1902	Knights of Labor expelled from TLC
1902	Expelled unions form the National Trades and Labour Congress (became the Canadian Federation of Labour [CFL] in 1908); purpose was to promote national unions instead of international ones
1902-1920	Rapid growth of union membership in both major unions (TLC and CFL)
1919	One Big Union formed; organized in opposition to the TLC
1919	Winnipeg General Strike
1921	Canadian Brotherhood of Railway Employees (CBRE) expelled from TLC
1921	Confédération des Travailleurs Catholiques du Canada (CTCC) organized by the Roman Catholic clergy in Quebec; goal was to keep French-Canadian workers from being unduly influenced by English-speaking and American trade unions
1927	All-Canadian Congress of Labour (ACCL)
	formed; objective was to achieve independence of the Canadian labor movement from foreign control; made up of One Big Union, the CFL, and the CBRE
1939	TLC expels industrial unions; Canadian Congress of Industrial Organization (CIO) Committee formed
1940	ACCL and the Canadian CIO Committee unite to form the Canadian Congress of Labour
1956	TLC and CCL merge to form the Canadian Labour Congress; remnants of One Big Union join new organization
1960	CTCC drops association with Roman Catholic Church and chooses a new name—Confédération des Syndicats Nationaux (CSN); in English, the Confederation of National Trade Unions (CNTU)
1960-1969	Rapid growth of CNTU in Quebec
1971	Centre for Democratic Unions formed as a result of secession from the CNTU by dissident members
1981	International building trades unions suspended from CLC
1982	Founding convention of Canadian Federation of Labour (CFL)
1985	Formation of United Auto Workers of Canada; formerly part of international UAW
1989	Merger of Candian Union of Postal Workers (CUPW) and Letter Carriers Union of Canada
1992	First-ever strike of NHL players
1994	Major league baseball players strike; no World Series played; NHL players also locked out, only half of hockey season played

Unionism Today

The growth of unions has slowed since the mid-1970s (see Figure 10.1). What has caused this change? Revelations of leadership corruption in the 1950s and 1960s tarnished the appeal of some unions. As well, since that time, foreign competition has prompted many heavily unionized industries, such as automobile and steel manufacturing, to cut back their work forces. The makeup of the work force has also changed. Most union members used to be white men in blue-collar jobs. But the work force is increasingly composed of women and minorities in white- or "pink"-collar (secretarial) positions.

At the same time, many nonunionized industries have developed strategies for avoiding unionization. Some companies have introduced new employee relations programs to keep their nonunionized facilities union free.

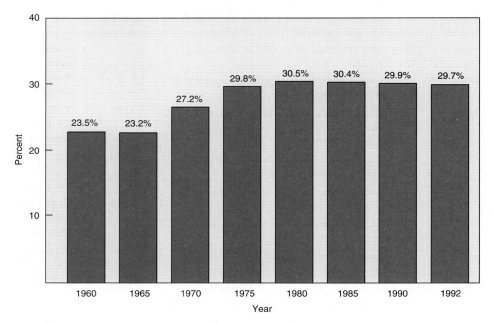

Figure 10.1
Union members as a proportion of the total work force.

Some work to create a "family feeling," setting aside company land for gardens, tennis courts, and other family activities. Some have used carefully managed campaigns to persuade workers not to form unions.

Even where union membership remains high, such as in the public sector, union power has declined. Growing international competition in certain private-sector industries has led employers to demand unprecedented concessions from unions. **Givebacks**, or sacrifices of previously won terms and conditions of employment, have become commonplace. These are turbulent times for unions and their leaders.

Nevertheless, labor unions remain a major factor in Canadian business. The labor organizations in the Canadian Labour Congress and independent major unions, such as the International Brotherhood of Teamsters and the Canadian Union of Public Employees, can disrupt the economy by refusing to work. The votes of their members are still sought by politicians at all levels. And the concessions they have won for their members—better pay, shorter working hours, safer working conditions, and benefits such as extended health insurance—now cover nonunion workers as well. The box "Workers of the World, Reorganize!" describes the environment for labor unions in several different countries.

givebacks

Union sacrifices of previously won wages and benefits in return for increased job security.

The Legal Environment for Unions in Canada

Political and legal barriers to collective bargaining existed until well into the twentieth century. Courts held that some unions were conspirators in restraint of trade. Employers viewed their employees' efforts to unionize as attempts to deprive the employers of their private property. The employment contract, employers contended, was between the individual worker and the employer—not between the employer and employees as a group. The balance of bargaining power was very much in favor of the employer.

International Report

WORKERS OF THE WORLD, REORGANIZE!

A tidal wave of political change has washed across the globe since the late 1980s. As market economies flourish and trading relations among nations grow more friendly, the role of unions is changing in many parts of the world, including countries as diverse as China, Poland, Mexico, and South Africa. In China, for instance, the government's market-oriented policies have resulted in both double-digit growth and an economic catch-22. On the one hand, Beijing is trying to reduce labor abuse through laws and decrees designed to spur union organization and regulate child labor. On the other hand, strict regulation could make foreign investors nervous about labor problems and send them in search of joint ventures elsewhere. Urban unemployment in 1994 was up 25 percent from the previous year. Although the government promises reform, the restructuring of state-owned enterprises has not yet taken place.

There is strong evidence that China also needs serious labor reform. Foreign investment, for example, has resulted in the hasty construction of thousands of new factories where profit is a priority over worker safety. Factories are plagued by fires and job-related accidents that have killed hundreds of workers in just a few short months. Wang Yuxian, director of the International Liaison Department of the government-run All-China Federation of Labor Unions (ACFLU) blames Asian investors in Hong Kong and Taiwan, citing "their emphasis on profits and their cavalier disregard for safety." In turn, foreign labor leaders call the ACFLU a "yellow union" for bowing to government pressures. "Yellow unions are totally useless," reports one labor official from Hong Kong. "Whenever management negotiates with the union, the union agrees with management."

Poland is experiencing similar troubles in its transition from a controlled economy. Solidarity—the Polish labor union that brought about the fall of Communism in that country in 1988—is no longer the powerful agent for change that it was in the 1980s. As foreign investors moved in to take over state-run enterprises, management styles have changed and Solidarity has had a hard time making the transition. For example, a strike at Huta Warszawa steel works, a former state enterprise, put Solidarity in the position of negotiating wages rather than leading social upheaval. "Before," complains Maciej Jankowski, leader of the union's Warsaw chapter, "we worked on everything: economic, political, and social. Now everything is strictly

wages." Of course, the union's most famous member, Lech Walesa, is now president of Poland. His popularity, however, has dropped, as has public support of Solidarity. Seventy percent of respondents to a poll taken in 1994 said that Solidarity, once in the forefront of progress in many aspects of Polish life, had deteriorated.

In Mexico, meanwhile, a unionization drive is being spearheaded by Americans opposed to the North American Free Trade Agreement (see Chapter 22). One goal is to increase pay in Mexico: For example, hourly wages for U.S. factory workers average $16, including benefits; Mexican workers' make about $8 per day. Another goal is leverage. Baldemar Velásquez, head of the Farm Labor Organizing Committee in the U.S., sees cross-border cooperation as a key to increased power among Mexican unions. "If we ever get into a big fight with a North American company that has operations in Mexico," says Velásquez, "I'm sure we're going to get good cooperation from the Mexican unions." Ironically, even though Mexican labor laws are more stringent than those in the United States, many of the large unions, like those in China, support official government positions rather than those of workers.

Finally, South African labor unions were instrumental in ending apartheid, and many observers expected Nelson Mandela's election in April 1994 to result in stronger unions: "It's our turn to be treated as human beings," announced Clara Monethi of the South African Clothing and Textile Workers Union. Unfortunately, economic realities are working against South African unions. Shortly after the election, for example, seven mills in the town of Kimberly were shut down by their Taiwanese owners, threatening to idle 1000 workers.

In addition, because South African workers had built up immense hostility toward employers during decades of white rule, post-apartheid unions pushed hard—and successfully—for higher and higher wages. Consequently, South African wage rates are now twice as high as those in Mexico and several times higher than wages in Thailand and China. Potential foreign investors are concerned that in addition to such high wages, South African unions are extremely powerful. The challenge, reports local labor expert Duncan Innes, is to make union members realize that a new era has begun: "They still see business as a kind of endless pot from which they can draw ever-increasing wages, and there is no end to the process."

The employer/employee relationship became much less direct as firms grew in size. Managers were themselves employees. Hired managers dealt with other employees. Communication among owners, managers, and workers became more formalized. Big business had more power than workers.

**Industrial Disputes
Investigation Act (1907)**
*Provided for compulsory inves-
tigation of labor disputes by a
government-appointed board
before a strike was allowed.*

**Privy Council Order 1003
(1943)**
*Recognized the right of employ-
ees to bargain collectively.*

Constitution Act, 1867
*Divided authority over labor
regulations between the federal
and provincial governments.*

Canada Labour Code
*Legislation that applies to the
labor practices of firms operating under the legislative authority of parliament.*

Because of mounting public concern, laws were passed to place the worker on a more even footing with the employer.

In 1900, government concern about labor disputes resulted in the passage of the *Conciliation Act*. The act was designed to help settle labor disputes through voluntary conciliation and was a first step in creating an environment more favorable to labor. A more comprehensive law, the 1907 ***Industrial Disputes Investigation Act***, provided for compulsory investigation of labor disputes by a government-appointed board before a strike was allowed. However, this act was later found to violate a fundamental provision of the *BNA Act* (see below).

The current positive environment for labor did not come into being until 1943 when ***Privy Council Order 1003*** was issued. This order recognized the right of employees to bargain collectively, prohibited unfair labor practices on the part of management, established a labor board to certify bargaining authority, and prohibited strikes and lockouts except in the course of negotiating collective agreements. Approximately 45 years of dealings among labor, management, and government were required before the labor movement achieved its fundamental goal of the right to bargain collectively.

The Constitution Act (originally the *BNA Act*), passed in 1867, has also affected labor legislation. This act allocated certain activities to the federal government (e.g., labor legislation for companies operating interprovincially) and others to individual provinces (labor relations regulations in general). Thus, labor legislation emanates from both the federal and provincial governments but is basically a provincial matter. That is why certain groups of similar employees might be allowed to go on strike in one province but not in another.

Federal Legislation—The Canada Labour Code

The ***Canada Labour Code*** is a comprehensive piece of legislation that applies to the labor practices of firms operating under the legislative authority of parliament. The code is composed of four major sections:

Fair Employment Practices.   This section prohibits an employer from either refusing employment on the basis of a person's race or religion or using an employment agency that discriminates against people on the basis of their race or religion. These prohibitions apply to trade unions as well, but not to nonprofit, charitable, and philanthropic organizations. Any individual who believes a violation has occurred may make a complaint in writing to Labour Canada. The allegation will then be investigated and if necessary, an Industrial Inquiry Commission will be appointed to make a recommendation in the case. (Since 1982, fair employment practices have been covered by the *Canadian Human Rights Act*; they are also covered by the Canadian Charter of Rights and Freedoms.)

Standard Hours, Wages, Vacations, and Holidays.   This section deals with a wide variety of mechanical issues such as standard hours of work (eight-hour day and 40-hour week), maximum hours of work per week (48), overtime pay (at least one and a half times the regular pay), minimum wages, equal wages for men and women doing the same jobs, vacations, general holidays, and maternity leave. The specific provisions are changed frequently to take into account changes in the economic and social structure of Canada, but their basic goal is to ensure consistent treatment of employees in these areas.

Safety of Employees.   This section requires that every person running a federal work project do so in a way that will not endanger the health or safety of any employee. It also requires that safety procedures and techniques be implemented to reduce the risk of employment injury. This section requires employees to exercise care to ensure their own safety; however, even if it can be shown that the employee did not exercise proper care, compensation must still be paid. This section also makes provisions for a safety officer whose overall duty is to assure that the provisions of the code are being fulfilled. The safety officer has the right to enter any federal project "at any reasonable time."

Canada Industrial Relations Regulations.   The final major section of the *Canada Labour Code* deals with all matters related to collective bargaining. It is subdivided into seven divisions:

- Division I—gives employees the right to join a trade union and gives employers the right to join an employers association.
- Division II—establishes the Canada Labour Relations Board whose role is to make decisions on a number of important issues (e.g., certification of trade unions).
- Division III—stipulates the procedures required to acquire or terminate bargaining rights.
- Division IV—establishes the rules and regulations that must be adhered to during bargaining; also presents guidelines for the content and interpretation of collective agreements.
- Division V—states the requirement that the Minister of Labour must appoint a conciliation officer if the parties in the dispute cannot reach a collective agreement.
- Division VI—stipulates the conditions under which strikes and lockouts are permitted.
- Division VII—a general conclusion giving methods that might be used to promote industrial peace.

Provincial Labor Legislation

Each province has enacted legislation to deal with the personnel practices covered in the *Canada Labour Code*. These laws vary across provinces and are frequently revised; however, their basic approach and substance is the same as in the *Canada Labour Code*. Certain provinces may exceed the minimum code requirements on some issues (e.g., minimum wage).

Each province also has a labor relations act. To give an indication of what these acts cover, the *Ontario Labour Relations Act* is briefly described below.

The Ontario Labour Relations Act.   The *Ontario Labour Relations Act* is a comprehensive document dealing with the conduct of labor relations in that province. Some illustrative provisions of the Ontario law are noted below.

- A trade union may apply at any time to the Ontario Labour Relations Board (OLRB) for certification as the sole bargaining agent for employees in a company.
- The OLRB has the right to call for a certification vote. If more than 50 percent of those voting are in favor of the trade union, the board certifies the union as the bargaining agent.
- Following certification, the union gives the employer written notification of its desire to bargain, with the goal being the signing of a collective agreement. The parties are required to begin bargaining within 15 days of the written notice.
- On request by either party, the Minister of Labour appoints a conciliation officer to confer with the parties and to help achieve a collective agreement. On joint request, the Minister of Labour can appoint a mediator.
- The parties may jointly agree to submit unresolved differences to voluntary binding arbitration. The decision of the arbitrator is final.
- Employers are required to deduct union dues from the union members and remit these dues directly to the union.

■ Every agreement must include a mechanism for settling grievances—differences between the parties arising from interpretation, application, or administration of the collective agreement.

■ If a person objects to belonging to a labor union because of religious beliefs, he or she is allowed to make a contribution equal to the amount of the union dues to a charitable organization.

■ If a trade union is not able to negotiate a collective agreement with management within one year of being certified, any of the employees in the union can apply to the OLRB for decertification of the union.

■ No employer can interfere with the formation of a union. The employer is, however, free to express an opinion about the matter.

■ No employer shall refuse to employ an individual because he or she is a member of a trade union.

The basic provisions of the Ontario Labour Relations Act are found in one form or another in the labor relations acts of all provinces, but the details and procedures vary from province to province. It is obvious that administering labor relations activity is complex and time-consuming. Company management, the union, and the government all expend much time and energy in an attempt to ensure reasonable relations between management and labor.

Union Organizing Strategy

A union might try to organize workers when a firm is trying to break into a new geographical area, when some workers in a firm are members and it wants to cover other workers, or when it is attempting to outdo a rival union. In some cases, a union might try to organize workers for purposes other than helping a group of employees to help themselves. The video case "Unions Growing" on p. 293 describes a new trend in union recruitment.

Management often becomes aware of a union organizing effort through gossip on the company grapevine. These rumblings may set off a countereffort by management to slow the drive. Management must know, however, what it can do legally. A do-nothing approach is rare today. An employer can exercise the right of free speech to present its side of the story to the workers.

Suppose that a union is trying to organize employees of a Manitoba company. If it can show that at least 50 percent of the employees are members of the union, it can apply to the Manitoba Labour Board (MLB) for certification as the bargaining agent for the employees.

A problem may arise regarding the right of different types of workers to join or not join the union. For example, supervisors may or may not be included in a bargaining unit along with nonmanagement workers. The **bargaining unit** includes those individuals deemed appropriate by the province. The MLB has final authority in determining the appropriateness of the bargaining unit. Professional and nonprofessional employees are generally not included in the same bargaining unit unless a majority of the professional employees wish to be included.

Once the MLB has determined that the unit is appropriate, it may order a **certification vote.** If a majority of those voting are in favor of the union, it is certified as the sole bargaining agent for the unit.

bargaining unit
Individuals grouped together for purposes of collective bargaining.

certification vote
A vote supervised by a government representative to determine whether a union will be certified.

craft unions
Unions organized by trades; usually composed of skilled workers.

Types of Unions

The two basic types of union are craft and industrial unions.

Craft unions are organized by crafts or trades—plumbers, barbers, airline pilots, etc. Craft unions restrict membership to workers with specific skills. In many cases, members of craft unions work for several different employers during the course of a year. For example, many construction workers are hired by their employers at union hiring halls. When the particular job for which they are hired is finished, these workers return to the hall to be hired by another employer.

Craft unions have a lot of power over the supply of skilled workers because they have apprenticeship programs. A person who wants to become a member of a plumber's union, for example, will have to go through a training program. He or she starts out as an apprentice. After the training, the apprentice is qualified as a journeyman plumber.

Industrial unions are organized according to industries, for example, steel, auto, clothing. Industrial unions include semiskilled and unskilled workers. They were originally started because industrial workers were not eligible to join craft unions. Industrial union members typically work for a particular employer for a much longer period of time than do craft union members. An industrial union has a lot of say regarding pay and human resource practices within unionized firms.

The **local union** (or local) is the basic unit of union organization. A local of a craft union is made up of artisans in the same craft in a relatively small geographical area. A local of an industrial union is made up of workers in a given industry or plant in a relatively small geographical area. Thus, plumbers in a local labor market may be members of the local plumbers' union. Truck drivers and warehouse workers in that same area may be members of a teamsters' local.

The functions of locals vary, depending not only on governance arrangements but also on bargaining patterns in particular industries. Some local unions bargain directly with management regarding wages, hours, and other terms and conditions of employment. Many local unions are also active in

industrial unions
Unions organized by industry; usually composed of semi-skilled and unskilled workers.

local union
The basic unit of union organization.

Unionized workers can be found in both manufacturing and service businesses. Here, a unionized VIA Rail employee serves a customer on a cross-country passenger train.

disciplining members for violations of contract standards and in pressing management to consider worker complaints.

A **national union** has members across Canada. These members belong to locals affiliated with the national union. There are many national unions in Canada, including the Canadian Union of Public Employees, the National Railway Union, and the Canadian Airline Pilots Union.

An **international union** is a union with members in more than one country. One example is the United Steelworkers of America, made up of locals in the United States and Canada.

An **independent local union** is one that is not formally affiliated with any labor organization. It conducts negotiations with management at a local level, and the collective agreement is binding at that location only. The University of Manitoba Faculty Association is an independent local union. Membership in local unions in 1992 was 3.2 percent of total union membership (see Table 10.2). Table 10.3 shows the ten largest unions in Canada.

national union
A union with members across Canada.

international union
A union with members in more than one country.

independent local union
One not formally affiliated with any labor organization.

TABLE 10.2   Characteristics of National and International Union Membership (1992)

Total union membership	4 088 626
Percentage in CLC/CTC	57.8
Percentage in American Federation of Labor (AFL)/CIO/CLC	20.8
Percentage in CSN/CNTU	6.2
Percentage in international unions	30.6
Percentage in national unions	65.1
Percentage in independent local unions	3.2

TABLE 10.3   The Ten Largest Unions in Canada (1992)

	Members
1. Canadian Union of Public Employees	406 600
2. National Union of Public and General Employees	307 500
3. United Food and Commercial Workers Union International	180 000
4. Public Service Alliance of Canada	165 000
5. United Steelworkers of America	160 000
6. National Auto, Aerospace, and Agricultural Implements Workers	153 600
7. Confédération des affaires sociales (CSN)	94 600
8. International Brotherhood of Teamsters, Chauffeurs, Warehousemen and Helpers of America	91 000
9. Confédération des enseignants et enseignantes des commissions scolaires du Québec (CEQ)	75 000
10. Service Employees International Union	75 000

Union Structure

Just as each organization has its own unique structure, so too does each union create a structure that best serves its own needs. As Figure 10.2 shows, however, there is a general structure that characterizes most national and international unions. A major function of unions is to provide service and support to both members and local affiliates. Most of these services are carried out by the types of specialized departments shown in Figure 10.2.

Officers and Functions. Each department or unit represented at the local level elects a **shop steward**—a regular employee who acts as a liaison between union members and supervisors. For example, if a worker has a grievance, he or she takes it to the steward, who tries to resolve the problem with the supervisor. If the local is very large, the union might hire a full-time **business agent** (or **business representative**) to play the same role.

Within a given union, the main governing bodies are the national union (or international union when members come from more than one country) and its officers. Among their other duties, national and international unions charter local affiliates and establish general standards of conduct and procedures for local operations. For example, they set dues assessments, arrange for the election of local officers, sanction strikes, and provide guidance in the collective bargaining process. Many national unions also engage in a variety of political activities, such as lobbying. They may also help coordinate organizing efforts and establish education programs.

Given the magnitude of their efforts, it is little wonder that unions often take on many of the same characteristics as the companies for which their members work. For example, almost all large unions have full-time administrators, formal organizational structures (see Figure 10.2), goals and strategic plans, and so forth.

shop steward
A regular employee who acts as a liaison between union members and supervisors.

business agent
In a large union, the business agent plays the same role as a shop steward.

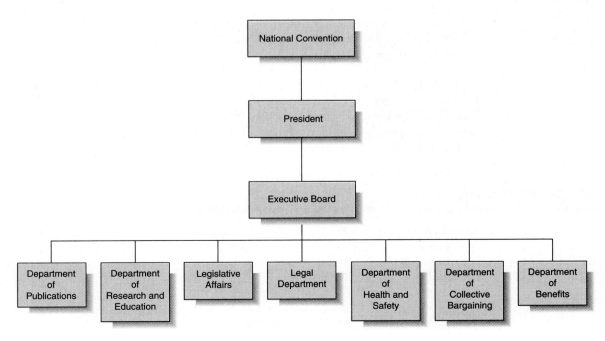

Figure 10.2
Organization of a large national union.

Union Security

The growing security consciousness of Canadian workers is reflected in union goals. The seniority provision in most contracts spells out the workers' rights when layoffs, transfers, and promotions occur. Employees are ranked by length of service. Those with longer service get better treatment.

Much conflict exists regarding seniority. For example, women and members of minority groups typically have less seniority and are the first to be laid off and the last to move up to higher jobs. These workers tend to oppose the tradition of seniority.

Union security refers to the means of ensuring the union's continued existence and the maintenance of its membership so that it can continue to meet the criteria for certification. There is always a danger—particularly in bad economic times—that the membership may drop below the required absolute majority. The union may then lose its certification.

The greatest union security is found in the closed shop. In a **closed shop**, an employer can hire only union members. For example, a plumbing or electrical contractor who hires workers through a union hiring hall can hire only union members.

In a **union shop**, an employer may hire nonunion workers even if the employer's current employees are unionized. New workers, however, must join the union within a stipulated period of time (usually 30 days).

In an **agency shop**, all employees for whom the union bargains must pay dues, but they need not join the union. This compromise between the union shop and the open shop is called the Rand Formula after the judge who proposed it. In the *Quebec Labour Code*, the Rand formula applies to all unions certified under this code.

In an **open shop**, an employer may hire union and/or non-union labor. Employees need not join or pay dues to a union in an open shop.

Another union security issue is job security, especially in highly automated industries. The guaranteed annual wage reflects workers' concerns about job security. The **guaranteed annual wage** is a provision in a labor contract that maintains the workers' income level during a year. Most labor contracts with this guarantee provide the worker with a minimum amount of work during the contract period. This provision lends stability to the worker's employment. Some contracts provide for early retirement, lengthy vacations, or sabbatical leaves for employees.

The security of unions themselves is also in question. The most unionized industries—steel, auto, transportation—are automating rapidly. Prospects for new members are not attractive. Furthermore, the stronghold of unions—blue-collar labor—is diminishing as a percentage of the labor force. On the other hand, unions have found new areas, such as government workers and white-collar workers, to organize.

union security
The maintenance of a union's membership so that it can continue to meet the criteria for certification.

closed shop
An employer can hire only union members.

union shop
An employer can hire nonunionized workers but they must join the union within a certain period.

agency shop
All employees for whom the union bargains must pay dues but they are not required to join the union.

open shop
An employer may hire union or nonunion workers.

guaranteed annual wage
A provision in a contract that guarantees the workers' income level during a year.

Collective Bargaining

Too often, people associate collective bargaining with the signing of a contract between a union and a company or industry. In fact, collective bargaining is an ongoing process involving not only the drafting but also the administering of the terms of a labor contract.

Reaching Agreement on the Contract's Terms

The collective bargaining process begins with the recognition of the union as the exclusive negotiator for its members. The *bargaining cycle* begins when union leaders meet with management representatives to agree on a new contract. By law, both parties must sit down at the bargaining table and negotiate "in good faith." Each side presents its demands. Ultimately, they reach some compromise and the new agreement is submitted to the union's membership for a *ratification vote.*

Most of the time this process will go smoothly. Sometimes, however, the two sides cannot—or will not—agree. Such an impasse is not illegal. How quickly and easily it is resolved depends in part on the nature of the demands made, the willingness of each side to use the weapons at its disposal, and the prospect for mediation or arbitration.

Contract Demands.   Contract negotiations may center on any number of issues. One common point of negotiation is compensation. For example, unions frequently fight for clauses ensuring a **cost-of-living adjustment (COLA)**, especially during times of high inflation. Such a clause specifies that wages will increase automatically in proportion to increases in the cost of living, usually as reflected in the *consumer price index,* a measure of inflation.

cost-of-living adjustment (COLA)
A contract clause specifying that wages will increase automatically with the rate of inflation.

Compensation was probably the dominant negotiation issue during the 1970s and 1980s. Business growth was producing large profits and labor wanted a portion of them. But as growth and inflation leveled off, compensation became a less critical part of most contract negotiations. In fact, as noted earlier, givebacks have become a topic for negotiation in recent years.

Instead of pushing for more money or benefits, union negotiators have increasingly made job security an important agenda item. In some cases, job-security issues may take the form of the demand that the company not relocate (see the box "Tough Choices"). The video case "Unions Growing" on p. 293 describes union demands in the 1990s.

The Canadian Business Scene

TOUGH CHOICES

Phillips Cables Ltd. makes industrial cables used in mining, oil-well pumping, and construction work. Until recently, the firm produced cables for the protected domestic Canadian market. But with the advent of free trade, tariffs on foreign cables are heading toward zero, and Canadian firms are going to have to become more competitive.

The cost of wages and benefits in Canadian plants is substantially higher than in the U.S. The Brockville plant of Phillips and a U.S. plant in Marion, Indiana, illustrate the problems. Because the Brockville plant had a union contract with automatic time-and-a-half pay for Saturday work, double time for Sunday work, and a 10 percent premium for evening work, it was extremely costly to run the plant seven days a week. Labor costs at Brockville were $6 per hour higher than in Marion. Interestingly, the Marion plant had similar work rules until the mid-1980s, but management there convinced the employees of the need to change.

David Foy, the CEO of Phillips, approached union leaders with the cost data and told them that the plant might have to close if costs were not brought into line. The union leaders were given a tour of a British cable plant where restrictive work rules had been abolished. By the time the workers were asked to vote on the proposals, 81 percent approved. The 10 percent night premium has been replaced by a straight one dollar per hour premium, and the Saturday and Sunday premiums have been eliminated. Workers will have more flexibility in the jobs they do, and more emphasis will be given to the team concept.

The Brockville employees hope that the increased efficiency brought about by the changes will mean that more product lines will be shifted from other plants to Brockville. There are also plans to invest more money in the Brockville plant to modernize and upgrade the facilities.

The trend to reducing the work force in return for job security is not restricted to North America. At British Steel Corp.'s Llanwern plant, the union agreed to a loss of 4454 jobs and the end of strict demarcations between jobs that prevented members of one union from doing the work of those in another union. In return, they received job security for the remaining workers at the plant. British Steel is now one of the lowest-cost producers of steel in the world.[3]

A final critical point of negotiation is management rights. Obviously, management wants as much control as possible over whom it hires, how it assigns work, and so forth. The union, on the other hand, often tries to limit management rights by specifying how hiring will be done, how work will be assigned, and other *work rules*. For example, at one automobile plant, the union contract specifies that three workers are to be used to change fuses in robots—a machinist to open the robot, an electrician to change the fuse, and a supervisor to oversee the process. Unions work to specify as many different job categories as possible. Workers in one category cannot perform work that falls into the domain of another category.

In general, the points bargained for may involve demands for mandatory and/or permissive items. *Mandatory items* are matters over which both parties must negotiate if either wishes to. Included in this category are wages, working hours, and benefits. *Permissive items* may be negotiated if both parties agree to do so. An example is a union demand to have veto power over the hiring and promotion of managerial personnel. In contrast, *illegal items* may not be legitimately brought to the negotiating table by either party. A management demand for a nonstrike clause would be an illegal item.

When Bargaining Fails

An impasse occurs when, after a series of bargaining sessions, management and labor fail to agree on a new contract or a contract to replace an agreement that is about to expire. Although it is generally agreed that both parties suffer when an impasse is reached and action is taken, each side can employ several tactics to support its cause until the impasse is resolved.

strike

A tactic of labor unions in which members temporarily walk off the job and refuse to work in order to win concessions from management.

Union Tactics.   Unions can take a variety of actions when their demands are not met. Chief among these tactics is the **strike**. Strikes triggered by impasses over mandatory bargaining items are called economic strikes, even if they occur over noneconomic issues such as working hours. Most strikes in Canada are economic strikes. The strike by National Hockey League players in 1992 and the lockout of players in 1994, as well as the strike by major league baseball players in 1994, were largely over economic issues.

During a strike, workers are not paid and the business is usually unable to produce its normal range of products and services. As the box "Strike is no Ball for Business" demonstrates, the impact of a strike goes far beyond the company and its employees.

After a strike is over, employees may exhibit low morale, anger, increased absenteeism, and decreased productivity. In these situations, care must be taken to improve communications between management and workers.[4]

Strikes may occur in response to an employer's unfair labor practices. A firm that refuses to recognize a duly certified union may find itself with a striking work force and having to explain its refusal to the provincial labor relations board. Such strikes are rare, however.

Not all strikes are legal. *Sympathy strikes* (also called *secondary strikes*), where one union strikes in sympathy with strikes initiated by another labor organization, may violate the sympathetic union's contract. *Wildcat strikes*, strikes unauthorized by the union that occur during the life of a contract, deprive strikers of their status as employees and thus of the protection of labor laws.

Postal workers picket the mail sorting plant in Toronto.

As part of or instead of a strike, unions faced with an impasse may picket or launch a boycott. **Picketing** involves having workers march at the entrance to the company with signs explaining their reasons for striking. A **boycott** occurs when union members agree not to buy the product of the firm that employs them. Workers may also urge other consumers to shun their firm's product. Another alternative to striking is a work **slowdown**: Instead of striking, workers perform their jobs at a much slower pace than normal. A variation is the "sickout," during which large numbers of workers call in sick.

Management Tactics.   Management can also respond forcefully to an impasse. To some extent, **lockouts** are the flip side of the strike coin. Lockouts occur when employers physically deny employees access to the work place. Lockouts are illegal if they are used as offensive weapons to give the firm an economic advantage in the bargaining process. They might be used, for example, if management wants to avoid a buildup of perishable inventory or in similar circumstances. Lockouts, though rare today, were used by major league baseball team owners (without success) in 1990.

As an alternative to a lockout, firms faced with a strike can hire temporary or permanent replacements (**strikebreakers**) for the absent employees. When players in the National Football League went out on strike during the 1987 season, the team owners hired free agents and went right on playing. In 1992, National Hockey League owners planned to use minor league hockey players if they could not reach an agreement with striking NHL players. Laws forbid companies from permanently replacing workers who strike because of the firm's unfair labor practices.

More and more firms are contracting out work as a way to blunt their unions' effects. Instead of doing all the assembly work they used to do themselves,

picketing
A tactic of labor unions in which members march at the entrance to the company with signs explaining their reasons for striking.

boycott
A tactic of labor unions in disputes with management in which members refuse to buy the products of the company and encourage other consumers to do the same.

slowdown
Instead of striking, workers perform their jobs at a much slower pace than normal.

lockout
A tactic of management in which the firm physically denies employees access to the workplace in order to pressure workers to agree to the company's latest contract offer.

strikebreaker
An individual hired by a firm to replace a worker on strike; a tactic of management in disputes with labor unions.

The Canadian Business Scene

STRIKE IS NO BALL FOR BUSINESS

When the major league baseball players went on strike in 1994, many other organizations were affected. Brewing giant John Labatt Ltd. was particularly hard-hit. Labatt owns 90 percent of the Toronto Blue Jays, 41 percent of the SkyDome where the team plays, and TSN (which broadcasts the games). The SkyDome alone was losing more than $100 000 per day during the strike. The strike also threatened Labatt's main product—beer—because baseball is such a high-profile arena for advertising this product.

But Labatt wasn't the only organization that suffered because of the strike. Broadcasters, advertisers, retailers, and restaurants had to scramble to save what remained of the summer after the strike began on August 12. Overall, the strike could have cost Toronto-area businesses more than $50 million in lost revenues of one sort or another. Montreal businesses could have lost $20 million.

Bitove Corp. is a hospitality company that handles catering at the SkyDome; it also operates food services at nearby restaurants, including Wayne Gretzky's and the Hard Rock Cafe. The company incurred substantial losses when games that were originally scheduled ended up not being played because of the strike. Well over 2000 jobs were lost at the SkyDome and Olympic Stadium as a result of the strike.

At CTV, losses approached $10 million because the network did not get to televise any post-season play. The losses were high because advertising rates for special events like the World Series are much higher than rates for regular movies or dramatic programs which CTV had to substitute when there were no games to televise.

The bad news for baseball is sometimes good news for people operating other types of businesses. Video rental chains reported increases in sales after the strike began, and The Second City, a Toronto comedy club, played to a full house every night the week after the strike started. Formerly the club had experienced low turnouts whenever the Blue Jays played.

The lockout of National Hockey League players in 1994 caused the same kinds of problems as the baseball strike. Molson Cos. Ltd. owns the Montreal Canadiens, the Montreal Forum, and the country's largest brewer, which advertises heavily at hockey games. Therefore they lost money on several ventures.

Maple Leaf Gardens also suffered during the strike. An entire season with no hockey would have resulted in a loss of $7 million. Layoffs and other cost-cutting measures would have been necessary, not only at Maple Leaf Gardens, but at every arena around the league.

The CBC was also hard hit because it had planned to start airing two hockey games instead of one in the fall of 1994 on Hockey Night in Canada. Saturday evening TV audiences, especially men, were down by as much as 50 percent during the lockout. While most of the money that was originally scheduled to be spent advertising hockey games was redirected, broadcasters worried that after the lockout ended they would have a tough time getting advertisers back.

Provincial governments stood to lose $75 million in profits because wagering on sports lotteries declined by as much as 50 percent during the hockey lockout. Ontario was the hardest hit because interest in sports betting is highest there. The Pro-Line lottery accounted for $65 million in 1993.

---

many firms now contract out work to nonunion contractors. This lessens the impact that the unions can have and results in fewer union workers.

Employers' associations are especially important in industries that have many small firms and one large union that represents all workers. Member firms sometimes contribute to a strike insurance fund. Such a fund could be used to help members whose workers have struck. They are similar in purpose to the strike funds built up by unions.

Employers are also increasingly using what unions refer to as "union-busting" consultants. These consultants assist management in improving their communications with the shop floor. They help management identify and eliminate the basic pressures that led to the prounion vote in the first place.

decertification

The process by which employees terminate their union's right to represent them.

The same law that grants employees the right to unionize also allows them to decertify. **Decertification** is the process by which employees legally terminate their union's right to represent them. In 1992, employees at Rogers Cablesystems

Ltd. voted to decertify the union that has represented them since 1975. The union charged that management had induced workers to leave the union.[5]

Decertification campaigns do not differ much from certification campaigns (those leading up to the initial election). The union organizes membership meetings, house-to-house visits, and other tactics to win the election. The employer uses meetings, letters, and improved working conditions to try to obtain a decertification vote.

Mediation and Arbitration.   Rather than using weapons on one another, labor and management can agree to call in a third party to help resolve the dispute. In **mediation**, the neutral third party (a mediator) can only advise—not impose—a settlement on the parties. In **voluntary arbitration**, the neutral third party (an arbitrator) dictates a settlement between two sides who have agreed to submit to outside judgment.

In some cases, arbitration is legally required to settle bargaining disputes. Such **compulsory arbitration** is used to settle disputes between government and public employees such as firefighters and police officers.

Administering the Contract's Terms

No matter how a contract is reached, once signed it must be administered and interpreted. Given the complexity of many contracts, this process can be difficult and controversial. To avoid recurring industrial conflicts over contract interpretations, unions and management typically negotiate grievance procedures into final contracts. A **grievance** is a complaint by a worker that a manager is violating the contract. Figure 10.3 traces a typical grievance procedure.

The union generally promises not to strike over disputes about contract interpretation. In return, unions get the right to file grievances in a formal procedure that culminates in binding arbitration. Most grievance arbitrations take place over disputes regarding the discipline or discharge of employees, but safety issues are a cause for arbitration in some industries.

mediation
A method of settling a contract dispute in which a neutral third party is asked to hear arguments from both the union and management and offer a suggested resolution.

voluntary arbitration
A method of settling a contract dispute in which the union and management ask a neutral third party to hear their arguments and issue a binding resolution.

compulsory arbitration
A method of settling a contract dispute in which the union and management are forced to explain their positions to a neutral third party who issues a binding resolution.

grievance
A complaint on the part of a union member that management is violating the terms of the contract in some way.

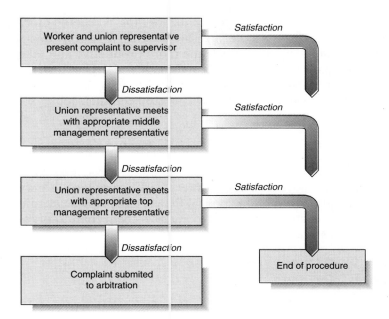

Figure 10.3
A typical grievance procedure.

The Future of Unionism in Canada

The union movement began in a period when the excesses of early capitalism placed the average worker at the mercy of the employer. For decades unions sought to bargain at arm's length with employers. This goal was met through legislation and the collective-bargaining process.

Many people considered unionism to be a worthwhile cause through the 1930s. But some people became critical of unions toward the end of the 1940s, and criticism has continued to mount. Unions are increasingly aware that they must cooperate with employers if they are both to survive. Critics of unions contend that excessive wage rates won through years of strikes and hard-nosed negotiation are partially to blame for the difficulties of large corporations. Others argue that excessively tight work rules limit the productivity of businesses in many industries. More and more often, however, unions are working with organizations to create effective partnerships in which managers and workers share the same goals—profitability, growth, and effectiveness with equitable rewards for everyone.

The future of unions depends on their ability to cope with the economic and social trends that threaten the labor movement. Some of these trends are

- the decline of the smokestack industries (e.g., steel, chemicals, metals)
- employment growth in the service industries
- deregulation
- a more competitive business environment
- changes in the overall health of the economy
- technological changes
- free trade.

The Decline of the Smokestack Industries

Competition from abroad is causing many of these industries to seek ways to become more productive. The drive to make Canadian firms competitive internationally makes Canadian labor leaders tremble. They believe that management inevitably asks for concessions in its attempt to become more competitive. Petromont Inc., for example, has said that it will shut its doors unless its unionized employees agree to become more productive and take pay cuts of up to 12 percent.[6] General Motors of Canada Ltd. has told workers at two assembly plants in Oshawa that they will have to make concessions and accept more flexible working rules if they want to keep their jobs.[7]

Employment Growth in the Service Industries

The majority of Canada's labor force is now employed in the service industries. Except for government employees, these workers have never been highly unionized. Many work part-time, and the typical firm is small. These factors make it harder and more costly for unions to organize them than to organize full-time workers in large factories.

Deregulation

Deregulation continues to have an impact on unions. Deregulation of the airline, railway, and trucking industries has forced firms to become more competitive. Mergers, layoffs, givebacks, and new nonunionized firms in these and other deregulated industries challenge unions. Just as these firms have to learn to survive under deregulation, so will their employees' unions.

The Business Environment

As domestic and international competition becomes more intense, management has introduced changes to increase corporate efficiency. But these changes have caused conflicts between labor and management. United Parcel Service, for example, has been trying to capture more of the light-trucking market, so it recently raised its maximum package weight from 70 pounds to 150 pounds. But unionized drivers and sorters revolted when asked to lift the increased weights without protective health and safety guarantees. Employees are also unhappy about the way the company is pressuring them to do more work.[8]

The Economy

The overall health of the economy will clearly play a major role in the future of unionism. Suppose labor and management negotiators continue to focus heavily on givebacks. More employers may find themselves setting up profit-sharing plans so that unions will believe they are getting something in return. Givebacks may also reduce the impact of national contracts if they are amended by concessions at local levels. Greater worker participation in quality-of-work-life programs may also lead unions to push for more profit sharing. It may also lead to narrower management rights clauses in labor contracts.

Technological Change

Technology will continue to challenge labor unions. Some clerical and professional workers, for example, now work at home on computer terminals linked to their employers' office computers. Instead of having to commute to work by car, bus, or train, these workers telecommute. Some unions oppose the work-at-home concept because it makes organizing workers harder.

Free Trade

Finally, organized labor is concerned about the potentially negative impact of free trade agreements. Their fear is that products made in the U.S. or Mexico will be shipped tariff-free into Canada, and business firms will put pressure on Canadian workers to work for lower wages. At the worst, companies may simply move out of Canada altogether and do all their production in the U.S. or Mexico. Many unionized jobs in Canada would be lost.

In 1994, for example, unionized workers at H.J. Heinz in Leamington, Ontario signed a new collective agreement that contained concessions such as a wage reduction of 50 cents per hour and a reduction in paid holidays. Workers agreed to this in return for a guarantee of job security. The company said it needed the concessions to remain competitive under the new conditions of free trade. Formerly the company had served a captive Canadian market with no competition from the U.S. The company threatened to close the plant if the workers did not accept the reductions; this would have put 450 employees out of work.[9]

Many companies, in fact, are moving south to the United States because they cannot compete with American companies that have much lower costs. Labor groups estimate that more than 200 000 jobs have been lost in Ontario alone as companies move south. Canadian companies have invested more than $400 million in the state of Tennessee alone. That investment has created more than 8000 jobs in the U.S.[10]

Summary of Key Points

Labor unions began developing in Canada early in the nineteenth century, but because the legal environment was unfavorable for unions, progress was slow. By the middle of the twentieth century, unions had secured the right to bargain collectively with businesses. Both the federal government and the provinces have labor relations acts that govern the relationship between management and labor in unionized firms.

The growth of unions has slowed dramatically in the last decade. Public sector white-collar unions continue to grow slowly, but traditional blue-collar unions are losing members as employment in industries such as steel, chemicals, and general manufacturing declines. Because of these changes, unions are increasingly concerned about job security for their members.

There are various categories of unions. Craft unions represent members with a certain craft—plumbers, airline pilots, electricians, barbers, etc. Industrial unions represent members from one industry who have general work skills. International unions have members in more than one country while national unions do not.

Collective bargaining is the process of negotiating a formal agreement between management and labor that spells out the terms and conditions of employment for the workers represented by the union. Labor's weapons during negotiations are the strike, picketing, and boycotts. Management's weapons include the lockout and using strikebreakers. If labor and management cannot agree on employment terms during negotiations, a strike or lockout may occur. Or the two parties may agree to call in a mediator, conciliator, or arbitrator to try to settle their differences.

Several recent trends may have a significant impact on the union movement. These are: 1) the decline of the smokestack industries (unions' historical base of strength); 2) employment growth in the service industries where unions are not strongly entrenched; 3) deregulation (less government involvement in business); 4) a more competitive business environment, which causes management to be more aggressive in dealing with unions; 5) changes in the overall health of the economy (in poor times, management offers less to workers); 6) technological changes (automation threatens union jobs); and 7) free trade agreements (manufacturers may move out of Canada and union jobs will be lost).

CONCLUDING CASE 10-1

What is the Role of Unions?

Jack Callahan is the president of Arco Manufacturing. He has always vigorously opposed unions and has fought them every time they tried to get a toehold in his firm. Until recently, he had succeeded in keeping his employees nonunion but, in 1995, the workers voted to join a union. Callahan was furious but, short of closing his plant, he did not see any alternative to dealing with the union.

At a recent social gathering, Callahan was introduced to the president of the new union, Bernie Pearson.

Callahan took an immediate dislike to Pearson and began to debate with him about the role of unions.

Callahan: The whole idea of unions really bothers me. Is it fair that a worker in a unionized plant should be forced to belong to the union even if he or she doesn't want to? A worker should not be forced to join your union in order to hold a job in my company. I'll accept the argument that employees have a right to form a union, but an employee should have a right not to join, too. But now that your union is certified as the exclusive bargaining agent for my production workers, even though not all of them voted to unionize, all of them have to join your union or be fired. They don't have freedom of choice.

Pearson: Well, it is true that a worker in a union plant must belong to the union. The majority rules, and the majority of your workers who voted wanted my union. Under the law, two people doing the same job must be paid the same wage and receive the same fringe benefits. It would be unfair for a person who doesn't pay union dues to enjoy the same benefits won by a union supported by members' dues. Freeloaders should have to pay their fair share.

Callahan: I'm against freeloaders as much as you are. But unions get all sorts of unfair advantages from the government. For example, I have to deduct union dues from my workers' wages and then pay them to your union. That's outrageous. The least you could do is collect your own dues. After all, it's your union and you should look after it.

Pearson: If we had to chase all the workers for union dues every month, we wouldn't have time for anything else. This province has passed legislation requiring you to deduct union dues. Your responsibility is to obey the law.

Callahan: But why should unions get a break like that? They've got too much power already. You can bring my whole operation to a halt just by calling a strike.

Pearson: That's an oversimplified view of reality. Look what's happened recently. Unions have had a lot of trouble getting wage increases for their members. In fact, a lot of workers seem to be unhappy with their unions for not getting them more money and better fringe benefits. If unions are so strong, why don't they obtain more money from management? I'll tell you why—we aren't that strong.

Callahan: Well, for being so weak, you can certainly cause me a lot of grief. You know, I really don't think that unions are necessary any more. I agree that unions did a lot for workers earlier in this century when management treated workers badly but, in this enlightened era, they are no longer necessary. Social insurance, workers' compensation, minimum wage laws, unemployment insurance, and job safety laws have eliminated the need for unions.

Pearson: To say that unions are unnecessary is hogwash. Do away with the union and see how employee-oriented most companies are. Business firms exist to make a profit. The less they have to pay their workers, the more profit they make. Keep in mind also that there is no law that requires workers to form a union. They get involved in unions because they think the union will help them get a better deal from management.

Callahan: But what if, after joining a union, the workers find that the union isn't doing anything for them? If a customer of mine doesn't like the products we make, he or she can simply stop buying from us. But a dissatisfied union member has to keep paying dues, even if the union isn't doing the job the worker expects.

Pearson: That's not true. If the employees don't consider that their union is benefiting them, they can have it decertified.

Callahan: I'm tired of arguing with you about this issue. You have a glib answer for every point I make. You're totally one-sided in your view. You think everything about unions is positive!

Pearson: You're not exactly open-minded yourself. You think everything about unions is negative!

CASE QUESTIONS
1. Assess the validity of each point made by Callahan and Pearson.
2. Why do workers join unions? Why do they decertify unions?
3. What are some difficulties legislators face when deciding on labor/management legislation?   ◆

CONCLUDING CASE 10-2

The New Job Title at United Airlines—"Owner"

In July 1994, United Airlines employees were finally successful in acquiring their employer through a $4.9 billion shareholder buyout. The action was hailed by many observers as perhaps a sign of a new era in labor-management relations. By the time the buyout was approved by the company's shareholders, United's unions—representing pilots, machinists and flight attendants—had been involved in a struggle with management for more than a decade.

The buyout process began in 1987, when union representatives of United pilots made two separate bids—both rejected by shareholders—to buy the company for more than $4 billion. In addition to two other unsuccessful employee buyout attempts, rumors of mergers, takeovers, and downsizing soon made the "United" company name a real contradiction. Divisions within the organization ran deeper than the traditional union-management schism. At times, even relations between United's unions were strained. United's union employees are drawn from the 8700-member Airline Pilots Association (ALPA), the International Association of Machinists (IAM) (representing 24 000 mechanics and ground-service workers), and the Association of Flight Attendants. Within each union, there are still members who disagree with the buyout agreement and its results. For example, a dissident group of ALPA members circulated a survey claiming that 1250 of 1700 pilots surveyed opposed the buyout. In fact, although the IAM had voted to support the buyout, the final tally was a narrow vote of 54 to 46 percent. IAM members opposed to the buyout were in court at the last minute trying to prevent the deal from going through.

Also affected by the buyout are 28 000 employees who are not union members or are not covered by union contracts—for example, ticket agents, crew members, schedulers, and sales employees. These workers complain that they have been forced to accept an agreement on which they never had a vote. They are especially unhappy because the buyout deal subjected them to a 8.25-percent pay cut. (It also included a 23.5-percent cut for pilots and a 15.7 percent cut for IAM employees.)

Arnie Canham, a United employee since 1969, sums up the feelings of many of her colleagues: "There's a lot of unhappiness, a lot of anxiety and underlying resentment. Taking a pay cut is not good news; you can't sugar coat that. I'm afraid that a lot of people are still looking at the situation as us vs. them—management vs. labor, non-union vs. union. There's a distinct emotional feeling among many people here," adds Canham, "that we don't need to be part of this deal, taking a pay cut.... Why are you taking 8.25 percent of my pay when I didn't contribute to this high-cost operation? That's a big hurdle for people like me to get over."

Supporters of the buyout admit that employees were required to make concessions—including pay cuts. They argue, however, that those concessions cut costs by about $5 billion. They also contend that job security is improved because the new contracts prevent management from laying off employees and from selling assets that could cut jobs. "For me," says James Kozar, a United mechanic since 1986, "it all comes down to job security. I got laid off at TWA after nine years, so I know what that's like. Basically, we are making a sacrifice, and that won't be easy. But we've got our jobs, and that means a lot these days."

The buyout also granted the unions' demand that United's top three executives, including CEO Stephen Wolf, be replaced. Gerald Greenwald, former vice chairman at Chrysler, is taking over the top job. He has his work cut out for him. Among his biggest tasks will obviously be healing rifts not only between unions and management but among United's unions themselves. In order to keep shareholders and employee-owners happy with their new deal, Greenwald must also boost profitability. In 1994, the numbers were promising: United made a $100 million profit on $16 billion in revenues. Unfortunately, the money is needed to balance big losses in recent years—$50 million in 1993, nearly $1 billion in 1992, and $332 million in 1991.

Employees still differ in their views of what UAL will become as a result of the changes. Reservations agent Melody Sadlier counts herself among the company's "Proud Owners," to borrow a phrase from a button worn by CEO Greenwald. "I'm going to make the best of this thing," she says, "and maybe we are going to weed out all the negative people, the people who complain and crab all the time. If people don't like what's happening, they can always leave. I'm used to change, and I like learning new things. The nice thing about all this is that now I own part of this company. It's like if I own my own house, I want to make sure it looks nice and the grass looks good."

On the other hand, some flight attendants still harbor resentment leftover from their treatment of the past. Says Kevin Lum, head of the Association of Flight Attendants master executive council and a United attendant since 1979: "We've always been treated like angry children who don't deserve what they get. Upper management has been adversarial and confrontational with us for over ten years now." He notes, for example, that attendants' hotels are frequently in less desirable locations than those of pilots who stay overnight. Attendants are also required to maintain their weight, while other groups of employees are not. "Attendants," charges Lum, "have always been singled out for this sort of treatment, and it has exacerbated our problems with management. The irony, of course, is that bosses ought to think a lot harder about how we feel if they want to keep their customers happy. We're the people who spend all the time with the passengers. To the public, we are United."

Finally, flight attendants and management are not the only groups perceived to be feuding. "Mechanics and pilots," admits 737 captain Dave Sharp, "have always had a rift between them. That's a conflict as old as aviation history. Hopefully, we can work together in quality management groups or whatever to establish some trust." Labor-management relations may be another matter. "As for management," says Sharp, "I don't know if they can change their culture. There are a lot of power struggles over there, and they worry more about those than they do running the airline. [Gerry Greenwald] has a track record for employee relations, and this trust thing is the key to the whole future."

CASE QUESTIONS:

1. What were some of the most important circumstances that led to the buyout at United?

2. Why have there traditionally been differences and disagreements between the various unions at United? Why do they persist?

3. How do you think employee ownership will affect worker attitudes toward United?

4. What recommendations would you make to Gerald Greenwald as CEO—that is, chief manager—of an employee-owned company?

◆

Key Terms

labor unions
collective bargaining
givebacks
Industrial Disputes
Investigation Act (1907)
Privy Council Order 1003
(1943)
Constitution Act, 1867
Canada Labour Code
bargaining unit

certification vote
craft unions
industrial unions
local union
national union
international union
independent local union
shop steward
business agent
union security

closed shop
union shop
agency shop
open shop
guaranteed annual wage
cost-of-living adjustment
(COLA)
strike
picketing
boycott

slowdown
lockout
strikebreaker
decertification
mediation
voluntary arbitration
compulsory arbitration
grievance

Study Questions and Exercises

Review Questions

1. Why do workers in some companies unionize while workers in other companies do not?
2. Why did it take so many years for the union movement to mature in Canada? Describe some of the key events along the way.
3. The proportion of the Canadian work force that is unionized has been constant for more than 15 years. Why hasn't the proportion increased or decreased?
4. Describe the kinds of employment issues that the Canada Labour Standards Code deals with.
5. How are craft and industrial unions different? How are international, national, and local unions different?

Analysis Questions

6. Workers at the Canadian plants of Ford, General Motors, and Chrysler are represented by the Canadian Auto Workers. Why are automobile workers at

Toyota's Cambridge, Ontario, plant—who are doing exactly the same kind of work—not unionized?
7. Suppose you are a manager in a nonunionized company. You have just heard a rumor that some of your workers are discussing forming a union. What would you do? Be specific.
8. What are the implications for management of a closed shop, a union shop, and an agency shop?

Application Questions

9. Interview the managers of two local companies, one unionized and one nonunionized. Compare and contrast the wage and salary levels, benefits, and working conditions of workers at the two firms.
10. With your instructor playing the role of management and a student playing the role of a union organizer, role play the processes involved in trying to form a union.

Building Your Business Skills

Goal

To help students understand the types of labor-management issues affecting various businesses.

Situation

Suppose you are the human-resources manager at a mid-sized firm where there has been some unrest among the unionized workforce. At issue are such things as pay and mandatory overtime. The president of the company wants to know whether the firm's problems are unique or whether similar issues arise at other companies. The president has asked you to prepare a report surveying labor issues confronting management today.

Method

Working in groups of four or five, make arrangements to conduct interviews at businesses near your college or university. Speak to members of management as well as workers or workers' representatives. Try to cover as many different types of businesses as possible—union and nonunion, service and manufacturing, large and small, and

so on. One group could conduct on-campus interviews with employees from your campus food service, physical plant, housekeeping, and clerical areas. In particular.

- At a union shop, interview a shop steward or the officer of a local union.
- Ask management whether the presence (or absence) of a union has an effect on company activities. If so, what kind of effects?
- Inquire about contract negotiations, personnel issues, pay issues, hiring and firing, and pressure from global competition.
- Ask what labor issues are facing the company in the next two to three years.

Circulate your findings to the other teams.

Follow-Up Questions:

1. In your research, did you find that one particular labor-management issue showed up repeatedly?
2. What differences, if any, arise in unionized businesses as opposed to nonunionized ones? In service firms as opposed to manufacturing companies?

WILL TRADITIONAL EMPLOYMENT PRACTICES IN JAPAN BECOME A THING OF THE PAST?

During the 1970s and 1980s, Japanese companies used employment practices such as lifetime employment, promotion through seniority, and company unions. These traditional employment practices (TEPs) were touted as one of the key reasons for the economic rise of Japan after World War II. But during the early 1990s, Japan experienced significant economic difficulties, and this has led some observers to conclude that these TEPs are in jeopardy. Others disagree and say that TEPs will remain firmly entrenched in Japan. Consider the arguments made by each side in this dispute.

Traditional Employment Practices Will Have to Change

The strongest argument against TEPs is that economic changes are occurring in Japan which are expected to make their use less feasible. The traditional employment system involves hiring young men directly out of college and bringing them along gradually (the hiring of women is increasing, but change is slow). These new workers learn about the firm and are promoted about once every two years.

While the seniority system does bolster the Japanese tradition of deferring to one's elders and working together as a team, it also means that office workers are expected to put in many hours of overtime; they frequently dine and drink with officemates late into the night. Such "salary-men" have little time for their wives and children. The result of this system is a work force of individuals with similar skills, a broad general knowledge of the firm, and an inclination to avoid risk taking.

But such avoidance of risk will be detrimental to the country. In recent years, less developed nations have filled many of the manufacturing roles formerly performed by Japanese workers. Korean companies can turn out automobiles and appliances at lower labor costs. Textile mills in the Philippines can easily undercut Japanese costs. Like Canada before it, Japan has seen its economy gradually shift toward a service economy aimed at the local citizenry.

In the new service economy, "think-alike" employees are a liability. As Japanese firms face increasing competition at home and abroad, they will need more and more creative and innovative employees. To obtain such employees, firms must offer incentives for performance—not simply seniority.

Critics of lifetime employment note that demographic changes are working against that tradition. The guaranteed lifetime employment system was created when Japan had a severe labor shortage and employers needed to hold on to workers. But Japan is now experiencing continuous growth in the work force. Part of this increase is a simple growth in population. Another part stems from the growing number of women entering and remaining in the work force. Yet another factor is the continued employment of older workers. Although workers with guaranteed employment are required to retire at age 55, Japanese pensions are low, so many older workers continue to work either part- or full-time for smaller firms.

Another factor working against a continuation of lifetime employment is the changing attitudes of younger Japanese workers. Traditionally, Japanese workers have put in more time on the job than those of any other industrialized nation. They also put in far more hours of overtime than their counterparts elsewhere. But younger workers are increasingly rebelling against these long hours and rigid working conditions. Between 10 and 20 percent of university graduates are now freelancing instead of accepting a corporate position.

The Japanese government is also pushing for a shorter workweek in an attempt to stimulate consumption of consumer goods. Firms are now encouraged to close both

Saturday and Sunday. The government hopes that with increased leisure time, Japanese consumers will purchase more goods and thereby give the economy a boost.

In addition to shorter hours, many young Japanese are attracted by the greater freedom and higher wages available in the areas of banking and finance. Western-owned brokerage houses and banks need Japanese graduates trained in mathematics, and they have shown themselves willing to pay a premium for such individuals. As a result, manufacturing firms are having trouble hiring graduates trained in mathematics from engineering and computer science programs. Job hopping, once considered taboo in Japan, is becoming more acceptable. With Western firms offering experienced individuals two or three times their normal salary *and* a say in what kinds of jobs they perform, many young Japanese are willing to take a chance.

To compete for highly trained workers, Japanese financial institutions have to raise their salary scales. Other companies, including the giant steel company Nippon Kokan, have instituted a pay system based on merit. To allow room to promote bright new employees, many firms are starting to force less competent senior executives to retire early or accept transfers.

A final factor undermining TEPs is the growing percentage of the work force who traditionally were not covered by TEPs in the first place—part-timers, retirees, women, and foreigners. Foreigners are a particularly difficult problem for Japanese employers. Over the centuries, Japan has consistently fought against any major influx of foreigners, determined not to upset the homogeneous nature of its populace. Yet the nation's Council for the Stabilization of National Life and its Economic Planning Board both say an influx of foreign technology and knowledge would benefit Japan.

Traditional Employment Practices Will Not Have To Change

Because TEPs run counter to free market ideals, Western observers are quick to predict their demise every time Japan runs into economic difficulties like it did in the early 1990s. But some observers of the Japanese systems predict that TEPs are here to stay, and they point to several peculiarities in the Japanese system in support of their arguments.

After World War II, informal employment cartels were formed in many industries. These required employers to refrain from hiring from each other's workers; this restricted competition for labor. Japanese workers are not as loyal to their firms as most Westerners suppose. Rather, they don't switch jobs because there are few opportunities to do so.

The passage of the *Employment Security Law* in 1947 allowed government officials to prevent employers from advertising for labor and from hiring workers if taking the new job required them to change their residence. But the law also made it illegal for companies to fire workers. So Japanese employers provide lifetime employment not be-

cause they want to, but because they have to.

In spite of this coercion of both companies and workers, the lifetime employment system has several significant advantages:

- Japanese firms rapidly introduce new technology—workers do not resist these changes because they have job security.
- Japanese companies are willing to spend heavily on employee training because they know employees will not leave and take jobs elsewhere. Thus, the organization that spent the money on the employees' training will benefit from that training.
- Corporations invest heavily in research and development. They know that employees will not change jobs and leak secrets to competitors.
- Japanese managers do not sweep problems under the carpet and let the next manager deal with them. Actions managers take are on the permanent record, and that record creates accountability.
- Union-management relations lead to unusually high productivity. A Japanese union's idea of a strike is stopping work for one hour over lunch so that productivity does not decline.
- Because workers have lifetime employment, the "we-they" attitude that exists in North America is almost nonexistent in Japan. Workers see the company's future as their future.
- Top executives in Japan earn about 10 times what the most junior worker earns, while in North America, top executives often earn up to 100 times what production workers earn. The much smaller salaries in Japan facilitates the team approach.
- Promotion by seniority motivates older managers to act as mentors to younger mangers. The senior managers, then, do not fear being "leapfrogged" by an aggressive younger person.

CASE QUESTIONS
1. What characteristics would the Japanese practices of lifetime employment and promotion based on seniority instill in Japanese employees that Canadian workers would be unlikely to have? What characteristics based on TEPs would Japanese workers have in common with Canadian workers?
2. How important are economic, demographic, and social changes in changing human resource management practices? Think, for example, about the labor movement described in Chapter 10.
3. Do you think Japan's problems in planning for and developing human resources differ greatly from those of Canada?
4. Are traditional employment practices on the way out in

Experiential Exercise: Establishing a Pay Policy

OBJECTIVE

To help students grasp the difficulties of creating an equitable system for paying employees and the inherent problems when the legality of such a system is questioned.

TIME REQUIRED

45 minutes
- Step 1: Individual activity (to be completed before class)
- Step 2: Small-group activity (25 minutes)
- Step 3: Class discussion (20 minutes)

PROCEDURE

Step 1: Read the following case regarding Hildebrandt Clothing Stores.

Hildebrandt Clothing Stores, long noted for their selection of men's suits, have recently branched out into sales of women's and children's clothing as well. The company's management feels that customers for men's and women's clothing are more comfortable buying their clothes from salespeople of the same sex and that both sexes are more comfortable buying children's clothing from saleswomen. Thus all salespeople in the men's department are male and all salespeople in the women's and children's departments are female.

All salespeople at Hildebrandt's stores are paid a flat salary and receive no commissions on the goods they sell. However, pay rates differ by department. The management at Hildebrandt gives the following rationale for this difference: men's suits (the biggest seller in the men's department) sell for higher prices—and also generate higher profit margins—than do dresses (the biggest seller in the women's department) or children's clothes. Thus salesmen bring in more revenue per person than do saleswomen (see table).

Hildebrandt's female workers resent the policy and have begun talks with local union organizers. Their success at getting this company policy spotlighted in the local newspaper has also led to a partial boycott of the stores by enraged citizens of both sexes. In addition, they are contemplating a lawsuit for possible discrimination. Hildebrandt's lawyers have advised that the company has a 50 percent chance of winning a lawsuit regarding possible discrimination in its hiring practices. They further advise, however, that the firm has virtually no chance of winning a lawsuit regarding its pay practices.

Should Hildebrandt Change Its Policy?

Step 2: The instructor will divide the class into small groups as follows:

a. Female workers at Hildebrandt
b. Male workers at Hildebrandt
c. Hildebrandt's management (to include persons of both sexes)
d. Union organizers (to include persons of both sexes)

Group members will then decide on a plan of action to meet their goals, completing the Decision-Making Grid on the facing page.

Step 3: One member of each small group will present the group's conclusions to the class.

QUESTIONS FOR DISCUSSION

1. If each group follows through on its decision, what will be the overall outcome eventually?
2. Regardless of their legality, how would you assess the ethics of Hildebrandt's employment practices?

SALES AND PROFITS FOR A TYPICAL HILDEBRANDT CLOTHING STORE

	Men's Department	Women's Department	Children's Department	% Excess Male/Female
Average sales per year/department	$647 000	$523 000	$519 000	23.78%
Average gross profits per year/department	$305 000	$197 000	$195 000	54.8%
Average percent profit per year/department	47.2%	37.6%	37.5%	——
Average sales per hour/individual	$150.46	$85.74	$84.39	75.5%
Average gross profits per hour/individual	$70.93	$32.30	$31.71	119.6%
Average wage per hour/individual	$7.20	$5.50	$5.50	31%
Wages as a percent of profits/hour	9.9%	17.0%	17.3%	——

DECISION-MAKING GRID

Group	How Proposed Plan Will Affect
Male Employees	
Female Employees	
Unionization efforts	
Protesting customers	
Management authority	
Overall wage rates	
Profits at Hildebrandt	

CAREERS IN BUSINESS
The Write Stuff

"The pen is mightier than the sword."
—Edward Bulwer-Lytton

No matter how well-conceived your career plan, how good your grades, or how much real-world experience you have, getting a job will take work...and a first-class cover letter and résumé. A cover letter introduces you and your qualifications to an organization and explains that you are seeking a position. Your résumé summarizes your qualifications.

PREPARING AN EFFECTIVE RESUME

A résumé is probably the most important factor in landing an interview with a firm. A résumé should be relatively brief (usually only a single page for applicants early in their careers), concise, clear, accurate, and professional.

Consider, for example, the sample résumé for Lee Fairfield—which is only one page long (Figure 1). Most employers get dozens of résumés. If yours is too long, it is likely to be discarded. Of course, if your credentials warrant two pages, then by all means include them all. But make sure that the information you include is relevant to the job you are seeking. *Never* exceed two pages.

The sample résumé shown here is just one of many different forms that you might use. Most libraries and many bookstores have books that contain a variety of sample résumés. In all cases, though, remember that the basic purpose of your résumé is to help you get a job. Thus, it should be structured to highlight your strengths while not calling undue attention to your weaknesses.

Regardless of its structure, most experts agree that your résumé should include the following:

■ Education, experience, honors and activities

In addition, experts recommend that you do not include:

■ Age, marital status/children, height and weight, health, a photo of yourself

Expert opinion is divided on the inclusion of either a statement of employment objective or a summary. An employment objective (for example, "A sales position for a major pharmaceutical manufacturer") is useful if you know just what you are looking for. But vague statements designed to cover a variety of positions can do you more harm than good. Unless you plan to have several

Figure 1   Lee Fairfield's Résumé

Lee Fairfield
1906 Meredith Lane
Toronto, Ontario
(416) 555-4239

EMPLOYMENT OBJECTIVE
A sales representative with a full-range consumer products firm.

EDUCATION
B. Comm., University of Toronto, 1994 (Marketing major)

EMPLOYMENT EXPERIENCE
Assistant manager for J. Riggins Clothing Store in Toronto (September, 1993 to April, 1994); assisted manager in scheduling sales clerks; supervised weekly ordering of merchandise; helped monitor inventory levels of basic merchandise lines.

Intern for Ensearch Corporation in Toronto (Summer, 1994); assisted a team of five managers developing a new marketing strategy.

Sales clerk for The Varsity Shop in Toronto (September, 1992 to August, 1993); helped customers in selecting clothing, finding correct sizes, matching colors, and ringing up sales.

OTHER EXPERIENCE
Coached youth ringette program in Toronto on a volunteer basis (Summer, 1992)
Worked as a United Way coordinator (1992)

HONORS AND ACTIVITIES
Deans List, 1993–94
James Collin Scholarship (1992–93)
Vice-President of the Marketing Club (1993–94)
Member of the Marketing Club (1991–94)

Be as specific as possible in your objective (if you include one).

List education with your most recent degree first. (*Note*: After many years on the job, education should follow, not precede, experience.)

List most recent experience first. Be sure to include dates, locations, and specific duties/achievements. Note use of action verbs (e.g., "assisted," "supervised," "helped").

List other experiences that show your leadership qualities, level of commitment, and other skills of value to an organization.

Focus on items that show a connection to areas of concern for the organization to which you are applying. *Warning*: Too many activities may imply that you have no time (or energy) for work.

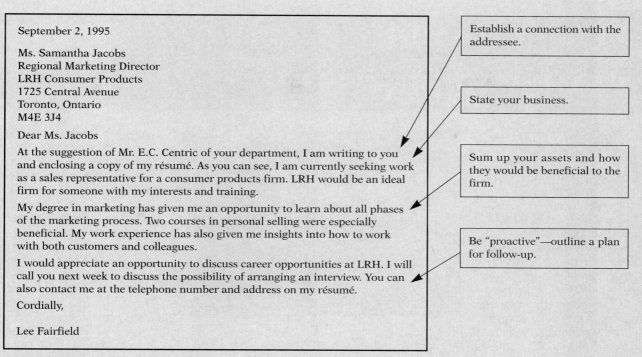

September 2, 1995

Ms. Samantha Jacobs
Regional Marketing Director
LRH Consumer Products
1725 Central Avenue
Toronto, Ontario
M4E 3J4

Dear Ms. Jacobs

At the suggestion of Mr. E.C. Centric of your department, I am writing to you and enclosing a copy of my résumé. As you can see, I am currently seeking work as a sales representative for a consumer products firm. LRH would be an ideal firm for someone with my interests and training.

My degree in marketing has given me an opportunity to learn about all phases of the marketing process. Two courses in personal selling were especially beneficial. My work experience has also given me insights into how to work with both customers and colleagues.

I would appreciate an opportunity to discuss career opportunities at LRH. I will call you next week to discuss the possibility of arranging an interview. You can also contact me at the telephone number and address on my résumé.

Cordially,

Lee Fairfield

Establish a connection with the addressee.

State your business.

Sum up your assets and how they would be beneficial to the firm.

Be "proactive"—outline a plan for follow-up.

Figure 2   Lee Fairfield's Cover Letter

variations of your résumé printed or have access to desktop publishing that makes such variations possible, you might want to skip an employment objective if you're flexible regarding what kind of job you'll accept. Those with a great deal of experience may choose to include a summary statement (for example, "An experienced marketing manager with a proven track record in developing and promoting new consumer products") instead.

Lee's résumé includes the key elements in a concise and clear fashion. Note, for example, that she lists two jobs and one internship under employment experience. Each listing includes the dates, location, and basic activities performed. This information helps a prospective employer better assess the nature of Lee's experiences and how they relate to both her employment objective and the type of work the firm has to offer.

While it should be obvious that a résumé must be accurate, some people exaggerate their accomplishments to make themselves look better. This tactic usually backfires. Prospective employers generally verify the content of résumés before making job offers. If they find a résumé to contain misleading or downright false statements, they will almost certainly reject the applicant immediately. Don't hesitate to blow your own horn about your accomplishments—if you led a task force that figured out how to save your employer $100 000 a year, then say so. But don't identify yourself as Warehouse and Distribution Manager if your real job was carrying merchandise from a small stockroom to the sales floor!

Over the past two decades, the availability of desktop publishing has also fostered explosive growth in résumé-writing services. Should you use one? Most experts say you shouldn't need to. But many people swear by their services for the help they offer in shaping a résumé,

ensuring that it looks professional, and offering encouragement to the struggling job hunter. If you opt for one of these services, don't abandon the basic principles of good résumé writing and presentation. And don't leave the proofreading to anyone else.

PREPARING A COVER LETTER

A cover letter should always be included with your résumé. The purpose of this letter is to introduce yourself, indicate your intentions, refer the reader to your résumé, and suggest a course of action.

Note, for example, the structure of Lee's cover letter (Figure 2). It begins with a brief mention of a mutual acquaintance. (If you don't write at someone's suggestion, be sure to say how you heard about a possible opening.) Next, Lee states her reason for writing. The letter goes on to note ways in which Lee (and her experience) may fit well into this company. (Caution: Do not repeat too much information from the résumé.) Be sure to phrase that fit in terms of what you have to offer the organization. Lee concludes her letter by describing the actions she will take—she will call the addressee, or the person receiving the letter can contact Lee first. If you ask the addressee to call you, ideally you should have an answering machine to take calls when you aren't there.

Cover letters should be brief. Unless you are sending your letter and résumé to a "blind" ad (one that does not indicate the name of the organization involved), your letters should always be addressed to a specific individual, as opposed to "Director of Human Resources" or (even worse) "To Whom It May Concern." As with résumés, always proofread your cover letters carefully to prevent errors.

Video Case III-I

CBC 🍁

FAMILY BUSINESS*

Wallace and Harrison McCain, brothers and co-owners of the $3 billion McCain food processing empire have recently gone public with their conflict over which of their offspring should lead the McCain empire once the two brothers are no longer holding the reins. To date they have brought in a variety of experts to assist them, beginning with management consultants and psychologists and, more recently, lawyers. While the McCains' very public fight threatens to tear their billion-dollar empire apart, the core issues involved in the struggle are extremely relevant to many working Canadians: family business succession.

According to recent estimates, approximately 4.5 million Canadians are employed by family-controlled businesses. In addition, family-controlled and closely-held businesses together account for about 85 percent of all new jobs. Recent estimates also report that as many as 75 percent of all family businesses fail to successfully pass the torch of business ownership and management to the next generation. Even more despairing, these studies also report that of the 25 percent that do survive the succession rapids, a whopping 90 percent fail to pass on the reins to the third generation.

One Canadian firm currently attempting to address this issue is Taillefer Construction in Edmonton, Alberta. While this firm is obviously much smaller than Canada's premiere family empires such as the Bronfmans, Irvings, and Eatons, the basic issues remain consistent across companies. Ray Taillefer, who founded the company 23 years ago, has built his construction company into a 100-employee operation that includes four of his sons. The oldest two have each been with the company for about half a dozen years. In the next few years Ray hopes to begin planning the management succession process at his company. According to noted family business expert and consultant, Leon Danco, one of Ray's central challenges will be to remain as objective as possible. This is an important priority because of how easily people's judgment gets steered by emotional attachments to family. Danco also advises family companies facing the types of decisions the Taillefers are working through to begin to work on these decisions as early as possible, before things get even more complicated. Given the less than encouraging succession statistics, the Taillefer business family will have their work cut out for them as they attempt to realize the dream of becoming a second-generation family business.

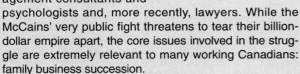

Study questions:

1. What are the basic steps in planning and developing human resources? In what ways are these activities carried out differently in family businesses? (Note: you may want to revisit Chapter 7).
2. What are orientation and employee training and development? In what ways are these two human resource activities often carried out differently in family businesses?
3. What, according to Abraham Maslow, are the basic needs that people seek to satisfy? In what ways can family businesses satisfy some of these needs in ways non-family businesses cannot?
4. What are performance appraisal and the basic steps by which it is carried out? In what ways might performance appraisal be different, and possibly more difficult, in family businesses?

---

* This case is based on the *Venture* episode first broadcast on November 20, 1994.

Video Case III-II

UNIONS GROWING*

The word "union" has been traditionally associated with jobs like steelmaking and automobile manufacturing and objectives like greater pay and increased worker benefits. But no more. A new breed of unions is reported in the Canadian workplace. A number of cross-Canada pro-union initiatives are reported among such diverse employee groups as taxi-drivers, hotel employees, and fast food "burger flippers." As a result of such interest, union officials report that the number of new bargaining units getting approval in Canada is up by over 50 percent.

The increase in interest in union membership comes at a most interesting time in Canada's history, with wage gains the lowest in 50 years and the number of strikes at an all-time low. In addition, Canadian manufacturing jobs are also at an all-time low. Virtually every new job that has been created in Canada since 1976 is in service areas such as retail, health care and transportation.

The surge in union enrollment comes as the result of a combination of several factors. First, unions have been devastated by the loss of manufacturing-related jobs. As a result, they have sought to replace lost manufacturing membership with members in the service sector. As second reason for this surge of interest comes in response to new pro-union legislation recently passed by the N.D.P. governments of Ontario and British Columbia that make it easier for workers to get organized. Such legislation explains, in part, the statistic that B.C. leads the country with a 400 percent increase in the number of new bargaining units.

A number of important differences are apparent between today's and earlier union movements. In the past unions typically initiated the process of union organizing; today union leaders report up to 80 percent of new union membership results from employee-sponsored initiatives. A second difference concerns the nature of the union's objectives. Whereas in the past emphasis was placed on getting maximum wage increases, today focus is on achieving fair treatment of employees. With many of the new unions yet to negotiate their first employee contract, the pressure will be on unions to deliver what they have promised their new members.

Study questions:

1. What is a union? What are the different types of unions and different levels of union security that exist?
2. What are the key laws and legislative orders that affect the formation and operation of labor unions?
3. What are the basic human needs identified by Professor Abraham Maslow? Which of these needs would it be most difficult for a union to satisfy for its members? Which would be least difficult?
4. What are the basic tactics available to a union? How do these compare to the tactics a company's management may use? In what ways could a union use its tactics to maximum effect?

* This case is based on the *Venture* episode first broadcast on January 16, 1994.

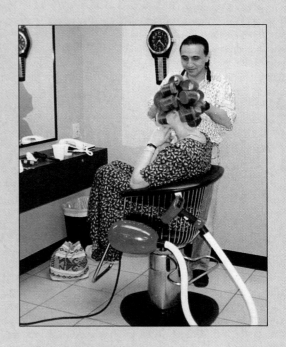

Part Four

*M*ANAGING PRODUCTION

Producing high quality goods and services is at the heart of all business operations. Business firms in Canada face increased international competition and the new reality of the Canada-U.S. Trade Agreement and the North American Free Trade Agreement. The opening cases of the chapters in this section show how business firms like Dorel Industries, Western Star Trucks, Ipsco Inc., Nova Scotia Power, and Jaguar have responded to increased competition and ever-increasing consumer expectations about quality and productivity.

Part Four, Managing Production, provides an overview of three aspects of business important to firms' existence: production of goods, production of services, and increasing productivity and quality.

■ We begin in **Chapter 11, Producing Goods**, by examining how firms manufacture goods, plan and schedule manufacturing processes, and control both the costs and quality of the final output.

■ Then, in **Chapter 12, Producing Services**, we explore the special nature of services and how their particular characteristics affect planning, scheduling, and quality control in service industries.

■ Finally, in **Chapter 13, Increasing Productivity and Quality**, we consider some of the ways by which companies can improve the productivity and the quality of their output, and thus their competitive position.

11

Producing Goods

OPENING CASE

The New Industrial Revolution

Canadians want a strong manufacturing sector because it makes us feel that we are more than simply hewers of wood and haulers of water. So, when jobs started to disappear from manufacturing in the early 1990s, everyone worried. In 1990 and 1991 in Ontario alone, more than 200 000 manufacturing jobs were lost to the U.S. after the Canada-U.S. Free Trade Agreement went into effect. Often the driving force behind the exodus was the promise of lower costs in the U.S. The average manufacturing wage in Tennessee, for example, was 30 percent lower than in Ontario. The cost of land, taxes, and transportation are also lower.

Firms like Tridon Ltd. and St. Lawrence Starch Co. were typical of firms that left. Tridon closed two auto parts manufacturing plants, putting 500 employees out of work. It moved to cope with its U.S. competitors, who had a lower cost structure. St. Lawrence Starch joined a strategic alliance with an Illinois firm because the Canadian government imposed a duty on U.S. corn, which also caused the price of Canadian corn to increase. The company said it couldn't pass the price increase on to consumers. So it moved to the U.S. and now ships its product into Canada under the provisions of the free trade agreement.

These and many other stories were a cause of deep concern just a few years ago. But the Canadian manufacturing sector is making a strong comeback. In 1992 and 1993, more than half of the growth in gross domestic product came from manufacturing. So did most of the growth in jobs. Manufacturing employment is now rising at five times the rate of Canadian business generally, and growth in Canadian manufacturing output has outpaced that of any other major industrial competitor.

Although the free trade agreement has indeed caused a "gutting" of the traditional manufacturing sector, for every firm that went out of business, another has rushed in to take its place. These new firms are building products that are more competitive and more suitable for the export market. In 1980, Canadian firms exported about 25 percent of their production to foreign markets; in 1993, the figure was almost 50 percent.

Consider these success stories. Dorel Industries Inc. of Montreal, a manufacturer of ready-to-assemble children's furniture, has quadrupled its sales by merging several Canadian companies and cracking the U.S. market. It now sells 70 percent of its output in the U.S. Ipsco Inc. recently achieved the highest profits in its history after adopting the latest technological improvements and selling its steel products in the U.S. Western Star Trucks Inc. is in the middle of a major expansion, and produces twice as many trucks per day as it did two years ago. SR Telecom, a manufacturer of microwave-telecommunications systems, sells its products in 73 countries and controls over 40 percent of the world market. Husky Injection Molding has in-

creased its productivity by more than 65 percent since 1990, and exports 88 percent of its output.

In spite of these success stories, critics can still be found. They point to the fact that the share of the Canadian market accounted for by Canadian firms dropped from 67 percent in 1981 to 59 percent in 1991. But for the huge U.S./Canadian market combined, Canada's share went from 1.9 percent before the free trade agreement to 2.6 percent since. Because the U.S. market is so large, this more than makes up for any losses of market share in Canada. And Canadian manufacturing firms have also been gaining an increasing share of the *growth* in this combined market.

It is true that many jobs in manufacturing have been lost. Employment peaked in 1989 at 2.1 million production workers; by 1993, there were just 1.7 million. But this drop in employment is one of the key reasons for the manufacturing sector's recent success. Output is back up to pre-recession levels, even though employment is down by 19 percent. In the wood products industry, for example, sales increased by 8 percent even though employment dropped by 2 percent. The same trend is evident in automotive, electrical products, and chemical firms. The labor cost gap with the U.S., which had reached 21 percent, is now only 3 percent.

Canadian manufacturing firms are also more competitive because they have aggressively adopted new technologies. Increases in labor productivity have outstripped those in the U.S. for the first time since 1985. Canadian firms have also adopted aggressive pricing strategies; the average price for manufactured goods was the same in 1993 as it was in 1989.

The future looks bright for Canadian manufacturing. The gains made in the last few years may be just the beginning. After learning some very tough lessons in the 1980s, Canadian manufacturers are not likely to fritter away their new-found advantages. The increased emphasis on worker training and an increased commitment to quality are likely to become mainstays of Canadian manufacturing for the foreseeable future.   ◆

The opening case gives some idea of just how complex and dynamic the Canadian manufacturing sector is. In this chapter, we will consider how firms involved in the production of goods deal with this complexity and with the rapid change with which they are continually faced. In the next chapter, we will do the same for the "production" of services, since many principles are common to both goods and services production. Both require management of the production process, including planning and control.

A Short History of Manufacturing

Before the Industrial Revolution began in England in the 18th century, the typical workplace was the small shop and the home. Leather and cloth were handmade, as were needles and other tools; clothing, harnesses, and other goods were made one at a time by craftsmen. In the late 1770s, however, a new institution emerged: Using machines, materials, industrial workers, and managers, the factory produced greater quantities of goods in an organized fashion. Throughout the 19th century, the factory remained the central institution for commerce. By then, it was using water, and then electricity, for power sources. The factory also relied on heavy machinery that was cumbersome, powerful, and it was often operated by children.

In the early 1900s in the U.S., two major developments took place: Frederick W. Taylor began his "scientific management" studies and Henry Ford revolutionized industry with the Ford "mass production" system. Production had become—at least in theory—the "science" of making products economically on a massive scale. Using specialization of labor for efficiency, the assembly line became the new tool for gaining economies of scale. Through the 1940s, the assembly line still depended heavily on human labor. By the 1960s, however, when mass production had reached its zenith, the factory culture had matured socially as well as commercially. As consumers continued to rely on access to the material goods that flooded from factories, attitudes toward production and production workers were changing. Children, of course, were no longer a part of the workforce, and such "radical" ideas as gender equality and ethnic diversity were soon to become accepted goals. Environmental concerns were also gaining in prominence.

More recently, other countries have joined the ranks of "developed" nations and benefited from new and better manufacturing methods. As a result, global competition has reshaped production into a fast-paced, challenging business activity. Although the factory remains the centerpiece for manufacturing, it is virtually unrecognizable when compared to its counterpart of even a decade ago. The noise, smoke, and danger have been replaced in many companies by glistening high-tech machines, computers, and "clean rooms" that are contaminant-free and carefully controlled for temperature.[1] Instead of the need to maintain continuous mass production, firms today face constant change. They must continually develop new technologies to respond to ever-changing consumer demands. They must produce varieties of different products at high quality levels. They must strive to design new products, get them into production, and deliver them to customers faster than their competitors.[2]

Production Management: An Overview

To understand the production processes of a firm, you need to understand the importance of products—both goods and services. Products provide businesses with both economic results (profits, wages, goods purchased

utility
The power of a product to satisfy a human want; something of value.

time utility
That quality of a product satisfying a human want because of the time at which it is made available.

place utility
That quality of a product satisfying a human want because of where it is made available.

ownership (possession) utility
That quality of a product satisfying a human want during its consumption or use.

form utility
That quality of a product satisfying a human want because of its form; requires raw materials to be transformed into a finished product.

operations (production) management
The systematic direction and control of the processes that transform resources into finished goods.

from other companies) and noneconomic results (new technology, innovations, pollution). And they provide consumers with what economists call **utility**—want satisfaction.

Four basic kinds of utility would not be possible without production. By making a product available at a time when consumers want it, production creates **time utility**, as when a company turns out ornaments in time for Christmas. By making a product available in a place convenient for consumers, production creates **place utility**, as when a local department store creates a "Trim-A-Tree" section. By making a product that consumers can take pleasure in owning, production creates **ownership (possession) utility**, as when you take a box of ornaments home and decorate your tree.

But above all, production makes products available in the first place. By turning raw materials into finished goods, production creates **form utility**, as when an ornament maker combines glass, plastic, and other materials to create tree decorations.

Because the term *production* has historically been associated with manufacturing, it has been replaced in recent years by *operations*, a term that reflects both services and goods production. **Operations** (or **production**) **management** is the systematic direction and control of the processes that transform resources into finished goods and services. Thus production managers are ultimately responsible for creating utility for customers.

As Figure 11.1 shows, production managers must bring raw materials, equipment, and labor together under a production plan that effectively uses all the resources available in the production facility. As demand for a good increases, they must schedule and control work to produce the amount required. Meanwhile, they must control costs, quality levels, inventory, and plant and equipment.

Not all production managers work in factories. Farmers are also production managers. They create form utility by converting soil, seeds, sweat, gas, and other inputs into beef cattle, tobacco, wheat, milk, cash, and other outputs. As production managers, farmers have the option of employing

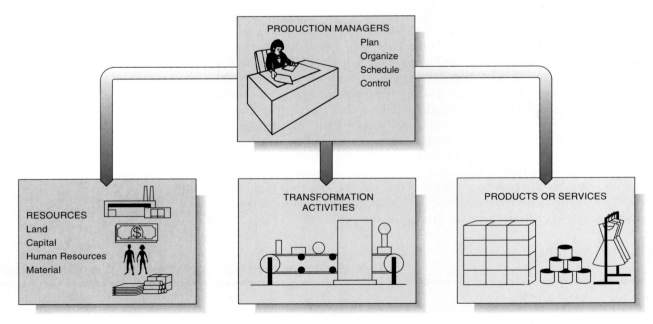

Figure 11.1
The transformation system.

TABLE 11.1   Inputs, Transformation, and Outputs in Production Systems

Production System	Inputs	Transformation	Outputs
Farm	Land, tractors and equipment, labor, buildings, fertilizer, farmer's management skills	Cultivation of plants and livestock	Food products, profit for owner, jobs for farmer's family
Jewelry store	Fashion-conscious customers, merchandise, sales clerks, showroom, fixtures, and equipment	Exchange of merchandise between buyer and seller	Satisfied jewelry customers
Tire producer	Rubber and chemical compounds, blending equipment, tire molds, factory, and human skills	Chemical reactions of raw materials	Tires for autos, airplanes, trucks, trailers, and other vehicles
Furniture manufacturer	Wood-working equipment fabrics, wood, nails and screws, factory, wood-working skills	Fabrication and assembly of materials	Furniture for homes and offices

many workers to plant and harvest their crops. Or they may decide to use automated machinery or some combination of workers and machinery. These decisions affect farmers' costs, the buildings and equipment they own, and the quality and quantity of goods they produce. Table 11.1 shows examples of different types of production management.

Classifying Operations Processes

Whether they are independent farmers or employees of a multinational manufacturer, production managers must control the process by which goods are produced. We can classify production processes in four different ways:

■ by the type of transformation technology used
■ by whether the process is analytic or synthetic
■ by the pattern of product flow during transformation
■ by the extent of labor use

Any process can be classified in any of these ways. The point of these different classification systems is to help managers analyze new or unfamiliar production processes by comparing them with familiar ones.

Transformation Technology.   Manufacturers use chemical, fabrication, assembly, transport, and clerical processes to transform raw materials into finished goods. In *chemical processes,* raw materials are chemically altered. Such techniques are common in the aluminum, steel, fertilizer, petroleum, and paint industries. In contrast, *fabrication processes* mechanically alter the basic shape or form of the product. Examples of fabrication abound in the metal-forming and machining industries, the wood-working industry, and the plastic-molding and plastic-forming industries.

As their name suggests, *assembly processes* involve putting together various components. These techniques are often used in the electronics, appliance, and automotive industries. *Transport processes*, in which goods acquire place utility by moving from one location to another, are also common in the appliance industry. For example, refrigerators are routinely moved from manufacturing plants to consumers through a series of regional warehouses and discount stores.

Finally, *clerical processes* transform information. Combining data on employee absences and machine breakdowns into a productivity report is a clerical process. One issue currently facing users of clerical transformation is whether too much information is being processed and presented. Methods for managing these information problems are discussed in Chapter 23.

analytic process

Any production process in which resources are broken down.

synthetic process

Any production process in which resources are combined.

continuous process

Any production process in which the flow of transformation from resources to finished product is fairly smooth, straight, and continuous.

Analytic versus Synthetic Processes.   A second way of classifying production processes is by the way resources are converted into finished goods. An **analytic process** breaks down the basic resources into components. For example, Alcan manufactures aluminum by extracting it from an ore called bauxite. The reverse approach, a **synthetic process**, combines a number of raw materials to produce a finished product such as fertilizer or paint.

Product Flow Pattern.   We can also classify production processes by how the plant is arranged and how the product moves through the plant.[3] In a **continuous process**, the flow is fairly smooth, straight, and continuous. A continuous-process pattern is usually found when a manufacturing operation is repetitive. Typically, such a plant turns out nearly identical finished products in production runs of several days, months, or even years. Toyota, Imperial Tobacco, and Labatt's all use continuous processes.

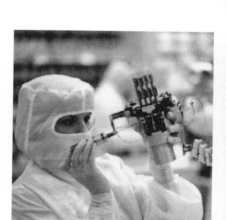

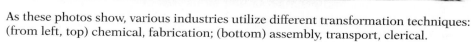
As these photos show, various industries utilize different transformation techniques: (from left, top) chemical, fabrication; (bottom) assembly, transport, clerical.

In contrast, material in an **intermittent process** flows through a plant in a stop-and-go fashion and a seemingly scattered arrangement of equipment and departments. The jumbled flows occur because such plants produce short runs of custom-made products, each requiring a unique set of operations. Printing shops are an example. As various jobs are routed through the necessary departments, machines are shut down frequently in order to set up for other jobs.

One other major characteristic of this process is that each job passes through specialized departments. Intermittent processes usually group similar machines—grinders in one department and milling machines in another, for example. But a continuous process would place grinders or mills wherever they are needed along an assembly line. Figure 11.2 illustrates some of the differences between continuous and intermittent processes.

Labor Use. Finally, processes vary in the amount of human input they need. **Labor-intensive processes** depend more on people than on machines. They are most likely to be used when labor is cheap or when there is an artistic element to the work. Many kinds of farming are still highly labor intensive. Producing cherries or lettuce is much more labor intensive than producing wheat or sugar beets.

intermittent process
Any production process in which the flow of transformation from resources to finished product starts and stops.

labor-intensive process
Any process that depends more on people than on machines.

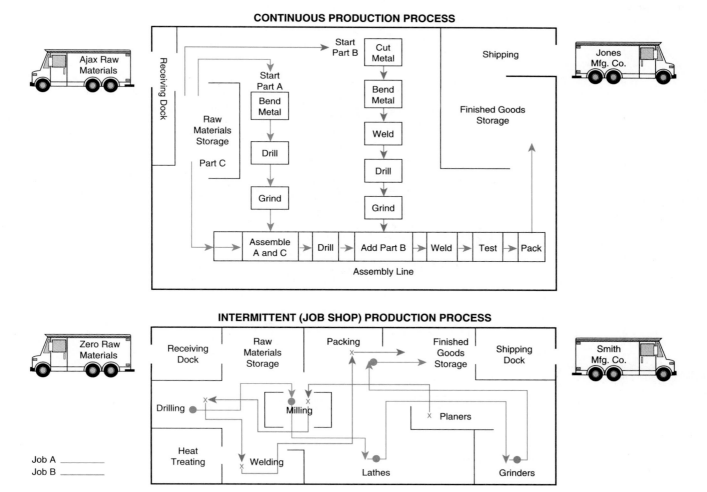

Figure 11.2
Continuous and intermittent processes.

capital-intensive process
Any process in which investment in machinery is great.

Capital-intensive processes are those in which investment in machinery is great. A huge petroleum refinery is a classic example of a capital-intensive process. A refinery that may cost hundreds of millions of dollars to build and equip may operate with fewer than 100 employees.

Operations Planning

Managers from many departments contribute to decisions about production management. As Figure 11.3 shows, however, no matter how many decision makers are involved, the process can be described as a series of logical steps. The success of any firm depends on the final result of this logical sequence of decisions.

The overall business plan developed by a company's top executives guides operations planning. This plan outlines the firm's goals and objectives, including the specific products and services that it will offer in the upcoming years. In this section, we will survey each of the major components of the business plan that directly affect operations planning. First, we will describe *forecasting* and then we will discuss the key planning and forecasting activities that fall into one of five major categories: *capacity, location, layout, quality,* and *methods planning.*

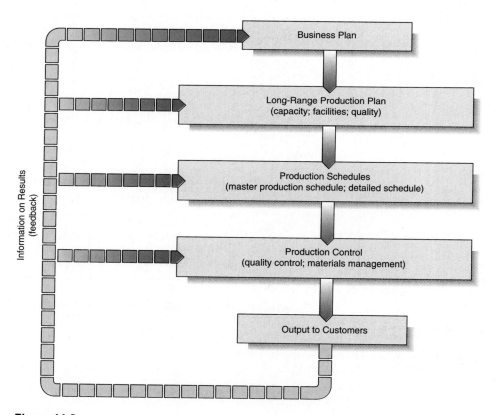

Figure 11.3
The steps in a production planning and control system ensure that production activities lead to customer satisfaction.

Forecasting

In addition to the business plan, managers develop the firm's *long-range production plan* through **forecasts** of future demand for both new and existing
products. This plan covers a two- to five-year period. It specifically details
the number of plants or service facilities, as well as labor, machinery, and
transportation and storage facilities, that will be needed to meet demand. It
also specifies how resources will be obtained.

    Forecasting uses both qualitative and quantitative methods. *Qualitative
forecasts* may come from an expert or group of experts who basically use
judgment and experience. *Quantitative forecasts* are statistical methods to
project future demand from past demand patterns. For example, in developing a new line of Memorex videotapes, Memtek Products might use quantitative methods to calculate demand three years hence at 4 million cassettes
per year. Its long-range production plan might translate this demand into a
need to build three new plants, lease another warehouse, acquire four new
tape-filling machines, and hire 2500 new employees.

forecasts
*Estimates of future demand for
both new and existing products.*

Capacity Planning

The amount of a product that a company can produce under normal working conditions is its **capacity**. A firm's capacity depends on how many people it employs and the number and size of its facilities. Long-range planing
must take into account both current and future capacity.

    Capacity planning means ensuring that a firm's capacity just *slightly*
exceeds the normal demand for its product. To see why this policy is best, consider the alternatives. If capacity is too small to meet demand, the company
must turn away customers—a situation that not only cuts into profits but
alienates both customers and salespeople. If capacity exceeds demand, the firm
is wasting money by maintaining a plant that is too large, by keeping excess
machinery on line, or by employing too many workers.

    When forecasts indicate a temporary business slowdown, companies
plan for ways to use existing capacity. For example, when demand for farm
machinery waned in the 1980s, John Deere found itself with excess production capacity. Rather than closing its plants, Deere used the extra capacity
to make engines for companies producing air compressors and irrigation
pumps as well as motor-home components for Winnebago. Capacity planning allowed Deere to use slack capacity while awaiting anticipated increases
in demand for traditional farm products.[4]

capacity
*The amount of a good that a
firm can produce under normal
working conditions.*

Adjusting Capacity.   Capacity adjustments are often made through the
make-versus-buy decision for production components. If a firm chooses to
manufacture (make) a needed item in its own facility, it will need *more*
production capacity. If it chooses to purchase (buy) that item from another
company, it will need *less* capacity. A clock maker, for example, can either
make the hands for its products or buy hands already made by another
company. If it decides to buy, it can adjust capacity downward.

    Instead of expanding capacity to meet peak demand, companies some-
times use pricing to shift peak demand to nonpeak periods. Golf club manufacturers, for example, will offer seasonal discounts to retailers during the
winter to encourage early ordering. This practice sustains production during
the winter months (an otherwise slow production period) and helps reduce
the peak demand for production in springtime.

Location Planning

Because facility location affects production costs and flexibility, sound location planning is crucial. Depending on the site of its facility, a company may either be capable of producing a low-cost product or may find itself at an extreme cost disadvantage. Such considerations weighed heavily on the decision-making process at Ford that resulted in the Mondeo—the so-called "world car" introduced in Europe in 1993 and (as the Ford Contour and Mercury Mystique) in the United States in 1994. Developed to be both manufactured and marketed around the world, the "world car" took advantage of design strengths in three separate engineering centers: Detroit (V-6 engine, automatic transmission, heating and air-conditioning units), London (4-cylinder engine, steering, suspension, electronics), and Cologne, Germany (basic structural engineering). To free its engineering workforce for other projects and facilities, Ford assigned a single 800-person team to design the Mondeo for both Europe and the United States and will employ identical production facilities to build the car at Genk, Belgium, and Kansas City, Missouri. By custom-building two production facilities on two continents, Ford has saved about 25 percent on customized factory machinery such as stamping dies and secured better prices for larger orders from its suppliers.[5]

As we can see from Ford's "world car" strategy, managers must consider many factors in location planning. Location attractiveness is influenced by proximity to raw materials and markets, availability of labor, energy and transportation costs, local and provincial regulations and taxes, and community living conditions.

Some location decisions are now being simplified by the rise of industrial parks. Created by cities interested in attracting new industry, these planned sites come with the necessary zoning, land, shipping facilities, utilities, and waste-disposal outlets already in place. Such sites offer flexibility, often allowing firms to open new facilities before competitors can get started in the same area. The ready-made site also provides faster construction startups because it entails no lead time in preparing the chosen site.

Layout Planning

Once a site has been selected, managers must decide on plant layout. Layout determines if a company can respond quickly and efficiently to customer requests for more and different products or if it finds itself unable to match competitors' production speed. Alternatives include *process, product, craft work, cellular,* and *fixed-position layouts.*

process layout

A way of organizing production activities such that equipment and people are grouped together according to their function.

Process Layouts.   In a **process layout**, equipment and people are grouped together according to function. In a custom-cake bakery, for instance, the blending of batters is done in an area devoted to mixing, baking occurs in the oven area, icing is prepared in the mixing area, and cakes are decorated on tables in a finishing area before boxing. The various tasks are each performed in specialized locations. Machine, woodworking, and dry cleaning shops usually feature process layouts.

Process layouts are well suited to *job shops*—firms that specialize in custom work. These companies do a variety of jobs for different customers. They rely on general-purpose machinery and skilled labor to respond to the needs of individual customers. For example, your local bakery can accommodate both your request for a wedding cake and your friend's request for a birthday cake.

product layout

A way of organizing production activities such that equipment and people are set up to produce only one type of good.

Product Layouts.   In a **product layout**, resources move through a fixed sequence of steps to become finished goods. Equipment and people are set up to produce only one type of good and are arranged according to its production requirements. Product layouts often use **assembly lines**—a partially finished product moves step by step through the plant on conveyor belts or other equipment, often in a straight line, until the product is completed. Automobile, food-processing, and computer-assembly plants use product layouts.

Product layouts can be efficient and inexpensive because they simplify work tasks and use unskilled labor. They tend, however, to be inflexible because they require a heavy investment in specialized equipment that is hard to re-arrange for new applications. In addition, workers are subject to boredom. Moreover, when workers at one end are absent or overworked, those farther down the line cannot help out.

Craft Work.   To address these problems, many Japanese companies have pioneered new ideas in job design on the assembly line. Both at home and in their Canadian and U.S. factories, NEC, Toyota, Sony, and other firms are finding alternatives to traditional conveyor belts and assembly lines. Instead of specialized jobs, workers are engaged in so-called "craft work" where each worker has the opportunity to assemble an entire product. Even when assembly lines are retained, as in automobile factories, employees are performing more tasks.

Much of the impetus for changes in job design came from Toyota, which is widely credited with developing "lean production" techniques to improve efficiency. Even in situations where assembly lines have been retained, Toyota has expanded employee responsibilities. In the past, for example, an employee's job might have been to install wheels and tires. If he or she discovered a flaw, the production process continued: Finding and fixing problems was not the wheel installer's job. Those tasks were handled by two workers farther down the line: a quality-control checker and a repairperson. However, in a modern Toyota facility like the plant in Cambridge, Ontario, employee responsibilities also include maintaining equipment and cleaning the work area, as well as monitoring overall quality control. If a wheel installer finds a flaw, he or she pulls a cord, which lights up the quality-control board. A team leader will then stop the line to repair the problem. Because workers up and down the line are flexible enough to perform whatever task arises, it can be stopped as often as necessary. Costs are thus lower for two reasons. First, fewer workers, of course, mean lower costs. Second, defective parts can be replaced immediately—and with little waste—because they are either manufactured or purchased in small quantities. Consequently, because both parts and partially finished cars can be held in small batches, inventory costs are also lower.[6]

Cellular Layouts.   Closely related to craft work are **cellular layouts** which are used when *families* of products can follow similar flowpaths. A clothing manufacturer, for example, may establish a "cell," or designated area, dedicated to making a family of clothing pockets—say, pockets for shirts, coats, blouses, trousers, and slacks. Although each type of pocket is unique in shape, size, and style, all go through the same production steps. Within the cell, therefore, various types of equipment (for cutting, trimming, sewing) are arranged close together in the appropriate sequence. All pockets pass, stage-by-stage, through the cell from beginning to end, in a nearly continuous flow. The cellular layout is similar to a product layout, except that product layouts usually are dedicated to single products instead of product families. Our clothing maker might also have cells for sleeves, collars, and so on. There may also be a separate area for final assembly.

Cellular layouts came into widescale use in the 1980s as an improvement over process layouts in some applications. They have several advantages. For example, because similar products require less machine adjustment, equipment setup time is reduced. Because flow distances are

assembly line
A type of product layout in which a partially finished product moves through a plant on a conveyor belt or other equipment.

cellular layouts
Used to produce goods when families of products can follow similar flowpaths.

usually shorter, materials handling and transit time is more efficient. Finally, inventories of goods in-process are lower—and paperwork is simpler—because material flows are more orderly.[7]

Developments in Flexibility.

U-shaped production lines

Machines are placed in a U-shape rather than a straight line so that a single worker can complete all the necessary tasks.

In addition to variations on the product layout, many companies have experimented with ways to make standard production lines more flexible. Some firms, for example, have adopted **U-shaped production lines**: Rather than stretching out in a straight line, machines are placed in a narrow *U*-shape, with workers operating them from within the *U*. Because machines are close together, in slow periods one worker can complete all the tasks needed to make a product by easily moving from one side of the *U* to the other. In busier times, more workers can be added until there is one worker per machine.[8]

flexible manufacturing system (FMS)

A production system in which automatic equipment produces small batches of different goods on the same production line.

Another tool for production flexibility is the **flexible manufacturing system (FMS)**—using computer information systems, a single factory can produce a wide variety of products. Production is adapted rapidly to changes in customer demand, product-by-product, by integrating sales information with the factory's production activities.

Many Japanese companies already have FMS facilities on line. At Toshiba, for instance, workers can make 9 different desktop and 20 different laptop computers on adjacent assembly lines. At each post, a laptop screen displays a drawing and gives instructions for the appropriate product. The goal is to produce sufficient numbers of products that sell while avoiding overproduction of those that do not. "Customers," explains Toshiba president Fumio Sato, "wanted choices. We needed variety, not mass production." The key, says Sato, is shorter production runs of smaller lots. "Every time I go to a plant," he stresses, "I tell the people, 'Smaller lot!'"

Similarly, Japan's largest soap and cosmetics company, Kao Corp., maintains a remarkable information-delivery system: A single system links information on everything, ranging from production and purchasing data to daily figures recorded on cash registers and salespeople's hand-held computers. Information is fed back into the company's R&D and manufacturing facilities, where decisions on how to respond to inventory buildup or competitor activity can be made within a single day. When Kao introduces a new product, information collected at point-of-sale locations is routed immediately to a test-marketing system which compares the data with input collected from customer calls and focus groups—a process much quicker than waiting for market surveys. Ultimately, production-line workers learn from posted signs what they will turn out each day to serve 280 000 stores with customized deliveries of goods.

soft manufacturing

Emphasizes computer software and computer networks instead of production machines.

But flexible manufacturing may soon be replaced by an even newer development. **Soft manufacturing** emphasizes computer software and computer networks instead of production machines. Soft manufacturing recognizes that complete automation of production processes may not be advisable and that humans are better at certain things than machines are. The box "The Latest Revolution in the Factory" gives more details about soft manufacturing.

Fixed-Position Layouts.

Sometimes, of course, the simplest layout is the most efficient. In a fixed-position layout, labor, materials, and equipment are brought to the work location. This layout is used in building ships, homes, skyscrapers, dams, and manufacturing facilities.

International Report

THE LATEST REVOLUTION IN THE FACTORY

During the 1980s, much was written about how Japan and Germany were leading the way in new production technology. But an amazing thing has happened: American manufacturing has regained its No. 1 position in manufactured exports for the first time since the mid-1980s. How did it happen?

Part of the answer is something called "soft manufacturing" (SM), which involves an emphasis on computer software and networks rather than production machines, where robots play only a supporting role, and where human workers are back in unexpectedly large numbers. SM plants, which can turn out customized products at mass-production speeds, will stabilize or even increase the number of jobs available in manufacturing.

How quickly times have changed. Just a few years ago, there was great alarm about the future of North American manufacturing. Japan was feared because of its flexible manufacturing system (FMS). Such a system emphasized computer-controlled machines, robots, and remotely guided carts to deliver materials to the production line. FMSs were supposed to lead to automatic factories that would be able to operate with very few workers.

But it didn't work out that way. Companies discovered that too much automation actually caused losses because large, complex systems are inherently vulnerable to failure. Robots were a real disappointment; they couldn't do the fine work needed in mass production assembly.

Under SM, robots are used only in jobs at which they excel (for example, spot welding). Humans are used in jobs that require high dexterity and judgment, like dealing with odd-size components and tight tolerances. Consider what happens at a Motorola plant that makes pagers. Orders come in from Motorola salespeople via an 800 line

or e-mail. The exact specifications desired for each pager (for example, color, type of beeper tone, etc.) are digitized and sent to the assembly line. Robots pick out the components, and humans assemble the pagers. The order is often completed within 80 minutes, and the customer may receive the pager on the same day it was ordered.

IBM does much the same thing in taking orders for PCs. Sales reps take orders from customers on an 800 phone line and enter the specifications desired by the customer. Finished orders are sent electronically to a nearby assembly plant, where workers receive them on hand-held bar code readers. The worker picks the right combination of parts like hard disks and memory boards from parts bins, and when a complete kit has been gathered together, it is taken to an assembly station. The assembler makes the computer and sends it down the line to be tested and packaged. The customer receives it the next day by airborne express.

SM has helped U.S. manufacturers outdistance their foreign rivals in such crucial measures as time to market and manufacturing flexibility. Hewlett-Packard, for example, recently embarrassed its Japanese rival NEC by beating it to the market with an ink-jet color printer. H-P's product was so good that the Japanese withdrew theirs a few months later.

Will the Japanese once again copy what the Americans are doing and beat them at their own game? Industry observers think not. They point out that Japanese business firms do not think in terms of customizing products for individual customers; rather, they emphasize the mass production of identical, high-quality items. Japanese business managers will have to make a major change in the way they think if they are going to be successful at SM.

Quality Planning

In planning production systems and facilities, managers must keep in mind the firm's quality goals.[9] Thus any complete production plan includes systems for ensuring that goods are produced to meet the firm's quality standards. The issues of productivity and quality are discussed in more detail in Chapter 13.

Methods Planning

In designing production systems, managers must clearly identify every production step and the specific methods for performing them. They can then work to reduce waste and inefficiency by examining procedures on a step-by-step basis—an approach sometimes called *methods improvement*.

Improvement begins when a manager documents the current method. A detailed description, often using a diagram called *process flow chart*, is usually helpful for organizing and recording all information. It identifies the sequence of production activities, movements of materials, and the work performed at each stage as the product flows through production. The flow can then be analyzed to identify wasteful activities, sources of delay in production flows, and other inefficiencies. The final step is implementing improvements.

Mercury Marine, for example, used methods improvement to streamline the production of stern-units for power boats. Examination of the process flow from raw materials to assembly (the final production step) revealed numerous wastes and inefficiencies. Each product, for instance, passed through 122 steps, traveled nearly 21 000 feet (almost four miles) in the factory, and was handled by 106 people. Analysis revealed that in the 122 steps through the factory, only 27 steps involved production that actually added value to the product (for example, drilling, painting). The remaining steps included handling, counting, checking, storing, and record-keeping. Work methods were thus revised to eliminate non-productive activities. Mercury ultimately realized savings in labor, inventory, paperwork, and space requirements. Because production lead time was also reduced, customer orders were filled faster.

Operations Scheduling

scheduling

Developing timetables for acquiring resources.

master production schedule

A general, rather than highly detailed, schedule of which product(s) will be produced, when production will occur, and what resources will be used in coming months.

Once plans identify the necessary resources and how to use those resources to reach a firm's quantity and quality goals, managers must develop timetables for acquiring the resources. This aspect of operations is called **scheduling**.

Scheduling occurs on many levels. A **master production schedule** shows which product(s) will be produced, when production will occur, and what resources will be used during the coming months. For example, the master schedule for Memtek might state that 70 000 Memorex tape cassettes should be produced in May, 60 000 in June, and 50 000 in July.

But this information does not tell the manufacturing people how many of the 70 000 cassettes in May should be standard videotapes, how many should be deluxe videotapes, or how many should be audio cassettes. Short-term *detailed schedules*, a type of tactical plan (see Chapter 6), answer questions of this kind on a daily or weekly basis. These schedules use incoming sales orders and weekly sales forecasts to determine what size and variation of cassettes to make in each of the next several days.

Tools for Scheduling

Production managers must sometimes schedule special projects, such as plant renovations or relocations, that require close coordination and timing. In these cases, project scheduling is facilitated by special tools like *Gantt and PERT charts*.

Gantt chart

A diagram laying out the steps in a production schedule along with the projected time to complete each step; used in production control.

Gantt Charts.   A **Gantt chart** diagrams the steps to be performed in a project and specifies the time required to complete each step. The manager lists all activities necessary to complete the work and then estimates the time required for each activity. To control production, the manager then checks the progress of the project against the chart. If the project is ahead of schedule, some workers may be shifted to another project. If behind schedule, workers may be added or completion of the job may be delayed.

Figure 11.4 shows a Gantt chart that has been prepared for the renovation of a college classroom. It serves both to show progress to date and to schedule remaining work. The current date is 5/11. Note that workers are about one-half week behind schedule in removing old floor tiles and reworking tables and chairs.

Pert Charts. *PERT*—short for *Program Evaluation and Review Technique*— is useful in managing major customized projects whose success means coordinating numerous activities. Like Gantt charts, **PERT charts** break down one large project into its necessary steps and specify the time required to perform each step. Unlike Gantt charts, however, PERT not only shows the necessary sequence of activities but identifies the *critical path* for accomplishing project goals.

Figure 11.5, for example, shows a PERT chart for the classroom renovation that we visited above. The critical path consists of activities *A*, *B*, *D*, *G*, *H*, and *I*. It is "critical" because any delay in completing any activity on it will cause workers to miss their completion deadline (9 1/2 weeks after startup). First, no activity can be started until all preceding activities are finished. For instance, chairs and tables cannot be returned to the classroom (*H*) until after they have been reworked (*G*) and after new tiles are installed (*F*). Second, the chart clearly identifies activities that will cause delays unless special action is taken at the right time. By reassigning workers and equipment, for example, potentially late activities can be speeded up to keep the project on schedule.

PERT (Program Evaluation and Review Technique)
A method of diagramming the steps in the production schedule along with the projected time to complete each step, taking into account the sequence of steps and the critical path of those steps.

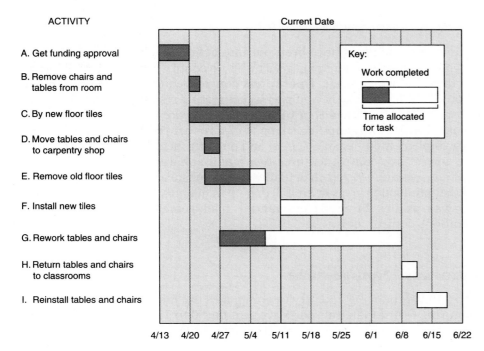

Figure 11.4
A Gantt chart for a classroom renovation shows the progress to date, as well as a schedule for the remaining work.

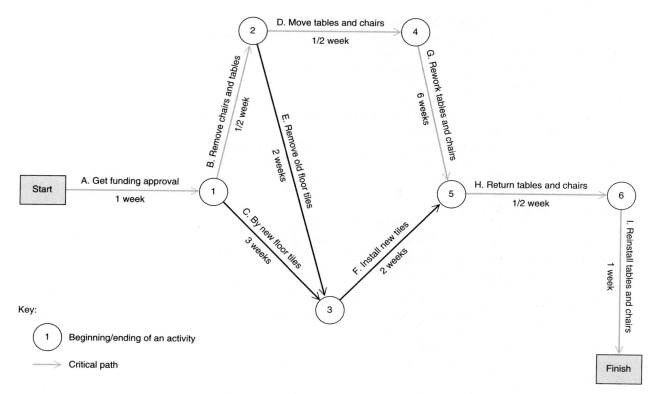

Figure 11.5
A PERT chart for a classroom renovation shows which activities must be completed before others can begin.

Operations Control

operations control
Managers monitor production performance by comparing results with plans and schedules.

follow-up
Checking to ensure that production decisions are being implemented.

Once long-range plans have been put into action and schedules have been drawn up, the production manager's task is to control production activities so that they conform to plans. **Operations control** requires managers to monitor production performance, in part by comparing results with detailed plans and schedules. If schedules or quality standards are not met, corrective action is needed. **Follow-up**—checking to ensure that production decisions are being implemented—is an essential and ongoing facet of operations control.

Operations control features two major subareas: *quality control* and *materials management*. Both activities seek to ensure that schedules are met and that production goals are fulfilled, both in quantity and quality. In this section, we consider the nature of materials management and some important operations-control tools.

materials management
Planning, organizing, and controlling the flow of materials from purchase through distribution of finished goods.

standardization
Using standard and uniform components in the production process.

Materials Management

Both goods-producing and service companies use materials. For some manufacturing firms, materials costs account for 50 to 75 percent of total product costs. For goods whose production uses little labor, such as petroleum refining, this percentage is even higher. Thus companies have good reasons to emphasize materials management.

Materials management involves not just controlling but also planning and organizing the flow of materials. Even before production starts, materials management focuses on product design by emphasizing materials **standardization**:

the use, where possible, of standard and uniform components rather than new or different components. Ford's engine plant in Romeo, Michigan, for instance, builds several different engine models. To save costs, the plant now uses common parts for several models rather than unique parts for each. One kind of piston, therefore, is now used in different engines. When components were standardized, the total number of different parts was reduced by 25 percent. Standardization also simplifies paperwork, reduces storage requirements, and eliminates unnecessary materials flows.

Once the product is designed, materials management purchases the necessary materials and monitors the production process through the distribution of finished goods. The four major areas of materials management are *transportation, warehousing, inventory control,* and *purchasing* (see Figure 11-6).

Transportation includes the means of transporting resources to the company and finished goods to buyers. *Warehousing* refers to the storage of both incoming materials for production and finished goods for physical distribution to customers. Because inventory control and purchasing are more specialized operations, we will explain each process in more detail.

Inventory Control.   **Inventory control** includes the receiving, storing, handling, and counting of all raw materials, partly finished goods, and finished

inventory control
The receiving, storing, handling, and counting of all resources, partly finished goods, and finished goods.

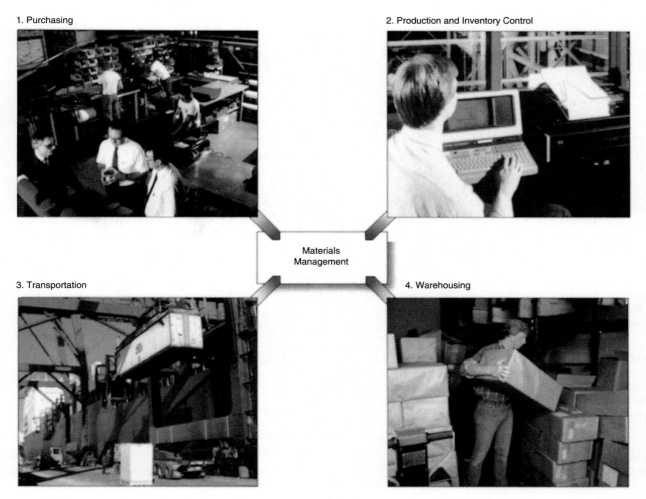

1. Purchasing

2. Production and Inventory Control

Materials Management

3. Transportation

4. Warehousing

Figure 11.6
Materials management begins with newly purchased materials and continues during production, transportation, and warehousing.

All kinds of products merit inspection. This quality inspector is testing new toilets during production to ensure proper performance and appearance.

goods. Inventory control of raw materials and finished goods is primarily a warehousing task. Production managers generally spend more time and effort controlling *materials inventory*—the stock of items needed during the production process, which might include such items as small components to be used in final assembly. Inventory control ensures that enough materials inventories are available to meet production schedules.

Purchasing.   Most companies have purchasing departments to buy proper materials in the amounts needed, both at reasonable prices and at the right time. The importance of purchasing can be seen in the relationship between buying practices and certain materials-management costs. For many years, purchasing departments practiced *forward buying*: That is, they routinely purchased quantities of materials large enough to fill their needs for long periods. The practice was popular because it can save money by allowing a firm to purchase materials at quantity discounts. Thus it may be advantageous for a crate manufacturer to buy truckloads of nails to satisfy its need for several weeks.

At the same time, however, purchasing agents must balance the need to hold enough materials in stock with the need to avoid excess supplies. Excess supplies entail increased **holding costs**—the costs of keeping extra supplies or materials on hand. These include the real costs of storage, handling, insurance, and obsolescence of the inventory as well as *opportunity costs*—additional earnings that the company must pass up because of the funds tied up in inventory.

In response to today's rising holding costs, many purchasing departments have adopted a so-called *hand-to-mouth pattern*—placing small orders frequently. This practice also requires shorter **lead time**—that is, the gap between the customer's placement of an order and the seller's shipping of merchandise. For example, a radio maker who uses hundreds or thousands

holding costs

Costs of keeping currently unsalable goods, or costs of money that could be otherwise invested.

lead time

The time between placing an order and actually receiving a shipment.

of standard components ranging from packaging materials to push buttons may significantly reduce holding costs by ordering only what it needs for the coming day or week.

Purchasing departments are responsible for **supplier selection**—finding and determining which suppliers to buy from.[10] Supplier selection typically follows a four-stage process. The purchaser first surveys possible suppliers. The purchaser then visits, evaluates, and narrows the list to the few suppliers who are best qualified to fill the company's needs. Purchaser and potential suppliers then negotiate terms of service, followed by the purchaser's final choice of a supplier. The fourth "stage" is actually an ongoing process: maintaining a continuing positive buyer-seller relationship. A good relationship ensures reliable and uninterrupted transactions that benefit both parties. Since maintaining relationships with multiple suppliers is expensive for the purchasing organization, most purchasers are working hard to reduce the number of their suppliers and vendors.

supplier selection
Finding and determining suppliers to buy from.

Tools for Operations Control

A wide variety of tools are available to help managers to make the necessary trade-offs for production control. Chief among these tools are just-in-time inventory systems, material requirements planning, and quality control.

Just-in-Time Inventory Systems. To minimize trade-offs between setup and holding costs, some production managers are using a **just-in-time (JIT) inventory system**. JIT brings together all materials and parts needed at each production step at the precise moment when they are required for the production process. At Toyota's Cambridge, Ontario, plant, delivery trucks constantly pull up at the plant to unload tires, batteries, steering wheels, seats, and many other items needed in the just-in-time production system.[11]

just-in-time (JIT) inventory system
A method of inventory control in which materials are acquired and put into production just as they are needed.

When the Oshawa assembly plant of General Motors of Canada needs seats for cars, it sends the order electronically to a local supplier. The supplier has four hours to make the seats and ship them to the plant. The supplier loads the truck in reverse order so that the last seat loaded is the first one that will be used on the assembly line. The supplier knows, for example, that the plant will be making five 4-door Luminas and then six 2-door Monte Carlo's.[12]

JIT saves money by replacing a stop-and-go production approach with a smooth movement. Everything flows from the arrival of raw materials to subassembly, final completion, and shipment of finished products. JIT reduces the number of goods *in process* (not yet finished) to practically nothing. It also helps to assure reliable quality levels. As the box "Managing Inventories Successfully" points out, however, using JIT takes planning.

Ironically, the problem of backlog orders has changed the minds of some production managers about the virtues of JIT. They have come to the conclusion that the JIT approach to lean inventories—both in terms of parts and finished goods—is not flexible enough to meet expanding orders. In some industries, therefore, inventory levels are creeping up again as insurance against such unexpected events as delays from key suppliers or the need to replace defective parts.

Winnebago Industries, the maker of recreational vehicles, has cyclical demand for its RVs; this means declining orders in the fall and winter. When it first moved to JIT, Winnebago cut its year-round full-time operations and hired workers and scheduled overtime only in the spring and summer. The result was disastrous: Parts were missing, poor fit meant leaks around windows and doors, and appliances inside the vehicles were often scratched.

The Canadian Business Scene

MANAGING INVENTORIES SUCCESSFULLY

You can't open a business magazine today without encountering the buzzword "JIT." Nearly everyone seems to agree that arranging to have on hand those components you need to make a product just when you need them makes financial sense. Inventories are expensive to carry, even if they do not deteriorate or become obsolete.

While JIT has been widely hailed, it is less widely practised because of the complexities involved. Successful implementation of these control systems requires thought and planning. Here are some suggestions:

Ask your workers for ideas. Even in the best-managed JIT system, parts will sometimes fail to be delivered when needed. Some of the people in the best position to set up contingency plans and prevent worker and machine downtime are the people who do the work and run the machines. Asking workers about both normal and abnormal work flows also helps them "buy into" the system.

Reassess "lowest cost." The JIT system leaves no room for error. With just enough components arriving just as they are needed, parts rejected for quality problems mean goods not produced and idled workers and machinery. In dealing with suppliers, companies must consider the *total* cost of a supply—including the cost of substandard parts.

Build a purchasing team. In most companies, one of two groups of people places orders for supplies: engineers and purchasing agents. Unfortunately, engineers may be too concerned with state-of-the-art technology and too little concerned with the commercial implications of their choices. In contrast, purchasing agents may not be able to evaluate the quality of a component or to determine which aspects of a component's specifications are flexible. By working together and involving management, engineers and purchasing agents can develop a flexible, low-cost design for suppliers to bid on.

Learn to work with suppliers. Companies contemplating a purchase need to be open with suppliers about their technical requirements and how the proposed component fits into the whole. With this information, suppliers may be able to suggest redesigned (or designed from scratch) parts that not only meet the company's needs but can be produced less expensively and/or with greater speed. Openness with suppliers can produce an additional benefit—goodwill. Goodwill is crucial in getting suppliers to schedule deliveries to suit the buyer's schedule and to be flexible in what they make and when they deliver it.

Be specific about your delivery needs. Despite a good relationship with its suppliers, Hewlett-Packard initially encountered severe delivery problems in instituting its JIT system. A study of various aspects of delivery revealed the root of the problem: unclear instructions to suppliers as to what date goods were due versus the date they were to be shipped. A simple change on the purchase order form clarified this distinction and more than doubled the percentage of shipments arriving on time.

Insist on quality. JIT requires suppliers of high-quality goods. Polaroid certifies suppliers only after three to six months of shipments with no defects. In some cases, companies must teach suppliers to use the same quality control standards and tests they themselves use.

The costs of fixing items covered by warranty skyrocketed, and relations with dealers deteriorated. Finally, Winnebago abandoned JIT. It smoothed out production schedules over the course of the year, and now allows vehicle inventories to build up during the off season.

material requirements planning (MRP)
A method of inventory control in which a computerized bill of materials is used to estimate production needs so that resources are acquired and put into production only as needed.

bill of materials
A "recipe" for production of a "batch" of a good that specifies the resources needed and the method of combining those resources.

Material Requirements Planning.   Like JIT, **material requirements planning (MRP)** also seeks to deliver the right amounts of materials to the right place at the right time. MRP uses a **bill of materials** that is basically a "recipe" for the finished product. It specifies the necessary ingredients (raw materials and components), the order in which they should be combined, and the quantity of each ingredient needed to make one "batch" of the product (say, 2000 finished telephones). The recipe is fed into a computer that controls inventory and schedules each stage of production. The result is fewer early arrivals, less frequent stock shortages, and lower storage costs. MRP is most popular among companies whose products require complicated assembly and fabrication activities, such as automobile manufacturers, appliance makers, and furniture companies.

Manufacturing resource planning, also called **MRP II**, is an advanced version of MRP that ties together all parts of the organization into the company's production activities. For example, MRP inventory and production schedules are translated into cost requirements for the financial management department and personnel requirements for the human resources department; information on capacity availability for new-customer orders goes to the marketing department.

MRP II (manufacturing resource planning)
An advanced version of MRP that ties together all parts of the organization into the company's production activities.

Quality Control.   Not all production-control tools focus on inventory control. Also important is **quality control**: the management of the production process so as to manufacture goods or supply services that meet specific quality standards. McDonald's, for example, has been a pioneer in quality control in the restaurant industry since the 1950s. The company oversees everything from the farming of potatoes for french fries to the packing of meat for Big Macs. Quality-assurance staffers even check standards for ketchup sweetness and french fry length.

quality control
The management of the production process so as to manufacture goods or supply services that meet specific quality standards.

In their quest for quality control, many businesses have adopted *quality-improvement teams* (patterned after the Japanese concept of *quality circles*): groups of employees from various work areas who define, analyze, and solve common production problems. Teams meet regularly to discuss problems and to keep management informed of the group's progress in addressing various issues.

Many companies report that improvement teams have not only raised quality levels but increased productivity and reduced costs. They have also improved job satisfaction. But improvement teams also involve risks. Not all employees, for example, want to participate. Moreover, management cannot always adopt group recommendations, no matter how much careful thought, hard work, and enthusiasm went into them. The challenge for production managers, then, is to make wise decisions about when and how to use quality-improvement teams. (Quality control and quality-improvement teams are discussed in more detail in Chapter 13.)

Completing the Operations Management Process: Feedback

Production management does not stop when the goods go out the door or even when they are purchased. Feedback from consumers, the final phase, influences every other part of production management. Comments from users may lead managers to plan smaller or larger production runs. Consumer enthusiasm may dictate a speed-up in master schedules that calls for opening new plants or hiring more workers. Negative criticism of quality may cause managers to seek new production methods and to tighten controls. Because it is consumers—and their "dollar votes"—who determine the success or failure of a company, managers have little choice but to heed customer feedback.

The Future of Operations Management

As Canadian businesses struggle to survive in fiercely competitive world markets, operations management becomes more and more crucial. As discussed in Chapter 3, lagging productivity put Canadian industries at a disadvantage in pricing their goods for world markets. In their battle for lower production costs, higher productivity, and higher quality, more and more managers are turning to mechanization and automation of the operations process, especially with computers.

Mechanization and Automation

Using machines to do work previously done by people is the process of **mechanization**. Its natural extension is **automation**, performing mechanical operations with either minimal or no human intervention. These techniques are not new, of course. The Industrial Revolution began with huge spinning and weaving machines that soon rendered handmade fabric obsolete. Nearly every company in the world uses some machinery in place of hand labor. Some of the most advanced firms are using sophisticated robots in production. Many small firms have automated at least to the degree that personal computer systems monitor production outcomes.

The replacement of manual labor by machinery has been a source of ethical controversy for years. Advocates of labor, for example, contend that jobs are sometimes replaced unnecessarily. Critics have also charged that businesses sometimes use the threat of mechanization to gain wage concessions.

Computers and Robotics

Computers stand at the forefront of modern automation. Companies use computers to construct detailed schedules, to monitor production, and to help determine raw material needs. In some firms, computers track customer orders as they move through the plant. Computers may also send production information to managers in various departments so that they know how much work is coming, what materials will be needed, and when each job must be completed. When Federal Express picks up a package, for example, the destination is read immediately by a portable scanner. This information then enters the Federal Express computer and is electronically transmitted to the central routing hub in Memphis. With this advance information, the facility can schedule its vehicles out of Memphis to other cities even before it receives incoming packages.

Robotics and Computer-Integrated Manufacturing.   Although Japanese companies pioneered their use, Canadian firms are becoming increasingly interested in **robotics**, the construction, maintenance, and use of computer-controlled machines in manufacturing operations. Automobile plants use robots to weld, assemble, paint, and inspect cars. Aircraft manufacturing plants are also using robotics to build planes faster and at less cost than humans can. Still, as the box "Robots: Mixed Success" discusses, robots have not yet found acceptance in many firms.

Robotics are only one part of a larger manufacturing automation system called **computer-integrated manufacturing (CIM)**. In addition to controlling robots, CIM can manage material requirements planning and just-in-time inventory systems.

Computer-Aided Design and Manufacturing.   The use of computers in manufacturing is not limited to robots and inventory control. Some of the most exciting uses of computers in production are in the areas of computer-aided design (CAD) and computer-aided manufacturing (CAM), known collectively as CAD/CAM.

As its name suggests, **computer-aided design** uses computers to design new products. Through the use of sophisticated analysis methods and graphics, CAD allows users to create a design and simulate conditions to test the performance of the design, all within the computer. Engineers use CAD to design planes and cars. CAD systems let designers see the result of changes in design without having to create costly prototype models and test them under real-world conditions.

The Canadian Business Scene

ROBOTS: MIXED SUCCESS

Industrial robots are not the glamorous creations usually pictured in science fiction movies. Rather, they are machines that are programmed to repeat tirelessly the chores common in industry. At present, robots are used most frequently in the automobile industry for such tasks as welding, painting, and metalworking.

The first fully computerized robotic paint shop for railroad cars in North America was opened on October 5, 1988, at Canadian National Railways' Winnipeg Transcona shops. The system cleans and repaints CN's 11 500 covered hopper cars which transport bulk commodities like grain and potash. The shops process about 1100 cars per year, four times more than under the old manual system.

Harber Manufacturing, a Fort Erie, Ontario, manufacturer of wood-burning stoves, uses several different types of robots in its manufacturing processes. Five arc-welding robot systems—each costing over $100 000—join metal seams together in a continuous weld. Programmable platforms are also used to move raw materials within the reach of the arc-welding robots.

Robots were supposed to revolutionize the work place, performing all the mundane and dangerous tasks from welding bolts to handling radioactive isotopes. Yet today, Canadian and American businesses employ only a fraction of the number used in Japan. Why so few electronic helpers? The answer lies in three problems: cost, complexity, and technical limitations.

Cost has kept robots out of many smaller enterprises. A hydraulic robot from Unimation, the leader in robotics, runs $30 000 to $200 000. Even smaller, less powerful robots from Japan can cost up to $40 000 each. With a price tag of $25 000 each, a HelpMate nurse's aid robot from TRC will pay for itself in two and a half years—if it's used 24 hours a day, 7 days a week, 52 weeks a year.

Larger companies have often found that the initial purchase cost is the cheapest part of robotics. A company installing robotics needs computer scientists to program and reprogram robots. And before that, it needs to perform exhaustive studies to determine the precise task to be accomplished. Workers must be trained to operate and work with robots.

Human beings are still vastly superior to robots in a great many regards, especially in tasks requiring sensory input and adaptation. The most sophisticated robots today cannot read handwriting or pick a single right part out of a box of wrong ones. A few can recognize about 20 slightly different shapes as airplanes. Humans can identify thousands of slightly different shapes as planes. As one researcher notes, one human eye has about "100 million vision cells and four layers of neurons, all capable of doing about 10 billion calculations a second." In other words, the visual calculations of a one-eyed human being would take 100 000 supercomputers to imitate.

Perhaps one reason why Japanese businesses use more robots is that they expect less of them. In Japan, robots are used for the most simple, most mindless, most limited of tasks. The preponderance of such tasks in the auto industry (along with the enormous economic and technical resources of such companies) may explain why more than 50 percent of robots in use in Canada are in auto plants versus 10 percent in Japan.

The future of robotics in Canada may depend on recognizing where it can be most useful. Already, robots are making inroads into fields dangerous to humans. Submersible robots are replacing divers in offshore oil and gas operations. They toil for hours in areas of nuclear power plants where once humans worked in very short relays to minimize their exposure to radiation. Cyberworks Inc. is a Canadian manufacturer of robots. While the growth in demand for industrial robots has been slower than expected, the company believes robots will eventually be widely used in space exploration, undersea work, underground mining, and in nuclear waste facilities.

As they become more aware of the special capabilities of robots, more mundane businesses may be willing to take a chance. Robots never get a backache from stooping. Their arms and wrists can twist around completely. A robot watchguard with microwave vision can see through nonmetallic walls and spot an intruder 40 metres away in the dark. And those challenged had better give the right password. Robots still have no sense of humor.

In a direct offshoot of computer-aided design, **computer-aided manufacturing** uses computers to design and control the equipment needed in the manufacturing process. For example, CAM systems can produce tapes to control all the machines and robots on a production line. Overall, CAD/CAM is useful for engineers in a manufacturing environment to design and test new products and then to design the machines and tools to manufacture the new product.

computer-aided manufacturing (CAM)
Computer systems used to design and control all the equipment and tools for producing goods.

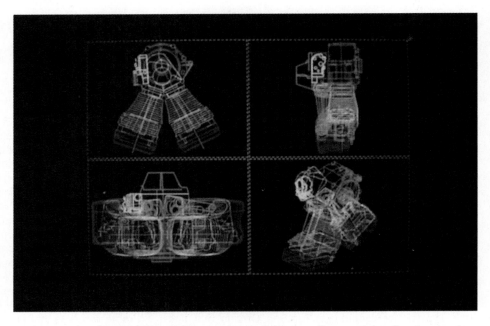

A CAD system displays four different views of this gasoline engine, allowing its design to be easily examined and modified.

decision support systems (DSS)

Computer systems used to help managers consider alternatives when making decisions on complicated problems.

Decision Support Systems.   A new development in the evolution of *management information systems*, which we will discuss in Chapter 23, has had an impact on manufacturing and production. Computer programs called **decision support systems (DSS)** give users easy access to decision models and data to help them make decisions on complicated problems. DSS allows users to investigate conveniently "What if?" questions. "What if the company decides to order twice as much raw material as needed—will we need more warehousing space?" "What if the company purchases ten additional robots—will we be able to cut some of our present work force?" "What if the company adds more flexible automation—will sales go up?"

Production and the Small Business Enterprise

As we noted in Chapter 7, manufacturing is the hardest industry for small businesses to break into because of the extensive resources it requires. But while large corporations continue to dominate this arena, small companies continue to enter—and succeed. Manufacturing giants increasingly find themselves overextended and close or sell off unprofitable companies. And small business people are moving in to fill market gaps and turn losing corporate subsidiaries into winners as independent small companies.

Precisely how do small companies succeed where larger ones have failed, in both goods and services production? Analysts cite the following advantages, among others:

- Many small firms offer higher product quality—a practice that makes them more competitive against foreign products than some bigger companies.
- Small businesses can frequently offer greater varieties of products because they have not committed themselves to the expensive, special-purpose equipment to which many large businesses have tied themselves.

- Small operations frequently offer more challenging work. They often give workers greater opportunities for advancing ideas and have better records in respecting and adopting those ideas. Indeed, surveys show that small businesses sometimes have a distinct competitive advantage because of favorable employee attitudes.

Of course, small businesses still face problems as manufacturers, especially with regard to equipment and inventories. Even general-purpose and small-volume equipment is expensive. And small businesses can more easily overextend themselves, both financially and with respect to the equipment's performance capabilities, than can large firms.

Inventories tend to be the single biggest problem area for small manufacturers. Too many resources on hand, rather than too few, is one of the most common and costly mistakes. Such surpluses can usually be traced to poor information about what and how many resources are on hand and what they will be used for. Since they have less capital than big companies, small manufacturers must maintain particularly close control over their inventories to succeed.

Summary of Key Points

Operations management focuses on the transformation of resources into finished goods. Production processes can be classified by the type of technology used (chemical, fabrication, assembly, transport, and clerical), by whether the process is analytic or synthetic, and by the pattern of product flow (continuous or intermittent). Production managers use these classifications to compare new production processes with old ones as they seek to plan, organize, and control the production process.

Long-range production plans determine a company's future production by identifying major resource needs, including capacity, facility location and layout, and quality of goods to be produced. These plans are translated into an intermediate-range master production schedule and short-range, detailed production schedules that designate when, where, and how much of a specific good will be produced.

Production control requires both quality control and materials management. Materials management focuses on the control of purchasing and inventory. To control purchasing, production managers must decide whether to use a forward-buying or a hand-to-mouth approach. To control inventory, they must balance holding costs with setup costs. Techniques such as just-in-time (JIT) inventory systems and materials requirement planning (MRP) can assist managers in inventory control. Gantt and PERT charts can assist in overall production planning, scheduling, and control.

Automation is changing the face of production operations in many areas. Computers drive robots that can perform many boring or dangerous tasks formerly requiring human labor in a process called computer-integrated manufacturing (CIM). CIM also integrates computer-aided design (CAD) and computer-aided manufacturing (CAM), allowing firms to send information back and forth between design engineers and production managers. Decision support systems (DSS) assist production managers in making decisions by allowing them to ask—and answer—"What if?" questions.

Small businesses have an advantage over larger manufacturers because they can offer their customers higher quality and greater product flexibility. They can also offer their employees more challenge and a chance to make a difference in the company. However, they face greater problems with inventories and equipment because of their limited funds.

Putting the Brakes on a Production Problem

Signal Automotive, a manufacturer of auto parts, wanted to crack the tough Japanese market. Signal's executives received a cool reception when they approached Nissan and Toyota, the giants of Japan's auto industry. Discussions with Nissan ended quickly when product samples didn't pass its critical examination.

Toyota's response was cautious but at least offered a glimmer of hope. The firm offered a modest order for 20 000 brake pads per month. However, it imposed more stringent product specifications than Signal was accustomed to. For example, Toyota required that all its pads be painted. (Apparently, the Japanese consider the appearance of the pads important even though auto drivers cannot see them.) In addition, Toyota's order specified that the pads would have to meet strict size criteria.

In taking the order, Signal's executives realized they were taking a major risk. To meet Toyota's demands for painted pads, Signal would have to make drastic and expensive changes in its production system. Buying equipment to paint the pads meant a substantial financial investment. Operating and maintaining the equipment meant hiring skilled people. Actually painting the pads meant working out new production processes. Shipping and storing the painted pads would also create new complications.

Toyota's strict size standards increased the risks. Could Signal's equipment and workers produce pads within the required size limits? What would happen if the pads were off just a bit?

Signal soon got the painful answer to these questions. Toyota rejected the first shipment of pads for failure to meet specifications. After the initial shock wore off, managers realized that they were dealing with a customer unlike any they had ever had before.

In the wake of Toyota's rejection, Signal's executives realized that to tap Japan's rich market potential they would have to abandon their traditional production style. The question remained: Was it worthwhile for only 20 000 pads a month? To Signal's managers, the answer was clearly "No, but if we can solve the problems we can get bigger orders that are worth the effort."

To get larger orders, though, they knew they would first have to show a willingness to provide quality and service over the long haul. To demonstrate its commitment, Signal sent the manager of its pad production plant to Japan to sort out the defective parts in the rejected shipment at Toyota. The manager was surprised to see what was rejected. Some of the "bad" parts were only a few thousandths of an inch outside the size standards. (Unlike Toyota, U.S. and Canadian customers accept pads unless they have flaws that affect performance.)

On returning home, the plant manager passed on these observations to top management. Gradually, the firm's managers put together a new production plan. The plan called for changes in worker skills and changes in attitudes of workers and managers. It also required better production processes, manufacturing equipment, and materials. More stringent planning for and control of quality were central to the new approach.

It took Signal a full year to make the adjustments to improve the quality of its brake pads. But the time, effort, and money paid off. Toyota approved later pad shipments. Eventually, satisfied that Signal would now meet the specifications, Toyota increased its purchases to 200 000 brake pads a month.

CASE QUESTIONS

1. Identify three ways Signal could reorient its employees toward manufacturing products of higher quality.
2. How might the plant layout requirements for making Toyota's brake pads differ from Signal's earlier plant layout?
3. What problems does Signal face in expanding capacity from 20 000 to 200 000 pads a month?
4. What factors led Signal's management to err initially in their production planning?
5. How might automation be used to better meet Toyota's demands? What problems might such automation create?

◆

Just-in-Time II

Just-in-time inventory systems were made famous by the Japanese in the 1980s. But in the 1990s, North American firms are carrying the concept even further. When JIT II is used, manufacturing firms treat their suppliers almost like their own employees. At some companies, sales representatives from suppliers even have desks next to the factory floor in the company they are supplying. They can go wherever they choose in the factory, attend production meetings, wander around the research lab, and even check the company's sales forecast.

Consider the JIT II works at Honeywell's Golden Valley, Minnesota plant. There are 15 representatives from 10 different suppliers who have offices in the plant. They think like Honeywell employees and are constantly trying to trim purchasing costs. Some are even allowed to place orders on Honeywell's behalf with their own competitors. Inventory levels at the plant are now measured in days instead of weeks, and Honeywell employs 25 percent fewer purchasing agents than it used to.

But JIT II is not always easy to introduce. The biggest problem is developing trust between the vendor and the manufacturer. Historically, the relationship between suppliers and manufacturers has been one of hard-nosed bargaining over prices. A substantial amount of mistrust is not uncommon. As a result, manufacturers are often not keen on the idea of letting one of their suppliers have confidential information about how the company operates.

For example, one purchasing manager at Honeywell, who oversees $180 million worth of purchases each year, didn't like the JIT II idea when it was initially proposed.

She was concerned that Honeywell's suppliers would find out about each other's prices by overhearing conversations between Honeywell's managers. But now, five suppliers work closely with her 20 buyers and there have been very few problems.

Suppliers may also be reluctant to get involved in JIT II because *they* may have to reveal their own costs. Suppliers have always been concerned that if the manufacturer found out their costs, that they would try to take advantage of them.

Bose Corp., the manufacturer of radio and stereo speakers, screens potential in-plant suppliers and requires them to sign a confidentiality agreement and stipulates certain guidelines. Purchases over a certain amount require a signature from a Bose manager.

One potential problem with JIT II concerns termination of agreements. Ball Corp., a manufacturer of baby food jars, had a plant right next door to a Gerber Baby Foods manufacturing plant. Ball always knew exactly how many jars to produce because workers from both plants interacted frequently. But when Gerber decided to shop around for a cheaper worldwide source of jars, it ended the relationship. Ball was forced to close its plant and lay off 350 workers.

CASE QUESTIONS
1. Why have companies started to move to JIT II?
2. What are the advantages of JIT II? Be specific.
3. What are the possible disadvantages of JIT II? Be specific.

◆

Key Terms

utility
time utility
place utility
ownership (possession)
  utility
form utility
operations (production)
  management
analytic process
synthetic process
continuous process
intermittent process
labor-intensive process
capital-intensive process
forecast

capacity
process layout
product layout
assembly line
cellular layouts
U-shaped production
  lines
flexible manufacturing
  system
soft manufacturing
scheduling
master production
  schedule
Gantt chart
(PERT) Program

Evaluation and
  Review Technique
operations control
follow-up
materials management
standardization
inventory control
holding costs
lead time
supplier selection
just-in-time (JIT)
  inventory system
material requirements
  planning (MRP)
bill of materials

MRP II (manufacturing
  resource planning)
quality control
mechanization
automation
robotics
computer-integrated
  manufacturing (CIM)
computer-aided design
  (CAD)
computer-aided
  manufacturing (CAM)
decision support systems
  (DSS)

Study Questions and Exercises

Review Questions

1. Explain how General Motors of Canada provides different forms of utility to its customers.
2. How does a process layout differ from a product layout? How does a fixed-position layout differ from a customer-oriented layout?
3. In what situations is forward buying most appropriate? In what situations is hand-to-mouth buying most appropriate?
4. What are the advantages of a flexible manufacturing system?
5. Why do small business people choose to go into manufacturing industries dominated by large companies?

Analysis Questions

6. Find examples of a synthetic production process and an analytic process. Then classify each according to whether it is chemical, fabrication, assembly, transport, or clerical. Explain your analysis.
7. In deciding to produce the first luxury minivan, the Town & Country, Chrysler had to develop long-range production plans. Outline as many of the major elements (production activities and resources) that they had to plan for as you can. Then, select any one of the elements and show the detailed aspects of it that would have to be investigated and considered before production could start.
8. Choose a simple project, such as giving a party, and draw a PERT chart that could be used to manage the project's progress.

Application Exercises

9. Select two manufacturers, a large one and a small one, in your community and compare the methods they use to get good quality in their products. Contrast the kinds of problems they face in assuring high product quality.
10. Interview the owner of a small manufacturing firm. Classify the firm's production processes, and then identify the major production problems of the firm and propose solutions for these problems.

Building Your Business Skills

Goal

To help students understand the just-in-time approach to inventory management of both components/raw materials and finished goods.

Situation

Suppose you work in the purchasing department at a manufacturing firm. Management is trying to decide whether just-in-time represents an approach that could help cut inventory costs and improve productivity. Your job is to find out what other companies are doing about JIT.

Method

Working groups of four or five, make arrangements to conduct interviews at various manufacturing companies near your college or university. Try to speak to a company executive as well as someone in purchasing or sales. In particular:

- ■ Determine which inventory method is used.
- ■ Assess attitudes toward JIT and ask about its strengths and weaknesses.
- ■ Ask whether the company's suppliers and customers are using JIT and find out what their experiences have been.

Prepare a brief report to summarize your findings and exchange reports with the other teams in the class.

Follow-Up Questions

1. Did your research reveal strong feelings, pro or con, about JIT? In particular, what aspect of JIT caused these feelings?
2. Can you make any generalizations about companies that look favorably on JIT compared to those that do not?

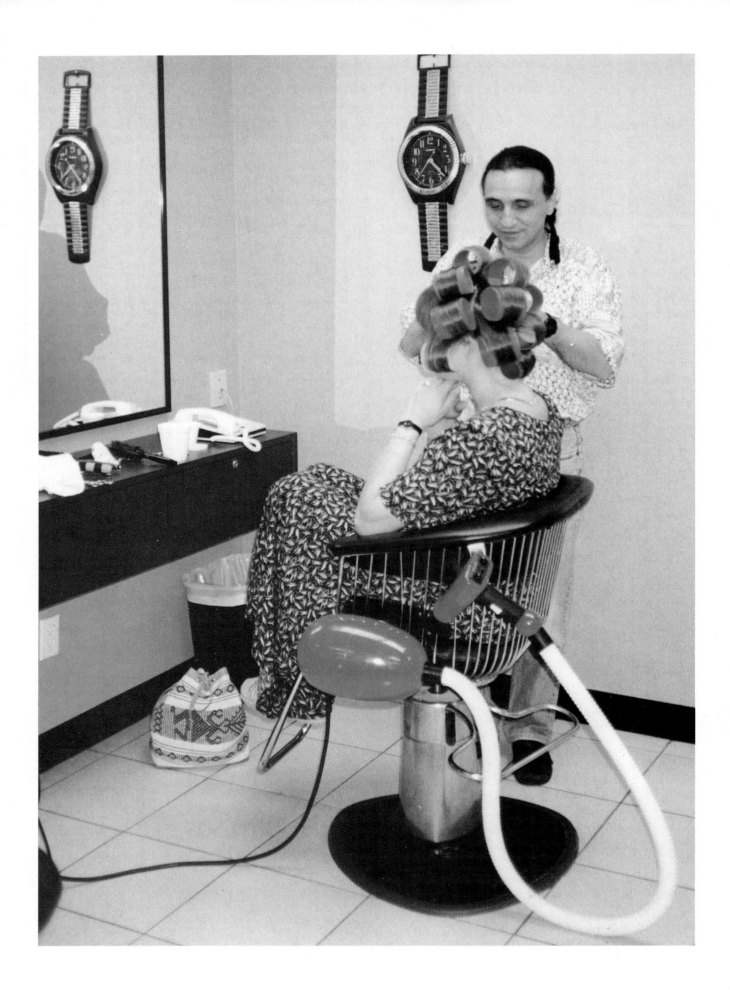

12

Producing Services

LEARNING OBJECTIVES

After studying this chapter, you will be able to

- Identify the characteristics of services that make their production different from that of goods.
- Classify services according to the extent of customer contact and their similarity to manufacturing.
- Describe the major decisions in service operations planning and scheduling.
- Explain how managers can control the quantity and quality of services offered.
- Identify ways to overcome the special problems of service operations management.

CHAPTER OUTLINE

OPENING CASE

Nova Scotia Power Is Customer Driven

Nova Scotia Power Inc. is a privatized utility with a near monopoly as a provider of electrical power in Nova Scotia. It is currently involved in "re-engineering"—a program to overhaul its work processes to reduce time and costs, and to boost the level of service to customers.

Utilities are not known for their service initiatives or for their efficiency. Nova Scotia Power's rates were as much as 40 percent above the national average in the mid-1980s, and big increases were expected in the 1990s. But the privatization of the the company made it less subject to political pressures, and gave it more freedom to do the things that were necessary to become more efficient. For example, the company informed its major coal supplier that it would go elsewhere for coal if the supplier's prices were not competitive.

In addition to these market moves, Nova Scotia Power has also instituted an internal "effectiveness program" that is designed to cut costs and improve service to customers. The initial step was to eliminate about one-quarter of the work force, mostly through retirements. This cut annual costs by $18 million, a big chunk of the targeted amount of $25 million. This will allow for the freezing of power rates until at least 1996.

The company also brought in management consultants to oversee a major re-engineering program. Four areas which promised the biggest improvements—fleet management, billing and meter reading, credit and collections, and capital work orders—were identified, and changes in work procedures were implemented. Improvements are already being noticed. The time required to get major capital projects approved has dropped from as much as 11 months to three weeks. Giving employees more say in decision making about vehicle maintenance has allowed reduction of the fleet by 12 percent.

Customer service initiatives are also being implemented. In 1994, a pilot project in the Halifax area gave customer service representatives the information and technology they needed to handle all aspects of customer service. This system replaced the old one where different aspects of customer service were handled by a maze of company offices.

Individual employees have seen significant changes in their jobs. Allan Farcey used to read meters. If a meter was broken, he would report it to the regional office. Eventually an installer would come to the home and put in a new one. Now, Farcey is a customer service representative, a job that combines meter reader, installer, and bill collector. He's also trained to replace broken meters himself. In his new role, he reads fewer meters, but he provides a much wider range of service to his customers.

The new approach to customer service has also given Farcey increased discretion in his work. For example, he has dealt with the unpleasant job of cutting off power to customers who haven't paid their bills by developing a new system that helps both the company and the customer. Twenty minutes before power is scheduled to be cut off, he phones the customer and offers one last chance for them to pay their bill. Typically, the customer pays the bill. This approach allows the customer to keep their electrical power, gives the utility a "human" touch, and saves Farcey two trips: one to cut off the power, and another to reconnect later. ◆

Firms like Nova Scotia power are in the business of providing services rather than physical products. In this chapter, we will consider what is involved in the provision of services, and why the services sector is growing so fast. We will see how the planning and controlling functions in business firms are influenced by the unique character of services, and how managers overcome the special problems associated with the "production" of services.

Service Operations: An Overview

service operations

Business activities that transform resources into services for customers.

Everywhere you go today, you encounter examples of **service operations**—business activities that provide services to their customers. You wake up in the morning to the sound of your favorite radio station. You stop at the newsstand on the corner for a newspaper on your way to the bus stop, where you catch the bus to work or school. Your instructors, the bus driver, the clerk at the 7-Eleven store, and the morning radio announcer are all examples of people who work in service operations. They provide you with tangible and intangible products: entertainment, transportation, education, and food preparation.

The Service Sector Explosion in Canada

Services are big business today. We saw in Chapter 3 that over 70 percent of employed Canadians work in service industries. Projections indicate that service sector employment will continue to grow at a faster rate than manufacturing sector employment. Much of the growth in the service sector is in the areas of finance, insurance, real estate, government, retailing, and health care. The video case "Radio Shack" on p. 378 describes the "production" of one kind of service—television advertisements.

Employment in service industries is also more stable than employment in manufacturing. As we saw in the opening case in Chapter 11, nearly 200 000 manufacturing jobs were lost in Ontario alone during 1990 and 1991. No such major losses are evident in the service sector. Apparently, consumers will stop buying many goods before they will sacrifice such essential services as education, telephones, banking, and police and fire protection.

The perception that the manufacturing sector offers high-paid jobs, while the service sector offers only low-paid, dead-end jobs is not correct. The service sector includes high paid people like doctors, lawyers, movie stars, and architects. It is as varied as the manufacturing sector. And the gap in wages between service and manufacturing jobs is narrowing.

All businesses are service operations to some extent.[1] Consider General Motors of Canada, a company that to many people is the epitome of manufacturing. Certainly GM produces cars. But it is also heavily involved with repairs and maintenance, warranty fulfillment, installation advice, operator training, and, through GMAC, lending funds. Without its attendant services, GM's automobile sales would shrivel.

Why Separate Out Services?

Service operations have features in common with manufacturing operations. For example, both involve transforming raw materials into finished goods. But the raw materials in services are not glass or steel. Rather, they are people with unsatisfied needs and people's possessions, which may need various kinds of care or alteration. The finished products are not goods like cars or houses. Rather, they are people with needs met and possessions serviced. Table 12.1 shows some examples of inputs, transformations, and outputs in the service sector.

Service operations differ from manufacturing operations in important ways. Probably the most obvious is that goods are *produced*, while services are *performed*. The focus of service operations is more complex. And services are more *intangible*, *customized*, and *perishable* than most products. There is also a unique link between production and consumption in service operations. Finally, consumers evaluate services differently than goods.

Focus on Process and Outcome.   Manufacturing operations focus on the *outcome* of the production process. But most services, because they are actually a combination of goods and services, focus on both the transformation *process* and its *outcome*. Thus, managing service operations requires some skills that differ from those required to manage manufacturing operations. For example, workers for a local gas company must possess interpersonal skills to calm and reassure frightened customers who have reported a

TABLE 12.1   Examples of Service Operation Inputs, Transformations, and Outputs

Service Operation	Inputs	Transformations	Outputs
Airline	Cold person in Toronto, jet, fuel, pilot and crew	Air travel	Warm person in Florida
Home security	House, family with fear of theft, home security system, tools, installer	Installation of system	Safe house, peace of mind
Hospital	Sick and injured people, supplies, nurses, doctors, utilities	Medical care and treatment	Healthy people
Jail	Convicted criminals, guards, wardens, teachers, food, clothing, utilities	Punishment, education	Responsible members of society
Lawn service	Overgrown lawn, lawn mower, worker work	Lawn mowing, yard	Neat yard
Pizza shop	Hungry person, truck, pizza, delivery person, fuel	Delivery of pizza	Satisfied person
Theater	Expectant people, actors, costumes, sets, utilities	Theatrical production	Entertained people
TV repair shop	Inoperable television set, replacement parts, tools, skilled technician, utilities	Television repair	Operable television set
University	High-school graduates, tuition, books, professors	Education	University graduate

leak. Their job is more than just repairing a problem with a pipe or valve. For factory workers installing gas pipes in mobile homes, in contrast, such interpersonal skills may not be important at all.

Intangibility.   Services often cannot be touched, tasted, smelled, or seen. An important part of their value may be subconscious, value that the individual doesn't consciously consider. For example, when you rent a hotel room for the night, you are purchasing the intangible quality of shelter. You may also be purchasing something even more intangible—a safe, homey, comfortable feeling—whether or not you are actually aware of it. All services have some degree of intangibility.[2]

Actually, tangible goods also have intangible aspects. Although a sofa is certainly a tangible good, it also provides comfort, an intangible, and its appearance may be aesthetically pleasing, another intangible. Figure 12.1 places a number of products on a scale from most to least tangible. Note that most products contain both tangible and intangible elements.

Customization.   Another characteristic of services is that they are typically *customized*. When you visit a therapist, you expect to be examined for the symptoms *you* are experiencing. Even a general diagnostic exam typically includes questions about your own unique problems. Similarly, when you buy insurance, get your favorite pet groomed, or have your hair cut, you expect these services to be customized to meet your needs.

Perishability.   Services are typically characterized by a high degree of perishability. Services such as garbage collection, transportation, child care, and house cleaning cannot be produced ahead of time and then stored. If a service is not used when it is available, it is wasted.

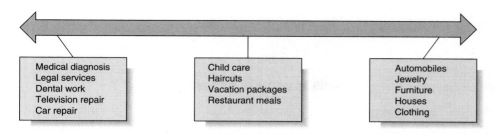

Figure 12.1
Tangible and intangible elements in services.

Link Between Consumer and Service.   Because services transform a customer or a customer's possessions, service operations must often contend with the fact that the customer is part of the production process. For example, unless you are a movie star or the prime minister, you must go to the barbershop or beauty salon to buy a haircut.

As part of the production process, consumers of services have a unique ability to affect that process. As the consumer, you expect the salon to be conveniently located, to be open for business at convenient times, to offer needed services at reasonable prices, and to provide prompt service. Accordingly, the manager adopts hours of operation, available services, and numbers of employees to meet the requirements of the customer.

Consumers of services also have an opportunity to comment on how well the service satisfies their needs. Indeed, managers of service operations often complain that everyone is an expert on services—or at least they think they are. Have you ever complained about the way your mail was delivered, the way checkout lines operated at the discount store, or the way your classes were taught? Probably. But have you given as much advice on how to manufacture a product? Probably not. The box "Customer Service in the Retail Store" gives additional information on the importance of service to customers.

Differing Quality Considerations.   Finally, consumers judge services on different bases than they do goods. Managers of service operations must understand that quality of work and quality of service are not necessarily synonymous. Your car could be flawlessly repaired, but if you had to wait a day past the time at which it was promised, you might feel that you had not received good service.

Classification of Service Operations

One way to classify service operations is according to how necessary it is for the customer to be a part of the system as the service is produced. A second way is based on how similar service operations are to a factory. Any service can be classified by either method. The point of classifications is to help managers determine the most appropriate strategy for managing services.

Extent of Customer Contact

A useful criterion for classifying service operations is the extent of customer contact.[3] Is it possible to provide the service without the customer being a part of the system?

The Canadian Business Scene

CUSTOMER SERVICE IN THE RETAIL STORE

The customer service revolution began in earnest a decade ago when books like *In Search of Excellence* were published. These books touted the importance of being obsessed with meeting customer needs. While this idea is undeniably correct, these books often fail to explain how companies can reconcile the conflicting demands of customer service, inventory control, employee efficiency, and profitability.

Consider the case of a clothing shop. It is now fashionable to stress customer service, and salesclerks are routinely sent to seminars to sharpen their skills in this area. At the same time, to counter theft, many shops have a rule that a customer cannot take more than two garments into the change room. Salesclerks spend excessive time watching the customers who are going in and out of change rooms and insufficient time with customers who have problems or want help.

Retail clerks are often caught in a catch-22 situation because exhortations about good service conflict with other rules of the business. In recessionary times, for example, retail stores may become less customer-oriented to improve the bottom line. Simultaneously, they are under pressure from competitors to improve customer service.

The retail sector must recognize that improving customer service requires a company-wide perspective, not just a focus on retail clerks. For example, Coopers & Lybrand Consulting Group created its Centre for Customer Satisfaction Excellence because it recognized the need for broad-based responses to customer demands. When a problem develops in customer service, resources from marketing, production, information technology, and human resources are involved to solve it.

Service excellence enthusiasts caution that the payoffs from improved service do not happen immediately, while the costs can be high. A full commitment to excellent service requires expenditures on employee training, incentive schemes, communications, and marketing. Excellence in service cannot overcome other weaknesses such as a poor product; rather, excellence in customer service is a potential competitive advantage.

Retail and Financial Consulting Services Inc. advises retailing firms on customer service and staff motivation programs. Their studies show that it is six times more expensive to attract a new customer to a store than it is to retain a current customer. Keeping the current customers is a matter of providing good service. To do that, staff enthusiasm is critical. Furthermore, by rewarding and recognizing staff properly, turnover is reduced. And when turnover is reduced, profits increase.

Toronto's SkyDome typifies the new emphasis on customer service. The 180 full-time and 500 part-time staff have to deal with as many as 68 000 people at once. To implement its philosophy of total guest satisfaction, the SkyDome requires 20 or more hours of training for each staff member. In 1991, "SkyDome U" was launched; each graduating class participates in a commencement ceremony. An employee incentive program has been set up to emphasize the goals of SkyDome's customer service strategy, and supervisors give out coupons to staffers who provide exceptional service to patrons. Lesley Chefero, human resources manager at Toronto Stadium Corp., says that none of this would have happened without the strong support of president Richard Peddie.

high-contact system

System in which the customer must be part of the system to receive the service.

low-contact system

System in which the customer need not be part of the system to receive the service.

Think of a public transit system. The service this business provides is transportation. It is impossible to provide transportation to a customer without the customer being a part of the system. The customer who purchases transportation must actually be on the bus. A public transit system is an example of a **high-contact system**. The customer must be a part of the system to receive the service. Other high-contact service providers include airlines, doctors, and car rental systems.

On the other hand, consider the cheque-processing operations at a bank. Workers sort the cheques that have been cashed that day and dispatch them to the banks on which they were drawn to receive a transfer of funds. This, too, is an example of a service operation. However, it is a **low-contact system**. Customers receive the service of having funds transferred to cover their cheques without ever setting foot in the cheque-processing center. Other low-contact systems include gas and electric utilities, auto repair shops, and lawn care services.

In some systems in both groups—for example, automatic car washes, computer time-sharing, and automatic bank teller machines—machines provide the

A public transit system, which is an example of a high-contact system, provides the service of transportation.

service. Substituting technology for the provider of the service may increase quality and efficiency (like the car wash). It can also lower consumer costs (computer time-sharing) or improve customer convenience (bank machines).

As you can imagine, it is much harder to manage a high-contact system than it is to manage a low-contact system. Having the customer in the system can lead to a number of uncertainties. For example, customers can affect the *timing* of when services must be performed, as when a restaurant must cope with a lunch or dinner rush. Since high-contact services cannot be inventoried, they can become overloaded in rush periods but sit idle during slow periods. Customers can also affect the exact *nature* of the service. A physician cannot provide exactly the same service to every patient, regardless of symptom!

In low-contact systems, the customer's interaction with the service production system is infrequent or very brief. Thus, the customer does not have much impact on the system during the production process. It is much easier for the company to conduct its business without interference from customers. In the sorting department of a parcel delivery service, for example, the workers who sift through the packages have no contact with the customers. So long as their packages are delivered on time, customers don't care how the sorters get the job done. But, for better efficiency, sorters in Toronto might fill a plane bound for the West Coast before one for Winnipeg, a procedure that would have offended Winnipeg customers if they had been first in line in a high-contact system.

Similarity to Manufacturing

Another way to classify service operations is by their similarity to manufacturing operations, as shown in Table 12.2. **Pure services** are high-contact services, such as hair styling or surgery. They have no inventoriable products. **Quasimanufacturing** services are much lower-contact and are in many ways similar to manufacturing.[4] **Mixed services** share some characteristics of both pure services and quasimanufacturing and involve moderate contact levels.

pure services
High-contact services in which the customer is part of the service production process.

quasimanufacturing
Low-contact services in which the customer need not be part of the service production process.

mixed services
Moderate-contact services in which the customer is involved in the service production process to a limited degree.

TABLE 12.2   Classification of Services by Similarity to Manufacturing Operations

Pure (High-Contact) Services	Mixed (Medium-Contact) Services	Quasimanufacturing (Low-Contact) Services
Medical clinics	Branch offices of banks and insurance companies	Home offices of banks and insurance companies
Schools	Real estate	Government
Apartments	Parcel delivery	Advertising agencies
Taxicabs	Dry-cleaning stores	Mail-order services
Restaurants	Home-cleaning services	News syndicates
Theaters	Repair shops	Research labs
Beauty parlors	Emergency departments Police Fire Ambulance	
Prisons	Moving Companies	

A main post office is a good example of quasimanufacturing because it is a lot like a factory. Machines and conveyors sort mail and people perform routine tasks, such as key-punching postal codes, very efficiently. This post office is providing a service: information delivery. But this service is not nearly as subject to uncertainties as pure services are. Whereas a barber cannot predict the arrival of a customer, shipments of mail arrive on a predictable schedule and can be briefly held in inventory when there is an overload. Automation can be applied to routine processes, and a number of the same production management techniques that apply to goods can be used to improve the efficiency of the post office operation.

In contrast, a branch post office is a mixed service operation. Bags of mail arrive and are delivered on a predictable schedule. Inventories of stamps and mailing supplies are maintained. Although usually not automated, preliminary mail sorting is routine and efficient, as in quasimanufacturing. However, the branch office is more like a pure service operation when it comes to customer service. Many customers stop at the post office during their lunch breaks or at the end of the day, creating peak periods of demand. They also affect the nature of the service. One customer may buy a few stamps. The next may have questions about sending mail to several overseas locations. A third may want to ship several packages. Dealing with this variety of demands is anything but routine, making it harder for managers to develop efficient procedures.

Service Operations Planning and Scheduling

Now that you know something about what services are, you can better understand how they can be managed. As with production, service operations management can be divided into planning, scheduling, and control phases. The planning phase includes not only deciding on the service to offer but also capacity planning and designing and laying out the service operation.

Capacity Planning

In low-contact systems, the presence of inventory enables managers to set capacity at the level of average demand. Orders that arrive faster than expected can be temporarily placed in inventory to be processed during an upcoming slower period. If you were planning a main post office, for example, you would logically use average demand to figure capacity for at least the sorting area.

In contrast, in high-contact systems, managers must plan capacity to meet peak demand. Your local supermarket has far more cash registers than it needs on an average day. But on a Saturday morning or during the three days before Christmas, all registers will be running full speed.

Location Planning

In low-contact services, the service is usually located near the firm's resource supply, labor, or transportation. For example, the mail sorting and processing facility of the post office is usually located downtown in an urban area. In this way, it is close to much of its supply (mail from downtown businesses). It is also usually near a highway, making it convenient for deliveries from suburban branches and for outgoing transport of mail.

On the other hand, high-contact services need to be located near their customers, who must be a part of the system. Have you ever noticed how several banks will be located close to each other? This pattern is the result of careful research by the banks' planning divisions, who have analyzed traffic flows, other businesses and schools in the area, and income patterns of local residents.

Sometimes high-contact services take to the road, bringing service to the customer. At small and large factories across the nation, canteen trucks pull up at coffee breaks and mealtimes each day. A bloodmobile that travels to schools and places of employment makes it easier for people to donate blood. Pizza delivery trucks traverse Canada's cities and towns to help satisfy our cravings.

The increasing globalization of business has led many service companies to consider international sites. Some foreign restaurants and banks, for example, have opened new facilities to serve customers in Canada. Similarly, many Canadian companies have expanded their services into international locations.

System Design

In a low-contact service system, the design process may resemble equipment planning in a manufacturing operation. The product is often a tangible item, such as a repaired television set, a legal document like a will, or a filled prescription.

In designing a high-contact service, managers must develop procedures that clearly spell out the ways in which workers interact with customers.[5] These procedures must cover information exchanges, delivery of material to and from the customer, exchanges of money, and physical contact. For example, people who work on patients in dental offices must follow strict procedures to avoid contact that can transmit disease. The next time you are at a dentist's office, notice that dental hygienists "scrub up" and wear disposable gloves. They also scrub after contact with a patient, even if they intend to work on equipment or do paperwork, and they rescrub before working on the next patient.

Service Flow Analysis. A useful way to design a service effectively is to develop a **service flow analysis**. Such analysis shows the flow of processes that make up the service and makes it easy to identify whether all the processes are necessary. Knowing what all the processes are also makes it easier to identify and isolate potential problems (known as *fail points*). Each process is a potential contributor to good or bad service.

service flow analysis
A method of improving services by identifying the flow of processes that make up the service.

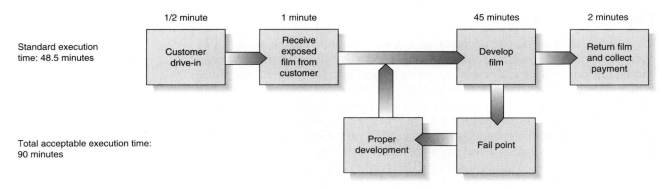

Figure 12.2
Service-flow analysis for quick photo-finishing.

A service flow analysis also makes scheduling easier. In the example in Figure 12.2, the shop manager has determined that the standard execution time for developing a roll of film is 48.5 minutes. Drive-in customers don't like to wait very long to get their finished photos from a "one-hour" photo finisher, but they will apparently tolerate up to a 90-minute wait before lowering their assessment of the quality of the service.

Facility Layout

In a low-contact system, the arrangement of the facility should be designed to enhance the production of the service. A mail processing facility at Federal Express looks very much like a factory. Machines and people are arranged in the order in which they are used in the processing of mail.

High-contact service systems are arranged to meet customer needs and expectations. Consider the cafeteria layout shown in Figure 12.3. Families enter and immediately find an array of high chairs and baby beds with wheels, so that it is convenient to wheel their children through the line with them. Waitresses carry trays for elderly people and those pushing high chairs. Hungry customers must walk past the whole serving line before they can begin making selections. Not only does this layout help customers make up their minds, but it also tempts them to select more.

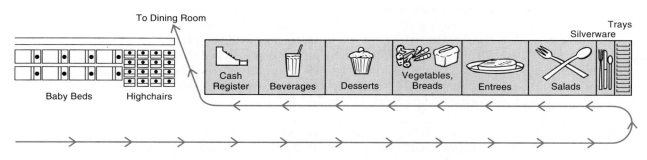

Figure 12.3
Layout of a cafeteria.

Applying Concepts from Goods Production Management

Some service industries lend themselves to the same techniques used in goods production management. Service operations can be carefully planned and controlled and sometimes even automated. They can be regularly reviewed for quality, performance improvement, and customer reaction.

McDonald's has done an outstanding job of treating the fast-food business as manufacturing, and many other fast-food franchisors have followed in its path. The byword at McDonald's is to substitute technology for discretion. By automating processes that otherwise would rely on judgment, McDonald's has been able to provide consistent service while using a staff with little specialized training.

For example, the hamburger patties at McDonald's are carefully premeasured and prepacked at a central supply house. Employees at a particular McDonald's outlet have no discretion in determining the size, shape, or quality of a hamburger patty. The drawers, shelves, and bins are designed to hold the ingredients for McDonald's standard product mix only. The scoop measures the same volume of french fries into each bag. Numerous trash cans in the parking lot remind customers where to dispose of their trash.

Sometimes, machines can substitute for employee discretion. For example, some hotels have a coffee machine in each guest's room. Guests feel they are getting something extra, while the coffee shop has more room for customers who want more than a cup of coffee for breakfast.

In other cases, special procedures are substituted for individual discretion. For instance, greeting-card displays often have a coded card that is sent to the greeting-card company when stock of an item is low. This approach eliminates the need for a salesperson to take inventory. Instead, the salesperson is notified that the order needs to be placed at the appropriate time.

A combination of equipment and procedures is most effective in some situations. Consider Midas Muffler shops. They combine special tools, procedures, and training to use them with limited service (exhaust, brake, and suspension system repairs and replacement only) to provide fast, low-priced repair services.

Scheduling Service Operations

Scheduling in service operations involves scheduling both work and workers. In a low-contact service, work scheduling is based on desired completion dates or on the time of arrival of orders. If a garage has several cars needing repairs and yours is not scheduled to be picked up until 5:00, it may sit idle for a while, even if it was the first to be dropped off. In such businesses, reservations and appointments systems can help to smooth demand.

On the other hand, in a high-contact service, the customer is in the system and must be accommodated. If a hospital emergency room is overloaded, patients cannot be asked to make an appointment to return at another time. Thus, scheduling of services may not be possible in high-contact systems.

In scheduling workers, managers must consider efficiency and costs. McDonald's, for example, guarantees workers that they will be scheduled for at least four hours at a time. To accomplish this goal without having workers idle, McDonald's uses *overlapping shifts*: The ending hours for some employees overlap the beginning hours for others. The overlap provides maximum coverage during peak periods. McDonald's also trains its employees to put off minor tasks, such as refilling napkin dispensers, until slow periods.

A 24-hour-a-day service operation, such as a hospital, can be an even greater scheduling challenge. Nurses must be on duty around the clock, seven days a week, yet few nurses want to work on weekends or during the wee hours of the morning. Enough nurses must be scheduled to meet emergencies, yet most hospitals are on a tight budget and cannot afford to have an overabundance of nurses. Incentives are often used to entice nurses to work at times they might not otherwise choose. For example, would you choose to work 12 hours a day, seven days a week? Probably not. But what if you were entitled to have every other week off in exchange for working such a schedule? A number of hospitals use just such a plan to attract nurses.

Service Operations Control

Is it possible to control the quantity and quality of services? Goods have constant, measurable characteristics. It is relatively easy to set a standard (for example, length or weight) and to measure items to determine whether that standard is being achieved. Services are more variable, and their quality is often in the eye of the beholder. Different customers want different services.

Because services are often performed by people, assuring a consistent quantity or quality of service may be difficult or impossible. Nevertheless every firm must have some standards and try to maintain some quality level.

Managing Demand and Supply

In Chapter 11, we discussed how important inventory control is in goods production. Keeping a suitable amount of inventory can help a business to meet uneven demand. But since high-contact services cannot be stored, they cannot be inventoried. There are ways, however, in which managers of service operations can control demand for and/or supply of services.

Managing Demand.   Some service operations use pricing to shift demand to nonpeak periods. This technique allows service-providing employees to be on a consistent schedule. Instead of hiring many employees to work a few hours a day or a few days a week, the company can hire fewer employees to work full-time schedules.

Examples of pricing to shift peak demand to nonpeak periods include matinee prices at movie theaters, weekday happy hours, and weekend rates at hotels frequented by business travellers. Evening and weekend long-distance telephone rates, peak-load pricing by utility companies, and two-for-one coupons at restaurants (good only Monday through Thursday) also represent demand shifting.

Special service offerings may also be used to stimulate demand during nonpeak periods. This approach is especially important for facilities with high fixed costs and low variable costs. For example, supermarkets have increased the number of hours they are open for business and have promoted it heavily. The additional hours of operation help cover the high fixed costs of the facility (such as mortgage, taxes, and insurance) at a low variable cost (few additional employees). In recent years, ski resorts have offered low-cost summer vacation packages. Many even provide special summer convention planning assistance.

Offering complimentary services during peak periods can temporarily soothe customers who are awaiting the service they desire. For example, many cocktail lounges provide free "munchies" for customers who are waiting to be seated in a busy restaurant. A mirror in the central lobby of each floor allows hotel patrons to check their appearance while waiting for a busy elevator.

Reservation systems can also be effective in managing demand. By pre-selling capacity, reservations force incoming demand into a predictable rate and pattern. A reservation system can be used to deflect excess demand to another slot at the same facility, for example, a later flight on the same airline.

Excess demand may also be deflected to another facility owned by the same company. There are, for example, two Road King motels in Grand Forks, North Dakota, to capitalize on Canadian demand for cross-border shopping. If the one next to Columbia Mall is full, the customer can usually be booked at the other one, just a few minutes up the road.

Controlling Supply.   Rather than trying to manage demand, some service organizations try to manage the supply of services available. For example, part-time employees can help meet variable demand. A company typically maintains a base of full-time employees to meet demand during nonrush periods and adds part-timers during peak demand periods. Part-time employees may be added during certain hours of the day (such as during the peaks at fast-food restaurants or transit services). They may also be added on certain days of the week (Fridays and Saturdays in a beauty parlor) or weeks of the month (the last week of each month at a bank). In some cases, companies even bring on part-time help for certain peak months of the year, such as income tax services during March and April.

The Canadian Passport Office is focusing more on the needs of customers. Business hours have been extended, a new system has been introduced that will speed up the process of completing customer files, and some passport offices have been moved to suburban locations which have more parking.[6]

A careful analysis of the service delivery system may show ways in which efficiency can be improved for a system to get the most supply during peak periods.[7] For example, during peaks, only essential services should be provided. In lawn-care companies, fertilizing, seeding, and insecticide applications are critical during the spring and autumn months. Equipment maintenance can wait.

Training employees to perform many jobs—**cross training**—can increase supply when one part of the delivery system is temporarily overloaded. Lawn-care businesses train their workers so that during a busy time a manager can help with the truck driving, drivers can help apply the lawn treatments, and so forth. Cross-training also provides variety in otherwise boring jobs. Rearranging the layout of a service system can also make it more efficient and increase its capacity. Supermarkets constantly rearrange their shelf displays to better use space, present more products, and increase sales.

cross training

Training employees to perform a variety of jobs as a way of increasing the supply of services.

Managers can also increase the supply of services by using **shared capacity**, especially when a major investment in equipment or labor is required. The executive suite concept is one example. A group of professionals—perhaps a lawyer, a psychologist, an accountant, and a public relations person—rent a group of offices together. They share a secretary, a duplicating machine, and a small computer. Because none of the professionals has enough work to justify a full-time secretary, this is a convenient arrangement. It may also free up funds for the lawyer to hire a paralegal aide, thereby increasing the supply of services within the law office.

shared capacity

A way of increasing the supply of services by having several individuals or companies share equipment, office space, or personnel.

Quality Control: Training Workers

An important factor to remember in service product design is that people deliver most services. Service system employees are both the producers of the product and the salespeople. Thus, human relations skills (see Chapter 5) are vital to anyone who has contact with the public.[8] In high-contact systems, the people are the service; your lawyer is the physical representation of the product you are receiving.

The wrong attitude from service employees can reduce sales of services. Conversely, the right attitude can increase sales, as the box "How's It Going in Moscow?" attests. Frequently, though, service employees receive low financial rewards, occupy low status positions in the organization, and receive little training. Some companies, however, remind top executives of the importance of the employee-customer relationship by having their executives perform the services. The president of Hyatt Hotels, for example, once worked as a doorman.

The Disney organization does a tremendous job of remembering that no matter what their jobs, all their service employees are links to the public. For example, Disney World has a team of sweepers constantly at work picking up bits of trash virtually as they fall to the ground. When visitors have questions about directions or time, they often ask one of the sweepers. Because their responses affect visitors' overall impressions of Disney World, sweepers

International Report

HOW'S IT GOING IN MOSCOW?

In 1976, George Cohon, president of McDonald's Canada, decided he wanted to open a McDonald's in Moscow. His idea has now become reality. Moscow-McDonald's is the largest McDonald's restaurant in the world. It seats 700, serves over 40 000 people a day, and has a staff of over 1000. The operation is a joint venture with the food service administration of Moscow's City Council, unlike McDonald's arrangements in all other countries which are with individual franchisees. Although demand is incredibly high, McDonald's is operating under nightmarish conditions because of the upheavals in Russian society. Marc Winer, McDonald's general director in Moscow, has discovered that doing even the simplest thing takes a lot of effort. Adhering to McDonald's rigid standards of quality, service, cleanliness, and value is extremely difficult.

In all of its other foreign operations, McDonald's relies on local suppliers for its food. McDonald's has also tied itself to the local food supply in Moscow because it uses the local currency, but the quality and quantity of that supply were very uncertain. Since local processors could not begin to meet McDonald's exacting standards for milk and beef, the firm had to hire outside expertise to help improve the local supply. McDonald's ended up building a huge complex to do the necessary processing of food that serves as the inputs to the restaurant.

McDonald's primary strengths—the commitment of its franchisees and the quality of its supplies—are both absent in Moscow. In addition, the idea of private enterprise and its rewards has, until recently, been unacceptable. But the biggest practical problem is ensuring that food items such as appropriate quality potatoes, beef, and milk are available when they are needed. The most demanding job in the entire McDonald's empire is probably that of quality assurance manager in a country that has one of the worst run agricultural sectors in the world. At one point, McDonald's workers had to be persuaded to go out and actually harvest potatoes. Rapid inflation and the difficulty of contracting with suppliers in rubles add to the firm's difficulties.

Soviet workers are completely unaccustomed to being polite—let alone friendly—to customers. In a land where shortages are the rule, the general attitude of shop workers seems to be "So do you want it or not?" Before McDonald's opened its doors in Moscow, however, its workers had learned to smile, say please and thank you, and tell each customer "priyatnovo appetita," Russian for "enjoy your meal." Customers were amazed. "Here my meal turned out to be just a supplement to the sincere smiles of the workers," said one woman.

To assure cleanliness, workers in the Soviet Union get a benefit denied their brethren elsewhere. Their uniforms are washed and pressed on the premises. Apparently this was the only way McDonald's could assure that its Russian workers would have clean clothes each day.

While a meal at McDonald's costs more than a meal at a nearby cafe, Russians seem to agree that they are getting value for their money. The tender meat, clean facilities, polite workers, and amenities such as soft toilet paper are appreciated. So are the short, fast-moving (by Soviet standards) lines.

Muscovites were a bit confused by the Big Mac at first. "It's a rather complicated sandwich," said one. Another commented, "It is a three-story sandwich!" But a 50-year-old engineer may have summed things up for everyone when he paused after his first bite and asked "Why can't we do this sort of thing?"

The political upheavals in what used to be the Soviet Union have caused McDonald's serious problems. The company is firm that it is in Moscow for the long haul, but there are some distressing financial considerations that cannot be ignored. The annual revenues of the Moscow outlet may be in the neighborhood of $5 million, but this amount is hardly enough to cover the interest on the firm's total investment there. It could be argued, however, that the opening day publicity alone was worth the cost.

All of this uncertainty has changed the timetable for opening additional McDonald's restaurants in Russia. The second one is more than a year behind schedule, and others that were planned may never be opened.

are trained to respond appropriately. Their work is evaluated and rewarded based on strict performance-appraisal standards.

In low-contact service operations, the technical skills of workers are more important than their human relations skills. As a consumer, you are not terribly concerned about how personable the individual who repairs your watch or television set is. But in high-contact service operations, human relations skills are more important. A student's counseling session can be made much more enjoyable by a cheerful, pleasant academic advisor. A pleased customer is more likely to return.

Quality Control: Motivating Workers

In addition to selecting and training the right workers, managers of service operations need to motivate their workers to offer the appropriate quality level of service. Positive and publicized recognition, such as employee-of-the-month awards, can be very effective, especially when based on customer feedback. Marriott hotels have evaluation slips in each room which guests are asked to fill out, indicating if they have received especially good service from a particular employee.

Monetary incentives, such as a bonus for being named employee of the month, are also effective. But other types of incentives may be equally effective and less costly. Examples include an employee badge that says "Employee of the Month" or "Superior Service Award" and special baseball caps or T-shirts to indicate superior service.

Making the deliverer of the service more visible to the customer makes the employee more aware of quality. At Ichi Ban restaurants, customers are seated around a large grill where a costumed chef puts on an elaborate show as he prepares their meals. This showcase promotes consistently high quality, and chefs are rewarded with consistently high tips. Similarly, quality in a repair garage may be improved if customers are allowed to speak directly with the mechanic who works on their car.

Handling the Special Problems of Service Operations

Although the production of goods and the production of services are similar in many ways, as noted at the beginning of this chapter, services have unique characteristics. These traits—intangibility, customization, and perishability, as well as the presence of customers within the production process—cause special challenges. In this section, we will consider some techniques for meeting these challenges. As you will see, each of these characteristics creates special problems for service operations managers and affects service management.

Intangibility

The often intangible nature of services makes them difficult for customers to evaluate before buying. When the product is a physical good, customers can see, feel, or touch its **search qualities**. These qualities may be determined before customers buy. Similarly, customers can determine **experience qualities** of goods, such as taste, after they have made their purchases. But with services, customers sometimes find it impossible to evaluate the **credence qualities**—the value you believe the service delivered—even after purchase or consumption. For example, most people have a difficult time evaluating the quality of the legal or psychological counseling services they buy.

Most services have few search qualities, so customers rely more on experience and credence qualities to evaluate services. That is, customers use

search qualities
Qualities in a product that can be perceived before buying by sight, feel, touch, or hearing.

experience qualities
Qualities in a product that can be perceived after buying by senses such as taste.

credence qualities
Qualities in a product that a purchaser believes exist but that are not subject to objective proof.

This highly skilled and diverting chef provides the quality food preparation and entertainment that keep customers coming back.

a different process to evaluate service products, such as a funeral, before buying than they do to evaluate goods before buying. Those charged with selling services thus have an interesting challenge.

One solution is to provide tangible evidence of the intangible, whenever possible. Lawyers and doctors display their diplomas on their office walls. Hotels provide evidence that the room has been specially cleaned and prepared for the new occupant: clean glasses in white paper bags, wrapped new bars of soap, a "sanitized" band across the toilet, a chocolate mint on the pillow.

Customization

The customized nature of services often makes their scheduling difficult or impossible. This difficulty is one reason why you often have to wait at your doctor's or dentist's office, even though you have an appointment. Because the patients before you also bought customized services, the receptionist could not know exactly when your appointment would begin.

In some services, scheduling can be improved by shifting the level of customer contact. High-contact service systems are harder to schedule than are low-contact systems. Thus, some services try to shift the level of customer contact downward. One way to lower the level of contact is to handle routine transactions by telephone or mail and to handle only exceptions face-to-face. L.L. Bean and Cabela's have built phenomenally successful mail-order catalogue businesses. Mailed orders can be "inventoried" for a day or two without a major effect on delivery times. Imagine being asked to wait a day or two at a department store!

Reservations or appointments-only systems can also help to reduce the level of customer contact. Only those customers who have an appointment are allowed into the system. These systems reduce the number of face-to-face contacts and simplify the scheduling of employees who have contact with customers.

Another strategy is to separate information-gathering from the provision of the service. For example, a well-run medical office will give you a medical history form to fill out while you wait. This system frees all the office personnel, including the doctor, for other duties.

Drop-off points away from the main facility also reduce the level of customer contact. Consider the success of automatic teller machines. Not only are they more convenient for the customer, but they also free bank tellers from processing routine deposits and withdrawals.

A final strategy for lowering the level of customer contact is to separate the high- and low-contact elements of a service. The purchase of some services may be divided into four phases: information, reservation, payment, and consumption. Often, the consumption phase must take place at a distant, specialized location, such as in an airplane or theater. But the other three elements can be separated from consumption and treated as low-contact services.

You may be familiar with this strategy from the entertainment service of a hockey or football game. Teams distribute *information* by publishing schedules in the newspaper and by making free pocket schedules widely available. When you have chosen a game to attend, you can make your *reservation* by calling the arena or stadium ticket office or by calling or visiting a nearby ticket outlet. You then make *payment* through the mail or by using a credit card, and the tickets are mailed to you. Only for the *consumption* phase do you actually need to be a part of the system (at the arena or stadium).

Perishability

Earlier in this chapter, we noted that the perishability of services means there is potential for waste. This characteristic causes many hotels to schedule more customer reservations than they have rooms for a given night. If some of the customers fail to keep their appointments, the hotel's ability to provide rooms has not been wasted (although they risk offending customers who are turned away.) Likewise, many airlines overbook flights, knowing that there will usually be some "no shows."

Customer Involvement

We have already seen that having customers as part of the process complicates the production of services. But some managers have found a way to turn

Self-service saves money for both the customer and the company providing the gasoline.

customer presence into an advantage. They actually get the customer more involved in the process. Direct long-distance dialing, for example, allows the customer to do the work that long-distance operators used to do. Some car washes provide the basic necessary equipment, but require the consumer to actually wash the car.

Shifting some of the productive effort to the customer frees employees for the tasks that require their special abilities. But some customers reject the idea of doing the work and paying for it too. This problem may be solved by offering financial incentives, such as reduced prices for self-service gasoline or bag-your-own groceries.

Summary of Key Points

Although the creation of services involves resources, transformations, and finished products, as does the production of goods, service operations differ from goods manufacturing in several important ways. Services are typically performed whereas goods are produced. Services are also predominantly intangible and perishable. They are more likely to be customized to meet the needs of the purchaser than are goods. And service production often requires the presence of the customer.

Services can be classified according to the degree of customer involvement in production and according to their similarity to manufacturing. In high-contact services, the customer must be within the service system as the service is performed. In low-contact systems, services may be performed independent of the customer, much like manufacturing. Quasimanufacturing is the most like manufacturing, with low customer contact and briefly inventoriable products. Pure services are the opposite, with high customer contact and noninventoriable products. Mixed services have some of the characteristics of both pure services and quasimanufacturing.

Planning for service operations requires decisions on the capacity, the location, and the layout of the service facilities. In designing the system, managers must pay special attention to the flow of activities involved in producing the service. Scheduling the work force in high-contact systems may involve overlapping shifts and other special scheduling strategies.

Service operations require control over both the quantity and the quality of the services offered. Quantity control in high-contact systems involves adjusting the supply of and the demand for services. Reservations systems and price incentives may smooth demand, while the use of part-time employees, cross-training, and shared capacity may smooth the supply of labor in service operations. To assure quality control, managers must focus on human relations aspects of the operations, hiring the right types of workers and then motivating them for quality performance.

Because of their unique characteristics, services need special management techniques. To overcome services' intangibility, managers need to provide as many tangible signs of their services' quality as possible. To minimize the scheduling problems that result from customized high-contact services, managers may try to lower the level of contact. To avoid the waste of perishable services, managers may elect to use reservations systems and even to "overbook" some services. To deal with the presence of customers in the production of high-contact services, managers may choose to involve customers further by running self-service operations.

Hold the Line!

Toronto-based Delrina Inc. is one of the hottest software companies in North America. Its most well-known product is Winfax Pro 3, a fax software. Its revenue soared from less than $50 million in 1992 to over $100 million in 1993. But it was growing faster than its ability to handle questions from customers. When an article appeared in *Info World* claiming that Delrina's technical support left much to be desired, the company's management knew it had to do something fast. The future of the company was at stake.

The mission statement of the company said that Delrina measured its success by how satisfied its customers were. But the company was failing to meet these expectations. Technical support services were not well organized and the company was chronically short-staffed in this important area. Customers who phoned in with questions about the company's software were often put on hold for a long time. By the time customers got to talk to a representative, they were often very angry. The average time a customer spent on hold was 10 minutes.

Enter Jim Moore, who took over as director of technical support in April of 1993. He first set out to create the right mentality and culture for a support call center. Because technical reps need to have a detailed understanding of software, Moore put a freeze on the transfer of anyone out of the technical support department until they had been there at least 9 months.

A more formal approach was adopted to get the right people into managerial positions. Previously, many people had just evolved into management positions based on their technical expertise, even if they had no managerial ability.

Moore also purchased a new Automatic Call Distribution (ACD) system to handle customer calls. The company now handles 2000 calls per day with the new system. A new customer management system was also installed. It keeps track of the kinds of questions and complaints that customers have and allows the new product development people to revise software quickly and accurately.

How successful has the company been in its attempts to improve customer satisfaction? The average time a customer was on hold in 1992 was 10 minutes; now it is less than 3 minutes. The ACD system has led to a reduction in the time it takes to get a revised version of software to the market; it has also led to a 40 percent reduction in the number of calls with complaints about revised software products. One customer was so delighted by the service level that he named his daughter Delrina.

CASE QUESTIONS
1. What steps were taken at Delrina to ensure that customer satisfaction was actually achieved?
2. Explain how the factors of intangibility, customization, and perishability manifest themselves in this kind of service business.
3. Is this a high- or low-contact service? Explain.
4. How does Delrina deal with the management of supply and demand?

Being Efficient Isn't Enough

Each day, more than 122 000 boxy, brown delivery trucks from United Parcel Service hit the streets in Canada, the U.S., Puerto Rico, Germany, and many other countries. The company, which was started in 1907, delivers 11.5 million packages (750 000 by air) for 2 million different business customers each day. The company has 162 airplanes working out of more than 500 airports.

Perhaps the most distinguishing feature of the company is the rigid control that it maintains over every aspect of its operations. Time-and-motion studies have been conducted on virtually every task that workers do. For example, delivery people are supposed to walk three feet per second, hold their key rings with their middle finger, and fold their money face up, sequentially ordered. Drivers are instructed to climb aboard their trucks with their left foot first to avoid wasted steps. Packages are arranged in a precise fashion in the trucks (which have overhead lights so the drivers can read the addresses better). Workers at sorting centers are carefully timed according to strict standards for each task. Drivers are closely timed also; each delivery is timed with a stopwatch. All trucks are washed every day, and they are kept on a strict maintenance schedule.

All these activities have resulted in a very efficient operation, and these efficiencies enabled UPS to achieve market success for more than 50 years.

Partly because of its emphasis on internal efficiency, UPS was reluctant to give discounts. Instead, it prided itself on charging the same rates to residential customers as it did for business customers. This policy alienated several large clients. Competitors who were willing to give discounts jumped in to fill the void. Roadway Package Systems Inc. began offering widespread discounts on large-volume shipments and now offers a package-tracking service to customers.

UPS's most formidable competitor is Federal Express, which gives volume discounts and tracks packages for customers. Federal controlled about 45 percent of the air cargo market in 1992, while UPS held about 25 percent.

After losing business to aggressive competitors like Federal Express and Roadway Package Systems, UPS has dramatically changed the way it does business. In 1990, CEO Kent Nelson ordered a sweeping examination of the company's business methods. The company's flaws were identified and fixed so that UPS could more effectively respond to competitive rivals.

The "we know what's best for the customer" attitude was one of the first casualties. Previously, UPS had the view that they knew what was best for their corporate customers. But in 1990, with Eastman Kodak thinking about dropping UPS because of its "bad attitude," things began to change. Now, UPS emphasizes customer satisfaction, offers flexible pickup and delivery times, customized shipment plans, and discount prices to volume shippers.

The head office marketing staff has been increased from 7 to 175, and face-to-face interviews have been conducted with 25 000 customers to find out what services they want. UPS increased its advertising budget from $75 000 in 1981 to $18 million in 1990. It is also trying to improve its image with the public. It launched a $35 million television advertising campaign (its first ever) focussing on the now well-known slogan "We run the tightest ship in the shipping business."

UPS has added to its air fleet and is matching technically advanced rivals with such devices as electronic scanners in its sorting centers and onboard computers in its delivery trucks. Between 1986 and 1991, UPS increased its spending on information technology almost tenfold, spending an average of $300 million per year. By 1996, the company will have spent an additional $3.2 billion on information technology. The company is in good shape financially, with only $114 million in debt, compared with $2.5 billion in employee equity.

In addition to its spending on advertising and equipment, UPS has also purchased a number of small foreign companies to get a foothold in the overseas package delivery market. It has also spent $1.4 billion on a system to efficiently track packages from door-to-door. A key part of the system is an in-house invention called a "dense code" which holds twice the information in a normal bar code. Scanners in the field and at sorting centers can read information on package origin, destination, and contents. The system is designed to leapfrog Federal Express's system. A system called GroundTrac has also been introduced; it allows shippers to get status reports on their ground packages 24 hours a day just by calling a toll-free number.

But with all of these changes, UPS is still committed to its emphasis on worker efficiency and commitment. That's the way the company achieved its success, and it will continue to bring new workers into a corporate culture where efficiency is a key word.

CASE QUESTIONS
1. Explain how each factor that distinguishes services production from goods production affects UPS's operations.
2. How would you classify UPS in terms of the degree of customer contact and its similarity to manufacturing?
3. If you were a senior UPS manager, with which aspect of planning and scheduling would you be most concerned? Why?
4. In what ways does UPS's management currently seek to control the quality of its service? The quantity of its service?

◆

Key Terms

service operations	pure services	service flow analysis	search qualities
high-contact system	quasimanufacturing	cross training	experience qualities
low-contact system	mixed services	shared capacity	credence qualities

Study Questions and Exercises

Review Questions

1. Why has employment in the service sector continued to grow, even during periods of overall unemployment and recession?
2. Identify pure services, quasimanufacturing services, and mixed services according to the degree of customer contact involved.
3. What factors must a manager consider when planning the layout of a service facility?
4. List three ways to deal with the unpredictable timing of demand in service organizations.
5. How does reducing the level of customer contact help managers schedule high-contact customized services?

Analysis Questions

6. What are the resources and finished products of the following services?
   - real-estate firm
   - child care facility
   - bank
   - municipal water department
   - hotel
7. Explain why the police department is a mixed service.
8. Develop a service flow analysis for some service you use frequently, such as buying lunch at a fast-food restaurant, having your hair cut, or riding a bus. Identify steps of potential quality or productivity failures in the process.

Application Questions

9. Interview the manager of a local service business, such as a laundry and/or dry cleaning shop. Identify the major decisions that were involved in planning for its service operations. Suggest areas for improvement.
10. Select a high-contact industry. Write an advertisement to hire workers for this business. Draw up a plan for motivating the hired workers to produce high-quality services for the firm.

Building Your Business Skills

Goal
To encourage students to assess the steps that service companies typically take in planning their operations.

Method

Step 1:
Working in groups of three, interview the manager of a local service business, such as a car service, laundry, or dry-cleaning shop. Identify the major decisions that were involved in planning for its service operation. Focus specific questions on the following planning elements:
- *Capacity planning* (How does the firm handle ebbs and flows in service demand?)
- *Location planning* (Did the firm conduct a detailed traffic and demographic analysis before choosing its current site?)
- *Layout planning* (How is the site laid out to meet customers' needs and expectations and to encourage sales?)
- *Quality planning* (What kind of quality controls are built into the system to maintain the highest standards?)
- *Methods planning* (Has the manager analyzed the steps involved in providing the service with the goal of improving the method of delivery?)

Step 2:
Compile your findings in the form of a memo to the manager. Your memo should point out the strengths and weaknesses in the planning process and suggest improvements. (Remember: Your memo is a working document and will not actually be sent to the store manager.)

Step 3:
Groups should share their memos with one another.

Analysis
Evaluate the common threads that run through the planning processes used by these local service companies. The following questions will help guide your analysis:
- Do the firms place greater emphasis on one aspect of planning over the others?
- Are some aspects of planning ongoing while others are responses to specific problems or circumstances?
- How do some planning elements influence others? For example, how does quality planning influence capacity, layout, and methods planning?

Follow-Up Questions
1. In your opinion, which aspects of a service company's operations planning are most responsible for its success? Which aspects are most responsible for the firm's problems?
2. If you were to open a service company in the community, how would you plan the operation to avoid the mistakes that you uncovered?

13

Increasing Productivity and Quality

LEARNING OBJECTIVES

After reading this chapter, you will be able to

- State the connection between productivity and quality.
- Describe the nature of the Canadian productivity problem and why some view it as a crisis.
- Illustrate total and partial measures for national, sector, and company productivity.
- Identify the functions needed for managing quality assurance and describe three tools for its management.
- Explain how companies can compete by improving productivity and quality.

CHAPTER OUTLINE

Ford Seeks New Way to Skin a Cat at Jaguar

Superstitious or not, executives at Britain's Jaguar Cars Ltd. apparently believe that cats have nine lives. In any case, they are hoping that the cat's proverbial good fortune applies to the world-famous automobiles named for one of nature's most powerful and graceful felines. So far, history is on their side. After nearly dying in the early 1980s, Jaguar is clawing its way back through a concentrated program of increased productivity and quality improvement. Its chances for survival increased dramatically in 1989, when Ford Motor Co. bought Jaguar for $2.5 billion and then invested another $700 million to breathe new life into its acquisition.

Despite the revival, however, Jaguar is not entirely out of danger. Plagued by serious quality and productivity problems, the company at one time lost $18 000 on every car it sold, and quality remains such a problem that some industry observers still joke that "Jaguar owners need two cars: one to drive and one for spare parts." Although quality has improved considerably since Ford took over, Jaguar still lags behind competitors in this crucial area. While Lexus, for instance, has an average of 0.66 defects per car, Jaguar owners face an average of 1.67.

Indeed, many problems in quality seem to be built into the Jaguar line. Introduced in 1986, for example, the pricy XJ6 sedan requires 20 000 parts—many of which are fragile and troublesome. By contrast, the Lincoln Town Car made by Jaguar's parent company uses only 5000 parts. Known in the company as the "problem child," Jaguar's second offering—the sleek and elegant XJS coupe—has proved to be even more prone to trouble.

How did such a once renowned company manage to saddle itself with such a problematic product line? Most analysts agree that Jaguar's quality and productivity problems can be traced, at least in part, to a corporate culture that stifled initiative. Discouraged from speaking up, for instance, managers and engineers became part of a grossly inefficient manufacturing system whose break-even point required more income than could actually be generated by the number of cars that the company built. Bitter labor-management relations and restrictive union practices made matters worse. Prior to 1990, when a new contract was signed, workers who met their daily quotas simply stopped working. Aging production facilities in Coventry, England, added to the problem.

Despite Jaguar's troubled history, Ford is by most accounts turning the company around. Largely as a result of rigorous quality checking, assembly-line defects have been cut by about 80 percent. Each week, engineers test

25 new cars to detect motor and electrical problems, leaks, and even bothersome squeaks. When problems are detected, a special squad of 25 inspectors works to fix these specific problems on the next cars coming down the line. Recurrent defects are referred to engineering for redesign.

Meanwhile, productivity is also improving. In 1991, for example, Jaguar required 418.6 person-hours to assemble a car. Two years later, it needed only 251.9. By 1997, Ford hopes to reduce that number to 126. Not surprisingly, as the manufacturing process has become more efficient, the company's workforce has shrunk—from 12 000 to 6500 in three years. Perhaps more surprisingly, these reductions have also been accompanied by a new spirit of labor-management cooperation. "Our members," explains union leader Chris Liddell, "have a new realization that they are the company, that customer satisfaction starts inside the factory."

Today, the confidence of Ford executives is up. They have reason to believe that with improved quality and productivity—plus design changes and exciting new models—consumers will be convinced to come back to Jaguar, a nameplate many still rank among the classiest on the road. For example, when the restyled XJ sedan was unveiled in the fall of 1994 with a base price of $53 450, Ford strategists predicted worldwide sales would rise by 7000 units the following year. Company forecasts call for Jaguar to sell 39 000 cars in 1995, although even a lower break-even point should allow Jaguar to eke out a slim profit on sales of $2.2 billion. Ford also hopes to broaden its market base by introducing a lower-priced, entry-level model—possibly designed and built in Japan by Mazda. Whether or not the company implements such a radical plan, it is clear that Ford sees Jaguar as a long-term investment and is willing to bide its time as it works toward the payoff in productivity. As Jaguar CEO Nick Steele says of the new XJ, "This is our opportunity to show people that we are world-class." ◆

Under the guidance of Ford, Jaguar is undergoing the growing pains of a company learning to appreciate the costliest and most valuable lessons about productivity and quality. It is a painful but necessary process—without vast improvements in both areas, Jaguar may soon use up what's left of its nine lives. It is no secret that *productivity* and *quality* are the watchwords of the 1990s. Companies are not only measuring productivity and insisting on improvements, they are also insisting that quality means bringing to market products that satisfy customers, improve sales, and boost profits.

The Productivity-Quality Connection

As we saw in Chapter 1, **productivity** is a measure of economic performance. It measures how much is produced relative to the resources used to produce it. The more we are able to produce the right things while using fewer resources, the more productivity grows and everyone—the economy, businesses, and workers—benefits.

productivity
A measure of efficiency that compares how much is produced with the resources used to produce it.

Notice that productivity considers both the amounts and the quality of what is produced. By using resources more efficiently, the quantity of output will be greater. But unless the resulting goods and services are of satisfactory quality (the "right things"), consumers will not want them. **Quality**, then, means fitness for use—offering features that consumers want.

The importance of quality in productivity cannot be overstated. Poor quality has created competitive problems for Canadian firms that have focused only on efficiency (quantity). Businesses in other countries have emphasized both efficiency and quality and consequently have increased productivity more rapidly than Canadian companies.

quality
A product's fitness for use in terms of offering the features that consumers want.

Meeting the Productivity Challenge

Productivity is an international issue with major domestic effects. A nation's productivity determines how large a piece of the global economic resource pie it gets. A country with more resources has more wealth to divide among its citizens. A country whose productivity fails to increase as rapidly as that of other countries will see its people's standard of living fall relative to the rest of the world.

Nations also care about domestic productivity regardless of their standing versus other nations. A country that makes more out of its existing resources (increases its productivity) can increase the wealth of all its inhabitants if it so chooses. But a productivity decline shrinks a nation's available resources so that any one person's increase in wealth can come only at the expense of others in the society. In addition, investors, suppliers, managers, and workers are all concerned about the productivity of specific industries, companies, departments, and individuals.

Canadian workers, managers, and investors are particularly concerned about recent trends in Canadian productivity. For decades, Canadian products have done well in world markets. Recently, however, foreign competitors have made significant inroads.

Productivity Trends

The United States remains the most productive nation in the world. In 1993, for instance, the value of goods and services produced by each U.S. worker was $46 500. This **level of productivity** was higher than that of any other country. In second place, French and Belgian workers produced $43 700 per worker, followed by Italian workers at $42 500. Canadian workers produced $42 000.[1]

level of productivity
The dollar value of goods and services produced versus the dollar value of resources used to produce them.

growth rate of productivity
The increase in productivity in a given year over the previous year.

Slower Growth Rates.   Many Canadians are alarmed by an important trend that persisted throughout the 1980s: a slowdown in our **growth rate of productivity**—the annual increase in a nation's output over the previous year. In short, Canadian productivity has not increased as fast as it did in the past. The growth of Canadian output has also slowed in comparison with other nations. Figure 13.1 shows how fast productivity is growing in various countries. Largely because of modernized facilities and work methods, Japan and South Korea have experienced especially strong growth spurts.

Difference Between the Manufacturing and Service Sectors.   Manufacturing productivity is higher than service productivity. Thus, manufacturing is primarily responsible for recent rises in the nation's overall productivity. With services growing as a proportion of Canadian businesses, productivity *must* increase more rapidly in that sector in the years ahead if Canada is to keep its edge. The box "Suggestions for Improving Canada's International Competitiveness" gives additional ideas for productivity improvements for Canada's industry in general.

Industry Productivity

In addition to differences between the manufacturing and service sectors, industries within these sectors differ vastly in terms of productivity. Agriculture is more productive in Canada than in many other nations because we use more sophisticated technology and superior natural resources. Technological advances have also given the computer industry a productivity edge in many areas. But investment in automated equipment—and thus productivity—in the automobile and steel industries has lagged behind that of other nations.

The productivity of specific industries concerns many people for different reasons. Labor unions need to take it into account in negotiating contracts, since highly productive industries can give raises more easily than can less productive industries. Investors and suppliers consider industry productivity when making loans, buying securities, and planning their own future production. Areas that have long depended on steel and auto plants have experienced economic and social devastation as a result of plant closings, layoffs, and closings of related businesses.

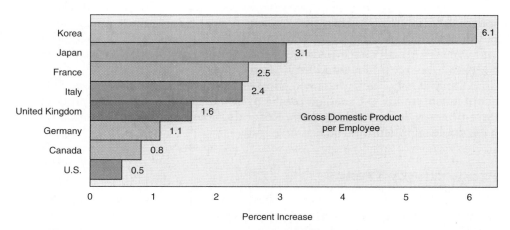

Figure 13.1
Growth in output per worker for selected countries.

International Report

SUGGESTIONS FOR IMPROVING CANADA'S INTERNATIONAL COMPETITIVENESS

In October 1991, Michael Porter, a business professor at Harvard University and an internationally recognized expert on competitiveness, released a report. In it he claims that Canada will have to stop living off its rich diet of natural resources and start emphasizing innovation and a more sophisticated mix of products if it hopes to be successful in international markets. He notes that one-third of Canada's total exports in 1989 were unprocessed or semi-processed natural resources. In other words, Canadian industry has not upgraded or extended its competitive advantage into processing technology and the marketing of more sophisticated resource-based products. The proportion of Canadian exports based on resources is higher than in many industrialized countries, including the U.S., Japan, Germany, Britain, Korea, and Sweden.

Porter points out that nostalgic thinking about the "good old days" before free trade is not productive, and that rescinding the Canada-U.S. free trade agreement will not make everything better. He says there can be no turning back and that old attitudes and practices inconsistent with international competitiveness will have to go.

The study criticizes Canadian business, government, and labor for their failure to abandon outdated ways of thinking regarding productivity and innovation. Porter makes the following recommendations to these groups:

To Business

- Compete based on innovation and cost, not simply cost.

- Concentrate on products with a lasting competitive edge.
- Spend more money on employee training.
- Finance university research to ensure that more of it is relevant.
- Base employee compensation on corporate performance.
- Stop relying on government assistance.

To Government

- Provide more training for the unemployed.
- Set higher national education standards.
- Finance university programs that are oriented toward competitiveness.
- Introduce stricter product standards to force Canadian companies to meet world product standards.
- Expand apprenticeship programs.

To Labor

- Recognize that, in the long run, the best guarantee of good wages is competitive corporate activities such as productivity enhancement programs.
- Help company management identify and remove barriers to productivity.
- Support broadening workers' skills.
- Take a more collaborative approach to union-management relations.

Company Productivity

High productivity gives a company a competitive edge because its costs are lower. As a result, it can offer its product at a lower price (and gain more customers), or it can make a greater profit on each item sold. Increased productivity also allows companies to pay workers higher wages without raising prices.

As a result, the productivity of individual companies is also important to investors, workers, and managers. Comparing the productivity of several companies in the same industry helps investors in buying and selling stocks. Employee profit-sharing plans are often based on the company's productivity improvements each year. And managers use information about productivity trends to plan for new products, factories, and funds to stay competitive in the years ahead.

Department and Individual Productivity

Within companies, managers are concerned with the productivity of various divisions, departments, workstations, and individuals. Improved productivity in any of these areas can improve a firm's overall productivity. An overemphasis on the performance of individuals and departments, however, tends to discourage working together as a team for overall company improvement. For this reason, many companies are cautious about using departmental and individual productivity measures.

Measuring Productivity

To improve productivity, we must first measure it. Otherwise, we will not be able to tell whether a program has increased productivity.

Total and Partial Measures of Productivity

Every productivity measure is a ratio of outputs to inputs. The outputs are the value of goods and services produced. The inputs are the value of the resources used to create the outputs. In selecting a productivity measure, managers must decide which inputs are most important for their business. The choice of inputs (factors) determines the specific measure.

In some cases, all inputs are equally important, so managers use a **total factor productivity ratio**, which can be expressed as

total factor productivity ratio
A measure of a firm's overall productivity calculated as outputs divided by all inputs.

$$\text{Productivity} = \frac{\text{Outputs}}{\text{Labor + Capital + Materials + Energy inputs}}$$

If an insurance company sold $10 million in policies and used $2 million of resources to do so, its total factor productivity would be 5.

Total factor measures can become complicated because of the different inputs involved. It is difficult to find comparable measures for energy consumption, capital, labor, and material. For some purposes, **partial productivity ratios**—which ignore some factors—may be best. For example, **materials productivity** (a partial productivity ratio) may be a fairly good measure of overall productivity in non-labor-intensive industries. Expenditures for equipment are also a more significant cost in many of these firms. Materials and equipment, not labor, constitute over 90 percent of operating costs in highly automated oil refineries, chemical companies, and manufacturing plants.

partial productivity ratio
A measure of a firm's overall productivity based on the productivity of its most significant input; calculated as total outputs divided by the selected input.

materials productivity
A partial productivity ratio calculated as total outputs divided by materials inputs.

$$\text{Productivity} = \frac{\text{Outputs}}{\text{Materials}}$$

If a chemical plant uses eight tonnes of chemicals to produce two tonnes of insecticide, its materials productivity is 0.25.

National Productivity Measures

labor productivity
A partial productivity ratio calculated as total outputs divided by labor inputs for a company and as gross domestic product divided by the total number of workers for a nation.

gross domestic product (GDP)
The value of all goods and services produced by an economy.

At one time, partial ratios of labor productivity were the measure typically used by most nations. A country's **labor productivity** is usually calculated as

$$\frac{\text{Gross domestic product}}{\text{Total number of workers}}$$

The total number of workers in this equation represents the nation's total labor input. (Sometimes the total hours worked, not the number of workers, is used as the input in figuring labor productivity.) **Gross domestic product (GDP)**—the value of all goods and services produced in the economy—represents the nation's total output.

An employee observes a robot's movements at a nuclear laboratory. Properly used, robots can perform dangerous tasks more safely than humans.

Labor productivity measures are popular because they are easy to calculate and compare. Most governments keep records on gross domestic product and adjust them for inflation. The resulting constant-dollar data permit reliable year-to-year comparisons of national and international productivity changes. But as labor-intensive industries become less important, other measures, such as materials productivity, capital productivity, and even total factor productivity are coming into wider use.

Sector and Industry Productivity Measures

In addition to national productivity measures, we need to determine the productivity of various sectors and industries in order to isolate and solve productivity problems.

The rise in labor productivity among manufacturing workers does not necessarily mean that they are working harder or better than service workers, whose productivity is stagnating. More often, labor productivity increases because other, nonlabor resources are added. The use of more capital—modernized trucks, machinery, and office equipment—often increases labor productivity by enabling fewer workers to accomplish more.

Is the additional capital investment worth the cost? To see, we need to look at capital productivity. **Capital productivity** is the ratio of outputs (the value of all goods and services) divided by the capital inputs for all firms.

capital productivity

A partial productivity ratio calculated as total outputs divided by capital inputs.

Company Productivity Measures

Many companies have established productivity measures for individual divisions, plants, departments, and even jobs. Goals for productivity improvements are set in the areas of greatest importance. They serve as guidelines for workplace changes and performance evaluations. For example, an automated, petroleum-fueled factory may place high priority on energy productivity. Its major goal, therefore, might be to raise the level of its sales per barrel of consumed fuel from $200 to $220. Employees would thus seek ways to conserve fuel while maintaining or increasing production and sales.

By contrast, a labor-intensive restaurant might use the dollar amount of food served per server as its main productivity measure. If it offers servers incentives to increase sales, they will encourage customers to order tempting (and highly profitable) specialties, drinks, and desserts.

Total Quality Management

It is no longer enough for businesses to simply measure productivity in terms of numbers of items produced. They must also take into account quality. But Canadian business has not always recognized the importance of quality.

In the decades after the Second World War, American business consultant W. Edwards Deming tried to persuade U.S. firms that they needed to improve quality at least as much as quantity. Like many a prophet, he was not honored in his homeland. But his arguments won over the Japanese. Through years of meticulous hard work, Japan's manufacturers have changed "Made in Japan" from a synonym for cheap, shoddy merchandise into a hallmark of reliability.

Many of the quality assurance programs that are integral to the modern Japanese production system were Deming's brainchildren. And Japan's highest honor for industrial achievement is the Deming Award for Quality. It took the economic troubles of the 1970s and 1980s for Deming's ideas to gain acceptance in Canada and the United States.

In the automobile industry in the 1980s, Japanese firms held a big lead in quality. North American manufacturers have closed that gap, but the Japanese are ahead once again in the area of customer service. Nissan, for example, has formed a Satisfaction Department that coordinates training for their 4000 Canadian dealers, salespeople, and employees. It even determines bonuses based on customer satisfaction ratings rather than sales volume.[2]

European businesses have also recognized the importance of the quality message. In 1988, executives from Olivetti, Renault, and other companies established the European Foundation for Quality Management (EFQM). The stated mission of the organization is to increase quality awareness and to promote quality in goods and services throughout European enterprise. Today, EFQM has more than 160 member companies that all face the difficult challenge of producing high-quality products and services for customers across a continent with diverse languages, cultures, and economies.

Emphasis on quality manufacturing in Canada is increasing, as is evidenced by the Gold Plant Quality Award given to the workers of Toyota's Cambridge, Ontario, plant in 1991. This award honors the plant as the top quality producer of automobiles in North America. The award is proof of Toyota's emphasis on *kaizen* (the continual search for improvement) and *jidoka* (defect detection). But there is still room for improvement. In a recent survey of consumers in 20 different countries, Canada came in sixth in the overall quality of its products. Japan was first, Germany second, and the U.S. third.[3]

The perception of quality is also important. Canadian wines are turned back at European ports because the Economic Community maintains that Canada does not have a proper quality control system for its wines. This happens despite the recent prestigious award won by Inniskillen Wines Inc. at the Bordeaux Vin Expo against more than 4000 entries.[4]

total quality management (TQM)

A concept that emphasizes that no defects are tolerable and that all employees are responsible for maintaining quality standards.

Today, many Canadian companies recognize that quality products are a must. But they have found that producing quality goods and services requires an effort from all parts of the business. **Total quality management (TQM)** emphasizes that no defects are tolerable and that employees are responsible for maintaining quality standards. At Toyota's Cambridge, Ontario, assembly plant, for example, workers can push a button or pull a rope to stop the production line when something is not up to standard.[5] The box "TQM at Standard Aero" shows how the concept was introduced at one Canadian company.

The Canadian Business Scene

TQM AT STANDARD AERO LTD.

In 1991, the U.S. Air Force visited Standard Aero in Winnipeg, Manitoba. Standard had submitted a bid to overhaul aircraft that undercut its competitors by more than 50 percent, and the Air Force wanted to see the firm's factory before it signed the contract. They must have liked what they saw, because Standard got the contract. What the Air Force didn't know was that the impetus for the bid came not from Standard's managers (who were concerned about the size of the contract), but from shop floor employees.

Standard Aero has made TQM work where other companies have failed because it is dedicated to an often overlooked tenet of TQM: the only definition of quality that really counts is "what the customer wants." Standard employees talk to customers to find out exactly what they expect from the firm's work. Top management is also committed to TQM, has spent $13 million on the program to date and has fired several top managers who would not commit to the program.

TQM became popular in the late 1980s, but has lately been greeted with increasing skepticism, with many companies being disappointed with the lack of fast results. Bob Hamaberg, CEO, says that there is nothing wrong with TQM; it has simply been applied badly in many companies.

The TQM process began at Aero in 1990 with the election of a "change council" consisting of Hamaberg and five senior managers. This council ensured that the TQM process received the money, equipment, and support necessary for success. A full-time "change manager" was appointed from within the company to make sure that the process didn't pull other managers from their regular duties.

Next, a nine-person task force was formed that consisted of employees who had done the full range of jobs on one of Standard's major overhaul contracts. Their first task was to find out what the customer wanted. To do this, the team designed a questionnaire and then visited customer plants around the world to gather information. Even though the cost of this part of the process was about $100 000, much new information was gathered and many old beliefs about customers were shattered. For example, Standard found that in spite of free trade some U.S. firms were reluctant to deal with them because of complex cross-border paperwork. So Standard now does the paperwork for the customer. As a result of these actions, the task force picked up $7 million in new business.

The task force also worked within Standard to determine exactly how the company did its aircraft overhaul work. After weeks of analysis, the team was able to reduce the flow and complexity of work dramatically. For example, one gearbox had previously required 213 steps as it moved through the plant; the task force reduced the distance travelled by 80 percent, and cut the number of times the component changed hands by 84 percent. Also, by reducing paperwork involved in tracking the item they saved the company $150 000 per year.

Training is a major feature of the TQM program. Workers receive training in technical areas like statistics and machine operation, as well as in team building. The price tag at Standard has been about $1.5 million per year. Getting workers to be enthusiastic about TQM was not easy at first. Hamaberg's pep talks were crucial in getting workers to try it.

Hamaberg says that implementing TQM has been very hard, but that the results have been impressive. The task force members worked 12 to 14 hours per day, and he was concerned that they would burn out. He also notes that you can't do TQM all at once; it must be implemented step by step because people can't handle large amounts of immediate change.

Any activity necessary for getting quality goods and services into the marketplace is a part of **quality assurance** (sometimes called quality management). Quality assurance is the management of the firm's quality efforts. Like any other management function, it involves planning, organizing, leading, and controlling.

quality assurance
Those activities necessary to get quality goods and services into the marketplace; also called quality management.

Planning for Quality

Planning for quality should begin before products are designed or redesigned. Managers need to set goals for both quality levels and quality reliability in the beginning. **Performance quality** refers to the features of a product and how well it performs. For example, Maytag gets a price premium because its washers and dryers offer a high level of performance quality. Customers perceive Maytags as having more advanced features and being more durable than other brands. (Everyone knows that the Maytag repairman is a lonely and idle person.)

performance quality
The overall degree of quality; how well the features of a product meet consumers' needs and how well the product performs.

quality reliability
The consistency of quality from unit to unit of a product.

Performance quality may or may not be related to quality reliability in a product. **Quality reliability** refers to the consistency or repeatability of performance. Toyota's small cars may not equal the overall quality level or have the luxury features of Rolls Royce; consequently, Toyota's prices are much lower. But Toyotas have high quality reliability. The firm has a reputation for producing very few "lemons."

Some products offer both high quality reliability and high performance quality. Kellogg has a reputation for consistent production of cereals made of good-quality ingredients. To achieve any form of high quality, however, managers must plan for production processes—equipment, methods, worker skills, and materials—that will result in quality products, as discussed in Chapter 11.

Organizing for Quality

Perhaps most important to the quality concept is the belief that producing quality goods and services requires an effort from all parts of the organization. The old idea of a separate "quality control" department is no longer enough. Everyone from the chairperson of the board to the part-time clerk—purchasers, engineers, janitors, marketers, machinists, and other personnel—must work to assure quality. In Germany's Messerschmitt-Boelkow-Blohm aerospace company, for example, all employees are responsible for inspecting their own work. The overall goal is to reduce eventual problems to a minimum by making the product right from the beginning. The same principle extends to teamwork practice at Heinz Co., where teams of workers are assigned to inspect virtually every activity in the company. Heinz has realized substantial cost savings by eliminating waste and rework.

At Motorola, the concept of teamwork as a key to organizational quality has resulted in an international event called the Total Customer Satisfaction Team Competition. Teams are composed of Motorola employees and also include customers and outside suppliers. Teams are judged on their success not only in promoting productivity but in sharing innovative ideas with people both inside and outside the company.

Although everyone in a company contributes to product quality, responsibility for specific aspects of total quality management is often assigned to specific departments and jobs. In fact, many companies have quality assurance, or quality control, departments staffed by quality experts. These people may be called in to help solve quality-related problems in any of the firm's other departments. They keep other departments informed of the latest developments in equipment and methods for maintaining quality. In addition, they monitor all quality control activities to identify areas for improvement.

Leading for Quality

quality ownership
The concept that quality belongs to each employee who creates or destroys it in producing a good or service; the idea that all workers must take responsibility for producing a quality product.

Too often, firms fail to take the initiative to make quality happen. Leading for quality means that managers must inspire and motivate employees throughout the company to achieve quality goals. They need to help employees see how they affect quality and how quality affects their jobs and their company. Leaders must continually find ways to foster a quality orientation by training employees, encouraging their involvement and tying wages to quality of work. If managers succeed, employees will ultimately accept **quality ownership**—the idea that quality belongs to each person who creates or destroys it while performing a job.

Controlling for Quality

By monitoring its products and services, a company can detect mistakes and make corrections. To do so, however, managers must first establish specific quality standards and measurements. Consider the following control system for a bank's teller services. Observant supervisors periodically evaluate transactions against a checklist. Specific aspects of each teller's work—appearance, courtesy, efficiency, and so on—are recorded. The results, reviewed with employees, either confirm proper performance or indicate changes that are needed to bring performance up to standards.

Tools for Quality Assurance

In managing for quality, many leading companies rely on assistance from proven tools. Often, ideas for improving both the product and the production process come from *competitive product analysis*. For example, Toshiba will take apart a Xerox photocopier and test each component. Test results help Toshiba's managers decide which Toshiba product features are satisfactory (in comparison to the competition), which product features need to be upgraded, or whether Toshiba's production processes need improvement.

Methods such as value-added analysis, statistical process control, quality/cost studies, quality circles, benchmarking, cause-and-effect diagrams, ISO 9000, and re-engineering provide different routes to quality. Each of these approaches is discussed briefly below.

Value-Added Analysis

One effective method of improving quality and productivity is **value-added analysis**: the evaluation of all work activities, materials flows, and paperwork to determine the value that they add for customers. Value-added analysis often reveals wasteful or unnecessary activities that can be eliminated without

value-added analysis
The evaluation of all work activities, material flows, and paperwork to determine the value they add for customers.

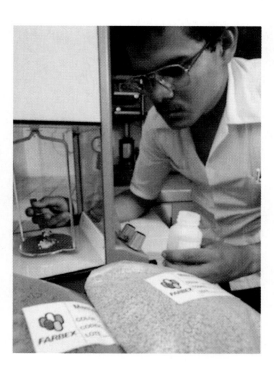

The quality control analyst at this plastics manufacturer is checking the weight of a sample of plastic pellets during the production process.

harming (and even improving) customer service. When Hewlett-Packard, for example, simplified its contracts and reduced them from 20 pages to as few as two pages for all customers, computer sales rose by more than 18 percent.

Statistical Process Control

statistical process control (SPC)

Statistical analysis techniques that allow managers to analyze variations in production data and to detect when adjustments are needed to create products with high quality reliability.

process variation

Any change in employees, materials, work methods, or equipment that affects output quality.

process capability study

A statistical process control method in which samples of the product are measured to determine the amount of process variation; shows the outputs' conformity with or deviation from specification limits.

specification limits

Limits defining acceptable and unacceptable quality in production of a good or service.

Every business experiences unit-to-unit variations in its products and services. Although every company would like complete uniformity in its outputs, this is an impossible quest. Companies can gain better control, however, by understanding the sources of variation. **Statistical process control (SPC)** methods—especially process variation studies and control charts—allow managers to analyze variations in production data.

Process Variation.   Variations in a firm's products may arise from the inputs in its production process. As people, materials, work methods, and equipment change, so do production outputs. While some amount of **process variation** is acceptable, too much can result in poor quality and excessive operating costs.

Consider the box-filling operation for Honey Nuggets cereal. Each automated machine fills two 400 gram boxes per second. Even under proper conditions, slight variations in cereal weight from box to box are normal. Equipment and tools wear out, the cereal may be overly moist, machinists make occasional adjustments. But how much variation is occurring? How much is acceptable?

Information about variation in a process can be obtained from a **process capability study.** Boxes are taken from the filling machines and weighed. The results are plotted, as in Figure 13.2, and compared with the upper and lower **specification limits** (quality limits) for weight. These limits define good and bad quality for box filling. Boxes with over 410 grams are a wasteful "giveaway." Underfilling has a cost because it is unlawful.

Looking at the results of the capability study, we see that none of machine A's output violates the quality limits. In fact, most of the boxes from

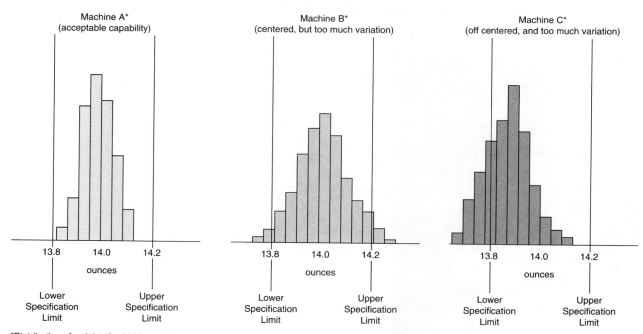

*Distribution of weights for 500 boxes from each machine

Figure 13.2
Process variation in box-filling for Honey Nuggets Cereal.

machine A are very close to the desired weight of 400 grams. In Figure 13.2, the shape of machine A's graph, high at the center and dropping sharply at the margins, is typical of many production processes. Machine A, then, is fully capable of meeting the company's quality standards.

But machines B and C have problems. In their present condition, they are "not capable." They cannot reliably meet Honey Nuggets' quality standards. The company must take special—and costly—actions to sort the good from the bad boxes before releasing the cereal for shipment. Unless machines B and C are renovated, substandard production quality will plague Honey Nuggets.

Control Charts.   Knowing that a process is capable of meeting quality standards is not enough. Managers must still monitor the process to prevent its drifting astray during production. To detect the beginning of bad conditions, managers can check production periodically and plot the results on a **control chart**. For example, several times a day a machine operator at Honey Nuggets might weigh several boxes of cereal together to ascertain the average weight.

Figure 13.3 shows the control chart for machine A, in which the first five points are randomly scattered around the center line, indicating that the machine was operating well. However, the points for samples 5 through 8 are all above the center line, indicating that something was causing the boxes to overfill. The last point falls outside the upper **control limit**, confirming that the process is out of control.

At this point, the machine must be shut down so that a manager and/or the operator can investigate what is causing the problem—equipment, people, materials, or work methods. Control is completed by correcting the problem and restoring the process to normal.

control chart

A statistical process control method in which results of test sampling of a product are plotted on a diagram that reveals when the process is beginning to depart from normal operating conditions.

control limit

The critical value on a control chart that indicates the level at which quality deviation is sufficiently unacceptable to merit investigation.

Quality/Cost Studies for Quality Improvement

Statistical process controls help keep operations up to *existing* capabilities. But in today's competitive environment, firms must consistently *raise* quality capabilities. Any improvement in products or production processes means additional costs, however, whether for new facilities, equipment, training, or other changes. Managers thus face the challenge of identifying those

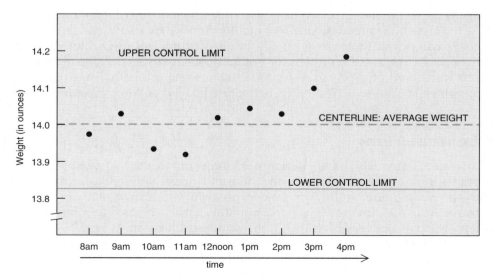

Figure 13.3
Honey Nuggets Cereal process control chart for machine A.

quality/cost study

A method of improving product quality by assessing a firm's current quality-related costs and identifying areas with the greatest cost-saving potential.

internal failures

Expenses incurred during production and before bad product leaves the plant.

external failures

Allowing defective products to leave the factory and get into consumers' hands.

improvements that offer the greatest promise. **Quality/cost studies** are useful because they not only identify a firm's current costs but also reveal areas with the largest cost-savings potential.

Quality costs are associated with making, finding, repairing, or preventing defective goods and services. All of these costs should be analyzed in a quality/cost study. For example, Honey Nuggets must determine its costs for **internal failures**. These are expenses—including the costs of overfilling boxes and the costs of sorting out bad boxes—incurred during production and before bad products leave the plant. Studies indicate that many manufacturers incur very high costs for internal failures—up to 50 percent of total costs.

Despite quality control procedures, however, some bad boxes may get out of the factory, reach the customer, and generate complaints from grocers and cereal eaters. These are **external failures** that occur outside the factory. The costs of correcting them—refunds to customers, transportation costs to return bad boxes to the factory, possible lawsuits, factory recalls—should also be tabulated in the quality/cost study.

The percentage of costs in the different categories varies widely from company to company. Thus every firm must conduct systematic quality/cost studies to identify the most costly—and often the most vital—areas of its operations. Not surprisingly, these areas should be targets for improvement. Too often, however, firms substitute hunches and guesswork for data and analysis.

Quality Circles

quality circle

A technique for maximizing quality of production by grouping employees into small teams who define, analyze, and solve quality and other process-related problems within their area.

As we noted in Chapter 11, one proven technique for improving quality is the use of **quality circles**, groups of employees who work in teams to improve their job environment. Meeting on company time in the facility, quality circles are a forum for quality improvement. Although the format varies in different companies, circle members are deeply involved in initiating changes in their work environment.

Quality circles organize their own efforts, choose a leader, and establish rules for discussion. Within the group, members identify aspects of their jobs that pose problems or are barriers to better quality and overall productivity. They gather data to evaluate the severity of problems and to identify improvement projects. The group's problem solving emphasizes brainstorming, group discussions, and tools such as process capability studies and cost analysis. Ultimately, the circle makes recommendations to management, identifying expected benefits, costs, and implementation timetables.

Perhaps the greatest benefit of quality circles, however, is not any direct cost savings, but their effect on employees' attitudes. Rather than viewing themselves as passive resources for production, employees develop a sense of self-worth and quality ownership. The talents and job knowledge of circle members are put to active, constructive use instead of lying dormant.

Benchmarking

benchmarking

Comparing the quality of the firm's output with the quality of the output of the industry's leaders.

An organization which uses **benchmarking** compares the quality of its output with the quality produced by the industry leaders. If differences are noted, the firm can figure out how the leaders are achieving their quality levels and then pursue the same strategy. Benchmarking can also be used to compare different departments or divisions in the same organization.

When Canon copiers first were sold in North America, they were priced below what it cost Xerox to make them. Canon could do this because it was far more efficient than Xerox. Xerox then embarked on a benchmarking exercise in order to regain its position as the most important company in the copier market. By using what it had learned about how other companies were making copiers, Xerox was able to cut its unit production cost in half and increase sales by 50 percent.[6]

Cause-and-Effect Diagrams

A **cause-and-effect diagram** summarizes the four possible causes of quality problems—materials, manpower, methods, and machines. For example, if car bodies are being produced with rippled paint, the problem might be thin paint (materials), poor training (manpower), a defective sprayer (machines), or a layer of paint that is too thick (methods). The cause-and-effect diagram is used to identify the source(s) of the problem. Once the source is identified, actions can be taken to resolve the problem.

cause-and-effect diagram
Summarizes the four possible causes of quality problems—materials, manpower, methods, and machines.

ISO 9000

The International Standards Organization in Geneva, Switzerland has developed a quality "scorecard" that is fast becoming a prerequisite for selling to the European Community. The aim of **ISO 9000** (pronounced ICE-O 9000) is to find the cause of product defects at the production line level. The North American automobile industry adopted the standard in 1994 in order to measure the performance of its suppliers. After Toronto Plastics was awarded the designation, defects fell to 15 000 part per million, down from 150 000 parts per million. About 600 Canadian firms have received the designation.[7] More information is contained in the box "ISO 9000: Seeking the Standard in Quality."

ISO 9000
A quality scorecard developed by the International Standards Organization.

International Report

ISO 9000: SEEKING THE STANDARD IN QUALITY

ISO 9000 standards enable firms to demonstrate that they follow documented procedures for testing products, training workers, keeping records, and fixing product defects. To become certified, companies must document the procedures that workers follow during every stage of production. They must also show that they have incorporated mechanisms to ensure that workers actually follow accepted practices. Not surprisingly, this approach leads to more reliable products with fewer defects. The purpose of ISO 9000 is "to ensure that a manufacturer's product is exactly the same today as it was yesterday, as it will be tomorrow." The goal of standardization is to guarantee that "goods will be produced at the same level of quality even if all the employees were replaced by a new set of workers."

Companies seeking ISO 9000 certification are audited by an elite group of quality-systems "registrars." These registrars focus on 20 different functions including design control, contract review, purchasing, inspection and testing, and training. For example, to pass order-processing requirements, a company must demonstrate procedures for guaranteeing on-time deliveries. Not surprisingly, the certification process is time-consuming and costly—it can take up to 18 months for a manufacturing plant employing 300 workers and cost more than $200 000.

Despite the interest in ISO 9000, however, it is not a cure-all for quality ailments. On the contrary, certification standards have little to do with customer satisfaction. Instead of imposing guarantee procedures, they focus on documenting a company's commitment to its *own* procedures. "With ISO 9000 you can still have terrible processes and products," complains Richard Buetow, director of corporate quality at Motorola. "You can certify a manufacturer that makes life jackets from concrete," says Buetow, "as long as those jackets are made according to the documented procedures and the company provides the next of kin with instructions on how to complain about defects. That's absurd."

Re-engineering

re-engineering
The process of rethinking and redesigning business processes in order to achieve dramatic improvements in productivity and quality.

Re-engineering is the process of rethinking and redesigning business processes in order to achieve dramatic improvements in productivity and quality. In effect, those engaged in re-engineering ask, "If this were a new company, how would we run it?" The bottom line in every re-engineering process is redesigning systems to better serve the needs of customers.

A re-engineering process at IBM Credit Corp., a financing subsidiary of IBM, is typical. The firm exists to provide a service—financing computers and software. But each financing request had to go through a cumbersome series of steps, even though most customers needed an immediate answer. After two managers decided to "walk through" a typical request, they discovered that the actual approval work took only 90 minutes. The rest of the time was spent shuffling forms around between the various people who worked on the process. Their solution was to put one person in charge of all the steps. The result? A hundredfold increase in the number of requests handled.[8]

Re-engineering is also underway at Novacor Chemicals in Sarnia. Over the past 10 years, the company acquired four different businesses, each with its own style, technology, and processes. It is now rethinking how it produces about two million tonnes of petrochemicals each year. In the process, it is finding that it can save millions of dollars by having the four businesses operate in a coordinated fashion rather than as separate entities. For example, when plants were shut down for maintenance, each one hired its own maintenance teams. Now, one team is hired and rotated among the four plants.[9]

Competing Through Productivity and Quality

While tools such as quality circles can help a firm improve product quality, they can enhance a company's ability to compete only when coupled with attention to all aspects of productivity. Both productivity and quality begin with attention to customers' needs. Also important are management's willingness to invest in innovation, its time perspective, its concern for quality of work life, how well it can streamline its service operations, and the size of the company.

Get Closer to the Customer

Many decaying businesses have lost sight of customers as the driving force for all business activity. With misplaced intentions, they waste resources designing products customers do not want. They ignore customers' reactions to existing products. They fail to keep up with changing consumer tastes, or they go beyond consumers' tastes. In contrast, the most successful businesses keep close to their customers and know what they want in the products they consume.

At Greyhound Lines of Canada, marketing and operations vice-president John Munro wanted to make a point about the importance of clean restrooms to customers. He warned regional managers that he would visit bus depots on one hour's notice to see if the restrooms were clean enough to eat dinner in them. Within weeks, photos of regional managers having dinner in the spotless restrooms began pouring into Munro's office.[10]

Invest in Innovation and Technology

Once companies know what their customers want, managers must find efficient ways to produce it. As we saw in Chapter 3, investment in research and development in Canada has lagged behind that in Europe and Japan. Rather than creating new products, more and more companies are choosing to copy innovations and market similar products to save innovation costs. Firms that have continued to invest in truly innovative technology have kept their productivity rising, along with their incomes. But firms that have merely copied the automation they see others using have not been as productive.[10]

Adopt a Long-Run Perspective

Part of the decline in innovation among Canadian firms reflects a common short-run perspective. Shareholders prefer short- and intermediate-term (less than five years), "sure thing" paybacks. Many companies reward managers with salaries and bonuses based on their quarterly or yearly performance. With owners and managers unwilling to wait for financial returns, many buildings, tools, and equipment have become old or obsolete. Canada is still a creative hothouse, but many businesses are shying away from long-term risks and are failing to convert their good new ideas into actual products.

By contrast, instead of emphasizing short-run results, many quality-oriented firms are committed to a long-run perspective for **continuous improvement**— the ongoing commitment to improving products and processes, step by step, in pursuit of ever-increasing customer satisfaction. Motorola is a good example of a company that emphasizes continuous, long-run improvement. In 1981, the firm adopted a five-year goal of a tenfold reduction of errors. In 1986, it extended that goal to a hundredfold reduction or errors by 1992. Despite initial hopes, however, Motorola missed its goal for 1992: At the start of that year, defects still ran at 40 per one million parts. Motorola managers had to be satisfied

continuous improvement
The ongoing commitment to improve products and processes, step by step, in pursuit of ever-increasing customer satisfaction.

Operators at Dofasco monitor the production of steel products with the latest in high technology monitoring devices.

with the reminder that five years earlier, the defect rate had been 6000 per one million parts. Moreover, Motorola continues to plan for still greater improvement. By 2001, say company officials, Motorola quality will be an unimaginable 1 defect per one *billion* parts. The focus on continuous improvement at another company is described in the box "SABRE-Toothed Tiger of the Skies."

Emphasize Quality-of-Work-Life Factors

Positive employee attitudes in small businesses have certainly made productivity growth better than it would otherwise have been. But big corporations represent so large a part of total national output that the reactions of their workers are central to improving productivity. Large firms can make their employees' jobs more challenging and interesting by enhancing their workers' physical and mental health through recreational facilities, counseling services, and other programs.

International Report

SABRE-TOOTHED TIGER OF THE SKIES

SABRE is the computerized reservation service of American Airlines. Most Canadians first heard about it when American Airlines offered to invest $246 million in troubled Canadian Airlines International if CAI would become part of SABRE. However, CAI was already a partner with Air Canada in the Gemini reservation system; therefore, it needed approval to join SABRE because doing so would doom Gemini.

SABRE has over 85 000 terminals in 47 countries. It allows travel agents to make reservations on virtually any airline and to book hotel rooms, rental cars, and even theatre tickets in many places. The system is just the latest development in American's ongoing dedication to continuous improvement.

The system got its start in the late 1950s, when reservations for American's flights exceeded the old system's (file cards and blackboards) capacity to handle them. By 1963, the original SABRE was in place, handling 85 000 phone calls, 40 000 confirmed reservations, and 20 000 ticket sales in its first year. (Today the system handles nearly 2000 messages *per second* during peak season.) By keeping track of passengers and passenger miles, SABRE also enabled American to launch the first comprehensive "frequent flier" program in the industry. By the mid-1970s, the system was also tracking spare parts, scheduling crews, and developing flight plans. In addition, the system enables the firm to maximize its revenues by shifting fares on each flight as necessary.

In 1976, SABRE moved beyond American's offices and into the offices of travel agents, enabling them not only to make reservations instantly but also to provide their clients with seat assignments (and even boarding passes) prior to their flights. Before SABRE, less than 40 percent of airline tickets were booked through travel agents. Today 80 percent are. On an average day, 40 000 new or changed fares are entered into the system. When "fare wars" break out, that number zooms to 1.5 million per day!

American continued to make changes in SABRE throughout the 1980s. Some of these changes, such as making the screen formats of all airlines' listings the same so that American was not unfairly favored, were the result of government regulations. But other changes—especially American's decision to sell copies of its software programs to anyone interested in buying them—came from within. Why? As the cost of developing and refining such software has risen, American wants to recoup some of its investment as quickly as possible. Moreover, the firm is convinced that it will still have an edge on its competition because it is better at interpreting and using the information that SABRE provides.

What lies ahead? Continued expansion worldwide is likely. But computer experts at American also argue that the current centralized system must be decentralized and that the system's reliance on the mainframe computer must be reduced if the system is to grow. American has also joined with a variety of other firms in the travel industry to create InterAAct, a system designed to list hotel and rental car options as methodically and comprehensively as SABRE does airline seats. If it succeeds, American will have another weapon against the competition.

Many firms are replacing the environments of yesterday, based on management-directed mass production, with worker-oriented environments that foster loyalty, teamwork, and commitment. Firms using this approach have found success in the concept of **employee empowerment**: the principle that all employees are valuable contributors to a business and should be entrusted with certain decisions regarding their work. Such confidence in employee involvement contrasts sharply with the traditional belief that managers are the primary source of decision making and problem solving.

employee empowerment
Principle that all employees are valuable contributors to business and should be entrusted with certain decisions regarding their work.

Employee Training.   For employee involvement to be effective, it must be implemented with preparation and intelligence. Training is one of the proven methods for avoiding judgments and actions that can lead to impaired rather than improved performance. In a recent survey, for example, insufficient training was the most-mentioned barrier encountered by work teams.

Improve the Service Sector

As important as employee attitude is to goods production, it is even more crucial to service production, since employees often *are* the service. The service sector has grown rapidly but this growth has often come at a cost of high inefficiency. Many newly created service jobs have not been streamlined. Some companies operate effectively, but many others are very inefficient, dragging down overall productivity. As new companies enter these markets, however, the increased need to compete should eventually force service producers to operate more productively.

Quality begins with listening to customers in order to determine what services they want. Companies in the temporary-services industry, for example, have long emphasized the needs of clients for clerical and light-industrial employees. More recently, however, temp services have realized the need for high-skilled, specialized temps like nurses, accountants, and scientists.

In trying to offer more satisfactory services, many providers have discovered five criteria that customers use to judge service quality:[12]

- *Reliability*: Perform the service as promised, both accurately and on time.
- *Responsiveness*: Be willing to help customers promptly.
- *Assurance*: Maintain knowledgeable and courteous employees who will earn the trust and confidence of customers.
- *Empathy*: Provide caring, individualized attention to customers.
- *Tangibles*: Maintain a pleasing appearance of personnel, materials, and facilities.

Smaller Can Be Better than Bigger

One bright spot in the productivity picture is small business. Many giant corporations have found themselves overextended. One department does not know what another is doing. Unnecessary duplication leads to wasted resources. By offering their customers higher product quality and tailored services, smaller companies have improved their overall productivity and have become more competitive.

In terms of job satisfaction, small businesses offer features that large ones cannot. Employees in small firms lag well behind their corporate counterparts in pay and benefits. But small companies offer employees more challenging, interesting work than do big firms. They give their employees more respect and greater chances of having their ideas adopted.

Summary of Key Points

Productivity is a measure of economic performance. It is a ratio of the amount produced relative to the resources used to produce it. Quality is a product's fitness for use. Competition in today's business world demands both productivity and quality.

Although the United States has the world's highest productivity (and Canada is close behind), other nations are closing the gap. The service sector is slowing the nation's productivity growth, while manufacturing's productivity is increasing. In addition, certain industries, companies, departments, and individuals are less productive than others.

Total factor productivity is a complex measurement. It includes all four types of input resources—labor, capital, materials, and energy. Partial productivity ratios use fewer input factors. Labor productivity is the most often used national productivity measure. Each company can develop its own measurements for partial and total productivity.

Quality assurance is the management (planning, organizing, leading, and controlling) of all the activities needed to get quality goods and services into the marketplace. It requires managers to set goals for and implement the performance quality and reliability of products. Statistical tools such as process capability studies and control charts can keep quality at an even level. Quality/cost studies, which identify potential savings, can help firms improve quality. Quality circles can also improve operations by more fully involving employees. Benchmarking allows an organization to compare the quality of its output with that of industry leaders and thereby determine whether improvements are needed. When specific problems emerge, cause-and-effect diagrams can be used to identify their sources. Another tool for identifying product defects at the production-line level is ISO 9000. Re-engineering is the process of rethinking and redesigning business processes in order to improve productivity and quality.

Among the lessons for increasing productivity, none is more important than staying close to customers, to better know their needs. Patience is required to reap the long-run potential rewards from investments in innovation and technology. Many smaller businesses have succeeded because they provide quality service and job satisfaction. Larger companies now are also putting greater emphasis on the quality of work life. Satisfied, motivated employees will be especially important in increasing productivity in the fast-growing service sector.

Jacking Up Quality and Competitiveness

Seeburn Metal Products Ltd. makes 34 models of scissor and vertical screw car jacks. In fact, it sells 43 percent of all jacks that go into cars that are assembled in North America. Sales in 1993 were $54 million and are expected to increase to $125 million by the end of the decade. The company has two manufacturing plants in Canada, and it is building a plant in Mexico that will take the place of a joint venture it formerly operated there. The key factor in the company's success is its strategy of making steady, incremental improvements in efficiency.

Making big changes all at once is not the Seeburn way. Rather, the company achieves higher productivity by adopting new technologies at a pace determined by workers' abilities to deal with them. Thousands of little changes have been made in the way things are done, and it is the sum of all these little changes that counts. This approach has led to productivity increases of 8 percent each year for the last five years.

Seeburn landed its first order for jacks from Toyota in 1987. That company's legendary emphasis on defect-free products made Seeburn adopt its new approach to continuous improvement of operations. Exports to Japan are growing rapidly, from 80 000 units in 1987 to 450 000 in 1993. The level could rise to over 800 000 units within a year or two. Over the past three years, the company has missed no deliveries to Japan, and no faulty parts have been shipped.

But Seeburn has bought into the Japanese management system only selectively. When the company received Toyota's first order, they almost built an entirely new plant to produce the jacks. But they ended up not building the plant, deciding instead to institute a new corporate culture based on a desire to eliminate waste and reduce costs. That led to numerous small changes that, when added together, have resulted in a major change in the way the company does business.

These changes include things like paying workers bonuses for not missing shifts (absenteeism is down from 4.3 percent to 1.5 percent as a result), better organization of start-up work on each shift so time is not wasted (set up times have been reduced from two-and-a-half days to two-and-a-half hours), and getting new work clothes for employees (paid for by the company). The company has not spent money on building new plants, and it has made no premature investment in Japanese-style inventory management systems. It has adopted the Japanese "pull" system, where inventory arrives at a work station just-in-time for when it is needed and not before.

CASE QUESTIONS

1. Contrast Seeburn's approach of incremental change with the alternate approach of building an entirely new state-of-the-art manufacturing plant. What are the advantages and disadvantages of each approach?
2. How has selling products in Japan affected Seeburn Metal Products?
3. To what extent has Seeburn adopted the suggestions for competitiveness that were made by Michael Porter?
4. Which of the techniques for improving quality that were discussed in this chapter could be useful at Seeburn? ◆

The Last Picture Show

The last cathode ray tube (CRT) manufacturing plant in Canada is in Midland, Ontario. Like many other manufacturing plants, it has had rough going in the last few years—high product defect rates, strained labor relations, increased global competition, price wars, and a threatened plant closure. But the plant is still operating, thanks to a combination of Japanese management, Canadian engineering, and perseverance.

The plant is owned by Mitsubishi Electronics Industries Canada Inc., which ships almost half its output to television assembly plants in Japan because the CRTs can be made cheaper in Canada than in Japan. But it wasn't always so. After Mitsubishi bought the plant in 1983, it embarked on a relentless pursuit of increased quality through automation and computerization. Because the plant was able to make far more CRTs than the Canadian market needed, the decision was made to ship tubes to Japan.

But reality soon hit home. When the Japanese plant rejected nearly a third of the Canadian plant's first shipment, management knew it had to make major changes in the way the plant operated. It decided that the top priority had to be the detection of defects *before* they left the plant. Assembly processes were therefore revised to prevent defects in the first place.

All of this required some high-powered new technology which the plant decided to purchase locally. To "align" a tube, for example, the CRTs three electron guns must be aimed precisely at the tube's red, green, and blue phosphor dots. Formerly, workers walked around each tube with a microscope to do the aligning, which was very time-consuming. Now, a computer monitor is used to do the job, and it takes only a fraction of the time. The plant also uses robots to unload TV screen assemblies. Reduced handling has saved more than $500 000 per year.

As a result of many changes, defect rates have fallen ten-fold since Mitsubishi took over the plant; production has nearly doubled, even though the plant now employs only half as many workers as it used to. The plant expects to turn its first profit in 1995.

But problems remain. Relations with the union are tense, partly because of the Japanese philosophy of *kaizen* (doing more with less). Recently the plant moved to a continuous operation with two 12-hour shifts each day, seven days a week. Union representatives say this has caused lower morale and an increase in repetitive strain injuries. Workers feel that the Japanese model has been imposed on them, except that workers are not allowed any input about operations.

CASE QUESTIONS

1. What are some reasons that a firm may not pursue quality in it products?
2. What difficulties has the Midland plant experienced as it pursues higher quality? Why has it experienced these problems?
3. How are productivity and quality related at this company?

◆

Key Terms

productivity
quality
level of productivity
growth rate of
  productivity
total factor productivity
  ratio
partial productivity ratio
materials productivity
labor productivity

gross domestic product
  (GDP)
capital productivity
total quality
  management (TQM)
quality assurance
performance quality
quality reliability
quality ownership
value-added analysis

statistical process
  control (SPC)
process variation
process capability study
specification limits
control chart
control limit
quality/cost studies
internal failures
external failures

quality circles
benchmarking
cause-and-effect
  diagram
ISO 9000
re-engineering
continuous
  improvement
employee empowerment

Study Questions and Exercises

Review Questions

1. What is the connection (relationship) between productivity and quality?
2. Why do labor unions care about the productivity of an industry?
3. How do total factor productivity ratios differ from partial factor ratios?
4. What activities are involved in quality assurance?
5. How do the purposes of statistical process controls and quality/cost studies differ?

Analysis Questions

6. How would you suggest the service sector increase productivity?
7. Some people argue that, while quality circles work well in Japan, Canadians lack the team orientation and management-labor trust to make them viable here. Do you agree or disagree? Why?

Application Exercises

8. Using a local company as an example, show how you would conduct a quality/cost study. Identify the cost categories and give some examples of costs in each category. Which categories do you expect will have the most and least costs? Why?
9. Select a company of interest to you and analyze it for productivity and quality improvements. Which of the "six suggestions for competing" detailed in the chapter apply to this company? What additional suggestions would you make to help this company improve its overall productivity?

Building Your Business Skills

Goal

To encourage students to evaluate the quality of the different goods and services they buy and to suggest ways to improve low-quality products.

Method

Step 1:

Working alone, think of a high-quality good and a high-quality service that you purchased recently. Then think of a good and a service with lesser quality. In each case, define the specific characteristics that led to your positive or negative assessment.

Step 2:

As a class, divide into groups of four or five and discuss your assessments. Where appropriate, try to focus on the following issues:

■ product reliability
■ process variation
■ customer service

Analysis

Choose one low-quality good and one low-quality service and analyze ways in which the following factors might be used to improve the final product. Some research may be needed to complete the analysis:

■ New production technologies: Can new or different technologies make a difference in product quality?
■ Improved quality of work life: Can an improved working environment improve employee performance and, ultimately, the quality of a good or service?

Follow-Up Questions

1. Is it possible for one consumer to consider a product to be of high quality and another to consider the same product inferior? What factors might be responsible for these differing perspectives?
2. Is it always in a firm's best interest to continue pursuing quality improvements?

DEVELOPING PRODUCTION EXPERTISE AT SAMSUNG

Samsung Group is South Korea's largest *chaebol* (conglomerate), with 1993 sales of $51 billion. Shares of Samsung Electronics stock increased over 200 percent during 1994. Technological expertise and rapid growth pushed Samsung Electronics to the top of the 1994 "Review 200" survey of Asia's leading companies headquartered in South Korea.

The electronics industry will enjoy strong growth in 1995. Total exports of electronic parts, industrial electronics, and consumer appliances from South Korea are expected to reach $35 billion in 1995; this accounts for more than one third of South Korea's total export goal of $105 billion.

Samsung was founded by Lee Byung-chull in 1938. It originally milled flour, brewed beer, and exported dried fish. By the end of the Korean War, Lee had stopped milling flour and exporting fish. He kept the brewery going and used profits from it to set up a sugar refinery. During the 1960s, Samsung started producing paper, fertilizer, and electronics; it also entered the retailing and insurance industries. In the 1970s and 1980s, profits came first from petrochemicals and construction and later from high-tech companies like aerospace, computers, genetic engineering, and semiconductors. In 1994 the company began producing automobiles, despite vehement protests from Hyundai and other South Korean producers.

Lee died in 1988 and the company is now headed by his son Lee Kun-hee. He acknowledges the difficulty of filling his father's shoes, but he is determined to keep the company headed into the future. He has introduced sweeping management innovations, ranging from changed office hours to a campaign for zero-defect production. Some of Lee's ideas are commonsensical—the need for globalization and quality products—and some are quirky—the idea that Samsung should develop its own language so that people outside the company do not understand it.

It has been a long road to Samsung's current position of power and influence. Consider the story of how Samsung developed its first microwave oven. The year was 1976, the place was Samsung's manufacturing facility in Suwon, Korea, and the situation was grim. Yun Soo Chu, a young engineer whose only previous assignment had been a failed attempt to create an electric skillet, received a new directive: develop a microwave oven. At the time, the market was about 2.2 million ovens a year, with Japanese ovens accounting for about a quarter of those sales.

No one in Korea had ever successfully built a microwave oven. Chu knew nothing much about microwaves. His "laboratory" was less well equipped than a high school science room. Nevertheless, he was determined to succeed. He began by ordering existing models from other companies and taking them apart. Although he remained mystified by the magnetron tube that generated the microwaves, he continued to tinker. After a year of 80-hour weeks, Chu had his first prototype—an awkward contraption held together by caulk and utilizing a Japanese-made magnetron tube. But when he turned it on, the plastic interior melted. His second microwave fared little better.

Despite these setbacks, neither Chu nor his superiors gave up. In June 1978, with the world market grown to 4 million microwave ovens a year, Chu finally got a model to run without melting. Although they knew the prototype was probably too crude to sell, Samsung managers set up a production line in case they were wrong. This decision underscores an ironclad corporate rule: NEVER keep the customer waiting.

The first week, the new production line turned out only one oven a day. By the end of the first year, total production was just under 1500 ovens. Five million microwave ovens were sold that year—none of them made by Samsung. Still, the firm's management persisted. Then, in 1979, things began to pick up. The firm got an order from Panama. With only 240 ovens ordered, Samsung would lose money on each one, but managers in Korea were ecstatic. Here was a chance to learn first-hand what customers did and didn't like about the unit and fine-tune it before moving on to bigger markets. Unlike most manufacturers, Samsung was more than ready to produce different ovens for different markets to please customers.

This willingness to adapt earned Samsung its breakthrough in 1980: an order from J.C. Penney in the United States. Penney wanted only a few thousand ovens. It needed to price them at $299. Hardest of all, its specifications meant that Chu and his team would have to design a whole new oven. Again, there was no hope of making money on the deal, but Samsung's managers eagerly agreed to supply the ovens anyway. Thanks to the support of the Korean government, they were also able to promise Chu the funds he needed.

With the expansion of production necessitated by Penney's order, Chu's boss, Kyung Pal Park, played a larger role. His first task was to set up a production team. To this team he gave only one absolute rule: it must make every delivery on time, not even one day late. Park's chief lieutenant, I.J. Jang, a production engineer, worked with members of the team and traveled across the globe to analyze the best features of competing microwaves and to hire outside vendors to complete some work. With the first delivery date just a few months away, the production "line" was still just an empty room. To meet their deadline, Park, Jang, Chu, and the other members of the team worked to produce units all day, then spent half the night ironing out the bugs. Producing 1500 ovens per month, they managed to make the delivery to Penney's on time.

No sooner had they made the first delivery than Penney's placed another order—this time for 5000 microwave ovens in a single month. That order filled, Penney's asked for 7000 more microwaves. Jubilant Samsung managers were only too happy to add more production lines to meet this demand. In 1982, Samsung produced 200 000 microwave ovens.

As Japanese microwave manufacturers continued to pare their prices—and thus Samsung's edge—Samsung managers began looking for ways to cut their costs. Far and away the most expensive component of the microwave was the magnetron tube. At the time, only two companies in the world made magnetron tubes: one in Japan and Amperex in the U.S. The Japanese firm refused to sell technical assistance to Samsung, and Amperex was folding, unable to compete with the Japanese. To Samsung's managers, the answer was clear: they bought every piece of Amperex's equipment and had it shipped to Korea.

In the 1980s, Samsung continued to expand its production of microwave ovens after it made a deal with General Electric: Samsung would make the ovens, and General Electric would put its name tag on the product. By 1984, Samsung was producing 4 million microwave ovens. Today it has about 20 percent of the world market.

But Samsung's managers are not resting on their laurels. They know that to continue to grow, they must expand the market for microwaves or find a new product. The executive now in charge of the division has begun to explore variations that will appeal to different European markets. Meanwhile, work on new products proceeds in the company's well-appointed new laboratory building.

The changes in Samsung's product line and production will need to be far-reaching, given the events of the late 1980s and early 1990s. Korea's leap toward democracy in 1987 was prodded in part by the nation's labor unions. Samsung has consistently avoided unionization of its work force, thanks to its superior wages, working conditions, and benefits. The company even throws in free housing for unmarried employees. Nevertheless, Samsung has not escaped the general increase in wages. With manufacturing workers' wages rising an average of almost 15 percent per year from 1987 to 1991, the cheap labor that gave Samsung and other Korean manufacturers a competitive edge is disappearing. At the same time, Korean citizens are beginning to demand greater regulation of the giant family-run conglomerates that dominate the nation's industry.

Recently, Samsung has begun to spend very large sums on research and development. Such investment has brought a new element into the picture: shareholders. Under pressure from the Korean government to free up bank capital for the use of smaller companies, Samsung has sold stock in 13 of its subsidiary companies to the public, raising hundreds of millions of dollars in the process. Lee Kunhee will need this cash to fulfill his dream of making Samsung one of the world's ten largest corporations.

CASE QUESTIONS

1. What do you think is the most important goods-production strategy Samsung practiced in the period covered by this case?
2. What do you think is the most important service-production strategy Samsung practiced in the period covered by this case?
3. As described in this case, Samsung has been used to responding to market demands as they arise and to customer demands as they are made. Do you think having shareholders will force changes in these practices?
4. What evidence do you find in this case that Samsung can achieve its goal of major growth?

Experiential Exercise:
Computing for More Timely Production

OBJECTIVE

To give students insight into the manufacturing process and the role for computers therein.

TIME REQUIRED

45 minutes
   Step 1: Individual activity (to be completed before class)
   Step 2: Small-group activity (30 minutes)
   Step 3: Class discussion (15 minutes)

PROCEDURE

Step 1: Read the following case regarding the Hall Company. (Students should read Chapter 23 before doing this exercise.)

Management at Hall, which manufactures clocks, knows that the firm needs to upgrade its computer system. However, they also know that choosing a new system will be difficult and time-consuming, since each department has its own set of problems it expects the new system to solve. A partial list of these problems follows:

Receiving Department: Currently logs in receipt of raw materials and shipment of finished goods by hand. Has trouble locating pertinent information when raw materials prove defective or finished goods are not received by the warehouse or a customer.

Manufacturing Department: Pays many of its personnel by piecework, but one person may perform several functions, each paid at a different rate. Pay is calculated by adding up "job tickets" collected by workers on completing a task. Manual collection and entry of this information into the current computer system is time-consuming and has a high potential error rate. This department also has trouble tracking work in process, that stage between raw materials and finished products. Scheduling is currently done on microcomputers in the department, with printouts of final schedules distributed. Delays or more rapid progress in production is not reflected in revised schedules until floor supervisors advise schedulers of this change. Floor supervisors, schedulers, and purchasing staff all complain that the existing system is inadequate for MRP and/or JIT.

Design Department: Current computer system allows reasonable CAD/CAM but does not hook into computer systems in other areas of the company. For example, the current system generates materials lists for new designs, but these must be printed out and manually sent to purchasing.

Finance: Like scheduling, finance has its own microcomputers and its own software, none of which interfaces with the mainframe computer or with other microcomputers in the company. Financial personnel spend a great deal of time taking mainframe reports (for example, on sales), microcomputer reports (for example, on materials costs), and handwritten reports (for example, on goods received and shipped and on employee pay rates and hours worked) and reentering this data.

Sales and Marketing: Terminals hooked into the mainframe allow quick access to sales figures, but managers cannot currently tell whether or how much sales representatives have actually been paid without asking the finance department for this information.

Warehousing: Current microcomputers do not interface with others in the company and cannot drive a roboticized system that automatically stores and ships bar-coded boxes on command.

Customer Service: Records on customer payment must be rekeyed from reports issued by the finance department. Lack of interface with manufacturing and warehousing means promised delivery dates are not always accurate.

Personnel Department: Current use of separate microcomputers means that information on employee earnings must be entered by hand.

What Does Hall Company Need In Its New Computer System?

Step 2: The instructor will divide the class into small groups and assign each group one or more departments in the Hall Company. Each group will complete the grid below with respect to its assigned department.

Department _____

Types of Software Needed: _____

Types of Hardware Needed: _____

Individuals to Be Questioned: _____

Type of Information Needed	Possible Source of Data	Process by Batch?	Other Depts. Involved

Type of system architecture recommended: Centralized _____

Decentralized _____

Networked _____

Step 3: One member of each small group will present the group's conclusions to the class.

QUESTIONS FOR DISCUSSION

1. What problems do you foresee for the Hall Company as it chooses a new computer system?
2. What areas of conflict emerged from the various presentations? How might some of these be resolved so that everyone wins?

Can We Talk?

"I should not talk so much about myself if there were anybody else whom I knew as well."
—Henry David Thoreau

The greatest résumé and the most persuasive cover letter in the world do not ensure that you will get the job. Rather, their purpose is to "get your foot in the door"—to get you an interview. Ultimately, it is the interview that will decide whether or not you get the job.

Interviewing for a job—whether it's your first or your twenty-first—is almost always a nerve-wracking experience. During an interview, recruiters and managers will talk to you, ask you questions, listen to your answers, and answer whatever questions you may have. They will then judge your qualifications based on this information. Because the interview is the basis on which most hiring decisions are made, it is very important that you understand how to prepare for an interview, how to handle yourself during an interview, and what to do after an interview.

PREPARING FOR AN INTERVIEW

The first step in preparing for an interview is to learn all you can about the company with which you'll be interviewing. Get a copy of the firm's annual report if time allows. Go to the library and check up on the company in business publications such as *Canadian Business* and the *Globe and Mail*. If such information is not available, prepare yourself by learning all you can about the industry or market.

The next step is to practice answering the questions you are likely to be asked. Friends or guidance counselors can help you here. For example, you should know ahead of time what you'll say when asked about your prior experience, reasons for wanting a job change, reasons for wanting this job, ability to do the job, strengths, weaknesses, and future goals. Other common questions include:

■ How would you describe the office politics in your current job and how do you handle them?
■ What's your personal work ethic?
■ How have you helped co-workers improve the productivity?
■ Would you buy stock in your current firm?

Be prepared to answer these questions, but don't be complacent. If you interview with several people, the chances are good that someone will ask you something you never dreamt of. One man reports being asked, "What would your co-workers say about you if I met them at a bar late on a Friday night?"

The third step in preparing for an interview is to develop questions of your own to ask your interviewers. These questions serve two purposes. First, they show your interest in the firm. Second, the answers to them can help you decide whether you want to work there—if you are offered the job. Questions you might consider asking include:

■ Does the company offer training for new employees, growth potential, and opportunities for advancement?
■ When was my predecessor promoted?
■ What skills and qualities do you believe are most important for this job?
■ How would you describe a typical day in this job?
■ What conditions in this job make it difficult to perform well?
■ Do most supervisors or managers have advanced degrees?
■ Are meetings an important part of the decision-making process on this job?

Warning: Do *not* ask about salary, benefits, or retirement plans until you are offered the job. Interviewers may interpret your concern as a desire to be comfortable—not productive.

Finally, assemble the materials you need to take with you: samples of your work (if appropriate), extra copies of your résumé, and written recommendations (if you have them). Also contact those you plan to use as references and let them know about your upcoming interview. This way they will be prepared to answer questions about you.

PRESENTING YOURSELF AT AN INTERVIEW

Answers—and questions—set, you are now ready to present yourself at the interview. When going to your interview, allow plenty of time to get there a few minutes early. Some experts suggest that you even do a "dry run" in advance so you can be sure how much time it will take. It's best to arrive about five minutes early. Over 70 percent of interviewers admit that a late applicant has little chance of getting the job, regardless of qualifications.

Dress conservatively for the interview. A dark suit is your best bet for most professional jobs, regardless of your sex or age. But if you are applying for a creative position such as designer or advertising copywriter, you may do better by dressing with a bit more dash. Whatever you wear, make it the best quality you can afford—it will pay off in the long run. Shined shoes and a well-groomed look also impress interviewers.

HANDLING YOURSELF DURING THE INTERVIEW

When meeting the interviewer, try to project an air of competence and assurance. Relax and remain calm. When the interviewer introduces himself or herself, state your own name as well and extend your hand for a handshake.

Speak clearly and directly as you are introduced. The interview will usually take place in a small room or office. Do not sit until the interviewer is ready to sit or at least indicates to you that you can sit. Sit up straight (do *not* slouch), but try not to be stiff. Likewise, don't fidget, but don't hold the arms of the chair in a death-grip either.

The interviewer will usually start by asking a few general questions, both to set the tone for the interview and to help you relax. When you answer questions, be honest, but don't bare your soul. Lies about what you have done probably won't get you the job, but *never* say you didn't get along with a previous boss. In fact, find something good to say about that person. If you were fired from a former job, admit it, but phrase it as a bad person-job fit—one you learned from.

Whatever the question, remember that your "job" at the moment is to sell yourself. Be upbeat and positive. Above all, try to present yourself as the right choice—the person who has:

- The skills to do the job.
- The commitment to do the job and to stay with the job.
- A personality that will enable you to get along with others on the job.
- The initiative to do the job—and even more than the job requires—without someone holding your hand.
- The ability to make the person who hired you look good.

Make your answers to the point, but don't be too brief—remember, the objective is to convey something about what you are like as a person. For example, if an interviewer asks you if you would consider relocating for a job, simply saying "Certainly" is not enough.

On the other hand, be careful not to talk too much. The old adage "Better to keep silent and be thought a fool than to open your mouth and remove all doubt" applies here. The more you talk, the better are the chances you'll say something that will disqualify you. For example, if asked whether you'd relocate, don't deliver a 30-minute travelogue about all the cities you would like to live in and why. Strike a happy medium: Indicate that you are willing to relocate and that you assume that an occasional move is necessary for advancement and to learn more about all aspects of the organization.

Some questions pose special problems. What if you are asked a question you don't know how to answer? If you are at all uncertain, ask the interviewer to clarify the question, but if you still don't know, *admit it*. Even more difficult is the situation in which an interviewer asks a question that is "out of bounds." Despite the fact that questions about a job applicant's age, ethnic background, religion, marital status, and personal life are illegal, a surprising number of interviewers continue to ask them. What should you do? You have two options: to answer or not to answer.

If it doesn't make you uncomfortable, you may choose to answer. Or you may respond with a "nonanswer" that shifts the topic back to job-related issues. For example, if asked whether you have a boy/girlfriend, you might try a nonanswer like the following: "I have many friends here, but I consider myself very adaptable and wouldn't expect to have difficulty making new friends wherever I was located. Would the job call for relocating me after the initial training session?"

What if you decide not to answer an illegal question? Certainly you risk losing the job if you point out to the interviewer that the question is inappropriate. You can report the firm, but you will need to prove that the purpose of the question was to discriminate against you—a difficult and time-consuming task indeed. And even if you win, you'll have to ask yourself whether you want to work for a company that supports such questioning. Turning the question back on the interviewer in the form of "Can you tell me how that question relates to this position?" may be some help, but the fact is that if you don't answer, or at least offer something resembling an answer, you probably won't get the job.

Regardless of how you perceive the interview to be going, remain calm and keep your sense of humor. Some interviewers may seem bored, others rude or distant. These attributes may have no bearing on how they are assessing you and your qualifications. The interviewer may be tired or cranky from traveling, or rudeness may just be her or his normal style. Some interviewers simply are not effective at what they do. A few interviewers may even push you a bit to see how you handle yourself under pressure. Remember that losing your temper will lose you the job for sure.

No matter how stressed you are and how much you want the job, try to keep things in perspective. The world will not end if the interview goes nowhere. In fact, having a sense of humor about the process can be a big asset. A vice president of a major brokerage house was once asked at an interview what he knew about foreign exchange. "After some thought," he recalled, "I said, 'I can spell both words.'" He got the job.

The interviewer will usually indicate to you when the interview is over. But the interviewer will seldom tell you whether or not you will be offered the job. There may be several applicants for the job, or the interviewer may need to discuss your qualifications with other managers before making a decision. But the interviewer should explain what will happen next—when the company will be in contact with you, what the next step will be if the company remains interested in hiring you, and so forth. If this information is not offered, ask before you leave.

FOLLOWING UP AFTER THE INTERVIEW

After any interview, be sure to write a letter to each person with whom you spoke. These letters are an opportunity not only to restate your interest and qualifications but also to resolve one of life's common annoyances. Almost everyone thinks of something they should have said, hours after the interview. Here's your chance to say it.

If you have applied for a managerial position, you can also expect more interviews before you get the job. You may be invited to the company's headquarters or regional office for more interviews with managers. So when you get contacted for a second interview, remember two things: (1) you'll need to do it all again, and (2) you did a good job of it the first time through!

" Advertising that's invisible really has no value whatsoever—its a squandering of the investment and it happens with far too much frequency."

—Vaughn Whelan

Vaughn Whelan knew he had his work cut out for him. Whelan, founder, owner, and general manager of Vaughn Whelan & Associates, a television commercial production agency, was on the first

day of an 18-day cross-Canada commercial shoot. As he looked out at the tour's first stop, St. John's, Newfoundland, he knew his objective was not an easy one: effectively differentiate Radio Shack from its competitors.

After eight years of working with big advertising agencies, Whelan had recently realized the long-held dream of starting his own agency. Now with a $3.5 million contract to produce a pre-Christmas campaign of 27 half-minute television spots for the Radio Shack electronics chain, he hoped the campaign would guarantee his agency's spot in the increasingly competitive Canadian advertising industry.

Whelan was no stranger to Newfoundland; the businessman had recently achieved local notoriety by producing an advertising campaign for Blue Star, one of Labatt's brands. Given the province's longstanding employment problems, part of Vaughn's advertising campaign included a contest that featured a first prize of ten weeks work—just enough to allow someone to re-file for unemployment insurance benefits. While the contest's sponsor eventually changed the campaign's prize, the contest served to launch Vaughn's reputation for producing advertising that got the public's attention.

Recently Whelan had approached the head offices of Radio Shack. The chain of consumer electronics stores, headquartered in Barrie, Ontario, had been taking a beating in recent years, in large part due to the recent entry of such players as Multitech, Future Shop and Majestic. In an effort to create customer enthusiasm for the company's

Christmas product offerings, Vaughn's company had been hired to create a series of pre-Christmas commercials for exclusive use in the Canadian market.

Together with comic Pat McCormick, Vaughn scheduled a tour of Radio Shack stores from coast to coast. In each store he planned to stage an impromptu skit involving McCormick and a local employee or customer. The core theme that would run across all 27 spots was simple but effective: *"This place is completely wired!"*

Vaughn had prided himself on his ability to empathize with the ultimate consumer of his company's product, the television viewer. Viewers, he remembered, basically hated commercials. The only exceptions were those commercials that, either through humor or pure novelty, piqued the viewer's interest. His objective for the Radio Shack campaign was to create several of these distinctive "must-see" commercials. With the northern maritime breeze blowing across the bluff from which he viewed St. John's, Vaughn wondered how to make his mark in this, his first national campaign.

Study questions:

1. What are the different ways in which to classify production processes? How do these classification techniques aid in classifying the production activities of Vaughn Whelan's company?
2. In what ways is the production of services different from the production of goods? In what ways is it similar?
3. What are the key issues that usually must be planned in offering a service? How would you explain these tasks in the context of producing a television commercial?
4. What is productivity? How is productivity usually measured? How might the productivity of a television commercial be measured?

---

* This case is based on the *Venture* episode first broadcast on January 16, 1994.

WAL-MART WIZARD*

❝The phrase that turns me off more than any other phrase I've heard...is that 'I've been doing business this way for 25 years. I don't see why I need to change now.'"

—Dr. Ken Stone
Iowa State Professor of Economics and small retail business consultant

Canada has recently experienced the entry of several giant warehouse discounters like the U.S. giant Wal-Mart. Wal-Mart's arrival in the Canadian retail marketplace is an important development because of the world-class competitive expertise the company commands in carrying out its merchandising task. The company features point-of-sale laser scanners that beam a continuous stream of sales information through a network of company-owned satellites back to the company's headquarters in Bentonville, Arkansas. With its over 2000 stores in the United States, the company has become the paradigm of operating efficiency. One of the implications of Wal-Mart's success is that smaller retailers, such as those that typically make up the Canadian marketplace, will have an increasingly hard time surviving.

One community of small retailers that has taken the initiative against the onslaughts of Wal-Mart is found in the American midwestern town of Greenup, Illinois. Merchants there have secured the services of Dr. Kenneth Stone, a retail consultant and professor of economics at Iowa State University. Stone, who has been observing Wal-Mart for over eight years, has been a consultant to over 300 small-town merchant groups that have faced the entry of one or more giant retailers such as Wal-Mart.

Stone counsels store owners on how to survive and hopefully thrive in the face of direct competition with these giants. According to Stone, Wal-Mart-type stores have a number of obvious advantages: longer hours of operation, economies of scale in purchasing, and more intensive advertising campaigns. As a result of such formidable advantages, smaller-scale, community-based retailers have taken a beating; Stone's research reports that discount

stores sales have grown by 20 percent while hardware stores are down in sales by 31 percent and in number by 37 percent.

However, behemoths like Wal-Mart are vulnerable in a number of key areas; these include product knowledge, product variety, and customer service. Therefore Professor Stone encourages small retailers to find one or more defensible niches that the giant retailers cannot fill. Three such niches include expanding the product line to include special products not found on the giants' shelves, offering technical advice in the proper use of products, and maintaining longer hours of operation than the giant stores. Accordingly, he also recommends abandoning the sale of low value-added products such as housewares and offering improved customer service, such as offering cash refunds on the spot. Stone also advises store owners to visit the giant retailers on a regular basis in order to become as familiar as possible with their "enemy." One objective of such visits is to monitor the 500-600 "price sensitive" products that people know the prices of by memory.

With the entry of Wal-Mart and other giant retailers in the Canadian economy, the implications for Canada's retail community are clear; no retailer can afford to sit still in the brave new world of the giant retailer.

Study questions:

1. What are the different pricing philosophies and strategies that a retailer can consider? Which of these best describes the strategy of Wal-Mart?
2. What are the 4 P's of marketing? How does Wal-Mart combine these four elements in its marketing strategy?
3. What is a distribution channel? What different types of channels exist? What is Wal-Mart's channel strategy?
4. What are the six basic types of retail stores identified in the text? Which of these stores would you expect to have the toughest time competing with Wal-Mart? Why?

*This case is based on the *Venture* episode first broadcast on December 5, 1993.

Part Five

MANAGING MARKETING

What is the first thing you think of when you hear the names Coffee Crisp, Post-It, Crest, and Eno? If you grew up in Canada, you probably didn't hesitate at all before picturing candy, little slips of paper with one sticky edge, toothpaste, and something to calm your stomach. Your rapid association of company names and the goods or services they provide is a tribute to the effectiveness of the marketing managers of the firms that produce these goods. These and many other names have become household words because companies have developed the right products to meet customers' needs, have priced those products appropriately, have made prospective customers aware of the products' existence and qualities, and have made the products readily available.

Part Five, **Managing Marketing**, provides an overview of the many elements of marketing, including developing, pricing, promoting, and distributing various types of goods and services.

■ We begin in **Chapter 14, Understanding Marketing Processes and Consumer Behavior**, by examining the ways in which companies distinguish their products, determine customer needs, and otherwise address consumer buying preferences.

■ Then, in **Chapter 15, Developing and Promoting Goods and Services**, we explore the development of different types of products, the effect of brand names and packaging, how promotion strategies help a firm meet its objectives, and the advantages and disadvantages of several promotional tools.

■ Finally, in **Chapter 16, Pricing and Distributing Goods and Services**, we look at the strategies firms use to price their products. We also consider the various outlets business firms use to distribute their products, and we discuss the problems of storing goods and transporting them to distributors.

14

Understanding Marketing Processes and Consumer Behavior

LEARNING OBJECTIVES

After reading this chapter you will be able to

■ Define marketing and explain its function in business.

■ Discuss how and why market segmentation is used for target marketing and how market research can help identify target markets.

■ Describe factors that influence consumer buying and the consumer buying process.

■ Explain how international differences affect marketing strategies.

■ Identify potential problems and strategies in marketing for small businesses.

CHAPTER OUTLINE

As Beauty Does

Most CEOs would kill to have Leonard Lauder's problems. Founded by his mother, the legendary Estée Lauder, his firm is at the top of the cosmetic heap, bringing in an estimated $2 billion each year. All of its product lines for women—Estée Lauder, Clinique, and Prescriptives—are doing well. Two—Clinique and Prescriptives—are growing rapidly in an industry where sales have been stagnant.

In recent years, however, demographic changes have presented Lauder with some new challenges. Most users of the Estée Lauder line discovered it in the early 1960s, when they were in their 20s and 30s, and have stayed with it. As a result, the typical Estée user is now in her 50s or 60s—and has very different cosmetic needs than she had when she was in her 20s.

An even greater challenge is the age of Estée Lauder herself. Estée Lauder refuses to reveal her exact age, but suggests that she is in her 70s. (Given the age of her sons, many believe 80s is closer to the truth.) An excellent advertisement for her products, she sometimes seems immortal. But Leonard Lauder is keenly aware that at some point his mother will die.

The death of a founder is not a problem for many companies. When, as at Estée Lauder, Inc., the founder has retired to a largely ceremonial role and day-to-day operations are being handled capably and even brilliantly by an heir such as Leonard, firms typically can go on without missing a beat when the founder dies. Such has not been the case in the cosmetics industry, though. Since the deaths of founders Helena Rubinstein, Elizabeth Arden, and Charles Revson (of Revlon), the cosmetics companies bearing their names have fallen prey to corporate buyouts and sagging sales.

Despite her age, Lauder remains a draw for Estée Lauder, Inc. and its products. Salespersons report positive response on telling customers that "There really is a Mrs. Lauder." When she gets up to speak, cameras snap. Her social contacts—ranging as high as the late Duchess of Windsor—lend a cachet to the firm and often provide free publicity.

Moreover, Estée Lauder has not always been a figurehead. Hers is the mind that conceived the marketing techniques that propelled the firm to the top. It all began in a tenement in Queens, New York, where young Josephine Esther Mentzer helped her uncle, John Schotz, a chemist, fill bottles with his "magic potion"—a skin cream. She then helped sell the cream by giving massages and beauty treatments to customers and employees of local beauty salons. To encourage women to buy her products, Lauder gave them free samples of other products when

The graceful and elegant Estée Lauder remains the greatest advertisement for the line of cosmetics that bears her name.

they bought one from her. "Charles of the Ritz said I'd never succeed by giving things away," she recalls. Charles was wrong, and Lauder's gift-with-purchase plan eventually changed the way cosmetics companies operate.

Not until she had to earn money during a separation from her husband Joseph Lauder did the woman now known as Estée Lauder charge into the business world full steam, though. Her first real order came in 1948, when she persuaded a buyer for Saks to stock some of her uncle's skin cream after demonstrating its effects on the troubled skin of the buyer's daughter. Later, she would train the sales staff who sold her products in department stores to "touch your customer." This strong personal sales approach is still visible in Estée Lauder employees today.

Just as Estée Lauder made her first sale by giving special attention to one buyer, so her company today never forgets its first "customer"—the retail stores. To keep major retailers happy, Lauder grants them exclusive promotions. Because of their high sales volumes, retailers are willing to give Estée Lauder, Clinique, and Prescriptives prime locations. Prime locations have meant prime profits. But with Estée Lauder herself past the so-called prime of life, what lies ahead?   ◆

The experience of Estée Lauder and her firm illustrates the importance of marketing in business today. By developing products that customers want, Estée Lauder is able to get more of what it wants—profits.

In the next three chapters, we will explore the major aspects of reaching a market. We begin in this chapter by considering how a company's marketing operations help it meet those needs, beginning with an exploration of the nature of marketing. As you will see, the marketing process is complex, requiring marketers to understand the nature of their product (and its place in the market) and the nature of their customers. The special problems of marketing internationally and of marketing for the small business are also addressed.

The Nature of Marketing

What do you think of when you think of marketing? If you are like most people, you probably think of advertising for something like detergent or soft drinks. But marketing is a much broader concept. **Marketing** is "the process of planning and executing the conception, pricing, promotion, and distribution of ideas, goods, and services to create exchanges that satisfy individual and organizational objectives."[1] In this section, we will dissect this definition to see what it encompasses.

marketing
Planning and executing the development, pricing, promotion, and distribution of ideas, goods, and services to create exchanges that satisfy both buyers' and sellers' objectives.

Marketing: Goods, Services, and Ideas

Marketing of tangible goods is obvious in our everyday life. You walk into a department store and a woman with a clipboard asks if you'd like to try a new cologne. A pharmaceutical company proclaims the virtues of its new cold medicine. Your local auto dealer offers an economy car at an economy price. These **consumer goods** are products that you, the consumer, buy for personal use. Firms that sell their products to the end user are engaged in *consumer marketing*.

consumer goods
Products purchased by individuals for their personal use.

Marketing is also applied to industrial goods. **Industrial goods** are items that are used by companies for production purposes or further assembly. Conveyors, lift trucks, and earth movers are all industrial goods, as are components and raw materials such as transistors, integrated circuits, coal, steel, and plastic. Firms that sell their products to other manufacturers are engaged in *industrial marketing*.

industrial goods
Products purchased by companies to use directly or indirectly to produce other products.

Marketing techniques can also be applied to services. *Service marketing* has become a major area of growth in the Canadian economy. Insurance companies, airlines, investment counselors, clinics, and exterminators all engage in service marketing to consumers. Some firms market their services to other companies, for example, security guards, janitors, and accountants.

Finally, marketing can be applied to *ideas* as well as to goods and services. Television advertising and other promotional activities have made "participaction" a symbol of a healthy lifestyle.

Planning and Executing Marketing Strategy

As a business activity, marketing requires management. Although many individuals also contribute to the marketing of a product, a company's **marketing managers** are typically responsible for planning and implementing all the marketing-mix activities that result in the transfer of goods or services to its customers. These activities culminate in the **marketing plan**: a detailed and focused strategy for gearing the marketing mix to meet consumer needs and wants. Marketing, therefore, begins when a company identifies a consumer need and develops a product to meet it. One way of identifying those needs,

marketing managers
Responsible for planning and implementing all the marketing mix activities that result in the transfer of goods or services to customers.

marketing plan
A detailed strategy for gearing the marketing mix to meet consumer needs and wants.

Each of these advertisements provides information about a specific product, service, or idea. Cott Cola, for example, is a consumer food *product* that can be consumed. The advertisement for the Metro Toronto Zoo promotes a *service* that can be enjoyed. The safer sex advertisement promotes the *idea* of changing behaviour as a way of combatting sexually transmitted diseases.

market research, is explored later in this chapter. Here, however, we begin by noting two important aspects of the larger market-planning process: developing the marketing plan and setting marketing goals.

Developing the Marketing Plan.   Marketing managers must realize that planning takes time. Indeed, the marketing-planning process may begin years before a product becomes available for sale. For example, the Dutch electronics firm Philips (its major label is Magnavox) developed such products as VCRs and compact discs years before these products actually hit the market. And although Philips has recently invested $1 billion in the planning and development of advanced semiconductor memory chips, the company is not assured of success. Without such planning and preparation, however, the electronics line would have little or no chance of success in a highly competitive market.[2]

Setting Goals for Performance.   Marketing managers—like all managers—must set objectives and goals and then establish ways to evaluate performance. An insurance company, for example, might establish the goal of increasing sales by 10 percent in its western and central Canadian sales districts. The district sales managers' performances will be evaluated against that goal. Or, a consumer products company might set a goal to reduce by 30 percent the time it takes to bring a new product to market.

The Marketing Concept

Increased competition and the growth of consumer discretionary income has given added impetus to an idea that had its beginnings early in the twentieth century. This idea or philosophy, known as the **marketing concept**, means that the whole firm is coordinated to achieve one goal—to serve its present and potential customers and to do so at a profit. This concept means that a firm must get to know what customers really want and to follow closely the changes in tastes that occur. The various departments of the firm—marketing, production, finance, and human resources—must operate as a system, well coordinated and unified in the pursuit of a common goal—customer satisfaction.

marketing concept
The idea that the whole firm is directed toward serving present and potential customers at a profit.

The importance of customer satisfaction has been recognized at IBM, which introduced a scheme that influences the pay of 350 managers. Up to 15 percent of their pay is tied to how satisfied their customers are. Bell Canada has a similar scheme; team awards are based partly on customer satisfaction.[3] Japan Air Lines' 747s are equipped with video monitors in the armrests so that passengers may choose exactly what they want to watch from a movie library. At Air France, a passenger who purchases a first-class ticket to Paris can upgrade to the Concorde at no extra cost.[4]

The Marketing Mix

In planning and implementing their marketing strategies, managers rely on the four principal elements of marketing. These four elements, often called the Four Ps of marketing, are *p*roduct (including developing goods, services, and ideas), *p*ricing, *p*romotion, and *p*lace (distribution).[5] Together, these elements are known as the **marketing mix**, depicted in Figure 14.1.

marketing mix
The combination of product, pricing, promotion, and distribution strategies used in marketing a product.

There are many possible combinations of the four elements in the marketing mix. Price might play a large role in selling fresh meat but a very small role in selling newspapers. Distribution might be crucial in marketing gasoline but not so important for lumber. Promotion could be vital in toy marketing but of little consequence in marketing nails. The product is important in every case but probably less so for toothpaste than for cars.

Figure 14.1
Choosing the marketing mix for a business.

product
A good, service, or idea that satisfies buyers' needs and demands.

product differentiation
The creation of a product or product image that differs enough from existing products to attract consumers.

pricing
That part of the marketing mix concerned with choosing the appropriate price for a product to meet the firm's profit objectives and buyers' purchasing objectives.

Product.   Clearly, no business can undertake marketing activities without a **product**—a good, service, or idea that attempts to fulfill consumers' wants. The conception or development of new products is a continual challenge. Businesses must take into account changing technology, consumer wants and needs, and economic conditions, among other factors. A recent survey showed the percentage of Canadian households that owned the following items: VCR (70 percent); home computer (20 percent); microwave oven (70 percent); CD player (20 percent).[6] These products did not even exist 20 years ago.

Having the product that consumers desire may mean changing existing products. For example, in the clothing industry, manufacturers must be alert to changes in fashion, which often occur rapidly and unpredictably. And as computer technology changes, so must many computer products, such as application programs.

Manufacturers may also develop new products and enter markets in which they have not previously competed. Consumer food giants such as Kraft Inc., General Mills, Sara Lee, and Quaker Oats have entered the institutional and restaurant food-service markets. They have modified consumer food mixes for the mass production needed in prisons, hospitals, schools, and restaurants.

Producers may develop new or "improved" goods and services for the sake of product differentiation. **Product differentiation** is the creation of a product or product image that differs enough from existing products to attract consumers. Product differentiation does not always mean a change in how a product functions. But when successful, it always means a change in how customers react. For example, early kitchen and laundry appliances were available only in white. Frigidaire capitalized on this situation, offering comparably priced and performing appliances, but in colors. Procter & Gamble is a master at product differentiation, working to make its products not only different from those of other firms but also from its own competing goods.

Services can also be sources of differentiation. One company has developed a computer system so that its customers at retail home centers and lumber yards can custom-design decks and shelving. As a result, the company has differentiated its commodity two-by-fours by turning them into premium products. We discuss product development in Chapter 15.

Pricing.   The second element of the marketing mix is the **pricing** of products. Deciding on the most appropriate price for the market is not easy. The price of the product must support the operating costs of the organization, administrative and research costs, and marketing costs such as advertising and sales salaries.

Both low or high price strategies may be appropriate for a company under various situations. Low prices will generally lead to a larger volume of sales. High prices will usually limit the size of the market, but will increase a firm's profits per unit. In some cases, however, high prices may actually attract customers by implying that the product is especially good or rare. We will discuss pricing in more detail in Chapter 16.

Promotion. The most visible component of the marketing mix is **promotion**, those techniques designed to sell a product to consumers. Promotional tools include advertising, personal selling, sales promotions, and public relations. Chapter 15 explores the promotion of products in more depth.

In marketing terms, **advertising** is any form of paid, nonpersonal communication used by an identified sponsor to persuade or inform certain audiences about a good, service, or idea. Advertising may be done through television, radio, magazines, newspapers, billboards or any other type of broadcast or print media.

Automobiles, appliances, and stereo equipment are often promoted through the use of **personal selling**—person-to-person sales. However, the bulk of personal selling occurs with industrial goods. Purchasing agents and other members of a business who require information about a product's technical qualities and price are usually referred to the selling company's sales representatives.

Less expensive items are often marketed through the use of **sales promotions**. Sales promotions can take many forms. Premiums (gifts included with the product), trading stamps, coupons, and package inserts are all sales promotions meant to tempt consumers to buy more of a product. Free samples, exhibits, and trade shows give customers an opportunity to try the product or talk with company representatives. The prevalence of self-service retail outlets has led marketers to think about package design—the "silent seller"—as an important sales promotion.

Public relations includes all promotional activities directed at building good relations with various sectors of the population. Many public relations activities are good deeds paid for by companies. Sponsorship of softball teams, Special Olympics, and automobile racing teams are examples of public relations efforts. Companies may also use public relations activities to boost employee morale.

Publicity also refers to a firm's efforts to communicate to the public, usually through mass media. Publicity, however, is not paid for by the firm, nor does the firm control the content of publicity. Publicity, therefore, can sometimes hurt a business. For example, Dun & Bradstreet received considerable negative publicity when newspapers and magazines reported that it was billing its customers for financial reports they did not need.

promotion

That part of the marketing mix concerned with selecting the appropriate technique for selling a product to a consumer.

advertising

Any promotional technique involving paid, nonpersonal communication used by an identified sponsor to persuade or inform a large number of people about a product.

personal selling

A promotional technique involving the use of person-to-person communication to sell products.

sales promotion

A promotional technique involving one-time direct inducements to buyers (such as coupons, sales displays, and contests) to purchase a product.

public relations

Any promotional activity directed at building good relations with various sectors of the population of buyers.

publicity

A promotional technique that involves nonpaid communication about a product or firm and that is outside the control of the firm.

By providing both distribution and advertising for Levi's, this truck plays a dual role in the company's marketing.

Place (Distribution).   Getting a product into a retail store requires transportation, decisions about direct sales, and a number of other **distribution** processes. Transportation options include moving merchandise by air, land, or pipeline, and, more specifically, by railroad, truck, air freight, or steamship.

Decisions about direct sales can affect a firm's overall marketing strategy. Many manufacturers sell their products to other companies who, in turn, distribute the goods to retailers. Some companies sell directly to major retailers such as Sears, K mart, and Safeway. Still others sell directly to the final consumer. Chapter 16 presents more detail on distribution decisions.

Marketing: Creating Exchanges

The last part of the definition of marketing focuses on the exchange process. An **exchange** is any transaction in which two or more parties trade things of value. In marketing, the typical exchange involves a business providing a good or service in return for payment from a buyer.

Although the exchange process always includes payment, the payment does not always involve money. It may involve barter, the trading of goods of equal value. Many people assume that barter survives as a means of exchange only in undeveloped economies, but it has become increasingly common throughout the world. Among companies, bartering takes several forms. In *countertrading*, multinational companies swap goods with companies in less developed countries. For example, Coca-Cola sold Coke to Eastern Europe and Asian countries and was paid in bathtubs and honey.

Another popular form of bartering occurs when companies with excess inventories of products trade them for advertising. Casio Inc., for example, disposed of surplus products (watches, calculators, musical keyboards) worth $25 million in return for advertising opportunities for its main products.[7] Although bartering may seem unusual, it is mutually satisfying to both parties and sometimes provides even better returns than cash sales.

Satisfaction and Utility.   One requirement of the exchange process, therefore, is that it should satisfy both buyers and sellers. If marketing managers provide an attractive mix of product, price, promotion, and placement, then sellers should earn satisfactory profits. Customers, meanwhile, should be getting satisfaction from the utility that the purchased product provides. If both buyers and sellers are satisfied, marketing operations will have contributed to the success of the exchange.

Recall from Chapter 11, for example, that production operations create *utility*, especially form and time utility, by transforming raw materials into products when buyers want them. Similarly, marketing operations create *time*, *place*, and *possession utilities*: Buyers not only obtain the product *when* and *where* they want it but receive the right to *use* it as they want. Figure 14.2 illustrates this relationship. Note that although it is convenient to distinguish between the roles of production and marketing management, product utility serves a common purpose: creating value for buyers

The need for the exchange process to satisfy both sellers and buyers underscores the importance of the marketing concept. To earn profits consistently, sellers must attempt to supply buyers' wants. Coca-Cola learned this lesson the hard way. In the 1980s, the firm tried to withdraw its original formula Coke and substitute a new formula it believed would have greater appeal. The company reckoned without its traditional customers, however. Their outcry eventually led Coca-Cola's management to reintroduce the original version as "Classic Coke."

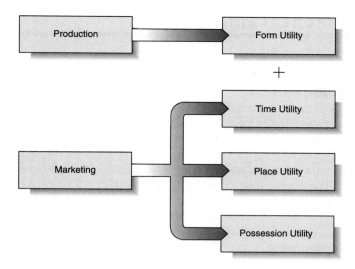

Figure 14.2
Production and marketing create utility for customers.

The Functions of Marketing

The definition of marketing, while lengthy, does not really address the question of what marketers *do*. In all, marketing has eight functions: buying, selling, transporting, storing, standardizing, financing, risk taking, and researching. The *transporting* and *storing* functions refer simply to the distribution portion of the marketing mix. The other six functions, however, require further explanation. We can better understand them by dividing them into *exchange* and *facilitating functions*.

Exchange Functions.   The buying and selling functions relate to the exchange portion of marketing. In *buying*, the role of marketing is to understand why and what customers buy. As we will see later in this chapter, understanding the behavior of consumers and industrial buyers can help a firm make better decisions about what to produce, how to price, how to promote, and where to sell. In *selling*, the role of marketing is to sell a product to someone. This role is largely a function of marketing's promotional activities, including personal selling.

Facilitating Functions.   The remaining functions are often called "facilitating" functions because they make exchange functions easier to perform. For example, *financing* programs, such as extension of credit to dealers, facilitate the selling process. *Standardizing* product features makes buyers more comfortable and likely to purchase. *Taking risks*—bringing out new products and spending money to promote them—makes it possible for customers to buy them in the first place. *Researching* consumer behavior enables a company to produce and sell products that customers will buy because they meet their needs.

At various times, marketers have focused more on some functions than on others. During the production era (see Chapter 2), marketing personnel were heavily involved in standardizing, transporting, and storing goods. More recently, the rise of the marketing concept has led marketers to focus on researching buyers' demands. Before we explore research in more detail, however, you need to understand the benefits of pinpointing those demands.

Target Marketing and Market Segmentation

target market
Any group of people who have similar wants and needs and may be expected to show interest in the same product(s).

market segmentation
Dividing a market into categories according to traits customers have in common.

positioning
The process of fixing, adapting, and communicating the nature of the product.

Marketing managers long ago recognized that they cannot be "all things to all people." People have different tastes, different interests, different goals, different lifestyles, and so on. The marketing concept's recognition of consumers' various needs and wants led marketing managers to think in terms of target marketing. **Target markets** are groups of people with similar wants and needs.

Target marketing clearly requires **market segmentation**, dividing a market into categories of customer types or "segments." For example, Mr. Big-and-Tall sells to men who are taller and heavier than average. Certain special interest magazines are oriented toward people with specific interests (see Table 14.1). The video case "Video Game Wars" on p. 493 describes the importance of identifying the target market in the highly competitive video game business. Once they have identified market segments, companies may adopt a variety of product strategies. Some firms decide to provide a range of products to the market in an attempt to market their products to more than one segment. For example, General Motors of Canada offers compact cars, vans, trucks, luxury cars, and sports cars with various features and prices. Their strategy is to provide an automobile for nearly every segment of the market.

In contrast, some businesses restrict production to one market segment. Rolls-Royce, for example, understands that only a relatively small number of people are willing to pay $310 000 for exclusive touring limousines. Rolls, therefore, makes no attempt to cover the entire range of possible products; instead, it markets only to a very small segment of the total automobile buyers market.

Table 14.2 shows how the radio market might be segmented by a marketer of home-electronic equipment. Note that segmentation is a strategy for analyzing consumers, not products. The analysis in Table 14.2, for example, identifies consumer-users—joggers, commuters, travelers. Only *indirectly*, then, does it focus on the uses of the product itself. In marketing, the process of fixing, adapting, and communicating the nature of the product itself is called **positioning**.

TABLE 14.1   Magazines with Specific Target Audiences

Accounting	Fishing/Hunting
CA Magazine	*Western Canada Outdoors*
CGA Magazine	*The Atlantic Salmon Journal*
CMA Update	*B.C. Outdoor Fishing Guide*
Agriculture	**Automotive**
Agro-Nouvelles	*Aftermarket Canada*
Canada Poultry	*Bodyshop*
Country Life in B.C.	*Canadian Automotive Trade*
Sports	**Boating**
B.C. Athletics Record	*Boating Business*
Canadian Squash	*Canadian Boating*
Athletics Canada	*Porthole Magazine*
Gardening	**Music**
Canadian Gardening News	*Billboard*
Prairie Landscape Magazine	*Guitar Player*
Landscape Ontario	*Rolling Stone*

Table 14.2   Possible Segmentation of the Radio Market

Segmentation	Product/Target Market
Age	Inexpensive, unbreakable, portable models for young children
	Inexpensive equipment—possibly portable—for teens
	Moderate-to-expensive equipment for adults
Consumer attitude	Sophisticated components for audio buffs
	All-in-one units in furniture cabinets for those concerned with room appearance
Product Use	Miniature models for joggers and commuters
	"Boom box" portables for taking outdoors
	Car stereo systems for traveling
	Components and all-in-one units for home use
Location	Battery-powered models for use where electricity is unavailable
	AC current for North American users
	DC current for other users

Identifying Market Segments

By definition, the members of a market segment must share some common traits or behaviors that will affect their purchasing decisions. In identifying market segments, researchers look at geographic, demographic, psychographic, and product-use variables.

Geographics.   In some cases, where people live affects their buying decisions. The heavy rainfall in British Columbia prompts its inhabitants to purchase more umbrellas than does Arizona's desert. Urban residents have less demand for four-wheel drive vehicles than do their rural counterparts. Sailboats sell better along both coasts than they do in the prairie provinces.

These patterns affect marketing decisions about what products to offer, at what price to sell them, how to promote them, and how to distribute them. For example, consider marketing down parkas in rural Saskatchewan. Demand will be high, price competition may be limited, local newspaper advertising may be very effective, and the best location may be one easily reached from several small towns.

Demographics.   A variety of demographic characteristics are important to marketers. As we noted in earlier chapters, demographics include traits such as age, income, gender, ethnic background, marital status, race, religion, and social class. Many marketers, for example, have discovered that university and community college students are an important market segment. Students across Canada have discretionary income totalling $4-$5 billion. Ford Motor of Canada has marketed to students since the mid-1980s, and gives graduates a $750 rebate on their first-time purchase of a car. Table 14.3 lists some demographic market segments. Note that these are objective criteria that cannot be altered. Marketers must work with or around them.

Demographics affect how a firm markets its product. For example, marketing managers may well divide a market into age groups such as 18-25, 26-35, 36-45 and so on. A number of general consumption characteristics that can be attributed to these age groups help marketing managers develop specific plans.[8] As a result, a community whose population is heavily dominated by young adults will most likely feature more fast-food restaurants

TABLE 14.3   Demographic Market Segmentation

Age	Under 5; 5–11; 12–19; 20–34; 35–49; 50–64; 65+
Education	Grade school or less; some high school; graduated high school; some college or university; college diploma or university degree; advanced degree
Family life cycle	Young single, young married without children; young married with children; older married with children under 18; older married without children under 18; older single; other
Family size	1, 2–3, 4–5, 6+
Income	Under $9000; $9000–$14 999; $15 000–$25 000; over $25 000
Nationality	Including but not limited to African, Asian, British, Eastern European, French, German, Irish, Italian, Latin American, Middle Eastern, and Scandinavian
Race	Including but not limited to Inuit, Asian, Black, and White
Religion	Including but not limited to Buddhist, Catholic, Hindu, Jewish, Muslim, and Protestant
Sex	Male, female
Language	Including but not limited to English, French, Inuktitut, Italian, Ukrainian, and German

and stores selling blue jeans and records than will a town with a high percentage of retirees. The box "Teenagers: An International Market Segment" describes similarities across countries in the 13–19 age group.

psychographics

A method of market segmentation involving psychological traits that a group has in common, including motives, attitudes, activities, interests, and opinions.

Psychographics. Members of a market can also be segmented according to **psychographic** (mental) traits such as their motives, attitudes, activities, interests, and opinions. Psychographics are of particular interest to marketers because, unlike demographics and geographics, they can be changed by marketing efforts. The box "Psychological Market Research" describes how consumers can be segmented by psychological variables.

Psychographics are particularly important to marketers because, unlike demographics and geographics, they can sometimes be changed by marketing efforts. For example, many companies have succeeded in changing at least some consumers' opinions by running ads highlighting products that have been improved directly in response to consumer desires. General Motors used this approach in the development and promotion of Saturns. GM gained an improved image by advertising its intended new design in conjunction with consumer-preferred features such as a one-price policy, careful selection of employees, high product quality, emphasis on quality, customer convenience during servicing, and extensive warranty coverage.

Product-Use Variables. This fourth way of segmenting looks at how group members use a good or service, their brand loyalty, and why they purchase the product. A woman's shoe maker, for example, might find three segments—athletic, casual, and dress shoes. Each market segment is looking for different benefits in a shoe. A woman buying an athletic shoe will probably not care much about its appearance, but she will care a great deal about arch support, traction offered by the sole, and sturdiness. In contrast, a woman buying a casual shoe will want it to look good but be comfortable, while a woman buying a dress shoe may require a specific color or style and accept some discomfort and a relatively fragile shoe.

International Report

TEENAGERS: AN INTERNATIONAL MARKET SEGMENT

We all know that trends spread rapidly through the ranks of teenagers. But that tendency is now accelerating internationally. Teens around the world have amazingly similar preferences for consumer products. BSB Worldwide, an advertising agency, videotaped teenagers' rooms in 25 different countries. From the items on display, it was hard to tell whether the room was in Mexico City, Tokyo, or Los Angeles.

The biggest beneficiary of this trend appears to be U.S. companies. The hot new trends in the U.S. often pop up in many other countries as well. Because the populations of Asia and Latin America are much younger than the population of North America, the teen market is big business. For example, the total number of 10- to 19-year-olds in Brazil, Argentina, and Mexico is 57 million; in the U.S., the total is only 35 million.

The most unifying force among teenagers is television. Satellite TV is helping to unify patchworks of domestic markets, and companies can mount Europe- or Asia-wide campaigns. No network is more popular than MTV, which is a monster hit in Europe and is watched by more households there than in the U.S. It broadcasts news and socially conscious programming, and is creating a Euro-language of simplified English.

MTV also promotes little-known European musicians and has the power to make them big stars in other countries. For example, it helped the Swedish group Ace of Base have a top ten hit in Germany, Italy, Britain, and the U.S. MTV has a roster of 200 advertisers, including Levi Strauss, Procter & Gamble, Johnson & Johnson, Apple Computer, and Pepsi Cola. These firms advertise on MTV because it reaches the market segment they want.

MTV may cause a revolution in worldwide marketing. At present, it is difficult to sell the same products to 35-year-olds in different countries because they never were exposed to anything but products from the country where they were raised. Not so for the upcoming generation of teenagers. They see (and buy) products from various countries and will probably continue to do so as they get older. Two famous brand names, Coke and Pepsi, are already competing vigorously to attract international teens to use their product.

Fashion fads are also spreading around the world. Hip-hop, first popularized by African-Americans, means wearing loose-fitting urban street wear, baggy jeans, sweat shirts, hiking boots, athletic shoes, and baseball caps (worn backwards). Within this fashion category, certain brands have become very popular. Levi jeans, Nike or Reebok athletic shoes, and Timberland boots are some of the brands that have profited.

Sports is the other universal language of teenagers. Basketball stars like Michael Jordan and Shaquille O'Neal have high name recognition overseas. In a poll of Chinese students in rural Shaanxi province, Michael Jordan tied with former Chinese premier Zhou En-lai for the title "World's Greatest Man." Not surprisingly, testimonial advertisements by big-name sports stars have a big impact on potential buyers. It is not uncommon for students to own multiple pairs of Nike Air Jordans.

Teen tastes in consumer electronics are also similar across countries. Kodak is developing an advertising campaign directed specifically at teenagers in the hope that when they have their own children they will use Kodak products to take pictures of them. Teens are also more comfortable with personal computers than their parents are. So, even if the parents are buying the machine, the teen determines what brand is purchased.

Market Segmentation: A Caution

Segmentation must be done carefully. A group of people may share an age category, income level, or some other segmentation variable, but their spending habits may be quite different. Look at your friends in school. You may all be approximately the same age, but you have different needs and wants. Some of you may wear cashmere sweaters while others wear sweatshirts. The same holds true for income. University professors and truck drivers frequently earn about the same level of income. However, their spending patterns, tastes, and wants are generally quite different.

In Canada, the two dominant cultures—English and French—show significant differences in consumer attitudes and behavior. Researchers have found, for example, that compared to English Canadians, French Canadians are more involved with home and family, attend ballet more often, travel

The Canadian Business Scene

PSYCHOLOGICAL MARKET RESEARCH

Psychological researchers try to determine consumers' subconscious desires so that companies (or political parties) can develop products (or candidates) that will appeal to them. During the Ontario election campaign in 1990, the NDP conducted psychological research using focus groups (discussed on pp. 399–400) which showed that the voters viewed their leader, Bob Rae, as a harmless-looking fellow. The research also showed that voters did not like the terms "the little man" or "the ordinary person." In response, the campaign avoided those terms and Rae developed a more commanding presence. The NDP won that election but was defeated in 1995.

Traditional market research focuses on quantitative data such as the number of people in certain age groups, the income levels of consumers, and structured responses from consumers about what they like or dislike. Qualitative research, on the other hand, is based on the assumption that consumers may be unwilling or unable to state exactly what it is about a product that attracts them (the product may calm their fears, increase their feelings of power or sexuality, make them feel competent, etc.).

Some of the techniques that marketers are currently using may seem strange. The most popular one at present is "let's pretend." Members of a focus group may, for example, be asked to pretend that a brand of beer is a car. They then state what car they think best represents the brand of beer. In one focus group, participants were asked to imagine that they were competing brands of dog food; they were then asked to come up with ways to entice the dog to eat the food they represented.

Although the techniques may seem bizarre, major companies including Lever Brothers Ltd., General Foods Inc., Sanyo Canada Inc., Procter & Gamble, Bell Canada, and Royal Trust have used them. It is estimated that marketers spend about $30 million per year in Canada on qualitative psychological research.

A typical success story of psychological research comes from Campbell's Soup. Campbell's was steadily losing market share. To counteract this trend, the company tried to develop a snappy image that stressed convenience. However, qualitative psychological research revealed that parental concern for children was a more promising theme. When advertisements began running that showed a loving mother preparing soup for her child, sales turned around.

less, eat more chocolate, and are less interested in convenience food. Obviously, prudent marketers should take these differences into account when developing marketing plans. This is, however, easier said than done.

It is one thing to know that consumers in Quebec buy large quantities of certain products; it is quite another to capitalize on these differences. One problem is that differences may not continue over time. Change is continually occurring in consumption patterns across Canada, and data may quickly become outdated. Another problem is that consumption patterns differ from region to region in Canada even where culture is not the main cause. The buying behavior of Quebec and Ontario consumers may be more similar than the behavior of British Columbia and Newfoundland consumers.

Market Research

market research

The systematic study of what buyers need and how best to meet those needs.

Market research can greatly improve the accuracy and effectiveness of market segmentation.[9] **Market research**, the study of what buyers need and how best to meet those needs, can address any element in the marketing mix. One marketer might study how consumers respond to an experimental paint formula. Another might explore how potential buyers will respond to a possible price reduction on calculators. Still another marketer might check audience response to a proposed advertising campaign with a humorous theme. A company manager might also try to learn whether customers will be more likely to buy a product in a store, a mall, or a special discount shop. But market research is no guarantee of success, as the video case "Flops" on p. 492 shows.

Most companies will benefit from market research, but they need not do the research themselves. O-Pee-Chee Co. Ltd. of London, Ontario (the bubble gum and candy manufacturer), does no market research and no product testing, yet it continues to be successful in a market where products change at a dizzying pace. By signing a licensing agreement with two U.S. giants, O-Pee-Chee simply has to look at what's hot in the U.S. and then start manufacturing those lines in Canada.[10]

The importance of selling products in today's international markets is expanding the role of market research into new areas. For example, when companies decide to sell their goods or services in other countries, they must decide whether to standardize products or to specialize them for new markets.

Consider the case of Pepsico when it entered a joint venture to market Cheetos in Guangdong province, China. Originally, Cheetos—crispy cheese puff snacks—did not "test well" in China. The Chinese, it seems, do not eat cheese and did not care for Cheetos' cheesy taste. Pepsico tested more than 600 flavors (including Roasted Cuttlefish) on more than 1000 Chinese consumers before arriving at two—Savory American Cream and Zesty Japanese Steak. Chinese packaging will bear the Chinese characters "qui duo," pronounced "CHEE dwaugh." "Luckily," explains the general manager of Pepsico Foods International, "the translation is 'new surprise,' instead of some phrase that might offend people."

The box "Romancing the Profits" describes the experience of Harlequin Enterprises in doing market research on customers in foreign countries.

The Research Process

Market research can occur at almost any point in a product's existence. Most commonly, however, it is used when a new or altered product is being considered. To see why, you need to understand the steps in performing market research illustrated in Figure 14.3 on page 399.

The process begins with a *study of the current situation*. In other words, what is the need and what is being done to meet it at this point? Such a study should note how well the firm is or is not doing in meeting the need.

The second step is to *select a research method*. As you will see shortly, marketing managers have a wide range of methods available. In choosing a method, marketers must bear in mind the effectiveness and costs of different methods.

The next step is to *collect data*. **Secondary data** are information already available as a result of previous research by the firm or other agencies. For example, Statistics Canada publishes a great deal of data which are useful for business firms.

Using secondary data can save time, effort, and money. But in some cases secondary data are unavailable or inadequate, so **primary data**—new research by the firm or its agents—must be obtained. Hostess Frito-Lay, the maker of Doritos, spent a year studying how to best reach its target market—teenagers. The researchers hung around shopping malls, schools, and fast-food outlets to watch teenagers.[11]

Once data have been collected, marketers need to *analyze the data*. As we shall see in Chapter 23, data are not useful until they have been organized into information.

Marketing personnel then need to share their analysis with others by *preparing a report*. This report should include a summary of the study's methodology and findings. It should also identify alternative solutions (where appropriate) and make recommendations for the appropriate course of action.

secondary data
Information already available to market researchers as a result of previous research by the firm or other agencies.

primary data
Information developed through new research by the firm or its agents.

The Canadian Business Scene

ROMANCING THE PROFITS

The largest romance publisher on earth occupies an uninspired office building in Toronto. Harlequin Enterprises Ltd., which started in Winnipeg in 1949, now has sales revenue exceeding $400 million annually. Its profits accounted for 83 percent of the total profits of its parent, Torstar Corp., the publisher of the *Toronto Star*. With the emergence of the women's liberation movement in the 1970s, skeptics predicted that romance novels were finished, but it hasn't worked out that way. Romance novels now account for 44 percent of all mass-market paperbacks sold in North America, and Harlequin controls 80 percent of that market.

The company also has a strong presence in overseas markets. By 1995, it will sell 45 million books in Eastern Europe alone; it also plans to start selling romances in China. Harlequin offers translations in 24 languages, and prints its books in 16 regions around the world. Interestingly, the book covers remain pretty much the same worldwide, including the emphasis on Caucasians.

When deciding whether to enter a foreign country, Harlequin looks for three things: First, there must be a distribution system already in place because it is prohibitively expensive to set one up. Second, there must be access to TV and print media so that demand can be stimulated through advertising. Third, the company must be able to convert the money it receives for books into dollars. The company has been reluctant to enter Russia because it does not really satisfy any of these criteria. In China, however, where the free market system is growing daily, the company has big plans.

How has Harlequin managed to achieve such success? A major reason is its emphasis on market research. The average reader is around 40, and half have a college education. Over half are employed. Research has shown that readers abroad have the same interests as North American readers. Focus groups and major surveys of North American consumers are a key part of Harlequin's strategic planning.

Readers of romance novels are not a demographic group to be trifled with. They want plot-driven books with lots of action. In all the romance books, the focal couple first meet, then have a misunderstanding, and then make up by the end of the book. Readers know there will be no violence and there will always be a happy ending.

The company has experienced some frustrations in gathering market research data. Because bookstores and other retail outlets take books on consignment, they can return any they don't sell. Thus, the publisher may ship products to retailers, but there is no guarantee of sales. Worse, it takes many months to determine how well a book is doing, and if it is selling particularly well or poorly. Executives at Harlequin say that if book sales could be accurately counted from week to week, Harlequin's books would take all 10 spots on the *New York Times* bestseller list.

Harlequin is developing new products by expanding into TV. For many years, film companies have courted the company, hoping to tap into its library and exploit its loyal readers. Now, the firm has signed a 50-50 partnership agreement with Alliance Communications Corp., Canada's largest independent film producer. Harlequin will supply the editorial work, and Alliance will produce the films. Six movies will be made in the first year of the arrangement, with 26 eventually being made each year. Eventually, the goal is to have a "Harlequin Night of the Week" on TV. The second part of the deal begins after several movies have been made. Then, Harlequin and Alliance will jointly market the movies on videocassettes.

Research Methods

observation

A market research technique involving viewing or otherwise monitoring consumer buying patterns.

The four basic types of methods used by market researchers are observation, survey, focus groups, and experimentation. Probably the oldest form of market research is simple **observation** of what is happening. A store owner notices that customers are buying red children's wagons, not green. The owner reorders more red wagons, the manufacturer's records show high sales of red wagons, and marketing concludes that customers want red wagons. Today, computerized systems allow marketers to "observe" consumers' preferences rapidly and with tremendous accuracy. For example, electronic scanners in supermarkets enable store owners to see what is and is not selling without having to check the shelves. Observation is also a popular research method because it is relatively low in cost, often drawing on data that must be collected for some other reason, such as reordering, anyway.

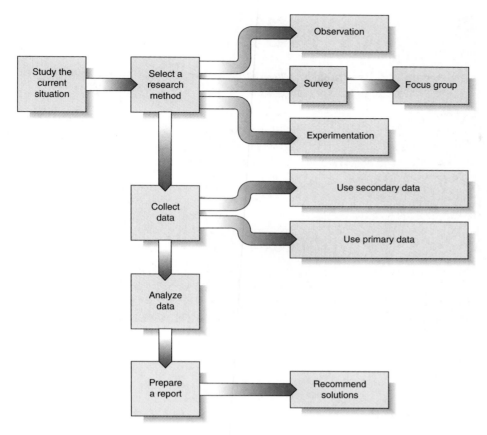

Figure 14.3
Steps in performing market research.

Sometimes, however, observation of current events is not enough. In many cases, marketers need to ask questions about new marketing ideas. One way to get answers is by conducting a **survey**. The heart of any survey is a questionnaire that is mailed to individuals for their completion or is used as the basis of telephone or personal interviews. Surveys can be expensive to carry out and may vary widely in their accuracy. Because no firm can afford to survey everyone, marketers must be careful to get a representative group of respondents. They must also construct their questions so that they get honest answers that address the specific issue being researched.

Some companies have their workers contact consumers directly to get information about how they feel about the company's product. Honda's "E.T. Phone Home Project" involved factory workers calling over 47 000 owners to find out if they were happy with the car and to get ideas for further improvements. The changes that were suggested will appear in the 1995 and 1996 Honda Accords. At Hewlett-Packard, every bit of customer feedback is assigned to an "owner" who must act on the information and report back to the consumer who called. For example, if a complaint about a printer is received, an employee checks the company's data base to see if the complaint is widespread and what the company is doing about it.[12]

Many firms also use **focus groups**, where six to 15 people are brought together to talk about a product or service. A moderator leads the group's discussion, and employees from the sponsoring company may observe the proceedings from behind a one-way mirror. The people in the focus group are not usually told which company is sponsoring the research. The comments of

survey
A market research technique based on questioning a representative sample of consumers about purchasing attitudes and practices.

focus group
A market research technique involving a small group of people brought together and allowed to discuss selected issues in depth.

Focus groups, used by many firms, bring people together to talk about a product or service. This market research technique allows selected issues to be discussed in depth.

people in the focus group are taped, and then researchers go through the data looking for common themes.

Union Gas Ltd. and Levi Strauss have set up focus groups to ask employees about their needs. John Deere uses focus groups of farmers to discuss its tractors. From these discussions have come many specific suggestions for changes in the product (for example, turning off the tractor with a key, different ways to change the oil filter, and making the steps up to the tractor cab wider).[13] The box "The Art of Listening" gives further information about focus groups.

At their best, focus groups allow researchers to explore issues too complex for questionnaires and can produce creative solutions. But because a focus group is small, its responses may not represent the larger market. Focus groups are most often used as a prelude to some other form of research.

experimentation

A market research technique in which the reactions of similar people are compared under different circumstances.

The last major form of market research, experimentation, also tries to get answers to questions that surveys cannot address. As in science, **experimentation** in market research attempts to compare the responses of the same or similar individuals under different circumstances. For example, a firm trying to decide whether or not to include walnuts in a new candy bar probably would not learn much by asking people what they thought of the idea. But if it made up some bars with nuts and some without and then asked people to try both, the responses could be very helpful. Experimentation is, however, very expensive. In deciding whether to use it or any other research method, marketers must carefully weigh the costs against the possible benefits.

Understanding Consumer Behavior

Market research in its many forms can be of great help to marketing managers in understanding how the common traits of a market segment affect consumers' purchasing decisions. Why do people buy VCRs? What desire are they fulfilling? Is there a psychological or sociological explanation for why

The Canadian Business Scene

THE ART OF LISTENING

Focus group research can yield remarkable insights into what consumers are really thinking. Insights, however, can go unnoticed if researchers lack the listening skills that enable them to hear—and interpret—meaning. Learning how to listen, therefore, is essential for every market researcher who plays an active role in focus group sessions.

Effective listening skills involve the ability to hear repeated patterns and "telling comments"—that is, remarks that may suggest new perspectives. For example, a female focus group member once reacted to a commercial that she had just watched with the criticism, "I'm not a cute mommy—I'm a busy mommy." That statement told researchers a great deal about the ways in which today's mothers perceive themselves.

Insights can also lead to new product ideas. For example, in a focus group comprised of parents of children aged two to five, a working mother once told researchers that there are "a lot of stressed-out kids today. We feel guilty and we spoil them with treats." Upon hearing the remark, researchers developed ideas for a new product: healthy snacks for kids.

Experienced focus group leaders understand that people often communicate their real feelings—and valuable messages—in nonverbal ways. Facial expressions, tone of voice, posture, and eye contact have the potential to reveal participants' true feelings. Nonverbal cues are especially important with children, whose body language is often the clearest barometer of what they actually think. "The information you gain from children," says Selma Guber, president of Children's Market Research, "is in not so much what they're saying, but how they're saying it."

Children provide a special challenge to focus group leaders, who realize that they must learn to understand how children think and express themselves. For example, although they can ask adults to list the foods they have eaten in the last month, asking a young child the same question would be fruitless: Many children do not know what a month is and have trouble dealing with long time frames. Similarly, children define words differently than adults. For example, they will tell researchers that a food is "crunchy" only if they can actually hear it make noise as they eat.

---

consumers purchase one product and not another? These questions and many others are addressed in the area of marketing known as consumer behavior. **Consumer behavior** focuses on the decision process by which customers come to purchase and consume a product or service.

consumer behavior

The study of the process by which customers come to purchase and consume a product or service.

Influences on Consumer Behavior

According to the not-so-surprising title of one classic study, we are very much "social animals."[14] To understand consumer behavior, then, marketers draw heavily on the fields of psychology and sociology. The result is a focus on four major influences on consumer behavior: *psychological, personal, social,* and *cultural.* By identifying the four influences that are most active, marketers try to explain consumer choices and predict future purchasing behavior:

- *Psychological influences* include an individual's motivations, perceptions, ability to learn, and attitudes.
- *Personal influences* include lifestyle, personality, economic status, and life-cycle stage.
- *Social influences* include family, opinion leaders (people whose opinions are sought by others), and reference groups such as friends, co-workers, and professional associates.
- *Cultural influences* include culture (the "way of living" that distinguishes one large group from another), subculture (smaller groups, such as ethnic groups, with shared values), and social class (the cultural ranking of groups according to criteria such as background, occupation, and income).

All these factors can have a strong impact on the products that people purchase—often in complex ways.

The purchase of some products is not influenced by psychosocial factors. Consumers with high brand loyalty are less subject to such influences—they stick with the brand of their preference. However, the clothes that you wear, the food that you eat, and the dishes you eat from often reflect social and psychological influences on your consuming behavior.

The Consumer Buying Process

Researchers who have studied consumer behavior have constructed models that help marketing managers understand how consumers come to purchase products. Figure 14.4 presents one such model. At the base of this and similar models is an awareness of the psychosocial influences that lead to consumption. Ultimately, marketing managers use this information to develop marketing plans.

Problem Recognition.   The buying process begins when a consumer becomes aware of a problem or need. After strenuous exercise, you may recognize that you are thirsty and need refreshment. After the birth of twins, you may find your one-bedroom apartment too small for comfort. After standing in the rain to buy movie tickets, you may decide to buy an umbrella.

Need recognition also occurs when you have a chance to change your purchasing habits. For example, the income from your first job after graduation will let you purchase items that were too expensive when you were a student. You may also discover a need for professional clothing, apartment furnishings, and cars. Visa and The Bay recognize this shift and market their credit cards to graduates.

Information Seeking.   Having recognized a need, consumers seek information. This search is not always extensive. If you are thirsty, you may ask where the soda pop machine is, but that may be the extent of your information search. Other times you simply rely on your memory for information.

What information is this shopper looking for to decide on his purchase? Marketers would like to know how and why he makes his choices.

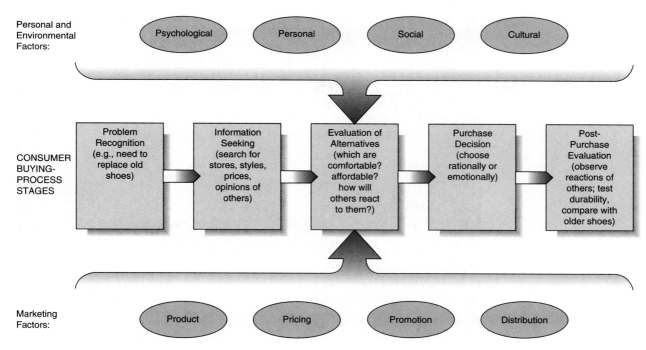

Figure 14.4
A model of the consumer buying process.

Before making major purchases, however, most people seek information from personal sources, marketing sources, public sources, and experience. For example, if you move to a new town, you will want to find out who is the best local dentist, physician, hair stylist, butcher, or pizza maker. To get this information, you may check with personal sources such as acquaintances, co-workers, and relatives. Before buying an exercise bike, you may go to the library and read the latest *Consumer Reports*—a public source of consumer ratings—on such equipment. You may also ask market sources such as the salesclerk or rely on direct experience. For example, you might test ride the bike to learn more before you buy.

Some sellers treat information as a value to be added to their products. For example, Body Shop International, a cosmetics manufacturer and retailer with no marketing or advertising department, has nevertheless been cited as a model of how to sell in the 1990s. The company's philosophy includes giving the customer product information rather than the traditional sales pitch. What makes this strategy work? The typical Body Shop customer is a skeptical consumer who generally distrusts advertising and sales hype, demands more product information, and is loyal to companies that, like the Body Shop, are perceived to be socially and environmentally responsible.[15]

Evaluation of Alternatives.   The next step in the consumer decision process is to evaluate your alternatives. If you are in the market for a set of golf clubs, you probably have some idea of who produces clubs and how they differ. You may have accumulated some of this knowledge during the information-seeking stage and combined it with what you knew before. Based on product attributes such as color, taste, price, prestige, quality, and service record, you will decide which product meets your needs most satisfactorily.

Purchase Decision.   Ultimately, you make a purchase decision. You may decide to defer the purchase until a later time or you may decide to buy now. "Buy" decisions are based on rational and emotional motives. **Rational motives**

rational motives
Those reasons for purchasing a product that involve a logical evaluation of product attributes such as cost, quality, and usefulness.

Body Shop International, which has no marketing or advertising department, is viewed by its loyal customers as socially and environmentally responsible.

emotional motives
Those reasons for purchasing a product that involve nonobjective factors.

involve a logical evaluation of product attributes: cost, quality, and usefulness. By definition, **emotional motives** lead to irrational decisions. Many spur-of-the-moment decisions are emotionally driven, though not all irrational decisions are sudden. Emotional motives include fear, sociability, imitation of others, and aesthetics. You might buy mouthwash to avoid ostracism. You might buy the same brand of jeans as your friends. And you might buy a chocolate milkshake because you like the taste.

Note that by "irrational" we do not mean insane or wrong, merely a decision based on nonobjective factors. Gratifying a sudden urge for ice cream may not require much thought and may produce lots of enjoyment. But in some cases, irrational decisions are bad. We have all purchased items, taken them home, and then wondered, "Why in the world did I buy this thing?"

Post-Purchase Evaluations.   Marketing does not stop with the sale of a product or service, but includes the process of consumption. What happens *after* the sale is very important. A marketer wants consumers to be happy after the consumption of the product so that they will buy the product again. In fact, since consumers do not want to go through a complex decision process for every purchase, they often choose a product they have used and liked.

Not all consumers are satisfied with their purchases, of course. Dissatisfied consumers may complain, file a lawsuit, or publicly criticize the product and the company. They are unlikely to purchase the product again. In addition, dissatisfied customers are much more likely to speak about their experience with a product than are satisfied customers. Dissatisfied customers can have a very negative impact on a company's marketing effort. In fact, word-of-mouth can be the most influential marketing tool and also the most devastating, since businesses cannot control it.[16]

purchase anxiety
A fear on the part of people who have made a purchase that their selection was wrong.

Doubts about the rationality of a purchase decision can cause **purchase anxiety**, sometimes called buyer's remorse. If you feel purchase anxiety after remodeling your home, you probably will not buy the services of the same interior designer again. Doing so would only perpetuate your anxiety. Reduction of purchase anxiety is important to marketers, particularly for expensive items like furniture and major appliances.

The Organizational Buying Process

Buying behavior is observable daily in the consumer market where marketing activities, including buying-selling transactions, are visible to the public. Equally important, however, and far less visible is the buying of goods and services by organizations which use them in creating and delivering consumer products. Organizational or commercial markets fall into three categories: *industrial, reseller,* and *government/institutional organizations*.

Industrial Market.   The **industrial market** includes businesses that buy goods falling into one of two categories: goods to be converted into other products and goods that are used up during production. This market includes farmers, manufacturers, and some retailers. For example, Seth Thomas purchases electronics, metal components, and glass to make clocks for the consumer market. The company also buys office supplies, tools, and factory equipment—items never seen by clock buyers—to be used during production.

industrial market
Businesses that buy goods to be converted into other products that will be sold to ultimate consumers.

Reseller Market.   Before products reach consumers, they pass through a **reseller market** consisting of intermediaries, including wholesalers and retailers, who buy the finished goods and resell them (wholesalers and retailers are discussed in Chapter 16.) Retailers like department stores, drug stores, and supermarkets buy clothing, appliances, foods, medicines, and other merchandise for resale to the consumer market. Retailers also buy such services as maintenance, housekeeping, and communications.

reseller market
Intermediaries like wholesalers and retailers who buy finished products and resell them.

Government and Institutional Market.   Federal, provincial, and municipal governments purchase millions of dollars worth of computer equipment, buildings, paper clips and other items. The **institutional market** consists of nongovernmental organizations, such as hospitals, churches, museums, and charitable organizations, that also comprise a substantial market for goods and services. Like organizations in other commercial markets, these institutions use supplies and equipment, as well as legal, accounting, and transportation services.

institutional market
Nongovernment organizations such as hospitals, churches, and schools.

   In many respects, industrial buying behavior bears little resemblance to consumer buying practices. For example, industrial product demand is stimulated by demand for consumer products and is less sensitive to price changes. Other differences include the buyers' purchasing skills, their decision-making activities, and buyer-seller relationships.

Differences in Demand.   Recall our definition of *demand* in Chapter 1: the willingness and ability of buyers to purchase a good or service. There are two major differences in demand between consumer and industrial products: *derived demand* and *inelasticity of demand*. The term **derived demand** refers to the fact that demand for industrial products often results from demand for related consumer products (that is, industrial demand is frequently *derived from* consumer demand). **Inelasticity of demand** exists when a price change for a product does not have much affect on demand. Take, for instance, the demand for cardboard used to package file cabinets. Because cardboard packaging is such a small part of the manufacturer's overall cabinet cost, an increase in cardboard prices will not lessen the demand for cardboard. In turn, because cabinet buyers will see little price increase, demand for filing cabinets—and for their accompanying cardboard packaging—will remain at about the same level.

derived demand
Demand for industrial products caused by (derived from) demand for consumer products.

inelasticity of demand
Exists when a price change for a product does not have much effect on demand.

Differences in Buyers.   Unlike most consumers, organizational buyers are professional, specialized, and expert (or at least well-informed):

- As *professionals*, organizational buyers are trained in arranging buyer-seller relationships and in methods for negotiating purchase terms. Once buyer-seller agreements have been reached, industrial buyers also arrange for formalized contracts.
- As a rule, industrial buyers are company *specialists* in a line of items. As one of several buyers for a large bakery, for example, you may specialize in food ingredients like flour, yeast, butter, and so on.
- Industrial buyers are often *experts* about the products that they are buying. On a regular basis, organizational buyers learn about competing products and alternative suppliers by attending trade shows, reading trade magazines, and conducting technical discussions with sellers' representatives.

Differences in Decision Making.   Recall that we illustrated the five stages in the consumer buying process in Figure 14.4. The organizational buyer's decision process differs in three important respects—*developing product specifications*, *evaluating alternatives*, and *making postpurchase evaluations*.

Following problem recognition, the first stage of the buying process, industrial buying takes an additional step—developing product specifications: A document is drawn up to describe the detailed product characteristics that are needed by the buyer and must be met by the supplier. These specifications are then used in the information-seeking stage, when buyers search for products and suppliers capable of meeting their specific needs.

In evaluating alternatives, buyers carefully measure prospective suppliers against the product specifications developed earlier. Only suppliers that can meet those requirements are considered further. Only thereafter are prospective vendors evaluated according to other factors, such as price, reliability, and service reputation.

The final stage, post-purchase evaluation, is more systematic in organizational buying than in consumer buying. The buyer's organization examines the product and compares it, feature-by-feature, for conformance to product specifications. Buyers retain records on product and service quality received from suppliers as the basis for evaluating suppliers' performance. These performance ratings become important considerations for selecting suppliers in the future.

Differences in the Buyer-Seller Relationship.   Consumer-seller relationships are often impersonal and fleeting—short-lived one-time interactions. In contrast, industrial situations often involve frequent, enduring buyer-seller relationships. Accordingly, industrial sellers emphasize personal selling by trained representatives who can better understand the needs of each customer. Through extensive interaction with numerous buyers, sellers are better prepared to make suggestions for improving products and services that will benefit their customers.

The International Marketing Mix

Marketing products internationally means mounting a strategy to support global business operations. Obviously, this is no easy task. Foreign customers, for example, differ from domestic buyers in language, customs, business practices, and consumer behavior. When they decide to go global, marketers must thus reconsider each element of the marketing mix: product, pricing, promotion, and place.

International Products

Some products, of course, can be sold abroad with virtually no changes. Budweiser, Coca-Cola, and Marlboros are exactly the same in Toronto, Tokyo, and Timbuktu. In other cases, firms have been obliged to create products with built-in flexibility—for instance, electric shavers that adapt to either 115- or 230-volt outlets.

At times only a redesigned—or completely different—product will meet the needs of foreign buyers, however. To sell the Macintosh in Japan, for example, Apple had to develop a Japanese-language operating system. Whether they are standard domestic products or custom-made products for foreign markets, however, the most globally competitive products are usually reliable, low-priced products with advanced features.

International Pricing

When pricing for international markets, marketers must handle all the considerations of domestic pricing while also considering the higher costs of transporting and selling products abroad. Some products cost more overseas than in Canada because of the added costs of delivery. Due to the higher costs of buildings, rent, equipment, and imported meat, a McDonald's Big Mac that sells for $2.99 in Canada has a price tag of over $10 in Japan. In contrast, products like jet airplanes are priced the same worldwide because delivery costs are incidental; the huge development and production costs are the major considerations regardless of customer location.

International Promotion

Some standard Canadian promotional devices do not always succeed in other countries. In fact, many Europeans believe that a product must be inherently shoddy if a company does *any* advertising.

International marketers must also be aware that cultural differences can cause negative reactions to products that are advertised improperly. Some Europeans, for example, are offended by television commercials that show weapons or violence. Advertising practices are regulated accordingly. Consequently, Dutch commercials for toys do not feature the guns and combat scenes that are commonplace on Saturday morning television in North America. Meanwhile, liquor and cigarette commercials that are banned from Canadian and U.S. television are thriving in many Asian and European markets.

Symbolism, too, is a sometimes surprising consideration. In France, for instance, yellow flowers suggest infidelity. In Mexico, they are signs of death—an association made in Brazil by the color purple. Clearly, product promotions must be carefully matched to the customs and cultural values of each country. The box "Pitfalls in Global Promotion" describes some difficulties companies have had when promoting their product in foreign markets.

International Distribution

Finally, international distribution presents several problems. In some industries, delays in starting new distribution networks can be costly. Therefore, companies with existing distribution systems often enjoy an advantage over new businesses. Several companies have gained advantages in time-based competition by buying existing businesses. Procter & Gamble, for example,

International Report

PITFALLS IN GLOBAL PROMOTION

Marketing products internationally can provide big payoffs to those who do their homework. As many firms have learned, careful research of both idiomatic nuances and cultural norms is critical to global success.

Some early attempts by Chinese marketers underscore this point. China had several products it wanted to market in the United States. But, as the manufacturers learned too late, brand names such as White Elephant batteries, Maxipuke playing cards, and Pansy brand men's underwear did not attract many U.S. customers.

But even careful research is not a guarantee of success. Japan's giant Toyota ran afoul in China with a marketing campaign targeted specifically to Chinese culture. Toyota launched an advertising campaign based on the old Chinese proverb, "When you get to the foot of the mountain, a road will appear." Toyota added "Wherever there is a road, there is a Toyota." In China, however, truth in advertising is taken very seriously. The Chinese hold to this tenet in their own advertising and expect foreign companies to do the same. A year after the slogan was used in print and TV ads, Chinese authorities told Toyota that it constituted false advertising. Toyota had to drop the campaign.

Ads sometimes backfire from miscalculating a country's sense of humor. Take the case of Luis Nasr, creative director of an ad agency in Ecuador, who designed an ad for a hairgrowth product called Regenal Forte. The ad featured a picture of Mikhail Gorbachev with the caption, "He didn't use Regenal Forte in time." The Russian ambassador was not amused. The uproar soon subsided, however, and the ad subsequently won a prize at the New York Print Festival.

Marketing managers are trying to avoid these kinds of problems with *global advertising*, a strategy in which the same basic ad campaign—with minor alterations from country to country—is used throughout the world. Peter S. Sealey, senior vice president and director of global marketing for Coca-Cola, puts it this way: "There is global media now, like MTV. And there is a global teenager. The same kid you see at the Ginza in Tokyo is in Picadilly Square in London, in Pushkin Square, at Notre Dame." So why not create an advertisement that will appeal to the universal teenager (or universal parent or universal businessperson)?

saved three years of start-up time by buying Revlon's Max Factor and Betrix cosmetics, both of which are well established in foreign markets. P&G can thus immediately use these companies' distribution and marketing networks for selling its own brands in the United Kingdom, Germany, and Japan.

Other companies contract with foreign firms or individuals to distribute and sell their products abroad. Foreign agents may perform personal selling and advertising, provide information about local markets, or serve as exporters' representatives. But having to manage interactions with foreign personnel complicates a marketing manager's responsibilities. In addition, packaging practices in Canada must sometimes be adapted to withstand the rigors of transport to foreign ports and storage under conditions that differ radically from domestic conditions.

Given the need to adjust the marketing mix, success in international markets is hard won. Even experienced firms can err in marketing to other countries. International success requires flexibility and a willingness to adapt to the nuances of other cultures. Whether a firm markets in domestic or international markets, however, the basic principles of marketing still apply. It is only the implementation of those principles that changes.

Small Business and the Marketing Mix

As we noted in Chapter 7, far more small businesses fail than succeed. Yet many of today's largest firms were yesterday's small businesses. McDonald's began with one restaurant, a concept, and one individual (Ray Kroc) who had foresight. Behind the success of many small firms lies a skillful application of the marketing concept and careful consideration of each element in the marketing mix.

Small Business Products

Some new products—and firms—are doomed at the start simply because few consumers want or need what they have to offer. Too often, enthusiastic entrepreneurs introduce products that they and their friends like, but they fail to estimate realistic market potential. Other small businesses offer new products before they have clear pictures of their target segments and how to reach them. They try to be everything to everyone, and they end up serving no one well. In contrast, sound product planning has paid off for many small firms. "Keep it simple" is a familiar key to success—that is, fulfill a specific need and do it efficiently.

Small Business Pricing

Haphazard pricing that is often little more than guesswork can sink even a firm with a good product. Most often, small business pricing errors result from a failure to project operating expenses accurately. Owners of failing businesses have often been heard to utter statements like "I didn't realize how much it costs to run the business!" and "If I price the product high enough to cover my expenses, no one will buy it!" But when small businesses set prices by carefully assessing costs, many earn very satisfactory profits—sometimes enough to expand or diversify.

Small Business Promotion

Many small businesses are also ignorant when it comes to the methods and costs of promotion. To save expenses, for example, they may avoid advertising and rely instead on personal selling. As a result, too many potential customers remain unaware of their products.

Successful small businesses plan for promotional expenses as part of start-up costs. Some hold down costs by taking advantage of less expensive promotional methods. Local newspapers, for example, are sources of publicity when they publish articles about new or unique businesses. Other small businesses have succeeded by identifying themselves and their products with associated groups, organizations, and events. Thus a custom-crafts gallery might join with a local art league and local artists to organize public showings of their combined products.

Small Business Distribution

Problems in arranging distribution can also make or break small businesses. Perhaps the most critical aspect of distribution is facility location, especially for new service businesses. The ability of many small businesses—retailers, veterinary clinics, gourmet coffee shops—to attract and retain customers depends partly on the choice of location.

In distribution, as in other aspects of the marketing mix, however, smaller companies may have advantages over larger competitors, even in highly complex industries. They may be quicker, for example, in applying service technologies. Everex Systems Inc. sells personal computers to wholesalers and dealers through a system the company calls "Zero Response Time." Phone orders are reviewed every two hours so that the factory can adjust assembly to match demand.

Summary of Key Points

In keeping with the marketing concept, marketers strive to earn profits for their firms by identifying and meeting the needs of buyers. The marketing process, which requires careful planning and execution, begins with the creation of a good, service, or idea. In addition to the product itself, the marketing mix must include strategies for pricing, promoting, and distributing the product. Successful marketing mixes create exchanges between buyers and sellers. In practice, marketing functions can be divided into exchange functions (buying and selling), distribution functions (transportation and storage), and facilitation functions (standardization, financing, risk taking, and researching).

Businesses have learned that their marketing is more successful when it is targeted toward specific market segments. Markets may be segmented based on geographic, demographic, psychographic, or product-use variables. Market research can help to identify target markets by studying consumer buying behavior and attitudes. This process involves a study of the current situation, selection of a research method, collection of data, analysis of data, and preparation of a report that includes recommendations for action. The four most common research methods are observation, survey, focus groups, and experimentation.

Market research can help marketers understand how the common traits of the segment affect consumers' purchasing decisions. A number of personal and psychological considerations, along with many social and cultural influences, determine consumers' behavior. When making buying decisions, consumers first determine their problem (need), then collect as much information as they think necessary before actually making a purchase. Post-purchase evaluations are also important to marketers, since they influence future buying patterns.

Organizations also purchase products and then use them to create consumer products. Organizational buying differs from consumer buying because it uses professional buyers, and the decision making process of organizational buyers is more formalized.

Because consumer behavior, languages, and customs in other nations differ from those of our country, international marketing—trade made across international boundaries—often requires marketers to reconsider the marketing mix. New products, prices that reflect higher transportation costs, culture-specific advertising, and the use of foreign firms to distribute the product may all be necessary.

Small businesses also face special marketing challenges if they are to survive and grow. Every aspect of the marketing mix must be addressed and planned for before a new business begins.

The Art and Science of Aisle-Traffic Control

There is nothing accidental about where products are placed on supermarket shelves. In fact, new marketing techniques are making aisle and shelf assignments more of a science than an art. Today's marketers use combinations of high-technology surveillance equipment and old-fashioned stakeouts to learn what they can about the aisles that shoppers travel and those they avoid. Naturally, they are adjusting product placement according to what they learn. The goal is to influence purchase decisions by placing *high-margin products*—those that produce the most revenue per unit sold—in high-traffic areas. Some stores also encourage sales through customized in-store video and audio ads, which direct consumers to specific products.

Executives at one supermarket knew that some items were moving faster than others, but they didn't really know how shoppers' habits affected purchase decisions. To gather some hard data, they placed a surveillance team on store catwalks. The team's mission: to observe the traffic patterns of 1600 shoppers. For one thing, they discovered that most shoppers were attracted to the periphery of the store—the produce, dairy, and meat aisles—but tended to avoid the store's center (the area consuming the greatest store space). So the store installed video monitors on the outskirts of the store to broadcast commercials for items shelved in the store's center. The theory is that after viewing a commercial for Quaker Oats cereals or Little Friskies cat food, shoppers venture into less-traveled aisles.

Another surveillance study showed that although greeting cards are high-volume items, fewer than one in five shoppers ever walk down the greeting-card aisle. When the cards were moved to a part of the store that regularly draws 62 percent of the traffic, quarterly sales jumped 40 percent. Undoubtedly, being next to the peanut butter and jelly helped boost sales. "We're no longer guessing if location really matters," explains Richard Blatt, executive director of the Point-of Purchase Advertising Institute. "We now have statistical proof."

Other analysts have found that audio ads supplied by Muzak also encourage purchase decisions. Some supermarket chains use audio advertising to pitch specific products to a captive audiences of shoppers. Moreover, nearly half of all regional chains and independent supermarkets promote products through a series of three 20-second point-of-purchase audio ads sandwiched between eight minutes of background music. Messages can be geared to local markets and even to specific stores.

However, although attempts to influence purchasing decisions have been largely successful, retailers face some built-in dangers. For example, harried shoppers who are used to finding items in specific places may balk when different, unrelated items are combined. According to food-retail consultant Willard Bishop, "a crazy-quilt pattern isn't consumer-friendly." Moreover, many consumers find audio ads intrusive and annoying and may decide not to buy promoted products because of the assault on their senses.

For marketers, of course, the bottom line is whether such techniques actually influence shoppers to make specific purchases. A recent incident involving Muzak advertising demonstrates that, at the very least, in-store messages are being heard. Using Muzak, one grocer broadcast a tip on how to tell the difference between fresh and stale eggs. However, instead of saying that fresh eggs *sink* in water, the announcer told shoppers that fresh eggs *float*. When large groups of customers began returning newly purchased eggs, Muzak marketers realized their mistake and pulled the ad. The incident was embarrassing, of course, but it showed that people were actually listening and, more importantly, acting on what they heard.

CASE QUESTIONS

1. When marketers watch shoppers' behavior, they are using the oldest form of market research—observation. Because marketers can use inventory data to determine what is selling and what is not, why is it important to observe the routes that shoppers take as they navigate a store?
2. Does observing shoppers without their knowledge raise any ethical concerns?
3. Because point-of-purchase advertising is trying to influence purchasing decisions in the moments before they are made, are marketers assuming that shoppers wait to the last minute to evaluate alternatives and decide what they want?
4. How do you feel about attempts by marketers to influence your supermarket purchasing decisions? Are you likely to be annoyed or grateful? ◆

CONCLUDING CASE 14-2

Marketing of Legal Services

Until recently, Canadian lawyers did not give much thought to marketing their services. But because there is now an abundance of lawyers, and because the recession has made many clients increasingly cost-conscious, the market for legal services has become extremely competitive. Lawyers used to sit back and wait for business to come to them. Now they must market themselves.

Traditionally, business firms knew little about the law and so trusted almost all of their legal business to one firm. But today over 5000 lawyers work for Canadian companies, and the firms know what they want and what it should cost. Their in-house lawyers do most of the routine work, and the companies go to outsiders only when they have special needs. It's a buyer's market. Law firms have responded by using cold calls, direct mail, billboards, and other advertising to attract clients.

Cassels Brock & Blackwell was one of the first law firms to hire a marketing director. And two of its lawyers—Ralph Lean and former Ontario premier David Peterson—spend most of their time developing new business. The secret to successful marketing of legal services is to deliver value for the money paid. Quick service and a first-rate "product" are essential, just as they are for firms selling a physical object.

Some firms, such as Stikeman Elliott, have opened offices overseas to develop international business. The firm decides on its target market and then develops a marketing campaign tailor-made to the industry or culture. A program in Hong Kong will differ from one in London. Individual lawyers are also encouraged to come up with ideas for developing new clients.

All this activity is a dramatic departure for a profession

that only a decade ago could have disbarred any lawyer who advertised or who approached a prospect. In 1979, the British Columbia law society disciplined a Vancouver lawyer for running a newspaper advertisement and for hanging an illuminated sign outside his office. He fought his case all the way to the Canadian Supreme Court but lost. The case did cause a loosening of the rules, but law societies in Saskatchewan and New Brunswick prohibited television and radio advertising until 1991. Such ads are still unacceptable in Prince Edward Island and Nova Scotia.

Canada is more conservative than the United States, where lawyers routinely use television, radio, and print advertising. In Canada, the leading marketing device at the moment is the Yellow Pages. One Toronto firm spends about $200 000 per year on Yellow Pages advertising; its main theme is "we listen."

Marketing and concern for the consumer are ideas that are still developing in the legal services industry. Art James, general counsel for IBM Canada, says that some firms never follow up to see how satisfied their client is with the job they did. But lawyers are in the same position as other organizations offering a service—they will have to increase their attention to the consumer or they will not survive.

CASE QUESTIONS

1. How is the marketing of legal services different from the marketing of other services? How is it similar?
2. Why are lawyers suddenly interested in advertising their services? Why did provincial law societies not allow lawyers to advertise until recently?
3. What problems might develop now that lawyers are allowed to advertise?   ◆

Key Terms

marketing	promotion	positioning	rational motives
consumer goods	advertising	psychographics	emotional motives
industrial goods	personal selling	market research	purchase anxiety
marketing managers	sales promotions	secondary data	industrial market
marketing plan	public relations	primary data	reseller market
marketing concept	publicity	observation	institutional market
marketing mix	distribution	survey	derived demand
product	exchange	focus group	inelasticity of demand
product differentiation	target market	experimentation	
pricing	market segmentation	consumer behavior	

Study Questions and Exercises

Review Questions

1. What are the similarities and differences between consumer marketing and industrial marketing?
2. Explain how and why market segmentation is used in target marketing.
3. Identify the steps in the consumer buying process.
4. What elements of the marketing mix may need to be adjusted to market a product internationally? Why?

Analysis Questions

5. Using examples of everyday products, explain why marketing plans must consider the marketing mix.
6. Pick an everyday product such as books, dog food, or shoes. Using your product as an example, show how different versions of it are aimed toward different market segments. Show how the marketing mix differs for each of the segments.

7. Select a readily available product and describe the steps you would expect to find in the consumer decision process about buying that product.
8. If you were starting your own new small business, what are the major pitfalls you would try to avoid as you put together your marketing plans?

Application Questions

9. Interview the marketing manager of a local business. Identify the degree to which this person's job is oriented toward each of the eight marketing functions.
10. Select a product made by a foreign company and sold in Canada. Compare it to a similar product made domestically in terms of its product features, price, promotion, and distribution. Which one of the two products do you believe will be more successful with Canadian buyers? Why?

Building Your Business Skills

Goal

To encourage students to understand how companies market similar products in different ways.

Method

Think of a specific good or service with a large number of competitors, such as Pizza Hut, Hertz Car Rental, or MasterCard. Keeping in mind the elements of the marketing mix—product, pricing, promotion, and place—write a short description of what, in your estimation, seems to be the company's marketing strategy.

Analysis

Pair off with another student and take turns analyzing each other's written description of the company's plan. Focus both on each company's current marketing strategy and on ideas that you have for improving it. Specifically, analyze the following factors:

- how product changes might affect consumer demand
- new methods for differentiating the company's product from those of competitors
- the effectiveness of the company's current pricing strategy
- the effectiveness of the company's product-promotion strategy
- ways in which you would change specific promotional activities
- the effectiveness of the company's current distribution channels.

Follow-Up Questions

1. Does your analysis show that one element of the marketing mix seems to be more important than the others in creating and satisfying consumer demand?
2. How do you think the marketing strategy would change if the company wanted to sell its products in Saudi Arabia, Mexico, Japan, and the U.S.?

15

Developing and Promoting Goods and Services

LEARNING OBJECTIVES

After reading this chapter, you will be able to

- Describe the nature of products and distinguish between consumer and industrial products in a product mix.
- Trace the steps in new product development and the stages of the product life cycle.
- Explain the importance of brand names, packaging, and labeling of products.
- Identify three objectives of promotion and three considerations in selecting a promotional mix.
- Describe advertising strategies and advertising media.
- Outline the situations and tasks associated with personal selling, and list the steps in the personal selling process.
- Discuss types of sales promotions.
- Show how publicity is used for promotion.
- Explain how small businesses use promotion.

CHAPTER OUTLINE

Developing a New Product for a Small Market

When you think of new product development, you often think of toothpaste, computers, or automobiles. But how about airplanes? Two new airplanes, aimed at the most elite market in the world will be flying before the year 2000. They are long-range corporate jets, and they will be able to carry eight passengers from New York to Tokyo in 13 hours without refueling. Only 350 to 800 of these planes will be sold, likely at a price of about $30 million each. The customers are multinational companies, a few billionaires, and a few heads of state.

Only two companies are developing this new product. One is a world-famous U.S. firm (Gulfstream) and the other is Bombardier Inc. of Montreal. This is going to be a David and Goliath struggle, but there is a big surprise: the Goliath is Bombardier. With annual sales of nearly $5 billion, 36 500 employees, manufacturing operations in eight countries, and markets in more than 60, Bombardier is the sixth largest aviation company in the world, and a major force in international transportation. The company has grown from its beginnings as a maker of snowmobiles to its present size by acquiring several firms, including Canadair, Learjet, Short Brothers PLC, and de Havilland. By contrast, Gulfstream is a small player and makes only top-of-the-line corporate jets. Its new jet is called the Gulfstream V.

In a football field-size room at its Montreal headquarters, a team of 250 Bombardier engineers sit at computer screens designing the new plane (called the Global Express). Part of the team is responsible for the wings and fuselage. Another part is building the engine. Next door, in a building so big its corridors have street names so that workers won't get lost, other parts of the new product development plan are being carried out.

The idea for an intercontinental business jet costing $30 million dollars started in 1989 when CEO Laurent Beaudoin called vice-president John Holding from his car phone and suggested that they leapfrog the competition. Bombardier's strategy has been to be a leader in selected market niches, and company executives agreed that with the increasing globalization of business, a global business jet was needed. In spite of the increased emphasis on electronic commuication and corporate efficiency, Bombardier is betting that it will continue to be necessary to conduct business face-to-face, particularly when new international deals are being put together. Hence, it will market the new jet on the basis that it economizes on the executive's most precious commodity—time.

Bombardier conducted market research on the new product by asking potential customers which pair of cities they most frequently travelled between. They found that New York-Tokyo was the key. Bombardier next asked customers if they would pay $28 million for a plane that could travel 12 000 kilometres at 850 kilometres per hour. They said yes. By the end of 1993, the company had 30

orders in hand, so the final go-ahead was given. Bombardier will break even when it sells the 100th plane.

At present, no corporate jet can match the speed of a commercial 747-400, which can fly from New York to Tokyo nonstop. But the Global Express will be able to fly the route in 13 hours nonstop *and* allow the executive to carry on business while in the air. Since executives on private jets move through customs much faster than those traveling on scheduled airlines, this will save further time.

Bombardier is shielded from a lot of financial risk in this new product venture because it isn't trying to carry the whole project. Although the total cost of the project is $1 billion, Bombardier has invested less than half that amount. It has generated the remaining funds by forming partnerships with several other firms like Mitsubishi and BMW Rolls Royce.

Compared to the Gulfstream V, the Global Express has the edge. It will be faster, enabling it to get to Tokyo an hour sooner. And it is roomier inside, with a higher, wider cabin that has 19 percent more floor area. The Gulfstream's advantage is that it will be on the market two years sooner. Because this is a critical new product for Gulfstream's future success, it is already aggressively competing against the Global Express. In late 1993, it took out a full page advertisement in *The Wall Street Journal* offering a $250 000 discount on its new plane to anyone who cancelled an order for the Global Express. But nobody took up the offer.

What other new products might Bombardier be introducing in the future? The most obvious is a supersonic corporate jet that could cut the flying time from New York to Tokyo to less than 6 hours. It's already technically feasible, but the product won't be developed until it makes financial sense. Bombardier always keeps in mind its two main goals: to make great aircraft, and to make money doing so. ◆

In the last chapter, we introduced the four components of the marketing mix: product, promotion, price, and distribution. In this chapter, we will look more closely at the first two of these components. In particular, we will look at the complex issue of what a product is and how it can best be promoted to customers. The opening case shows that developing a new product is a risky and time-consuming activity, but it must be done if a company is to survive and prosper in the long run.

What Is a Product?

In developing the marketing mix for any products—whether ideas, goods, or services—marketers must consider what consumers really buy when they purchase products. Only then can they plan their strategies effectively. We will begin this section where product strategy begins—with an understanding of product *features* and *benefits*. Next, we will describe the major *classifications of products*, both consumer and industrial. Finally, we will discuss the most important component in the offerings of any business—its *product mix*.

Features and Benefits

Customers do not buy products simply because they like the products themselves—they buy products because they like what the products can *do* for them, either physically or emotionally. As one marketing expert has observed, "Consumers don't buy quarter-inch drills; they buy quarter-inch holes." This observation goes to the heart of any effort to analyze products and product success: Companies must base the approach to products (quarter-inch drills) on providing consumers with products that *do* what customers want *done* (drill quarter-inch holes).

To succeed, then, a product must include the right features and offer the right benefits. Product features are the qualities, tangible and intangible, that a company "builds into" its products, such as a 12-horsepower motor on a lawn mower, an improved accounting system, pH balance in a shampoo, or a 60-40 fibre blend in a shirt. To be saleable, however, a product's features also must provide *benefits*: The mower must provide an attractive lawn; the accounting system, better information for making decisions; pH balance, clean and healthy hair; and a 60-40 blend, a good-looking, easy-care shirt.

Obviously, features and benefits play extremely important roles in the pricing of products. Products are much more than just *visible* features and benefits. In buying a product, consumers are also buying an image and a reputation. The marketers of Swatch Chrono watch, for example, are well aware that brand name, packaging, labeling, and after-purchase service are also indispensable parts of their product. Advertisements remind consumers that such "real" features as shock and water resistance, quartz precision, and Swiss manufacture come hand-in-hand with Swatch's commitment to three "concept" features: young and trendy, active and sporty, and stylistically cool and clean.

Classifying Goods and Services

One way to classify a product is according to expected buyers. Buyers fall into two groups: buyers of *consumer* products and buyers of *industrial* products. As we saw in Chapter 14, the consumer and industrial buying processes differ significantly. Not surprisingly, then, marketing products to consumers is vastly different from marketing them to other companies.

Classifying Consumer Products.   Consumer products are commonly divided into three categories that reflect buyers' behavior: convenience, shopping, and specialty products.

convenience goods/services

Relatively inexpensive consumer goods or services that are bought and used rapidly and regularly, causing consumers to spend little time looking for them or comparing their prices.

shopping goods/services

Moderately expensive consumer goods or services that are purchased infrequently, causing consumers to spend some time comparing their prices.

specialty goods/services

Very expensive consumer goods or services that are purchased rarely, causing consumers to spend a great deal of time locating the exact item desired.

expense items

Relatively inexpensive industrial goods that are consumed rapidly and regularly.

■ **Convenience goods** (such as milk and newspapers) and **convenience services** (such as those offered by fast-food restaurants) are consumed rapidly and regularly. They are relatively inexpensive and are purchased frequently and with little expenditure of time and effort.

■ **Shopping goods** (such as stereos and tires) and **shopping services** (such as insurance) are more expensive and are purchased less frequently than convenience goods and services. Consumers often compare brands, sometimes in different stores. They may also evaluate alternatives in terms of style, performance, color, price, and other criteria.

■ **Specialty goods** (such as wedding gowns) and **specialty services** (such as catering for wedding receptions) are extremely important and expensive purchases. Consumers usually decide on precisely what they want and will accept no substitutes. They will often go from store to store, sometimes spending a great deal of money and time to get a specific product.

Classifying Industrial Products.   Depending on how much they cost and how they will be used, industrial products can be divided into two categories: *expense items* and *capital items*.

Expense items are any materials and services that are consumed within a year by firms producing other goods or supplying services. The most obvious expense items are industrial goods used directly in the production process, for example, bulkloads of tea processed into tea bags. In addition, *support materials* help to keep a business running without directly entering the production process. Oil, for instance, keeps the tea-bagging machines running but is not used in the tea bags. Similarly, *supplies*—pencils, brooms, gloves, paint—are consumed quickly and regularly by every business. Finally, *services* such as window cleaning, equipment installation, and temporary office help are essential to daily operations. Because these items are used frequently, purchases are often automatic or require little decision making.

capital items

Expensive, long-lasting industrial goods that are used in producing other goods or services and have a long life.

Capital items are "permanent"—that is, expensive and long-lasting—goods and services. All these items have expected lives of more than a year—typically up to several years. Expensive buildings (offices, factories), fixed equipment (water towers, baking ovens), and accessory equipment (computers, airplanes) are capital goods. Capital services are those for which long-term commitments are made. These may include purchases for employee food services, building and equipment maintenance, or legal services. Because capital items are expensive and purchased infrequently, they often involve decisions by high-level managers.

The Product Mix

product mix

The group of products a company has available for sale.

The group of products a company has available for sale, be they consumer or industrial, is known as the firm's **product mix**. Black and Decker, for example, makes toasters, vacuum cleaners, electric drills, and a variety of other appliances and tools. 3M makes everything from Post-Its to laser optics.

Most companies begin with a single product. Over time, successful companies may find that the initial product does not suit all consumers shopping for the product type. So they often introduce similar products designed to reach other consumers. Apple computer introduced the first successful personal computer. Shortly thereafter, Apple produced a range of personal computers for various applications—for example, the Apple 2C, 2E, 2GS, Macintosh Plus, and Macintosh SE. A group of similar products intended for a similar group of buyers who will use them in similar fashions is known as a **product line**.

Companies may also extend their horizons and identify opportunities outside of their existing product line. The result—multiple (or diversified) product lines—is evident in firms like Procter & Gamble. This firm began by making soap, but it now also produces paper products, foods, coffee, and baby products. Multiple product lines allow a company to grow more rapidly and minimize the consequences of slow sales in any one product line.

product line

A group of similar products intended for a similar group of buyers who will use them in a similar fashion.

Developing New Products

To expand or diversify product lines—indeed, just to survive—firms must develop and successfully introduce streams of new products. Faced with competition and shifting consumer preferences, no firm can count on a single successful product to carry them forever. The video case "Video Game Wars" on p. 493 illustrates the extreme importance of new products for business firms. Even basic products that have been widely purchased for decades require nearly constant renewal. Consider the unassuming facial tissue. The white tissue in the rectangular box has been joined (if not replaced) by tissues of many different colors and patterns. They arrive in boxes shaped and decorated for nearly every room in the house, and they are made to be placed or carried not only in the bathroom but in the purse, the briefcase, and the car.

Finding a market for a new product may be difficult. Terry Knight and Al Robinson learned a tough lesson. They sat around over coffee and dreamed up gadgets that they thought everyone would want. But hardly anyone wanted the "neat" stuff their company, Inuktun Services Ltd., made during its first few years. So they had to figure out where the demand was.

Prior to forming their company, both partners had worked in developing underwater technology. They developed a product called Seamor and its successor, Scallop—both small, submersible, remotely operated vehicles (ROVs) equipped with lights and a video camera. The idea was that boat owners could guide these devices down into the water and view the bottom of their boat on a TV monitor. Boat owners weren't interested, but the nuclear industry was. Now Inuktun's ROVs travel up and down stairs, around corners, over obstacles, in water up to 30 metres deep, and through ducts and pipes as little as six inches in diameter.[1] The box "Henry Wong Is Rolling in the Dough" describes another entrepreneur's struggle to get a new product accepted.

The New Product Development Process

In January 1990, General Electric announced its five-year program for the revolutionary GE90, a cleaner, quieter jet engine. GE has already spent its $2 billion development budget and, in December 1993, celebrated the maiden flight of its test engine. Still, GE has no advance assurances that the engine will be certified in time for commercial service later in the decade. That is the basic risk. The opportunity, however, is also great. If completed on time and certified, the GE90 will dominate the commercial jet market for years while other engine manufacturers are still working to develop competing engines.[2]

Like GE, many firms maintain research and development departments—even divisions—for exploring new product possibilities. Why do they devote so many resources to thinking about products and "exploring" their possibilities—and rejecting many a seemingly good idea along the way? How do they conduct these early explorations into new product possibilities?

The Canadian Business Scene

HENRY WONG IS ROLLING IN THE DOUGH

Henry Wong came to Canada from Hong Kong at age 12. Through most of the 1970s, he managed the Cozy Restaurant and Tavern in St. Catharines. He also started an import-export company, but the venture failed after two years. One day in 1985, he overheard someone raving about some pizza finger food, which they described as "an Italian egg roll or Chinese pizza."

Henry and an Italian friend experimented with various combinations of ingredients until they came up with the pizza roll—spaghetti sauce, vegetables, pepperoni, and mozzarella cheese in an egg roll that is deep fried. Henry gave out samples to local restaurants and they liked them. Soon he was delivering the pizza rolls from his Honda Civic.

Later, Henry raised $100 000 from 10 investors and bought a food processing plant in Niagara Falls. He also got a $275 000 loan from the Federal Business Development Bank. But Henry made some mistakes in pricing his product and found that in spite of paying large sums of money to retailers to display his product, it simply wasn't selling very well. He therefore lost money in his attempt to enter the U.S. market and the Quebec market. His company was good at manufacturing, but weak in the marketing area.

To make matters worse, Henry also got into a dispute with the giant Pillsbury Co. about the name "pizza rolls." To try to settle the issue, Henry met with the Pillsbury Canada president, Robert Hawthorne. The two men hit it off after they discovered that they lived in the same area as youngsters and that Hawthorne had actually hung around the restaurant owned by Henry's father. Henry finally decided to sign a deal with Pillsbury to supply products for Pillsbury's own label. In return, Henry would own the "pizza roll" trademark in Canada.

Henry Wong now sells pizza rolls to a variety of companies. Annual revenue for his firm is nearly $3 million, and he is making a profit. Pillsbury now buys 50 percent of Henry's output. Henry must adhere to Pillsbury's way of manufacturing, but he has gained a high-quality customer that pays its bills. He also avoids paying steep listing fees (money to chains to display the product).

We will address these questions in this section. We will see, for instance, that the high *mortality rate* for new ideas means that only a few new products eventually reach commercialization. Moreover, as in the case of the GE90, *speed to market* with a product is often as important as care in developing it. Finally, product development is a long and complex (and expensive) process. Companies do not dream up new products one day and ship them to retailers the next. In fact, new products usually involve carefully planned—and sometimes risky—commitments of time and resources.

Product Mortality Rates.   Typically, new products move through a series of stages, beginning with the search for ideas and culminating in introduction to consumers. At each stage of this process, potential products fall from further consideration as the company pursues more attractive alternatives. In fact, it is estimated that it takes 50 new product ideas to generate one product that finally reaches the marketplace. Even then, of course, only a few of those survivors become *successful* products. Many seemingly great *ideas* have failed as *products*. Indeed, creating a successful new product has become more and more difficult. The video case "Flops" on p. 492 describes several new products that failed in the marketplace.

Speed to Market.   The principle is quite simple: The more rapidly a product moves from the laboratory to the marketplace, the more likely it is to survive. By introducing new products ahead of competitors, companies quickly establish market leaders. They become entrenched in the market before being challenged by late-arriving competitors.

How important is **speed to market**—that is, a firm's success in responding to customer demand or market changes? One study has estimated that a product which is only three months late to market (that is, three months behind the leader) sacrifices 12 percent of its lifetime profit potential. A product that is six months late will lose 33 percent.

speed to market
The rate at which a business firm responds to consumer demands or market changes.

The Seven-Step Development Process. To increase their chances of developing a successful new product, many firms adopt some variation on a basic seven-step process (see Figure 15.1).

1. Product Ideas. Product development begins with a search for ideas for new products. Product ideas can come from consumers, the sales force, research and development people, or engineering personnel. The key is to actively seek out ideas and to reward those whose ideas become successful products.

2. Screening. This second stage is an attempt to eliminate all product ideas that do not mesh with the firm's abilities, expertise, or objectives. Representatives from marketing, engineering, and production must have input at this stage.

3. Concept Testing. Once ideas have been culled, companies use market research to solicit consumers' input. In this way, firms can identify benefits that the product must provide as well as an appropriate price level for the product.

Figure 15.1
The new product development process.

4. Business Analysis.   This stage involves developing an early comparison of costs versus benefits for the proposed product. Preliminary sales projections are compared with cost projections from finance and production. The aim is not to determine precisely how much money the product will make but to see whether the product can meet minimum profitability goals.

5. Prototype Development.   At this stage, product ideas begin to take shape. Using input from the concept-testing phase, engineering and/or research and development produce a preliminary version of the product. Prototypes can be extremely expensive, often requiring extensive hand crafting, tooling, and development of components. But this phase can help identify potential production problems.

6. Product Testing and Test Marketing.   Using what it learned from the prototype, the company goes into limited production of the item. The product is then tested internally to see if it meets performance requirements. If it does, it is made available for sale in limited areas. This stage is very costly, since promotional campaigns and distribution channels must be established for test markets. But test marketing gives a company its first information on how consumers will respond to a product under real market conditions.

7. Commercialization.   If test-marketing results are positive, the company will begin full-scale production and marketing of the product. Gradual commercialization, with the firm providing the product to more and more areas over time, prevents undue strain on the firm's initial production capabilities. But extensive delays in commercialization may give competitors a chance to bring out their own version.

The development of services (both for consumers and industrial buyers) involves many of the same stages as goods development. Basically, Steps 2, 3, 4, 6, and 7 are the same. There are, however, some important differences in Steps 1 and 5:

definition of the service package
Identification of the tangible and intangible features that define the service.

■ *Service Ideas*. The search for service ideas includes a task called **definition of the service package**, which involves identification of the tangible and intangible features that define the service (see Chapter 12).[3] This definition includes *service specifications*. For example, a firm that wants to offer year-end cleaning services to office buildings might commit itself to the following specifications: "The building interior will be cleaned by midnight, January 5, including floor polishing of all aisles, carpets swept free of all dust and debris, polished washbowls and lavatory equipment, with no interruption or interference to customer."

service process design
Selecting the process, identifying worker requirements, and determining facilities requirements so the service can be effectively provided.

■ *Service Process Design*. Instead of protype development, services require a **service process design**. This step involves selecting the process, identifying worker requirements, and determining facilities requirements so that the service can be provided as promised in the service specifications. *Process selection* identifies each step in the service, including the sequence and the timing. *Worker requirements* specify employee behaviors, skills capabilities, and interactions with customers during the service encounter. *Facilities requirements* designate all the equipment that supports delivery of the service. All three of these areas must be coordinated.[4]

The Product Life Cycle

Products that reach the commercialization stage begin a new series of stages known as the product life cycle. **Product life cycle (PLC)** is the concept that products have a limited profit-producing life for a company. This life may be a matter of months, years, or decades, depending on the ability of the product to attract customers over time. Strong products such as Kellogg's Corn Flakes, Coca-Cola, Ivory soap, Argo corn starch, and Caramilk candy bars have had extremely long productive lives.

product life cycle (PLC)

The concept that the profit-producing life of any product goes through a cycle of introduction, growth, maturity (leveling off), and decline.

Stages in the Product Life Cycle

The product life cycle is a natural process in which products are born, grow in stature, mature, and finally decline and die. The life cycle is typically divided into four states through which products pass as they "age" on the market:

1. *Introduction.* The introduction stage begins when the product reaches the marketplace. During this stage, marketers focus on making potential consumers aware of the product and its benefits. Because of extensive promotional and development costs, profits are nonexistent.
2. *Growth.* If the new product attracts and satisfies enough consumers, sales begin to climb rapidly. During this stage, the product begins to show a profit. Other firms in the industry move rapidly to introduce their own versions.
3. *Maturity.* Sales growth begins to slow. Although the product earns its highest profit level early in this stage, increased competition eventually leads to price cutting and lower profits. Toward the end of the stage, sales start to fall.
4. *Decline.* During this final stage, sales and profits continue to fall. New products in the introduction stage take away sales. Companies remove or reduce promotional support (ads and salespeople) but may let the product linger to provide some profits.

Figure 15.2 shows the four stages of the cycle—not yet complete—for VCRs. The product was introduced in the late 1970s and is, of course, widely used today. (Notice that profits lag behind sales because of the extensive costs of developing new products.) If the market becomes saturated, sales will begin to decline. Sales will also fall if new products, such as laser discs, send the VCR the way of the eight-track audio player.

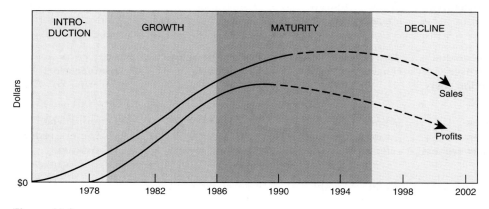

Figure 15.2
The product life cycle for VCRs. Note that profits lag behind sales due to the extensive development costs to create the new product.

Service products also have life cycles. Consider the management advice offered by consulting firms. Most major companies purchase advice for designing and implementing new management practices. For example, advice on appropriate wage-incentive systems flourished through the 1950s and then went into decline by the 1970s. Advice on how to implement "Management by Objectives" (see Chapter 6) was introduced in the 1960s, passed through the maturity stage during the 1970s, and today is in the decline stage. A more recent product, advice on "Total Quality Management" (see Chapter 13), has been introduced for firms that want assistance in implementing TQM. TQM advisory service is now offered by major accounting firms like Deloitte & Touche. This service is in transition from growth to maturity.

Adjusting Marketing Strategy During the Life Cycle

As a product passes from stage to stage, marketing strategy changes, too. Each aspect of the marketing mix—product, price, promotion, place (distribution)—is reexamined for each stage of the life cycle. Changes in strategy for all four life-cycle stages are summarized in Table 15.1. Here, however, we will pause to describe in more detail the differences in marketing a product during its introduction and maturity stages:

■ *Introduction Stage.* Overall strategy emphasizes market development. *Product strategy*, of course, has already focused on new product introduction—on seeking and testing new ideas. *Pricing strategy* seeks a high price, both to capitalize on the product's uniqueness and to cover startup costs. *Promotional strategy* emphasizes product awareness, using sales promotions to encourage trial use. *Distribution strategy* uses selective, scattered outlets to get the product started on its way to larger and larger markets.

■ *Maturity Stage.* Now strategy emphasizes the defense of market share against competing products that have entered the market. To keep customers, pricing strategy aims to set a price at or below competitors'.

TABLE 15.1   Marketing Strategy over the Life Cycle

Stage	Introduction	Growth	Maturity	Decline
Marketing Strategy Emphasis	Market development	Increase market share	Defend market share	Maintain efficiency in exploiting product
Pricing Strategy	High price, unique product/cover introduction costs	Lower price with passage of time	Price at or below competitors'	Set price to stay profitable or decrease to liquidate
Promotion Strategy	Mount sales promotion for product awareness	Appeal to mass market; emphasize features, brand	Emphasize brand differences, benefits, loyalty	Reinforce loyal customers; reduce promotion expenditures
Place Strategy	Distribute through selective outlets	Build intensive network of outlets	Enlarge distribution network	Be selective in distribution; trim away unprofitable outlets

Product strategy calls for diversifying the product and differentiating it from competing products. Promotional strategy emphasizes brand differences, brand benefits, and brand loyalty, often through advertising. Distribution strategy works to enlarge the distribution network.

Extending Product Life

Not surprisingly, companies wish they could maintain a product's position in the maturity stage for longer periods of time. Many creative companies have successfully and profitably achieved this feat.[5] Cheez-Whiz experienced a rapid increase in sales when its maker used the popularity of microwave ovens to promote it as a "one-minute cheese sauce." Sales of television sets have been revitalized time and time again by introducing changes such as color, portability, and stereo capability.

The beginning of a sales downturn in the maturity stage is not necessarily the time to start abandoning a product. Often, it is a time to realize that the old approach is starting to fade and to search for a new approach.

The Growth-Share Matrix. Companies with multiple product lines typically have various products at each point in the PLC. To decide how best to market each product, many marketers rely on the growth-share matrix, which classifies products according to market share and growth potential. Figure 15.3 shows the four categories into which products may be grouped: *question marks, stars, cash cows,* and *dogs.*

■ Most products start as *question marks*—low market share, high growth potential—because they are entering new markets that may grow but have not yet captured consumers' attention.

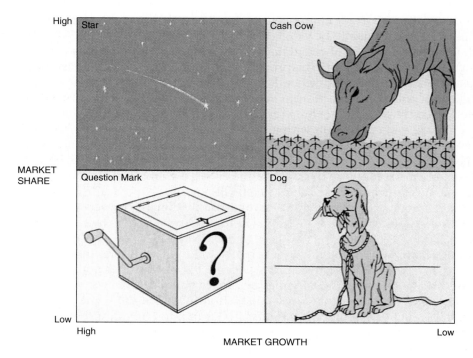

Figure 15.3
Growth-share matrix.

- During the growth stage, products often become *stars* with high market share and high growth potential. Stars have large shares of still-growing markets.
- In the maturity stage, products serve as *cash cows*—high market share, low growth potential—because their large market share makes them profitable even while market growth slows.
- Products in the decline stage are *dogs*—low market share, low growth potential—whose profits and sales signal that the life cycle is nearly complete.

When developing marketing plans, managers must consider not only the product's location on the growth-share matrix but also the direction in which it is moving. For example, while a question mark with increasing market share may be headed for stardom, a question mark with decreasing market share may require major changes or elimination.

In addition, companies always seek balance and continuity in the product mix. A company loaded with cash cows, for example, has a great present but may have a questionable future. Because they require a lot of attention, a firm loaded with stars may be focusing its managers' energies too narrowly. On the other hand, a firm with mostly cash cows and stars, some question marks, and a couple of unavoidable dogs has developed a strong product pipeline and a balanced product mix.

Identifying Products

As noted earlier in the chapter, developing the features of a product is only part of a marketer's battle. Identifying that product in consumers' minds through the use of brand names, packaging, and labeling is also important.

Branding Products

An especially important component of product development is deciding on a name for the product. The video case "Video Game Wars" on p. 493 demonstrates the importance of brand names for products. **Brand names** were introduced to try to simplify the process of product selection for consumers. Customers try a product, remember its name, and go back to it next time. Millions of dollars have been spent developing names like Noxzema, Prudential, and Minute Maid and attaching meaning to them in consumers' minds.

brand names

Those specific names of products associated with a manufacturer, wholesaler, and/or retailer that are designed to distinguish products from those of competitors and are promoted as part of the product.

The key in coming up with a brand name for a product is to keep the name simple. As few letters and numbers as possible make the name sound "good" and easy to remember. The brand must also be consistent with current lifestyles. Post recently changed the name of Sugar Smacks to Honey Smacks and its mascot from Sugar Bear to Honey Bear. In today's health conscious market, a honey cereal is viewed more favorably than a sugar-coated one.

An issue of growing importance in branding strategy is faced by firms that sell products internationally. They must also consider how product names will translate in various languages. In Spanish, for example, the name of Chevrolet's now-defunct Nova simply became *no va*—"it does not go." Sales were particularly poor in South America. Similarly, Rolls-Royce was once going to name a new touring car "Silver Mist." Rolls changed the name to "Silver Shadow" when it discovered that *mist* is German for "manure."[6] Naturally, foreign companies hoping to sell in Canada must be equally careful. The box "Building Brands at Nestlé" describes that company's brand strategy.

International Report

BUILDING BRANDS AT NESTLÉ

Nestlé is the world's most successful international food company. It is the market leader in instant coffee in Australia (71 percent), France (67 percent), Japan (74 percent), and Mexico (85 percent). In powdered milk, it is the leader in the Phillipines (66 percent) and Brazil (58 percent). In Chile, Nestlé has 73 percent of the cookie market and 70 percent of the soups and juices market.

Although Nestlé is a global company, it lives on local brands. It achieves much of its growth in the developing countries simply by getting there before other companies do. Once in a country, it builds both a manufacturing and a political presence. Nestlé already gets one-quarter of its worldwide sales from the Far East and Latin America. About one-third of company profits come from products sold outside the developed countries.

Nestlé owns nearly 8000 brands worldwide, but you won't see hundreds of their brands in a store near you. Only about 750 are registered in more than one country, and only 80 brands are registered in more than 10 countries. Nestlé thus rejects the "one-world, one-brand" school of marketing thought that companies like Coca-Cola and Pepsico embrace.

In the developed world, Nestlé pursues a strategy of acquiring well-known brands. For example, it owns Stouffer's, Perrier, and Carnation. In the developing countries, it grows by building up brand loyalty to a local brand—for example, Bear Brand condensed milk in Asia. By developing only a few brands in each country, Nestlé is able to highly focus its advertising money and thereby achieve big market shares. The executive vice-president in charge of marketing says the company does not believe in life cycles for brands; he says that a well-managed brand will outlive any manager.

Nestlé's experience selling coffee in Thailand demonstrates their attitude toward brand development. How does a Swiss company sell a hot beverage in the tropics? The general manager of Nestlé Thailand decided that coffee was the perfect product to capitalize on the growth that Thailand was experiencing in the late 1980s. He and his team decided to forget advertising coffee based on traditional taste and aroma. Instead, the advertisements emphasized coffee as a stress reducer and as a promoter of romance. When one of the team members saw a Nestlé promotion on cold coffee from Nestlé Greece, they quickly adopted that idea. Coffee sales jumped from $25 million in 1987 to $100 million in 1994.

An extreme example of Nestlé's strategy of local brand development is found in China. After 13 years of talks, Nestlé was finally invited into China in 1987 because the government wanted to increase milk production. Nestlé opened a powdered milk plant in 1990, but then it had a tough choice to make: use the overburdened local network of trains and roads to collect milk, or build its own roads. It chose the latter, even though it was very costly. Farmers now follow Nestlé's "milk roads" when they bring their milk to the chilling centers for weighing and analysis.

Nestlé pays the farmers promptly, something the government didn't always do, so farmers now have an incentive to produce more milk (the district cow population has increased 50 percent in the last 18 months). Nestlé also brought in experts to train farmers in animal health and hygiene. In its first year, the factory produced 316 tonnes of powdered milk; by 1994 it produced 10 000 tonnes. Nestlé now has exclusive rights to sell the product across China for 15 years. The company predicts that sales will reach $700 million by the year 2000.

Types of Brands

Virtually every product has a brand name of some form. However, different types of brand names tell the alert consumer something about the product's origin.

National Brands.   Brand name products that are produced and distributed by the manufacturer are called **national brands**. These brands, such as Scotch tape, are often widely recognized by consumers because of large national advertising campaigns. The costs of developing a positive image for a national brand are high, so some companies use their national brand on several related products. Procter & Gamble now markets Ivory shampoo, capitalizing on the widely recognized name of its soaps.

national brands
Products distributed by and carrying a name associated with the manufacturer.

licensed brands
Selling the right to use a brand name, a celebrity's name, or some other well-known identification mark to another company to use on a product.

Licensed Brands.   More and more nationally recognized companies and personalities have sold other companies the right to place their names on products, which are **licensed brands**. Licensing has become big business. Coca-Cola Company, Guns 'N Roses, and Hard Rock Cafe will make millions on licensed apparel sales this year. Free advertising from T-shirts and sweatshirts worn primarily by young people—an age group in which cola consumption is heavy—is just an added bonus.

Tie-ins with movies and other entertainment vehicles are popular forms of licensing. In 1994, the surprise hit *Forrest Gump*, for instance, climbed to number five on the all-time box-office list. In the process, it generated nearly 30 different licensing agreements, with products ranging from T-shirts and baseball caps to a line of shrimp foods from the Bubba Gump Seafood Co. The movie's owner, Viacom Inc., will be paid anywhere from 5 to 12 percent of the wholesale price of every licensed item.[7]

private brands
Products promoted by and carrying a name associated with the retailer or wholesaler, not the manufacturer.

Private Brands.   When a wholesaler or retailer develops a brand and has the manufacturer place that brand name on the product, the resulting product name is a **private brand**. One of the best-known purveyors of private brands is Sears, with its Craftsman tools and Kenmore appliances.

J. Sainsbury PLC, the largest supermarket chain in Britain, recently introduced its own private brand of cola in a can that looks strikingly like the one used by Coke. The two products are stocked side by side on store shelves, and Sainsbury's offering is noticeably cheaper than Coke. The product is made by Cott Corp. of Toronto, which has successfully won market share

The Toronto Blue Jays benefit both from the licensing fees they receive as well as from the free advertising whenever these shirts are worn.

from Coca-Cola in Canada.[8] The story is much the same in North America. Under the Sam's American Choice label, Cott sells a billion cans of soft drinks each year at Wal-Mart.

Meanwhile, Loblaw Cos. Ltd. has created a line of upscale private brands called President's Choice (PC). Clever advertising, fancy labels, and exotic product names differentiate the line and draw consumer attention to items like peanut butter and cookies. The success of PC is one reason why the private-label share of the Canadian soft-drink market grew from 5 percent to 25 percent between 1990 and 1993.[9]

U.S. companies are having trouble in Japan, too. After prolonged trade negotiations, Dole, Tropicana, and other American orange juice brands finally went on sale in Japan in 1992. Japan's Daiei supermarket chain immediately launched its own Savings line of private label juices. Daiei's products include juice made from Brazilian oranges and are priced 40 percent below American brands, and a pint of Daiei's premium ice cream sells for half the price of Lady Borden. Daiei buys its ice cream from the same supplier and packages it in cartons quite similar to Lady Borden's.

Generic Products.   "No-name" products in very plain packages with black lettering describing the contents were first introduced in the 1970s. For a while their lower prices attracted consumers. Supermarkets began devoting entire aisles to **generic products** such as paper towels, green beans, and shampoo. But concern over consistent product quality has resulted in a deemphasis of generic products in recent years.

generic products
Products carrying no brand or producer name and sold at lower prices.

Trademarks.   Because brand development is very expensive, a company does not want another company using its name and confusing consumers into buying a substitute product. Many companies apply to the Canadian government and receive a **trademark**, the exclusive legal right to use a brand name. Trademarks are granted for 15 years and may be renewed for further periods of 15 years, but only if the company continues to protect its brand name.

Just what can be trademarked is not always clear, however. If the company allows the name to lapse into common usage, the courts may take away protection. Common usage occurs when the company fails to use the ® symbol for its brand. It also occurs if the company fails to correct those who do not acknowledge the brand as a trademark. Recently Windsurfer (a popular brand of sailboards by WSI Inc.) lost its trademark. Like the trampoline, yo-yo, and thermos, the brand name has become the common term for the product and can now be used by any sailboard company. But companies like Xerox, Coke, Jello, and Scotch tape have successfully defended their brand names.

trademark
The exclusive legal right to use a brand name.

Brand Loyalty

Companies that spend the large amount of money it takes to develop a brand are looking for one thing from consumers: **brand loyalty**. That is, they want to develop customers who, when they need a particular item, will go back to the same brand and buy the company's products. The video case "Video Game Wars" on p. 493 describes the brand loyalty strategy that Sega and Nintendo have developed for their products.

Brand loyalty is measured in three stages. First, the company wants *brand recognition*. By putting the brand in front of consumers many times and associating it with a type of product, the producer hopes that consumers will become aware of its existence.

Recognition is not enough, however. The owner of the brand wants consumers to start showing *brand preference* when they make a purchase. Brand preference requires not only awareness that the brand exists but also a favorable attitude toward the ability of the brand to provide benefits.

brand loyalty
Customers' recognition of, preference for, and insistence on buying a product with a certain brand name.

Finally, because a brand may be unavailable in a store from time to time, companies seek *brand insistence*. Brand insistence is highly valued by brand owners, but it is very difficult to achieve. For all convenience and many shopping products, consumers will freely substitute another brand when they need a product. Usually, only specialty products have much potential for developing brand insistence in a large group of consumers. For example, a family wanting to buy or sell a home might insist on using a trusted local realtor.

Packaging Products

packaging

The physical container in which a product is sold, including the label.

With a few exceptions, including fresh fruits and vegetables, structural steel, and some other industrial products, products need some form of **packaging** in which to be carried to the market. A package also serves as an in-store advertisement that makes the product attractive, clearly displays the brand, and identifies product features and benefits.

A growing number of companies are shifting their promotional spending from advertising to packaging. The trend is to lighter, brighter colors that stand out more on grocery store shelves. The package is the marketer's last chance to say "buy it" to the consumer.[10]

Packaging reduces the risk of damage, breakage, or spoilage, and it increases the difficulty of stealing smaller products. But once a product is opened and used, expensive packaging may become waste.

The year 1982 marked a turning point for the packaging industry. In that year seven people were killed when they took Tylenol that had been contaminated with cyanide after the capsules left the factory. In response to this and other incidents, consumers have begun to demand product packaging that provides some safety insurance. The packaging industry has responded with tamper-resistant package designs.

One marketing technique that has been criticized is the practice of keeping the price the same but reducing the size of the package. For example, Huggies has reduced the number of disposable diapers in a box from ten to six, and Kleenex boxes have fewer tissues than they used to. But the price remains the same.[11]

Labeling Products

label

That part of a product's packaging that identifies the product's name and contents and sometimes its benefits.

Consumer Packaging and Labelling Act

A federal law that provides comprehensive rules for packaging and labeling of consumer products.

Every product has a **label** on its package. Packaging and labeling can help market the product. The information on package labels is regulated by the federal government. The ***Consumer Packaging and Labelling Act*** has two main purposes: the first is to provide a comprehensive set of rules for packaging and labeling of consumer products, and the second is to ensure that the manufacturer provides full and factual information on labels. All prepackaged products must state in French and English the quantity enclosed in metric and imperial units. The name and description of the product must also appear on the label in both French and English.

In recent years labels have begun to display the Universal Product Code (UPC) bar code. This series of bars of various lengths and widths and spaces helps identify and keep track of merchandise. It also enables retailers to speed up the check-out process by using special bar-code scanners.

Promoting Products and Services

It is no secret to anyone who watches television, reads magazines, or even surveys the urban landscape that businesses rely on advertising, publicity, and other techniques in the battle to attract the attention of customers and maintain their loyalty. In many businesses, promotion can be the key either to establishing a new product or keeping an established product in the public eye.

The Importance of Promotion

Let's begin our look at promotion by observing how one company responded to threats in its marketing environment. For years, Burger King had declined to follow industry leaders McDonald's and Wendy's in introducing discounted products like "value meals." Like many franchisers, BK feared that discounting would cut into profit margins. But profits languished anyway, and in October 1993, new CEO James B. Adamson rolled out the "value menu," which offers breakfast, lunch, and dinner specials at 99¢, $1.99, and $2.99. He also informed the company's ad agency that he was putting the account up for review and seeking a refreshing campaign to replace the MTV-modeled "BK Tee Vee" spots that had alienated longtime old customers. Finally, Adamson redistributed BK's advertising expenditures: Whereas the company customarily spent about $180 million of its $250 million annual marketing budget on TV and radio spots, Adamson reduced the amount to 40 percent and earmarked the rest for national discounts and local-market promotions.[12]

Burger King perceived its problem to lie in its *communications mix*—the total message that it was sending to consumers about its product. In particular, the company reacted to competitive pressures by adjusting its promotional practices, relying less on advertising and more on two other elements of marketing strategy: pricing and sales promotions.

As we noted in Chapter 14, *promotion* is any technique designed to sell a product. As part of the communications mix designed for products, promotional techniques—especially advertising—must communicate the uses, features, and benefits of products. Sales promotions, however, also include various programs that add further value beyond the benefits inherent in the product. It is nice, for example, to get a high-quality product at a reasonable price but even better when the seller offers, say, a rebate or a bonus pack with "20 percent more FREE." In promoting products, then, marketers have an array of tools at their disposal.

In free market systems, a business uses promotional methods to communicate information about itself and its products to consumers, industrial buyers, or both. The purpose, of course, is to influence purchase decisions. From an *information* standpoint, promotions seek to accomplish four things with potential customers:

- make them *aware* of products
- make them *knowledgable* about products
- *persuade* them to like the products
- persuade them to *purchase* products.

In terms of the marketing *exchange relationship*, the firm hopes that marketing promotions will make its product more attractive. The buyer therefore gains more from the exchange (a more attractive product), as does the seller (more unit sales or higher prices).

Successful promotions provide communications about the product and create exchanges that satisfy both the consumer's and organization's objectives. At the same time, however, because promotions are expensive, choosing the best promotional mix becomes critical. The promotional program, then, whether at the introduction stage (promoting for new product awareness) or maturity stage (promoting brand benefits and customer loyalty) can determine the success or failure of any business or product.

Promotional Objectives

The ultimate objective of any promotion is to increase sales. However, marketers also use promotion to communicate information, position products, add value, and control sales volume.[13]

Communication of Information.   Consumers cannot buy a product unless they have been informed about it. Information can advise customers about the availability of a product, educate them on the latest technological advances, or announce the candidacy of someone running for a government office. Information may be communicated in writing (newspapers and magazines), verbally (in person or over the telephone), or visually (television, a matchbook cover, or a billboard). Today, the communication of information regarding a company's products or services is so important that marketers try to place it wherever consumers may be. If you are an average consumer, you come in contact with approximately 1500 bits of promotional communication a day![14]

product positioning

The establishment of an easily identifiable image of a product in the minds of consumers.

Product Positioning.   Another objective of promotion, **product positioning**, is to establish an easily identifiable image of a product in the minds of consumers. For example, by selling only in department stores, Estée Lauder products have positioned themselves as more upscale than cosmetics sold in drugstores. With product positioning, the company is trying to appeal to a specific segment of the market rather than to the market as a whole.

Adding Value.   Today's value-conscious customers gain benefits when the promotional mix is shifted and when it communicates value-increased products. Earlier we saw how Burger King shifted its promotional mix by cutting back on advertising and using those funds instead for customer discounts. Similarly, Compaq Computer countered increased pressure from low-priced competitors by introducing its own lower-priced desktop computers with enhanced capabilities.[15]

In addition to adding value, promotion is the main way to establish a product's perceived value. It means creating communications and directing them to value-conscious customers. Whether or not they make emotional appeals, effective advertising promotions are clear and factual. Customers, for example, must be given information about the value-adding characteristics— say, warranties, repair contracts, and after-purchase service—by which a product provides greater value than its competitors. Lexus, for example, prides itself on adding value by providing superb treatment of customers. Sales representatives don't pry, solicit, or hover over buyers in the showroom. The first two scheduled maintenances are free. Waiting customers can use offices, desks, or phones and can borrow cars or get rides. "We try to make it very hard for you leave us," explains General Manager George Borst. "When you buy a Lexus, you don't buy a product. You buy a luxury package."[16]

Controlling Sales Volume.   Sales volume control is also an objective of promotions. Many companies, such as Hallmark Cards, experience seasonal

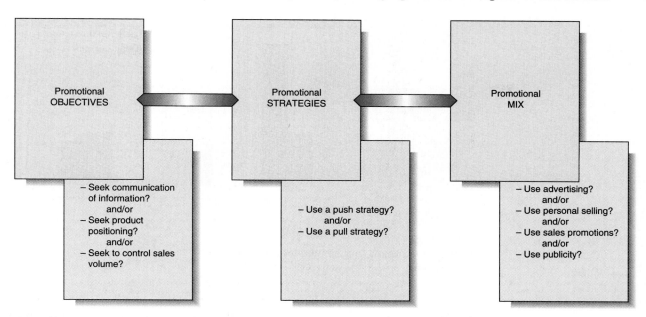

Figure 15.4
Developing the promotional plan.

sales patterns. By increasing its promotional activities in slow periods, the firm can achieve a more stable sales volume throughout the year. As a result, it can keep its production and distribution systems running evenly.

Promotional Strategies

Once a firm's promotional objectives are clear, it must develop a promotional strategy to achieve these objectives. Promotional strategies may be of the push or pull variety. A company with a **push strategy** will aggressively "push" its product through wholesalers and retailers, who persuade customers to buy it. In contrast, a company with a **pull strategy** appeals directly to customers, who demand the product from retailers, who in turn demand the product from wholesalers. Advertising "pulls" while personal selling "pushes."

Makers of industrial products most often use a push strategy, and makers of consumer products most often use a pull strategy. Many large firms use a combination of the two strategies. For example, General Foods uses advertising to create consumer demand (pull) for its cereals. It also pushes wholesalers and retailers to stock these products.

The Promotional Mix

As we noted in Chapter 14, there are four basic types of promotional tools: advertising, personal selling, sales promotions, and publicity and public relations. Figure 15.5 shows the relative usage of these tools by consumer- and industrial-goods businesses.

The best combination of these tools—the best **promotional mix**—depends on many factors. The company's product, the costs of different tools versus the promotions budget, and characteristics in the target audience all play a role. Figure 15.6 shows different combinations of products, promotional tools, and target consumers.

push strategy

A promotional strategy in which a company aggressively pushes its product through wholesalers and retailers, who persuade customers to buy it.

pull strategy

A promotional strategy in which a company appeals directly to customers, who demand the product from retailers, who demand the product from wholesalers.

promotional mix

That portion of marketing concerned with choosing the best combination of advertising, personal selling, sales promotions, and publicity to sell a product.

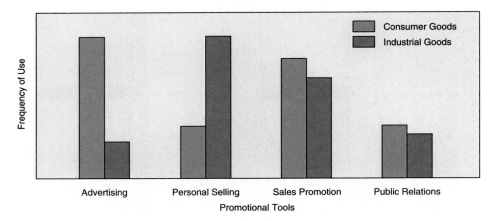

Figure 15.5
The relative importance of promotional tools.

The Product.   The nature of the product being promoted affects the mix greatly. For example, advertising can reach a large number of widely dispersed consumers. It is used by makers of products that might be bought by anyone, like sunglasses, radios, and snack foods. Companies introducing new products also favor advertising because it reaches a large number of people quickly and can repeat a message many times. Personal selling, on the other hand, is important when the product appeals to a specific audience, such as piping or pressure gauges for industrial customers.

Cost of the Tools.   The cost of communication tools is important. Because personal selling is an expensive communication tool, it is most appropriate in marketing high-priced goods such as computers for industrial customers and homes for consumers. In contrast, advertising reaches more customers per dollar spent.

A promotional mix that is good for one company may not be good for another. A large firm can afford to spend millions of dollars on national advertising, but a local firm must rely on personal selling and publicity to promote its products.

Promotion and the Buyer Decision Process.   Another consideration in establishing the promotional mix is the stage of the buyer decision process that customers are in. As noted in Chapter 14, customers must first recognize the need to make a purchase. At this stage, marketers need to make sure the buyer is aware that their products exist. Thus, advertising and publicity, which can reach a large number of people quickly, are important.

At the next stage, customers want to learn more about possible products. Advertising and personal selling are important because they both can educate the customer about the product.

During the third stage, customers will evaluate and compare competing products. Personal selling is vital at this point because sales representatives can demonstrate their product's quality and performance in direct relation to the competition's product.

Next, customers decide on a specific product and buy it. Sales promotion is effective at this stage because it can give consumers an incentive to buy. Personal selling can also help by bringing the product to convenient locations for the consumer.

Finally, consumers evaluate the product after buying it. Advertising, or even personal selling, is sometimes used after the sale to remind consumers

Goods Promotion: House (real estate)
Tool: Personal selling
Consumer: House buyer

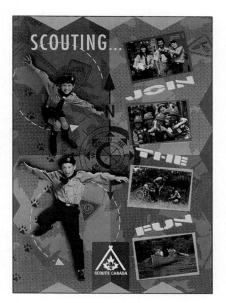

Organizational Promotion: Boy Scouts of Canada
Tool: Publicity
Consumer: Young men

Service Promotion: Weight-loss program
Tool: Sales promotion (coupon)
Consumer: Overweight person

Event Promotion: Rock concert
Tool: Advertising
Consumer: Cheering fan

Person or Idea Promotion: Candidate for Prime Minister
Tool: Publicity/advertising/personal sales
Consumer: Voter

Figure 15.6
Each promotional tool should be properly matched with the product being promoted and the target customer.

that they made wise and prudent purchases. Figure 15.7 summarizes effective promotional tools for each stage of the consumer buying process.

The Promotional Mix Decision. Choosing the promotional mix begins by determining the promotional budget—one of the marketing manager's most difficult decisions. The budget specifies how much of the firm's total resources will be spent on promotions. The combined costs of personal selling, advertising, sales promotion, and public relations must fall within the budgeted amount. Moreover, the elements of the mix, collectively, must be *balanced* if they are to have the desired effect on attitudes and purchasing decisions.

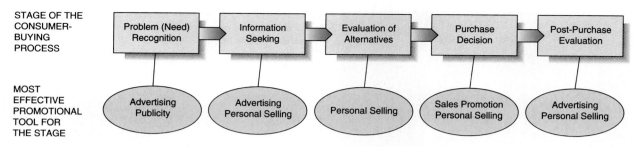

Figure 15.7
The promotional mix and the consumer buying process.

The stage in the product's life cycle influences the promotional balance. New product introductions, for instance, may call for expensive personal sales promotions concentrated on a limited audience of early adopters and dealers. Personal sales may also be combined with direct mail to instill product awareness in the selected audience. The maturity stage, on the other hand, may call for mass-media advertising that emphasizes brand features and lower prices. Advertising may be used with sales promotions—say, coupons to get buyers to try the seller's product instead of competitors'.

Now that you have a general understanding of promotional tools, let's look more closely at each.

Advertising Promotions

What candy bar is "a nice light snack"? What soap is "99 and 44/100% pure"? What is the store where "the lowest price is the law"? What product is "only available in Canada? Pity." If you are like most Canadians, you can answer these questions because of advertising. (The answers are Coffee Crisp, Ivory Soap, Zellers, and Red Rose Tea.) Figure 15.8 shows the top ten advertisers in Canada.

informative advertising

An advertising strategy, appropriate to the introduction stage of the product life cycle, in which the goal is to make potential customers aware that a product exists.

persuasive advertising

An advertising strategy, appropriate to the growth stage of the product life cycle, in which the goal is to influence the customer to buy the firm's product rather than the similar product of a competitor.

comparative advertising

An advertising strategy, appropriate to the growth stage of the product life cycle, in which the goal is to influence the customer to switch from a competitor's similar product to the firm's product by directly comparing the two products.

Advertising Strategies

Advertising strategies most often depend on which stage of the product life cycle their product is in. During the introduction stage, **informative advertising** can help develop an awareness of the company and its product among buyers and can establish a primary demand for the product. For example, before a new textbook is published, instructors receive direct-mail advertisements notifying them of the book's contents and availability.

As products become established, advertising strategies must change. During the growth stage, **persuasive advertising** can influence consumers to buy the company's products rather than those of its rivals. Persuasive advertising is also important during the maturity stage to maintain the product's level of sales. **Comparative advertising** involves comparing the sponsoring company's brand name with a competitor's brand name in such a way that the competitor's brand looks inferior. The box "Battery Giants Get a Jolt" describes a recent example of comparative advertising in Canada. The video case "Video Game Wars" describes how Sega and Nintendo use comparative advertising which focuses on the alleged weaknesses in their competitors' products.

In many countries (for example, Japan), advertisements that knock a competitor's product are frowned on. But not so in Canada or the U.S. In the European Union comparative advertising became legal in 1993, but advertisers must meet several limiting conditions.[17]

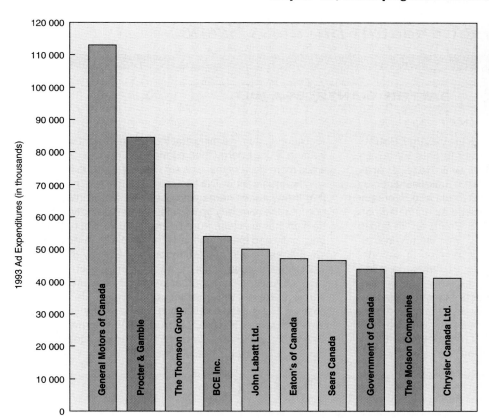

Figure 15.8
The top ten advertisers in Canada.

During the latter part of the maturity stage and all of the decline stage, **reminder advertising** keeps the product's name in front of the consumer.

Whatever the product's life cycle stage, advertising strategies must consider *timing*. Should the organization advertise continually throughout the year or seasonally? Companies such as banks space ads evenly throughout the year. In contrast, H&R Block Inc. runs advertisements in one major spurt during the tax season.

reminder advertising
An advertising strategy, appropriate to the latter part of the maturity stage of the product life cycle, in which the goal is to keep the product's name in the minds of customers.

Advertising Media

In developing advertising strategies, marketers must consider the best **advertising medium** for their message. IBM, for example, uses television ads to keep its name fresh in consumers' minds. But it also uses newspaper and magazine ads to educate consumers on products' abilities and trade publications to introduce new software.

An advertiser selects media with a number of factors in mind. The marketer must first ask: Which medium will reach the people I want to reach? If a firm is selling hog breeding equipment, it might choose *Playboar*, a business magazine read mostly by hog farmers. If it is selling silverware, it might choose a magazine for brides. If it is selling toothpaste, the choice might be a general audience television program or a general audience magazine such as *Reader's Digest* (or *Sélection*, for exposure to a similar audience of francophones).

Each advertising medium has its own advantages and disadvantages. The relative importance of different media is shown in Figure 15.9.

advertising medium
The specific communication device—television, radio, newspapers, direct mail, magazines, billboards—used to carry a firm's advertising message to potential customers.

The Canadian Business Scene

BATTERY GIANTS GET A JOLT

Just before Christmas in 1994, Pure Energy Battery Corp. of Mississauga launched high-profile TV advertisements that compared their new Pure Energy Rechargeable alkaline battery with the batteries made by the two market leaders (Duracell Canada and Eveready Canada). The advertisements showed an animated battery taunting "Mr. Duracell" and "Mr. Energizer" to "move over" and make room for Canada's first mercury-free alkaline battery. The advertisement went on to say that Pure Energy's battery had "at least 25 times more life" than the other two batteries.

Eveready (the one with the pink bunny it its advertisements) had a lawyer's letter sent to Pure Energy, threatening legal action over the advertisement. And Duracell (the copper-top battery) launched a complaint with the Canadian Advertising Foundation, an industry self-regulatory group, claiming that the advertisement was misleading. Pure Energy then changed its claim to "up to 25 times more life," but that was still not acceptable to Duracell.

The president of Duracell said that he was not upset that the Duracell name was used in the advertisement, because the company appreciates the free publicity. Rather, he said that the claim Pure Energy made for its battery is physically and mathematically impossible. The vice-president of sales and marketing for Pure Energy (a former Duracell employee) says the claims can be documented.

Disputes between companies about comparative advertising are not new. Earlier in 1994, an Ontario court ordered Robin Hood Multifoods Inc. to stop airing comparative advertisements naming Tenderflake and Gainsborough pie crusts by name. These products are made by rival Maple Leaf Foods.

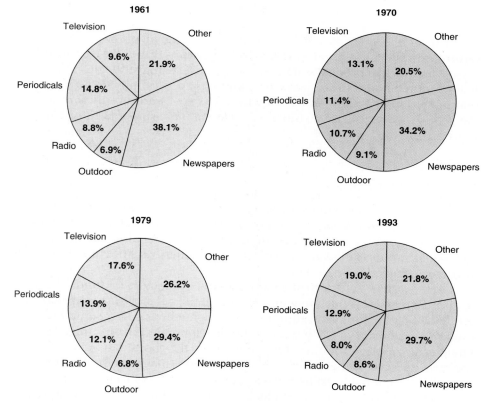

Figure 15.9
Relative importance of various media; 1961, 1970, 1979, 1993.

Newspapers. Newspapers remain the most widely used advertising medium. They offer excellent coverage, since each local market has at least one daily newspaper, and many people read the paper every day. This medium offers flexible, rapid coverage, since ads can change from day to day. It also offers believable coverage, since ads are presented side by side with news. However, newspapers are generally thrown out after one day, often do not print in color, and have poor reproduction quality. Moreover, newspapers do not usually allow advertisers to target their audience well.

Television. Television allows advertisers to combine sight, sound, and motion, thus appealing to almost all the viewer's senses. Information on viewer demographics for a particular program allows advertisers to promote to their target audiences. National advertising is done on television because it reaches more people than any other medium.

In 1991, Pepsi Cola Canada Ltd. asked for amateur videos for the best rendition of its jingle: "Diet Pepsi: You Got The Right One Baby, Uh-Huh" (a takeoff on the Ray Charles commercial for regular Pepsi). After judging 500 videos, the company awarded the $10 000 first prize to the firefighters of Cole Harbour, Nova Scotia. Their video showed them walking over cans of Diet Coke to save a Diet Pepsi machine from a burning building.[18] The video was then shown as part of a television advertising campaign.

One disadvantage of television is that too many commercials cause viewers to confuse products. Most people, for example, can't recall whether a tire commercial was sponsored by Firestone, Goodyear, or B.F. Goodrich. In addition, VCR viewers often fast-forward past the ads of TV shows that they have recorded. Moreover, because "commercial spots" last only a short time (usually 30 seconds), the impact of the commercial is lost if the viewer is not paying attention. The brevity of TV ads also makes television a poor medium in which to educate viewers about complex products. Finally, television is the most expensive medium in which to advertise. A 30-second commercial during the NFL Super Bowl costs about $1 000 000.

Direct Mail. **Direct mail** involves fliers or other types of printed advertisements mailed directly to consumers' homes or places of business. Direct mail allows the company to select its audience and personalize its message. Although many people discard "junk mail," targeted recipients with stronger-than-average interest are more likely to buy. Although direct mail involves the largest advance costs of any advertising technique, it does appear to have the highest cost effectiveness. Particularly effective have been "fax attacks," in which advertisers send their "mail" messages electronically via fax machines and get higher response rates than they would if they used Canada Post.

direct mail
Printed advertisements, such as flyers, mailed directly to consumers' homes or places of business.

The rise of mailing lists and the high cost of developing them have led to a thriving industry: the swapping and selling of mailing lists and consumer data among businesses for use in direct-mail advertising. Such practices present an ethical question for many businesses, whose customers resent having their names and addresses bought and sold or their fax machines tied up. As a result of consumer protests, many companies now promise not to sell the customer's name if the customer asks them not to.

Radio. A tremendous number of people listen to the radio each day, and radio ads are inexpensive. In addition, since most radio is programmed locally, this medium gives advertisers a high degree of customer selectivity. For example, radio stations are already segmented into listening categories such as rock and roll, country and western, jazz, talk shows, news, and religious programming.

Like television, however, radio ads are over quickly. And radio permits only an audio presentation. As well, people tend to use the radio as "background" while they are doing other things, paying little attention to advertisements.

Magazines.   The many different magazines on the market provide a high level of consumer selectivity. The person who reads *Popular Photography* is more likely to be interested in the latest specialized lenses from Canon than is a *Gourmet* magazine subscriber. Magazine advertising allows for excellent reproduction of photographs and artwork that not only grab buyers' attention but may also convince them of the product's value. And magazines allow advertisers plenty of space for detailed product information. Magazines have a long life and tend to be passed from person to person, thus doubling and tripling the number of exposures. The latest gimmick in print advertising is to catch the reader's eye by having the top half of an advertisement printed right side up and the bottom half upside down.[19]

One problem with magazine advertising is that ads must be submitted well in advance to be included in a certain issue. Often there is no guarantee of where within a magazine an ad will appear. Naturally, a company prefers to have its advertisement appear near the front of the magazine or within a feature article.

Outdoor.   Outdoor advertising—billboards, signs, and advertisements on buses, taxis, and subways—is relatively inexpensive, faces little competition for customers' attention, and is subject to high repeat exposure. Unfortunately, companies have little control over who will see their advertisements. Because roadside billboards are prohibited on some major Ontario arteries, Moving Impressions Inc. has introduced "rolling billboards"—advertisements attached to the sides of large freight trucks. The truck companies get a piece of the action.[20]

Word of Mouth.   Consumers form very strong opinions about products as a result of conversations with friends and acquaintances. If **word-of-mouth** says that a product is good, higher product sales are very likely. Of course, word-of-mouth will also spread bad news about a product.

Some companies rely heavily on word-of-mouth advertising. Big Rock Brewery does no advertising, but relies on word of mouth to expand its market share. It already has a 7 percent share of Alberta's draft beer market, and its exports to the U.S. are increasing rapidly.[21]

word-of-mouth
Opinions about the value of products passed among consumers in informal discussions.

Other Advertising Channels.   A combination of many additional media, including catalogues, sidewalk handouts, *Yellow Pages*, skywriting, telephone calls, special events, and door-to-door communications, make up the remaining advertisements that Canadians are exposed to. Each of these media is specialized and used selectively, often locally by small businesses, political campaigners, and special-interest groups.

The combination of media that a company chooses to advertise its products is called its **media mix**. Although different industries use different mixes, most depend on multiple media to advertise their products and services (see Table 15.2).

media mix
The combination of media through which a company chooses to advertise its products.

TABLE 15.2   Media Mix by Industry

Industry	Magazines	Newspapers	Outdoor	Television	Radio
Retail Stores	4.2%	61.1%	1.9%	27.8%	5.0%
Industrial materials	29.3	7.8	0.3	52.8	9.8
Insurance and real estate	11.1	53.5	2.2	29.3	3.9
Food	14.9	0.7	0.3	80.5	3.6
Apparel	50.5	1.8	0.5	45.8	1.4

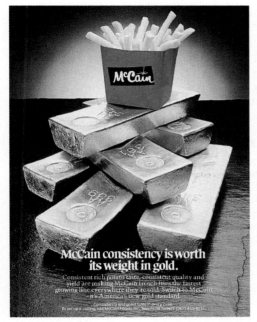

The McCain advertisement is an example of brand advertising because it promotes a specific brand. The Imagine advertisement is an example of advocacy advertising because it promotes a particular viewpoint about charitable giving.

Types of Advertising

Regardless of the media used, advertisements fall into one of several categories. **Brand advertising** promotes a specific brand, such as Kodak 126 film, Air Canada, or Nike Air Jordan basketball shoes. A variation on brand advertising, **product advertising** promotes a general type of product or service like milk or dental services. **Advocacy advertising** promotes a particular candidate or viewpoint, as in ads for political candidates at election time and antidrug commercials. **Institutional advertising** promotes a firm's long-term image rather than a specific product.

In consumer markets, local stores usually sponsor **retail advertising** to encourage consumers to visit the store and buy its products and services. Larger retailers, like K-mart and The Bay, use retail advertising both locally and nationally. Often retail advertising is actually **cooperative advertising**, with the cost of the advertising shared by the retailer and the manufacturer.

In industrial markets, to communicate with companies that distribute its products, some firms use **trade advertising** publications. For example, a firm that makes plumbing fixtures might advertise in *Hardware Retailer* to persuade large hardware stores to carry its products. And to reach the professional purchasing agent and managers at firms buying raw materials or components, companies use **industrial advertising**.

Advertising Agencies

An **advertising agency** is a firm that specializes in planning, producing, and placing advertisements in the media for clients. Ad agencies work together with the client company to determine the campaign's central message, create the detailed message content, identify the ad media, and negotiate media purchases. The advantage that ad agencies offer is expertise that many clients

brand advertising
Advertising that promotes a specific brand-name product.

product advertising
A variation on brand advertising that promotes a general type of product or service.

advocacy advertising
Advertising that promotes a particular viewpoint or candidate.

institutional advertising
Advertising that promotes a firm's long-term image, not a specific product.

retail advertising
Advertising by retailers designed to reach end-users of a consumer product.

cooperative advertising
Advertising in which a manufacturer together with a retailer or wholesaler advertise to reach customers.

trade advertising
Advertising by manufacturers designed to reach potential wholesalers and retailers.

industrial advertising
Advertising by manufacturers designed to reach other manufacturers' professional purchasing agents and managers of firms buying raw materials or components.

advertising agency
A firm that specializes in creating and placing advertisements in the media for clients.

do not possess on their own staffs—expertise in developing ad themes, message content, and artwork, as well as expertise in coordinating ad production and advising on relevant legal matters.

Agencies are normally paid a 15 percent commission based on the dollar amount of advertising placed in the media. (See Table 15.3 for a list of the top ten advertising agencies in Canada.)

TABLE 15.3   The Top Ten Advertising Agencies in Canada, 1994 (ranked by revenues)

Company	Revenues (in millions)
1. BBDO Canada Inc.	$52.2
2. Cossette Comm.-Marketing	43.1
3. Young & Rubicam Ltd.	37.2
4. MacLaren: Lintas Inc.	29.6
5. Leo Burnett Co. Ltd.	23.2
6. FCB Canada Ltd.	23.1
7. Ogilvy & Mather Canada Ltd.	20.2
8. DDB Needham Worldwide Ltd.	17.8
9. J. Walter Thompson Co. Ltd.	17.6
10. Grey Canada	15.1

Advertising agencies such as Baker Lovick use "account planning," which means doing exhaustive research to help decide how an advertising campaign should be conceived. This kind of planning helped the firm win the $54 million Federal Express account.[22]

The globalization of business has impacted advertising agencies, both in Canada and elsewhere. In 1994, IBM abandoned its practice of using over 40 different advertising agencies around the world and replaced them with one single agency—Ogilvy & Mather. Since IBM spends over $400 million on advertising each year, this was a major windfall for Ogilvy & Mather. Other large U.S.-based multinational advertisers such as Ford and Coca-Cola have also dropped Canadian agencies. By giving all their advertising business to one agency, these firms hope to cut costs and deliver a uniform global message about their products.[23]

The box "Making It on Madison Avenues" describes how several Canadians have made it to the top of advertising.

The 18-member Association of Quebec Advertising Agencies says that big U.S. companies often bypass Montreal-based advertising agencies when they are developing advertising campaigns for Quebec. The group says that it is pointless to try to simply translate into French a campaign that is developed by a New York or Toronto agency for the rest of Canada. As an example of the right way to do it, consider advertisements for Pepsi. In the rest of English-speaking North America, big name singers and movie stars were used to promote the product, but in Quebec, successful commercials featured popular local comedian Claude Meunier to make Pepsi the number one soft drink in the province.[24]

The Canadian Business Scene

MAKING IT ON MADISON AVENUE

Frank Anfield was born in Alert Bay, B.C. and is now the CEO of Young & Rubicam, a large advertising agency located in New York. He is one of many Canadians who are making their mark on Madison Avenue, the home of the major advertising agencies in the U.S. Six months before Anfield went to New York, Lintas Worldwide named Tony Miller (former CEO at MacLaren Lintas Inc. in Toronto) as CEO of its prestigious New York office. Two months after that, Peter Mills, who had been president of Baker Lovick, was named chief operating officer of BBDO North America. And finally, Allan Kazmer, the creative director of DDB Needham Ltd. of Toronto, was named international creative director at DDB Needham Worldwide Inc.

Why are Canadians so popular in U.S. advertising agencies? Part of the reason is the globalization of the world's advertising business. A more homogenous business world has resulted in more managers moving from country to country, and some Canadian managers are going to the U.S. Another reason is Canada's closeness to the U.S. and the increasing control of Canadian advertising firms by foreign companies. Just 10 years ago, seven of the top 10 advertising agencies in Canada were Canadian-owned; now only one is. Canada is a great place to work because it is possible for someone who is ambitious and wants to move up to head office to get noticed.

But the most important reason for the success of Canadian advertising executives is the challenging business climate in Canada. Peter Georgescu, president of Young & Rubicam, thinks that managers benefit from working in Canada because it's harder to succeed here. Those managers who do well have finely honed their business skills.

Steve Brown, a Toronto native who became executive management director at J. Walter Thompson in 1992, noted that he has a 20-person research unit that he can call on to develop data about a client's brand. But in Canada he had no such resource, so he had to become more entrepreneurial to get the job done. Peter Mills says that Canadian managers are expected to produce the same results as their American counterparts with budgets one-tenth the size. Finding ways to do so develops their skills to a high level.

Julian Clopet spent 15 years at Ogilvy & Mather Canada before he was appointed president of Ogilvy & Mather's North American operations. He says that anyone who succeeds in Canada is an "all-rounder" with a wide breadth of experience. In Toronto, he was in charge of three major accounts, while in New York he was given only a portion of one account. He didn't even meet the client until six months after he was assigned to the account.

Canadians are also perceived as having a more wordly outlook than Americans. The experience with a bilingual culture, for example, is seen as a plus for agencies which are pursuing cross-cultural and global marketing strategies. Ironically, Canada's much lamented "branch plant economy" has helped managers here because Canada is seen as a great training ground for the best and brightest.

Will the continuing exodus of talented Canadians be bad for the advertising business in Canada? Apparently not. The same sort of business climate that developed Anfield, Mills, Kazmer, and Miller will continue to bring new faces to the forefront. And if that doesn't work, Canadian firms can hire Americans. Kazmer says he gets at least three calls a week from people in the U.S. who want to know about working in Canada.

Personal Selling Promotions

Virtually everyone has done some selling. Perhaps you had a lemonade stand or sold candy for the drama club. Or you may have gone on a job interview, selling your abilities and service as an employee to the interviewer's company. In personal selling, a salesperson communicates one-to-one with a potential customer to identify the customer's need and match that need with the seller's product.

Personal selling—the oldest form of selling—provides the personal link between seller and buyer. It adds to a firm's credibility because it provides buyers with someone to interact with and to answer their questions. Because it involves personal interaction, personal selling requires a level of trust between the buyer and the seller. When a buyer feels cheated by the seller, that trust has been broken and a negative attitude toward salespeople in general can develop. Consider the image of the sleazy used car dealer. To counteract this reputation, many companies are emphasizing customer satisfaction and generally striving to improve the effectiveness of whatever personal selling they undertake.

Personal selling is the most expensive form of promotion per contact because presentations are generally made to one or two individuals at a time. Personal selling expenses include salespeople's compensation and their overhead, usually travel, food, and lodging. The average cost of an industrial sales call has been estimated at nearly $300.[25]

telemarketing
The use of the telephone to carry out many marketing activities, including sales and research.

Such high costs have prompted many companies to turn to **telemarketing**: using telephone solicitations to carry out the personal selling process. Telemarketing can be used to handle any stage of the personal selling process or to set up appointments for outside salespeople. For example, it saves the cost of personal sales visits to industrial customers. Each industrial buyer requires an average of nearly four visits to complete a sale; some companies have thus realized savings in sales visits of $1000 or more. Not surprisingly, such savings are stimulating the growth of telemarketing.

Types of Personal Selling Situations

retail selling
Selling a consumer product for the buyer's own personal or household use.

industrial selling
Selling products to other businesses, either for manufacturing other products or for resale.

Managers of both telemarketing and traditional personal salespeople must always consider how personal sales are affected by the differences between consumer products and industrial products that we discussed earlier in this chapter. **Retail selling** involves selling a consumer product for the buyer's own personal or household use. **Industrial selling** deals with selling products to other businesses, either for manufacturing other products or for resale. For example, Levi's wholesales its jeans to the retail clothing operation The Gap (industrial selling). Consumers purchase these jeans at one of The Gap's stores (retail selling).

salesforce management
Setting goals at top levels of an organization; setting practical objectives for salespeople; organizing a salesforce to meet those objectives; implementing and evaluating the success of a sales plan.

Each situation has its own distinct characteristics. In retail selling the buyer usually comes to the seller. The industrial salesperson almost always goes to the prospect's place of business. The industrial decision process also may take longer than a retail decision because more money, decision makers, and weighing of alternatives are involved. And industrial buyers are professional purchasing agents accustomed to dealing with salespeople. Consumers in retail stores, on the other hand, may be intimidated by salespeople.

Salesforce management means setting goals at top levels of the organization, setting practical objectives for salespeople, organizing a salesforce that can meet those objectives, and implementing and evaluating the success of the overall sales plan. Obviously, then, sales management is an important factor in meeting the marketing objectives of any large company.

Personal Selling Tasks

Improving sales efficiency requires marketers to consider salespeople's tasks. Three basic tasks are generally associated with selling: order processing, creative selling, and missionary selling. Sales jobs usually require salespeople to perform all three tasks to some degree, depending on the product and the company.

order processing
In personal sales, the receiving and follow-through on handling and delivery of an order by a salesperson.

Order Processing.   At selling's most basic level, **order processing**, a salesperson receives an order and sees to the handling and delivery of that order. Route salespeople are often order processors. They call on regular customers to check the customer's supply of bread, milk, snack foods, or soft drinks. Then, with the customer's consent, they determine the size of the reorder, fill the order from their trucks, and stack the customer's shelves.

creative selling
In personal sales, the use of techniques designed to persuade a customer to buy a product when the benefits of the product are not readily apparent or the item is very expensive.

Creative Selling.   When the benefits of a product are not clear, **creative selling** may persuade buyers. Most industrial products involve creative selling because the buyer has not used the product before or may not be familiar with the features and uses of a specific brand. Personal selling is also crucial for high-priced consumer products, such as homes, where buyers comparison shop. Any new product can benefit from creative selling that differentiates it from other products. Finally, creative selling can help to create a need.

Missionary Selling.   A company may also use **missionary selling** to promote itself and its products. Drug company representatives promote their companies' drugs to doctors who, in turn, prescribe them to their patients. The sale is actually made at the drugstore. In this case, the goal of missionary selling is to promote the company's long-term image rather than to make a quick sale.

missionary selling
In personal sales, the indirect promotion of a product by offering technical assistance and/or promoting the company's image.

The Personal Selling Process

Although all three sales tasks are important to an organization using personal selling, perhaps the most complicated is creative selling. It is the creative salesperson who is responsible for most of the steps in the personal selling process described here.

Prospecting and Qualifying.   To sell, a salesperson must first have a potential customer or *prospect*. **Prospecting** is the process of identifying potential customers. Salespeople find prospects through past company records, customers, friends, relatives, company personnel, and business associates. Prospects must then be **qualified** to determine whether they have the authority to buy and the ability to pay.

prospecting
In personal sales, the process of identifying potential customers.

qualifying
In personal sales, the process of determining whether potential customers have the authority to buy and the ability to pay for a product.

Approaching.   The first few minutes that a salesperson has contact with a qualified prospect are called the *approach*. The success of later stages depends on the prospect's first impression of the salesperson, since this impression affects the salesperson's credibility. Salespeople need to present a neat, professional appearance and to greet prospects in a strong, confident manner.

Presenting and Demonstrating.   Next, the salesperson must *present* the promotional message to the prospect. A presentation is a full explanation of the product, its features, and its uses. It links the product's benefits to the prospect's needs. A presentation may or may not include a *demonstration* of the product. But it is wise to demonstrate a product whenever possible, since most people have trouble visualizing what they have been told.

Handling Objections.   No matter what the product, prospects will have some *objections*. At the very least, prospects will object to a product's price, hoping to get a discount. Objections show the salesperson that the buyer is interested in the presentation and which parts of the presentation the buyer is unsure of or has a problem with. They tell the salesperson what customers feel is important and, essentially, how to sell them.

Closing.   The most critical part of the selling process is the **close**, in which the salesperson asks the prospective customer to buy the product. Successful salespeople recognize the signs that a customer is ready to buy. For example, prospects who start to figure out monthly payments for the product are clearly indicating that they are ready to buy. The salesperson should then attempt to close the sale.

closing
In personal sales, the process of asking the customer to buy the product.

Salespeople can ask directly for the sale or they can indirectly imply a close. Questions such as "Could you take delivery Tuesday?" and "Why don't we start you off with an initial order of ten cases?" are implied closes. Such indirect closes place the burden of rejecting the sale on the prospect, who will often find it hard to say no.

These customers have raised some questions that the salesperson is answering before they reach an agreed price for closing the sale of this car.

Following Up. The sales process does not end with the close of the sale. Most companies want customers to come back again. Sales *follow-up* activities include fast processing of the customer's order and on-time delivery. Training in the proper care and use of the product and speedy service if repairs are needed may also be part of the follow-up.

Sales Promotions

sales promotion

Short-term promotional activities designed to stimulate consumer buying or cooperation from distributors and other members of the trade.

Sales promotions are short-term promotional activities designed to stimulate consumer buying or cooperation from distributors, sales agents, or other members of the trade. They are important because they increase the likelihood that buyers will try products. They also enhance product recognition and can increase purchase size and amount. For example, soap is often bound into packages of four with the promotion. "Buy three and get one free."

To be successful, sales promotions must be convenient and accessible when the decision to purchase occurs. If Harley-Davidson has a one-week motorcycle promotion and you have no local dealer, the promotion is neither convenient nor accessible to you, and you will not buy. But if The Bay offers a 20-percent-off coupon that you can save for use later, the promotion is convenient and accessible.

Types of Sales Promotions

The best known sales promotions are coupons, point-of-purchase displays, purchasing incentives (such as free samples, trading stamps, and premiums), trade shows, and contests and sweepstakes.

coupon

A sales-promotion method featuring a certificate that entitles the bearer to a stated savings off a product's regular price.

Coupons. Any certificate that entitles the bearer to a stated savings off a product's regular price is a **coupon**. Coupons may be used to encourage customers to try new products, to attract customers away from competitors, or to induce current customers to buy more of a product. They appear in newspapers and magazines and are often sent through direct mail.

Point-of-Purchase Displays.   To grab customers' attention as they walk through a store, some companies use **point-of-purchase (POP) displays**.[26] Displays located at the end of the aisles or near the checkout in supermarkets are POP displays. POP displays often coincide with a sale on the item(s) being displayed. They make it easier for customers to find a product and easier for manufacturers to eliminate competitors from consideration. The cost of shelf and display space, however, is becoming more and more expensive.[27]

point-of-purchase (POP) display

A sales-promotion method in which a product display is so located in a retail store as to encourage consumers to buy the product.

Purchasing Incentives.   Purchasing incentives such as free samples, trading stamps, and premiums are used by many manufacturers and retailers. Free samples allow customers to try a product for a few days without any risk. They may be given out at local retail outlets or sent by manufacturers to consumers via direct mail.

Although the use of free samples is commonplace in Canada, it is very unusual in some other countries, especially those that are changing over to free-market economies. Procter & Gamble's marketing team was greeted with thanks and even tears when it gave free shampoo samples to grateful shoppers in Warsaw, who were stunned at getting a valued product without having to pay for it or even wait in a long line.[28]

Some retail outlets offer trading stamps as a bonus for patronizing a particular store. Finally, **premiums** are gifts, such as pens, pencils, calendars, and coffee mugs, that are given away to consumers in return for buying a specified product. Retailers and wholesalers also receive premiums for carrying some products.

premium

A sales-promotion method in which some item is offered free or at a bargain price to customers in return for buying a specified product.

Trade Shows.   Periodically, industries sponsor **trade shows** for their members and customers. Trade shows allow companies to rent booths to display and demonstrate their products to customers who have a special interest in the products or who are ready to buy. Trade shows are relatively inexpensive and are very effective, since the buyer comes to the seller already interested in a given type of product. International trade shows are becoming more important.

trade shows

A sales-promotion method in which members of a particular industry gather for displays and product demonstrations designed to sell products to customers.

Contests and Sweepstakes.   Customers, distributors, and sales representatives may all be persuaded to increase sales of a product through the use of contests. Distributors and sales agents may win a trip to Hawaii for selling the most pillows in the month of March. Although sweepstakes cannot legally require consumers to buy a product to enter, they may increase sales by stimulating buyers' interest in a product.

Publicity and Public Relations

Much to the delight of marketing managers with tight budgets, *publicity* is free. Moreover, because it is presented in a news format, consumers see publicity as objective and highly believable. Thus, it is an important part of the promotional mix. However, marketers often have little control over publicity. For example, when a critic rates a movie or a restaurant, there is no guarantee that the review will present the product favorably.[29]

In contrast, *public relations* is company-influenced publicity. It attempts to establish a sense of goodwill between the company and its customers through public-service announcements that enhance the company's image. For example, a bank may announce that senior citizens' groups can have free use of a meeting room for their social activities.

Most large firms have a department to manage their relations with the public and to present desired company images. As well, company executives may make appearances as guest speakers representing their companies at professional meetings and civic events. They may also serve as leaders in civic activities like the United Way campaign and university fundraising. Through PR offices, many companies produce audio-visual materials about company activities and make them available to interested groups, other companies, or the general public.

Companies can also take steps to exercise some control over publicity by press releases and press conferences. A *press release* is a written announcement sent to news agencies describing a new product, an event, or information about the company that may be of interest to the general public. In a *press conference*, a firm's representative meets face-to-face with the press to communicate information that the media may then publish or broadcast publicly.

Promotional Practices in Small Business

From our discussion so far, you might think that only large companies can afford to promote their goods and services. Although small businesses generally have fewer resources, cost-effective promotions can improve sales and enable small firms to compete with much larger firms.

Small Business Advertising

Advertising in non-prime-time slots on local television or cable TV offers great impact at a cost many small firms can afford. More commonly, though, small businesses with a local market use newspaper and radio advertising and, increasingly, direct mail. Billboards are beyond the means of many small businesses, but outdoor store signs can draw a strong response from passers-by.

The timing of advertising can be critical for generating revenues for a small business. For year-round advertising, the *Yellow Pages* are a widely used medium for advertising both industrial and consumer products in local markets. However, many small businesses, especially those selling to consumer markets, rely more on seasonal advertising. Retail stores advertise for the holidays; ads for lawn care and home maintenance services begin to appear in the early spring; and ads for tax preparation services become more visible at the beginning of the year.

Television, radio, and newspapers are seldom viable promotional options for reaching international markets because of their high costs and their limited availability. The market research needed to determine the best message and style for reaching the target audience is costly. Additional costs are incurred in developing broadcast and newsprint advertisements with the necessary variations in language and cultural appeal. Limited availability—the inaccessibility of the intended audience—is a problem in nations that have underdeveloped mass media or high illiteracy rates, or that place severe restrictions on advertising by private companies. In these situations, broadcast and newsprint media will not be feasible options for the international advertising mix. Instead, most small firms find direct mail and carefully targeted magazine advertising the most effective promotional tools.

The Role of Personal Selling in Small Business

Some small firms maintain a salesforce to promote and sell their products locally. Your local newspapers and television and radio stations, for example, use personal selling to attract advertisements by individuals and businesses. As part of the personal selling process, they provide complete information about the audiences ads will reach. Other small firms prefer not to do their own selling, but instead contract with a sales agency—a company that handles the products of several companies—to act on their behalf. Insurance agents who sell insurance for several different companies are sales agencies.

Because of the high costs of operating a national salesforce, many small companies have established telemarketing staffs. By combining telemarketing with a catalog or other educational product literature, small companies can sell their products nationally and compete against much larger companies.

Most small companies cannot afford to establish international offices, though some entrepreneurs, such as Art de Fehr of Palliser Furniture, do visit prospective customers in other countries. However, for most small businesses, even sending sales representatives overseas is expensive. Thus many small companies have combined telemarketing with direct mail in order to expand internationally.

Small Business Promotions

Small companies use the same sales promotion incentives that larger companies use. The difference is that larger firms tend to use more coupons, POP displays, and sales contests. Smaller firms rely on premiums and special sales, since coupons and sales contests are more expensive and more difficult to manage. For example, some automobile dealerships offer fishing reels at a bargain price if you just "come on down and road-test" a new four-wheel-drive vehicle. Gas stations use premiums by offering a free car wash with each fillup. Special sales prices are commonly offered by many service companies, including martial arts centers, remodeling companies, and dry cleaners.

Small Business Publicity

Publicity is very important to small businesses with local markets. Small firms often have an easier time getting local publicity than do national firms. Readers of local papers like to read about local companies, so local papers like to write about such businesses. However, fierce competition for coverage in national and international publications limits the access small businesses have to those markets.

Summary of Key Points

Products are a firm's reason for being; their features offer benefits to buyers whose purchases are the source of business profits. In developing products, marketers must take into account whether their market is individual consumers or other firms. Marketers must also recognize that buyers will pay less for, and worry less about, the exact nature of convenience goods than about shopping and specialty goods. In industrial markets, expense items are generally less expensive and more rapidly consumed than are capital items.

The seven stages of product development are development of ideas, screening, concept testing, business analysis, prototype development, product testing (test marketing), and commercialization. Few ideas for new products survive to the commercialization stage.

When new products are launched, they have a life cycle that begins with their introduction and progresses through stages of growth, maturity, and decline. Sales increase during the growth stage and level off in the maturity stage.

Each product is given a visible identity by its brand and the way it is packaged and labeled. National, licensed, and private brands are developed to create brand loyalty. Packaging provides an attractive container and advertises the product. The label informs the consumer of the package contents.

Promotion—any of a number of techniques designed to sell products to customers—involves communicating information about those products. Promotion may also help to position products or control sales volume. To meet these objectives, marketers must choose push or pull strategies. They must also select the best combination of tools—advertising, personal selling, sales promotion, and/or publicity and public relations—for the promotional mix.

Advertising strategies include informing and persuading potential buyers, comparing different firms' products, and reminding consumers about a product's existence. To implement these strategies, marketers may use various media—newspapers, television, direct mail, radio, magazines, and outdoor advertising. These media differ in their cost and ability to segment target markets. Advertising may also differ in its focus on a brand, viewpoint, or company image and in the target market, consumer or industrial, at which it is aimed.

Personal selling is the oldest form of selling, as well as the most expensive. In both retail and industrial situations, it may involve order processing, creative selling, and/or missionary selling. In the personal selling process, salespeople first identify and qualify prospective buyers and then approach these individuals and present information about the product. If salespeople are able to overcome a customer's objections, they may be able to close the sale. Follow-up after the sale is important to ensure repeat business.

Sales promotions, such as coupons, point-of-purchase (POP) displays, and trade shows, increase the chances that customers will recognize and try a product. Publicity differs from the other types of promotions in that it is free, but it is often uncontrollable.

Promotion activity is important to both small and large businesses. Small business firms conduct advertising campaigns (usually on a local scale), maintain a sales force (and perhaps telemarketers) to promote their products, use promotional tools like coupons and incentives, and use publicity in their local market.

CONCLUDING CASE 15-1

Beer Battles

Summer is the make-it-or-break-it time for Canadian brewers like Labatt and Molson. It is the time when beer drinkers are most likely to switch brands. As a result, beer companies spend up to half their annual advertising budgets in the three summer months.

During the 1970s and 1980s, the famous Labatt's Blue balloon was frequently seen on Canadian TV. Advertisements showed groups of happy Canadians enjoying various social events to the background music of "When You're Smiling." Blue dominated the market. In the early 1980s, Molson decided to target a specific market segment—males between 19 and 23—and begin marketing to them in an effort to "grow a market." Molson knew this strategy would take a while. By the late 1980s, there was evidence that Molson was, in fact, catching up to Blue. By 1992, Molson had pulled to within one percentage point of Labatt in the battle for market share between Blue and Canadian.

In recent years, several new beer products—notably ice beer and light beer—have been introduced, and these have taken sales away from the old standby brands of both Labatt and Molson. By the end of 1993, Labatt's Blue held 15 percent of the market, but Molson Canadian had declined to just 7 percent. Labatt controls 35.5 percent of the total beer market, Molson 26.5 percent, and all others, 38 percent.

Industry observers think that Molson spends about $40 million each year to advertise its products, while Labatt spends about $30 million. Molson recently increased advertising on Canadian in an attempt to recover some of the market share it lost during 1993. New television commercials used the line "I am" and showed the diverse cultures and regions of Canada. The latest TV advertisements of both Labatt and Molson are a departure from the stereotyped advertisements showing young people mindlessly partying.

Advertising agencies like beer accounts because, first of all, they make the agency a lot of money, and, second, the correlation between the campaigns the agencies develop and sales is pretty clear. Because the government strictly controls other factors that normally influence product sales (pricing, packaging, and distribution), promotion is extremely important. Furthermore, the fact is, competing beers taste pretty much alike. Thus, beer accounts prove how good an advertising agency is.

In addition to their own competitive rivalry, both Labatt and Molson have had to scramble in the past few years to ward off competition from small breweries, from low-priced beer, and from imports. They were also disappointed that light beers did not sell as well as they had hoped. Industry observers think that there are simply too many beer brands on the market. Big brewers like Labatt and Molson would like to get consumers to return to just a few tried-and-true brands because it costs less to pitch fewer brands.

CASE QUESTIONS
1. What type of product is beer (convenience, shopping, or speciality)?
2. In what stage of the product life cycle is beer? Does this product have unique characteristics that make normal life cycle considerations irrelevant?
3. How does brand loyalty in the beer market influence advertising strategies?
4. Why is personal selling not used in the marketing of beer?
5. Discuss each of the four elements in the promotional mix as they relate to beer. ◆

CONCLUDING CASE 15-2

Brand Battles

Coca-Cola is one of the most famous brands in the world. For many years it has been number one in the cola wars, closely followed by Pepsi. But lately, Cott Corp. of Toronto has been causing trouble for both Coke and Pepsi by making private brand cola for a variety of supermarkets.

Cott was started in the 1950s and sold its own branded cola with the slogan "It's Cott to be Good." But it wasn't very successful. In 1991, the company struck a deal with Royal Crown Cola (another also-ran in the cola wars) to buy its concentrate. Now Cott uses that concentrate to make private label pop that sells throughout North America. At Safeway, for example, Cott's private label is called "President's Choice," at A & P it is called "Master Choice," and at Wal-Mart it is called "Sam's American Choice." Cott has signed up 60 major U.S. retailers and now controls 2 percent of the $30 billion soft drink market. Sales revenue in 1994 was over $600 million, and profits were over $9 million. The company's goal is to achieve 5 percent of the market and sales revenue of $1.5 billion.

The CEO of Coca-Cola claims that private labels do not pose much of a threat to either Coke or Pepsi. But both companies have been blitzing supermarkets with studies claiming, among other things, that customers who purchase major brands spend significantly more money on each trip to the store than people who buy private labels. The major brands will have to reduce their prices to compete with Cott (and they can do that), but whether they can make any money selling their product at lower prices remains to be seen.

The most dramatic threat to Coke occurred when J. Sainsbury PLC, Britain's largest supermarket chain, introduced its own private brand cola, made by Cott, in a can that is strikingly similar to Coke's can. What has caught the media's attention is the fact that Cott's quality is high enough and its packaging similar enough to be mistaken for the "Real Thing." Sainsbury stocks its private brand label (simply labelled "cola") right next to Coca-Cola, and prices it at only three-quarters the price of Coke.

It is not clear what Coca-Cola should do about all of this. They are reluctant to get into a fight with Sainsbury because suppliers like Coke must maintain good relations with retail outlets that stock their products.

CASE QUESTIONS
1. What type of consumer good is cola?
2. Discuss each of the four elements in the promotion mix as they relate to the promotion of cola.
3. In what stage of the product life cycle is cola? How does the stage in the life cycle influence promotional strategy?
4. How important is brand loyalty in the sale of cola? Why have private brands been more successful recently? ◆

Key Terms

convenience goods/services	private brands	reminder advertising	retail selling
shopping goods/services	generic products	advertising medium	industrial selling
specialty goods/services	trademark	direct mail	salesforce management
expense items	brand loyalty	word of mouth	order processing
capital items	packaging	media mix	creative selling
product mix	label	brand advertising	missionary selling
product line	*Consumer Packaging and*	product advertising	prospecting
speed to market	*Labelling Act*	advocacy advertising	qualifying
definition of the service	product positioning	institutional advertising	closing
package	push strategy	retail advertising	sales promotion
service process design	pull strategy	cooperative advertising	coupon
product life cycle (PLC)	promotional mix	trade advertising	point-of-purchase (POP)
brand names	informative advertising	industrial advertising	display
national brands	persuasive advertising	advertising agency	premium
licensed brands	comparative advertising	telemarketing	trade shows

Study Questions and Exercises

Review Questions

1. What are the various classifications of consumer and industrial products? Give an example of a good and a service for each category different from the examples given in the text.
2. List the seven stages of the product development process. Give an example showing how or why a new product can fail or succeed at each stage.
3. Distinguish between national brands, licensed brands, and private brands. Give examples of at least two competing products for each type of brand.
4. Describe the differences between the push and pull promotional strategies. Why would a company choose one rather than the other?
5. Compare and contrast the advantages and disadvantages of the different advertising media.
6. What is the advantage of personal selling over the other communication tools?
7. How do creative and missionary selling differ? Give three examples of products for which each might be used, other than those listed in the chapter.
8. Is publicity more or less readily available to small firms than to large ones? Why?

Analysis Questions

9. How would you expect the naming, packaging, and labeling of convenience, shopping, and specialty goods to differ? Why? Give examples to illustrate your answers.

10. Take a look at some of the television advertising that is being done by small local businesses in your area. What differences can you see between those commercials and the ones done by large national companies?
11. Pick a consumer product and trace the steps in the personal selling process for this item. Do the same for an industrial product.
12. Find some examples of publicity about some local and national businesses. Do you think the publicity had positive or negative consequences for the businesses? Why?

Application Exercises

13. Interview a manager of a local manufacturing firm. Identify the company's products according to where they stand in the product life cycle.
14. Choose a product with which you are familiar and analyze various pricing objectives for it. What information would you want to have if you were to adopt a profit-maximizing objective? A market-share objective? An image objective?
15. Choose a product sold nationally. Identify as many media used in its promotion as you can. Which medium is used most? Why? Do you believe the promotion is successful? Why or why not?
16. Interview the owner of a local small business. Identify the promotional objectives and strategies of the firm as well as the elements in the promotional mix. What (if any) changes would you suggest? Why?

Building Your Business Skills

Goal

To encourage students to to think about new product development and pricing issues from the standpoint of both marketers and consumers.

Method

Each student should write down the name and approximate price of one new product or service that has been introduced during the past year or so. Also write down the name of the company that markets the product. The product should be one about which the student has formed an opinion or a perception. For example, are you interested in purchasing or not interested in purchasing? Do you find any product features attractive? Do you find the marketer's claim about a benefit to be reasonable or unreasonable?

Analysis

Team with two or three other students. Each student should describe the product that he or she has identified.

This description should include the writer's opinion(s) about the product, plus his or her perception about price: Is it high, low, or just right? Each student should now comment on all the other products by offering his or her own opinions or perceptions, including attitude toward price. If time permits, each team should share its findings with the rest of the class.

Follow-up Questions

1. How many of your teammates were aware of the product that you chose? In general, were some students familiar with certain new products while others had not yet heard about them? Are marketers doing enough to build awareness?
2. How many of the products identified in your group were genuinely new products as opposed to line extensions or new versions of existing products?
3. Do perceptions about product prices vary widely or very little? Why do people vary in their willingness to pay a given price for a product?

16

Pricing and Distributing Goods and Services

LEARNING OBJECTIVES

After reading this chapter, you will be able to

- Identify the various business objectives that can govern pricing decisions and the tools used in making these decisions.
- Discuss pricing strategies and tactics for existing and new products.
- Outline and discuss the channels of distribution in the distribution mix and distribution strategies.
- Explain how merchant wholesalers and agents/brokers differ in their activities.
- Identify the different types of retail outlets.
- Describe the three major activities in the physical distribution process.
- Compare the five basic forms of transportation used in the distribution of goods and identify the types of firms that provide such transportation.

CHAPTER OUTLINE

OPENING CASE

Dramatic Changes in Retailing

For most Canadian retailers, the 1990s have been a trying time. Free trade, the recession, the goods and services tax, cross-border shopping, and tough new competition from U.S.-based retailers have been a source of deep concern. At the start of the decade, The Bay, Eaton's, and Sears lost money (and they were the lucky ones). Retailers like Simpson's, Henry Birks & Sons, Peoples Jewellers, Woodward's, and Bargain Harolds all went bankrupt or into receivership. To make matters worse, department stores have come under attack from discount chains like Office Depot, Price/Costco, and Wal-Mart. In 1993, the sales of discount and warehouse outlets exceeded those of traditional department stores for the first time.

Customers aren't cooperating, either. They used to be willing to pay higher prices for brand-name merchandise that had been heavily advertised, but not anymore. They are now much more value- and price-conscious. Canadian department stores may be hurt by this trend because they are less competitive than their U.S. counterparts and have not had to operate in such a fiercely competitive environment until recently.

Eaton's is one of the most famous Canadian retailers. But that has not spared it from the problems facing other retailers. The company is presently divided into three divisions: T. Eaton Realty Co. Ltd. (which handles the firm's property holdings); T. Eaton Acceptance Co. Ltd. (which manages credit card operations); and T. Eaton Co. Ltd. (which operates the department store). The first two divisions made money, while the department store has been losing money. Just how much money is unclear. Estimates range from $20 million to $100 million annually for the past few years. (Because Eaton's is a private company, it does not have to disclose its financial figures, and its management is renowned for its unwillingness to talk about the financial affairs of the company.)

In the view of some analysts, the main deterrent to the company's success is not financial, but personal. Tom Reid, chief operating officer, and CEO George Eaton are regarded by industry insiders as lacking the skills needed to inspire employees to be excited about the company. While one of the strengths of the company is the family continuity that has characterized the firm since its begin-

ning, the firm may have become too inward looking and unaware of major changes that are occurring in retailing.

Eaton's current strategy is twofold: to emphasize "everyday low prices" and to be a store where consumers can buy *anything*. The company doesn't claim that it has the lowest prices in town, but rather that it has a commitment to year-round lower prices. The store's long-standing "goods satisfactory or money refunded" policy has been handed down through four generations from its founder, Timothy Eaton. Eaton's continues to concentrate on solid, middle-of-the-road merchandise, but has instituted some major changes in its marketing strategy as of late. For example, the TransCanada sales, which were a national institution, are gone. So too are the stores' coupon events, which generated high sales volume. Eaton's has had to spend heavily on advertising to convince shoppers that it realy means what is says about low prices.

While some industry observers think that traditional department stores are dinosaurs, Eaton's is opening new ones. At a time when retailers have decided that people skills are the key to retailing success, Eaton's continues to pay its executives 25 percent below the industry norm. At a time when stores are narrowing their focus, Eaton's continues with its strategy of trying to sell everything to everybody. Does Eaton's need a new visionary? Where is the Timothy Eaton of the 1990s? ◆

In this chapter, we complete our look at the marketing function by examining the role of pricing and distribution. The opening case describes how one of the most famous Canadian distributors is trying to meet the price challenges from foreign discounters.

The first part of the chapter examines the pricing objectives of business firms, as well as the various methods they use to decide what to charge for the goods and services they produce. The second part of the chapter describes how producers get their goods and services into consumers' hands. Should the company sell directly to consumers? Or should some type of intermediary like a retailer be used? How will the merchandise be moved from the factory to the consumer?

Pricing Objectives and Tools

Price is becoming an increasingly important part of the marketing mix. During the last 10 years, companies have increased their emphasis on quality, so quality across products is now very similar. As a result, consumers now focus more on price as a way to decide which products to buy. In grocery stores, for example, private brands are increasingly su c-cessful because they sell for 15 to 40 percent less than the name brands. Successful stores like Wal-Mart realize the importance of price, so they have adopted an "everyday low price" (EDLP) policy.[1]

In **pricing**, managers decide what the company will receive in exchange for its products. In this section, we first discuss the objectives that influence a firm's pricing decisions. Then we describe the major tools that companies use to meet those objectives.

pricing
Deciding what the company will receive in exchange for its product.

Pricing to Meet Business Objectives

Companies often price products to maximize profits. But other objectives can also be involved. Some firms, for example, are more interested in dominating the market or securing high market share than in maximizing profits. Pricing decisions are also influenced by the need to survive in competitive marketplaces, by social and ethical concerns, and even by corporate image.

Profit-Maximizing Objectives.   Pricing to maximize profits is tricky. If prices are set too low, the company will probably sell many units of its product. But it may miss the opportunity to make additional profit on each unit—and may indeed lose money on each exchange. Conversely, if prices are set too high, the company will make a large profit on each item but will sell fewer units. Again, the firm loses money. In addition, it may be left with excess inventory and may have to reduce or even close production operations. To avoid these problems, companies try to set prices to sell the number of units that will generate the highest possible total profits.

In calculating profits, managers weigh receipts against costs for materials and labor to create the product. But they also consider the capital resources (plant and equipment) that the company must tie up to generate that level of profit. The costs of marketing (such as maintaining a large sales staff) can also be substantial. Concern over the efficient use of these resources has led many firms to set prices so as to achieve a targeted level of return on sales or capital investment.[2]

Market-Share Objectives.   In the long run, of course, a business must make a profit to survive. Nevertheless, many companies initially set low prices for new products. They are willing to accept minimal profits—even losses—to get buyers to try products. In other words, they use pricing to establish **market share**: a company's percentage of the total market sales for a specific product. Even with established products, market share may outweigh profits as a pricing objective. For a product like Philadelphia Brand Cream Cheese, dominating a market means that consumers are more likely to buy it because they are familiar with a well-known, highly visible product.

market share
A company's percentage of the total market sales for a specific product.

Other Pricing Objectives.   Profit-maximizing and market-share objectives may not be appropriate in some instances. During difficult economic times, many firms go out of business. Loss containment and survival replace profit maximization when a company in distress attempts to right itself. In the mid-1980s, John Deere priced its agricultural equipment for survival in a depressed farm economy.

Social and ethical concerns may also affect pricing for some types of products. In 1987, drugmaker Burroughs Wellcome received approval to begin selling AZT, the first drug shown to help in combating AIDS. A storm of protest erupted when Burroughs announced that a year's supply of AZT would cost $10 000. After months of relentless pressure, Burroughs reduced the price to about $3000.[3]

Pricing decisions may also reflect a company's image. Retailers such as Braemar's and Holt-Renfrew will not sell a $10 shirt or $20 dress, and Kmart will not carry $500 men's suits, regardless of quality.

Tools for Price Determination

Whatever the company's pricing objective, managers must measure the business impact before they can set prices. Three basic tools are used for this purpose: economic demand-supply comparisons, cost-oriented pricing, and break-even analysis. Rarely is one of these tools sufficient. Most often, they are used together to identify prices that allow the company to reach its objectives.

Economic Demand-Supply Comparisons.   Economic theory helps firms maximize profits. This approach looks at the total market for a product, identifying the amount that consumers will demand and producers will supply at various prices.

Figure 16.1 compares demand for and supply of movie tickets at various prices. As prices go up, the number of tickets sought goes down, causing the downward-sloping demand curve. But theater owners would

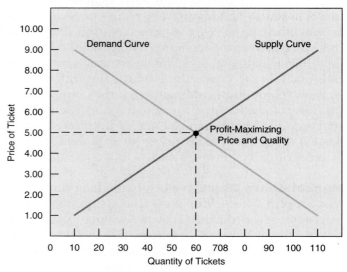

(a) Demand and Supply Schedules for Movie Ticket

Price (dollars)	Ticket Demanded (units of tickets)	Ticket Supplied (units of tickets)
$1.00	108	10
3.00	80	32
5.00	60	60
7.00	35	87
9.00	10	110

Figure 16.1
Demand and supply schedules for movie tickets (a) and demand and supply curves for movie tickets (b).

be willing to supply more tickets when prices are higher, as shown in the upward-sloping supply curve.

Considering the two curves together tells us the best (profit-maximizing) price for movie tickets: $5.00. At this price, the number of tickets demanded and the number of tickets supplied are the same. According to economic theory, in the long run, the market price will *always* settle where the demand and supply curves meet.

Cost-Oriented Pricing. The major weakness of the demand-and-supply approach to pricing is that it focuses entirely on identifying a market price for a product. It does not consider whether companies can make money at this price. As well, it treats the products of all suppliers as identical, which is not always true. In contrast, cost-oriented pricing takes into account the firm's need to cover its costs of producing the product.

A music store manager would begin using the cost-oriented approach to pricing records by calculating the cost of making compact discs (CDs) available to shoppers. Included in this figure would be store rent, sales clerks' wages, utilities, CD displays, insurance, and the cost of the CDs. Assume that the cost of a CD comes to $9.00. If the store sold the CD for this price, it would not make any profit. The manager must add in an amount for profit called **markup**. A markup of $6.00 over cost in this case would result in a selling price of $15.00.

Profit is usually evaluated based on a percentage of the selling price. The manager calculates the markup percentage as follows:

markup
The amount added to the cost of an item to earn a profit for the retailer or wholesaler.

$$\text{Markup percentage} = \frac{\text{Markup}}{\text{Sales price}}$$

$$\text{Markup percentage} = \frac{\$6.00}{\$15.00} = 40.0\%$$

That is, out of every dollar taken in, 40 cents will be gross profit for the store. However, out of this profit still must come store rent, utilities, insurance, and all those other costs.

Another way to express the markup is as a percentage of cost instead of a percentage of sales price. The $6.00 markup is 66.7 percent of the $9.00 cost of a CD ($6.00 ÷ $9.00). Some retailers prefer to express the markup using this cost-based method. Others, however, prefer the sales-price approach.

Break-Even Analysis: Cost-Volume-Profit Relationships. A company that uses cost-oriented pricing can count on covering its **variable costs** (materials and labor primarily) for each item sold. It will also make some money toward **fixed costs** such as equipment, rent, management salaries, and insurance. But without a **break-even analysis**, the company does not know how many units it must sell before all its fixed costs are covered and it truly begins to make a profit.

Continuing on with the music store example, suppose the variable costs for each CD (basically, the cost of buying the CD from the producer) are $8.00. Fixed costs for keeping the store open for one year are $100 000. The **break-even point**, the number of CDs that must be sold to cover both fixed and variable costs and thus for the store to start to make some profit, will be 14 286 CDs, calculated as follows:

variable costs
Those costs that change with the number of goods or services produced or sold.

fixed costs
Those costs unaffected by the number of goods or services produced or sold.

break-even analysis
An assessment of how many units must be sold at a given price before the company begins to make a profit.

break-even point
The number of units that must be sold at a given price before the company covers all its variable and fixed costs.

$$\text{Break-even point (in units)} = \frac{\text{Total fixed costs}}{\text{Price} - \text{variable cost}}$$

$$= \frac{\$100\ 000}{\$15.00 - \$8.00}$$

$$= 14\ 286\ \text{CDs}$$

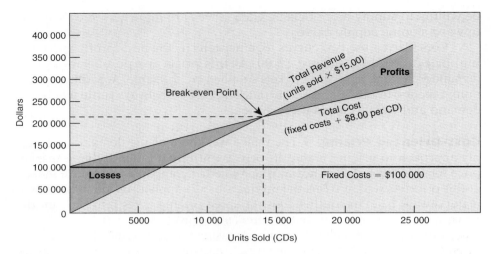

Figure 16.2
Break-even analysis: 14 286 CDs is the break-even point.

Figure 16.2 shows the break-even point graphically. Note that if sales are below 14 286 CDs, the store loses money for the year. If sales exceed 14 286 CDs, profits grow by $7.00 for each CD sold.

In reality, managers calculate break-even points for each of several possible price levels. As the price per CD increases, the number of units that must be sold before the break-even point is reached decreases. As prices fall, the number of units that must be sold before the break-even point is reached increases. Table 16.1 shows this relationship for a variety of prices. Prices below $8.00 are not considered because, if the price does not exceed the item's variable cost, the break-even point will never occur.

The music store owner would certainly like to hit the break-even quantity as early as possible so that profits will start rolling in. Why not charge $20.00 per CD, then, and reach break-even earlier? The answer lies in the downward-sloping demand curve we discussed earlier. At a price of $20.00 per CD, CD sales at the store would drop. In setting a price, the manager must consider how much CD buyers will pay and what the store's local competitors charge.

TABLE 16.1   Comparison of Break-Even Quantities for Various Price Levels

Price ($)	Number of CDs for Break-Even Quantity	Total Cost and Revenue at Break-Even Quantity
$ 8.00	*	*
$10.00	50 000	$500 000
$12.00	25 000	$300 000
$14.00	16 667	$233 340
$15.00	14 286	$214 290
$16.00	12 500	$200 000
$18.00	10 000	$180 000
$20.00	5 000	$100 000

*Does not exist at this price.

Pricing Strategies and Tactics

The pricing tools discussed in the previous section provide a valuable guide for managers trying to set prices on specific goods. But they do not provide general direction for managers trying to set a pricing philosophy for their company. In this section, we discuss *pricing strategy*—that is, pricing as a planning activity that affects the marketing mix. We then describe some basic *pricing tactics*—ways in which managers implement a firm's pricing strategies.

Pricing Philosophies and Strategies

Given our earlier discussion, you might think that a manager can identify a single "best" price for a product. But a study of prices for popular nonaspirin pain relievers (such as Tylenol and Advil) found variations of 100 percent.[4] These price differences may reflect some differences in product costs, but even more they reflect differing brand images that attract different customers. These images in turn reflect vastly different pricing philosophies and strategies. In this section, we will consider how pricing strategies for both existing and new products can cause widely differing prices for similar products.

Pricing Existing Products.   A firm basically has three options available in pricing its existing products. It can set prices for its product above prevailing market prices charged for similar products. It can set prices below market. Or it can set prices at or near the market price.

Companies pricing above the market play on customers' beliefs that higher price means higher quality. Curtis Mathes, a maker of televisions, VCRs, and stereos, promotes itself as the most expensive television set "but worth it." Companies such as Godiva chocolates and Rolls Royce have also succeeded with this pricing philosophy.

In contrast, both Budget and Discount car rental companies promote themselves as low-priced alternatives to Hertz and Avis. Ads for Suave hair-care products argue that "Suave does what theirs does—for a lot less." Pricing below the prevailing market price can succeed if the firm can offer a product of acceptable quality while keeping costs below those of higher-priced options.

Finally, in some industries, a dominant firm establishes product prices and other companies follow along. This is called **price leadership**. (Don't confuse this approach with *price fixing*, the illegal process of producers agreeing among themselves what prices will be charged.) Price leadership is often evident in products such as structural steel, gasoline, and many processed foods. These products differ little in quality from one firm to another. Companies compete through advertising campaigns, personal selling, and service, not price.

price leadership
The dominant firm in the industry establishes product prices and other companies follow suit.

Pricing New Products: Skimming and Penetration Pricing.   Companies introducing new products into the market have to consider two contrasting pricing policy options: coming in with either a very high price or a very low one. The former is known as a **price-skimming strategy** and the latter is a **penetration-pricing strategy**.

Skimming may allow a firm to earn a large profit on each item sold. This cash is often needed to cover product development and introduction costs. But skimming is possible only as long as the company can convince consumers that the product is truly different from existing products on the market. Eventually, the initial high profits will attract competition. Microwave ovens, calculators, and VCRs were introduced at comparatively high prices and prices fell as new companies entered the market.

price-skimming strategy
The decision to price a new product as high as possible to earn the maximum profit on each unit sold.

penetration-pricing strategy
The decision to price a new product very low to sell the most units possible and to build customer loyalty.

On the other hand, the low initial prices of a penetration-pricing strategy seek to generate consumer interest and stimulate trial purchases of the new product. New food products—convenience foods, cookies, and snacks—are often promoted at special low prices that stimulate brisk early sales of the product. Penetration pricing provides for minimal, if any, profit. This strategy can only succeed if the company can raise its price as consumer acceptance grows. Such price increases must be managed carefully to avoid alienating future customers.

Pricing Tactics

No matter what philosophy a company uses to price existing or new products, its managers may adopt one or more pricing *tactics* such as price lining or psychological pricing. Managers must also decide on what, if any, discounting tactics to use.

price lining

The practice of offering all items in certain categories at a limited number of predetermined price points.

psychological pricing

The practice of setting prices to take advantage of the nonlogical reactions of consumers to certain types of prices.

odd-even psychological pricing

A form of psychological pricing in which prices are not stated in even dollar amounts.

threshold pricing

A form of psychological pricing in which prices are set at what appears to be the maximum price consumers will pay for an item.

discount

Any price reduction offered by the seller in order to persuade customers to purchase a product.

cash discount

A form of discount in which customers paying cash, rather than buying on credit, pay lower prices.

seasonal discount

A form of discount in which lower prices are offered to customers making a purchase at a time of year when sales are traditionally slow.

trade discount

Discount given to firms involved

Price Lining.   Companies selling multiple items in a product category use price lining. For example, a department store carries literally thousands of products. To set a separate price for each brand and style of suit, plate, or couch would take many hours. By using **price lining**, the store can predetermine three or four price points at which a particular product will be sold. For men's suits, the price points might be $175, $250, and $400. All men's suits in the store will be priced at one of these three points. Buyers for the store must choose suits that can be purchased and sold profitably for one of these three prices.

Price lining requires managers to set each price level with a specific type of customer in mind and to display and sell the products accordingly. For example, Sears offers three lines of power tools, batteries, and appliances. "Sears Good" is for novice or occasional users. "Sears Better" is for avid users. And "Sears Best" is for professional users.

Psychological Pricing.   Another pricing tactic, **psychological pricing**, takes advantage of the fact that customers are not completely rational when making buying decisions.[5] **Odd-even psychological pricing** proposes that customers prefer prices that are not stated in even dollar amounts. That is, customers see prices of $1000, $100, $50, and $10 as much higher than prices of $999.95, $99.95, $49.95, and $9.95, respectively. One common explanation for this widely recognized process is that the consumer looks at the whole dollar figure, ignores the cents, and rounds down.

Closely related to odd-even pricing, **threshold pricing** argues that consumers set maximum prices they will pay for a particular item. Many gift shops, for example, will carry a supply of gifts in the $20-or-under price range. The feeling is that gift-givers often place an upper limit of $20 on gifts they buy.

Discounting.   The price that is eventually set for a product is not always the price at which all items are sold. Many times a company has to offer a price reduction—a **discount**—to stimulate sales. Cash, seasonal, trade, and quantity discounts are the most common forms.

In recent years, **cash discounts** have become popular, even at retail stores. Stores may offer **seasonal discounts** to stimulate the sales of products during times of the year when most customers do not normally buy the product. Travellers can find low prices on summer trips to tropical islands and July shoppers can get sale prices on winter coats thanks to seasonal discounts. Airlines use a computer-based system called yield management to predict the number of empty seats likely to exist on future flights. The system then juggles the prices in an attempt to attract bargain travellers.[6] **Trade discounts** are available only to those companies or individuals involved in a product's

These teens are as concerned with the price tag as with the style of the clothing they might buy on this shopping trip.

distribution. Thus, wholesalers, retailers, and interior designers pay less for fabric than the typical consumer does. Related to trade discounts are **quantity discounts**—lower prices for purchases in large quantities. Case price discounts for motor oil or soft drinks at retail stores are examples of quantity discounts.

quantity discount
A form of discount in which customers buying large amounts of a product pay lower prices.

The Distribution Mix

We have already seen that a company needs an appropriate product mix. But the success of any product also depends in part on its **distribution mix**: the combination of distribution channels that a firm selects to get a product to end users. In this section, we will consider some of the many factors that enter into the distribution mix. First, we will explain the need for *intermediaries*. We will then discuss the basic *distribution strategies*. Finally, we will consider some special issues in channel relationships—namely, conflict and leadership.

distribution mix
The combination of distribution channels a firm selects to get a product to end users.

Intermediaries and Distribution Channels

Once called *middlemen*, **intermediaries** are the individuals and firms who help to distribute a producer's goods. They are generally classified as *wholesalers* or *retailers*. **Wholesalers** sell products to other businesses, who resell them to final consumers. **Retailers** sell products directly to consumers. While some firms rely on independent intermediaries, others employ their own distribution networks and sales forces. The decision normally hinges on three factors:

- the company's target markets
- the nature of its products
- the costs of maintaining distribution and sales networks.

We examine these factors more closely below by describing some of the distribution decisions that go into the marketing of consumer products.

intermediary
Any individual or firm other than the producer who participates in a product's distribution.

wholesalers
Intermediaries who sell products to other businesses, who in turn resell them to the end-users.

retailers
Intermediaries who sell products to the end-users.

Distribution of Consumer Products

Figure 16.3 shows six primary **distribution channels** aimed at different target audiences and product types. Note that *all* channels *must* begin with a manufacturer and end with a consumer or an industrial user. Channels 1 through 4 are most often used for the distribution of consumer goods and services.

Channel 1.   In this **direct channel**, the product travels from the producer to the consumer with no intermediaries. Companies such as Avon, Fuller Brush, Tupperware, and many encyclopedia distributors use this channel. Direct channel distribution is also popular with craftspeople who sell their wares through word-of-mouth reference or from booths at local flea markets or craft shows. Roadside vegetable stands also use the direct channel.

Channel 2.   In this channel, manufacturers distribute their products through retailers. Goodyear Tire and Rubber has set up its own system of retail outlets. The perfume and fragrance industry uses its own sales force to sell many of its products to retailers who, in turn, sell them across the counter to consumers.

Channel 3.   Until the mid-1960s, Channel 2 was a widely used method of retail distribution. But that channel requires a large amount of floor space both for storing merchandise and for displaying it in retail stores. As the cost of retail space rose, retailers found that they could not afford to buy space to store goods. Thus wholesalers have increasingly entered the distribution network. They have taken over more and more of the storage service. A good example of this philosophy in practice is convenience food/gas stores. Approximately 90 percent of the space in these stores is devoted to merchandise displays. Only about 10 percent is used for storage and office facilities.

Wholesalers have always played a role in distributing some products. Many manufacturers only distribute their products in large quantities. Small businesses that cannot afford to purchase large quantities of goods rely on wholesalers to hold inventories of such products and to supply them on short notice. For example, a family-owned grocery store that sells only 12 cases of canned spinach in a year cannot afford to buy a truckload (perhaps 500

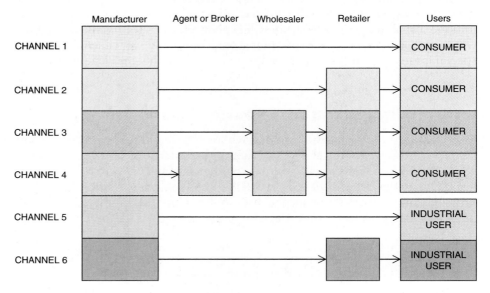

Figure 16.3
Channels of distribution: How the product travels from manufacturer to consumer.

cases) in a single order. Instead, it orders one case a month from a local wholesaler, which buys large lots of spinach and other goods from the makers, stores them, and resells them in small quantities to various retailers.

Channel 4. This complex channel uses **sales agents**, or **brokers**, who represent manufacturers and sell to wholesalers, retailers, or both. They receive commissions based on the price of goods they sell. Agents generally deal in the related product lines of a few producers, serving as their sales representatives on a relatively permanent basis. Travel agents, for example, represent the airlines, car-rental companies, and hotels. In contrast, brokers are hired to assist in buying and selling temporarily, matching sellers and buyers as needed. This channel is often used in the food and clothing industries. The real estate industry and the stock market also rely on brokers for matching buyers and sellers.

agent/broker

An independent businessperson who represents a business and receives a commission in return, but never takes legal possession of the product.

Indirect distribution channels do mean higher prices to the end consumer. The more members involved in the channel, the higher the final price to the purchaser. After all, each link in the distribution chain must charge a markup or commission to make a profit. Figure 16.4 shows typical markup growth through the distribution channel.

Ernst & Young conducted a study of the competitiveness of distribution channels which showed that Canada often has an extra layer of wholesale distribution compared to American distribution channels and higher markups at the retail level. But the Canadian retail sector is becoming more like the U.S., with larger stores, more items, and fewer intermediaries.[7]

Intermediaries add to the visible dollar cost of a product but, in many ways, they save the consumer time and thus money. A manufacturer would not sell you one calculator for the same price it charges wholesalers who buy truckloads of them. In other ways, intermediaries actually save you money.

Consider Figure 16.5, which illustrates the problem of making chili without an intermediary—the supermarket. You would probably spend a lot more time (and a lot of money on gas) if you had to get all the necessary ingredients on your own. In fact, intermediaries can add form, place, and time utility by making the right quantities available where and when you need them.

Distribution of Industrial Products

Industrial channels are important because each company is itself a customer that buys other companies' products. The Kellogg Co. buys grain to make breakfast cereals, Stone Container Corp. buys rolls of paper and vats of glue to make corrugated boxes, and Victoria Hospital buys medicines and other supplies

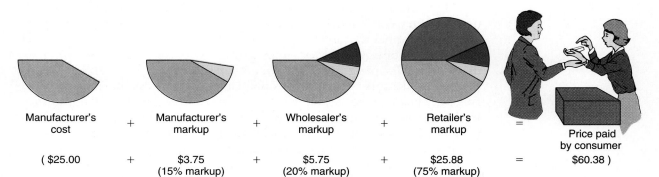

Manufacturer's cost	+	Manufacturer's markup	+	Wholesaler's markup	+	Retailer's markup	=	Price paid by consumer
($25.00	+	$3.75 (15% markup)	+	$5.75 (20% markup)	+	$25.88 (75% markup)	=	$60.38)

Figure 16.4
Where your dollar goes in the distribution channel for an electronic calculator.

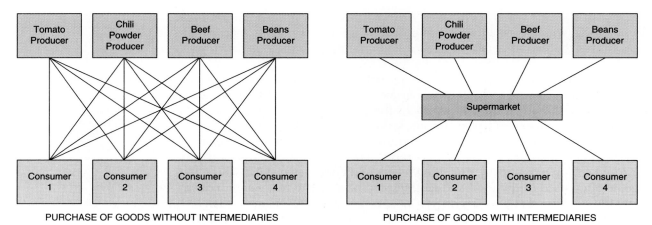

PURCHASE OF GOODS WITHOUT INTERMEDIARIES   PURCHASE OF GOODS WITH INTERMEDIARIES

Figure 16.5
Advantages of intermediaries.

to provide medical services. Industrial distribution, therefore, refers to the network of channel members involved in the flow of manufactured goods to industrial customers. Unlike consumer products, industrial products are traditionally distributed through Channels 5 or 6 (refer back to Figure 16.3).

sales offices

Offices maintained by sellers of industrial goods to provide points of contact with their customers.

Channel 5.   Most industrial goods are sold directly by the manufacturer to the industrial buyer. As contact points with their customers, manufacturers maintain **sales offices**. These offices provide all services for the company's customers and serve as headquarters for its salespeople.

Steel, transistors, and conveyors are all distributed through Channel 5. Because such goods are usually purchased in large quantities, intermediaries are often unnecessary. In some cases, however, brokers or agents may enter the distribution chain between manufacturer and buyer.

Channel 6.   Wholesalers function as intermediaries between manufacturers and users in only a very small percentage of industrial channels. Brokers and agents are even rarer. Channel 6 is most often used for accessory equipment (computer terminals, office equipment) and supplies (floppy disks, copier paper). While manufacturers produce these items in large quantities, companies buy them in small quantities. Few companies, for example, order truckloads of paper clips. As with consumer goods, then, intermediaries help end users by representing manufacturers or by breaking down large quantities into smaller sales units.

In some areas, however, relationships are changing. In the office-products industry, for instance, Channel 6 is being displaced by the emergence of a new channel that looks very much like Channel 3 for consumer products: Instead of buying office supplies from wholesalers (Channel 6), many users are shopping at office discount stores such as Office Depot. Warehouselike superstores target small- and medium-sized businesses, which generally buy supplies at retail stores, much as they target retail consumers. In these new "discount stores for industrial users," customers stroll down the aisles behind shopping carts, selecting from 7000 items at prices 20 to 75 percent lower than manufacturers' suggested prices.

Distribution Strategies

Choosing a distribution network is a vital consideration for a company. It can make the firm succeed or fail. The choice of distribution strategy determines the amount of market exposure the product gets and the cost of that exposure.

The appropriate strategy depends on the product class. The goal is to make a product accessible in just enough locations to satisfy customers' needs. Milk can be purchased at many retail outlets (high exposure). But there is only one distributor for Rolls Royce in a given city.

Different degrees of market exposure are available through intensive distribution, exclusive distribution, and selective distribution. **Intensive distribution** means distributing a product through as many channels and channel members (using both wholesalers and retailers) as possible. For example, as Figure 16.6 shows, Caramilk bars flood the market through all suitable outlets. Intensive distribution is normally used for low-cost, consumer goods such as candy and magazines.

In contrast, **exclusive distribution** occurs when a manufacturer grants the exclusive right to distribute or sell a product to one wholesaler or retailer in a given geographic area. Exclusive distribution agreements are most common in high-cost, prestige products. For example, Jaguar automobiles are sold by only a single dealer servicing a large metropolitan area.

Selective distribution falls between intensive and exclusive distribution. A company that uses this strategy carefully selects only wholesalers and retailers who will give special attention to the product in terms of sales efforts, display position, etc. Selective distribution policies have been applied to virtually every type of consumer product. It is usually embraced by companies like Black & Decker whose product lines do not require intense market exposure to increase sales.

intensive distribution

A distribution strategy in which a product is distributed in nearly every possible outlet, using many channels and channel members.

exclusive distribution

A distribution strategy in which a product's distribution is limited to only one wholesaler or retailer in a given geographic area.

selective distribution

A distribution strategy that falls between intensive and exclusive distribution, calling for the use of a limited number of outlets for a product.

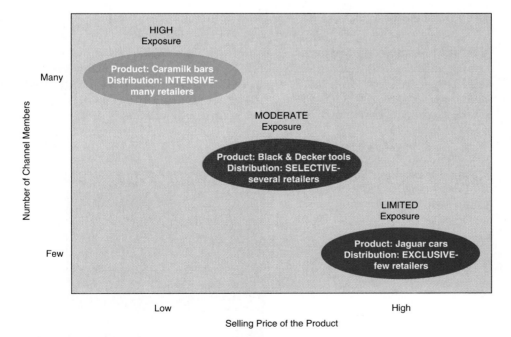

Figure 16.6
Amounts of market exposure from three kinds of distribution.

Channel Conflict and Channel Leadership

Manufacturers can choose to distribute through more than one channel or wholesaler. They can also choose to make new uses of existing channels. Similarly, most retailers are free to strike agreements with as many producers as capacity permits. In such cases, *channel conflict* may arise. Conflicts are resolved when members' efforts are better coordinated. A key factor in coordinating the activities of independent organizations is *channel leadership*. Another strategy for improving coordination is known as the *vertical marketing system*.

Channel Conflict.   Channel conflict occurs when members of the channel disagree over the roles they should play or the rewards they should receive. John Deere, for example, would no doubt object if its dealers began distributing Russian and Japanese tractors. Similarly, when a manufacturer-owned factory outlet store discounts the company's apparel or housewares, it runs the risk of alienating the manufacturer's retail accounts. Channel conflict may also arise if one member has more power than the others or is viewed as receiving preferential treatment. Needless to say, such conflicts defeat the purpose of the system by disrupting the flow of goods to their destinations.

Consider the case of IBM, which sells both through wholesalers and retailers and directly to major corporations. When IBM makes a direct sale, its dealers point out that they have lost a chance to earn money by making the sale themselves. If this pattern repeatedly frustrates one particular dealer, that dealer may take action—switching, for example, from IBM to Apple products.[8]

Channel Leadership.   Usually, one channel member is most powerful in determining the roles and rewards of other members. That member is the channel captain. Often, the channel captain is a manufacturer, particularly if the manufacturer's product is in high demand. In some industries, an influential wholesaler or a large retailer like Wal-Mart or Sears may emerge as channel captain because of large sales volumes.

vertical marketing system
A system in which there is a high degree of coordination among all the units in the distribution channel so that a product moves efficiently from manufacturer to consumer.

Vertical Marketing Systems.   To overcome problems posed by channel conflict and issues of channel leadership, the **vertical marketing system (VMS)** has emerged. In a VMS, separate businesses join to form a unified distribution channel, with one member coordinating the activities of the whole channel. There are three types of VMS arrangements:

The intense competition between IBM and Apple has led to rapid technological advances in personal computers.

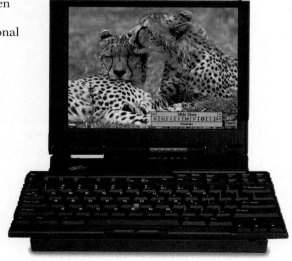

■ In a *corporate VMS*, all stages in the channel are under single owner-ship. The Limited, for example, owns both the production facilities that manufacture its apparel and the retail stores that sell it.

■ In a *contractual VMS*, channel members sign contracts agreeing to spe-cific duties and rewards. The Independent Grocers' Alliance (IGA), for example, consists of independent retail grocers joined with a whole-saler who contractually leads—but does not own—the VMS. Most fran-chises are contractual VMSs.

■ In an *administered VMS*, channel members are less formally coordi-nated than in a corporate or contractual VMS. Instead, one or more of the members emerge as leader(s) and maintain control as a result of power and influence. Although the administered VMS is more fragile than the corporate and contractual forms, it is more unified than chan-nels relying on independent members.

Wholesaling

Now that you know something about distribution channels, we can consider the broader role played by intermediaries. Wholesalers provide a variety of functions for their customers, who are buying products for resale or for busi-ness use. In addition to storing products and providing an assortment of products for their customers, wholesalers offer delivery, credit, and infor-mation about products. Not all wholesalers provide all of these functions. The specific services they offer depend on the type of intermediary involved: mer-chant wholesalers or agents/brokers.

Merchant Wholesalers

Most wholesalers are independent operators who derive their income from sales of goods produced by a variety of manufacturers. All **merchant whole-salers** take title to merchandise. That is, merchant wholesalers buy and own the goods they resell to other businesses. They usually provide storage and a means of delivery.

A **full-service merchant wholesaler** provides credit, marketing, and merchandising services. Approximately 80 percent of all merchant whole-salers are full-service wholesalers.

Limited-function merchant wholesalers provide only a few services, sometimes merely storage. Their customers are normally small operations that pay cash and pick up their own goods. One such wholesaler, the **drop ship-per**, does not even carry inventory or handle the product. Drop shippers re-ceive orders from customers, negotiate with producers to supply goods, take title to them, and arrange for shipment to customers. The drop shipper bears the risks of the transaction until the costumer takes title to the goods.

Other limited-function wholesalers, known as **rack jobbers**, market consumer goods—mostly nonfood items—directly to retail stores.[9] Procter & Gamble, for example, uses rack jobbers to distribute products like Pampers diapers. After marking prices, setting up display racks, and displaying dia-pers in one store, the rack jobber moves on to another outlet to check in-ventories and shelve products.

Agents and Brokers

Agents and brokers serve as sales forces for various manufacturers. They are independent representatives of many companies' products. They work on

merchant wholesaler
An independent wholesaler who buys and takes legal posses-sion of goods before selling them to customers.

full-service merchant wholesaler
A merchant wholesaler who pro-vides storage and delivery in addition to wholesaling services.

limited-function merchant wholesaler
An independent wholesaler who provides only wholesaling—not warehousing or transportation—services.

drop shipper
A type of wholesaler who does not carry inventory or handle the product.

rack jobber
A full-function merchant whole-saler specializing in nonfood merchandise who sets up and maintains display racks of some products in retail stores.

commissions, usually about 4 to 5 percent of net sales. Unlike merchant wholesalers, they do not take title to—that is, they do not own—the merchandise they sell. Rather, they serve as the sales and merchandising arms of manufacturers who do not have their own sales forces.

The value of agents and brokers lies primarily in their knowledge of markets and their merchandising expertise. They also provide a wide range of services, including shelf and display merchandising and advertising layout. Finally, they maintain product saleability by removing open, torn, or dirty packages, arranging products neatly, and generally keeping them attractively displayed. Many supermarket products are handled through brokers.

Trends in Intermediary-Customer Relationships

Like so many relationships in today's environment, intermediary-customer relationships are undergoing a variety of changes. Two emerging trends are the use of fewer intermediaries and more customer-supplier partnerships. In some industries, intermediaries are losing sales because customers with access to new information sources are locating new channels for the products they want. Travel agents, for example, still sell about four-fifths of all U.S. air-travel tickets (a service for which they are paid by airlines.) This service, however, is now threatened with displacement by consumers who have such services as Prodigy and CompuServe, which give them direct computer access to airline reservations systems.[10]

Likewise, readers can order books factory-direct by fax or toll-free telephone. Buyers of electronics products, too, now have direct access to sellers via 800 lines and e-mail. Orders received electronically can be transmitted to the factory floor, where each unit can actually be earmarked for a specific customer. At its Erskine, Scotland, plant, for example, Compaq Computer is testing an automatic restocking system: For some customers, Compaq will build to order instead of producing ahead and placing products in inventory to await buyer demand. Similarly, telephone orders for Motorola pagers and IBM PCs can be placed for made-to-order customers.[11]

Even in industries where intermediaries are still thriving, new information technologies are altering relationships with industrial customers. For example, Bailey Controls, an Ohio manufacturer of control systems for factories, has close team relationships with two distributors that supply it with parts. One distributor, Future Electronics in Montreal, is electronically connected with Bailey: When Bailey's parts supply drops below a certain level, a laser scanner instantly notifies Future to send replacements at once. Bailey stocks only enough inventory to meet immediate needs and relies on quick service from Future.

Retailing

You probably have had little contact with merchant wholesalers, merchandise brokers, or manufacturers. If you are like most Canadians, you buy nearly all the goods and services you consume from retailers. Most retailers are small operations, often consisting of just the owners and part-time help. But there are a few very large retailers, and these account for billions of dollars of sales each year (see Table 16.2 for a top-10 listing of retailers in Canada and the world.

In the past few years, U.S. retailers have become very aggressive in expanding into Canada and Europe. This has created problems for retailers in those countries, but bargains for consumers (see the box "U.S. Discounters Making Waves in Canada and Europe").

TABLE 16.2

The Top Ten Retailers in Canada, 1994 (ranked by sales)		The Top Ten Retailers in the World, 1994 (ranked by sales)	
Company	**Sales (in billions)**	**Company**	**Sales (in billions)**
1. George Weston Ltd.	$13.6	1. Wal-Mart (U.S.)	$67.3
2. Provigo Inc.	6.1	2. Sears Roebuck (U.S.)	54.8
3. The Oshawa Group Ltd.	6.0	3. Kmart (U.S.)	34.1
4. Hudson's Bay Co.	5.8	4. Ito-Yokado (Japan)	26.4
5. Canada Safeway Ltd.	4.6	5. Daiei (Japan)	24.3
6. Sears Canada	4.0	6. Kroger (U.S.)	22.3
7. Canadian Tire Corp. Ltd	3.5	7. Carrefour (France)	21.7
8. Shoppers Drug Mart Ltd.	3.2	8. J.C. Penney (U.S.)	19.5
9. Metro-Richelieu Inc.	2.9	9. Dayton Hudson (U.S.)	19.2
10. Empire Co. Ltd.	2.5	10. American Stores (U.S.)	18.7

Types of Retail Outlets

The major categories of retail stores are department, speciality, discount (bargain), convenience, supermarkets, warehouse clubs, and hypermarkets. Some retailing is also done without stores.

Department Stores.   As the name implies, **department stores** are organized into specialized departments—shoes, furniture, appliances, etc. Department stores began in the 1800s and were initially located in downtown districts, although most now have suburban branches. Generally, department stores are quite large and handle a wide range of goods. They usually offer a variety of services as well, such as generous merchandise return policies, credit plans, and delivery. The largest department stores—Hudson's Bay and Sears—have combined annual sales over $9 billion.

department stores
Large retail stores that offer a wide variety of high-quality items divided into specialized departments.

Specialty Stores.   In sharp contrast to department stores are **specialty stores**, small stores that carry one line of related products. These stores serve a carefully defined market segment by offering a full product line in a narrow product field, along with knowledgeable sales personnel. For example, most golf courses have a pro shop that carries golf clubs, as well as apparel, shoes, and other accessories for golfing. Other examples of specialty stores are The Fishin' Hole, Radio Shack, and Jiffy Lube.

specialty stores
Small retail stores that carry one line of related products.

Particularly in the apparel industry, the 1980s were the decade of the specialty store. Between 1980 and 1990, retailers like The Gap, The Limited, and Ann Taylor spearheaded the growth spurt of a multi-billion dollar industry in stylish upscale clothing. More apparel manufacturers are entering the retail industry. Companies like Timberland (outdoor wear), Tommy Hilfinger (casual clothing), OshKosh B'Gosh (children's clothes), and Speedo (swim and athletic wear) have all opened showcase outlets in specialty shopping centers and large malls.

Retailers who carry an extremely deep selection of goods in a relatively narrow product line and hire technical experts to give customers advice are called **category killers**. They are so named because they carry virtually everything within a certain category. Home Depot, which recently purchased 75 percent of Aikenhead's Home Improvement Warehouse from Molson, is an example of a category killer. It sells building materials, lawn and garden supplies, and home improvement products.

category killers
Retailers who carry a deep selection of goods in a narrow product line.

International Report

U.S. DISCOUNTERS MAKING WAVES IN CANADA AND EUROPE

During the last five years, several U.S. retail giants have invaded the Canadian market. Why has this happened now? Most U.S. executives say that the Canada-U.S. free trade agreement had a lot to do with it. Large U.S. retailers feel that the Canadian retail industry is five to ten years behind the U.S. in terms of purchasing, distribution, and technology. Since Canada is no longer a protected market, these retailers see good profit possibilities in Canada.

Since 1985, Price/Costco has opened 47 stores in Canada. Wal-Mart purchased 122 stores from Woolco and opened them as Wal-Marts in 1994. The video case "Wal-Mart Wizard" on p. 379 gives additional information about this very successful retailer. The Gap expanded from 34 outlets to 64. Home Depot, which came to Canada in 1994, plans to open 50 stores in the next five years. One Canadian retail consultant predicts that only half of all Canadian retailers will survive to 2000.

Because high prices are the rule rather than the exception in Europe, U.S. discounters like Price/Costco, Toys 'R' Us, and Kmart are also starting to compete there. Bargain-hungry Europeans are welcoming these discounters with open arms. For example, at the grand opening of England's first factory outlet mall, 25 000 people showed up (some having travelled great distances) to pay discount prices for apparel by Wrangler, Benetton, and Pierre Cardin.

These changes are very threatening to European retailers, and some have already gone out of business. Some have gone to court in an attempt to defend their turf. The three largest grocery chains in Britain took legal action to keep Price/Costco out (they failed). In both Germany and France, merchants have banded together to oppose changes—like late-night hours—that American discounters bring with them. But these responses simply highlight the vulnerability of retail outlets that are not responsive to consumer needs.

U.S. discounters feel that the European market is a place where they can deliver bargains to consumers and in the process make fat profit margins for themselves.

Canadian retailers have also pursued a strategy of entering foreign markets, particularly in the U.S. Unfortunately, their success has been limited. Consider these examples:

- Canadian Tire tried twice to enter the retail market (once with Auto Source in the north-central U.S., and once with White Stores in Texas). The company lost over $300 million in the two ventures.

- Imasco, the owner of Shopper's Drug Mart, purchased Peoples Drug Stores in the U.S. The stores did not do well and were sold off.

- Dylex operates several well-known retail stores in Canada (Tip Top Tailors, Big Steel Man, Bi-Way). It also operated Foxmoor Specialty Stores in the U.S., but had to file for bankruptcy on those stores.

A study team at the University of Western Ontario found that fewer than one-third of Canadian retailers who tried to enter the U.S. market were successful. By contrast, nearly all of the U.S. retailers who entered Canada were successful. Why? The research suggested four reasons. First, the U.S. firms were larger and therefore had more clout in the market place. Second, U.S. retailers provide more service and selection. Third, CEOs of U.S. retailers were older, more experienced, and had more education than Canadian CEOs. Finally, the competitive environment is tougher in the U.S. For example, the typical response of a U.S. retailer to foreign competition is to drive it out of business.

---

discount houses

Bargain retail stores that offer major items such as televisions and large appliances at discount prices.

Discount Houses.   After the Second World War, some retailers began offering discounts to certain customers. These **discount houses** sold items like televisions and other appliances at substantial reductions in price in order to sell large volumes of products. As name-brand items became more plentiful in the early 1950s, discounters offered better assortments to customers while still embracing a basic philosophy of low-rent facilities and cash-only sales. But as discount houses became more firmly entrenched in the marketplace, they began moving to better locations, improving in-store decor and selling better quality merchandise at higher prices. They also began offering some of the services of a department store, such as credit plans and non-cash sales. Kmart, Zellers, and Wal-Mart are discount stores. The box "The Wal-Mart Invasion" describes how this much publicized retailer operates.

This furniture shopper has chosen a specialty store that carries a complete line of furnishings and offers interior decorating services.

Catalogue showrooms mail catalogues with color pictures of products, product descriptions, and prices to customers' homes and businesses. In the showroom, customers view samples on display, place orders, and wait briefly while clerks retrieve their orders from the warehouse attached to the showroom. Consumers Distributing has many such catalogue showrooms.

Factory outlets sell merchandise directly from the factory to consumers, thereby avoiding wholesalers and retailers. The first factory outlets featured products such as apparel, linens, food items, and furniture. Located next to the factories in warehouse-like facilities, their distribution costs were very low. Consequently, they could offer their products at lower costs.

Convenience Stores.   While selection is the lure of department stores and price the lure of discount stores, **convenience stores**, as their name implies, offer ease of purchase. They stress an easily accessible location with parking, extended store hours (in many cases 24 hours), and fast service. Neighborhood gasoline/food retailers like 7-Eleven stores are convenience stores.

Supermarkets.   Beginning in the last half of the 1930s, a radical shift began to occur in the grocery business from the small corner grocery store to supermarkets. Like department stores, **supermarkets** are divided into departments of related food and household paper and cleaning products. The emphasis is on low prices, self-service, and wide selection. The largest supermarkets are chain stores such as Safeway, Loblaws, and Provigo.

Warehouse Clubs.   One of the newer innovations in retailing is the **warehouse club** (also called wholesale clubs). These are huge, membership-only, combination retail-wholesale operations that sell all kinds of brand-name merchandise. They carry groceries, appliances, tires, clothing, and countless other items at very low prices.

catalogue showrooms
Bargain retail stores in which customers place orders for items described in a catalogue and pick up those items from an on-premises warehouse.

factory outlets
Bargain retail stores that are owned by the manufacturers whose products they sell.

convenience stores
Retail stores that offer high accessibility, extended hours, and fast service on selected items.

supermarkets
Large retail stores that offer a variety of food and food-related items divided into specialized departments.

warehouse clubs
Huge, membership-only, combined retail-wholesale operations that sell brand-name merchandise.

The Canadian Business Scene

THE WAL-MART INVASION

Big, bad Wal-Mart has come to Canada. While Canadian retailers are worried, retailing experts say that in the long run everyone will benefit. They point to the experience of the domestic automobile industry in the 1980s when Japanese firms invaded North America in a big way. Eventually General Motors, Chrysler, and Ford stopped complaining about foreign competition, pulled up their socks, and became more competitive. Now, domestic automobiles are a better value (and are selling better) than Japanese cars. The same thing is going to happen in the retail business.

In the short-run, however, Wal-Mart's entrance into Canada has a lot of people worried. It will change a lot of things in Canada, including manufacturing and distribution processes. And it will shake up an industry that is still in turmoil after the recent recession. It will probably cause a lot of little retailers to go under, and perhaps a national chain as well. But it will not destroy Canadian retailing, just mediocre retailers. In short, Wal-Mart (and other innovations like warehouse clubs) will do to Canadian retailing what the Japanese threat did to automobile manufacturing. The video case "Wal-Mart Wizard" on p. 379 describes some of the strategies small retailers can use to cope with retail giants like Wal-Mart.

Wal-Mart gives consumers what they want: low prices, convenience, good selection, no stock-outs, and fast in-and-out time. But Wal-Mart is not alone in changing the face of Canadian retailing. Warehouse clubs and "category killers" like Office Depot and Home Depot are also challenging traditional retailing and distribution practices.

Each of these three kinds of retailers has a slightly different strategy. Warehouse clubs keep prices low by offering minimal service, limited selection, and no guarantee that the same brand will be available next week. They pursue high volume and are content with low margins. Category killers offer a deep selection of a narrow range of goods and have higher margins, which allows them to provide much more customer service. Wal-Mart, Kmart, and Zellers lie somewhere in between these two formats, providing a wide range of products at low prices.

The success of these three retailing formats shows just how much Canadian consumers have changed over the years. In the 1960s, Canadian families spent more than 80 percent of their income on consumption; now it is 72 percent. Real disposable income has been falling and is now down to the level it was in 1980. Because of this, consumers are very price-conscious. They are also time-conscious; one study showed that shoppers now spend 20 minutes less on the average trip to a shopping mall than they did in 1982.

The success of Wal-Mart bears looking into. Its annual sales revenue of nearly $70 billion is five times greater than the total of all Canadian department and discount stores combined. How does it achieve this? Wal-Mart has figured out how business operates *and* how consumers think, and it successfully manipulated both of these. A large part of its success is attributed to its inventory and distribution systems. Checkout scanners feed information to distribution centers where products move on high speed conveyers. Most of its stores are within a day's drive of a distribution center, and many stores are replenished daily. It is really just-in-time retailing. Information technology allows Wal-Mart's suppliers to better plan their production schedules because they know almost instantaneously what is going on at the retail level.

The system ensures that products will not be out of stock and that they will be the lowest price possible, a big advantage in an industry where small margins are the rule. Wal-Mart has a policy of everyday-low prices; it has no sales except on items that are being closed out. But its big advantage comes with the use of something called variable pricing—maintaining unusually low prices on goods like motor oil, paper towels, and laundry detergent that are frequently purchased by customers. Local Wal-Mart managers have authority to lower prices on these goods to below that of their competitors. Because of the low prices on these sensitive goods, customers often think that Wal-Mart has the lowest prices on everything (it doesn't). Wal-Mart stores have sales of about $300 per square foot, which is about 50 percent higher than discount competitors like Kmart and Zellers.

Some Canadian retailers are in denial about the changes that are coming in retailing. They say that Wal-Mart, the warehouse clubs, and the category killers won't be able to achieve really low prices here because doing business in Canada is simply a higher cost proposition because of a smaller population, a large country, and higher taxes. But this is wishful thinking. New era retailers don't have to offer absolutely low prices; they simply have to beat the prices charged by the traditional Canadian retailers. And it won't stop there. The new retailers will also cause reductions in the activity of wholesalers by dealing directly with manufacturers. The new retailers even will change manufacturing as they continually question whether manufacturers are producing goods at the lowest possible cost.

Traditional retailers like Canada Safeway generate 80 percent of their sales from just 20 percent of the products they carry. By contrast, warehouse clubs stock only the 20 percent and sell huge volumes of it at low margins. Supermarkets carry about 20 000 items, but warehouse clubs carry only about 3500. The typical warehouse club margin is 8 percent, while at more traditional discount stores the margin can be up to 40 percent. By carrying only the top-selling brands, warehouse clubs have been able to expand their product lines into non-grocery items like appliances, consumer electronics, tools, and office supplies.

Some traditional retailers have also experimented with the "warehouse format." Canadian Tire, for example, opened a warehouse format store in St. Hubert, Quebec in 1991. The company's strategy is to convince consumers that it can match the low prices at warehouse clubs like Price/Costco.[12]

Hypermarkets.   **Hypermarkets** are also large institutions with broad merchandise offerings, but they have somewhat higher prices than warehouse clubs. Hypermarkets may also include service departments such as cafeterias and beauty salons. Meijer's Thrifty Acres near Detroit and Hypermarché Laval near Montreal are examples of hypermarkets. These firms practise **scrambled merchandising**, carrying any product—whether similar or dissimilar to the store's original product offering—they feel will sell.

Other retail variations exist. Liquidation World, with locations in Calgary, Edmonton, and Surrey, B.C., does not carry a standard product line. Instead, it gets deals on merchandise from insurance companies, receivers, and bankruptcy trustees and then sells the products at low prices. And McDonald's opens a mobile outlet during the summer months in Grand Bend, Ontario. The company is thinking of using mobile units at special events like concerts.[13]

Nonstore Retailing

Not all goods and services are offered for sale in stores. In fact, some retailers sell all or most of their products without stores. Examples of nonstore retailing include mail order, vending machines, video marketing, telemarketing, electronic shopping, and direct selling.

Mail Order.   Firms that sell by **mail order** typically send out splashy catalogues describing a variety of merchandise. Singer-actress Cher calls her catalogue "a coffeetable book you can order from." Called *Sanctuary*, it features a medieval theme—lamps with chain mail shades, wrought-iron bedsteads, and velvet pillows with Gothic church designs.[14]

Some firms sell solely through the mail. Others, such as Sears and Consumers Distributing, have a combination marketing strategy and distribute merchandise through both catalogue sales and retail outlets. Although mail-order firms have existed for a long time, computer technology and telephone-charge transactions have helped this industry boom in recent years.

Vending Machines.   Certain types of consumer goods—most notably candy, soft drinks, and cigarettes—lend themselves to distribution through **vending machines**. Vending machine sales have increased in recent years, but they still represent only a small proportion of retail sales.

Video Marketing.   More and more companies have begun using television to sell consumer commodities such as jewelry and kitchen accessories. Many cable systems now offer **video marketing** through home shopping channels that display and demonstrate products and allow viewers to phone in orders. One weekend in 1993, Ivana Trump's appearance on the Home Shopping Club netted $2 million in orders for her high fashion apparel.

hypermarkets
Large institutions with broad product offerings but with somewhat higher prices than warehouse clubs.

scrambled merchandising
The retail practice of carrying any product expected to sell well, regardless of whether it fits into the store's original product offering.

mail order
A form of nonstore retailing in which customers place orders for merchandise shown in catalogues and receive their orders via mail.

vending machine
Machine which dispenses mostly convenience goods like candy, cigarettes, and soft drinks.

video marketing
Selling to consumers by showing products on television that consumers can buy by telephone or mail.

telemarketing

Use of the telephone to sell directly to consumers.

Telemarketing.   **Telemarketing** is the use of the telephone to sell directly to consumers. WATS (Wide Area Telephone Service) lines can be used to receive toll-free calls from consumers in response to television and radio advertisements. Offering live or automated dialing, message delivery, and order taking, telemarketers can use WATS lines to call consumers to promote products and services. Telemarketing is used for both consumer and industrial goods, and it is experiencing rapid growth in Canada, the U.S., and Great Britain.

electronic shopping

Using computer information systems to help sellers connect with buyers' computers with information about products and services.

Electronic Shopping.   **Electronic shopping** is made possible by computer information systems that allow sellers to connect into consumers' computers with information about products and services. The member's computer video display shows the available products, which range from plane reservations to consumer goods. Viewers can examine detailed product descriptions, compare brands, send for free information, or purchase by credit card—all at home. Prodigy, a joint venture of IBM and Sears, is the largest of the home networks.

direct selling

A form of nonstore selling sometimes called door-to-door sales.

Direct Selling.   The oldest form of retailing, **direct selling** is still used by companies that sell door-to-door or through *home-selling parties*. Most of us have talked with salespeople from World Book, Avon, or Fuller Brush as they make their door-to-door sales calls.

Direct selling is also common in the wholesaling of such industrial goods as commercial photocopying equipment. Although direct selling is convenient and gives customers one-on-one attention, prices are usually driven up by labor costs (salespeople often receive commissions of 40 to 50 cents on every sales dollar). Worldwide, 9 million direct salespeople now generate annual sales of $35 billion. In Japan alone, for instance, 1.2 million distributors have made Amway Corp. second only to Coca-Cola as the most profitable foreign retailer.[15]

multi-level marketing

A system in which a salesperson earns a commission on their own sales and on the sales of any other salespeople they recruit.

Some door-to-door firms use **multi-level marketing**, which attracts both buyers and sellers. The company convinces people to sell the product to anyone they can. In return the salesperson gets a commission. Salespeople also get a commission on the sales of any person they recruit to work for the business. Amway and Mary Kay Cosmetics are two of the most well-known multi-level marketing firms. The box "Selling Big Dreams" describes multi-level marketing in more detail.

Changes in Retailing: The Wheel of Retailing

wheel of retailing

The idea that retail stores evolve over time from low-priced stores that provide few services in simple surroundings to higher-priced stores that provide many services in more upscale surroundings.

The **wheel of retailing** concept shows how retail stores evolve over time. The "wheel" works like this: A new retailer emerges primarily because existing stores have become overpriced. The new retailer initially keeps prices down by providing fewer services, selling unknown brands, or locating in a low-rent area. But as the new retailer gets a foothold in the market, it wants to expand its market share. So it begins to offer more services, sells name-brand merchandise, and upgrades its stores facilities. But this increases costs, so it begins charging higher prices to consumers. This, in turn, creates a gap in the low-price end of the market, and even newer retailers move in to fill that gap.

Kmart is a good example of the wheel of retailing concept. It initially offered low priced products in converted warehouses. But over the years it built new stores, remodeled others, and began offering higher-quality merchandise. In response, a large number of "bargain barns" have sprung up to fill the gap that was created as Kmart moved up.

The Canadian Business Scene

SELLING BIG DREAMS

A typical promotional meeting for a multilevel marketing operation goes something like this: About 50 people come to a meeting room in a hotel to hear a sales pitch about how much money they can make in direct selling. Any product will do, but perfume, smoke alarms, and vitamin products are popular at the moment. During the meeting, an enthusiastic speaker tells the audience how precarious it has become working for someone else, and that to gain personal freedom and financial security, you should go to work for yourself in sales. Various other people then get up and describe how much money they have made selling the product. Participants are told that they can do it, too.

In multi-level marketing the recruiter receives a cut of all sales made by people the person recruits. If the new people also recruit, the person gets a cut of that, too. Commissions can travel five or six layers up the network of distributors.

This method of selling dates back to Amway Corp., which started it all in the 1960s. Multi-level marketing is not the same as the illegal pyramid scheme, which generates money almost totally from recruiting new people rather than selling products. But multi-level marketing has suffered an image problem because it is similar. Critics say multi-level marketing results in too much money going to people at the top and not enough to people at the bottom. In addition, they say that multi-level marketing is selling a dream that few people will ever realize.

Supporters claim it is a genuine entrepreneurial opportunity that allows almost anyone to make a lot of money if they work hard. Marta Chiappori was one such person. On top of her full-time job, she began selling Perfect Scents perfume everywhere she went. Initially, she did fairly well—about $400 per week in commissions. But within six months, her commissions declined to about $20 per week as sales declined and many of the people she recruited drifted away. She now regrets her involvement and says she was brainwashed into thinking she could become a millionaire. Another disenchanted person who was formerly involved says that multi-level marketing is just like a cult.

About 750 000 Canadians are involved in multi-level marketing at any one time. Three to four hundred multi-level companies are in operation at any one time, some just starting up, some chugging along, and some fizzling out. Seventy percent of these companies collapse before they are eight months old. Because there have been so many complaints about multi-level marketing, the federal government amended provisions in the Competition Act relevant to this form of selling. Among other things, the new rules state that a company cannot require product purchase as a condition of participation, nor can they "load up" distributors with more product than they can sell. Companies must disclose the earnings of a "typical participant," and they cannot pay fees to distributors for recruiting.

Physical Distribution

Physical distribution refers to the activities needed to move products efficiently from manufacturer to consumer. The goals of physical distribution are to keep customers satisfied, to make goods available when and where consumers want them, and to keep costs low. Thus physical distribution includes *customer-service operations* like order processing, as well as *warehousing* and *transporting operations*.

physical distribution
Those activities needed to move a product from the manufacturer to the end consumer.

Customer-Service Operations

Often the customer's only direct contact with the seller is to place an order. Thus **order processing**—filling orders as they are received—strongly affects how customers view the firm's efficiency and cooperation. The behavior of order-entry personnel can make or break a firm's reputation.

To please customers and assure repeat business, companies need to offer fast, convenient, and polite service. Bass Pro Shops' (offering a complete line of fishing and recreational products) catalogue sales has a toll-free number that is answered quickly by courteous, knowledgeable employees.

order processing
In a product's distribution, the receiving and filling of orders.

They offer customers different methods of paying for purchases and indicate when and how an order will arrive.

Many companies set standards for order-cycle times. **Order-cycle time** is the total amount of time from when the order is placed to when the customer receives the goods. Companies that can achieve rapid order-cycle times may have a competitive edge over less efficient firms. Some customers are willing to pay extra to receive their purchases faster, rather than having to wait.

Warehousing Operations

Storing or **warehousing** products is a major function of distribution management. In selecting a warehousing strategy, managers must keep in mind the characteristics and costs of warehousing operations.

Types of Warehouses.   There are two basic types of warehouses: private and public. Within these categories, we can further divide warehouses according to their use as storage sites or as distribution centers.

The first type, **private warehouses**, are owned by and provide storage for just one company, be it a manufacturer, a wholesaler, or a retailer. Most are used by large firms that deal in mass quantities and need storage regularly.

Public warehouses are independently owned and operated. Companies that use these warehouses pay for the actual space used. Public warehouses are popular with firms that need such storage only during peak business periods. They are also used by manufacturers who want to maintain stock in numerous locations in order to get their products to many markets quickly.

Storage warehouses provide storage for extended periods of time. Producers of seasonal items, such as agricultural crops, most often use this type of warehouse. In contrast, **distribution centers** store products whose market demand is constant and quite high. They are used by retail chains, wholesalers, and manufacturers that need to break large quantities produced or bought into the smaller quantities their stores or customers demand.

Warehousing Costs.   All warehouse types involve costs. These costs include obvious expenses such as storage space rental or mortgage payments (usually computed by square foot), insurance, and wages. They also include the costs of inventory control and materials handling. **Inventory control** is a vital part of warehouse operations. It goes beyond keeping track of what is on hand at any time and involves planning to ensure that an adequate supply of a product is in stock at all times—a tricky balancing act.

Materials handling is the transportation, arrangement, and orderly retrieval of goods in inventory. Most warehouse personnel are employed in materials handling. Keeping materials handling costs down requires managers to develop a strategy for storing a company's products that takes into account product locations within the warehouse. One strategy for managing materials is **unitization**, a method that standardizes the weight and form of materials and makes storage and handling more systematic. To reduce the high costs of materials handling, more and more warehouses are automating. Computerized systems can move, store, and retrieve items from storage in the warehouse.

Transportation Operations

Transportation, for both passengers and freight is big business. In 1993, the world's 50 largest transportation companies had revenues totalling $380 billion. Revenues for the top 10 transportation companies in the world are shown in Table 16.3.

order-cycle time
The total amount of time from order placement to when the customer actually receives the order.

warehousing
That part of the distribution process concerned with storing goods.

private warehouses
Warehouses owned and used by just one company.

public warehouses
Independently owned and operated warehouses that store the goods of many firms.

storage warehouses
Warehouses used to provide storage of goods for extended periods of time.

distribution centers
Warehouses used to provide storage of goods for only short periods before they are shipped to retail stores.

inventory control
The part of warehouse operations that keeps track of what is on hand and ensures adequate supplies of products in stock at all times.

materials handling
The transportation and arrangement of goods within a warehouse and orderly retrieval of goods from inventory.

unitization
A materials-handling strategy in which goods are transported and stored in containers with a uniform size, shape, and/or weight.

TABLE 16.3   The World's Largest Transportation Companies

Company	Country	Revenues (in billions)
East Japan Railway	Japan	$21.7
United Parcel Service	U.S.	17.7
AMR	U.S.	15.8
Nippon Express	Japan	15.3
UAL	U.S.	14.5
Delta Air Lines	U.S.	11.9
Japan Airlines	Japan	11.6
Air France Group	France	11.0
Lufthansa Group	Germany	10.7
Central Japan Railway	Japan	10.3

The major transportation modes are rail, water, truck, air, and pipelines. In the early part of the 20th century, railroads dominated the Canadian transportation system, but by the 1970s, truck and air transportation had become much more important. Using operating revenue as the basis for comparison, in 1993 the most important modes of transportation in Canada were trucks, air, and rail (in that order).

Cost is a major factor when a company chooses a transportation method. The difference in cost among the various transportation modes is directly related to the speed of delivery. The higher the speed of delivery, the greater the cost. But cost is not the only consideration. A company must also consider the nature of its products, the distance the product must travel, timeliness, and customers' needs and wants. A company shipping orchids or other perishable goods will probably use air transport, while a company shipping sand or coal will use rail or water transport.

Trucks.   The advantages of trucks include flexibility, fast service, and dependability. Nearly all sections of Canada, except the far north, can be reached by truck. Trucks are a particularly good choice for short-distance distribution and more expensive products. Large furniture and appliance retailers in major cities, for example, use trucks to shuttle merchandise between their stores and to make deliveries to customers. Trucks can, however, be delayed by bad weather. They also are limited in the volume they can carry in a single load.

More and more manufacturers are using **expedited transportation**, which involves paying a higher-than-normal fee for truck delivery in return for guaranteed delivery times. Even this higher fee is still cheaper than air freight.[16]

expedited transportation
Paying a higher-than-normal fee for truck delivery for guaranteed delivery times.

Planes.   Air is the fastest available transportation mode. In Canada's far north, it may be the only available transportation. Other advantages include greatly reduced costs in packing, handling, unpacking, and final preparations necessary for sale to the consumer. Also, inventory-carrying costs can be reduced by eliminating the need to store certain commodities. Fresh fish, for example, can be flown to restaurants each day, avoiding the risk of spoilage that comes with packaging and storing a supply of fish. However, air freight is the most expensive form of transportation. In recent years a whole new industry has evolved to meet the customer's need to receive important business papers and supplies "overnight."

Railroads.   Railroads have been the backbone of our transportation system since the late 1800s. Until the 1960s, when trucking firms lowered their rates and attracted many customers, railroads were fairly profitable. They are now used primarily to transport heavy, bulky items such as cars, steel, and coal.

A container train crosses the Salmon River bridge in New Brunswick.

Water Carriers.   Of all the transportation modes, water transportation is the least expensive. Unfortunately, water transportation is also the slowest way to ship. Boats and barges are mainly used for extremely heavy, bulky materials and products (like sand, gravel, oil, and steel) for which transit times are unimportant. Manufacturers are beginning to use water carriers more often because many ships are now specially constructed to load and store large standardized containers. The St. Lawrence Seaway is a vital link in Canada's water transportation system.

Water transportation is particularly important in Canada's far north. Northern Transportation Co. Ltd. has 90 barges, nine seagoing tugboats, and 250 employees. The company uses barges to deliver commodities like fuel oil to various isolated hamlets along the western edge of Hudson's Bay during the summer months. Each barge has a capacity of 4000 tonnes.[17]

Pipelines.   Like water transportation, pipelines are slow in terms of overall delivery time. They are also completely inflexible, but they do provide a constant flow of the product and are unaffected by weather conditions. Traditionally, this delivery system has transported liquids and gases. Lack of adaptability to other products and limited routes make pipelines a relatively unimportant transportation method for most industries.

intermodal transportation

The combined use of different modes of transportation.

containerization

The use of standardized heavy-duty containers in which many items are sealed at the point of shipment and opened only at the final destination.

Intermodal Transportation.   Intermodal **transportation**—the combined use of different modes of transportation—has come into widespread use. For example, shipping by a combination of truck and rail ("piggy-back"), water and rail ("fishy back"), or air and rail ("birdyback") has improved flexibility and reduced costs.

To make intermodal transport more efficient, **containerization** uses standardized heavy-duty containers in which many items are sealed at points of shipment and opened only at final destinations. On the trip, containers may be loaded onto ships for ocean trans t, transferred onto trucks, loaded on railcars, and delivered to final destinations by other trucks. The containers are then unloaded and returned for future use. International Cargo Management Systems has developed a device that is attached to the inside of containers being shipped. The device pulls in signals from global positioning satellites to determine the container's latitude and longitude. The device then transmits this information to computers at a tracking center. Customers can call the tracking center to determine where their package is at any moment.[18]

Companies Specializing in Transportation

The major modes of transportation are available from one or more of four types of transporting companies: common carriers, freight forwarders, contract carriers, and private carriers. Table 16.4 shows the top ten transportation companies in Canada.

TABLE 16.4   The Top Ten Transportation Companies in Canada, 1994 (ranked by sales)

Company	Sales (in millions)
1. Canadian National Railways	$4670
2. Air Canada	4024
3. PWA Corp.	2953
4. Laidlaw Inc.	2884
5. Trimac Ltd.	687
6. Fednav Ltd.	595
7. Transat A.T. Inc.	522
8. VIA Rail Canada Inc.	451
9. British Columbia Railway Co.	388
10. Newfoundland Capital Corp. Ltd.	263

The nation's **common carriers** transport merchandise for any shipper—manufacturers, wholesalers, retailers, and even individual consumers. They maintain regular schedules and charge competitive prices. The best examples of common carriers are truck lines and railroads.

In 1897, the *Crow's Nest Pass Agreement* established the rate that railways could charge for hauling grain. This agreement was essentially a freight subsidy that helped prairie farmers pay some of their transportation costs to distant ports. But in 1995, the Liberal government abolished the Crow subsidy. Freight rates will increase from $10 to $40 per tonne for Manitoba farmers by 1996. The loss of the subsidy will likely cause farmers in Manitoba and Saskatchewan to stop growing wheat and to start raising livestock.[19]

Not all transportation companies own their own vehicles. A **freight forwarder** is a common carrier that leases bulk space from other carriers, such as railroads or airlines. It then resells parts of that space to smaller shippers. Once it has enough contracts to fill the bulk space, the freight forwarder picks up whatever merchandise is to be shipped. It then transports the goods to the bulk carrier, which makes delivery to an agreed-on destination, and handles billing and any inquiries concerning the shipment.

Some transportation companies will transport products for any firm for a contracted amount and time period. These **contract carriers** are usually self-employed operators who own the vehicle that transports the products. When they have delivered a contracted load to its destination, they generally try to locate another contract shipment (often with a different manufacturer) for the return trip.

A few manufacturers and retailers maintain their own transportation systems (usually a fleet of trucks) to carry their own products. The use of such **private carriers** is generally limited to very large manufacturers such as Kraft Foods and Canada Safeway.

common carriers
Transportation companies that transport goods for any firm or individual wishing to make a shipment.

freight forwarders
Common carriers that lease bulk space from other carriers and resell that space to firms making small shipments.

contract carriers
Independent transporters who contract to serve as transporters for industrial customers only.

private carriers
Transportation systems owned by the shipper.

Summary of Key Points

The pricing of a product will determine its business success, depending on the business objectives being sought. Profit maximization, market share, and other business objectives may be relevant to the pricing decision. Economic theory, cost-oriented pricing, and break-even analysis are used as tools in determining prices.

Pricing also involves choosing a basic pricing strategy. Either a skimming or a penetration strategy can be used for new products. Existing products may be priced at, above, or below prevailing prices for similar products, depending on the other elements in the marketing mix. Within a firm's pricing strategies, managers set prices using tactics such as price lining, psychological pricing, and discounting.

In selecting a distribution mix for getting its products to customers, a firm may use any or all of six distribution channels. The first four are aimed at consumers and the last two at industrial customers. Channel 1 involves a direct sale to the consumer. Channel 2 includes a retailer. Channel 3 also includes one wholesaler, while Channel 4 includes an agent or broker before the wholesaler. Distribution strategies include intensive, exclusive, and selective distribution.

Wholesalers act as distribution intermediaries, extending credit and storing, repackaging, and delivering the product to other members of the distribution channel. Full-service and limited-service merchant wholesalers differ in the number of distribution functions they offer. Agents and brokers never take legal possession of the product.

Retailing involves direct interaction with the final consumer. The major types of retail stores are department, specialty, bargain, and convenience stores and supermarkets and hypermarkets. They differ in terms of size, services and product types they offer, and in how they price products. Some retailing also takes place without stores, through the use of catalogues, vending machines, direct selling, video marketing, telemarketing, and electronic shopping.

Distribution ultimately depends on physically getting the product to the buyer. Physical distribution includes customer-service operations such as order-processing. It also includes warehousing and transportation of products. Warehouses may be public or private and may be used for long-term storage or serve as distribution centers. Costs of warehousing include inventory control and materials handling.

Truck, plane, railroad, water, and pipeline transportation differ in cost, availability, reliability of delivery, and speed. Air is the fastest but most expensive. Water carriers are the slowest but least expensive. Most products are moved by truck at some point. Transportation in any form may be supplied by common carriers, freight forwarders, contract carriers, or private carriers.

"This Is Not a Product for Computer Nerds"

William "Trip" Hawkins had a lot riding on the Christmas 1994 shopping season. Hawkins is the founder of 3DO, a company whose namesake product is a sophisticated videogame player. Several years ago, Hawkins set out to develop the world's most technologically advanced home gaming system. As a result, 3DO's processor is twice as powerful—32 bits instead of 16—as those found in competing game systems from Sega and Nintendo. Moreover, 3DO software comes on CD-ROM instead of cartridges. 3DO can thus boast 3-D realism and even allows video games to incorporate actual video clips from movies and TV shows.

Despite the avowed sophistication of his brainchild, Hawkins was hoping for broad consumer appeal from the outset of his marketing campaign. "This is not a product for computer nerds," he promised. "It's for the masses." The first 3DO players went on sale in October 1993. Manufactured in Japan by Matsushita and bearing the Panasonic brand, they carried a hefty price tag of $699. A year later, about 300 000 units had been sold worldwide.

When Hawkins first conceived of 3DO, he realized the "razors" would never sell unless plenty of "blades" were available: In other words, he knew that he could drive sales of 3DO machines only if he could convince software developers to create popular games to be played on them. To do that, he took advantage of developers' resentment at the exorbitant fees—as much as $12 per cartridge—that they had to pay to Sega and Nintendo for every piece of software sold. Hawkins offered a licensing deal stipulating a fee of only $3 per game. Developers were also attracted by the fact that 3DO's disc format was cheaper to manufacture than game cartridges.

However, despite Hawkins' success at lining up hundreds of software developers, only about 50 game titles were available during the first few months that 3DO was on sale. None of them was an instant hit along the lines of, say, *Sonic the Hedgehog*, the game that helped propel sales of Sega's Genesis player. Then there was the issue of price: With Sega and Nintendo players selling for less than $100, even consumers who wanted to own 3DO players were hard-pressed to justify the premium price. Before long, limited consumer demand had put a severe financial strain on Hawkins' company; 3DO posted a $51 million loss for the year that ended March 31, 1994.

This dismal performance prompted one industry analyst to declare that "3DO is going to fail. It will be a footnote in the history of the business." And in fact, by May the stock price of 3DO Co. had sunk to the mid-teens—down from on October 1993 high of $47. In mid-December, 1994, the price dipped below $11 per share. The picture was further clouded after Hawkins made several decisions that angered suppliers. First, he launched an in-house software-development program that put the company in direct competition with its own outside developers. Even more damaging was his announcement that in order to help cover manufacturing and advertising costs, the $3-per-unit licensing fee would be doubled. After vendors expressed outrage, however, Hawkins was forced to scale back the increase to $1 instead of $3.

As the Christmas shopping season got under way in 1994, there was some basis for optimism that 3DO might make a solid showing. For one thing, Korea's Goldstar began marketing a 3DO unit, and players became available in about 6000 stores—three times the number of outlets as in 1993. In addition, 100 game titles were now available, including *Demolition Man*, a possible breakout title featuring actual footage from the Sylvestor Stallone movie of the same name. An aggressive TV advertising campaign showed competing machines being dumped in a coffin as an announcer urged videogame fans to "put away your toys." Perhaps most important, however, was a 40-percent cut in the list price of 3DO machines, down to $399.

Still a number of lower-priced competitors are waiting in the wings: By Christmas 1995, Sega, Nintendo, and Sony are all expected to be selling powerful new game players to compete directly with 3DO. Industry consultant Paul Saffo sums up the latest in expert opinion on Trip Hawkins' 3DO venture: "Trip's cleared the runway," says Saffo, "but he hasn't cleared the trees."

CASE QUESTIONS
1. What pricing strategy did Hawkins use when 3DO was first released?
2. What are some of 3DO's key product features?
3. Do you agree with Hawkins' 1994 decision to alter the fee arrangement with his software suppliers?
4. How might 3DO be classified in terms of the growth-share matrix?
5. Do you think that 3DO will succeed during the next few years? Why or why not?

◆

CONCLUDING CASE 16-2

Partners in the North

The North West Company's store in Sandy Lake, Ontario opened in 1993. The company knows it is operating as a guest of the Sandy Lake First Nation, and it must bargain the terms of its continued presence. The store is a joint venture, with profits shared between the company and the band. Native people make up 90 percent of North West's customers and a lot of its employees. Thirty-five of the 38 employees at Sandy Lake are aboriginal.

Len Flett, a Cree from Saskatchewan, is the company's store development director. He says that management realizes the need to become more culturally sensitive, and to be careful that the company's goals don't clash with those of its customers. Nearly half of the employees of the company are aboriginal, making the North West Company the largest private employer of aboriginal people in Canada. During the Royal Commission on Aboriginal Peoples, the company supported the entrenchment of aboriginal self-government as an inherent right.

In most of the remote communities in which it operates, North West is the only retailer, so it has a captive market. This makes the business fairly recession-proof, but since customers are increasingly plugged into southern

lifestyles through television, the store must keep up to date in the products it sells.

While a lot has changed in retailing in Canada's north, one long-time challenge never seems to change—supplying merchandise to isolated communities. One of the quintessential Canadian responses to distribution challenges is the "winter road." For example, each winter, the road between Pickle Lake, Ontario and Sandy Lake opens once the muskeg has frozen to a sufficient depth to allow heavy trucks to drive over it. These trucks will deliver a year's supply of all sorts of commodities needed at the community. The rest of the year the community is accessible only by air, and this is an expensive way of shipping goods.

CASE QUESTIONS
1. How is the relationship between North West and its customers different than the relationship between, say, a Kmart and its customers in Winnipeg? What implications do these differences have for the way in which the company is run?
2. What type of retail outlet is the North West store in Sandy Bay?

◆

Key Terms

pricing
market share
markup
variable costs
fixed costs
break-even analysis
break-even point
price leadership
price-skimming strategy
penetration-pricing
   strategy
price lining
psychological pricing
odd-even psychological
   pricing
threshold pricing
discount
cash discount
seasonal discount
trade discount

quantity discount
distribution mix
intermediaries
wholesalers
retailers
distribution channel
direct channel
agent/broker
sales offices
intensive distribution
exclusive distribution
selective distribution
vertical marketing
   system
merchant wholesalers
full-service merchant
   wholesaler
limited-function
   merchant wholesaler
drop shipper

rack jobber
department stores
specialty stores
category killers
discount houses
catalogue showrooms
factory outlets
convenience stores
supermarkets
warehouse clubs
hypermarkets
scrambled
   merchandising
mail order
vending machines
video marketing
telemarketing
electronic shopping
direct selling
multi-level marketing

wheel of retailing
physical distribution
order processing
order-cycle time
warehousing
private warehouses
public warehouses
storage warehouses
distribution centers
inventory control
materials handling
unitization
expedited transportation
intermodal
   transportation
containerization
common carriers
freight forwarders
contract carriers
private carriers

Study Questions and Exercises

Review Questions

1. List five objectives a firm might have in setting its prices.
2. Identify four types of discounting and give an example for each that is different from the examples in the text.
3. From the manufacturer's point of view, what are the advantages and disadvantages of using intermediaries to distribute a product? From the end buyer's view?
4. How do the six distribution channels cited in the chapter differ from one another?
5. How do manufacturer-owned, merchant, and agent wholesalers differ? How are they the same?
6. Compare and contrast the five types of bargain stores listed in the text. Give an example of each in your town or city.

Analysis Questions

7. Suppose that a book company selling to book distributors has fixed operating costs of $600 000 per year and variable costs of $3.00 per book. How many books must the firm sell to break even if the selling price is $6.00? If the company expects to sell 50 000 books next year and decides on a 40 percent markup, what will the selling price be?

8. Under what competitive conditions would you price your existing product at the prevailing market price for similar products? Above the prevailing price? Below the prevailing price?
9. Give three examples (other than those in the chapter) of products that use intensive distribution. Do the same for products that use exclusive distribution and selective distribution. For which category was it easiest to find examples? Why?
10. If you could own a firm in the business of transporting products, what type of firm would you prefer to own (truck, air, shipping, etc.)? Why?

Application Exercises

11. Interview the manager of a local manufacturing firm. Identify the firm's distribution strategy and the channels of distribution it uses. Where applicable, describe the types of wholesalers and/or retail stores the firm uses to distribute its products.
12. Choose any consumer item at a supermarket and trace the chain of physical distribution activities that brought it to the store's shelf.

Building Your Business Skills

Goal
To encourage students to evaluate their local retailers in terms of product lines, customer service, and pricing strategies.

Method
Step 1
Working alone, visit ten different retailers in your community. If possible, choose at least one each: department store, supermarket, hypermarket, specialty store, discount house, off-price store, catalogue showroom, factory outlet, warehouse club, and convenience store. Compare the stores in terms of the following criteria:

- atmosphere
- prices for identical or similar items
- merchandise quality
- selection at different price points
- level of customer service, including presence and helpfulness of sales staff and return policy

- forms of accepted payment, including cash, cheque, and national and store credit cards
- location

Step 2
Now rate each retailer in terms of popularity or consumer preference in the community. Which retailers are *you* most likely to patronize? Why?

Follow-Up Questions

1. In many communities, bargain retailers are replacing product-line retailers in sales volume. As the bargain retailers in your community have become more successful, have they changed their approach to pricing and service? Have they improved the retailing atmosphere in their stores?
2. Judging both from your own shopping habits and from what you observe in your community, how is your choice of retailer influenced by general economic conditions? For example, are you more likely to shop at a bargain retailer during an economic recession than during a period of prosperity?

IKEA: SITTING PRETTY AROUND THE WORLD

Winters in Sweden are long and dark. On the family farm, Elmtaryd, in Agunnaryd County, young Ingvar Kamprad started a small mail-order business in 1947, partly as a way to pass the time. Beginning with seeds and ballpoint pens, Kamprad gradually added a wide array of items to his catalog. Then, in 1950, he introduced a line of inexpensive "knockdown" (assemble-it-yourself) furniture and IKEA—short for Ingvar Kamprad Elmtaryd Agunnaryd—took off. In 1953, Kamprad opened IKEA's first store in Stockholm. In 1954, IKEA gave out 285 000 catalogs and racked up sales of 3 million kroner (about $500 000 US). By 1994, sales were $4.5 billion.

Behind this growth is IKEA's unique approach to the "four Ps" of marketing:

- *Product.* IKEA's emphasis has been not on product, but on products. Every IKEA store carries a staggering 12 000 products, ranging from plants to housewares to decorator accents to furniture—virtually everything you need to set up housekeeping except major appliances. (You can even purchase a fresh-cut Christmas tree and get a $10 rebate by bringing it back after the holiday and having IKEA chop it into mulch.) IKEA's specialty is contemporary furnishings, although some Scandinavian country influence is also visible in its offerings.

  IKEA stands out from most of its competitors for several reasons. First, it designs and arranges for the manufacture of virtually all the furnishings it sells. In all, some 20 in-house designers and 1800 suppliers in 50 countries are needed to create IKEA's products.

  Second, much of IKEA's furniture still is of the knockdown variety—sold disassembled in boxes. IKEA pulls together the components for these furnishings, which usually come from a variety of suppliers. Thus, a table might have legs made in Lithuania, a top made in Taiwan, and bolts made in Brazil.

Finally, while many furniture stores emphasize their ability to provide customized furniture (for example, you pick a style and a fabric you like and the store has the item custom made for you), IKEA's furnishings are strictly take-it-or-leave-it. Customers seem happy to take it.

- *Price.* From the beginning, IKEA has priced its products at least 10 percent below those of the competition and generally 25 to 50 percent below those of other concerns. In fact, when Kamprad first entered the furniture business, Swedish furniture dealers attempted to drive him out of business by threatening IKEA's suppliers. Their tactic backfired, however. Forced to look outside of his home nation, Kamprad discovered he could get the quality he wanted—at even lower prices—by ordering goods from Eastern European nations.

  Using the lowest-cost producers who can meet its standards and buying in tremendous bulk remain the linchpins of IKEA's success, and the company knows it. A walk around any IKEA store underscores the emphasis on price, as signs proclaim "Impossible Price: $1094!!!" for a roomful of furniture including a sofabed, armchair, wall unit, coffee table, and endtable.

- *Promotion.* Appealing as its products and prices are, IKEA could not have achieved its current success without a major investment in advertising. A television advertisement produced by Deutsch Inc. for IKEA was selected as one of the best advertisements of March 1994 by *Adweek.*

  IKEA has historically pursued people aged 25–40 with higher-than-average income and education. This market is more apt to try something new, and more likely to be interested in the contemporary styles IKEA offers. More recently, IKEA has been creating advertising directed at people in the 50–64 age bracket.

These "pre-baby boomer" consumers have the highest average household income. If the company is successful with this group, it will be in a good position to reach the baby boomers that are following.

The sheer size (60 940 square metres) and color (bright yellow and blue) of IKEA's retail outlets is another major component of IKEA's promotional strategy. These outlets are strategically located to be visible from major highways.

One aspect of the typical furniture store's promotional activities that is distinctly missing at IKEA is the salesperson. Instead, IKEA has "information clerks" who stand ready to answer questions for customers. If you don't want to speak to an IKEA employee the whole time you're in the store, you don't have to. The result: IKEA saves the cost of a large, commission-based salesforce and customers are spared one frequently expressed complaint about furniture shopping: the pushy salesperson.

■ *Place (Distribution)*. If IKEA is different from its competitors in its handling of product, price, and promotion, it is positively unique in its distribution. On entering the store, customers are given pencils and paper on which to make notes, tape measures to check sizes, and catalogs listing and describing each item in the store. Customers are then funneled into IKEA's furniture showroom. To help shoppers compare prices between similar items and visualize how one particular item might look at home, the showroom includes two types of displays: decorated "rooms" of furniture and areas showing all sofas, all chairs, and so forth.

In addition to the large furniture showroom and an equally large "marketplace" of other goods for the home, every IKEA store has an attached warehouse where customers go to pick up larger items. Handcarts are available to wheel such items out to the parking lot, and IKEA will lend you roof racks to help you get your purchase home. By staying out of the delivery business (although it does contract with an outside delivery firm to cart large items for an additional charge), IKEA saves money and the customer gets the "instant gratification" of having the new furnishing immediately—without the hassle of having to take time off from work to wait for delivery.

Tying the whole IKEA package together are many "extras" that the company's management has found cost far less than they bring in. For example, IKEA found that most couples prefer to shop for furnishings together. When the couple has children, however, the results can be dismal: children rampaging through the showroom and parents who can't stay long enough to make a decision. To nip these problems in the bud, IKEA offers child care for all children aged three to ten. You simply "check" your children at the IKEA-attended playroom (you even get a claim check), where they can play games, watch videos, and revel in the store's roomful of colored balls. Meanwhile, you can shop to your heart's content, and then pick up your children on the way out. Shoppers with infants can take advantage of the store's changing areas and free disposable diapers.

Knowing that furniture shopping takes time and requires deliberation, IKEA has also incorporated restaurants (self-service, of course) into its stores. Thus, customers can weigh the merits of the blue-striped sofa versus the dusty rose armchair while refueling with such popular Swedish specialties as Swedish meatballs and lingonberries.

Despite IKEA's success, there have been some problems. The chief complaint by IKEA customers is that some items are out of stock, particularly when a new store first opens. This problem was caused by IKEA's underestimation of sales levels. To counteract this problem, IKEA has increased the size of its orders.

Over the next ten years, the company plans to open new stores in several different countries. IKEA announced in 1994 its intention to expand into Italy, Germany, China, and Russia. IKEA has closed some units in Canada and the former Yugoslavia, but is optimistic about its sales potential elsewhere.

CASE QUESTIONS

1. Describe the probable motives of IKEA consumers.
2. If you were suddenly to become the CEO of IKEA, what changes would you make in the firm's product development and pricing policies? What would you keep the same? Why?
3. What is your opinion of IKEA's promotional policies? Would the absence of salespeople make you more or less likely to purchase furniture from IKEA? Why?
4. In view of its distribution problems, what approach do you think IKEA should take relative to opening new stores? Why?
5. What problems do you foresee for IKEA in the future and how might the company take steps to prevent them?

Experiential Exercise:
Setting Up a Promotional Plan

OBJECTIVE

To give students experience in using promotional strategies to overcome drawbacks in sales of new products and to make the most of the new products' assets.

TIME REQUIRED

45 minutes
  Step 1: Individual activity (15 minutes)
  Step 2: Small-group activity (15 minutes)
  Step 3: Class discussion (15 minutes)

PROCEDURE

Step 1: Read the following case regarding Supershop.

The Supershop Company owns a chain of successful supermarkets in eastern Canada. Managers at Supershop headquarters are currently contemplating a startling proposal from the marketing department: drive-through service.

As proposed, this system would require a sophisticated new computer system. Customers with personal computers at home or at work would be able to use them to tap directly into Supershop's system. Others would simply phone in their orders to store employees who would enter the specified items into the store's computer. The computer would generate a list—and a receipt. Other store employees would take the lists, pull the items from the shelves, and bag them. Customers would then pull into a special area at one end of the store and pay their bill at a drive-through window while their groceries were being loaded into the car.

Proponents of the new plan argue that it has several virtues:

a. The service would meet the needs of the two-career couples with families, who are the mainstay of Supershop's business. These individuals are typically attracted to services that save them time. At the same time, it should attract individuals more likely to shop at convenience stores and fast food restaurants.

b. The service would distinguish Supershop's offerings from those of its competition and give it a promotional advantage.

c. A fee of 2 percent of the total order would not deter most of Supershop's customers but would cover ongoing costs of the new system.

d. Customers could put in their orders hours ahead of time (with a one-hour minimum). Employees could pull nonperishable items from the shelves during slack times, increasing labor productivity. Placing items directly into bags as they were gathered would further improve productivity and efficiency.

e. If the service does well, eventually it could be run from a warehouse-type structure, mechanization of which would increase productivity and efficiency still further.

Opponents of the new plan argue that it has several drawbacks:

a. Glitches in the computer system and human error in picking items by store employees could result in customer dissatisfaction with Supershop in general. In particular, employee selection of fresh fruits and vegetables poses a high risk of customer dissatisfaction.

b. Start-up costs for the computer system and customer pick-up would be high—too high to be covered by a 2 percent fee.

c. The stores would lose "impulse sales," since customers would not be trapped in line near, or even just pass by, displays of high-profit items.

d. The plan could create trouble with the union workers employed by Supershop. Union representatives would probably fight the new job classifications that would be necessary and would probably strike over any reduction in employees due to greater productivity.

e. Producers of new goods, beverages, etc., might object that consumers are not exposed to and thus will not buy these items. They might in turn refuse to sell to Supershop at the highest discount rate, which would drive up costs and drive away customers.

How Can Supershop Use Promotion To Make The Most Of This Plan's Virtues And Minimize Its Drawbacks?

Step 2: The instructor will divide the class into small groups and will assign each group one strong point and one weak point of the plan. Each group will then develop an advertising slogan to stress the strength and downplay the weakness. Each group should also complete the following grid, rating possible promotional tools from 1 (very effective at reaching/persuading target market) to 5 (very ineffective at reaching/persuading target market) and divide a promotions budget of $1 million among these tools.

Promotional Tool	1	2	3	4	5 $ Allocated
Advertising:					
Newspapers					
Television					
Direct mail					
Radio					
Magazines					
Billboards					
Personal Selling					
Sales Promotions:					
Coupons					
Premiums					
Contests					
Publicity/Public Relations					

Step 3: One member of each small group will present the group's conclusions to the class.

QUESTIONS FOR DISCUSSION

1. Would you or members of your family consider using a drive-through service like the one proposed by Supershop's marketing staff? Why or why not?
2. What do you consider to be the greatest virtue of the proposed service? What do you consider to be the greatest drawback? Overall, do you think Supershop would be wise to go ahead with this plan?

The Choice is Yours

"The difficulty in life is the choice...
The wrong way always seems the more reasonable."
—George Moore, "The Bending of the Bough"

You did it! You got the job offer! Despite the tight job market, your impressive combination of sound coursework (and good grades), practical experience, and successful interviewing has garnered you not one but several job offers. You are now faced with the problem many job seekers would like to have—how to select one of these offers.

There are six major considerations to take into account when making your choice:

- Job responsibilities.
- Person-job fit.
- Firm image or quality.
- Quality of training and development.
- Career opportunities.
- Compensation.

Of course, all people will have additional factors to consider, and each individual will weigh each factor differently.

JOB RESPONSIBILITIES

The first question that will cross your mind as you evaluate various job offers will probably be: Which job will I enjoy most? As a general rule, you should avoid signing on with any company that thrusts too much responsibility on new managers too quickly. In these types of organizations, lack of both experience and the necessary job-specific skills will probably doom you to failure. Organizations that overextend newcomers may do so because they want to "stretch" them, because they are understaffed, or because they don't truly understand the strengths and weaknesses of new managers. You should also stay away from firms that tend to underutilize new managers, assigning them menial and/or routine assignments. Such practices may reflect a lack of trust in the capabilities of new managers or a lack of meaningful work in the organization.

What you should be looking for, clearly, is a balanced approach—one that will give you a chance to gain experience, but one that will also utilize your existing skills while giving you the opportunity to master new ones. The ideal assignment in this regard is one that has well-defined boundaries in a setting in which you can get advice and assistance from others in the organization.

PERSON-JOB FIT

Another factor to take into account when selecting among job offers is the fit between your own interests, aspirations, and preferences and the requirements and opportunities of the jobs you are considering. For example, if you have always wanted a career in retailing, then you will probably have no trouble choosing The Bay over Dofasco. But if you prefer a career in manufacturing, you are likely to find Dofasco a better fit.

The job itself is only one part of the person-job fit story, however. Other considerations include:

- *Location.* Will one job require you to live in a big city and another in a small town? If cities make you claustrophobic, you'd probably be better off taking the job in Regina instead of the one in Toronto. But if your favorite forms of entertainment are art museums, opera, major-league baseball, and ethnic restaurants, you should probably head for Toronto instead. Many single people also prefer urban locations because of the greater opportunities they provide for meeting people and developing romantic relationships.
- *Ambiance.* Did you feel more comfortable with the people and/or physical environment at one firm than you did at the other? Remember, you'll be spending between a quarter and a third of your life at work. Those hours can be miserable or pleasant, depending on how well you fit in.
- *Travel required by the job.* Some people look forward to the chance to travel, while others prefer to stay close to home. Do the jobs offered differ in their travel requirements? If the difference is a substantial one, give this factor serious consideration. You won't be happy for long if you're constantly on the go and hate being on the road . . . or if you're tied to a desk but itching to get out of the office.
- *Family consideration.* Children, spouses, other relations, and close friendships may also influence your ultimate choice. It is essential that you take into account the quality of the local schools for your children and the local job market for your spouse or "significant other." It's hard to be happy at work—and to do your best work—if you're worrying about things at home. If you have elderly parents, you may find it less stressful to live where you can be on hand in case of emergency. On the other hand, you may view a cross-country move as an opportunity to explore new aspects of your life and personality far away from the place where everyone knows everything about you.

QUALITY OF TRAINING AND DEVELOPMENT

Especially when choosing a first job, but also throughout your career, you should seriously weigh the value of the training and development that a firm offers its new employees. Although anecdotes from established managers about "How I survived in a 'sink or swim' situation" may be amusing, trial by fire is frequently frustrating, often counterproductive, and always stressful.

Your education is providing you with the fundamental information and skills you will need to succeed in the business world. But because each organization is unique, and because each values and expects different things from its employees, most large firms provide a systematic program to help them become more effective in performing their jobs.

Large firms like Proctor & Gamble, General Foods, IBM, and General Mills are all known to have outstanding training programs. Indeed, some firms actively seek to hire people who have successfully completed the training programs of these and similar firms. Although smaller firms generally do not offer such structured programs, at these organizations you my benefit greatly from the opportunity to work directly with upper-level management and from exposure to many areas of the firm's operations.

Finally, be sure to weigh the company's attitudes toward further education. Some companies pay all or part of tuition costs for those who take technical and/or advanced college courses and underwrite the costs of taking professional certification examinations. Some firms will even give you a paid "sabbatical" after a number of years on the job so that you can complete an advanced degree. Remember that in this fast-changing world, to stand still is to be left behind. To stay ahead, you must *constantly* sharpen your skills.

CAREER OPPORTUNITIES

Clearly, career opportunities and prospects with each of your potential employers will play a major role in your decision. Where will you go in a firm that has just laid off hundreds of managers? Will you be subject to the same degree of job insecurity? If another firm is hiring hundreds of new people each year but provides advancement opportunities for only a few, what are your chances of succeeding?

Most large organizations have clearly formulated career paths to help people understand where they can expect to be at different points in their career. Be wary if a large firm has not given consideration to these issues. But also be wary if its career paths are highly programmed and regimented. Ideally, your new employer will have several clear, well-developed career paths but still offer sufficient flexibility for you to pursue new opportunities.

COMPENSATION

Finally, give careful consideration to the compensation package that you are offered. You can get salary data for comparative purposes from your campus placement office, your friends, and similar sources. Most firms know what others are paying, so there probably will not be wide variation in the salary offers you receive. If you have excellent grades, a strong résumé, and solid references, you may be able to start at a somewhat higher salary than someone with average grades, a mediocre résumé, and weak references.

What if you like everything about the job—the fit, the location, the responsibilities, the prospects—except the pay? You may try to negotiate a higher salary, but experts agree that attempting to negotiate too much on salary can backfire. Most firms have a predefined salary structure for new employees and may react negatively to a request for a higher salary. If the company you really want to work for is offering less than the other firms, you might subtly point out the differences and ask if there is any *flexibility* in the offer. But always be both honest and discreet. If you tell your preferred employer that another firm has offered you $10 000 more than it really has, you might be advised to take the other job!

Finally, don't get too hung up on the starting salary itself. You also need to factor in such items as the value of benefits (such as insurance, retirement plans, etc.), perks (car, office, etc.), the cost of living where you will be working, and prospects for salary increases. Look at the *whole* package—and the *whole* job—before you say "Yes."

In the small upstate New York town of Ithaca stands a monument to the trials and tribulations of new product development: the New Products Showcase and Learning Center. The center is an interesting place because of the thousands of failed products that stock its shelves. The center evolved out of the product testing efforts of its curator, Robert McMath, who admits to never having thrown away any of the products his market research company was asked to test.

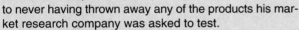

McMath estimates that about 90 percent of all new products fail in the consumer marketplace. Countless examples of such well-intended failures line the display cases of the New Products Showcase and Learning Center. Some of the odder products warrant mention: toaster eggs, Harley Davidson heavy beer, R.J. Reynold's smokeless Premier cigarette, and toaster chicken patties whose fat drippings succeeded in setting toasters afire.

According to McMath, product failure can often be traced back to three basic reasons: launch timing, product name, and product concept. An example of an ill-timed product launch is the Short 'N Sassy shampoo line developed by Clairol. According to McMath, Clairol missed the boat by introducing the product only after hairstyles had gone long. The problem of timing also explains the failure of many copy cat wine cooler products; according to McMath over 300 cooler products were offered on the heels of the first California wine coolers in hopes of cashing in on a temporary surge in consumer demand.

Product failure can also be explained by bad product names and/or packaging; examples include Campbell's Soups marketing blue cans of low-salt soups and a flatulence-minimization product for pets named Curtail. Furthermore, cases also abound of product concepts being inherently flawed from square one. Examples include tomato ketchup packaged in aerosol cans and a high power toothpaste named Monday morning for those wanting to only brush their teeth once a week.

The New Products and Showcase and Learning Center provides countless examples of the unpredictable nature of consumer marketing where what seem like "sure hits" in the board room turn into "doomed duds" in the marketplace. In looking out over the number of repeat failures McMath also infers a second key lesson for would-be marketeers; in reflecting on the thousands of oddball products his center contains, he concludes that this collection of duds, flops and failures teaches us that we either learn from history or become doomed to repeat it.

Study questions:

1. What is marketing and the marketing concept? What lessons do the flops mentioned in this case suggest about how difficult it can be to market a product to the consumer?
2. What is meant by market segmentation? What are the different way to segment a market? What are the requirements of effective segmentation? What do the products mentioned in this case suggest about mistakes in market segmentation?
3. What is market research? What are the different ways in which market research can be done? How might market research have prevented the occurrence of some of the flops mentioned in this case study?
4. What is brand loyalty? What do the list of flops suggest about the nature of brand loyalty?

*This case is based on the *Venture* episode first broadcast on January 20, 1994.

VIDEO GAME WARS*

Video games have come a long way since "Pong" was marketed by Atari in the late 1970s. Today, two Japanese companies—Sega and Nintendo—are dominant, and they are locked in a fierce battle for supremacy of this $10 billion market. The stakes are high and so is profitability.

The video game business is much like the movie business, only more profitable. Only a small proportion of films—or video games—are big hits. But one hit can make up for a bunch of flops. For example, the film *Interview with the Vampire*, starring Tom Cruise, cost $55 million to make and generated gross revenues of $150 million. A typical video game costs only $2 million to develop, and can bring in as much as $240 million in revenue.

Until recently, Nintendo was the clear leader in the industry. Donkey Kong and Mario Brothers are legendary names from the 1980s which put Nintendo in a commanding position. But in the early 1990s, Nintendo couldn't seem to get a hit video. Its market share, which dropped from 80 percent to 55 percent, was largely scooped up by Sega using a brash, aggressive television advertising campaign which promoted hot new titles.

But Nintendo is now becoming more aggressive itself. A new game—Donkey Kong Country—was developed in Nintendo's ultra-secret "war room." It features an 800 lb. gorilla and improved graphics. Nintendo also sent a "teaser" video to 200,000 game players in Canada and spent $25 million on advertisements which directly challenged Sega. Publicity using characters from the videos has also been part of its marketing strategy.

Sega retaliated with a crazed hedgehog (Sonic) and an Australian anteater (Knuckles) and a marketing budget of $10 million. The new videos were launched at the famed Alcatraz prison in San Fransisco. In a publicity stunt, kids were flown in and pretended to be prisoners.

The basic marketing strategy being employed by both Nintendo and Sega is to get young males interested to their products and then keep them as customers as they grow older. Both companies spend millions on television advertising, and each company's advertisements point out the shortcomings in their competitor's product. Video counsellors field telephone calls from users who are playing the games and have questions about them. Most advertising is directed at young males, but recently Sega introduced a video game for girls.

In this business, new product development is critical. Each company pours big dollars into new product development, but Sega is currently allocating more dollars of profit than Nintendo is. Sega has its own "think-tank" in California where new ideas for video games are conceived and developed into finished products. It employs many Japanese artists who must learn about North American tastes as they try to develop games that will interest their target marget.

In an attempt to maintain momentum, Sega is developing toys and video games for girls, video game theme parks, and Sega TV network. Nintendo continues to market to boys; its president says he would like to expand sales by reaching other market segments (e.g., girls and adults), but he is not sure if this is feasible given the nature of the product.

Study questions:

1. Describe the relative importance of the four elements of the marketing mix in the video game business.
2. Who is the target market for video games? Can video games be marketed to other market segments? If so, explain how this might be done.
3. Compare and contrast the new product development process at Sega and Nintendo with that at Bombardier Inc. and Coca-Cola.
4. In what stage of the product life cycle are video games in the mid-1990s? Explain.

*This case is based on the *Venture* episode first broadcast on April 12, 1994.

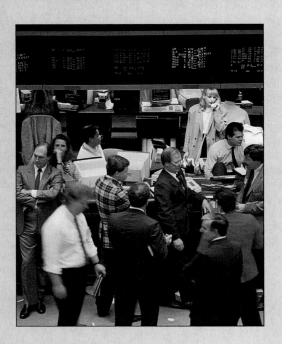

Part Six

*M*ANAGING
FINANCIAL ISSUES

Management of the financial transactions of a business firm are absolutely critical to its survival. Whether it involves properly accounting for costs, raising money to start a new firm, having an accurate view of the riskiness of the firm's investments, or monitoring the firm's activities in securities markets, financial management is a key business activity. The opening cases of the chapters in this section are diverse, yet they all deal specifically with the important function of financial management.

Part Six, Managing Financial Issues, provides an overview of accounting and business finance, including how firms develop and use financial information, how they raise and manage money, how they define and manage risk, and how they use Canadian securities markets to meet their financial needs.

- We begin in **Chapter 17, Understanding Accounting Issues,** by examining the role of accountants in gathering, assembling, and presenting financial information about a firm. We also look at the tools accountants use and the statements they prepare to report a firm's financial standing.

- Then, in **Chapter 18, Understanding Money and Banking,** we explore the nature of money, its creation through the banking system, and the role of the Bank of Canada in the nation's financial system.

- Next, in **Chapter 19, Financial Decisions and Risk Management,** we look at the reasons businesses need funds and how financial managers raise both long- and short-term funds. We also examine the kinds of risks businesses encounter and the ways in which they deal with such risks.

- Finally, in **Chapter 20, Understanding Securities Markets,** we consider the markets in which firms raise long-term funds by examining how these markets operate and how they are regulated.

17

Understanding Accounting Issues

LEARNING OBJECTIVES

After reading this chapter, you will be able to

- Identify the role of accountants and distinguish between the kinds of work done by public and private accountants.
- Explain how journals and double-entry accounting ledgers are useful tools for financial analysis.
- Describe the three basic financial statements and how they reflect the financial condition and activities of a business.
- Explain how computing key ratios for information in financial statements can help in analyzing a business's financial strengths.
- Discuss how budgets are developed and used for internal planning and control.
- Describe some ways in which companies use computers to handle accounting functions.

CHAPTER OUTLINE

Accounting for Costs

Traditional cost accounting methods used by Canadian business firms are based on the idea that the primary value in a product is generated by the direct labor of production workers. To determine costs, accountants add together the cost of materials, labor, and overhead (things like R&D, rent, administration expense, etc.) to get a total cost figure. To determine unit cost, total costs are divided by the number of units that are produced.

That accounting system worked well when labor was the biggest part of cost. But today, overhead can be as much as 70 percent of the total cost of a product. The primary value in the product is now usually generated by knowledge workers, not production line workers. Whereas direct labor used to be as high as 35 percent of the cost of goods sold, it is now often less than 10 percent.

A new cost accounting system called *activity-based costing* (ABC) has been developed to help managers figure out how much it actually costs to make specific products or services. Here's how it works: First, all the activities that are necessary to get the product from the raw materials stage to the shipping dock are identified. After the list of activities is developed, ABC focuses on the events that stimulate the activity. For example, an event may be the number of invoices issued, the number of people supervised, the number of sales calls completed, or the number of pallets loaded onto a truck. Then data are gathered on these events and plugged into computer software like NetProphet II. The "bottom line" stays the same, but previously unknown information about costs usually emerges.

To see how ABC works, consider a production line where two kinds of pens are being made—black in high volume and purple in low volume. The total cost includes supplies (which are the same for both kinds of pens), the direct labor of the production line workers who make the pens, and overhead. The most significant overhead cost is the time it takes to switch over from making black to purple or purple to black. Under traditional cost accounting systems, if ten times as many black pens are made as purple pens, then ten times the cost of each changeover will be allocated to the black pens. But this obviously understates the cost of producing the low-volume pens. ABC, on the other hand, recognizes the importance of the changeover activity, and charges it against each batch of pens that is made, regardless of the size of the production run. This will clearly yield a higher unit cost for the low volume purple pens.

The ABC system can generate information that causes managers to agonize over some tough decisions. One bakery found that 86 percent of its output was purchased by just 16 percent of its customers. Deliveries to small, owner-operated stores were costing the bakery a fortune. An ABC analysis showed that if the bakery dropped 84 percent of its customers, its profits would triple. But this might not be a wise move strategically. The bakery has not yet decided what to do about this information generated by ABC.

Other firms, faced with the same type of dilemma, have taken decisive action. When Northern Telecom discovered that making a red telephone with French-language packaging cost four times what it thought, it did not stop making the product. Rather, it took action to reduce activity costs. In the process, the company discovered that purchasing 20 percent of the plant's raw materials ate up 80 percent of the purchasing budget. So they decided to pay a little more and get everything from one supplier, thus saving about half a million dollars a year on purchasing activities.

Thorlo Inc. is another company that changed its work processes after an ABC analysis showed that it was losing money on 80 percent of its customers. But Thorlo was loyal to its customers and didn't want to stop selling to them. So, it revised its procedures for dealing with small customers, including the setting up of an entirely separate warehouse that is designed to efficiently deal with small orders. After introducing this system, profits rose 40 percent in one year.   ◆

In the 1990s, business firms are facing intense competition, both domestically and internationally. As the opening case demonstrates, business firms must be able to accurately compute their business costs or they will not be able to compete. Accounting occupies a central place in the determination of these costs. But that is not all that accounting involves. In this chapter, we will consider who accountants are, what they do, what concepts and rules they apply, and how these rules are developed. Then we will explore the most important part of accounting—the basic financial reports of business activity that are the primary reason for accounting.

What Is Accounting?

Accounting is a comprehensive information system for collecting, analyzing, and communicating financial information. As such, it is a system for measuring business performance and translating those measures into information for management decisions. Accounting also uses performance measures to prepare performance reports for owners, the public, and regulatory agencies. To meet these objectives, accountants keep records of such transactions as taxes paid, income received, and expenses incurred, and they analyze the effects of these transactions on particular business activities. By sorting, analyzing, and recording thousands of transactions, accountants can determine how well a business is being managed and how financially strong it is.

accounting

A comprehensive system for collecting, analyzing, and communicating financial information.

Bookkeeping, a term that is sometimes confused with accounting, is just one phase of accounting—the recording of accounting transactions. Clearly, accounting is much more comprehensive than bookkeeping because accounting involves more than just the recording of information.

bookkeeping

Recording accounting transactions.

Because businesses engage in many thousands of transactions, ensuring consistent, dependable financial information is mandatory. This is the job of the **accounting system**: an organized procedure for identifying, measuring, recording, and retaining financial information so that it can be used in accounting statements and management reports. The system includes all the people, reports, computers, procedures, and resources for compiling financial transactions.[1]

accounting system

An organized procedure for identifying, measuring, recording, and retaining financial information so that it can be used in accounting statements and management reports.

Users of Accounting Information

There are numerous users of accounting information:

- *Business managers* use accounting information to set goals, develop plans, set budgets, and evaluate future prospects.
- *Employees and unions* use accounting information to get paid and to plan for and receive such benefits as health care, insurance, vacation time, and retirement pay.
- *Investors and creditors* use accounting information to estimate returns to stockholders, to determine a company's growth prospects, and to decide if it is a good credit risk before investing or lending.
- *Taxing authorities* use accounting information to plan for tax inflows, to determine the tax liabilities of individuals and businesses, and to ensure that correct amounts are paid in a timely fashion.
- *Government regulatory agencies* rely on accounting information to fulfill their duties; the provincial securities commissions, for example, requires firms to file financial disclosures so that potential investors have valid information about a company's financial status.

Who Are Accountants and What Do They Do?

controller

The individual who manages all the firm's accounting activities.

At the head of the accounting system is the **controller**, who manages all the firm's accounting activities. As chief accounting officer, the controller ensures that the accounting system provides the reports and statements needed for planning, controlling, and decision-making activities. This broad range of activities requires different types of accounting specialists. In this section, we will begin by distinguishing between the two main fields of accounting, *financial* and *managerial*. Then we will discuss the different functions and activities of *chartered accountants* and *private accountants*.

Financial and Managerial Accounting

In any company, two fields of accounting—financial and managerial—can be distinguished by the different users they serve. As we have just seen, it is both convenient and accurate to classify users of accounting information as users outside the company and users inside the company. This same distinction allows us to categorize accounting systems as either *financial* or *managerial*.

financial accounting system

The process whereby interested groups are kept informed about the financial condition of a firm.

Financial Accounting.   A firm's **financial accounting system** is concerned with *external* users of information—consumer groups, unions, shareholders, and government agencies. It prepares and publishes income statements and balance sheets at regular intervals. All of these documents focus on the activities of *the company as a whole*, rather than on individual departments or divisions.

In reporting data, financial accountants must conform to standard reporting formats and procedures imposed by both the accounting profession and government regulatory agencies. This requirement helps ensure that users can clearly compare information, whether from many different companies or from the same company at different times. The information in such reports is mostly *historical*: That is, it summarizes financial transactions that have occurred during past accounting periods.

A financial report is an integral component of the financial accounting system.

The Canadian Business Scene

CERTIFICATION PROGRAMS IN ACCOUNTING AND FINANCE

Not too long ago, a professional certificate in accounting meant the CA or Chartered Accountant. To become a CA, a person must earn a university degree, complete an accounting-oriented education program, and then pass a national exam. About half of all CAs work in public accounting firms (CA firms). These firms give external opinions on their clients' financial statements. The other half work in business, government, and nonprofit organizations. The main emphasis in CA work is on financial accounting, auditing, and taxation accounting.

In recent years, accounting and financial skills have become increasingly specialized. In addition to the CA, the following certification programs are now available.

■ *Certified General Accountant (CGA).* To become a CGA, a person must complete an education program and pass a national exam. A university degree is not required for admission to the program. To be eligible, a person must have an accounting job with a company. There are fewer CGAs than

CAs, and in most provinces they are not allowed to give opinions on financial statements of publicly held companies. Almost all CGAs work in private companies, but there are a few CGA firms. Some CGAs work in CA firms.

■ *Certified Management Accountant (CMA).* The goal of the CMA program is to train accountants for industry. To become a CMA, a person must have an accounting position with a company and must complete an education program; a university degree is not required for admission. Unlike CAs, CMAs have management accounting as their focus. That is, they are concerned about internal uses of accounting data rather than their external uses, as are CAs.

■ *Certified Financial Analyst (CFA).* This program is relevant for people in investment jobs. To earn the CFA designation, a person must complete an education program and pass a national exam dealing with securities regulations, investments, and related topics.

Managerial Accounting.   In contrast, **managerial** (or **management**) **accounting** serves *internal* users. Managers at all levels need information to make decisions for their departments, to monitor current projects, and to plan for future activities. Other employees, too, need accounting information. Engineers, for instance, want to know costs for materials and production so they can make product or operations improvements. To set performance goals, salespeople need data on past sales by geographic region. Purchasing agents use information on materials costs to negotiate terms with suppliers.

Reports to these users serve *the company's individual units*, whether departments, projects, plants, or divisions. Internal reports may be designed in any form that will assist internal users in planning, decision making, and controlling. Furthermore, as *projections and forecasts* of both financial data and business activities, internal reports are an extremely important part of the management accounting system: They are forward-looking rather than historical in nature.

managerial accounting
Internal procedures that alert managers to problems and aid them in planning and decision making.

Public Accountants

Although public accountants are not the most common type of accountants, they are probably the best known. **Chartered accountants** (CAs) derive their name from the fact that they are members of firms who offer their accounting services to the public. They are also licensed provincially based on the results of a rigorous examination.[2] The Canadian Institute of Chartered Accountants prepares the CA examination. It also provides technical support to its members and discipline in matters of professional ethics.

chartered accountant (CA)
An individual who has met certain experience and education requirements and has passed a licensing examination; acts as an outside accountant for other firms.

While some CAs work as individual practitioners, many join with one or more other CAs in a partnership. Table 17.1 lists the ten largest CA firms in Canada.

TABLE 17.1   The Top Ten Accounting Firms in Canada, 1994 (ranked by revenues)

Company	Revenue (in millions)
1. KPMG	$475.1
2. Deloitte & Touche	406.0
3. Ernst & Young	366.0
4. Coopers & Lybrand	266.4
5. Arthur Andersen & Co.	252.0
6. Price Waterhouse	240.0
7. Doane Raymond Grant Thornton	204.4
8. BDO Dunwoody	119.1
9. Richter Usher & Vineberg	49.0
10. Collins Barrow	27.9

Virtually all CA firms—whether they boast 10 000 employees and 100 offices or just one person in a tiny office—provide three types of services: audit services, tax services, and management services. The larger CA firms earn about 60 percent to 70 percent of their revenue from audit services. Smaller firms typically earn most of their income from tax and management services.

audit

An accountant's examination of a company's financial records to determine if it used proper procedures to prepare its financial reports.

Auditing.   In an **audit**, the accountant examines a company's accounting system to determine whether the company's financial reports fairly present its financial operations. Companies normally must provide audited financial reports when applying for loans or when selling stock.

The audit will determine if the firm has controls to prevent errors or fraud from going undetected. Auditors also examine receipts such as shipping documents, cancelled cheques, payroll records, and cash receipts records. In some cases, an auditor may physically check inventories, equipment, or other assets, even if it means descending 200 metres underground in a lead mine.

One of the auditor's responsibilities is to make sure the client's accounting system adheres to generally accepted accounting principles. **Generally accepted accounting principles** (**GAAP**) are a body of theory and procedure developed and monitored by the Canadian Institute of Chartered Accountants (CICA), a professional accounting organization. At the end of an audit, the auditor will certify whether or not the client's financial reports comply with GAAP. The box "Who Can We Blame For This Mess?" describes some of the practical problems in auditing.

generally accepted accounting principles (GAAP)

Standard rules and methods used by accountants in preparing financial reports.

Recently, some non-profit organizations like churches and universities have said that they felt pressured by their auditors to use GAAP. They argue, however, that GAAP principles are designed for profit-seeking business firms, not non-profit organizations. Non-profits should be judged on how well they meet their goals—for example, helping people—rather than on a financial criterion like profit.[3]

Tax Services.   Tax services include helping clients not only with preparing their tax returns but also in their tax planning. Tax laws are complex. A CA's advice can help a business structure (or restructure) its operations and investments and save millions of dollars in taxes. To best serve their clients, of course, accountants must stay abreast of changes in tax laws—no simple matter.

The Canadian Business Scene

WHO CAN WE BLAME FOR THIS MESS?

The accounting profession has come under increased pressure during the 1990s, partly as a result of fallout from the unexpected failures of the Canadian Commercial Bank and the Northland Bank. It now seems that every time a business firm fails, there is talk of suing the CA firm that audited its books. The average person simply does not understand how a business firm can suddenly fail right after it has just been audited by a CA firm, particularly after the CA firm certifies that the business adhered to generally accepted accounting principles.

Some people think that auditors should expand their reports or clarify their language so that readers of financial statements will have a better idea of how a company is doing before they invest in it. Others suggest that auditors should give more consideration to the users of financial statements, and perhaps provide specific financial reporting for different user groups. Perhaps auditors should be charged with detecting fraud and reporting it when they find it.

Individuals in the accounting profession recognize that there is a "chummy" relationship between CA firms and their clients. There is also considerable elasticity in the application of generally accepted accounting principles. Some critics argue that business firms should be required to change their auditors every five years to prevent these relationships from developing.

One of the outcomes of several visible business failures in Canada and the U.S. is a sharp rise in the liability insurance premiums that are being paid by the big accounting firms. Insurance premiums have increased tenfold in the past two years, coverage has been reduced, and deductability limits have been increased. Interestingly, the smaller accounting firms have not faced big increases, mainly because they do not generally audit the books of large firms (the ones who get sued for megabucks).

Big firms attract big clients, and when a big firm is sued, the suit frequently names the firm's auditor as well. At the end of 1992, for example, outstanding claims against the six biggest accounting firms in the U.S. totalled $30 billion. The most notable Canadian case involved Coopers & Lybrand, with claims against that firm totalling $500 million.

In 1993, the Canadian Life & Health Insurance Compensation Corp. (better known as Comp-Corp.), which was set up to protect holders of policies issued by insolvent companies, sued the CA firm of Mallette Maheu for negligence. It claimed Mallette made errors that forced Comp-Corp. to pay over $93 million in claims to policyholders of Les Cooperants, the failed insurance company. (For a description of the Les Cooperants debacle, see Chapter 19.) Comp-Corp. claimed that Mallette employees made errors that allowed Les Cooperants Insurance Group to report a profit of over $3 million in 1989, whereas the company actually lost $21 million. Mallette Maheu said the suit was frivolous and unfounded.

There are interesting legal ramifications of these lawsuits. In the simplest case, both a corporation and its auditor may be sued. But even if they are both found negligent, and if the courts decide that the auditor is 20 percent responsible, the accounting firm may have to pay the entire bill if the business firm has no money (which is likely, since it went bankrupt). And its gets worse. In theory, since accounting firms are partnerships, the partners have unlimited liability. In a big settlement, the partners' personal assets could be seized to pay the legal judgment.

Management Services.   Management services range from personal financial planning to planning corporate mergers. Other services include plant layout and design, marketing studies, production scheduling, computer feasibility studies, and design and implementation of accounting systems. Some CA firms even assist in executive recruitment. Small wonder that the staffs of CA firms include engineers, architects, mathematicians, and even psychologists.

Private Accountants

To assure the fairness of their reports, CAs must be independent of the firms they audit. They are employees of accounting firms and provide services for many clients. But businesses also hire their own private accountants as salaried employees to deal with the company's day-to-day accounting needs.

This advertisement by the chartered accountant and management consulting firm of Deloitte & Touche is directed toward services which will help small businesses that are managed by their owners.

Private accountants perform an amazing diversity of accounting jobs. Large businesses employ specialized accountants in such areas as budgets, financial planning, internal auditing, payroll, and taxation. Each accounting area has its own challenges and excitement. In small businesses, a single individual may handle all accounting tasks—and approve credit terms, too!

The nature of an accounting job depends on the specific business. For example, the accounting and reporting systems and needs of the Toronto Blue Jays differ considerably from those of Air Canada. An internal auditor for Imperial Oil might fly to an offshore drilling platform to confirm the accuracy of oil flow meters. But an accounts payable supervisor responsible for $2 billion a month in payments to vendors and employees may travel no further than the executive suite.

Tools of the Accounting Trade

All accountants, whether public or private, rely on record-keeping. Private accountants use journals and ledgers to enter and keep track of business transactions for their company. Underlying these records are the two key concepts of accounting: the accounting equation and double-entry bookkeeping.[4]

Record-Keeping with Journals and Ledgers

As Figure 17.1 shows, record-keeping begins with initial records of the firm's financial transactions. Examples include sales orders, invoices for incoming materials, employee time cards, and customer payments on installment purchases. Large companies receive and process tens of thousands of these documents every day. But unless they are analyzed and classified in an orderly fashion, managers cannot keep track of the business's progress.

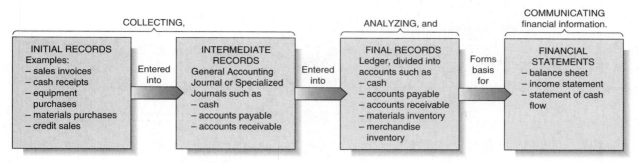

Figure 17.1
Accounting and record-keeping.

Notations of the sorted records are entered into a journal, an intermediate form of record, as the initial records are received. A **journal** is just a
chronological record of financial transactions along with a brief description
of the transaction. Some companies keep only a single (general) journal.
Others keep specialized journals for cash receipts, sales, purchases, and the
like. For centuries, journals were kept by hand but, today, many firms use
computers for their record-keeping.

Transactions from a company's journal(s) are brought together and summarized, usually monthly, in final records called **ledgers**. Ledgers are divided
into categories (accounts) similar to those of specialized journals. Unlike journals, accounts in a ledger contain only minimal descriptions of transactions. But
they do contain an important additional column, labeled "Balance," as shown
in Figure 17.3 (see page 507). (We will explore the meaning of the debit and
credit columns shortly.) Because of this column, ledgers enable managers to tell
at a glance where the company stands. If the balance is unexpectedly high or
low, accountants and other managers can track backward to the correspond-
ing journal entry to see what has caused the unexpected balance.

Finally, at the end of the year, accountants total up all the accounts in a
firm's ledger and assess the business's financial status. This summation is
the basis for annual financial reports. With the preparation of financial reports,
the old *accounting cycle* ends and a new cycle begins.

To clarify this record-keeping process, consider Figure 17.2, which illustrates a portion of the process for Perfect Posters Inc. Notice how the
cheque from Eye Poppers (an initial record) has been entered in the firm's
general accounting journal (an intermediate record). As you can see, this entry
eventually turns up in Perfect Poster's ledgers (a final record). And as we will
discuss in the next section, these ledger entries are ultimately reflected in the
financial reports that Perfect Posters needs for its shareholders and bank.

journal
*A chronological record of a
firm's financial transactions
along with a brief description of
each transaction.*

ledger
*Summations of journal entries,
by category, that show the effects of transactions on the balance in each account.*

The Accounting Equation

At various points in the year, public and private accountants balance the data
in journals and ledgers by using the following accounting equation:

$$\text{Assets} = \text{Liabilities} + \text{Owners' equity}$$

To understand why this equation is important, you must first understand what accountants mean by assets, liabilities, and owners' equity.

You are probably familiar with the first two terms in their general sense.
Charm and intelligence are often said to be "assets." Someone who cannot

```
Eye-Poppers, Inc.                                    CHEQUE NUMBER
702 Willow St.                                          09006
Don Mills, Ontario
                                          September 29    ,19 94

Pay to the
Order of _____ Perfect Posters Inc. _____    $  245.00
                                                        xx
         _____ Two Hundred forty five and _____   100   Dollars

BANK

_____                             Joan Little
                                             Authorized Signature
: 200 5268474  264  1223                     Ivan Itsch, Treasurer
```

Figure 17.2
Record-keeping at Perfect Posters Inc. traces the path of every financial transaction, such as this cheque from a customer, showing how it affects each financial category.

asset

Anything of economic value owned by a firm or individual.

liability

Any debt owed by a firm or individual to others.

owners' equity

Any positive difference between a firm's assets and its liabilities; what would remain for a firm's owners if the company were liquidated, all its assets sold, and all its debts paid.

swim may be a "liability" on a boat trip. Accountants apply these terms more narrowly, focusing on items with quantifiable value. Thus an **asset**, in the accounting sense, is anything of economic value owned by the firm. Examples include land, buildings, equipment, inventory, and payments due the company. In contrast, a **liability** is a debt owed by the firm to others.

Finally, you may have heard people speak of the "equity" they have in their home, meaning the amount of money they would get if they sold the house and paid off the mortgage. Similarly, **owners' equity** refers to the amount of money a firm's owners would receive if they sold all the company's assets and paid off all its liabilities (*liquidated* the company). We can rewrite the accounting equation to show this definition:

$$\text{Assets} - \text{Liabilities} = \text{Owners' equity}$$

If a company's assets exceed its liabilities, owners' equity is positive: If the company goes out of business, the owners will receive some cash (a gain) after selling assets and paying off liabilities. If liabilities outweigh assets, however, owners' equity is negative: There are insufficient assets to pay off all debts. If the company goes out of business, the owners will get no cash and some creditors will not be paid. Finally, owners' equity is also a meaningful number of both investors and lenders. For example, before lending money to owners, lenders want to know the amount of owners' equity existing in a business.

Owners' equity consists of two sources of capital:

- the amount that the owners originally invested
- profits earned by and reinvested in the company.

For example, when a company operates profitably, its assets increase faster than its liabilities. Owners' equity, therefore, will increase if profits are kept in the business instead of paid out as dividends to shareholders. Owners' equity can also increase if owners invest more of their own money to increase assets. However, owners' equity can shrink if the company operates at a loss or if the owners withdraw assets.

Double-Entry Accounting

If your business purchases inventory with cash, you do *two* things: (1) decrease your cash and (2) increase your inventory. Similarly, if you purchase supplies on credit, you (1) increase your supplies and (2) increase your accounts payable. If you invest more money in your business, you (1) increase your cash and (2) increase your owners' equity. In other words, *every transaction affects two accounts*. Accountants thus use a **double-entry accounting system** to record the *dual effects* of financial transactions.

Recording dual effects ensures that the accounting equation always balances. As the term implies, the double-entry system requires at least two bookkeeping entries for each transaction. This practice keeps the accounting equation in balance.

Debits and Credits: The T-Account

Another accounting tool uses *debits* and *credits* as a universal method for keeping accounting records. To understand debits and credits, we first need to understand the **T-account**. The format for recording transactions takes the shape of a **T** whose vertical line divides the account into two sides. The **T** format for Perfect Posters' General Accounting Journal is shown in Figure 17.3.

In bookkeeping, *debit* and *credit* refer to the side on which account information is to be entered: The left column of any T-account is called the *debit* side, and the right column is the *credit* side:

debit = left side
credit = right side

When an asset increases, it is entered as a **debit**. When it decreases, it is entered as a **credit**. Thus when Perfect Posters received payment from Eye-Poppers, it received more cash—an asset. It thus debited the General Accounting Journal (Figure 17.4) by placing $245 on the left side of that T-account.

Figure 17.5 shows how the rules of the T-account are consistent with the terms of the accounting equation. Debits and credits provide a system of checks and balances. Every debit entry in a journal must have an offsetting credit entry elsewhere (not shown here). If not, the books will not balance because some error (or deliberate deception) has been introduced in the record keeping. To ensure accurate financial records, accountants must find and correct such errors.

The double-entry system, therefore, provides an important method of accounting control: At the end of the accounting cycle, debits and credits must balance. In other words, total debits must equal total credits in the account balances recorded in the general ledger. An imbalance indicates improper accounting that must be corrected. "Balancing the books," then, is a control procedure to ensure that proper accounting has been used.

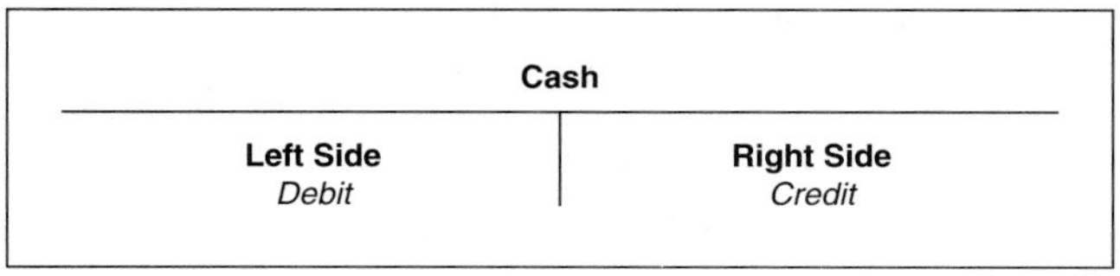

double-entry accounting system

A bookkeeping system, developed in the fifteenth century and still in use, that requires every transaction to be entered in two ways—how it affects assets and how it affects liabilities and owners' equity—so that the accounting equation is always in balance.

T-account

An accounting format that divides an account into a debit and a credit side.

debit

In bookkeeping, any transaction that increases assets or decreases liabilities or owners' equity; always entered in the left column.

credit

In bookkeeping, any transaction that decreases assets or increases liabilities or owners' equity; always entered in the right column.

Cash	
Left Side *Debit*	**Right Side** *Credit*

Figure 17.3
This unnumbered/unlabeled general accounting journal
T format divides an account into two sides.

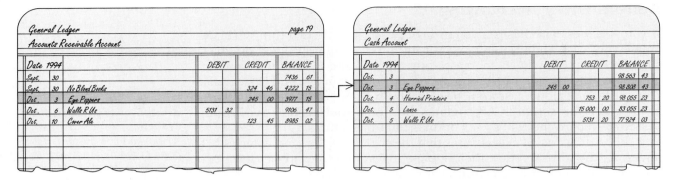

Figure 17.4
Under the double-entry accounting system, this cheque from a customer increases the Cash Balance and decreases the Accounts Receivable Balance.

Accounting Equation Rules of the T-Account	**Assets**		=	**Liabilities**		+	**Owner's Equity**	
	Debit for Increase	Credit for Decrease		Debit for Decrease	Credit for Increase		Debit for Decrease	Credit for Increase

Figure 17.5
In both the T-account and the accounting equation, debits and credits provide a system of checks and balances.

Financial Statements

As we noted earlier, the primary purpose of accounting is to summarize the results of a business's transactions and to issue reports that can help managers and others make informed decisions. Some of the most important reports, called **financial statements**, fall into several broad categories: balance sheets, income statements, and statements of cash flows. Balance sheets are sometimes called statements of financial position because they show the financial condition of a firm at one time. Other financial statements summarize the economic activities that have occurred during a specified period, usually one year. Together, these statements provide a picture of a business's financial health: what it is worth, how much it earns, and how it spends its resources.[5] Misleading financial statements can be very costly to investors.

financial statement

Any of several types of broad reports regarding a company's financial status; most often used in reference to balance sheets, income statements, and/or statements of cash flows.

Balance Sheets

At one time, the only financial statement released to external users (such as shareholders and lenders) was the **balance sheet**. Early balance sheets provided sketchy information. Today, balance sheets supply a considerable amount of information including detailed, technical descriptions of complex accounts and transactions. Balance sheets present the accounting equation factors: a company's assets, its liabilities, and its owners' equity. Figure 17.6 shows a balance sheet for Perfect Posters.

balance sheet

A type of financial statement that summarizes a firm's financial position on a particular date in terms of its assets, liabilities, and owners' equity.

🗆🗆🗆🗆🗆🗆🗆🗆🗆 **Perfect Posters, Inc.**
555 Riverview, Toronto, Ontario

Perfect Posters, Inc.
Balance Sheet
As of December 31, 1994

Assets

Current Assets:		
Cash		$7,050
Marketable securities		2,300
Accounts receivable	$26,210	
Less: Allowance of doubtful accounts	(650)	25,560
Merchandise inventory		21,250
Prepaid expenses		1,050
Total current assets		**$57,210**
Fixed Assets:		18,000
Building	65,000	
Less: Accumulated depreciation	(22,500)	42,500
Equipment	72,195	
Less: Accumulated depreciation	(24,815)	47,380
Total fixed assets		**107,880**
Intangible assets:		
Patents	7,100	
Trademarks	900	
Total intangible Assets		**8,000**
Total assets		**$173,090**

Liabilities and Owners' Equity

Current liabilities:		
Accounts payable	$16,315	
Wages payable	3,700	
Taxes payable	1,920	
Total current liabilities		**$21,935**
Long-term liabilities:		
Notes payable, 8% due 1997	10,000	
Bonds payable, 9% due 2001	30,000	
Total long-term liabilities		**40,000**
Total liabilities		**$61,935**
Owners' Equity		
Common stock, $5 par	40,000	
Additional paid-in capital	15,000	
Retained earnings	56,155	
Total owners' equity		**111,155**
Total liabilities and owners' equity		**$173,090**

Figure 17.6
Perfect Posters, Inc. balance sheet as of December 31, 1994.

Assets.   Most companies have three types of assets from an accounting standpoint: current, fixed, and intangible. **Current assets** include cash and assets that can or will be converted into cash in the following year. They are normally listed in order of **liquidity**, which refers to how quickly they can be converted into cash or used up. Business debts normally can be satisfied only through payments of cash. A company that cannot generate cash easily as needed (in other words, a company that is not liquid) may be forced to sell assets at sacrifice prices or even to go out of business.

Cash is, by definition, completely liquid. Marketable securities are slightly less liquid but can be sold quickly if there is a need for additional cash. Stocks or bonds of other companies and government securities such as treasury bills are all marketable securities. **Accounts receivable** are amounts due from customers who have purchased goods on credit. Most businesses expect to receive payment within 30 days of a sale.

Following accounts receivable is merchandise inventory, the cost of merchandise that has been acquired for sale to customers but is still on hand. Merchandise inventory is two steps removed from cash: first the inventory must be sold, generating accounts receivable, and then the accounts receivable must be collected to obtain cash.

The final current asset listed is prepaid expenses. Included in this category would be supplies on hand and rent paid for the period to come. In all, Perfect Posters's current assets as of December 31, 1994, totaled $57 210.

current assets
Cash and other assets that can be converted into cash in the following year.

liquidity
The ease and speed with which an asset can be converted to cash; cash is said to be perfectly liquid.

accounts receivable
Amounts due to the firm from customers who have purchased goods or services on credit; a form of current asset.

fixed assets

Assets that have long-term use or value to the firm such as land, buildings, and machinery.

depreciation

Distributing the cost of a major asset over the years in which it produces revenues; calculated by each year subtracting the asset's original value divided by the number of years in its productive life.

intangible assets

Nonphysical assets such as patents, trademarks, copyrights, and franchise fees, that have economic value but whose precise value is difficult to calcu-

current liabilities

Any debts owed by the firm that must be repaid within the year.

accounts payable

Amounts due from the firm to its suppliers for goods and/or services purchased on credit; a form of current liability.

long-term liabilities

Any debts owed by the firm that need not be repaid within the year.

retained earnings

A company's net profits less any dividend payments to shareholders.

Normally, the next major balance sheet classification is **fixed assets**. Items in this category have long-term use or value, for example, land, buildings, and equipment. Because buildings and equipment do eventually wear out or become obsolete, however, the accountant has depreciated them. **Depreciation** means calculating the useful life of the asset, dividing its worth by that many years, and then subtracting the resulting amount each year. That is, the asset's remaining value on the books goes down each year. In Figure 17.6, Perfect Posters has fixed assets of $107 880 after depreciation.

Despite their name, intangible assets are not without monetary value, although their worth is hard to set. **Intangible assets** usually consist of the cost to obtain rights or privileges such as patents, trademarks, copyrights, and franchise fees. Another intangible asset, *goodwill*, can be recorded only when a business is being bought. It is the amount paid for an existing business over and above the value of its other assets because the firm has a particularly good reputation or good location. Perfect Posters has intangible assets of $8000 in patents for specialized equipment it designed to store posters vertically in the warehouse and for trademarks it owns.

Liabilities.   Like assets, liabilities are separated into different categories, in this case, current liabilities and long-term liabilities. **Current liabilities** are debts that must be paid within the year. They include unpaid bills to suppliers for materials (**accounts payable**) as well as wages and taxes that will have to be paid in the coming year. Note in Figure 17.6 that Perfect Posters has current liabilities of $21 935.

Debts that are not due within one year are called **long-term liabilities**. They normally represent borrowed funds on which the company must pay interest. Perfect Posters's long-term liabilities are $40 000.

Owners' Equity.   The final section of the balance sheet shows owners' equity broken down into common stock, paid-in capital, and retained earnings. When Perfect Posters was formed, the declared legal value of stock was $5 per share. By law, this $40 000 ($5 × 8000 shares) cannot be distributed as dividends. Paid-in capital is additional money invested in the firm by the owners.

A company's net profits less dividend payments to shareholders are its **retained earnings**. Retained earnings accumulate when profits, which could have been distributed to shareholders, are instead kept for use by the company. Perfect Posters has total paid-in capital of $55 000 (from common stock plus additional paid-in capital) and retained earnings of $56 155.

Fixed assets at this Coca-Cola bottling plant include the building and equipment that fills the bottles and moves them through production.

Income Statements

Perhaps the most popular form of financial statement is the **income statement**. It is sometimes called a **profit-and-loss statement** because its description of a company's revenues and expenses results in a figure of the firm's profit or loss. That is,

Revenues − Expenses = Profit (or Loss)

An income statement enables the reader to assess how effectively management is using the resources entrusted to it. Figure 17.7 shows an income statement for Perfect Posters.

Revenues. The first major category shown on an income statement is revenues. **Revenues** are the value of the resources that flow into a business from selling products or providing services. The $250 a law firm receives for preparing a will and the $65 a supermarket receives from a customer for groceries are both revenue. Perfect Posters reported revenues of $256 425 from the sale of the art prints and other posters it supplies to retailers.

income (profit-and-loss) statement

A type of financial statement that describes a firm's revenues and expenses and indicates whether the firm has earned a profit or suffered a loss during a given period.

revenues

Any monies received by a firm as a result of selling a good or service or from other sources such as interest, rent, and licensing fees.

❏❏❏❏❏❏❏❏❏❏❏❏❏❏ **Perfect Posters, Inc.**
555 Riverview, Toronto, Ontario

Perfect Posters, Inc.
Income Statement
Year ended December 31, 1994

Revenues (gross sales)		**$256,425**
Costs of goods sold:		
Merchandise inventory,		
January 1, 1994	$22,380	
Merchandise purchases during year	103,635	
Goods available for sale		$126,015
Less: Merchandise inventory, December 31, 1994		21,250
Cost of goods sold		104,765
Gross profit		151,660
Operating expenses:		
Selling and repackaging expenses:		
Salaries and wages	49,750	
Advertising	6,380	
Depreciation-warehouse and repackaging equipment	3,350	
Total selling and repackaging expenses		59,480
Administrative expenses:		
Salaries and wages	55,100	
Supplies	4,150	
Utilities	3,800	
Depreciation-office equipment	3,420	
Interest expense	2,900	
Miscellaneous expenses	1,835	
Total administration expenses		71,205
Total operating expenses		130,685
Income before taxes		20,975
Income taxes		8,390
Net income		**$12,585**

Figure 17.7
Perfect Posters, Inc. income statement for year ended December 31, 1994.

cost of goods sold

Any expenses directly involved in producing or selling a good or service during a given time period.

gross profit (gross margin)

A firm's revenues (gross sales) less its cost of goods sold.

operating expenses

Costs incurred by a firm other than those included in cost of goods sold.

net income (net profit or net earnings)

A firm's gross profit less its operating expenses and income taxes.

statement of cash flows

A financial statement that describes a firm's generation and use of cash during a given period.

Cost of Goods Sold.   The next section of the income statement details expenses involved in producing goods—the **cost of goods sold**. This category shows the costs of obtaining materials to make the products that were sold during the year. Perfect Posters, for example, started the year with posters valued at $22 380 in the warehouse. During the year it bought $103 635 more of these posters for a total of $126 015 worth of merchandise available to sell during 1994. By the end of the year it had sold all but $21 250 of the posters, which remained as "merchandise inventory" on December 31. So the firm's cost to obtain the goods it sold was $104 765.

Subtracting cost of goods sold from revenues gives us **gross profit** (or **gross margin**). Perfect Posters's gross profit was $151 660 ($256 425–$104 765).

Operating Expenses.   In addition to costs directly related to acquiring the goods it sells, every company has general operating expenses, ranging from erasers to the president's salary. Like cost of goods sold, **operating expenses** are resources that must flow out of a company for it to earn revenues. Perfect Posters had operating expenses of $59 480 in selling and repackaging expenses and $71 205 in administrative expenses for a total of $130 685.

Subtracting operating expenses and income taxes from gross margin yields **net income** (also called **net profit** or **net earnings**). As Figure 17.7 shows, in 1994, Perfect Posters's net income was $12 585. Remember that the net income figure can only be computed after many assumptions have been made and much data analyzed. The box "How Well Is Four Seasons Really Doing?" shows how controversy can arise when auditors try to determine a business firm's financial condition.

Statement of Changes in Cash Flows

A balance sheet and an income statement are the only financial reports some companies prepare. But a third report, a **statement of cash flows**, is also important. This statement describes a company's cash receipts and cash payments for the year. Since it provides the most detail about the company's ability to generate and use cash, some investors and creditors consider it the most important statement of all. A statement of cash flows, like that in Figure 17.8 for Perfect Posters, shows the effects on cash of three aspects of the business: operations, investing, and financing.

Cash Flows from Operations.   The first section of the statement is concerned with the firm's main operating activities—cash transactions in buying and selling goods and services. Starting with net income (from the income statement), accountants must make several adjustments to reveal true cash flows (rather than paper transactions). Depreciation of $6770 from the income statement is an example of an item that must be added back. Although it was an expense in determining net income, it did not reduce Perfect Posters's cash.

Three additional operating activities—inventories, accounts receivable, and accounts payable—also require adjustments. The income statement showed an $1130 inventory reduction for the year. Inventory was, in effect, converted into additional cash. Accounts receivable, however, absorbed some of the company's cash. Receivables (from the balance sheet) for 1994 were $2165 higher than in 1993, depriving Perfect Posters of cash. But the increased accounts payable for the year yielded a $3215 cash savings. After making these adjustments to net income, Perfect Posters's main operations provided cash of $21 535.

Cash Flows from Investing.   This section reports net cash used in or provided by investing. It includes cash receipts and payments from buying and

The Canadian Business Scene

HOW WELL IS FOUR SEASONS REALLY DOING?

Four Seasons Hotels and Resorts, which operates luxury hotels around the world, has developed a reputation for great personal service to its customers. This "product" is difficult to deliver to customers because it depends on so many front-line individuals, including bellhops, bartenders, desk clerks, and cleaning staff. Some industry analysts think that the financial difficulties that Four Seasons has recently experienced are the result of an overemphasis on personal service.

But there is great debate about Four Seasons' financial condition. Some analysts say that the company stretches accounting loopholes and uses accounting practices in such a way that financial performance is hard to judge. Four Seasons' CEO, Isadore Sharp, says that is ludicrous.

There are several accounting practices that critics are concerned about. First, concerns arose when Four Seasons converted a big ownership position in six hotels into a small, passive stake by transferring the six hotels to a partnership. The six hotels now appear nowhere on Four Seasons' income statements. Thus, these hotels could be losing money and none of the shareholders would know it. While the company defends this on the basis that the hotels that are now in the partnership were "sold," observers point out that this was a strange kind of sale—both partners in the partnership are still fully responsible for any losses that might occur on the property they contributed to the partnership.

Second, prior to 1992, Four Seasons depreciated its hotel assets before calculating operating margins. After 1992, it lumped depreciation costs into administrative costs so that its operating margin would not be affected.

Third, some assets listed on Four Seasons' balance sheet appear questionable. On its 1993 balance sheet, for example, are assets labeled "notes and mortgages receivable." But this account represents money that Four Seasons advanced to hotels that it manages and that were in financial difficulty. The problem with this arrangement is that the more money Four Seasons advances to hotels that are in difficulty, the larger its "assets" become on its balance sheet. In a similar vein, when Four Seasons advances money to the six hotels it put in the partnership, it lists that as an asset called "investment in hotel partnerships." This account has also been increasing. Four Seasons says that all this money will come back to the company eventually just like any other receivables would, but skeptics think these "assets" may not really represent a future benefit at all.

In February, 1993 a Toronto analyst published a 28-page report on Four Seasons and concluded that investors should sell their shares. The stock was then selling for $17.50 per share; by May, 1994 the stock had dropped to $11 per share.

---

selling stocks, bonds, property, equipment, and other productive assets. Perfect Posters's purchases of land and equipment used $23 495 of net cash in 1994.

Cash Flows from Financing.   This final section reports the net cash from all financing activities. It includes cash inflows from borrowing or issuing stock as well as outflows for payment of dividends and repayment of borrowings. Perfect Posters received $10 000 from issuing long-term notes. Dividend payments used $6000.

The overall change in cash from the three sources—operations, investing, and financing—is an increase of $2040 for the year. This amount is added to the beginning cash (from the 1993 balance sheet) to arrive at 1994's ending cash position of $7050.

The Budget: An Internal Financial Statement

In addition to financial statements, managers need other types of accounting information to aid in internal planning, controlling, and decision making. Probably the most crucial *internal* financial statement is the budget. A **budget** is a detailed statement of estimated receipts and expenditures for a period of

budget
A detailed financial plan for estimated receipts and expenditures for a period of time in the future, usually one year.

☐☐☐☐☐☐☐☐☐☐☐☐   **Perfect Posters, Inc.**
555 Riverview, Toronto, Ontario

Perfect Posters, Inc.
Statement of Cash Flows
Year ended December 31, 1994
Increase (Decrease) in Cash

Cash flows from operating activities:		
Net income		$12,585
Adjustments to reconcile net income to		
net cash provided by operating activities:		
Depreciation	$ 6,770	
Decrease in merchandise inventory	1,130	
Increase in accounts receivable	(2,165)	
Increase in accounts payable	3,215	
Total adjustments		8,950
Net cash provided by		
operating activities		**21,535**
Cash flows from investing activities:		
Payment for purchase of land	(10,000)	
Payment for purchase of equipment	(13,495)	
Net cash used in investing activities		**(25,495)**
Cash flows from financing activities		
Proceeds from issuance of long-term note	10,000	
Dividends paid	(6,000)	
Net cash provided by financing		
activities		**4,000**
Net increase in cash		2,040
Cash at beginning of year		5,010
Cash at end of year		**$ 7,050**

Figure 17.8
Perfect Posters, Inc. statement of cash flows for year ended
December 31, 1994. Increase (decrease) in cash.

time in the future. Although that period is usually one year, some companies also prepare budgets for three- or five-year periods, especially when considering major capital expenditures.

Budgets are also useful for keeping track of weekly or monthly performance. Procter & Gamble, for example, evaluates all its business units monthly by comparing actual financial results with monthly budgeted amounts. Discrepancies in "actual versus budget" totals signal potential problems and initiate action to get financial performance back on track.

Although the accounting staff coordinates the budget process, it requires input from many people in the company regarding proposed activities, needed resources, and input sources.[6] Figure 17.9, for example, is a sample sales budget. In preparing such a budget, the accounting department must obtain from the sales group both its projections for units to be sold and expected expenses for each quarter of the coming year. Accountants then draw up the final budget, and throughout the year, the accounting department compares the budget to actual expenditures and revenues.

□□□□□□□□□□□□□ **Perfect Posters, Inc.**
555 Riverview, Toronto, Ontario

Perfect Posters, Inc.
Sales Budget
First Quarter, 1995

	January	February	March	Quarter
Budgeted sales (units)	7,500	6,000	6,500	20,000
Budgeted selling price per unit	$3.50	$3.50	$3.50	$3.50
Budgeted sales revenue	**$26,250**	**$21,000**	**$22,750**	**$70,000**
Expected cash receipts:				
From December sales	$26,210[a]			$26,210
From January sales	$17,500[b]	$8,750		26,250
From February sales		14,000	$7,000	21,000
From March sales			15,200	15,200
Total cash receipts:	**$43,710**	**$22,750**	**$22,200**	**$88,660**

[a] This cash from December sales represents a collection of the Account Receivable appearing on the December 31, 1994, Balance Sheet.
[b] The company estimates that two-thirds of each month's sales revenues will result in cash receipts during the same month. The remaining one-third is collected during the following month.

Figure 17.9
Perfect Posters, Inc. sales budget, First Quarter 1995.

Analyzing Financial Statements

The financial statements discussed above present a great deal of information. But what does it all mean? How can these statements help investors decide what stock to buy or managers to decide whether to extend credit to another firm? By using statistics and ratios, we can analyze and compare financial statements from various companies and help answer these questions. We can also check a firm's progress by comparing its current and past statements.

A **key ratio** is a value obtained by dividing one value on a financial statement by another value. A business firm's financial condition can be assessed by comparing several important key ratios of items from its financial statements with key ratios for similar types of firms. Dun & Bradstreet Canada publishes key ratios for a variety of industries, including retail trade, wholesale trade, manufacturing, construction, services, and so on.

Ratios are normally grouped into four major classifications based on what they measure. As summarized in Table 17.2, these groups are (1) short-term solvency ratios, (2) long-term solvency ratios, (3) profitability ratios, and (4) activity ratios. Solvency ratios estimate risk; profitability ratios measure potential earnings; and activity ratios reflect management's use of assets. Depending on the types of decisions to be made, a user may apply none, some, or all the ratios in a particular group.

key ratio
A value obtained by dividing one value on a financial statement by another value.

TABLE 17.2   Financial Ratios

Overall Type	What Measured	Specific Types	Formula
Short-Term Solvency (Liquidity Ratios)	Potential Risk	Current Ratio	$\dfrac{\text{Current assets}}{\text{Current liabilities}}$
		Quick (Acid-test) Ratio	$\dfrac{\text{Quick assets}}{\text{Current liabilities}}$
Long-Term Solvency (Debt) Ratios	Potential Risk	Debt-to-Owners'-Equity Ratio	$\dfrac{\text{Debt}}{\text{Owners' equity}}$
Profitability Ratios	Potential Rewards	Return on Sales	$\dfrac{\text{Net income}}{\text{Sales}}$
		Return on Investment	$\dfrac{\text{Net income}}{\text{Total owners' equity}}$
		Earnings Per Share	$\dfrac{\text{Net income}}{\text{Number of common shares outstanding}}$
Activity Ratios	Efficient Use of Resources	Inventory Turnover Ratio	$\dfrac{\text{Cost of goods sold}}{\text{Average inventory}}$

Short-Term Solvency Ratios

In the short run, a company's survival depends on its ability to pay its immediate debts. As noted earlier, such payments require cash. Short-term solvency ratios measure a company's relative liquidity. The higher a firm's **liquidity ratios**, the lower the risks involved for investors. The two most commonly used liquidity ratios are the current ratio and the quick (or acid-test) ratio.

liquidity ratios
Measures of a firm's ability to meet its immediate debts; used to analyze the risks of investing in the firm.

Current Ratio.   This ratio has been called the bankers' ratio because it is used by those concerned with a firm's creditworthiness. By dividing current assets by current liabilities, the **current ratio** measures a company's ability to meet its current obligations out of its current assets. It reflects a firm's ability to generate cash to meet obligations through the normal, orderly process of selling inventories and collecting accounts receivable.

current ratio
A form of liquidity ratio calculated as current assets divided by current liabilities.

As a rule of thumb, a current ratio of 2:1 is satisfactory. A larger current ratio may imply that assets are not being used productively and should be invested elsewhere, rather than in current assets. A smaller current ratio may indicate that a company will have difficulty paying its bills.

How does Perfect Posters measure up? Judging from its current assets and liabilities at the end of 1994, we see that

$$\frac{\text{Current assets}}{\text{Current liabilities}} = \frac{\$57\ 210}{\$21\ 935} = 2.61$$

The firm may be holding too much cash, but it is a good credit risk.

quick ratio (acid-test ratio)
A form of liquidity ratio calculated as quick assets (cash plus marketable securities and accounts receivable) divided by current liabilities.

Quick (Acid-Test) Ratio.   The current ratio represents a company's ability to meet expected demands for cash. In contrast, the **quick ratio**, or **acid-test ratio**, which divides quick assets by current liabilities, measures a firm's ability to meet emergency demands for cash. *Quick assets* include cash and assets just one step removed from being converted into cash: marketable securities and accounts receivable. Inventory is excluded from this measure because it can be liquidated quickly only at sacrifice prices. Thus, the quick ratio is a more stringent test than is the current ratio. As a rule of thumb, a quick ratio of 1.0 is satisfactory.

If we again consider Perfect Posters's position at the end of 1994, we see that

$$\frac{\text{Quick assets}}{\text{Current liabilities}} = \frac{\$7050 + 2300 + 26\,210 - 650}{\$21\,935} = 1.59$$

In an emergency, the firm apparently can pay off all current obligations without having to liquidate its inventory.

Long-Term Solvency Ratios

If a company is to survive in the long run, it must be able to meet both its short-term (current) and long-term liabilities. These debts, as we have seen, usually involve interest payments. A firm that cannot meet these payments is in serious danger of collapse or takeover—a risk that makes creditors and investors alike very cautious. To measure this risk, we use long-term solvency ratios—**debt ratios**—like the debt-to-equity ratio.

debt ratios

Measures of a firm's ability to meet its long-term debts; used to analyze the risks of investing in the firm.

The Debt-to-Owners'-Equity Ratio.   Calculated as debt (total liabilities) divided by owner's equity, the **debt-to-owners'-equity ratio** describes the extent to which a firm is financed through borrowings. This ratio is commonly used in industry financial statistical reports so that a reader can compare a company's ratio with industry averages. Companies with debt-to-equity ratios above 1 are probably relying too much on debt.

In the case of Perfect Posters, this ratio works out to

$$\frac{\text{Debt}}{\text{Owners' equity}} = \frac{\$61\,935}{\$111\,155} = .56$$

debt-to-owners' ratio

A form of debt ratio calculated as total liabilities divided by owners' equity.

If this firm developed disastrous business difficulties and had to liquidate, all of the creditors would be protected. The owners' equity is more than sufficient for meeting all debts.

Sometimes, however, a fairly high debt-to-owners'-equity-ratio may be not only acceptable but desirable. Borrowing funds gives companies or individuals **leverage**, the ability to make a purchase they otherwise could not afford. You have probably read about a "leveraged buyout" (LBO) in the newspapers. In these instances, firms have borrowed (taken on debt) in order to buy out another company. When the purchased company allows the buying company to earn profits that exceed the cost of the borrowed funds, leveraging makes sound financial sense, even if it raises the debt-to-owners'-equity ratio. Unfortunately, many LBOs have gotten into financial trouble when actual profits fell short of anticipated levels or interest payments ballooned due to rising rates.

leverage

Using borrowed funds to make purchases, thus increasing the user's purchasing power, potential rate of return, and risk of loss.

Profitability Ratios

Although it is important for investors to know that a company is solvent in both the long and short term, safety or risk alone is not an adequate criterion for investment decisions. To decide which company's stock to buy, investors also need to have some measure of what returns they can expect. Return on sales, return on investment, and earnings per share are three commonly used **profitability ratios**.

Return on Sales.   Also called the **net profit margin**, **return on sales** is calculated as net income divided by sales. It indicates the percentage of income

profitability ratios

Measures of a firm's overall financial performance in terms of its likely profits; used by investors to assess their probable returns.

return on sales (net profit margin)

A form of profitability ratio calculated as net income divided by net sales.

that is profit to the company. There is no single right net profit margin. The figure for any one company must be compared to figures for other firms in the industry to determine how well a business is doing. Typical returns on sales ratios are 1 percent for meat-packing plants, 3 percent for wholesalers such as Perfect Posters, and 6 percent for machinery manufacturers.

In the case of Perfect Posters, return on sales for 1994 was

$$\frac{\text{Net income}}{\text{Sales}} = \frac{\$12\ 585}{\$256\ 425} = .049 = 4.9\%$$

That is, the business realized a 4.9 cent profit on each dollar of sales. Thus, if someone shoplifted a $15.00 item from the warehouse, $306 in sales would be required ($15.00/.049) to make up the loss.

Return on Investment.   Owners are interested in how much net income the business earns for each dollar invested by the owners. **Return on investment** (sometimes called **return on equity**) gives them the desired measure by dividing net income by total owners' equity.

For Perfect Posters, the ratio in 1994 was

return on investment (return on equity)

A form of profitability ratio calculated as net income divided by total owners' equity.

$$\frac{\text{Net income}}{\text{Total owners' equity}} = \frac{\$12\ 585}{\$111\ 155} = 11.3\%$$

Is this figure good or bad? There is no set answer. If the firm's ratio for 1994 is higher than for previous years, then owners and potential investors should be encouraged. But if 11.3 percent is lower than the ratios of other companies in the same industry, they should be concerned.

Earnings per Share.   This ratio is one of the most quoted financial statistics. Defined as net income divided by the number of shares of common stock outstanding, **earnings per share** determines how large a dividend a company can pay its shareholders. It also indicates how much the company can reinvest in itself instead of paying dividends—that is, how much it can grow. Investors watch this ratio and use it to decide whether to buy or sell the company's stock. Often, a company's stock will lose market value when its latest financial statements report a decline in earnings per share.

earnings per share

A form of profitability ratio calculated as net income divided by the number of common shares outstanding.

If we assume that Perfect Posters has only one class of stock, we can calculate its earnings per share as

$$\frac{\text{Net income}}{\substack{\text{Number of common}\\ \text{shares outstanding}}} = \frac{\$12\ 585}{8000} = \$1.57 \text{ per share}$$

Earnings per share is easy to calculate in the abstract. But in real life the computation is quite complex, in part because of the many classes of stock available.

Activity Ratios

Obviously, the efficiency with which a firm uses resources is linked to profitability. As a potential investor, then, you want to know which company "gets more mileage" from its resources. **Activity ratios** measure this efficiency. For example, say that two firms use the same amount of resources or assets. If Firm A generates greater profits or sales, it is more efficient and thus has a better activity ratio.

activity ratios

Measures of how efficiently a firm uses its resources; used by investors to assess their probable returns.

By the same token, if a firm needs more resources to make products comparable to its competitors', it has a worse activity ratio. In June 1994, for instance, the consulting firm of Harbour & Associates Inc. released a study showing that in order to match Ford's efficiency, General Motors would have to cut 20 000 workers. According to the report, production inefficiency at its plants costs GM $2.2 billion annually in excess labor costs. On the upside, however, GM is making substantial progress. A similar report issued two years earlier had concluded that GM needed to cut 70 000 workers because excess labor costs were $4 billion.[7]

Inventory Turnover Ratio. Perhaps the most widely used typical activity ratio is the **inventory turnover ratio**. This ratio measures the average number of times inventory is sold and restocked during the year. It is expressed as the cost of goods sold divided by the average inventory. A high ratio means efficient operations—a smaller amount of investment is tied up in inventory. The company's funds can then be put to work elsewhere, earning greater returns.

Inventory turnover rates must be compared with earlier years and with industry averages. An inventory turnover rate of 5 might be excellent for an auto-supply store, but it would be disastrous for a supermarket, where a ratio of about 15 is common.

Perfect Posters's inventory turnover ratio for 1994 was

$$\frac{\text{Cost of goods sold}}{\text{Average inventory*}} = \frac{\$104\ 765}{(\$21\ 250 + \$22\ 380)/2} = 4.8 \text{ times}$$

Average Inventory is the average of inventory value on January 1, 1994, and December 31, 1994.

The firm's new merchandise replaces old merchandise every 76 days (365 days/4.8). This ratio of 4.8 is below the average of 7 for comparable wholesaling operations, indicating that the business is slightly inefficient. So, although Perfect Posters is highly profitable and low risk, it is not truly a "perfect" company!

inventory turnover ratio
An activity ratio that measures the average number of times inventory is sold and restocked during the year.

International Accounting

More and more companies are buying and selling goods and services in other countries. Accounting for foreign transactions is therefore increasing in importance. One of the key activities in international accounting is translating the values of the currencies of different countries.

The value of any country's currency is subject to occasional change. Political and economic conditions, for instance, affect the stability of a nation's currency and its value relative to the currencies of other countries. The Swiss franc, for example, has a long history of stability, while the Brazilian real has a history of instability.

Any currency's value is determined by market forces—what buyers and sellers are willing to pay for it. The resulting values are called *foreign-currency exchange rates*. These rates can be very volatile. The Mexican peso, for example, began a disastrous plunge in December 1994. The peso is thus regarded as a *weak currency*. On the other hand, the Japanese yen is a *strong currency* because its value is rising in comparison to the Canadian dollar. As exchange rate changes occur, they must be considered by accountants for their firm's international transactions.

International Purchases

Accounting for international transactions involves two steps: (1) translating from one currency to another and (2) reflecting gains or losses due to exchange-rate changes. Let's explain these two steps by using an illustration. Suppose that on March 7, an American firm called Village Wine and Cheese

Shops imports Bordeaux wine from Pierre Bourgeois in France. The price is 32 000 francs, and the exchange rate on March 7 is $0.18 per French franc.

The first step for Village's accountant is to translate the price of the transaction into U.S. dollars:

$$\text{price in French francs} = 32\ 000\ \text{Fr}$$
$$\text{price in U.S. dollars} = (32\ 000\ \text{Fr}) \times (\$0.18) = \$5760$$

Next, the transaction must be recorded in Village's books. Assume that Village purchases on credit and that Bourgeois requires payment within 30 days. Village's accounting records will then appear as follows:

		Debit	Credit
March 7	Inventory	5760	
	Accounts payable		5760

Then, on April 1 when Village pays Bourgeois, the payment entry will appear this way:

		Debit	Credit
April 1	Accounts payable	5760	
	Cash		5760

Thus far, our bookkeeping has been straightforward because Village's accountants have assumed a constant exchange rate of $0.18 per franc. The above entries, then, are correct *if the exchange rate for francs on April 1 is the same as it was on March 7* ($0.18 per franc). However, because exchange rates rise and fall daily, some change will no doubt occur during the month in question.

Let's say, for example, that on April 1 the value of the French franc has fallen below $0.18. Village Cheese, therefore, will enjoy a *foreign-currency transaction gain*: It can pay its debt with fewer dollars. Suppose that the franc has fallen to $0.17 by the time Village pays Bouregois on April 1. The payment entry, therefore, will appear as follows:

		Debit	Credit
April 1	Accounts payable	5760	
	Cash (32 000 × $0.17).......		5440
	Foreign-currency transaction gain........		320

In other words, when the value of the franc decreased, Village needed only $5440 to pay the original account payable of $5760. Of course, had the franc *increased* to a value above $0.18, Village would have paid more than the original $5760. It would have suffered a *foreign-currency transaction loss*.

International Sales

Sales made to customers in other countries can also be recorded to reflect both translations from foreign currency and changes in currency exchange rates. Suppose, for instance, that on June 1, Motorola sells some cellular phones on credit to the Japanese distributor Hirotsu. The total price of the phones is 50 million yen, and the exchange rate is $0.01 per yen. Motorola's transaction is thus recorded as follows:

	Debit	Credit
April 1 Accounts receivable		
(50 000 000 × $0.01)	500 000	
Sales revenue		500 000

Let's suppose that when Hirotsu pays Motorola—say, on June 30—the exchange rate has fallen to $0.0095 per yen. Motorola, therefore will receive *fewer* dollars than were recorded in its June 1 accounts-receivable entry. It will suffer the foreign-currency transaction loss shown in the following entry:

	Debit	Credit
June 30 Cash (50 000 000 × $0.0095) ...	475 000	
Foreign-currency		
transaction loss	25 000	
Accounts receivable		500 000

At the end of an accounting period, all exchange rate gains and losses are combined to reveal a net gain or loss. This net gain or loss can then be shown on the income statement as "other revenue and expense."

Summary of Key Points

Accounting is a comprehensive information system for collecting, analyzing, and communicating financial information. The firm's financial accounting system identifies, measures, records, and retains financial information for external users like consumer groups, unions, shareholders, and government agencies. The managerial accounting system provides information for the firm's managers and employees.

Chartered accountants are licensed professionals who provide auditing, tax, and management services to other firms and individuals. Private accountants provide diverse specialized services for the firm that employs them.

The use of journals and double-entry accounting ledgers provides for standardized, accurate record-keeping. Journals form a chronological log of transactions, while ledgers allow managers to assess the firm's current state of finances. Using double-entry accounting in ledgers provides a system of checks and balances against errors.

The accuracy of information in a firm's journals and ledgers affects the accuracy of its financial statements—balance sheet, income statement, and statement of cash flows. A balance sheet summarizes a company's assets, liabilities, and owners' equity at a given time. An income statement details a company's revenues and expenses for a given period and identifies any profit or loss. A statement of cash flows reports cash receipts and payments from operating, investing, and financing activities.

To ensure the overall efficient use of resources, accountants and other managers develop budgets. A budget shows where funds will be obtained (the sources) and where they will be spent (the uses).

Using data from the financial statements, ratios can help creditors, investors, and managers assess a firm's finances. The current ratio, the quick ratio, and the debt-to-owners'-equity ratio all measure solvency—the firm's ability to pay its debts in the short and long run. Return on sales, return on investment, and earnings per share all measure profitability. Inventory turnover ratios show how efficiently funds are being used for inventories.

Because more and more firms are selling internationally, accounting for international transactions is becoming increasingly important. Accounting for international transactions—whether buying or selling goods—requires accountants to translate from one currency to another and to report gains or losses due to exchange rates.

CONCLUDING CASE 17-1

Who Should Have the Right to Audit

Canada has three major accounting groups—Chartered Accountants (CAs), Certified General Accountants (CGAs), and Certified Management Accountants (CMAs). CAs are the only group allowed to audit public companies in most provinces (British Columbia and Saskatchewan allow all three groups to conduct audits). The Toronto Stock Exchange will accept only financial statements audited by CAs.

For some years, CGAs and CMAs have argued that CAs have an unfair monopoly on auditing public companies. They claim that the policy inhibits their ability to earn a livelihood. In June, 1992, the Alberta Securities Commission began reviewing its policy that limits the auditing field to CAs. And the CA monopoly is also under attack in Prince Edward Island.

Lawyers for the CMAs and the CGAs argue that the public interest is not served by restricting auditing rights to CAs. But the Alberta Securities Commission is not eager to see additional accounting groups given the right to conduct audits. It is concerned that too much varia-

tion in practical experience and training standards exists and that this will create problems. The CMA program, for example, requires students to complete one auditing course, while the CGA program requires three. The CA program requires 1250 hours of audit and review work. CMAs and CGAs argue that their standards are identical to those in the CA program.

CASE QUESTIONS
1. Why might the situation have developed that, in most provinces, only CAs can audit public companies?
2. The CGAs and the CMAs claim that their programs are identical to the CA program. How would you go about determining whether their claim is valid?
3. In recent years, CA firms have been sued in several cases for not warning a firm or its investors that the firm was in trouble (see, for example, Case 17-2). How could the CGAs and CMAs use these cases to argue that they should be allowed to audit public companies? ◆

Who's to Blame Here?

When it went bankrupt in 1991, Standard Trustco Ltd. was Canada's eighth largest trust company. Several members of the board of directors of Standard Trustco are now suing the CA firm of Peat Marwick Thorne (the firm's auditors), accusing the accountants of negligence and of failing to disclose that the firm was insolvent two years before it actually collapsed. Chairperson Helen Roman-Barber maintains that Standard's board would have taken immediate action had the auditing firm warned the directors that financial problems existed. She says that a review of corporate financial statements has convinced the directors that Peat Marwick Thorne failed to convey appropriate warnings to the directors. A spokesperson for Peat Marwick says the firm was blameless; he is confident the auditing firm will be vindicated.

The directors launched their lawsuit against Peat Marwick one day after the Ontario Securities Commission (OSC) concluded a probe of Standard Trustco. The OSC accused Mrs. Roman-Barber and several other directors of issuing a misleading news release in 1990 which failed to state that federal regulators had concerns about the firm. The release painted a rosy picture of the firm and claimed it was profitable. Later, an audited statement showing extremely large losses replaced this unaudited one.

At the hearings, the OSC said the directors either knew of the firm's problems or they were willfully blind to them. It noted that Standard had made loans on construction projects for condominiums, and that the directors knew these were riskier than loans on single-family houses. The OSC also pointed out that Michael Mackenzie, the Superintendent of Financial Institutions, had conveyed serious reservations about some of the firm's accounting policies. He believed the company would experience a cash shortfall, and that the firm was understating loan losses. The board of Standard did nothing about these concerns.

But Standard's directors place the blame for their inaction on Peat Marwick. They claim that the auditor failed to tell the company to set aside adequate amounts to cover loan losses on its deteriorating real estate loans. The directors argue that, if Peat Marwick had taken this action, it would have been obvious in 1988 that Standard Trustco was insolvent.

CASE QUESTIONS
1. What kind of evidence is needed to show that a CA firm has been negligent? Do you think there is such evidence in this case?
2. What kind of evidence is needed to show that members of a firm's board of directors have been negligent? Do you think there is such evidence in this case? ◆

Key Terms

accounting
bookkeeping
accounting system
controller
financial accounting
   system
managerial accounting
chartered accountant (CA)
audit
generally accepted
   accounting pri··ciples
   (GAAP)
journal
ledger
asset

liability
owners' equity
double-entry accounting
   system
T-account
debit
credit
financial statement
balance sheet
current assets
liquidity
accounts receivable
fixed assets
depreciation
intangible assets

current liabilities
accounts payable
long-term liabilities
retained earnings
income (profit-and-loss)
   statement
revenues
cost of goods sold
gross profit (gross margin)
operating expenses
net income (net profit or
   net earnings)
statement of cash flows
budget
key ratio

liquidity ratios
current ratio
quick ratio (acid-test ratio)
debt ratios
debt-to-owners'-equity
   ratio
leverage
profitability ratios
return on sales (net
   profit margin)
return on investment
   (return on equity)
earnings per share
activity ratios
inventory turnover ratio

Study Questions and Exercises

Review Questions

1. Identify the three types of services that CAs perform.
2. How does the double-entry system reduce the chances of mistakes or fraud in accounting?
3. What are the three basic financial statements and what major types of information does each contain?
4. Identify the four major classifications of financial statement ratios and give an example of one ratio in each category.
5. In what ways does an electronic spreadsheet simplify the budgeting process?

Analysis Questions

6. Suppose Inflatables Inc., makers of air mattresses for swimming pools, has the following transactions one week:
   ■ Sale of three deluxe mattresses to Al Wett (paid cash—$75) on 7/16
   ■ Received cheque from Ima Flote in payment for mattresses bought on credit ($90) on 7/13
   ■ Received new shipment of 200 mattresses from Airheads Mfg. (total cost $2000) on 7/17
   Construct a journal for Inflatables Inc.
7. If you were planning to invest in a company, which of the three types of financial statements would you most want to see? Why?

8. Dasar Company reports the following data in its September 30, 1995, financial statements:
   ■ Gross sales $225 000
   ■ Current assets   40 000
   ■ Long-term assets   100 000
   ■ Current liabilities   16 000
   ■ Long-term liabilities   44 000
   ■ Owners' equity   80 000
   ■ Net income   7 200
   a. Compute the current ratio.
   b. Compute the debt-to-equity ratio.
   c. Compute the return on sales.
   d. Compute the return on owners' equity.

Application Exercises

9. Interview an accountant at a local manufacturing firm. Trace the process by which budgets are developed in that company. How does the firm use budgets? How does budgeting help its managers plan business activities? How does budgeting help them control business activities? Give examples.
10. Interview the manager of a local retail or wholesale business about taking inventory. What is the firm's primary purpose in taking inventory? How often is it done?

Building Your Business Skills

Goal

To encourage students to understand the purpose of financial statements and to understand the functions of each of the three broad categories of financial statements.

Method

At the library, look through the financial statements of a local company or of some well-known company. For each category listed below, list the company's main item and its dollar amount from its financial statements. From which financial statement did you obtain each item?

Follow-Up Questions

1. Which financial statement provides the most complete picture of the company's finances?
2. How are the various financial ratios—solvency, profitability, and activity ratios—used in the financial statements that you examined?

| | Financial Statement | | |
Category	Item	Dollar Amount	From which Financial Statement
Current assets			
Fixed assets			
Intangible assets			
Revenues			
Expenses			
Current liabilities			
Long-term liabilities			
Owners' equity			

18

Understanding Money and Banking

LEARNING OBJECTIVES

After studying this chapter, you will be able to

- Identify the characteristics that money must possess and the different forms of money in the nation's money supply.
- Discuss the different kinds of financial institutions that make up the Canadian financial system and the services they offer.
- Explain how banks create money and how they are regulated as a result.
- Describe the Bank of Canada's mission and the tools it uses to accomplish its mission.
- Explain how nonbank financial intermediaries complement the chartered banking system in Canada.

CHAPTER OUTLINE

OPENING CASE

A Start-Up Star

Ed Rygiel is rewriting the book on how to invest in start-up companies. Venture capitalists—those people who put money into risky new ventures in return for a piece of the action—have a rule of thumb which says that 8 out of 10 investments don't pan out. But Rygiel has made 20 start-up investments, and only two have not lived up to expectations. What is he doing right?

First, some background. Ed Rygiel is senior vice-president of corporate development at MDS Health Group Ltd., a $450 million conglomerate of medical laboratories and other health-related companies. He is also CEO of MDS Health Ventures Inc., the venture capital arm of MDS. Health Ventures makes investments in fledgling companies making all sorts of new products, ranging from new drugs for healing tissue damage to a system of out-patient care for pregnant mothers.

Health Ventures Inc. is not like most venture capital firms. While MDS Health Group owns the biggest piece, Health Ventures also has several other owners, including the Alberta Government Treasury, the Manitoba Teachers Federation, the Molson Cos. Ltd., and Ontario Hydro. Its first and foremost aim is to satisfy its investors by getting a good return on investment for them. The projects that Health Ventures Inc. gets involved in may not be of immediate use to MDS Health Group, but the parent company accepts that. (This approach was not acceptable at Northern Telecom and BCE, both of which folded their venture capital groups in frustration.)

Health Ventures also violates several other traditional venture capital axioms. First, it is not very diversified in its investments, but gets involved only in new, health-care related companies. Second, it buys larger-than-usual stakes in these new companies. Third, it does not charge the usual 2 percent to 2.5 percent investment fee; instead, it takes extra equity up-front. Finally, it does not accept the idea that an experienced manager must reside in the new company. While it doesn't deny the importance of good management, it recognizes that a new company may be headed by a person with a good idea, rather than lots of management talent. With MDSs influence in the health care business, it can usually find someone with the required management expertise to give the new company a guiding hand.

Health Venture's stake in Disys Corp., a manufacturer of smoke detectors, is typical of its approach to venture capital investing. Health Ventures took a 55 percent piece in 1991; now Disys makes radio-frequency indentification

tags for hospitals and nursing homes that track medical equipment, patients, visitors, and even babies. CEO Steven Chepa says that Health Ventures enabled his company to expand its horizons to think in terms of medical applications of the technology the company knew about.

Health Venture's track record in four different companies is shown in the table below. For the longer-term, Health Ventures wants to invest in areas that will help the overburdened Canadian health care system. Rygiel lists solutions to problems like low back pain, drug side-effects, and chronic fatigue as promising areas for investment. Given that pharmaceuticals, medicines, and health care services have grown 35 percent over the last decade, and given that they now account for 10 percent of Canada's GNP, the industry looks promising for future venture capital investing. But there is one downside: it can take many years to determine whether an investment will work out. Because new drugs and technologies will be used on humans, extensive testing (up to seven years) may be required. At the end of this time, there is no guarantee of success. But if Health Venture's early successes continue, the company will have found a way around the usual problems facing venture capital firms.

Company	Amount Invested	Current Value
Disys Corp.	$2.4 million	$ 9.4 million
ISG Technologies	$3.3 million	$16.8 million
Access Health Mktg.	$1.4 million	$ 3.2 million
Hemosol	$2.5 million	$ 8.1 million

◆

Business firms rely on all sorts of financial institutions for money. A venture capital company like MDS Health Ventures is just one of the many sources of money for business firms. In this chapter, we describe what money is, the different definitions of the money supply, and why money is essential for every business. We also describe the major financial institutions in Canada, and the way they facilitate business activity. The recent failures of firms such as Bargain Harold's, Olympia & York, Royal Trustco, and Canadian Commercial Bank underscore the importance of stability in Canada's economic system.

Money

When someone asks you how much money you have, what do you say? Do you count the bills and coins in your pockets? Do you mention the funds in your chequing and savings accounts? What about stocks, bonds, your car? Taken together, the value of everything you own is your personal *wealth*. Not all of it, however, is *money*. In this section, we will consider what money is and what it does.

What Is Money?

The bills and coins you carry every day are money. So are U.S. dollars, British pound notes, French francs, and Japanese yen. Modern money often takes the form of printed paper or stamped metal issued by a government. But over the centuries, items as diverse as stone wheels, salt, wool, livestock, shells, and spices have been used as money. **Money** is any object generally accepted by people as payment for goods and services.

     Thousands of years ago, people began to accept certain agreed-upon objects in exchange for goods or services. As early as 1100 B.C., the Chinese were using metal money that represented the objects they were exchanging (for example, bronze spades and knives). Coins probably came into use sometime around 600 B.C. and paper money around 1200 A.D.

money
Any object generally accepted by people as payment for goods and services.

Desirable Characteristics of Money

Any object can serve as money if it is portable, divisible, durable, and stable.[1] To understand why these qualities are important, imagine using as money something valuable that lacks them—a 35 kilogram salmon, for example.

Throughout the ages, humans have used many monetary devices. Two interesting ones that were in common circulation are the Iroquois wampum belt (early nineteenth century) from eastern North America and this ancient Greek coin (circa 375 B.C.).

Portability of Money.   If you wanted to use the salmon to buy goods and services, you would have to lug a 35 kilogram fish from shop to shop. Modern currency, by contrast, is lightweight and easy to handle.

Divisibility of Money.   Suppose you wanted to buy a hat, a book, and some milk from three different stores—all using the salmon as money. How would you divide the fish? First, out comes a cleaver at each store. Then, you would have to determine whether a kilogram of its head is worth as much as a kilogram from the middle. Modern currency is easily divisible into smaller parts with fixed value for each unit. In Canada, for example, a dollar can be exchanged for 4 quarters, 10 dimes, 20 nickels, 100 pennies, or any combination of these coins. It is easy to match units of money with the value of all goods.

Durability of Money.   Fish seriously fails the durability test. Each day, whether or not you "spend" it, the salmon will be losing value (and gaining scents). Modern currency, on the other hand, does not spoil, it does not die, and, if it wears out, it can be replaced with new coins and paper money.

Stability of Money.   Fish are not stable enough to serve as money. If salmon were in short supply, you might be able to make quite a deal for yourself. But in the middle of a salmon run, the market would be flooded with fish. Since sellers would have many opportunities to exchange their wares for salmon, they would soon have enough fish and refuse to trade for salmon. While the value of the paper money we use today has fluctuated over the years, it is considerably more stable than salmon.

The Functions of Money

Imagine a successful fisherman who needs a new sail for his boat. In a _barter economy_—one in which goods are exchanged directly for one another—he would have to find someone who not only needs fish but who is willing to exchange a sail for it. If no sailmaker wants fish, the fisherman must find someone else—say, a shoemaker—who wants fish and will trade for it. Then the fisherman must hope that the sailmaker will trade for his new shoes. Clearly, barter is quite inefficient in comparison to money. In a money economy, the fisherman would sell his catch, receive money, and exchange the money for such goods as a new sail.

In broad terms, money serves three functions:

- _Medium of exchange_. Like the fisherman "trading" money for a new sail, we use money as a way of buying and selling things. Without money, we would be bogged down in a system of barter.
- _Store of value_. Pity the fisherman who catches a fish on Monday and wants to buy a few bars of candy on, say, the following Saturday. By then, the fish would have spoiled and be of no value. In the form of _currency_, however, money can be used for future purchases and so "stores" value.
- _Unit of account_. Finally, money lets us measure the _relative_ values of goods and services. It acts as a unit of account because all products can be valued and accounted for in terms of money. For example, the concepts of "$1000 worth of clothes" or "$500 in labor costs" have universal meaning because everyone deals with money every day.

The Money Supply: M-1

For money to serve as a medium of exchange, a store of value, or a unit of account, buyers and sellers must agree on its value. The value of money, in turn, depends in part on its supply, that is, how much money is in circulation. When the money supply is high, the value of money drops. When the money supply is low, the value of money increases.

Unfortunately, it is not easy to measure the supply of money, nor is there complete agreement on exactly how it should be measured. The "narrow" definition of the money supply is called **M-1**. **M-1** counts only the most liquid forms of money: currency and demand deposits (chequing accounts) in banks.

Currency.   **Currency** is paper money and coins issued by the Canadian government. It is widely used to pay small bills. Canadian currency states clearly: "This note is legal tender." Legal tender is money the law requires a creditor to accept in payment of a debt.

Demand Deposits.   The majority of Canadian households have chequing accounts against which millions of cheques are written each year. A **cheque** is an order instructing the bank to pay a given sum to a specified person or firm. Although not all sellers accept cheques in payment for goods and services, many do. Cheques enable buyers to make large purchases without having to carry large amounts of cash. Sellers gain a measure of safety because the cheques they receive are valuable only to them and can later be exchanged for cash. Money in chequing accounts, known as **demand deposits**, is counted in M-1 because such funds may be withdrawn at any time without notice.

The Money Supply: M-2

M-2 includes everything in M-1 plus items that cannot be spent directly but that are easily converted to spendable forms: *time deposits, money market mutual funds*, and *savings deposits*. M-2 accounts for nearly all the nation's money supply. It thus measures the store of monetary value that is available for financial transactions. As this overall level of money increases, more is available for consumer purchases and business investment. When the supply is tightened, less money is available; financial transactions, spending, and business activity thus slow down.

Time Deposits.   Unlike demand deposits, **time deposits** require prior notice of withdrawal and cannot be transferred by cheque. On the other hand, time deposits pay higher interest rates. Thus the supply of money in time deposits—such as *certificates of deposit (CDs)* and *savings certificates*—grew rapidly in the 1970s and 1980s as interest rates rose to levels never before seen in Canada.

Money Market Mutual Funds.   **Money market mutual funds** are operated by investment companies that bring together pools of assets from many investors. The fund buys a collection of short-term, low-risk financial securities. Ownership of and profits (or losses) from the sale of these securities are shared among the fund's investors.

These funds attracted many investors in the 1980s because of high pay-offs and because they often allow investors to write checks against their shares. Mutual funds pay higher returns than most individuals can get on their own because:

1. Funds can buy into higher-paying securities that require larger investments than most individuals can afford.
2. They are managed by professionals who monitor changing investment opportunities.

Savings Deposits.   In the wake of new, more attractive investments, traditional savings deposits, such as passbook savings accounts, have declined in popularity.

M-1
Only the most liquid forms of money (currency and demand deposits).

currency
Paper money and coins issued by the government.

cheque
An order instructing the bank to pay a given sum to a specified person or firm.

demand deposit
Money in chequing accounts; counted as M-1 because such funds may be withdrawn at any time without notice.

M-2
Everything in M-1 plus savings deposits, time deposits, and money market mutual funds.

time deposit
A deposit that requires prior notice to make a withdrawal; cannot be transferred to others by cheque.

money market mutual funds
Funds operated by investment companies that bring together pools of assets from many investors.

Plastic Money

Although not included in M-1 or M-2, credit—especially credit cards—has become a major factor in the purchase of consumer goods in Canada. The use of MasterCard, Visa, American Express, Discover, and credit cards issued by individual businesses has become so widespread that many people refer to credit cards as "plastic money." Nevertheless, credit cards do not qualify as money. Rather, they are a *money substitute*; they serve as a temporary medium of exchange but are not a store of value. The box "To Catch a Credit Card Thief" describes an interesting development in credit card fraud detection.

Credit cards are big business for two reasons. First, they are quite convenient—and about to become both more convenient and more reliable:

- Visa, for instance, has already modified the software used at its processing centers and can now attach a special "transaction identifier" to every transaction. This digital code stays with the transaction from the time the consumer uses the card until the time everyone in the system has been paid. Visa says that the number of erroneous charges has already been greatly reduced.
- MasterCard is experimenting with real-time auditing of charges filed by merchants: Every transaction will be completed as soon as it is made rather than, as now, at the end of the day with 20 million others. Merchants will be paid more quickly, and chances of both error and fraud will be reduced significantly.[2]

The Canadian Business Scene

TO CATCH A CREDIT-CARD THIEF

Imagine a computer technology that could find relationships among hundreds of unrelated variables and, in the process, recognize patterns, make associations, generalize about new problems, and even learn from the experience. This technology, which roughly mimics the activity of the human brain, is currently operational in the form of *neural networks*. Not surprisingly, companies that have incorporated these networks into their computer systems are already experiencing significant productivity gains.

Neural network chips will soon be part of all computers. Over the next five years, neural network chips not only will be integrated into every PC but will also control the ordinary tasks of everyday life, including microwave cookery (the oven will know how long to cook a chicken without being told) and balancing the shifting load in a washing machine.

Meanwhile, banks and other credit-card issuers are already using neural networks to detect credit-card fraud. Before the development of neural networks, companies relied on specialized computer programs to detect sudden, obvious changes in cardholders' spending patterns.

For example, a cardholder who normally purchased no more than $500 at a time would be notified if thousands of dollars in jewelry and furs were suddenly charged to the account. The relatively crude nature of these early systems often created more problems than solutions, however. Computers often flagged innocent cardholders as well as those who had lost their cards. Consumers who may have altered their spending habits even slightly were notified, a practice that annoyed many and wasted the time and resources of fraud detectors.

Faced with an inefficient system, one bank began using a neural network. Its old system had alerted it to as many as 1000 potential frauds each day (many of which were false alarms), but the neural network flagged only about 100—each of which was likely to signal an actual case of fraud. Using the neural network, bank personnel can now focus on fewer cases and complete investigations within hours rather than days. In one case, the bank notified a customer that her credit card has been stolen only hours after the theft had taken place and before she realized that it was gone.

Second, credit cards are extremely profitable for issuing companies. Profits derive from two sources:

1. Some cards charge annual fees to holders. All charge interest on unpaid balances. Depending on the issuer, cardholders pay interest rates ranging from 11 to 20 percent.
2. Merchants who accept credit cards pay fees to card issuers. Depending on the merchant's agreement with the issuer, 2 to 5 percent of total credit-sales dollars goes to card issuers.

Annually, more than 25 million cards are used in Canada, 28 million in the United Kingdom, and over 1 billion in the U.S. The accompanying problems are international in scope. The number of cards issued in Japan, for instance, doubled (to 166 million) from 1985 to 1990—and so did the number of delinquencies. Many younger Japanese have incurred large debts by using credit cards to purchase high-ticket items like travel packages and automobiles. In South Korea, because heavy spending by young people is contributing to higher inflation, the Finance Minister has actually curbed the issuance of credit cards: No more cards can be issued to college students, to people younger than 20, or to workers holding jobs less than one year.[3]

International Currency Valuation

Each nation tries to influence its currency exchange rates for economic advantage in international trade. The subsequent country-to-country transactions result in an *international payments process* that moves money among buyers and sellers on different continents.

The value of a given currency—say, the Canadian dollar—reflects the overall supply and demand for Canadian dollars both at home and abroad. This value, of course, changes with economic conditions. Worldwide, therefore, firms will watch those trends. What is the current exchange rate between their own currencies and our Canadian dollar? Decisions about whether or not to do business in Canada will be affected by more or less favorable exchange rates. How do firms determine favorable exchange rates?

The Law of One Price. When a country's currency becomes *overvalued*, its exchange rate is higher than warranted by its economic conditions. Its high costs make it less competitive: Because its products are too expensive to make and buy, fewer are purchased by other countries. The likely result is a *trade deficit*. In contrast, an *undervalued* currency means low costs and low prices. It attracts purchases by other countries, usually leading to a *trade surplus*.

How do we know if a currency is overvalued or undervalued? One method involves a simple concept called the **law of one price**: the principle that identical products should sell for the same price in all countries. In other words, if the different prices of a Rolex watch in different countries were converted into a common currency, the common-denominator price should be the same everywhere.

law of one price
The principle that identical products should sell for the same price in all countries.

But what if prices are not equal? In theory, the pursuit of profits should equalize them: Sellers in high-priced countries will have to reduce prices if they are to compete successfully and make profits. As prices adjust, so, too, should the exchange rates between different currencies until the Rolex can be purchased for the same price everywhere.

A simple example that illustrates over- and undervalued currencies is the "Big MacCurrencies," an index published in the British magazine *The Economist*. The "identical product" here is always McDonald's Big Mac, which is made locally in 68 countries. The first two columns in Table 18.1 list several countries and Big Mac prices in terms of local currencies. Each country's price is then converted into U.S. dollars (based on recent exchange rates). As you can see, while the Swiss price (SFr5.70) is most expensive, the Chinese yuan is the cheapest.

TABLE 18.1   The "Big Mac" Currency Index

Country	Big Mac Prices in Local Currency	Big Mac Prices in Equivalent U.S. Dollars	Local Currency Overvaluation (+) or Undervaluation (–)
United States	**$2.30**	**$2.30**	
Switzerland	5.70 francs	3.96	+72%
Denmark	25.75 krone	3.85	+67
Argentina	3.60 pesos	3.60	+57
Belgium	109 francs	3.10	+35
S. Korea	2300 won	2.84	+24
Greece	620 drachma	2.47	+8
Taiwan	$62 Taiwanese	2.35	+2
Chile	948 pesos	2.28	–1
Canada	**$2.86 Canadian**	**2.06**	**–10**
Australia	$2.45 Australia	1.72	–25
Poland	31000 zloty	1.40	–40
China	9.00 yuan	1.03	–55

According to the Big Mac index, then, the Swiss franc is the most overvalued currency (against the U.S. dollar), while the Chinese yuan is the most undervalued. In theory, this means that you could buy Big Macs in China (using yuan) and resell them in Switzerland (for Swiss francs) at a handsome profit. In China, therefore, the demand for burgers would increase, driving the price up toward the higher prices in the other countries. In other words, the law of one price would set in. The index also indicates that the exchange rates of Greece, Taiwan, Chile, and Canada are barely overvalued or undervalued against the U.S. dollar.[4]

Government Influences on Exchange Rates.   What happens—in reality—when a currency becomes overvalued or undervalued? A nation's economic authorities may take action to correct its balance-of-payments conditions. Typically, they will *devalue* or *revalue* the nation's currency, as Mexico did in 1994. The purpose of *devaluing* is to cause a decrease in the home country's exchange value. It will then be less expensive for other countries to buy the home country's products. As more of its products are purchased, the home country's payment deficit goes down. The purpose of revaluation is the reverse: to increase the exchange value and reduce the home country's payment surplus.

The Canadian Financial System

The financial system is central to business firms in Canada. A financial system is made up of organizations and individuals who are sources and users of funds, and/or who help funds flow from sources to users. (See Figure 18.1.) People or organizations with surplus funds will want to earn a return on them. An individual may put his or her money into a savings deposit, buy a bond or a life insurance policy, or invest in the stock market. A business firm may deposit its money in a bank in the short term, buy treasury bills, or buy

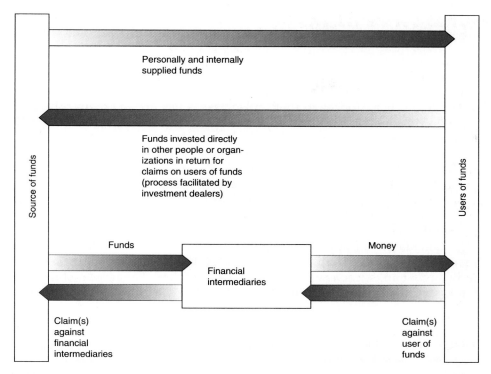

Figure 18.1
Sources of funds, users of funds, financial intermediaries, and investment dealers.

long-term securities. Charitable organizations and governments may also have surplus funds they wish to invest for certain periods of time.

All people and organizations are users of funds. Sometimes they are unable to raise all the funds they require from personal or internal sources. Money must then be raised from other people or institutions that have surplus funds. Individuals borrow money for certain purposes. Business firms raise money to finance projects, as do governments.

Financial institutions facilitate the flow of funds from sources to users. Their services are important both to organizations that have surplus funds to invest and to those that are in a deficit position and must raise funds.

Financial Intermediaries

There are a variety of financial intermediaries in Canada. They vary in size, in importance, in the types of sources they appeal to, in the form of the claim they give to sources of funds, in the users they supply credit to, and in the type of claim they make against the users of funds.

Until recently, the financial community in Canada was divided rather clearly into four distinct legal areas. Often called the "four financial pillars," they were: (1) chartered banks; (2) alternate banks, such as trust companies and *caisses populaires* or credit unions; (3) life insurance companies and other specialized lending and saving intermediaries, such as factors, finance companies, venture capital firms, mutual funds, and pension funds; and (4) investment dealers. Although we will discuss the roles of these four financial divisions, the legal barriers between them are gradually coming down. For example, the 1980 *Bank Act* permits banks to engage in factoring and leasing through subsidiaries. This act also permits the alternate banks to create a Schedule B Bank subsidiary. Since 1987 deregulation has also allowed banks to sell commercial paper.

Financial Pillar #1—Chartered Banks

chartered bank

A privately owned, profit-seeking firm that serves individuals, nonbusiness organizations, and businesses as a financial intermediary.

A **chartered bank** is a privately owned, profit-seeking firm that serves individuals, nonbusiness organizations, and businesses as a financial intermediary. Chartered banks offer chequing and savings accounts, make loans, and provide many other services to their customers. They are the main source of short-term loans for business firms. The video case "Bank Battle" on p. 620 describes one entrepreneur's difficulties with a bank loan.

Chartered banks are the largest and most important financial institution in Canada. They offer a unique service. Their liability instruments (the claims against their assets) are generally accepted by the public and by business as money or as legal tender. Initially, these liability instruments took the form of bank notes issued by individual banks. The *Bank Act* amendments of 1944 removed the right to issue bank notes.

Canada has a branch banking system. Unlike the United States, where there are hundreds of banks, each with a few branches, in Canada there are only a few banks, each with hundreds of branches. The largest chartered banks in Canada are shown in Table 18.2.

TABLE 18.2   The Top Ten Banks in Canada, 1994 (ranked by assets)

Bank	Assets (in billions)
1. Royal Bank of Canada	$173.0
2. Canadian Imperial Bank of Commerce	151.0
3. Bank of Montreal	138.1
4. Bank of Nova Scotia	132.9
5. Toronto-Dominion Bank	99.7
6. National Bank of Canada	44.7
7. Hongkong Bank of Canada	16.0
8. Laurentian Bank of Canada	10.4
9. Province of Alberta Treasury Branches	8.1
10. Citibank Canada	4.2

The 1980 *Bank Act* requires Schedule A banks to be Canadian-owned and have no more than 10 percent of voting shares controlled by a single interest. It also permits Schedule B banks, which may be domestically owned banks that do not meet the 10 percent limit or may be foreign-controlled. Schedule B banks are initially limited to one main office and one branch. Since the passing of the act, several foreign banks have set up Schedule B subsidiaries. The act limits foreign-controlled banks to deposits that do not exceed 8 percent of the total domestic assets of all banks in Canada.

The five largest Schedule A banks account for about 90 percent of total bank assets. Some of them also have branches in other countries. There are thousands of branch bank offices in Canada, about one for every 3300 people.

Services Offered by Banks

The banking business today is a highly competitive industry. No longer is it enough for banks to accept deposits and make loans. Most, for example, now offer bank-issued credit cards and safe-deposit boxes. In addition, many offer pension, trust, international, and financial advice, and electronic money transfer.

Pension Services.   Most banks help customers establish savings plans for retirement. Banks serve as financial intermediaries by receiving funds and investing them as directed by customers. They also provide customers with information on investment possibilities.

Trust Services.   Many banks offer **trust services**—the management of funds left "in the bank's trust." In return for a fee, the trust department will perform such tasks as making your monthly bill payments and managing your investment portfolio. Trust departments also manage the estates of deceased persons.

trust services
The management of funds left in the bank's trust.

International Services.   The three main international services offered by banks are *currency exchange, letters of credit,* and *banker's acceptances.* Suppose, for example, that a Canadian company wants to buy a product from a French supplier. For a fee, it can use one or more of three services offered by its bank:

1. It can exchange Canadian dollars for French francs at a Canadian bank and then pay the French supplier in francs.
2. It can pay its bank to issue a **letter of credit**—a promise by the bank to pay the French firm a certain amount if specified conditions are met.
3. It can pay its bank to draw up a **banker's acceptance**, which promises that the bank will pay some specified amount at a future date.

letter of credit
A promise by a bank to pay money to a business firm if certain conditions are met.

banker's acceptance
Promises that the bank will pay a specified amount of money at a future date.

A banker's acceptance requires payment by a particular date; letters of credit are payable only after certain conditions are met. The French supplier, for example, may not be paid until shipping documents prove that the merchandise has been shipped from France.

Financial Advice.   Many banks, both large and small, help their customers manage their money. Depending on the customer's situation, the bank may recommend different investment opportunities. The recommended mix might include guaranteed investment certificates, mutual funds, stocks, and bonds. Today, bank advertisements often stress the role of banks as financial advisers.

Electronic Funds Transfer.   Chartered banks and some other financial institutions now use electronic funds transfer (EFT) to provide many basic financial services. **Electronic funds transfer** combines computer and communication technology to transfer funds or information into, from, within, and among financial institutions. Examples include the following:

electronic funds transfer (EFT)
A combination of computer and communications technology that transfers funds or information into, from, within, and among financial institutions.

- Automated teller machines (ATMs), or 24-hour tellers, are electronic terminals that let you bank at almost any time of day or night. Generally, you insert a special card and enter your own secret identification number to withdraw cash, make deposits, or transfer funds between accounts.
- Pay-by-phone systems let you telephone your financial institution and instruct it to pay certain bills or to transfer funds between accounts merely by pushing the proper buttons on your phone.
- Direct deposits or withdrawals allow you to authorize in advance specific, regular deposits and withdrawals. You can arrange to have pay cheques and social assistance cheques automatically deposited and recurring expenses, such as insurance premiums and utility bills, automatically paid.
- Point-of-sale transfers let you pay for retail purchases with your debit card. A **debit card** is a type of plastic money that immediately reduces the balance in the user's bank account when it is used. For example, if you use a debit card at a grocery store, the clerk simply runs the card through the machine and asks you to punch in a personal identification number on a keypad next to the cash register. The price of the groceries is then deducted electronically from your chequing account, and money moves from your chequing account to the grocery store's account. The box "The Debit Card Comes to Ontario" describes the increasing popularity of the debit card.

debit card
A type of plastic money that immediately on use reduces the balance in the user's bank account and transfers it to the store's account.

The Canadian Business Scene

THE DEBIT CARD COMES TO ONTARIO

In 1992, consumers in Quebec and B.C. were the first to get widespread access to the debit card. Over the next year it was made available in the Prairie Provinces. Finally, in 1994, the debit card was officially launched in Ontario by Interac. Interac's members—banks and trust companies—want to sign up as many retailers as possible to use the debit card because the more transactions there are, the more money the banks make.

A Royal Bank study in the early 1990s found that 90 percent of retail transactions were then in cash, 6 percent were credit cards, and 3 percent were cheques. The bank predicted that the use of debit cards would increase to 100 million transactions per year by 1995. By early 1994, debit cards already accounted for approximately 11 million transactions per month. The latest estimate is that there will be 700 million transactions per year by 1998, a level that will exceed that for credit cards. A lot of the usage will be in places that do not do a large credit card business now—for example, grocery stores.

Once usage reaches 500 million transactions per year, Canadian banks will start making money on the system. They will receive $30-$40 per month rental fees from retailers who will need terminals to hook into the network. They will also receive a fee of about 40 cents for every transaction at every retailer using the system—25 cents paid by the customer and about 15 cents paid by the retailer.

Some big retailers like grocery stores have already signed up to be on the debit card system, but others are still deciding. In Manitoba, the provincially controlled liquor commission was allowed to sign on to Interac, but in Ontario the government was slower to act because of the political sensitivity surrounding decisions about alcoholic beverages.

The Retail Council of Canada is skeptical about all the hype for debit cards because the financial institutions have by far the most to gain from them. The Council feels that the transaction fees are excessive because debit cards will simply displace cheques in most transactions, and will not bring retailers any additional business. The Council notes that this was not the case when credit cards were introduced in the late 1960s. Then, retailers were able to make more sales because customers had gained more purchasing power. The Consumers Association of Canada is more positive, largely because introduction of the debit card will allow customers to shop without having to actually carry large amounts of cash. This reduces the risk of theft.

Automated Teller Machines (ATMs) have revolutionized the way we do our banking. Now we have access to our money almost everywhere we go—shopping malls, grocery stores, even roadside "minibanks."

Figure 18.2
Examples of services provided by many chartered banks and trust companies.

Figure 18.2 summarizes the services that chartered banks offer. Banks are chartered by the federal government and are closely regulated when they provide these services. As the box "Promoting Banking Services" describes, banks have recently begun to promote their services more actively.

Bank Deposits

Chartered banks provide a financial intermediary service by accepting deposits and making loans with this money. Banks make various types of loans to businesses. When applying for a business loan, it is wise for the manager to remember that the banker is interested in making money for the bank through the loan. The banker is also interested in how the loan will be repaid and how it will be secured. A brief written statement accompanied by a cash-flow analysis is a useful approach when applying for a loan.

One type of deposit a customer can make in a bank is a chequable, or demand, deposit. A **chequable deposit** is a chequing account. Customers who deposit coins, paper currency, or other cheques in their chequing accounts can write cheques against the balance in their accounts. Their banks must honor these cheques immediately; this is why chequing accounts are also called demand deposits.

chequable deposit
A chequing account.

The other type of deposit a customer can make in a chartered bank is a term deposit. A **term deposit** is one that remains with the bank for a period of time. Interest is paid to depositors for the use of their funds. There are two types of term deposits. The most popular is the regular passbook savings account. Although banks can require notice before withdrawals can be made, they seldom do. These accounts are intended primarily for small individual savers and nonprofit organizations.

term deposit
Money that remains with the bank for a period of time with interest paid to the depositor.

Another type of term deposit is the guaranteed investment certificate. This deposit is made for a specified period of time ranging from 28 days to several years. These certificates are available to all savers. The interest rate paid on a guaranteed investment certificate is higher than that paid on a regular savings account, but a depositor must give up interest if the certificate is cashed in before its maturity date.

The Canadian Business Scene

PROMOTING BANKING SERVICES

Years ago, banks did virtually no advertising. Apparently their managers held the view that advertising was somehow inconsistent with the image of stability and security that banks wanted to project. During the last couple of decades, banks became more involved in advertising but always with a conservative, tasteful, business-like approach. All this is changing as banks turn away from some of the commercial activities that have occupied their minds for the last decade (for example, loaning money to high-risk developing countries and building major office complexes) and begin to refocus on the consumer.

As the competition for the small consumer's business intensifies, banks are beginning to spend large sums of money on advertising, sales promotion, and market research. Their goal is to increase customer loyalty; they do this through "relationship banking" (emphasizing a renewed commitment to personal service) and by giving incentives to customers who remain with one bank.

At Toronto-Dominion, the emphasis is on customer service. More than 7000 of TD's front-line staff are taking a customer-service workshop designed to sensitize them to customers' feelings.

The Bank of Montreal is combining new television advertisements designed to improve the bank's image with practical innovations at the branch level. For example, mortgagees no longer automatically get a nasty letter when they miss a payment. Instead, a staff member phones and tactfully asks if there is a problem with the payment. The overall goal is to empower branch staff to manage customer relationships better.

Banks are trying to target more precise market segments. The Royal Bank's seniors banking center in Toronto is located next to a senior citizens' home. It features a push-button door opener, sit-down service, and large-print withdrawal slips. Staff at the center make house calls on shut-ins, and generally keep an eye out for their clients, many of whom live alone.

Mass advertising plays a role at many banks as part of their overall strategy of increasing customer loyalty:

- CIBC advertisements show bank personnel talking to customers about how the bank can deliver a better product or service than the competition can.
- National Trust developed commercials that spoof the frustrating situations consumers encounter at an unnamed rival financial institution. The ads stress that National Trust never forgets whose money it is they are working with.
- The Bank of Montreal has developed a series of advertisements that features the slogan "We pay attention."

All of these campaigns are aimed at reducing the "bank-as-bad-guy" image that Canadian banks have. Gregory White, president of Insight Canada Research, says that bank-bashing is the second-most popular sport in Canada after politician-bashing. Consumers feel that banks have done a poor job of listening to their concerns and of caring about their financial problems. White's research shows that 80 percent of Canadians think all banks are alike in the products and services they offer.

Research shows that the main reason Canadians close a bank account is poor service. So banks are responding with the above-noted advertising campaigns, as well as other promotions designed to convince Canadians that things are going to change. Skeptics point out that certain problems remain. For example, banks have not addressed some long-standing, high-profile irritants. They still charge 20 percent interest on credit cards for their supposedly important customers. Some banks are quietly charging up to 21 percent interest on loans under $3000, precisely the kind needed by small consumers. Moreover, there is still tremendous turnover among tellers, which will inhibit attempts to improve service to customers.

Bank Loans

Banks are the major source of short-term loans for business. Although banks make long-term loans to some firms, they prefer to specialize in providing short-term funds to finance inventories and accounts receivable. Many loans made to businesses are secured by inventory under section 83 of the *Bank Act*. Section 86 of the *Bank Act* allows banks to make loans against the security of bills of lading and warehouse receipts. Section 82 allows banks to take as security hydrocarbons in store or under the ground.

A secured loan is backed by collateral such as accounts receivable or a life insurance policy. If the borrower cannot repay the loan, the bank sells the collateral. An unsecured loan is backed only by the borrower's promise to repay it. Only the most creditworthy borrowers can get unsecured loans.

Borrowers pay interest on their loans. Large firms with excellent credit records pay the prime rate of interest. The **prime rate of interest** is the lowest rate charged to borrowers. This rate changes from time to time owing to changes in the demand for and supply of loanable funds as well as to policies of the Bank of Canada. The so-called "Big 6" Canadian banks (Royal Bank, CIBC, Bank of Montreal, Bank of Nova Scotia, Toronto-Dominion, and National Bank of Canada) typically act in concert with respect to the prime rate.

prime rate of interest
The lowest rate charged to borrowers.

Banks as Creators of Money

In the course of their activities, financial institutions provide a special service to the economy—they create money. This is not to say that they mint bills and coins. Rather, by taking in deposits and making loans, they *expand the money supply*.

Suppose you saved $100, took it to a bank, and opened a chequing account. Some portion of your $100 is likely to stay in your account. Your bank can earn interest by lending some of it to borrowers.

A chartered bank must keep some portion of its chequable deposits in vault cash or as deposits with the Bank of Canada. These are legal reserves. Let's assume that the reserve requirement is 10 percent. Your bank must keep $10 of your $100 deposit in legal reserves. Therefore, it has $90 to lend.

Now, suppose Jennifer Leclerc borrows the $90 from your bank. Leclerc has $90 added to her chequing account. Assume that she writes a cheque for $90 payable to Canadian Tire. Canadian Tire's bank ends up with a $90 deposit and is required to keep 10 percent ($9.00) in legal reserves. The bank can lend out $81.00.

This process is called deposit expansion, and it can continue, as shown in Figure 18.3. The banking system creates money in the form of chequable deposits. Of course, the process of deposit expansion is much more complex in practice. General economic conditions, for example, influence the willingness of bankers to make loans and of borrowers to borrow.

As you can see from Figure 18.3, your original deposit of $100 could result in an increase of $1000 in new deposits for all banks in the banking system. Remember to assume a reserve requirement of 10 percent. Thus, your original deposit of $100 could expand by 10 times (the reciprocal of the reserve requirement, 100/10), or to $1000. This example assumes that no borrower takes part of his or her loan in cash and that the banks want to lend as much as they legally can. Otherwise, the increase would be less than $1000.

Changes in Banking

Because of deregulation, banks are shifting away from their historical role as intermediaries between depositors and borrowers. Canada's banks are diversifying to provide a wider array of financial products to their clients. Training bankers to be effective in this environment is necessary. For example, over 100 executives at Toronto-Dominion Bank attended a Harvard University course that taught them to think like investment bankers. The Bank of Montreal conducted a similar course for over 400 executives.

In the last few years, large companies have reduced their use of bank loans. To compensate for this loss, banks are setting up money market operations. For example, until deregulation, only securities firms were allowed to sell commercial paper (see Chapter 19), but banks expect to dominate in this area before too long. (Commercial paper is usually issued by blue-chip companies that pay a fee to investment dealers or banks to sell the security.)

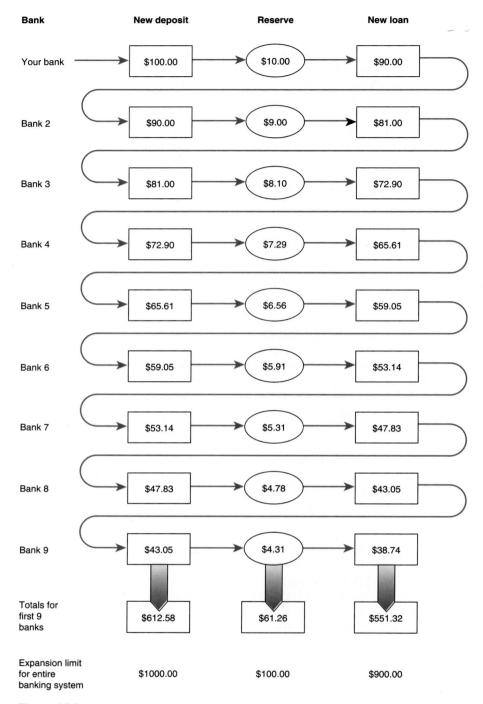

Bank	New deposit	Reserve	New loan
Your bank	$100.00	$10.00	$90.00
Bank 2	$90.00	$9.00	$81.00
Bank 3	$81.00	$8.10	$72.90
Bank 4	$72.90	$7.29	$65.61
Bank 5	$65.61	$6.56	$59.05
Bank 6	$59.05	$5.91	$53.14
Bank 7	$53.14	$5.31	$47.83
Bank 8	$47.83	$4.78	$43.05
Bank 9	$43.05	$4.31	$38.74
Totals for first 9 banks	$612.58	$61.26	$551.32
Expansion limit for entire banking system	$1000.00	$100.00	$900.00

Figure 18.3
How the chartered banking system creates money.

Banks have been allowed to sell commercial paper only since June 1987, when deregulation opened up this possibility. The Bank of Montreal and the Toronto-Dominion Bank have been the most active in this new market.

In Canada, about 200 companies have a credit rating good enough for commercial paper. Banks want to use commercial paper more because they do not have to keep capital reserves on hand for commercial paper as they do for acceptances.

Changes are also taking place in banking because consumers are no longer content to simply keep money in a bank when they can get more for it elsewhere. Banks are responding by selling a growing array of corporate and government securities through their branches.

All of this activity is transforming the profit base of banks. In the past, they made most of their money from the spread between interest rates paid to depositors and the rates charged on loans. Investment banking, on the other hand, is fee-based. Banks are making a larger proportion of their profits from fees, and this is blurring the traditional boundary between banks and securities firms.

Another change concerns international banking. Since Ottawa lifted the barriers to foreign banks, many American banks have begun to do business in Canada, along with most of the world's largest banks. But they have not done well. Many of them have lost large sums of money and most are now reducing the size of their staffs.[5]

Canadian banks had also planned to invade the U.S. However, these plans have been put on hold because share prices of U.S. banks have increased rapidly. As a result, it is difficult to pick up bargains.[6]

The Bank of Canada

The **Bank of Canada**, formed in 1935, is Canada's central bank. It has a crucial role to play in managing the Canadian economy and in regulating certain aspects of chartered bank operations.

Bank of Canada
Canada's central bank; formed in 1935.

The Bank of Canada is managed by a board of governors composed of a governor, a deputy governor, and 12 directors appointed from different regions of Canada. The directors, with cabinet approval, appoint the governor and deputy governor. The deputy minister of finance is also a nonvoting member of the board. Between meetings of the board, normally held eight times a year, an executive committee acts for the board. This committee is composed of the governor, the deputy governor, two directors, and the deputy minister of finance. The executive committee meets at least once a week.

Operation of the Bank of Canada.   The Bank of Canada plays an important role in managing the money supply in Canada. (See Figure 18.4.) If the Bank of Canada wants to increase the money supply, it can buy government securities. The people selling these bonds deposit the proceeds in their banks. These deposits increase banks' reserves and their ability to make loans. The Bank of Canada can also lower the bank rate and lower the reserve requirement; both of these actions allow banks to loan more money to business and consumers.

If the Bank of Canada wants to decrease the money supply, it can sell government securities. People spend money to buy bonds, and these withdrawals bring down banks' reserves and reduce their ability to make loans. The Bank of Canada can also raise the bank rate and raise the reserve requirement; both of these actions cause banks to loan less money.

Member Bank Borrowing from the Bank of Canada.   The Bank of Canada is the lender of last resort for chartered banks. The rate at which chartered banks can borrow from the Bank of Canada is called the **bank**, or rediscount, **rate**. It serves as the basis for establishing the chartered banks' prime interest rates. By raising the bank rate, the Bank of Canada depresses the demand for money; by lowering it, the demand for money increases. In practice, chartered banks seldom have to borrow from the Bank of Canada. However, the bank rate is an important instrument of monetary policy as a determinant of interest rates.

bank rate
The rate at which chartered banks can borrow from the Bank of Canada.

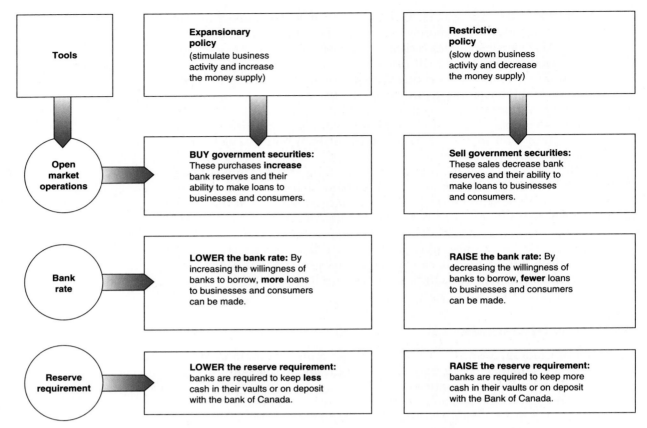

Figure 18.4
Bank of Canada monetary policy actions.

In 1985, two Schedule A Alberta-based banks, Canadian Commercial Bank and Northland Bank, failed. These were the first bank failures in Canada since the Home Bank failed in 1923. Because of these failures, some smaller regional banks had difficulty maintaining their deposit bases. To ease this banking crisis, the Bank of Canada lent over $4 billion to chartered banks.

primary reserve requirement

The percentage of a chartered bank's deposits that it must keep in vault cash or as deposits with the Bank of Canada.

Reserve Requirements.   The **primary reserve requirement** is the percentage of its various deposits that a chartered bank must keep in vault cash or as deposits with the Bank of Canada. The 1980 *Bank Act* specifies that the banks on average must hold reserves of 10 percent of Canadian dollar chequable deposits, 3 percent of term deposits, and 3 percent of foreign currency deposits booked in Canada by Canadian residents.

In addition to the primary reserve requirement, the Bank of Canada sets a secondary reserve requirement. The 1980 *Bank Act* permits the Bank of Canada to vary the secondary requirement from 0 to 12 percent. The **secondary reserve requirement** is the percentage of Canadian dollar deposits to be held in the form of cash, treasury bills, or day loans to securities dealers.

secondary reserve requirement

The percentage of Canadian dollar deposits to be held in the form of cash, treasury bills, or day loans to securities dealers.

The International Bank Structure

There is no worldwide banking system that is comparable, in terms of policy-making and regulatory power, to the system of any one industrialized nation. Rather, worldwide banking stability relies on a loose structure of agreements among individual countries or groups of countries.

The World Bank and the IMF.   Two United Nations agencies, the World Bank and the International Monetary Fund, help to finance international trade. Unlike true banks, the **World Bank** (technically the International Bank for Reconstruction and Development) actually provides only a very limited scope of services. For instance, it funds national improvements by making loans to build roads, schools, power plants, and hospitals. The resulting improvements eventually enable borrowing countries to increase productive capacity and international trade.

The **International Monetary Fund** is a group of some 150 nations that have combined resources for the following purposes:

- To promote the stability of exchange rates
- To provide temporary, short-term loans to member countries
- To encourage members to cooperate on international monetary issues
- To encourage development of a system for international payments.

The IMF makes loans to nations suffering from temporary negative trade balances. By making it possible for these countries to continue buying products from other countries, the IMF facilitates international trade. Some nations, however, have declined IMF funds rather than accept the economic changes that the IMF demands. For example, some developing countries reject the IMF's requirement that they cut back social programs and spending in order to bring inflation under control.

World Bank
Funds national improvements by making loans to build schools, roads, power plants, and hospitals.

International Monetary Fund
A group of 150 nations that have combined resources to stabilize the world's currencies.

Financial Pillar #2—Alternate Banks

Trust Companies

Another financial intermediary that serves individuals and businesses is the alternate, or near, bank: the trust company. A **trust company** safeguards property—funds and estates—entrusted to it; it may also serve as trustee, transfer agent, and registrar for corporations and provide other services.

A corporation selling bonds to many investors appoints a trustee, usually a trust company, to protect the bondholders' interests. A trust company can also serve as a transfer agent and registrar for corporations. A transfer agent records changes in ownership of a corporation's shares of stock. A registrar certifies to the investing public that stock issues are correctly stated and comply with the corporate charter. Other services include preparing and issuing dividend cheques to shareholders and serving as trustee for employee profit-sharing funds. Trust companies also accept deposits and pay interest on them. The box "A Classic Case of Mismanagement" describes the collapse of Royal Trustco, one of Canada's largest trust companies.

trust company
Safeguards funds and estates entrusted to it; may also serve as trustee, transfer agent, and registrar for corporations.

Credit Unions/Caisses Populaires

Credit unions (called *caisses populaires* in Quebec) are also alternate banks. They are important to business because they lend money to consumers to buy durable goods such as cars and furniture. They also lend money to businesses. **Credit unions** and *caisses populaires* are cooperative savings and lending associations formed by a group with common interests. Members (owners) can add to their savings accounts by authorizing deductions from their pay cheques or by making direct deposits. They can borrow short-term, long-term, or mortgage funds from the credit union. Credit unions also invest substantial amounts of money in corporate and government securities. The largest credit unions in Canada are listed in Table 18.3.

credit union
Cooperative savings and lending association formed by a group with common interests.

TABLE 18.3	The Top Ten Credit Unions in Canada, 1994 (ranked by assets)	
Company		**Assets (in billions)**
1. Caisse centrale Desjardins		$5.4
2. Vancouver City Savings Credit Union		4.0
3. B.C. Central Credit Union		2.3
4. Credit Union Central of Saskatchewan		1.4
5. Surrey Metro Savings Credit Union		1.4
6. Richmond Savings Credit Union		1.2
7. Credit Union Central of Ontario Ltd.		1.2
8. Pacific Coast Savings Credit Union		1.1
9. Credit Union Central of Canada Ltd.		.9
10. Civil Service Co-operative Credit Society		.8

The Canadian Business Scene

A CLASSIC CASE OF MISMANAGEMENT

Royal Trustco Ltd., the holding company for Canada's second-largest trust company, disintegrated in 1993. Its brewing troubles became evident in 1990, when it incurred its first loss ever. Much of the blame is put on CEO Michael Cornelissen, who took three specific actions that later came back to haunt him: he acquired the financial services holdings of Dow Chemical, made major investments in the U.S. savings and loan industry, and moved into the British mortgage market. All of these initiatives caused big problems for Royal Trust.

When Cornelissen became CEO at Royal Trustco in 1983, he introduced major changes in the laid-back way the firm operated. He expected all executives to arrive at 7 a.m., and left nasty notes on the desks of executives who didn't comply. He berated people publicly in front of others and called his new colleagues "turkeys." He was impatient with the slow pace of decision making at management meetings.

Not surprisingly, many managers who had been with the firm for years decided to leave. Cornelissen then brought in new people more to his liking. He tried to make Royal Trustco an entrepreneurial, decentralized organization, an objective that clashed with the culture of most banks, which are bureaucratic and hierarchical. No one questioned his commitment and hard work, and there was strong loyalty to him within his new top man-

agement team. But he received little sympathy in financial circles, partly because he had a short fuse and because some people he dealt with considered him arrogant. And industry analysts expressed concern that Royal Trustco's emphasis on entrepreneurialism would lead to a lack of discipline and the financial controls that are critical in a financial institution.

Their fears were well founded. In 1993, the company disintegrated from superficial good health to near collapse and was sold to the Royal Bank of Canada (Cornelissen had already left as CEO). At the company's annual meeting in June, 1993, company officials gave shareholders a humble presentation explaining how things had gone so wrong and why they had decided to sell the company's best assets to the Royal Bank. In a nutshell, the company had made too many real estate loans in markets like London, Los Angeles, and Toronto. When those markets collapsed, loan losses began. Once that happened, investor confidence declined and the company started losing depositors.

The shareholders at the meeting were not impressed. Today, these investors are left holding shares in Gentra Inc., the renamed company that was left behind after most of Royal Trustco's assets were sold. The shares are trading for about 40 cents (Royal Trustco's shares were trading for $36 in 1986).

Credit unions (caisses populaires) are cooperative saving and lending organizations that loan money to both consumers and businesses.

Financial Pillar #3—Specialized Lending and Savings Intermediaries

Life Insurance Companies

An important source of funds for individuals, nonbusiness organizations, and businesses is the life insurance company. A **life insurance company** is a mutual or stock company that shares risk with its policyholders in return for payment of a premium. It lends some of the money it collects from premiums to borrowers. Life insurance companies are substantial investors in real estate mortgages and in corporate and government bonds. Next to chartered banks, they are the largest financial intermediaries in Canada. We discuss insurance companies in more detail in Chapter 19.

life insurance company
A mutual or stock company that shares risk with its policyholders for payment of premiums.

Factoring Companies

An important source of short-term funds for many firms is factoring companies. A **factoring company** (or factor) buys accounts receivable (amounts due from credit customers) from a firm. It pays less than the face value of the accounts but collects the face value of the accounts. The difference, minus the cost of doing business, is the factor's profit.

A firm that sells its accounts receivable to a factor without recourse shifts the risk of credit loss to the factor. If an account turns out to be uncollectable, the factor suffers the loss. However, a factor is a specialist in credit and collection activities. Using a factor may enable a business firm to expand sales beyond what would be practical without the factor. The firm trades accounts receivable for cash. The factor notifies the firm's customers to make their overdue payments to the factor.

factoring company
Buys accounts receivable from a firm for less than their face value, and then collects the face value of the receivables.

Financial Corporations

There are two types of financial corporations: sales finance companies and consumer finance companies.

sales finance company
Specializes in financing installment purchases made by individuals or firms.

A major source of credit for many firms and their customers is the sales finance company. A **sales finance company** specializes in financing installment purchases made by individuals and firms. When you buy durable goods from a retailer on an installment plan with a sales finance company, the loan is made directly to you. The item itself serves as security for the loan. Sales finance companies enable many firms to sell on credit, even though the firms could not afford to finance credit sales on their own.

General Motors Acceptance Corporation (GMAC) is a sales finance company. It is a captive company because it exists to finance installment contracts resulting from sales made by General Motors. Industrial Acceptance Corporation is a large Canadian sales finance company.

Sales finance companies also finance installment sales to business firms. Many banks have installment loan departments.

consumer finance company
Makes personal loans to consumers.

An important source of credit for many consumers is the consumer finance company. A **consumer finance company** makes personal loans to consumers. Often the borrower pledges no security (collateral) for the loan. For larger loans, collateral may be required, such as a car or furniture.

These companies do not make loans to businesses but they do provide the financing that turns many people into actual paying customers. Household Finance Corporation is an example of a consumer finance company.

Venture Capital or Development Firms

venture capital firm
Provides funds for new or expanding firms thought to have significant potential.

A **venture capital firm**, or development firm, will provide funds for new or expanding firms thought to have significant potential. Venture capital firms obtain their funds from initial capital subscriptions, from loans from other financial intermediaries, and from retained earnings. The company profiled in the opening case—MDS Health Ventures Inc.—is a venture capital company.

Venture capital firms may provide either equity or debt funds to firms. Financing new, untested businesses is risky, so venture capital firms want to earn a higher-than-normal return on their investment. The ideal situation is an equity investment in a company that becomes very successful and experiences substantial increases in its stock value.

Pension Funds

pension fund
Accumulates money that will be paid out to plan subscribers in the future.

A **pension plan** accumulates money that will be paid out to plan subscribers at some time in the future. The money collected is invested in corporate stocks and bonds, government bonds, or mortgages until it is to be paid out.

Financial Pillar #4—Investment Dealers

Investment dealers (called stockbrokers or underwriters) perform two important financial functions. First, they are the primary distributors of new stock and bond issues (underwriting). Second, they facilitate secondary trading of stocks and bonds, both on stock exchanges and on over-the-counter stock and bond markets (the brokerage function). These functions are discussed in more detail in Chapter 20.

Other Sources of Funds

Government Financial Institutions and Granting Agencies

In Canada, a number of government suppliers of funds are important to business. In general, they supply funds to new and/or growing companies. However, established firms can also use some of them.

The **Industrial Development Bank (IDB)**, a subsidiary of the Bank of Canada, was created to make loans to business firms. The **Federal Business Development Bank (FBDB)** took over operation of the IDB in 1975. The IDB was set up to make term loans, primarily to smaller firms judged to have growth potential but unable to secure funds at reasonable terms from traditional sources. Its services were expanded by providing proportionally more equity financing and more management counselling services. The FBDB has been especially active in providing loans for small businesses.

A variety of provincial industrial development corporations provide funds to developing business firms in the hope that they will provide jobs in the province. These were discussed in Chapter 7.

The federal government's Export Development Corporation can finance and insure export sales for Canadian companies. The Canada Mortgage and Housing Corporation (CMHC) is involved in providing and guaranteeing mortgages. The CMHC is particularly important to the construction industry.

A number of federal and provincial programs are specifically designed to provide loans to agricultural operators. Most of these, with the exception of farm improvement loans which guarantee bank loans to farmers, are long-term loans for land purchase.

In addition to these activities, governments are involved in providing grants to business operations. For example, the federal government, through the Department of Regional Industrial Expansion (DRIE), gives grants for certain types of business expansion in designated areas of the country. Other federal government grants are available for activities such as new product development.

Industrial Development Bank (IDB)

A subsidiary of the Bank of Canada created to make loans to business firms.

Federal Business Development Bank (FBDB)

Took over operation of the IDB in 1975; particularly active in lending money to small businesses.

International Sources of Funds

Not all of the financing requirements of Canadian businesses and governments are met from within Canada. Foreign sources of funds are also important. The financial institutions of Canada play a role in facilitating the flow of funds into the country.

The Canadian capital market is one part of the international capital market. Canadian provinces borrow extensively in foreign markets such as those in London and in New York. Canadian corporations likewise find it attractive to borrow in foreign markets.

Foreign sources of funds have been significant to the economic development of Canada. Although many groups and individuals have expressed concern about foreign ownership of Canadian firms, projections of Canada's future capital requirements indicate that it will continue to need foreign sources of funds. Canadian financial institutions will continue to play a large role in making these funds available.

Summary of Key Points

Money is anything that people generally accept as payment for goods and services. The three primary functions of money are to serve as a medium of exchange, a store of value, and a unit of account. To perform these functions, money should be durable, portable, divisible, and stable. In our economic system, financial institutions can actually create money. A chequing account, for example, is money.

The designation "M-1" includes only the most liquid forms of money such as currency and demand deposits (chequing accounts). M-2 is a broader definition of money and includes everything in M-1 plus items like time deposits and savings deposits which are easily converted to spendable form.

The value of a currency like the Canadian dollar reflects the overall supply and demand for Canadian dollars both at home and abroad. When a country's currency is overvalued (undervalued), its exchange rate is higher (lower) than warranted by economic conditions. Governments devalue (revalue) the nation's currency to make it less (more) expensive for other countries to buy the home country's products.

The financial intermediaries that form the "four financial pillars" in Canada are banks, alternate banks, life insurance companies, and investment dealers. The chartered banks, which are at the heart of our financial system, are the most important source of short-term funds for business firms. The chartered banking system creates money in the form of expanding demand deposits. The Bank of Canada is the central bank of Canada; its main job is to control the nation's money supply.

There is no worldwide banking system that is comparable to the banking system of any one nation. Two United Nations agencies—the World Bank and the International Monetary Fund (IMF)—help to finance international trade. The World Bank funds national improvements like roads, schools, and power plants, while the IMF promotes stability in exchange rates and encourages international cooperation on monetary issues.

In addition to chartered banks, other financial intermediaries include the near banks (trust companies and *caisses populaires*/credit unions), life insurance companies, sales and consumer finance companies, venture capital funds, mutual funds, pension funds, and investment dealers. While the others are not as important to businesses as the chartered bank, they play a significant role in providing services to their business and nonbusiness customers.

CONCLUDING CASE 18-1

Dollar Fluctuations: Good or Bad News for Canada?

For most of the 1980s, the Canadian dollar declined sharply. It dropped as low as $.69 (U.S.), but rebounded to a high of $.89 by 1991. More recently, the dollar has been trading at around $.73. When the dollar began its decline, some analysts claimed a low dollar was good for Canada while others claimed it was bad.

One school of thought argues that a high dollar is good. It means lower prices for imports, lower interest rates, faster growth, and more jobs. A low dollar is bad because it increases the price of imports, boosts inflation, deflates income, and harms Canadian competitiveness. Holders of this view stress that Canada's relentless attack on inflation during the 1980s impressed money managers in foreign countries and convinced them that Canada was a good place to invest, even though our economy was not doing very well.

Those who argue for a cheaper Canadian dollar, such as David West of DRI/McGraw-Hill, say that the dollar's sharp increase in the late 1980s caused the decline of Canada's international competitiveness. These opponents of a high dollar argue that an inflated dollar causes demand for our exports to drop. They also argue that, if the dollar were to be at $.80 (U.S.) rather than climbing higher, our competitiveness relative to the U.S. would be higher.

Other analysts at DRI/McGraw-Hill considered two scenarios for the Canadian dollar: one at $.75 (U.S.) and one at $.95. With the dollar at $.75, Canada will sell more abroad, but imports will also cost more. Since imports constitute 25 percent of gross domestic product, inflation will increase. Capital spending will go down because of the increased cost of imported machinery. As a result, productivity will also decline. Annual growth will be less than 3 percent.

If the Canadian dollar is at $.95, our exports will be more expensive to foreigners, so we will sell less abroad. However, our imports will be much cheaper. Capital spending will go up, as will productivity. Inflation will be down because of the lower price of imported goods. In this scenario, inflation will be beaten because the Canadian economy will become more efficient. Annual growth will be about 4 percent.

So who is right? In the middle of 1990, David West predicted that the Canadian dollar would decline to $.81 (U.S.) by the end of 1990. This obviously did not happen. In fact, the dollar rose to $.91 by late 1991. But it did happen by the fall of 1992. Like a company's stock, the value of a country's currency depends on a variety of factors that are hard to pin down. A big factor is consumer confidence, in this case foreign consumers, that is hard to measure. Perhaps we can comfort ourselves with this fact: During the last 20 years, the Canadian dollar has fluctuated widely and much has been written about the benefits and costs of a high or a low dollar. Yet our economic system continues to function.

CASE QUESTIONS
1. What are the benefits of a "high" Canadian dollar? The drawbacks?
2. What are the benefits of a "low" Canadian dollar? The drawbacks.
3. Compare the level of the Canadian dollar over the last 15 years with Canada's pattern of imports and exports. Is there any relationship among imports, exports, and the level of the Canadian dollar? (The *Bank of Canada Review* contains the information you need to answer this question.)
4. Should the government of Canada intervene to influence the level of the Canadian dollar? Defend your answer. ◆

CONCLUDING CASE 18-2

Fallout from the Fall of the Mexican Peso

In late 1994 and early 1995, the Mexican peso was devalued by 40 percent. This devaluation has had a serious impact on domestic activities in Mexico. Prices on nearly all products have increased sharply, as merchants try to recover profits lost because of the devaluation. Even the wealthiest people in Mexico are feeling the pinch. The net worth of the richest person in the country, Carlos Slim, has declined from about $8 billion to just over $4 billion.

The average Mexican has a lower standard of living now than before free market reforms were introduced in Mexico. Middle class incomes have now regressed to their 1982 level. The minimum wage has lost half its buying power, and more than 40 million people—half the population—live in poverty. The middle class is also disappointed because they had expectations of a steadily improving standard of living. Foreign-made products bought by middle class consumers have now become much more expensive.

The problem has been aggravated because companies that sell goods produced in Mexico have seized the opportunity to raise their prices, even though the devaluation should have little effect on them. McDonald's, which uses mostly domestic ingredients, is one of the companies that has raised its prices. Thousands of complaints of price-gouging have been received at the government's consumer protection agency, and some stores have been forced by the government to close temporarily.

CASE QUESTIONS
1. Why did the Mexican peso decline so sharply in value?
2. Are there any potential benefits associated with the decline in the peso?
3. Does the decline of the peso have any implications for Canadian business firms? Explain. ◆

Key Terms

money

M-1

currency

cheque

demand deposit

M-2

time deposit

money market mutual
funds

law of one price

chartered bank

trust services

letter of credit

banker's acceptance

electronic funds transfer
(EFT)

debit card

chequable deposit

term deposit

prime rate of interest

Bank of Canada

bank rate

primary reserve
requirement

secondary reserve
requirement

World Bank

International Monetary
Fund

trust company

credit union

life insurance company

factoring company

sales finance company

consumer finance
company

venture capital firm

pension fund

Industrial Development
Bank (IDB)

Federal Business
Development Bank
(FBDB)

Study Questions and Exercises

Review Questions

1. What is money? What are its ideal characteristics?
2. What are the components of M-1? Of M-2?
3. Describe the structure and operation of the Bank of Canada.
4. List and describe the sources of short-term funds for business firms.

Analysis Questions

5. What kinds of changes in banking are shifting banks away from their historical role?
6. Do we really need all the different types of financial institutions we have in Canada? Could we make do with just chartered banks? Why or why not?

7. Should credit cards be counted in the money supply? Why or why not?
8. Should chartered banks be regulated or should market forces be allowed to set the money supply? Defend your answer.

Application Exercises

9. Beginning with a $1000 deposit and assuming a reserve requirement of 15 percent, trace the amount of money created by the banking system after five lending cycles.
10. Interview the manager of a local chartered bank. Identify the ways in which the Bank of Canada helps the bank and the ways in which it limits the bank.

Building Your Business Skills

Goal

To encourage students to understand how credit-card companies have responded to an economic environment characterized by falling and low interest rates.

Method

Step 1:

Working alone, choose any one of the major credit card companies (e.g., Bank of Montreal MasterCard, CIBC Visa, etc.). Research the ways in which the credit card issuer responded to falling interest rates between 1992 and 1993. Specifically, which actions did it take?

■ Did it drop its rates considerably for all customers? For some customers? If it lowered rates to some customers but not others, what criteria did it use to select favored customers?

■ Did it eliminate or reduce its yearly fee to all or some customers?

■ Did it offer inducements for customers to use the card? What bonus plan or incentive did it use?

■ Did it offer inducements for merchants to encourage customers to use the card?

■ Did it change its new-cardmember application requirements?

Step 2:

Join in teams with students who researched other cards to compare and contrast your findings.

Follow-Up Questions

1. In what ways did falling interest rates affect the entire credit-card marketing environment?
2. What card offers the most favorable terms to consumers? To merchants? The least favorable terms?

19

Financial Decisions and Risk Management

LEARNING OBJECTIVES

After studying this chapter, you will be able to

- Describe the ways in which financial managers meet businesses' needs for funds.
- Identify five sources of short-term financing for businesses.
- Distinguish between various sources of long-term financing and their financial risks.
- Describe how financial returns to investors are related to the financial risks they take.
- Identify areas of financial management of particular concern to small businesses.
- Describe how risk affects business operations.
- Discuss the role of risk management in dealing with risk.
- Explain the insurance mechanism and how it works.
- Distinguish among the different types of insurers.
- Describe the various insurance products that exist for business firms and how firms use them.

CHAPTER OUTLINE

OPENING CASE

Risky Decisions in the Insurance Business

As recently as 1990, the prevailing view in Canada was that life insurance companies were models of safety and prudence. They simply couldn't fail; they never had and they never would. But since 1992, two large insurance companies have failed—Cooperants Mutual Life and Confederation Life.

Cooperants Mutual   Cooperants Mutual Life Insurance Society started out as a tiny, but profitable, mutual life insurer owned by its rural and blue-collar policyholders. By the mid-1980s, the outlook of the firm had changed dramatically. It went on a buying spree, becoming involved in stock brokerage, real estate, trust companies, and financial planning. By 1991, the firm had 2400 employees, 30 subsidiaries, and more than $3 billion in assets. It also built a gleaming new head office in Montreal.

For a time, things seemed to be going well, but by 1987 profits had dropped to only $3 million. In 1991, the firm lost nearly $60 million. Over two-thirds of the firm's assets were invested in businesses other than traditional life insurance, and the firm was stressing growth at the expense of profitability. In 1992, Cooperants achieved the dubious distinction of being the first-ever Canadian insurance company to go bankrupt.

Confederation Life   The story at Confed is similar. A conservative company that started in 1871, Confed operated successfully for over 100 years. In the 1980s, it became heavily involved in real estate investments, and when the real estate boom ended, the company found itself in trouble. In 1992, the company was barely profitable, and in 1993 it lost $29 million. Its credit rating was questioned by review agencies, and it began looking for a partner to inject new capital into the company. After policyholders and investors began pulling their money out in 1994, the company was granted court protection under the Companies' Creditors Arrangement Act, a bankruptcy statute.

At the time of its demise, Confed held interests in 69 different Canadian, U.S., and British properties, most of which were purchased during the real estate boom of the 1980s under its second-last CEO, Patrick Burns. In 1989, an alarming 71 percent of Confed's assets were in real estate. Confed's liquidator, Peat Marwick Thorne Inc., is now in the process of trying to sell all these buildings, most of which are worth less than what it cost to build them.

Why was Confed so heavily into real estate? In 1987, regulators in the office of the Suprintendent of Financial Institutions adopted a policy that allowed insurance companies to record as profits one-tenth of any paper gains they made on real estate. So, for example, if an insurance company bought a building for $1 million and it appreciated in value to $2 million, the insurance company could declare a $100 000 profit on the building, even if they still owned it. Confed therefore had an incentive to be into real estate in a big way.

P.D. Burns, President and Chief Executive Officer, Confederation Life Insurance Company

In the end, control of Confed passed to Great-West Life, which pumped millions of dollars into the company and will control a majority of the seats on Confed's board of directors. Great-West, which is Canada's largest group life underwriter, also purchased Confed's valuable group health and life insurance operations. All of this activity should result in about $400 million in cash coming in to Confed.

The collapse of Confed will cause Comp-Corp. (the industry-financed consumer protection plan) to charge all other insurance companies a fee to cover needed payouts to Confed's policyholders. The ten biggest life insurance companies, for example, will have to kick in about $25-$30 million apiece.

The big losers in the Confed liquidation are the banks and other institutional holders of Confed's commercial paper, banker's acceptances, and long-term debt. These creditors held $1.7 billion worth of Confed investments. They will receive payment only after policyholders and depositors have received their money.

In the wake of the Confed collapse, the Dominion Bond Rating Service called for major changes to Comp-Corp. It said the insurance industry needs a Crown corporation backing it, just as banks and trust companies have the Canada Deposit Insurance Corp. backing them.   ◆

As the Confederation and Cooperants cases show, how a company handles it finances can mean the difference between life and death for the firm. It can also affect the level of interest that investors show in the firm. These fundamental facts apply to both established firms and those which are just starting up.

In this chapter, we will examine the role of financial managers and show why businesses need financial management. We will discuss the sources of short-term funds and how they are put to use, as well as sources and uses of long-term financing. As you will see, using funds involves risks and so requires management to protect the firm from unnecessary financial losses.

The Role of the Financial Manager

We have seen that production managers are responsible for planning and controlling the output of goods and services. We have noted that marketing managers must plan and control the development and marketing of products. Similarly, **financial managers** plan and control the acquisition and dispersal of the company's financial assets.

The business activity known as **finance** (or **corporate finance**) typically entails four responsibilities:

- determining a firm's long-term investments
- obtaining funds to pay for those investments
- conducting the firm's everyday financial activities
- helping to manage the risks that the firm takes.

financial managers
Those managers responsible for planning and overseeing the financial resources of a firm.

finance
The business function involving decisions about a firm's long-term investments and obtaining the funds to pay for those investments.

Objectives of the Financial Manager

The overall objective of financial managers is to increase the value of the firm and thus to increase shareholder wealth. To reach this goal, financial managers must ensure that the company's earnings exceed its costs—in other words, that the company earns a profit. For a proprietorship or partnership, profits translate into an increase in the owners' wealth. For a corporation, profits translate into an increase in the value of its common stock.

The various responsibilities of the financial manager in increasing a firm's wealth fall into three general categories: *cash-flow management, financial control,* and *financial planning.*

Cash-Flow Management.   To increase a firm's value, financial managers must ensure that it always has enough funds on hand to purchase the materials and human resources that it needs to produce goods and services. At the same time, of course, there may be funds that are not needed immediately. These must be invested to earn more money for a firm. This activity—**cash flow management**—requires careful planning. If excess cash balances are allowed to sit idle instead of invested, a firm loses the cash returns that it could have earned.

cash flow management
Managing the pattern in which cash flows into the firm in the form of revenues and out of the firm in the form of debt payments.

Financial Control.   Because things never go exactly as planned, financial managers must be prepared to make adjustments for actual financial changes that occur each day. **Financial control** is the process of checking actual performance against plans to ensure that the desired financial status occurs. For example, planned revenues based on forecasts usually turn out to be higher or lower than actual revenues. Why? Simply because sales are unpredictable. Control involves monitoring revenue inflows and making appropriate financial adjustments. Excessively high revenues, for instance, may be deposited in short-term interest-bearing accounts. Or they may be used to pay off short-term debt. Otherwise earmarked resources can be saved or put to better use. In contrast, lower-than-expected revenues may necessitate short-term borrowing to meet current debt obligations.

Budgets (as we saw in Chapter 17) are often the backbone of financial control. The budget provides the "measuring stick" against which performance

financial control
The process of checking actual performance against plans to ensure that the desired financial status is achieved.

is evaluated. The cash flows, debts, and assets not only of the whole company but of each department are compared at regular intervals against budgeted amounts. Discrepancies indicate the need for financial adjustments so that resources are used to the best advantage.

financial plan

A description of how a business will reach some financial position it seeks for the future; includes projections for sources and uses of funds.

Financial Planning.   The cornerstone of effective financial management is the development of a **financial plan**. A financial plan describes a firm's strategies for reaching some future financial position. In constructing the plan, a financial manager must ask several questions:

- What amount of funds does the company need to meet immediate plans?
- When will it need more funds?
- Where can it get the funds to meet both its short- and long-term needs?

To answer these questions, a financial manager must develop a clear picture of *why* a firm needs funds. Managers must also assess the relative costs and benefits of potential funding sources. In the sections that follow, we will examine the main reasons for which companies generate funds and describe the main sources of business funding, both for the short and long term.

Why Businesses Need Funds

Every company needs money to survive. Failure to make a contractually obligated payment can lead to bankruptcy and the dissolution of the firm. But the successful financial manager must distinguish between two different kinds of financial outlays: short-term operating expenditures and long-term capital expenditures.

Short-Term (Operating) Expenditures

A firm incurs short-term expenditures regularly in its everyday business activities. To handle these expenditures, financial managers must pay attention to accounts payable and receivable and to inventories.

Accounts Payable.   In drawing up a financial plan, financial managers must pay special attention to accounts payable, for it is the largest single category of short-term debt for most companies. But they must rely on other managers for accurate information about the quantity of supplies that will be required in an upcoming period. Financial managers also need to consider the time period in which they must pay various suppliers. For example, a financial manager for *Maclean's* magazine needs information from production about both the amount of ink and paper needed to print the magazine and when it will be needed. Obviously, it is in the firm's interest to withhold payment as long as it can without jeopardizing its credit rating.

Accounts Receivable.   A sound financial plan requires financial managers to project accurately both the amounts buyers will pay to the firm and when they will make those payments. For example, a manager at Kraft Foods needs to know how many dollars worth of cheddar cheese Safeway supermarkets will order each month and how quickly it pays its bills. Because they represent an investment in products on which the firm has not yet received payment, accounts receivable temporarily tie up some of the firm's funds. It is in the firm's interest to receive payment as quickly as possible.

Given that it is in the self-interest of buyers to delay payment as long as possible, how can a financial manager predict payment times? The answer lies in the development of a *credit policy*, the set of rules governing the extension of credit to customers. The credit policy sets standards as to which buyers are eligible for what type of credit. Financial managers extend credit to customers who have the ability to pay and honor their obligations to pay. They deny credit to firms with poor repayment histories.

The credit policy also sets payment terms. For example, credit terms of "2/10; net 30" mean that the selling company offers a 2 percent discount if the customer pays within 10 days. The customer has 30 days to pay the regular price. Thus, on a $1000 invoice, the buyer would have to pay only $980 on days 1 to 10 but all $1000 on days 11 to 30. The higher the discount, the more incentive buyers have to pay early. Sellers can thus adjust credit terms to influence when customers pay their bills. Often, however, credit terms can be adjusted only slightly without giving competitors an edge.

inventory
Materials and goods currently held by the company that will be sold within the year.

Inventories.   Between the time a firm buys raw materials and the time it sells finished products, it has funds tied up in **inventory**, materials and goods that it will sell within the year. There are three basic types of inventories: raw materials, work-in-process, and finished goods.

The basic supplies a firm buys to use in its production process are its **raw materials inventory**. Levi Strauss's raw materials inventory includes huge rolls of denim. **Work-in-process inventory** consists of goods partway through the production process. Cut out but not yet sewn jeans are part of the work-in-process inventory at Levi's. Finally, the **finished goods inventory** is those items ready for sale. Completed blue jeans ready for shipment to dealers in Levi jeans are finished goods inventory.

raw materials inventory
That portion of a firm's inventory consisting of basic supplies used to manufacture products for sale.

work-in-process inventory
That portion of a firm's inventory consisting of goods partway through the production process.

finished goods inventory
That portion of a firm's inventory consisting of completed goods ready for sale.

International Report

A SHORT-SIGHTED APPROACH TO INVENTORY

In extreme cases, companies may look upon inventory as a source of creative accountancy. In December 1993, executives at Bausch & Lomb's contact lens division instructed the company's 32 distributors to boost inventories in preparation for a major sales push. There were some strings attached, however: Lenses had to be ordered by December 23, when B&L closed its books for 1993, and distributors had to pay wholesale prices 50-percent higher than those they had paid just a few months earlier. Even though many still had several months' worth of inventory on hand, most distributors agreed. The $25 million transaction provided a 20-percent revenue boost for B&L's contact lens unit and represented about half of its 1993 total earnings of $15 million.

It was not until B&L reported poor financial results in 1994 that the terms of the sale came under scrutiny. At mid-year, B&L announced that high levels of contact lens inventory among distributors would hurt 1994 profits. Indeed, third-quarter 1994 profits slid 86 percent, with fully half of the decline due to distributors' contact lens inventories. Meanwhile, several distributors reported that B&L had not required them to make payment for the lenses until they were sold. That revelation prompted ac-

counting experts to question the 1993 arrangement: Was it really a financial-management gimmick that allowed B&L to inflate 1993 sales? "If the distributors were told they didn't have to pay for inventory until they sold it," contends one professor of accounting, "the company is supposed to hold off booking the revenues." Says one contact lens marketer of the deal: "It was just a blatant attempt to make their numbers." B&L's controller insists that the transaction was cleared with outside auditors.

For much of 1994, distributors had a hard time moving stockpiled lenses. Part of the problem was B&L's practice of competing with its own distributors by making direct sales to high-volume vision professionals. In mid-1994, Harold O. Johnson, the B&L executive who had presented the original 1993 deal to distributors, left his position. In an effort to end the controversy, Johnson's replacement authorized distributors to return unsold lenses. Distributors generally responded favorably to the offer. "They've been fair," conceded an executive at one distributor. "They saw they made a mistake and tried to rectify it." Now, however, B&L must deal with angry shareholders, who launched a class-action lawsuit alleging that B&L executives received excessive 1993 bonuses based on overstated sales.

Failure to manage inventory can have grave financial consequences. Too little inventory of any kind can cost the firm sales. Too much inventory means that the firm has funds tied up that it cannot use elsewhere. In extreme cases, too much inventory may force a company to sell merchandise at low profits simply to obtain needed cash. The box "A Short-Sighted Approach to Inventory" describes a related situation.

Long-Term Expenditures

Companies need funds to cover long-term expenditures for fixed assets. As noted in Chapter 17, fixed assets are items that have a lasting use or value, such as land, buildings, and machinery. The Hudson Bay Oil and Gas plant in Flin Flon, Manitoba, is a fixed asset.

Because they are so crucial to business success, long-term expenditures are usually planned more carefully than are short-term expenditures. But long-term expenditures pose special problems for the financial manager because they differ from short-term expenditures in several ways. First, unlike inventories and other short-term assets, they are not normally sold or converted into cash. Second, their acquisition requires a very large investment in funds. Third, they represent an ongoing tie-up of the company's funds. All these features influence how long-term expenditures are funded.

Short-Term Sources of Funds

Just as firms have many short-term expenditures, so they can call on many short-term sources for the funds to finance day-to-day operations and to implement short-term plans. These sources include trade credit, secured and unsecured loans, commercial paper, and factoring accounts receivable.

trade credit
The granting of credit by a selling firm to a buying firm.

open-book credit
A form of trade credit in which buyers receive their merchandise along with an invoice stating the terms of credit, but in which no formal promissory note is signed.

promissory note
A written commitment to pay a stated sum of money on a given date; a form of trade credit in which the buyer signs an agreement regarding payment terms before receiving the merchandise.

trade draft
A form of trade credit in which the seller draws up a statement of payment terms and attaches it to the merchandise; the buyer must sign this agreement to take delivery of the merchandise.

trade acceptance
A trade draft that has been signed by the buyer.

Trade Credit

Accounts payable are not merely an expenditure. They are also a source of funds to the company, which has the use of both the product purchased and the price of the product until the time it pays its bill. **Trade credit**, the granting of credit by one firm to another, is effectively a short-term loan.

The most common forms of trade credit are open-book accounts, promissory notes, and trade drafts and trade acceptances. **Open-book credit** is essentially a "gentlemen's agreement." Buyers receive their merchandise along with an invoice stating the terms of credit. Sellers ship the products on faith that payment will be forthcoming.

When sellers want more reassurance, they may insist on a legally binding written document called a **promissory note**. Buyers must sign a promissory note before the merchandise is shipped. The agreement states when and how much money will be paid to the seller in return for immediate credit.

Another type of credit agreement, the **trade draft**, is written by sellers, not buyers. Attached to the shipment of merchandise, a trade draft states the promised date and amount of repayment due the seller. The buyer must sign the draft to take possession of the merchandise. Once signed by the buyer, the document is called a **trade acceptance**. Trade drafts and trade acceptances are useful forms of credit in international transactions.

Trade credit is not without problems. During the recession of 1990-92, many large firms did not pay their bills for 90 days or more. Much of this money was owed to small firms who were afraid to hound the big firms for the money. But the small firms desperately needed the cash and many of them were pushed to the brink of insolvency.[1]

Secured Short-Term Loans

For most firms, bank loans are a vital source of short-term funding. As the video case "Bank Battle" on p. 620 shows, John Banka took out a loan from the Toronto Dominion Bank in an attempt to develop a new product. Such loans almost always involve a promissory note in which the borrower promises to repay the loan plus interest. In **secured loans**, banks also require the borrower to put up **collateral**—to give the bank the right to seize certain assets if payments are not made as promised. Inventories, accounts receivable, and other assets may serve as collateral for a secured loan.

Perhaps the biggest disadvantage of secured borrowing is the paperwork and administrative costs. Agreements must be written, collateral evaluated, and the terms of the loans enforced. But secured loans do enable borrowers to get funds when they might not qualify for unsecured credit. And even creditworthy borrowers benefit by borrowing at lower rates than with unsecured loans.

Inventory Loans.   When a loan is made with inventory as a collateral asset, the lender loans the borrower some portion of the stated value of the inventory. Inventory is more attractive as collateral when it provides the lender with real security for the loan amount: For example, if the inventory can be readily converted into cash, it is relatively more valuable as collateral. Other inventory—say, boxes full of expensive, partially completed lenses for eyeglasses—is of little value on the open market. Meanwhile, a thousand crates of boxed, safely stored canned tomatoes might well be convertible into cash.

secured loan
A short-term loan in which the borrower is required to put up collateral.

collateral
Any asset that a lender has the right to seize if a borrower does not repay a loan.

The inventory in this auto parts warehouse is good collateral because it is neatly stored, accessible, can be readily evaluated, and is quickly disposable.

pledging accounts receivable

Using accounts receivable as collateral for a loan.

Accounts Receivable.   When accounts receivable are used as collateral, the process is called **pledging accounts receivable**. In the event of nonpayment, the lender may seize the receivables—that is, funds owed the borrower by its customers. If these assets are not enough to cover the loan, the borrower must make up the difference. This option is especially important to service companies such as accounting firms and law offices. Because they do not maintain inventories, accounts receivable are their main source of collateral.

Typically, lenders who will accept accounts receivable as collateral are financial institutions with credit departments capable of evaluating the quality of the receivables. Loans are granted only when lenders are confident that they can recover funds from the borrower's debtors. (We will discuss the companies that specialize in these loans, called *factors*, later in the chapter.)

Unsecured Short-Term Loans

unsecured loan

A short-term loan in which the borrower is not required to put up collateral.

With an **unsecured loan**, the borrower does not have to put up collateral. In many cases, however, the bank requires the borrower to maintain a *compensating balance*: The borrower must keep a portion of the loan amount on deposit with the bank in a non-interest-bearing account.

The terms of the loan—amount, duration, interest rate, and payment schedule—are negotiated between the bank and the borrower. To receive an unsecured loan, then, a firm must ordinarily have a good banking relationship with the lender. Once an agreement is made, a promissory note will be executed and the funds transferred to the borrower. Although some unsecured loans are one-time-only arrangements, many take the form of *lines of credit, revolving credit agreements*, or *commercial paper*.

line of credit

A standing agreement between a bank and a firm in which the bank specifies the maximum amount it will make available to the borrower for a short-term unsecured loan; the borrower can then draw on those funds, when available.

Lines of Credit.   A standing agreement with a bank to lend a firm a maximum amount of funds on request is called a **line of credit**. With a line of credit, the firm knows the maximum amount it will be allowed to borrow if the bank has sufficient funds. The bank does not guarantee that the funds will be available when requested, however.

For example, suppose the Toronto-Dominion Bank gives Sunshine Tanning Inc., a $100 000 line of credit for the coming year. By signing promissory notes, Sunshine's borrowings can total up to $100 000 at any time. The bank may not always have sufficient funds when Sunshine needs them. But Sunshine benefits from the arrangement by knowing in advance that the bank regards the firm as creditworthy and will loan funds to it on short notice.

revolving credit agreement

A guaranteed line of credit for which the firm pays the bank interest on funds borrowed as well as a fee for extending the line of credit.

Revolving Credit Agreements.   Revolving credit agreements are similar to bank credit cards for consumers. Under a **revolving credit agreement**, a lender agrees to make some amount of funds available on demand to a firm for continuing short-term loans. The lending institution guarantees that funds will be available when sought by the borrower. In return, the bank charges a *commitment fee*—a charge for holding open a line of credit for a customer even if the customer does not borrow any funds. The commitment fee is often expressed as a percentage of the loan amount, usually one-half to 1 percent of the committed amount.

For example, suppose the Toronto-Dominion Bank agrees to lend Sunshine Tanning up to $100 000 under a revolving credit agreement. If Sunshine borrows $80 000, it still has access to $20 000. If it pays off $50 000 of the debt, reducing its debt to $30 000, then it has $70 000 available to it. Sunshine pays interest on the borrowed funds and also pays a fee on the unused funds in the line of credit.

Commercial Paper. Some firms can raise funds in the short run by issuing commercial paper. Since **commercial paper** is backed solely by the issuing firm's promise to pay, it is an option for only the largest and most creditworthy firms.

How does commercial paper work? Corporations issue commercial paper with a face value. Companies that buy commercial paper pay less than that value. At the end of a specified period (usually 30 to 90 days but legally up to 270 days), the issuing company buys back the paper—*at the face value*. The difference between the price the buying company paid and the face value is the buyer's profit.

For example, if Noranda needs to borrow $10 million for 90 days it might issue commercial paper with a face value of $10.2 million. Insurance companies with $10 million excess cash will buy the paper. After 90 days, Noranda would pay $10.2 million to the insurance companies.

Commercial paper offers those few corporations able to issue it several advantages. Its cost is usually lower than prevailing interest rates on short-term loans. And it gives the issuing company access to a wide range of lenders, not just financial institutions.

commercial paper
A method of short-run fundraising in which a firm sells unsecured notes for less than the face value and then repurchases them at the face value within 270 days; buyers' profits are the difference between the original price paid and the face value.

Factoring Accounts Receivable

One way to raise funds rapidly is **factoring**, that is, selling the firm's accounts receivable. In this process, the purchaser of the receivables, usually a financial institution, is known as the *factor*. The factor pays some percentage of the full amount of receivables to the selling firm. The seller gets money immediately.

For example, a factor might buy $40 000 worth of receivables for 60 percent of that sum ($24 000). The factor profits to the extent that the money it eventually collects exceeds the amount it paid. This profit depends on the quality of the receivables, the costs of collecting the receivables, the time until the receivables are due, and interest rates.

factoring
Selling a firm's accounts receivable to another company for some percentage of their face value in order to realize immediate cash; the buyer's profits depend on its ability to collect the receivables.

Long-Term Sources of Funds

Just as firms need short-term sources of funds to cover their short-term expenditures, so they need long-term sources to finance long-term expenditures for fixed assets. Firms need funds for buildings and equipment necessary for conducting their business. Companies may seek long-term funds from outside the firm (debt financing), or they may draw on internal financial sources (equity financing).

Debt Financing

Long-term borrowing from outside the company—**debt financing**—is a major component of most firms' long-term financial planning. The two primary sources of such funding are long-term loans and the sale of bonds.

Long-Term Loans. In some respects, a long-term loan is like a short-term loan. The major difference is that a long-term loan extends for three to ten years, while short-term loans must generally be paid off in a few years or less. Most corporations get their long-term loans from a chartered bank, usually one with which the firm has developed a long-standing relationship. But credit companies, insurance companies, and pension funds also grant long-term business loans.

debt financing
Raising money to meet long-term expenditures by borrowing from outside the company; usually takes the form of long-term loans or the sale of corporate bonds.

Interest rates on long-term loans are negotiated between borrower and lender. Although some bank loans have fixed rates, others have *floating rates* tied to the prime rate (see Chapter 18). A loan at "1 percent above prime," then, is payable at 1 percentage point higher than the prime rate. This rate may fluctuate—"float"—because the prime rate itself goes up and down as market conditions change.

Long-term loans are attractive to borrowing companies for several reasons. First, because the number of parties involved is limited, long-term loans can often be arranged quickly. Second, the firm need not make a public disclosure of its business plans or the purpose for which it is acquiring the loan. Third, the duration of a long-term loan can easily be matched to the borrower's needs. Finally, if the firm's needs change, long-term loans usually contain clauses making it possible to change the loan's terms.

Long-term loans also have some disadvantages. Large borrowers may have trouble finding lenders to supply enough funds. Long-term borrowers may also have restrictions placed on them as conditions of the loan. They may have to pledge long-term assets as collateral. And they may have to agree not to take on any more debt until the borrowed funds are repaid.

corporate bond

A promise by the issuing company to pay the holder a certain amount of money on a specified date, with stated interest payments in the interim; a form of long-term debt financing.

Corporate Bonds.   Like commercial paper, a **corporate bond** is a contract—a promise by the issuing company or organization to pay the holder a certain amount of money on a specified date. Unlike commercial paper, however, bond issuers do not pay off quickly. In many cases, bonds may not be redeemed for 30 years from the time of issue. In addition, unlike commercial paper, most bonds pay the bondholder a stipulated sum of interest semiannually or annually. If it fails to make a bond payment, the company is in default.

The terms of a bond, including the amount to be paid, the interest rate, and the **maturity** (payoff) **date**, differ from company to company and from issue to issue. They are spelled out in the bond contract, or *bond indenture*. The indenture also identifies which of the firm's assets, if any, are pledged as collateral for the bonds.

maturity date

The date on or before which a company must pay off the principal of a particular bond issue.

Corporate bonds are the major source of long-term debt financing for most corporations. Bonds are attractive when companies need large amounts of funds for long periods of time. The issuing company gets access to large numbers of lenders through nationwide bond markets and stock exchanges.

But bonds involve expensive administrative and selling costs. They also may require very high interest payments if the issuing company has a poor credit rating. We will return to these characteristics when we consider the market for bonds in more detail in Chapter 20.

Equity Financing

Although debt financing has strong appeal in some cases, looking inside the company for long-term funding is preferable under other circumstances. In small companies, the founders may increase their personal investment in the firm. In most cases, however, **equity financing** takes the form of issuing common stock or of retaining the firm's earnings. As you will see, both options involve putting the owners' capital to work.

equity financing

Raising money to meet long-term expenditures by issuing common stock or by retaining earnings.

Common Stock.   As noted in Chapter 2, when shareholders purchase common stock, they seek profits in the form of both dividends and appreciation. Overall, shareholders hope for an increase in the market value of their stock because the firm has profited and grown. By selling shares of stock, the company gets the funds it needs for buying land, buildings, and equipment.

For example, suppose Sunshine Tanning's founders invested $10 000 by buying the original 500 shares of common stock (at $20 per share) in 1992. If the company used these funds to buy equipment and succeeded financially, by 1994 it might need funds for expansion. A pattern of profitable operations and regularly paid dividends might allow Sunshine to raise $50 000 by selling 500 new shares of stock for $100 per share. This additional paid-in capital would increase the total shareholders' equity to $60 000, as shown in Table 19.1.

It should be noted that the use of equity financing via common stock can be expensive because paying dividends is more expensive than paying bond interest. Why? Interest paid to bondholders is a business expense and, hence, a tax deduction for the firm. Stock dividends are not tax-deductible.

TABLE 19.1 Shareholders' Equity for Sunshine Tanning Inc.

Common Shareholders' Equity, 1989:

Initial common stock (500 shares issued @ $20 per share, 1989)	$10 000
Total shareholders' equity	$10 000

Common Shareholders' Equity, 1994:

Initial common stock (500 shares issued @ $20 per share, 1989)	$10 000
Additional paid-in capital (500 shares issued @ $100 per share, 1994)	50 000
Total shareholders' equity	$60 000

Retained Earnings. Another approach to equity financing is to use retained earnings. As we saw in Chapter 17, these earnings represent profits not paid out in dividends. Using retained earnings means that the firm will not have to borrow money and pay interest on loans or bonds. A firm that has a history of eventually reaping much higher profits by successfully reinvesting retained earnings may be attractive to some investors. But the smaller dividends that can be paid to shareholders as a result of retained earnings may decrease demand for—and thus the price of—the company's stock.

For example, if Sunshine Tanning had net earnings of $50 000 in 1994, it could pay a $50-per-share dividend on its 1000 shares of common stock. But if it plans to remodel at a cost of $30 000 and retains $30 000 of earnings to finance the project, only $20 000 is left to distribute for stock dividends ($20 per share).

Financial Burden on the Firm. If equity funding can be so expensive, why don't firms rely instead on debt capital? Because long-term loans and bonds carry fixed interest rates and represent a fixed promise to pay, regardless of economic changes. If the firm defaults on its obligations, it may lose its assets and even go into bankruptcy.

Because of this risk, debt financing appeals most strongly to companies in industries that have predictable profits and cash flow patterns. For example, demand for electric power is steady from year to year and predictable from month to month. So provincial electric utility companies, with their stable stream of income, can carry a substantial amount of debt.

Hybrid Financing: Preferred Stock

Falling somewhere between debt and equity financing is the *preferred stock* (see Chapter 2). Preferred stock is a hybrid because it has some of the features of corporate bonds and some features of common stocks. As with bonds, payments on preferred stock are for fixed amounts, such as $6 per share year. Unlike bonds, however, preferred stock never matures. It can be held indefinitely, like common stock. And dividends need not be paid if the company makes no profit. If dividends are paid, preferred shareholders receive them first in preference to dividends on common stock.

A major advantage of preferred stock to the issuing corporation is its flexibility. It secures funds for the firm without relinquishing control, since preferred shareholders have no voting rights. It does not require repayment of principal or the payment of dividends in lean times.

Choosing Between Debt and Equity Financing

Part of financial planning involves striking a balance between debt and equity financing to meet the firm's long-term need for funds (see the box "Debt Strategy at B.C. Hydro"). Because the mix of debt versus equity provides the firm's financial base, it is called the *capital structure* of the firm. Financial plans contain targets for the capital structure, such as 40 percent debt and 60 percent equity. But choosing a target is not easy. A wide range of debt-versus-equity mixes is possible.

The most conservative strategy would be to use all equity financing and no debt. Under this strategy, a company has no formal obligations for finan-

The Canadian Business Scene

DEBT STRATEGY AT B.C. HYDRO

British Columbia Hydro and Power Authority is Canada's fifth largest utility. Over the last few decades the company has built a debt portfolio of more than $8 billion. With the decline of interest rates, the company has been left with excessively high debt service payments at a time when the recession has caused revenues to slump. In the late 1980s, when Larry Bell was appointed chairman, over 50 percent of the utility's operating expenses was consumed by debt service payments.

Rather than simply doing an interest rate swap (replacing high interest bonds with lower interest bonds), Bell hired financial risk management consultants Bridgewater Associates Inc. B.C. Hydro wanted to develop a continuing process for managing risk rather than only trying to solve current problems.

Before it could restructure its debt and bring debt service charges in line with revenue, B.C. Hydro had to understand what drove its long-term sales growth. The utility refined its understanding of its two basic types of customers—residential and small business users (60 percent) and major manufacturers (40 percent). The former group's use of hydroelectric power was stable, but the latter group's demand varied widely.

The next step for B.C. Hydro was to figure out what caused the wide fluctuations in demand by the major manufacturers. General commodity prices had a big impact because most of the firms were in the pulp and paper, chemical, and mining industries. A 30-year analysis of trends showed an almost perfect correlation between sales, general industrial production, and commodity prices.

To reduce its interest expenses when revenues dropped, Hydro needed some short-term debt. To determine the appropriate level of short-term debt, Bridgewater urged Hydro to picture itself as two separate businesses with separate financing structures. Ideally, the 60 percent of revenues from residential consumers should have its own financing structure (long-term, fixed-rate debt), while the 40 percent from industrial customers should have its own short-term financing structure. In practice, Hydro is keeping short-term debt between 15 and 30 percent of total debt.

The new system has reduced Hydro's debt load from its one-time high of $8.6 billion to $6.6 billion. Interest expense has declined from $880 million per year to about $750 million.

cial payouts. But equity is a very expensive source of capital. The most risk-filled strategy would be to use all debt financing. While less expensive than equity funding, indebtedness increases the risk that a firm will be unable to meet its obligations and will go bankrupt. Magna International, for example, has had a high debt to equity ratio in the recent past. Industry analysts believe increased demand for automobiles will allow the firm to make large profits and pay off much of the debt, causing its debt/equity ratio to fall.[2] Somewhere between the two extremes, financial planners try to find a mix that will maximize shareholders' wealth. Figure 19.1 summarizes the factors management must take into account when deciding between debt and equity financing.

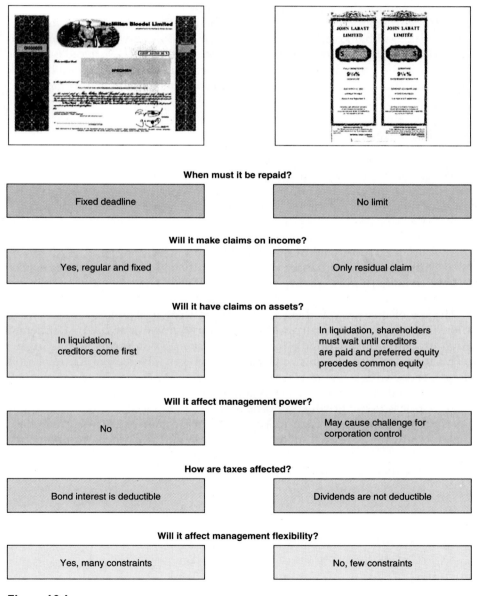

Figure 19.1
Comparing debt and equity financing.

Indexes of Financial Risk.   To help understand and measure the amount of financial risk they face, financial managers often rely on indexes for various investments. *Financial World*, for example, publishes independent appraisals of mutual funds (see Chapter 20) using ratings of 1 to 5. A fund rated "1" is least volatile (stable price), while a "5" has the greatest volatility (a highly fluctuating price) compared to all others. Similarly, Standard & Poor's has volatility indexes for mutual funds and for stocks that are available for purchase by financial managers.[3] By using these indexes, financial managers can determine how stable a particular investment is compared to other investment opportunities.

Firms go into debt (both long- and short-term) in the hope of being able to pay the interest and principal out of earnings. If this does not work out over the period of indebtedness, the firm is in trouble. A firm that cannot meet its maturing financial obligations is insolvent. If, in addition, its liabilities are greater than its assets, the firm is said to be in **bankruptcy**.

bankruptcy

When a firm's liabilities exceed its assets and it cannot meet its maturing financial obligations.

Under voluntary bankruptcy, a person or firm files a petition in court claiming inability to pay debts because the debts exceed available assets. This petition asserts willingness to make all assets available to creditors under the supervision of a court-appointed trustee.

Under involuntary bankruptcy, a person or firm's creditors seek to have a debtor declared bankrupt by proving that the debtor committed one or more acts of bankruptcy as defined in the law. Once a defendant is declared bankrupt by a court, the procedure is the same as for voluntary bankruptcy. The box "Bankruptcy at Olympia & York" describes a recent Canadian example.

The Risk-Return Relationship

While developing plans for raising capital, financial managers must be aware of the different motivations of individual investors. Why, for example, do some individuals and firms invest in stocks while others invest only in bonds? Investor motivations, of course, determine who is willing to buy a given company's stocks or bonds. Everyone who invests money is expressing a personal preference for safety versus risk. Investors give money to firms and, in return, anticipate receiving future cash flows.

Some cash flows are more certain than others. Investors generally expect to receive higher payments for higher uncertainty. They do not generally expect large returns for secure investments such as government-insured bonds. Each type of investment, then, has a **risk-return relationship**. Figure 19.2 shows the general risk-return *relationship* for various financial instruments. High-grade corporate bonds, for example, rate low in terms of risk on future returns but also low on size of expected returns. The reverse is true of junk bonds, those with a higher risk of default.

risk-return relationship

Shows the amount of risk and the likely rate of return on various financial instruments.

Risk-return differences are recognized by financial planners, who try to gain access to the greatest funding at the lowest possible cost. By gauging investors' perceptions of their riskiness, a firm's managers can estimate how much it must pay to attract funds to their offerings. Over time, a company can reposition itself on the risk continuum by improving its record on dividends, interest payments, and debt repayment.

The Canadian Business Scene

BANKRUPTCY AT OLYMPIA & YORK

Olympia & York Developments Ltd. is a real estate and natural resources conglomerate that sought bankruptcy protection under the *Companies' Creditors Arrangement Act* in May, 1992. O & Y had been hailed in the mid-1980s as a pioneer in new financial techniques when it issued short-term debt (commercial paper) to finance some of its office buildings. The firm believed it could issue short-term debt during the double-digit inflation of the early 1980s and replace it with lower cost long-term debt later.

In adopting this strategy, O & Y departed from the industry's traditional practice of paying for skyscrapers with 20- or 30-year mortgages. By 1990, O & Y had borrowed more than $1 billion in short-term financial instruments such as commercial paper as well as an additional $1 billion in five- and ten-year bonds. O & Y's major mistake, according to investment bankers, was to finance long-term assets with short-term debt.

When the recession caused a steep decline in real estate prices in 1991, investors began to back away from buying further commercial paper from O & Y. The company was left short of cash to pay the interest on other loans it had taken out from nearly 100 banks worldwide. In turn, investors threatened to seize O & Y's assets for nonpayment of interest. Eventually, the cracks in the O & Y empire became so great that the firm had to file for protection under bankruptcy laws. Had O & Y used long-term bonds to finance its real estate activities, it might have averted many of its difficulties.

A brief summary of the events leading to O & Y's bankruptcy is presented below.

February, 1992
- Dominion Bond Rating Service downgrades its rating on O & Y's bonds.
- Bank stocks decline as investors worry about bank exposure to O & Y loans.
- CIBC and Royal Bank each have more than $500 million in outstanding loans to O & Y.
- Rumors begin to circulate that O & Y is in danger of collapse. The $7 billion Canary Wharf project in London, England, is seen as the big drain on the company.

March 6, 1992
- O & Y retreats further from the commercial paper market.

- O & Y denies it is headed for bankruptcy.
- O & Y sells its interest in Interprovincial Pipeline Inc. for $665 million and begins retiring $500 million in commercial paper.

March 25, 1992
- Thomas Johnson replaces Paul Reichmann as president of O & Y; he is hired to work out restructuring on debt of $14.3 billion.
- O & Y discusses the possibility of loan guarantees from the federal government.

March 28, 1992
- Albert Reichmann personally buys O & Y's interest in Damdev Corp. (the former Campeau Corp.).
- Company executives meet with bankers to begin discussions on restructuring; lenders asked to extend deadlines on debt falling due.

April 23, 1992
- O & Y states that it has no intention of applying for bankruptcy protection in Britain, the U.S., or Canada.

May, 1992
- O & Y has a difficult series of meetings with bankers. They finally agree to lend enough money to keep the Canary Wharf project going for just one month.

May 14, 1992
- U.S. court rules that O & Y must pay Morgan Stanley International $231 million for its building at Canary Wharf; if O & Y does not make the payment, Morgan Stanley can seize the asset.
- Investors threaten to seize O & Y's First Canadian Place in Toronto unless the company pays $17 million in interest due.

May 15, 1992
- O & Y files for bankruptcy protection in Canada and the U.S. as it continues to try to restructure $14.9 billion in debt; investors increasingly threaten to seize O & Y's assets because the firm failed to make interest payments on loans.
- Documents show the company's assets equal its liabilities; under bankruptcy, O & Y must develop a plan for restructuring and talk with investors about its plan.

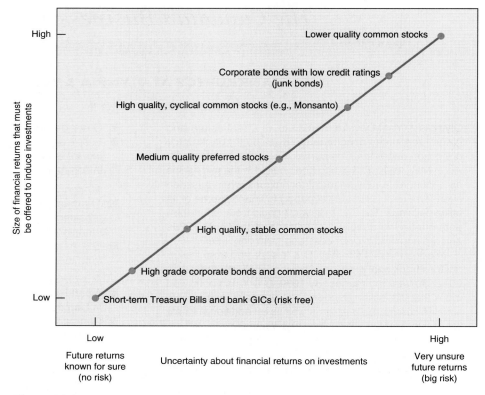

Figure 19.2
Investors expect a chance at greater financial returns for riskier investments.

Financial Management for Small Businesses

Most new businesses have inadequate funding. An Ontario government report stated that the average investment needed to start a new enterprise was about $58 000, but that more than half of all new companies have less than $15 000 invested.[4] Another study of nearly 3000 new companies revealed a survival rate of 84 percent for new businesses with initial investments of at least $50 000. Unfortunately, those with less funding have a much lower survival rate.[5] Why are so many startups underfunded? For one thing, entrepreneurs often underestimate the value of establishing *bank credit* as a source of funds and use *trade credit* ineffectively. In addition, they often fail to consider *venture capital* as a source of funding, and they are notorious for not *planning cash-flow needs* properly.

Establishing Bank Credit and Trade Credit

Banks differ greatly in willingness to assume risk, ability to give professional advice, loyalty to customers, and maximum size of loans offered.[6] Some have liberal credit policies. Some offer financial analysis, cash-flow planning, and suggestions based on experience with other local small businesses. Some provide loans to small businesses in bad times and work to keep them going. Others do not.

Credit-seekers must be prepared to show they are worthy of the bank's help. A sound financial plan, a good credit history, and proven capability on the part of the entrepreneur can all convince bankers and other potential financiers that the business can succeed.

Once it has obtained a line of credit, the small business can then attempt to gain more liberal credit policies from other businesses. Sometimes, suppliers will give customers longer credit periods, such as 45 or 60 days net rather than 30 days. Such liberal trade credit terms with suppliers let the firm increase its own short-term funds and avoid additional borrowing from banks.

Planning Cash for Requirements

Although all businesses should plan for their cash flows, it is especially important for small businesses to do so. Success or failure may hinge on anticipating times when cash will be short and when excess cash is expected.

Figure 19.3 shows possible cash inflows, cash outflows, and net cash position (inflows minus outflows), month by month, for Slippery Fish Bait Supply. In this highly seasonal business, bait stores buy heavily from Slippery during the spring and summer months. Revenues outpace expenses, leaving surplus funds that can be invested. During the fall and winter, expenses exceed revenues. Slippery must borrow funds to keep going until sales revenues pick up again in the spring. Comparing predicted cash inflows from sales with outflows for expenses shows the firm's monthly cash-flow position.

By anticipating shortfalls, a financial manager can seek funds in advance and minimize their cost. By anticipating excess cash, a manager can plan to put the funds to work in short-term, interest-earning investments.

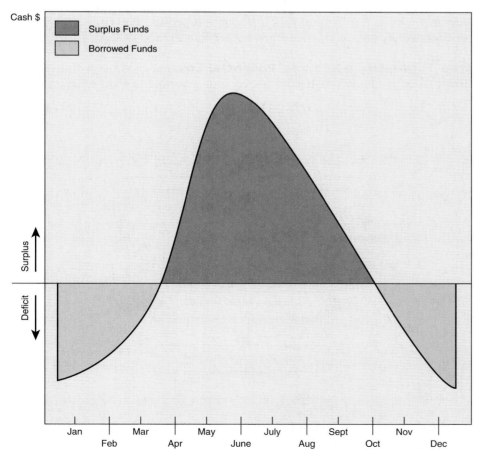

Figure 19.3
Cash flow for Slippery Fish Bait Supply Company.

Emcor Treasury Consultancy Inc. advises corporate and government clients on financial risk management. For example, if a client has money under a previously arranged credit deal but does not currently have a use for the money, the consultants ensure that the client earns a profit from the money until suitable assets are found as an investment.[7]

Risk Management

Financial risks are not the only risks faced every day by companies (and individuals). In this section, we will describe various other types of risks that businesses face and analyze some of the ways in which they typically manage them.

Coping with Risk

risk
Uncertainty about future events.

speculative risk
An event that offers the chance for either a gain or a loss.

pure risk
An event that offers no possibility of gain; it offers only the chance of a loss.

risk management
Conserving a firm's (or an individual's) financial power or assets by minimizing the financial effect of accidental losses.

Businesses constantly face two basic types of **risk**—that is, uncertainty about future events. **Speculative risks**, such as financial investments, involve the possibility of gain or loss. **Pure risks** involve only the possibility of loss or no loss. Designing and distributing a new product, for example, is a speculative risk: The product may fail or it may succeed and earn high profits. The chance of a warehouse fire is a pure risk.

For a company to survive and prosper, it must manage both types of risk in a cost-effective manner. We can thus define the process of **risk management** as "conserving the firm's earning power and assets by reducing the threat of losses due to uncontrollable events."[8] In every company, each manager must be alert for risks to the firm and their impact on profits. The risk-management process usually entails the five steps outlined in Figure 19.4.

Step 1: Identify Risks and Potential Losses.   Managers analyze a firm's risks to identify potential losses. For example, a firm with a fleet of

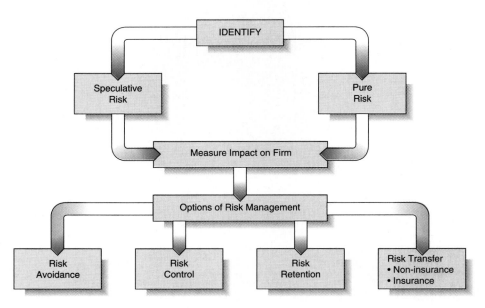

Figure 19.4
The risk management process.

delivery trucks can expect that one of them will eventually be involved in an accident. The accident may cause bodily injury to the driver or others, may cause physical damage to the truck or other vehicles, or both.

Step 2: Measure the Frequency and Severity of Losses and Their Impact.

To measure the frequency and severity of losses, managers must consider both past history and current activities. How often can the firm expect the loss to occur? What is the likely size of the loss in dollars? For example, our firm with the fleet of delivery trucks may have had two accidents per year in the past. If it adds trucks, however, it may reasonably expect the frequency of accidents to increase.

Step 3: Evaluate Alternatives and Choose the Techniques That Will Best Handle the Losses.

Having identified and measured potential losses, managers are in a better position to decide how to handle them. With this third step, they generally have four choices: *risk avoidance, control, retention,* or *transfer.*

A firm opts for **risk avoidance** by declining to enter or by ceasing to participate in a risky activity. For example, our firm with the delivery trucks could avoid any risk of physical damage or bodily injury by closing down its delivery service. Similarly, a pharmaceutical maker may withdraw a new drug for fear of liability suits.

By definition, risk avoidance is always successful. It is not, however, always practical. A manager who avoids a certain risk may be acting inconsistently with the firm's strategic direction. For example, if a speedy, centrally controlled delivery system gives our company a competitive edge, risk avoidance may be the wrong choice.

When avoidance is not practical or desirable, firms can practice **risk control**—say, the use of loss-prevention techniques to minimize the frequency of losses. A delivery service, for instance, can prevent losses by training its drivers in defensive-driving techniques, mapping out safe routes, and conscientiously maintaining its trucks.

Unfortunately, loss-prevention techniques cannot guarantee that losses will not occur. Rather, they concede that losses may occur while trying to minimize their severity. Seat belts or air bags, for example, can minimize injuries to truck drivers when accidents do happen. Many firms use fire extinguishers, fire alarms, or buglar alarms to reduce loss.

All risk-control techniques involve costs. The risk manager's job, therefore, is to find techniques whose benefits exceed their costs. For example, a new sprinkler system may cost $100 000. However, if it reduces fire losses by $150 000, it is money well spent.

When losses cannot be avoided or controlled, firms must cope with the consequences. When such losses are manageable and predictable, they may decide to cover them out of company funds. The firm is thus said to "assume" or "retain" the financial consequences of the loss: hence the practice known as **risk retention**. For example, the firm with the fleet of trucks may find that vehicles suffer vandalism totaling $100 to $500 per year. Depending on its coverage, the company may find it cheaper to pay for repairs out of pocket rather than to submit claims to its insurance company.

Some large organizations choose to build up their own pools of funds as a reserve to cover losses that would otherwise be covered by commercial insurance. This type of coverage is called **self-insurance**.

The primary motive for self-insurance is to avoid the high cost of buying coverage from private insurers. For example, part of a firm's paid premiums go to cover the insurer's administrative, advertising, and sales costs. Self-insurance avoids these costs. Suppose, for instance, that an athletic club pays $100 000 in premiums annually but experiences average losses of only

risk avoidance
Stopping participation in or refusing to participate in ventures that carry any risk.

risk control
Techniques to prevent, minimize, or reduce losses or the consequences of losses.

risk retention
The covering of a firm's unavoidable losses with its own funds.

self-insurance
Occurs when a company chooses to build up a pool of its own funds as a reserve to cover losses that would otherwise be covered by insurance.

risk transfer

The transfer of risk to another individual or firm, often by contract.

insurance policy

A written contract between an individual or firm and an insurance company transferring financial liability in the event of some loss to the insurance company in return for a fee.

deductible

A previously agreed-upon amount of loss the insured must absorb before reimbursement from the insurer.

$20 000. Let's say, however, that the club decides instead to set up its own reserve fund of $50 000 annually. If it also establishes efficient procedures for handling damages and other losses, it might achieve comparable coverage through self-insurance *and* save $50 000 in annual premiums.

As a practical matter, self-insurance is not a reasonable alternative for smaller or new companies (even large ones) that have not yet built up sizable reserves. What would happen if our athletic club suffers a $1 million fire loss when its reserve fund has grown to only $100 000? It may be forced to close. Had its previous commercial coverage been in effect, however, the entire loss might have been covered. Then it could have resumed operations after the club was renovated.

When the potential for large risks cannot be avoided or controlled, managers often opt for **risk transfer**: They transfer the risk to another firm—namely, an insurance company. In transferring risk to an insurance company, a firm pays a sum called a *premium*. In return, the insurance company issues an **insurance policy**—a formal agreement to pay the policyholder a specified amount in the event of certain losses. In some cases, the insured party must also pay a **deductible**—an agreed-upon amount of the loss that the insured must absorb prior to reimbursement. Thus, our delivery service may buy insurance to protect itself against theft, physical damage to trucks, and bodily injury to drivers and others involved in an accident. Similarly, retail stores buy protection in case customers are injured on their premises. (We discuss insurance more fully later in this chapter.)

Step 4: Implement the Risk-Management Program. The means of implementing risk-management decisions depends on both the technique

Losses are reduced or prevented when this security specialist uses electronic surveillance (below), when valuables are stored under lock and key (top right), and when workers are reminded to wear safety gear at this construction site (bottom right).

chosen and the activity being managed. For example, risk avoidance for certain activities can be implemented by purchasing those activities from outside providers, such as hiring delivery services instead of operating delivery vehicles. Risk control might be implemented by training employees and designing new work methods and equipment for on-the-job safety. For situations in which risk retention is preferred, reserve funds can be set aside out of revenues. When risk transfer is needed, implementation means selecting an insurance company and buying the right policies.

Step 5: Monitor Results.   Because risk management is an ongoing activity, follow-up is always essential. New types of risks, for example, emerge with changes in customers, facilities, employees, and products. Insurance regulations change, and new types of insurance become available. Consequently, managers must continually monitor a company's risks, reevaluate the methods used for handling them, and revise them as necessary.

The Contemporary Risk-Management Program

Virtually all business decisions involve risks having financial consequences. As a result, the company's chief financial officer, along with managers in other areas, usually has a major voice in applying the risk management process. The box "Changes in Risk Management" describes the activities of risk managers. In some industries, most notably insurance, the companies' main line of business revolves around risk-taking and risk management for themselves and their clients.

Today, many firms are taking a new approach to risk management.[9] The key to that approach is developing a program that is both comprehensive

The Canadian Business Scene

CHANGES IN RISK MANAGEMENT

What do risk managers do? Buy insurance policies and keep them filed away, right? Wrong. Like all other areas of business, risk managers have to work smarter and add value. They no longer sit around and mechanically renew policies. Instead, they focus more on loss control and risk financing than on purchasing insurance. Because companies are increasingly concerned about their liability in the areas of the environment and employee health & safety, risk managers are upgrading their knowledge in these areas as well.

In these new activities, risk managers are supported by the international Risk and Insurance Management Society (RIMS). The society has a staff of 50 in New York and a Canadian coordinator working out of Ottawa. It offers its members courses, legislation updates, and educational publications. The society's annual conference attracts up to 10 000 people from 4500 different firms. With such a large number of risk managers in one place at one time, a great deal of information is traded back and forth.

Because so many companies have overseas operations, risk management is a global concern. RIMS is connected to the International Federation of Risk and Insurance Management Associations. Risk managers from 21 countries attend its annual conference.

To be effective, risk managers must know what is going on in their company's operations. Don Barrett, the manager of corporate affairs and risk management for Newfoundland and Labrador Hydro says risk managers should travel to their company's various locations to see exactly how things are done. Once there, they can sensitize workers to potential losses, and they can encourage them to work safely. He also thinks it is important for insurance brokers to see how the company operates. The brokers will be able to write a more reasonable policy if they see exactly what activities they are covering in their policy for the company.

and companywide. In the past, risk management was often conducted by different departments or by narrowly focused financial officers. Now, however, more and more firms have not only created high-level risk-management positions, but, at the same time, stressed the need for middle managers to practice risk management on a daily basis.

Why Insurance Companies Exist—and Thrive

The reason why companies often find insurance appealing is clear—in return for a sum of money, they are protected against certain potentially devastating losses. But why are insurance companies willing to accept these risks for other companies?

Like all firms, insurance companies are in business to make a profit (see Table 19.2 for a list of the ten largest life insurance companies in Canada). They do so by taking in more premiums than they pay out to cover policyholder losses. They profit because they have many policyholders paying them for protection against the same type of loss, yet not all policyholders will experience a loss.

TABLE 19.2   The Top Ten Life Insurance Companies in Canada, 1994 (ranked by assets)

Company	Assets (in billions)
1. Manulife Financial	$40.2
2. Sun Life Assurance Co. of Canada	40.2
3. The Great-West Life Assurance Co.	27.1
4. Canada Life Assurance Co.	19.5
5. The Mutual Group	18.9
6. London Insurance Group Inc.	17.8
7. North American Life Assurance Group	9.2
8. Desjardins-Laurentien Life Group	8.8
9. Crown Life Insurance Co.	6.7
10. Industrial-Alliance Life Insurance Co.	6.6

The Statistical Basis of Insurance

For example, consider a town with 5000 insured houses. Based on past history, insurers know that about 50 of these will be involved in a fire each year and that damages will average $40 000 per house involved. That is, insurance companies can expect to pay $2 000 000 ($40 000 x 50) to cover their policyholders. By charging each household in the town $500 a year for fire insurance the company effectively spreads out the risk. It also earns a gross profit of $500 000 ($2 500 000 in premiums versus $2 000 000 in damages). This is the insurer's gain for providing risk-spreading services.

To earn a profit, insurance companies must know the likelihood of a particular loss. The more they know, the better their predictions and the fairer the rates they set will be. Insurance companies also benefit from a statistical principle called the **law of large numbers**. As the number of people who seek insurance rises, so does the chance that the actual loss rate will be the same as the statistically calculated rate.

law of large numbers

The statistical principle that the larger the number of cases involved, the more closely the actual rate will match the statistically calculated rate.

To help them properly price insurance policies, insurers use a system of classification that rates possible losses based on certain characteristics. The frequency of loss from an automobile accident varies with the number of kilometres driven per year, whether the driving is done in a rural or urban area, and the driver's experience. An individual driving under 5000 kilometres per year on uncongested roads with many years of experience will probably have fewer accidents than someone in the opposite situation. Therefore, individuals with a lower probability of accidents as determined by these classification characteristics should pay a relatively lower premium. If insurance companies did not try to make rates equitable, so few customers might buy policies that the insurance company could not cover its costs.

The ultimate purpose of insurance is to *indemnify* policyholders. That is, policyholders should be brought back to their financial position before the loss. No policyholder should gain financially from insurance. To remain financially viable, an insurance company must be sure never to pay for losses not covered by the policy nor to pay too much for each loss.

Insurable versus Uninsurable Risks

Like every business, insurance companies avoid certain risks. Toward this end, insurers divide potential sources of loss into insurable risks and uninsurable risks and issue policies only for insurable risks. While some policies provide certain exemptions, in general, to qualify as an insurable risk, the risk should be predictable, outside the control of the insured, spread geographically, and verifiable. As the box "Risky Business" indicates some insurable risks are quite interesting.

Predictable. The insurance company must be able to use statistical tools to forecast the likelihood of a loss. For example, the insurer needs information about the number of car accidents in the past year to estimate the expected accidents for the following year. Translating the expected level of accidents into expected dollar losses helps determine the premium.

Outside the Control of the Policyholder. The loss must result from an accident, not from an intentional act by the policyholder. Insurers do not have to cover the damages if a policyholder deliberately sets fire to an office building. To avoid paying in cases of fraud, insurers may refuse to cover losses when they cannot determine whether the policyholder's action contributed to the loss.

Spread over a Large Geographic Area. One insurance company would not want to have all of the hail coverage in Saskatchewan or all of the earthquake coverage in Vancouver. Through selective underwriting of risks, the insurance company can dilute its chances of a large loss.

Verifiable. Did an employee develop emphysema due to a chemical he worked with in his job or because he smoked two packs of cigarettes a day for thirty years? Did the policyholder pay the renewal premium *before* the fire destroyed her home? Were the goods stolen from company offices or the president's home? What was the insurable value of the destroyed inventory?

Types of Insurance Companies

Insurance firms can be either private or public (government).

Private Insurance Companies. Private insurers may be shareholder-owned or mutually owned. **Stock insurance companies**, as the former are

stock insurance company
Any insurance company whose stock is held by members of the public, who may or may not be policyholders of the company.

International Report

RISKY BUSINESS

"Excuse me," says one man to another. "Did you give the Pope to someone else?" No, these are not armed guards wondering who is standing beside the pontiff right now. They are insurance brokers for the world's most famous insurance company, Lloyd's of London. To understand the first broker's question, you must first understand the unusual operations of Lloyd's.

Technically, Lloyd's is not an insurance company but an insurance market. Customers usually come to Lloyd's to seek insurance on items most insurance companies do not deem insurable (see the list below). At Lloyd's their requests are turned over to brokers, like the men above, who attempt to persuade one of the 366 syndicates that make up Lloyd's to underwrite the risk. Underwriters for the syndicates look over the risks and, if they decide they are interested, quote a premium. Brokers may accept the first quote they get or try several underwriters to get a lower premium price.

While the underwriters set the premiums, they do not insure the risks. The actual funds for insuring come from the 31 000 members ("Names") of Lloyd's who make up the syndicates. These individuals, who must meet stringent financial qualifications and invest a minimum of 28 000 pounds sterling, can reap profits of over 30 percent per year. However, because Lloyd's Names face *unlimited* liability, they could lose their entire fortunes if a major risk were realized. To avoid such a cataclysm, most Names purchase stop-loss insurance from outside insurance companies.

The range of items insured with Lloyd's over the years is both instructive and amusing. The syndicates got their start by insuring against maritime losses, which still represent a major portion of Lloyd's activities today. In fact, the business took its name from Lloyd's Coffee House in London where shipowners, ship captains, and seamen gathered at the turn of the seventeenth century, and anyone looking to insure a ship could always find someone to take on the risk.

In the years that followed, Lloyd's became a pioneer in what is now commonplace insurance: burglary, earthquake, and hurricane protection. It is one of the few private companies in the world to offer "political-risk insurance." This insurance protects clients against possible problems abroad ranging from government takeovers of private industry to kidnapping and hijacking.

But above all, Lloyd's has remained noteworthy for policies unusual even today. Among these are policies protecting

- Elizabeth Taylor's eyes and Bruce Springsteen's voice;
- R2D2 from the *Star Wars* movies;
- all the art objects held for sale by Christie's, the big London art auction house;
- shipments of diamonds from the former Soviet Union to the West;
- the Boeing 707s of a Middle Eastern airline against war risks;
- a vast number of thoroughbred horses (Lloyd's is the largest insurer of horse flesh in the world) against injury, death, infertility, and even a stallion whose "romantic advances succeed less than 60 percent of the time."

Oh yes, among other ventures, Lloyd's now insures the life of Pope John Paul II.

---

mutual insurance company

Any insurance company that is owned by its policyholders, who share in its profits.

known, are like any other corporation. They sell stock to the public, which hopes to earn a profit on its investment. Shareholders can be, but do not have to be, policyholders of the insurance company.

Mutual insurance companies are owned by their policyholders, for whom they seek to provide insurance at lower rates. As *cooperative* operations, they divide profits among policyholders, either by issuing dividends or by reducing premiums. In other words, the company's profits are generated for the direct benefit of policyholders rather than for outside shareholders. As nonprofit operations, they divide any profit among policyholders at the end of the year.

Two of the most important activities of private insurers are the underwriting and marketing of insurance offerings. **Underwriting** involves two basic tasks:

underwriting

Determining which applications for insurance to accept and deciding what rates the insurer will charge.

1. determining which applications for insurance to accept and which ones to reject
2. deciding what rates the insurer will charge.

These decisions are made by *underwriters*—experts who gather information and tabulate data, assess loss probabilities, and decide which applications will be accepted. The purpose of all these functions, of course, is to maximize the insurer's profits.

Agents and brokers are the people who market insurance. An **insurance agent** represents and is paid a commission by an insurance company. The agent, then, represents the insurance seller. An **insurance broker**, on the other hand, is a freelance agent who represents insurance buyers rather than sellers. Brokers work for clients by seeking the best coverage for them. They are then paid commissions by the insurers whom they recommend to their clients. Some brokers also offer risk-management advice for clients.

Public Insurers.   Most insurance that businesses buy is written by private insurance companies. But some—and a great deal of individual insurance—is issued by government agencies.

Provincial governments administer workers' compensation insurance and the federal government administers the unemployment insurance program. Employers, employees, and the government share the cost of these programs. The federal government also operates the Social Insurance program. It has become an important part of our economic life and is a major means of protecting older, disabled, and poor citizens from economic hardship.

insurance agent
A person who markets insurance and is paid a commission by the insurance company.

insurance broker
A freelance agent who represents insurance buyers rather than insurance sellers.

Insurance Products to Meet Diverse Needs

Insurance companies are often distinguished by the types of insurance coverage they offer. While some insurers offer only one area of coverage—life insurance, for example—others offer a broad range. In this section, we describe three major categories of business insurance: *liability, property,* and *life*. Each of these broad categories includes a wide variety of coverage plans and options.

Liability Insurance

As we saw in Chapter 4, *liability* means responsibility for damages in case of accidental or deliberate harm to individuals or property. Who, for example, might be financially responsible—liable—for the medical expenses, lost wages, and pain and suffering incurred by an individual temporarily or permanently disabled because of another's actions? **Liability insurance** covers losses resulting from damage to people or property when the insured party is judged liable.

To meet this growing need, insurance companies now offer a wide variety of liability insurance policies. All policies, however, offer two basic types of coverage:

1. The insurer promises to defend the policyholder in a court of law.
2. The insurer promises to pay damages assessed against the policyholder if the policyholder is held to be legally liable.

General Liability.   General liability policies protect business policyholders in cases involving four types of problems:

- **Personal liability** coverage would protect a firm if one of its truck drivers runs over a customer's foot.
- **Professional liability** coverage would protect a surgeon who leaves a pair of scissors inside a patient.
- **Product liability** coverage would protect the maker of a new hair conditioner that causes users' hair to fall out.

liability insurance
Insurance covering losses resulting from damage to persons or property of other people or firms.

personal liability
For a business, responsibility for certain actions of those who work for the business.

professional liability
For a business or a business person, responsibility for an individual's actions in working at the business or profession.

product liability
For a business, responsibility for the actions of its products.

premises liability

For a business, responsibility for occurrences on its premises.

■ **Premises liability** coverage would protect a firm if a customer slips on a wet floor and suffers a severe concussion.

Selected Types of Liability Coverage.   Businesses often choose to purchase comprehensive general liability policies, which provide coverage for all these problems and more. In this section, we will focus on three types of such coverage: *umbrella policies, automobile policies*, and *workers' compensation*.

Umbrella Policies.   Because the dollar value of a liability loss can be huge, many insurers will write coverage only up to a certain limit. Moreover, many liability contracts exclude certain types of losses. To cover financial consequences that exceed the coverage of standard policies, some businesses buy **umbrella insurance**: insurance intended to cover losses in addition to or excluded by an underlying policy.

For example, suppose that a business has an automobile policy with the following coverage:

umbrella insurance

Insurance that covers losses over and above those covered by a standard policy as well as losses excluded by a standard policy.

■ a limit of $500 000 for bodily injury and property damage
■ a premises liability policy with a limit of $500 000
■ a product liability policy with a limit of $750 000.

Figure 19.1 shows how an umbrella policy might double the coverage in each area. Another umbrella policy might extend product liability coverage to items not covered by the firm's existing policy.

Automobile Policies.   A firm that owns and maintains automobiles for business use needs a *business automobile policy*. This policy will protect it against liability for bodily injury and property damage inflicted by its vehicles. Typically, such policies provide the following types of coverage:

■ *Bodily injury and property damage*. Coverage that pays the firm if it is held legally liable for bodily injury or property damage.

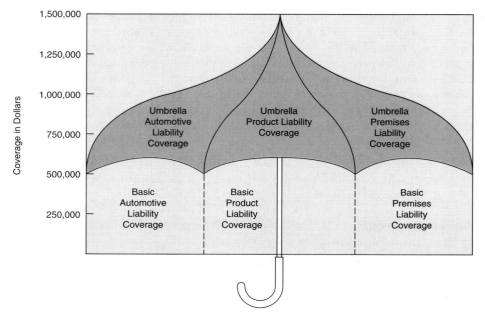

Figure 19.5
Umbrella insurance coverage.

Machines and people sometimes don't mix well, as this employee discovered when his wrist was caught in a conveyor sleeve. Industrial accidents are an undesirable risk.

- *Medical.* Coverage that pays for medical expenses incurred by persons in an insured vehicle.
- *Uninsured motorists.* Coverage that pays bodily-injury expenses when injury to an insured driver is caused by an uninsured motorist, a hit-and-run driver, or a driver whose employer is insolvent.

Workers' Compensation.   A business is liable for any injury to an employee when the injury arises from activities related to occupation. When workers are permanently or temporarily disabled by job-related accidents or disease, employers are required by law to provide **workers' compensation** coverage for medical expenses, loss of wages, and rehabilitation services.

workers' compensation
A business's liability for injury to its employee(s) resulting from any activities related to the occupation.

Property Insurance

Firms purchase **property insurance** to cover injuries to themselves resulting from physical damage to or loss of real personal property. Property losses might result from fire, lightning, wind, hail, explosion, theft, vandalism, or other destructive forces. Many different forms of property insurance exist to cover the many types of property losses.

property insurance
Insurance covering losses resulting from physical damage to real estate or personal property.

Fire and Allied Lines.   The typical fire insurance policy covers damage to specified property caused by fire, lightning, or theft. Coverage can be extended to cover other perils such as windstorm, hail, riot, smoke, aircraft, vehicles, explosion, vandalism, malicious mischief, and sonic boom. Some policies also include special provisions insuring the firm's property against sprinkler leakage, earthquake, or flood.

Marine Insurance.   Another area of property insurance is **marine insurance**, a form of transportation insurance. Marine insurance includes two distinct areas: ocean marine and inland marine. *Ocean marine insurance* has been around for more than 500 years. Medieval shippers used a system of insurance to protect their cargoes from loss. As commerce grew, so did the need for specialized services to guarantee financial solvency in the face of

marine insurance
A form of transportation insurance covering both the act of transportation (by water, land, or air) and the transported goods.

navigation disasters.[10] Today's ocean marine insurance covers the liability and loss of or damage to ships and their cargo.

Waterborne commerce was the most important method of transporting goods for centuries. As industry moved inland, land transportation of cargo became important and the *inland marine policies* were created. Although inland marine insurance sounds like a contradiction in terms, it is truly an extension of the ocean marine form, since it covers transportation (whether by truck, rail, or plane) and transported property. There are four main categories of inland marine insurance: property in transit (such as parcel post), bailee liability (such as dry cleaners), instrumentalities of transportation (such as bridges), and mobile property (such as farm animals).

title insurance

Insurance that guarantees a seller has clear title to a property.

Title Insurance.   When real property is purchased, it is customary to research the *title* (ownership) of that property to determine whether it is free of defects such as tax liens. The easiest way for a purchaser to verify that the seller has a clear legal right to convey the property is through the purchase of **title insurance**. A title insurance company will search a variety of sources and guarantee that the seller is the proper owner and that there are no unknown debts or liens against the property. For instance, if the person selling the property owned it with a former spouse, a title search would verify whether the seller has the legal right to sell the property. If the title insurance company erroneously indicates that the title is free of defects and the policyholder subsequently suffers a loss, then the insurance company must reimburse the insured to an amount specified in the policy.

Business Interruption Insurance.   In some cases the loss to property may be minimal in comparison to the loss of income suffered as a result of the property damage. A manufacturer may be required to close down for an extended period of time while repairs are being completed. During that time the company is not generating income. However, certain expenses—taxes, insurance premiums, and salaries for key personnel—may continue to accrue. The company may also need to keep running advertisements to make customers aware that repairs are progressing so they do not take their business elsewhere permanently. To cover these potential losses a firm may buy **business interruption insurance**.

business interruption insurance

Insurance to cover potential losses incurred during times when a company is unable to conduct its business.

credit insurance

Insurance to protect against customers' failure to pay their bills.

Credit Insurance.   In addition to protecting its physical assets, a firm may be interested in **credit insurance** to protect its financial assets. For example, if one or more of a business's customers cannot or do not pay their debts to the firm, the firm loses the value of the goods or services it provided the customers on credit. Even firms that manage their credit policies well will sometimes experience such losses. A customer that is well managed and a fine credit risk may fail if it experiences property losses from natural disasters such as tornadoes, flood, or fire. Credit insurance can protect companies from many kinds of accounts receivable losses.

Coinsurance.   Because a total loss of property is not likely, property owners have traditionally bought less than the total value in coverage. This practice results in coverage of losses on all parts of the property, but the insurer receives a premium for only a fraction of the property's value. To counter this problem, policies include a coinsurance provision requiring policyholders to insure to a certain minimum percentage of the total value of the property. If the policyholder fails to insure to the required percentage, the insurance company's payment will not cover the entire loss. Instead, insurance pays a smaller amount, as determined by the following formula:

$$\frac{\text{Amount of}}{\text{insurance owned}} \times \frac{\text{Amount of}}{\text{property loss}} = \frac{\text{Insurance company's}}{\text{payment}}$$

If, for example, a building has a replacement value of $80 000 and the insurance policy has an 80 percent coinsurance requirement, the required amount of insurance coverage is $64 000 ($80 000 × .80). If the owner carries $64 000 worth of insurance coverage, then a $25 000 loss will be paid in full, as will any other loss up to $64 000. However, if the owner carries only $50 000 of insurance coverage, the insurance company will pay only $19 531.25 of the $25 000 loss, as the following calculation shows:

$$\frac{\$50\ 000}{\$64\ 000} \times \$25\ 000 = \$19\ 531.25$$

The policyholder bears the remainder of the loss ($25 000 − $19 531.25 = $5468.75), in effect, a penalty for underinsuring the property.

Multi-Line Policies

Because companies have many risks, they may need many kinds of insurance. Rather than purchasing many separate policies, firms may elect to buy one of the *multi-line package policies* now offered. These policies combine coverage for property losses with coverage for liability losses. Examples of multi-line policies include the Special Multi-Peril Policy (SMP) for owners of large businesses and the Business Owners Policy (BOP) designed for small- to medium-size retail stores, office buildings, apartment buildings, and similar firms.

Life Insurance

Insurance can protect not only a company's physical and capital assets but its labor assets as well. As part of their benefits packages, many businesses buy **life insurance** for their employees. Life insurance companies accept premiums from policyholders in return for the promise to pay a **beneficiary** after the death of the policyholder. A portion of the premium is used for current losses and expenses. The remainder is invested in various types of financial instruments such as corporate bonds and stocks. A portion of the investment income generated offsets the premium paid by the policyholder. Therefore, an insurance company with a high investment return theoretically should charge less than one with a lower investment return, assuming that both companies have similar loss experience and expenses.

Life insurance is a profitable business in Canada. In 1994, the top ten insurance companies received over $28.9 billion in premiums from policyholders; net profit for the top 10 firms combined was almost $1.4 billion.[11] Among the many products life insurance companies offer are whole life, term insurance, endowment, and universal life policies.

Whole Life Insurance.   In **whole life insurance**, a business or individual pays a sum that is sufficient to keep the policy in force for the whole of the person's life. This sum can be paid every year for life or for a stated period of years (such as 20 years). For example, Evita Guard may pay $115 each year and be assured that her beneficiary, her husband, will receive the stated face value upon her death. Alternatively, she could pay $198 each year for 20 years and receive the same benefit. In both cases, the policy is said to be paid-up.

Whole life policies have an internal build-up called a *cash value*. This value can never be forfeited even if the policyholder chooses to stop paying

life insurance
Insurance that pays benefits to survivors of a policyholder.

beneficiary
The person to whom benefits of a life insurance policy are paid.

whole life insurance
Insurance coverage in force for the whole of a person's life, with a build-up of cash value.

the premium. In some cases, the policyholder can borrow against this value. Or a policyholder can surrender (discontinue) the insurance policy and receive its cash value from the insurance company. Cash value makes whole life policies attractive to some insurance purchasers.

term insurance

Insurance coverage for a fixed period of time, often one, five, ten, or twenty years.

Term Insurance.   As its name suggests, **term insurance** provides coverage for a term (a temporary time period) stated in the policy. The term can be for one, five, ten or twenty years. Term insurance has no cash value and is less expensive than any of the other forms discussed in this section. A policyholder receives maximum death protection for the premium paid. An individual who has a limited insurance budget but a significant need for death protection should consider term insurance. Term insurance is also the form of life insurance companies supply most often to their employees.

endowment

Insurance that pays face value after a fixed period of time whether the policyholder is alive or dead.

Endowments.   A type of policy called an **endowment** pays the face value of the policy whether the policyholder is dead or alive. The purpose of an endowment is to allow accumulation of a fund. For example, a father might buy a $20 000, ten-year endowment in order to accumulate $20 000 within a ten-year period for his daughter's university education. If he dies before the ten years are up, the insurance company will pay his beneficiary (his daughter). However, if the father lives to the tenth year, the company turns the accumulated $20 000 over to him. Table 19.3 compares these three policies with regard to premiums, benefits, and use.

Universal Life Insurance.   The life insurance industry was very profitable for many years selling only the three policies described above. Whole life was the backbone of the industry. But as interest rates spiraled in the 1960s and 1970s, many policyholders became disillusioned with the very low rate of interest they earned in whole life and endowment policies. Policyholders began surrendering their policies and investing their funds in higher yielding instruments such as guaranteed investment certificates. This withdrawal of funds, coupled with the difficulty of selling new policies, caused serious problems for life insurance companies. They responded by developing a new product to lure policyholders back to buying insurance: **universal life policies**.

universal life policy

A term insurance policy with a savings component.

Universal life policies combine a term insurance product with a savings component. Although this product may require a high initial premium, premium payments are flexible and interest earned on the savings component is competitive with other money market instruments.

variable life insurance (VLI)

A modified form of life insurance where the policyholder chooses the minimum face value of the policy.

Variable Life Insurance.   Another new form of life insurance is a modified form of whole life insurance. **Variable life insurance** (**VLI**) allows flexibility regarding the minimum face value of the policy, the types of investments supporting it, and even the amount and timing of the premiums.

How does VLI work? Instead of buying a whole life policy with a fixed face value of $100 000, a policyholder may choose a variable life policy with a $100 000 *minimum* face value. The actual face value can exceed the minimum, depending on the market performance of the VLI investment portfolio. VLI policyholders can stipulate the portfolio mix, choosing among a variety of investment instruments such as common stocks, short-term bonds, and high-yield money market securities. The increase in the policy's face value depends on the success of the underlying investments. VLIs are a growing segment of the insurance market because they offer more flexibility than traditional policies.

group life insurance

Life insurance written for a group of people rather than an individual.

Group Life Insurance.   Most companies buy **group life insurance**, which is underwritten for groups as a whole rather than for each individual member. The insurer's assessment of potential losses and its pricing of premiums are based on the characteristics of the whole group. Johnson &

Johnson's benefit plan, for example, includes group life coverage with a standard program of protection and benefits—a master policy purchased by J&J—that applies equally to all employees.

Key Insurance.   Many businesses choose to protect themselves against the loss of the talents and skills of key employees. If a salesperson who brings in $2.5 million in sales every year dies or takes a new job elsewhere, the firm will suffer loss. Moreover, the firm will incur recruitment costs to find a replacement and training expenses once a replacement is hired. *Key person insurance* can offset the lost income and the additional expenses.

A related matter is who takes control of a business when a partner or associate dies. At issue is whether the surviving business partners are willing to accept an inexperienced heir as a management partner in the business. Business continuation agreements are traditionally used to plan for this situation. The business owners can plan to buy the ownership interest of the deceased associate from his or her heirs. The value of the ownership interest is determined when the agreement is made. Special business insurance policies can provide the funds needed to make the purchase.

TABLE 19.3   Comparison of Basic and Common Life Insurance Contracts

Basic type	Protection period	Approximate costs for when benefits are payable	How long $10 000 at age 20*	Premiums are paid	Uses
1. Whole Life	Permanent	At death, any time	—	—	Combination of moderate savings and protection
a. Straight or ordinary life	"	"	$115	Throughout life	"
b. 20-payment life	"	"	$198	For 20 years	Paying up premiums during working life
c. Life paid up at 65	"	"	$127	To age 65	
2. Term	Temporary	At death, only during term	—	—	Protection only
a. Yearly renewable term	"	"	$25 increasing each year	Varies—can be to age 60-70	Maximum protection
b. Five-year level term (renewable and convertible)	"	"	$53	5 years	Very high protection for limited period
3. Endowment	Temporary or long term	At death, or if living, at end of endowment period	—	—	Combination of higher savings and protection
a. 20-year endowment	"	"	$426	20 years	"
b. Retirement income at 65	"	"	$177	To age 65	"

*Costs are necessarily approximate for such general comparisons. Participating policies would be slightly higher, with net costs reduced by annual dividends. Nonparticipating policies would be somewhat lower. Smaller policies under $10 000 will be slightly higher; those over this amount may have a lower rate per $1000. Those insuring women will also be somewhat lower in cost. Extra policy features such as waiver of premium, accidental death benefits, and so on, would increase these estimates.

Summary of Key Points

To increase the firm's value for its owners, financial managers must develop plans that identify the funds a company needs, when it needs them, and how it can obtain them. In the short run, firms need funds to cover accounts payable, accounts receivable, and inventories. In the long run, they need funds to cover purchases of land, buildings and equipment.

To finance their short-term expenditures, firms rely on credit extended by suppliers and on secured and unsecured loans. Some very large firms are able to issue commercial paper. Smaller firms may choose to factor their accounts receivable.

Long-term sources of funds include debt financing, equity financing, and preferred stock financing. Debt financing uses long-term loans and corporate bonds that obligate the firm to pay interest regularly. Equity financing involves the use of the owners' capital, either from the sale of the firm's common stock or from retained earnings. Preferred stock funding has some of the features of both common stock and bonds. Financial planners must choose the proper mix of debt, equity, and preferred stock funding. The most conservative strategy is to use all equity financing. The most speculative option is to use all debt funding. The ultimate choice depends on investors' attitudes and the costs and risks of the various forms of funding.

Financial managers and investors consider how safe or hazardous different investments can be. If the financial return in the future is certain, investors are willing to invest for a lower financial return. But if the future return has more chance of not being paid, then investors demand a greater return before they will invest.

Finance and risk management are especially important for small businesses. They must establish bank and trade credit by taking steps to show they are creditworthy. They also need to use cash-flow planning to gain credit and use it wisely in meeting needs for funds.

Businesses operate in an environment pervaded by risk. Speculative risks involve the prospect of gain or loss. Pure risks involve the prospect of loss or no loss. Business firms must manage their risks by identifying risks, measuring possible losses, evaluating alternatives, implementing chosen techniques, and monitoring the program continually.

Insurance companies earn profits by charging customers a premium that, on average, exceeds the losses the insurer must cover for policyholders. To minimize their own risks, insurers will provide coverage only for risks that are generally predictable, outside the control of the insured, spread geographically, and verifiable. Insurance companies may be organized as private stock insurance companies, private mutual insurance companies, or public agencies. Government insurers provide protection in some social welfare areas (for example, workers' compensation, Social Insurance).

Most insurance purchased by businesses includes coverage of liability, property, and the life of employees. Liability insurance protects a firm from costs in the case of personal, professional, product, or premises liability. Property insurance protects a firm's building, equipment, and financial assets. Life insurance is often purchased by the business for at least some of its employees. Key employee insurance and business continuation insurance can minimize loss due to the death or departure of key personnel.

Barings Trader's Big Bet Breaks Bank

Twenty-eight-year-old Nicolas Leeson had certainly contributed his share to the bottom line of Barings PLC, the venerable British merchant bank. In less than two years as manager of Barings' futures-trading subsidiary in Singapore, Leeson had boosted profits from $1.2 million in 1992 to $30 million by the first seven months of 1994. Leeson's job involved buying and selling futures contracts, particularly investments known as *derivatives*. His specialties were trades in three markets: the Japanese stock index, known as the Nikkei 225; the futures market in Osaka, Japan; and the Singapore International Monetary Exchange (Simex). For example, Leeson exploited small price differences by buying contracts on Simex and selling them for slightly higher prices in Osaka. He was not, however, engaging in these low-risk trades on behalf of Barings' clients; rather, his trades were in-house transactions using the bank's own money. Many of Barings' 4000 employees enjoyed the fruits of Leeson's labors. In 1994, for example, a bonus pool of more than $160 million was paid out. Leeson's 1994 own bonus was more than half a million dollars, twice what he had received in 1993.

As one might expect for a British investment bank founded in 1762, Barings was widely regarded as a conservative institution. Indeed, its clients include the Queen herself. Thus the financial world was astounded in February 1995, when it was revealed that Leeson had incurred staggering trading losses of nearly $1 billion. In the aftermath of the disclosure, the Bank of England refused to come to the rescue by providing financial backing. Barings had no alternative but to declare bankruptcy. The problem, experts agreed, was a lack of internal risk-management controls. As one British banking official put it: "I always feared that the biggest danger to the banking system would be a rogue derivatives trader, but I never believed it could be on this scale."

In fact, the Barings fiasco was just one in a series of stories from around the globe in the mid-1990s, all with a common theme: stunning financial losses. Procter & Gamble, for example, lost more than $100 million on derivatives purchased from Bankers Trust Co. Officials in Orange County, California, were forced to declare bankruptcy following huge investment losses incurred by the county treasurer. And of course many investors suffered losses when the government of Mexico was forced to seek $50 billion to prop up its economy in the wake of the peso's devaluation. "Whether it's Mexico or Barings," argues economist Henry Kaufman "these problems reflect inadequate monitoring and supervision." Adds Eddie George, Governor of the Bank of England:

"What happened to Barings could happen to any financial institution in the world."

What did happen to Barings? Over a three-week period, Leeson apparently bought $27 billion in futures contracts. In doing so, he wagered—very heavily—that the sluggish Japanese stock market would stage a rally. If the Nikkei 225—an index of Japanese stocks—rose as he predicted, Leeson would cash in and profit. How? The contract price on which he had originally agreed would be lower than the actual level of the index when the contract came due. He would profit by the amount of the difference. In fact, however, the Nikkei fell *below* Leeson's contract price—whereby Barings was obligated to *pay* the difference. The young trader tried desperately to reverse his losses, but he was forced to put up cash for margin calls. In other words, he had to pay to maintain a certain percentage of the daily value of his contract—which was dropping along with the Nikkei. Where did Leeson get the money? Investigators believe that he convinced Barings officials back in London to advance him more cash by claiming that he was trading on behalf of a client who would soon be depositing funds with the bank.

The ploy failed. After leaving a note saying simply, "I'm sorry," Leeson disappeared. Several days later, he was apprehended by German police. If he is returned to Singapore, he may face a variety of criminal charges.

How could a single trader have racked up such losses? After all, Leeson's activities were subject to oversight by risk-management officials at Barings. Indeed, computers could have provided a warning when Leeson's trades exceeded pre-set amounts (as one financial expert notes, "There's widely available software for this type of risk management"). Barings officials, however, were slow to catch on, partly because Leeson was, in essence, supervising and settling his own trading activities. Despite warnings about lax controls over Leeson's trading following an internal audit in mid-1994, recommended changes were not made. For one thing, the same audit stressed Leeson's indispensability to the firm: "Without Leeson," advised internal auditors, Barings' Singapore operations "would lack a trader with the right combination of experience in trading sizable lots, a detailed appreciation of trading strategies, familiarity with local traders' limits and practices, and contacts among traders and officials."

Another reason may have been internal rivalries and turf battles pitting Barings' London-based banking operations against the company's trading divisions in other parts of the world. In the weeks following Leeson's arrest, there was a flurry of accusations regarding which Barings executive should have been responsible for preventing the fiasco. "The great shame," lamented one Barings official, "is that we're very conservatively run. The one thing that we were trying to minimize—risk taking—is what blew us out of the water."

Ultimately, the fate of Barings PLC was determined within a matter of days. A Dutch banking and insurance company, Internationale Nederlanden Groep NV (ING), paid a nominal sum of one British pound in exchange for all of Barings' liabilities and assets. The purchase came after ING officials carefully inspected Barings' books. "Don't forget, we're Dutch after all," explained a spokesperson for ING. "We've got a well-deserved reputation for caution and thriftiness." Still, ING announced that it would provide an immediate cash infusion of more than $1 billion to allow Barings to continue its operations.

CASE QUESTIONS:
1. Discuss Leeson's trading activities in terms of the risk-reward relationship.
2. Explain the type of risk that Leeson was facing in his financial dealings.
3. The Bank of England might have intervened to prevent Barings from falling into bankruptcy. What did Bank of England officials hope to achieve by not coming to the rescue?
4. Using the framework developed in the chapter, explain how a proper risk-management plan could help a financial institution prevent a disaster of the magnitude described in this case.
5. What are some of the risks and challenges ING might face as the new owner of Barings?   ◆

CONCLUDING CASE 19-2

Lake Trout Ltd.

Don Braden was an avid fisherman. While pursuing his favorite sport, he experimented with many different fishing lures, always trying to find the ideal one. But he gradually came to the conclusion that what was available in tackle stores just wasn't quite right.

After some years of frustration, he began to think about making his own lures. His first efforts were rather crude but, because he was highly motivated and had some mechanical skill, he eventually produced three first-rate fishing lures. Initially, he concentrated on developing lures for pickerel (walleye) and lake trout because he was interested in catching them. During a couple of fishing seasons, he gave some of his new lures to several fishing buddies.

Although Don never intended to start a business, he soon began receiving inquiries about where his lures could be purchased. Because of this "natural demand," he began to think about getting into serious production of his products. In 1982, Don Braden decided to go full-time into the production and marketing of the three fishing lures he had developed. In 1985, he also got involved in the manufacture and sale of fishing rods. To date, the company's performance has exceeded his expectations. It has expanded dramatically and now has 28 employees. He has hired a production supervisor, and Don now concentrates on finance and marketing.

There are five shareholders in the firm. Don owns 65 percent of the company's shares. Three other investors each own 10 percent of the shares, and Don's sister owns 5 percent. Sales in 1989 were $4 600 000. This figure represents sales of about 400 000 fishing lures at an average price of $4.00 each, plus 100 000 fishing rods at an average price of $30 each. Demand continues to exceed the company's ability to supply it.

Lake Trout Ltd. has a good credit rating, and an analysis of its financial statements by a local CA firm indicates that it is a good prospect for further growth if it can obtain the capital it needs for expansion. Bonds currently outstanding total $1 million, with one quarter of that amount coming due within one year. Including the retirement of the maturing bonds and capital needed for expansion, Don estimates that Lake Trout Ltd. will need about $2 million in long-term capital funds over the next five years.

Don's sister recently proposed that the way to get this money was to issue $1 million in 12 percent bonds maturing in 20 years, and to sell 40 000 shares of stock at $25 per share. (This would double the number of shares outstanding.) Don is concerned about this proposal because he does not have sufficient funds to maintain majority ownership under such a plan. But he also sees the advantages of the plan. The three investors who each own 10 percent have indicated that they would be interested in purchasing 10 000 additional shares each. Financial advisors whom Don has talked to have indicated that he could probably sell up to $2 million in 12 percent bonds.

CASE QUESTIONS
1. Assume that you are Don Braden. Would you oppose your sister's plan? Why or why not?
2. What are the advantages of the proposed stock plan? The disadvantages?
3. What are the advantages of selling $2 million in bonds?
4. What market information is needed before making this decision?   ◆

Key Terms

financial managers
finance
cash flow management
financial control
financial plan
inventory
raw materials inventory
work-in-process inventory
finished goods inventory
trade credit
open-book credit
promissory note
trade draft
trade acceptance
secured loan
collateral
pledging accounts
  receivable

unsecured loan
line of credit
revolving credit agreement
commercial paper
factoring
debt financing
corporate bond
maturity date
equity financing
bankruptcy
risk-return relationship
risk
speculative risk
pure risk
risk management
risk avoidance
risk control
risk retention

self-insurance
risk transfer
insurance policy
deductible
law of large numbers
stock insurance
  company
mutual insurance
  company
underwriting
insurance agent
insurance broker
liability insurance
personal liability
professional liability
product liability
premises liability
umbrella insurance

worker's compensation
property insurance
marine insurance
title insurance
business interruption
  insurance
credit insurance
life insurance
beneficiary
whole life insurance
term insurance
endowment
universal life policy
variable life insurance
  (VLI)
group life insurance

Study Questions and Exercises

Review Questions

1. What questions must a financial manager answer when constructing a financial plan?
2. In what ways do the two sources for debt financing differ from each other? How do they differ from the two sources of equity financing?
3. What is the main source of credit for small businesses? Why?
4. Describe the risk management process. What role does the risk manager play in the firm?
5. What requirements must a risk meet to be considered insurable?

Analysis Questions

6. Which of the life insurance products described in the chapter would you buy for yourself? Why?

7. How would you decide the best mix of debt and equity financing for a company?
8. If you were a financial manager for a large firm, what types of short-term funding would you use most? Why?

Application Exercises

9. Interview the owner of a local small business. Identify the types of short-term and long-term funding used by the firm. As well, ask the owner to describe the risk management process he or she uses in the business. Determine the reasons behind both these decisions.
10. Choose two well-known firms in different industries and compare their financial structures. Using public records and financial reports, determine each company's short-term debt, long-term debt, common equity, and preferred stock funding.

Building Your Business Skills

Goal

To encourage students to gain a better understanding of the major financial and risk-management issues that have faced large companies in the mid-1990s.

Method

In 1994, all of the following companies reported financial problems relating to risk management:

- Gibson Greetings
- Procter & Gamble
- Federal Paper Board
- Chemical Bank
- Metallgesellschaft AG

Step 1:
Working alone, research one of the companies listed above to learn more about the financial risks that were reported in the news.

Step 2:
Make sure that you can explain in your own words the risks and financial-management issues that were faced by the firm that you researched.

Step 3:
Join in teams with students who researched other companies and compare your findings.

Follow-Up Questions

1. Were there common themes in the "big stories" in financial management?
2. What have the various companies done to minimize future risks and losses?

20

Understanding Securities and Investments

LEARNING OBJECTIVES

After studying this chapter, you will be able to

- Explain what is meant by the primary and secondary markets for securities and who buys securities.
- Discuss the value to shareholders of common stock and preferred stock and describe the secondary market for these securities.
- Distinguish among various types of bonds available to securities investors in terms of their issuers, safety, and retirement.
- Describe the types of investment opportunities offered by mutual funds, commodities, and options.
- Explain how securities are bought and sold and how the transactions of the securities markets are reported in the financial information services.
- Identify the reasons why the securities markets are regulated.

CHAPTER OUTLINE

OPENING CASE

Helping Investors Get the Facts about Mutual Funds

During the last few years, many Canadians have invested their money in mutual funds. Billions of dollars have flooded into mutual funds in spite of the fact that buyers don't know very much about the fund managers who invest their money or about the risks and rewards of such investing. By the end of 1994, assets in mutual funds exceeded $127 billion.

In an attempt to keep up with the rapid increase in mutual fund investment, the Ontario Securities Commission appointed Glorianne Stromberg to conduct a review of the mutual fund industry. Her report commented on a variety of concerns, including (1) disclosure laws, (2) soft-dollar transactions, and (3) reciprocal commissions.

Disclosure Laws   Under provincial securities rules, individuals and companies must reveal when they own 10 percent or more of a company's stock. But mutual fund managers argue that this law shouldn't apply to them because they hold the shares in several funds, and the 10 percent limit is exceeded only on an aggregate basis. The OSC is now deciding whether to require fund managers to stick to the 10 percent guideline.

The problem with the current lack of disclosure is that a fund manager could make the fund's performance look good by buying large blocks of shares in companies with only a small number of shares on the market. This type of buying could drive up the price of the stock and make the fund look good. But it is also risky, because if there is a downturn in the market, the fund manager will have difficulty selling so much stock from one company. Investors in the fund would then be stuck with a poorly performing fund.

Soft-dollar Transactions   In these deals, brokerage firms play the role of intermediary between various kinds of money managers, including mutual fund managers. For example, a mutual fund manager may purchase a consulting report and then pay for it by routing trading commissions through a brokerage firm. The brokerage firm may get a substantial markup over the actual cost of the report.

The problem here is that the cost of these "soft-dollar" deals is borne by the investor (through commissions paid by the mutual fund). There is potential for abuse here

because investors don't know what funds are buying with soft dollars and whether or not these expenses should rightfully be charged to the fund.

Reciprocal Commissions   This occurs when a stockbroker recommends that a client invest in a certain mutual fund. The mutual fund manager then buys and sells securities through the same broker. What is essentially happening is that the mutual fund manager is channeling commissions to the broker in return for the broker pushing the mutual fund. Critics point out that "sweetheart" deals like this work to the detriment of investors by raising the cost of doing business. (The ethics of this practice are examined later in the chapter.)

In its report issued on February 1, 1995, the Ontario Securities Commission made the following recommendations about the operation of mutual funds:

■ provide more information to buyers of mutual funds so they will better understand what they are buying

■ create an industry self-regulating organization that would be responsible for setting rules and monitoring conduct

■ eliminate controversial practices such as reciprocal transactions and soft-dollar transactions

■ increase training for mutual fund managers and introduce an apprenticeship program.   ◆

Thousands of Canadians regularly invest their money in stocks and bonds. As the opening case demonstrates, this can be costly for investors, especially when the brokers who are involved in the actual buying and selling of stocks and bonds do not behave properly. In this chapter, we will consider the types of markets in which stocks and bonds are sold. You will then be better able to understand the nature of interactions between buyers and sellers in these markets and the reasons for government regulation of them.

What Are Securities Markets?

Stocks and bonds are both known as **securities** because they represent a secured (asset-based) claim on the part of investors. But while stocks are a claim on all the assets of a corporation (because they represent a part-ownership of the business), bonds are strictly a financial claim on the business. Collectively, the market in which stocks and bonds are sold is called the *securities market.*

securities
Stocks and bonds (which represent a secured-asset-based claim on the part of investors) that can be bought and sold.

Primary and Secondary Markets for Securities

Primary securities markets handle the buying and selling of new stocks and bonds by firms or governments. New securities are sometimes sold to one buyer or a small group of buyers. These so-called private placements allow the businesses that use them to keep their plans confidential. But because such offerings cannot be resold, buyers demand higher returns from them.

primary securities market
The sale and purchase of newly issued stocks and bonds by firms or governments.

Most new stocks and some bonds are sold to the wider public market. To bring a new security to market, the issuing corporation must obtain approval from a provincial securities commission. It also needs the services of an investment banker. **Investment bankers** serve as financial specialists in issuing new securities. Such well-known firms as RBC Dominion Securities and Wood Gundy provide three types of investment banking services. They advise the company on the timing and financial terms for the new issue. By *underwriting* (buying) the new securities, investment bankers bear some of the risk of issuing the new security. And, finally, they create the distribution network that moves the new securities through groups of other banks and brokers into the hands of individual investors.

investment banker
Any financial institution engaged in purchasing and reselling new stocks and bonds.

New securities represent only a small portion of securities traded, however. The market for existing stocks and bonds, the **secondary securities market**, is handled by organizations like the Toronto Stock Exchange. We will consider the activities of these markets later in this chapter, after you know more about stocks and bonds and who buys them.

secondary securities market
The sale and purchase of previously issued stocks and bonds.

Who Invests in Securities Markets?

A variety of investors, ranging from average working citizens to huge cash-rich institutions, buy and sell securities. **Institutional investors**—organizations that invest for themselves and their clients (for example, a mutual fund)—may have the greatest influence on securities markets. But individual investors hold a substantial portion of the stock in Canadian companies.

institutional investors
Organizations whose investments for themselves and their clients are so large that they can influence prices on securities markets.

All investors, large and small, have unique motives and goals that affect their investment *portfolios* (the mix of securities they hold). Young people may be saving for college or university, a car, or a first house. They want relatively safe investments that will preserve their accumulated savings. They also want investments with some liquidity, so that the necessary funds are available when needed.

But people also have long-term goals, such as preparing for retirement. Such individuals are most interested in maximizing their wealth during the next 20 or 30 years. They are largely unconcerned about the ups and downs of investments in any particular year.

Personality differences, too, affect investment decisions. Some people are uncomfortable about taking chances with money, while some *speculators* thrive on the excitement of large gains and losses. Thus, the best types of investments differ depending on investors' goals and attitudes toward the need for safety, income, and growth. As you will see, each type of security offers its own mix of these traits.

Stocks

Each year, financial managers, along with millions of individual investors, buy and sell the stocks of thousands of companies. This widespread ownership has become possible because of the availability of different types of stocks and because markets have been established for conveniently buying and selling them. In this section, we will focus on the value of *common* and *preferred stock* as securities. We will also describe the *stock exchanges* where they are bought and sold.

Common Stock

Individuals and other companies buy a firm's common stock in the hope that the stock will increase in value, affording them a capital gain, and/or will provide dividend income. But what is the value of a common stock? Stock values are expressed in three different ways: as par value, as market value, and as book value.

par value

The arbitrary value of a stock set by the issuing company's board of directors and stated on stock certificates; used by accountants but of little significance to investors.

Par Value.   The face value of a share of stock, its **par value**, is set by the issuing company's board of directors. But this arbitrary accounting value has almost nothing to do with the real value of the share.

market value

The current price of one share of a stock in the secondary securities market; the real value of a stock.

Market Value.   The real value of a stock is its **market value**, the current price of a share in the stock market. Because it reflects buyers' willingness to invest, market value depends on a firm's history of dividend payments as well as expectations of **capital gains**, profits from selling the stock for more than it cost. Investors are primarily concerned with a stock's market value. Attempts are often made to influence the price of a stock (see the box "The Art of Influencing a Company's Stock Price").

capital gains

Profits from the sale of an asset (such as stock) for a higher price than that at which it was purchased.

Book Value.   Another commonly cited value, **book value**, represents shareholders' equity divided by the number of shares of common stock. Shareholders' equity is the sum of all common stock, retained earnings, and additional paid-in capital. While book value is often published in financial reports, its usefulness is also limited.

book value

The value of a stock expressed as the total shareholders' equity (assets minus liabilities and preferred stock) divided by the number of shares of common stock outstanding; used by accountants but of little significance to investors.

Investment Traits of Common Stock.   Common stocks are among the riskiest of securities. When companies have unprofitable years, they cannot pay dividends. Shareholder income—and perhaps share price too—drops. Even companies with solid reputations sometimes have downturns. IBM is an example. Cash dividends have been paid continuously to shareholders every year since 1916. Revenues per share grew steadily from the 1970s to 1990, then began falling until 1993, when IBM showed a financial loss rather than a profit. Along with lower earnings per share during 1990-1993, IBM paid smaller dividends to shareholders each year. During this period, IBM's stock price fell steadily, from a 1990 high of $123 per share to a 1993 low of $41.[1]

The Canadian Business Scene

THE ART OF INFLUENCING A COMPANY'S STOCK PRICE

What determines the price of a company's stock? There are some obvious financial things like a company's sales and earnings, or the number of promising new products it is bringing to the market. But other factors like stock market rumors, investor relations, and the activities of individual stockbrokers can also play a part.

Rumors One of the most well-known stock exchanges in Canada is the Vancouver Stock Exchange, not because it is large or successful, but because numerous charges have been made that stock swindles and market manipulations are not adequately controlled. Overall, the exchange is viewed by many as a place where highly speculative stocks are traded, where rumor and speculation abound, and investors have a good chance of losing their shirt. This is especially true for the so-called "penny mine" stocks— those which cost less than a dollar per share and are very high risk. A 1994 report (the latest of several which have been critical of the exchange) recommended that investors be given more information about the market, that stock promoters be more tightly regulated, and that more restrictions should be placed on traders' activities.

Investor Relations This is the art of disseminating information about a company's financial condition through activities like annual meetings, corporate reports, road shows, site tours, contacts with stock analysts, and properly timing the release of financial information. While public relations tries to make the company look good to the general public, investor relations tries to play up the positive aspects of a company's finances to a sophisticated audience of stockbrokers, financial analysts, and financial institutions. The video case "French Fries" on p. 621 illustrates some investor relations activities that were carried out by Harvard International Technologies.

There is a fine line between investor relations and mere hype. Done poorly, it can cause the price of the company's stock to decline, which in turn impacts on the earnings of company executives, since part of their compensation package is made up of stock options. A reduced stock price also makes it harder for the firm to raise funds.

American Barrick Resources Corp. is a Toronto-based company that is well-known for its investor relations. The company's CEO meets with financial analysts over a lunch buffet to spread the good word about his company. He communicates openly with the financial community and conducts a question-and-answer period at the end of the lunch. In addition, the company publishes a detailed account of its various gold mining operations and also conducts site tours for interested analysts.

Stockbrokers Individuals who buy and sell stock for their clients are also part of the equation that determines stock prices. Positive recommendations to customers can increase the demand for certain stock, and negative recommendations can reduce it. The brokerage industry has something of an image problem at the moment, due in part to the insider trading scandals of the late 1980s.

The general public has always worried that stockbrokers will put their own financial interests ahead of their customers'. Most brokers receive a combination of percentage of gross commissions (usually 30-45 percent) plus transaction size. A broker who grosses $150 000 annually in commissions with an average commission of $100 is lucky to take home $45 000. Because of these pressures, many brokers are not interested in customers with less than $20 000 in their account. To increase their earnings, brokers may be tempted to pursue a "churn and burn" strategy (buying and selling stocks frequently) to increase their commissions.

Customers who have large accounts may be able to negotiate discounts. A full-service broker (one that buys and sells stocks and performs other services like conducting research on companies) will charge an average of 2 percent of the total share price per trade. But a good customer could ask for a 10 percent discount on a $10 000 transaction, and a 20 percent discount on a $50 000 transaction. Discount brokers (those who provide few services beyond buying and selling shares of stock) charge about $40 per transaction.

On the other hand, common stocks offer high growth potential for investors. In particular, the common stocks of pollution control, medical technology, natural gas, financial services, and high technology firms can yield high returns. And the "blue-chip" stocks of some well-established firms like General Electric and Imperial Oil offer investors a history of secure income.

Preferred Stock

Preferred stock is usually issued with a stated par value, such as $100. Dividends paid on preferred stock are usually expressed as a percentage of the par value. For example, if a preferred stock with a $100 par value pays a 6 percent dividend, shareholders would receive an annual dividend of $6 on each share.

Some preferred stock is *callable*. The issuing firm can require the preferred shareholders to surrender their shares in exchange for a cash payment. The amount of this cash payment, known as the *call price*, is specified in the agreement between the preferred shareholders and the firm.

cumulative preferred stock

Preferred stock on which dividends not paid in the past must first be paid up before the firm may pay dividends to common shareholders.

Investment Traits of Preferred Stock.   Because of its preference on dividends, preferred stock's income is less risky than the common stock of the same company. Moreover, most preferred stock is cumulative. With **cumulative preferred stock**, any dividend payments the firm misses must be paid later, as soon as the firm is able. Typically, the firm cannot pay any dividends to its common shareholders until it has made up all late payments to preferred shareholders. If a firm with preferred stock having a $100 par value and paying a 6 percent dividend fails to pay that dividend for two years, it must make up the arrears of $12 per share before it can pay dividends to common shareholders.

Nevertheless, even the income from cumulative preferred stock is not as certain as the corporate bonds of the same company. The company cannot pay dividends if it does not make a profit. The purchase price of the preferred stock can also fluctuate, leading to a capital gain or loss for the shareholder. And the growth potential of preferred stock is limited due to its fixed dividend.

Stock Exchanges

Most of the secondary market for stocks is handled by organized stock exchanges. In addition, a so-called "dealer," or the over-the-counter, market handles the exchange of some stocks. A **stock exchange** is an organization of individuals formed to provide an institutional setting in which stock can be bought and sold. The exchange enforces certain rules to govern its members' trading activities. Most exchanges are nonprofit corporations established to serve their members.

stock exchange

A voluntary organization of individuals formed to provide an institutional setting where members can buy and sell stock for themselves and their clients in accordance with the exchange's rules.

To become a member, an individual must purchase one of a limited number of memberships—called "seats"—on the exchange. Only members (or their representatives) are allowed to trade on the exchange. In this sense, because all orders to buy or sell must flow through members, they have a legal monopoly. Memberships can be bought and sold like other assets.

The Trading Floor.   Each exchange regulates the places and times at which trading may occur. Trading is allowed only at an actual physical location called the *trading floor*. The floor is equipped with a vast array of electronic communications equipment for conveying buy and sell orders or confirming completed trades. A variety of news services furnish important up-to-the-minute information about world events as well as business developments. Any change in these factors, then, may be swiftly reflected in share prices.

Information is critical on securities exchanges. A software glitch in March 1992 caused computers at the Toronto Stock Exchange to go berserk and print inaccurate information on stock prices. The exchange was closed for four hours before the problem was solved.

program trading

The purchase or sale of stocks by computerized trading programs that can be launched without human supervision or control.

One oft-cited cause of the 1987 panic on the Toronto Stock Exchange is **program trading**—the purchase or sale of a group of stocks valued at $1 million or more, often triggered by computerized trading programs that can be launched without human supervision or control.[2] As market values change during the course of a day, computer programs are busy recalculating the future values of stocks. Once a calculated value reaches a critical point, the program automatically signals a buy or sell order. Program trading could conceivably cause the market to spiral out of control. One way to avoid this is to set up "circuit breakers" that suspend trading for a preset length of time (for example, one hour). The interruption provides a "cooling-off" period that slows down trading activity and allows computer programs to be revised or shut down.

Brokers.   Some of the people working on the trading floor are employed by the exchange; others trade stocks for themselves. But a large number of those working on the trading floor are brokers. A **broker** receives buy and sell orders from those who are not members of the exchange and executes the orders. In return, the broker earns a commission from the order placer.

broker
An individual licensed to buy and sell securities for customers in the secondary market; may also provide other financial services.

The New York Stock Exchange.   For many people, "the stock market" means the New York Stock Exchange (NYSE). Founded in 1792 and located at the corner of Wall and Broad Streets in New York City, the largest of all U.S. exchanges is in fact the model for exchanges worldwide. With an average of 264 million shares changing hands each day, about 50 percent of all shares traded on U.S. exchanges are traded there.

Only firms meeting certain minimum requirements—earning power, total value of outstanding stock, and number of shareholders—are eligible for listing on the NYSE. About 2400 listings are traded on the NYSE with total market values of $4.5 trillion. Currently, Exxon Corp.'s common shares have the highest market value —$114 billion. NYSE trading volume in 1993 was over 67 billion shares.[3]

The Toronto Stock Exchange.   The largest stock exchange in Canada is the Toronto Stock Exchange (TSE). It is made up of about 100 individual members who hold seats. The securities of most major corporations are listed here. A company must pay a fee before it can list its security on the exchange. In addition to the TSE, there are stock exchanges in Winnipeg, Calgary, Vancouver, and Montreal.

The Toronto Stock Exchange is one of several in Canada where shares of stock in Canadian companies are bought and sold.

The Montreal Stock Exchange.   In recent years, the Montreal Exchange has been aggressively promoting itself and improving its trading systems. It now accounts for nearly 24 percent of the combined Montreal-Toronto trading value. The Montreal Exchange has a sizable market share in many of Canada's blue-chip companies. It handles more than 50 percent of the shares traded in companies like Bombardier, Provigo, Memotec Data, and Power Corporation.

Foreign Stock Exchanges.   In 1980, the U.S. stock market accounted for over half the market value of the world market. In 1975, the equity of IBM alone was greater than the national market equities of all but four countries! Market activities, however, have shifted as the value of shares listed on foreign exchanges continues to grow. The annual dollar value of trades on exchanges in London, Tokyo, and other cities is in the trillions. In fact, the London exchange exceeds even the NYSE in number of stocks listed; in market value, transactions on U.S. exchanges are now second to those on Japanese exchanges.

New exchanges are beginning to flourish in cities from Shanghai, China, to Warsaw, Poland. Founded in 1991, for example, the Chinese exchange now trades about $350 million in shares on a good day—more than the bustling Hong Kong exchange on a slow day. China now has about 2 million shareholders in various companies, with the number growing about 50 000 every week.

Meanwhile, many analysts currently regard the Polish exchange as the world's strongest-performing market. Although it lists only 22 stocks, the Polish index increased in volume by 700 percent in 1993. In countries like both China and Poland, thriving stock exchanges have contributed, among other things, to more efficient, profit-conscious companies (many of them once or still state-owned).[4]

Foreign stock exchanges have become increasingly important to portfolio managers. Foreign exchanges allow investors to *diversify* (spread investable funds among a variety of investments to reduce risk). Astute managers have also been able to achieve higher returns by investing internationally.

The Over-the-Counter (OTC) Market.   Many securities are not listed on any of the organized securities exchanges. Making a market in these securities is one of the functions of investment dealers. These securities are traded in the over-the-counter (OTC) market. (In reality, it is an over-the-telephone market.) The **over-the-counter market** is a complex of dealers in constant touch with one another. Stocks and bonds of some smaller corporations are traded on the OTC market as well as all fixed-income securities, including bonds and debentures.

Security dealers in the OTC market often buy securities in their own names. They must maintain an inventory of securities to make a market in them. They hope to sell them to their clients at a higher price. These dealers also buy shares at the request of their clients for a commission. Dealers selling to one another charge a wholesale price and sell to their customers at a retail price.

over-the-counter (OTC) market

A complex of dealers in constant touch with each other who trade stocks and bonds of some smaller corporations and all fixed-income securities (bonds and debentures).

Bonds

bond

A written promise that the borrower will pay the lender, at a stated future date, the principal plus a stated rate of interest.

A **bond** is a written promise that the borrower will pay the lender, at some stated future date, a sum of money (the principal) and a stated rate of interest. Bondholders have a claim on a corporation's assets and earnings that comes before the claims of common and preferred shareholders. Bonds differ from one another in terms of maturity, tax status, and level of risk versus potential yield (the interest rate). Potential investors must take these factors into consideration to evaluate which particular bond to buy.

To help bond investors make assessments, several services rate the quality of bonds from different issuers. Table 20.1 shows ratings by three principal rating services: Standard & Poor's, Moody's, and the Canadian Bond Rating Service. The rating measures the bond's *default risk*—the chance that one or more promised payments will be deferred or missed altogether.

TABLE 20.1   Bond Ratings

	High Grade	Medium Grade (Investment Grade)	Speculative	Poor Grade
Moody's	Aaa Aa	A Baa	Ba B	Caa to C
Standard & Poors	AAA AA	A BBB	BB B	CCC to D
Canadian Bond Rating Service	A++	B++	C	B

Although all corporations issue common stock, not all issue bonds. Shareholders provide equity (ownership) capital, while bondholders are lenders (although they are also considered "investors" as far as the securities market is concerned). Stock certificates represent ownership, while bond certificates represent indebtedness. Federal, provincial, and city governments as well as nonprofit organizations also issue bonds.

Government Bonds

Government bonds—for example, Canada Savings Bonds—are among the safest investments available. However, securities with longer maturities are somewhat riskier than short-term issues because their longer lives expose

Private corporations are not the only organizations that issue bonds. The government of Canada issues Canada Savings Bonds to finance its debt.

them to more political, social, and economic changes. All federal bonds, however, are backed by the Canadian government. Government securities are sold in large blocks to institutional investors who buy them to ensure desired levels of safety in portfolios. As their needs change, they may buy or sell government securities to other investors.

Provincial and local governments also issue bonds (called municipal bonds) to finance school and transportation systems and a variety of other projects. The most attractive feature of municipal bonds is the fact that investors do not pay taxes on interest received. Banks invest in bonds nearing maturity because they are relatively safe, liquid investments. Pension funds, insurance companies, and private citizens also make longer-term investments in municipals. But, as the box "Investment Turns Sour in Orange County" shows, even these bonds can be risky.

International Report

INVESTMENT TURNS SOUR IN ORANGE COUNTY

Like that of many county treasurers, Robert Citron's job was to invest tax revenues and money raised through municipal bond offerings. Investment proceeds were used for such expenses as education, construction projects, and public employee salaries. As the treasurer of Orange County, California, Citron had amassed an impressive track record: In the ten-year period between 1984 and 1994, income from Orange County's investment portfolio nearly quadrupled, to $666 million. In 1993, Orange County's 2.6 million residents were the beneficiaries of an 8.5-percent investment return, compared with 4.7 percent for the state of California as a whole.

How did Citron achieve such phenomenal results? Since he had become treasurer in 1973, Californians' increasing anti-tax sentiment led to regulatory changes that had allowed Citron to gradually make more risky investments promising higher returns. Citron was particularly fond of an investment called a "reverse repurchase" — an arrangement whereby the county sold short-term securities with the promise to buy them back for a higher price. Meanwhile, Citron invested the proceeds from the sales in longer-term securities at higher rates of interest. It is basically a sound idea: The difference between the higher returns and the contracted buyback price allowed Citron to repurchase the county's securities with money left over. Moreover, Citron was fond of exotic *derivatives*—investment instruments whose value is literally "derived" from the value of a variety of other assets—say, stocks, bonds, or mortgages.

The strategy was hugely successful—as long as interest rates fell. This they did in the late 1980s and early 1990s. Meanwhile, Citron also borrowed money from Wall Street brokers (in particular, Merrill Lynch). In other words, he purchased securities—including derivatives—by borrowing money from brokers, who, in turn, got the money from banks. The collateral for these loans consisted of the purchased securities—whose values, of course, were subject to change. Using the county's $7.4 billion as collateral, Citron built a portfolio valued at $20 billion. For many years, he was a local hero because his dealings helped finance Orange County's growing needs without substantially raising taxes.

Eventually, however, the inherent risks of Citron's strategy became apparent. Early in 1994, interest rates began to rise. When that happens, the share prices of the underlying assets shrink. What if your securities-purchase agreement requires you to secure your loans with higher collateral? In the case of Orange County, lenders began to demand more collateral to back up the portfolio assets that the county had purchased with borrowed money. Meeting those demands drained hundreds of millions from the county treasury. On December 1, county representatives announced that the value of Orange County's portfolio had dropped $1.5 billion. A few days later, unable to make a scheduled debt payment, Orange County declared bankruptcy in U.S. Federal court. To one market observer, the reason for the fiasco was painfully simple: "This county has taken a market hit. And then they borrowed to do that, so it's even worse."

Who stands to lose from the Orange County debacle? For one thing, investors holding $500 million in tax-exempt Orange County bonds may have trouble getting their money back—the county may not have the money to redeem them. Overall, the bond market was shaken by fears that other municipalities might be in the same situation as Orange County.

Immediately after the bankruptcy filing, Orange County was able to meet its payroll expenses only amid concerns about future cutbacks in municipal services—and, of course, tax increases. Not least among those directly affected was Citron himself, who was forced to resign.

Corporate Bonds

Corporate bonds are a major source of long-term financing for Canadian corporations. They have traditionally been issued with maturities ranging from 20 to 30 years. In the 1980s, ten-year maturities came into wider use. As with government bonds, longer-term corporate bonds are somewhat riskier than shorter-term bonds. Bond ratings of new and proposed corporate issues are published to keep investors informed of the latest risk evaluations on many bonds. Negative ratings do not preclude a bond's success, but they do raise the interest rate that issuers must offer.

Corporate bonds may be categorized in one of two ways: (1) according to methods of interest payment and (2) according to whether they are *secured* or *unsecured*.

Interest Payment: Registered and Bearer Bonds. **Registered Bonds** register the names of holders with the company, which simply mails out cheques. Certificates are of value only to registered holders. **Bearer** (or **coupon**) **bonds** require bondholders to clip coupons from certificates and send them to the issuer in order to receive payment. Coupons can be redeemed by anyone, regardless of ownership.

registered bond
Names of holders are registered with the company.

bearer (coupon) bond
Require bondholders to clip coupons from certificates and send them to the issuer in order to receive interest payments.

Secured Bonds. Borrowers can reduce the risk of their bonds by pledging assets to bondholders in the event of default. **Secured bonds** can be backed by first mortgages, other mortgages, or other specific assets. If the corporation does not pay interest when it is due, the firm's assets can be sold and the proceeds used to pay the bondholders.

secured bonds
Bonds issued by borrowers who pledge assets as collateral in the event of nonpayment.

Unsecured Bonds. Unsecured bonds are called **debentures**. No specific property is pledged as security for these bonds. Holders of unsecured bonds generally have claims against property not otherwise pledged in the company's other bonds. Accordingly, debentures have inferior claims on the corporation's assets. Financially strong corporations often use debentures.

debentures
Unsecured bonds.

The Retirement of Bonds

Maturity dates on bonds of all kinds may be very long. But all bonds must be paid off—*retired*—at some point. Most bonds are callable, but others are serial or convertible.

Callable Bonds. Many corporate bonds are callable. The issuer of a **callable bond** has the right at almost any time to call the bonds in and pay them off at a price stipulated in the bond indenture (contract). Usually the issuer cannot call the bond for a certain period of time after issue, but some are callable at any time.

callable bond
A bond that may be paid off by the issuer before the maturity date.

Issuers are most likely to call in existing bonds when the prevailing interest rate is lower than the rate being paid on the bond. But the price the issuer must pay to call in the bond, the *call price*, usually gives a premium to the bondholder. For example, a bond might have a $100 face value and be callable by the firm for $108.67 anytime during the first year after being issued. The call price and the premium decrease annually as the bonds near maturity.

A Notice of Redemption calls for certain bonds to be turned in and paid off by the issuer. The accrual of interest on the selected bonds stops upon the redemption date.

sinking-fund provision
A clause in the bond indenture (contract) that requires the issuing company to put enough money into a special bank account each year to cover the retirement of the bond issue on schedule.

Sinking Funds. Bonds are often retired by the use of a **sinking-fund provision** in the bond indenture. This method requires the issuing company to put a certain amount of money into a special bank account each year. At the end of a number of years, the money in this account (including interest) is sufficient to redeem the bonds. Failure to meet the sinking-fund provision places the bond issue in default. Bonds with sinking funds are generally regarded as safer investments than bonds without them.

Serial and Convertible Bonds.   As an alternative to sinking funds, some corporations issue serial or convertible bonds. In a **serial bond** issue, the firm retires portions of the bond issue at different predetermined dates. In a $100 million serial bond issue maturing in 20 years, for example, the company may retire $5 million of the issue each year.

serial bond

A bond issue in which redemption dates are staggered so that a firm pays off portions of the issue at different predetermined dates.

Convertible bonds can be paid off in (converted to) common stock of the issuing company, at the option of the bondholder, instead of in cash. Since bondholders have a chance for capital gains, the company can offer lower interest rates when issuing the bonds. However, since bondholders cannot be forced to accept stock in lieu of money, conversion will work only if the corporation is considered a good investment.

convertible bond

Any bond that offers bondholders the option of accepting common stock instead of cash in repayment.

To draw a clearer picture of how convertible bonds work, let's consider the following example. In 1993, Lowe's Companies Inc. sold a $250 million issue of 4 1/2 percent convertible bonds. The bonds were issued in $1000 denominations; they mature in 2003 and are called after 1996. At any time before maturity, each debenture of $1000 is convertible into 19 1/8 shares of the company's common stock. Between October 1993 and March 1994, the stock price ranged from a low of $28 to a high of $67. In that time, then, 19 1/8 common shares had a market value ranging from $535 to $1281.[5] In other words, the holder could have exchanged the $1000 bond in return for stock to be kept or sold at a possible profit (or loss).

Secondary Securities Markets for Bonds

Unlike stocks, nearly all secondary trading in bonds occurs in the over-the-counter market rather than on any organized exchange. As a result, precise statistics about annual trading volumes are not recorded.

Like stocks, however, market values and prices of bonds change from day to day. Prices of bonds with average risks tend to move up or down until the interest rate they yield generally reflects the prevailing interest rate of the economy. That is, the direction of bond prices moves opposite to interest rate changes—as interest rates move up, bond prices tend to go down. The prices of riskier bonds fluctuate more than those of higher-grade bonds and often exceed the interest rate of the economy.

Other Investments

Although stocks and bonds are very important, they are not the only marketable securities for businesses. Financial managers are also concerned with investment opportunities in mutual funds, commodities, and options.

Mutual Funds

mutual fund

Any company that pools the resources of many investors and uses those funds to purchase various types of financial securities, depending on the fund's financial goals.

Companies called **mutual funds** pool investments from individuals and other firms to purchase a portfolio of stocks, bonds, and short-term securities. Investors are part-owners of this portfolio. For example, if you invest $1000 in a mutual fund that has a portfolio worth $100 000, you own 1 percent of the portfolio. Mutual funds usually have portfolios worth many millions of dollars. The video case "French Fries" on p. 621 describes how a mutual fund called Altamira bought stock in a new company called Harvard International Technologies.

Like stocks and bonds, there are many types of mutual funds. Investors in **no-load funds** are not charged a sales commission when they buy into or sell out of the mutual fund. **Load funds** carry a charge of between 2 and 8 percent of the invested funds.

Mutual funds vary by the investment goals they stress. Some stress safety. The portfolios of these mutual funds include treasury bills and other safe issues that offer immediate income (liquidity). Short-term municipal bond funds emphasize tax-exempt, immediate income.

Other funds seek higher current income and are willing to sacrifice some safety. Long-term municipal bond mutual funds, corporate bond mutual funds, and income mutual funds (which invest in common stocks with good dividend-paying records) all fall into this category.

Still other funds stress growth. Examples include balanced mutual funds, which hold a mixture of bonds, preferred stocks, and common stocks. Growth mutual funds stress common stocks of established firms. Aggressive growth mutual funds seek maximum capital appreciation. To get it, these funds sacrifice current income and safety. They invest in stocks of new companies, troubled companies, and other high-risk securities.

Mutual funds give small investors access to professional financial management. Their managers have up-to-date information about market conditions and the best large-scale investment opportunities. The box "Are Reciprocal Commissions Ethical?" describes a potential problem in this area.

no-load fund
A mutual fund in which investors are not charged a sales commission when they buy into or sell out of the fund.

load fund
A mutual fund in which investors are charged a sales commission when they buy into or sell out of the fund.

The Canadian Business Scene

ARE RECIPROCAL COMMISSIONS ETHICAL?

Reciprocal commissions (called "recips" in the trade) work as follows: A broker may recommend that a client invest in a certain mutual fund. The fund's manager then buys and sells securities through that broker's trading desk. Essentially, the fund manager channels commissions to an investment dealer in return for sales of the fund. Several mutual fund companies, including Fidelity Investments Canada, Mackenzie Financial Corp., and Elliott & Page Ltd., pay recips. The Ontario Securities Commission allows the practice of paying recips, so companies that do it are not breaking the law.

Investors are often unaware that their stockbrokers have "sweetheart" incentive deals with some fund managers. People in the mutual fund business are split in their opinions about the practice. Some feel that it's O.K. as long as customers know it is being done. Others feel it is completely unacceptable.

Some fairly large amounts of money may be involved. For example, Richardson Greenshields of Canada Ltd. received over $350 000 in recips from Mackenzie's Industrial Growth Fund (35 percent of all the commissions paid by that fund), and over $86 000 from Mackenzie's Industrial Balanced Fund (33 percent of all commissions paid by that fund). Officials at mutual funds argue that the practice of paying recips is perfectly

reasonable since brokers invest in their funds because of the fund's performance, not recips.

Opponents of the practice have three concerns. First, recips raise the cost of doing business, and the customer is the one who comes out on the short end. Allan Marple, the president of Spectrum Bulloch Financial Services (a mutual fund which does not pay recips) says that it is inappropriate to spend investors' money to increase sales. Second, there is concern that mutual fund managers will not negotiate as hard as they can to get transaction costs down if they have an incentive arrangement with a broker. Third, recips may encourage brokers to give clients something less than objective advice about mutual funds (for example, not recommending mutual funds that don't direct stock trades through that broker).

Interestingly, there are few complaints from investors about the practice of paying recips. Interviews with over 1000 buyers of mutual funds by the firm Marketing Solutions yielded no mention about the practice. Critics argue that this is because securities rules allow fund managers to make only minimal disclosure about the practice. A prospectus typically says something like "the fund manager may direct brokerage transactions to a registered dealer in compensation for that dealer selling the fund's securities."

Commodities

futures contract

An agreement to purchase a specified amount of a commodity at a given price on a set date in the future.

commodities market

The market in which investors can buy and sell contracts for a variety of goods.

In addition to buying and selling bonds, individuals and businesses may elect to buy and sell commodities as an investment. **Futures contracts** —agreements to purchase a specified amount of a commodity at a given price on a set date in the future—can be bought and sold in the **commodities market**. Futures contracts are available for commodities ranging from coffee beans and live hogs to propane and platinum, as well as for stocks. Since selling prices reflect traders' beliefs about the future, prices of such contracts are very volatile, and futures trading is very risky. The Chicago Board of Trade is the world's largest commodity exchange. The Winnipeg Commodity Exchange is the largest commodity exchange in Canada.

To clarify the workings of the commodities market, let's look at an example. On March 14, 1994, the price of gold on the open market was $386.50 per ounce. Futures contracts for October 1994 gold were selling for $394.60 per ounce. This price reflected investors' estimates in March that gold prices would be higher the following October. Now suppose that you purchased a 100-ounce gold contract in March for $39 460 ($394.60 x 100). If in May 1994 the October gold futures sold for $419.60, you could sell your contract for $41 960. Your profit after the two months would be $2500.

margin

The percentage of the total sales price that a buyer must put up to place an order for stock or a futures contract.

Margins.   Usually, buyers of futures contracts need not put up full purchase amounts. Rather, the buyer posts a smaller amount—the **margin**—that may be as small as $3000 for contracts up to $100 000. Let's look again at our gold futures example. As we saw, if you had posted a $3000 margin for your October gold contract, you would have earned a $2500 profit on that investment of $3000 in only two months.

However, you also took a big risk involving two big *ifs*:

1. If you had held onto your contract, and
2. if gold had dropped to a value of only $377 in October 1994,

Gold is one of the many commodities for which futures contracts can be bought.

you would have lost $1760. If you had posted a $3000 margin to buy the contract, you would receive only $1240. In fact, between 75 and 90 percent of all small-time investors lose money in the futures market. For one thing, the action is fast and furious, with small investors trying to keep up with professionals ensconced in seats on the major exchanges. Although the profit potential is also exciting, experts recommend that most novices retreat to safer stock markets. Of course, as one veteran financial planner puts it, commodities are tempting: "After trading commodities," he reports, "trading stocks is like watching the grass grow."[6]

Most investors in commodities markets never intend to take possession of the commodity in question. They merely buy and sell the futures contracts. But some companies buy futures to protect the price of commodities important to their businesses, as when Canada Packers trades in hog futures.

More than 400 "commodity exchanges" have opened up in the former Soviet Union. These exchanges bring together buyers and sellers of many different types of goods. Although they call themselves commodity exchanges, they are in fact far more primitive than commodity exchanges in Canada and the U.S. One trader says they are more like flea markets than commodity exchanges.[7]

stock option

The purchased right to buy or sell a stock.

call option

The purchased right to buy a particular stock at a certain price until a specified date.

Stock Options

Trading in stock options has become a popular investment activity. A **stock option** is the right to buy or sell a stock. More specifically, a **call option** gives its owner the right to *buy* a particular stock at a certain price, with that right lasting until a particular date. A **put option** gives its owner the right to *sell* a particular stock at a specified price, with that right lasting until a particular date. These options are traded on several stock exchanges.

Suppose you thought the price of Alcan (which sold for $37 5/8 on April 5, 1995) was going to go up. You might buy a call option giving you the right to buy 100 shares of Alcan anytime in the next two months at a so-called strike price of $55. If the stock rose to $65 before June, you would exercise your call option. Your profit would be $10 per share ($65 – $55) less the price you paid to buy the option. However, if the stock price fell instead of rising, you would not exercise your call option because Alcan would be available on the open market for less than $55 per share. You would lose whatever you paid for the option.

In contrast, if you thought the price of Alcan would fall below $37 5/8 sometime during the two months after April 5, 1995, you might buy a put option. This option would give you the right to sell 100 shares for $42 5/8 per share anytime before June 1995. If the stock price fell to $32 5/8, your profit would be $10 per share ($42 5/8 – $32 5/8), less whatever you paid for the option. Assume that the price of a put option was $2 3/4 per share at that time. If the stock price increased, you would not exercise your option to sell, and you would lose what you paid for the put option. The daily prices of put and call options are listed in the financial press.

put option
The purchased right to sell a particular stock at a certain price until a specified date.

Buying and Selling Securities

The process of buying and selling stocks, bonds, and other financial instruments is complex. To start, you need to find out about possible investments and match them to your investment objectives. Then you can select a broker and open an account. Only when you have a broker can you place different types of orders and make different types of transactions.

Using Financial Information Services

Have you ever looked at the financial section of your daily newspaper and found yourself wondering what all those tables and numbers mean? If you cannot read stock and bond quotations, you probably should not invest in these issues. Fortunately, this skill is easily mastered. More complicated but also important is some grasp of market indexes.

Stock Quotations. Figure 20.1 shows the type of information newspapers give about daily market transactions of individual stocks. The corporation's name is shown along with the number of shares sold (expressed in board lots). Prices are quoted in dollars and fractions of a dollar ranging from 1/8 to 7/8. A quote of 50 5/8 means that the price per share is $50.625.

Bond Quotations. Bond prices also change from day to day. These changes form the *coupon rate*, which provides information for firms about the cost of borrowing funds.

Prices of domestic corporation bonds, Canadian government bonds, and foreign bonds are reported separately. Bond prices are expressed in terms of 100, even though most have a face value of $1000. Thus, a quote of 85 means that the bond's price is 85 percent of its face value, or $850.

A corporation bond selling at 155 1/4 would cost a buyer $1552.50 ($1000 face value × 1.5525), plus commission. The interest rate on bonds is also quoted as a percentage of par, or face, value. Thus "6 1/2s" pay 6.5 percent of par value per year. Typically, interest is paid semiannually at half of the stated interest or coupon rate.

- Stock
  ***Inco* (Name of company)**
- Sales
  62 701
  Total number of shares traded this date. There were 62 701 shares sold.
- High *16⅛* Low *15⅝*
  During the trading day highest price was $16.125 and the lowest was $15.6725.
- Close
  16
  At the close of trading on this date the last price paid per share was $16.00.
- Net Change
  –⅜
  Difference between today's closing price and previous day's closing price. Price decreased by $0.375.

Stock	Sales	High	Low	Close	Net Change
H Bay Mng	1 557	$ 21	20¾	21	+½
H Bay Co	1 440	$ 21⅞	21½	21⅞	+⅜
HBC pr	5 388	$ 15½	15¼	15½	
Hu-Pam o	1 600	55	52	52	–10
Husky Oil	17 520	$ –8 ⅞	8 ⅝	8¾	+⅛
Husky 13p	9 605	$40½	39	40¼	+1
Hydra Ex o	4 000	80	74	80	+10
ITL Ind	2 000	60	60	60	+5
IU Intl	622	$22¾	22	22¾	+½
Imasco	26 511	$ 37	36	36⅞	+34
Imasco A p	200	350	350	350	+25
Imasco B p	350	$ 74	73	74	+1¾
Imp Life p	400	$ 27¾	27¾	27¾	
Imp Oil A	18 390	$ 28⅜	27¾	28¼	+⅜
Imp Oil B	z6	$ 27½	27½	27½	
Inca o	46 285	$ 6⅜	5⅞	6⅜	+¾
Inca w	28 100	275	246	255	+25
Inco	***62 701***	***$ 16⅛***	***15⅝***	***16***	***–⅜***
Inco 7.85	400	$ 18	17½	17½	–½
Inco wt	14 600	$ 6¼	6⅛	6¼	–½
Indal	z75	$ 17½	17¼	17½	
Inland Gas	5 580	$ 13⅜	13	13	–⅜
Inland G p	z17	$ 9	9	9	
Inter-City	24 500	$ 11	10⅝	11	+⅜
IBM	908	$124⅝	123⅜	124⅝	+2⅛

Figure 20.1
How to read a stock quotation.

The market value (selling price) of a bond at any given time depends on its stated interest rate, the "going rate" of interest in the market, and its redemption or maturity date.

A bond with a higher stated interest rate than the going rate on similar quality bonds will probably sell at a premium above its face value—its selling price will be above its redemption price. A bond with a lower stated interest rate than the going rate on similar quality bonds will probably sell at a discount—its selling price will be below its redemption price. How much the premium or discount is depends largely on how far in the future the maturity date is. The maturity date is shown after the interest rate. When more than one year is given, the bond is either retractable or extendible.

Figure 20.2 shows the type of information daily newspapers give about bond transactions.

Bond Yield. Suppose you bought a $1000 par-value bond in 1977 for $650. Its stated interest rate is 6 percent, and its maturity or redemption date is 1997. You therefore receive $60 per year in interest. Based on your actual investment of $650, your yield is 9.2 percent. If you hold it to maturity, you get $1000 for a bond that originally cost you only $650. This extra $350 increases your true, or effective, yield.

market index
A measure of the market value of stocks; provides a summary of price trends in a specific industry or of the stock market as a whole.

Market Indexes. Although they do not indicate how particular securities are doing, **market indexes** provide a useful summary of trends in specific industries and the stock market as a whole. Such information can be

		Price	Yield	Change
• *Dofasco* Company name is Dofasco Ltd.	**Government of Canada**			
	Canada 13 May 1-01	100.62	12.22	+¼
• *17* Annual rate of interest at face value is 17 percent	Canada 9½ Oct 15-01	86.00	11.33	+¼
	Canada 15½ Mar 15-02	122.75	12.35	+½
	Canada 11¼ Dec 15-02	94.87	11.93	+¼
• *May 1-97* Maturity date. In this case, May 1, 1997	Canada 11¾ Feb 1-03	98.75	11.92	+¼
	Canada 10¼ Feb 1-04	89.75	11.567	+⅛
• *117.00* On this date, this was the price of the last transaction	**Provincials and Guaranteed**			
	Alta 12¼ Dec 15-02	99.00	12.38	+¼
	BC Hy 14½ Apr 14-06	109.25	13.21	+¼
• *14.17* Annual interest paid divided by current market price	NS 15½ Apr 15-87-97	117.25	12.82	...
	Ont Hy 17 Mar 3-02	123.25	13.56	+¼
	Ont Hy 14¼ Apr 21-06	109.50	12.94	...
• *+¼* The closing price on this day was up $0.25 from the closing price on the previous day.	Que 16¼-½ Mar 22-87-97	119.00	13.40	...
	Corporates			
	Bel 11 Oct 15-04	90.50	12.26	+½
	CIL 14½ Apr 15-96	105.75	13.45	+¼
	Cdn Util 17½ Mar 15-97	119.00	13.40	...
	Dofasco 17 May 1-97	***117.00***	***14.17***	***+¼***
	Nova 17¾ Feb 15-97	118.00	14.68	...

Figure 20.2
How to read a bond quotation.

crucial in choosing appropriate investments. For example, market indexes reveal bull and bear market trends. **Bull markets** are periods of upward-moving stock prices. The years 1981 to 1989 featured a strong bull market. Periods of falling stock prices, such as 1972 to 1974, are called **bear markets**.

The most widely cited market index is the **Dow Jones Industrial Average**. The "Dow," as it is sometimes called, is the sum of market prices for 30 of the largest industrial firms listed on the NYSE. By tradition, the Dow is an indicator of blue-chip stock price movements. Because of the limited number of firms it considers, however, it is a limited gauge of the overall stock market.

Standard & Poor's Composite Index is a broader report than the Dow. It consists of 500 stocks: 400 industrial firms, 40 utilities, 40 financial institutions, and 20 transportation companies. Other widely publicized indexes are the NYSE Index, the TSE 300 Index, and the Tokyo Index.

Selecting a Broker

In choosing a broker, you must consider what services you need. All brokerages execute customers' orders for securities purchases and sales. **Discount brokerage houses** do little beyond this minimum. But their low commissions make them popular with some investors.

In contrast, **full-service brokerages** offer a variety of services, including investment advice to meet individuals' financial goals. They suggest the best mix of debt versus equity for corporate investors. One service that some brokerages use as a tool in competing with other houses is research. Firms that offer research services provide clients with assessments on the quality and investment prospects of different industries, companies, and securities. Such reports are supplied free of charge, but brokerage fees are higher at these houses.

bull market
A period of rising stock prices; a period in which investors act on a belief that stock prices will rise.

bear market
A period of falling stock prices; a period in which investors act on a belief that stock prices will fall.

Dow Jones industrial average
An overall market index based on stock prices of 30 of the largest industrial, transportation, and utility firms listed on the New York Stock Exchange.

discount brokerage house
A stock brokerage that charges a minimal fee for executing clients' orders but offers only limited services.

full-service brokerage
A stock brokerage that offers a variety of services, including investment advice, to help clients reach their financial goals.

One service that full-service brokerage houses offer is investment advice to clients.

Placing an Order

Based on your own investigations and/or recommendations from your broker, you can place many types of orders. A **market order** requests the broker to buy or sell a certain security at the prevailing market price at the time. For example, your broker would have sold your Alcan stock for between $37.62 and $38.00 per share on April 5, 1995. When you gave the order to sell, however, you did not know exactly what the market price would be.

In contrast, both limit and stop orders allow for buying and selling of securities only if certain price conditions are met. A **limit order** authorizes the purchase of a stock only if its price is less than or equal to a given limit. For example, a limit order to buy a stock at $80 per share means that the broker is to buy it if and only if the stock becomes available for a price of $80 or less. Similarly, a **stop order** instructs the broker to sell a stock if its price falls to a certain level. For example, a stop order of $85 on a particular stock means that the broker is to sell it if and only if its price falls to $85 or below.

You can also place orders of different sizes. A **round lot** order requests 100 shares or some multiple thereof. Fractions of a round lot are called **odd lots**. Trading odd lots is usually more expensive than trading round lots, because an intermediary called an odd-lot broker is often involved, which increases brokerage fees.

Financing Securities Purchases

When you place a buy order of any kind, you must tell your broker how you will pay for the purchase. You might maintain a cash account with your broker. Then, as stocks are bought and sold, proceeds are added into the account and commissions and costs of purchases are withdrawn by the broker. In addition, as with almost every good in today's economy, you can buy shares on credit.

Margin Trading. As with futures contracts, you can buy stocks on *margin*—putting down only a portion of the stock's price. You borrow the rest

---

market order

An order to a broker to buy or sell a certain security at the current market price.

limit order

An order to a broker to buy a certain security only if its price is less than or equal to a given limit.

stop order

An order to a broker to sell a certain security if its price falls to a certain level or below.

round lot

The purchase or sale of stock in units of 100 shares.

odd lots

The purchase or sale of stock in units other than 100 shares.

from your broker, who, in turn, borrows from the banks at a special rate and secures the loans with stock.

Margin trading offers clear advantages to buyers. Suppose you purchased $100 000 worth of stock in Alcan, paying $50 000 of your own money and borrowing the other $50 000 from your broker at 10 percent interest. If, after one year, the shares have risen in value to $115 000, you could sell them, pay your broker $55 000 ($50 000 principal plus $5000 interest), and have $60 000 left over. Your original investment of $50 000 would have earned a 20 percent profit of $10 000. If you had paid the entire price of the stock from your own funds, your investment would have earned only a 15 percent return.

Brokerages benefit from margin trading in two ways. First, it encourages more people to buy more stock, which means more commissions to the brokerage. And, second, the firm earns a profit on its loans, since it charges buyers a higher interest rate than it pays the bank.

Short Sales.   In addition to money, brokerages also lend buyers securities. A **short sale** begins when you borrow a security from your broker and sell it (one of the few times it is legal to sell what you do not own). At a given time in the future, you must restore an equal number of shares of that issue to the brokerage, along with a fee.

short sale
Selling borrowed shares of stock in the expectation that their price will fall before they must be replaced, so that replacement shares can be bought for less than the original shares were sold for.

For example, suppose that in June you believe the price of Alcan stock will soon fall. You order your broker to sell short 100 shares at the market price of $38 per share. Your broker will make the sale and credit $3800 to your account. If Alcan's price falls to $32 per share in July, you can buy 100 shares for $3200 and give them to your broker, leaving you with a $600 profit (before commissions). The risk is that Alcan's price will not fall but will hold steady or rise, leaving you with a loss.

Securities Regulation

Canada, unlike the United States with its Securities and Exchange Commission (SEC), does not have comprehensive federal securities legislation or a federal regulatory body. Government regulation is primarily provincial and there is a degree of self-regulation through the various securities exchanges.

In 1912, the Manitoba government pioneered in Canada laws applying mainly to the sale of new securities. Under these "**blue-sky laws**," corporations issuing securities must back them up with something more than the blue sky. Similar laws were passed in other provinces. The video case "French Fries" on p. 621 describes a situation which blue sky laws will usually (but not always) prevent. Provincial laws also generally require that stockbrokers be licensed and securities be registered before they can be sold. In each province, issuers of proposed new securities must file a prospectus with the provincial securities exchange. A **prospectus** is a detailed registration statement that includes information about the firm, its operation, its management, the purpose of the proposed issue, and any other data helpful to a potential buyer of these securities. The prospectus must be made available to prospective investors.

blue-sky laws
Laws regulating how corporations must back up securities.

prospectus
A detailed registration statement about a new stock filed with a provincial securities exchange; must include any data helpful to a potential buyer.

Ontario is regarded as having the most progressive securities legislation in Canada. The Ontario Securities Act contains disclosure provisions for new and existing issues, prevention of fraud, regulation of the Toronto Stock Exchange, and takeover bids. It also prohibits **insider trading**, which is the use of special knowledge about a firm to make a profit in the stock market.

The Toronto Stock Exchange provides an example of self-regulation by the industry. The TSE has regulations concerning listing and delisting of securities, disclosure requirements, and issuing of prospectuses for new securities.

insider trading
The use of special knowledge about a firm to make a profit on the stock market.

Summary of Key Points

The securities markets for stocks and bonds are an important source of long-term financing for businesses. Primary securities markets involve buying and selling new securities, either in a public offering or with a private placement. The secondary markets involve the trading of existing stocks and bonds. Within these markets, investors, who range from average workers to powerful businesses, choose securities with the safety, income, and growth characteristics that match their investment goals and attitudes toward risk.

Common stock affords investors the prospect of capital gains and/or dividend income. Common stock has par value, market value, and book value. Of these, market value is most important to would-be investors. Preferred stock is less risky than common stock and offers steadier income prospects. Preferred shareholders must be paid dividends (including arrears in the case of shareholders of cumulative preferred stock) before shareholders of common stock can receive dividends.

Common and preferred stock are traded on stock exchanges and in the over-the-counter markets. Holders of seats on the exchanges act as brokers for individuals wishing to trade in such exchanges. These exchanges include the Toronto, Vancouver, and Montreal Exchanges, as well as foreign exchanges. Licensed traders serve a similar function in the over-the-counter market.

A bond is a written promise that the borrower will pay the lender a certain amount of money, plus a stated amount of interest, at a certain time in the future. The safety of bonds issued by various borrowers is rated by services such as the Canadian Bond Rating Service, Moody's, and Standard & Poor's. Government bonds are very safe because they are backed by the federal or provincial government. Corporate bonds may be secured or unsecured, offering varying degrees of safety to investors. To reassure investors and keep their interest payments low, some firms issue serial or convertible bonds or bonds that contain a sinking-fund provision.

Like stocks and bonds, mutual funds offer investors different levels of risk and growth potential. Some mutual funds emphasize safety and liquidity while others seek maximum capital appreciation with high-risk securities. Even riskier than mutual funds are commodities trading in the futures market and options trading.

Investors can match their goals to specific securities by following the activities of organized stock and bond exchanges and the over-the-counter market as reported in the financial section of the newspaper. After settling on a discount or full-service broker, investors can place different types of orders, including market orders, limit orders, and stop orders. Rather than immediately paying in full for a security, some investors buy stocks and bonds on margin or as part of a short sale.

Because of the potential for abuse in securities trading, each province has a securities commission which regulates the sale of new and existing securities, the licensing of stockbrokers, and the disclosure of information.

Wham! Bang! Pow! The Marvel of Going Public

In 1991, Marvel Comics announced plans to sell 3.5 million common shares at $14 to $16 each. Before the shares could even get to market, demand was so great that the company decided instead to issue 4.2 million shares at $16 to $17 each. The stock promptly sold out, grossing $69.3 million for the comic-book company. About one-third of the money went to pay down the $70 million debt incurred during the 1989 takeover by financier Ronald Perelman. In the form of special dividends, the rest went to various other Perelman enterprises. By early 1992, the price of the stock had skyrocketed to $65 per share.

Was everybody happy? Not by a long shot. In mid-February 1992, *Barron's* magazine ran an article highly critical of Marvel. Among the potential pitfalls noted:

- Roughly 85 percent of the firm's revenues come from publishing; 80 percent of publishing revenues come from comic books.
- Because of rising prices and the general economic downturn, comic-book sales have been leveling off.
- Recent increases in Marvel revenues can be traced largely to price increases, which are now meeting resistance from both consumers and retailers.
- Collector interest in comic books is waning, further depressing the company's ability to raise more money from comic-book sales.
- The recession of 1991-93 hit many of the U.S.'s specialty comic-book stores—which account for 73 percent of sales. This loss is especially troubling because these stores (unlike newsstands) buy comics with no option to return unsold copies. (Each month, newsstands return about two-thirds of their orders for refunds.)
- The remaining 15 percent of Marvel's revenues come from licensing its characters—a revenue source that may have reached the saturation point.
- Marvel's biggest licensing opportunity is an agreement with Carolco Pictures to produce a Spiderman movie. But with the movie studio in financial trouble of its own, the film may not get made. If so, licensed manufacturers will not produce Spiderman dolls and costumes—or, of course, pay licensing fees to Marvel.
- Although dominant with 45 percent of the $400 million annual market, Marvel faces serious challenges. Number-two DC Comics, for example, can look both to such popular characters as Batman and to its affluent parent company, Time Warner, for resources.

Moreover, many small companies are cutting into the market with innovative characters and artwork.

The stock market responded quickly to the *Barron's* analysis: After a one-day New York Stock Exchange holiday, Marvel's stock fell from $66 to $54.625. Marvel executives criticized the article, arguing that the company would be free from debt by year's end and that its prospects for growth remained high. One day later, however, the company had to deal with the announcement that eight of its key writers and illustrators were leaving to join competitor Malibu Graphics.

However, although the results of his efforts are still inconclusive, Ron Perelman has shown his confidence by upping his investment in Marvel to 80 percent. He now draws a comparison between Marvel and entertainment colossus Disney: "We are a developer of characters just as Disney is," he explains. "Disney's got much more highly recognized characters and 'softer' characters, whereas our characters are termed as action heroes. But at Marvel we are now in the creation and marketing of characters." Perelman also notes that comic books now represent only about 15 percent of Marvel's business, and his new strategy calls for stepping up the pace of licensing ventures. The Spider Man movie, for example, is now at Twentieth-Century Fox, and characters like X-Men are showing up in TV shows, movies, and other merchandise, both in the U.S. and abroad. In the fall of 1994, Marvel previewed its X-men spinoff, Generation X, on several online computer services. In the span of a few weeks, more than 44 000 Generation X files were downloaded from the Internet.

CASE QUESTIONS

1. Who do you think were the major investors in Marvel's 1991 stock offering? Why?
2. If you had purchased Marvel stock in 1991, how would you have felt about its use of the monies raised in the offering?
3. Because of the flood of sell orders, the New York Stock Exchange initially delayed trading of Marvel stock following the Barron's article. Do you think this action was justified?
4. Not all brokers advised against purchasing Marvel stock following the appearance of the Barron's article. Why might some have recommended buying instead?
5. Would you buy stock in Marvel today? Why or why not?

◆

CONCLUDING CASE 20-2

Institutional Investors Are Getting More Demanding

Not too many years ago, institutional investors were usually content to let management run the companies they had bought shares in. But it has become increasingly common for pension fund managers to flex their muscles and try to influence management decisions. In fact, intervention has become so common that when the Caisse de dêpot et placement du Québec decided *not* to intervene in a takeover fight for Connaught BioSciences Inc., its decision made headlines.

A fundamental power struggle is being fought between management and the agents who invest the savings of millions of Canadians. The capital pool controlled by organizations such as Jarislowsky Fraser & Co., Canadian National Pension Trust Fund, and the Ontario Municipal Employees Retirement System (OMERS) keeps growing. It now totals over $1 trillion. Because takeovers and mergers have reduced the number of companies they can invest in, institutional investors have taken to watching their investments very closely.

Stanley Beck, former chairman of the Ontario Securities Commission, sees institutional investors and provincial securities commissions as allies—they both want to see responsible corporate behavior regarding shareholders. The OSC does not have the time or personnel to police all management activity. They are happy that the institutional investors are doing some of it.

The institutions win some fights and lose others. OMERS holds 6 percent of the common shares of Xerox Canada Inc. When the U.S. head office decided to exchange one common share of the U.S. company for three of the Canadian company, OMERS complained that the price was too low. The plan was approved anyway and OMERS sued Xerox. Since then, the OSC has developed more stringent rules on directors' responsibilities to shareholders during takeovers.

Sometimes institutional investors have had their representatives elected to the board of directors of companies they are concerned about. Royal Trust Energy Corp. nominated two of its officials to sit on the board of the near-bankrupt Oakwoods Petroleum Ltd. When it became clear that two pension funds—CN's and Central Trust's— would support the Royal Trust nominees, two incumbent management-supported nominees withdrew their names.

Major battles between pension funds and company management often shape up over the issue of poison pills. Poison pills usually give shareholders the right to buy company stock at a below-market price if a would-be purchaser's holdings go beyond a certain level. Management favors poison pills, but institutional investors usually oppose them. In the case of Inco, the institutional investors were major losers when the company persuaded shareholders to adopt the poison pill by offering them a $10 dividend if they would approve the plan.

Management often resents institutional investors, arguing that they do not know how a specific company should be run yet they insist on input anyway. They want institutional investors simply to pick stocks for their clients, not try to tell company management what to do. They point out that institutions generally have no positive advice to offer; rather, they just veto management plans. When the pension funds of CBC and Investors Group torpedoed a restructuring plan at Unicorp Canada Ltd., they did not offer an alternative. Instead they insisted that the company come up with proposals for them to accept or reject. Unicorp finally abandoned the restructuring.

Pension fund managers counter by stressing that they are preventing company management from taking advantage of small investors. Companies, they argue, too often view small shareholders as a source of cheap money rather than as equal partners in the enterprise.

CASE QUESTIONS

1. What motivates pension fund managers to try to influence the management decisions of companies they hold stock in?
2. What are the pros and cons of pension fund managers trying to influence management decisions of the companies the pension fund holds stock in?
3. Why do institutional investors such as pension funds oppose "poison pills"?
4. Imagine that you are a top manager in a company whose stock is often bought by institutional investors. What kinds of complaints about institutional investors are you likely to have? ◆

Key Terms

securities	secondary securities	par value	book value
primary securities market	market	market value	cumulative preferred
investment banker	institutional investors	capital gains	stock

stock exchange	callable bond	stock option	full-service brokerage
program trading	sinking-fund provision	call option	market order
broker	serial bond	put option	limit order
over-the-counter (OTC)	convertible bond	market index	stop order
market	mutual fund	bull market	round lot
bond	no-load fund	bear market	odd lots
registered bond	load fund	Dow Jones Industrial	short sale
bearer (coupon) bond	futures contract	Average	blue-sky laws
secured bonds	commodities market	discount brokerage	prospectus
debentures	margin	house	insider trading

Study Questions and Exercises

Review Questions

1. What are the purposes of the primary and secondary markets for securities?
2. Which of the three measures of common stock value is most important? Why?
3. What is the difference between callable and convertible bonds?
4. How might an investor lose money in a commodities trade?
5. How do the provincial securities commissions regulate securities markets?

Analysis Questions

6. Which type of stock or bond would be most appropriate for your investment purposes at this time? Why?
7. Which type of mutual fund would be most appropriate for your investment purposes at this time? Why?

8. Choose from a newspaper an example listing of a recent day's transactions for each of the following: a stock on the NYSE; a stock on the TSE; an OTC stock; a bond on the NYSE. Explain what each element in the listing means.

Application Exercises

9. Interview the financial manager of a local business or your school. What are the investment goals of this organization? What mix of securities does it use? What advantages and disadvantages do you see in its portfolio?
10. Contact a broker for information about setting up a personal account for trading securities. Prepare a report on the broker's requirements for placing buy/sell orders, credit terms, cash account requirements, services available to investors, and commissions/fees schedules.

Building Your Business Skills

Goal
To encourage students to understand how a company's internal and external environment affects the price of its common stock.

Method

Step 1
Research the activity of *one* of the following common stocks during 1995. In addition, research the internal and external events that affected the company during the year:

- IBM
- Canadian National Railway
- Bank of Montreal
- Viacom
- General Motors of Canada
- Air Canada
- Apple Computer
- Borden

Step 2
Based on your analysis, answer the following sets of questions:

- What happened to the stock price during the period? What was the high during the year? What was the low?
- What events affected the stock price?
- Which of these events involved internal changes—say, reorganizations, layoffs, a new CEO, a new labor contract, dramatic changes in sales? What were the effects of these events?
- Which of these events involved external factors—say, changes in the competitive environment or an economic downturn? What were the effects of these events?

Follow-up Questions

1. What were the main factors that influenced the company's stock price?
2. Based on what you learned, can you predict how well the stock will perform over the coming year?

WHAT HAPPENED TO MEXICO'S CURRENCY?

Since the late 1980s, Mexico has attracted foreign investment with the promise of a stable exchange rate and solid economic growth. But Mexico had a trade deficit of $17 billion in 1994 because Mexican exports and savings weren't generating enough money to pay for consumers' desires for foreign-made products like computers and running shoes. Because the country needed large inflows of short-term foreign investment, it borrowed money, mostly in the bond markets. But interest rates were going up around the world, so Mexico had to offer ever-higher interest rates on its bonds in order to attract foreign investment. (Canada has had to do the same thing.)

In early 1994, it took about 3.1 pesos to purchase a U.S. dollar. During the first 11 months of 1994, the peso slowly declined in value to about 3.7 to the dollar. The Mexican government maintained a policy of supporting the peso in an attempt to convey to other countries that Mexico had a stable economy and was a good place to invest. But in December 1994, the pressure on the peso became too great.

On December 20, 1994 Mexico reversed its long-standing policy and allowed the peso to drop nearly 13 percent in relation to the U.S. dollar. Within a week, it took 5.5 pesos to buy one U.S. dollar. The devaluation caused large losses for foreign investors, who held over $75 billion worth of Mexican securities. When the trouble started with the peso, Mexican finance officials frantically activated a $6 billion line of credit with the U.S. Federal Reserve and a $1.5 billion line of credit with the Bank of Canada. Also, Mexican Finance Minister Jaime Serra Puche flew to New York to make a pitch to investors to keep investing in Mexico. Serra spent much of the meeting apologizing for the way the situation was being handled. (He went on Mexican radio to announce the float of the peso rather than making a formal announcement or calling foreign investors directly. Only hours before the announcement, president Zedillo had stated that the peso would not be devalued.)

The government initially blamed a rebel uprising in the southern state of Chiapas for scaring off foreign investors and limiting economic growth. Troops were dispatched to the area to prevent further trouble. But many other factors were involved, including interest rate increases in the U.S. and elsewhere, competition from other emerging Latin American countries, and the assassination of the leading contender for the Mexican presidency. All of these things contributed to a perception of instability in Mexico.

In early 1995, the peso rallied to as high as 4.9 to the U.S. dollar. But in the following weeks, it plunged once more. By March 6, 1995 the peso had declined to about 7 to the dollar. On March 9, it dropped as low as 7.7 at one point. The decline in the value of the peso affected the Mexican economy in several areas:

- *Interest rates.* When the peso was devalued, interest rates increased because foreign investors wanted higher returns for investing in a riskier situation. Short-term interest rates in Mexico rose to a staggering 85 percent as the government attempted to attract new investment. But with interest rates that high, foreign investors began to assume that Mexico was headed for a major economic downturn, and that further dampened investor interest in Mexico.
- *Corporations.* Mexican companies with dollar-denominated debts had to use more pesos to pay off their debt, and this reduced their profits. On February 16,1995 a large Mexican conglomerate defaulted on some of its short-term debt (commercial paper). This is considered worse then defaulting on a long-term debt because commercial paper is thought to be more secure. Fears about the solvency of other Mexican companies have also been expressed.
- *Emigration.* A lower peso makes wages in the U.S. look more attractive to Mexican workers and increases the likelihood of illegal border crossings into the U.S.

- *Inflation.* A currency devaluation is likely to cause increased inflation. Workers ask for higher wages in order to maintain their purchasing power, and businesses charge higher prices to pay for the increased cost of production. Inflation surged from 7 percent in 1994 to an annualized rate of 64 percent in February 1995.

    In an attempt to cope with past inflation in Mexico, the government established a pact with labor and corporations. Labor would keep wage demands down, business would not raise prices, and the government would do what it could to keep inflation down. The devaluation of the peso has put that plan in jeopardy. A wage-price spiral could now occur, which would lead to much higher inflation rates and put the economy into a recession.

- *Stock markets.* The devaluation of the peso caused the Mexican stock market to decline sharply. In the weeks following the devaluation, the Bolsa IPC index declined more than 30 percent. Investors also showed nervousness about investing in other Latin American countries. Prices on the Argentine and Brazilian stock exchanges dropped after the peso was devalued.

- *Foreign investment.* At the same time the peso was losing so much of its value, the U.S. dollar was also losing ground to the German mark and the Japanese yen. The decline in the value of the U.S. dollar should make plants and factories in Mexico look very cheap to German and Japanese investors. This should result in increased foreign investment.

Recent Developments

In 1995, the U.S., Canada, and several other countries reached an agreement with Mexico on a $52 billion rescue plan. This money was used to help Mexico retire billions of short-term dollar-denominated securities. The plan included $21.5 billion from the U.S. and Canada, $17.8 billion from the International Monetary Fund and $10 billion in short-term central bank loans made available through the Bank of International Settlements.

On March 9, 1995 Mexico announced an austerity plan which called for big tax increases coupled with spending cuts designed to rein in inflationary pressures. But the plan will inflict additional burdens on workers who are already suffering from widespread layoffs and credit shortages. It could also increase business failures and fuel social unrest. Gasoline prices are scheduled to go up 35 percent, and electricity prices will rise 20 percent. Government spending will be reduced and there will be no raises for government employees. Many government businesses are scheduled to be privatized.

By the end of April 1995, the peso had staged a comeback, trading for about 6 per U.S. dollar. The stock market closed up as well. Agustin Carstens, senior director at the Bank of Mexico, said that the government economic plan calls for the peso to trade at about 6 to the dollar. That would be a 42% devaluation in the peso since December 20, 1994.

The good news is that a rise in the peso should reduce the risk of more inflation, and improve the financial condition of companies that have dollar debt. The bad news is that a stronger peso could endanger Mexican exports by making them more expensive. This will reduce revenues which are needed to supply Mexico with its dollar needs.

Until the fluctuations in the peso are brought under control, the climate for foreign investment will be poor. What foreign investors want is political stability, a stable exchange rate, a clear understanding of the government's long-term plans for the peso, and revised economic targets developed by the government of Mexico. Given the recent volatility in the exchange rate, foreign investors are reluctant to invest in Mexico because they cannot estimate the returns they will earn.

CASE QUESTIONS
1. Why did the Mexican peso decline in value?
2. Describe the costs and benefits that are associated with this decline.
3. What actions did the government of Mexico take in an attempt to influence the currency exchange rate for the peso? Indicate how these actions may help (or hinder) economic growth in Mexico.
4. What can Mexico do to restore confidence in the peso?

Experiential Exercise:
Going to Bat for Financing

OBJECTIVE

To help students understand how many aspects of a company's operations contribute to its financial standing and its access to capital.

TIME REQUIRED

45 minutes
  Step 1: Individual activity (15 minutes)
  Step 2: Small-group activity (15 minutes)
  Step 3: Class discussion (15 minutes)

PROCEDURE

Step 1: Read the following case regarding the Hickory Sport Company.

The Hickory Sport Company, manufacturer of aluminum baseball bats, has been doing a booming business. In each of the last five years, company sales and profits have risen by at least 20 percent:

Year	Sales	Profits
1990	$231 000	$29 000
1991	$307 000	$40 000
1992	$456 000	$59 000
1993	$610 000	$88 000
1994	$772 000	$106 000

Dan Bowers, cofounder and owner of Hickory Sport, is pleased with the growth of his business and expects it to grow further still. One element hampering his growth, however, is a loan limit of $200 000 at his bank, Batch National Bank. In considering his application for a $500 000 line of credit, the bank investigated Bowers and Hickory Sport thoroughly and learned the following:
  Company History. The firm was founded by Bowers and his sister. In late 1993, Bowers bought his sister's share in the business for $150 000, mortgaging the firm's plant to raise part of the money needed. He is now the sole proprietor of the company.
  Personal History. Bowers, now 37 years old, has a B.A. in economics and an MBA. A long-time sports enthusiast, he received a full athletic scholarship for playing baseball and played local softball after university. Over the last five years, however, he has given up softball and put in long hours at Hickory Sport. His suppliers and current bankers think highly of his knowledge of the business and willingness to do whatever needs to be done—typing and filing or running a lathe. His personal assets are limited to a $150 000 home with a $100 000 mortgage.
  Employees. Bowers has a well-trained assistant who has been with the company since its inception, as well as three other office employees. His hard work and upbeat attitude have contributed to high productivity and a low turnover rate among the firm's 25 employees.
  Financial Management. The company has a reputation for wise use of capital. Before Bowers bought out his sister, the firm paid its bills within the discount period. Since that time, mortgage payments and loan limits have forced Hickory Sport to delay payments to an average of 45 days. A recent financial report appears on the facing page.

Hickory Sport Company
Balance Sheet
As of December 31, 1994

Current Assets

Cash		21 150
Accounts receivable		86 600
Merchandise inventory		63 750
Prepaid expenses		3 150

Fixed Assets

Land		54 000
Building		195 000
Equipment		216 585
(Less depreciation)	141 945	
Total assets		529 270

Current Liabilities

Accounts payable	48 945	
Wages payable	11 100	
Taxes payable	5 760	

Long-term Liabilities

Notes payable, 11.25% due 1999	120 000	

Owner's Equity

Retained Earnings		333 465
Total Liabilities and Owner's Equity		529 270

Should The Bank Approve A Line Of Credit For Hickory Sport?

Step 2: The instructor will divide the class into small groups, each of which will complete the following grid ranking Hickory Sport from 1 (highly favorable in loan-making) to 5 (highly unfavorable), and decide whether the bank should extend a $500 000 line of credit to Hickory Sport.

Decision-Making Grid

Characteristic	1	2	3	4	5
Form of ownership					
Qualities of owner					
Quality of employees					
Management of assets					
Current financial health					
Future prospects					

Step 3: One member of each small group will present the group's conclusions to the class.

QUESTIONS FOR DISCUSSION

1. What factor most influenced your decision to approve or not to approve a new credit line for Hickory Sport?
2. If turned down by the bank, what other methods of financing might Dan Bowers use to fund future growth at Hickory Sport?

CAREERS IN BUSINESS
Reality Check

Landing a job is a major accomplishment. But keeping one—and advancing in the organization—is no less important and often considerably more difficult. While no one can guarantee you success on the job, following these seven guidelines can put you on the inside track to career success.

- Be a problem solver.
- Pay attention to details.
- Be a team player.
- Impress your peers.
- Do your own thing.
- Know how you're doing.
- Find a mentor.

BE A PROBLEM SOLVER

It's easy to identify and point out problems—sales are going down; turnover is too high; too many customers are complaining; quality is poor; productivity is low. It is much more difficult to be a *constructive* problem solver—one who not only points out problems but also identifies new, creative, and effective ways to remedy those problems.

After you have identified a problem, go ahead and solve it yourself—if you have the responsibility and authority. But don't go too far. If you don't have the responsibility and authority, write your boss a memo explaining the problem and recommending a solution. Even if the boss does not accept your recommendations, she or he will still be impressed by your initiative.

PAY ATTENTION TO DETAILS

It is important that you pay close attention to the "little things," the details. For example, when you submit your first report to your boss, check, double-check, and then check again to make sure that all calculations are correct and that there are no errors in your report. Also eliminate any misspelled words and/or grammatical errors.

Likewise, if you are making a presentation—whether to a group of managers, investors, or customers—don't allow mistakes to distract from your message. Be sure that your slides or overhead transparencies are just as error-free as that first report you submitted. If time permits, set the room up yourself. (At least give it a quick once-over before anyone else arrives.) Is the volume on the microphone correctly adjusted? Are your slides in the correct order? Is the projector properly focused? How do you dim the lights? Is there a spare bulb for the projector? If you will be operating the projector or any other mechanical device, make sure you can run the equipment flawlessly and smoothly. Always rehearse every element of your presentation several times.

BE A TEAM PLAYER

In school you will probably be awarded at least a few grades that are higher than you deserve. But overall, everything will equal out. The same is true on the job. You will no doubt have some great ideas for which others will be given credit. But you will sometimes get credit for other people's ideas.

Today's organizations want people who will be part of the team. Work hard at getting along with others in the organization—your boss, your peers, and your subordinates. And spread the credit around to everyone. Remember that organizations are most likely to succeed when people work together. Take joy and pride in the success of others, and recognize that no organization can function if people don't work together.

What if someone else claims credit for your ideas? If that someone is your boss, pat yourself on the back—if your boss rises because of your work, chances are good that you'll rise with that individual. If a peer deliberately misleads others and takes credit for your idea, you are likely to feel anger and resentment. Keep your mouth closed and keep doing your best. Chances are that over time your boss and everyone else in the organization will see who is really pulling the weight. As Figure 1 illustrates, a sour attitude can put a damper on your career faster than any rival can.

IMPRESS YOUR PEERS

Closely related to teamwork is the idea of impressing your peers. Obviously, it is important to impress your boss. But if you ignore your co-workers, downgrade their abilities and accomplishments, and work only to advance yourself, you will eventually become an outcast in the organization.

You will be far better served if you can earn the respect, trust, and support of your co-workers. Working well with them is sure to pay you dividends in the future. If you find yourself as their boss one day, you will have already earned their respect. And if one of them should someday become your boss, he or she will still respect you.

DO YOUR OWN THING

While it's important to be a team player and to get along with your peers, don't get dragged blindly into the herd. Part of the reason the company hired you is that you are you. Your job may dictate that you dress and behave in certain ways. But don't be a robot—be your own person.

Your success in the business world (or whatever career path you take) will depend in great measure on your abilities to determine what you are good at and to build a career around those skills. Are you good with statistics, or do your talents lie in more artistic directions? The answer may indicate whether you would be better off in the financial department or the advertising division. Are you

Figure I   Attitdes That Can Sabotage Your Career

Attitude	Example	Solution
"They owe me."	Deprived of a promised raise because of a financial pinch, you decide to stay at the best hotels and eat in the best restaurants while traveling—and put it all on your expense account.	Speak to your manager about your disappointment with a small raise. Get a commitment for another review soon or start hunting for a new job.
"I'm too good for them. They don't deserve me."	Assigned to write a two-page press release on a new bug spray, you, a *summa cum laude* graduate, write a memo on why such a release was a waste of time, then reject advice from a colleague on how to format it.	Remember that everyone has to start somewhere and that you still have a lot to learn. Ask a peer for advice—it could be the start of a lifelong friendship and/or working relationship. Use the opportunity to learn about the firm's products so you can talk about them intelligently in meetings.
"Why should I help *you*?"	When your assistant notes for the fifth time that he just can't get that spreadsheet of yours to run, you dismiss him curtly, saying, "Never mind, I'll do it myself."	Helping others in the organization, whether above or below you, is part of your job. Show your assistant how to use the spreadsheet again—and make arrangements for him to take a course in using computers.
"Now I can coast a little."	After months of 60-hour weeks to launch a new advertising campaign, you start routinely coming in a little late and taking long lunches to "recapture" the extra hours you put in earlier.	Never make it a habit to come in late, leave early, or take long, nonworking lunches. Keep up the appearance of hard work by being visible—just slow down the pace of what you do on the job when the situation doesn't call for haste.

adept at getting groups of people to work well together, or are you happier completing a project on your own? One path leads to management, while the other takes you to a more "technical" career. You chose your major at least in part because you were interested in the subject. Now that you're on the job, remember your love for that subject and try to use it every day in what you do.

KNOW HOW YOU'RE DOING

It's important for you to know at all times how the organization rates your efforts and achievements. A formal performance appraisal is one key source of feedback. Pay close attention to your boss's comments and suggestions at this time, *don't get defensive*, and work hard to improve in those areas in which you are perceived to be deficient.

In addition to the formal performance appraisal, you should seek actively your supervisor's feedback on other daily activities. When you submit your first report, ask your boss to critique it for you. When you solve your first problem, ask your boss if you handled it right. And after you make that first presentation, ask people who attended for their reactions. (One note of caution: Assuming all goes well with your first report, presentation, etc., do not seek constant reassurance. This may cause you to be viewed as insecure, not effective.)

Also pay attention to more subtle forms of feedback. Suppose you are given a routine project and complete it in what you think is a satisfactory manner. If your next several assignments are equally routine, your boss may

not be as impressed with your work as you thought. If you sense that you are "falling behind" others who entered the organization at the same time as you, again seek feedback from your boss and co-workers and ask for suggestions on how you can improve your performance.

FIND A MENTOR

A final bit of advice: Find a mentor. As we noted in the text, a mentor is a senior person in the organization who is willing to help you with your career. In looking for a mentor, try to identify someone who has succeeded in the organization and who is respected by others. Things will be easier if the individual is someone you both respect professionally and like personally.

Start establishing a relationship with your prospective mentor by getting to know him or her. You don't want to waste anyone's time, but do drop by occasionally to ask advice and seek council. Be open, but not pushy, in your quest for a mentor. You will be able to detect fairly early if the person you've chosen is too busy or is not interested in helping you—in which case you should start looking for someone else.

Once you have found a mentor, she or he will be a valuable source of information throughout your career. You can ask for technical advice and career advice, or just talk about problems and opportunities. In addition, your mentor can be a champion for your interests in the organization by pointing out your positive qualities and recommending you to others.

Video Case VI-I

BANK BATTLE*

Could Argord Industries be saved? The question ran through John Banka's mind over and over. Banka, the president of Argord Industries and principal owner, had just finished an exhausting day meeting with bankers, employees, politicians, and media in an effort to save his company from the bankruptcy receiver and ultimately the auction block now only a few days away.

Argord Industries was a Canadian-owned company which manufactured small electric motors for products like hedge trimmers and kitchen blenders. The company employed 45 people and had just developed a new motor design that had resulted in $600 000 of orders. Although Banka realized the design and production of this motor would stretch the company's finances, he had opted to gamble on it.

In recent weeks the risks inherent in this decision became painfully apparent. Argord Industries now owed the Toronto-Dominion Bank about $180 000. The bank, fearful of Argord's overextension, had begun withholding 25 percent of the firm's deposits. To make matters worse the bank had just called the company's loan, making the $180 000 immediately due and payable. Since Banka was unable to pay off the loan, the bank began receivership procedures against the company. Complicating the matter further were personal loan guarantees given the bank by both Banka and his mother.

After the bank foreclosed the company, plans were made to schedule an auction of the company's assets. With the auction about to take place, Banka decided to go on the offensive. His first step was to launch a one-man media blitz. With the assistance of the Global Television Network he was able to raise significant public awareness for his plight; thanks to an insensitive and heartless billion dollar financial corporation, another small and struggling Canadian manufacturer would be forced out of business even though it had more than enough orders in hand to pay off the bank. Shortly after Banka's media heroics, the Toronto-Dominion announced that it would give the businessman 12 days to make good on the outstanding debt as well as an additional $80 000 for the receiver's bill.

Given this window of opportunity Banka proceeded to call one of his biggest accounts. His reason for phoning was simply to reassure the account of his company's in- tention to fill the order; the continued commitment of such customers was absolutely essential if Banka was to secure the necessary finances to recommence operations.

Banka then began searching for another bank. Early leads pointed to the Bank of Nova Scotia as a possible ally. In order to bolster the company's financial resource base, Banka also began to probe the possibility of one or more private investors taking an equity position in Argord Industries. While this was not his preferred course of action, he recognized that such an alternative might be necessary as a back-up option. Two other key stakeholders Banka had to appease were his company's landlord, who was owed $200 000 in back rent, and his employees, who had not received six weeks in back wages. After meeting with both the landlord and the senior employees he began to sense the possibility of a turnaround being a long, but possible, shot.

It was just before 6 a.m., and John awoke as exhausted as he'd fallen asleep only four hours earlier. With only two days to go he wondered what else he could do to keep alive his hopes of regaining control over Argord Industries. Bankers, customers, employees, investors, landlords — was there anyone else he should, or more appropriately could, call?

Study questions:

1. What are assets, liabilities, and equities? How would you explain the current crisis at Argord Industries using these three concepts? What is an income statement? How would you explain the current crisis at Argord Industries in terms of the company's income statement?
2. What are the different types of financial ratios that can be used to measure a company's financial health? What does each ratio contribute to understanding a company's financial health? Which of these ratios would best explain the troubles Argord Industries is currently going through?
3. What are the different pillars of the Canadian financial system? Which of these pillars might John Banka turn to in order to get help in saving his company from the auction block?

*This case is based on the *Venture* episode first broadcast on January 23, 1994.

"People get sucked in by the thought that they might be in on a quick-moving stock."

– Michael Ryan,
*former Chairman,
Vancouver Stock Exchange*

Buying and selling shares in different publicly-traded companies is often a risky and speculative experience. The recent history of Harvard International Technologies highlights this truth all too painfully. In the early 1990s the company offered its shares for sale on Canadian, and later, American, stock exchanges. The company marketed itself to potential investors as the manufacturer of a revolutionary vending machine, named the "Spud Stop," that made fresh french fries. The allure of the company's product was understandable; according to recent estimates, french fries accounted for almost 25 percent of all fast food purchases, while vending machines generated about $27 billion in annual sales.

In announcing its shares for public sale, Harvard International Technologies undertook a number of strategic initiatives to increase its perceived credibility in the securities marketplace. One such initiative was its June 1992 decision to locate its corporate headquarters in a posh downtown Vancouver business complex. Another image-enhancing initiative was to appoint former Canadian Prime Minister John Turner as the company's chairman.

In response to such actions a number of reputable investors, such as mutual fund giant Altamira and corporate raider Sam Belzberg, took out significant equity positions early on in the stock's trading history. Thanks to the company's efforts and such early investment responses the company's stock quickly soared from $2.00 to over $23.00 per share by the end of summer 1993.

However, it soon became apparent that Harvard International Technology offered its investors more sizzle than steak (or in this case potatoes) in promoting the company and its product. External reports suggested that the company had not sufficiently tested the safety of its product. One documented incident reported one of the company's french fry vending machines bursting into flames after being installed at the University of British Columbia in August 1992.

In an effort to head off the detrimental effects of such adverse publicity, the company announced hundreds of millions in foreign sales contracts in May 1993. Purchases included companies in such countries as Brazil, Spain, Korea, and Saudi Arabia, even though the firm had been all but unable to market its product domestically. Upon closer investigation it became apparent that the company had misrepresented these sales contracts to its investors. Investigators attempting to verify the existence of the firm's customers in Spain and Brazil discovered the alleged companies to be nonexistent. As a result of such investigations the company admitted in a August 1993 article in the influential financial newspaper *Barrons* that the million dollar deals were not as solid as originally reported.

As a result of such admissions a class action suit has been launched by investors In the United States. Several hundred shareholders now claim the company misrepresented itself to its shareholders. In response, Harvard has attempted to settle the suit quietly out of court. More recently the president of the company, Edgar Kaiser, has resigned, but only after receiving over $1 million in compensation. While a new CEO has recently been appointed, John Turner remains as the company's chairman. After announcing 1993 losses of $12 million the company's stock has recently been trading back around $2 per share. Sadly, the company stands as a sorry example of one Canadian company whose aspirations outstripped its capabilities.

Study questions:

1. What is a 'blue sky law' and a prospectus? In what ways do they protect investors? In what ways are they limited in the protection they provide?
2. What are the different financial ratios that can be used to assess a company's financial health? Which of these ratios would be particularly useful in detecting the problems that occurred at Harvard International Technologies?
3. What is meant by margin trading and short sales? How could trading on margin or selling short be especially risky in dealing with a stock like Harvard International Technologies?
4. Revisit Chapter 4's sections on corporate social responsibility. How would you assess the manner in which Harvard International Technologies carried out its social responsibilities?

*This case is based on the *Venture* episode first broadcast on May 15, 1994.

Part Seven

M*EETING BUSINESS CHALLENGES*

The modern business world is a complicated place. Companies must comply with a host of government laws regulating their interactions with competitors, the environment, customers, employees, and investors. To compound these complexities, more and more firms have decided to do business in and with other countries. At the same time, businesses must keep up with the latest developments in computer technology so that their operations run at peak efficiency.

Part Seven, Meeting Business Challenges, provides an overview of several major concerns of business firms, including the need to deal with all levels of government, to respond to the globalization of business, and to apply the latest in computer technology.

- We begin in **Chapter 21, Business-Government Relations**, by examining the structure of government in Canada, how government laws affect business firms, and how business and government interact.

- Then, in **Chapter 22, Understanding International Business**, we look at why countries engage in international trade, how companies organize to operate internationally, the development of free trade agreements, and factors that help and hinder international trade.

- Finally, in **Chapter 23, Managing Computers in Business**, we consider the growing need for companies to manage information and how different types of computers have evolved to help.

21

Business-Government Relations

LEARNING OBJECTIVES

After reading this chapter, you will be able to

■ Discuss the various levels of government and their responsibilities.

■ Explain how governments can influence business decision making.

■ Discuss how government and business interact in the day-to-day administration of government programs.

■ Describe the various roles government plays in Canada's economic system.

■ Describe the stages involved in government policy formulation.

■ Describe the ways business executives can get involved in changing government policy.

CHAPTER OUTLINE

OPENING CASE

A Question of Ethics?

Henry Jackman is the Lieutenant-Governor of Ontario. He is also the honorary chairman of National Trustco Inc. and owns 47 percent of the company. In 1995, Jackman became involved in a dispute with the federal Ethics Counsellor Howard Wilson about his continued attendance at National Trustco board meetings. The Counsellor argued that Jackman was violating the province's conflict-of-interest guidelines, which state that a lieutenant-governor may not practice a profession or take part in the day-to-day management of a business or financial corporation. Wilson argued that because Jackman has such a large ownership stake in the company and because he is very involved in the board of directors, he is taking part in day-to-day decision making.

Wilson warned Jackman to stop attending meetings twice in 1994, but he has no disciplinary powers when it comes to dealing with lieutenant-governors. For his part, Jackman says he is not in a conflict-of-interest situation. He also says he feels responsible for the company, given that he has such a large ownership share. Jackman has gotten a legal opinion that his behavior is acceptable from none other than former Liberal Prime Minister John Turner, who is now with a Toronto law firm.

Observers of the conflict are divided about the importance of the conflict. Some say that Jackman is bringing disrepute to the lieutenant-governor's office by his actions; others say those opposing Jackman are simply trying to make him look bad because he is rich and powerful. Michael McDonald, who is the director of the Centre for Applied Ethics at UBC, said that ethics is about the "spirit of things," and that more than a narrow legal opinion is necessary. He feels that in the case of a highly visible,

symbolic office like lieutenant-governor, the person must make every effort to avoid the appearance of impropriety.

Jeffrey Gandz of the University of Western Ontario also thinks that the Ethics Counsellor's view is correct. He said that public servants must make some difficult choices about their private business practice before they decide to take a position like that of lieutenant-governor.

Michael Deck, the associate director of the Centre for Corporate Social Performance and Ethics at the University of Toronto, has a slightly different view. He says that the real question here is whether Jackman is doing anything wrong. But he also added that it would have been better if Jackman had simply put his stock holdings in a blind trust, even though in practical terms this would not lessen his influence at National Trustco—at least he would be seen to be doing the right thing. ◆

Governments in Canada influence many of the decisions discussed in Chapter 1—what to produce, how to produce, and how to distribute income. Government makes some of these decisions directly; others are made indirectly through private sector firms influenced by government policies.

We begin this chapter by describing how the government of Canada is organized and discussing the importance of government as a decision maker in the economic system. We then describe the major roles the government plays in our economic system. We conclude with a brief discussion of how changes in government policy are made and put into practice.

The Government of Canada

The government of Canada includes the Canadian federal government, the provincial (or territorial) governments, and nearly 5000 municipal governments. All three levels of government influence business activity.

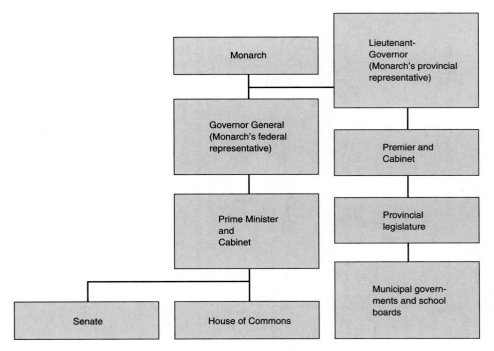

Figure 21.1
Structure of the Canadian parliamentary system.

The Canadian Parliamentary System

Canada's federal and provincial governments operate under a parliamentary system of government. There is an executive branch of government nominally headed by the monarch. The monarch's representative in Canada is the governor general. (See Figure 21.1.) The monarch's representative in each province is the lieutenant-governor. The positions of governor general and lieutenant-governor are largely ceremonial, but they do play a role in transferring power to a new government after an election. Federally, the prime minister and the cabinet are formally the monarch's advisors. In actual fact, they are the prime determiners of the Canadian government's policies. In the provinces, the provincial premier and the cabinet perform this function.

Both federally and provincially, the cabinet determines what executive actions the government will take. It also places legislative proposals before the House of Commons, Senate, or provincial legislatures.

The unit of local government is usually the municipality, normally incorporated as a city, town, village, district, or township. The powers and responsibilities of municipalities are delegated to them by the provincial governments.

The Structure of Government

Canada has a federal structure of government, outlined in *The Constitution Act, 1867*. The **distribution of government powers** means that different levels of government have responsibilities for different matters. The federal government has legislative jurisdiction over all matters of general or common interest. Provincial governments have jurisdiction over all matters of local or common interest. The specific areas of jurisdiction for federal and provincial governments are described in Table 21.1.

The sharing of responsibilities between federal and provincial governments has been controversial. The tasks outlined in Table 21.1 sometimes overlap, as in the cases of agriculture, immigration, and old-age pensions.

distribution of government powers
The responsibility different levels of government hold for different matters.

628

TABLE 21.1   Examples of Federal and Provincial Constitutional Responsibilities

FEDERAL GOVERNMENT

The legislative authority of parliament includes

- the amendment of the constitution of Canada
- the public debt and property
- the regulation of trade and commerce
- unemployment insurance
- the raising of money by any mode or system of taxation
- the borrowing of money on the public credit
- postal service
- the census and statistics
- militia, military and naval services, and defence
- the fixing of and providing for the salaries and allowances of civil and other officers of the government of Canada
- beacons, buoys, lighthouses, and Sable Island
- navigation and shipping
- quarantine and the establishment and maintenance of marine hospitals
- seacoast and inland fisheries
- ferries between a province and any British or foreign country or between two provinces
- currency and coinage, banking, incorporation of banks, and the issue of paper money
- savings banks
- weights and measures
- bills of exchange and promissory notes—interest
- legal tender
- bankruptcy and insolvency
- patents of invention and discovery
- copyrights
- Native peoples and lands reserved for them
- naturalization and aliens
- marriage and divorce
- the criminal law except the constitution of courts of criminal jurisdiction but including the procedures in criminal matters
- the establishment, maintenance, and management of penitentiaries
- agriculture and immigration
- old-age pensions

PROVINCIAL GOVERNMENTS

The legislature of each province may make laws in relation to the following:

- amendment of the constitution of the province except as regards the lieutenant-governor
- direct taxation within the province
- borrowing of money on the credit of the province
- establishment and tenure of provincial offices and appointment and payment of provincial officers
- the management and sale of public lands belonging to the province and of the timber and wood thereon
- the establishment, maintenance, and management of public and reformatory prisons in and for the province
- the establishment, maintenance, and management of hospitals, asylums, charities, and eleemosynary institutions in and for the province, other than marine hospitals
- municipal institutions in the province
- shop, saloon, tavern, auctioneer, and other licences issued for the raising of provincial or municipal revenue
- local works and undertakings other than interprovincial or international lines of ships, railways, canals, telegraphs, etc., or works which, although wholly situated within one province, are declared by the federal parliament to be for the general advantage either of Canada or of two or more provinces
- the incorporation of companies with provincial objects
- the solemnization of marriage in the province
- property and civil rights in the province
- the administration of justice in the province, including the constitution, maintenance, and organization of provincial courts, both of civil and of criminal jurisdiction, including procedure in civil matters in these courts
- the imposition of punishment by fine, penalty, or imprisonment in enforcing any law of the province relating to any of the aforesaid subjects
- generally all matters of a merely local or private nature in the province
- education
- agriculture and immigration

One of the major sources of revenue for local governments is property tax on agricultural, residential, and commercial property. This farmer pays property taxes but is also the recipient of federal aid to farmers.

Social, technological, economic, and political developments have created new problems to be dealt with, including aviation, payment for medical services, telecommunications, and energy shortages.

Problems have had to be resolved over provincial control of natural resources. In addition, disputes have arisen about how mining tax revenues are to be collected and allocated between the federal and provincial governments.

Broadcasting is another area of concern. The Quebec government, in particular, wants provincial control over broadcasting to assure consistency between programming and the cultural aspirations of Quebec citizens. The government of Canada, on the other hand, refuses to give up control of broadcasting in that province.

The federal government has far more extensive taxing powers than the provincial governments. Since the costs of some provincial responsibilities, such as education and health care, exceed their revenue-raising capabilities, the federal government has instituted revenue sharing. For example, the federal, provincial, and municipal governments share education expenses.

The federal government, through the Department of Regional Industrial Expansion, also makes funds available in various provinces for economic development. Examples of other programs for which the federal government transfers money to the provinces include medical care, agriculture, tourism, crop insurance, and pest control.

The major source of revenue for local governments is taxation of real property. Revenue is also obtained from licences, permits, rents, concessions, franchises, fines, and surplus revenue from such municipal enterprises as transit systems.

How Government Influences Business Decisions

A business decision has four elements: the decision maker(s), the options available to the decision maker(s), the criterion by which the options are judged, and the pay-offs for each option. Consider the case of Christine Beliveau, who has to choose one of two competing products to sell in her store. Her objective is to make as much profit on the product as possible. The criteria she will apply in judging the two brands will be the anticipated profitability of each. Based on her knowledge of the brand, image, price, quality of product, and sales in other stores, she estimates that she can sell 12 000 units of Product *A* at an average profit per unit of $2.73. She estimates that she can sell 15 000 units of product *B* at an average profit per unit of $1.68. Total profit from Product *A* would be $32 760. Total profit from Product *B* would be $25 200. Christine would therefore choose Product *A* (see Table 21.2).

The government can influence the way this decision is made. It can change the decision maker, the options available to the decision maker, the criteria used to make the decision, or the anticipated pay-offs from one or more of the decision options. Let's look at each of these possibilities.

TABLE 21.2   Four Elements of the Decision About What Products to Sell

The Decision Maker	The Options	The Criterion	The Anticipated Pay-Offs
Christine Beliveau	1. Product *A*	Profit for the	12 000 × $2.73 = $32 760
	2. Product *B*	store	15 000 × $1.68 = $25 200

Governments Can Change the Decision Maker

In the example above, Christine Beliveau is the only decision maker. This would change if, for example, a government decided to nationalize the sale of the product, as is done with liquor in most provinces. The decision maker in that case would not be Christine. She would simply be a representative of the government. The authority and responsibility to make the decision would shift from the private sector to the public sector.

The authority and responsibility for making the decision would also shift away from Christine if a government-appointed board or tribunal reviewed and approved decisions about what products could be sold. If this type of body existed, Christine would no longer be free to decide what product to sell. The government, through its board, would have control over the decision. When government control over the decision increases, so does government responsibility for the decision.

A government might not completely ban the sale of a product, but it might place certain restrictions on it. For example, in 1988, the federal government passed the *Tobacco Products Control Act.* It was designed to discourage Canadians from smoking, and it bans all cigarette advertising. Tobacco companies argue that the ban violates their right of freedom of expression. Consumption of cigarettes has dropped by 25 percent since 1988, the largest drop in any developed country.[1]

Governments Can Change Options

The options currently available to Christine Beliveau are to sell either Product *A* or Product *B.* Government action could make it illegal to sell one or the other or both of the products; this action might be taken if, for instance, the product was considered unsafe.

Governments Can Change Decision Criteria

Government actions can change the criteria applied to the making of economic decisions. This occurs when government becomes involved as a decision maker, either through Crown corporation ownership or through a regulatory board or tribunal.

The traditional decision criteria or goals for private economic activity are some combination of profit, growth, and survival. We have assumed in Christine Beliveau's case that her primary goal is profitability.

Imagine a situation in which Christine went to a government agency and received a grant for hiring three new employees. After she hired them, some circumstance occurred that made it necessary to lay off two of the people and cancel the positions. Because the government grant had helped create the jobs, the employees cannot be laid off without at least considering the likely reaction from the relevant government agency, that part of the grant may be revoked. On its own and without the government grant, the decision about how to handle the layoff is less complicated than it is when the government agency must also be taken into account.

Governments Can Affect Pay-Offs

Many government policies can affect the anticipated pay-offs from decision options, including taxes, incentive grants, and tariffs. Government purchasing decisions can also affect the anticipated pay-offs.

Let's assume that Product B was imported from France, and the federal government decided to impose an import tariff of $1.00 per unit on it. This would have the effect of reducing the profit per unit by $1.00, assuming the selling price was not raised by $1.00. This tariff would reduce the potential on Product B to $10 200. making it even less attractive in relation to Product A than it had previously been.

Assume that Christine has just received an order from the government for 12 000 units of Product B in addition to the initial 15 000 units she had estimated could be sold. Suppose also that she could make the same profit per unit on these 12 000 units as she could on the initial 15 000. She is also aware that the government will not buy Product A. Christine has to recalculate the estimated profitability of Product B. Instead of $1.68 $\times$ 15 000 units or $25 000, it is now $1.68 $\times$ 27 000 units or $45 360. This will make Product B more profitable than Product A, and Christine will decide to sell it if she wishes to maximize profits.

In addition to such specific policies, government policies can have a general influence on the pay-offs of decision options, in particular, in two ways—the cost of implementing government regulations and the cost of collecting statistics on business activity.

Government intervention in the macroeconomy also affects pay-offs. The exchange rate can influence costs. In this example, Product B is imported. If the value of the Canadian dollar decreases, the cost of Product B to Canadian firms increases. Interest rate changes influenced by the government through the Bank of Canada can also affect the anticipated pay-offs of decisions. If a firm is borrowing money, interest rate fluctuations affect its interest costs.

The Role of Government in Our Economic System

To this point, our discussion has focused on the general impact that government has on business decisions. We now turn our attention to the many specific roles government plays in our economic system. These roles directly influence decisions made by business firms. Government can have the following roles:

- competitor
- economic administrator
- regulator
- taxation agent
- provider of incentive programs
- customer
- housekeeper

Each of these is discussed below.

Government as a Competitor

Crown corporation

One that is accountable through a minister to parliament for the conduct of its affairs.

The most obvious way that government competes with business is through Crown corporations. A **Crown corporation** is one that is accountable, through a minister, to parliament for the conduct of its affairs. The federal government has three types of Crown corporations: departmental corporations, agency corporations, and proprietary corporations (see Table 21.3).

Crown corporations exist provincially as well. The majority of the electricity in Canada is generated by provincial government utilities. A number of

When Via Rail Canada provides passenger service, it is competing with other, private-sector firms such as bus lines and airlines.

TABLE 21.3   Types of Crown Corporations

Type of Corporation	Definition	Examples
1. Departmental	Responsible for administrative, supervisory, and/or regulatory government services	Atomic Energy Control Board, Unemployment Insurance Commission
2. Agency	Management of trading or service operations on a quasi-commercial basis	Atomic Energy of Canada Ltd., Lotto Canada, Royal Canadian Mint
3. Proprietary	Management of lending or financial operations; management of commercial or industrial operations	CBC, Central Mortgage & Housing Corp., St. Lawrence Seaway Authority

provinces own the telephone utilities within their borders. In addition, various provincial governments own and operate other types of businesses. The Manitoba, Saskatchewan, British Columbia, and Quebec governments own all or part of the provincial automobile insurance operations in their provinces. Government-owned and government-operated enterprises account for a significant amount of economic activity in Canada. (See Tables 21.4 and 21.5.)

TABLE 21.4   The Top Ten Federal Crown Corporations, 1994
(ranked by revenues)

Corporation	Revenues (in millions)
1. Canadian National Railways	$4670
2. Petro-Canada*	4581
3. Canada Post	4115
4. Canadian Wheat Board	3873
5. Canadian Commercial Corporation	880
6. Via Rail Canada	451
7. Atomic Energy of Canada	375
8. Canadian Broadcasting Corporation	374
9. Cape Breton Development Corporation	271
10. **	

* 70 percent owned by the federal government.
** There were only 9 federal crown corporations listed in the *Financial Post 500*.

TABLE 21.5   The Top Ten Provincial Crown Corporations, 1994
(ranked by revenues)

Corporation	Revenues (in millions)
1. Ontario Hydro	$8732
2. Hydro-Québec	7297
3. B.C. Hydro	2185
4. Liquor Control Board of Ontario	2054
5. Société des alcools du Québec	969
6. Manitoba Hydro	924
7. New Brunswick Power Corporation	895
8. Saskatchewan Power Corporation	836
9. Toronto Electric Commissioners	764
10. SaskTel	626

Government as an Economic Administrator

Governments wishing to control business decisions have alternatives to Crown corporations. Governments can, for example, use administrative boards, tribunals, or commissions to screen decisions of private companies before they can be implemented.

The **Canadian Radio-television and Telecommunications Commission (CRTC)**, for example, regulates the Canadian broadcasting system. The CRTC issues broadcasting licences and renews licences of existing broadcasting outlets subject to certain conditions. For example, a licence may stipulate the

Canadian Radio-television and Telecommunications Commission (CRTC)
Regulates and supervises all aspects of the Canadian broadcasting system.

type of programming, the power of the station, or the minutes of commercial messages that can be broadcast. The CRTC, for example, handed out a one-year licence renewal (the next thing to revocation) to station CHIK-FM in Quebec City because it was playing too little French-language music.[2] The CRTC also decides on applications for rate changes submitted to it by federally regulated telecommunications carriers such as Bell Canada. In June, 1992, the CRTC decided to end Bell Canada's long-standing monopoly on long-distance telephone service by allowing total competition in that market.

The advent of the much-publicized *information highway* has complicated the work of the CTRC. Hearings began in 1993 to determine how the convergence of telephone, television, cable, computer, and satellite technologies should be regulated. The CRTC is trying to reduce the regulatory burden where effective competition already exists; it also wants to streamline regulations so that Canadian companies in the telecommunications industry are not at a disadvantage in dealing with increasing competition in Canada and abroad.[3]

The **Canadian Transport Commission (CTC)** makes decisions about route and rate applications for commercial air and railway companies. For example, before rail service can be expanded or contracted, the CTC must approve the change. The same holds true for other transportation activities (for example, trucking lines and airlines). Proposed changes in rates must also be approved.

The **National Energy Board (NEB)** is responsible for regulating the construction and operation of oil and gas pipelines under the jurisdiction of the Canadian government. This includes decisions about routes of pipelines and the size of pipe to be used in the lines. The NEB also decides on the tolls to be charged for transmission by oil and gas pipelines and levels of export and import of oil and gas. It issues guidelines on internal company accounting procedures and allowable rates of return. In recent years, deregulation has meant less control by the National Energy Board.

Certain **provincial boards** consider and judge proposed decisions by private companies, for example, provincial liquor boards or commissions. They authorize price changes by breweries within their province. Milk prices charged by farmers, dairies, and supermarkets are also regulated in a number of provinces. Other marketing boards for commodities such as pork, eggs, and vegetables have important roles in establishing prices and/or production levels of producers.

The power of marketing boards is likely to decrease in the coming years as free market ideas become more widely accepted. One of the most famous of all boards, the Canadian Wheat Board, came under fire in 1994 from farmers who wanted the freedom to sell their grain directly into the U.S. market instead of having to go through the Wheat Board.[4]

Government as a Regulator

As we saw in Chapter 3, there has been a strong movement toward deregulation of industries such as banking, airlines, and trucking. However, government still regulates many aspects of business activity, and about one third of all federal and provincial statutes are regulatory. These statutes try to alter the economic behavior of individuals in the private sector.

Three important areas of regulation are competition policy, consumer protection, and ecological policies.

Competition Policy.   Canada's competition policy has been the subject of much discussion—supporters argue it is necessary for a healthy economy and critics claim it is not effective. **Competition policy** seeks to eliminate restrictive trade practices and thereby stimulate maximum production, distribution, and employment through open competition.

Canadian Transport Commission (CTC)
Makes decisions about route and rate applications for commercial air and railway companies.

National Energy Board (NEB)
Responsible for regulating the building and operation of oil and gas pipelines under the jurisdiction of the federal government.

provincial boards
Consider and judge proposed decisions by private companies.

competition policy
Tries to eliminate restrictive trade practices in order to stimulate maximum business activity.

The guidelines for competition policy are contained in the *Competition Act*, a comprehensive document that regulates the practices of Canadian business firms. It does not apply to labor unions. The act is divided into 49 sections that deal either with the actual laws or with activities necessary to administer them. The box "The Competition Act" describes selected sections of the act.

Over the years, many business firms have been charged with activity illegal under the *Competition Act*. For example, it is illegal to refuse to supply buyers with the company's product. Chrysler Canada, Ltd. was charged with refusing to supply parts to R. Brunet Co. of Montreal. A major Canadian film distributor was charged for refusing to supply movies to Cineplex Odeon. And three gasoline companies were charged when they cut off gasoline supplies to a dairy company.[5]

Consumer Protection.   The Canadian government has implemented a number of government programs related to consumer protection, many of them administered by Consumer and Corporate Affairs Canada. The department initiates programs to promote the interests of Canadian consumers.

The **Hazardous Products Act** regulates two categories of products. The first comprises products that are banned because they are dangerous. Some examples are toys and other children's articles painted with coatings containing harmful amounts of lead or other chemical compounds, certain highly flammable textile products, and baby pacifiers containing contaminated liquids. The second category comprises products that can be sold but must be labeled as hazardous. Standard symbols that denote poisonous, flammable, explosive, or corrosive properties must be attached to certain products.

Hazardous Products Act
Regulates banned products and products that can be sold but must be labeled hazardous.

The Canadian Business Scene

THE COMPETITION ACT

Section 32. Prohibits conspiracies and combinations formed for the purpose of unduly lessening competition in the production, transportation, or storage of goods. Persons convicted may be imprisoned for up to five years or fined up to $1 million or both.

Section 33. Prohibits mergers and monopolies that substantially lessen competition. Individuals who assist in the formation of such a monopoly or merger may be imprisoned for up to two years.

Section 34. Prohibits illegal trade practices. A company may not, for example, cut prices in one region of Canada while selling at a higher price everywhere else if this substantially lessens competition. A company may not sell at "unreasonably low prices" if this substantially lessens competition. (This section does not prohibit credit unions from returning surpluses to their members.)

Section 35. Prohibits giving allowances and rebates to buyers to cover their advertising expenses, unless these allowances are made available proportionally to other purchasers who are in competition with the buyer given the rebate.

Section 36. Prohibits misleading advertising including (1) false statements about the performance of a product, (2) misleading guarantees, (3) pyramid selling, (4) charging the higher price when two prices are marked on an item, and (5) referral selling.

Section 37. Prohibits bait-and-switch selling. No person can advertise a product at a bargain price, if there is no supply of the product available to the consumer. (This tactic baits prospects into the store, where salespeople switch them to higher-priced goods.) This section also controls the use of contests to sell goods, and prohibits the sale of goods at a price higher than the advertised one.

Section 38. Prohibits resale price maintenance. No person who produces or supplies a product can attempt to influence upward, or discourage reduction of, the price of the good in question. It is also illegal for the producer to refuse to supply a product to a reseller simply because the producer believes the reseller will cut the price.

Food and Drug Act

Prohibits the sale of food unfit for human consumption and regulates food advertising.

Weights and Measures Act

Sets standards of accuracy for weighing and measuring devices.

Textile Labelling Act

Regulates the labeling, sale, importation, and advertising of consumer textile articles.

Food and drug regulations are designed to protect the public from possible risk to health, fraud, and deception in relation to food, drugs, cosmetics, and therapeutic devices. For example, the ***Food and Drug Act*** prohibits the sale of a food that contains any poisonous or harmful substances, is unfit for human consumption, consists in whole or in part of any rotten substances, is adulterated, or was manufactured under unsanitary conditions. The act also provides that no person can sell or advertise a food in a misleading or deceptive manner with respect to its value, quantity, composition, or safety.

Regulations under the *Weights and Measures Act* complement the packaging and labeling regulations. The ***Weights and Measures Act*** sets standards of accuracy for weighing and measuring devices. The ***Textile Labelling Act*** regulates the labeling, sale, importation, and advertising of consumer textile articles. The *National Trade Mark and True Labelling Act* provides that products authorized under the regulations can be designated by the term "Canada Standard." A familiar application is children's garments that bear the Canada Standard trademark.

Ecological Regulations.   Most industrial sources of environmental pollution are subject to provincial regulation. The federal role is limited to areas in which there are interprovincial or international implications.

One of the major pieces of federal environmental legislation is the *Canada Water Act.* The federal government can control water quality in fresh and marine waters when there is a formal federal-provincial agreement, when federal waters are involved, or when there is sufficient national urgency to warrant federal action. The federal government handles the acid rain situation because international negotiation is necessary.

Two other important environmental regulations are the *Fisheries Act,* which controls the discharge of any harmful substance into any water, and the *Environmental Contaminants Act,* which establishes regulations for airborne substances that are a danger to human health or the environment.

Many business managers in Canada feel that government regulates business too closely. They feel that government regulation inhibits business activity when it should be facilitating it. But, compared to the way that some foreign governments regulate business firms, the Canadian government seems quite orderly and reasonable (see the box "Business-Government Relations in Russia").

Government as a Taxation Agent

revenue taxes

Taxes whose main purpose is to fund government services and programs.

restrictive taxes

Levied to control certain activities that legislators believe should be controlled.

income tax

Tax paid by individuals and corporations on income received in a given tax year.

progressive tax

A tax levied at a higher rate on higher-income taxpayers and at a lower rate on lower-income taxpayers.

Taxes are imposed and collected by federal, provincial and local governments. **Revenue taxes** are taxes whose main purpose is to fund government services and programs. These represent the majority of taxes at all levels of government in Canada. **Restrictive taxes** are levied to control certain activities that legislative bodies believe should be controlled.

Revenue Taxes.   The three main forms of revenue taxes are income taxes, property taxes, and sales taxes. **Income tax** is a tax paid by individuals and corporations on income received in a given tax year and is the primary taxing device federally. All three types are used in different combinations provincially and locally.

Both federal and provincial income taxes are examples of progressive taxes. A **progressive tax** is one levied at a higher rate on higher-income taxpayers and at a lower rate on lower-income taxpayers. A progressive income tax has the effect of increasing total consumption because poorer people spend more of their income than do richer people. Tax policy, however, must avoid being so progressive that little incentive remains for wealthy people to invest.

International Report

BUSINESS-GOVERNMENT RELATIONS IN RUSSIA

Before the collapse of communism, entrepreneurial activity was illegal in Russia. The entire economic system was biased against thinking in enrepreneurial terms. Children were not encouraged to earn money. The parents of one child, who was collecting glass bottles and jars in order to get a small refund from a state store, were criticized by their neighbors for allowing such activity. One Russian banker says the problem with Russia is that "… no one ever had a paper route." Even though entrepreneurial activity is now legal, businesspeople are still known colloquially as *speculyant* (meaning speculator) or *zhulyik* (which means thief).

Evgeny Poletsky is one such speculator. In the 1980s, he was arrested for buying Scottish woollen scarves from sailors at the port of Tallinn and reselling them to gypsy traders in Novosibirsk. For his "crime," he was sentenced to two years hard labor in a steel mill. When Mikhail Gorbachev instituted major economic reforms a few years later, Poletsky decided to go into business for himself.

He started with a small construction business and parlayed that into a fishing fleet of five boats. He also bought a factory ship that the government was selling for scrap. He then borrowed money from a state-run poultry farm and promised to pay them back in fish meal (which can be used for animal feed). Since there is always a shortage of fish meal, Poletsky does not have money problems.

But he does have one big problem—government bureaucrats who demand "commissions" before they will approve the permits he needs. The Western media give a lot of coverage to the Russian Mafia (which kidnaps, bombs, and extorts money from businesspeople), but Poletsky says his biggest problem is poorly paid government bureaucrats who are trying to line their pockets at his expense.

In trying to run his fish meal processing business, Poletsky has discovered that government bureaucrats have a lot of power because he must get permission for all sorts of things—fishing quotas, fishing licences, opening a bank account, and even building a new fishing boat. His refusal to pay bribes to get these permissions has resulted in permit delays and many dirty tricks. For example, his factory ship was seized by the Azerbaijani government, an act Poletsky is convinced was engineered by Moscow bureaucrats. The entire fish meal cargo on the ship disappeared sometime after the boat was seized. Now he is trying to get restitution for his losses.

Like most entrepreneurs, Poletsky does not give up easily. He has ordered another five fishing boats from a shipyard that would have folded without his business. He feels that he has achieved a lot in the last few years, but he says he would have achieved even more if he didn't have to fight with government bureaucrats all the time.

Most provinces have a sales tax that is paid through retail stores, which act as collection agents when they sell their merchandise. The rate of sales tax varies across provinces. It also applies to different groups of products in different areas. Food and drug sales are often exempted. A sales tax is an example of a regressive tax. A **regressive tax** causes poorer people to pay a higher percentage of income than richer people pay. All pay the same percent of the selling price. But poorer people spend a much higher percentage of their income in retail stores than middle-income and rich people do.

regressive tax
A tax that causes poorer people to pay a higher percentage of income than richer people pay.

Restrictive Taxes.   Two major taxes are levied not just for their revenue. They are excise taxes on alcohol, tobacco, and gasoline, and import duties. Excise taxes serve both as a "deterrent to excesses"—to discourage what many regard as behavior the government should curtail—and as a revenue source. Import duties were once a major revenue source as well as a kind of protection for home industries. The growth of free trade in the post-World War II era has resulted in a reduction of this revenue source.

Government as a Provider of Incentive Programs

Federal, provincial, and municipal governments offer incentive programs that help stimulate economic development. The video case "Trepassey III" on

incentive programs

Programs to encourage managers to make certain decisions desired by governments.

p. 720 describes how one town in Newfoundland has spent money it received from the federal government. **Incentive programs** are designed to encourage managers to make certain decisions and take certain actions desired by governments. For example, they are designed to encourage managers to locate in one (underdeveloped) region rather than another, to invest in new product development, or to engage in export activities. Because incentive programs can improve the pay-offs for a firm, they encourage a manager to choose that option.

One example of a grant incentive program is the Industrial and Regional Development Program (IRDP) offered by the federal Department of Regional Industrial Expansion. The IRDP is designed to deliver federal assistance to manufacturers throughout Canada. Four tiers of assistance are offered, with the greatest support (Tier IV) available for firms in the most disadvantaged areas of the country.

The IRDP is intended to support private sector firms that show the greatest potential for economic return, growth, and international competitiveness. It is oriented particularly toward small- and medium-sized firms, and it complements other federal programs, such as those offered by the Federal Business Development Bank (see Chapter 18). The four main encouragements the program gives are innovation (developing new products and processes), establishment (of new production facilities), modernization (improving and expanding existing manufacturing facilities, and marketing (developing and exploiting domestic and international marketing opportunities).

An example of a grant program that encourages development of pollution control equipment is administered by Fisheries Canada and Environment Canada. This program, called Development and Demonstration of Pollution Abatement Technology, is intended to help develop new methods, procedures, processes, and equipment to prevent, eliminate, or reduce the release of pollutants into the air, soil, and water. The program pays a percentage of the capital and operating costs incurred by firms and municipalities in such developments.

There are many other examples of grant programs. Some include municipal tax rebates for locating in certain areas, design assistance programs, and remission of tariffs on certain advanced technology production equipment. Government incentive programs may or may not have the effect intended. See the box "Government Involvement in the Wine Industry."

Information on incentive programs is available from the various provincial and municipal governments. CCH Canadian Limited publishes a book entitled *Industrial Assistance Programs in Canada*, which is updated regularly.

Many people are critical of government incentive programs for business. They argue that private sector firms should have to make it on their own in a free market society. They also say that government money taken from taxpayers should not be given to business firms.

Government involvement at Hyundai Motor's plant in Bromont, Quebec illustrates these concerns. Workers at the plant were paid $4.2 million in 1992 under a special unemployment insurance program; the company received another $682 000 to pay for training employees. That money is in addition to the $6.4 million that the federal and provincial governments gave Hyundai to build the plant in the first place. On top of all that, the government has forgiven over $28 million in customs duties on cars and parts imported from South Korea. In 1993, Hyundai closed the plant and laid off the workers while it retooled the plant. In 1994, Hyundi announced that it is putting on hold any plans to reopen the plant, which has lost $400 million since it opened in 1988.[6]

Government Services.   Governments also offer incentives through the many services they provide to business firms. One example of such a program is the Trade Commissioner Service of the federal government. External Affairs Canada has approximately 300 trade commissioners in 70 countries. The Trade Commissioner Service responds to requests for assistance from

The Canadian Business Scene

GOVERNMENT INVOLVEMENT IN THE WINE INDUSTRY

Because of its harsh climate, Canada is not a country particularly suited to growing grapes. The main vine that can be grown here—*vitis labrusca*—produces grapes that are low in sugar, high in acid, and have a particular tang. While these grapes are suitable for jellies or juice, they don't make good wine. Given that fact, it is easy to question the enthusiasm for a viable wine industry in Ontario. The answer lies in government policy.

Until the advent of free trade, the government of Ontario had tried to halt the declining popularity of Canadian wines by imposing duties on imported wines. Under free trade, the predictable has happened—consumers are drinking a lot less Ontario wine. The total amount bought was down 8 million litres between March, 1989, and March, 1990. To ease the shock, the provincial government has allocated $100 million to grape growers, including $50 million to rip out unwanted grape vines and $45 million to help Ontario wineries improve marketing and productivity.

The cash injection only partially addresses the industry's problems. *Labrusca* has now been banned from Ontario wines, but not much else is being done to ensure that more suitable grapes are grown. To date, Ontario grape growers have been reluctant to plant higher quality vines voluntarily because the process is time-consuming and expensive.

The government assistance program involves a lot of money, given that there are only 800 grape growers in

Ontario and only half of their production is for wine. For some firms, their government grant equals nearly one quarter the value of the company. But even these large amounts of money will not solve the problem because the government continues to force wineries to use Ontario grapes, which cannot measure up to the quality of foreign grapes.

The province not only holds monopoly power over grape supply and prices through the Grape Marketing Board, it is virtually the sole retailer of wine in the province through its Liquor Control Board of Ontario (LCBO). As consumer tastes began to move to lighter wines in the 1960s and 1970s, the Ontario wineries found it increasingly hard to produce what consumers wanted. Beginning in 1976, wineries were allowed to use up to 30 percent foreign grapes in their wines to improve the taste. At the same time, the LCBO ruled that Ontario wines did not have to meet the same standards as foreign wines. As a result of these and other actions, the Ontario wine industry suffered some serious image problems.

A 1986 task force report blamed the decline in demand on yuppies who had a taste for foreign products. In spite of the problems already caused by government involvement, the task force recommended that government agencies such as hospitals, universities, and prisons be forced to use Ontario wines, and that the LCBO restrict imports. It appears that the basic lesson of business—satisfying consumers—has not been learned.

Canadian exporters and helps foreign importers to find Canadian sources of supply for products they wish to buy. Trade commissioners also participate in developing programs to improve Canadian exports. This service includes identifying market opportunities.

The Export Development Corporation was designed to assist Canadian exports by offering export insurance against nonpayment by foreign buyers; long-term loans or guarantees of private loans to foreign buyers of Canadian products; and insurance against loss of or damage to a Canadian firm's investment abroad arising from expropriation, revolution, or war.

Energy, Mines and Resources Canada provides geological maps of Canada's potential mineral-producing areas. This service gives companies interested in mineral exploration much better geological information about Canada than is available about most other countries. Provincial governments also provide geological services to the mining industry.

Statistics Canada is yet another valuable government service to business firms. Its data and analysis describe almost every aspect of social and economic life in Canada, and provide information used in government policy formulation and decision making by the private sector. The Census of Population and Housing, taken every five years, is a high-profile Statistics Canada activity. This census produces a range of key social and economic

The federal and provincial governments provide a variety of services that facilitate business activities. The construction of roads, ports, and harbors, for example, helps business firms move goods that are vital to our economy.

data describing all Canadians. The Labour Force Survey, which monitors the labor force activities of Canadians, and the Consumer Price Index, which measures price changes for consumer goods and services, are among the agency's other major programs.

Statistics Canada's information is available in publications, on microfiche and microfilm, on computer tape, and through CANSIM, the agency's electronic data bank. Special tabulations and a considerable volume of unpublished data can be obtained on request.

Government as a Customer

Government spending for its own needs can also influence business decisions such as where to locate or what type of product to produce. Government buys many services as well as products, ranging from paper clips and pencils to warships, highways, and high-rise office buildings. Many firms and industries depend on government purchasing decisions, if not for their survival, at least for their level of prosperity. Examples include construction and architectural firms and companies in the aerospace industry. Government expenditure on goods and services amounts to billions of dollars per year.

Government as a Housekeeper

The federal, provincial, and municipal governments facilitate business activity through the wide variety of services they supply. The federal government provides highways, the postal service, the minting of money, the armed forces, and statistical data on which to base business decisions. It also tries to maintain stability through fiscal and economic policy.

Provincial and municipal governments provide streets, sewage and sanitation systems, police and fire departments, utilities, hospitals, and education. All these activities create the kind of stability that encourages business activity.

Changes in Government Policy

One important type of interaction between business and government occurs when government policy is discussed and changed. **Government policy formulation** is the process by which changes are made in current government policies.

government policy formulation
The process by which changes are made in current government policies.

The Process of Government Policy Formulation

The process of changing government policy is long and complicated, but some general features can be identified. First, there are a number of stages. Second, there are usually a number of people involved who change at different stages of the process. Third, decisions will be made at each stage which will depend on the power of the people involved in the given stage (see Figure 21.2).

No one person controls the process through all stages. The key people vary from politicians at the decision-to-proceed-with-legislation stage to civil servants at the drafting-of-legislation stage. Similarly, the opportunity to influence the decision makers varies from stage to stage.

Understanding the process of change in government policy is important for business managers who want to influence government policy. Business people should attempt to be influential at all stages of the process because decisions made at an early stage in the process can have a profound effect on the ultimate outcome.

The people who are involved at different stages must be identified, and the appropriate method by which to approach them must be considered. Recognizing the process of government policy formulation and thinking about the best way to participate at each stage can result in increased influence. Such influence is called lobbying, which was discussed in Chapter 3.

Administration of Government Programs

The role of government in the economic system was described in an earlier section, and some of the many government programs available to business were discussed. For these programs to be effective, they must be put into practice and managed properly. **Administration of government programs** involves the day-to-day activities required to implement government programs. This creates the need for communication between business decision makers and those responsible for implementing government programs.

administration of government programs
The day-to-day activities required to implement the programs.

Government representatives need to understand business strategy and how it is formulated and implemented. They must also design efficient systems to comply with government regulations. Business managers, on the other hand, must have a thorough knowledge of government programs and how they are implemented. Then, business can deal effectively with government and keep its costs for this activity as low as possible.

Stage of process	Outcome of stage	Primary determiner of outcome (decision maker)	Possible influencers
1. Societal need	The existence of a problem	Created by changes in technology or attitudes (economic or ecological)	
2. Perception of need	General awareness of a problem	Researchers, media, politicians	
3. Articulation of demand	Different groups with different ideas about what to do	Leaders of different groups: e.g., political parties, media, interest groups, businesses	Members of various groups
4. Decision to proceed with legislation	Government commitment to deal with the problem	Cabinet ministers	Political party members, civil servants, public, media, researchers, interest groups
5. Determination of the nature of the legislation	A decision about what type of legislation to introduce	Civil servant teams, cabinet	(Same influencers as for No. 4)
6. Drafting of legislation	A draft of new legislation	Public service drafting expert	Cabinet minister, civil servant study team
7. Legislative consideration	Royal assent to legislation	Parliament or legislative assembly	Party loyalties, pressure groups, media
8. Formulation of regulations	The completed set of regulations	Civil servants	Industry representatives politicians, interest groups
9. Implementation	The new policy in practice	Civil servants	Groups being affected

Figure 21.2
The process of government policy formulation.

Summary of Key Points

The government of Canada includes the federal, provincial, and municipal governments. Canada operates under a parliamentary system. The prime minister and the cabinet are the prime determiners of the federal government's policy direction. The federal government has jurisdiction over certain matters, and the provincial governments over other matters (see Table 21.1).

Governments can participate in and influence economic decisions by actually making the decision (by using a Crown corporation or a regulatory agency), by limiting the options available to business managers, by specifying goals for the decision, or by influencing the pay-offs associated with available options. The wide range of tools available to governments to influence economic decisions include Crown corporations, administrative (regulatory) agencies, regulations, taxes, tariffs, incentive programs, government purchases, and information collection.

The government has seven major roles in Canada's economic system. It can act in the role of (1) competitor (selling the same kinds of goods and services as private sector firms), (2) economic administrator (approving or denying certain business decisions), (3) regulator (passing laws that restrict certain business activities), (4) taxation agent (collecting income, sales, and other taxes), (5) provider of incentive programs (to encourage business managers to make certain decisions desired by the government), (6) customer (buying goods and services produced by private sector firms), and (7) housekeeper (providing services like fire and police protection).

Government policy formulation is the process by which changes are made in current government policy. The steps in the process include societal need, perception of need, articulation of demand, decision to proceed with legislation, determining the nature of the new legislation, drafting of legislation, legislative consideration, formulation of regulations, and implementation.

CONCLUDING CASE 21-1

Trading Places

There is a new program designed to prove that Pierre Trudeau's two solitudes—business and government—can, at least occasionally, reach out and touch each other. The goal of the Business-Government Executive Exchange program, begun in 1987, is to provide a place for an exchange of ideas and expertise between business and government. It places senior public servants in key private sector jobs for up to two years, and takes promising young private sector managers and gives them challenging government assignments.

Since its inception, 30 men and women have "graduated" from the program, and another 30 are currently enrolled. A program advisory committee made up of 17 industry chiefs and 10 federal deputy ministers coordinates the program. Senior government officials from the Treasury Board, Secretary of State, Supply and Services Canada, and the Department of Finance have gone to work for firms such as IBM, Coles Book Stores, DuPont, and the Royal Bank of Canada. Executives from IBM, Canadian Airlines International, DuPont, and Bell Canada have taken positions with the Department of National Defence, Transport Canada, and Revenue Canada.

Bob Weese, one of nine senior government officials currently in the program, is a typical program member. He had been an assistant deputy minister with Supply and Services Canada for six years and supervised a staff of 150. He was transferred to General Electric Canada as manager of corporate business development programs. He says the most striking difference between a large public organization and an even larger private sector one is the amount of paperwork. At General Electric, decisions on problems may be made based on a five or six page report, and it may take as little as one week to make the decision. In government, in contrast, such a decision would involve hundreds of people, thousands of pages of analysis, and perhaps years before the decision is reached.

Weese also notes that General Electric has reduced its work force by 100 000 over the last five years. He does not think that kind of downsizing will ever happen in government. But Weese's private sector experience reinforces his belief that public sector managers are hard-working and conscientious. Unfortunately, they work in a rigid, bureaucratic system that frustrates them because it is too control-oriented.

But private sector firms have shortcomings, too. In Weese's view, General Electric has not done enough to convey to the public all the different business lines it is involved in. The company is the world's largest manufacturer of diesel locomotives and commercial aircraft engines, and GE Capital Canada is one of the fastest-growing, nonbank financial institutions in Canada. Weese is also surprised by the lack of women in private sector management. He is used to seeing women around the management table and was shocked when he attended a company meeting with 30 others, all of whom were men.

Another member of the program, Victor Shantora, found that, when he moved from government to a private sector firm, he had to live with the very regulations he had helped develop while in government. Shantora was a director with Environment Canada, and his staff developed environmental regulations affecting industry. He then moved to DuPont Canada as environmental affairs manager. He notes that the industry is responding to environmental concerns more favorably than it did in the 1960s and 1970s. For example, DuPont tackled the problem of chlorofluorocarbons by building a plant that now produces an alternative chemical.

Shantora experienced some culture shock when he went to DuPont. He says that objectives are much clearer in the private sector, and individuals know exactly what they are expected to do. When top management sets a goal, they expect it to be reached. When a government minister gives a direction, it may take an octopus to pull things together.

Russell Bula was production manager at DuPont before spending two years in Ottawa as a manager at Industry, Science, and Technology Canada. He too was impressed with the motivation and commitment of public servants—at least at the top levels. Below middle management, he saw too many uncommitted people. He discovered that the lines of communication between business and government were better than he had expected, but he also saw government taking excessive time to make decisions.

CASE QUESTIONS
1. What are the advantages of the Business-Government Executive Exchange program? Are there any disadvantages?
2. Managers report that, compared to private sector organizations, there is much more paperwork and decisions take much longer to make in government. Why might this be so?
3. One government official reports being shocked that so few women are senior managers at the private sector firm he worked for. Why might there be more women in top management in the public sector? ◆

CONCLUDING CASE 21-2

Cosy Relations Between Business and Government

When the Liberals were the opposition party in the early 1990s, they vowed that once they were in power, they would "clean up" the way in which the federal government awarded advertising, polling, and public relations contracts to private sector firms. But the Liberals have been in power since 1993, and not much has changed.

Consider these examples:

■ The very first major government advertising contract went to two advertising agencies that have strong Liberal ties; these two firms did not get much work when the Conservatives were in power.
■ In the public relations area, Groupe Columbia Inc. of Montreal was successful in bidding on two contracts worth $290 000 that will launch the Youth Services Corps; this small company, which had done very little work for the Conservatives, is owned by the son of a former Quebec Liberal cabinet minister.
■ In the polling area, Insight Research of Toronto, which handled Liberal polling during the election, is the Liberals' pollster of choice; Decima Research, the Conservatives' pollster, does no work for the Liberals.

Ottawa insiders do not appear at all surprised at these developments. One pollster admitted that his firm had done very well under the Conservatives and was now having difficulty getting business from the Liberals. But he said he understood that was the way it would be.

All of this is not to say that government advertising, public relations, or polling contracts are easy to get or easy to carry out. The real issue, some argue, is whether the government is spending less money on these ventures than it used to. The federal government spent about $40 million in advertising in 1994-95, down sharply from the $126 million spent in 1992-93. Spending on polling is also down from $8 million in 1994 to $6.5 million in 1995.

CASE QUESTIONS
1. Why might the Liberals and Conservatives use different advertising and polling companies?
2. The chapter discusses the various roles that government plays in our society. What role is the government playing when it awards contracts to private sector firms?
3. Is it possible to make the awarding of government contracts more "rational" and less political? Explain how this might be done. What are the possible benefits and drawbacks of your suggestions? ◆

Key Terms

distribution of
government powers
Crown corporation
Canadian
Radio-television and
Telecommunications
Commission (CRTC)

Canadian Transport
Commission (CTC)
National Energy Board
(NEB)
provincial boards
competition policy
Hazardous Products Act

Food and Drug Act
*Weights and Measures
Act*
Textile Labelling Act
revenue taxes
restrictive taxes
income tax

progressive tax
regressive tax
incentive programs
government policy
formulation
administration of
government programs

Study Questions and Exercises

Review Questions

1. Briefly explain the structure of the Canadian government.
2. What are the responsibilities of the federal and provincial governments?
3. What are the elements of a business decision? How can government influence these elements?
4. Briefly describe each of the seven roles the government plays in Canada.
5. What are the stages in the formulation of government policy?

Analysis Questions

6. Should the use of Crown corporations be limited? Why or why not?

7. What are the advantages and disadvantages of having regulatory agencies such as the National Energy Board?
8. Describe two specific examples (beyond those in the text) that illustrate government's role as a competitor to business firms.

Application Exercises

9. Ask a manager you are acquainted with to give you several examples of how government helps (and hinders) private sector business managers.
10. Form two teams and formally debate the question: "Government should not regulate business other than formulating some basic ground rules about business operations."

Building Your Business Skills

Goal

To increase student awareness and appreciation for the complexity of the relationship between business and government.

Situation

You are talking to two friends at a social gathering. One is a manager in a government regulatory agency, and the other is a marketing manager in a private sector business firm. These two friends are having a rather serious debate about the pros and cons of government regulation of business. The business manager argues that there is far too much government regulation of business and that this regulation is inhibiting business efficiency and effectiveness. The manager in the government regulatory agency argues that businesses must be regulated or they would do all sorts of things that are bad for the environment and bad for consumers.

Method

Divide the class into teams of three or four. Designate half of the teams as "government" teams and half as "business" teams. Have each of the government teams inter-

view one manager working in a government regulatory agency. Have each of the business teams interview one marketing manager in a private sector firm. Both types of teams should get answers to the following questions:

1. Is it necessary for government to regulate business firms? Why or why not?
2. What are the costs associated with regulation of business firms? Give a specific example.
3. What are the benefits associated with regulation of business firms? Give a specific example.
4. What changes in regulations should be implemented in order to make the regulatory system more effective?

Follow-up Questions

1. For each of the four questions above, compare the answers of the government regulatory managers with those of the marketing managers in the private sector firms. What are the main differences? Is there any common ground where agreement exists?
2. Assuming that there is agreement that some form of government regulation is necessary, suggest ways to make this regulation positive for consumers and the environment without it being unduly restricting for business firms.

22

Understanding International Business

LEARNING OBJECTIVES

After reading this chapter, you will be able to

- List the approaches a company can use to manage internationally.
- Understand the importance to Canadian managers of thinking internationally.
- Define trade and describe its importance in the Canadian economy.
- Identify and describe the challenges in world markets for Canadian business.
- Describe the main forms of organization used by corporations operating internationally.

CHAPTER OUTLINE

OPENING CASE

Glegg Makes International Splash

Robert Glegg graduated from McGill University in 1976 with degrees in engineering and business. He first went to work as a sales engineer for Gaco-Sternson Ltd., a water purification company. But within a year, he saw that the market for water purification systems was booming, so he started Glegg Water Conditioning Inc. by renting an office in a manufacturing plant that had excess space. In 1982, he built his own factory.

His company builds large purification systems that can deliver specially treated tap water for industrial uses at rates up to 19 000 litres per minute. Ordinary tap water, which is fine for human consumption, cannot be used by some manufacturing firms because the minerals in the water gum up their machinery. Glegg's systems can reduce impurities in water to only 20 parts per *trillion*. Water purified to this extent will pull particles out of even stainless steel pipes, so it has to be sent through special pipes.

Sales exceeded $50 million in 1994. The company does all the design and engineering work at its Guelph factory, but it contracts out most of the manufacturing to keep its costs low. The emphasis on low-cost, high-quality products has allowed Glegg to become well-established in a market where many larger competitors have struggled.

Glegg is a good example of a Canadian firm that has a truly international outlook—96 percent of its sales are outside of Canada. Most sales are in the U.S., but the company also sells in Europe, Latin America, and Asia. It also has plans for expansion into Chile, Venezuela, Mexico, Thailand, China, and Taiwan. Glegg views the U.S. and Canada as one market; his company has established itself as a leader in supplying equipment to U.S. firms. One survey estimated that Glegg accounted for 20 percent of the U.S market for heavy industrial water purifiers.

The company's long-term goal is to make 70 percent of its sales in offshore markets, with the remainder in the U.S. and Canada. Robert Glegg says it is absolutely essential for the company to sell internationally because there is not enough domestic volume to satisfy the firm.

The company's international sales are supported by a network of independent manufacturing representatives. The reps work on commission, and they sell to a specific industry and geographic area. These reps provide Glegg with local contacts and an understanding of businesses in the area where they work. Glegg also has close ties with several large engineering firms. When Glegg does a good job at one site, the engineering firm will often use the company at another site. Executives of Glegg also travel extensively and meet customers face to face.

In spite of all this focus on international sales, Robert Glegg intends to keep the core functions of the business in Guelph. "We're a Canadian company," he says. ◆

Glegg Water Conditioning is one of the new breed of Canadian companies that have adopted an international focus in their operations. Increasingly, Canadian firms will have to look beyond the domestic Canadian market in their business dealings.

In this chapter, we examine international business by first looking at the contemporary global economy, including the key players in it and some fundamental ideas about international business. We then explain the various levels of involvement that are possible for Canadian business firms in international business. Barriers to international trade are noted, as well as strategies for overcoming these barriers, particularly free trade agreements. The chapter concludes with a description of the challenges facing Canadian business firms in international markets.

The Rise of International Business

The total volume of world trade today is immense—around $7 trillion each year. As more and more firms engage in international business, the world economy is fast becoming a single interdependent system—a process called **globalization**. Even so, we often take for granted the diversity of goods and services available today as a result of international trade. Your television set, your shoes, and even the roast lamb on your dinner table may all be **imports**—that is, products made or grown abroad but sold in Canada. At the same time, the success of many Canadian firms depends in large part on **exports**—products made or grown domestically and shipped for sale abroad.

globalization
The integration of markets globally.

imports
Products that are made or grown abroad and sold in Canada.

exports
Products made or grown in Canada that are sold abroad.

The Contemporary Global Economy

The global economy in which Canadian business firms must operate has four basic features:

- international trade in goods and services
- international movement of labor
- international flow of money
- international flow of information

Although the international trade in goods and the international flow of money is not new, the international movement of services, labor, and information is.

We noted in Chapter 3 that two-thirds of all Canadians are employed in service industries. Yet the majority of services cannot be directly exchanged for another product in the international market. In spite of this, services are becoming increasingly important in international trade, as shown by the examples in Table 22.1.

Major World Marketplaces

The contemporary world economy revolves around three major marketplaces: North America, the Pacific Rim, and Western Europe. But business activity is not limited to these three markets. The World Bank notes, for example, that 77 percent of the world's people live in so-called "developing" areas. Economies in those areas are expanding 5 to 6 percent annually.

TABLE 22.1   Examples of Trade in Services

Exports of Services

- An advertising agency in Toronto develops television commercials for an American client.
- A taxi takes a Japanese manager from the Toronto airport to the hotel.
- An Australian corporation hires a Canadian accountant to prepare its financial statements.
- A Canadian engineer designs a bridge to be built in Zambia.
- A television show produced in Canada is broadcast in England.

Imports of Services

- A Canadian takes a vacation in Hawaii.
- A Vancouver resident buys a ticket to see a performance by a foreign artist.
- Excalibur Corp. accesses and extracts information from a foreign data base.
- A Canadian tourist in Italy has her camera repaired there.
- A Regina resident buys shares of stock on a foreign stock exchange.

There are 300 million consumers in Eastern Europe and another 300 million in South America. In India alone, estimates of the size of the middle class run from 100 million to 300 million.[1]

North America.   The United States dominates the North American business region. It is the single largest marketplace and enjoys the most stable and sound economy in the world. Many U.S. firms, such as General Motors and Procter & Gamble, have had successful Canadian operations for years, and Canadian firms like Northern Telecom and Alcan Aluminum are major competitors.

Mexico has also become a major manufacturing center. Cheap labor and low transportation costs have encouraged many foreign firms to build plants in Mexico. Both Chrysler and General Motors, for instance, are building new assembly plants, as are suppliers like Rockwell International Corp. Nissan opened an engine and transmission plant in 1983 and a car-making plant in 1992. Mexican forecasters expect 200 000 workers to be in the automobile industry by 1998.

Western Europe.   Europe is often divided into two regions. Western Europe, dominated by Germany, the United Kingdom, France, and Italy, has been a mature but fragmented marketplace for years. The evolution of the European Union in 1992 into a unified marketplace has further increased the importance of this marketplace. Major international firms like Unilever, Renault, Royal Dutch Shell, Michelin, Siemens, and Nestlé are all headquartered in this region.

Eastern Europe, which was until recently primarily communist, has also gained in importance, both as a marketplace and a producer. In May 1994, for example, Albania became the 197th country in which Coca-Cola is produced, as Coke opened a new $10 million bottling plant outside the capital city of Tirana. Meanwhile, Kellogg has opened a new plant in Riga, capital of the former Soviet republic of Latvia. Kellogg has also launched a vigorous campaign of television ads and in-store demonstrations to capitalize on one of the world's few remaining cereal frontiers.[2]

The Pacific Rim.   The Pacific Rim consists of Japan, the People's Republic of China, Thailand, Malaysia, Singapore, Indonesia, South Korea, Taiwan, Hong Kong, the Philippines, and Australia. Fueled by strong entries in the automobile, electronics, and banking industries, the economies of these countries grew rapidly in the 1970s and 1980s. Today, the Pacific Rim is an important force in the world economy and a major source of competition for North American firms. Japan, led by companies like Toyota, Toshiba, and Nippon Steel, dominates the region. In addition, South Korea (with such firms as Samsung and Hyundai), Taiwan (owner of Chinese Petroleum and manufacturing home of many foreign firms), and Hong Kong (a major financial center) are also successful players in the international economy. China, the most densely populated country in the world, continues to emerge as an important market in its own right. In fact, the International Monetary Fund concluded in 1993 that the Chinese economy is now the world's third largest, behind the United States and only slightly behind Japan.[3] The video case "Batam Island" on p. 721 describes the aggressive actions of Singapore and Indonesia as they attempt to become more prominent players on the world business scene.

Forms of Competitive Advantage

No country can produce all the goods and services that its people need. Thus countries tend to export those things that they can produce better or less expensively than other countries. The proceeds are then used to import things that they cannot produce effectively. However, this very general principle does not fully explain why nations export and import what they do. Such decisions hinge, among other things, on whether a country enjoys an absolute or a comparative advantage in the production of different goods and services.[4]

An **absolute advantage** exists when a country can produce something more cheaply than any other country. Saudi oil and Canadian timber approximate absolute advantage, but examples of true absolute advantage are rare. In reality, "absolute" advantages are always relative. Brazil, for instance, produces about one-third of the world's coffee. However, because its high-quality coffees are preferred by Canadians and Americans, the impact of Brazil's production is widely felt. Consider what happened when a severe frost in the winter of 1994 destroyed nearly half of the 1995-96 harvest. First, commodities prices—prices paid by producers, roasters, and speculators— jumped to their highest levels in 10 years. Then, the three largest coffee producers—Procter & Gamble, Kraft, and Nestlé—raised retail prices by 45 percent. With the threat to worldwide supplies, prices for lower-quality African coffees also went up. Forecasters predict that the prices paid by consumers will continue to reflect the damage to the 1995-96 Brazilian crop.[5]

A country has a **comparative advantage** in goods that it can make more cheaply or better than other goods. For example, if businesses in a country can make computers more cheaply than automobiles, then computers represent a comparative advantage for its firms. The United States has a comparative advantage in the computer industry because of technological sophistication. Canada has a comparative advantage in farming because of fertile land. South Korea has a comparative advantage in electronics manufacturing because of efficient operations and cheap labor.

absolute advantage
A nation's ability to produce something more cheaply or better than any other country.

comparative advantage
A nation's ability to produce some products more cheaply or better than it can others.

The Balance of Trade and the Balance of Payments

A country's **balance of trade** is the difference in value between its total exports and its total imports. A country that exports more than it imports has a *favorable* balance of trade, or a surplus. A country that imports more than it exports has an *unfavorable* balance of trade, or a deficit.

Canada has enjoyed a favorable balance of merchandise trade since 1975 (see Figure 22.1). However, the trade balance is favorable only because Canada exports so much more to the U.S. than it imports from the U.S. Canada's trade balance with its other major trading partners (e.g., Japan, the U.K., and other EEC countries) is unfavorable. Our trade balance with all remaining countries of the world taken together as a group is also unfavorable (see Table 22.2).

balance of trade
The difference in value between a country's total exports and its total imports.

TABLE 22.2   Exports and Imports, Selected Countries, 1992

	Exports to (billions)	Imports from (billions)
United States	$118.4	$90.4
Japan	7.4	10.7
United Kingdom	3.0	4.1
Germany	2.1	3.5
South Korea	1.4	2.0
France	1.4	2.7
Taiwan	0.95	2.4
Hong Kong	0.85	1.1

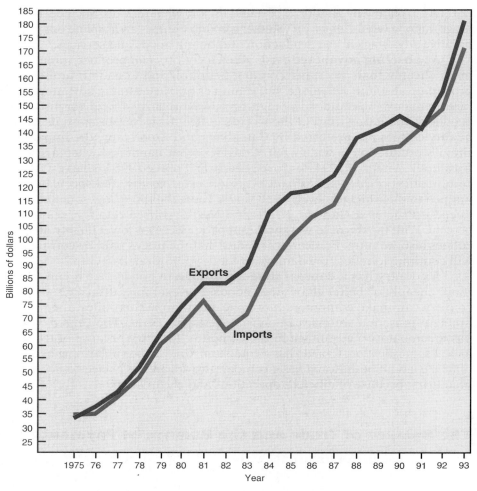

Figure 22.1
Canadian imports and exports of merchandise.

balance of payments

The difference between money flowing into and out of a country as a result of trade and other transactions.

Even if a country has a favorable balance of trade, it can still have an unfavorable balance of payments. A country's **balance of payments** is the difference between money flowing into the country and money flowing out of the country as a result of trade and other transactions. An unfavorable balance means more money is flowing out than in. For Canada to have a favorable balance of payments for a given year, the total of our exports, foreign tourist spending in this country, foreign investments here, and earnings from overseas investments must be greater than the total of our imports, Canadian tourist spending overseas, our foreign aid grants, our military spending abroad, the investments made by Canadian firms abroad, and the earnings of foreigners from their investments in Canada. (See Figure 22.2.) Canada has had an unfavorable balance of payments for about the last 20 years.

The Rate of Exchange

foreign exchange rate

The ratio of one currency to another.

The **foreign exchange rate** is the ratio of one currency to another; it tells how much a unit of one currency is worth in terms of a unit of another currency. Canada's exchange rate has a significant effect on imports and exports. If the exchange rate decreases (that is, the value of the Canadian dollar falls in relation to other currencies), two things happen: our exports become less

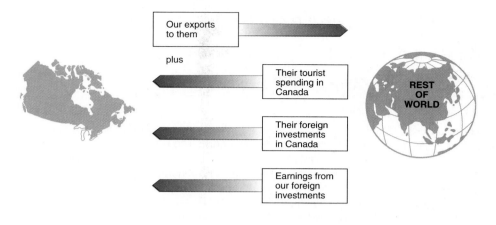

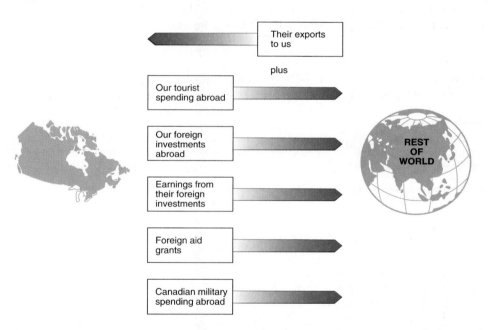

Figure 22.2
Requirements for Canada to have a favorable balance of payments. (The arrows indicate the direction of the flow.)

expensive to other countries, so they will want to buy more of what we produce; and prices of the goods other countries export to Canada will become more expensive, so we will buy less of them. If the exchange rate increases (that is, the value of the Canadian dollar increases), two things also happen: our exports become more expensive to other countries, so they will want to buy less of what we produce; and prices of the goods other countries export to Canada will become less expensive, so we will buy more of them.

During the last 20 years, the value of the Canadian dollar has fluctuated a great deal in relation to the currencies of other countries, including the U.S. Since the U.S. is our biggest trading partner, the fluctuations of our currency

International Report

RUSSIA'S RAMBLING RUBLE

After the fall of communism, things were supposed to get a lot better for the average Russian. But staggering problems have plagued Russia as it attempts to make the transition from a command economy to a market economy. Nowhere are these problems more evident than in the wild fluctuations that have occurred in the Russian currency, the ruble.

During the many years of the communist reign, the value of the ruble was artificially controlled by the government. Although the ruble was used by Russians in everday business activities, no one outside Russia wanted rubles because the currency was seen as worthless.

Since the fall of communism, the weaknesses in the Russian currency have come to light. In 1992, the government introduced a new ruble in an attempt to rein in inflation. Shortly after the introduction, the ruble was trading at about 1000 to a U.S. dollar. But the new ruble had problems almost immediately, and by the fall of 1994 it had declined in value to about 3000 to a U.S. dollar. Then the real decline started. In just one day, the value of the ruble fell 27 percent, going from 3081 to 3926 to the dollar. In six weeks, the ruble lost 78 percent of its value. Long lines of people appeared at currency exchanges to dump their rubles before they lost even more value.

These changes have had a big impact on Russian consumers. In the time it took one shopper to pick out a telephone and take it to the checkout, its price had increased from 75 000 to 100 000 rubles. On Moscow's subway, a ride that had cost five-hundreths of a ruble for the last 40 years has now increased to 250 rubles.

It is a great irony after all the years of the Cold War between the U.S. and Russia that American dollars are now a big item in Russia. An official at the St. Petersburg Hard Currency Stock Exchange estimates that 90 percent of Russians have at least some U.S. dollars tucked away. Russian retailers often value their goods in U.S. dollars and then convert that amount to rubles at the cash register so they don't violate a Russian law requiring retailers to sell in rubles.

But even this tactic doesn't insulate sellers from hyperinflation. Wholesalers, for example, lose money while they wait for retailers to pay for goods. One wholesaler sent a shipment of mugs for 2000 rubles each to a retailer. But by the time he got paid, he lost all the money he might have made because the value of the ruble had declined so fast.

To put all of this in perspective, consider how this currency uncertainty affects the McDonald's in Moscow, which buys and sells in rubles. A hamburger now costs about 4900 rubles, up from 3 rubles when the restaurant first opened in 1990. That is the equivalent of a hamburger in Canada increasing from $2.00 in 1990 to well over $2000 in 1994!

compared to the U.S. dollar have a big impact on our economy. During the mid-1970s, the Canadian dollar was worth slightly more than the U.S. dollar. By the late 1970s, however, it started on a steady downward path that eventually led to a value of only $0.69 U.S. By 1990, it had risen substantially, and was worth about $0.89 U.S. More recently, it has declined again to $0.73.

The fluctuations in the Canadian dollar are small compared to fluctuations that other countries have experienced (see the box "Russia's Rambling Ruble").

In the late 1980s and early 1990s, Canadians frequently crossed the border and shopped in the U.S. But times have changed, due to the decline of the Canadian dollar. During 1994, same-day car trips to the U.S. dropped 20 percent from 1993. In the same period same-day car trips to Canada by Americans rose about 8 percent.[6] The new trend is hurting U.S. shopping centers that located close to the Canadian border to take advantage of the willingness of Canadians to spend in the U.S. With the sharp drop in the dollar, customer traffic from Canada is way down.

International Business Management

Wherever it is located, the success of any firm depends largely on how well it is managed. International business is so challenging because the basic management responsibilities—planning, organizing, directing, and controlling—

are much more difficult to carry out when a business operates in several markets scattered around the globe.

It is not surprising, then, that business abounds with legends about managers who made foolish decisions because they failed to familiarize themselves with the foreign markets in which they hoped to do business. Estée Lauder, for example, launched an Italian cosmetics line with a picture of a model holding some flowers. The approach was conventional—and seemingly harmless. Unfortunately, the flowers chosen were the kind traditionally used at Italian funerals—hardly the image that Lauder intended to communicate.

Planning difficulties are compounded by difficulties in organizing, directing, and controlling. An organizational structure that works well in one country may fail in others. Management techniques that lead to high worker productivity in Canada may offend workers in Japan or the United Kingdom. Accounting and other control systems that are well-developed in Canada, may be unsophisticated or even nonexistent in developing nations.

"Going International"

The world economy is becoming globalized, and more and more firms are conducting international operations. This route, however, is not appropriate for every company. For example, companies that buy and sell fresh produce and fish may find it most profitable to confine their activities to a limited geographic area because storage and transport costs may be too high to make international operations worthwhile.

As Figure 22.3 shows, several factors enter into the decision to go international. One overriding factor is the business climate of other nations.

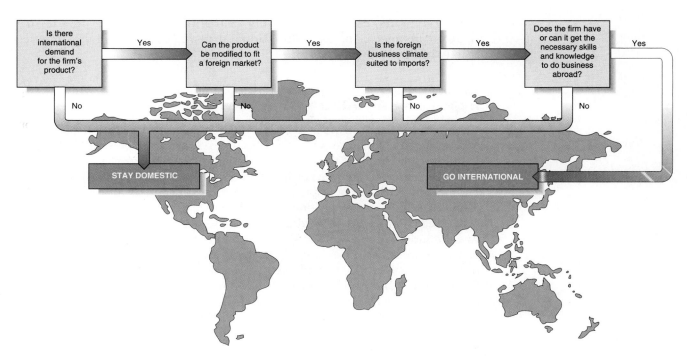

Figure 22.3
The decision to go international.

Even experienced firms have encountered cultural, legal, and economic road-blocks. (These problems are discussed in more detail later in this chapter.) In considering international expansion, a company should also consider at least two other questions: Is there a demand for its products abroad? If so, must those products be adapted for international consumption?

Gauging International Demand.   Products that are seen as vital in one country may be useless in another. Snowmobiles, for example, are not only popular for transportation and recreation in Canada and the northern United States, but actually revolutionized reindeer herding in Lapland. But there would be no demand at all for this product in Central America. Although this is an extreme example, the point is quite basic to the decision to go international: namely, that foreign demand for a company's product may be greater than, the same as, or weaker than domestic demand.

Adapting to Customer Needs.   If there is international demand for its product, a firm must consider whether and how to adapt that product to meet the special demands of foreign customers. For example, in Mexico, GM's Chevrolet division sells a Spanish-made subcompact called the Joy. Chevy prices the Joy $1500 to $2000 more than Volkswagen's old-fashioned Beetle, which still sells well in Mexico. GM has upped its price because it has found that in a country where 60 percent of the population is under 25, there is a huge market of younger buyers who will pay for stylish, more powerful vehicles. In the Czech Republic, however, GM markets the same car—known as the Opel Corsa—to potential buyers in their 30s. Here, says GM's director of sales for Central Europe, "younger buyers can't even afford bicycles."[7]

Levels of Involvement in International Business

Canadian business firms are involved in international business at many different levels, including importing and exporting goods and services, licensing agreements, establishing foreign subsidiaries, product mandating, strategic alliances, and as multinational firms. Each approach is discussed briefly in the following sections.

Exporting Goods and Services

Canadian business firms sell goods and services to many other countries. McCain Foods Ltd., for example, has become a formidable presence in Europe. It holds 75 percent of the "oven fries" market in Germany, and dominates the frozen French fry market in France and England.[8] MacMillan-Bloedel and Abitibi-Price sell newsprint and other forest products around the world. Small firms also export products and services. Seagull Pewter & Silversmiths Ltd., Magic Pantry Foods, and Lovat Tunnel Equipment Inc. have all recently won Canada Export Awards. Sabian Cymbals sells 90 percent of its products to 80 different countries outside Canada. Electrovert Ltd. does 95 percent of its business outside Canada. As we saw in the opening case, Glegg Water Conditioning Inc. sells almost all of its products in export markets. These companies have little in common with firms that concentrate on the Canadian market and then unload what is left somewhere else.[9]

A Canadian firm may not even have to send salespeople to foreign countries because some foreign firms have set up international procurement offices (IPOs) in Canada. These IPOs buy Canadian parts and incorporate them into products they make and sell abroad. Horn Plastics Ltd. supplies plastic parts to IBM and Hewlett-Packard under an IPO arrangement.[10]

An **independent agent** is a foreign individual or organization who agrees to represent an exporter's interests in foreign markets. Independent agents often sell the exporter's products, collect payment, and make sure that customers are satisfied. They often represent several firms at once and usually do not specialize in any one product or market. Levi Strauss uses agents to market clothing products in many smaller countries in Africa, Asia, and South America.

Exporting increases sales volume and generates a flow of funds that can lead to profits. Exporting also reduces the unit cost of production because of the increased volume, allows for greater use of plant capacity, lessens the dependence on a single traditional market, offers some protection against a downturn in Canadian sales, and provides an opportunity to gain a knowledge of and experience with other products and potential markets. But there are also disadvantages to exporting, such as the expense required to develop export markets, the modifications to products necessary to meet government regulations, the acquisition of further financing, and the obligation to learn about the customs, culture, language, local standards, and government regulations of the new customers.

Improvements can be made in Canada's export record. Canada sells only 9 percent of its exports to developing countries. We export eight times as much to the U.S. alone as we do to *all* developing countries combined. In every developing area of the world, Canada ranks last among the G7 countries in exports.[11] Table 22.3 lists the top 10 importing and exporting countries of the world.

independent agent

A foreign individual, or organization, who agrees to represent an exporter's interests in foreign markets.

TABLE 22.3   The Top 10 Importing and Exporting Countries

	Exporting		
Rank	**Country**	**$ Value (billions)**	**Share**
1	United States	465	12.6
2	Germany	362	9.8
3	Japan	361	9.8
4	France	209	5.7
5	Britain	183	5.0
6	Italy	168	4.6
7	**Canada**	**145**	**3.9**
8	Hong Kong	136	3.7
9	Netherlands	134	3.6
10	Belgium/Luxembourg	116	3.1
	All Others	1409	38.2
	Total	3687	100.0

	Importing		
Rank	**Country**	**$ Value (billions)**	**Share**
1	United States	603	15.9
2	Germany	327	8.6
3	Japan	241	6.3
4	Britain	210	5.5
5	France	201	5.3
6	Italy	147	3.9
7	Hong Kong	143	3.8
8	**Canada**	**139**	**3.7**
9	Netherlands	126	3.3
10	Belgium/Luxembourg	118	3.1
	All Others	1541	40.6
	Total	3796	100.0

Importing Goods and Services

While many enterprises sell Canadian goods and services abroad, others are involved in buying goods and services in foreign countries for resale to Canadians. For example, Gendis Inc., a large Winnipeg-based corporation, distributes Sony electronic products throughout Canada. Locally, most large shopping malls have a retail outlet selling wicker goods, brass objects, carpeting, and similar products imported from India and various Far Eastern countries. Canadian importing businesses employ buyers who travel around the world seeking out goods that can be sold here. Foreign suppliers might have salespeople or representatives based in Canada to market these products.

Licensing Agreements

licensing agreement

An agreement by an owner of a process or product to allow another business to produce, distribute, or market it for a fee or royalty.

Licensing agreements exist when the owner of a product or process allows another business to produce, distribute, or market the product or process for a fee or royalty. Such agreements can mean a Canadian enterprise licenses another enterprise in a foreign country to produce, distribute, or market its products in that area. Or the agreement could work the other way, and foreign enterprises allow Canadian firms to produce, distribute, and market their products in Canada. For example, Can-Eng Manufacturing, Canada's largest supplier of industrial furnaces, exports its furnaces under licensing agreements with Japan, Brazil, Germany, Korea, Taiwan, and Mexico.[12]

Licensing agreements are used when a company does not wish to establish a plant or marketing network in another country. They avoid the need to manage operations in foreign countries, and allow the owner of the product or process to concentrate on further technological research and development, financed, in part, from the royalties received.

Establishing Subsidiaries

If the volume of business to be conducted is large and ongoing, Canadian enterprises may choose to establish subsidiary or branch operations in foreign countries through which they can market goods and services. Other reasons for establishing a subsidiary are that a foreign government requires it or it may increase sales because locally operated branches can respond more quickly to delivery and service requests. Sometimes branches are established by forming an operation where none previously existed. Another approach is to buy a business in the foreign country. Of course, this process works both ways, with foreign enterprises doing the same in Canada. The establishment of subsidiaries can lead to the sensitive issue of foreign ownership and the analysis of its benefits and drawbacks.

world product mandating

The assignment by a multinational of a product responsibility to a particular branch.

Product Mandating.   When a business operates branches, plants, or subsidiaries in several countries, it may assign to one plant or subsidiary the responsibility for researching, developing, manufacturing, and marketing one product or line of products. This approach allows the business to achieve optimum levels of efficiency because economies of scale are possible through specialization. The assignment of a product responsibility to a particular branch is known as **world product mandating**.

At Northern Telecom, for example, the company's Belleville, Ontario plant was chosen as the one to produce a new business telephone system designed for the world market. The plant won out in a competition with two other Northern Telecom plants, one in Calgary and one in Santa Clara, California. The Belleville plant also has global mandates for several other product lines.

About 100 Canadian-based subsidiaries are now involved in some form of world product mandates. Some examples are the following:

- Pratt & Whitney Canada produces small gas turbine engines.
- Black and Decker Canada makes orbital sanders, the "Workmate" work bench, the "Workwheel" power stripper, and the "Workhorse" scaffold.
- Westinghouse Canada produces steam and gas turbines, airport lighting, and digital-video converters and displays.

Strategic Alliances

Strategic alliances involve two or more enterprises cooperating in researching, developing, manufacturing, or marketing a product. The relationship is more subtle than the usual supplier-customer relations, yet less formal than ownership. These relationships, which have become more popular in the last decade, take many forms and are also called cooperative strategies, joint ventures, strategic networks, and strategic partners. There are various reasons for entering into a strategic alliance, such as gaining access to new markets or customers, acquiring advanced or new technology, sharing the costs and risks of new ventures, obtaining financing to supplement a firm's debt capacity, and sharing production facilities to avoid wasteful duplication. Northern Telecom, for example, has strategic alliances with several firms, including Daewoo (Korea), Tong Guang (China), and Ascom Hasler (Switzerland). A strategic alliance between the governments of Indonesia and Singapore is described in the video case "Batam Island" on p. 721.

strategic alliances
Two or more enterprises that cooperate in researching, developing, manufacturing, or marketing a product.

Multinational Firms

Multinational firms do not ordinarily think of themselves as having specific domestic and international divisions. Rather, planning and decision making are geared to international markets. Headquarters locations are almost irrelevant. Northern Telecom, Royal Dutch Shell, Nestlé, IBM, and Ford are well-known multinational firms.

multinational firm
Controls assets, factories, mines, sales offices, and affiliates in two or more foreign countries.

The British firm Imperial Chemical Industries is one of the 50 largest industrial firms in the world, with nine major business units, four of which are headquartered outside of Britain. Until 1982, all 16 of its directors were British; today, the board includes two Americans, a Canadian, a Japanese, and a German. ICI has major operations in 25 different countries, and rather than managing businesses that are located and active within given countries, ICI managers are now in charge of business units that compete around the world.[13]

Fewer than 5000 of Nestlé Food Corp.'s 200 000-plus employees are stationed in its home country of Switzerland. The giant food-products company has manufacturing facilities in 50 countries and owns suppliers and distributors around the globe. Nestlé markets products worldwide by taking advantage of all possible levels of international involvement. In 1991, for instance, Nestlé entered a strategic alliance with the U.S. food-products company General Mills to create a new company called Cereal Partners Worldwide. General Mills initiated the joint venture with a European partner in an effort to cut into Kellogg's commanding lead in ready-to-eat cereals. For its part, Nestlé sees the venture as an opportunity to affirm its leadership in the $550 billion European food industry.

Multinational firms have encouraged economic growth in many areas of the world by providing financing, technological expertise, and the managerial know-how to operate industry. Financing is not always available locally, and the multinational firms can provide funds from other sectors of their operations. They bring technological expertise to less developed areas. The

Nestlé, a multinational firm, has its headquarters in Switzerland. Northern Telecom also carries out business activities in various countries. The bottom photo shows the company's plant in San Diego, California.

management capabilities of multinational firms are also used to organize and operate business enterprises in parts of the world other than the corporation's home country. By facilitating international trade and the transfer of capital, technology, and managerial know-how, multinational firms further international economic development and cooperation.

Managers of multinational corporations face many challenges, but the greatest is the need to respond to criticisms. These criticisms include the multinational firm's alleged nonallegiance to the host country, transferring profits from the host country, failing to promote research and development activities, exporting jobs by not producing finished products, and not hiring local personnel. The managers in the head office find it difficult to control and coordinate the activities of the branches located in foreign countries, while the managers sent to the foreign country must cope with different cultural, social, and economic environments. They may be restricted in many ways, for example, by local laws and religious practices.

Barriers to Trade

Whether a business is selling to just a few foreign markets or is a true multinational, a number of differences between countries will affect its international operations. How a firm responds to and manages social, economic, and political issues will go a long way toward determining its success.

Social and Cultural Differences

Any firm involved in international business needs to understand something about the society and culture of the countries in which it plans to operate. Unless a firm understands these cultural differences—either itself or by acquiring a partner that does—it will probably not be successful in its international business activities.

Some differences are relatively obvious. We have already seen how language barriers can cause inappropriate naming of products. In addition, the physical stature of people in different countries can make a difference. For example, the Japanese and French are slimmer and shorter on average than Canadians, an important consideration for firms that intend to sell clothes in these markets.

Differences in the average ages of the local population can also have ramifications for product development and marketing. Countries with growing populations tend to have a high percentage of young people. Thus, electronics and fashionable clothing would likely do well. Countries with stable or declining populations tend to have more old people. Generic pharmaceuticals might be more successful in such markets.

In addition to such obvious differences, a wide range of subtle value differences can have an important impact on international business. For example, many Europeans shop daily. To Canadians used to weekly trips to the supermarket, the European pattern may seem like a waste of time. But for Europeans, shopping is not just "buying food." It is also meeting friends, exchanging political views, gossiping, and socializing. The box "Faux Pas in Foreign Lands" describes how North Americans can make embarrassing mistakes in both business and politics when they are in a foreign country.

What implications does this kind of shopping have for firms selling in European markets? First, those who go shopping each day do not need the large refrigerators and freezers common in North America. Second, the large supermarkets one sees in Canada are not an appropriate retail outlet in Europe. Finally, the kinds of food Europeans buy differ from those Canadians buy. While in Canada prepared and frozen foods are important, Europeans often prefer to buy fresh ingredients to do their own food preparation "from scratch." These differences are gradually disappearing, however, so firms need to be on the lookout for future opportunities as they emerge.

Economic Differences

Although cultural differences are often subtle, economic differences can be fairly pronounced. In dealing with economies like those of France and Sweden, for example, firms must be aware of when—and to what extent—the government is involved in a given industry. The French government, for example, is heavily involved in all aspects of airplane design and manufacturing.

Similarly, a foreign firm doing business in a planned economy must understand the unfamiliar relationship of government to business, including a host of idiosyncratic practices. General Motors, which entered a $100 mil-

International Report

FAUX PAS IN FOREIGN LANDS

Politicians and business executives in both Canada and the U.S. frequently find it necessary to go to a foreign country to transact business. On occasion, these people fail to "do their homework" and do not learn enough about the country to which they are travelling. Then they do something that creates embarrassment.

When U.S. president Bill Clinton travelled to Russia in 1994, his trip was generally a hit with the media and the folks back home. But at the end of one town-hall style meeting, a beaming Clinton gave the audience the North American high-sign, a circle made with the thumb and forefinger. Oops! That gesture would likely have started a brawl in a Moscow pub, because in Russia it is the equivalent of our middle finger salute. Former U.S. president George Bush had the same problem when he visited Australia a few years earlier. There, he gave a "thumbs-up" sign, which unfortunately is the Australian equivalent of the same middle finger salute.

These gaffes are not limited to visiting politicians. Business executives also have to be aware of local etiquette and how this impacts business negotiations. Consider these examples:

- Crossing your legs in a business meeting in Saudi Arabia is considered an insult, because when you do that you are showing the sole of your foot; this is an insult to the other people in the room.
- In Portugal, it is considered rude to discuss business during dinner.
- In Taiwan, tapping your fingers on the table is a sign of appreciation for a meal.

Because the difference between proper and improper behavior can be so subtle, some companies hire local individuals to make sure that negotiations go smoothly. One such company is Dominion Bridge, which successfully concluded a deal to supply a subway/light rail system, a hydroelectric power station, and a cement plant in Chengdu, China. Interestingly, the man that Dominion hired also was working for the city of Chengdu. This would be considered a blatant conflict of interest in Canada, but not in China.

Business negotiation in China is a finely tuned waltz of etiquette and politics, and if everything doesn't go just right, the deal will fall flat. It is therefore important to have someone orchestrating all of the activities leading up to the signing of the deal. The president of Dominion Bridge says that it would take 100 years for a Canadian to develop the subtle understanding of the Chinese culture that their Chinese business agent has.

lion joint venture to build pickup trucks in China, found itself faced with an economic system that favored state-owned companies over foreign investors. So, while its Chinese suppliers passed on inflation-based price increases for steel and energy, GM could not in turn pass increases on to Chinese consumers. With subsidized state-owned automakers charging considerably less per truck, GM had no choice but to hold its own prices—and lose money on each sale.

Despite such problems, however, not all companies have had entirely negative experiences in China. For example, when Motorola opened a factory to manufacture paging devices, it planned to export most of the pagers because it forecasted limited internal demand. In a pleasant surprise, Motorola was forced to reassess the Chinese market after repeatedly selling out its weekly output of 10 000 units. This experience helped convince Motorola to build a $120 million plant in the northern port city of Tianjin, where it will manufacture pagers, simple integrated circuits, and cellular phones. As part of the largest manufacturing venture in Canada, it will also involve Chinese technicians in the production process. Chinese designers and engineers will play key roles in creating an operation that integrates manufacturing, sales, research, and development.

Legal and Political Differences

Closely linked to the structure of the economic systems in different countries are the legal and political issues that confront businesses as they try to expand internationally. These issues include tariffs and quotas, local-content laws, and business-practice laws. An awareness of differences in these areas can be crucial to a business's success.

Quotas and Tariffs. Even free-market economies often use some form of quota and/or tariff that affects the prices and quantities of foreign-made products in those nations. A **quota** restricts the total number of certain products that can be imported into a country. It indirectly raises the prices of those imports by reducing their supply.

The ultimate form of quota is an **embargo**: a government order forbidding exportation and/or importation of a particular product—or even all the products—of a particular country. For example, many countries control bacteria and disease by banning certain plants and agricultural products.

In contrast, a **tariff** is a tax charged on imported products. Tariffs directly affect the prices of products, effectively raising the price of imports to consumers who must pay not only for the products but also for the tariff. Tariffs may take either of two forms. A **revenue tariff** is imposed strictly to raise money for the government. But most tariffs in effect today are **protectionist tariffs** meant to discourage the import of a particular product.

Governments impose quotas and tariffs for a wide variety of reasons. For example, the U.S. government restricts the number of Japanese automobiles that can be imported into that country. The United States is not the only country that uses tariffs and quotas. Italy, for example, imposes high tariffs on imported electronic goods. Consequently, Sony Walkmans cost almost $150, and CD players are prohibitively expensive. Canada also imposes tariffs on many imported goods.

The customs duties that Canadians must pay after shopping in the U.S. yield revenue for the federal government and may also deter Canadians from buying some goods in the U.S. But if prices are low enough in the U.S., consumers will shop there. In the late 1980s and early 1990s, price differentials became so great that cross-border shopping increased dramatically. Canadian retailers are beginning to lower prices in response. When Cineplex Odeon reduced general admission prices from $7 to $4, attendance went up substantially. And Bata Shoes announced in 1991 that it would match any U.S. price on a comparable brand.[14]

Protectionism has both advocates and critics. Supporters argue that tariffs and quotas protect domestic firms and jobs. In particular, they protect new industries until they are truly able to compete internationally. Some claim that, since other nations have such measures, so must we. Still others justify protectionism in the name of national security. They argue that a nation must be able to produce goods needed for its survival in the event of war and that advanced technology should not be sold to potential enemies.

But opponents of protectionism are equally vocal. They note that protectionism reduces competition and drives up prices to consumers. They cite it as a cause of friction between nations. They maintain that, while jobs in some industries would be lost if protectionism ceased, jobs in other industries would expand if all countries abolished tariffs and quotas.

Local-Content Laws. A country can affect how a foreign firm does business there by enacting local-content laws. **Local-content laws** require that products sold in a particular country be at least partly made in that country. These laws typically mean that firms seeking to do business in a country must either invest directly in that country or have a joint-venture partner from that country. In this way, some of the profits from doing business in a foreign country are shared with the people who live there.

Many countries have local-content laws. In a fairly extreme case, Venezuela forbids the import of any product if a like product is made in

quota
A restriction by one nation on the total number of products of a certain type that can be imported from another nation.

embargo
A government order forbidding exportation and/or importation of a particular product.

tariff
A tax levied on imported products.

revenue tariff
A tariff imposed solely to raise money for the government that imposes it.

protectionist tariff
A tariff imposed at least in part to discourage imports of a par-

local-content laws
Laws requiring that products sold in a particular country be at least partly made in that country.

Local-content laws require that products sold in a particular country be at least partly made in that country.

Venezuela. Even when an item is not made in Venezuela, many companies choose to begin making their product in Venezuela both to drive out competitors and to prevent being forced out by local firms.

Local-content laws may even exist within a country; when they do, they act just like trade barriers. In Canada, for example, a low bid on a bridge in British Columbia was rejected because the company that made the bid was from Alberta. The job was given to a B.C. company. A New Brunswick window manufacturer lost a contract in Nova Scotia despite having made the lowest bid, and the job went to a Nova Scotia company. Recognizing that these interprovincial barriers are not helping Canada's international competitiveness, the federal government has committed itself to removing such barriers.

Business Practice Laws.   A final influence on how a company does business abroad stems from laws both abroad and in the firm's home nation. Sometimes, what is legal—and even accepted—business practice in one country is illegal in another. For example, in some countries it is perfectly legal to obtain business by paying bribes to government officials.

cartel

Any association of producers whose purpose is to control supply of and prices for a given product; illegal in Canada.

The formation of **cartels**—an association of producers whose purpose is to control supply and prices—gave the oil-producing countries belonging to OPEC a great deal of power in the 1970s and 1980s. In 1994, the major aluminum producing countries, including Canada, worked out a deal to curb world production. Government officials said the deal did not violate competition laws in either the U.S. or Canada, but it will probably result in higher aluminum prices.[15]

Cartels have historically not been very effective. In the 1970s, Canadian uranium producers banded together to restrict supply, but the cartel was challenged in U.S. courts and defeated. The power of OPEC has declined in the 1990s because of internal dissension in that cartel. The only effective cartel at present is in diamonds.

dumping

Selling a product for less abroad than in the producing nation; illegal in Canada.

Many countries forbid **dumping**—selling a product abroad for less than the comparable price charged at home. Antidumping legislation typically views dumping as occurring if

- products are being priced at "less than fair value," or
- the result unfairly harms domestic industry.

Overcoming Barriers to Trade

Despite the barriers described so far, world trade is flourishing. A number of world organizations and treaties have as their primary reason for being the promotion of international business.

Trade Agreements

Virtually every nation in the world has formal treaties with other nations regarding trade. One of the largest such treaties, the **General Agreement on Tariffs and Trade (GATT)**, was signed shortly after the end of the Second World War. But while the 92 countries that have signed GATT have agreed to reduce taxes on imported goods to 5 percent, not all have complied. One of the worst offenders is the United States.

Other GATT signatories who often do not live up to the terms of this treaty include the members of the **European Union.** The EU includes most western European nations, most notably Belgium, Denmark, France, Greece, Ireland, Italy, Luxembourg, the Netherlands, the United Kingdom, and Germany. These nations continue to place quotas and high tariffs on goods imported from non-member nations. But they have eliminated most quotas and set uniform tariff levels on products imported and exported within their group, encouraging intracontinental trade. In 1992, virtually all internal trade barriers were eliminated, making western Europe the largest free marketplace in the world.

On January 1, 1995, the new World Trade Organization came into existence. It will oversee a one-third reduction in import duties on thousands of products that are traded between countries. The reductions will be phased in over the next few years. Canada, the U.S., and the European Union are founding members of the WTO.[16]

General Agreement on Tariffs and Trade (GATT)

An international trade accord in which the 92 signatories agreed to reduce tariffs; often ignored by signatories.

European Union (EU)

An agreement among twelve western European nations to eliminate quotas and keep tariffs low on products traded among themselves, but to impose high tariffs and low quotas on goods imported from other nations.

The Canada–U.S. Free Trade Agreement

On January 1, 1989, a far-reaching free trade agreement between Canada and the U.S. came into effect. This agreement was the result of extensive negotiation between the U.S. and Canada, with each side showing concern for how it would fare under the agreement. In Canada, there was particularly vigorous debate in 1988, culminating in heated rhetoric during the election called because of the issue. The Liberals and NDP strongly opposed the deal, while the Conservatives supported it. With the election of a Conservative majority on November 21, 1988, the passage of the free trade agreement was assured.

The agreement represents the culmination of a long series of trade agreements made with the U.S. over the last 100 years. The first free trade agreement between Canada and the U.S. was signed in 1854 but broken by the U.S. in 1866. In the latter half of the nineteenth century, several other attempts at trade agreements were made, but none was successful.

This situation existed until 1935 when Canada ratified a modest "most-favored nation" agreement with the U.S. This agreement marked the start of serious trade liberalization between the U.S. and Canada. In 1948, Canada became part of GATT, which laid the foundation for a dramatic expansion of world trade. GATT negotiations between 1948 and 1979 gradually lowered trade barriers between countries and established trading rules. GATT agreements also helped reduce trade barriers between Canada and the U.S.

In 1965, Canada and the U.S. concluded the Auto Pact, which provided for duty-free trade in cars, trucks, buses, and auto parts at the manufacturing level. With the success of this "sectoral" free trade agreement, the Canadian government developed an interest in gaining more secure access to the large

U.S. market. In 1983, the Trudeau government began exploring the possibility of more agreements like the Auto Pact. In 1985, Prime Minister Brian Mulroney and U.S. President Ronald Reagan met to begin serious discussions on a new trade treaty. Several months later, the two governments agreed to conclude a comprehensive new agreement.

Canada-U.S. Free Trade Agreement
An agreement to eliminate over time tariffs on goods and services that move between the two countries.

The Nature of the Free Trade Agreement.   The **Canada-U.S. Free Trade Agreement** has as its goal the elimination over time of tariffs on products and services that move between the two countries. It is a *trade* agreement whose objective is to improve the employment rate and living standards in both Canada and the U.S. Its goal is to strengthen each country's ability to compete in international markets. The free trade agreement is an ambitious undertaking. Because it covers such a wide variety of issues, and because it cannot be known for certain how it will affect the two countries, the agreement is lengthy. The summary alone runs to 60 pages. It contains various provisions for the agreement to be reviewed and changed along the way.

The Free Trade Timetable.   Because the free trade agreement is complex, the two sides agreed to implement its provisions gradually. On the first day the agreement was in force, tariffs were totally eliminated on about 15 percent of all goods traded between the U.S. and Canada. For the remaining 85 percent, tariffs are being phased out over five or ten years, depending on the product. By January 1, 1998 tariffs will be eliminated on almost all goods traded between the U.S. and Canada.

Arguments For and Against Free Trade.   The basic arguments for and against the agreement are shown in Figure 22.4.

The North American Free Trade Agreement

North American Free Trade Agreement (NAFTA)
A trade agreement signed by Canada, the U.S., Mexico, and, later, Chile, whose purpose is to create a free trade area.

On January 1, 1994, the **North American Free Trade Agreement (NAFTA)** took effect. The objective of NAFTA is to create a free trade area for Canada, the U.S., and Mexico. It eliminates trade barriers, promotes fair competition, and increases investment opportunities. Chile became the fourth member of NAFTA later in 1994.

Surveys showed that a majority of Canadians originally opposed NAFTA. Labor leaders argued that the agreement did not go far enough to protect jobs in Canada. They feared that Canada would be flooded with products manufactured in Mexico, where wages are much lower than in Canada. Once tariffs are removed from these products because of NAFTA, they will be much cheaper than Canadian-made goods, and will likely be purchased instead of goods made in Canada. For example, clothing manufacturers in Quebec and Ontario are likely to be hurt by NAFTA because limits have been set on the amount of clothing that can be exported to the U.S. The Canadian Apparel Federation predicts that 30 000 jobs will be lost in the industry because of NAFTA.[17]

On the positive side, the agreement will open up Mexico's protected automobile market to Canadian exports over a ten-year period. In return for this concession, Canada agreed to increase the North American content required in auto parts from 50 to 60 percent. The Canadian textile industry may also benefit because the U.S. has agreed to substantial increases in the amount of textiles they are willing to import. The box "The Effect of Free Trade Agreements" describes the overall effect of NAFTA and the FTA.

Other Free Trade Agreements in the Americas

The Canada-U.S. free trade agreement and NAFTA are the most publicized trade agreements in the Americas, but there has recently been a flurry of activ-

Arguments in Favor of Free Trade	**Arguments Against Free Trade**
1. *Employment*. Canada needs open access to the U.S. market. To protect our employment we must get involved in free trade deals as other countries are doing. Canadian companies are already competing successfully with U.S. firms in industries in which there are no tariffs.	1. *Employment*. Canadian workers in a variety of industries will be laid off because U.S. firms will reduce their manufacturing activities here and simply send in goods from their duty-free U.S. plants.
2. *Social programs*. Canada already has over 200 agreements and understandings with the U.S. and none of these has ever threatened social services such as unemployment insurance and universal medical care. If Canada does not have a free trade deal with the U.S., the performance of our economy will be so poor that we will not be able to afford the current levels of social programs.	2. *Social programs*. Business firms in Canada will pressure the government to reduce social programs in order to lower their level of income tax. This will mean the end of universal access to services such as unemployment insurance and medicare.
3. *Takeovers*. Controls remain on foreign investment. Canada's corporate assets will remain subject to government approval before a takeover is allowed.	3. *Takeovers*. U.S. corporations can come into Canada and buy almost any Canadian company. Foreign ownership of Canada will increase.
4. *Energy*. There is nothing specific in the free trade agreement regarding energy or natural resources (e.g., water). There are, however, specific articles giving the Canadian government the right to act to protect health, safety, essential security, the environment, or consumer interest.	4. *Energy*. The free trade agreement will allow the U.S. to take the same percentage of our natural resources (e.g., oil) that they have taken in the past. If there is a shortage, Canadians will suffer.
5. *Effect on women*. Women are heavily employed in the service sector. Since many of the new jobs that will be created by the free trade deal will be in the service sector, women will benefit.	5. *Effect on women*. Women are heavily involved in the service sector. Since the free trade deal allows U.S. firms to deal in services, many of these jobs will be lost to the U.S.
6. *Environment*. Is not covered in the agreement. The federal government retains its right to take whatever actions are necessary to protect health, safety, essential services, the environment, and consumer interests.	6. *Environment*. Standards of all kinds must be harmonized with the U.S. This will mean that Canada will lose its right to control environmental standards.
7. *Culture*. The free trade agreement is about trade and tariffs. Canadian culture is not mentioned in the deal. European countries did not lose their culture when the Economic Community was formed, and Canada will not lose its culture because of a free trade deal with the U.S.	7. *Culture, Sovereignty, and Identity*. Because of all of the changes that will be required in the free trade deal, Canada will no longer be an independent country, but merely an economic subsidiary of the U.S.

Figure 22.4
Arguments for and against free trade.

ity among other countries as well. (The box "Moving Toward Free Trade in South America" describes this development.) On January 1, 1995, a free trade agreement known as Mercosur went into effect between Argentina, Brazil, Uruguay, and Paraguay. By 2005, tariffs will be eliminated on 80 percent of the goods traded between those four countries. Brazil has proposed enlarging Mercosur into a South American Free Trade Area (SAFTA), which might eventually negotiate with NAFTA to form an Americas Free Trade Area (AFTA).

There are several other free trade areas already in existence in the Americas: The Andean Pact (Bolivia, Ecuador, Colombia, Peru, and Venezuela), The Central American Common Market (Costa Rica, El Salvador, Guatemala, Honduras, and Nicaragua), and The Caribbean Common Market (many of the island nations of the Caribbean).[18]

International Report

THE EFFECT OF FREE TRADE AGREEMENTS

The Canada-U.S. Free Trade Agreement (FTA) and the North American Free Trade Agreement (NAFTA) are doing what supporters said they would—increasing the amount of trade between the U.S., Canada, and Mexico. Consider these figures:

- Canada's exports to the U.S. increased over 20 percent in 1994, and U.S. exports to Canada increased over 19 percent.
- Since 1989, when the FTA went into effect, trade between Canada and the U.S. has increased 75 percent (versus a 10 percent increase in Canada's trade with the rest of the world).
- Trade with the U.S. now represents 78 percent of Canada's total trade (the figure was 69 percent in 1988).
- Canada's exports to Mexico increased 25 percent in 1994, and Mexico's exports to Canada increased 23 percent.
- U.S. exports to Mexico rose 22 percent in 1994, and Mexico's exports to the U.S. rose 23 percent.
- Canada remains the number one trading partner with the U.S., but Mexico is now vying for the number two spot.

All this sounds pretty positive. But some people are concerned about the not-so-obvious effects of free trade agreements. Take jobs, for example. The Canadian government hasn't yet published an analysis of the effect of free trade on jobs, but one U.S. study estimates that about 100 000 new jobs were created by NAFTA. Another study estimated that NAFTA caused a small decline in the number of jobs. Even if the first study is accurate, the creation of 100 000 jobs isn't much in an economy like the U.S. (which added 2 million new jobs in 1994).

Critics of free trade are also worried about how it affects income distribution. In all three NAFTA countries, the percentage of gross domestic product going to the top one-fifth of income-earners has risen at the expense of those at the lower end of the income scale. In Mexico, for example, the richest 20 percent of the population earns 60 percent of national income. Economic instability is evident, unemployment has risen, and there is growing inequality and poverty.

Mexico has apparently been most negatively affected by NAFTA. Entire industries are under severe competitive attack from companies in Canada and the U.S. The large number of "mom and pop" stores is Mexico seem particularly vulnerable.

What is the future of the FTA and NAFTA? Just prior to the time that both these free trade agreements were passed, there was much vocal objection to them. In the U.S., for example, union leaders complained loudly about NAFTA and threatened to get revenge at the polls by voting pro-NAFTA politicians out of office. But in the 1994 election, there was no evidence that voters were unhappy with NAFTA. In Canada, the Liberal party fought the proposed FTA in the months before the 1988 election, but now that same party seems very committed to free trade. It appears that free trade is here to stay.

And maybe that's good. Free trade supporters argue that free trade helps the average working person because it expands the level of trade that is going on. This, in turn, gives consumers greater choices, lower prices on imported goods, and jobs in industries that are involved in exporting. Trade protectionism, on the other hand, favors narrow business, government, and labor interests.

International Report

MOVING TOWARD FREE TRADE IN SOUTH AMERICA

Canadians hear a lot about the Canada-U.S. free trade agreement and the North American Free Trade Agreement (NAFTA). But there has recently been a flurry of free trade activity in South America, too.

For many years, South American countries were run by military dicators who spent a lot of money on weapons of war and encouraged nationalistic tensions. Mistrust among countries like Argentina, Brazil, and Chile was very high. Brazilian engineers at one time designed bridges so that they would collapse when Argentine tanks drove over them. Brazil and Argentina also built their rail systems with different track gauges so the enemy's trains couldn't run on them if an invasion occurred.

With many South American countries now run by civilians, military tensions have eased and interest in international trade has increased. Now the emphasis is on facilitating movement between the various countries. A railway tunnel, a gas pipeline, and an oil pipeline connecting Argentina and Chile were cut through the Andes in 1994. Brazilian engineers are drawing up plans for a 2400-kilometre highway to speed the movement of goods between Sao Paulo and Buenos Aires. And plans are in place for major improvements in water transportation to further connect Bolivia, Brazil, and Argentina.

South American countries are realizing that their key trading partners are no longer European countries, but other close-by South American countries. Brazil's trade with Paraguay, for example, now exceeds its trade with France, and its trade with Uruguay is equal to its trade with Britain. Since 1990, trade between Argentina and Brazil has tripled, and so has trade between Chile and Argentina.

Trade Challenges for Canadian Business

Many challenges confront Canadian companies as they become involved in international trade. Four areas where challenges must be met are
1. increasing the effectiveness of government involvement in promoting exports
2. improving Canadian competitiveness in world markets
3. meeting competitive challenges from other countries
4. monitoring the level of foreign investment in Canada.

Increasing the Effectiveness of Government Involvement

The federal and provincial governments recognize the importance of international trade for the Canadian economy. As a result, they are trying to encourage trade by helping those business firms that are interested. Table 22.4 lists some selected services that are available to businesses. Some provinces have trade offices similar to the federal government's trade services, and provincial premiers sometimes visit foreign countries to promote trade.

While the government provides assistance in one way, it sometimes restricts international business in another. The government levies tariffs on imports and introduces nontariff barriers such as quotas and strict testing requirements to protect Canadian industry from foreign competitors. Canadian businesses wishing to import goods and services must sometimes pay duties and other charges that increase the price Canadians pay for these products. In some cases, imports are prevented from entering the country. Potential sales for businesses relying on foreign suppliers are therefore reduced.

TABLE 22.4   Examples of Government Assistance for Exports

Program	Function
Program for Export Market Development	Assists in export promotion activities. Shares financial risks of entering new foreign markets.
Technology Inflow Program	Facilitates the flow of foreign technology into Canada. Helps Canadian scientists in gaining technological knowledge.
Trade Commissioner Service	Promotes export trade and represents and protects Canadian interests abroad.
Export Development Corporation	A Crown corporation that facilitates and develops Canada's export trade through provision of insurance, guarantees, and loans.

Improving Canadian Competitiveness in World Markets

Canada's share of world trade is declining. This is partly caused by the increased competitiveness of other countries, as well as the decline in competitiveness of Canadian business firms. High-tech imports surpass exports, meaning that we rely on other countries for technological innovation. Canadian labor costs are also rising more quickly than elsewhere, and Canadian companies do not spend as much on on either R & D or training employees as firms in many other countries. Some critics claim that Canada lacks a "competitive culture."

The world competitiveness index is published each year by the International Institute for Management Development in Switzerland. **International competitiveness** refers to the ability of a country to proportionally generate more wealth than its competitors in world markets. In 1994, the U.S., Singapore, and Japan ranked first, second, and third in international competitiveness. Canada has been steadily losing ground during the past decade, dropping from fourth in 1989 to 14th in 1994. Canada's weaknesses include over-involvement of government in the economy, high debt levels, poor peformance by Canadian managers in new product development and entrepreneurship, and excessively high taxes.[19]

international competitiveness

The ability of a country to generate more wealth than its competitors in world markets.

Meeting Competitive Challenges from Other Countries

Canadian business firms face aggressive competition from several economic entities, including the European Union, the Asian countries, the developing countries, and the former communist countries.

The European Union.   The European Union means the economic integration of 12 nations: Belgium, Denmark, France, Germany, Greece, Ireland, Italy, Luxembourg, the Netherlands, Portugal, Spain, and the United Kingdom. The EU comprises 320 million people, compared to the U.S.'s 250 million and Japan's 120 million, and has thus become a strong trading block.

The EU is based on the following premises:

- The removal of barriers through about 300 legislative actions to create one internal market allowing for the free movement of goods, services, people, and capital.
- The standardization and harmonization of national laws and regulations so that they no longer interfere with the free trade of goods and services within the community.

- The opening of government purchases to all companies within the community.
- Companies are free to develop cooperative arrangements with companies in other member states allowing industry to organize on a large scale.
- An attempt to harmonize consumer sales and excise tax rates.[20]

Although the EU forms one market, cultural distinctions will continue. Nine languages will be spoken, a common currency is unlikely, and different taxation policies will remain. National identities and national preferences or tastes will not be obliterated. For example, British consumers will still prefer front-loading washing machines while French consumers will continue to like top-loading machines.

Many challenges for Canadian business emerge from this new trade block. The businesses within the EU that survive will be more efficient, more aggressive and more likely to compete around the world, including in Canada. It has become more difficult for Canadian enterprises to export to the EU, unless they are already established in Europe, as there is protection for EU enterprises from "outsiders."

The Asian Countries. The Asian trading block comprises four units: Japan; the newly industrialized countries (NICs) of Hong Kong, South Korea, Singapore, and Taiwan; the emerging NICs of Indonesia, Malaysia, Thailand, and the Philippines; and China.

Much has been written about Japanese business and how it operates.[21] Japanese enterprises have been very successful at exporting manufactured goods around the world, and have made huge inroads into Canadian markets. Japanese businesses have invested directly in Canadian business, including owning pulp and paper mills in Alberta and automobile plants in Ontario. Japanese portfolio investment, which includes holdings of federal and provincial bonds and corporate bonds and stocks, was estimated to be about $40 billion in 1988.[22]

Canadian business enterprises have been most successful at selling Japan commodities such as pulp and paper, coal, and iron ore. Little progress has been made in selling manufactured and high technology goods. Part of the problem is Japan's protectionist policies, but others suggest that Canadian business people fail in their business dealings because they are not as effective at managing business enterprises as the Japanese.

Canadian business enterprises face a formidable challenge when competing with the **keiretsu** companies of Japan.[23] These are loosely affiliated groups in industry and banking and can encompass hundreds of companies. Of the 1612 companies on the Tokyo stock exchange, 1100 belong to a *keiretsu* and the six major *keiretsu* companies account for 78 percent of the total capitalization of the exchange. The Mitsubishi *keiretsu* alone accounts for 11 percent of the capitalization. The main features of a *keiretsu* are

keiretsu

Loosely affiliated Japanese companies in industry and banking.

- The existence of cross-shareholdings. That is, companies own shares in each other, but no one company dominates ownership.
- The formation of a presidents' club. Top executives meet regularly to exchange information.
- Joint investment among member companies.
- *Keiretsu* member banks provide financing arrangements to member companies.
- Extensive buying and selling relationships exist among member companies.

Sometimes *keiretsu* companies are called cartels, that is, a group of companies that behave as a monopoly. They are hostile to outsiders, especially to foreign enterprises. They are demanding of new recruits, they extract special deals or cheap loans, and they expect obedience from all members. Their philosophy toward business differs from that of western companies. Western

The Japanese have been very successful in the mass production of consumer electronic products like televisions, VCRs, and video cameras.

multinationals emphasize profits, and shareholders are the most powerful stakeholders. With *keiretsu* companies, profits and the interests of shareholders are subordinate to long-range goals.

The newly industrialized nations and emerging NICs of Asia present other challenges for Canadian business. Enterprises in these nations produce consumer goods, such as clothing and electronics, at much lower costs than can be achieved in Canada. In Indonesia, for example, workers who make running shoes are paid less than $10 a week. The government wants to keep labor costs down because it knows that foreign manufacturers will set up plants there if wages are low. The video case "Batam Island" on p. 721 shows how the governments of Indonesia and Singapore are working together to create jobs in manufacturing and to increase the export of manufactured goods from Batam Island.

China is a huge market that is experiencing change. Canada used to sell large amounts of grain to China but recently this market has been lost to other grain producers. With its unstable political situation, Canadian business people are not sure how involved they should become in this market.

Some companies are now making their first tentative moves into China. Manulife Financial, for example, began selling life insurance in China in 1995. The company invested about $20 million in China, and expects to reach the breakeven point on operations early in the next century. China is potentially the world's largest market for life insurance, even though no insurance was sold there between 1947 and 1983.[25]

The Developing Countries.   Canadian business cannot ignore developing countries, or less developed countries (LDCs), as future markets. Approximately 77 percent of the world's population lives in these 142 nations, principally in South America, Africa, and Asia. These countries are buyers, suppliers, competitors, and capital users and are becoming increasingly important players in international business. They account for about 25 percent of the world's imports and 28 percent of exports.

The Former Communist Countries.   With the emergence of more market-based economic systems in many eastern European countries and the republics emerging from the former Soviet Union, Canadian business may have opportunities to conduct more trade with or to invest in business enterprises in these areas. One of the first Canadian enterprises to operate a business in the Soviet Union was McDonald's of Canada, which operates a fast food outlet in Moscow.

Glasnost and *perestroika* have led to the demise of the "socialist planned economy" of the Soviet Union. The progress and the form of the economic liberalization in that region are not clear, and many pros and cons face the Canadian enterprise that wishes to do business there.[26] Canadian companies may still encounter bureaucratic red tape and political instability.

Doing business in eastern Europe is also a challenge.[27] Not all the communist systems are changing at the same rate. East and West Germany are now integrated, and Poland and Hungary are introducing market mechanisms, but other countries are not as progressive.

Foreign Investment in Canada

Canada's manufacturing economy has developed behind a protective tariff barrier, which made it attractive for foreign firms to establish or acquire subsidiaries in Canada to supply the Canadian market. Foreign firms were able to supply goods to the Canadian market less expensively than by exporting to Canada and paying the tariff on the product. This situation is now changing rapidly as the free trade agreement takes effect.

Canada's rich natural resources—minerals and petroleum—also attracted money from abroad. Canada leads the world in the value of its mineral exports. It ranks first in the production of uranium, zinc, and nickel; second in asbestos, potash, sulphur, and gypsum; and third in gold, aluminum, and platinum.

Foreign firms that invested in Canada because of the tariff barriers often built small, inefficient plants to serve only the Canadian market. The cost of production, as well as the tariff barriers erected by other countries and the fact that head offices of foreign companies made most export allocations, made it difficult for these firms to compete actively as exporters.

The market size and the tendency for much technological development work done by foreign-owned companies to be conducted outside Canada means that Canadian subsidiaries do not do much new product development work. This, it has been argued, is one major disadvantage of the high degree of foreign ownership of Canadian corporations. The other side of the argument, of course, is that Canadian firms would have less access to technological developments were it not for foreign ownership.

Concern about foreign ownership in Canada has prompted several government studies. The first was the Gordon Commission Report in 1957. It pointed out that there were dangers to foreign investment, in particular, the possibility that U.S. subsidiaries in Canada, faced with a conflict between U.S. and Canadian positions, would choose to support the U.S. position. A key recommendation, subsequently acted on, was that financial intermediaries, such as banks, should be in Canadian hands.

The Watkins Report in 1968 dealt with **extraterritoriality**, that is, the application of one country's laws to the subsidiaries of its companies in other countries. Major recommendations of the Watkins Report were to create a government agency to survey multinational activities in Canada, to compel foreign subsidiaries to disclose more of their activities in Canada, to encourage nationalization of Canadian industry, to subsidize research and development and management education in Canada, to form the Canada Development Corporation, and to forbid the application of foreign laws in Canada.

extraterritoriality
The application of one country's laws to the subsidiaries of its companies in other countries.

The 1970 Wahn Committee investigation examined Canada-United States relations. Much of its work was based on the Watkins Report. One of its recommendations was that, over time, all foreign-owned firms in Canada should allow Canadians to own at least 51 percent of their shares.

The Gray Report in 1972, *Foreign Direct Investment in Canada*, attempted to determine the economic forces that promoted foreign investment and to measure its benefits and costs. The report saw the major benefits of foreign direct investment as access to new technology, resulting in increased productivity in Canada, and the introduction of new and improved products in Canada. The Gray Report recommended a foreign investment review agency to screen new foreign direct investments in Canada to determine their effect. As a result of that recommendation, the Liberal government of Canada established the **Foreign Investment Review Agency (FIRA)**. Its purpose was to ensure that significant benefits accrued to Canada from new foreign direct investment. In 1985, under a Conservative government, FIRA's title was changed to **Investment Canada**. The new federal organization is designed primarily to attract and facilitate foreign investment in Canada. During the 1970s and 1980s, in fact, U.S. ownership of Canadian assets declined steadily.

Foreign Investment Review Agency (FIRA)
Established in 1973 to screen new foreign direct investment in Canada; supposed to ensure that significant benefits accrued to Canada.

Investment Canada
Replaced FIRA in 1985; designed primarily to attract and facilitate foreign investment in Canada.

Summary of Key Points

The three major marketplaces for international business are North America, Europe, and the Pacific Rim. Goods and services are imported and exported from these areas to meet the needs of consumers worldwide.

Nations trade with each other because they cannot supply all the products and services that their citizens want. Countries may engage in trade because they can produce a good or service more cheaply than any other nation (absolute advantage). More often, they trade because they can produce some items more cheaply or better than other goods (comparative advantage). Canadian business firms are actively involved in exporting and importing goods and services, but our share of world trade declined during the 1980s.

A country's balance of trade is the difference in value between its total exports and its total imports. If a country exports more than it imports, it has a favorable balance of trade. Canada has had a favorable balance of trade since 1975. A country's balance of payments is the difference between money flowing into the country and money flowing out of the country as a result of trade and other transactions. Canada's balance of payments has been unfavorable for about the last 20 years.

In deciding whether to do business internationally, a firm must determine whether a market for its product exists abroad, and, if so, whether the firm has the skills and knowledge to manage such a business. It must also assess the business climate of other nations to make sure that they are conducive to international operations. Several levels of international business operation are possible: exporting and importing goods and services, licensing agreements, establishing subsidiaries in foreign countries, strategic alliances, and becoming a multinational corporation.

Numerous barriers to trade exist, including social and cultural differences between countries, economic differences, legal/political differences, tariffs and quotas, local content laws, and business-practice laws. Many countries are trying to overcome barriers to trade by signing free trade agreements such as the Canada-U.S. Free Trade Agreement and the North American Free Trade Agreement.

Canadian businesses face four challenges in international business: increasing the effectiveness of government involvement in encouraging exports, improving the competitiveness of Canadian business firms in international markets, meeting the competitive challenge from business firms in other countries, and monitoring the amount of foreign investment in Canada.

Even Wal-Mart Has Its Problems

When the first Wal-Mart store opened in Mexico City, big crowds showed up and sales were strong. But interest soon waned, and customers complained that the chain's prices were too high. Some Mexicans living near the U.S. border cross it to shop at Wal-Marts in the U.S. When Wal-Mart opened a store in Monterey, the local press soon was publicizing the fact that prices were 15 to 20 percent higher than at the Wal-Mart in Laredo, Texas (a two-hour drive to the north). Wal-Mart is now admitting that it has a long way to go in establishing itself in Mexico.

Wal-Mart's experience should serve as a warning to any retailer who is thinking about entering a foreign market as a result of the North American Free Trade Agreement (NAFTA). Industry analysts say that retail outlets in Mexico are growing far faster than the buying power of their potential customers. The big problem is that Mexico's middle class is not very large by Canadian or U.S. standards, and it will take 10 to 20 years for such a group of consumers to develop.

Wal-Mart faces the following problems in Mexico:

- It does not have the same clout with Mexican suppliers that it has with U.S. suppliers because it is not a major presence in Mexico.
- Distribution systems in Mexico are different—suppliers ship directly to stores rather than to retailer warehouses—thus nullifying Wal-Mart's efficient control of distribution.

- The appeal of well-known U.S. brand names is fading.
- Mexicans continue to shop for food at small neighborhood shops, not at big discount stores, because they feel the food is fresher at local markets.
- Most Mexicans do not own cars, so the geographic "reach" of a particular store is limited.

Kmart, one of Wal-Mart's major competitors in the U.S. and Canada, is also operating in Mexico. Unlike Wal-Mart (which shipped a manager from the U.S. to Mexico), Kmart hired a Mexican who was formerly director of store development for a Mexican department store chain. Juan Suberville knows all about Mexican shopping habits and has used this knowledge to advantage. For example, Kmart stores have a bank inside so that customers can easily get cash (there are few credit sales in Mexico). Also, each Kmart has a walk-in refrigerator where customers can go in and choose the cut of beef they want. Even hot dogs are wrapped in front of customers to convey a sense of freshness.

CASE QUESTIONS

1. What social, cultural, and economic differences has Wal-Mart had to cope with while trying to enter the Mexican market?
2. What level of involvement in international business has Wal-Mart demonstrated in its move into Mexico?
3. Is Wal-Mart a multinational company? Explain. ◆

CONCLUDING CASE 22-2

AST Computes the Odds in China

With domestic computer makers bumping up against one another to snag local customers, AST Research Inc., a personal computer manufacturer, decided to take a chance in China. Although industry giants, including IBM, Apple, and Compaq, were convinced that China was not yet ready for PCs, AST believed that the Chinese market held unlimited—and immediate—opportunity. For one thing, statistical data convinced the company that it was right. When AST first entered China in 1987, the country had only one computer for every 6000 people, and forecasters projected annual growth rates of more than 22 percent.

AST began its marketing effort by advertising in Chinese computer magazines and flying in its managers to conduct demonstrations. By 1992, its pioneering efforts had paid off: It had captured 25 percent of China's PC market and was optimistic about future growth. With the political climate in China allowing some semblance of a market economy, AST felt confident that demand would rise in such fields as finance, heavy industry, and transportation. It also felt sure that foreign companies would continue to capture the lion's share of the growing market.

Adhering to a better-late-than-never philosophy, other PC makers finally noticed both AST's success and China's largely untapped market potential. Compaq, for instance, joined forces with Beijing Stone Corp., China's leading computer company, to build and distribute 30 000 PCs a year. Apple, IBM, and Hewlett-Packard are involved in ventures to develop the Chinese-language software programs that all three companies believe crucial to long-term success.

Operating in a climate that will not allow it to rest on its laurels, AST is meanwhile establishing its own production and design capacity inside China. Through a recent joint venture, it will build a $16 million plant to produce 100 000 PCs annually. It is also targeting small businesses, schools, and hospitals—millions of untapped users who need computer products. At the same time, in order to accommodate the thousands of characters in the Chinese alphabet, AST is moving rapidly to introduce tablet-based PCs that will allow users to write on the screen instead of typing.

AST's 1993 purchase of Tandy Corp.'s computer-making business doubled its own plant capacity nearly overnight and placed it in an even better position to maintain its hold on the Chinese market. According to Safi U. Qureshey, AST's president and CEO, "This [acquisition] gives us economies of scale that we need in order to compete with the big guys." As the competition heats up in China, AST remains confident that its pioneering efforts will pay off and that it is already one of the "big guys" on Chinese soil. We have planted "our roots," says Qureshey, "so that we can lead the development of the [Chinese] market."

CASE QUESTIONS

1. Why do you think IBM, Apple, and Compaq misread market forces in the mid-1980s and decided not to establish a marketing presence in China? Why do you think it is more difficult to forecast market trends in China than it is in Canada?
2. How is AST's continuing success connected to the political climate in China?
3. Why do you think a joint venture is an important part of AST's expansion plans?
4. Although several Japanese computer makers are also trying to enter the Chinese market, American firms are far ahead in software and microprocessor technology. In your opinion, are these technological advantages likely to make a difference in the years ahead? In your answer, consider Japan's natural advantage as a Pacific Rim country doing business with another Pacific Rim country.   ◆

Key Terms

globalization	licensing agreements	protectionist tariff	North American Free
imports	world product	local content laws	Trade Agreement
exports	mandating	cartels	international
absolute advantage	strategic alliances	dumping	competitiveness
comparative advantage	multinational firms	General Agreement on	*keiretsu*
balance of trade	quota	Tariffs and Trade (GATT)	extraterritoriality
balance of payments	embargo	European Union (EU)	Foreign Investment
foreign exchange rate	tariff	Canada-U.S. Free Trade	Review Agency (FIRA)
independent agent	revenue tariff	Agreement	Investment Canada

Study Questions and Exercises

Review Questions

1. Explain the difference between a nation's balance of trade and balance of payments.
2. What are the possible ways that Canadian firms can be involved in international business?
3. What are the advantages and disadvantages of multinational corporations?
4. How does the economic system of a country affect foreign firms interested in doing business there?

Analysis Questions

5. Make a list of all the major items in your bedroom. Identify the country in which each item was made. Give possible reasons why that nation might have a comparative advantage in producing this good.
6. Do you support protectionist tariffs for Canada? If so, in what instances and for what reasons? If not, why not?

7. Is the Canada-U.S. free trade agreement good for Canada? Give supporting reasons for your answer.
8. The EC includes much of western Europe, but some countries, such as Switzerland, have chosen not to join. Why might that be?

Application Exercises

9. Interview the manager of a local firm that does at least some business internationally. Identify reasons why the company decided to "go international," as well as the level of the firm's international involvement and the organizational structure it uses for its international operations.
10. Select a product familiar to you. Using library reference works to learn something about the culture of India, identify the problems that might arise in trying to market this product to India's citizens.

Building Your Business Skills

Goal

To encourage students to understand the cultural differences that affect international business.

Situation

Imagine that you are the head of marketing for an international consumer products company. Your assignment is to sell the company's line of diapers in the Far East.

Method

Develop a strategy for marketing diapers in Japan and China.

Step 1

As you work, keep in mind the following characteristics that define the cultures of these two countries:

■ Japanese mothers change their babies' diapers more than twice as often as Canadian mothers—up to 14 times a day.
■ Sexism is a fact of life in China; girls have less value in society than boys.

Step 2

With this cultural information in mind, ask yourself the following questions. Your answers will help define your marketing strategy:

■ Considering how frequently they change their children's diapers, would Japanese mothers be more likely to buy

a thin or a thick diaper? Keep in mind the need to store large numbers of diapers in homes that are relatively small compared with Canadian homes.
■ With the prejudice against female babies a pervasive part of their culture, would Chinese mothers be likely to buy color-coded diapers (pink for girls, blue for boys) or white unisex diapers? Keep in mind that every time a Chinese mother bought a package of pink diapers, she would be telling the world that she has a daughter.

Step 3

Join with groups of four or five students to analyze ways in which your answers to these questions would affect your marketing approach.

Follow-Up Questions

1. How should a Canadian-based company act when the cultural norms of the country with which it is doing business are considered discriminatory—and even repugnant—in Canada?
2. How important is it to acquaint yourself with a country's culture before doing business there? Based on your marketing analysis in this exercise, explain how cultural mistakes can doom a product to failure.

23

Managing Computers in Business

LEARNING OBJECTIVES

After studying this chapter, you will be able to

- Discuss the reasons why a business needs to manage information as a resource and why computers have revolutionized information management.
- Identify the five components of a computer system and four major types of business applications programs.
- Categorize computer systems by size and structure.
- Trace the development of computers.
- Discuss future trends in business information management.

CHAPTER OUTLINE

OPENING CASE

Software Piracy

For many Canadians, copying software is no big deal. They feel that computer companies are rich and that software is overpriced, so they think it is O.K. to copy software and thereby avoid paying for it. People who would never dream of shoplifting, evading income taxes, or embezzling money seem quite willing to copy software illegally.

The Canadian Copyright Act of 1988 prohibits the unlicensed copying of software, and software piracy is taken quite seriously by our judicial system. Maximum fines of $1 million and up to five years in prison are possible. In two recent high-profile cases of software piracy, Ali Computers of Ottawa was convicted and fined and the Vancouver Island Business College settled out of court. These cases may deter some people from illegally copying software.

Increasingly, software companies are deciding to prosecute individuals and organizations that illegally copy software. They have chosen to do so for two reasons: they are losing revenue to software pirates, and companies who legally purchased their software are complaining that other companies who pirated it have an unfair advantage.

Software piracy is a worldwide phenomenon, but it appears to be particularly bad in some foreign countries. One firm which had sold only two registered copies of a software package in Russia found to its dismay that hundreds of thousands of copies were circulating a short while later. A study of software usage found that legal software accounted for more than half the software in use in countries like the U.S., Britain, Austria, Italy, South Africa, and Switzerland. But legal software accounted for less than 1 percent of the software in countries like the United Arab Emirates, Pakistan, Thailand, and Indonesia. In Canada, about 60 percent of the software in use has been copied illegally.

The Canadian Alliance Against Software Theft (CAAST) estimates that unauthorized copying of software programs is costing the industry approximately $17 *billion* worldwide. The estimate for Canada alone is well over $300 million. Pirating not only denies companies legitimate sales revenues for their products, it also makes no contribution to the Canadian economy, creates no jobs, and generates no tax revenue. CAAST estimates that for every $1 million of revenue lost to piracy, one

job is not created that otherwise would have been. And that doesn't count the jobs that would have been created by dealers and distributors of software.

A Canadian company has developed an anti-piracy technology called SoftCop that could dramatically cut down on software piracy. This clever system works by "thumbprinting" the software to the authorized user's computer so it will not run on another computer. It will cost software manufacturers about $10 per package to implement. It also allows detection of attempts to tamper with the protection system.

In another clever twist, the company selling the software will *encourage* the purchaser to make copies of the software and distribute it to friends. When the friends try to use the software, they will, of course, find that it won't work unless they get it activated by Bell Sygma (a subsidiary of Bell Canada) through the phone system and a modem. After that, the new user will get a free period in which to try out the software. At the end of the trial period, the software will no longer work unless the new user purchases his or her own copy.

Surprisingly, one of the biggest and most well-known software companies, Microsoft, has not shown any interest in the system. But even if Microsoft doesn't buy into the idea initially, many smaller companies have already expressed interest. And Microsoft is not as big as some people think. Its microprocessor-based applications software revenue in 1992 was $1.35 billion in a market worth a total of $17.8 billion. ◆

As the opening case demonstrates, software piracy is just one of the many computer-related issues that business firms have to cope with if they are to be effective. The computer revolution is all about the management of information—information about customers, employees, competitors, government, suppliers, and many others. The list is endless. Such information has always been important to business, but the advent of the computer has allowed businesses to analyze this information much more quickly than before. If one firm discovers an even better way to analyze information, all other firms must adopt it in order to keep up in the competitive race.

In this chapter, we will explore the ways in which companies use computers to manage information. Information management requires that you first understand what information is and what it is not. Only then can you appreciate what computers can do and how they do it. As you will see, the computer systems in use today are just the latest step in the evolution of information management.

Information Management: An Overview

People in business today are bombarded with facts and figures. Modern communications enable businesses to hear from plants, branches, or sales offices at remote locations daily—or even more often. Despite predictions of paperless offices, managers are receiving more and more computer-generated reports and memos. One president of an electronics firm says he receives 97 reports a month![1] How can a manager sift through all the reports, memos, magazines, and phone calls to find the information needed to make critical decisions? How can businesses get useful information to the right person at the right time?

Most businesses regard their information as a resource and an asset that they plan, develop, and protect. It is not surprising that companies have information-management departments, just as they have production, marketing, and finance departments. As you will see in this chapter, information management is one of the operations that determines how well a business performs.

Data versus Information

Although business people often complain that they receive too much information, they usually mean that they get too much data. **Data** are raw facts and figures. **Information** is based on data, but it is a meaningful, useful interpretation of that data (see Figure 23.1).

Consider the following data: 50 million tubes of toothpaste were sold last year; the birth rate is rising; 35 million tubes of toothpaste were sold the year before last; advertising for toothpaste increased 57 percent; a major dentists' group recently came out in favor of brushing three times a day. If all these data can be put together in a meaningful way, they may produce *information* about what sells toothpaste and whether manufacturers should build new plants. The challenge for businesses is to turn a flood of data into information and to manage that information to their best advantage.

data
Raw facts and figures.

information
A meaningful, useful interpretation of data.

Management Information Systems

One response to this challenge has been the growth of **management information systems (MIS)** designed to transform data into information that can be used for decision making. Those charged with the company's MIS services must determine what information will be needed, then gather the data and provide ways to convert them into the desired information. They must also *control* the flow of information so that only those who need or are entitled to certain information receive it. Information supplied to employees and managers varies, depending on the functional area in which they work (such as accounting or marketing) and on their level in management.

management information system (MIS)
An organized method of transforming data into information that can be used for decision making.

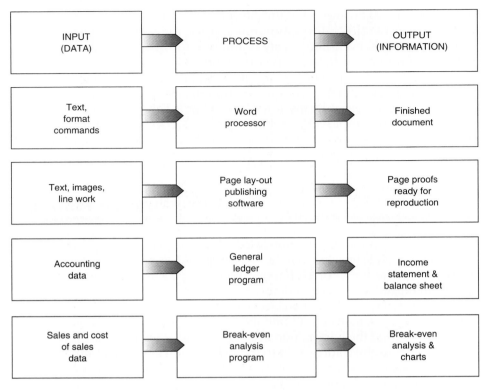

Figure 23.1
From data to information and knowledge.

Levels of Management.   First-line managers need information for the day-to-day operations of the business. Middle managers need summaries and analyses to help them set intermediate- and long-range goals and to plan strategies for reaching these goals. Top management needs even more sophisticated analyses to meet its responsibilities for long-range and corporate planning.

Consider the needs of various managers of a flooring manufacturer. Sales managers (first-line managers) supervise salespeople, assign territories to the sales force, and handle customer-service and delivery problems. To do their job well, they need current and accurate information on the sales and delivery of flooring products to customers in their branches. Regional managers (middle managers) set sales quotas for each sales manager, prepare budgets, and plan staffing needs for the next year. They need total monthly sales by product and by branch, as opposed to an itemized sales report. Finally, top management will need sales data summarized by product, customer type, and geographic region, and analyzed in comparison to previous years' and competitors' sales. Environmental (external) information such as consumer behavior patterns, the competition's record, and related economic forecasts are as important as internal operations information.

Figure 23.2 illustrates the need for information at the different levels of management. As you can see, information is increasingly condensed and summarized as it moves up through the management hierarchy.

Top management may turn to outside companies to manage the firm's information systems. This is called *outsourcing*. In 1990, Andersen Consulting began providing a service that allows clients to modify, enhance, and maintain their existing MIS. Kodak Canada has such an arrangement with **IBM**. Businesses outsource because they lack the technical expertise to deal with rapid changes in computer technology.

Management information systems are becoming increasingly important as managers try to cope with the flood of data they are confronted with.

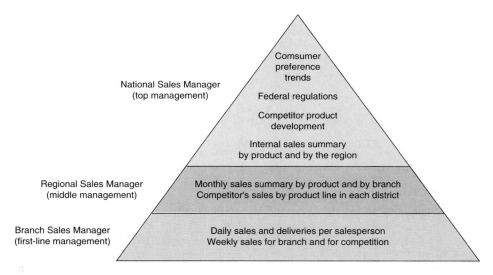

Figure 23.2
Different information needs at various managerial levels.

The Computer Revolution

Today, more than ever before, information management requires managing computers as an information tool. Changes in computer technology have revolutionized the way businesses manage information. As little as fifteen years ago, automated banking machines were virtually unheard of. Now national banking networks like Circuit, Interac, and Cirrus mean that a customer of a Toronto bank can run out of cash in Caesar's Palace in Las Vegas and withdraw money from a teller machine in the hotel lobby.

Computers also offer businesses a wide range of capabilities. Airlines use reservation systems not only to book flight reservations but also to plan marketing programs for frequent travellers and airplane maintenance schedules.

On a smaller scale, companies like the Artists' Frame Service, a custom picture framer, may use a computer to keep track of customers' addresses and also to decide when to order more framing materials.

The Outaouais Regional Community Transit Commission has equipped buses in Hull, Gatineau, and Aylmer with a special microprocessor that transmits information on the location of all 150 buses every 20 seconds. It also monitors important operational characteristics like brakes, air and oil pressure, and engine temperature. The driver of a bus with a potential problem can be notified before a breakdown occurs.[2]

Diamond Taxi of Toronto has equipped its cabs with computers. The computer lets each driver know when a fare is waiting, and it displays the name and address of the fare on a small screen. The company is now responding about 20 percent faster to calls than it did before.[3]

As we saw in the opening case, computer technology has made possible the development of many new businesses. The development of the "Softcop" software would not have been possible or necessary without computer technology.

The areas in which computers can help improve operations are almost endless. The box "The Paper Chase" describes how the computer helps manage information at the Canadian Patent Office.

Why are computers having such an impact on business? Although it is really nothing more than a machine, the computer boasts four features that make it especially useful:

- *Speed of Processing.* The computer is fast—very fast. Calculations requiring several lifetimes if done by hand can be performed in less than one second by today's most powerful computers.

The Canadian Business Scene

THE PAPER CHASE

The Canadian Patent Office receives a steady flow of patent applications for everything from cattle fences to computer anti-piracy devices. These applications are on top of the 1.3 million patents it has already granted since 1920. Paper files now occupy 12 kilometres of shelf space in various buildings around the Ottawa area.

How does the patent office know if the application it just received duplicates some idea that is already patented? Someone at the patent office has to do a lot of searching through files to see if something similar is already patented. Since this is a very time-consuming activity, the patent office is looking for a way to streamline the work. Enter the computer.

The patent office has embarked on a major project to put all of its files, abstracts, diagrams, and chemical formulas on computer. When the project is completed in 1996, the patent office will have spent $76 million.

Under the old system, when a patent application was received, an examiner filled out a form requesting files of previous designs in a certain area. The examiner then had to wait while a clerk found the relevant files. With the new computerized system, the examiner uses the computer to rapidly find the needed information. For example, when an examiner like Isaac Ho receives an application file labelled CO7K, he knows (based on an international coding system) that the application deals with a chemical formula. He then uses the computer to determine how many patents have been filed in that chemical field (the answer is 2289). He then uses different search terms to narrow the field down to just a handful of applications. Next he examines these few files to determine if the most recent application is breaking new ground. The process is complete when he decides whether or not a patent should be issued.

Inventors of ideas that are granted patents must supply a write-up of how their invention was created, and this information is made available to the public. Under the old system, interested parties had to come to the patent office to read the information, but with computerization, the information will be widely available. This may stimulate further creativity and more valuable patents. It will also help inventors avoid re-inventing the wheel.

- *Accuracy of Processing.* Modern computers have built-in error-checking ability that allows them to perform billions of literally error-free calculations.
- *Ability to Store Programs.* One of the most important breakthroughs of the computer revolution is the *stored-program concept*: Computers store and handle not only the data that need processing, but also the instructions (program) needed to process the data.
- *Ability to Make Comparisons.* Although computers cannot yet "think," they can make comparisons. More important, based on the results of those comparisons, they can take different courses of action—that is, they can execute a huge variety of programmed instructions.

Remember, however, that, for all its virtues, the computer is far from perfect. Unfortunately, the computer can and will process incorrect data just as quickly and accurately as it can process correct data. The accuracy of what you receive from the computer depends on the accuracy of what you put in. People in the computer field have coined a term for this phenomenon— *GIGO: Garbage In, Garbage Out.* In other words, if the computer is given the wrong data to process, it is likely to give you back the wrong answer.

Elements of a Computer System

The computer is a powerful electronic machine. But it is only part of the **computer system**. Every computer system has five parts: (1) hardware (2) software (3) people (4) control and (5) data. All five components must be present and properly coordinated for a computer system to function properly.

computer system

An electronic method of turning data into information; its five parts are hardware, software, people, control, and data.

Hardware

Figure 23.3 shows the various systems and components that make up the **hardware** of a computer system. The functioning of a computer's hardware is not as complicated as it might look. To get a bird's-eye view of how it works, suppose you are a very simple piece of data—the number "3."

hardware

The physical components of a computer system.

Inputting.   To get into the computer, you must be entered by an **input device**. A punch card, magnetic tape, and a "mouse" are all input devices (see Figure 23.4), but let's assume that you are entered by a friend using the most common input device, a keyboard. When your friend presses the number "3" on the keyboard, an electronic signal is sent to the computer's **central processing unit (CPU)**, where the actual processing of data takes place.

input device

Hardware that gets data into the computer in a form the computer can understand.

central processing unit (CPU)

Hardware in which the actual transforming of data into information takes place; contains the primary storage unit, the control unit, and the arithmetic logic unit.

Bits and Bytes.   Actually, the CPU does not receive a signal that *is* "3." Rather, it receives a special code that *stands for* "3." This code consists of eight binary digits—**bits**—which together form a **byte**. A bit is either the digit *0* or the digit *1*. To understand how bits and bytes work, remember that the earliest computers had mechanical switches, much like the on/off light switches in your home. Although modern computers have no mechanical switches, the principle remains the same: The electronic signals tell the computer to set a particular switch in one of two positions (*binary* means *two*)—"on" or "off." In a computer, these two positions represent the flow— or lack of flow—of electricity.

bit

A way of representing data in a computer as one of two digits (0 or 1); abbreviation for binary digit.

Obviously, however, we need to signal many different letters, digits, and other symbols. A single "switch" (bit), therefore, is not enough. Taken together, a series of eight bits—a single byte—can represent any character on the computer keyboard. As the number "3," for example, you would be sent to the computer as a command to turn bits *1, 2, 3, 4, 7,* and *8* "on" and bits *5* and *6* "off." The binary code for "3" thus works out as *11110011*.

byte

A series of eight bits that, together, represent a character in a computer.

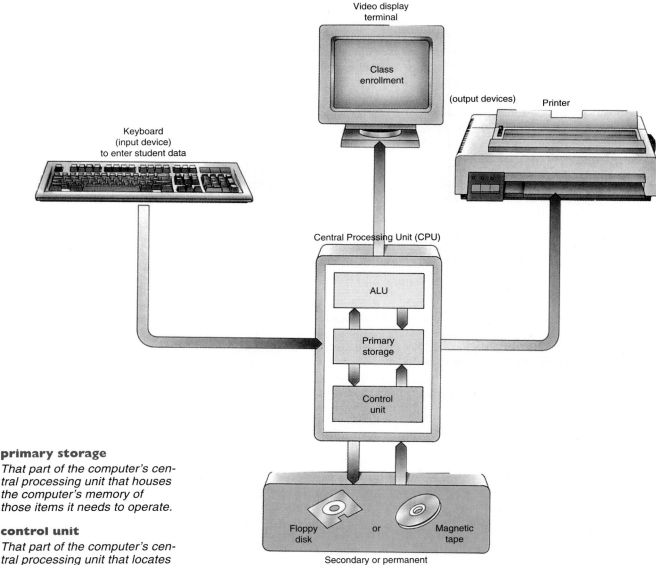

Figure 23.3
Components of a computer system.

primary storage

That part of the computer's central processing unit that houses the computer's memory of those items it needs to operate.

control unit

That part of the computer's central processing unit that locates instructions, transfers data to the arithmetic logic unit for processing, and transmits results to an output device.

program

Any sequence of instructions to a computer.

arithmetic logic unit (ALU)

That part of the computer's central processing unit that performs logical and mathematical operations such as addition, subtraction, multiplication, and division.

output device

That part of a computer's hardware that presents results to users; common forms include printers and cathode ray tube (CRT)/video display terminals (VDTs).

Primary Storage.   You are now inside the CPU in a form that the computer can handle. Now what happens? If you look around the inside of the CPU, you will find three major objects: the computer's primary storage, its control unit, and its arithmetic logic unit. As a piece of data, you must go first to **primary storage**—the part of the computer's CPU that houses its memory of those items that it needs in order operate.

Programs.   At this point, the computer's **control unit** searches through its memory for instructions—**programs**—on what to do with you. Using the appropriate instructions, it then sends you to the **arithmetic logic unit (ALU)**, where (as the name implies) logical functions and calculations (addition, subtraction, multiplication, and division) take place. When the ALU is done with you, the control unit again takes over. It sends the results into one or more **output devices**—a cathode ray tube (CRT) more appropriately known as a *video display terminal (VDT)* and/or a printer.

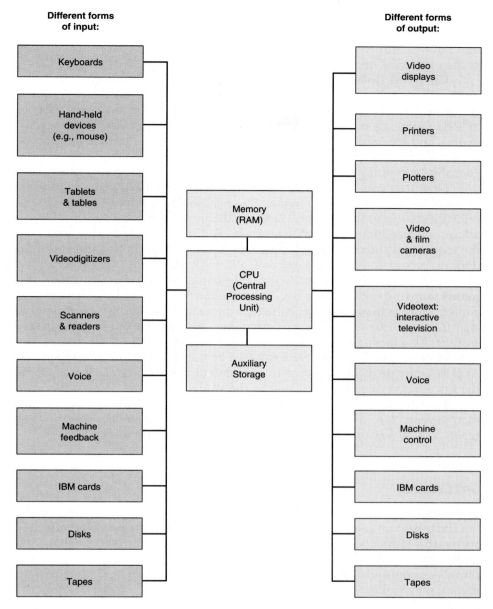

Different forms of input:

- Keyboards
- Hand-held devices (e.g., mouse)
- Tablets & tables
- Videodigitizers
- Scanners & readers
- Voice
- Machine feedback
- IBM cards
- Disks
- Tapes

Memory (RAM)

CPU (Central Processing Unit)

Auxiliary Storage

Different forms of output:

- Video displays
- Printers
- Plotters
- Video & film cameras
- Videotext: interactive television
- Voice
- Machine control
- IBM cards
- Disks
- Tapes

Figure 23.4
An overview of input and output.

random-access memory (RAM)
The computer's short term active memory that lasts only as long as the computer stays on.

secondary storage
Any medium that can be used to store computerized data and information outside the computer's primary storage mechanism; magnetic tape, floppy disks, and hard disks are common forms.

hard disks
Rigid metal disks permanently enclosed in the computer.

floppy disks
Portable disks that can be easily inserted into and removed from the computer.

Secondary Storage. If someone turned off the computer at this point, it would "forget" both the data (you) and information that resulted. Why? The computer's active memory is a short-term form of memory that lasts only as long as the computer stays on. This short-term memory is the main memory that is active when the computer does its work. It is also called **random-access memory (RAM)** because any part of it can be called upon for processing at any time.

Disks and ROM. For long-term memory, however, we need **secondary storage**. Magnetic tape, hard disks, and floppy disks can all be used for secondary storage. Digital data can be written into storage and retrieved (that is, "read") from storage by the user. **Hard disks** are rigid metal disks permanently enclosed in the computer. **Floppy disks** are portable and can be

read-only memory (ROM)
A portion of computer memory that can hold instructions that have been read by the computer; does not permit instructions to be written in.

CD-ROM disks
Look like music CDs but can hold as much data as 400 regular floppy disks.

easily inserted and removed. Another kind of data storage uses **read-only memory (ROM)**: a portion of computer memory which can hold instructions that have been *read* by the computer but which does not accept instructions *written* into that memory.

CD-ROM disks (for *compact disk—read only memory*) look just like music CDs and can hold as much data as 400 regular floppy disks. They are convenient for storing sound and video data but do not allow users to write new data onto them. Popular CD-ROMs include library materials, encyclopedias, and specialized scientific, medical, and technical tutorials that can be activated on newer PCs. For example, Microsoft's *Encarta* disc contains the complete text of the 29-volume Funk & Wagnall's New Encyclopedia.

Now that you have an inside view of computer hardware operations, let's look at things from the outside. Suppose you have a part-time job in the registrar's office at your school. Let's say that a student requests information about an introductory accounting class. You insert a floppy disk and type the request on your keyboard—your link to the CPU. Although the keyboard does no processing itself, it lets you "talk" with the CPU.

Inside the CPU, the control unit takes over. It issues an electronic command that finds data about accounting classes in secondary storage and copies it into primary storage. Note that information is available for use *only after it has been transferred into primary storage*, never while it is in secondary storage. Also moved to primary storage is a program that tells the computer how to search through course listings. The control unit then instructs the ALU to locate the necessary data in primary storage and search through it for the introductory course requested by the student.

Finally, the control unit transfers the results to primary storage and then to your VDT. In a matter of seconds, you can tell the student that the class meets at 8:30 A.M. every day and that three seats are still open.

Software

software
Programs that instruct the computer in what to do and how to do it.

system program
A program that tells a computer what resources to use and how to use them.

application program
A program that actually processes data according to a particular user's specific needs.

While hardware is a vital component of a computer system, it is useless without the other components. As you have just seen, hardware needs programs—**software**—to function. Canada's software industry made profits of about $500 million in 1991, but it may also have lost as much as $200 million to software pirates—people who make illegal copies of computer software. The problem is that, with millions of individuals copying software, it is hard to know the magnitude of the problem or to catch anyone.[4]

There are basically two types of programs: system programs and application programs. **System programs** tell the computer what resources to use and how to use them. For example, an operating system program tells the computer how and when to transfer data from secondary storage to primary storage and return information to the user. You have probably heard of DOS, the *d*isk *o*perating *s*ystem used by the IBM PC and its clones.

Language programs, another type of system program, allow computer users to give the machine their own instructions. Table 23.1 lists some of the most common computer languages and their primary fields of use.

In contrast, **application programs** actually process data according to the special needs of the particular user. A computer system usually has only one operating system program, but it may use many application programs. Application programs run payroll, act as word processors, and play games. Programs such as Lotus 1-2-3 and WordPerfect are application programs. (See Figure 23.5 for an example.) We will consider the types of application programs most often used in business later in this chapter.

Writing software programs requires painstaking work and thousands of lines of commands. As software programs have become more complex, the time needed to write all these commands is becoming excessive. **Object-oriented technology** reduces these demands by dividing programs into small, reusable chunks of code (objects) with standard interfaces. Programmers can fit the objects together in different configurations as they write different programs. It's like building a house with Lego blocks instead of doing it molecule by molecule.[5]

object-oriented technology
Reduces the complexity of writing software programs by dividing the programs into reusable chunks with standard interfaces.

Graphic User Interface.   One of the most popular software developments in recent years is the **graphic user interface (GUI)**—the user-friendly visual display that helps users select from among the many possible applications on the computer. Typically, the screen displays numerous bright boxes with animated characters representing such choices as Word Processing, Graphics, DOS, Fax, Printing, or Games. A pointing device (usually an arrow) is moved around the screen to activate the desired box. Colorful printed text presents simple instructions for using activated features.

    Before the Macintosh first popularized the GUI, new users were often frustrated in their attempts to *interface* with computers—that is, in figuring out how to copy a disk, write a program in a given language, create graphs, or use the computer's many other capabilities. Prior to GUI, interfaces were standard letters, numbers, and keyboard symbols that appeared on the video screen. For most people, they required long hours of computer practice and extensive reading of users manuals to become familiar with computers. Today, just one of the GUI software packages, Microsoft Windows, has found 55 million customers because it simplifies computer use while actually making it fun.

graphic user interface (GUI)
The user-friendly display that helps users select from among the many possible applications of the computer.

TABLE 23.1   Computer Languages and Fields of Use

Language	Primarily Used By	Advantages	Disadvantages
ADA	Military, government	Efficient, meets govt. standard	Complex; still experimental
BASIC	Education, business, hobbyists	Very easy to learn and run; good on systems with many users	Not powerful; not flexible; cumbersome in solving complex problems
C	System programming	Fast, powerful; created by a programmer for programmers	Hard for beginners; few helps to correct errors
COBOL	Business	Organizes data for easy access and manipulation	Limited math function; not easy for nonprogrammers to use
FORTRAN	Engineering, science	Rapid calculation of large numbers	Awkward, difficult to learn
LOGO	Education	Users can create own commands; good graphics	No standard version; often considered a "child's language"
LISP	Artificial intelligence	Good symbol manipulation; imitates human thought better than most	Expensive; existence of many dialects makes it hard to read program written by others
PASCAL	Education	Structured nature teaches good programming habits; makes reviewing and debugging easy	Primarily taught to teach idea of programming, not used for much actual programming
PL/1	Science, business	Designed to meet needs of general-purpose audience	Unwieldy; difficult to use; cannot handle logic programming

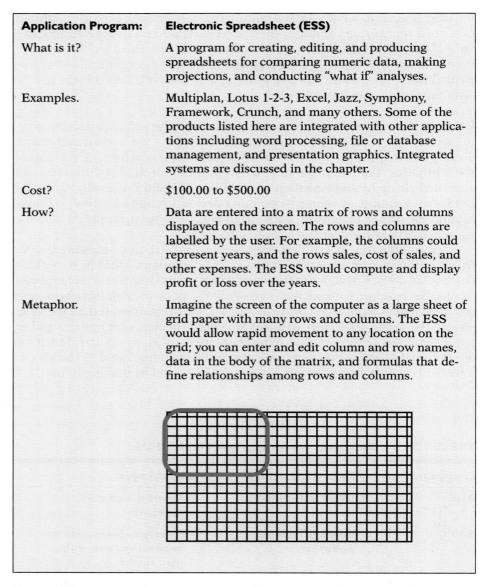

Application Program:	Electronic Spreadsheet (ESS)
What is it?	A program for creating, editing, and producing spreadsheets for comparing numeric data, making projections, and conducting "what if" analyses.
Examples.	Multiplan, Lotus 1-2-3, Excel, Jazz, Symphony, Framework, Crunch, and many others. Some of the products listed here are integrated with other applications including word processing, file or database management, and presentation graphics. Integrated systems are discussed in the chapter.
Cost?	$100.00 to $500.00
How?	Data are entered into a matrix of rows and columns displayed on the screen. The rows and columns are labelled by the user. For example, the columns could represent years, and the rows sales, cost of sales, and other expenses. The ESS would compute and display profit or loss over the years.
Metaphor.	Imagine the screen of the computer as a large sheet of grid paper with many rows and columns. The ESS would allow rapid movement to any location on the grid; you can enter and edit column and row names, data in the body of the matrix, and formulas that define relationships among rows and columns.

Figure 23.5
Creating spreadsheets with applications software.

People

We think—and speak—of computer systems as if they were only hardware and software. In large part, however, a computer system is a function of the people who construct and use it. The people in a computer system can be divided into three categories: *programming personnel, operations personnel,* and *end users*.

Programming Personnel.   Programming personnel include both systems analysts and applications or systems programmers:

- *Systems analysts* deal with the entire computer system. They work with users to learn their requirements and then design systems to meet them. Generally, they decide upon the type of computer, its size, and how to link it to all the users who will use the system.
- Using various language programs, *programmers* write the instructions that tell computers what to do. *Applications programmers*, for example,

write the instructions to address particular problems. *Systems programmers* ensure that a system can handle the requests made by various applications programs.

Operations Personnel.   Individuals who run the computer equipment are called *operations personnel*: They make sure that the right programs are run in the correct sequence and monitor equipment to ensure that it is operating properly. Many organizations also have *data-entry clerks* who key data into the system for processing.

End Users.   Finally, *end users* employ the system to obtain information needed for their jobs. For example, a marketing manager who needs weekly reports on expenses for personal selling promotions is an end user of a company's system. As we noted earlier, many programmers today realize that effective systems can be created only if intended users play a part in designing them.

Although programming personnel, operations personnel, and end users are the people inside the computer system, other people benefit from computers. For example, you benefit when your bank teller can tell you your balance quickly. And individuals who service computers benefit from the employment. But many employees are concerned about what impact computers will have on them (see Table 23.2). Management must address these concerns.

TABLE 23.2   Attitudes Toward Computer Technology

The Technology	Attitude Expressed
1. May replace me.	Obsolescence
2. May be used to exploit me.	Exploitation
3. May be used to invade my privacy.	Privacy
4. Is vaguely threatening.	Technophobia
5. May involve me too deeply.	Technophilia
6. May become a "crutch."	Dependence
7. May generate too much information.	Overload
8. May depersonalize me.	Informediation[*]
9. May change me.	Media-as-message
10. May take too much time.	Opportunity-cost

[*]A term coined to refer to human communication mediated by information technology (telephone, computer).

Control

The fourth component of a computer system is control. *Control* ensures that the system is operating according to specific procedures and within specific guidelines. These procedures include guidelines for operating the system, the responsibilities of the personnel involved with it, and plans for dealing with system failure. For example, a key aspect of information management is controlling two groups of individuals: those who have access to input or change its data and those who receive the output from it. Thus most firms limit access to salary information. Control procedures are usually detailed in company manuals and often designate protected "passwords" for gaining system access.

Problems of Privacy.   "Breaking and entering" no longer refers merely to physical intrusions into one's home or business. Today, it applies to computer-system intrusions as well. In this section, we will describe the three most common forms of computer intrusion: *privacy invasion, viruses,* and *piracy.* We will also discuss some of the methods that companies use to provide security for their information systems.[6]

privacy invasion

Intruders gain unauthorized access to computers in order to steal information or tamper with data.

In the computer world, **privacy invasion** occurs in two forms. First, intruders gain unauthorized access, either to steal information, money, or property or to tamper with data. We have all read, for instance, about computer "hackers" who have gained access to school systems to change grades. Others have invaded government databases to sabotage data, and still others have broken into stock brokerage databases to access the private transaction records of individual clients. One high school student stole more than $1 million in software from AT&T's computer system, and it is estimated that billions of dollars are embezzled electronically every year by intruders who alter data and shift funds from corporate and government accounts. One such intruder illegally transferred $10 million from one bank to another. Other intruders have been convicted of taking unauthorized information from computers and selling it to other governments and companies.

A second form of intrusion involves passing a computer "virus" into the system. **Viruses** are harmful programs created and spread by vandals seeking to destroy or disrupt computer operations. In effect, the virus is an unwanted "disease" that spreads from computer to computer, damaging data, programs, and even hardware.

viruses

Harmful programs created and spread by vandals seeking to destroy or disrupt computer operations.

While some viruses erase databases or programs immediately, others spread slowly like a cancer. Some may even lie dormant for weeks before suddenly activating. Viruses can be transmitted electronically from one system to another and can be distributed by virus-infected disks. Today, virus-protecting software is widely available for scanning incoming computer disks before they are introduced into a user's system.

computer piracy

The unauthorized copying of software programs.

Piracy.   **Computer piracy** is the unauthorized copying of software. As we saw in the opening case, some users ignore the law, illegally copying programs for friends and family who then do not have to purchase the software.

Another form of piracy involves proprietary software for special applications. For example one company's computer staff may develop its own program for computer-aided design. Piracy occurs when it stolen from the developer company and illegally sold to other firms. A third form of piracy occurs when a buyer distributes unauthorized copies of software throughout the company. Most software suppliers offer **site-license agreements** that authorize companywide use of software in return for a fee.

site-license agreement

Authorizes company-wide use of a software package in return for a fee.

Security.   Security measures for protection against intrusion and piracy are a constant challenge for many firms. To prevent unlawful modification of software, codewords allowing access to it can be changed periodically. The activities of users can also be monitored, and some procedures require second-person confirmation before any one person can make changes in software programs.

Protection for data files and databases is not foolproof and typically involves making backup copies to be stored outside the computer system, usually in a safe. Thus if system files are damaged, they can be replaced by backup. Data communications can be intercepted during transit from one location to another. To prevent interception, transmission signals can be *scrambled* so that only those with deciphering codes can read them. The most common measure for virus protection is a program called a *vaccine.*

Finally, the most important factor in communications security is the *people* in the system. At most firms, therefore, procedures carefully control access to the system's components. Personnel are trained in the responsibilities of computer use and often apprised of the penalties for violating system security. For example, each time the computer boots up, a notice displays the warning that software and data are protected and spells out penalties for unauthorized use.

Data

Chunks of data—numbers, words, and sentences—are stored in fields, records, and files. Figure 23.6 presents the various levels of data as they might be structured for customers of Artists' Frame Service. All the files together are the **data base**—a centralized collection of related data.

Once data are entered into the data base, they can be *processed*—manipulated, sorted, combined, and/or compared. Data can be processed in a batch mode or a real-time mode. Neither mode is generally superior to the other. The "better" mode depends on the characteristics of the particular problem to be solved. In fact, many companies use both modes at different times.

In **batch processing**, operations personnel collect data over some time period and then process that data as a group or batch. The key aspect of batch processing is that the data are not processed at the time they are collected. For example, payroll is usually run in a batch mode. Few of us get paid the same hour or even the same day we earn the money. Rather, we get paid weekly, biweekly, or monthly. The data (hours) are accumulated over the pay period and processed all at one time. Batch processing was the only mode available on early computers and is still widely used.

Today, however, companies have choices about processing modes. Instead of batch processing, they can use a real-time (on-line) system. End users feed data into the computer in **real-time processing**, and the data are processed instantly. Real-time processing is always used when the results of each entry affect subsequent entries. For example, if you book seat F6 on Air Canada flight 253 on December 23, the computer must thereafter keep other passengers from booking the same seat.

data base
A centralized, organized collection of related data.

batch processing
A method of transforming data into information in which data are collected over a period of time and then processed as a group or batch.

real-time processing
A method of transforming data into information in which data are entered and processed immediately.

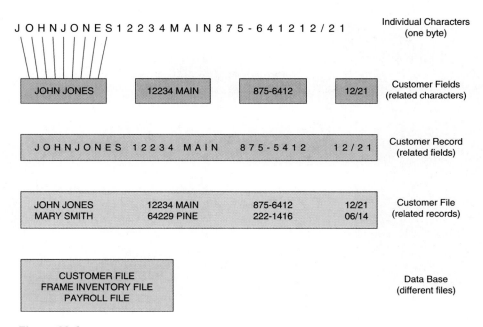

Figure 23.6
Levels of data for a data base.

Computer Application Programs for Business

Increasingly inexpensive equipment and software have made computers an irresistible option for businesses of all types and sizes. Programs are available for a huge variety of business-related tasks. Some of these programs address such common, long-standing needs as accounting, payroll, and inventory control. Others have been developed for application to an endless variety of specialized needs. Most applications programs used by businesses fall into one of four categories: *word processing, spreadsheets, database management,* and *graphics*. Seventy percent of all PC software applications are designed for the first three types of programs.[7]

Word Processing Programs

word processing

Application programs that allow the computer to act as a sophisticated typewriter to store, edit, and print letters and numbers.

Many companies use **word processing**, which allows the computer to act as a sophisticated typewriter. Word processing programs make it easy to correct mistakes or revise quickly. Sentences or paragraphs can be added or deleted without retyping or restructuring the entire document. Word processing has greatly increased productivity in many companies.

Word processing also means that mailing lists and form letters can be prepared quickly and easily. As a result, you and millions of other consumers now get letters from advertisers that appear to be directed specifically at you. Word, WordPerfect, and DisplayWrite are three popular word-processing programs.

Spreadsheet Programs

electronic spreadsheet

Application programs that allow the user to enter categories of data and determine the effect of changes in one category (e.g., sales) on other categories (e.g., profits).

Worksheets called **electronic spreadsheets** spread across and down a page in columns and rows. The user enters data, including formulas, at row and column intersections, and the computer automatically does the calculations. Balance sheets, income statements, and a host of other financial reports can be prepared using these programs.

These are some of the most widely used computer application programs.

	A	B
1	EXPENSES %	60
2	TAX %	20
3	SALES $	300.00
4		
5	SALES $	300.00
6	EXPENSES $	180.00
7	INCOME $	120.00
8	TAX $	24.00
9	NET PROFIT $	96.00

	A	B
1	EXPENSES %	70
2	TAX %	20
3	SALES $	300.00
4		
5	SALES $	300.00
6	EXPENSES $	210.00
7	INCOME $	90.00
8	TAX $	18.00
9	NET PROFIT $	72.00

Figure 23.7
This spreadsheet shows what happens to income, taxes, and net profit if operating expenses rise from 60 to 70 percent of sales.

Spreadsheets are also a useful planning tool, because they allow managers to see how changing one item will affect other related items. For example, as Figure 23.7 shows, a manager can insert various operating cost percentages, tax rates, or sales revenues. The computer will automatically recalculate all of the other figures and determine net profit.

Since they are helpful for investigating changes, spreadsheets can be used in building *decision support systems* (see Chapter 11). Popular spreadsheet packages include Lotus 1-2-3 and Excel.

Data-base Management Programs

As the name implies, **data-base management** programs can keep track of all relevant data in a business. They can sort and search through data and integrate a single piece of data into several files. For example, Figure 23.8 illustrates a small data base integrating customer picture-framing orders and an inventory file for Artists' Frame Service.

In addition to producing standardized reports, data-base management programs can supply answers to one-time questions such as "What are the names of the students who failed English Composition last term?" or "What was our most popular product last year?" Examples of data-base management programs include DBase IV and RBase System V for personal computers and Total and IMS for mainframes.

In addition to "home grown" or *primary data bases*, a company may decide to use external, or *secondary data bases*. Secondary data bases can be broad or narrow. Nexis is a secondary data base of news and financial information that draws on over 100 newspapers, newsletters, magazines, and wire services such as Associated Press. Lexis is a secondary data base that deals solely with legal materials. Dow Jones News/Retrieval offers business and economic news headlines, including highlights from *The Wall Street Journal*.

The popularity of secondary data bases has grown because they are easy to use and can provide information on factors outside the company. Using a personal computer with a **modem**, a computer-to-computer link via telephone lines, a user can search for articles based on key words. A restaurant chain, for example, could query Nexis to locate information on consumer preferences for Mexican food.

data-base management
Application programs that keep track of and manipulate the relevant data of a business.

modem
A hardware device permitting the user of a personal computer to link up with other computer systems via telephone lines.

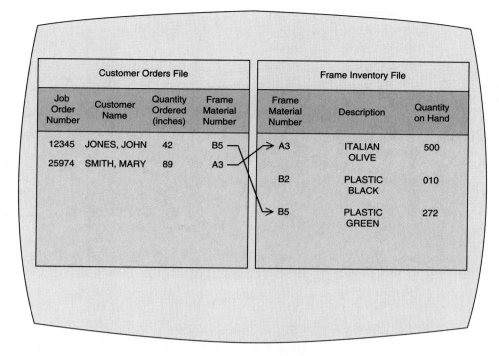

Figure 23.8
The two files are integrated in the data base. New customer orders reduce the on-hand inventories of frame materials.

Graphics

computer graphics programs
Application programs that convert numerical and character data into pictorial forms.

desktop publishing
Combines word processing and graphics capability in producing typeset-quality text from personal computers.

Computer-graphics programs convert numeric and character data into pictorial information such as charts and graphs. These programs make computerized information easier to use and understand in two ways. First, graphs and charts summarize data and allow managers to detect problems, opportunities, and relationships more easily. Second, graphics are valuable in creating clearer and more persuasive reports and presentations.

Some of the latest software for **desktop publishing** combines word-processing and graphics capability in producing typeset-quality text from personal computers. Quark XPress, for example, is able to manipulate text, graphics, and full-color photographs. Desktop publishing eliminates costly printing services for reports and proposals, and Quark is also used by advertising agencies where computer-generated designs offer greater control over color and format.

Two of the most common graphics displays are the pie chart and the bar graph. As Figure 23.9 shows, both types of graphics can convey different kinds of information—in this case, the type of framing materials that should be ordered by a picture-framing shop like Artists' Frame Service. Both types of graphs are more likely to help a manager make decisions than the stack of numbers on which they are based.

Computer graphics capabilities extend beyond mere data presentation. They also include stand-alone programs for artists, designers, and special effects designers. Everything from simple drawings to fine art, television commercials, and motion-picture special effects are now created by computer graphics-software.[8] The realism of the dinosaurs in *Jurassic Park* and the physical appearance of the legless Vietnam veteran in *Forrest Gump* are special effects created with computer graphics.

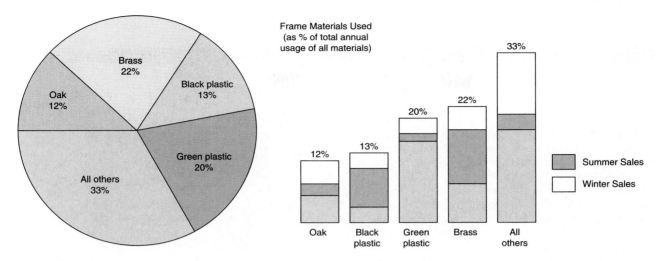

Figure 23.9
Both the pie chart and the bar graph show that four frame materials are the most used, but the bar graph also shows that brass and black plastic are most popular in winter.

Types of Computer Systems

Although all computer systems share the common elements of hardware, software, control, people, and data, not all computer systems are alike. Computer systems vary dramatically in their overall size, capacity, and cost, as well as in how their elements are put together.

Categorizing Computer Systems

One way of grouping computer systems is by their cost, capacity, and capability. This approach results in four basic categories of computer systems: microcomputers, minicomputers, mainframes, and supercomputers.

Microcomputers.   The smallest computers, **microcomputers** (also called personal computers), range in cost from a few hundred dollars to around $25 000. Most of the computers you see sitting on desks are micros. Well-known brands include the IBM-PC, the Apple Macintosh, and the Compaq. Rapid changes have already led to even smaller computers (see the box "A Different Type of Downsizing").

Floppy disks were originally the only form of secondary storage available on micros. Now, virtually any microcomputer system can have a hard disk attached to it. Hard disks offer several advantages over floppies. First, they are more convenient. Each time you run a different program or application using floppy disks, you must physically take one disk out and replace it with another. A hard disk can store multiple programs and a simple command can call up the one you need for a particular application. Moreover, while the typical floppy holds only 720 000 to 1.4 million characters, hard disks hold up to 400 million characters. Hard disks can also retrieve and process data faster than a floppy disk. Because of these advantages, many firms are replacing their larger computers with smaller ones, shifting the balance of computer power to smaller systems.[9]

Minicomputers.   Larger, faster, and more sophisticated than microcomputers, **minicomputers** range in cost from around $25 000 upward. While

microcomputer
The smallest, slowest, and least expensive form of computer available today; sometimes called a personal computer.

minicomputer
A computer whose capacity, speed, and cost fall between those of microcomputers and mainframes.

The Canadian Business Scene

A DIFFERENT TYPE OF DOWNSIZING

In a way, you could view the history of computers as an "incredible shrinking story." The earliest computers, despite their limited abilities, were huge—about the size of an average house. But over the years, machines have become smaller and smaller, and many companies have moved from mainframes to minicomputers to the micro-computers (PCs) found on desks in most companies.

Yet the trend toward "downsizing" continues, with the latest crop of computerized wonders making the standard PC look like an elephant. First came the *laptops*, computers weighing between 8 and 20 pounds and about the size of a small briefcase. With laptops, businesspeople could for the first time literally take their offices with them. Sales staff could hook into their firms' main computers via modem and get the latest prices and place orders.

Laptops had barely begun to get a foothold in the market when the next wave of even smaller machines hit. Called *notebooks*, these variations on the microcomputer are about the size of a notebook—approximately 8 1/2 by 11 inches—and weigh 4 to 7 pounds. Despite the difficulties of typing on a somewhat smaller keyboard, many businesspeople have embraced notebook computers, thrilled to be able to tuck the units into a briefcase and avoid carrying an extra piece of luggage on trips.

The future appears to be even smaller. Consider the latest in computer miniaturization—*palmtops*. As the name implies, these mini-minicomputers fit into the palm of your hand, measuring as little as 8 inches by 4 inches by 1 inch thick and weighing in at only 11 to 19 *ounces*. Yet these miniature marvels offer standard (albeit tiny) 25-line-by-80-character screens. They come with 512 RAM, hard drives, and a host of built-in programs (including the popular Lotus 1-2-3). And with the aid of special connecting cables, palmtops can be connected to other computers, printers, and modems. While their miniature keyboards make touch typ-

ing impossible, palmtops can be tucked into a jacket pocket and taken anywhere—from the oil fields to the board room—and can be used to make notes, revise spreadsheets, and check important data on the spot. Fold-up keyboards are now available which allow the computer to be very small, but which still permit standard touch typing once the keyboard is unfolded.

Can computers get much smaller? Improvements in computer chips mean that some further reductions in the size of the processing operation may be possible, even as tiny computers become more and more powerful. Furthermore, the introduction of pen-based technologies—in which users just "write" information into the computer—may banish keyboard size as an issue. Screens probably cannot be made much smaller (though they may get thinner and lighter), but with scientists at work teaching computers to accept spoken commands and data, perhaps someday the computer will simply talk back.

---

micros typically process only tens of thousands of instructions per second, minis can process over a million instructions per second (MIPS.) Minis can also support multiple users and provide much more storage than micros do.

mainframe
A computer whose capacity, speed, and cost fall between those of minicomputers and supercomputers.

Mainframes. Still bigger and faster are **mainframes**. Costing a million or more dollars, they can store and access billions of characters, not the thousands or millions of characters in micros and minis. Mainframes also process tens of millions of instructions per second. Because of their speed and capacity, mainframes are most often found in banks, other large commercial organizations, and universities where large volumes of data must be processed.

supercomputer
The largest, fastest, and most expensive form of computer available today.

Supercomputers. The largest, fastest, and most expensive of all computers are the **supercomputers**. They are used mainly in scientific applications where large numbers of complex calculations need to be performed quickly. In part because of their cost—over 5 million dollars—fewer than 150 of these systems are currently in actual operation. Table 23.3 summarizes the distinctions between the four categories of computer systems.

TABLE 23.3   Classes of Computers

Size	Example	Processing Range (instructions per second)	Operating Speed
Micro	Apple-Macintosh; IBM PC-XT; HP-85	Up to .1 MIPS*	Milliseconds
Mini	DEC VAX-11/780; HP 3000/64	.1 to 3 MIPS	Microseconds
Mainframe	IBM 370/158; NCR 9300	.5 to 30 MIPS	Nanoseconds
Supercomputer	CYBER 205	20 MIPS and up	Nanoseconds, picaseconds

*Million instructions per second

Systems Architecture

While differences in computer capacity and ability are shrinking, systems *architecture* has remained a fairly constant feature. **Systems architecture** refers to the location of the various parts of the system—its data-entry and data-processing operations, database, data output, and computer staff. System architecture is classified according to the organization of a system's parts.

Centralized Systems.   In a **centralized system**, most of the processing is done in one location. For example, all of a bank's branch teller machines need the same information. Thus they are all hooked up to the main-office mainframe, which houses all customer-information files in a central database. Centralized systems do have drawbacks: For example, when the central computer fails or communication lines to it go down, all the branches also go down.

Decentralized Systems.   In a **decentralized system**, each location determines the needs of its own system—physical components, programs, databases, personnel. Locations are independent of centralized mainframes, and there are no communication links between locations. A drawback arises when different locations independently adopt incompatible components and/or programs. It may then become difficult or impossible for systems at separate locations to share important data.

Networks.   At the same time, however, *networking* now allows computers to exchange data quickly and easily. A **computer network** is a group of interconnected systems that can exchange information among several different locations. Networks may link computers statewide or even nationwide through telephone wires or satellites, as in **wide area networks**. Wal-Mart stores, for example, invested more than $20 million on a satellite network that links more than 2000 retail stores to its Bentonville, Arkansas, headquarters.

Internal networks may link computers through cables, as in **local area networks** (**LANs**). The computers in internal networks share processing duties,

systems architecture
The way in which a computer system's data entry, data processing, data base, data output, and computer staff are located.

centralized system
A form of computer system architecture in which all processing is done in one location using a centralized data base and computer staff.

decentralized system
A form of computer system architecture in which processing is done in many locations using separate data bases and computer staffs.

computer network
A form of computer system architecture in which computers at different locations can function independently but are also interconnected and able to exchange information with one another.

wide area network
System to link computers across the country through telephone wires or satellites.

local area network (LAN)
System to link computers in one building or in a small geographical area by cable.

software, storage areas, and data. On television's *Home Shopping Network*, for example, hundreds of operators seated at monitors in a large room are united by a LAN for entering call-in orders from customers. This arrangement allows the use of a single computer system with one database and software system.

Combination systems using local and wide area networks are also possible. For example, separate plants or offices might handle orders locally while electronically transmitting sales summaries to a corporate office. Computer networks thus give companies the advantages of both centralized and decentralized processing.

Server-Client Systems. Over the years, components and features were simply added on to mainframe systems, increasing capacity without meeting the need for greater flexibility. Consequently, many companies now find their old mainframe systems outmoded. In addition, systems have become overcustomized, and reprogramming mainframes to respond to new formats is expensive and time-consuming. In order to construct systems that will support such innovative management techniques as just-in-time inventory and total quality management, many companies are thus "downsizing"— switching from mainframe to more adaptable, cost-effective LANs systems.

Although some LANs systems are specialized, they are shared to avoid costly, unnecessary duplication. Any component that can be shared by LAN users is called a **server**. The powerful minicomputer at the network hub, for example, may be the server for the surrounding **client PCs** in the network.

server
Any component that can be shared by LAN users.

client PC
Personal computers that are part of a LAN.

More specifically, it may act as either a *file server* or a *print server*. As a file server, the mini has a large-capacity disk for storing the programs and data shared by all the PCs in the network. It will thus contain customer files plus the database, word-processing, and spreadsheet programs that may be called upon when needed by clients. As a print server, the mini controls the printer, stores printing requests from client PCs, and routes jobs to the printer as it becomes available. Only one main memory and one printer, therefore, are needed for an entire system.

A Short History of Computer Systems

The kinds of computer systems and architecture we have just described are only the latest in a long line. Computer systems have changed greatly over the years, both in their physical appearance and in their abilities.

The Earliest Calculating Machines

Computers as we know them have existed for fewer than fifty years, but the concept of a mechanical device to aid humans in computations is much older. In 1823, British mathematician Charles Babbage, often known as the Father of Computers, invented his "differential engine," a simple mechanical device designed to do calculations. Although Babbage never got a model of his idea actually to work, his design was the basis of later, successful, computers.

The first working calculating machine was developed by Herman Hollerith to tabulate the results of the 1890 U.S. census. Results from the 1880 census had not become available until 1888. Clearly, the census bureau needed a way to count the 1890 census faster and more accurately. Hollerith responded with an electromechanical device that used punched holes to represent data and processed the 1890 census in only six weeks. Hollerith eventually sold his invention to a company that became IBM.

The First Generation

After Hollerith's success, other inventors built bigger, faster electromechanical machines, culminating in the Mark I computer developed by IBM's Howard Aiken and the U.S. Navy. But the first true electronic (nonmechanical) computer did not come until 1946, when the *Electronic Numerical Integrator and Computer* (ENIAC) was completed. During the period 1947 to 1951, scientists at the University of Toronto, funded by the National Research Council, built UTEC (University of Toronto Electronic Computer).

Like other machines in the *first generation* of computers, ENIAC replaced mechanical switches with glass vacuum tubes. Dubbed the "giant brain" by the newspapers, it was certainly a giant in size. It used 17 468 vacuum tubes, took up 170 square metres—about as much space as an average house—and weighed in at 27 tonnes. It was also 1600 times faster than any previous machine (though much slower than a modern personal computer)—when it worked. Problems with the vacuum tubes were common. One problem actually added a new term to the field, **debugging**. It seems that programmers of the ENIAC had to remove bugs—the bodies of moths attracted to the warm vacuum tubes—before the computer would function. Today debugging simply refers to removing problems from a program so that it runs smoothly.

An even greater problem with ENIAC's vacuum tubes was their tendency to burn out completely. In developing its UNIVAC computer, Sperry was able to reduce, but not eliminate, this burnout. Nevertheless, in 1954, the UNIVAC became the first computer installed by a business, when General Electric purchased a unit for one of its plants.

debugging
Removing problems from a program.

The Second Generation

Another hardware advance brought into being the next generation of computers. In 1959, scientists at Bell Laboratories developed the **transistor**. Far more reliable than vacuum tubes, transistors also made *second-generation* computers many times faster than their predecessors. In addition, these machines had much more memory available. Programming was made easier by more sophisticated languages such as Cobol. The IBM 1401 was the most popular second-generation computer.

transistor
A compact electronic switch that amplifies and controls electric current; its application marked the start of the second generation of computers.

The Third Generation

Hardware changes also led to a *third computer generation*. In 1969, IBM unveiled the first computer in its 460 line. Transistors had given way to **integrated circuits** as the state-of-the-art technology. A single integrated circuit could replace a large number of transistors in a *silicon chip* less than 30 millimetres square! Besides reducing the bulk of computers, the silicon chip sped up processing, reduced computer manufacturing costs, and made the computer even more reliable. Software for third-generation machines made use of their increased speed and memory.

integrated circuit
A group of transistors and circuits embedded in a silicon chip; its application marked the start of the third generation of computers.

The Fourth Generation

In 1971 the *fourth generation* of computers arrived with the first commercial introduction of the **microprocessor chip**. This chip contains the computer's central processing unit. Before this time, computers had specialized chips for logic, programming, etc. Intel Corporation's development of the microprocessor enabled all the computer's functions to be put on a single chip. Today many cars, watches, and televisions, among other items, use microprocessors.

microprocessor chip
A single silicon chip containing the central processing unit of a computer; its application marked the start of the fourth generation of computers.

large-scale integration (LSI)

The inclusion of many circuits with different functions on a single chip; its use is characteristic of fourth-generation computers.

very large-scale integration (VLSI)

The process of reducing the size of circuits on a silicon chip, enabling a small chip to hold many more circuits; VLSI chips are used in fourth-generation computers.

Continued miniaturization made it possible to put even more circuits on a single chip. The result is what is known as **large scale integration** (LSI) and **very large scale integration** (VLSI). LSI and VLSI enable software and printers to react more quickly with each other and with the computer. LSI and VLSI, coupled with improvements in software, have made fourth-generation computers faster, easier, and more appealing for nonprogrammers to use. In addition, the microprocessor made possible microcomputers, such as the Compaq, which have revolutionized the role of computers in business.[10] Figure 23.10 summarizes the four generations of computers. Table 23.4 lists the top ten high-tech companies in Canada.

Miniaturization: A First Step toward the Fifth Generation.   Although no one is sure what the next generation of computing will be like, the continuing miniaturizing of transistor circuits is creating—almost daily—new possibilities in both speed and storage capacity. A microprocessor's speed determines how fast

TABLE 23.4   The Top Ten High-Tech Companies in Canada, 1994 (ranked by sales)

Company	Sales (in millions)
1. IBM Canada Ltd.	$8449
2. Digital Equipment of Canada Ltd.	1563
3. Xerox Canada Inc.	1171
4. SHL Systemhouse Inc.	1160
5. Hewlett-Packard Canada Ltd.	1004
6. Newbridge Networks Corp.	736
7. Spar Aerospace Ltd.	571
8. Mitel Corp.	496
9. Apple Canada Inc.	416
10. AT&T Global Information Solutions Canada	297

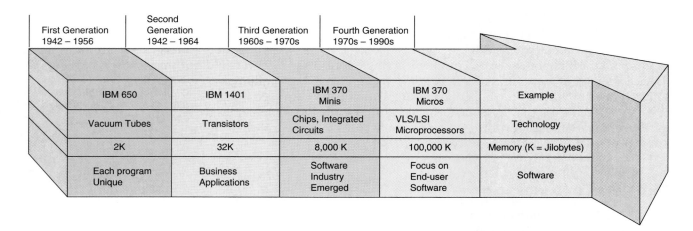

First Generation 1942 – 1956	Second Generation 1942 – 1964	Third Generation 1960s – 1970s	Fourth Generation 1970s – 1990s	
IBM 650	IBM 1401	IBM 370 Minis	IBM 370 Micros	Example
Vacuum Tubes	Transistors	Chips, Integrated Circuits	VLS/LSI Microprocessors	Technology
2K	32K	8,000 K	100,000 K	Memory (K = Jilobytes)
Each program Unique	Business Applications	Software Industry Emerged	Focus on End-user Software	Software

Figure 23.10
Rapid progress in computing places businesses under continual pressure to upgrade their computer systems.

it can process software instructions. Smaller circuit sizes mean that more transistors can be placed on a single silicon chip. They can also be placed closer together, and reduced distance means faster processing. If downsizing continues at current rates, even today's transistor sizes of less than a *micron* (one-millionth of a meter) will be goliaths compared to those expected in the future.

With miniaturization, the transistor circuits in memory chips are also smaller. More circuits per chip means much larger memory capacity. While today's capacities are measured in *megabits* (millions of bits), chip technology is fast approaching the *gigabit* (billion-bit) range. The 486-class chip common in today's PCs is more powerful than the mainframes of 1985. It is just one product of a computing power "explosion" that has been growing by a factor of four every three years since 1979; in other words, the performance of this year's PC is about four times that of the PC of just three years ago. And today's PC is priced lower.[11]

The Fifth Generation: The Marriage of Information and Communications Technology

Although the fifth generation of computing has not yet arrived, some of its foundation elements are here: *artificial intelligence, natural language dialogue between computers and users, expert systems, office automation*, and *executive information systems*. However, the most powerful vehicle for exploiting these elements to their full potential is the marriage of computers to communications technologies. Thanks to lower-cost, higher-capacity networks, the joining of computers, communications, and the mass media is already in its first stages.

This marriage promises to change the future face of business—indeed, of society itself. "Personal computing," observes Microsoft's Bill Gates, "was qualitatively a very, very different thing than the computing that came before. The advances in communication likewise will create new ways of using communication for learning, education, and commerce that go far beyond anything done to date." Thus both independently and through joint ventures, companies like Microsoft, AT&T, Oracle Corp., and Telecommunications Inc. are pursuing such products as personal digital assistants, digital TVs, and devices for tapping into high-band-width networks, multimedia information, and online services.[12] In this section, we will briefly discuss the progress of some of these projects that are already realities.

Artificial Intelligence

Artificial intelligence (**AI**) is the construction and programming of computers to imitate human thought processes. In developing components and programs for artificial intelligence, computer scientists are trying to design computers capable of reasoning so that computers, instead of people, can perform useful activities.

Robotics is just one category of AI. For example, IBM's Tape Library Dataserver, which is designed to serve giant companies that must store immense amounts of information, stores 42 trillion bytes of data. Data requests can be made from terminals in various departments. Cameras mounted on each robotic "hand" locate one out of almost 19 000 numbered tape cartridges. The robot then loads the cartridge into a reader that projects the information on the personal computer screen of a manager needing data on inventory, transactions, employees, or customers.[13]

artificial intelligence
The construction and/or programming of computers to imitate human thought processes.

IBM's Tape Library Dataserver stores 42 trillion bytes of data.

With their "reasoning" capabilities, such robots can "learn" repetitive tasks such as painting, assembling components, and inserting screws. Furthermore, they avoid repeating mistakes by "remembering" the causes of past mistakes and, when those causes reappear, adjusting or stopping until adjustments are made.

Computer scientists are also designing AI systems which possess sensory capabilities (vision with lasers, as well as hearing and feeling). In addition, when machines are ultimately able to process natural languages, humans will be able to give instructions and ask questions without learning special computer languages. In fact, Oracle Corp., the leading supplier of database software for minicomputers and servers, has already introduced software, called ConText, that understands such natural-language instructions as "Get my broker on the phone." When machines learn to reason on the basis of natural-language inputs, they may even be able to learn from experience and apply their learning to solve new problems.[14]

Expert Systems

expert system

A form of artificial intelligence in which a program draws on the rules an expert in a given field has laid out in order to arrive at a solution for a problem.

A special form of artificial intelligence programs, **expert systems** try to imitate the behavior of human experts in a particular field. Expert systems thus make available the rules that an expert applies to specific types of problems. In effect, they supply everyday users with "instant expertise."

Many firms already use expert systems for training and analysis:

- The Digital Equipment salesforce, for example, uses a system called Xcon to match customer needs with the most appropriate combination of computer input, output, and memory devices. Almost as if they were accompanied by expert sales advisors, salespeople receive one-of-a-kind equipment suggestions that the system has tailored to each customer's specific requirements.[15]
- Northern Telecom uses a system called Engineering Change Manager to simplify and speed up product design changes. The system considers such factors as a component's strength requirements, shape, appearance, and cost. It then creates the suggested redesigns to meet all the requirements. The new designs are then given to engineers, who can compare them to their own designs for better, faster product improvements.[16]

Office Automation

Office automation refers to the computer-based devices and applications whose function is to enhance the performance of general office activities.[17] In this section, we will survey three of the most solidly entrenched innovations in today's automated office: *fax machines, voice mail,* and *e-mail.*

Fax Machines.   **Fax machines** (short for *facsimile-transceiver machines*) can transmit text documents (and even drawings) over telephone lines in a matter of seconds, thus permitting written communication over long distances. Fax machines are popular with both large and small firms because of speed and low cost.

fax machine
A machine that can quickly transmit a copy of documents or graphics over telephone lines.

Voice Mail.   **Voice mail** is a computer-based system for receiving and delivering incoming telephone calls. Incoming calls are never missed when the phone owner is absent because a voice responds to the caller and invites a message, stores it, and delivers it when instructed to do so by the callee. A company with voice mail has each employee's phone networked for receiving, storing, and forwarding calls.

Voice mail consists of software that links the communications device (telephone) with the computer. The input from the telephone is sent to the computer, which digitizes the voice data and stores it on a disk. The employee can then call the voice-mail center to retrieve from storage a recording of waiting calls and voice messages.

voice mail
A computer-based system for receiving and delivering incoming telephone calls.

E-Mail.   An **electronic mail** (or **e-mail**) system electronically transmits letters, reports, and other information between computers, whether in the same building or across the country. Thus they substitute for the flood of paper and telephone calls that threatens to engulf many offices. They are, however, expensive and generally found only in large, technically sophisticated companies. Some potential problems with e-mail are described in the box "Information Overload on E-mail."

A new type of software—called **groupware**—is changing the nature of personal computing. The simplest and most familiar groupware is e-mail, but more sophisticated groupware programs function like an electronic conference room where many people can converse at once. Groupware allows people from all levels in the organization to "talk" together, and people may be judged more on what they say than on their rank in the hierarchy. Groupware may therefore end up changing corporate culture and reducing the impact of the classic organizational hierarchy.[18]

electronic mail (e-mail)
Electronic transmission of letters, reports, and other information between computers.

groupware
System that allows two or more individuals to communicate electronically between desktop PCs.

Executive Information Systems

Executive information systems (EIS) are quick-reference, easy-access information clusters especially designed for instant access by upper-level managers. Business planning, strategy sessions, and competitive evaluations depend on retrieving information conveniently by senior-level managers who, typically, are not computer-oriented and do not possess technical computer skills. An EIS is easily accessible with simple, unintimidating keyboard strokes or even voice commands. The system predetermines and prepares for access the types of data of special interest to the senior manager—for instance, sales summarized by geographic regions and company divisions, competitive sales trends, market shares among different product lines, costs of operation in various profit centers.

Upon retrieval, EIS data are organized into menus allowing for selective access and manipulation. You might, for example, retrieve data on geographic sales and then instruct the computer to provide a further breakdown year-by-year

executive information systems (EIS)
Easy-access information clusters especially designed for instant access by upper-level managers

The Canadian Business Scene

INFORMATION OVERLOAD ON E-MAIL

The Electronic Messaging Association estimates that 50-60 million people sent e-mail messages in North America in 1994. This form of communication has taken the business world by storm by speeding up communication and giving workers and managers easy access to interesting and important information. But it has its downside too, as companies are beginning to discover.

The biggest problem is information overload. Because e-mail messages can be easily constructed and then copied to just about anybody with a single stroke of a key, the amount of information that is being electronically sent is escalating dramatically. More and more managers and workers are spending more and more time reading and responding to an increasing number of e-mail messages, many of which are either trivial or, worse, have nothing to do with their work.

Andrew Grove, CEO of Intel Corp., has told employees to stop broadcasting non-essential memos such as notices of softball practice or pets for sale. And Bill Gates, CEO of Microsoft, fired an employee who used his Microsoft e-mail address to complain about Ukrainian communists. After the firing, Gates (who is an avid e-mail person) was bombarded with e-mail protests about his actions. Charles Wang, CEO of Computer Associates International, no longer sends or reads e-mail, even though his company sells an e-mail package. He shuts down the company's e-mail system for five hours each day so employees can get their work done.

The introduction of e-mail was supposed to increase workplace democracy by giving everyone increased access to important information. And so it has. But here's the rub: In hierarchical organizations, this may be threatening to those near the top of the hierarchy who are used to being more isolated from those who are lower in the hierarchy. To counter this problem, some top executives use a "bozo filter," which is special software that culls e-mail from strangers and puts it into an electronic archive where it sits, unread. Maybe corporations aren't ready for democracy yet.

A final problem concerns the impersonality of e-mail. The ease of sending messages motivates some people to conduct much of their communication through the e-mail system. This is efficient and can be positive, at least up to a point. But the written word can easily be misinterpreted, and nasty disputes have broken out between workers who fire written salvos back and forth on e-mail instead of walking down the hall and talking through the problem face-to-face. E-mail has also been used by subordinates to criticize managerial competence, especially in companies that are going through downsizing. Managers can retaliate by snooping on an employee's e-mail, even after it has supposedly been erased from the system.

---

for each competing firm. With fingertip access, the manager can request needed information in the midst of executive sessions, when new questions arise, as plans are being developed, or at the time decisions are being made.

Manufacturing Information Systems

As we saw in Chapter 11, computer technology is already having a major impact on manufacturing through the use of *computer-aided design* (*CAD*), *computer-aided manufacturing* (*CAM*), and *computer-integrated manufacturing* (*CIM*). In their competition for world markets, companies are continuing to develop more sophisticated variations of these computer systems in order to increase productivity.[19]

multimedia communications systems
Connected networks of communications appliances like faxes, televisions, sound equipment, printing machines, and photocopiers that may also be linked with mass media such as TV.

Multimedia Communications Systems

Today's information systems include not just computers, but **multimedia communications systems**: connected networks of communications appliances like faxes, televisions, sound equipment, printing machines, and photocopiers that may also be linked with such mass media as TV and radio

The Canadian Business Scene

SURFING THE INTERNET

The popularity of the Internet (or "the Net," for short) has skyrocketed in recent years. Originally commissioned by the Pentagon in the U.S. as a communication tool for use during war, the Internet allows personal computers in virtually any location to be linked together by means of large computers known as *network servers*. The Net has gained in popularity because it makes available an immense wealth of academic, technical, and business information. Another major attraction is the Net's capacity to transmit electronic mail, or e-mail. In addition, such popular on-line services as Prodigy and CompuServe provide e-mail gateways to the Net.

For thousands of businesses, therefore, the Net is joining—and even replacing—the telephone, the fax machine, and express mail as a standard means of communication. In 1994, the number of Net users doubled, to 15 million, with links to more than 138 countries. "If you're not an active Internet citizen by the mid-1990s," proclaims one computer-industry consultant, "you're likely to be out of business by the year 2000." Many companies have already gotten the message: By the end of 1994, nearly 22 000 businesses were connected to the Internet.

Moreover, thanks to a subsystem of 7000 computers known as the World Wide Web (WWW, or simply "the Web"), the Internet is easier to use than ever before. "The Web," explains investment analyst Stephen Franco, "has made the Internet usable to a general audience, rather than the technical users who had been the only ones using it for years and years." The computers linked by the Web are known as "Web servers"; they are owned by corporations, colleges, government agencies, and other large or-ganizations. The individual user can connect with the Web by means of so-called "browser" software, such as Mosaic. The user must simply "point and click," and experts predict that as more people become familiar with "browsers," the number of Net users will grow by 10 to 15 percent a month.

The Net's power to change the way business is conducted has already been amply demonstrated. Digital Equipment Corp., for instance, is a heavy Internet user: With more than 31 000 computers connected to the network, DEC's monthly e-mail volume has jumped to an average of 700 000 messages. DEC has also linked its new Alpha AXP high-speed business computer to the Internet so that potential buyers and software developers can spend time using and evaluating it. Gail Grant, the Internet administrator at DEC, reports that in just a few months, 2500 computer users in 27 countries have taken advantage of the opportunity to explore the Aplha AXP.

The Net has also benefited small companies. For example, one florist shop has used the Net to establish an international presence. Its owner reports that the Net now generates nearly as many orders as FTD.

Of course, the advent of such services has accelerated to a fairly heady pace by the mid-1990s. What can the average company do to keep up with constant, sometimes dramatic changes in the Internet era? For one thing, seminars and workshops provide uninitiated members of the business community with in-depth looks at the Net and its potential applications. A 1994 Internet conference in New York attracted 1750 attendees and 40 vendors; in 1992, the same conference attracted only 600 people and 13 vendors.

---

broadcast programming, news and other print publications, and library collections. Not surprisingly, the integration of these elements is changing the way we live our lives and manage our businesses.

Data Communications Networks.   Also gaining popularity on both home and business computers are public and private **data communications networks**: global networks that permit users to send electronic messages, documents, and other forms of video and audio information quickly and economically. Internet is the largest public network, serving thousands of computers in North America with information on business, science, and government and providing communications flows with certain private networks, including CompuServe and MCI Mail.[20] (See the box "Surfing the Internet" for more information.)

Communications Channels.   *Communications channels* refer to the media that make all these transmissions possible. These include coaxial and fiber-optic

data communication networks
Global networks that permit users to send electronic messages quickly and economically.

After the telephone receiver is positioned in its cradle, this fax machine will electronically read, transmit, and receive paper documents.

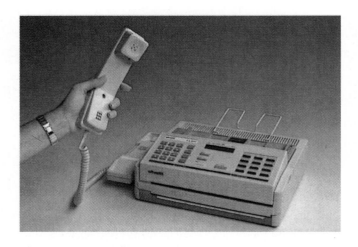

cable and infrared, microwave, and satellite transmission. In particular, the use of satellite channels is increasing to meet the growing demand for wireless transmission. For example, Teledesic Corp. plans to create a major global wireless telephone network by launching 840 satellites. One new application for wireless systems is electronic terminals installed on seatbacks of airplanes so that you can access your e-mail during business travel.[21]

Most of us, of course, use communications channels when we use some type of telephone system. Even today, however, the bulk of telephone transmissions are data, not conversations. Fax data, for instance, account for 90 percent of all telephone signals between North America and Japan.

"Smart" Software.   Software for many multimedia components actually permits them to perform some activities automatically. "Smart" modems, for example, perform such functions as dialing, answering the phone, and transmitting. "Smart" TVs remember your program preferences, make suggestions for your viewing pleasure, and remind you of upcoming programs. Similar software is available for watches, ovens, automobiles, airplanes, and air conditioners. New software is also emerging to integrate the activities of the multimedia hardware. Microsoft at Work, for example, can be installed in office equipment hardware—phones, fax machines, copiers—so they can all be controlled by PCs.[22]

Changing Lifestyles: The Virtual Office.   The impact of communications technologies on lifestyles is nowhere more evident than in the so-called "virtual office"—the mobile office-like working environment that is replacing the traditional, fixed-location office housing hundreds of employees side-by-side. Are you one of the growing number of employees who want to work more at home? Today, the technology is available for more and more people to communicate electronically with the office, lab, or factory by means of their home PCs. On the road, a portable computer can communicate with either the PC at home or the mainframe at headquarters. Wireless faxes can transmit written communications from computer to computer, while voice mail and e-mail provide most of the work-related interaction with headquarters that is ever needed by many employees.

The Use of Computers in Small Businesses

In the past, retail stores, medical offices, restaurants, and farms had manual systems or used a data processing service bureau. Today, many of these businesses own their own computer systems. Personal computer systems offer small businesses the advantage of better inventory control, more accurate sales analysis, and improved financial planning. Several new software programs are aimed specifically at the needs of emerging businesses.[23] The Quattro Pro spreadsheet, for example, is available for less than $50. Quicken, the personal-finance software that tracks cheques, bills, credit-card accounts, and anything else that passes through a wallet or cash register, is already used in more than 5 million homes and business.[24]

Computer ownership, of course, is not without challenges. For example, many small business owners and managers have trouble choosing programs. In addition, they may lack the time and expertise needed to set up programs to handle such data as payroll records, customer payment schedules, and inventory control. An alternative approach is using programs developed for specific applications. General accounting packages like Dac-Easy Accounting and the IBM Accounting Assistant Series are designed for small businesses and contain programs for all of the major accounting functions.

A business such as a real estate company or a medical office may be able to buy even more specific software designed for its industry. A real estate office package will maintain client lists, keep sales records, and hook into a multiple-listing service for the city. A medical office package will schedule patients and create and maintain a data base for patient medical records. Small businesses have also found the combination of data-base and word-processing programs valuable for mailing list management. Advertisements and notices of special sales or new merchandise can be targeted to specific clientele by using an appropriate customer data base.

Summary of Key Points

Businesses today abound with data and information about their customers, their competitors, their competitors' environment, and their own internal operations. The ability to manage this information resource can mean the difference between success and failure. Computers, because of their speed, accuracy, storage capabilities, and ability to make comparisons, have emerged as a powerful tool for information management.

Management information systems transform data into information that is useful for management decision making. Managers at all levels make use of a firm's information system, but information is condensed and summarized as it moves up the hierarchy.

Every computer system consists of five components: hardware, software, people, control, and data. Hardware includes input, processing, and output devices. Software programs tell the computer what resources to use and how to use them; they also process data according to the particular needs of the user. People include the programming personnel, operations personnel, and end users of computers. The fourth component, control, ensures that the system is operating according to specific procedures and within specific guidelines. Computer piracy is a growing problem in the area of computer control. The final component is the data, which are entered into the computer and processed in such a way as to be useful to managers when they make decisions.

The most popular application programs for computers are word processing, electronic spreadsheets, data-base management, and graphics. Word processing allows the computer to act as a sophisticated typewriter. Electronic spreadsheets allow the user to enter data across rows and down columns, and then quickly do a variety of calculations. Data-base management programs are used by managers to keep track of all relevant data for a business. Graphics programs convert numerical data into graphs and charts, making information easier to understand.

Computers can be categorized according to their capacity, speed, and cost. The smallest, slowest, and least expensive option is microcomputers. The largest, fastest, and most expensive option is supercomputers. Minicomputers and mainframes fall in between, but all such lines of distinction are beginning to blur. In contrast, computer systems differ sharply in their architecture. In centralized systems, all processing is done from one location using a centralized data base. In decentralized systems, each location handles its own processing and has its own data base. Computer networks allow branch computers to communicate, offering some of the advantages of both centralized and decentralized systems.

The computers in use today are just the latest in a long line. First-generation computers were large and somewhat unreliable because of their use of vacuum tubes. Second-generation computers replaced those tubes with more reliable transistors. Third-generation computers reduced transistors to tiny integrated circuits on silicon chips. Fourth-generation computers continued with further miniaturization and used the microprocessor chip. The result was greater speed and the microcomputer revolution.

The next (fifth) generation of computers promises even more exciting developments in information management. Artificial intelligence, expert systems, and manufacturing-information systems offer managers help in making business decisions and in solving difficult business problems.

CONCLUDING CASE 23-1

Computerized Cattle

What comes to mind when you hear the phrase "cattle auction?" A bunch of bawling steers in a smelly corral? Think again, because the computer revolution has come to the cattle business. Calgary Stockyards Ltd. conducts most of its business on the "open range of cyberspace" instead of the confined space of the old auction barn.

In the 1970s, the stockyards sold all their cattle at a complex of corrals, loading pens, and barns along the CPR track in Calgary. By 1994, two-thirds of the cattle were marketed by modem from places like Douglas Lake, B.C. Cattle are moved by an on-line system called TEAM (The Electronic Auction Method).

Here's how it works: A single PC is connected by phone lines and modems to buyers in various locations. Buyers get a detailed description of the cattle for sale, but they don't actually see the cattle. Don Danard, president of Calgary Stockyards, sets the starting price, which drops every five seconds until someone makes a bid by hitting the ENTER key. When that happens, the price rises one-quarter of a cent with every bid. After 15 seconds have passed without another bid, the seller can accept or reject the last offer on the screen.

As you can imagine, this type of auction is a lot quicker and quieter than the old-fashioned kind. At one recent computer auction, 3600 cattle were sold in two hours; a "live auction" at nearby Strathmore took eight hours to sell just 2500 cattle.

There are other advantages as well. Under the old system, a rancher had to pay to transport cattle to a live auction without knowing what price the cattle would fetch. Now ranchers know the price they will get before their cattle are moved. The system has also allowed large ranchers to avoid rounding up the 2000 or so cattle needed for on-ranch auctions (a practice that caused the animals stress and reduced the prices they would bring). Now, ranchers can sell smaller lots of cattle—normally 300 to 500—when conditions are right and a good price can be obtained. The rancher rounds up cattle only if a sale is made. Small ranchers also benefit because their cattle are exposed to a larger number of buyers in a computer auction than they would be in a live auction. Another advantage: On a day when it's minus twenty degrees, cattle buyers would rather be looking at a computer screen in a comfortable room than standing out in a corral with a cold wind blowing down their neck.

Some buyers are still suspicious of computer auctions. They feel that buying cattle this way is risky because the person writing up the computer description of the cattle may exaggerate. The operators of TEAM deal with this concern by constantly weeding out individuals who write exaggerated descriptions of their cattle. Other cattle markets are not happy with Calgary Stockyards because they fear the company will take away their business with its new technology. Some of these smaller markets got together and formed the Canadian Satellite Livestock Auction. It shows video clips of cattle to prospective buyers who phone in their bids.

CASE QUESTIONS
1. What type of computer hardware and software is used in computer auctions?
2. Which of the attitudes toward computer technology (see Table 23.2) are likely to be evident in computer auctions? How will these attitudes affect acceptance of the system?
3. Summarize the advantages and disadvantages of computer auctions as noted in the case study. What other advantages and disadvantages might exist? ◆

CONCLUDING CASE 23-2

Computing Flower Power

G.A. Vantreight & Sons has grown daffodils on Vancouver Island's Saanich peninsula since the 1930s. Each spring, about 12 million yellow daffodils are picked by seasonal laborers. Vantreight's sells about half of its daffodils to the Canadian Cancer Society, which uses them for its Daffodil Day fundraiser that kicks off its annual April campaign. Other flowers grown by Vantreight are sold to Canada Safeway, wholesale florists, and other retailers.

As serene and slow moving as this business might seem, it has been changed dramatically by computers in the last few years. The big change is a recently-introduced automated payroll system that tracks each worker's production in the field. With the new system, the average worker's output has doubled, labor and production costs have declined, and profits are up.

The system uses 12 portable, hand-held computers, bar-coded packaging tags, bar-coded employee identification badges, and a customized software package called FieldManager designed especially for the company. Under the old system, the names of workers were scribbled on notepads before they were sent to various fields to pick. Errors in keeping track of workers were common. And when it rained (which was often), the notepads got soaked. At the end of the day, the notepads were turned in to the office staff so they could figure out how much each worker should get paid.

With the new system, most of these problems have disappeared. Supervisors now record the output of each worker right in the field by scanning each worker's bar-coded identification that is attached to each bunch of flowers the worker picks. By 3 p.m. each day, the company knows how many flowers have been picked that day. Under the old system, all the company could do was make an educated guess.

The new system has also meant a change in the way workers are paid. Workers, who used to receive a flat $6.50 per hour, are now paid 14 cents for each bunch of 10 flowers they pick. A fast worker can pick enough flowers to earn the equivalent of $11.50 per hour, a big improvement over the flat wage amount. This payment system has reduced the number of pickers employed, but those that do work are much more productive. It has also reduced the farm's unit costs—from 22 cents per bunch to 18 cents per bunch.

The use of computers is just beginning at Vantreight's. The next step is to start tracking bulb production and relate it to actual flower production.

CASE QUESTIONS
1. How has computerization improved productivity and profits at Vantreight's?
2. From the workers's perspective, what are the disadvantages of the new computer system?
3. Which of the attitudes toward computer technology (see Table 23.2) might field workers exhibit regarding the introduction of the new computer system? What about supervisors and office workers? ◆

Key Terms

data	floppy disks	computer graphics	large scale integration
information	read-only memory	programs	(LSI)
management information	CD-ROM disks	desktop publishing	very large scale
system (MIS)	software	microcomputer	integration (VLSI)
computer system	system program	minicomputer	artificial intelligence (AI)
hardware	application program	mainframe	expert system
input device	object-oriented technology	supercomputer	fax machines
central processing unit	graphic user interface	systems architecture	voice mail
(CPU)	privacy invasion	centralized system	e-mail
bit	viruses	decentralized system	groupware
byte	computer piracy	computer network	executive information
primary storage	site-license agreement	wide area network	systems
control unit	data base	local area network	multimedia
program	batch processing	server	communication systems
arithmetic logic unit (ALU)	real-time processing	client PCs	data communication
output device	word processing	debugging	networks
random access memory	electronic spreadsheet	transistor	
secondary storage	data-base management	integrated circuit	
hard disks	modem	microprocessor chip	

Study Questions and Exercises

Review Questions
1. Why does a business need to manage information as a resource?
2. Describe the components of a computer system. Explain how each part is related to the others.
3. Rank microcomputers, minicomputers, mainframes, and supercomputers according to their cost, speed of processing, and capacity.
4. What features distinguish each of the first four generations of computers?
5. How can an e-mail system increase office productivity and efficiency?

Analysis Questions
6. Give two examples not in this chapter for each of the four major types of application programs used in businesses.

7. Describe the types of work or activities for which a local department store might choose to use batch processing. Do the same for real-time processing.
8. Choose a simple, everyday problem and prepare an artificial intelligence system to help solve it.

Application Exercises
9. Describe the computer system at your college or university. Identify the components of the system (including specific examples of some of the fields, records, and files in its data base), the capacity/speed of the system, and its architecture.
10. Visit a small business in your community to investigate how it uses computers and how it plans to use them in the future. Prepare a report to present to your class.

Building Your Business Skills

Goal

To help students understand how organizations use technology and information systems in their day-to-day operations.

Method

Visit a small business in your community—perhaps an insurance agency, a travel agency, or an auto-parts dealer. Determine the various organizational activities linked to the company's information system. Ask employees about the particular uses to which they put the system in order to do their jobs. Ask them whether they have experienced any diffculties using the system. Ask them to describe any significant changes that have occurred in the company's operations since the installation or last upgrade of the system.

Follow-up Questions

1. What information is available on the computer system that you examined? Is it available to everyone in the company?
2. To what extent is the computer system that you examined linked to other computers (for example, to a database at the home office of an insurance company)?

THE EUROPEAN UNION: IT'S COME A LONG WAY

For thousands of years, people have tried to unite Europe. The Romans probably came closest, but eventually fell victim to the Goths, Vandals, and other northern tribes. Napoleon made a major effort, but a Russian winter and a British lord ultimately limited his rule to the island of Elba. But where military minds have failed, the economists and bureaucrats hope to succeed with their version of a united Europe: the European Union (EU).

The EU is not really new. At its root is the old Common Market, founded in 1958 by Belgium, France, Italy, Luxembourg, the Netherlands, and West Germany. In 1967, the Common Market merged with two other groups—the European Coal and Steel Community and the European Atomic Energy Commission—to form the European Community. Unlike the Common Market, the EU's goals go well beyond the elimination of trade barriers, the development of common price levels, and a common currency. To those spearheading the EU, the goal is to create a Europe unified in virtually all regards: no mean feat for a group of countries with a total population of 340 million. Accordingly, the EU has an (executive) European Commission composed of the heads of state of each nation that meets twice a year in different locations. It also boasts a European Parliament (based in Strasbourg, Germany) that was elected by direct vote of all citizens in the member nations for the first time in 1979.

Given centuries of independent—and often unique—approaches on the part of the EU's member nations, reaching agreement on even the slightest issues has proved a major undertaking. It took over a decade just to agree on the appropriate decibel level of noise made by power lawn mowers, for example. Nevertheless, since 1967, EU members have reached agreement on a number of points:

■ Tariffs on goods sold among EU countries have been abolished.
■ Banks approved for operation in one EU country are automatically allowed to open branches in other EU countries, provided they meet minimum capital and solvency requirements.
■ Restrictions on employing individuals from other EU nations have been lifted, as have many laws governing foreign residency.
■ Professionals, such as doctors and engineers, who have been licensed in one EU nation are free to practice in any other EU nation without further certification.
■ Insurance companies are free to sell their products (except life insurance) throughout the EU, subject only to the regulations of their home country.
■ "Buy national" policies in areas such as energy supply and waste management have been eliminated.
■ Drugs patented in one EU nation will automatically be patented in all other EU nations, and new drugs approved by one EU nation will be automatically accepted for use by the other member nations.
■ Border-crossing posts between EU nations will be dismantled, speeding the passage of individuals (as well as trucks and trains carrying goods) from one EU nation to another.
■ Airlines have been decontrolled.
■ Creation of Eurolist, a cross-listing of 250 companies in the EU, will enable investors in one nation to purchase the stocks of another. Listed companies will not have to pay separate fees to each exchange on which they are listed.

Despite these ambitious efforts, as this book goes to press, Europe is far from unified. Many of the Eastern European nations, free from communist rule, are either trying to construct free-market economies or are engaged in violent civil wars.

Even among the nations in the EU, there is great dispute over some proposed plans. Among the points of contention are:

- *Transportation of livestock*: Britain and Ireland are worried about reimporting rabies, which they have eliminated.
- *Brokerage and investment firms*: Several nations oppose universal licensing of such firms and their employees.
- *Standardization of products*: With 10 different kinds of electrical plugs and 29 different kinds of wall outlets, total standardization may be impossible.
- *Standardization of taxes*: Member nations have been unable to agree on a common value-added tax, the most common type of tax in Europe.
- *Labor laws*: Britain opposes the adoption of minimum wage laws and hours of work based on Germany's current system, arguing that these would undermine competition and deprive nations with lower-cost labor of the chance to garner business and thus improve their lot.
- *Government supports*: France and Italy, especially, do not want to see supports for industry cut off. Farmers in Spain and Portugal took to the streets to protest proposed cuts in agricultural supports.
- *A European army*: France wants it; the rest of Europe so far prefers separate forces and NATO (the North Atlantic Treaty Organization) as a unifying force.
- *Judicial powers*: Britain wants the EU's Court of Justice to be able to punish those who break the EU's rules; France doesn't.
- *Capital markets*: While many companies and investors would like to see a unified stock and bond market, the relative technological backwardness of some EU nations' stock exchanges (notably Italy's) and differing accounting practices remain obstacles.
- *Corporate management*: Britain opposes regulations that would require seats for employees on corporate boards, the present practice in Germany.

One particular issue—the European Currency Unit—is so hotly contested that it merits detailed discussion. At present, the *concept* of the ECU, based on an average of member nations' currencies, is used by some European businesses to set prices, but as yet the actual currency does not exist. The proposed common currency unit is strongly opposed by Britain, which argues that individual currency units ensure competitiveness—that is, businesses favor selling to nations that remain strong and are eager to purchase the labor of weaker nations. Proponents of the ECU note that it would save businesses millions of dollars in accounting costs and could lower prices, since firms would no longer feel compelled to hedge against foreign currency fluctuations. European banks would also have to become more competitive, since companies would no longer need multiple banks to handle multiple currencies.

Given the radically different views of the nations involved, especially pro-free-trade Britain and pro-socialist France, no one expects agreement on most of these issues to come quickly or easily. Nevertheless, the advances toward European economic union made in recent years are impressive and offer substantial opportunities for businesses around the world. Already, hundreds of European companies have merged to form larger industries capable of producing and distributing goods throughout the EU.

European consumers also stand to benefit in a variety of ways. First, consumer prices of many items will fall in response to lowered tariffs and speedier transit of goods among EU nations. Competition among banks and insurance companies will likely lower the costs of such services. As more companies around the world are attracted to this huge potential market, Europeans will also have more choices about what to buy. Particularly apt to benefit are U.S. and Canadian firms in the health-care and medical supply industries. Outside of the United States, the EU will be the largest market for health-care services and products, and the new era of cross-approval should benefit firms in those businesses.

Finally, Europe itself stands to benefit from establishing free trade. As small firms merge to form larger ones, these new firms may be better able to compete, not just in the EU, but also in global markets. At the same time, the many government-subsidized industries that run far below their capacity (at great cost) will be compressed. For example, there are now 37 locomotive makers in EU nations, a number experts predict will fall to 10 by the end of the decade. EU nations can then use these resources elsewhere.

CASE QUESTIONS
1. In what ways will the new legal and regulatory environment in the EU benefit Canadian firms seeking to do business there? In what ways will it hurt those firms?
2. How does the formation of the EU illustrate the nature of absolute and competitive advantage?
3. Who do you think will be most helped by the removal of barriers to trade in the EU? Do you think Canada should lower its barriers in exchange for lower barriers in selling to Europe?
4. In what ways will the productivity of European firms be affected by the EU?
5. In an article entitled "Europe's Coming Decline," scholar Michael Novak wrote: "...as an inventor of new technologies, a cheaper producer, a swifter competitor, Europe is no dire threat....In products of exquisite taste and styling, European producers will probably always offer special pleasures to those who love the best. The world honors Europeans for living well, more than for

Experiential Exercise:
Coping with an International Crisis

OBJECTIVE

To give students a better understanding of the complexities involved in operating an international business and the need for long-range planning to cope with potential disasters.

TIME REQUIRED

45 minutes
   Step 1: Individual activity (to be completed before class)
   Step 2: Small-group activity (30 minutes)
   Step 3: Class discussion (15 minutes)

PROCEDURE

Step 1: At the library, consult encyclopedias and other sources to learn about petroleum and its use in creating other products.

Step 2: Read the following case about Webb Enterprises Inc.

Like many large, multinational organizations, Webb Enterprises owns a host of businesses that are only loosely connected to one another. Among Webb's vast holdings are

*   Keypon Trucking, a major international freight carrier in Africa.
*   Wanee's Stores, a group of up-scale department stores located in the northeastern and southwestern portions of the United States.
*   Pool Service Stations, a chain of full-service stations offering not only gasoline and diesel fuel but also mechanical repairs for all models of cars.
*   Grad Plastics, manufacturer of a variety of plastics.
*   Rapid Packaging, maker of packaging products ranging from cardboard boxes to machinery used by supermarkets to seal freshly cut meat in plastic wrap.
*   Creed Petroleum, which buys and sells petroleum products internationally and is also a major oil producer, with drilling operations in 14 countries, including the United States, Mexico, Argentina, the North Sea, and several Arab nations.
*   Fly Asian Airlines, with service throughout the Far East.
*   Paint Your Wagon, which specializes in repainting cars and trucks using the finest paints and enamels.
*   Webber Electric, providing electrical service in Southeast Asia through a series of petroleum-fired generators.
*   Vital Sessions, manufacturers of cosmetics and hair care products made from natural and chemical ingredients.
*   Featherflight Boats, makers of superlight power racing boats with a patented "Featherflight" plastic hull.
*   Color Coordinated, producers of dyes for the textile industry.

Over the years, Webb Enterprises has had to deal with a variety of problems, many of them related to the rise in oil prices, first following the Arab-Israeli War in 1973 and again following the fall of the Shah of Iran in 1979. Neither event, however, totally prepared Webb's management for the events of 1990, when Saddam Hussein and the Iraqi military invaded Kuwait, one of the world's largest oil producers, and stood poised near the oil fields of Saudi Arabia, which supply over 10 percent of the world's crude oil. Eleven of Webb's employees were caught in Kuwait or Iraq when Hussein closed the borders. Nearly all of Webb's businesses were affected to some degree by the nearly 15 percent increase in oil prices in the first month after the invasion.

How Could Webb Have Coped With The Crisis?

How Could Webb Minimize The Impact Of Another Such Event In The Future?

At this point the instructor should divide the class into small groups and assign each group one or more of the subsidiary companies listed above. Each group should identify at least five problems the assigned subsidiaries may have possibly faced as a result of the Iraqi invasion of Kuwait and complete the following grid.

Subsidiary _____

Problem	Best Action At Time of Crisis	How to Avoid/Limit Future Impact
1.		
2.		
3.		
4.		
5.		

Step 3: One member of each small group will present the group's conclusions to the class.

QUESTIONS FOR DISCUSSION

1. Which of the companies assigned do you think faced the greatest problems in the wake of the Iraqi invasion of Kuwait? Why?
2. Which of the companies assigned do you think faced the fewest problems in the wake of the Iraqi invasion of Kuwait? Why?

CAREERS IN BUSINESS
Starting Over

*"All is flux, nothing stays still....
Nothing endures but change."*

The Greek philosopher Heraclitus wrote these words nearly 2500 years ago, but they remain as true today as they were then. If anything, the rate of change in our modern world seems to be accelerating continually.

If you are like most of your classmates, the chances are very strong indeed that you will change jobs—even change professions—at some point in your career. In this section, we consider some of the reasons people change jobs and offer some suggestions on how to go about it.

WHY CHANGE JOBS?

During your career, you may find yourself changing what you do and where you do it for a variety of reasons. As the vast number of Baby Boomers reach the "upper-executive" years, the number of upper-management jobs is sure to fall short of demand, a trend that may well drive some managers in pursuit of better opportunities. Moreover, in today's uncertain economic climate, many people have found themselves out of a job as their firms cut back or went under. The demand for some positions is growing, while demand for others is declining. And, increasingly, people are opting for self-employment, setting up as consultants, and opening the new small businesses that are projected to be the major source of growth in the twenty-first century.

The most common reason of all, however, is an inappropriate person-job fit. Though many people find their first job interesting, challenging, and rewarding, many others find their first jobs to be much different than they expected. Some experts estimate that as many as 20 percent of all new graduates change jobs within 12 months of starting their careers.

People sometimes find that they chose the wrong job because they did not truly understand their own interests and abilities. The young man who got into sales after enjoying jobs as a paperboy and counterman at McDonald's may find that what he really liked was the independence of being a paperboy and the camaraderie of working with schoolmates at McDonald's—neither of which is part of selling cosmetics to Kmart. The young woman who chose her job because she wanted the highest possible salary, because she did not want to be too far away from home, or because her father worked for the company before he retired may find that the high salary carries with it too many unpleasant working conditions or that she would actually prefer to live farther from home.

SHOULD YOU CHANGE JOBS?

If you have just taken your first job and find yourself unhappy with it—for whatever reason—experts have a few words of advice: HANG IN THERE. No organization is perfect, nor is any job. And no matter how well you thought you understood what you would be doing, there will always be some surprises in store. Moreover, it may not be the job that's making you unhappy. The upheaval and stress of being independent and coping with the myriad problems of everyday life may be partially to blame for your frustration.

Resist moving too quickly; try to last at least a year. Why a year? Because leaving much earlier than that can be interpreted as a sign of impatience, or a lack of commitment or maturity, on your part. One year is usually perceived to be a long time for a person to make an informed and professional decision about staying or leaving. A year will also give you a chance to reassess what you like and don't like about the job while giving you valuable experience that can help you in your next job.

Even if it's not your first job, experts recommend that you stay at least a year—or even two—so as not to create an impression of instability. While employers today are much more open to hiring individuals who have worked for several companies, a job hopper's résumé is more likely than most to hop into the circular file.

HOW TO LOOK FOR A NEW JOB

If you are sure that you made the wrong decision in selecting an occupation or employer, or if changes in the organization are simply too great for your comfort, you may very well decide to look for another job. If you do decide to look around, you should keep several things in mind. Remember, you are not starting over, but simply making a change. You made a decision, it turned out to be the wrong one, and now you want to correct it.

Spend some time thinking about why you want to change jobs. Is it because of location? Or pay? Or company policies? Or is it the actual work you are doing? Make sure that a new job will actually correct the problems you are experiencing. Table 1 lists some of the right—and wrong—reasons for changing careers.

Second, compile a list of your strengths and weaknesses, goals, and aspirations. Also develop a list of the things you like and don't like about your current job. Why do you want to keep it and why do you want to leave it? Use this information to determine exactly what kind of new job you want.

Third, revise your résumé and start job-hunting. If you graduated from college or university less than five years ago, your campus placement office may still be willing to assist you. If you want to stay in the same line of work, contact the companies you interviewed with before—especially any firm that offered you a job. Use personal contacts, the local newspaper, employment agencies—anything and anyone you can think of to turn up leads on job openings.

The library can be an excellent source of leads for job hunters. Scan the newspapers of other cities in which you might like to work. And don't forget to look in trade publications and journals in your field for positions that are open.

Prospective new employers will be very interested in why you want to leave your current job. Be honest, but don't wear your heart on your sleeve. Don't blame your current employer—doing so may make you look like a complainer or malcontent. But don't blame yourself too much either. Explain why you made a mistake in taking the job, then explain that you are now trying to correct it.

What should you tell your current employer when you decide it's time to go? Some experts recommend that you advise your employer of your unhappiness and your plans to seek employment elsewhere. You should be aware, however, that by doing so you are effectively "giving notice." Some firms may make an effort to find a different position for you, but most will start looking for someone else to fill your job. Thus, many people choose to keep the job-hunting activities a secret until they have found a new position. Whichever way you choose to handle the situation, be sure to give your current employer adequate notice—it's the professional thing to do, and it can influence the references you get from that employer in years to come.

EXCELSIOR! (ONWARD AND UPWARD)

Job hunting is never easy, but it can be highly profitable. Many studies have found that changing jobs offers the best chance for middle-level managers to improve their positions and salaries. As Figure 1 shows, moving is essential to career development in some careers, so if you don't like your job or don't see a future in it—go for a change.

Table 1   Reasons to Change—and Not to Change—Careers

Reasons to Change

- Your job or industry is becoming obsolete because of changes in technology.
- The personal costs of your job—long hours, too much travel—outweigh its benefits.
- You've been fired because you were not well suited for the work.
- Your financial needs have changed.
- You feel bored or burned-out.
- You don't fit in.

Reasons Not to Change

- Eyeing your friend's profitable career without giving any thought to the day-to-day activities involved.
- Considering a field where job security or money is the only plus.
- Entering a field because it's what your father, mother, sister, or brother does.
- Hearing that a certain field is growing, but ignoring that it doesn't fit you.

Figure 1   Optimal Time in Job, by Occupation

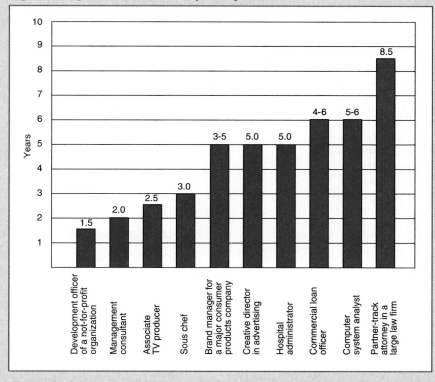

TREPASSEY*

> "People don't want to leave here. They want to stay here. But they're not going to stay if there's no jobs."
>
> —Colin Chader, Mayor of Trepassey, Newfoundland

For many decades the island of Newfoundland has been acknowledged as one of Canada's have-not provinces. As a result of this longstanding condition new government-sponsored initiatives are underway to foster a new private sector in the province. One example of such an initiative is found in the small coastal town of Trepassey, where town mayor Colin Chader is currently screening job creation proposals from such varied places as Norway and the People's Republic of China. After the town was hit with a loss of 625 jobs when its fish processing plant closed in 1990, the government gave the town $7 million to spend over five years in new job creation. To date the town has used about $4 million but has succeeded in creating only a few dozen jobs. New jobs attributable to these efforts include a water bottler, a florist, and a custom window manufacturer. In addition, a new cedar wood products factory is expected to employ between 20 and 25 by the end of 1995.

The presence of government start-up funding has attracted a diverse range of business venture proposals. One of the more far-fetched proposals envisioned making Trepassey the gold capital of the world; another offered to manufacture car seats for pets. On a more realistic note, applications have also been received for a caribou interpretation center, a tourist campground, and a blueberry farm.

With government support soon to end, the townspeople recognize that some hard choices are ahead of them. One such choice centers on a proposal from the People's Republic of China—an investor is reportedly interested in opening up a Dim Sum factory in Trepassey that would make dumplings. This proposal is particularly attractive because it would create hundreds of jobs. One of the difficult aspects of this proposal is that it would require the entire $3 million left in Trepassey's community development fund. At recent town council meetings town residents have begun to reckon with the hard choice of "betting the farm" on the dumpling proposal or diversifying among a number of different business proposals.

Study questions:

1. What roles does government play in our economic system? Which of these roles is the government attempting to play in this case? When does government operate as a customer? How could the people of Trepassey create products and services that the government might be interested in acquiring from them?
2. What are the different ways in which government can influence business decisions? How does the government appear to be attempting to influence business decisions in this case?
3. What are the different steps of government policy formulation? How would you explain these steps in the context of the decisions the government reached in this case?
4. What is an incentive program? In what ways can government offer incentives in the development of private enterprise? In what ways is government ill-equipped to aid in this process?

*This case is based on the *Venture* episode first broadcast on May 1, 1994.

A "business haven" is being created 20 kilometres offshore from Singapore on tiny Batam Island. On this island, which is one-tenth the size of Prince Edward Island, companies can concentrate on manufacturing their product in a very favorable environment for business. Property taxes, duties, and worker wages are extremely low, and all kinds of services (phones, electricity) and security are available to

business firms who set up shop here. Businesses simply bring their technology and production machinery, and the Batamindo Industrial Management Group looks after the rest.

Batam Island is a partnership between Indonesia (whose economy is growing at six times the rate of Canada's) and Singapore (one of the strongest economies in the world). These two countries are blurring their borders to create a new country devoted entirely to business. Labor, which is in short supply in Singapore, is abundant in densely-populated Indonesia. So, Indonesia provides cheap labor and Singapore provides managerial expertise and business know-how.

Batam Island is designed to be a global village serving markets around the world. Within Asia, competition among countries for investment is fierce; this partnership between Singapore and Indonesia is designed to attract business investment to the area.

The centrepiece of the island is a modern industrial park where 20 000 people work producing electronic equipment. The park has already attracted companies from Japan, France, and the U.S. with a "one-stop shopping" approach to business development. Assistance is available in many areas, including cutting through government red tape in getting business permits, delivering tax-free materials to manufacturing plants, getting finished goods to port, and providing production workers. The industrial park also has

a market, restaurants, a clinic, and a mosque.

Single women who work at the manufacturing plants in the industrial park live in dorms right next to the factories. Most of them are from rural villages in Indonesia, and they have experienced culture shock as they are put into a factory environment. The leap from the third world to the first is daunting. Human resource policies are very strict—if a woman get pregnant, she is terminated.

Everywhere you look there is growth. Construction on Batam Island is proceeding at a furious pace. A new highway is being constructed, and six new bridges are being built to connect Batam Island to the mainland. All of this activity is to be completed by 1996. Construction is also underway on a new golf course, a new town center, additional industrial parks, and new residential housing for managers of multinational firms.

Asia, which is already the world's economic hotspot, may have just pushed global competition up another notch.

Study questions:

1. How is the climate for business different on Batam Island than it is in a typical Canadian city?
2. What are the implications for international competitiveness of the business firms that set up operations on Batam Island?
3. What kind of relationship do business and government apparently have on this island? Support your answer by referring to facts from the case.
4. From an employee's perspective, what are the advantages and disadvantages of working on Batam Island?

*This case is based on the *Venture* episode first broadcast on February 20, 1994.

GLOSSARY

A

absolute advantage   A nation's ability to produce something more cheaply or better than any other country can. (651)

accountability   A subordinate's liability in the event of non-performance of a task. (160)

accounting   A comprehensive system for collecting, analyzing, and communicating financial information. (499)

accounting system   An organized procedure for identifying, measuring, recording, and retaining financial information so that it can be used in accounting statements and management reports. (499)

accounts payable   Amounts due from a firm to its suppliers for goods and/or services bought on credit; a form of current liability. (510)

accounts receivable   Amounts due to a firm from customers who have bought goods or services on credit; a form of current asset. (509)

acid rain   A form of pollution affecting the eastern United States and central and eastern Canada as a result of sulphur expelled into the air by power and manufacturing plants. (89)

acquisition   The purchase of one company by another, usually larger firm that absorbs the smaller company into its operations. (60)

activity ratios   Measures of how efficiently a firm uses its resources; used by investors to assess their probable returns. (518)

administrative law   The rules and regulations developed by government agencies and commissions based on their interpretations of statutory laws. (99)

administration of government programs   The day-to-day activities that are required to implement government programs. (641)

advertising   Any promotional technique involving paid, nonpersonal communication used by an identified sponsor to persuade or inform a large number of people about a product. (389)

advertising agency   A firm that specializes in planning, producing, and placing advertisements in different media for clients. (441)

advertising medium   The specific communication device—television, radio, newspapers, direct mail, magazines, billboards—used to carry a firm's advertising message to potential customers. (437)

advocacy advertising   Advertising that promotes a particular viewpoint or candidate. (441)

agency-principal relationship   Established when one party (the agent) is authorized to act on behalf of another party (the principal). (101)

agency shop   A work place in which nonunion employees must pay dues to the union. (274)

agent/broker   An independent business person who represents a business and receives a commission in return but never takes legal possession of the product. (465)

alternate dispute resolution   The employee and the company agree to submit things like wrongful dismissal claims to binding arbitration. (222)

analytic process   Any production process in which resources are broken down. (302)

application programs   Computer programs that actually process data according to a particular user's specific needs. (698)

arithmetic logic unit (ALU)   That part of the computer's central processing unit that performs logical and mathematical operations such as comparisons and addition, subtraction, multiplication, and division. (686)

artificial intelligence   The construction and/or programming of computers to imitate human thought processes. (703)

assembly line   A type of product layout in which a partially finished product moves through a plant on a conveyor belt or other equipment. (307)

assessment center   A series of exercises in which management candidates perform realistic management tasks under the supervision of expert appraisers. (220)

asset   Anything of economic value owned by a firm or an individual. (505)

audit   An accountant's examination of a company's financial records to determine if the company used proper procedures to prepare its financial reports. (502)

authority   The power to make decisions necessary to accomplish certain tasks. (160)

autocratic style   A management style characterized by the manager making all decisions and issuing orders for work to be completed without the input of subordinates. (135)

automation   The process of performing mechanical operations with minimal or no human involvement. (318)

B

bailor-bailee relationship   Established when one party (the bailor) gives possession of his or her property to another party (the bailee) but retains ownership. (101)

balance of payments   The difference between the money flowing into a country and the money flowing out of a country. (652)

balance of trade   The difference in value between a nation's total exports and its total imports. (23: 651)

balance sheet   A type of financial statement that summarizes a firm's financial position on a particular date in terms of its assets, liabilities, and owners' equity. (508)

Bank of Canada   Canada's central bank. (543)

bank rate   The rate at which chartered banks can borrow from the Bank of Canada. (543)

banker's acceptance   Promises that the bank will pay a specified amount of money at a future date. (537)

bankruptcy   Permission granted by the courts to individuals and businesses not to pay some or all of their debts. (568)

bargaining unit   Includes in the union those individuals whom a provincial labor board deems appropriate. (270)

batch processing   A method of transforming data into information in which data are collected over a period of time and then processed as a group or batch. (693)

bear market   A period of falling stock prices; a period in which investors act on a belief that stock prices will fall. (607)

bearer (coupon) bond   Requires bondholders to clip coupons from certificates and send them to the issuer in order to receive interest paymnets. (601)

benchmarking   Comparing the quality of the firm's output with the quality of the output of the industry's leaders. (362)

beneficiary   The person to whom benefits of a life insurance policy are paid. (583)

benefits   What a firm offers its workers in return for their labors *other than* wages and salaries. (226)

bill of materials A "recipe" for production of a "batch" of a good that specifies the resources needed and the method of combining those resources. (316)

bit A way of representing data in a computer as one of two digits (0 or 1); abbreviation for *bi*nary digi*t*. (685)

blue-sky laws Legislation that requires corporations issuing securities to back them up with something more than the "blue sky." (609)

board of directors A group of individuals elected by a firm's shareholders and charged with overseeing and taking legal responsibility for the firm's actions. (38)

bona fide occupational requirement Allows an employer to choose one person over another based on overriding characteristics of the job in question. (213)

bond A written promise that the borrower will pay the lender a sum of money and a stated rate of interest. (598)

book value The value of a stock expressed as the total shareholders' equity (assets minus liabilities and preferred stock) divided by the number of shares of common stock outstanding; used by accountants but of little significance to investors. (594)

bookkeeping Recording accounting transactions. (499)

boycott A weapon of labor unions in disputes with management in which members refuse to buy the products of the company and encourage consumers to do the same. (277)

brand advertising Advertising that promotes a specific brand-name product. (441)

brand loyalty Customers' recognition of, preference for, and insistence on buying a product with a certain brand name. (429)

brand names Those specific names of products associated with a manufacturer, wholesaler, and/or retailer that are designed to distinguish products from those of competitors and are promoted as part of the product. (426)

breach of contract Occurs when one party in an agreement fails to live up to the provisions of the agreement without having a legal reason to do so. (101)

break-even analysis An assessment of how many units must be sold at a given price before the company begins to make a profit. (459)

break-even point The number of units that must be sold at a given price before the company covers all its variable and fixed costs. (459)

broker An individual licensed to buy and sell securities for customers in the secondary market; may also provide other financial services. (597)

budget A detailed financial plan for estimated receipts and expenditures for a period of time in the future, usually one year. (513)

budget deficit Occurs when the government spends more in one year than it takes in during that year. (23)

bull market A period of rising stock prices; a period in which investors act on a belief that stock prices will rise. (607)

business An organization that seeks to earn profits by providing goods and services. (7)

business agent In a large union, the business agent plays the same role as a shop steward. (273)

business cycle The fluctuations in the level of activity that an economy goes through. (14)

business interruption insurance Insurance to cover potential losses incurred during times when a company is unable to conduct its business. (582)

business law Those aspects of law that specifically affect the way business firms are managed. (99)

byte A series of eight bits that together represent a character in a computer. (685)

C

cafeteria benefits A flexible approach to providing benefits in which employees are allocated a certain sum to cover benefits and can "spend" this allocation on the specific benefits they prefer. (227)

call option The purchased right to buy a particular stock at a certain price until a specified date. (604)

callable bond A bond that may be paid off by the issuer before the maturity date. (601)

Canada Labour Code Legislation that applies to the labor practices of firms operating under the legislative authority of parliament. (268)

Canada-U.S. Free Trade Agreement An agreement to gradually eliminate tariffs on goods and services moving between Canada and the U.S. (666)

Canadian Federation of Independent Business (CFIB) A nonprofit, nonpartisan lobby group representing small and medium-sized businesses. (179)

Canadian Human Rights Act Ensures that any individual who wishes to obtain a job has an equal opportunity to compete for it. (213)

Canadian Radio-television and Telecommunications Commission Regulates all aspects of the Canadian broadcasting system. (633)

Canadian Transport Commission Makes decisions about route and rate applications for commercial air and railway companies. (634)

capacity In production, the amount of a good that a firm can produce under normal working conditions. (305)

capital The funds needed to operate an enterprise. (8)

capital gains Profits from the sale of an asset (such as stock) for a higher price than that at which it was purchased. (594)

capital items Expensive, long-lasting industrial goods that are used in producing other goods or services and have a long life. (418)

capital-intensive process Manufacturing or service processes in which investment in machinery is great. (304)

capital productivity A partial productivity ratio calculated as total outputs divided by capital inputs. (355)

capitalism A market economy; an economic system in which markets decide what, when, and for whom to produce. (12)

cartel Any association of producers for the purpose of controlling supply of and prices for a given product; illegal in Canada. (664)

cash discount A form of discount in which customers paying cash, rather than buying on credit, pay lower prices. (462)

cash flow management Managing the pattern in which cash comes into the firm in the form of revenues and goes out of the firm in the form of debt payments. (557)

catalogue showrooms Bargain retail stores in which customers place orders for items described in a catalogue and pick up those items from an on-premises warehouse. (473)

category killers Retailers who carry an extremely deep selection of goods in a relatively narrow product line. (471)

cause-and-effect diagram Summarizes the four possible causes of quality problems—materials, manpower, methods, and machines. (363)

CD-ROM disks Look like music CDs but can hold as much data as 400 regular floppy disks. (688)

cellular layouts Used to produce goods when families of products can follow similar flowpaths. (307)

central processing unit (CPU) That part of a computer's hardware in which the actual transforming of data into information takes place; it contains the primary storage unit, the control unit, and the arithmetic logic unit. (685)

centralization Occurs when top management retains most decision-making rights for itself. (161)

centralized system A form of computer system architecture in which all processing is done in one location using a centralized data base and computer staff. (699)

certification vote A vote to determine whether a union can represent a group of employees. (270)

chain of command Reporting relationships within a business; the flow of decision-making power in a firm. (154)

chartered accountant (CA) An individual who has met certain experience and education requirements and has passed a licensing examination. (501)

chartered bank A privately owned, profit-seeking firm that serves individuals, nonbusiness organizations, and businesses as a financial intermediary. (536)

chequable deposit A chequing account. (539)

cheque An order instructing a bank to pay a given sum to a specified person or firm. (531)

cheque kiting Writing cheques against money that has not yet arrived at the bank on which the cheque has been drawn. (94)

chief executive officer (CEO) The person responsible for the firm's overall performance. (39)

classical theory of motivation A theory of motivation that presumes that workers are motivated almost solely by money. (239)

chief executive officer (CEO) The person responsible for the firm's overall performance. (39)

client PCs Personal computers that are part of a LAN. (700)

closed promotion system A promotion system in which managers choose from inside the firm the workers who will be considered for a promotion. (217)

closed shop A work place in which only those who already belong to the appropriate union may be hired by the company. (274)

closing In personal sales, the process of asking the customer to buy the product. (445)

collateral Any asset that a lender has the right to seize in the event of nonrepayment of a loan. (561)

collective bargaining The process in which union leaders and management personnel negotiate common terms and conditions of employment for those workers represented by the unions. (263)

collusion An illegal agreement among companies in an industry to set ("fix") prices for their products. (92)

commercial paper A method of short-run fund-raising in which a firm sells unsecured notes for less than the set face value and then repurchases them at face value within 270 days; buyers' profits are the difference between the original price paid and the face value. (563)

committee and **team authority** Authority granted to committees or work teams that play central roles in the firm's operations. (162)

commodities market The market in which investors can buy and sell contracts for a variety of goods. (604)

common carriers Trucking companies that transport goods for any firm or individual wishing to make a shipment. (481)

common law The unwritten law of England; built on precedents, or the previous legal opinions of judges. (99)

common stock Shares whose owners have last claim on the corporation's assets (after creditors and owners of preferred stock) but who have voting rights in the firm. (37)

communism A kind of planned economy in which the government owns and operates all industries. (9)

comparable worth The concept that individuals whose jobs require similar levels of education, training, and skills—although they do not involve the same tasks—should be compensated in the same manner. (224)

comparative advantage A nation's ability to produce some products more cheaply or better than it can others. (651)

comparative advertising An advertising strategy, appropriate to the growth stage of the product life cycle, in which the goal is to influence the customer to switch from a competitor's similar product to the firm's product by directly comparing the two products. (436)

compensation system What a firm offers its employees in return for their labor. (223)

competition The vying among businesses in a particular market or industry to best satisfy consumer demands and earn profits. (16)

competition policy Seeks to eliminate restrictive trade practices and stimulate production and employment. (634)

compressed workweek Employees work fewer days per week, but more hours on the days they do work. (253)

compulsory arbitration A method of settling a contract dispute in which labor unions and management are forced to explain their positions to a neutral third party who issues a binding resolution. (279)

computer graphics programs Applications programs that convert numerical and character data into pictorial form. (696)

computer network A form of computer system architecture in which computers at different locations function independently but are also interconnected and able to exchange information with one another. (699)

computer piracy The unauthorized copying of software programs. (692)

computer-aided design (CAD) Computer analysis and graphics programs that are used to create new products. (318)

computer-aided manufacturing (CAM) Computer systems used to design and control all the equipment and tools for producing goods. (319)

computer-integrated manufacturing (CIM) Computer systems that drive robots and control the flow of materials and supplies in the goods- production process. (318)

concentric diversification Involves adding new but related products or services to the existing business. (151)

conceptual skills Skills associated with abstract thinking, problem diagnosis and analysis, and future planning. (130)

conglomerate diversification Involves adding unrelated products or services to the existing business. (152)

conglomerate merger A merger of two firms in completely unrelated businesses. (61)

Constitution Act, 1867 Divided authority over labor regulations between the federal and provincial governments. (268)

consumer behavior The study of the process by which customers come to purchase and consume a product or service. (401)

consumer goods Products purchased by individuals for their personal use. (385)

consumer finance company Makes personal loans to consumers. (548)

consumer movement Activism on the part of consumers seeking better value from businesses. (70)

Consumer Packaging and Labelling Act A federal law that provides comprehensive rules for packaging and labeling of consumer products. (431)

consumer rights The legally protected rights of consumers to choose products, to safety from those products, to be informed about any potential risks from a product, and to be heard in the event of problems with a product. (70)

consumerism A social movement that seeks to protect and expand the rights of consumers in their dealings with businesses. (92)

containerization The use of standardized heavy-duty containers in which many items are sealed at the point of shipment and opened only at the final destination. (480)

contingency approach The philosophy that the appropriate managerial behavior in any situation is dependent (contingent) on the unique characteristics of the situation. (136)

contingency planning A plan that attempts to identify in advance important aspects of a business or its market that might change and to define how the firm will respond in the event of those changes. (147)

continuous improvement The ongoing commitment to improve products and processes, step by step, in pursuit of ever-increasing customer satisfaction. (365)

continuous process Any production process in which the flow of transformation from resources to finished product is fairly smooth, straight, and continuous. (302)

contract An agreement between two parties to act in a specified way or to perform certain acts. (100)

contract carriers Independent transporters who contract to serve as transporters for industrial customers only. (481)

control chart A statistical process control method in which results of test sampling of a product are plotted on a diagram that reveals when the process is beginning to depart from normal operating conditions. (361)

control limit The critical value on a control chart that indicates the level at which quality deviation is sufficiently unacceptable to merit investigation. (361)

control unit That part of the computer's central processing unit that locates instructions, transfers data to the arithmetic logic unit for processing, and transmits results to an output device. (686)

controller The individual who manages all the firm's accounting activities. (500)

controlling   That portion of a manager's job concerned with monitoring the firm's performance and, if necessary, acting to bring it in line with the firm's goals. (123)

convenience goods services   Relatively inexpensive consumer goods that are bought and used rapidly and regularly, causing consumers to spend little time looking for them or comparing their prices. (418)

convenience stores   Retail stores that offer high accessibility, extended hours, and fast service on a usually limited selection of items. (473)

convertible bond   Any bond that offers bondholders the option of accepting common stock instead of cash in repayment. (602)

cooperative   A group of individuals or businesses that joins forces to act as one large company for marketing and/or purchasing purposes. (42)

cooperative advertising   Advertising in which a manufacturer together with a retailer or wholesaler advertises in order to reach customers. (441)

cooperative strategies   Joint ventures, alliances, networks, strategic partnering, and strategic networks. (152)

corporate bond   A promise by the issuing company to pay the holder a certain amount of money on a specified date, with stated interest payments in the interim; a form of long-term debt financing. (564)

corporate culture   The shared experiences, stories, beliefs, and norms that characterize a firm. (132)

corporate strategy   A strategy concerned with what businesses a corporation does and does not wish to enter. (148)

corporation   A business considered by law to be a legal entity separate from its owners with many of the legal rights and privileges of a person; a form of business organization in which the liability of the owners is limited to their investment in the firm. (35)

cost leadership   Striving to have the lowest costs in the industry. (151)

cost of goods sold   Any expenses directly involved in producing or selling a good or service during a given time period. (512)

cost-of-living adjustment (COLA)   A contract clause specifying that wages will increase automatically with the rate of inflation. (275)

coupon   A sales-promotion method featuring a certificate that entitles the bearer to a stated savings off a product's regular price. (446)

craft unions   Unions organized by trades; usually composed of skilled workers. (270)

creative selling   In personal sales, the use of techniques designed to persuade a customer to buy a product when the benefits of the product are not readily apparent or the item is very expensive. (444)

credence qualities   Qualities in a product that a purchaser believes to exist but that are not subject to objective proof. (341)

credit   In bookkeeping, any transaction that decreases assets or increases liabilities or owner's equity; always entered in the right column. (507)

credit insurance   Insurance to protect against customers' failure to pay their bills. (582)

credit union   Cooperative savings and lending associations that are owned by their members. (545)

crisis management   Managing an unexpected emergency by making an immediate response to it. (148)

cross training   Training employees to perform a variety of jobs as a way of increasing the supply of services. (339)

Crown corporation   One that is accountable to parliament or a provincial legislature for the conduct of its affairs. (632)

cumulative preferred stock   Preferred stock on which dividends not paid in the past must first be paid up before the firm may pay dividends to common shareholders. (596)

currency   Paper money and coins issued by the Canadian government. (531)

current assets   Cash and other assets that can be converted into cash in the following year. (509)

current liabilities   Any debts owed by the firm that must be repaid within the year. (510)

current ratio   A form of liquidity ratio calculated as current assets divided by current liabilities. (516)

customer departmentalization   Departmentaliza-tion according to the type of customer likely to buy a given product. (157)

D

data   Raw facts and figures. (681)

data base   A centralized, organized collection of related data. (693)

data-base management   Applications programs that keep track of and manipulate the relevant data of a business. (695)

data communication networks   Global networks that permit users to send electronic messages quickly and economically. (707)

debentures   Unsecured bonds. (601)

debit   In bookkeeping, any transaction that increases assets or decreases liabilities or owners' equity; always entered in the left column. (507)

debit card   An encoded plastic card that enables an individual to transfer money from one bank account to another or from the individual's bank account to a store's account to pay for merchandise. (537)

debt   Borrowed funds that require interest payments and must be repaid. (187)

debt financing   Raising money to meet long-term expenditures by borrowing from outside the company; usually takes the form of long-term loans and the sale of corporate bonds. (563)

debt ratios   Measures of a firm's ability to meet its long-term debts; used to analyze the risks of investing in the firm. (517)

debt-to-owners'-equity ratio   A form of debt ratio calculated as total liabilities divided by owners' equity. (517)

debugging   Removing problems from a program. (701)

decentralization   Occurs when lower- and middle-level managers are allowed to make significant decisions. (161)

decentralized system   A form of computer system architecture in which processing is done in many locations using separate data bases and computer personnel. (699)

decertification   The process by which employees terminate their union's right to represent them. (278)

decision making   That portion of a manager's job concerned with choosing among alternative courses of action to reach a desired goal. (122)

decision support systems (DSS)   Computer systems used to help managers consider alternatives when making decisions on complicated problems. (320)

deductible   A previously agreed-on amount of loss the insured must absorb before reimbursement from the insurer. (574)

deed   A document showing ownership of real property. (102)

definition of the service package   Involves identification of the tangible and intangible features that define the service. (422)

delegation   The assignment of a task, responsibility, and/or authority by a manager to a subordinate. (160)

demand   The willingness and ability of buyers to purchase a product. (12)

demand deposits   Money in chequing accounts. (531)

democratic style   A management style characterized by the manager making decisions that take into account the input of subordinates. (136)

demotion   Reducing the rank of a person who is not performing up to standard. (222)

department stores   Large retail stores that offer a wide variety of high-quality, mainly nonfood items divided into specialized departments. (469)

departmentalization   The grouping of jobs into logical units. (157)

depreciation   Distributing the cost of a major asset over the years in which it produces revenues; calculated by subtracting each year the asset's original value divided by the number of years in its productive life. (510)

depression   A particularly severe and long-lasting recession like the one that affected the world in the 1930s. (20)

deregulation   The removal or easing of government-imposed laws or restrictions on business operations. (64)

derived demand Demand for industrial products that is caused by (derived from) demand for related consumer products. (405)

desktop publishing Combines word processing and graphics capabilities in producing typeset-quality text from personal computers. (700)

differentiation Striving to provide products that are distinctive from those of competitors. (151)

direct channel A distribution channel in which the product travels from the producer to the consumer without passing through any intermediary. (464)

direct mail Involves fliers or other types of printed advertisements mailed directly to consumers' homes or places of business. (439)

direct selling Marketing products and services to customers door-to-door. (476)

discount Any price reduction offered by the seller to persuade customers to buy a product. (462)

discount brokerage houses A stock brokerage that charges a minimal fee for executing clients' orders but offers limited services. (607)

discount houses Bargain retail stores that offer major items such as televisions and large appliances at discount prices. (472)

distribution That part of the marketing mix concerned with getting products from the producer to the buyer, including physical transportation and choice of sales outlets. (390)

distribution centers Warehouses used to provide storage of goods for only short periods before they are shipped to retail stores. (478)

distribution channel The path that a product follows from the producer to the end-user. (464)

distribution of government powers Different levels of government have responsibility for different matters. (627)

distribution mix The combination of distribution channels that a firm selects to get a product to end users. (463)

dividend A part of a corporation's profits paid out per share to those who hold its stock. (37)

divisional structure Divides the organization into several divisions, each of which operates as a semi-autonomous unit and profit center. (155)

double-entry accounting system A bookkeeping system, developed in the fifteenth century and still in use, that requires every transaction to be entered in two ways—how it affects assets and how it affects liabilities and owners' equity—so that the accounting equation is always in balance. (507)

double taxation A corporation must pay taxes on its profits, and the shareholders must pay personal income taxes on the dividends they receive. (41)

Dow Jones Industrial Average An overall market index based on stock prices of 30 of the largest industrial, transportation, and utility firms listed on the New York Stock Exchange. (607)

drop shipper A type of wholesaler which does not carry inventory or handle the product. (469)

dumping Selling a product for less abroad than in the producing nation; illegal in Canada. (664)

E

earnings per share A form of profitability ratio calculated as net income divided by the number of common shares outstanding. (518)

ecology The relationship between living things and their environment. (73)

economic system The way in which a nation allocates its resources among its citizens. (7)

electronic funds transfer (EFT) Combines computer and communications technology to transfer funds or information into, from, within, and among financial institutions. (537)

electronic mail (e-mail) The electronic transmission of letters, reports, and other information between computers. (705)

electronic shopping Using computer information systems to help sellers connect with buyers' computers with information about products and services. (476)

electronic spreadsheet Applications programs that allow the user to enter categories of data and determine the effect of changes in one category (e.g., sales) on other categories (e.g., profits). (694)

embargo A government order forbidding exportation and/or importation of a particular product. (663)

emotional motives Those reasons for purchasing a product that involve nonobjective factors. (404)

employee empowerment Principle that all employees are valuable contributors to business and should be entrusted with certain decisions regarding their work. (367)

employee stock ownership plan (ESOP) An arrangement whereby a corporation buys its own stock with loaned funds and holds it in trust for its employees. Employees "earn" the stock based on some condition such as seniority. The business's profits pay off the loan used to buy the stock. (44)

Employment Equity Act of 1986 Designates four groups as employment disadvantaged—women, visible minorities, aboriginal people, and people with disabilities. (214)

empowerment Motivating and energizing employees to create product quality and bend-over-backwards service to customers. (237)

endorsement Signing your name to a negotiable instrument, which makes it transferable to another person or organization. (102)

endowment Insurance that pays face value after a fixed period of time whether the policyholder is alive or dead. (584)

entrepreneur An individual who organizes and manages natural resources, labor, and capital in order to produce goods and services to earn a profit, but who also runs the risks of failure. (9; 177)

entrepreneurship An individual's willingness to take advantage of business opportunities and to assume the risk of establishing and operating a business. (177)

environmental analysis The second step in strategy formulation; it involves scanning the environment for threats and opportunities. (148)

equilibrium The price and quality of a product at which the quantities demanded and supplied are equal. (13)

equity Capital invested in an enterprise by individuals or companies who become owners. (187)

equity financing Raising money to meet long-term expenditures by issuing common stock or retaining earnings. (564)

equity theory Suggests that people compare what they contribute to their job with what they get in return; they then compare their input/outcome ratio with that of other employees. (246)

ethics Individual standards or moral values regarding what is right and wrong or good and bad. (83)

European Union (EU) An agreement among ten Western European nations to eliminate quotas and keep tariffs low on products traded among themselves and to impose high tariffs and low quotas on goods imported from other nations. (665)

exchange Any transaction in which two or more parties interchange something of value. (390)

exclusive distribution A distribution strategy in which a product's distribution is limited to only one wholesaler or retailer in a given geographic area. (467)

executive information systems Easy-access information clusters especially designed for instant access by upper-level managers. (705)

expectancy theory Suggests that people are motivated to work toward rewards which they want *and* which they believe they have a reasonable chance of obtaining. (245)

expedited transportation Paying a higher-than-normal fee for truck delivery for guaranteed delivery times. (479)

expense items Relatively inexpensive industrial goods that are consumed rapidly and regularly. (418)

experience qualities Qualities in a product that can be perceived after purchase by senses such as taste. (341)

experimentation A market research technique in which the reactions of similar people are compared under different circumstances. (400)

expert system A form of artificial intelligence in which a program draws on the rules an expert in a given field has laid out to arrive at a solution to a problem. (704)

exports Products made or grown in Canada which are sold abroad. (649)

express warranty A specific claim about a product made by the manufacturer. (102)

external failures Allowing defective products to leave the factory and get into consumers' hands. (362)

extraterritoriality The application of one country's laws to the subsidiaries of its companies in another country. (673)

F

factoring Selling a firm's accounts receivable to another company for some percentage of their face value to realize immediate cash; the buyer's profits depend on its ability to collect the receivables. (563)

factoring company A firm that buys accounts receivable from a firm for less than their face value and collects those receivables for their full value. (547)

factors of production The resources used to produce goods and services: natural resources, labor, capital, and entrepreneurs. (8)

factory outlets Bargain retail stores that are owned by the manufacturers whose products they sell. (473)

factory system A process in which all the machinery, materials, and workers required to produce a good in large quantities are brought together in one place. (48)

fax machine A machine that can quickly transmit a copy of documents or graphics over telephone lines. (705)

Federal Business Development Bank Took over the operations of the Industrial Development Bank in 1975; particularly active in lending money to small business. (549)

federal deficit Occurs when federal expenditures are greater than federal revenues in a given year. (71)

finance The business function involving decisions about a firm's long-term investments and obtaining the funds to pay for those investments. (557)

finance era The period during the 1980s when there were many mergers and much buying and selling of business enterprises. (51)

financial accounting system The process whereby interested groups are kept informed about the financial condition of a business firm. (500)

financial control The process of checking actual performance against plans to ensure that the desired financial status is achieved. (557)

financial managers Those managers responsible for planning and overseeing the financial resources of a firm. (557)

financial plan A description of how a business will reach some financial position it seeks for the future; includes projections for sources and uses of funds. (558)

financial statement Any of several types of broad reports regarding a company's financial status; most often used in reference to balance sheets, income statements, and/or statements of cash flows. (508)

finished goods inventory That portion of a firm's inventory consisting of completed goods ready for sale. (559)

first-line managers Those managers responsible for supervising the work of employees. (125)

fiscal policies Refer to the collection and spending of government revenues. (23)

fixed assets Assets that have long-term use or value to the firm, such as land, buildings, and machinery. (510)

fixed costs Those costs unaffected by the number of goods or services produced or sold. (459)

flexible manufacturing system (FMS) A production system in which automatic equipment produces small batches of different goods on the same production line. (308)

flextime A method of increasing employees' job satisfaction by allowing them some choice in the hours they work. (252)

focus Concentrating on serving a particular market segment. (151)

focus group A market research technique involving a small group of people brought together and allowed to discuss selected issues in depth. (399)

Food and Drug Act Establishes quality levels for food and drugs. (636)

follow-up Checking to ensure that production decisions are being implemented. (312)

floppy disks Portable disks which can be easily inserted into and removed from the computer. (687)

forecasts Estimates of future demand for new and existing products. (305)

foreign exchange rate The ratio of one currency to another. (652)

Foreign Investment Review Agency (FIRA) Government agency set up to screen new foreign direct investment in Canada; supposed to ensure that significant benefits accrue to Canada. (674)

form utility That quality of a product satisfying a human want because of its form; requires raw materials to be transformed into a finished product. (300)

formal organization The specified relationship between individuals, their jobs, and their authority, as shown in the company's organizational chart. (164)

franchisee A person who agrees to sell the product or service of a manufacturer under certain specified conditions. (183)

franchising A legal arrangement under which a buyer (franchisee) purchases the right to sell the good or service of the seller (franchisor) as well as certain management and financial aid supplied by the seller. (183)

franchisor A manufacturer who allows a person to sell the manufacturer's products or services under certain specified conditions. (183)

freedom of choice The right to choose what to buy or sell, including one's labor. (16)

free-rein style A management style characterized by the manager allowing subordinates to make most decisions. (136)

freight forwarders Common carriers that lease bulk space from other carriers and resell that space to firms making small shipments. (481)

friendly takeover An acquisition in which the management of the acquired company welcomes the firm's buyout by another company. (61)

full-service brokerage A stock brokerage that offers a variety of services, including investment advice, to help clients reach their financial goals. (607)

full-service merchant wholesaler A merchant wholesaler who provides storage and delivery in addition to wholesaling services. (469)

functional departmentalization Departmentaliza-tion according to a group's functions or activities. (159)

functional structure Various units in an organization are formed based on the functions that must be carried out to reach the organization's goals. (155)

futures contract An agreement to purchase a specified amount of a commodity at a given price on a set date in the future. (604)

G

gain-sharing plan An incentive program in which employees receive a bonus if the firm's costs are reduced because of greater worker efficiency and/or productivity. (224)

Gantt chart A diagram laying out the steps in the production schedule along with the projected time to complete each step; used in production control. (310)

General Agreement on Tariffs and Trade (GATT) An international trade accord in which 92 signatories agreed to reduce tariffs; often ignored by signatories. (665)

general partnership   A business with two or more owners who share in the operation of the firm and in financial responsibility for the firm's debts. (33)

generally accepted accounting principles (GAAP)   Those standard rules and methods used by accountants in preparing financial reports. (502)

generic products   Products carrying no brand or producer name and sold at lower prices. (429)

geographic departmentalization   Departmentalization according to the area of the country or world supplied. (159)

givebacks   Union sacrifices of previously won wages and benefits in return for increased job security. (266)

globalization   The process by which the world economy is becoming a single interdependent system. (649)

goal setting theory   Suggests that when people set specific, quantified, time-framed goals they perform better. (247)

goals   Results the organization wants to achieve. (143)

government policy formulation   The process by which changes are made in current government policies. (641)

grapevine   An informal communication network that carries gossip and other information throughout an organization. (164)

graphic user interface   The user-friendly display that helps users select from among the many possible applications of the computer. (689)

greenmail   A process in which a group of investors proposes a hostile takeover of a firm but allows the firm to buy back its stock at a large profit to the investors. (63)

grievance   A complaint on the part of a union member that management is in some way violating the terms of the contract. (279)

gross domestic product (GDP)   The value of all goods and services produced by an economy. (354)

gross national product (GNP)   The total of all completed goods and services produced by an economic system during a one-year period. (23)

gross profit (gross margin)   A firm's revenues (net sales) less its cost of goods sold. (512)

group life insurance   Life insurance written for a group of people rather than an individual. (584)

groupware   A system that allows two or more individuals to communicate electronically between desktop PCs. (705)

growth   An increase in the amount of goods and services produced using the same resources. (21)

growth rate of productivity   The increase in productivity in a given year over the previous year. (352)

guaranteed annual wage   A provision in a labor contract that maintains the workers' income level during a year. (274)

H

hard disks   Rigid metal disks permanently enclosed in the computer. (687)

hardware   The physical components of a computer system. (685)

Hawthorne effect   The tendency for workers' productivity to increase when workers feel they are receiving special attention from management. (241)

Hazardous Products Act   Regulates or completely bans dangerous products. (635)

high technology   As applied to businesses, a firm that spends twice as much on research and development and employees twice as many technical personnel as the average manufacturing firm. (59)

high-contact system   Service system in which the customer must be part of the system to receive the service. (332)

holding costs   Costs of keeping currently unsalable goods, or costs of money that could be otherwise invested. (314)

horizontal integration   Occurs when a corporation purchases or obtains control over another enterprise in the same business. (151)

horizontal merger   A merger of two firms that have previously been direct competitors in the same industry. (61)

hostile takeover   An acquisition in which the management of the acquired company fights the firm's buyout by another company. (62)

human relations   Interactions between employers and employees and their attitudes toward one another. (237)

human relations skills   Skills associated with understanding and working well with other employees. (128)

human-resource management   The development, administration, and evaluation of programs to acquire and enhance the quality and performance of people in a business. (209)

human-resource managers   Those managers responsible for hiring, training, evaluating, and compensating employees. (127)

hypermarkets   Very large retail stores that offer a variety of food and nonfood items divided into specialized departments. (475)

I

implied warranty   A suggestion that a product will perform in the way the manufacturer claims. (102)

imports   Products sold in Canada that are made or grown abroad. (649)

incentive program   Designed to encourage managers to make certain decisions and take certain actions desired by government. (224, 638)

income (profit-and-loss) statement   A type of financial statement that describes a firm's revenues and expenses and indicates whether the firm has earned a profit or suffered a loss during a given period. (511)

income tax   A tax paid by individuals and corporations on income received in a given tax year. (636)

independent agent   A foreign individual or organization who agrees to represent an exporter's interests in a foreign market. (657)

independent local union   One that is not formally affiliated with any labor organization. (272)

industrial advertising   Advertising by manufacturers designed to reach other manufacturers' professional purchasing agents and managers of firms buying raw materials and/or components. (441)

Industrial Development Bank   Created to make loans to business firms; a subsidiary to the Bank of Canada. (549)

Industrial Disputes Investigation Act (1907)   Provided for compulsory investigation of labor disputes by a government-appointed board before a strike was allowed. (268)

industrial goods   Products purchased by companies to use directly or indirectly to produce other products. (385)

industrial market   Includes businesses which buy goods to convert into other products that will be sold to ultimate consumers. (405)

Industrial Revolution   A major change in goods production that began in England in the mid- eighteenth century and was characterized by a shift to the factory system, mass production, and specialization of labor. (48)

industrial selling   Selling products to other businesses, either for manufacturing other products or for resale. (444)

industrial union   A union composed of all workers in a particular industry, regardless of their skills or specific jobs. (271)

inelasticity of demand   Exists when a price change for a product does not have much effect on demand. (405)

inflation   A period of widespread price increases throughout an economic system. (19)

informal organization   A network of personal interactions and relationships among employees unrelated to the firm's formal authority structure as shown in its organizational chart. (164)

information   A meaningful, useful interpretation of data. (681)

information managers   Those managers responsible for the design and implementation of systems to gather, process, and disseminate information. (128)

information services   Service industries that provide information in return for a fee. Examples include law, accounting, and computer processing. (59)

informative advertising   An advertising strategy, appropriate to the introduction stage of the product life cycle, in which the goal is to make potential customers aware that a product exists. (436)

input device   That part of a computer's hardware concerned with getting data into the computer in a form the computer can understand; common forms include the keyboard, punch cards, magnetic tape, and the "mouse." (685)

inside directors   Members of a corporation's board of directors who are also full-time employees of the corporation. (38)

insider trading   The use of special knowledge about a firm to make a profit on the stock market. (94; 609)

institutional advertising   Advertising that promotes a firm's long-term image rather than a specific product. (441)

institutional investors   Organizations like mutual and pension funds which purchase large blocks of company stock. (46; 592)

institutional market   Consists of nongovernment organizations such as hospitals, churches, and schools. (405)

insurance   A way to share risk in which many individuals contribute to a fund out of which those who suffer losses are paid. (524)

insurance agent   A person who markets insurance and is paid a commission by the insurance company. (579)

insurance broker   A freelance agent who represents insurance buyers rather than insurance sellers. (579)

insurance policy   A written contract between an individual or firm and an insurance company transferring financial liability in the event of some loss to the insurance company in return for a fee. (574)

intangible assets   Nonphysical assets such as patents, trademarks, copyrights, and franchise fees that have economic value, but whose precise value is difficult to calculate. (510)

integrated circuit   A group of transistors and circuits embedded in a silicon chip; its application marked the start of the third generation of computers. (705)

intensive distribution   A distribution strategy in which a product is distributed in nearly every possible outlet, using many channels and channel members. (467)

intentional tort   A wrongful act that is purposefully committed. (102)

intermediary   Any individual or firm other than the producer who participates in a product's distribution. (463)

intermediate goals   Goals dealing with a period one to five years in the future. (144)

intermittent process   Any production process in which the flow of transformation from resources to finished product starts and stops. (303)

intermodal transportation   The combined use of different modes of transportation. (480)

internal failures   Expenses incurred during production and before bad product leaves the plant. (362)

international competitiveness   The ability of a country to generate more wealth than its competitors in world markets. (670)

International Monetary Fund   A group of 150 nations that have combined resources to stabilize the world's currencies. (545)

international union   A union with members in more than one country. (272)

inventory   Materials and goods currently held by the company that will be sold within the year. (559)

inventory control   The receiving, storing, handling, and counting of all resources, partly finished goods, and finished goods; the planning to ensure that an adequate supply of a product is in stock at all times. (313; 478)

inventory turnover ratio   An activity ratio that measures the average number of times inventory is sold and restocked during the year. (519)

investment banker   Any financial institution engaged in buying and reselling new stocks and bonds. (593)

Investment Canada   Replaced the Foreign Investment Review Agency in 1985; designed primarily to attract and facilitate foreign investment in Canada. (674)

ISO 9000   A quality scorecard developed by the International Standards Organization. (363)

J

job analysis   A detailed study of the specific duties entailed in a particular job and the human qualities required for that job. (209)

job description   The objectives, responsibilities, and key tasks of a job, the conditions under which it will be done, its relationship to other positions, and the skills needed to perform it. (209)

job enrichment   A method of increasing employees' job satisfaction by extending or adding motivating factors such as responsibility or growth. (251)

job redesign   A method of increasing employees' job satisfaction by improving the worker-job fit through the combining of tasks, the creation of natural work groups, and/or the establishment of client relationships. (251)

job-relatedness   The principle that all personnel decisions, policies, and programs should be based on the requirements of a position. (209)

job satisfaction   The pleasure and feeling of accomplishment employees derive from performing their jobs well. (237)

job specialization   The use of individuals with specialized skills to perform specialized tasks within a business. (157)

job specification   The specific skills, education, and experience needed to perform a job. (210)

journal   A chronological record of a firm's financial transactions, along with a brief description of each transaction. (505)

just-in-time (JIT) inventory system   A method of inventory control in which materials are acquired and put into production just as they are needed. (315)

K

keiretsu   Loosely affiliated groups of companies in Japan in the banking and manufacturing industries. (671)

key ratio   A value obtained by dividing one value on a financial statement by another value. (515)

L

label   That part of a product's packaging that identifies the product's name and contents and sometimes its benefits. (430)

labor   The mental and physical training and talents of people; sometimes called human resources. (8)

labor-intensive process   Manufacturing or service processes that depend more on people than on machines. (303)

labor productivity   A partial productivity ratio calculated as total outputs divided by labor inputs for a company and as gross domestic product divided by the total number of workers for a nation. (354)

labor unions   Groups of individuals who work together to achieve shared job-related goals. (263)

large scale integration (LSI)   The inclusion of many circuits with different functions on a single chip; its use is characteristic of fourth-generation computers. (702)

law   The set of rules and standards that a society agrees upon to govern the behavior of its citizens. (99)

law of demand   The principle that buyers will purchase (demand) more of a product as price drops. (12)

law of large numbers   The statistical principle that the larger the number of cases involved, the more closely the actual rate will be to the statistically calculated rate. (578)

law of one price   The principle that identical products should sell for the same price in all countries. (532)

law of supply   The principle that producers will offer (supply) more of a product as price rises. (12)

lead time   The time between placing an order and actually receiving it. (314)

leading   That portion of a manager's job concerned with guiding and motivating employees to meet the firm's objectives. (123)

lease   Grants the use of an asset for a specified period of time in return for payment. (102)

ledger   Summations of journal entries, by category, that show the effects of transactions on the balance in each account. (505)

letter of credit   A promise by a bank to pay money to a business firm if certain conditions are met. (537)

level of productivity   The dollar value of goods and services produced versus the dollar value of resources used to produce them. (351)

leverage Using borrowed funds to make purchases, thus increasing the user's purchasing power, potential rate of return, and risk of loss. (517)

liability Any debt owed by a firm or individual to others. (506)

liability insurance Insurance covering losses resulting from damage to the persons or property of other people or firms. (579)

licensed brands Products promoted by and carrying a name associated with the retailer or wholesaler, not the manufacturer. (428)

licensing agreement The owner of a product or process allows another business to produce or distribute the product for a fee. (658)

life insurance Insurance that pays benefits to survivors of a policyholder. (583)

life insurance company A mutual or stock company that shares risks with its policyholders in return for payment of a premium. (547)

limit order An order to a broker to buy a certain security only if its price is less than or equal to a given limit. (608)

limited-function merchant wholesaler An independent wholesaler who provides only wholesaling—not warehousing or transportation—services. (469)

line managers Managers in the regular chain of command of an organization. (162)

line of credit A standing agreement between a bank and a firm in which the bank specifies the maximum amount it will make available to the borrower for a short-term unsecured loan; the borrower can then draw on these funds when available. (562)

line organization An organization in which all positions are line positions and no staff experts are employed. (162)

line-staff organization An organization that employs both line managers and staff experts. (162)

liquidate Sell the assets of a business. (32)

liquidation A strategic option involving selling the business's assets and ceasing to do business. (152)

liquidity The ease and speed with which an asset can be converted to cash; cash is said to be perfectly liquid. (509)

liquidity ratios Measures of a firm's ability to meet its immediate debts; used to analyze the risks of investing in the firm. (516)

load fund A mutual fund in which investors are charged a sales commission when they buy into or sell out of the fund. (602)

lobbyist A person hired by a company or an industry to represent its interests with government officials. (66)

local area network (LAN) A system linking computers in one building or in a small geographical area by cable. (703)

local-content laws Laws requiring that products sold in a particular country be at least partly made in that country. (663)

local unions Unions organized at the level of a single company, plant, or small geographic region. (271)

lockout A weapon of management in which the firm physically denies employees access to the work place to pressure workers to agree to the company's latest contract offer. (277)

long-term goals Goals dealing with extended periods of time, usually five or more years into the future. (144)

long-term liabilities Any debts owed by the firm that need not be repaid within the year. (510)

low-contact system Service system in which the customer need not be a part of the system to receive the service. (332)

M

M-1 A measure of the money supply that counts only currency and demand deposits. (531)

M-2 A measure of the money supply that includes everything in M-1 plus time deposits, money market mutual funds, and savings deposits. (531)

mail order A form of nonstore retailing in which customers place orders for merchandise shown in catalogues and receive their orders via mail. (475)

mainframe A computer whose capacity, speed, and cost fall between those of minicomputers and supercomputers (698)

management The process of planning, organizing, leading, and controlling a business's financial, physical, human, and information resources in order to achieve its goals. (121)

management by objectives (MBO) An approach to management control and employee motivation in which a manager and an employee cooperatively establish goals against which the employee is later evaluated. (145)

management development programs Those development programs in which current and prospective managers gain new conceptual, analytical, and problem-solving skills. (220)

management information system (MIS) An organized method of transforming data into information that can be used for decision making. (681)

managerial accounting Calls attention to problems and helps managers in their planning, decision making, and controlling of the firm's operations. (501)

margin The percentage of the total sales price that a buyer must put up in order to place an order for stock or a futures contract. (604)

marine insurance A form of transportation insurance covering both the act of transportation (by water, land, or air) and the transported goods. (581)

market An exchange process between buyers and sellers of a particular good or service. (12)

market development Introducing existing products into new geographic areas. (151)

market economy An economic system in which individuals control all or most factors of production and make all or most production decisions. (9)

market index A measure of the market value of stocks; provides a summary of price trends in a specific industry or of the stock market as a whole. (606)

market order An order to a broker to buy or sell a certain security at the current market price. (608)

market penetration Seeking to increase market share in the firm's present markets. (151)

market research The systematic study of what buyers need and how best to meet those needs. (396)

market share A company's percentage of the total market sales for a specific product. (457)

market segmentation Dividing a market into categories according to traits customers have in common. (392)

market value The current price of one share of a stock in the secondary securities market; the real value of a stock. (594)

marketing Planning and executing the development, pricing, promotion, and distribution of ideas, goods, and services to create exchanges that satisfy both buyers' and sellers' objectives. (385)

marketing concept The philosophy that a business must identify and meet consumer wants to make a profit. (387)

marketing era The period during the 1950s and 1960s when business began to identify and meet consumer wants in order to make a profit. (50)

marketing managers Responsible for planning and implementing all the marketing mix activities that result in the transfer of goods or services to customers. (125; 385)

marketing mix The combination of product, pricing, promotion, and distribution strategies used in marketing a product. (387)

marketing plan A detailed strategy for gearing the marketing mix to meet consumer need and wants. (385)

markup The amount added to the cost of an item in order to earn a profit for the retailer or wholesaler. (459)

mass production The manufacture of a good of uniform quality in large quantities. (48)

master production schedule A general, rather than highly detailed, schedule of which product(s) will be produced, when production will occur, and what resources will be used in coming months. (310)

material requirements planning (MRP) A method of inventory control in which a computerized bill of materials is used to estimate production needs so that resources are acquired and put into production only as needed. (316)

materials handling The transportation and arrangement of goods within a warehouse and orderly retrieval of goods from inventory. (478)

materials management Planning, organizing, and controlling of the flow of materials from purchase through distribution of finished goods. (312)

materials productivity A partial productivity ratio calculated as total outputs divided by materials inputs. (354)

matrix organization A project structure in which the project manager nad the regular line managers share authority until the project is concluded. (163)

maturity date The date on or before which a company must pay off the principal of a particular bond issue. (564)

mechanization The process of using machines instead of people to perform certain tasks. (318)

media mix The combination of media chosen by a company to advertise its product. (440)

mediation A method of settling a contract dispute in which a neutral third party is asked to hear arguments from both labor unions and management and offer a suggested solution. (279)

mentor A manager who guides the careers of subordinates by offering them advice, providing them training and expanded responsibility, and otherwise assisting them in gaining promotions. (166)

merchant wholesaler An independent wholesaler who buys and takes legal possession of goods before selling them to customers. (469)

merger The union of two companies to form a single new business. (60)

microcomputer The smallest, slowest, and least expensive form of computer available today; sometimes called a personal computer. (697)

microenterprise An enterprise operating from the home part-time while the entrepreneur continues working as a regular employee of another organization. (182)

microprocessor chip A single silicon chip containing the central processing unit of a computer; its application marked the start of the fourth generation of computers. (701)

middle managers Those managers responsible for implementing the decisions made by top-level managers. (124)

minicomputer A computer whose capacity, speed, and cost fall between those of microcomputers and mainframes. (697)

mission How the company will achieve its purpose. (144)

missionary selling In personal sales, the indirect promotion of a product by offering technical assistance and/or promoting the company's image. (445)

mixed economy An economic system with elements of both a planned economy and a market economy; in practice, typical of most nations' economies. (12)

mixed services Moderate-contact services in which the customer is involved in the service production process to a limited degree. (333)

modem A hardware device permitting the user of a personal computer to link up with other computer systems via telephone lines. (695)

monetary policies Control the size of the nation's money supply. (23)

money Any object that serves as a medium of exchange, a store of value, and a unit of account in a country's economy; must be portable, divisible, durable, and stable. (529)

money-market mutual funds Funds operated by investment companies that bring together pools of assets from many investors. (531)

monopolistic competition A market or industry characterized by a large number of firms supplying products that are similar but distinctive enough from one another to give firms some ability to influence price. (17)

monopoly A market or industry with only one producer who can set the price of its product and/or resources. (18)

morale The generally positive or negative mental attitude of employees toward their work and work place. (237)

motivation The set of forces that cause people to behave in certain ways. (238)

MRP II (manufacuring resource planning) An advanced version of MRP that ties all parts of the organization into the company's production activities. (317)

multi-level marketing A system in which a salesperson earns a commission on their own sales and on the sales of any other salespeople they recruit. (476)

multimedia communications systems Connected networks of communications appliances like faxes, televisions, sound equipment, printing machines, and

photocopiers that may also be linked with mass media such as TV. (706)

multinational firm Controls assets, factories, mines, sales offices, and affiliates in two or more countries. (659)

mutual fund Any company that pools the resources of many investors and uses those funds to purchase various types of financial securities. (602)

mutual insurance company Any insurance company that is owned by its policyholders, who share in its profits. (578)

N

national debt The total amount of money that Canada owes its creditors (presently over $550 billion). (23)

national brands Products distributed by and carrying a name associated with the manufacturer. (427)

National Energy Board Responsible for regulating the construction and operation of oil and gas pipelines that are under the jurisdiction of the Canadian government. (634)

national union A union with members across Canada. (272)

natural monopoly A market or industry in which having only one producer is most efficient because it can meet all of consumers' demand for the product. (18)

natural resources Items in their natural state, including land, water, minerals, and trees, used in the production of goods and services. (8)

negligence A wrongful act that inadvertently causes injury to another person. (102)

negotiable instrument Types of commercial paper that can be transferred among individuals and business firms. (102)

net income (net profit or net earnings) A firm's gross profit less its operating expenses and income taxes. (512)

networking Informal interactions among managers for the purpose of discussing mutual problems, solutions, and opportunities. (220)

no-load fund A mutual fund in which investors are not charged a sales commission when they buy into or sell out of the fund. (602)

North American Free Trade Agreement (NAFTA) A trade agreement signed by Canada, the U.S., Mexico, and, later, Chile, whose purpose is to create a free trade area. (666)

O

object-oriented technology Reduces the complexity of writing software programs by dividing the programs into reusable chunks with standard interfaces. (609)

observation A market research technique involving viewing or otherwise monitoring consumer buying patterns. (398)

odd-even psychological pricing A form of psychological pricing in which prices are not stated in even dollar amounts. (462)

odd lots The purchase or sale of stock in units other than 100 shares. (608)

off-the-job training Those development programs in which employees gain new skills at a location away from the normal work site. (219)

oligopoly A market or industry characterized by a small number of very large firms that have the power to influence the price of their product and/or resources. (17)

on-the-job training Those development programs in which employees gain new skills while performing them at work. (219)

open-book credit A form of trade credit in which buyers receive their merchandise along with an invoice stating the terms of credit, but in which no formal promissory note is signed. (560)

open promotion system An internal promotion system in which all employees are advised of open positions and may apply for those positions if they so desire. (217)

open shop A work place in which union membership has no effect on the hiring or retaining of an individual. (274)

operating expenses Costs incurred by a firm other than those included in cost of goods sold. (512)

operational plan   Highly detailed short-run plan for performing specific tasks necessary to the achievement of strategic goals. (152)

operations control   Managers monitor production performance by comparing results with plans and schedules. (312)

operations production management   The systematic direction and control of the processes that transform resources into finished goods. (300)

operations managers   Those managers responsible for controlling production, inventory, and quality of a firm's products. (127)

order-cycle time   The total amount of time from order placement to the customer actually receiving the order. (478)

order processing   In personal sales, the receiving and follow-through on handling and delivery of an order by a salesperson; in a product's distribution, the receiving and filling of orders for an item. (444; 477)

organizational analysis   The third step in strategy formulation; it involves analyzing the firm's strengths and weaknesses. (148)

organizational chart   A physical depiction of the company's structure showing employee titles and their relationship to one another. (154)

organizational structure   The specification of the jobs to be done within a business and how those jobs relate to one another. (154)

organizing   That portion of a manager's job concerned with structuring the necessary resources to achieve a particular goal. (123)

orientation   The initial acquainting of new employees with the company's policies and programs, with personnel with whom new employees will be interacting, and with the nature of the job. (218)

output device   That part of a computer's hardware that presents results to users; common forms include printers and cathode ray tube (CRT)/video display terminals (VDTs). (686)

outside directors   Members of a corporation's board of directors who are not also day-to-day employees of the corporation. (39)

over-the-counter market   A complex of securities dealers who are informally in constant touch with one another. (598)

owners' equity   Any positive difference between a firm's assets and its liabilities; what would remain for a firm's owners if the company were liquidated, all its assets sold, and all its debts paid. (506)

ownership (possession) utility   That quality of a product satisfying a human want during its consumption or use. (300)

P

packaging   The physical container in which a product is sold, including the label. (430)

par value   The arbitrary value of a stock set by the issuing company's board of directors and stated on some stock certificates; used by accountants but of little significance to investors. (594)

parent corporation   A corporation that owns a subsidiary. (45)

parking   The illegal and complex practice of shifting funds between countries to avoid taxes. (94)

partial productivity ratio   A measure of a firm's overall productivity based on the productivity of its most significant input; calculated as total outputs divided by the selected input. (354)

participative management   A method of increasing employees' job satisfaction by giving them a voice in how they do their jobs and how the company is managed. (248)

penetration-pricing strategy   The decision to price a new product very low in order to sell the most units possible, build customer loyalty, and ultimately raise prices. (461)

pension fund   Accumulates money that will be paid out to plan subscribers at some time in the future. (548)

performance appraisal   A formal program for comparing employees' actual performance with expected performance; used in making decisions about training, promotions, compensation, and firing. (220)

performance quality   The overall degree of quality; how well the features of a product meet consumers' needs and how well the product performs. (357)

personal liability   For a business, responsibility for certain actions of those who work for the business. (579)

personal property   Tangible or intangible assets other than real property. (101)

personal selling   A promotional technique involving the use of person-to-person communication to sell products. (389)

persuasive advertising   An advertising strategy, appropriate to the growth stage of the product life cycle, in which the goal is to influence the customer to buy the firm's product rather than the similar product of a competitor. (436)

PERT (Program Evaluation and Review Technique)   A method of diagramming the steps in the production schedule along with the projected time to complete each step, taking into account the sequence of steps and the critical path of those steps. (311)

physical distribution   Those activities needed to move a product from the manufacturer to the ultimate consumer. (477)

picketing   A weapon of labor unions in which members march at the entrance to the company with signs outlining their complaints about management. (277)

piecework system   Paying workers a set rate for each piece of work produced. (240)

place utility   That quality of a product satisfying a human want because of where it is made available. (300)

planned economy   An economic system in which the government controls all or most factors of production and makes all or most production decisions. (9)

planning   That portion of a manager's job concerned with determining what the business needs to do and the best way to do it. (121)

plans   Activities that must be performed if a business is to achieve its goals. (145)

pledging accounts receivable   Using accounts receivable as collateral for a loan. (562)

point-of-purchase (POP) display   A sales promotion method in which a product display is so located in a retail store as to encourage buying of the product. (447)

poison pill   A defence management adopts to make its firm less attractive to a current or potential hostile suitor in a takeover attempt. (62)

pollution   The injection of harmful substances into the environment. (73; 88)

positioning   In marketing, the process of fixing, adapting, and communicating the nature of the product. (392)

preferred stock   Shares whose owners have first claim on the corporation's assets and profits but who have no voting rights in the firm. (37)

premises liability   For a business, responsibility for occurrences on its premises. (580)

premium   A sales promotion method in which some item is offered free or at a bargain price to customers in return for buying a specified product, or a fee paid by a company or individual to an insurance company in return for the insurance company accepting a certain risk. (447)

price leadership   The dominant firm in the industry establishes product prices and other companies follow along. (461)

price lining   The practice of offering all items in certain categories at a limited number of predetermined price points. (462)

price-skimming strategy   The decision to price a new product as high as possible to earn the maximum profit on each unit sold. (461)

pricing   Deciding what the company will receive in exchange for its products. (388; 457)

primary data   Information developed through new research by the firm or its agents. (397)

primary reserve requirement   The percentage of its various deposits that a chartered bank must keep in vault cash or as deposits with the Bank of Canada. (544)

primary securities market   The sale and purchase of newly issued stocks and bonds by firms or governments. (593)

primary storage   That part of the computer's central processing unit that houses the computer's memory of those items it needs to operate. (686)

prime rate of interest   The lowest rate charged to borrowers. (541)

privacy invasion   Intruders gain unauthorized access to computers in order to steal information or tamper with data. (692)

private brands   Products promoted by and carrying a name associated with the retailer or wholesaler, not the manufacturer. (428)

private carriers   Transportation systems owned by the shipper. (481)

private corporation   A business whose stock is held by a small group of individuals and is not usually available for sale to the general public. (39)

private enterprise   An economic system characterized by private property rights, freedom of choice, profits, and competition. (14)

private property   The right to buy, own, use, and sell an item. (16)

private warehouses   Warehouses owned and used by just one company. (478)

privatization   The transfer of business activities from the government to the private sector. (65)

Privy Council Order 1003 (1943)   Recognized the right of employees to bargain collectively. (268)

process capability study   A statistical process control method in which samples of the product are measured to determine the amount of process variations; shows the outputs' conformity with or deviation from specification limits. (360)

process departmentalization   Departmentalization according to the preduction process used to make a good. (158)

process layout   A way of organizing production activities such that equipment and people are grouped together according to their function. (306)

process variation   Any change in employees, materials, work methods, or equipment that affects output quality. (360)

product   A good, service, or idea that satisfies buyers' needs and demands. (388)

product advertising   Promotes a general type of product or service like milk or dental services. (441)

product departmentalization   Departmentalization according to the specific good produced. (158)

product development   Improving existing products for existing or new customers. (151)

product differentiation   The creation of a product or product image that differs enough from existing products to attract consumers. (388)

product layout   A way of organizing production activities such that equipment and people are set up to produce only one type of good and are arranged according to that good's production requirements. (306)

product liability   For businesses, responsibility for injuries caused to users because of negligence in designing and manufacturing a product. (102; 579)

product life cycle (PLC)   The concept that the profit-producing life of any product goes through a cycle of introduction, growth, maturity (leveling off), and decline. (423)

product line   A group of similar products intended for a similar group of buyers who will use them in a similar fashion. (418)

product mix   The group of products a company has available for sale. (418)

product positioning   The establishment of an easily identifiable image of a product in the minds of consumers. (432)

production era   The period during the early twentieth century when North American businesses focused almost exclusively on improving productivity and manufacturing methods. (50)

productivity   A measure of efficiency that compares how much is produced with the resources used to produce it. (23; 351)

professional liability   For a business or a business person, responsibility for an individual's actions in working at the business or profession. (579)

profit   What remains (if anything) after a business's expenses are subtracted from its sales revenues. (7)

profit center   Treatment of a division of a corporation as if it were a separate company with regard to its individual profitability. (159)

profit-sharing plan   An incentive program in which employees receive a bonus depending on the firm's profits. (224)

profitability ratios   Measures of a firm's overall financial performance in terms of it likely profits; used by investors to assess their probable returns. (517)

program   Any sequence of instructions to a computer. (686)

program trading   The purchase or sale of stocks by computerized trading programs that can be launched without human supervision or control. (596)

progressive tax   One that is levied at a higher rate on higher-income taxpayers and at a lower rate on lower-income taxpayers. (636)

project organization   An organization that uses teams of specialists to complete specific projects. (163)

promissory note   A written commitment to pay a stated sum of money on a given date; a form of trade credit in which the buyer signs an agreement regarding payment terms before receiving the merchandise. (560)

promotion   That part of the marketing mix concerned with choosing the appropriate technique for selling a product to a consumer. (389)

promotional mix   That portion of marketing concerned with selecting the best combination of advertising, personal selling, sales promotions, and publicity to sell a product. (433)

property   Anything of tangible or intangible value that the owner has the right to possess and use. (101)

property insurance   Insurance covering losses resulting from physical damage to real estate or personal property. (581)

prospecting   In personal sales, the process of identifying potential customers. (445)

prospectus   A registration statement which includes information about a firm that is proposing to issue securities. (609)

protectionist tariff   A tariff imposed at least in part to discourage imports of a particular product. (663)

provincial boards   Government bodies that pass judgment on proposed decisions by private companies. (634)

proxy   A legal document that temporarily transfers the voting rights of a shareholder to another person. (37)

psychographics   A method of market segmentation involving psychological traits a group has in common, including motives, attitudes, activities, interests, and opinions. (396)

psychological pricing   The practice of setting prices to take advantage of the nonlogical reactions of consumers to certain types of prices. (462)

public corporation   A business whose stock is widely held and available for sale to the general public. (39)

public relations   Any promotional activity directed at building good relations with various sectors of the population of buyers. (389)

public warehouses   Independently owned and operated warehouses that store the goods of many firms. (478)

publicity   A promotional technique that involves nonpaid communication about a product or firm and that is outside the control of the firm. (389)

pull strategy   A promotional strategy in which a company appeals directly to customers, who demand the product from retailers, who demand the product from wholesalers. (433)

purchase anxiety   A fear on the part of people who have made a purchase that their selection was wrong. (404)

pure competition   A market or industry characterized by a very large number of small firms producing an identical product so that none of the firms has any ability to influence price. (16)

pure risk   An event that offers no possibility of gain; it offers only the chance of a loss. (572)

pure services   High-contact services in which the customer is part of the service production process. (333)

purpose   The company's reason for being in business. (143)

push strategy   A promotional strategy in which a company aggressively pushes its product through wholesalers and retailers who persuade customers to buy it. (433)

put option   The purchased right to sell a particular stock at a certain price until a specified date. (605)

Q

qualifying In personal sales, the process of determining whether potential customers have the authority to buy and the ability to pay for a product. (445)

quality A product's fitness for use in terms of offering the features that consumers want. (351)

quality assurance Those activities necessary to get quality goods and services into the marketplace; also called quality management. (357)

quality circle A technique for maximizing quality of production. Employees are grouped into small teams who define, analyze, and solve quality and other problems within their areas. (251; 362)

quality control The management of the production process so as to manufacture goods or supply services that meet specific quality standards. (317)

quality/cost study A method of improving product quality by assessing a firm's current quality-related costs and identifying areas with the greatest cost-saving potential. (362)

quality ownership The concept that quality belongs to each employee who creates or destroys it in producing a good or service. (358)

quality reliability The consistency of quality from unit to unit of a product. (358)

quantity discount A form of discount in which customers buying large amounts of a product pay lower prices. (463)

quasimanufacturing Low-contact services in which the customer need not be part of the service production process. (333)

quick ratio (acid-test ratio) A form of liquidity ratio calculated as quick assets (cash plus marketable securities and accounts receivable) divided by current liabilities. (516)

quota A restriction by one nation on the total number of products of a certain type that can be imported from another nation. (663)

R

rack jobber A full-function merchant wholesaler specializing in nonfood merchandise who sets up and maintains display racks of some products in retail stores. (469)

random access memory The computer's short-term active memory, which lasts only as long as the computer stays on. (687)

rational motives Those reasons for purchasing a product that involve a logical evaluation of product attributes such as cost, quality, and usefulness. (403)

raw materials inventory That portion of a firm's inventory consisting of basic supplies used to manufacture products for sale. (559)

read-only memory A portion of computer memory which can hold instructions that have been read by the computer; does not accept instructions written into that memory. (688)

real gross national product Gross national product adjusted for inflation and changes in the value of a country's currency. (23)

real property Land and any permanent buildings attached to that land. (101)

real-time processing A method of transforming data into information in which data are entered and processed immediately. (693)

recession Part of the business cycle characterized by a decrease in employment, income, and production. (20)

recruitment The phase in the staffing of a company in which the firm seeks to develop a pool of interested, qualified applicants for a position. (212)

recycling The reconversion of waste materials into useful products. (89)

re-engineering The process of rethinking and redesigning business processes in order to achieve dramatic improvements in productivity and quality. (364)

registered bond Names of holders are registered with the company. (601)

regressive tax One that causes poorer people to pay a higher percentage of income than higher-income people. (637)

reminder advertising An advertising strategy, appropriate to the latter part of the maturity stage of the product life cycle, in which the goal is to keep the product's name in the minds of customers. (437)

repetitive strain injury Occurs when a worker performs the same function over and over again. (227)

research and development (R&D) Activities intended to provide new products, services, and processes. (74)

reseller market Consists of intermediaries like retailers and wholesalers who buy finished products and resell them. (405)

responsibility A duty to accomplish assigned tasks. (160)

restrictive taxes Levied to control certain activities that legislative bodies feel should be controlled. (636)

retail advertising Advertising by retailers designed to reach end users of a consumer product. (441)

retail selling Selling a consumer product for the buyer's own personal or household use. (444)

retailers Intermediaries who sell products to the end users. (463)

retained earnings A company's net profits less any dividend payments to shareholders. (187; 510)

retrenchment A strategic option designed to increase efficiency through asset reduction or cost cutting. (152)

return on investment (return on equity) A form of profitability ratio calculated as net income divided by total owners' equity. (518)

return on sales (net profit margin) A form of profitability ratio calculated as net income divided by net sales. (517)

revenue tariff A tariff imposed solely to raise money for the government that imposes it. (663)

revenue taxes Taxes whose main purpose is to fund government programs. (636)

revenues Any monies received by a firm as a result of selling a good or service or from other sources such as interest, rent, and licensing fees. (511)

revolving credit agreement A guaranteed line of credit for which the firm pays the bank interest on funds borrowed as well as a fee for extending the line of credit. (562)

risk Uncertainty about future events. (572)

risk avoidance Stopping participation in or refusing to participate in ventures that carry any risk. (573)

risk control Techniques to prevent, minimize, or reduce losses or the consequences of losses. (573)

risk management Conserving a firm's (or an individual's) financial power or assets by minimizing the financial effect of accidental losses. (572)

risk retention The covering of a firm's unavoidable losses with its own funds. (572)

risk transfer The transfer of risk to another individual or firm, often by contract. (574)

risk-return relationship Shows the amount of risk and the likely rate of return in various financial instruments. (568)

robotics The use of computer-controlled machines that perform production tasks. (318)

round lot The purchase or sale of stock in units of 100 shares. (608)

S

salary Dollars paid at regular intervals in return for doing a job, regardless of the time or output involved. (224)

sales era The period during the 1930s when North American businesses focused on sales forces, advertising, and making sure products were readily available. (50)

sales finance company A company that specializes in financing installment purchases made by individuals and firms. (548)

salesforce management Setting goals at top levels of the organization, setting practical objectives for salespeople, organizing the salesforce, and implementing and evaluating the success of the overall sales plan. (444)

sales office Offices maintained by sellers of industrial goods to provide points of contract with their customers. (466)

sales promotion Short-term promotional activities designed to stimulate consumer buying or cooperation from distributors and other members of the trade. (389; 446)

scheduling Developing timetables for acquiring resources. (310)

scientific management Analyzing jobs and finding better, more efficient ways to perform them. (239)

scrambled merchandising The retail practice of carrying any product expected to sell well, regardless of whether it fits into the store's original product offering. (475)

search qualities Qualities in a product that can be perceived before purchase by sight, feel, touch, or hearing. (341)

seasonal discount A form of discount in which lower prices are offered to customers making a purchase at a time of year when sales are traditionally slow. (462)

secondary data Information already available to market researchers as a result of previous research by the firm or other agencies. (397)

secondary reserve requirement The percentage of Canadian dollar deposits to be held in the form of cash, treasury bills, or day loans to securities dealers. (544)

secondary securities market The sale and purchase of previously issued stocks and bonds. (593)

secondary storage Any medium that can be used to store computerized data and information outside the computer's primary storage mechanism; magnetic tape, floppy disks, and hard disks are common forms. (687)

secured bonds Bonds issued by borrowers who pledge assets as collateral in the event of nonpayment. (601)

secured loan A short-term loan in which the borrower is required to put up collateral. (561)

securities Stocks and bonds (which represent a secured-asset-based claim on the part of investors) that can be bought and sold. (593)

selection The process of sorting through a pool of candidates to choose the best one for a job. (214)

selective distribution A distribution strategy that falls between intensive and exclusive distribution, calling for the use of a limited number of outlets for a product. (467)

self-insurance Occurs when a company chooses to build up a pool of its own funds as a reserve to cover losses that would otherwise be covered by insurance. (573)

serial bond A bond issue in which redemption dates are staggered so that a firm pays off portions of the issue at different predetermined dates. (602)

server Any component that can be shared by LAN users. (700)

service economy A reference to the growing importance of services, rather than products, as the major contributor to the North American economy. (59)

service flow analysis A method of improving services by identifying the flow of processes that make up the service. (335)

service operations Business activities that transform resources into services for customers. (328)

service process design Involves selecting the process, identifying worker requirements, and determining facilities requirements so the service can be effectively provided. (422)

shareholders Those who own shares of stock in a company. (37)

shared capacity A way of increasing the supply of services in which several individuals or companies share equipment, office space, or personnel. (339)

shop steward A regular employee who acts as a liaison between union members and supervisors. (273)

shopping goods/services Moderately expensive consumer goods that are purchased infrequently, causing consumers to spend some time comparing their prices. (418)

short sale Selling borrowed shares of stock in the expectation that their price will fall before they must be replaced so that replacement shares can be bought for less than the original shares were sold for. (609)

short-term goal A goal for the very near future, usually less than one year in the future. (145)

shortage A situation in which demand exceeds supply at a given price. (13)

single-use plan Operational plan for carrying out activities not likely to be repeated in the future, such as a program or a project. (152)

sinking-fund provision A clause in the bond indenture (contract) that requires the issuing company to put enough money into a special bank account each year to cover the retirement of the bond issue on schedule. (601)

site-license agreement Authorizes company-wide use of a software package in return for a fee. (692)

slowdown Instead of striking, workers perform their jobs at a much slower pace than normal. (277)

small business A business that is independently owned and operated and does not dominate its field. (176)

social audit A systematic analysis of how a firm is using funds earmarked for social-responsibility goals and how effective these expenditures have been. (98)

social-obligation approach A conservative approach to social responsibility in which a company does only the minimum required by law. (96)

social-opposition approach The position of a firm that makes a conscious decision not to observe regulatory and standard business practice guidelines to social responsibility. (96)

social-reaction approach A moderate approach to social responsibility in which a company, by request, sometimes goes beyond the minimum required by law. (96)

social-response approach A liberal approach to social responsibility in which a company actively seeks opportunities to contribute to the well-being of society. (96)

social responsibility A business's collective code of ethical behavior toward the environment, its customers, its employees, and its investors. (86)

socialism A kind of planned economy in which the government owns and operates the main industries, while individuals own and operate less crucial industries. (10)

soft manufacturing Emphasizes computer software and computer networks instead of production machines. (308)

software Programs that instruct the computer in what to do and how to do it. (692)

sole proprietorship A business owned (and usually operated) by one person who is personally responsible for the firm's debts. (31)

span of control The number of people managed by one manager. (161)

specialization The breaking down of complex operations into simple tasks that are easily learned and performed. (48)

specialty goods/services Very expensive consumer goods that are rarely purchased, causing consumers to spend a great deal of time locating the exact item desired. (418)

specialty stores Small retail stores that carry one line of related products. (471)

specification limits Limits defining acceptable and unacceptable quality in production of a good or service. (360)

speculative risk An event that offers the chance for either a gain or a loss to result. (572)

speed to market The rate at which a business firm responds to consumer demands or market changes. (421)

stability A situation in which the relationship between the supply of money and of goods, services, and labor remains constant. (19)

stabilization A strategic option designed to maintain revenues and profits. (152)

staff experts People with technical training in areas such as accounting or law. (162)

standard of living A measure of a society's economic well-being. (22)

standardization Using standard and uniform components in the production process. (312)

standing plans Operational plans for carrying out activities that are a regular part of a business's operations. (154)

statement of cash flows A financial statement that describes a firm's generation and use of cash during a given period; required of all firms issuing stock publicly. (512)

statistical process control (SPC) Statistical analysis techniques that allow managers to analyze variations in production data and to detect when adjustments are needed in order to create products with high quality reliability. (360)

statutory law   Law developed by city councils, provincial legislatures, and parliament. (99)

stock   A share of ownership in a corporation. (37)

stock exchange   A voluntary organization of individuals formed to provide an institutional setting in which members can buy and sell stock for themselves and their clients in accordance with the exchange's rules. (596)

stock insurance company   Any insurance company whose stock is held by members of the public who may or may not be policyholders of the company. (577)

stock option   The purchased right to buy or sell a stock at a predetermined price. (604)

stop order   An order to a broker to sell a certain security if its price falls to a certain level. (608)

storage warehouses   Warehouses used to provide storage of goods for extended periods of time. (478)

strategic alliance   Involves two or more enterprises cooperating in the research, development, manufacture, or marketing of a product. (45; 659)

strategic business unit   The smallest operating division of an enterprise that is given authority to make its own strategic decisions within corporate guidelines. (150)

strategic goals   Long-term goals derived directly from the firm's mission; their determination is the first step in strategy formulation. (148)

strategy formulation   The developing of a long-range plan for meeting a goal. (148)

strict product liability   A business is liable for injuries caused by their products even if there is no evidence of negligence in the design and manufacture of the product. (102)

strike   A weapon of labor unions in which members temporarily walk off the job and refuse to work in order to win concessions from management. (276)

strikebreaker   An individual hired by a firm to temporarily or permanently replace a worker on strike; a weapon of management in disputes with labor unions. (277)

subsidiary corporation   One that is owned by another corporation. (45)

supercomputer   The largest, fastest, and most expensive form of computer available today. (698)

supermarkets   Large retail stores that offer a variety of food and food-related items divided into specialized departments. (473)

supplier selection   Finding suppliers and determining which ones to buy from. (315)

supply   The willingness and ability of producers to offer a good or service for sale. (12)

surplus   A situation in which supply exceeds demand at a given price. (13)

survey   A market research technique based on questioning a representative sample of consumers about purchasing attitudes and practices. (399)

synthetic process   Any production process in which resources are combined. (302)

systems architecture   The way in which a computer system's data entry, data processing, data base, data output, and computer staff are located. (679)

system programs   Programs that tell a computer what resources to use and how to use them. (688)

T

T-account   An accounting format that divides an account into a debit and a credit side. (507)

tactical plan   Specific short-run to intermediate action plans for achieving strategic goals. (152)

target market   Any group of people who have similar wants and needs and may be expected to show interest in the same product(s). (392)

tariff   A tax levied on imported products. (663)

technical skills   Skills associated with performing specialized tasks within a firm. (128)

technology   The application of science to enable people to do entirely new things or perform established tasks in new and better ways. (74)

telecommuting   Allowing employees to do all or some of their work away from the office. (254)

telemarketing   Use of the telephone to sell directly to consumers. (446; 476)

term deposit   Money that remains with the bank for a period of time with interest paid to the depositor. (539)

term insurance   Insurance coverage for a fixed period of time, often one, five, ten, or twenty years. (584)

termination   Firing an employee who is not performing up to standard. (222)

Textile Labelling Act   Regulates the labeling, sale, importation, and advertising of consumer textile articles. (636)

Theory X   A management approach based on the belief that people must be forced to be productive because they are naturally lazy, irresponsible, and uncooperative. (242)

Theory Y   A management approach based on the belief that people want to be productive because they are naturally energetic, responsible, and cooperative. (242)

threshold pricing   A form of psychological pricing in which prices are set at what appears to be the maximum price consumers will pay for an item. (462)

time-and-motion studies   The use of industrial-engineering techniques to study every aspect of a specific job to determine how to perform it most efficiently. (239)

time deposits   That part of the M-2 money supply consisting of funds deposited in savings accounts that require notice before withdrawal and against which cheques cannot be drawn. (531)

time utility   That quality of a product satisfying a human want because of the time at which it is made available. (300)

title   Shows legal possession of personal property. (102)

title insurance   A guarantee by the insuring company that the seller of property is its owner and the property itself is free of debts or liens or other defects that prevent it from being sold. (582)

top managers   Those managers responsible for a firm's overall performance and effectiveness and for developing long-range plans for the company. (124)

tort   A wrongful civil act that one party inflicts on another and which results in injury to the person, to the person's property, or to the person's good name. (102)

total factor productivity ratio   A measure of a firm's overall productivity calculated as outputs divided by all inputs. (354)

total quality management (TQM)   A concept that emphasizes that no defects are tolerable and that all employees are responsible for maintaining quality standards. (356)

toxic waste   Pollution resulting from the emission of chemical and/or radioactive byproducts of various manufacturing processes into the air, water, or land. (89)

trade acceptance   A trade draft that has been signed by the buyer. (560)

trade advertising   Advertising by manufacturers designed to reach potential wholesalers and retailers. (441)

trade association   An organization dedicated to promoting the interests and assisting the members of a particular industry. (67)

trade credit   The granting of credit by a selling firm to a buying firm. (560)

trade discount   A form of discount in which companies involved in a product's distribution pay lower prices for the product. (462)

trade draft   A form of trade credit in which the seller draws up a statement of payment terms and attaches it to the merchandise; the buyer must sign this agreement to take delivery of the merchandise. (560)

trade shows   A sales promotion method in which members of a particular industry gather for displays and product demonstrations designed to sell products to customers. (447)

trademark   The exclusive legal right to use a brand name. (429)

transistor   A compact electronic switch that amplifies and controls electric current; its application marked the start of the second generation of computers. (701)

trust company   An organization that safeguards property—funds and estates—entrusted to it; may also serve as trustee, transfer agent, and registrar for corporations. (545)

trust services   The management of funds left in the bank's trust. (537)

two-factor theory   A theory of human relations developed by Frederick Herzberg that identifies factors that must be present for employees to be satisfied with their jobs, and factors that if increased lead employees to work harder. (244)

U

U-shaped production line   Machines are placed in a narrow U-shape, with workers operating them from within the U. (308)

umbrella insurance   Insurance that covers losses over and above those covered by a standard policy as well as losses excluded by a standard policy. (580)

underwriting   Determining which applications for insurance to accept and deciding what rates the insurer will charge. (578)

union security   The means of ensuring the continued existence of the union and the maintenance of its membership so that it can continue to meet the requirements for certification. (274)

union shop   A work place in which employees must join the union within a specified period after being hired. (274)

unitization   A materials handling strategy in which goods are transported and stored in containers with a uniform size, shape, and/or weight. (478)

universal life policy   A term insurance policy with a savings component. (584)

unlimited liability   A person who invests in a business liable for all debts incurred by the business; personal possessions can be taken to pay debts. (32)

unsecured loan   A short-term loan in which the borrower is not required to put up collateral. (562)

utility   The power of a product to satisfy a human want; something of value. (300)

V

value added analysis   The evaluation of all work activities, material flows, and paperwork to determine the value they add for customers. (359)

variable costs   Those costs that change with the number of goods or services produced or sold. (459)

variable life insurance (VLI)   A modified form of life insurance where the policyholder chooses the minimum face value of the policy. (584)

vending machine   Machine which dispenses mostly convenience goods like candy, cigarettes, and soft drinks. (475)

venture capital firm   Provides funds for new or expanding firms thought to have significant potential. (548)

vertical integration   Occurs when a corporation attains ownership or control of a supplier. (151)

vertical marketing system   A system in which there is a high degree of coordination among all the units in the distribution channel so that a product moves efficiently from manufacturer to consumer. (468)

vertical merger   A merger of two firms that have previously had a buyer-seller relationship. (61)

very large scale integration (VLSI)   The process of reducing the size of circuits on a silicon chip enabling a small chip to hold many more circuits; VLSI chips are used in fourth-generation computers. (702)

video marketing   Selling to consumers by showing products on television that consumers can purchase by telephone or mail. (475)

viruses   Harmful programs created and spread by vandals seeking to destroy or disrupt computer operations. (692)

voice mail   A computer-based system for receiving and delivering incoming telephone calls. (705)

voluntary arbitration   A method of settling a contract dispute in which a labor union and management ask a neutral third party to hear their arguments and issue a binding resolution. (279)

W

wages   Dollars paid based on the number of hours worked or the number of units produced. (223)

warehouse club   Large, membership-only, retail/wholesale operations that sell large quantities of limited lines of goods at low prices. (473)

warehousing   That part of the distribution process concerned with the storage of goods. (478)

warranty   A promise that a product or service will perform in the manner promised by the seller. (102)

Weights and Measures Act   Sets standards of accuracy for weighing and measuring devices. (636)

wheel of retailing   The idea that retail stores evolve over time from low-priced stores that provide few services in simple surroundings to higher-priced stores that provide many services in more upscale surroundings. (476)

whistle-blower   An individual who calls attention to an unethical, illegal, and/or socially irresponsible practice on the part of a business or other organization. (93)

whole life insurance   Insurance coverage in force for the whole of a person's life, with a build-up of cash value. (582)

wholesalers   Intermediaries who sell products to other businesses who in turn resell them to the end users. (463)

wide area network   System to link computers across the country through telephone wires or satellites. (703)

word-of-mouth   Opinions about the value of products passed between consumers in informal discussions. (440)

word processing   Applications programs that allow the computer to store, edit, and print letters and numbers like a very sophisticated typewriter. (694)

workers' compensation   A business's liability for injury to its employee(s) resulting from any activities related to the occupation. (581)

work-in-process inventory   That portion of a firm's inventory consisting of goods partway through the production process. (559)

World Bank   Funds national improvements by making loans to build schools, roads, power plants, and hospitals. (545)

world product mandating   The assignment of product responsibility to a particular branch plant of a multinational corporation. (660)

worksharing (job sharing)   A method of increasing employees' job satisfaction by allowing two people to share one job. (254)

NOTES, SOURCES, AND CREDITS

Reference Notes

Chapter 1

1. Larry Peppers and Dale G. Gails, *Managerial Economics: Theory and Applications for Decision Making* (Englewood Cliffs, NJ: Prentice-Hall, 1987).
2. Howard W. French, "On the street, Cubans fondly embrace capitalism," *The New York Times*, February 3, 1994, p. A4.
3. Robert Stone, "China's old guard holds on to power as the system slowly changes," *Winnipeg Free Press*, November 13, 1991, p. A7.
4. Richard I. Kirkland, Jr., "The death of socialism," *Fortune*, January 4, 1988, pp. 64-72.
5. Patrick Martin, "Cash-strapped kibbutz jettisons socialist values," *The Globe and Mail*, September 14, 1992, pp. A1-A2.
6. Page Smith, *The Rise of Industrial America* (New York: Viking Penguin, 1990).
7. Marina Strauss, "Business travel comes down to earth," *The Globe and Mail*, March 21, 1991, pp. B1-B2.
8. Adam Smith, *The Wealth of Nations* (New York: Modern Library, 1937; originally published in 1776).
9. Nicholas C. Siropolis, *Small Business Management*, 4th ed. (Boston: Houghton Mifflin, 1990).
10. Andrew Coyne, "Whatever happened to profitability?" *Canadian Business*, June, 1991, pp. 71-92.
11. "Big G is growing fat on oat cuisine," *Business Week*, September 18, 1989, p. 29.
12. John Partridge and Lawrence Surtees, "Rogers faces assault from Telcos," *The Globe and Mail*, March 28, 1994, pp. B1-B2.
13. "Where global growth is going," *Fortune*, July 31, 1989, pp. 71-92.
14. Peter Cook, "Nation's living standards under growing pressure," *The Globe and Mail*, August 31, 1991, pp. B1-B2.

Chapter 2

1. U.S. Small Business Administration, "Selecting the legal structure for your firm," *Management Aid No. 6.004* (Washington, D.C.: U.S. Government Printing Office, 1985).
2. Quoted in Lowell B. Howard, *Business Law* (Woodbury, NY: Barron's Woodbury Press, 1965), p. 332.
3. See "A seat on the board is getting hotter," *Business Week*, July 3, 1989, p. 72.
4. "A seat on the board is getting hotter." See note 3.
5. John Heinzl, "The battling McCain's show signs of softening," *The Globe and Mail*, August 27, 1994, p. B1.
6. Stratford P. Sherman, "How Philip Morris diversified right," *Fortune*, October 23, 1989, pp. 120-128.
7. Bill Redekop, "Co-op withers as pool goes public," *Winnipeg Free Press*, July 15, 1994, p. 1.
8. Robin Sidel, "Employee ownership seen as industry trend," *The Globe and Mail*, December 24, 1993, p. B5.
9. Madelaine Drohan, "Ottawa targets interprovincial barriers," *The Globe and Mail*, May 14, 1991, p. B5.

Chapter 3

1. See Daniel McCarthy, Francis C. Spital, and Milton C. Lauenstein, "Managing growth at high-technology companies: A view from the top," *Academy of Management Executive*, August, 1987, pp. 313-322, for an overview of high-tech companies and their management.

2. Ann Gibbon, "CN, CP on track to merger goal," *The Globe and Mail*, March 1, 1994, p. B22; also "Price/Costco merger gets OK," *The Financial Post*, October 23, 1993, p. 11; also "Martin Marietta, Lockheed strike $10 billion merger," *The Globe and Mail*, August 31, 1994, pp. B1, B8.
3. "Beyond Marlboro country," *Business Week*, August 8, 1988, pp. 54-58.
4. Alan Freeman, "Takeovers no cure," *The Globe and Mail*, June 13, 1991, p. B13.
5. Mark Evans, "Maple Leaf's Newton a turnaround artist," *The Financial Post*, December 6, 1991, p. 8.
6. Pauline Comeau, "Deregulated industry hits turbulence," *Winnipeg Free Press*, December 3, 1988, pp. 1-2.
7. Peter Foster, "Choked by the invisible hand," *Canadian Business*, December, 1991, pp. 552-559.
8. Barrie McKenna, "The heat is on for Hydro Quebec," *The Globe and Mail*, November 24, 1993, pp. B1, B9.
9. John Stackhouse, "Missing the market," *Report on Business Magazine*, January, 1992, p. 38; also Karen Lynch, "Wave of privatization sweeps the globe," *The Financial Post*, November 11, 1991, p. 42.
10. "Privatization bug bites in France as leaders try to prime economy," *The Financial Post*, November 27, 1993, p. 22; also "Privatization a global revolution," *The Globe and Mail*, September 3, 1993, p. B2.
11. Martin Mittelstaedt, "Canada gets deficit wake-up call," *The Globe and Mail*, September 7, 1994, pp. B1, B16.
12. Dan Lett and John Douglas, "Too often to the well," *Winnipeg Free Press*, February 17, 1995, p. B10.
13. Eduardo Lachina, "Saving the earth: U.S. asks World Bank to make safeguarding environment a priority, " *Wall Street Journal*, July 3, 1987, p. 1.
14. Bruce McDougall, "Driven by design," *Canadian Business*, January, 1991, pp. 49-53.
15. "Engine efficiency boosted," *The Globe and Mail*, July 31, 1991.
16. Barrie McKenna, "Alcan aims to be No. 1 with a 'bullet'," *The Globe and Mail*, July 31, 1991.
17. Victor Fung, "New system aims to revolutionize mining," *The Financial Post*, July 29, 1991, p. 5.

Chapter 4

1. Michael Stern, "Ethical standards begin at the top," *The Globe and Mail*, November 11, 1991, p. B4.
2. Richard p. Nielsen, "Changing unethical organizational behavior," *Academy of Management Executive*, May, 1989, pp. 123-130.
3. See Archie Carroll, *Business and Society: Ethics and Stakeholder Management* (Cincinnati: Southwestern, 1989).
4. Jeremy Main, "Here comes the big new cleanup," *Fortune*, November 21, 1988, pp. 102-118.
5. Catherine Collins, "The race for zero," *Canadian Business*, March, 1991, pp. 52-56.
6. Charles Davies, "Strategy session 1990," *Canadian Business*, January 1990, p. 48.
7. "Room service and the recyclable rubber chicken," *Canadian Business*, May, 1991, p. 19.
8. Casey Mahood, "Bell zeros in on waste," *The Globe and Mail*, May 4, 1992, p. B1.
9. Martin Mittelstaedt, "Greenpeace takes on Cameco shares," *The Globe and Mail*, June 10, 1991, p. B10.
10. John Fox, "No eluding the enviro-sleuths—not even abroad," *The Financial Post*, April 8, 1991, p. 5.

11. See note 10.
12. Bruce Livesey, "Stuck with the cleanup," *Canadian Business*, February, 1991, pp. 92-96.
13. Geoffrey Scotton, "Cleanups can hurt, companies warned," *The Financial Post*, June 25, 1991, p. 4.
14. Marc Huber, "A double-edged endorsement," *Canadian Business*, January, 1990, pp. 69-71.
15. "Breast implant production halted," *The Globe and Mail*, January 15, 1992, p. B9.
16. John Saunders, "Polar plastic plot flops," *The Globe and Mail*, June 10, 1994, p. B1.
17. Shona McKay, "Willing and able," *Report on Business*, October, 1991, pp. 58-63.
18. "Why business is hiring the mentally abled," *Canadian Business*, May, 1991, p. 19.
19. J. Southerst, "In pursuit of drugs," *Canadian Transportation*, November, 1989, pp. 58-65.
20. G. Bylinsky, "How companies spy on employees," *Fortune*, November 4, 1991, pp. 131-140.
21. Michael McHugh, "Blowing whistle on company can be a risky venture," *The Financial Post*, August 26, 1991, p. 2.
22. "Is Ivan Boesky just the tip of the insider iceberg?" *Dun's Business Month*, January, 1987, p. 22.
23. Daniel Stoffman, "Good behavior and the bottom line," *Canadian Business*, May, 1991, pp. 28-32.
24. Michael Valpy, "A clear conscience can also make money," *The Globe and Mail*, August 25, 1989, p. A8; also Mark Evans, "Wildlife preservation a corporate issue," *The Financial Post*, June 25, 1991, p. 13.
25. Tom Kierans, "Charity begins at work," *Report on Business Magazine*, June, 1990, p. 23.

Chapter 5

1. Alex Taylor III, "How a top boss manages his day," *Fortune*, June 19, 1989, pp. 95-100.
2. John Lorinc, "Managing when there's no middle," *Canadian Business*, June, 1991, pp. 86-94.
3. Kenneth Labich, "Making over middle managers," *Fortune*, May 8, 1989, pp. 58-64.
4. "MBAs are hotter than ever," *Business Week*, March 9, 1987, pp. 46-48.
5. Terrence Deal and Allen Kennedy, *Corporate Cultures: The Rites and Rituals of Corporate Life* (Reading, MA: Addison-Wesley, 1982).
6. Bruce McDougall, "The thinking man's assembly line," *Canadian Business*, November, 1991, pp. 40-44.
7. Paul M. Eng and Evan I. Schwartz, "The games people play in the office," *Business Week*, October 11, 1993, p. 40.
8. Marina Strauss, "Baker's brassy style may rub off on McKim," *The Globe and Mail*, January 27, 1992, pp. B1, B6.
9. Harvey Enchin, "Consensus management? Not for Bombardier's CEO," *The Globe and Mail*, April 16, 1990, p. B1; also Margaret Philp, Campeau executives offered a carrot," *The Globe and Mail*, June 27, 1990, p. B9.
10. John Schreiner, "Green war and Greenpeace," *The Financial Post*, 1994 Annual Issue, p. 45.
11. Alan Freedman, "Passports to profits," *The Globe and Mail*, December 14, 1993, p. B 24.

Chapter 6

1. Lawrence Surtees, "Unitel must sell itself: survey," *The Globe and Mail*, October 22, 1990, p. B10.
2. Geoffrey Rowan, "Xerox launches document processing products," *The Globe and Mail*, October 3, 1990, p. B7.
3. Andre Picard, "Turn green or wilt, business told," *The Globe and Mail*, October 13, 1990, p. B6.
4. Stephen Carroll and Henry L. Tosi, *Management by Objectives* (New York: Macmillan, 1973).
5. John Schreiner, "Green war and Greenpeace," *The Financial Post*, 1994 Annual Issue, pp. 44-48.
6. Charles Hill and Gareth Jones, *Strategic Management: An Analytical View* (Boston: Houghton Mifflin, 1989).
7. Peter Nulty, "Kodak grabs for growth again," *Fortune*, May 16, 1994, pp. 76-78.
8. Dave Ulrich and Dale Lake, "Organizational capability: Creating competitive advantage," *Academy of Management Executive*, February 1991, pp. 77-83.
9. Michael Porter, *Competitive Strategy: Techniques for Analyzing Industries and Competitors* (New York: The Free Press, 1980).
10. Barnaby J. Feder, "The Tech exec who also brings home the bacon," *New York Times*, August 21, 1994, Sec. 3, p. 4.
11. See John A. Wagner and John R. Hollenbeck, *Management of Organizational Behavior* (Englewood Cliffs, NJ: Prentice Hall, 1992), pp. 563-565.
12. Jacquie McNish, "A chairman with worries lots of others would like," *The Globe and Mail*, April 14, 1990, p. B6.

13. Peter Larson, "Winning strategies," *Canadian Business Review*, Summer, 1989, p. 41.
14. Ian Allaby, "The search for quality," *Canadian Business*, May, 1990, pp. 31-42.
15. J. Galbraith, "Matrix organization designs: How to combine functional and project forms," *Business Horizons*, 1971, pp. 29-40; also H.F. Kolodny, "Evolution to a matrix organization," *Academy of Management Review*, 4, 1979, pp. 543-553.
16. Lawton R. Burns, "Matrix management in hospitals: Testing theories of matrix structure and development," *Administrative Science Quarterly*, 34, 1989, pp. 48-50.
17. Glenn Rifkin, "Digital dumps matrix management," *The Globe and Mail*, July 21, 1994, pp. B1, B4.
18. Thomas Peters and Robert Waterman, *In Search of Excellence* (New York: Harper & Row, 1982).

Chapter 7

1. Bruce Little, "Statscan economists give nod to the little guys in long-standing debate," *The Globe and Mail*, November 22, 1994, pp. B1, B8.
2. *The State of Small Business 1989, Annual Report on Small Business in Ontario* (Toronto: Ministry of Industry, Trade and Technology, 1990), pp. 3-4.
3. Murray McNeill, "Women step out on their own," *Winnipeg Free Press*, December 8, 1994, p. C10; also *The State of Small Business*, p. 8, see note 2.
4. Alan M. Cohen, "Entrepreneur and Entrepreneurship: The Definition Dilemma," Working Paper Series No. NC89-08, National Centre for Management Research and Development, The University of Western Ontario, London, February, 1989.
5. *The State of Small Business*, pp. 24-27. See note 2.
6. *The State of Small Business*, p. 29. See note 2.
7. Recent Canadian textbooks include D. Wesley Balderson, *Canadian Small Business Management: Text, Cases and Incidents* (Homewood, IL: Richard D. Irwin, 1990); Raymond W.Y. Kao, *Entrepreneurship and Enterprise Development* (Toronto: Holt, Rinehart and Winston of Canada, 1989); and Andrew J. Szonyi and Dan Steinhoff, *Small Business Management Fundamentals*, 3rd Canadian ed. (Scarborough, Ont.: McGraw-Hill Ryerson, 1987).
8. Allan Gould, *The New Entrepreneurs: 80 Canadian Success Stories* (Toronto: Seal Books, 1986); also Kenneth Barnes and Everett Banning, *Money Makers: The Secrets of Canada's Most Successful Entrepreneurs* (Toronto: McClelland and Stewart, 1985); also Matthew Fraser, *Quebec Inc.: French-Canadian Entrepreneurs and the New Business Elite* (Toronto: Key Porter Books, 1987).
9. Many models of organizational growth have been developed. One that is often described in management books is in Larry E. Greiner, "Evolution and revolutuon as organizations grow," *Harvard Business Review*, 50, No. 4 July/August 1972, pp. 37-46. One example of a growth model developed for small business is Mel Scott and Richard Bruce, "Five stages of growth in small business," *Long Range Planning*, 20, No. 3, 1987, pp. 45-52.
10. The statistics in this section are from *Small Business in Canada: Growing to Meet Tomorrow* (Ottawa: Supply and Services Canada), Cat. No. C28-12 1989E; also The State of Small Business, see note 2.
11. Paul Waldie, "Small business hits out," *The Financial Post*, September 4-6, 1993, pp. 1, 10-11.

Chapter 8

1. John Partridge, "B of M lauded for promoting women's careers," *The Globe and Mail*, January 7, 1994, p. B3.
2. Vivian Smith, "Breaking down the barriers," *The Globe and Mail*, November 17, 1992, p. B24.
3. "More firms use personality tests for entry-level blue collar jobs," *Wall Street Journal*, January 16, 1986, p. 25.
4. Bruce McDougall, "The thinking man's assembly line," *Canadian Business*, November, p. 40.
5. "Testing for drug use: Handle with care," *Business Week*, March 28, 1988, p. 65.
6. Jacquie McNish, "Akers out as IBM CEO," *The Globe and Mail*, January 27, 1993, pp. B1-B2.
7. Jane Allan, "Literacy at work," *Canadian Business*, February, 1991, pp. 70-73.
8. Harvey Enchin, "Employee training a must," *The Globe and Mail*, May 15, 1991, p. B6.
9. John Southerst, "Kenworth's gray revolution," *Canadian Business*, September, 1992, p. 74.
10. I.L. Goldstein, *Training in Organizations: Needs Assessment, Development, and Evaluation*, 2nd ed. (Monterey, CA: Brooks/Cole, 1986).
11. Jerry Zeidenberg, "Extra-curricular," *Canadian Business*, February, 1991, pp. 66-69.
12. Charles Davies, "Strategy session 1990," *Canadian Business*, January, 1990, p. 50.

13. Scott Feschuk, "Phi Beta Cuppa," *The Globe and Mail*, March 6, 1993, pp. B1, B4.
14. Ann Gibbon, "How training primed the pump," *The Globe and Mail*, November 16, 1993, p. B26.
15. Margot Gibb-Clark, "Alternate mechanism solves work disputes," *The Globe and Mail*, November 7, 1994, pp. B1-B2.
16. Thomas Claridge, "Fired jumbo boss awarded $226,000," *The Globe and Mail*, May 31, 1993, p. B5.
17. "Well-paid workers, low-paid bosses?" *Canadian Business*, December, 1992, p. 17.
18. David Roberts, "A long way from Cambodia," *The Globe and Mail*, July 5, 1994, p. B18.
19. C.D. Fisher, L. Schoenfeldt, and B. Shaw, *Personnel/Human Resources Management* (Boston: Houghton-Mifflin, 1990).
20. Bob Cox, "Women gaining on men's wages," *The Globe and Mail*, January 18, 1994, p. B4.
21. Gordon Pitts, "Equal pay issue: Business uneasy," *The Financial Post*, August 31, 1985, pp. 1-2.
22. "Ouch! The squeeze on your health benefits," *Business Week*, November 20, 1989, pp. 110-116.
23. McDougall, "The thinking man's assembly line." See note 4.
24. Ted Kennedy, "Beware of health and safety law: It could bite you," *Canadian Business*, December, 1990, p. 19.
25. Wilfred List, "Under the gun about safety," *The Globe and Mail*, January 4, 1994, P. B14.
26. Margot Gibb-Clark, "Harrassment cases can also hurt employees," *The Globe and Mail*, September 16, 1991, p. B4.

Chapter 9

1. Michael Stern, "Empowerment empowers employees," *The Globe and Mail*, December 9. 1991, p. B4.
2. Margot Gibb-Clark, "Canadian workers need some respect," *The Globe and Mail*, September 4, 1991, pp. B1, B6.
3. Margot Gibb-Clark, "Frustrated workers seek goals," *The Globe and Mail*, May 2. 1991, p. B7.
4. Margot Gibb-Clark, "Family ties limit workers," *The Globe and Mail*, January 22, 1991, pp. B1-B2.
5. Frederick W. Taylor, *Principles of Scientific Management* (New York: Harper and Brothers, 1911).
6. Fritz J. Roethlisberger and William J. Dickson, *Management and the Worker* (Cambridge, MA: Harvard University Press, 1939).
7. Douglas McGregor, *The Human Side of Enterprise* (New York: McGraw-Hill, 1960).
8. Abraham Maslow, "A theory of human motivation," *Psychological Review*, July 1943, pp. 370-396.
9. Frederick Herzberg, Bernard Mausner, and Barbara Bloch Snydeman, *The Motivation to Work* (New York: Wiley, 1959).
10. Victor Vroom, *Work and Motivation* (New York: Wiley, 1964); Craig Pinder, *Work Motivation* (Glenview, IL: Scott, Foresman, 1984).
11. J. Stacy Adams, "Toward an understanding of inequity," *Journal of Abnormal and Social Psychology*, Vol. 75, No. 5 (1963), pp. 422-436.
12. Edwin Locke, "Toward a theory of task performance and incentives," *Organizational Behavior and Human Performance*, Vol. 3 (1968), pp. 157-189.
13. Margot Gibb-Clark, "BC Telecom managers get an overhaul," *The Globe and Mail*, July 23, 1994, p. B3.
14. Wilfred List, "On the road to profit," *The Globe and Mail*, July 10, 1991, pp. B1, B3.
15. Ricky Griffin, *Task Design* (Glenview, IL: Scott, Foresman, 1982).
16. Richard J. Hackman and Greg Oldham, *Work Redesign* (Reading, MA: Addison-Wesley, 1980).
17. Robert White, "Changing needs of work and family: A union response," *Canadian Business Review*, Autumn, 1989, pp. 31-33.
18. Margot Gibb-Clark, "Banks' short work week improves service," *The Globe and Mail*, September 23, 1991, p. B4.
19. "Escape from the office," *Newsweek*, April 24, 1989, pp. 58-60.
20. Margot Gibb-Clark, "Satellite office a hit with staff," *The Globe and Mail*, November 18, 1991, p. B4.

Chapter 10

1. Homer, *The Iliad*, Book XIII, Line 237.
2. Gary Dessler, *Personnel Management*, 4th ed. (Englewood Cliffs, NJ: Prentice-Hall, 1988).
3. Madelaine Drohan, "Steel hands try velvet gloves," *The Globe and Mail*, p. B26.
4. Margot Gibb-Clark, "Wounds left by strike require healing," *The Globe and Mail*, September 30, 1991, p. B4.
5. Margot Gibb-Glark, "Rogers workers abandon union," *The Globe and Mail*, January 22, 1992, p. B7.
6. Barrie McKenna, "Petromont gives employees grim choice," *The Globe and Mail*, December 17, 1991, p. B6.

7. Timothy Pritchard, "GM sends union clear signals," *The Globe and Mail*, February 26, 1992, pp. B1, B21.
8. Robert Frank, "UPS and downs," *The Globe and Mail*, June 7, 1994, p. B24.
9. Susanne Craig, "Free trade puts heat on unions," *The Financial Post*, May 28, 1994, p. 15.
10. Jacquie McNish, "Throng of firms move to U.S. to slash costs," *The Globe and Mail*, July 2, 1991, pp. B1-B6.

Chapter 11

1. Gene Bylinsky, "The digital factory," *Fortune*, November 14, 1994, pp. 92-96+.
2. Christopher Farrell, "A wellspring of innovation," *Business Week*, Enterprise 1993, pp. 57-62.
3. Roger G. Schroeder, *Operations Management: Decision Making in the Operations Function*, 3rd ed.)New York: McGraw-Hill, 1989), pp. 234-264.
4. John R. Dorfman, "Deere's stock is attractive to those who see farmers about to splurge on new equipment," *Wall Street Journal*, July 1, 1991, p. C2; Steven Weiner, "Staying on top in a tough business in a tough Year," *Forbes*, May 27, 1991, p. 38.
5. Alex Taylor III, "Ford's $6 billion baby," *Fortune*, June 28, 1993, pp. 76-77+; Richard W. Stevenson, "Ford sets its sights on a world car," *New York Times*, September 27, 1993, pp. D1, D4; James B. Treece. "Motown's struggle to shift on the fly," *Business Week*, July 11, 1994, pp. 111-112.
6. Michael Williams, "Back to the past: Some plants tear out long assembly lines, switch to craft work," *Wall Street Journal*, October 24, 1994, pp. A1, A4; Doron P. Leven, "Toyota plant in Kentucky provides a font of ideas for U.S. manufacturers," *New York Times*, May 5, 1992, Sec. 3, pp. C1, C6.
7. Richard J. Schonberger and Edward M. Knod, Jr., *Operations Management*, 5th ed. (Burr Ridge, IL: Irwin, 1994), Chapter 11.
8. Hirano Hiroyuki and J.T. Black, *JIT Factory Revolution* (Cambridge, MA: Productivity Press, 1988), p. 126; James B. Dilworth, *Production and Operations Management*, 5th ed. (New York: McGraw-Hill, 1993), p. 567.
9. Don Marshall, "Time for just in time," *P&IM Review*, June 1991, pp. 20-22. See also Gregg Stocker, "Quality function deployment: Listening to the voice of the customer," *APICS: The Performance Advantage*, September 1991, pp. 44-48.
10. Schonberger and Knod, *Operations Management*, Chapter 11. See note 7.
11. Bruce McDougall, "The thinking man's assembly line," *Canadian Business*, November, 1991, p. 40.
12. Alan Freeman, "Why firms avoid taking inventory," *The Globe and Mail*, December 12, 1994, pp. B1, B4.

Chapter 12

1. Richard B. Chase and Warren J. Erickson, "The service factory," *Academy of Management Executive*, August, 1988, pp. 191-196.
2. Theodore Levitt, "Marketing intangible products and product intangibles," *Harvard Business Review*, May-June, 1981, pp. 94-102.
3. Richard B. Chase, "Where does the customer fit in a service organization?" *Harvard Business Review*, November-December, 1978, pp. 137-142.
4. Theodore Levitt, "Production-line approach to service," *Harvard Business Review*, September-October, 1972, pp. 41-52.
5. Richard B. Chase, "The 10 commandments of service system management," *Interfaces*, 15(3), pp. 68-72.
6. Alan Freedman, "Passports to profits," *The Globe and Mail*, December 14, 1993, p. B24.
7. Stanley Harris, "Improving customer support," *Management Today*, August, 1986, pp. 67-90.
8. G.M. Hostage, "Quality control in a service business," *Harvard Business Review*, July-August, 1975, pp. 98-106.

Chapter 13

1. Estimated from *Monthly Labor Review* (Washington, DC: U.S. Dept. of Labor, October 1994), p. 87; *Survey of Current Business* (Washington, DC: U.S. Dept. of Commerce, February 1994), p. 9; Carl G. Thor, *Perspectives '94* (Houston: American Productivity and Quality Center, 1994), p. 17.
2. Bruce McDougall, "The next battleground," *Canadian Business*, February, 1992, pp.52-57.
3. Marina Strauss, "Canada rated 6th in quality of its manufactured goods," *The Globe and Mail*, February 10, 1994.
4. "A feisty domestic with a chip on its shoulder," *Canadian Business*, November, 1991, p. 15.
5. Bruce McDougall, "The thinking man's assembly line," *Canadian Business*, November, 1991, p. 40.

6. Jeremy Main, "How to steal the best ideas around," *Fortune*, October 19, 1992, pp. 102-106; also Otis Port and Geoffrey Smith, "Beg, borrow—and benchmark," *Business Week*, November 30, 1992, pp. 74-75; also Howard Rothman, "You need not be big to benchmark," *Nation's Business*, December, 1992, pp. 64-65.

7. Gordon Pitts, "Stepping on the quality ladder," *The Globe and Mail*, June 30, 1992, p. B20; also Timothy Pritchard, "Big three adopt new standard," *The Globe and Mail*, March 28, 1994, p. B3.

8. Michael Hammer and James Champy, "The promise of reengineering," *Fortune*, May 3, 1993, pp. 94-97; also Thomas A. Stewart, "Reengineering: The hot new managing tool," *Fortune*, August 23, 1993, pp. 41-48; also Ronald Henkoff, "The hot new seal of quality," *Fortune*, August 23, 1993, pp. 116-118.

9. Cathryn Motherwell, "How to fix a model of a muddle," *The Globe and Mail*, November 22, 1994, p. B30.

10. "Customer service you can taste," *Canadian Business*, July, 1991, pp. 19-20.

11. *Business Week*, Special 1989 Issue: "Innovation in America," p. 177.

12. Leonard L. Berry, A. Parasuraman, and Valarie A. Zeithaml, "Improving service quality in America: Lessons learned," *Academy of Management Executive*, Vol. 8, No. 2, 1994, pp. 32-45.

Chapter 14

1. From "AMA board approves new marketing definition," *Marketing News*, March 31, 1985, p. 1, published by the American Marketing Association.

2. Jonathan Kapstein, Thaine Peterson and Lois Therrien, "Look out world, Philips is on a war footing," *Business Week*, January 15, 1990, pp. 44-45.

3. Margot Gibb-Clark, "Customers have a say on IBM managers' pay," *The Globe and Mail*, April 1, 1991, p. B4.

4. "Above the crowd," *Canadian Business*, April, 1990, p. 76.

5. Philip Kotler, *Marketing Management: Analysis, Planning, Implementation, and Control*, 7th ed. (Englewood Cliffs, NJ: Prentice-Hall, 1991).

6. "What Canadians own," *Winnipeg Free Press*, November 14, 1991, p. A4.

7. Stephen Barr, "Trading places: Barter re-enters corporate America," *Management Review*, August, 1993, p. 30; John J. McDonald, "Barter can work," *Chief Executive (U.S.)*, June, 1994, p. 40.

8. Charles D. Scheive, "Effective communication with our aging population," *Business Horizons*, January-February, 1989, pp. 19-25.

9. John Morton, "How to spot the really important prospects," *Business Marketing*, January, 1990, pp. 62-67.

10. Paul Sutter, "How to succeed in bubble gum without really trying," *Canadian Business*, January, 1992, pp. 48-50.

11. Marina Strauss, "First you have to get their attention," *The Globe and Mail*, July 12, 1991, p. B1.

12. Terence Pare, "How to find out what they want," *Fortune*, Autumn/Winter, 1993, pp. 39-41.

13. Oliver Bertin, "John Deere reaps the fruits of its labors," *Globe and Mail*, September 2, 1991, pp. B1, B3.

14. Stephen Barr, "Trading places: Barter re-enters corporate America," *Management Review*, August, 1993, p. 30; John J. McDonald, "Barter can work," *Chief Executive (U.S.)*, June, 1994, p. 40.

15. William J. Stanton, Michael J. Etzel, and Bruce J. Walker, *Fundamentals of Marketing*, 10th ed. (New York: McGraw-Hill, 1994), Chapter 5.

16. Thomas Russell, Glenn Verrill, and W. Ronald Lane, *Kleppner's Advertising Procedure*, 11th ed. (Englewood Cliffs, NJ: Prentice-Hall, 1990; also James Engel, Martin Warshaw, and Thomas Kinnear, *Promotional Strategy*, 6th ed. (Homewood, IL: Richard D. Irwin, 1987).

Chapter 15

1. Patricia Lush, "From pipe dream to profit," *The Globe and Mail*, December 12, 1994, p. B6.

2. Todd Vogel, "Will GE's new jet engine ever get off the ground?" *Business Week*, February 4, 1991, pp. 98-99; Tim Smart et al., "Clash of the flying titans," *Business Week*, November 22, 1993, pp. 64-66.

3. Richard Chase and Nick Aquilano, *Production and Operations Management*, 6th ed. (Homewood, IL: Irwin, 1992), Chapter 4.

4. Leonard E. Berry, A. Parasuraman, and Valerie A. Zeithaml, "Improving service quality in America," *Academy of Management Executive*, Vol. 8, No. 2, 1994, pp. 37-38.

5. Joel Baumwell, "Life cycle for brands? Forget it!" *Advertising Age*, March 17, 1986, p. 18.

6. Cyndee Miller, "Little relief seen for new product failure rate," *Marketing News*, June 21, 1993, p. 1; Nancy J. Kim, "Back to the drawing board, *The Bergen (New Jersey) Record*, December 4, 1994, pp. B1, B4.

7. Stuart Elliott, "'Gump' sells, to Viacom's surprise," *New York Times*, October 7, 1994, pp. D1, D16.

8. Madelaine Drohan, "British await Coke's reply to grocer's look-alike cola," *The Globe and Mail*, April 29, 1994, p. B5.

9. William C. Symonds and Paula Dwyer, "A third front in the cola wars," *Business Week*, December 12, 1994, pp. 66-68; Richard Gibson, "Pitch, panache buoy fancy private label," *Wall Street Journal*, January 27, 1994, p. B1; Eleena De Lisser and Kevin Helliker, "Private labels reign in British groceries," *Wall Street Journal*, March 3, 1994 p. B4; E.S. Browning, "Europeans witness proliferation of private labels," *Wall Street Journal*, October 20, 1992, p. B1; Yumiko Ono, "The rising sun shines on private labels," *Wall Street Journal*, April 26, 1993, pp. B1, B6.

10. Marina Strauss, "Packaging is a marketer's last chance to say `Buy me'," *The Globe and Mail*, September 17, 1991, p. B4.

11. Marina Strauss, "Packages shrink but not their price," *The Globe and Mail*, March 30, 1991, pp. B1-B2.

12. Gail Degeorge with Julia Flynn, "Turning up the gas at Burger King," *Business Week*, November 15, 1993, pp. 62, 66-67.

13. William Pride and O.C. Ferrell, *Marketing*, 5th ed. (Boston: Houghton Mifflin, 1987).

14. John B. Clark, *Marketing Today: Successes, Failures, and Turnarounds* (Englewood Cliffs, NJ: Prentice-Hall, 1987), p. 32.

15. Michael Allen, "Developing new line of low-priced PCs shakes up Compaq," *Wall Street Journal*, June 15, 1992, pp. A1, A4.

16. Ronald Henkoff, "Service is everybody's business," *Fortune*, June 27, 1994, p. 52.

17. "Regulators wary of ads rapping rivals," *The Globe and Mail*, May 23, 1991, p. B4.

18. "Pepsi got the right one for promoting itself," *The Globe and Mail*, January 30, 1992, p. B4.

19. Stuart Elliot, "Topsy-turvey becomes darling of print ads," *The Globe and Mail*, February 25, 1992, pp. B1, B6.

20. Marina Strauss, "This billboard wants to pass you by," *The Globe and Mail*, February 27, 1992, p. B4.

21. Laurie Ward, "Big rock brews strong U.S. growth," *The Financial Post*, September 25, 1993, p. 7.

22. Marina Strauss, "Trend to foreign-made ads a severe blow to Canadian firms," *The Globe and Mail*, January 6, 1992, pp. B1-B2.

23. Marina Strauss, "Small shops quake over IBM's earth-shaking move," *The Globe and Mail*, May 26, 1994, p. B4.

24. Ann Gibbon, "Ad group tries to demystify Quebec," *Globe and Mail*, November 25, 1993, p. B6.

25. "Regulators wary of ads rapping rivals," *The Globe and Mail*, May 23, 1991, p. B4.

26. "Point-of-purchase rush is on," *Advertising Age*, February 8, 1988, p. 47.

27. Lois Therrien, "Want shelf space at the supermarket? Ante up," *Business Week*, August 7, 1989, pp. 60-61.

28. Jennifer Lawrence, "Free samples get emotional reaction," *Advertising Age*, September 30, 1991, p. 10.

29. Michael L. Rothschild, *Marketing Communications* (Lexington, MA: D.C. Heath, 1987).

Chapter 16

1. Rahul Jacob, "Beyond quality and value," *Fortune*, Autumn/Winter, 1993, pp. 8-11.

2. Stephen Kindel, "Tortoise gains on hare," *Financial World*, February 23, 1988, pp. 18-20.

3. Bruce Nussbaum, *Good Intentions* (New York: Atlantic Monthly Press, 1990), pp. 176+; Brian O'Reilly, "The inside story of the AIDS drug," *Fortune*, November 5, 1990, pp. 112+; Julia Flynn with John Carey, "Wellcome's AZT faces attacks on two fronts," *Business Week*, July 26, 1993, p. 36.

4. Stewart Washburn, "Establishing strategy and determining costs in the pricing decision," *Business Marketing*, July, 1985, pp. 64-78.

5. "Odd prices hurt image of prices," *Business Month*, July, 1987, p. 23.

6. Geoffrey Rowan, "Airlines try to lure bargain travellers," *The Globe and Mail*, May 7, 1991, pp. B1-B2.

7. Randall Litchfield, "The pressure on prices," *Canadian Business*, February, 1992, pp. 30-35.

8. Stephanie Anderson Forest, "The education of Michael Dell," *Business Week*, March 22, 1993, pp. 82-86; Lois Therrien, "Why gateway is racing to answer on the first ring," *Business Week*, September 13, 1993, pp. 92-93; Peter Burrows, "The computer is in the mail (really)," *Business Week*, January 23, 1995, pp. 76-77; Scott McCartney, "Michael Dell—and his company—grow up," *Wall Street Journal*, January 31, 1994, pp. B1, B2.

9. Dale M. Lewison, *Retailing*, 5th ed. (New York: Macmillan, 1994), p. 454; Louis Stern and Adel I. El-Ansary, *Marketing Channels*, 4th ed. (Englewood Cliffs, NJ: Prentice Hall, 1992), pp. 129-130.

10. Zachary Schiller and Wendy Zellner, "Making the middleman an endangered species," *Business Week*, June 6, 1994, pp. 114-115.

11. Ronald Henkoff, "Delivering the goods," *Fortune*, November 28, 1994, pp. 64-66+; Gene Bylinsky, "The digital factory," *Fortune*, November 14, 1994, pp. 92-95+.

12. Kenneth Kidd, "Canadian Tire opts for austerity," *The Globe and Mail*, July 17, 1991, pp. B1-B2; also John Heinzl, "Canadian Tire

treads new ground in warehouse stores," *The Globe and Mail*, October 7, 1991, pp. B1-B2.

13. Barnaby Feder, "McDonald's makes a comeback," *The Globe and Mail*, January 22, 1994, p. B8.

14. Julie Iovine, "Cher's gothic look, by mail," *New York Times*, September 8, 1994, p. C8.

15. Philip Kotler and Gary Armstrong, *Marketing: An Introduction*, 3rd ed. (Englewood Cliffs, NJ: Prentice Hall, 1993), p. 362; Scott Donaton and Joe Mandese, "GM, Hachette to test TV show," *Advertising Age*, September 13, 1993, p. 1.

16. Andrew Tausz, "Getting there fast—by truck," *The Globe and Mail*, March 1, 1994, p. B23.

17. Andrew Allentuck, "Arctic delivery tough sailing," *The Globe and Mail*, March 1, 1994, p. B23.

18. Rick Tetzeli, "Cargo that phones home," *Fortune*, November 15, 1993, p. 143.

19. Bill Redekop, "The crow subsidy is history," *Winnipeg Free Press*, February 28, 1995, p. 1.

Chapter 17

1. Ronald Hilton, *Managerial Accounting*, 2nd ed. (New York: McGraw-Hill, 1994), p. 7.

2. M. Rothkopf, "No more easy questions on the uniform CPA examination," *Accounting Horizons*, Vol. 1, No. 4, December, 1987, pp. 79-85.

3. Philip Mathias, "Non-profits fight move to GAAP accounting," *The Financial Post*, March 5, 1994, p. 15.

4. L.A. Nikolai, J.D. Bazley, and J.C. Stallman, *Principles of Accounting*, 3rd ed. (Boston: PWS-Kent, 1990).

5. C.T. Horngren and G.I. Sundem, *Introduction to Financial Accounting* (Englewood Cliffs, NJ: Prentice-Hall, 1987).

6. Ronald Hilton, *Managerial Accounting*, 2nd ed. (New York: McGraw-Hill, 1994), pp. 402-403.

7. Douglas Lavin, "GM would have to cut 20,000 workers to match Ford efficiency, report says," *Wall Street Journal*, June 24, 1994, p. C22.

Chapter 18

1. P.S. Rose and D.R. Fraser, *Financial Institutions*, 3rd ed. (Plano, TX: Business Publications, Inc., 1988).

2. Robert E. Calem, "Taking the worry out of paying with plastic," *New York Times*, November 14, 1993, Sec. 3, p. 9.

3. William Cantrell, "Why are all of those Canadian issuers selling?" *Credit Card Management*, December 1991, pp. 26-31; Thomas Holden, "The Japanese discover the perils of plastic," *Business Week*, February 10, 1992, p. 42; Richard L. Holman, "Korea curbs credit cards," *Wall Street Journal*, December 22, 1994, p. A10.

4. "Big MacCurrencies," *The Economist*, April 9, 1994, p. 88.

5. Brian Milner, "Canada tough on foreign banks," *The Globe and Mail*, February 25, 1992, pp. B1, B20.

6. Eric Reguly, "Big 6 Canadian banks forced to reconsider buying U.S. operations," *The Financial Post*, September 16, 1991, pp. 35, 37.

Chapter 19

1. Jerry Zeidenberg, "Suppliers at mercy of big companies," *The Globe and Mail*, June 10, 1991, p. B10.

2. John Heinzl, "Good strategy gone awry, top retailer's tale of woe," *The Globe and Mail*, March 7, 1992, pp. B1, B4.

3. *Financial World*, April 4, 1989, p. 106; also *Mutual Fund Profiles* (New York: Standard and Poor's Corp., May, 1989), p. ix; also *Stock Reports Index* (New York: Standard and Poor's Corp., November, 1989), p. 38.

4. *The State of Small Business, 1989 Annual Report on Small Business in Ontario* (Toronto: Ministry of Industry, Trade and Technology, 1990).

5. J.W. Duncan, *D&B Reports*, September-October 1991, p. 8.

6. E.F. Brigham, *Fundamentals of Financial Management*, 5th ed. (Chicago: Dryden, 1989).

7. Barry Critchley, "Risk management now Bhalla's full-time business," *The Financial Post*, September 17, 1990, p. 29.

8. Thomas P. Fitch, *Dictionary of Banking Terms*, 2nd ed. (Hauppauge, NY: Barron's 1993), p. 531.

9. This section is based on Phillip L. Zweig et al., "Managing risk," *Fortune*, October 31, 1994, pp. 86-90+.

10. Figure estimated from *1988-89 Property/Casualty Fact Book*, p. 19.

11. *The Financial Post*, July, 1995, p. 172.

Chapter 20

1. *The Value Line Investment Survey*, January 28, 1994, p. 1095.

2. George G. Kaufman, *The U.S. Financial System: Money, Markets, and Institutions*, 6th ed. (Englewood Cliffs, NJ: Prentice Hall, 1995), p. 432.

3. *New York Stock Exchange Fact Book 1994*, pp. 26, 39.

4. Nicholas D. Kristof, "Don't joke about this stock market," *New York Times*, May 9, 1993, Sec. 3, pp. 1, 6; Jane Perlez, "Warsaw's exuberant exchange," *New York Times*, December 25, 1993, pp. 47-48.

5. *Moody's Bond Survey*, August 2, 1993, p. 4138.

6. Amey Stone, "Futures: Dare you defy the odds?" *Business Week*, February 28, 1994, pp. 12-13.

7. Steven Greenhouse, "Exchanges thrive as Russians pursue market economy," *Winnipeg Free Press*, November 3, 1991, p. B13.

Chapter 21

1. Barrie McKenna, "Just another round in cigarette ad fight," *The Globe and Mail*, July 26, 1991, pp. B1, B5.

2. "CRTC clamps down on eight wayward FM stations," *Winnipeg Free Press*, September 28, 1985, p. 48.

3. Harvey Enchin, "CRTC heads down new road," *The Globe and Mail*, November 1, 1993, pp. B1, B8.

4. Ashley Geddes, "Marketing boards under fire," *The Financial Post*, October 9, 1993, p. 6.

5. John Kohut, "Chrysler facing federal tribunal for refusing to supply car parts," *The Globe and Mail*, December 16, 1988, p. B5.

6. Barrie McKenna, "Hyundai gorged on federal funds," *The Globe and Mail*, March 25, 1994, p. B3.

Chapter 22

1. Bill Saporito, "Where the global action is," *Fortune*, Autumn/Winter 1993, pp. 62-65.

2. John Tagliabue, "Coca-Cola reaches into impoverished Albania," *New York Times*, May 20, 1994, pp. D1, D3; Joseph B. Treaster, "Kellogg seeks to reset Latvia's breakfast table," *New York Times*, May 19, 1994, pp. D1, D8.

3. Brenton R. Schlender et al., "Special Report/Pacific Rim: The battle for Asia," *Fortune*, November 1, 1993, pp. 126-156; Philip Shenon, "Missing out on a glittering market," *New York Times*, September 12, 1993, Sec. 3, pp. 1, 6; Steven Greenhouse, "New tally of world's economies catapults China into third place," *New York Times*, May 20, 1993, pp. A1, A8.

4. Michael Porter, "Why nations triumph," *Fortune*, March 12, 1990, pp. 94-108.

5. Jeffrey Taylor and Neil Behrmann, "Coffee prices surge after frost hits Brazil," *Wall Street Journal*, June 28, 1994, pp. C1, C16; Dori Jones Yang with Bill Hinchberger, "Trouble brewing at the coffee bar," *Business Week*, August 1, 1994, p. 62.

6. John Heinzl, "U.S. shoppers flock to Canada," *The Globe and Mail*, February 7, 1995, pp. B1, B16.

7. Anthony DePalma, "G.M. gives Mexico its own 'Chevy'" *The New York Times*, May 12, 1994, pp. D1, D6; James B. Treece et al., "New worlds to conquer," *Business Week*, February 28, 1994, p. 51.

8. Peggy Berkowitz, "You say potato, they say McCain," *Canadian Business*, December, 1991, pp. 44-48.

9. Daniel Stoffman, "Cross-border selling," *Report on Business Magazine*, November, 1991, pp. 61-68.

10. "Cracking world markets without leaving home," *Canadian Business*, January, 1992, pp. 13-14.

11. John Stackhouse, "Missing the market," *Report on Business Magazine*, January, 1992, p. 38.

12. "In hot pursuit of international markets," *Innovation*, Summer, 1990, pp. 11-13.

13. Jeremy Main, "How to go global—and why," *Fortune*, December 17, 1990, pp. 70-73; see p. 72.

14. Randall Litchfield, "The pressure on prices," *Canadian Business*, February, 1992, pp. 30-35.

15. Barrie McKenna, "Aluminum producers whispering dirty word," *The Globe and Mail*, March 5, 1994, pp. B1, B4.

16. "New global trade regulator starts operations tomorrow," *Winnipeg Free Press*, December 31, 1994, p. A5.

17. Barrie McKenna, "Threat won't force changes," *The Globe and Mail*, January 1, 1994, pp. B1, B5.

18. Peter Cook, "Free trade free-for-all causes confusion," *Globe and Mail*, December 5, 1994, p. B7.

19. Bruce Little, "Canada slips in world rankings," *The Globe and Mail*, September 7, 1994, pp. B1, B16.

20. Herman Daems, "The strategic implications of Europe 1992," *Long Range Planning*, 23, No. 3, 1990, pp. 41-48.

21. For example, see James C. Abegglen and George Stalk, *Kaisha: The Japanese Corporation* (New York: Basic Books, 1986).

22. Tim Richardson, "Reaping the yen," Canadian Business, August, 1990, pp. 49-57.

23. See Edith Terry's series on *keiretsu* in *The Globe and Mail*: "The land of the rising cartels," September 22, 1990, pp. B1-B2; "The ties that bind," September 24, 1990, pp. B1, B4; and "Looking in from the outside," September 25, 1990, pp. B1-B2.

24. "Indonesia mixes delicate labour brew for foreign audience," *The Globe and Mail*, March 11, 1994, p. B10.

25. Michael Bociurkiw, "Manulife braces for push into China," *The Globe and Mail*, March 10, 1994, p. B3.

26. For a discussion of doing business in the (former) Soviet Union, refer to Carl H. McMillan, "Eastward ho! Tackling the last frontier," *Canadian Business Review*, Summer, 1990, pp. 17-26.

27. For a discussion of practical ideas and useful information on surviving and succeeding in eastern Europe, refer to Tarif Korabi and David G. Grieve, "Doing business in Eastern Europe: A survival guide," *Canadian Business Review*, Summer, 1990, pp. 22-25.

Chapter 23

1. John Rockart, "Chief executives define their own data needs," *Harvard Business Review*, March-April, 1979, pp. 81-93.

2. Andrew McIntosh, "Computerized bus system set for Hull region," *The Globe and Mail*, July 5, 1985, p. B10.

3. Patrick Conlon, "Use of computer dispatching means fewer squawks for taxis," *The Globe and Mail*, December 5, 1988, p. B7.

4. Bruce Gates, "Hard-to-police software pirates cost industry millions," *The Financial Post*, March 11, 1991, p. 13.

5. Geoffrey Rowan, "Speed is object of new technology," *The Globe and Mail*, June 15, 1994, pp. B1, B19.

6. This section is based on Larry Long, *Computers and Information Systems*, 4th ed. (Englewood Cliffs, NJ: Prentice Hall, 1994), pp. 450-51.

7. Catherine Arnst et al., "The Information Appliance," *Business Week*, November 22, 1993, p. 98-102+.

8. Jack B. Rochester, *Computers: Tools for Knowledge Workers* (Homewood, IL: Irwin, 1993), pp. 164, 167; Robert D. Hof with Neil Gross, "The Gee-Whiz Company," *Business Week*, July 18, 1994, pp. 56-59+.

9. "Zoom! Here comes the new micros," *Business Week*, December 1, 1986, p. 82.

10. Donald Sanders, *Computers Today*, 3rd ed. (New York: McGraw-Hill, 1988).

11. Otis Port et al., "Wonder chips," *Business Week*, July 4, 1994, pp. 86-92.

12. Richard Brandt, "Bill Gates's vision," *Business Week*, June 27, 1994, pp. 56-62.

13. Bruce Nussbaum et al., "Winners: The best product designs of the year," *Business Week*, June 7, 1993, p. 68; Long and Long, *Computers*, pp. 27-29, 473-74.

14. Gary McWilliams, "Computers are finally learning to listen," *Business Week*, November 1, 1993, pp. 100-101; Gene Bylinski, "At last! Computers you can talk to," *Fortune*, May 3, 1993, pp. 88-91; Brandt, "Bill Gates's vision," p. 60.

15. Andrzej J. Taramina, "Expert systems in manufacturing," *P&IM Review with APICS News*, December 1990, pp. 42, 45.

16. Deidre A. Depke and Richard Brandt, "PCs: What the future holds," *Business Week*, August 12, 1991, pp. 58-64.

17. Long and Long, *Computers*, p. 470.

18. John Wilke, "Togetherness, the PC way," *The Globe and Mail*, December 11, 1993, pp. B1, B5.

19. David Caruso, "Making sense of new information technologies," *APICS—The Performance Advantage*, October 1991, pp. 32-35; John J. Kanet, "Real decision support for production scheduling and support," *Production and Inventory Management*, September 1991, pp. 24-25; Gene Bylinsky, "The payoff from 3-D computing," *Fortune*, Autumn 1993, pp. 32-34+.

20. Rochester, *Computers*, pp. 449-50.

21. Brandt, "Bill Gates's vision," p. 62; Arnst et al., "The information appliance," p. 100.

22. Brandt, "Bill Gates's vision," p. 58.

23. "Small business computing," *Nation's Business*, December, 1989, pp. 34-35; also Deidre A. Depke, "Software's big guns take aim at small business," *Business Week*, September 25, 1989, pp. 216-218.

24. Kirkpatrick, "How PCs will take over your home," p. 101; Barbara Kantrowitz, "In Quicken they trust," *Newsweek*, May 2, 1994, pp. 65-66.

Source Notes

Chapter 1

Opening Case John Milward, "Joy in Mudville," *Rolling Stone*, September 22, 1994, pp. 61+; Karen Schoemer, "Woodstock '94: Back to the garden," *Newsweek*, August 8, 1994, pp. 44-45; John Pareles, "This Woodstock won't inhale," *The New York Times*, August 7, 1994, Sec. 2, pp. 1, 24; Emily DeNitto, "Pepsi, Haagen-Dazs find harmony at Woodstock '94," *Advertising Age*, August 22, 1994, p. 13. **Figure 1.6** *Bank of Canada Review*, Autumn 1994, p. A1. **International Report** Summarized from Peter Cook, "Brazil campaigns against inflation," *The Globe and Mail*, May 16, 1994, p. B1; also Katherine Ellison, "Heart attacks price of Brazil's chaotic economy," *The Financial Post*, January 17, 1994, p. C8; also Peter Cook, "Brazil's inflation fight gets real," *The Globe and Mail*, July 4, 1994, p. B1; also Isabel Vincent, "Argentina's miracle more of a paradox," *The Globe and Mail*, March 17, 1994, p. B1; also Bruce Little, "Deflation returns after 40 years," *The Globe and Mail*, June 18, 1994, pp. B1, B3; also Barrie McKenna, "Is it the last gasp for inflation?" *The Globe and Mail*, February 17, 1994, pp. B1, B8. **Figure 1.7** *Bank of Canada Review*, Autumn 1994, p. S85. **The Canadian Business Scene** Randall Litchfield, "The Contrarian Case for Canada," *Canadian Business*, December, 1991, pp. 33-38. **The Canadian Business Scene** Summarized from Geoffrey Rowan, "CN productivity right off the tracks," *The Globe and Mail*, October 9, 1991, pp. B1, B4.

Chapter 2

Opening Case Summarized from Gail Lem, "Algoma chief shares pain, gives up $400,000 bonus," *The Globe and Mail*, May 4, 1994, pp. B1-B2; also Patricia Commins, "United Airlines unions bet on success," *The Globe and Mail*, December 24, 1993, p. B5; also Robin Sidel, "Employee ownership seen as industry trend," *The Globe and Mail*, December 24, 1993, p. B5; also David Roberts, "The brew crew takes over," *The Globe and Mail*, December 21, 1993, p. B20; also Hugh McBride, "How to lose freedom and gain the world," *The Globe and Mail*, January 25, 1994; also Kimberley Noble, "Can the workers make a go of it?" *The Globe and Mail*, August 17, 1991, p. B18. **International Report** Adapted from Madelaine Drohan, "Lloyd's ends tradition of unlimited liability," *The Globe and Mail*, April 30, 1993, pp. B1, B8; also "Investors revel in Lloyd's suit win," *Winnipeg Free Press*, October 5, 1994, p. C12. **Figure 2.3** Statistics Canada, multiple years, catalogue number 31-203. **Table 2.2** *The Financial Post 500*, 1995 edition, p. 102. Used with permission. **The Canadian Business Scene** Summarized from Gayle MacDonald, "Board seat a hotter place to sit," *The Financial Post*, November 19, 1990, p. 36; see also Arthur Johnson, "Directors: New breed in a hot seat," *Canadian Business*, June 1991, pp. 74-83; see also Patricia Lush, "Being a director means being a worker," *The Globe and Mail*, March 16, 1987, pp. B1, B8; see also Drew Fagan, "Despite recent gains, women still a rare breed on company boards," *The Globe and Mail*, May 2, 1990, p. B7. **Table 2.4** *The Financial Post 500*, 1995 edition, pp. 102-116. Used with permission. **International Report** Gale Eisenstodt, "Bullies on the farm," *Forbes*, July 22, 1991, pp. 84+; "Knocking the Nokyo." *The Economist*, June 18, 1988, p. 73; "When the salt of the earth loses its savour," *The Economist*, February 10, 1986, pp. 31+. **International Report** Summarized from John Lorinc, "Alliances: going global made simple," *Canadian Business*, November 1990, pp. 126-137; see also Laura Fowlie, "Strategic alliances wave of the future," *The Financial Post*, October 22, 1990, pp. 37-38; see also Gordon Pitts, "Why foreign joint ventures end in divorce," *The Financial Post*, November 13, 1989, p. 7. **Concluding Case 2.1** Randall Forsyth, "Dig this gig: Hard Rock Cafe goes public," *Barron's*, March 30, 1987, pp. 16+; see also Floyd Norris, "The trader," *Barron's*, August 8, 1988, pp. 111+; see also Laura Sanderson and Michael Small, "New York shakes, rattles, and rolls as London's Hard Rock Cafe brings home the burgers," *People*, March 26, 1984, pp. 40+; see also Jeffrey Trachtenberg, "Ballad of a Made Cafe," *Forbes*, November 19, 1984, pp. 288+. **Concluding Case 2.2** Adapted from Peter Foster, "Bill Hopper's first (and last) annual meeting," *The Globe and Mail*, January 30, 1993, p. B4.

Chapter 3

Opening Case Summarized from Kevin Cox, "Sea change," *The Globe and Mail*, May 17, 1994, p. B24. **Figure 3.1** *Historical Statistics of Canada*, F.H. Leacy (ed), Series D266-317 (1950-1975); see also *The Labour Force*, 71-001 (1980 and 1985). Used by permission of the Minister of Supply and Services Canada; also *The Bank of Canada Review*, "General Economic Statistics Section, Catalogue Number FB12-1. **The Canadian Business Scene** Summarized from Allan Robinson and Kimberley Noble, "Lac makes a deal," *The Globe and Mail*, August 25, 1994, pp. B1, B4; also Allan Robinson, "Lac rivals await poison pill ruling," *The Globe and Mail*, August 20, 1994, p. B1; also Allan Robinson, "Royal Oak asked to extend offer," *The Globe and Mail*, August 19, 1994, pp. B1, B6; also Allan Robinson, "Lac slams bid from Royal Oak," *The Globe and Mail*, July 19, 1994, p. B1; also Jacquie McNish, "Time pops poison pill; Seagram gets headache," *The Globe and Mail*, January 21, 1994, pp. B1, B5; also Casey Mahood, "MDC challenges Regal poison pill," *The Globe and Mail*, August 27, 1994, p. B18; also Kimberley Noble, "Cangene resisting takeover bid," *The Globe and Mail*, July 9, 1994, p. B18; also John Partridge, "Poison pill a sore point between Nova, Fairvest," *The Globe and Mail*, June 27, 1994; also Harvey Enchin, "Emerson targets old client," *The Globe and Mail*, February 14, 1994, pp. B1, B4; also Marina Strauss, "Labatt shareholders reject poison pill," *The Globe and Mail*, September 14, 1994, pp. B1, B5. **The Canadian Business Scene** Summarized from Brian Hutchinson, "Cheers!" *Canadian Business*, November 1994, pp. 23-28. **Figure 3.4 (a)** *Historical Statistics of Canada*, F.H. Leacy (ed.), Series D8-55 (1911-1971); see also *The Labour Force*, 71-001 (1981 and 1986); see also Cansim data base. Used by permission of the Minister of Supply and Services Canada. **(b)** Cansim data base. **(c)** *Historical Statistics of Canada*, F.H. Leacy (ed.), Series C85-97 (1921-1971); see also *The Labour Force*, 71-001 (1981, 1986, and 1992). Used by permission of the Minister of Supply and Services Canada. **The Canadian Business Scene** Summarized from Michael Posner, "The death of leisure," *The Globe and Mail*, May 25, 1991, pp. D1, D4. **Figure 3.6** *Bank of Canada Review*, Autumn 1994, p. S74. **Figure 3.7** Statistics Canada *Industrial R & D Statistics*, catalogue number 88-202, p. 21 (1983); see also chart 1.1, 1989, p. 15. **Concluding Case 3.1** Summarized from Geoffrey Rowan, "Airline deal signals a new era," *The Globe and Mail*, April 26, 1994, pp. B1, B8. **Concluding Case 3.2** Summarized from Janice Castro, "From walkman to showman," *Time*, October 9, 1989, pp. 70+; see also Neil Gross and William Holstein, "Why Sony is plugging into Columbia," *Business Week*, October 16, 1989, pp. 56+; see also Ronald Grover et al., "Invasion of the studio snatchers," *Business Week*, October 16, 1989, pp. 52+; Ronald Grover, "When Conlumbia Met Sony . . . A Love Story," *Business Week*, October 9, 1989, pp. 44+; see also Gene Kobetz, "Which country is buying the most U.S. companies? Wrong," *Business Week*, February 13, 1989, p. 22; see also John Schwartz et al., "Japan Goes Hollywood," *Newsweek*, October 9, 1989, pp. 62+.

Chapter 4

Opening Case Summarized from Mark Stevenson, "Waste not," *Canadian Business*, January 1994, pp. 20-26. **The Canadian Business Scene** Kenneth Andrews, "Ethics in practice," *Harvard Business Review*, September/October 1989, pp. 99+; see also Jefferson Grigsby, "Unethical behavior," *Financial World*, June 27, 1989, p. 20; see also James Strodes, "Mr. Diogenes, call your office," *Financial World*, June 27, 1989, pp. 24+. **International Report** Summarized from Madelaine Drohan, "To bribe or not to bribe," *The Globe and Mail*, February 14, 1994, p. B7; see also Margaret Shapiro, "A Country on the Take," *Winnipeg Free Press*, November 21, 1994, p. A7. **Figure 4.2** Guiding Principles of Great West Life Assurance Company, Winnipeg, Manitoba. Reproduced with permission. **The Canadian Business Scene** Summarized from Catherine Collins, "The Greening of Dow," *Report on Business Magazine*, November 1991, pp. 21-35; see also Jeb Blount, "Battle of the Clamshell," *Report on Business Magazine*, April 1991, pp. 40-47. **Concluding Case 4.1**

Kevin Kelly and Kathleen Kerwin, "There's another side to the López saga," *Business Week*, August 23, 1993, p. 26; John Templeman and Peggy Salz-Trautman, "VW figures its best defense may be a good offense," *Business Week*, August 9, 1993, p. 29; Templeman and David Woodruff, "The aftershock from the López affair," *Business Week*, August 19, 1993, p. 31; Doron Levin, "Executive who left G.M. denies taking documents and sues," *The New York Times*, May 25, 1993, pp. A1, D21; Ferdinand Protzman, "VW hums tightfisted López tune," *The New York Times*, April 30, 1994, pp. 39, 47. **Concluding Case 4.2** Summarized from John Schreiner, "Green war and Greenpeace," *The Financial Post*, Annual Issue, 1994, pp. 44-48.

Part One

International Case This case was written by Professor Reg Litz of the University of Manitoba. Used with permission.

Chapter 5

Opening Case Summarized from Mark Stevenson, "Indomitable Showman," *Canadian Business*, October 1994, pp. 23-32. **The Canadian Business Scene** Summarized from Henry Mintzberg, *The Nature of Managerial Work* (New York: Harper and Row, 1973), Chapter 3. **The Canadian Business Scene** Summarized from Gail Lem, "Bell to slash 5,000 jobs," *The Globe and Mail*, September 29, 1993, p. B1; also Lawrence Surtees, "NorTel starts swinging the axe," *The Globe and Mail*, September 2, 1993, p. B1; "Royal Bank cuts 4,100 jobs," *Winnipeg Free Press*," November 25, 1993, p. A4; also "Coca-Cola Spares City in Cuts," *Winnipeg Free Press*, November 25, 1993, p. A4; also Larry Johnsrue, "Klein warns of layoffs unless salary cuts OK'd," *Winnipeg Free Press*, November 25, 1993, p. A4; also W. Cascio, "Downsizing: What do we know? What have we learned?" *Academy of Management Executive*, 7, 1993, pp. 95-104; also Carol Hymnowitz, "When firms slash middle management, those spared often bear a heavy load," *Wall Street Journal*, April 5, 1990, pp. B1+; also Kenneth Labich, "Making over middle managers," *Fortune*, May 8, 1989, pp. 58-64; also Thomas O'Boyle, "From Pyramid to Pancake," *Wall Street Journal*, June 4, 1990, pp. R37+; also Edith Terry, "Japan lives with tradition," *The Globe and Mail*, May 14, 1994, B1, B4. **International Report** Beth Brophy, "Out of sight—but not mind," *U.S. News and World Report*, July 18, 1988, pp. 33+; see also Jim Impoco, "You think it's bad here . . . ," *U.S. News and World Report*, July 18, 1988, pp. 34+; see also Joann Lublin, "Grappling with the expatriate issue: Companies try to cut subsidies for employees," *Wall Street Journal*, December 11, 1989, pp. B1+; see also Thomas O'Boyle, "Little benefit to careers seen in foreign stints," *Wall Street Journal*, December 11, 1989, pp. B1+. **The Canadian Business Scene** Summarized from Margot Gibb-Clark, "New crew on board," *The Globe and Mail*, June 14, 1994, p. B25; also Hugh McBride, "How to lose freedom and gain the world," *The Globe and Mail*, January 25, 1994, p. B22. **Concluding Case 5.1** Summarized from David Napier, "Beeston plays hardball," *The Financial Post Magazine*, September 1992, pp. 28-32. **Concluding Case 5.2** Starke/Sexty, *Contemporary Management in Canada* (Scarborough, ON: Prentice Hall Canada, 1992), p. 541.

Chapter 6

Opening Case Summarized from Geoffrey Rowan, "Airline deal signals new era," *The Globe and Mail*, April 26, 1994, pp. B1, B8; also Arthur Johnson, "Up in the Air," *Canadian Business*, November 1993, pp. 45-48; also Geoffrey Rowan, "JAL bows out of link with Canadian," *The Globe and Mail*, January 15, 1993, pp. B1, B12; also Drew Fagan, "Showdown for Canadian," *The Globe and Mail*, February 2, 1993, pp. B1, B6; also Geoffrey Rowan, "Judge scolds Air Canada, gives AMR hefty award," *The Globe and Mail*, February 13, 1993, p. B5; also "The PWA Videotape," *The Financial Post*, April 1, 1991, p. 7; also Donald Campbell, "Airlines holding pattern," *Winnipeg Free Press*, November 14, 1992, p. 1; also John Douglas, "Tories raise ante in airline bailout," *Winnipeg Free Press*, November 20, 1991, p. 1; also Alex Binkley, "Key advice in transport study spurned," *Winnipeg Free Press*, November 20, 1992, p. A8; also John Douglas, "Number of flights to be cut," *Winnipeg Free Press*, November 24, 1992, p. 1; also Brad Oswald, "Air deal approval stirs joy, anxiety," *Winnipeg*

Free Press, May 28, 1993, p. 1; also J. Douglas and Bonnie Bridge, "Ruling may kill gemini," *Winnipeg Free Press*, November 25, 1993, p. 1. **The Canadian Business Scene** Interviews with Sterling McLeod and Wayne Walker, senior vice-presidents of sales for Investors. **The Canadian Business Scene** John Case, "The Enemy Within," reprinted with permission, *Inc.*, magazine (April 1987), pp. 32+. Copyright 1993 by Goldhirsh Group, Inc., 38 Commercial Wharf, Boston, MA 02110; see also Tom Herman, "Running Around," *Wall Street Journal*, June 10, 1988, p. 17R. **The Canadian Business Scene** Interview with Tom Ward, Operations Manager for Genstar Shipyards Ltd. **The Canadian Business Scene** Summarized from Owen Edwards, "Leak soup," *GQ*, April 1989, pp. 224+; see also Beatryce Nivens, "When to Listen to the office grapevine," *Essence*, March 1989, p. 102; John S. Tompkins, "Gossip: Silicon Valley's secret weapon," *Science Digest*, August 1986, pp. 58+; see also "Why you need the grapevine," *Glamour*, August 1986, pp. 126+. **Concluding Case 6.1** Joseph Weber, "A big company that works," *Business Week*, May 4, 1994, pp. 124-33. **Concluding Case 6.2** Summarized from Robert Collison, "How Bata rules the world," *Canadian Business*, September 1990, pp. 28-34.

Chapter 7

Opening Case Adapted from Cathryn Motherwell, "Ice cream team scoops success," *The Globe and Mail*, August 15, 1994, p. B4. **Figure 7.1** *Quality of Work in the Service Sector*, Statistics Canada, 11-612E, No. 6, 1992. **The Canadian Business Scene** Diane Francis, "What makes Jim Pattison run—and whistle," *The Financial Post*, March 5, 1994, p. S3. **Figure 7.2** Allan J. Magrath, "The thorny management issues in family-owned business," *Business Quarterly*, Spring 1988, p. 73. Reprinted with permission of *Business Quarterly*, published by the Western Business School, The University of Western Ontario, London, Ontario. **The Canadian Business Scene** Summarized from Al Emid, "Trend to micro-enterprises helps neophytes," *The Globe and Mail*, March 13, 1990, p. C5; see also Laura Fowlie, "How to feel at home in your home office," *The Financial Post*, June 25, 1990, p. 34; see also Douglas and Diana Lynn Gray, *Home Inc.: The Canadian Home-Based Business Guide* (Toronto: McGraw-Hill Ryerson, 1990). **International Report** Summarized from Richard T. Ashman, "Born in the U.S.A.," *Nation's Business*, November 1986, pp. 41+; see also "Canadian franchisees start to fight abuses," *Wall Street Journal*, October 6, 1988, p. B1; see also Ted Holden et al., "Who says you can't break into japan?" *Business Week*, October 16, 1989, p. 49; see also Joann S. Lublin, "For U.S. franchisers, a common tongue isn't a guarantee of success in the U.K.," *Wall Street Journal*, August 16, 1988, p. 25; see also Matt Moffitt, "For U.S. firms, franchising in Mexico gets more appetizing, thanks to Michael Selz, *Wall Street Journal*, January 3, 1991, p. A6; see also Michael Selz "Europe offers expanding opportunities to franchisers," *Wall Street Journal*, July 20, 1991, p. B2; see also Jeffrey A. Tannenbaum, "Franchisers see a future in East Bloc," *Wall Street Journal*, June 5, 1990, pp.B1+; see also Jeffrey A. Tannenbaum, "Small businesses join franchise push in Japan," *Wall Street Journal*, May 17, 1989, p. B1; see also Andrew Tanzer, "A form of flattery," *Forbes*, June 2, 1986, pp. 110+; see also Russell G. Todd, "U.S. fast-food franchises go East in American international venture," *Wall Street Journal*, November 15, 1988, p. B2; see also Meg Whittemore, "International franchising," *Inc.*, April 1988, pp.116+. **International Report** Ebert/Griffin, *Business Essentials* (Englewood Cliffs, NJ: Prentice Hall, 1995), p. 166 and Wilton Woods, "Products to watch: Heavy artillery," *Fortune*, May 30, 1994, p. 163; David Whitford, "Opposite attractions," *Inc.*, December 1994, pp. 60-64+. **Table 7.3** Mel Scott and Richard Bruce, "Five stages of growth in small business," *Long Range Planning*, 20, 1987, p. 48. **Table 7.5** Starke/Sexty, *Contemporary Management in Canada*, Scarborough: Prentice Hall Canada (1995). **Concluding Case 7.1** Ellen Roseman, "Flowering firm faces branch battles," *The Globe and Mail*," November 1, 1994, p. B6. **Concluding Case 7.2** Starke/Sexty, *Contemporary Management in Canada*, Scarborough: Prentice Hall Canada (1995).

Part Two

International Case Ebert/Griffin, *Business*, Third Edition (Englewood Cliffs, NJ: Prentice Hall, 1993), pp. 200-201. Oneal, "Just what is an entrepreneur?" p. 105.

Chapter 8

Opening Case Summarized from Cathryn Motherwell, "Life in greener fields," *The Globe and Mail*, August 2, 1994, p. B18. **The Canadian Business Scene** Bruce Little, "Employment sweepstakes requires flexible ticket," *The Globe and Mail*, January 13, 1993, pp. B1, B6. **The Canadian Business Scene** Summarized from Rose Fisher, "Screen Test," *Canadian Business*, May 1992, pp. 62-64. **The Canadian Business Scene** Summarized from Diane Forrest, "Guess who you can't fire," *Canadian Business*, November 1991, pp. 97-100; see also Margot Gibb-Clark, "Campeau faces hurdles in lawsuit," *The Globe and Mail*, July 13, 1991, p. B1. **International Report** Ebert/Griffin, *Business Essentials* (Englewood Cliffs, NJ: Prentice Hall, 1995), pp. 214-215. **The Canadian Business Scene** John Partridge, "Shareholder activism brewing," *The Globe and Mail*, December 24, 1993, pp. B1, B4; also Karen Howlett, "Teacher wins battle with board," *The Globe and Mail*, May 16, 1994. **The Canadian Business Scene** Summarized from Wilfred List, "Under the gun about safety," *The Globe and Mail*, January 4, 1994, p. B14; also Doron Levin, "Industry counts on the thin, grey line," *The Globe and Mail*, March 1, 1994, p. B9. **Concluding Case 8.1** Starke/Sexty, *Contemporary Management in Canada* (Scarborough, ON: Prentice Hall Canada, 1992), p. 351. **Concluding Case 8.2** Summarized from Mark Brender, "Free isn't easy," *The Globe and Mail*, August 9, 1994, p.B18; also Margot Gibb-Clark, "Temps take on new tasks," *The Globe and Mail*, December 22, 1993, p. B1; also Merle MacIsaac, "New broom sweeps schools," *The Globe and Mail*, March 22, 1994, p. B22; also Robert Williamson, "Tradition gives way to world of freelancers," *The Globe and Mail*, January 15, 1993, pp. B1, B4; also Sally Ritchie, "Rent-a-manager," *The Globe and Mail*, August 17, 1993, p. B22.

Chapter 9

Opening Case Mark Stevenson, "Be nice for a change," *Canadian Business*, November 1993, pp. 81-85; also Michael Smyth, "Union leaders claim violence was a setup," *Winnipeg Free Press*, November 26, 1994, p. C6. **The Canadian Business Scene** Alan Farnham, "The trust gap," *Fortune*, December 4, 1989, pp. 56+; Anne B. Fisher, "Morale crisis," *Fortune*, November 18, 1991, pp. 70+; Anne B. Fisher, "CEOs think that morale is dandy," *Fortune*, November 18, 1991, pp. 83+; Walter Kiechell III, "How important is morale, really?" *Fortune*, February 13, 1989, pp. 121+. **The Canadian Business Scene** Summarized from Arthur Bragg, "Should you make a lateral move?" *Sales & Marketing Management*, June 1989, pp. 70+; Carey W. English, "Money Isn't Everything," *U.S. News & World Report*, June 23, 1986, pp. 64+; see also "Family Ties," *Inc.*, August, 1989, p. 112; see also Curtis Hartman and Steven Pearlstein, "The joy of working," *Inc.*, November 1987, pp. 61+; see also John Naisbitt and Patricia Aburdene, "When companies are great places to work," *Reader's Digest*," January 1987, pp. 141+. **Figure 9.2** Griffin/Ebert, *Business*, Second Edition (Englewood Cliffs, NJ: Prentice Hall, 1996). **Figure 9.3** Griffin/Ebert, *Business*, Second Edition (Englewood Cliffs, NJ: Prentice Hall, 1996). **International Report** Summarized from Brenton Schlender, "Japan's white collar blues," *Fortune*, March 21, 1994, pp. 97-100; also Brenton Schlender, "Japan: Is it changing for good?" *Fortune*, June 13, 1994, pp. 124-134; also Edith Terry, "Japan lives with tradition," *The Globe and Mail*, May 14, 1994, pp. B1, B4; also William Ouchi, *Theory Z* (Reading, Mass.: Addison-Wesley, 1981); also Suzanne McGee, "How Japanese managers are trained," *The Financial Post*, June 1, 1985, p. 25; also Chalmers Johnson, "Japanese-style management in America," *California Management Review*, Summer 1988, pp. 34-45; N. Coates, "Determinants of Japan's business success: Some Japanese executives' views," *Academy of Management Executive*, February 1988, 2, pp. 69-72. **The Canadian Business Scene** Summarized from Bruce McDougall, "Perks with pizzazz," *Canadian Business*, June 1990, pp. 78-79; see also Don Champion, "Quality—a way of life at B.C. Tel," *Canadian Business Review*, Spring 1990, p. 33; see also Margot Gibb-Clark, "Companies find merit in using pay as a carrot," *The Globe and Mail*, May 9, 1990, p. B1; also Margot Gibb-Clark, "The right reward," *The Globe and Mail*, August 10, 1990, p. B5; see also Peter Matthews, "Just rewards—the lure of pay for performance," *Canadian Business*, February, 1990, pp. 78-79; also Ian Allaby, "Just Rewards," *Canadian Business*, May 1990, p. 39; see also David Evans, "The myth of customer service," *Canadian Business*, March 1991, pp. 34-39; also Bud Jorgensen, "Do bonuses unscrupulous brokers make?" *The Globe and Mail*, May

28, 1990, p. B5; also Wayne Gooding, "Ownership is the best motivator," *Customer Business*, March 1990, p. 6. **The Canadian Business Scene** Summarized from Warren Bennis, "How to be the leader they'll follow," *Working Woman*, March 1990, pp. 75+; see also Sherry Suib Cohen, "How to Be a Leader," *Reader's Digest*, August 1989, pp. 98+; see also Peter Drucker, "Leadership: More doing than dash," *Wall Street Journal*, January 1, 1988, p. 14; see also Jack Falvey, "Before spending $3 million on leadership, read this," *Wall Street Journal*, October 3, 1988, p. A22; see also Sharon King, "The leading edge," *Black Enterprise*, May 1988, pp. 87+; see also Kenneth Labich, "The seven keys to business leadership," *Fortune*, October 24, 1988, pp. 58+; see also Jeremy Main, "Wanted: Leaders who can make a difference," *Fortune*, September 28,1987, pp. 92+; see also Miller, "Lorenzo, you're no nelson," *New York Times*, March 30, 1989, p. A25. **Concluding Case 9.1** Summarized from Alan Farnham, "Mary Kay's lesson in Leadership," *Fortune*, September 20, 1993, pp. 68-77. **Concluding Case 9.2** Summarized from Aaron Bernstein and Wendy Zellner, "Detroit vs. the UAW: At odds over teamwork," *Business Week*, August 24, 1987, pp. 54+; see also Peter Downs, "Drudgery at Wentzville: The team concept strikes out," *Commonweal*, September 9, 1988, pp. 453+; see also John Hoerr, "Is teamwork," *Business Week*, July 10, 1989, pp. 56+; see also John Holusha, "A new spirit at U.S. auto plants," *New York Times*, December 29, 1987, p. D1+.

Chapter 10

Opening Case Summarized from John Lorinc, "Crossing the line," *Canadian Business*, September, 1993, pp. 68-73; also Jeb Blount, "Behind the lines," *Canadian Business*, January 1990, p. 63; also Casey Mahood, "Whirlpool closing Inglis factory in Ontario," *The Globe and Mail*, November 16, 194, pp. B1, B8; also Virginia Galt, "Skills made to order," *The Globe and Mail*, January 22, 1992, p. B7. **Table 10.1** Labour Canada, *Labour Organizations in Canada*, 1989, pp. xiii and xiv. Used by permission of the Minister of Supply and Services Canada. **International Report** Joyce Barnathan and Matt Forney, "Damping labor's fires," *Business Week*, August 1, 1994, p. 41; Jane Perlez, "Solidarity forever? Well, it's not the 80's anymore," *The New York Times*, July 20, 1994, p. A4; Allen R. Myerson, "Big labor's strategic raid in Mexico," *The New York Times*, September 12, 1994, pp. D1, D4; Bill Keller, "The revolution won, workers are still unhappy," *The New York Times*, July 23, 1994, p. A2. **Table 10.2** Labour Canada, *Labour Organizations in Canada*, 1992. Used by permission of the Minister of Supply and Services Canada. **Table 10.3** Labour Canada, *Labour Organizations in Canada*, 1992. Used by permission of the Minister of Supply and Services Canada. **Figure 10.2** Griffin/Ebert, *Business*, Second Edition (Englewood Cliffs, NJ: Prentice Hall, 1996). **The Canadian Business Scene** Summarized from Alan Freeman, "Philips gets ready for a tough new era," *The Globe and Mail*, October 26, 1991, pp. B1-B2. **The Canadian Business Scene** Summarized from Marina Strauss and Harvey Enchin, "Strike is no ball for business," *The Globe and Mail*, August 22, 1994, pp. B1, B5; also Marina Strauss, "Broadcasters bodychecked," *The Globe and Mail*, October 1, 1994, pp. B1, B2; also Scott Feschuk, "Hockey shutout costs provinces millions," *The Globe and Mail*, December 8, 1994, pp. B1, B10; also Marina Stauss, "Broadcasters worry: When the games return, will advertisers follow?" *The Globe and Mail*, December 3, 1994, pp. B1, B7; also Harvey Enchin, "Hockey loss crosschecks Maple Leaf Gardens," *The Globe and Mail*, November 11, 1994, pp. B1, B4. **Figure 10.3** Labour Canada, *Labour Organizations in Canada*, 1991, p. xxv. Used by permission of the Minister of Supply and Services Canada. **Concluding Case 10.2** Kennith Labich, "Will United fly?" *Fortune*, August 22, 1994, pp. 70+; Adam Bryant, "After seven years, employees win United Airlines," *The New York Times*, July 13, 1994, pp. A1, D13; Bryant, "Buyout of UAL by its unions looks like winning alternative," *The New York Times*, May 13, 1994, p. D6; Aaron Bernstein and Kevin Kelly, "This give-and take may actually fly," *Business Week*, December 27, 1993, p. 37; Susan Chandler, "United: So many cuts, so little relief," *Business Week*, December 5, 1994, p. 42; "United Airlines' parent posts first yearly profit since 1990," *The New York Times*, January 25, 1995, p. D8.

Part Three

International Case Summarized from Eamonn Fingleton, "Jobs for life: Why Japan won't give them up," *Fortune*, March 20, 1995, pp. 119-125; also Larry Armstrong, "Japan's newest import: U.S.—style layoffs," *Business Week*, March 9, 1987, pp. 57+; see also Amy Borrus and Sayaka Shinoda, "Japan Inc. hangs out a help-wanted sign," *Business Week*, July 24, 1989, p. 32; see also James Fallows, "The hard life," *Atlantic*, pp. 16+; see also Nagaharu Hayabusa, "A necessary farewell to tradition," *World Press Review*, September, 1988, p. 50; see also Ted Holden, "Big bucks vs. a job for life: Why top talent is defecting," *Business Week*, January 9, 1989, p. 58; see also Yjko Inoue and Hisayuki Mitsusada, "Japan's new job hoppers,'" *World Press Review*, January, 1988, p. 50; see also "Jobs for Japan's next generation," *The Economist*, February 27, 1988, pp. 51+; see also "Put your feet up," *The Economist*, March 19, 1988, pp. 35+; see also "Situations not quite vacant," *The Economist*, April 16, 1988, p. 42; see also "Yoshio Stakhanov on Holiday," *The Economist*, March 26, 1989, 70+.

Chapter 11

Opening Case Summarized from Alexander Ross and Randall Litchfield, "The new industrial revolution," *Canadian Business*, December 1993, pp. 23-33; also Jacquie McNish, "Throng of firms moves to the U.S. to slash costs," *The Globe and Mail*, July 2, 1991, pp. B1, B4; also Ian Allaby, "Why everybody's flying south," *Canadian Business*, December 1990, pp. 2-47. **International Report** Summarized from Gene Bylinsky, "The digital factory," *Fortune*, November 14, 1994, pp. 92-110. **The Canadian Business Scene** Summarized from David N. Burt, "Managing suppliers up to speed," *Harvard Business Review*, July-August, 1989, p. 127+; see also Uday Karmarkar, "Getting control of just-in-time," *Harvard Business Review*, September-October, 1989, p. 133; see also Dan Marshall, "HP helps deliver just-in-time," *Harvard Business Review*, July-August, 1989, p. 133; see also Peter C. Reid, *Well Made in America* (McGraw-Hill, 1989), excerpted in "How Harley beat back the Japanese," *Fortune*, September 25, 1989, pp. 155+. **The Canadian Business Scene** Summarized from Gordon Bock, "Limping along in robot land," *Time*, July 13, 1987, pp. 46+; see also Gene Bylinsky, "Invasion of the service robots," *Fortune*, September 14, 1987, pp. 81+; "*Ecce Robo*," *The Economist*, October 15, 1988, pp. 19+; see also Bill Lawren, "Humans make a comeback," *Omni*, August 1987, pp. 32+; see also "Living with smart machines," *The Economist*, May 21, 1988, pp. 79+; see also Wally Dennison, "Robotics paint system makes splash at CN," *Winnipeg Free Press*, October 6, 1988, p. 30; see also "Robots aren't for burning," *Canadian Business*, September 1984, p. 45; see also Renate Lerch, "More firms finding place for robots on factory floor," *The Financial Post*, June 29, 1985, p. C6; see also Carolyn Leitch, "When boxes have brains," *The Globe and Mail*, April 12, 1994, p. B26. **Concluding Case 11.1** Summarized from "How to beat the Japanese at home," *Fortune*, August 31, 1987, pp. 80+; see also "Maybe this time . . . ," *Forbes*, September 7, 1987, p. 34. **Concluding Case 11.2** Summarized from Fred Bleakley, "Who's that on the factory floor?" *The Globe and Mail*, January 31, 1995, p. B26.

Chapter 12

Opening Case Summarized from Alfred LeBlanc, "Power play," *The Globe and Mail*, June 21, 1994, p. B24. **The Canadian Business Scene** Summarized from David Evans, "The myth of customer service," *Canadian Business*, March 1991, pp. 34-39. **Table 12.2** Adapted from Richard Chase, "Where does the customer fit in a service operation?" *Harvard Business Review*, November/December 1978, pp. 137-142. **International Report** Summarized from Peter Foster, "McDonald's excellent Soviet venture?" *Canadian Business*, May 1991, pp. 51-64. **Concluding Case 12.1** Summarized from Geoffrey Rowan, "How software star solved service slips," *The Globe and Mail*, December 13, 1994, p. B24. **Concluding Case 12.2** Starke/Sexty, *Contemporary Management in Canada*, Second Edition (Scarborough, ON: Prentice Hall Canada, 1995), pp. 31-2.

Chapter 13

Opening Case Alex Taylor III, "Shaking up Jaguar," *Fortune*, September 6, 1993, pp. 65-68; John Templeman, "These repair jobs are taking a little longer than expected," *Business Week*, April 27, 1992, pp. 117, 121; "Will your next Jaguar be built at Von Braun's lane?" *Road & Track*, May 1993, pp. 39-40; Julia Flynn and James B. Treece, "Is the jinx finally off Jaguar?"

Business Week, October 10, 1994, p. 62; Valerie Reitman and Oscar Suris, "Can the very British Jaguar be made in Japan?" *The Wall Street Journal*, December 9, 1994, p. B1; Michael Clements, "Jaguar has a lot riding on XJ series," *USA Today*, December 19, 1994, pp. B1, B2. **Figure 13.1** Reprinted from *Perspectives '90* (1994) with permission from the Houston-based American productivity and Quality Center. **International Report** Summarized from Harvey Enchin, "Canada urged to stop living off fat of the land," *The Globe and Mail*, October 25, 1991, pp. B1, B6. **The Canadian Business Scene** Starke/Sexty, *Contemporary Management in Canada*, Second Edition (Scarborough, ON: Prentice Hall Canada, 1995), p. 564. **International Report** Ebert/Griffin, *Business Essentials* (Englewood Cliffs, NJ: Prentice Hall, 1995), pp. 272-3. **International Report** "Air reservation merger is off," *The New York Times*, October 16, 1991, p. D3; "Best practice companies;" *Financial World*, September 17, 1991, pp. 36+; "The computer network that keeps American flying," *Fortune*, September 24, 1990, p. 46; Max D. Hopper, "Rattling SABRE—New ways to compete on information," *Harvard Business Review*, May-June 1990, pp. 188+; "Hotels find better lodging in airline reservation systems," *Business Week*, July 10, 1989, p. 84E; Kenneth Lambich, "American takes on the world," *Fortune*, September 24, 1990, pp. 40+. **Concluding Case 13.1** Summarized from Timothy Pritchard, "King of Jacks," *The Globe and Mail*, February 8, 1994, p. B28. **Concluding Case 13.2** Summarized from Scott Rankine, "The last picture show," *The Globe and Mail*, July 26, 1994, p. B22.

Part Four

International Case Summarized from Michael Newman, "Chips ahoy," *Far Eastern Economic Review*, December 29, 1994/January 5, 1995, pp. 66-67; also Kathleen Morris, "Sitting duck," *Financial World*, November 22, 1994, pp. 50-55; also "A giant with wings?," *Business Korea*, December 1994, pp. 21-23; also "Semiconductor exports to continue healthy growth," *Business Korea*, January 1995, pp. 27-28; also Peter McGill, "Tomorrow belongs to Lee," *Euromoney*, October 1994, pp. 98-99, also Louis Krarr, "Tough comeback artist," *Fortune*, August 3, 1987, p. 53; see also Ira C. Magaziner and Mark Patinkin, "Fast heat: How Korea won the microwave war," *Harvard Business Review*, January-February, 1989, pp. 83+; see also Laxmi Nakarmi, "Roh cracks his whip at the Chaebol," *Business Week*, May 28, 1990, p. 40; see also Andrew Tanzer, "Samsung: South Korea marches to its own drummer," *Forbes*, May 16, 1988, pp. 84+.

Chapter 14

Opening Case "Public relations, store tie-ins launch 'green' cosmetics line," *Public Relations Journal*, April 1991, pp. 24+; P. Born, "Spellbound's moving image," *Women's Wear Daily*, August 16, 1991, p. 10; Subrata N. Chakravarty, "Acceptably sexy," *Forbes*, November 13, 1989, pp. 122+; Alan Deutschman, "Nudes for Lauder," *Fortune*, March 12, 1990, p. 129; Kathleen Deveny, "How Leonard Lauder is making his Mom proud," *Business Week*, September 4, 1989, pp. 68+; M. Duffy, "The war of the noses," *Time*, September 30, 1991, p. 50; Walter Guzzardi. Jr., "The U.S. business hall of Fame." *Fortune*, March 14, 1988, pp. 142+; C. Miller, "Cosmetics Industry's marketing approach says 'color me green." *Marketing News*, June 10, 1991, p. 2; C. Trueheart, "Video scent-station: for discriminating customers, a taped ad for perfume," *The Washington Post*, August 19, 1991, p. B1. **International Report** Summarized from Shawn Tully, "Teens: The most global market of all," *Fortune*, May 16, 1994, pp. 90-97. **The Canadian Business Scene** Summarized from Suanne Kelman, "Consumers on the couch," *Report on Business Magazine*, February 1991, pp. 50-53. **The Canadian Business Scene** Summarized from Gina Mallet, "Greatest romance on earth," *Canadian Business*, August 1993, pp. 19-23. **The Canadian Business Scene** Ebert/Griffin, *Business Essentials*, pp. 328-9. **International Report** Griffin/Ebert, *Business*, Third Edition. **Concluding Case 14.2** Summarized from Michael Crawford, "The law and the jungle," *Canadian Business*, February 1992, pp. 42-47.

Chapter 15

Opening Case Summarized from Daniel Stoffman, "Bombardier's billion-dollar space race," *Canadian Business*, June 1994, pp. 91-101. **The Canadian Business Scene** Summarized from Shirley Won, "A roll player wins the pie," *The Globe and Mail*, November 15, 1993, p. B4. **Table 15.1** Philip Kotler and Gary Armstrong, *Marketing: An Introduction*, 3rd ed. (Englewood Cliffs, NJ: Prentice Hall), p. 274; William J. Stanton, Michael J. Etzel, and Bruce J. Walker; *Fundamentals of Marketing*, 10th ed. (New York: McGraw-Hill, 1994), p. 247; William P. Pride and O.C. Ferrell, *Marketing: Concepts and Strategies*, 9th ed. (Boston: Houghton Mifflin, 1995), pp. 307-13. **International Report** Summarized from Carla Rapaport, "Nestle's brand building machine," *Fortune*, September 19, 1994, pp. 147-156. **Figure 15.8** *Marketing Magazine*, 02/05/94. **Figure 15.9** 1994 *Canadian Advertising Rates and Data*. Maclean Hunter Publishing Ltd., Used with permission. **The Canadian Business Scene** Marina Strauss, "Battery companies battle over ads," *The Globe and Mail*, November 29, 1994, pp. B1, B10; also Marina Strauss, "Frozen pie crust ruling puts chill on comparative ads," *The Globe and Mail*, October 6, 1994, p. B4. **Table 15.2** "Total measured U.S. ad spending by category and media," *Advertising Age*, September 28, 1994, p. 8. **Table 15.3** *The Financial Post 500*, 1995 edition, pp. 102-116. Used with permission. **The Canadian Business Scene** Summarized from Shona McKay, "Make room, Madison Avenue," *Canadian Business*, January 1993, pp. 33-36. **Concluding Case 15.1** Summarized from Marina Strauss, "Brewers concentrate on the flagship labels," *The Globe and Mail*, June 9, 1994, p.B6; also Patricia Davies, "Labatt's Blues," *Report on Business Magazine*, June 1991, pp. 41-47; also Jan Matthews and Greg Boyd, "The Hardest Sell," *Canadian Business*, April 1991, pp. 60-65. **Concluding Case 15.2** Summarized from Gail Lem, "Cott profit soars as revenues double," *The Globe and Mail*, April 9, 1994, p. B18; also Patricia Sellers, "Brands: It's thrive or die," *Fortune*, August 23, 1993, pp. 52-56; also Madelaine Drohan, "British await Coke's reply to grocer's look-alike cola," *The Globe and Mail*, August 29, 1994.

Chapter 16

Opening Case Summarized from Alexander Ross, "The Eaton's nobody knows," *Canadian Business*, May 1993, pp. 47-59. **Table 16.2** *The Financial Post 500*, 1995 edition, p. 142. Used with permission; also *Fortune*, August 22, 1994, p. 189. **International Report** Summarized from John Heinzl, "Canadian Tire pulls out of U.S.," *The Globe and Mail*, December 2, 1994, pp. B1, B6; also William C. Symonds, "Invasion of the retail snatchers," *Business Week*, May 9, 1994, pp. 72-73; also Carla Rapaport, "The new U.S. push into Europe," *Fortune*, January 10, 1994, pp. 73-74; also Marina Strauss, "Imasco sells stores," *The Globe and Mail*, June 26, 1990, pp. B1-B2; also Karen Howlett, "Once bitten in the U.S. market, Canadian Tire not shy about re-entering," *The Globe and Mail*, May 6, 1988, p. B3; also Kenneth Kidd, "Success breeds prudence as Canadian Tire peers over 49th parallel," *The Globe and Mail*, January 31, 1990, p. 36; also Frances Phillips, "Canadian Tire finds Texas trails a bit bumpy," *The Financial Post*, March 26, 1983, p. 18; also Jean Matthews and Greg Boyd, "Can Lionel Robbins rescue Dylex?" *Canadian Business*, November 1990, pp. 106-114; also Beppi Crosariol, "What makes the U.S. so tough," *Financial Times of Canada*, October 8, 1990, p. 14; also *The Financial Post* Information Service, History Sections on Canadian Tire Corporation and Dylex Ltd. **The Canadian Business Scene** Summarized from Mark Stevenson, "The store to end all stores," *Canadian Business*, May 1994, pp. 20-29. **The Canadian Business Scene** Summarized from Tamsen Tillson, "Multilevel marketing sells costly dreams," *The Globe and Mail*, October 8, 1994, pp. B1, B6. **Table 16.3** *Fortune*, August 22, 1994, p. 190. **Table 16.4** *The Financial Post 500*, 1995 edition, p. 144. Used with permission. **Concluding Case 16.1** Summarized from John Markoff, "For 3DO, a make-or-break season," *The New York Times*, December 11, 1994, Sec. 3, pp. 1, 6; Ralph T. King, Jr., "3DO faces struggle to keep video-game player alive," *The Wall Street Journal*, May 19, 1994, p. B4; Jim Carlton, "3DO faces revolt by game developers over fee to cut manufacturers' losses," *The Wall Street Journal*, October 24, 1994, p. B4; Cleveland Horton and Ira Teinowitz, "Video goes 3DO," *Advertising Age*, January 11, 1993, pp. 1, 43. **Concluding Case 16.2** Summarized from David Roberts, "41 below but getting warmer," *The Globe and Mail*, February 1, 1994, p. B24.

Part Five

International Case Summarized from Laurie Freeman, "Completing the span of 'bridge' to boomers, *Advertising Age*,

November 7, 1994, p. S-8; also Angela Morgan, "Habitat International to hit Italy and Germany," *European Retail*, December 6, 1994, p. 1; also "Management Brief: Furnishing the World," *Economist*, November 19, 1994, pp. 79-80; also Jonathan Bell, "IKEA successfully penetrates East European consumer markets," *Central European*, June 1994, pp. 13-14; also Helen Pike, "IKEA still committed to U.S., despite uncertain economy," *Discount Store News*, April 18, 1994, pp. 17-19; also "March: Best spots," *Adweek*, April 11, 1994, pp. 40-42.

Chapter 17

Opening Case Summarized from John Southerst, "Suddenly, it all makes sense," *Canadian Business*, March, 1994, pp. 39-42; also Bruce Little, "A foundry finds its way," *The Globe and Mail*, October 5, 1993, p. B28; also Terence Pare, "A new tool for managing costs," *Fortune*, June 14, 1993, pp. 124-129. **Table 17.1** *The Financial Post 500*, 1995 edition, p. 175. Used with permission. **The Canadian Business Scene** Summarized from Edward Clifford, "Big accounting firms face insurance crunch," *The Globe and Mail*, November 13, 1993, p. B3; also "Cooperants' Auditors Sued," *The Financial Post*, October 30, 1993, p. 8; also Patricia Lush, "Gap widens between views on auditor's role in Canada," *The Globe and Mail*, February 14, 1986, p. B3; also Chris Robinson, "Auditors' Role Raises Tough Questions," *The Financial Post*, June 22, 1985. **The Canadian Business Scene** Summarized from Carolyn Leitch, "Four Seasons' accounting queried," *The Globe and Mail*, January 25, 1994, pp. B1-B2; also John Saunders and Carolyn Leitch, "Sharp seeks graceful checkout," *The Globe and Mail*, May 21, 1994, pp. B1, B14. **Concluding Case 17.1** Summarized from Cathryn Motherwell, "Accounting fight spills over into Alberta," *The Globe and Mail*, June 4, 1992, p. B6. **Concluding Case 17.2** Summarized from Karen Howlett and Murray Wood, "Standard directors sue Peat Marwick," *The Globe and Mail*, June 5, 1992, pp. B1, B10; see also Allan Robinson, "OSC says Standard ignored warning signals," *The Globe and Mail*, June 2, 1992, p. B10.

Chapter 18

Opening Case Summarized from John Southerst, "The start-up star who bats .900," *Canadian Business*, March 1993, pp. 66-72. **The Canadian Business Scene**, Ebert/Griffin, *Business Essentials*, p. 252. **Table 18.1** *The Economist*, April 9, 1994, p. 88. **Table 18.2** *The Financial Post 500*, 1995 edition, p. 170. Used with permission. **The Canadian Business Scene** Summarized from John Partridge, "Debit cards move into Ontario," *The Globe and Mail*, April 25, 1994, pp. B1, B2; also Virginia Galt, "Debit cards: You may be unable to leave home without them," *The Globe and Mail*, April 14, 1989, pp. B1, B2; also Bruce Cheadle, "Debit card shopping a success," *Winnipeg Free Press*, November 14, 1991, p. E53. **The Canadian Business Scene** Summarized from Sandy Fife, "Have a nice day," *Report on Business Magazine*, October 1991, pp. 49-57. **The Canadian Business Scene** Summarized from Janet McFarland, "A royal loss of trust: 1993s sorriest debacle," *The Financial Post*, December 25, 1993, p. 9; also Gordon Pitts, "The Man on Royal Trustco's Hot Seat," *The Financial Post*, November 25, 1991, p. 7. **Table 18.3** *The Financial Post 500*, 1995 edition, p. 170. Used with permission. **Concluding Case 18.1** Summarized from David West, "Why we need a cheaper buck," *Canadian Business*, July 1990, p. 21; see also Randall Litchfield, "Our Strong Dollar: The right medicine," *Canadian Business*, January 1992, p. B10. **Concluding Case 2** Summarized from Drew Fagan, "Living standards plunge with peso," *The Globe and Mail*, February 20, 1995, p. B7.

Chapter 19

Opening Case Summarized from Barrie McKenna, "A perfect reflection," *The Globe and Mail*, January 22, 1992, pp. B1, B3; also Ann Gibbon, "Cooperants collapses after bailout plan fails," *The Globe and Mail*, January 7, 1992, pp. B1-B2; also John Saunders, "Confed bestows property legacy," *The Globe and Mail*, August 29, 1994, pp. B1, B8; also Janet McFarland, "Great-West takes control of Confed," *The Financial Post*, April 30-May 2, 1994, p. 1; also John Partridge and Dennis Slocum, "Damage control at Confed," *The Globe and Mail*, August 13, 1994, pp. B1, B3; also Terence Corcoran, "One man's mixed legacy at Confederation," *The Globe and Mail*, August 16, 1994,

p. B2; also Dennis Slocum, "Confed failure costly for industry," *The Globe and Mail*, August 16, 1994, pp. B1-B2; also Barrie McKenna, "Insurance plan reconsidered," *The Globe and Mail*, September 5, 1994, pp. B1-B2; also Dennis Slocum, "Insurance industry gets harsh review," *The Globe and Mail*, August 23, 1994, pp. B1, B6. **The Canadian Business Scene** Summarized from Barrie McKenna, "A perfect reflection," *The Globe and Mail*, January 22, 1992, pp. B1, B3; also Ann Gibbon, "Cooperants collapses after bailout plan fails," *The Globe and Mail*, January 7, 1992, pp. B1-B2; also Barrie McKenna, "Insurance plan reconsidered," *The Globe and Mail*, September 5, 1994, pp. B1-B2. **The Canadian Business Scene** Summarized from Jacquie McNish and Margaret Philp, "O & Y backs away from commercial paper," *The Globe and Mail*, March 6, 1992, pp. B1, B7; see also Brian Milner, Margaret Philp, Alan Freeman, Drew Fagan, and John Saunders, "Reichmanns call in cavalry; U.S. banker to head O & Y," *The Globe and Mail*, March 25, 1992, pp. B1, B4; see also Brian Milner and Margaret Philp, "Reichmann shuffle gives Camdev stake to Albert," *The Globe and Mail*, March 28, 1992, pp. B1, B8; see also Jacquie McNish, Margaret Philp, and Brian Milner, "O & Y's hard times stem from shift to short-term debt," *The Globe and Mail*, April 4, 1992, pp. B1, B8; see also Madelaine Drohan, "O & Y has no plans for bankruptcy filing," *The Globe and Mail*, April 23, 1992, pp. B1, B6; see also Madelaine Drohan and Jacquie McNish, "O & Y reported on verge of bankruptcy protection," *The Globe and Mail*, May 15, 1992, pp. B1, B5; see also Brian Milner and Margaret Philp, "O & Y puts on brave face to mask predicament," *The Globe and Mail*, May 16, 1992, pp. B1, B4. **The Canadian Business Scene** Summarized from "Taking risk into their own hands," *The Financial Post*, September 11, 1993, pp. S13-S14. **Table 19.2** *The Financial Post 500*, 1995 edition, p. 172. Used with permission. **International Report** Summarized from Kerry Hannon, "High Stakes," *Forbes*, May 29, 1989, pp. 326+; see also Godfrey Hodgson, *Lloyd's of London* (New York: Viking, 1984); see also Peter D. Lawrence, "Trying Your Luck at Lloyd's," *Esquire*, February 1988, p. 66; "Premiumstroika," *The Economist*, January 20, 1990, p. 95. **Concluding Case 19.1** Sara Webb et al., "A royal mess: Britain's Barings PLC bets on derivatives—and the cost is dear," *The Wall Street Journal*, February 27, 1995, pp. A1, A6; Marcus W. Brauchli, Nicholas Bray, and Michael R. Sesit, "Broken bank: Barings PLC officials may have been aware of trader's position," *The Wall Street Journal*, March 6, 1995, pp. A1, A7; Richard W. Stevenson, "Markets shaken as a British bank takes a big loss," *The New York Times*, February 27, 1995; pp. A1, D5; Paula Dwyer et al., "The lesson from Barings' straits," *Business Week*, March 13, 1995, pp. 30-32. Glenn Whitney, "Dutch concern agrees to buy Barings assets," *The Wall Street Journal*, March 5, 1995, pp. A3, A5.

Chapter 20

Opening Case Summarized from Karen Howlett, "Funds told to inform public," *The Globe and Mail*, February 1, 1995, pp. B1, B12; also Karen Howlett, "Mutual fund industry put under spotlight," *The Globe and Mail*, January 30, 1995, pp. B1-B2. **The Canadian Business Scene** Summarized from Patricia Lush, "Matkin lowers the boom on VSE," *The Globe and Mail*, January 26, 1994, pp. B1, B7; also Douglas Gould, "Who needs brokers?" *Report on Business Magazine*, June 1990, pp. 35-37; also John Lorinc, "Making your firm a stock market star," *Canadian Business*, January 1992, pp. 51-54. **The Canadian Business Scene** Summarized from Karen Howlett, "Critics call for ban on sweetheart incentives," *The Globe and Mail*, February 14, 1994, pp. B1-B2. **Concluding Case 20.1** David J. Jefferson, "Bam! Aargh! Little comics get trounced," *The Wall Street Journal*, January 22, 1990, pp. B1+; Douglas A. Kass, "Pow! Smash! Kerplash!" *Barron's*, February 17, 1992, pp. 14+; Floyd Norris, "Boom in comic books lifts new marvel stock offering," *The New York Times*, July 15, 1991, pp. D1, D8; Mark Landler with Laura Zinn, "The new Ron Perelman has an old problem," *Business Week*, June 14, 1993, pp. 94-95; Gene G. Marcial, "Ron Perelman: Vegas or bust?" *Business Week*, January 16, 1995, p. 72; Marvin Shankin, "Interview: Ron Perelman," *Cigar Aficionado*, Spring, 1995, p. 65; Jeff Jensen, "Comics' high-tech weapons," *Advertising Age*, September 12, 1994, pp. 20, 24. **Concluding Case 20.2** Summarized from Daniel Stoffman, "Look who's calling the shots," *Canadian Business*, July 1990, pp. 45-47.

Part Six

International Case Summarized from Craig Torres, "Battered peso stages surprising rebound," *The World Street Journal*, April 25, 1994, p. A14, also Craig Torres and Dianne Solis, "Mexico's Central Bank might raise interest rates even more to help peso," *The Wall Street Journal*, March 24, 1995, p. A10; also Paul Carroll and Craig Torres, "Mexico unveils program of harsh fiscal medicine," *The Wall Street Journal*, March 10, 1995, pp. A3, A11; also Craig Torres, "Mexican peso plunges 10 percent before Central Bank acts," *The Wall Street Journal*, March 7, 1995, p. A3; also Tim Carrington and Craig Torres, "U.S. unveils rescue plan for Mexico," *The Wall Street Journal*, February 22, 1995, pp. A3-A4; also Craig Torres, "Mexican markets are hit by fresh blows," *The Wall Street Journal*, February 15, 1995, p. A11; also Craig Torres and David Wessel, "Mexico creates rescue plan featuring credit, austerity," *The Wall Street Journal*, January 3, 1995, pp. 3, 40; also Craig Torres and David Wessel, "U.S. considers additional aid for Mexico," *The Wall Street Journal*, December 29, 1994, p. A12; also Craig Torres, "Mexico's goal for '95 growth may be tough," *The Wall Street Journal*, December 16, 1994, p. A8; also Craig Torres and Paul Carroll, "Mexico reverses currency policy," *The Wall Street Journal*, December 21, 1994, pp. A3, A6; also Craig Torres, "Mexico's devaluation stuns Latin America—and U.S. investors," *The Wall Street Journal*, December 22, 1994, pp. A1, A6; also "Mexico drops efforts to prop up peso, spurring 15 percent fall and eroding credibility," *The Wall Street Journal*, December 23, 1994, pp. A3, A4; also Craig Torres and Paul Carroll, "Mexico puts economic steps on hold until fallout from peso's plunge settles," *The Wall Street Journal*, December 27, 1994, pp. A3, A6.

Chapter 21

Opening Case Summarized from John Partridge, "Jackman challenges ethics warning," *The Globe and Mail*, February 5, 1995, pp. B1, B16; also John Partridge, "Blind trust could have solved Jackman's woes," *The Globe and Mail*, February 6, 1995, p. B3. **Table 21.1** Reproduced by permission of the Minister of Supply and Services Canada. **Tables 21.4 and 21.5** *The Financial Post 500*, 1995 edition, pp. 102-127. Used with permission. **International Report** Summarized from Madelaine Drohan, "Corrupt officials line road to capitalism," *The Globe and Mail*, May 2, 1994, p. B8; also "Entrepreneurship still viewed as a criminal activity by some," *The Globe and Mail*, May 26, 1994, p. B8. **The Canadian Business Scene** Summarized from Peter Foster, "Harvest of hangovers," *Report on Business Magazine*, February 1991, pp. 55-59. **Figure 21.2** Summarized from Brian Owen, "Business managers' influence (or lack of influence) on government," *Business Quarterly*, Autumn 1976. **Concluding Case 21.1** Summarized from Paul King, "Trading Places," *Canadian Business*, May 1991, pp. 78-81; see also Douglas Forster, "Trading Places," *Report on Business Magazine*, March 1992, pp. 17-27. **Concluding Case 21.2** Summarized from Barrie McKenna, "Ad firms find a friend in Liberals," *The Globe and Mail*, February 11, 1995, p. B7.

Chapter 22

Opening Case Summarized from Casey Mahood, "Glegg makes a splash abroad," *The Globe and Mail*, April 12, 1994, pp. B1-B2. **Table 22.2** Statistics Canada, publication 63-224, 1993-94, p. 46. **Figure 22.1** Bank of Canada Review, Autumn 1994, p. 100. **International Report** Summarized from Michael Urlocker and Frances Misutka, "Russians learn to love the greenback," *The Financial Post*, September 11, 1993, p. 9; also "Russia tumbles, Russia reels," *The Globe and Mail*, October 12, 1994, pp. B1, B20. **Figure 22.3** Griffin/Ebert, *Business*, Fourth Edition (Englewood Cliffs, NJ: Prentice Hall, 1996). **Table 22.3** GATT, April 1994. **International Report** Summarized from Phillip Day, "A-OK? Not for this Moscow Crowd, after Clinton Gives 'em the Finger," *Winnipeg Free Press*, June 18, 1994, p. C6; also Tamsen Tillson, "The art of the deal in China," *The Globe and Mail*, September 5, 1994, pp. B1-B2. **International Report** Summarized from Drew Fagan, "NAFTA tightens ties that bind," *The Globe and Mail*, December 30, 1994, pp. B1-B2. **International Report** Summarized from James Brooke, "South America's quiet revolution," *The Globe and Mail*, April 25, 1994, p. B5. **Concluding Case 22.1** Summarized from Bob Ortega, "Wal-Mart's invasion of Mexico far from a revolution," *The Globe and Mail*, August 4, 1994, p. B1.

Chapter 23

Opening Case Summarized from Mark Anderson, "Software piracy robbing Canadian economy," *The Financial Post*, May 28, 1994, p. S18; also Jonathan Chevreau, "SoftCop tackles the software pirates," *The Financial Post*, March 12, 1994, p. 16; also Frank Lenk, "Piracy costs software firms billions," *The Globe and Mail*, May 18, 1994, p. B5. **The Canadian Business Scene** Summarized from Carolyn Leitch, "Paper chase goes high tech," *The Globe and Mail*, October 11, 1994, p. B26. **Figure 23.6** Based on a study by W. Lambert Gardiner, GAMMA, Montreal, Quebec. Reproduced by permission. **The Canadian Business Scene** James Kaminsky, "Computers that fly," *Vis a Vis*, October 1991, pp. 39+; Peter H. Lewis, "One day, laptops could rule the world," *The New York Times*, March 31, 1991, p. F4; Thayer C. Taylor, ed., "Small is beautiful: Making laptops easier to love," *Sales & Marketing Management*, May 1990, p. 103; Thayer C. Taylor, ed., "The PC evolution: desktop...laptop...palmtop...? Top," *Sales & Marketing Management*, February 1991, pp. 50+. **Table 23.4** *The Financial Post 500*, 1995 edition. p. 140. Used with permission. **The Canadian Business Scene** Summarized from G. Pascal Zachary, "Executives jam e-mail signals," *The Globe and Mail*, June 23, 1994, p. B7; also John Wilke, "Togetherness, the PC way," *The Globe and Mail*, December 11, 1993, pp. B1, B5. **The Canadian Business Scene** Peter H. Lewis, "Getting down to business on the Net," *The New York Times*, June 19, 1994, Sec. 3, p. 1; John W. Verity and Robert D. Hof, "The Internet: How it will change the way you do business," *Business Week*, November 14, 1994, pp. 80-86+; Steven Dickman, "Catching customers on the Web," *Inc. Technology*, Summer 1995, pp. 56-60; Stephen D. Solomon, "Staking a claim on the Internet," *Inc. Technology*, March 1995, pp. 87-90+; Alan R. Earls, "Incubators of agility," *Computerworld*, January 23, 1995, pp. 81-82; Hof, "From the man who brought you silicon graphics...," *Business Week*, October 24, 1994, pp. 90-91; Lewis, "Netscape knows fame and aspires to fortune," *The New York Times*, March 1, 1995, pp. D1, D6. **Concluding Case 23.1** Summarized from Victoria Burrus, "The virtual stockyard," *The Globe and Mail*, September 27, 1994, p. B28. **Concluding Case 23.2** Summarized from Gary Lamphier, "Flower power," *The Globe and Mail*, March 29, 1994, p. B30.

Part Seven

International Case Griffin/Ebert, *Business*, Third Edition, pp. 730-731.

Photo Credits

Chapter 1
Page 4, Inco Limited; Page 6, Reuter Bettmann; Page 5, Dick Hemingway; Al Harvey/The Slide Farm; Page 10, Susan McCartney; Bettmann Archives; Junebug Clark; David R. Frazier, Paolo Koch/Photo Researchers; Page 13, Ontario Ministry of Agriculture and Food; Page 15, Angelika Baur; Al Harvey/The Slide Farm; Page 18, Kathleen Bellesiles/Little Apple Studio

Chapter 2
Page 28, Bank of Montreal; Page 32, Wendell Mentzen/Bruce Coleman, Inc.; Page 35, Reprinted with permission - The Toronto Star Syndicate; Page 38, Imperial Oil Limited; Page 41, Al Harvey/The Slide Farm; Page 49, The Granger Collection

Chapter 3
Page 56, Canapress; Page 59, Allelix Biopharmaceuticals Inc., Mississauga, Ontario; Page 61, Courtesy IBM; Courtesy BASF; George Haling/Photo Researchers; Page 64, Dave Repp/Black Star; Page 69, Ontario Hydro

Chapter 4
Page 80, Al Harvey/The Slide Farm; Page 84, Al Harvey/The Slide Farm; Kathleen Bellesiles; Page 90, David R. Frazier/Photo Researchers; Page 95, Courtesy of Construction Association of Ontario; Page 97, McDonald's Restaurant; Page 100, Supreme Court of Canada

Chapter 5
Page 118, Canada Wide; Page 120, Canapress; Page 125, Will McIntyre; Blair Seitz; Hank Morgan/Photo Researchers; Page 127, Henley & Savage/The Stock Market; Jan Feingersh/The Stock Market; Courtesy Control Data Corporation; Al Harvey/The Slide Farm; Federal Express Customer Service; Page 129, Tom Hollyman/Photo Researchers; Page 130, Tom Hollyman/Photo Researchers; Page 134, International Verifact; Takeshi Takahara, Richard Hutchings; Spencer Grant/Photo Researchers; Page 135, Craig Abel Photography; Courtesy Hewlett-Packard Company; Tim Davis/Photo Researchers

Chapter 6
Page 140, Al Harvey/The Slide Farm; Page 142, Lockheed Air Terminal of Canada Inc.; Page 147, Gabe Palmer/The Stock Market; Page 158, Eaton's; Page 165, Renee Lynn/Photo Researchers

Chapter 7
Page 172, Dick Hemingway; Page 174, Mackay's Cochrane Ice Cream; Page 177, S. Houston; Page 183, Midas Canada Inc.; Page 186, Robert Semeniuk Photography

Chapter 8
Page 206, Courtesy of Centennial College; Page 208, Crown Life Insurance Company; Page 212, Hunt Personnel; Pages 226, 228, David Starrett/The Cove Studios

Chapter 9
Page 234, Deborah Starks; Page 241, Courtesy Western Electric; Page 244, Dick Hemingway; Ed Bock/The Stock Market; Page 248, Al Harvey/The Slide Farm; Page 252, David Starrett/The Cover Studios

Chapter 10
Page 260, Canada Post Corporation; Page 264, Prentice Hall Archives; Page 271, VIA Rail Canada Inc.; Page 277; Canapress Photo Service/Bill Becker

Chapter 11
Page 296, Norco Bicycles; Page 298, Canapress Photo Service; Page 304, Bettye Lane/Photo Researchers; Page 313, Jay Freis/The Image Bank; Courtesy Jervis B. Webb; Courtesy Atlantic Container Line; Page 314, Larry Mulvehill/Photo Researchers; Page 320, Courtesy Calma Company

Chapter 12
Page 326, Courtesy of Massimo's, Steeles Avenue, Woodbridge, Ontario; Page 333, Al Harvey/The Slide Farm; Page 342, Courtesy of Four Seasons Hotels and Resorts; Page 343, Dave Starrett/The Cover Studios

Chapter 13
Page 348, Magna International Inc.; Page 350, Jaguar Canada Inc.; Page 355, Hank Morgan/Photo Researchers; Page 359, Chris Jones/The Stock Market; Page 365, Dofasco Canada

Chapter 14
Page 382, Al Harvey/The Slide Farm; Page 384, Bettman Archive; Page 386, Watt Group; Agency Chiat/Day/Mojo, Creative Director Marty Cooke, and the AIDS Committee of Toronto; Page 389, Will McIntyre, Photo Research; Page 400, Al Harvey/The Slide Farm; Page 402, Prentice Hall Archives; 404, The Body Shop Canada

Chapter 15
Page 414, Canapress; Page 416, Bombardier Canadair; Page 428, Warner Bros. Canada, photo courtesy of Angelika Baur; Page 435, Boy Scouts of Canada; Joseph Rodriguez/Black Star; Duncan Roban/Alpha, Prime Minister's Office; Page 441, McCain Foods Limited, and The Canadian Centre for Philanthropy; Page 446, Paul Barton/ The Stock Market

Chapter 16
Page 454, Trudy Woodcock's Image Network/Al Harvey; Page 456, Canapress; Page 463, Richard Hutchings/Photo Researchers; Page 468, IBM Canada Limited; Page 473, Larry Mulvehill/Photo Researchers; Page 480, Canadian National

Chapter 17
Page 496, Trudy Woodcock's Image Network/Kharen Hill; Page 498, Walt Hodges/Tony Stone Images; Page 500, Al Harvey/The Slide Farm; Page 504, Deloitte & Touche; Page 510, Courtesy The Coca-Cola Company

Chapter 18
Page 526, Trudy Woodcock's Image Network/Al Harvey; Page 528, Courtesy of MDS Health Group Limited; Page 529, The Granger Collection; Page 538, Kathleen Bellesiles; Page 539, Courtesy of Canada Trust; Page 547, Prentice Hall Archives

Chapter 19
Page 554, Canapress; Page 556, Canapress; Page 561, David Pollack/The Stock Market; Page 574, Lawrence Migdale, Ulrich Welch, Eunice Harris/Photo Researchers; Page 581, Kent and Donna Dannen/Photo Researchers

Chapter 20
Page 590, Dick Hemingway; Page 592; Royal Bank; Page 597, Dick Hemingway; Page 599, Bank of Canada; Page 604, Canapress Photo Services; Page 608, Trudy Woodcock's Image Network/Kharen Hill

Chapter 21
Page 624, Canapress; Page 626, Canada Wide; Page 629, Ontario Ministry of Natural Resources; Page 632, VIA Rail Canada Inc.; Page 640, Ports Canada

Chapter 22
Page 646, Canapress; Page 648, Courtesy of Glegg Water Conditioning; Page 660, Nestle Limited of Vevey, Switzerland, and Northern Telecom; Page 664, Prentice Hall Canada Inc.; Page 672, Courtesy of Sony Canada

Chapter 23
Page 678, Al Harvey/The Slide Farm; Page 680, Softcop International Inc.; Page 683, Northern Telecom; Page 694, Courtesy of QUE Books; Page 698, Courtesy of IBM Canada Limited; Page 704, Courtesy of IBM Canada Limited

All photos for the video cases provided courtesy of the CBC.

INDEX

Subject Index

Name and Company Index